THE CAMBRIDGE LEGAL HISTORY OF

AUSTRALIA

Featuring contributions from leading lawyers, historians and social scientists, this path-breaking volume explores encounters of laws, people and places in Australia since 1788. Its chapters address three major themes: the development of Australian settler law in the shadow of the British Empire; the interaction between settler law and First Nations people and the possibility of meaningful encounter between First laws and settler legal regimes in Australia. Several chapters explore the limited space provided by Australian settler law for respectful encounters, particularly in light of the High Court's particular concerns about the fragility of Australian sovereignty. Tracing the development of a uniquely Australian law and the various contexts that shaped it, this volume is concerned with the complexity, plurality and ambiguity of Australia's legal history.

Peter Cane has written widely in areas of public law, private law and legal theory. He is co-editor (with H. Kumarasingham) of *The Cambridge Constitutional History of the United Kingdom* and author of *Controlling Administrative Power: An Historical Comparison* (2016). He is a Corresponding Fellow of the British Academy and a Fellow of the Academy of the Social Sciences in Australia.

Lisa Ford is Professor of History at UNSW, Sydney. A prize-winning legal historian whose work explores jurisdictional politics in the United States and the British Empire to 1850, she is author of *Settler Sovereignty* (2010) and *The King's Peace* (2021), and co-author (with L. Benton) of *Rage for Order* (2016). She is a Fellow of the Academy of Humanities in Australia.

Dr Mark McMillan is a Wiradjuri man from Trangie in New South Wales, who was NAIDOC scholar of the year in 2013. Dr McMillan has published widely on the achievement of human rights for Australian Indigenous people, recovering Indigenous self-governance and promoting settler recognition for Indigenous law in Australia.

THE CAMBRIDGE LEGAL HISTORY OF AUSTRALIA

*

Edited by
PETER CANE
University of Cambridge

LISA FORD
University of New South Wales, Sydney

MARK MCMILLAN
Independent Scholar

CAMBRIDGE
UNIVERSITY PRESS

Shaftesbury Road, Cambridge CB2 8EA, United Kingdom

One Liberty Plaza, 20th Floor, New York, NY 10006, USA

477 Williamstown Road, Port Melbourne, VIC 3207, Australia

314–321, 3rd Floor, Plot 3, Splendor Forum, Jasola District Centre, New Delhi – 110025, India

103 Penang Road, #05–06/07, Visioncrest Commercial, Singapore 238467

Cambridge University Press is part of Cambridge University Press & Assessment,
a department of the University of Cambridge.

We share the University's mission to contribute to society through the pursuit of
education, learning and research at the highest international levels of excellence.

www.cambridge.org
Information on this title: www.cambridge.org/9781108499224

DOI: 10.1017/9781108633949

First published 2022

A catalogue record for this publication is available from the British Library

Library of Congress Cataloging-in-Publication data
NAMES: Cane, Peter, 1950– editor. | Ford, Lisa, 1974– editor. | McMillan, Mark David, 1969– editor.
TITLE: The Cambridge legal history of Australia / edited by Peter Cane, University of Cambridge; Lisa Ford, University of New South Wales, Sydney; Mark McMillan, independent scholar.
DESCRIPTION: Cambridge, United Kingdom; New York, NY : Cambridge University Press, 2022.
IDENTIFIERS: LCCN 2021970034 (print) | LCCN 2021058742 (ebook) | ISBN 9781108499224 (hardback) | ISBN 9781108633949 (ebook)
SUBJECTS: LCSH: Law – Australia – History.
CLASSIFICATION: LCC KU120 .C36 2022 (print) | LCC KU120 (ebook) | DDC 349.94–dc23/eng/20220429
LC record available at https://lccn.loc.gov/2021970034
LC ebook record available at https://lccn.loc.gov/2021970104

ISBN 978-1-108-49922-4 Hardback

Contents

Figures

Maps

Contributors

JASON BEHRENDT is an Indigenous lawyer and Director at Chalk & Behrendt, Lawyers & Consultants. He has over twenty-five years' experience in representing Aboriginal Land Councils, Indigenous communities and Indigenous corporations in relation to land rights, native title and cultural heritage matters.

SHAUN BERG is the principal of Berg Lawyers, a specialist Commercial Law and Intellectual Property firm. Berg works closely with the Ngarrindjeri Nation, and was their principal negotiator in treaty negotiations with the State of South Australia. Berg was counsel and solicitor in the significant High Court decision in *Karpany v Dietman* [2013] HCA 47.

FRANK BONGIORNO is Professor of History at the Australian National University. He writes on Australian political history, and is a Fellow of the Royal Historical Society, the Academy of the Social Sciences in Australia and the Australian Academy of Humanities.

KATHY BOWREY is a Professor in the Faculty of Law and Justice, University of New South Wales. She is a legal historian and socio-legal researcher whose research explores laws and practices that inform knowledge creation and the production, distribution and reception of technology and culture.

SEAN BRENNAN is an Associate Professor at the UNSW Faculty of Law and Justice. He has worked with a variety of Aboriginal and other community organisations and his teaching, writing and external engagement focus mainly on constitutional law, native title and land rights.

PETER CANE is a Senior Research Fellow at Christ's College, Cambridge and Emeritus Distinguished Professor at The Australian National University. He has researched and written in public law, the law of obligations and legal theory. With Harshan Kumarasingham, he is co-editor of *The Cambridge Constitutional History of the United Kingdom*.

EDDIE CUBILLO is an Aboriginal man with strong family links throughout the Northern Territory. He is a descendant of the Larrakia, Wadjigan and Central Arrernte peoples. He is undertaking a PhD in law at the University of Technology of Sydney and is a Senior Fellow at Melbourne Law School.

ANN CURTHOYS is Professor Emerita at The Australian National University. She has published on many aspects of Australian history and on historical writing and theory. Her publications include *Freedom Ride: A Freedomrider Remembers* (2002); (with John Docker) *Is History Fiction?* (2005, revised 2010); and (with Jessie Mitchell) *Taking Liberty: Indigenous Rights and Settler Self-Government in Colonial Australia, 1830–1890* (2018).

SHAUNNAGH DORSETT is Distinguished Professor of Law in the Faculty of Law at the University of Technology Sydney. Much of her work centres on questions of authority and jurisdiction, particularly in the context of Crown-First Nations legal relations. Her most recent book is *Juridical Encounters: Māori and the Settler Courts, 1840–1852* (2017).

KATHERINE ELLINGHAUS is an Associate Professor of History in the School of Archaeology and History at La Trobe University. Dr Ellinghaus is of Irish, Scottish and German descent and has researched and written extensively on Indigenous assimilation policies in Australia and the United States.

MARK FINNANE FAAH FASSA is Professor of History at Griffith University, where he directs the Prosecution Project, a database on the history of the criminal trial in Australia. He has published widely on the history of criminal justice, policing, punishment, and criminal law in both Australia and Ireland.

GARY FOLEY PhD is a Professor of History and head of the Aboriginal History Archive at Victoria University.

LISA FORD is Professor of History at the University of New South Wales. Her work explores the interface of sovereignty, constitutional law, and jurisdiction with everyday legal practice in the late eighteenth- and early nineteenth-century British Empire and United States.

KIRSTY GOVER is a first-generation New Zealander who grew up on Kati Mamoe-Ngai Tahu land. She is a Professor and Associate Dean (Indigenous Recognition) at Melbourne Law School and writes about settler law affecting Indigenous peoples in Australia, Aotearoa New Zealand, Canada and the United States.

PAUL GRAY (WIRADJURI) is Associate Professor at the University of Technology Sydney Jumbunna Institute for Indigenous Education and Research. Dr Gray has over a decade's experience in the NSW child protection sector, as a psychologist and in policy and project roles. Paul has led the development of Aboriginal child and family systems and policy frameworks and contributed to state and national advocacy.

JENNIFER GREEN is a postdoctoral research fellow in the School of Languages and Linguistics at the University of Melbourne. Since the mid-1970s she has collaborated with Indigenous people in Central and Northern Australia documenting spoken and signed languages, cultural history and visual arts. Her publications include *Drawn from the Ground: Sound, Sign and Inscription in Central Australian Sand Stories* (2014).

STEVE HEMMING contributes to the development of strategic and collaborative Indigenous research programs in the Indigenous Nations and Collaborative Futures (INCF) research hub at Jumbunna Institute for Indigenous Education and Research, UTS. Associate Professor Hemming has worked with Indigenous communities since the

1980s, with a primary research focus on Indigenous nation-building, environmental management and cultural heritage management.

MIRANDA JOHNSON is a senior lecturer in the history program at the University of Otago. The author of *The Land Is Our History: Indigeneity, Law and the Settler State* (2016), her current research explores entanglements of Australasian empire and Indigenous political innovation in the nineteenth-century South Pacific.

JUDITH S. JONES is an Associate Professor of Law at the ANU College of Law, The Australian National University, where she researches and teaches in environmental law and colonial legal history.

MIRIAM JORGENSEN is Research Director of both the University of Arizona Native Nations Institute and the Harvard Project on American Indian Economic Development. Professor Jorgensen co-founded the University of Arizona Indigenous Governance program, and has worked extensively in the areas of Indigenous governance and economic development in the United States, Canada and Australia.

ANDY KALADELFOS is Senior Lecturer in the Faculty of Law and Justice at the University of New South Wales. Dr Kaladelfos's research examines sexual and gender-based violence and queer criminology. Originally trained in history, Andy's research is interdisciplinary, using methods from history, law, criminology and psychology to analyse the shifting relationship between law and society.

AMANDA KEARNEY is Honorary Professorial Fellow, School of Culture and Communication, University of Melbourne. Her work is distinguished by a two-decade-long commitment to collaboration and ethnographic fieldwork with Indigenous families and their communities in Australia and African descendant communities in northern Brazil. Her research specialty is cultural wounding, healing, land security and interculturalism in Australia. Her research has developed with the kind support and intellectual generosity of Yanyuwa families, the Indigenous owners of land and sea in the southwest Gulf of Carpentaria, Australia. In collaboration with Yanyuwa, Amanda has written a series of books, *Before the Old People and Still Today*, *Cultural Wounding, Healing and Emerging Ethnicities*, *Violence in Place* and *Reflexive Ethnographic Practice*. Her current book project is titled, *Keeping Company: An Anthropology of Being-in-Relation.*

BRUCE KERCHER is Emeritus Professor of Law at Macquarie University. He is particularly interested in the adaptation of English law to Australian conditions during the nineteenth century. His publications include *An Unruly Child: A History of Law in Australia* (1995) and *Debt, Seduction and Other Disasters: The Birth of Civil Law in Convict New South Wales* (1996). He is President of the Francis Forbes Society for Australian Legal History.

COEL KIRKBY is a Lecturer at the University of Sydney Law School. Before that he was the Smuts Research Fellow in Commonwealth Studies at the University of Cambridge. He also completed his PhD in Law at the University of Cambridge.

DIANE KIRKBY FAAH, FASSA and Fellow ASLH is Professor of Law and Humanities, University of Technology Sydney and Research Professor (Emeritus) in History at La Trobe University. She has been active in the ANZ Law and History Society since its foundation. Her research on women's, and maritime, labour history is funded by the Australian Research Council.

SHINO KONISHI is an Aboriginal historian and identifies with the Yawuru people of Broome, Western Australia. She is an Associate Professor in the Institute for Humanities and Social Sciences at the Australian Catholic University.

TERRI LIBESMAN is an Associate Professor in the Law Faculty at the University of Technology Sydney. Dr Libesman has researched and advocated for more than two decades with First Nations children's organisations nationally and internationally and published widely in the field.

DAVID LIEBERMAN is the James W. and Isabel Coffroth Professor of Jurisprudence at the University of California, Berkeley School of Law, where he teaches in the Jurisprudence and Social Policy Program. He is the author of *The Province of Legislation Determined: Legal Theory in Eighteenth-century Britain* and many other studies of law, jurisprudence and political ideas in the eighteenth and nineteenth centuries.

BRENDAN LIM is a barrister at Eleven Wentworth Chambers in Sydney and a Centre Fellow at the Gilbert + Tobin Centre of Public Law at the University of New South Wales. He practises principally in public and commercial law and has published widely on constitutional law and statutory interpretation.

MARK LUNNEY is a Professor at the School of Law at the University of New England in Armidale, Australia, and a Professor at the Dickson Poon School of Law, King's College London. He is a Fellow of the Australian Academy of Law.

CRYSTAL MCKINNON PhD is a Senior Lecturer in the Social and Global Studies Centre at RMIT University. She is an Amangu woman, and an historian whose work is underpinned by Indigenous critical theory.

MARK MCMILLAN is a Wiradjuri man from Trangie in New South Wales who was National Aboriginal and Islanders Day Observance Committee (NAIDOC) scholar of the year in 2013. Dr McMillan has published widely on the achievement of human rights for Australian Indigenous people, recovering Indigenous self-governance and promoting settler recognition for Indigenous law in Australia.

JESSIE MITCHELL holds a doctorate in history from the Australian National University. She has published on the histories of Aboriginal policy, self-government and missionary work in colonial Australia, including *In Good Faith? Governing Indigenous Australia through God, Charity and Empire, 1825–1855* (2011) and (with Ann Curthoys) *Taking Liberty: Indigenous Rights and Settler Self-Government in Colonial Australia, 1830–1890* (2018).

RUTH A. MORGAN is Director of the Centre for Environmental History at the Australian National University. She is the author of the award-winning book, *Running Out? Water in Western Australia* (2015), and she is currently preparing her next monograph, *Climate Change and International History*, for publication by Bloomsbury.

AMANDA NETTELBECK is a Professor of the Institute of Humanities and Social Sciences, Australian Catholic University, and Professor of History at the University of Adelaide. Her most recent book *Indigenous Rights and Colonial Subjecthood* (2019) received the 2020 ANZLHS Annual Prize in Legal History.

Anne O'Brien is Professor of History in the School of Humanities and Languages at the University of New South Wales, Sydney. She has published widely on the histories of poverty, welfare, women, gender and religion and is currently writing a history of homelessness and homeless people.

Alana Piper is a Chancellor's Postdoctoral Research Fellow at the Australian Centre for Public History at the University of Technology Sydney. Dr Piper's research interests draw together the social and cultural history of crime with legal history, criminology and digital humanities approaches.

Daryle Rigney is a citizen of the Ngarrindjeri Nation. Professor Rigney is Director of the Indigenous Nations and Collaborative Futures (INCF) research hub at Jumbunna Institute for Indigenous Education and Research, University of Technology Sydney. Rigney is one of Australia's foremost Indigenous nation-building scholars and practitioners, and has been a critical strategist for the Ngarrindjeri Nation.

David Andrew Roberts teaches History at the University of New England (New South Wales) where he edits the Journal of Australian Colonial History. His interests range widely across the history of early colonial Australia, but he is particularly focused on the nature and legacies of the convict period.

Denis Rose is a Gunditjmara Elder and spear-headed the Gunditjmara People's nomination of the Budj Bim Cultural Landscape for UNESCO World Heritage status. Rose is the project manager for the Budj Bim Sustainable Development Partnership with the Gunditj Mirring Traditional Owners Aboriginal Corporation. He served earlier as CEO of Winda-Mara Aboriginal Corporation and played a key role in the development of Australia's Indigenous Protected Areas Program.

Tim Rowse holds honorary appointments at the Australian National University and Western Sydney University. His books include *White Flour, White Power: From Rations to Citizenship in Central Australia* (1998). He lived in Alice Springs between 1987 and 1995 and has researched Indigenous topics since the early 1980s.

Cheryl Saunders is a Laureate Professor Emeritus at Melbourne Law School, with specialist interests in Australian and comparative constitutional law, theory and practice. She was the founding Director of the Centre for Comparative Constitutional Studies and is a President Emeritus of the International Association of Constitutional Law. She is a convenor of the Constitution Transformation Network and a senior technical adviser to the Constitution building program of International IDEA.

Alecia Simmonds is a senior lecturer in law at the University of Technology Sydney. She has published on the relationship between intimacy, imperialism and law and gender and emotions in a range of scholarly journals. Her current project examines the legal regulation of love through the lens of breach of promise of marriage cases from 1806 to 1975. It will be published by Black Inc/La Trobe Scholarly Press in 2022. Her books include: *Transnationalism and Nationalism in Australian History* (2017) and *Wild Man: A True Story of a Police Killing, Mental Illness and the Law* (2015), which won the 2016 Davitt prize for best crime non-fiction.

Cait Storr is a Chancellor's Postdoctoral Research Fellow at the University of Technology Sydney. She researches the relationship between the domestic law of property and the international law of territory in colonial and imperial history, with a focus on decolonial struggles for control over natural resources.

Maureen Tehan is a Principal Fellow at the Melbourne Law School, University of Melbourne. She is a researcher, teacher and legal practitioner in the fields of property and land law, primarily their colonial and contemporary relationship with systems of First Nations knowledges, land law, native title and statutory land rights schemes.

Rayner Thwaites is a Senior Lecturer at Sydney Law School. His research analyses citizenship, and the interaction between domestic and international law. In 2021 he will start on 'Citizenship and Claims of Belonging in Australian Law and History' with Elisa Arcioni and Helen Irving, funded by the Australia Research Council.

Alison Vivian is a lawyer and Senior Researcher in the INCF research hub at Jumbunna Institute for Indigenous Education and Research, University of Technology Sydney. Dr Vivian has practised native title, refugee and humanitarian law, and has a primary research focus on Indigenous nation-building and governance as an exercise of Indigenous sovereignty and self-determination.

Nicole Watson is Associate Professor and Director of Academic Programs at Nura Gili, UNSW Sydney. She is a member of the Birri-Gubba People and the Yugambeh language group. Nicole has published extensively on issues relating to Indigenous Australians and the law, especially in relation to the Northern Territory Intervention, land ownership and connection to country, and difficulties particularly facing Aboriginal women. At the 2018 Dreamtime Awards, she was named Educator of the Year for her outstanding work in law affecting Indigenous people and her support for Indigenous students.

Mary Spiers Williams is Sub-Dean of Australian Indigenous Studies, College of Arts and Social Sciences and member of the Law School, The Australian National University, legal practitioner, descended from sandstone country – including that of the Darkiñung – and European coloniser-settlers.

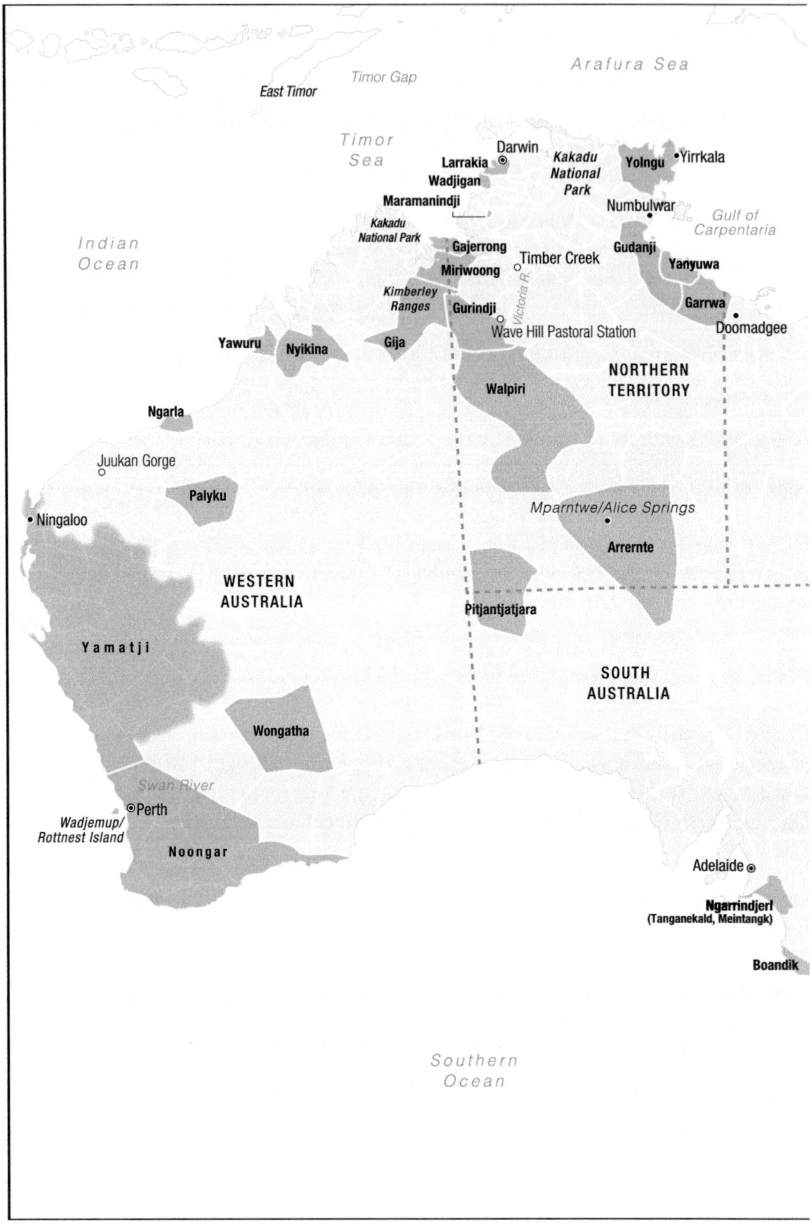

Map 0.1: Australia – Place and Peoples Mentioned (For the colour version, please refer to the plate section)

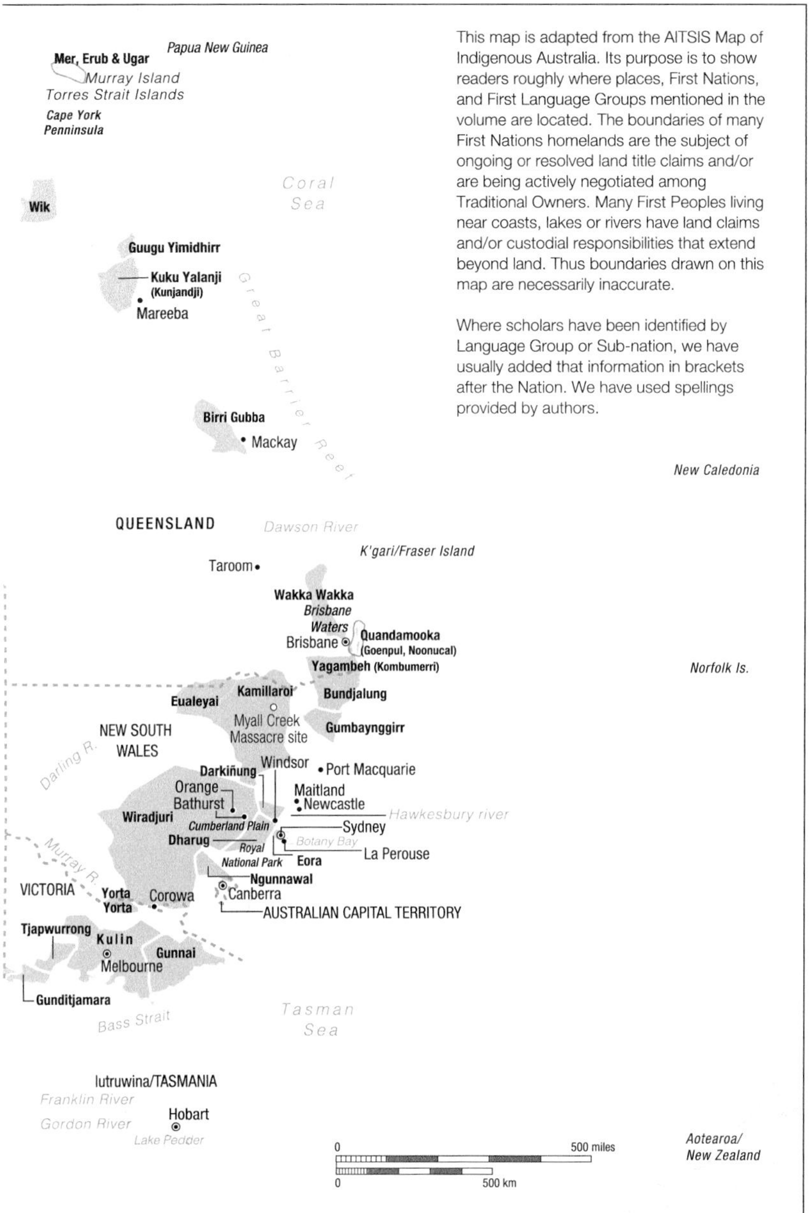
This map is adapted from the AITSIS Map of Indigenous Australia. Its purpose is to show readers roughly where places, First Nations, and First Language Groups mentioned in the volume are located. The boundaries of many First Nations homelands are the subject of ongoing or resolved land title claims and/or are being actively negotiated among Traditional Owners. Many First Peoples living near coasts, lakes or rivers have land claims and/or custodial responsibilities that extend beyond land. Thus boundaries drawn on this map are necessarily inaccurate.
Where scholars have been identified by Language Group or Sub-nation, we have usually added that information in brackets after the Nation. We have used spellings provided by authors.
Papua New Guinea
Mer, Erub & Ugar
Murray Island
Torres Strait Islands
Cape York
Penninsula
Wik
Coral
Sea
Guugu Yimidhirr
Kuku Yalanji
(Kunjandji)
Mareeba
Great Barrier Reef
Birri Gubba
Mackay
New Caledonia
QUEENSLAND
Dawson River
K'gari/Fraser Island
Taroom
Wakka Wakka
Brisbane
Waters
Brisbane
Quandamooka
(Goenpul, Noonucal)
Yagambeh (Kombumerri)
Norfolk Is.
Kamillaroi
Eualeyai
Bundjalung
Myall Creek
Massacre site
Gumbaynggirr
NEW SOUTH
WALES
Darling R.
Darkiñung
Windsor
Port Macquarie
Orange
Bathurst
Maitland
Newcastle
Hawkesbury river
Wiradjuri
Cumberland Plain
Sydney
Dharug
Royal
National Park
Botany Bay
La Perouse
Eora
Murray R.
Ngunnawal
VICTORIA
Yorta
Yorta
Corowa
Canberra
AUSTRALIAN CAPITAL TERRITORY
Tjapwurrong
Kulin
Melbourne
Gunnai
Gunditjamara
Bass Strait
Tasman
Sea
lutruwina/TASMANIA
Franklin River
Gordon River
Hobart
Lake Pedder
0
500 miles
0
500 km
Aotearoa/
New Zealand

Map 0.1: (cont.)

1

Editors' Introduction

PETER CANE, LISA FORD AND MARK MCMILLAN

The editorial project we set for ourselves was to assemble a legal history of Australia. As this continent has been occupied by human communities for more than 60,000 years, this is, of course, an impossible task. We have approached it cautiously and partially. The chapters in this volume explore encounters of laws, people and place in Australia since 1788. They address at least three distinct aspects of this broad topic. One concerns the complex unfolding of Australian settler law in the shadow of the British Empire. It begins with the fundamental tenet of British imperial law – that English law applied in settled colonies to the extent that it was appropriate to local circumstances and conditions.[1] Many of the chapters in the volume go on to explore the employment and adaptation of inherited laws and ideologies for the legal project of settler nation-building after federation. A second aspect of the broad theme of encounter concerns interaction between settler law and First Nations people: it concerns ways in which and the extent to which introduced and adapted laws were applied to Aboriginal and Torres Strait Islander peoples. The third, most difficult and undeveloped aspect explores the possibility of meaningful encounter between First Laws and settler legal regimes in Australia. A number of chapters explore the limited space provided by Australian settler law for respectful encounters, particularly in light of the High Court's particular concerns with the fragility of Australian sovereignty.

We owe special thanks to Professors Shaunnagh Dorsett and Kirsty Gover who helped enormously in planning and troubleshooting this volume. It could not have happened without their enormous kindness, collegiality and generosity.

1 For a recent discussion of the adaptation in the British Empire, see Lisa Ford, *The King's Peace: Empire and Order in the British Empire* (Cambridge, MA: Harvard University Press, 2021). For the law of reception, see, Alex Castles, 'The Reception and Status of English Law in Australia' *Adelaide Law Review* 2 (1963): 1–31; B. H. McPherson, *The Reception of English Law Abroad* (Brisbane: Supreme Court of Queensland Library, 2007), 235–55.

We originally set out to create a counterpart to the three-volume *Cambridge History of Law in America*, edited by Michael Grossberg and Christopher Tomlins. However, we have ended up in a very different place. The *Cambridge Legal History of Australia* is distinctive in its sustained attention to the encounter of First Peoples and their laws with settler law. Second, we have attempted to bring into the project a large number of Indigenous scholars – lawyers, historians, anthropologists and activists, involved in both understanding and assessing settler-Indigenous legal engagement in Australia and actively building local governance structures. Third, by conceiving of Australian legal history as a three-way encounter between English, Australian and Aboriginal and Torres Strait Islander legal regimes, we make the point that all legal systems are porous, particularly when they co-exist in the 'social field'.[2] *The Cambridge Legal History of Australia* contributes to the understanding of the nature and limits of legal plurality and pluralism as explanatory frameworks for legal history at the local, national and transnational/imperial level.

This *Cambridge Legal History* is not only innovative in its focus on legal encounter: its approach to legal history is also decidedly interdisciplinary. The chapters that focus on the law of Aboriginal and Torres Strait Islanders in particular, have a theoretical or empirical cast: they describe unfolding institution-building efforts, future projects and principles of lawfulness. Other chapters focus on the development of legal doctrine and the substance of the law as historical phenomena worthy of attention in their own right. Yet others adopt a more 'socio-legal' stance that understands law as an interwoven set of rules and practices that are crafted and unfold in social, political and temporal contexts. By and large, these differences are only of degree and emphasis. Historically sensitive study of the nature and substance of law is necessarily located in various temporal contexts that reflect distinct moments in a community's legal life. On the other hand, the socio-legal and historical approaches in this volume do not ignore or discount the norms and rules created by judges and legislators but seek, rather, to highlight the political, economic and social conditions in which they were made and applied. In short, we aspire to bypass barriers between different understandings of law – as normative social practice, as a body of doctrine, and as politics. Law is all these things and more. Its history is integral to histories of society, economics, politics and so on.

2 Sally Falk Moore, 'Law and Social Change: The Semi-autonomous Social Field as an Appropriate Subject of Study' *Law and Society Review* 7 (1973): 719–46.

The Plan of the Book

Of our three themes of encounter, the first – between English legal traditions and the project of Australian settlement and nation-building – receives most attention in this volume. David Lieberman argues in his framing chapter that in the late eighteenth century, English legal culture was characterised by a complex interaction between, on the one hand, an undigested mass of inherited institutions and rules of court-focused 'common law'; and, on the other, legislative attempts to update that inheritance by statute in the light of changed social, economic and political circumstances both at home and in British colonies scattered around the globe. In his chapter, Bruce Kercher shows that in New South Wales, adaptation of English law to local conditions, including the fact of a convict majority and the reality of settler-Indigenous violence, was an inevitable feature of law and its administration in the colony from the very start. Focusing on the theme of adaptation, Mark Lunney tells the story of civil wrongs, taking us from early colonial days well into the twentieth century. He finds the ongoing process of adaptation masked by a rhetoric of 'one common law' for the whole Anglosphere and a judicial tradition of what he calls 'British race nationalism'.

David Roberts's chapter on early criminal law shows that the penal purpose and population of the colony of New South Wales presented a raft of problems for the administration of justice and the maintenance of discipline in the colonial period. Colonial authorities saw the need for a simplified and more coercive system of law for the colony that fitted awkwardly with metropolitan legal reforms. The pursuit of this dual goal produced tension, compromise and chaotic informality that the authorities were slow to address. Andy Kaladelfos and Alana Piper trace the history of criminal law beyond the colonial period into the twentieth century, noting both major transformation – in relation to criminal process, for instance – but also continuity in, for example, the use of the prison as a major instrument of state power.

After the need to keep order, the settler state's highest priority was the allocation and use of land. The story begins with the obvious fact that the First Peoples already occupied, used and managed the land within a complex framework of religious and cultural beliefs, and social norms and expectations. At first, as Lisa Ford and David Roberts point out, appropriation of land by settlers, in total disregard of the interests and claims of First Peoples, was a fact of colonial life, a mix of opportunism and force; only later did the settlers formalise and (in their own eyes) legitimise systematic dispossession by adopting the fiction of *terra nullius*. Maureen Tehan shows that, in the course of the nineteenth century, settler land law evolved in various ways that modified and departed from the highly technical and arcane English law the settlers had brought with them. Some of these changes were prompted by the facts of First Peoples' continued presence on and use of the land of which they had been 'dispossessed'. Tehan argues, for example, that repudiation of the *terra nullius* myth in the late twentieth century shook the theoretical foundations of land law in Australia, placing an adapted doctrine of land tenure at its centre. Title to land is, of course, inextricably tied up with its use. Ruth Morgan and Judith Jones point to a sharp contrast between the interests of settlers in exploiting the land and the concept of caring for Country, on which First Peoples' law, culture and praxis is based. They suggest that the settlers' focus on development has almost always impeded Australia's genuine engagement with environmental imperatives.

Alongside issues of crime, law and order, and of land ownership and use, various chapters explore other sites of adaptation of English law to Australian circumstances. The centre of gravity of Diane Kirkby's chapter on labour law is the contract of employment, which she tracks from convict labour regimes to the gig economy. She also explores distinctively Australian approaches such as the system of compulsory arbitration. Anne O'Brien contrasts family and kin-based models of welfare characteristic of Indigenous societies with the imported English model of state provision combined with elements of social control. She argues that the imported approach worked quite well for settlers but much less well for First Peoples, among whom it has caused significant social and economic disruption and degradation. On the other hand, at the start of this century, she also detects increasing dissemination of First Peoples' ideas of well-being which, she hopes, may contribute to addressing the welfare challenges of what she calls 'the post-work future'. Alecia Simmonds's account of the history of conjugality chronicles shifting settler practices and values that have established marriage as the dominant legal form but have also brought increasing tolerance and recognition of other types of intimate relationship. Hers is not just an Australian story but one that tracks similar changes within Western societies.

Kathy Bowrey focuses on copyright. Copyright law, she tells us, concerns the production and circulation of commodities that have helped define Australian culture. Through a case study of artist and illustrator, May Gibbs, the chapter tracks the slow emergence of Australian copyright law from its English and imperial cocoon; and, through a case study of the life and work of Albert Namatjira, it explores the impact of race on Australian copyright law.

Chapters in Parts II and III tell stories of the development of settler government, politics and public law. Building on Kercher's account of the first years of colonial settlement, Ann Curthoys and Jessie Mitchell trace the transition from remote rule by the metropolitan authorities in Britain to local self-government, a shift that occurred in most colonies in the 1850s. They find that self-government was implemented in different ways in the various colonies, with varying consequences for class and gender relations. The authors also explore the negative impacts of colonial self-government on Aboriginal sovereignty and self-determination. The six settler colonies came together in the federated Commonwealth of Australia in 1901. Brendan Lim traces the emergence of quasi-federal arrangements in the later nineteenth-century British Empire and chronicles the encounter of Australian constitution-makers with American federalism and constitutionalism. Lim speculates that in the flexibility and adaptability of Australian federalism may be found fruitful approaches to constitutional recognition of First Peoples. On the other hand, Kirsty Gover and Eddie Cubillo argue that the constitutional mischaracterisation of First Peoples in racial terms continues to present a significant obstacle to the realisation of their aspirations for self-determination and self-governance.

Nation-building is a multi-faceted activity. One facet involves the definition of membership. In his chapter, Rayner Thwaites analyses Australian membership statuses in the period since Federation: British subject, non-immigrant, citizen and non-alien. Australia's halting move away from the centrality of membership in the British Empire towards a more distinct and self-sufficient national citizenship lies at the centre of this story. This historical trajectory overlaps with the operation and long, slow demise of the White Australia policy. The chapter also analyses current issues challenging and changing our understanding of Australian citizenship, including the recent ruling of the High Court that Aboriginal Australians have a relationship with the continent that is not bound by citizenship: accordingly, Aboriginal non-citizens are not vulnerable to deportation.

Though a key characteristic of nation-building since the late eighteenth century has been the inclusion in written constitutions of bills of rights, as Frank Bongiorno notes, this is not true of Australia. However, from early colonial days settlers, including convicts, had a well-developed sense of their civil and political rights as freeborn Britons. These rights were not extended to First Peoples. Through the first half of the twentieth century, the British basis of rights claims remained dominant in Australia; but from the 1940s, Australia was gradually drawn into an international human rights order in a manner that strengthened the ability of marginalised groups to make rights claims through appeals to international standards and covenants. Cheryl Saunders's chapter brings together various strands of these stories by exploring a framing concept of constitutionalism, the sometimes-distinctively Australian approach to polity and nation-building, and the challenges it faces in the twenty-first century.

In contrast to the focus in these chapters on the importation of European technologies of governance into Australia, their development by settlers, and the largely negative impacts of settler nation-building on Australia's First Peoples, Miranda Johnson and Cait Storr explore Australia's role as an agent as well as a product of empire. They track Australia's attempt to colonise the Pacific – a late nineteenth- and twentieth-century project that shapes Australia's continuing influence in the region. In this context, it may be observed that significant aspects of the relationship between settler Australia and its imperial parent remain post-colonial. Relations between settler Australia and its First Nations have not yet made the transition from the colonial to the post-colonial. Coel Kirkby brings these various threads together into a story of encounter between settler Australia and three different worlds. The first world is that of the ancient and ongoing history of international relationships between First Nations, and the unfinished business of relations between them and the settler state. The second world is the British Empire, a global state that aimed to impose a single legal order over its imperial jurisdictions. The third world is the international system of sovereign states that covers the globe today. Law is a prominent feature of each of these encounters and the tensions they embody.

Much important historical work has addressed the second strand of this volume: the encounter of Aboriginal and Torres Strait Islanders with Australian settler law. The chapters in this strand draw together elements of an already rich historical literature about entanglements of First Peoples with settler law, including projects as diverse as Mark Finnane's and Heather Douglas's agenda-setting work on persistent plurality in Australian criminal law,[3] and Amanda Nettelbeck's foundational work on the interplay of policing and protection.[4] Genocide, dispossession and assimilationist

3 Heather Douglas and Mark Finnane, *Indigenous Crime and Settler Law: White Sovereignty after Empire* (London: Palgrave Macmillan Limited, 2012).

4 Amanda Nettelbeck, *Indigenous Rights and Colonial Subjecthood: Protection and Reform in the Nineteenth-century British Empire* (Cambridge: Cambridge University Press, 2019).

'protectionism' preoccupy a number of the chapters in this volume. They tell big stories of settler law's dispossession of Indigenous peoples, exercises of criminal jurisdiction, the violence of protection regimes, the legal assault on Aboriginal and Torres Strait Islander families and their demands for civil rights.

One of the most heart-breaking of these contributions is the chapter on Indigenous families by Terri Libesman, Katherine Ellinghaus and Paul Gray. These authors explore ongoing settler state violence against Aboriginal and Torres Strait Islander families from first contact to contemporary child welfare interventions. Such interventions have been authorised by laws and policies that have forcibly separated children from their families and communities legally and illegally, and separated kin by exerting control over where Aboriginal people could live, whom they could marry, and how their identity was legally defined. Amanda Nettelbeck's chapter traces the tortuous interface of Aboriginal Australians with protection and welfare regimes in Australian legal history. She traces Australia's history of protection, from its nineteenth-century origins as a program designed to build Indigenous peoples' status as British subjects, to its twentieth-century expressions as a legally empowered system of state guardianship that granted state governments wide-ranging powers of control over Indigenous lives, purportedly for their own good. Mark Finnane explores the interface of settler criminal law with Aboriginal Australians since 1836 – a topic of immense contemporary importance as Aboriginal Australians are among the world's most incarcerated populations. In tracking the long history of Aboriginal criminalisation from nineteenth-century debates about the admissibility and translation of their evidence to more recent patterns of prosecution and punishment, Finnane shows that, over time, the legal system's professed principles of justice and fairness have compounded discrimination against and disadvantage of Aboriginal Australians.

In their chapter on 'Civil Rights and Indigenous People', Gary Foley and Crystal McKinnon explore several key moments in the Aboriginal and Torres Strait Islanders' crusade to end discriminatory laws in Australia. They track the formation of the Aborigines Progressive Association in 1837, and its role in launching a national movement for civil rights in Australia, culminating in the Constitutional Referendum in 1967 that destroyed the exclusive power of states to legislate for Aboriginal and Torres Strait Islander people. But, as Foley and McKinnon note, the end of formal discrimination did not transform the lives of many Aboriginal Australians and, by the 1960s, Indigenous participants struggled to have their voices heard in the civil rights movement. A new generation of activists combined some of the tenets of the US Black Power movement with demands for recognition for the special group rights of First Peoples, a foundational shift that underpins a range of contemporary demands, spanning land rights and constitutional recognition. In her wide-ranging and deeply researched reflection on the volume's attempt to foreground the encounter of settler laws with Aboriginal people and their law, Shino Konishi emphasises the ongoing struggle of Indigenous people to reckon with the ideology of *terra nullius* and the ongoing impact of discriminatory law.

The third aspect of encounter in this volume, between settler society and law on the one hand and Aboriginal and Torres Strait Islander legal systems on the other, is, perhaps, the most difficult and elusive of the three to explore in a *Cambridge Legal History*. Aboriginal and Torres Strait Islander law and legal cultures are dynamic and adaptive both in their own right and in their encounter with settler-colonial law and culture.[5] However, as Mary Spiers Williams points out, they are difficult for settler scholars and officials to see. There are several reasons for this. First, although the British settlers did eventually classify Australia as *terra nullius*, in practice, from the start, they realised (and for a good while accepted) that Australian Indigenous communities had their own laws. However, settler law has long marginalised and refused to engage meaningfully and substantively with Indigenous law and legal traditions. As Pueblo judge Christina Zuni Cruz noted, 'suppression of Indigenous legal traditions was, and in many cases continues to be, a formal policy objective of many nations in their attempts to assimilate Indigenous peoples'.[6] Second, while much of the substance of English law and Australian law is embodied, more or less determinately and accessibly, in written documents, most Aboriginal and Torres Strait Islander laws are not. Though some of our

5 See Carwyn Jones on the difficulty of disentangling internal dynamism and forced legal change in Māori legal orders: Carwyn Jones, 'Whakaeke I Nga Ngaru: Riding the Waves: Maori Legal Traditions in New Zealand Public Life', in Lisa Ford and Tim Rowse (eds), *Between Indigenous and Settler Governance* (New York: Routledge, 2012), 174–86, 176. On the syncretism of Indigenous laws, see John Borrows, *Canada's Indigenous Constitution* (Toronto: University of Toronto Press, 2010), 28; and John Borrows, 'Heroes, Tricksters, Monsters, and Caretakers: Indigenous Law and Legal Education' *McGill Law Journal* 61, no. 4 (2016): 815.

6 Christina Zuni Cruz, 'Law of the Land – Recognition and Resurgence in Indigenous Law and Justice Systems', in Benjamin J. Richardson, Shin Imai and Kent McNeil (eds), *Indigenous Peoples and the Law: Comparative and Critical Perspectives* (Oxford: Hart Publishing, 2009), 319.

more creative historians, along with anthropologists, archaeologists and Indigenous legal scholars, are finding ways to fill the gaps and fissures of the written archive with the reality of living law, most are still subject to its tyranny.[7] Third, the Australian continent houses hundreds of Indigenous peoples and nations, each with distinctive legal traditions, whose members live in widely varied contexts – rural, urban and suburban – in all parts of the Australian landmass. This multi-national order generates significant plurality of laws and legal systems, many of which are closely kept within communities, or entrusted only to certain people within a community.[8]

Despite this complexity, native title and many statutory land rights regimes grapple with Aboriginal and Torres Strait Islander laws. A significant number of chapters in this volume explore the lopsided nature of that encounter, most demonstrating that the nooks and crannies provided for First Law in Australian settler law are not adequate to structure meaningful engagement. Amanda Kearney's chapter exploring the Yanyuwa encounter with Northern Territory statutory land shows how the processes of parsing First Law to support land claims works its own colonial alchemy. Shaunnagh Dorsett (with Shaun McVeigh) has elsewhere explored the grudgingly created place for legal encounter in statutory native title law.[9] Jason Behrendt and Sean Brennan show in their chapter that all regimes based on historical claims-making in Australia place narrow limits on what counts as recognisable Indigenous law in that encounter. These chapters, on Aboriginal title to land, form a particularly illuminating set because they cut across English legal heritage, its Australian variants, and the laws and practices of Australia's First Peoples. Kirsty Gover and Eddie Cubillo explore the challenges faced by Aboriginal and Torres Strait Islander peoples determined to fill the awkward spaces left for Indigenous representation in governance bodies, many designed more to tame than to empower Indigenous voices, while Tim Rowse and Jennifer Green show how Arrernte people have mobilised mundane legislative instruments, including heritage law, to exercise some halting jurisdiction over settler development on Country.

7 Ann Laura Stoler, *Along the Archival Grain: Epistemic Anxieties and Colonial Common Sense* (Princeton, NJ: Princeton University Press, 2008), 27–55.

8 Kirsty Gover, 'Legal Pluralism & Indigenous Legal Traditions', Paul Schiff Bierman (ed.), *The Oxford Handbook of Global Legal Pluralism* (Oxford: Oxford University Press, 2020) 847–75, 861.

9 Shaunnagh Dorsett and Shaun McVeigh, 'Conduct of Laws: Native Title, Responsibility, and Some Limits of Jurisdictional Thinking', *Melbourne University Law Review* (2012–2013): 470–93.

These stories of encounter include remarkable (if fragile) successes, as Daryle Rigney, Denis Rose, Alison Vivian, Miriam Jorgensen, Steve Hemming and Shaun Berg show. Building on their own principles of governance, but also responding to the pressures of institutional encounter, the Ngarrindjeri and Gunditjamara peoples have formed and transformed local institutions, asserting control over land management in and around their Country, emerging as significant interlocutors of government. In such encounters, as Kirsty Gover observes, 'arguably the political arrangements devised by Indigenous peoples and settler states (governing the allocation of power and property) have outpaced much canonic Western legal theory'.[10] However, as Dorsett notes in this volume, the Australian High Court strives constantly to close down larger conversations about First Law and sovereignty. For example, when, in 2020, the High Court decided (in the *Love-Thoms* case) that Aboriginal Australians who were non-citizens could not be deported because their connection to Australian land and waters survived any 'assertion of sovereignty', the minority fretted that the decision might conjure 'the kind of [Aboriginal] sovereignty . . . rejected by *Mabo*'. The court's repeated insistence on perfect sovereignty is very modern, peculiarly mired in the anxieties of Australian settler-colonialism, and imperilled by the compelling claims of the litigants in the *Mabo (No. 2)* and *Love-Thoms* cases.

Meanwhile, understanding First Laws in their own right, rather than as matters of fact to be proved for the purposes of Australian law, presents ethical and methodological challenges. As a result, few chapters in our volume take this on and none of the chapters on this subject treats First Law as purely a matter of history. When this volume was originally conceived, we thought it might be possible to make Aboriginal law legible by accounting for it in established categories, including family law (which has been discussed recently by Ann McGrath) and criminal law (which Douglas and Finnane and others have discussed).[11] However, in her chapter, Mary Spiers Williams alerts us to the risks and perils of such a project. In her discussion of a similar attempt to account scientifically for Cheyenne law by using 'cases of trouble', Zuni Cruz argues that to present the contents of Indigenous law in social-scientific taxonomic terms is decidedly 'Eurocentric' and therefore 'useful but problematic'.[12] The key risk that such a project

10 Gover, 'Legal Pluralism & Indigenous Legal Theory', 860.

11 Ann McGrath, *Illicit Love: Interracial Sex and Marriage in the United States and Australia* (Lincoln: University of Nebraska Press, 2015); Douglas and Finnane, *Indigenous Crime and Settler Law*.

12 Cruz, 'Law of the Land', 317.

poses is internal encroachment – colonising First Law by trying to make it legible, leaving the Western organising framework intact and uninterrogated. Similarly, Williams argues that just as land rights regimes typically accept only the representations of Aboriginal and Torres Strait Islander law that fit settler-colonial imaginations of 'tradition', 'custom' and 'continuous connection', the invitation to reduce Aboriginal law to existing Western categories is another settler-colonial project.[13]

These writers contend that such approaches misrecognise (and, so, do not lawfully engage with) the ontological distinctiveness of Aboriginal law in Australia. Williams reminds us, as do other scholars of Indigenous law, that Country lies at the centre of the law of Aboriginal and Torres Strait Islander communities. In terms that would be somewhat familiar to Zuni Cruz and scholars of comparative First Law, Williams tells us that lawfulness and lawful behaviour stress the interdependency and interrelatedness of everyone, settler and Indigenous; that relationships bind people into human and more than human communities; and that learning First Law is not about reading books about Indigenous knowledge: rather, it requires listening to, watching and practising lawful behaviour in place. Understanding First Law is not an exercise in ethnography or translation; rather, lawful behaviour is constitutive of identity and belonging.[14] As Irene Watson put it nearly twenty years ago, 'Our laws are lived as a way of life, they are not written down because the knowledge of the law comes through the living of it, as law is lived, sung, danced, painted, eaten, walked upon, and loved; law lives in all things. It is law that holds the world together as it lives inside and outside of all things.'[15]

13 Kirsty Gover articulates the risk thus: 'Given that the inextricable connection between people and the natural world is a tenet of many Indigenous legal systems, there is a particular risk that writing about Indigenous law using a non-Indigenous lexicon can contribute to its deracination, approximating meanings in written words that are far removed from the places, people, and activities that give the law its authority. The proper articulation of Indigenous law on its own terms may require, for example, requisite affect and feeling toward one's environment, proximity to law's sources in particular lands, waters, plants, and animals, an appropriate relationship to a person or persons who are able to name and speak about law, participation in practices of shared ceremony, eating, and singing; or one's presence in other legal rituals and sites of law.' Gover, 'Legal Pluralism & Indigenous Legal Theory', 871.

14 These relate to three of the six characteristics of 'Indigenous ways of knowing' laid out by Battiste and Henderson, M. Battiste and J. Y. Henderson, *Protecting Indigenous Knowledge and Heritage: A Global Challenge* (Saskatoon: Purich, 2003), 42, discussed in Cruz, 'Law of the Land', 318. See also Gover, 'Legal Pluralism & Indigenous Legal Theory', 863–70.

15 Irene Watson, 'Buried Alive' *Law and Critique* 13 (2002): 255; for other powerful articulations of the nature of Indigenous law in Australia, see Mary Graham, 'Some Thoughts About the Philosophical Underpinnings of Aboriginal Worldviews' *Australian Humanities Review* 3, no. 2 (2008): 181–94; C. F. Black, *The Land Is the Source*

In contrast, Nicole Watson's chapter starts to imagine what the project of identifying and describing principles of Australian First Law might look like. In doing so she engages with Hadley Friedland's and Val Napoleon's work in Canada, which applies something like a common law (but also collaborative) method to analyse the stories of a number of participating First Nations and to extract their core messages.[16] Friedland and Napoleon argue that being too cautious about describing First Law can prevent genuine engagement with the vibrant field of Indigenous legal theory, 'perpetuating the colonial myth of an absence of Indigenous legal thought'. They also make the point that, in the shadow of centuries of settler-colonialism, 'articulation and recognition' are not enough, 'mindful and intentional acts of recovery and revitalization' are also required.[17] This, Watson thinks, might provide a promising pathway: the sharing of stories has the 'potential to create a bridge between Indigenous communities and legal scholars', breaking down the monologic nature of Australian legal education, and providing resources to bolster Aboriginal and Torres Strait Islander communities. This project may also transform settler law: Gover embraces the 'transformative potential' of pivoting towards the focus of Aboriginal and Torres Strait Islander legal culture on interdependency and the environment and away from the Anglo-American focus on individual contract and property rights.[18] On the other hand, as Dorsett and McVeigh have argued, embracing a reconciliatory plurality in Australia does not require us to encode the content of Indigenous law in print or reduce it to cognate legal categories. What it requires is the creation of lawful meeting grounds, legal spaces where regimes can meet.[19] In such spaces, James Tully argues, Aboriginal and Torres Strait Islander peoples would not be 'constrained to speak within the institutions and traditions of interpretation of the imperial constitutions that have been imposed over them'.[20] As Christine Black puts it, plurality requires that meeting places be governed by 'the Law of Relationship . . . Any relationship demands the witnessing of

of the Law: A Dialogic Encounter with Indigenous Jurisprudence (New York: Routledge, 2011), 184.

16 Hadley Friedland and Val Napoleon, 'Gathering the Threads: Developing a Methodology for Researching and Rebuilding Indigenous Legal Traditions' *Lakehead Law Journal* 1, no. 1 (2015–2016), 24.

17 Ibid, 31, 17–18.

18 Gover, 'Legal Pluralism & Indigenous Legal Theory', 873.

19 Dorsett and McVeigh, 'Conduct of Laws', 470–93; see also Jeremy Webber, 'Legal Pluralism and Human Agency' *Osgoode Hall Law Journal* 44 (2006): 167–98.

20 James Tully, *Strange Multiplicity: Constitutionalism in an Age of Diversity* (Cambridge: Cambridge University Press, 1995), 24, quoted in Kirsty Gover, 'Legal Pluralism & Indigenous Legal Traditions', 859.

another – that other being another way of seeing the world'.[21] This volume does not explore how such aspirations might be turned into political and institutional realities.

From the beginning, as editors, we realised that a single volume *Cambridge Legal History of Australia* was an enormously – some might say, impossibly – ambitious project. Our volume aims to give Indigenous law and legal culture a larger part in the legal history of Australia than it is typically allocated. It aims to be self-consciously pluralistic, examining the intertwined lives of First Law, English law, settler law and, to a lesser but significant extent, US constitutional law (particularly relevant to the chapters contributed by Brendan Lim and Cheryl Saunders) and international law (particularly relevant to the contributions of Miranda Johnson and Cait Storr, and Coel Kirkby). It encourages lawyers to think more carefully about how they understand and use history, and historians to appreciate the centrality of law to social, economic and political history. It aspires to stimulate and encourage new methods of legal-historical study. It will be obvious to the close reader that many, significant areas of law are not covered in this volume. We have made no attempt to be 'comprehensive'. We are extremely grateful to all our authors for responding so fruitfully to our methodological and intellectual demands. In doing so they have, together, produced what we always wanted – a provocation and encouragement to others to think about and do Australian legal history pluralistically, with interdisciplinary sensitivity and with a deep understanding of law and legal institutions as integral to social, economic and political life.

21 Black, *The Land is the Source of Law*, 184.

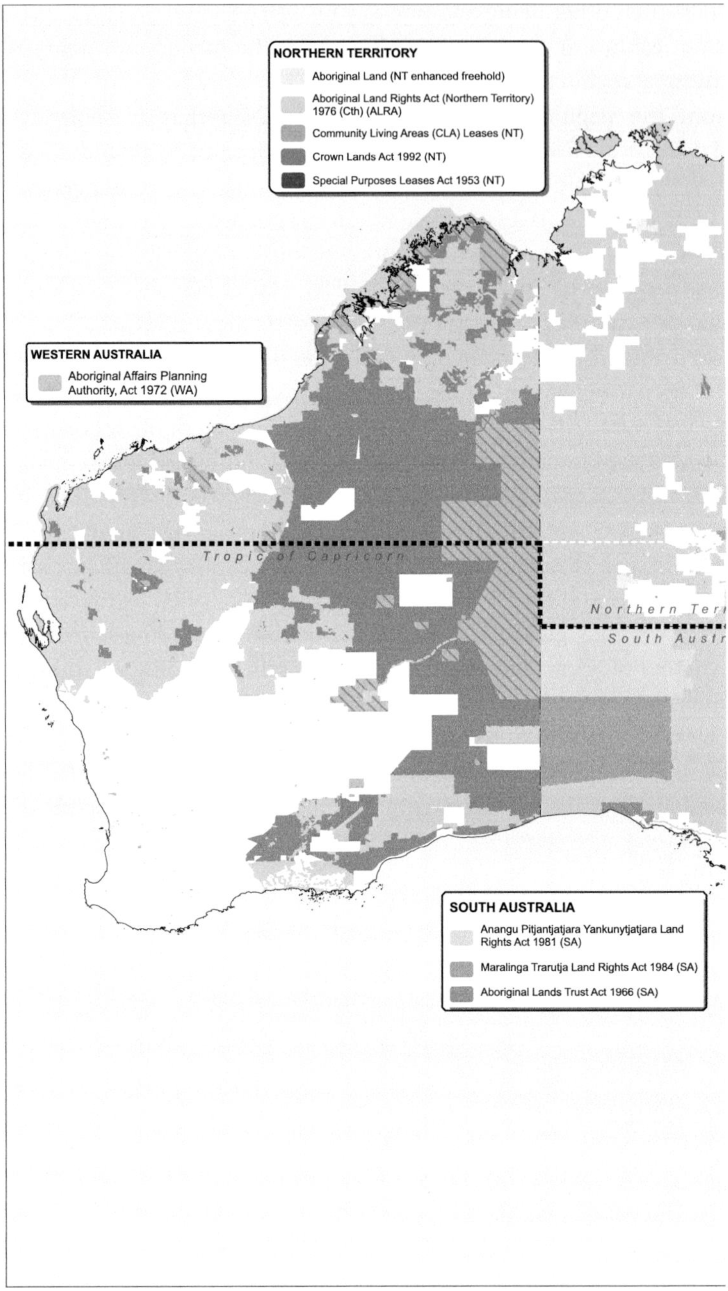

Map 1.1 Indigenous Estates as at 1 January 2021 (For the colour version, please refer to the plate section)

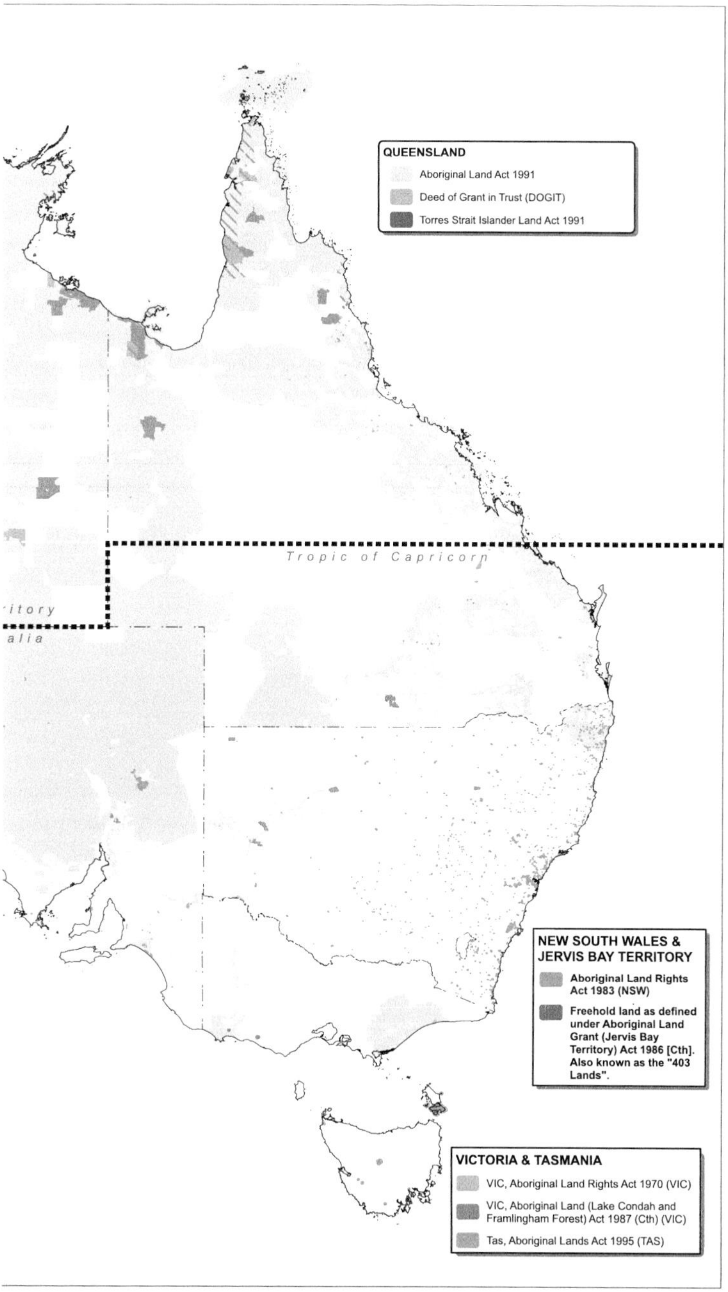
QUEENSLAND
Aboriginal Land Act 1991
Deed of Grant in Trust (DOGIT)
Torres Strait Islander Land Act 1991
Tropic of Capricorn
itory
alia
NEW SOUTH WALES & JERVIS BAY TERRITORY
Aboriginal Land Rights Act 1983 (NSW)
Freehold land as defined under Aboriginal Land Grant (Jervis Bay Territory) Act 1986 [Cth]. Also known as the "403 Lands".
VICTORIA & TASMANIA
VIC, Aboriginal Land Rights Act 1970 (VIC)
VIC, Aboriginal Land (Lake Condah and Framlingham Forest) Act 1987 (Cth) (VIC)
Tas, Aboriginal Lands Act 1995 (TAS)

Map 1.1 (cont.)

I

*

CULTURES OF LAW

2

Plural Legal Orders: Concept and Practice

SHAUNNAGH DORSETT

Introduction

In early 2020 the High Court of Australia handed down its decision in *Love v Commonwealth; Thoms v Commonwealth* ('*Love*').[1] This case concerned the citizenship status of two Aboriginal men. Both were born overseas (Papua New Guinea and New Zealand respectively). Both had lived in Australia most of their lives on Australian residency visas. Neither had taken out Australian citizenship. Each had one parent who was/is both Indigenous and an Australian citizen. Mr Thoms identifies as Gunggari and is a native title holder. Mr Love identifies as Kamilaroi. Both had been convicted of assault charges. Following their release from gaol the Commonwealth cancelled their visas and determined to deport them. Both men resisted. Love and Thoms argued that by virtue of their Aboriginality ('by descent, self-identification and community acceptance') and deep ongoing connection with Country they could not be deported. They could not be considered as 'aliens' (i.e. neither subjects nor citizens) under the *Constitution*. In effect their connection to Country meant that they could not be 'strangers nor foreigners to Australia'.[2] Rather, they argued, they fell into a new category of status: 'non-citizen, non-aliens'.

By a narrow majority, the High Court held that Aboriginal Australians could not be considered 'aliens' and hence could not be deported. The majority based their decisions on a recognition of First Nations' deep connection to Country. For Gordon J the 'fundamental premise from which the decision in *Mabo v Queensland (No. 2)* proceeds – the deeper truth – is that the Indigenous peoples of Australia are the first peoples of this country ...

Many thanks to Rachel Bolton for the invaluable help with research for this chapter and to Shaun McVeigh for the conversations and collaborations over many years, all of which underpin much of the thinking in this chapter.

1 [2020] HCA 3. 2 Summary of arguments by Kiefel CJ, ibid, para [21].

European settlement did not abolish traditional laws and customs . . . Assertion of sovereignty did not sever that connection.'[3] Nevertheless, this finding did not lead Gordon J or the other members of the majority to any recognition of Aboriginal sovereignty or polities or, even, to make any comment on the status or nature of those 'traditional laws and customs'. They were content to recognise the connections to Country within the existing Australian polity and legal framework. For the minority, however, a deeper matter was at stake: to recognise the plaintiffs as 'non-citizen, non-aliens' would be to potentially disrupt the narrative of singular national sovereignty. According to Kiefel CJ if to be a 'non-citizen, non-alien' required a decision by the Elders that a person was Aboriginal and held that status, then to allow this would effectively be to give credence to their laws as determinative, and to therefore attribute to the group 'the kind of sovereignty which was implicitly rejected by *Mabo [No. 2]* . . . and explicitly rejected in subsequent cases'. Gageler J similarly rejected parts of the plaintiffs' 'argument [which] come perilously close to an assertion of Aboriginal and Torres Strait Islander sovereignty'.[4] In the end, all the judgments either skirted around or, more straightforwardly, rejected any recognition of legal plurality.

The history of legal plurality in Australia has not simply been one of the recognition or not of Indigenous jurisdictions.[5] The modern Australian nation is a place of significant plurality, and always has been. Chinese immigrants, arriving in numbers from the mid-nineteenth century, diverse European immigrants and, more latterly, those from the Middle East and beyond, have brought varied traditions, cultures and laws with them. These also raise questions about whether and how we conceptualise and incorporate varying laws within the Australian legal system. The chapter, however, focuses on the relations between Indigenous laws and that law brought with

3 Ibid, para [289] (Gordon J). 4 Ibid, para [25] (Kiefel CJ); Gageler J at para [125].

5 In this chapter the word 'plurality' is preferred to 'pluralism'. The latter is intimately connected with a particular understanding of legal pluralism that emerged from the work of anthropologists and sociologists in the mid-twentieth century. The word 'plurality' and the phrase 'plural legal order' return the language to that of the law. Halliday also argues for the use of 'plurality' rather than 'pluralism'. He similarly locates the history of 'legal pluralism' in that era and scholarship. For Halliday the word 'plurality' better reflects the kind of concrete, granular, highly contextual histories undertaken in recent years by historians, while avoiding specific connections with some of the problems of legal pluralism scholarship, particularly related to the broad, often a-contextual, meaning of 'law' and to a 'bounded' notion of the state: P. Halliday, 'Laws' Histories: Pluralism, Plurality, Diversity', in L. Benton and R. J. Ross (eds), *Legal Pluralism and Empires, 1500–1850* (New York: New York University Press, 2013), 261–77, 268.

the first colonists – the common law. This is because it is the relations between these laws which has been an ongoing matter of contestation across the period of white colonisation and which continues to provide the clearest lens through which to examine how legal plurality has been conceptualised, practised and contained (or not) as a matter of law and of history.[6] Over the period since first white settlement, courts and law-makers have struggled to articulate the relations between Indigenous laws and settler law. Despite initial attempts to do so in the first part of the nineteenth century, much of Australia's legal history has been characterised by either, at best, attempts to contain Indigenous jurisdictions or, at worst, a simple denial of their existence and force.

In the twenty-first century the gap between the ongoing narrative of a singular national law under singular sovereignty, and the reality of continuing Indigenous legal orders, has become increasingly difficult to maintain. Moreover, the legal story of our origins and of that singular law is becoming ever less tenable in the face of detailed and careful histories of (legal) engagement between Indigenous and settler laws. It is primarily the 'problem' of the containment of Indigenous laws which has continued to pressure the modern vision of singular sovereignty and singular law which courts still insist underpins the Australian polity. The concern of all the judges in *Love* – in stepping around or directly engaging with sovereignty – is testament to this. It is in the continued care to reinscribe the sole sovereignty (and hence jurisdiction) of the Commonwealth of Australia that we find the displacement or obfuscation of Indigenous jurisdictions and hence of plural legal orders.

This chapter considers how we have approached legal plurality through the specific lens of thinking with jurisdiction – conceptually and practically. Jurisdiction is one of the persistent technologies of law, and hence of colonial governance, which have worked to displace or obscure First Nations laws. Underneath the legal regime established by the assertion of sovereignty by the British a raft of other laws continued. The chapter opens by explaining why jurisdiction is the lens through which this chapter examines that plurality; it considers the shift in the mid-nineteenth century to thinking not of jurisdiction but of 'customary laws' and the problems of containing those laws; and finishes with an examination of the movement back to jurisdiction in the twenty-first century and the increasing divide between the way in

6 The word 'contained' is adopted from Halliday, 'Laws' Histories: Pluralism, Plurality, Diversity', 267.

which courts think about plurality and the careful histories of plurality being undertaken by historians. Throughout, the chapter points to the ongoing problems posed to any recognition of plural legal orders by the constant re-inscription of a particular construct of singular sovereignty and territorial jurisdiction.

Plurality in the Nineteenth Century: Taking Jurisdiction

In 1788 the Australian continent was a place of diverse legal plurality. This was so in a number of ways. First, there were hundreds of language groups and Indigenous nations, each with their own laws and with their own ways of organising relations between those laws. Second, New South Wales may have been the newest colony in the Empire, but in becoming part of the British Empire it became part of an Empire itself characterised by considerable legal diversity. Moreover, the Colonial Office was familiar and, more importantly, comfortable with legal plurality in colonies (including Indigenous plurality). Third, those who arrived with the First Fleet brought with them their law – in particular the common law – from England, a place which at the time was itself one of diverse legal plurality. As Tamahana puts it 'legal pluralism . . . is a common historical condition'.[7] As are plural legal orders. Thus, laws and legal traditions, both local and from across the globe, met in the new place of the colony of New South Wales. As Douglas and Finnane have noted, while European settlement may have commenced in 1788, the story of the assertion of jurisdiction over Indigenous Australians was a predominantly nineteenth-century story.[8]

Yet for many years legal histories of Australia supposed the opposite. It was assumed that British law (and in particular the English common law) was the only law of the colony; Indigenous peoples had no laws recognisable as such. Histories of New South Wales were rarely situated within the broader frame of the British Empire, let alone as part of a global history of encounter. Even if it was conceded that Australia's First Nations had laws recognisable as such to the British at European colonisation, the legal orthodoxy for many years was that they were long gone, extinguished – along with any rights to land – by the forces of that colonisation. Rather, the

7 B. Z. Tamahana, 'Understanding Legal Pluralism: Past to Present, Local to Global' *Sydney Law Review* 30 (2008): 375–411, 376.

8 H. Douglas and M. Finnane, *Indigenous Crime and Settler Law: White Sovereignty after Empire* (Basingstoke: Palgrave Macmillan, 2012).

Australian continent was, so the story went, one of no law, into which the common law arrived and became the only law of the land, and in which Britain's sovereignty was uninterrupted.

Thinking with Jurisdiction

In 1998 Bruce Kercher's Colonial Case Law Project reintroduced scholars to long-forgotten decisions of early courts concerning the status of Aboriginal Australians and their amenability to the common law.[9] As Kercher revealed, over a twenty year period the courts in New South Wales heard a number of cases, all involving crime, in which the court considered whether or not Indigenous Australians could be tried at common law. The re-discovery of these decisions came at an opportune moment. Just a few years before, the High Court of Australia had, in *Mabo v Queensland (No. 2)* (*'Mabo (No. 2)'*), finally recognised that a form of enforceable rights to land, vested in Indigenous Australians, and to be known as native title, had survived the annexation of New South Wales by Great Britain.[10] However, in *Mabo (No. 2)*, Brennan J also held that on acquisition of sovereignty the common law had become the law of the new colony and of all within it. While native title rights might have survived annexation (or to put it another way, not been extinguished) the Court made it clear that this was really an exception. It did not purport to suggest that Indigenous laws generally should be recognised.

The decision in *Mabo (No. 2)* was critical in three ways for recent scholarship on legal plurality. First, although the High Court of Australia did recognise that enforceable native title rights had survived annexation, it did so in a way which stepped around any recognition of Indigenous sovereignty or laws more broadly. In so doing, *Mabo (No. 2)* not only reinforced the orthodox account of our legal origins, but more deeply embedded it. Second, the story of the legal origins of New South Wales in *Mabo (No. 2)* caused historians to pause. Was the orthodoxy of *Mabo (No. 2)* really an account which reflected our origins? Did it really accord with the practices of law in the early colony? These issues, and indeed the early cases presented by Kercher, had been considered before, but the confluence of the decision in *Mabo (No. 2)* and Kercher's presentation of new material on these cases gave new impetus to legal historians to revisit

9 B. Kercher, 'R v Ballard, R v Murrell, R v Bonjon' *Australian Indigenous Law Reporter* 3, no. 3 (1998): 410–25; B. Kercher, 'Recognition of Indigenous Legal Autonomy in Nineteenth Century New South Wales' *Indigenous Law Bulletin* 4, no. 13 (1998): 7–9.

10 (1992) 175 CLR 1.

the early colonial period.[11] Third, for many, this confluence reoriented the frame through which legal historians considered the relations between peoples and laws in the colonies. It did so through a returning of questions of legal plurality to a traditional language and technology of the common law: jurisdiction.

In the late 1990s and 2000s a variety of scholarship brought jurisdictional thinking to the fore. Rush returned us to the language of jurisdiction in *Mabo* and *Wik* even before Kercher's discoveries; McHugh discussed jurisdiction in the early period in a comparative context in *Aboriginal Societies and the Common Law*. Dorsett, and Dorsett and McVeigh, re-connected the questions of jurisdiction and sovereignty in different historical periods with contemporary native title cases. Ford's work carefully unpacked the colonial period in New South Wales and Georgia and introduced the language of jurisdiction to a new generation of historians. Her *Settler Sovereignty* brought to the fore the importance of the assertion by colonial administrators and judges of jurisdiction over *inter se* crime to the project of sovereignty formation in the Australian colonies. Douglas and Finnane added a careful examination of jurisdiction and sovereignty in the later period through a consideration of criminal law and colonial violence.[12] Kombumerri / Munaljahlai jurisprudent Christine Black reminded us that Indigenous laws are laws of relationships.[13] At the same time, world historian Lauren Benton introduced the idea of 'jurisdictional politics' in her key work *Law and Colonial Cultures*.[14] Benton

11 S. Davies, 'Aborigines, Murder and the Criminal Law in Early Port Phillip, 1841–1851' *Historical Studies* 22 (1987): 313–35; B. Bridges, 'The Extension of English Law to the Aborigines for Offences Committed Inter Se, 1829–1842' *Journal of the Royal Australian Historical Society* 59 (1973): 264–69; S. Cooke, 'Arguments for the Survival of Aboriginal Customary Law in Victoria: A Casenote on R v. Peter (1860) and R. v. Jemmy (1860)' *Australian Journal of Legal History* 5 (1999): 201–41; H. Reynolds, *Aboriginal Sovereignty: Three Nations, One Australia?* (Sydney: Allen and Unwin, 1996), 70–1.

12 P. Rush, 'An Altered Jurisdiction: Corporeal Traces of Law' *Griffith Law Review* 6 (1997): 144–68; S. Dorsett, 'Since Time Immemorial: Jurisdiction, Native Title and the Case of Tanistry' *Melbourne University Law Review* 26 (2002): 32–59; P. McHugh, *Aboriginal Societies and the Common Law: A History of Sovereignty, Status, and Self-Determination* (Oxford: Oxford University Press, 2004); S. Dorsett and S. McVeigh, 'Just So: "The Law Which Governs Australia is Australian Law"' *Law and Critique* 13 (2002): 289–309; S. Dorsett and S. McVeigh, *Jurisdiction* (London: Routledge, 2012); L. Ford, *Settler Sovereignty: Jurisdiction and Indigenous People in America and Australia, 1788–1836* (Cambridge, MA: Harvard University Press, 2010); Douglas and Finnane, *Indigenous Crime and Settler Law*.

13 C. Black, *The Land is the Source of the Law: A Dialogic Encounter with Indigenous Jurisprudence* (London: Routledge, 2010), 184.

14 L. Benton, *Law and Colonial Cultures: Legal Regimes in World History, 1400–1900* (Cambridge: Cambridge University Press, 2001). While this work introduced the term to many scholars it was not the first or only use of the term by Benton. See, for example, L. Benton, 'Making Order Out of Trouble: Jurisdictional Politics in the

described the ways in which, in the early modern period (and beyond), 'jurisdictional jockeying' of imperial legal orders provided rhetorical and legal strategies through which actors could position themselves, in various ways, in and against these orders. She described how jurisdictional regimes were never static and how conflicts between them changed jurisdictional boundaries. This fluidity, and the conflicts it could engender, were productive of different legal orders. Each scholar, through slightly different frameworks, and responding to slightly different concerns, reoriented or returned matters of plurality and plural legal orders to the first question of law: that of jurisdiction.

Early Cases

Prior to Kercher's recovery of early New South Wales court decisions, our understanding of the early period had been dominated by the decision of the Supreme Court of New South Wales in 1836 in *R v Murrell* (*'Murrell'*).[15] *Murrell* was the case best remembered from the early period, mainly because it had been published in a series of nominate reports by Legge, although not until 1896.[16] When Kercher uncovered the early decisions of *R v Ballard* (*'Ballard'*) and *R v Boatman* (*'Boatman'*) he also published new versions of the decision in *Murrell*, based on a wider range of sources.[17] This did not change what we understood the outcomes of the case to have been, but these newer accounts were more nuanced and detailed, and provided more grist for historians' mills.

In *Ballard*, the Attorney General sought the direction of the Supreme Court as to whether an Aboriginal person could be prosecuted for the murder of another Aboriginal person, 'both having been in a savage state at the time of the transaction in question'.[18] Ballard had allegedly killed another Aboriginal man called Borrondire, or Dirty Dick, near the Domain, not far from Sydney. While Indigenous Australians had been prosecuted in the years prior to this case, this was the first prosecution of an Indigenous defendant for the murder of another Indigenous person. The previous cases (few though they were) were not *inter se* and had involved at least one European. In those decisions, the Court was of the

Spanish Colonial Borderlands' *Law and Social Inquiry* 26 (2001): 373–401 and, more latterly, L. Benton, *A Search for Sovereignty: Law and Geography in European Empires, 1400–1800* (Cambridge: Cambridge University Press, 2010).

15 (1836) 1 Legge 72 (*'Murrell'*). 16 Ibid.

17 *R v Ballard* [1829] NSWSupC 26 (*'Ballard'*); *R v Boatman* [1832] NSWSupC 4 (*'Boatman'*); *R v Murrell and Bummaree* [1836] NSWSupC 35.

18 *Ballard*, unpaginated.

opinion that the common law applied.[19] Some three years later, the same question again came before the Court, in the case of *R v Boatman*. In both *Ballard* and *Boatman*, the Court took the same approach to the matter: that the prisoner ought to be discharged for want of jurisdiction. That the matter was one of jurisdiction was clear to the Court in both cases. In *Boatman*, Dowling J commenced by asking counsel 'if he renewed his objection to the jurisdiction of the court in this case?' When Counsel indicated that he did because it was 'in his opinion, a most important question, whether the aboriginal natives were subject to our laws', Dowling J responded that 'the regular course of proceedings was to plead to the jurisdiction'.[20]

Ballard and *Boatman* were decided in an early period, not just in the history of New South Wales, but in terms of global jurisprudence on the subject. The New South Wales Supreme Court had little guidance on the matter. Even had they been decided, cases such as those of the United States Supreme Court in *Cherokee Nation* would not yet have been available in New South Wales.[21] Very few colonies in North America, for example, claimed jurisdiction over Indigenous peoples, and certainly not with any consistency.[22] Forbes CJ noted in *Ballard* that this 'is a case sui generis, and the Court must deal with it upon general principles, in the absence of any fixed known rule upon the subject'.[23] That the matter was one of jurisdiction, then, was hardly surprising. The English common law had always existed alongside a multiplicity of other jurisdictions and their courts: not just the well-known courts of Chancery, Admiralty or Ecclesiastical but a myriad of others – feudal courts such as manorial courts, borough courts in towns, palatinate courts and topically specific courts such as the stannary courts, which regulated tin mining in Cornwall, and the courts of the forest. At the time of the annexation of the colony of New South Wales, the jurisdiction of the common law had achieved considerable dominance in England, but it is often forgotten that many of these other jurisdictions continued to function well into the nineteenth century. In the late eighteenth century there were still hundreds of local courts and, as Arthurs

19 *R v Lowe* [1827] NSWKR 4; *R v Tibbs* [1824] TasSupC 1. See also *R v Mow-watty* [1816] NSWKR 2. On this see L. Ford and B. Salter, 'From Pluralism to Territorial Sovereignty: The 1816 Trial of Mow-watty in the Superior Court of New South Wales' *Indigenous Law Journal* 7 (2008): 69–86.

20 *Boatman*, unpaginated. See also McHugh, *Aboriginal Societies*, 161; Ford, *Settler Sovereignty*.

21 *Cherokee Nation v Georgia*, 30 U.S. (5 Pet.) 1 (1831).

22 See Ford, *Settler Sovereignty*.

23 *Ballard*, unpaginated.

reminds us, altogether these bodies disposed of many more cases than the central Westminster courts.[24] England was a place of plural laws.

Plurality of laws, and the contestations between them, were, therefore, familiar territory for the legal fraternity in the late eighteenth and early nineteenth centuries. It is hardly surprising, then, that in considering the meeting of laws in the new colony of New South Wales, the judges simply reiterated the same questions as characterised practice in England: did the common law have jurisdiction, or did that more properly belong to another law? This, of course, raised questions about the nature of Aboriginal laws. If there were no other 'law' then the common law properly had jurisdiction. This matter proved difficult for the early judges. Aboriginal laws were clearly so foreign that they could not be said to be 'laws' within the understandings of English trained judges. But neither did they believe that they had an automatic right to intrude on the 'customs and habits' of other peoples. As Forbes CJ noted in *Ballard*:

> It is known as a matter of experience that the savages of this part of the globe, have a mode of dressing [sic] wrongs committed amongst themselves, which is perfectly agreeable to their own natures & dispositions, and is productive, amongst themselves, of as much good, as any novel or strange institution which might be imparted to them.[25]

If relations between laws, and hence legal plurality, is thought of as a question of jurisdiction, how do we define jurisdiction? In modern law we tend to think of jurisdiction as being a simple matter of procedure – in which court, for example, should I commence my action? The answer to this might simply be a prosaic matter of determining the monetary limit of the particular court. But engaging jurisdiction is more meaningful than simply bringing something within the business of that court. Jurisdiction is key to the ordering of law (and laws). Jurisdiction is about the authority of law: it is about who or what speaks in the name of the law. For the common law, the key site from which the law has always spoken is the courts. Thus, for a court to declare that it has jurisdiction has the effect of bringing someone or something to the law administered by that court. It binds those persons or things to that law.[26] For the courts in *Ballard* and *Boatman* to declare they did not have jurisdiction was to say that the matter did not belong to the common law: it more

24 See generally, H. Arthurs, 'Special Courts, Special Law: Legal Pluralism in Nineteenth Century England', in G. Rubin and D. Sugarman (eds), *Law, Economy and Society: 1750–1914: Essays in the History of English Law* (Abingdon: Professional Books, 1984).

25 *Ballard*, unpaginated.

26 Dorsett and McVeigh, *Jurisdiction*.

properly belonged to another law (regardless of how they viewed that law as somehow less 'civilised' than that of the colonisers).

Boatman and *Ballard* demonstrate another important matter about jurisdiction and plurality. In both cases the dominant modality through which jurisdiction was conceived was that of personal jurisdiction. For the court, the colonisers brought the common law with them, as their personal law and the laws of the First Nations remained personal to First Nations peoples. It was only when these laws met that issues arose of how to manage legal encounter. A system based predominantly on personal jurisdiction clearly makes plurality easier to observe: there are multiple bodies of law. A shift to another mode – that of territorial jurisdiction – does not necessarily result in a loss of plurality, but it can make that plurality harder to see.

This shift in mode of jurisdiction is most clearly seen in the 1836 decision in *Murrell*. When Jack Congo Murrell was charged with the murder of another Aboriginal man, Bill Jabbingee (or Jabingi, or Jabenguy), his counsel pleaded that the court had no jurisdiction to try the matter. Unlike in *Ballard* and *Boatman*, the argument was not successful. Burton J delivered the judgment of the court. Burton was of the opinion that most of the eastern half of the Australian continent was in the actual possession of the Crown and therefore that as the 'English Nation has obtained and exercised for many years the rights of Domain and Empire over the country thus possessed . . . the law of England is the law of the land'.[27] This left no room for another law. Thus, in enacting the Australian Courts Act 1828 (Imp), the British Parliament had, as an act of sovereignty, he maintained, asserted jurisdiction over a defined area with respect to a range of matters which included crime. *Murrell* therefore signalled an important shift – from a mode predominantly of personal jurisdiction to a preferred mode of territorial jurisdiction. Importantly for subsequent developments, the judgment also assumed that territorial jurisdiction followed the acquisition of sovereignty.[28] That *Murrell* would take this path was not a foregone conclusion. In other parts of the British Empire, imperial and local administrators had recognised that plural jurisdictions, including those of the Indigenous inhabitants, were compatible with British sovereignty. India and New Zealand are examples.[29] What set Australia apart

27 *Murrell*, unpaginated.

28 A similar conclusion was reached by the Court of Civil Jurisdiction in Western Australia in *R v We-war* [1842] WASupC 7, sourced from *The Perth Gazette and Western Australian Journal*, 8 January 1842, 2–3, although that court did not often choose to exercise its jurisdiction over crime *inter se*.

29 S. Dorsett, *Juridical Encounters: Maori and the Colonial Courts, 1840–1852* (Auckland: Auckland University Press, 2017).

was the view of Burton J (and others, including the Colonial Office) that Indigenous Australians were lower on the scale of civilisation compared to their counterparts in other places in the Empire. For jurisdictional purposes, therefore, there was no other relevant law. Thus, in one movement, Burton J both instituted the common law as the only law of the territory and inscribed a model of singular sovereignty.

None of this meant that plurality somehow went away. The decision in *Murrell*, that Aboriginal Australians were amenable to the common law, did not mean that Indigenous laws ceased to exist or, to use more modern terminology, were extinguished. Burton J's decision had nothing to say (and nor could it have) about the continuance of laws within other jurisdictions; it simply meant that the common law would not recognise them. There is little doubt that the effects of colonisation on Indigenous culture and laws was drastic, but the damage done does not mean that Indigenous jurisdictions did not in many places survive, even if compromised. As Noel Pearson once put it, for Indigenous Australians their law is simply a 'social reality'.[30] Nor did the decision in *Murrell* mean that challenges to the jurisdiction of the common law courts suddenly ended. But they waned and eventually more or less ceased.[31] From the point of view of settler law, therefore, the effect of *Murrell* was to obscure Indigenous jurisdictions – not to extinguish them, but to remove them from easy (legal) sight. The construct of territorial jurisdiction made it hard to see a law other than the common law, while the shift to sovereignty rather than jurisdiction as the predominant idiom through which to consider Indigenous claims made it more difficult to find a language through which to articulate legal encounter. As the century wore on, courts found it increasingly difficult to think with jurisdiction without also assuming a co-extensive sovereignty. It is this elision which has proven so problematic for legal plurality.

Containing Plurality

The demise of challenges to the jurisdiction of the courts did not end questions about plurality; nor did it end plural practices. It did, however, change the terms of jurisdictional engagement. From the mid-nineteenth

30 N. Pearson, 'The Concept of Native Title at Common Law' *Australian Humanities Review* 5 (1997), online at www.australianhumanitiesreview.org/1997/03/01/the-concept-of-native-title-at-common-law/, accessed 23 November 2021.

31 See, for example, *R v Jemmy* (1860); *R v Peter* (1860), both in Cooke 'Arguments for the Survival of Aboriginal Customary Law in Victoria'.

century until well into the twentieth century the most significant way we thought about legal relations between laws was through the accommodation of 'customary law'. The use of the term 'customary law' was clearly pejorative – while anthropologists acknowledged the continued existence of tribal laws and ways of life (they could hardly do other as it was clear that Indigenous practices were alive and well across country) that acknowledgment did not mean that, for most, 'customary laws' were considered to have the same status as the Australian common law or that this acknowledgment included the idea that these practices amounted to, or flowed from, legally autonomous Aboriginal jurisdictions.

Customary Law

From the mid-nineteenth century, across many parts of the north of Western Australia, the northern parts of Queensland and the Northern Territory in particular, it was clear that the assertion of jurisdiction over crime was in itself not sufficient to manage high levels of inter-racial conflict. From the 1840s onwards, particularly in Western Australia, an increasingly interventionist approach was taken towards dealing with Aboriginal offenders. Having established jurisdiction over Indigenous offenders, including over *inter se* crime, some states, such as Western Australia, took the opportunity to fashion regimes for managing this crime. In 1849, for example, Western Australia introduced summary jurisdiction regimes for dealing with Aboriginal offenders.[32] As Douglas and Finnane relate, one way in which 'custom' emerged as important as the nineteenth century progressed was as a factor mitigating culpability for crime. By the late part of the century it was accepted in Western Australia, for example, that Indigenous custom was a reason for mitigating punishment, most commonly in the form of commuting death sentences, particularly in *inter se* cases.[33] This recognition was, of course, a further example of exercising jurisdiction over Indigenous offenders in *inter se* matters. Allowances for custom were made at the discretion of the state legal system and its administrators. As Douglas and Finnane further relate, the content of the custom was not particularly relevant; a reference to custom sufficed as a mitigating factor.

In other places, the extent to which custom was taken into account depended on how far Aboriginal crime intruded into settler space. In

32 Douglas and Finnane, *Indigenous Crime and Settler Law*, 78–9. See An Ordinance to Provide for the Summary Trial and Punishment of Aboriginal Native Offenders in Certain Cases 1849 (WA).

33 Douglas and Finnane, *Indigenous Crime and Settler Law*, 80–1.

Queensland, the greater the intrusion the 'less interest there was in identifying some customary force as impelling Aboriginal actions'. Douglas and Finnane suggest that South-east Queensland, for example, 'still hosted spaces of shared jurisdiction and different custom'. And that '[c]riminal cases may be seen as the places where those competing jurisdictions and ways of life were brought into uneasy confrontation'.[34] Importantly, however, the decision of settler authorities to prosecute or not, or to take into account jury suggestions of leniency was determined by colonial authorities. Whatever recognition was given to custom, however perfunctory, was, in an era when sovereignty and jurisdiction were largely uncontested, a matter for the colonisers. Nevertheless, the ways in which Aboriginal peoples across Australia experienced the exercise of jurisdiction varied significantly as did the effect of the exercise of that jurisdiction on Aboriginal laws.

As Halliday has noted, the late nineteenth century was a time of containment of plurality.[35] In many diverse locations around the Empire, early legal recognition of Indigenous jurisdictions had fallen away. As McHugh relates, in the 'settler' colonies, Aboriginal societies were increasingly 'contained within specific statutory regimes' as policies of protection and assimilation were increasingly imposed.[36] McHugh charts the rise, particularly post-Federation, of statutory regimes applying to Indigenous Australians. As he outlines, these statutory regimes regulated Indigenous lives, but did not acknowledge any collective form of Aboriginal organisation. This was not surprising, given the low view most administrators held of the levels of 'civilisation' of First Nations peoples in Australia.[37] Such views, of course, ensured that the second half of the nineteenth century and first half of the twentieth remained not only an era in which little or no evidence of thinking about legal plurality could be seen in legal policy-making, but in which 'customary law' was generally suppressed, left to the arena of sentencing law.

In the 1970s, debates over legal pluralism intersected with renewed engagement with 'customary law'. As Douglas and Finnane note, positive political support for 'land rights and (limited) self-determination was the context for the emergence of customary law as a governmental object,

34 Ibid, 83. 35 Halliday, 'Laws' Histories: Pluralism, Plurality, Diversity', 267.

36 McHugh, *Aboriginal Societies and the Common Law*, 215; A. Nettelbeck, *Indigenous Rights and Colonial Subjecthood: Protection and Reform in the 19th Century British Empire* (Cambridge: Cambridge University Press, 2019).

37 McHugh, *Aboriginal Societies and the Common Law*, 277. For a detailed picture of this period see Douglas and Finnane, *Indigenous Crime and Settler Law*.

a possible sphere of recognition'.[38] One of the most significant institutional responses to this re-engagement was the 1986 Report of the Australian Law Reform Commission (ALRC) into the 'Recognition of Aboriginal Customary Laws'. Although many of its recommendations were never implemented, the Report continued to be influential for several decades, and to provide a point of engagement for scholars from a variety of disciplines. As suggested by the title, the remit of the ALRC was to consider whether it was desirable to 'apply Aboriginal customary law to Indigenous people, generally or in particular areas or to those living in tribal communities only'.[39]

If legal pluralists at the time contested how we might understand 'law', the ALRC was largely content to assume that it was unnecessary to define it, simply stating that while Indigenous laws differed across the continent, 'some basic generalisations can be made. In particular, it can be said that mechanisms for the maintenance of order and resolution of disputes, that is, a system of law, existed within Aboriginal groups.'[40] Moreover, extensive public hearings, often undertaken in remote communities, confirmed for the Commissioners that 'there are many indications that Aboriginal customary laws and traditions continue as a real controlling force in the lives of many Aborigines'.[41] The ALRC further pointed to the first land rights case, the 1971 decision in *Milirrpum v Nabalco*, and the judgment of Blackburn J, as authority for the premise that 'customary law' and 'law' were to be understood broadly and that the institutions and traditions of the Aboriginal plaintiffs indeed amounted to a system of law.[42] This was not the view of all contributors. The well-known anthropologist T. G. H. Strehlow told the ALRC that '"[t]rue tribal law" is probably dead everywhere. It could not change, for there were no aboriginal agencies that had the power to change any of the traditional norms'.[43] What was left, it seemed, for Strelow, was some kind of synthetic law. This was a view rejected by many who gave evidence to the ALRC and which would be unlikely to find favour now.

38 Douglas and Finnane, *Indigenous Crime and Settler Law*, 4–5, citing J. M. D. Kirby, 'TGH Strehlow and Aboriginal Customary Laws' *Adelaide Law Review* 7 (1980): 172–99.

39 Australian Law Reform Commission, *Recognition of Aboriginal Customary Laws* (ALRC Report 31, 1986), online at www.alrc.gov.au/publication/recognition-of-aboriginal-customary-laws-alrc-report-31/terms-of-reference-2/, accessed 23 November 2021, Terms of Reference.

40 Ibid, para [37].

41 Ibid, paras [38] and [100].

42 Ibid, para [102] citing *Milirrpum v Nabalco Pty Ltd* (1971) 17 FLR 141, 266–8 (Blackburn J).

43 Ibid, para [119].

The ALRC recommended that customary laws be recognised: because it in turn recognised the reality of Indigenous lives lived according to their laws; because of the inherent justice of doing so; and because it mattered to those whose laws had been long denied.[44] In the end, however, while the ALRC Report was broad and suggested significant change, few recommendations were instituted. The Report suggested a number of ways in which recognition could occur: by incorporation of specific customary laws into the general law in some form; by allowing Indigenous Australians to live according to their own laws, unless a matter is specifically excluded; by recognition as accommodation (e.g. in sentencing); or by codification of customary law.[45] Each of these, of course, suggests a different scope for the accommodation or recognition of (in the ALRC's terms) 'customary laws', and hence different degrees of legal plurality. All, however, remind us that the degree to which legal plurality is acknowledged, accommodated, recognised or given space in which to operate remains a matter within the jurisdiction of the state and is shaped by that jurisdiction.

Reinscribing Sovereignty

In the second half of the twentieth century Indigenous plaintiffs again began to challenge the jurisdiction of the courts and to argue that they were not amenable to the common law. Rather, plaintiffs argued, they should be subject to their own laws. While not phrased in quite the same manner, these challenges were essentially the same as those in the early cases of *Ballard*, *Boatman* and *Murrell*. The same technique is evident: an argument for denial of jurisdiction based on there being 'another law'. Only one of these cases, the decision of Rath J, in *R v Wedge*, referred to *Murrell*. Rath J dismissed an argument that Wedge was not subject to the jurisdiction of the New South Wales Supreme Court on a charge of murder. Not only did Rath J find the arguments in *Murrell* convincing, but he also saw the challenge to jurisdiction as a challenge to the authority of the Supreme Court of New South Wales, and the body of law it administers – the Australian common law.[46]

What is arguably the most important decision on jurisdiction and sovereignty was not, however, about criminal law. Rather, it concerned land. As previously noted, in 1992, in *Mabo (No. 2)*, the High Court of Australia determined that enforceable rights to land, to be known as native title, had survived the annexation of the Australian continent by Great Britain. That

44 Ibid, para [127]. 45 Ibid, paras [198]–[208]. 46 *R v Wedge* [1976] 1 NSWLR 581, 586–7.

case laid down the rules for recognition of native title and for its extinguishment. The finding that native title existed, however, did not result in any concurrent recognition of legal plurality. Quite the opposite. The trick for the judges was to craft a decision which recognised native title, but did so in a way which allowed no cracks in the construct of singular sovereignty of the Australian nation. Thus, sovereignty – and a particular model of sovereignty – lay at the heart of the case.

At the outset, the Court made it clear that sovereignty was non-justiciable: in other words that it did not have the power to reconsider any matters relating to the lawfulness of Britain's acquisition of sovereignty. However, while it could not question this, the consequences of that acquisition of sovereignty were within the remit of the Court and the judgment was structured around these consequences. According to the Court, all rights to land – both Indigenous and non-Indigenous – flow from the moment of assertion of sovereignty. Most pertinently, at the moment of acquisition of sovereignty the imported common law became the law of the territory, not just the personal law of the colonists, but of all, including First Nations. The description of sovereignty offered by the High Court, and by Brennan J in particular, was similar to that in *Murrell* and was that which is now considered the orthodox account: sovereignty (and hence jurisdiction) is co-extensive with the modern state, and indivisible – the entire power of the state has to be vested in a single locus, a centralised legal authority. This left no room for any recognition of First Nations sovereignty or, it seems, law.

While sovereignty lay at the heart of the decision in *Mabo*, the case is not conducted through the language of jurisdiction. This was a consequence of determining that the common law became the law of the territory. For the High Court singular sovereignty equated to singular law. There was, therefore, no need to consider the jurisdictional relations between laws. Despite the absence of the language of jurisdiction, as noted, one result of the decision in *Mabo* was a resurgence in thinking about and with jurisdiction. This resurgence was not just evident in the work of scholars. In the years immediately following *Mabo* a number of cases were brought challenging the jurisdiction of Australian law. In each case those challenges were not only dismissed, but the High Court was quick to reiterate its particular model of singular sovereignty and co-extensive territorial jurisdiction. *Walker v New South Wales*, for example, concerned an application by summons to dismiss a statement of claim by which Walker, a member of the Noonuccal Nation, claimed that his actions should be governed by customary Aboriginal criminal law, rather than Australian criminal law. Hearing the application at first instance, Mason CJ dismissed any suggestion that customary criminal law survived either English 'settlement' or the introduction of the general provisions of English criminal law. Specifically, he noted that 'English criminal law did not, and Australian criminal law does not, accommodate an alternative body of law operating alongside it'.[47] Thus, while, across the nineteenth and twentieth centuries, courts had commonly referred to customary law, at least for mitigation of sentences, it was clear that that law held no real juridical status for the courts. Rather, the relations between laws could, at best, be understood as adjectival. In other words, where the settler courts exercised jurisdiction over crime, any reference to custom simply described it as a matter of evidential fact, rather than giving it any recognition as an autonomous body, or autonomous bodies, of law.

What was begun in *Mabo (No. 2)* was entrenched a decade later in *Members of the Yorta Yorta Community v Victoria* ('*Yorta Yorta*').[48] As in *Mabo (No. 2)*, in *Yorta Yorta* sovereignty was the linchpin of the court's reasoning. In that case, concerns to delimit the power of Indigenous laws vis-à-vis the colonising power led to the re-inscription of singular national sovereignty and an emphatic denial of legal pluralism in the Australian legal system. *Yorta Yorta* concerned an application for native title over an area which straddled the New South Wales/Victorian border. For the majority in the case, the key point of departure was again the assertion of sovereignty by Great Britain. This was so for two reasons. First, native title is evidentially based on those customs and traditions of the claimant which existed at sovereignty and which survived the change in legal regime and which continue to be practised.[49] Second, although there were multiple normative systems at sovereignty – Indigenous and non-Indigenous – thereafter one must be dominant. The logic of state sovereignty requires this. Further there can be no 'parallel law-making':

> [u]pon the Crown acquiring sovereignty, the normative or law-making system which then existed could not thereafter validly create new rights, duties or interests. Rights or interests in land created after sovereignty and which owed their origin and continued existence only to a normative system other than that of the new sovereign power, would not and will not be given effect by the legal order of the new sovereign.[50]

47 *Walker v New South Wales* (1994) 182 CLR 45, [6].

48 *Members of the Yorta Yorta Community v Victoria* (2002) 214 CLR 422 ('*Yorta Yorta*').

49 This was prefigured some months earlier in *Western Australia v Ward* (2002) 213 CLR 1 ('*Ward*'), where the majority noted that '[t]he assertion of sovereignty marked the imposition of a new source of authority over the land': 94 (Gleeson CJ, Gaudron, Gummow and Hayne JJ).

50 *Yorta Yorta*, [43].

In *Yorta Yorta* the narrative of sovereignty was presented in stark terms. The assertion of sovereignty by the British Crown 'necessarily entailed' that thereafter there could be 'no parallel law-making system in the territory over which it asserted sovereignty. To hold otherwise would be to deny the acquisition of sovereignty and . . . that is not permissible.'[51] The question never addressed is that of what is the status of Indigenous laws or, as the court puts it, other normative orders, post-British sovereignty? The inevitable conclusion remains that 'customary law' is simply not viewed as law in the way that the common law is. Such a stark conclusion reflected the increased concerns of the High Court in the decade post-*Mabo* to inscribe and control its narrative of singular sovereignty. The majority opinion in *Yorta Yorta* virtually precluded serious curial consideration about how to rethink relations of laws in Australia for almost two decades.

Post-*Yorta Yorta*, therefore, there were two possible ways to imagine legal plurality. The first is that as a result of that decision there is no Indigenous or Aboriginal law as such post-sovereignty, merely a normative system which is less than law, maybe 'custom', in which case no meeting point between laws is possible. Or, second, there are laws, but they run in parallel to the common law, and hence never meet unless a meeting point is built between them.[52] Caught by the original determination in *Mabo* that native title originated in Indigenous laws and customs, not the common law, the High Court was forced to find an intersection between laws: one which remained faithful to *Mabo*, but also to *Yorta Yorta*. The High Court took a hybrid approach – Indigenous custom or norms were denied law-making capacity, but nevertheless native title required a meeting point between Indigenous law and the Australian common law. While once that meeting place might have been the common law itself, the High Court preferred to locate that meeting point in the Native Title Act 1993 (Cth). In both *Western Australia v Ward* and *Yorta Yorta*, the High Court mandated that post the enactment of the Native Title Act '[a]n application for determination of native title requires the location of that intersection [between common law and Indigenous law and custom], and it requires that it be located by reference to the *Native Title Act*'.[53] Over the last almost twenty years the Native Title Act, and in particular

51 S. Dorsett and S. McVeigh, 'An Essay on Jurisdiction, Jurisprudence and Authority: The High Court of Australia in Yorta Yorta' *Northern Ireland Legal Quarterly* 59 (2005): 1–20.

52 This section relies in part on S. Dorsett and S. McVeigh, 'Section 223 and the Shape of Native Title: The Limits of Jurisdictional Thinking', in L. Ford and T. Rowse (eds), *Between Indigenous and Settler Governance* (London: Routledge, 2014), 162–73.

53 *Yorta Yorta*, 439 (Gleeson CJ, Gummow and Hayne JJ); *Ward*, 65–6, 69 (Gleeson CJ, Gaudron, Gummow and Hayne JJ).

Section 223, has provided the intersection between laws. Section 223 defines 'native title' for the purposes of the Act and, therefore, defines what the meeting point can look like and what native title can encompass. The relocation of the intersection from the common law to statute, however, does not change the quality of that meeting: it is still one of jurisdiction and of the jurisdictional practices of the Australian common law. As it defines native title Section 223 functions as a jurisdictional device. As any claim must be for rights and interests that meet the definition in that section, it is the words in Section 223 (and how they have been interpreted by the courts) which ultimately determines what can and what cannot belong to law, in this case to Australian law.[54] To locate the intersection in Section 223 reinscribes the Australian nation as the relevant sovereign body: it is according to Australian law, and specifically that section, that the determination of the character, nature and extent of native title is determined.

Ironically, *Yorta Yorta* was decided at the same moment that historians were increasingly turning to re-examining and reconsidering histories of legal plurality. Just four years after Kercher's publication of *Ballard* and *Boatman* and the same year as Benton placed 'jurisdictional politics' at the centre of imperial legal histories, the decision in *Yorta Yorta* signalled an increasing bifurcation between the history set out in court decisions and the granular, detailed, work of legal historians. At the same time as scholars, such as Kercher and Ford, were uncovering our plural past, the High Court was reinscribing a neat tale of our legal origins which left out the story of the messy, complicated uneven nature of the assertion of jurisdiction and sovereignty over the Australian continent, let alone the continuing reality of Indigenous jurisdictions. This story is predicated on an elision of jurisdiction with sovereignty that has shaped the way we characterise legal relations between laws since *Murrell*. The Court's refusal to acknowledge that there is a meeting of laws – Indigenous and non-Indigenous – does not, of course, mean that there is no meeting. It merely means that it is one that the High Court refuses to acknowledge.

Conclusion

In Australia, relations between laws are conducted through the idiom of sovereignty. The modern model of singular sovereignty, co-extensive with

54 For one history of how this section was interpreted over its first almost twenty years see P. G. McHugh, *Aboriginal Title: The Modern Jurisprudence of Tribal Land Rights* (Oxford: Oxford University Press, 2011).

territorial jurisdiction, works to obscure legal plurality. Legal relations could, as previously mentioned, be organised in other ways. Around the British Empire multiple jurisdictions frequently sat under singular sovereignty and in other places, such as Canada, legal regimes from different traditions – there civil law and common law – work side by side today. Undoubtedly this jurisdictional plurality has also led and continues to lead to difficult questions about how to organise relations between those laws, but it also reminds us of the contingency of the way Australian courts have, since *Murrell*, chosen to inscribe a particular understanding of sovereignty and territorial jurisdiction. Yet, despite continued re-inscription plural legal orders refuse to remain contained. The loss of the language of jurisdiction has left courts with no way of giving a voice to Indigenous legal orders and, it seems, in any case they have no willingness to do so. Moreover, there is an inherent instability built into the High Court's edifice of singular sovereignty. This is amply demonstrated by the decision in *Love*, the case with which this chapter opened. In *Yorta Yorta* the High Court maintained that post-sovereignty there could only be one law-making entity; the Australian common law. This left, as we saw, questions as to how we might understand the juridical nature of First Nations laws, Aboriginal jurisdictions having been largely reduced to an adjectival relationship with Australian law. Yet at the same time, in *Love*, that a decision might need to be made by an elder as to membership of their community was enough to ensure that the three judges in the minority refused the claimant's case because the capacity to make such a decision might imply that they were doing so according to another law. That would amount to a crack in the nation's singular sovereignty. In effect, this constituted a recognition and simultaneous denial of another legal order. By contrast, the majority simply ignored the possibility of plurality. They contained plurality by refusing to acknowledge that any other legal order might be at stake. In some ways the characterisation of sovereignty and consequent legal order in *Mabo (No. 2)* was not surprising. As noted once by Tully, uniformity was a hallmark of the 'liberal promise' of modern constitutionalism in the late twentieth century.[55] What is more surprising, however, is the clinging to that model in the twenty-first century, against the intellectual force of post-colonial consciousness and the persistent calls for reconciliation.

Can we then find a way of thinking about relations between laws that allows us to genuinely reconcile plural legal orders? It seems that this may not be possible without questioning the sole sovereignty of the Australian nation

55 J. Tully, *Strange Multiplicity: Constitutionalism in an Age of Diversity* (Cambridge: Cambridge University Press, 1995).

and the pre-eminence of territorial jurisdiction. It may be that the era prior to *Murrell*, in which modern modes of sovereignty and jurisdiction were not set, remain the closest we will get to achieving that legal plurality. There are, of course, many practical measures that can be taken – the ALRC Report outlined some ways in which Indigenous jurisdictions could, in part at least, be integrated into the Australian legal system. However, without an acknowledgment that sovereignty was never ceded and a commensurate recognition of the force of Indigenous jurisdictions, any mechanisms for such integration will always ultimately remain within the remit and jurisdiction of the state. For the foreseeable future, however, plural legal orders may well continue to be obscured by the ongoing task of containing that plurality. Legal plurality will continue, as in *Love*, to be hidden in the interstices of decisions concerning Indigenous Australians and the legal regimes which support those decisions.

3

English Legal Culture in the Late Eighteenth Century: Institutions and Values

DAVID LIEBERMAN

England's Gothic Castle

David Neal opens his valuable study of law and power during the first decades of British settlement in New South Wales with an intriguing episode. Within months of their arrival in Sydney Harbour in 1788, Henry and Susannah Cable successfully prosecuted a claim for lost property against the captain of the ship that had taken them on the eight-month voyage from Plymouth, England. This was the first civil case held in the new settlement, heard before its Court of Civil Jurisdiction. Like innumerable other English subjects of the period, the Cables turned to the institutions of law to redress their injuries and vindicate their rights, particularly rights of property. Nonetheless, much of their personal story was highly unusual. In legal terms, the success of their claim violated settled common law doctrine. Henry and Susannah Cable were both convicted felons, who had escaped capital sentences on condition of transportation. As a result, they were technically 'already dead in law' and, therefore, incapable of pursuing any claim in a court of English justice.[1]

In addition to much else, the case of the Cables alerts us to the enormous complexity of eighteenth-century England's legal culture and of the ambiguities between its formal institutions and its routine practices. In a revealing passage of his long-influential *Commentaries on the Laws of England*, Sir William Blackstone maintained that in their law, the English 'inherit an old Gothic Castle, erected in the days of chivalry, but fitted up for a modern inhabitant',[2] notwithstanding that its technicality 'is apt at our first

1 David Neal, *The Rule of Law in a Penal Colony* (Cambridge: Cambridge University Press, 1991), 1–7.

2 William Blackstone, *Commentaries on the Laws of England, The Oxford Edition of Blackstone*, general editor Wilfrid Prest (4 volumes, Oxford: Oxford University Press, 2016), 3: 178.

acquaintance to breed a confusion of ideas and a kind of distraction in the memory'.[3] Such 'confusion' and 'distraction' easily could be prompted by the baffling catalogue of tribunals through which justice was administered. Blackstone, for example, acknowledged England's 'prodigious variety of courts' of varying jurisdictions, legal capacities and procedures.[4] His presentation of these institutions required lengthy exposition, spread out over seven separate chapters. He began by identifying a structure of common law courts that operated locally throughout the kingdom. Next described were the central royal courts of Westminster Hall that exercised jurisdiction over the entire kingdom, as well as the House of Lords, which exercised appellate jurisdiction over these tribunals. Last, he discussed courts of assize and *nisi prius* by which the judges of the central courts or their delegates decided cases in the localities.[5]

Blackstone then turned to another large set of tribunals that exercised jurisdiction throughout the entire kingdom over specific kinds of disputes and injuries – 'ecclesiastical courts' (seven kinds), 'courts military' and 'maritime courts'.[6] Next were 'courts of a special jurisdiction'; that is, tribunals whose jurisdiction was limited to particular territorial areas or to particular kinds of disputes. This diffuse and lengthy list included well over twenty different courts, supplemented by the many courts in London and other towns and boroughs, as well as the numerous 'courts of requests' operating throughout the kingdom for the recovery of small debts.

This multitude of institutions handling 'private injuries' operated in addition to a set of tribunals dealing with 'public wrongs', or misdemeanours and felonies. Blackstone here surveyed previously described courts in terms of their criminal jurisdictions, and then introduced previously untreated tribunals.[7] He next described at length the various bodies that operated in the locality to enforce public order. The 'court of *oyer* and *terminer* and general *gaol delivery*' extended the circuit jurisdiction of the judges of Westminster Hall. The court of 'general quarter sessions', comprising two or more justices of the peace, handled a wide variety of misdemeanours 'and especially offences relating to the game, highways, alehouses, bastard children, the settlement and provision for the poor, vagrants, servants' wages, apprentices and popish recusants'. Justice in the locality was further served by a network of historically older tribunals operating under the authority of

3 Blackstone, *Commentaries*, 3: 176.
4 Blackstone, *Commentaries*, 3: 16.
5 Blackstone, *Commentaries*, 3: 30–40.
6 Blackstone, *Commentaries*, 3: 41–7.
7 Blackstone, *Commentaries*, 4: 171.

county and local officials, such as the *sheriff's tourn*, the *court-leet*, and the court of the *coroner*.[8]

Because of his general concern to be comprehensive, Blackstone provided little indication of which of England's tribunals were largely moribund and which were active, or which social groups were most affected by which tribunals. His presentation of the crucial institution of the justice of the peace aggravated the problem. England's unpaid magistrates discharged a wide range of critical administrative and legal responsibilities at the local level, responsibilities that were steadily enlarged in the eighteenth century through parliamentary statute. In most areas, the justices' 'quarter sessions' had largely supplanted the older structure of manorial courts and local officials. In addition, legislation gave new legal powers to pairs of magistrates acting in 'petty sessions' or to individual justices acting alone. Blackstone's fullest acknowledgment of these developments came in the form of critique of the increasing reliance on 'summary convictions' (the procedure by which individual justices decided cases without juries) and the resulting decay of the 'king's ancient courts of common law'.[9]

Blackstone's protracted account of England's 'prodigious variety of courts' reflected the manner in which legal innovation layered new jurisdictions and practices on top of older structures rather than replacing them outright. New and older institutions alike sustained a centuries-long pattern in which law and governance, especially outside metropolitan London, depended upon and sustained the authority of landed wealth and local elites. The resulting variation, moreover, also preserved high levels of discretion that operated routinely in the mechanisms of public justice. Critics of English justice, however, disparaged a body of law that contained such unfathomable complexity, enabled such routine variation in application, and preserved arcane and burdensome forms. John Stuart Mill, discussing the contributions of Jeremy Bentham, the period's great advocate of comprehensive law reform, thus compared the condition of English law to 'the costume of a full grown man who had never put off the clothes made for him when he went to school. Band after band had burst, and . . . then, without removing anything except what might drop off of itself, the whole was darned, or patches of fresh law were brought from the nearest shop and stuck on'.[10] By such lights, Blackstone's 'Gothic Castle' appeared a much shabbier and ramshackle artefact.

8 Blackstone, *Commentaries*, 4: 176–9.
9 Blackstone, *Commentaries*, 4: 184.
10 John Stuart Mill, *Essays on Ethics, Religion and Society*, edited by J. M. Robson, *Collected Works of John Stuart Mill* (London: University of Toronto Press, 1969), 101.

Legal complexity generated one more vital complication. Critics and supporters could each invoke the institution of law and refer to quite different elements of the same system. Was the essence of English law a system of ancient rights and privileges, as the defenders of legal custom ardently insisted, or rather a stable structure of sovereign power, as establishment defenders of the constitutional order celebrated? Did the exacting procedural requirements of English justice operate to preserve the liberty and property of the kingdom, as jurists championed, or to secure the professional interests and fees of lawyers and judges, as critics charged? Did the distinctive excellence of English law reside in its system of jury trials, designed to protect the weak and innocent, or in its obscure rules concerning estates and descent that preserved the dynastic fortunes of a ruling elite? Were the representative agents of the law the untrained and unpaid magistrates and officers in the locality, or the remote, elevated and well-rewarded justices of Westminster Hall? England's complex legal inheritance, in this sense, was a polychrest, available to support any number of competing values and causes.

Common Law and English Liberty

Notwithstanding the variation and complexity of England's legal inheritance, the legal order contained two powerful unifying elements: the legislative authority of the British Parliament and the idea and practice of the common law. Together, in theory at least, they insured the unity and central direction of law in and beyond England.

In contrast to the statutes enacted by Parliament, common law formed a body of 'unwritten law'. As the seventeenth-century jurist, Matthew Hale, explained in an influential discussion, 'I style those parts of the law, *Leges non Scriptae*, because their Authoritative and Original institutions are not set down in Writing ... but ... have acquired their binding Power and Force of Laws by a long and immemorial Usage and by the Strength of Custom and a Reception in this Kingdom.'[11] Lacking authoritative written expression, the practice of the common law courts provided evidence of which rules and norms were in fact constitutive of the common law.

Of course, as Blackstone's survey of tribunals made clear, England's law included many legal institutions that were not common law. The ecclesiastical courts, for example, utilised canon law; military and other courts

11 Matthew Hale, *The History of the Common Law of England*, edited by Charles M. Gray (Chicago, IL: University of Chicago Press, 1971), 17.

adopted civil (Roman) law; mercantile courts practised a transnational law merchant. As Shaunnagh Dorsett explains in her contribution to this volume, England maintained a plural legal order; a plurality that was even more dramatic in the case of British rule beyond the kingdom. The 1707 Acts of Union preserved Scots law in the northern kingdom, so that the new political entity of Great Britain contained two different bodies of national law. English law was transplanted and imposed in many settings, such as Ireland and British North America. But in an increasingly global empire, other bodies of law were recognised in specific territories – French civil law, in the case of Québec; Hindu and Islamic law in the case of British India. Such plurality, as Dorsett emphasises, made questions of jurisdiction basic to the operation of legal authority and determinations of right. According to the orthodoxies of the jurists, what gave England's law its ultimate unity and coordination was the 'Superintendency' of the common law, which kept its heterogeneous laws and tribunals 'within the Limits and Bounds of their several Jurisdictions'.[12]

Common law itself comprised a system of legal custom. 'Custom', however, like many other basic legal terms, was a capacious category, encompassing a number of distinct ideas and references. It is helpful to distinguish and highlight two especially important usages. The first is the idea of legal custom as denoting the particular usages and practices of the courts of common law, such as the central courts of King's Bench and Common Pleas. Captured here were some of the most technical and intricate features of the processes through which common law courts adjudicated private disputes and vindicated legal rights: writs and forms of action; intricate rules concerning special pleading and evidence gathering; procedures for authenticating legally relevant facts and competing claims.

The meaning of 'custom' here conformed to a more general understanding in which what we now treat as fields of substantive law were instead identified and determined according to the practices and procedures of various types of tribunals. Thus, 'ecclesiastical law' denoted the law of the ecclesiastical courts; 'maritime law' denoted the law of the maritime courts; 'manorial law' denoted the law of the manor courts; and 'common law' denoted the law of the common law courts. In the case of common law, the idea that there was indeed a body of law 'common' to the entire kingdom testified to the success of a set of courts and officials in consolidating and

12 Hale, *History of the Common Law*, 28.

extending a central system of royal justice throughout England and Wales during the formative period of medieval development.

Equally important, however, was the idea of common law 'custom' as the legal expression of the customary practices of the community itself. This idea of legal custom was by no means particular to the common law. Classical Roman law recognised custom as a source of law. Early modern jurists, both in England as well as on the continent, utilised the spacious category of 'local custom' to explain the wide regional variation of rules found in the legal systems of individual kingdoms and polities.[13] The link between common law and community usage performed important ideological work in standard celebrations of England's law. The English jurist, Sir John Davies, in his 1612 collection of Irish *Reports*, traced the origins of England's law to those 'reasonable act(s)' and 'practice(s)' which, through 'often iteration and multiplication', became settled as 'custome' and finally endowed with 'the force of a *Law*'.[14] On this understanding, the typical function of the institutions of the common law was to settle precisely and authoritatively which of the customary practices of the community enjoyed or warranted legal validity. This function served to explain the vital connectedness between law and community that jurists praised as a distinctive strength and achievement of the common law. It also helped explain the nature of the processes of gradual alteration and refinement that comprised common law development: as the usages and practices of the community altered through time, so too did the law change in response to these altered social conditions.

Given this process of refinement and development over time, the common law itself came to be, in Blackstone's phrase, 'fraught with the accumulated wisdom of ages'.[15] The same historical process tightly bound the law itself with the social experience of the kingdom. The cumulative result, Davies explained, was a legal system 'so framed and fitted to the nature and disposition of this people' that it became 'connatural to the Nation', making it impossible to imagine this community 'ruled by any other Law'.[16] Crucially, the identification of legal custom and communal practice served to sustain the political value in terms of which common lawyers most ardently celebrated their legal order: English liberty. Since common law derived from the customs of the community, it embodied the independently developed usages and expectations of the society itself. 'And indeed', enthused Blackstone, 'it is

13 This theme receives helpful summary in Tamar Herzog, *A Short History of European Law* (Cambridge, MA: Harvard University Press, 2018), 119–30, 134–48.

14 John Davies, *Reports of Cases and Matters in Law* (Dublin, 1762), Preface, 3.

15 Blackstone, *Commentaries*, 4: 442.

16 Davies, *Reports*, Preface, 5–6.

one of the characteristic marks of English liberty that our common law depends upon custom; which carries this internal evidence of freedom along with it, that it probably was introduced by the voluntary consent of the people'.[17] The important implication for political liberty was that all law in England evinced this form of political freedom. In the case of parliamentary legislation, the constitution maintained the consent of the community through the participation of the elected representatives in the House of Commons. In the case of the common law, the community authored the social custom from which the law itself derived.

This ideologically charged reading of the common law was largely a product of the momentous seventeenth-century political conflicts over the pretensions of Stuart absolutism. These battles generated rival accounts of the law's historical origins and orientation, and the relationship between the power of the Crown and the authority of the law. It was in this setting that common lawyers developed tendentious claims concerning the antiquity and continuity of England's law and constitution, the insularity of its legal experience, and the centrality of historical liberties to its legal inheritance. On this reading of England's past, Parliament had played a critical role in preserving the historical liberties of the community. The maintenance of liberty had been marked by a series of famous enactments – the thirteenth-century Magna Carta and Charter of Forests (and their subsequent re-enactments), the 1628 Petition of Right, the 1679 Habeas Corpus Act, the 1689 Bill of Rights – that preserved ancient liberties and the integrity of the law through a specific set of legal procedures and political guarantees.[18]

Political controversy over these matters scarcely vanished in the eighteenth century. For many commentators, however, the constitutional settlement that emerged in the aftermath of the Glorious Revolution of 1688 effectively vindicated the legal case against royal absolutism. The case for English liberties brought together both notions of custom: legally validated social practice and the practice of courts. The appeal to custom and customary right was pervasive in the treatment of a wide range of social and economic relations, especially when these came under threat or challenge. Conditions of work and employment concerned the customs of the trade;

17 Blackstone, *Commentaries*, 1: 55.

18 The classic discussion of these issues remains J. G. A. Pocock's (1957) *The Ancient Constitution and the Feudal Law*. More recent contributions include Pocock's own 'Retrospect' to the second edition (Cambridge: Cambridge University Press, 1987), and Glenn Burgess, *The Politics of the Ancient Constitution* (University Park, PA: Penn State University Press, 1993).

collective rights to pasturage and gleaning concerned the customs of the commons; the regulation of sales, exchange and the setting prices concerned the customs of markets and fairs. And historical custom figured prominently in the legal right that received lavish attention in English jurisprudence and political debate: the right of property.

For English jurists, the law governing estates and tenures was recognised as central and defining. Whereas students of Roman law began with the Rights of Persons, English law began with tenures, and the training of legal practitioners properly began with this notoriously intricate and technical body of law.[19] Its rules reflected a long process of historical development and adaptation through which the restrictive doctrines associated with feudal dominion and military tenures gave way to more flexible powers of alienation and exchange. Under feudal law (as then understood), the Crown stood as the original proprietor of the kingdom, and the landed estates which secured the wealth and social standing of England's governing elite began as gifts of the king, granted under conditions of service. According to a conventional counter-narrative, English tenures originated in a pre-feudal form of freehold (or allodial) tenures found in the ancient customs of the Saxons. Military tenures and feudal law had not become widespread until the Norman defeat of the Saxons. Royal power under Norman kingship was thereafter advanced by the machinations of their jurists and priests through the vehicles of feudal law and canon law. Just as Parliament had endured and triumphed over royal absolutism, so the historical common law had endured and triumphed over the centuries-long threat of the feudal law.[20]

The 'customs' of the courts were no less central and decisive to the survival of English liberties. Indeed, common law procedures and remedies not only functioned instrumentally to protect English liberties; they were, in themselves, constitutive of English liberty. No feature of legal process received such extensive praise and prominence as common law juries. Trial by jury, the influential Genevan commentator, Jean Louis De Lolme, reported at mid-century, was 'that part of their liberty to which the people of England are most thoroughly and universally wedded'.[21] Trial by one's peers – standardly treated as a Saxon practice reaffirmed in Magna Carta and

19 For a fuller discussion, see my, 'Mapping Criminal Law: Blackstone and the Categories of English Jurisprudence', in Norma Landau (ed.), *Law, Crime and English Society, 1660–1830* (Cambridge: Cambridge University Press, 2002), 144–5.

20 See, for example, Blackstone's characterisation of the legal legacies of the Norman Conquest in *Commentaries*, 4: 270–1.

21 Jean Louis De Lolme, *The Constitution of England* (Indianapolis, IN: Liberty Fund, 2007), 164.

subsequent enactments – was, for Hale, 'the best Trial in the World'. According to Blackstone, juries constituted 'the glory of the English law' and 'the most transcendent privilege which any subject can enjoy or wish for'.[22]

Common law process included multiple forms of jury, beyond the familiar twelve-person 'petit jury', for the trial of civil and criminal cases. Composed of untrained and unpaid laypersons, jurors – like constables, coroners, justices of the peace – were emblematic of the form of participatory governance through which justice operated in the localities. What rendered the common law jury such a prominent element in this legal order was its political function in protecting the innocent from the machinations of power. The jury was expressly recognised to provide a 'democratic' dimension to the legal process and to supply a potent check against threats to English liberties. As such, for conservative commentators and radical critics alike, the strength of the jury served as a measure of the health of the legal system overall.

Opponents of the Hanoverian political establishment found in the common law a rich resource for advancing their cause. Common law juries and open courts proved a fruitful public setting for publicising issues and airing grievances. In the 1760s, John Wilkes and his followers celebrated the common law jury as a representative body against which to measure the failings of the unreformed parliamentary representatives. Then and in following decades, ministerial attempts to silence opposition critics often foundered in well-publicised prosecutions for seditious libel in which recalcitrant jurors resisted the legal doctrines urged by government prosecutors and the courts. The same radical utilisation of common law weapons continued well into the nineteenth century.[23]

Colonial opposition to British rule in North America provided a classic setting for the startling mixture of legal antiquarianism and moral argument that framed so much of the period's political debate. The contributions of two early-career colonial lawyers and future US presidents, John Adams and Thomas Jefferson, supply distinguished examples. Adams composed his earliest political writings in criticism of the 1765 Stamp Act, the novel revenue measure imposed on British North America to help defray the wartime debt

22 Hale, *History of the Common Law*, 160; Blackstone, *Commentaries*, 3: 249.

23 For these episodes see, John Brewer, 'The Wilkite's and the Law', in John Brewer and John Styles (eds), *An Ungovernable People: The English and their Law in the 17th and 18th Centuries* (London: Hutchinson, 1980); Thomas A. Greene, *Verdict According to Conscience* (Chicago: University of Chicago Press, 1988); James A. Epstein, *The Radical Expression* (Oxford: Oxford University Press, 1994).

from the Seven Years' War. Like other colonial critics, Adams was clear that the measure was 'inconsistent with the spirit of the common law and of the essential fundamental principles of the British Constitution'. The Stamp Act violated the common law by placing jurisdiction for enforcement in the Admiralty courts, where 'no juries have any concern', as was 'directly repugnant to the Great Charter itself'. And it violated the Constitution by disregarding 'grand and fundamental principle' that 'no freeman should be subject to any tax to which he has not given his own consent'.[24] His most substantial contribution to the agitation against the Stamp Act, however, proceeded less directly, through a tendentious exercise in legal history. The 1765 *Dissertation on the Canon and Feudal Law* placed the colonial predicament in the long narrative of English liberty. Canon and feudal law, and especially the 'confederacy between the two systems', Adams maintained, comprised 'the two greatest systems of tyranny' since 'the promulgation of Christianity'. The original settlers in British North America formed their systems of ecclesiastical and civil government 'in direct opposition to the canon and the feudal systems'; and in so doing, sustained the same project of liberty 'which denounced hostilities against John till Magna Carta was signed, which severed the head of Charles I from his body, and drove James II from his kingdom'. Against this background, the recent Stamp Act threatened nothing less than 'an entire subversion of the whole system of our fathers, by the introduction of the canon and feudal law into America'.[25] To the modern reader, Adams's efforts to establish a direct linkage between the mid-eighteenth century revenue measure and the medieval jurisprudential enemies of ancient English liberties can seem an esoteric and even exotic exercise. However, for a common lawyer, trained to understand legal institutions as a customary inheritance, the pressing relevance of this history was unmistakable.

Jefferson's own treatment of the political situation, his 1774 *A Summary View of the Rights of British America*, focused on another thread of common law antiquarianism: the nature of English tenures. In addition to opposing the record of British policy since the passage of the 1765 Stamp Act, Jefferson strove to combat the general presumption that colonial 'lands and title' were

24 John Adams, 'Instructions of the Town of Braintree . . ., 1765', in *Revolutionary Writings of John Adams*, edited by C. Bradley Thompson (Indianapolis, IN: Liberty Fund, 2000), 40.

25 John Adams, *A Dissertation on the Canon and Feudal Law*, in *Revolutionary Writings of John Adams*, edited by C. Bradley Thompson (Indianapolis, IN: Liberty Fund, 2000) 22–3, 32, 34.

received as grants from the British Crown. The error was quickly disclosed by examining the 'Saxon laws of possession' that formed 'the basis, or groundwork, of the common law'. According to the customs of the Saxons, lands were held 'in absolute dominion, disencumbered with any superior, answering nearly to the nature of those possessions which the feudalists term allodial'. 'William the Norman' introduced feudal tenures; and despite the best efforts of 'the Norman lawyers', these tenures remained restricted exceptions to the mainstay 'Saxon laws of possession'. The lessons of this history for British North America were clear. 'America was not conquered by William the Norman, nor its lands surrendered to him' and therefore, 'Possessions there [in colonial North America] are undoubtedly of the allodial nature.'[26] For later generations, Jefferson's revolutionary principles became better associated with the universalist claims of the opening of the Declaration of Independence than with common law of the *Summary View*. Still, the Declaration's detailed litany of abuses justifying political independence included the charge that the king had 'endeavored to prevent the population of these States ... [by] raising the conditions of new Appropriations of Lands'.[27]

Modern legal historians often yoke together the founding of the independent North American state republics and the later French Revolution as decisive moments of rupture in the long pattern of royal governments and legally privileged nobility. At the same time, as the contributions of Adams and Jefferson disclose, the weapons of North American protest against British authority were forged in the tendentiously rendered history of common law custom. Like the English legal order itself, common law was a heterogeneous entity, more the creature of central royal courts and elite lawyers than the product of community practice. Nonetheless, common law custom and the authority of the established institutions of common law justice gave the legal order a distinctive identity and source of unity.

Legislation and State Capacities

Colonial North America also provided the site for some of the most robust statements of legislative capacity presented by the British Parliament. In 1765,

26 Thomas Jefferson, 'A Summary View of the Rights of British America', in *Thomas Jefferson Writings*, edited by Merrill D. Peterson (New York: Library of America, 1984), 118–9.

27 US Congress, *Declaration of Independence* (1776), www.archives.gov/founding-docs/declaration-transcript, accessed 5 January 2022.

for example, Parliament repealed the stamp duties that had attracted such fierce criticism in colonial North America. However, as part of the political compromise to secure the repeal, the next year it enacted a Declaratory Act, repudiating the colonial denials of parliamentary authority to impose taxes on colonies in the absence of direct electoral representation in the legislature. The British Parliament, the Declaratory Act countered, held 'full power and authority to make laws and statutes of sufficient force and validity to bind the colonies and people of America, subjects of the Crown of Great Britain, in all cases whatsoever'.[28]

Parliament's claimed authority to create valid law 'in all cases whatsoever', itself modelled on earlier like-minded legislation for Ireland, combined a mix of conventional and more recent ideas. Parliamentary statute, as we have seen, was long recognised along with legal custom to be a principal component of England's law. Moreover, the status of the 'High Court of Parliament' as the pinnacle of political authority in the kingdom was no less orthodox. The idea that legislative authority of the King-in-Parliament was unlimited in its extent and application – as the terms of the Declaratory Act concerning North America insisted – was more novel and controversial. Blackstone provided a particularly robust rehearsal of this conception of parliamentary sovereignty. Parliament, he maintained, 'hath sovereign and uncontrollable authority in making ... laws, concerning matters of all possible denominations ... this being the place where that absolute despotic power, which must in all governments reside somewhere, is entrusted by the constitution of these kingdoms'.[29] Blackstone's critics sharply protested that this formulation ignored the enduring rights of the community over which this parliamentary authority was exercised, just as it neglected those established usages and constitutional arrangements that guided its exercise.[30]

Controversies concerning the nature and limits of parliamentary authority, and the relationship between constitutional norms and legislative capacity, proved a major and long-influential feature of eighteenth-century political theory in and beyond Britain and its empire. Nonetheless, for the legal history of the period, the abstractions of parliamentary supremacy were of less significance than the cumulative impacts of its actual law-making. In

28 6 Geo. 3 c 12; https://avalon.law.yale.edu/18th_century/declaratory_act_1766.asp, accessed 21 April 2021.
29 Blackstone, *Commentaries*, 1: 107.
30 For a fuller discussion, see David Lieberman, 'The Mixed Constitution and the Common Law', in Mark Goldie and Robert Wokler (eds), *The Cambridge History of Eighteenth-century Political Thought* (Cambridge: Cambridge University Press, 2006).

the period after 1688, the succession of costly foreign wars, financed through ever-increasing levels of public debt, led to a series of major changes in the size and politics of Britain's executive government. The annual need for legislation to maintain the military and renew taxation made Parliament and the annual parliamentary session for conducting business a regular feature of political life. The routine direction of royal government shifted from the Privy Council to a ministerial cabinet and powerful state ministries, such as the Treasury and Board of Trade, all headed by party leaders who could deliver legislative majorities to support bellicose policies and the fiscal measures required to sustain them. Initiatives previously authorised by prerogative powers, royal proclamations and Letters Patent increasingly gave way to parliamentary statutes. Regular parliamentary sessions, in turn, enabled the enactment of ever-greater numbers of statutes and drove further changes in legislative procedure. The same developments altered the political dynamic between central government and locality. The availability of statutory relief stimulated local elites and officeholders to turn to Parliament to redress grievances and grant legal powers for schemes of improvement.[31]

The net result of all these developments was an ever-expanding body of legislation. In the period between 1688 and 1801, Britain's legislators enacted nearly 14,000 statutes.[32] Studying the nature and impacts of this production poses considerable challenges for the legal historian. The major part of English law concerning what Matthew Hale termed 'the common administration of justice between party and party' and comprising such basic fields as property, inheritance, exchange, credit and debt, were all settled by common law. 'The judgments of Westminster Hall', as was explained in 1834, 'are the only authority that we have for by far the greatest part of the law of England'.[33] Yet, at the same time, traditional understandings of the limited functions of statutes to clarify contested points of law and to supply defects of existing law no longer captured a legal reality in which parliament legislated routinely and frequently. Certainly, the sheer scale of the development drew

31 In this and the following paragraphs, I draw heavily on several important studies, including: John Brewer, *The Sinews of Power: War, Money in the English State 1688–1783* (Cambridge, MA: Harvard University Press, 1989); Paul Langford, *Public Life and the Propertied Englishman 1689–1798* (Oxford: Oxford University Press, 1991); Joanna Innes, *Inferior Politics: Social Problems and Social Policies in Eighteenth-century Britain* (Oxford: Oxford University Press, 2009).

32 David Lemmings, *Law and Government in England during the Long Eighteenth Century* (London: Palgrave Macmillan, 2011), 126.

33 Hale, *History of the Common Law*, 102; James Ram, *The Science of Legal Judgment* (London, 1834), title page.

frequent complaint, particularly from professional lawyers who despaired of the resulting bulk and frequent inconsistency of England's legislation. At mid-century, an alarmed Lord Chancellor Hardwicke declared to his fellow peers in the House of Lords that the statutes 'have of late years increased to such an enormous size, that no lawyer . . . can pretend to be master of all the statutes that relate to any one case that comes before him'.[34]

A major reason for the number of statutes was the particularity with which the eighteenth-century Parliament typically legislated. The bulk of this legislation comprised so-called 'private acts' which authorised a wide range of local innovations: individual land enclosures; highway and turnpike trusts; canal construction; and regulatory powers granted to new bodies or to established local corporations. Added to such 'improvement' legislation was a further body of private acts granting individuals naturalisation, divorces, debt relief or estate reorganisation. Statutes of more general scope frequently contained expiration clauses, which created a further body of legislative work for future Parliaments. Over a third of the enacted local statutes 'continued, amended, or repealed previous local acts'.[35] Legal reformers decried such legislative myopia and the style of law-making that facilitated it. A youthful Jeremy Bentham, writing in the 1770s, thundered, 'the country gentleman who has had his turnips stolen, goes to work and gets some bloody law against stealing Turnips: it exceeds the utmost stretch of his comprehension to conceive that the next year the same catastrophe may happen to his Potatoes'.[36]

It has been the work of current scholarship to take the fuller measure of eighteenth-century statute law.[37] One significant area of investigation reveals greater levels of care, competence and regularity in Parliament's law-making. England's legislators were largely drawn from a small, traditional cohort of privileged elites. The electorate remained small and restricted; new areas of population lacked representation, while unpopulated 'rotten boroughs' continued to send members to the House of Commons. Nevertheless, in its legislative practice, law-makers displayed their readiness to support propertied interests beyond the landed elite, and to authorise projects of

34 Hardwicke's speech to the House of Lords, cited in William Holdsworth, *A History of English Law* (16 volumes, London: Methuen, 1922–66), 11: 374.
35 Innes, *Inferior Politics*, 96.
36 Bentham Mss., University College London, Box cxl, fol. 92.
37 See Sheila Lambert, *Bills and Acts: Legislative Procedure in 18th-century England* (Cambridge: Cambridge University Press, 1971); Innes, *Inferior Politics*, 21–105; J. Hoppit and J. Innes, 'Introduction' to *Failed Legislation, 1660–1800*, edited by Julian Hoppit (London: Hambledon Continuum, 1997).

improvement in unrepresented and under-represented locales. Where consensus had been achieved among local propertied interests and the sources of revenue required for projects had been secured, Parliament proved ready to grant legislative authorisation. The limited and seemingly ad hoc nature of the resulting statute book reflected the reliability of the legislature in responding to local initiatives and needs.

At the same time, parliament's political supremacy altered the terms and responsibilities of parliamentary service. Active members with no connection to the networks of government patronage cultivated particular areas of expertise, and House of Commons emerged as a crucial investigator and collector of national intelligence concerning population, industries, employment and poverty. Not all parliamentary legislation was local and facilitative. In areas where previous Parliaments had legislated generally, as in the case of poor relief and settlement laws, it was ready to legislate on a more comprehensive basis.[38] At the same time, powerful corporate entities, such as the Bank of England and the East India Company, as well as older borough corporations, originally the handiwork of royal charters, were now regulated and modified through legislative enactment. Colonial affairs were supervised by the standing Board of Trade, the Privy Council and, less frequently, the courts of Westminster Hall. Nonetheless, major policy decisions, as embodied in such measures as the 1774 Québec Act and the succession of East India Company Acts, were properly a matter of parliamentary debate and action. Business groups, colonial elites and city merchants employed agents to monitor parliamentary deliberations, while a select group of metropolitan attorneys developed the practice of preparing bills and guiding their progress to enactment.

In particular areas, the cumulative impact of this legislative particularism can be readily discerned. Paul Langford furnishes an instructive example in the statutes establishing Courts of Requests, small debts courts that offered summary procedures for debts of less than forty shillings in value. In the 1730s and 1740s, Parliament considered but rejected general legislation for establishing such courts. 'But what Parliament would not accept as a matter of general policy', Langford explains, 'it was quite prepared to implement

38 General law reform efforts are described by Wilfrid Prest, 'Law Reform in Eighteenth Century England', in Peter Birks (ed.), *Life of the Law: Proceedings of the 10th British Legal History Conference* (London: Hambledon Continuum, 1991) and Barbara J. Shapiro, *Law Reform in Early Modern England* (Oxford: Hart, 2019). Developments in legislative practice receive extensive discussion in Lambert, *Bills and Acts*; Innes, *Inferior Politics*, 21–105; Hoppit and Innes, 'Introduction'.

piecemeal.' Through a series of fifty separate and more limited enactments, these courts were established throughout 'large tracts of the country'.[39]

Elsewhere, however, discerning the larger pattern of eighteenth-century statute requires greater care. A leading example is found in the era's most notorious arena of legislative craft: the enactment of a ferocious volume of capital statutes. The severity of parliament's penal legislation figured prominently in reform advocacy from mid-century onwards. Thomas Fowell Buxton in 1819 tendentiously informed fellow members of the House of Commons that the statute book contained 223 capital offences, 150 of which had been 'made capital during the last century'.[40] The blunt numbers were designed to shock, but were misleading as well. The increase of capital statutes conformed to the growth of legislative enactments and reflected the same kind of particularism that characterised parliament's law-making overall. English law, by the early nineteenth century, did not have 223 categories of capital crime. Rather, capital sanctions had been assigned to highly specific offences attached to legislative authorisations for individual projects or outbreaks of disorder in particular localities.[41]

More important than the numbers of capital statutes were the policies promoted through this law-making. The purpose, like that of so much other eighteenth-century English law, was the protection of property and the rights of property-holders. According to the influential formulations of E. P. Thompson and his successors, the period witnessed a steady entrenchment of exclusive property rights and the accompanying destruction of customary rights guiding relations among land-owners, tenants and agrarian workers, and among masters and servants. Thus, the criminal law became a crucial site of social conflict driven by new wealth, commercial growth and economic change.[42] Certainly, in many instances the association between economic development and capital sanctions is apparent. The death penalty was extended to cover damage to costly investments, such as turnpikes and coalmines. A series of statutes transformed the

39 Langford, *Public Life and the Propertied Englishman*, 158–60.

40 Buxton's speech to the House of Commons, cited in Leon Radzinowicz, *A History of English Criminal Law and Its Administration from 1750* (5 volumes, London, 1948–86), I: 4–5.

41 See Joanna Innes and John Styles, 'The Crime Wave: Recent Writing on Crime and Criminal Justice in Eighteenth-century England' *Journal of British Studies* 25 (1986): 425.

42 Thompson's treatment of these issues developed over a series of important articles subsequently incorporated in E. P. Thompson, *Customs in Common* (New York: New Press, 1993). A valuable supplement appears in Douglas Hay and Nicholas Rogers, *Eighteenth-century English Society* (Oxford: Oxford University Press, 1997).

forgery of the major forms of commercial credit, such as Bank of England notes, into capital crimes. (In conspicuous contrast to most of the capital statutes, conviction for these types of forgery routinely led to public execution.) The dramatic growth of London, new populations of poor and unattached labourers, and the concentration of large stores of merchandise and commodities, particularly in the crowded warehouses and ships of the River Thames, led to repeated public preoccupation with anonymous crime and significant government experiments in policing, prevention and prosecution.[43] Nonetheless, it is difficult to chart changes in criminal justice exclusively in terms of legislative innovations driven by economic transformation and social conflict. Throughout the century, most prosecutions and executions were for crimes that had been made capital centuries before – murder, robbery, burglary, horse theft and forms of housebreaking. Even in the case of forgery, Parliament did not extend capital sanctions to private instruments, such as promissory notes and bills of exchange, upon which eighteenth-century credit chiefly depended.

At the same time that Parliament enlarged the number of property crimes eligible for the death penalty, the proportion of those convicted of capital felonies who actually were executed decreased through the century. The contrasting dynamics served to increase the amount of discretion in the processes of criminal punishment. Discretion, in fact, attended every stage of criminal justice – victims determined whether or not to initiate charges, magistrates selected cases for indictment, juries might mitigate the severity of law through a purposeful under-valuation of the worth of stolen goods, and felons convicted of capital crimes were most often pardoned from execution. The resulting patterns of discretion have likewise become the object of sustained historical reconstruction and interpretation. Periods of dearth and high food prices led to increases in indictments, as did the demobilisation and return of underpaid and now-unemployed soldiers and seamen at the conclusion of wars. Periods of warfare led to a decrease in indictments, as those accused of crime could escape prosecution by agreeing to enter into military service. Perhaps the most notable innovation in the levels of prosecution followed from the emergence of a metropolitan and provincial press eager to secure readers through frequent reports of crime, criminal gangs and threats of lawlessness. For the

43 See J. M. Beattie, *Policing and Punishment in London 1660–1750* (Oxford: Oxford University Press, 2001); Bruce Smith, 'The Emergence of Public Prosecution in London, 1790–1850' *Yale Journal of Law and the Humanities* 29 (2006) and 'The Presumption of Guilt and the English Law of Theft 1750–1850' *Law and History Review* 23 (2005).

first time, the public response to crime's dangerousness was a manipulated product of new forms of commercial media and communication.[44]

Discretion and the technical machinery of criminal justice figures in the deservedly influential studies of John Beattie. These researchers revealed a major transformation in eighteenth-century criminal justice that operated in an indirect relationship to capital felonies. This was the emergence of transportation as the preferred secondary punishment for those convicted of serious crimes. With Parliament's enactment of the 1718 Transportation Act, the British state accepted the need to practice, and subsidise the costs of, penal exile for large numbers of felons; and transportation emerged as the institutional alternative to fines and corporal penalties or capital sentences. However, in a manner reflecting the characteristic intricacy of English legal procedures, transportation itself was not standardly specified as the statutory penalty for the commission of serious crime. Instead, those convicted of capital felonies, upon successful recommendation to the Crown, had their sentences commuted to a period of penal exile. In this way, the creation of capital crimes through particular statutes legally enabled the use of transportation as a penal alternative.[45]

In contrast to its enactments concerning crime and punishment, the rest of the parliamentary statute book has received much less sustained attention. A recent survey by David Lemmings offers an ambitious interpretation of the character and cumulative impacts of this legislation. Here, changes in criminal justice form part of a much broader pattern in which the coercive and executive capacities of England's law strengthened at the expense of common law's traditional customary and participatory practices. Parliament's enhanced legislative output served not only to protect property interests, but equally to advance local administrative and disciplinary power.

A key component of the development were the changes to powers and authority of justices of the peace. Throughout the century, local magistrates continued in their traditional functions of keeping the peace, administering

44 Douglas Hay's 'Property, Authority and the Criminal Law', in Douglas Hay et al., *Albion's Fatal Tree: Crime and Society in 18th-century England* (London: Pantheon, 1975), initiated an important line of inquiry concerning the ideological and class-based dimensions of 18th-century criminal justice. In addition to John Langbein's critique, 'Albion's Fatal Flaws' *Past and Present* 97 (1983), see D. Hay, 'War, Dearth and Theft in the 18th Century: The Record of the English Courts' *Past and Present* 95 (1982): 117–60; and Peter King, *Crime, Justice and Discretion in England 1740–1820* (Oxford: Oxford University Press, 2000) and *Crime and Law in England 1750–1840* (Cambridge; Cambridge University Press, 2006).

45 J. M. Beattie, *Crime and the Courts in England 1600–1800* (Oxford: Clarendon, 1986), 450–519.

the poor law and monitoring the maintenance of local facilities, such as roads, gaols and houses of correction. At the same time, as we have seen, statutes increased the justices' authority to bring charges and impose sanctions in the absence of juries, a power that was regularly exercised in the case of minor property offences. Parliament additionally passed legislation to block traditional legal actions to challenge summary convictions and the central courts broadly supported these measures. Administrative discretion and control were equally enhanced through the legislative creation of new poor law corporations, urban authorities, enclosures and turnpike trusts, each of which enjoyed wide powers to undertake public works, impose rates and determine boundaries and rights-of-way. Such costly initiatives might attract popular protest. However, the investments were now protected through capital statutes and summary process.[46] Finally, parliamentary legislation gave the counties' courts of Quarter Sessions (the quarterly meeting of two or more justices) new executive powers to levy rates, undertake capital improvements and appoint salaried officers to implement its initiatives. 'With the encouragement of Parliament', Lemmings maintains, 'the "court of quarter sessions" had begun to assume the proportions of the county executive, rather than a judicial body.' The cumulative effects of such changes, coupled with the declining use of traditional legal structures for plebeian disputes, produced a major reorientation of English law and governance. 'The dynamic and reciprocal, socially embedded state of the sixteenth and seventeenth centuries atrophied in the eighteenth, and the business of government became more linear and one-dimensional as parliamentary statute, rather than the culture of common law, became the principal instrument of government.'[47]

Empire and colonies were never far removed from the dynamics of eighteenth-century English law and British governance. As we have seen, colonial resistance to British policy in North America furnished the opportunity for lavish rehearsals of the customary liberties of English subjects, the sanctity of common law juries and freehold tenures, and rights of political representation. Overall, however, the British government simultaneously developed the legal tools to preserve metropolitan authority and imperial domination. In the 1770s, two major parliamentary enactments – the 1773 East

46 Lemmings, *Law and Government in England*, 32–7, 151–4.

47 Lemmings, *Law and Government in England*, 52–3, 11. A contrasting timeline and account of the transformation in local government is presented by David Eastwood, *Governing Rural England: Tradition and Transformation in Local Government 1780–1840* (Oxford: Oxford University Press, 1994).

India Company (Regulating) Act and the 1774 Québec Act – specified a distinctive form of governance for each possession. British rule was now maintained by a Crown-appointed governor (or, alternatively, military commander) who exercised broad executive and legislative powers in conjunction with a small Crown-appointed Legislative Council; their broad powers subject to the review of the Crown and the legislative supremacy of the British Parliament. The Québec Act, which applied to the entire territory of formerly French North America, transplanted English criminal law, but preserved French civil law for the determination of property rights and titles. (Most controversially, the Act granted 'the free Exercise of the Religion of the Church of Rome' for Canada's Catholic subjects.) The Regulating Act created a new Supreme Court of Judicature for British subjects in the East India Company's territories, and granted the summary powers of justices of the peace and Quarter Sessions to the judges, the new Governor General and members of the Legislative Council. This form of strong centralised authority, equipped with legal instruments for its parliamentary-sanctioned powers, in turn provided a model for imperial governance in the convict colony of New South Wales and well beyond.

Each of these enactments was a product of a variety of immediate and contested imperatives, not least of which involved decisions concerning the kind of economy each colonial setting was intended to sustain.[48] In the case of Québec, there was the pressing need to strengthen British authority in the face of the resistance being mobilised by colonial elites on the Atlantic seaboard. In the case of British India, the 1770 statute was one of a series of measures by which Parliament and the Crown established greater controls over the administration of the East India Company. Nevertheless, all such projects confronted blunt realities influencing which features of English liberty and the common law could safely be extended beyond the kingdom. As it was candidly expressed by an anonymous 1773 commentator on legal arrangements for Bengal, 'if the natives should be actually endowed with the red cap of liberty in the jury room . . . there is a certainty that they would make bold to wear it elsewhere; and then, adieu to the British dominion in Bengal'.[49]

48 This is the leading argument of Christian R. Burset, 'Why Didn't the Common Law Follow the Flag?' *Virginia Law Review* 105 (2019): 483–542.

49 *The Present State of the British Interest in India: With a Plan for Establishing a Regular System of Government in That Country* (London, 1773), 46, quoted in Christian R. Burset, *A Common Law? Legal Pluralism in the Eighteenth-Century British Empire* (Yale University PhD thesis, 2018), 323.

Imperial dynamics, moreover, were never a simple matter of the metropole exporting terms to colonies and settlements. In his illuminating study of habeas corpus, Paul Halliday provides a telling illustration of the larger dynamic for English law of relations between Britain and her increasingly global dominions.[50] The writ of habeas corpus, through which royal prerogative policed the conduct of inferior officials, emerged by the early modern period into a celebrated marker of English liberty. The 1679 Habeas Corpus Act, which Halliday shows provided somewhat modest administrative improvements to the execution of the common law writ, was nonetheless extolled by the defenders of liberty as a milestone event. Blackstone celebrated the statute as 'a second Magna Carta, as beneficial and effectual as that of Running-Mead'.[51] Once again, Parliament reassuringly legislated in support of common law liberty. Yet, as Halliday further emphasises, while the statute strengthened the writ, it simultaneously helped create the means to curtail its operation. To deal with armed resistance in North America, Parliament adopted the expedient of suspending habeas corpus in the rebellious colonies for an unprecedented period of six years (1777–83). Suspension Acts later became a staple device for British authority facing unrest throughout the major outposts of empire. Most strikingly, the practice, in turn, was domesticated for the purposes of maintaining authority within Britain itself. During the protracted wars against revolutionary France, Parliament suspended habeas corpus from 1794–5 and again from 1798–1801. 'Beginning in the 1790s', Halliday observes, 'suspension became just one part of wider statutory campaigns against political dissent in all its forms.'[52] By such means, the governance of empire had become firmly embedded in the legal history of England itself.

50 Paul D. Halliday, *Habeas Corpus: From England to Empire* (Cambridge, MA: Harvard University Press, 2010). In what follows I draw especially on the discussion at 237–58.

51 Blackstone, *Commentaries*, 4: 283. In this characterisation, Blackstone twinned the Act with concurrent legislation abolishing the principal vestiges of military tenures.

52 Halliday, *Habeas Corpus*, 255.

4

Challenging Settler State Legal Fantasies: Basic Precepts of First Law

MARY SPIERS WILLIAMS

Lawful

Some time ago now, there was some trouble and a man – a senior law man – was required to enforce his law. After it was done, when everyone had gone, he waited for the police. Because he was a lawful man and the policeman's law was in this Country, he reasoned that he ought to follow their law too. Finally, the police arrived. When asked, he told the police what he had done.

Weeks maybe months later, he walked into a courthouse in a big town a long way from his home. He was in other peoples' Country, but he knew how to be there. He had been summoned to appear, charged with a criminal offence. It was the first time that he had been in a courthouse. When he entered the courthouse foyer, he was struck by an array of paintings depicting local law, *tjukurrpa*. He could read this law. These were stories that travelled through his Country too.

He entered the courtroom proper to await the beginning of the colonising-state lawyers' ceremony and sat in the public seats. He noticed high on the wall in front of him an image of two kangaroos facing each other. Over the kangaroos flew a wedge-tailed eagle; he recognised the wedge-tail, an important teacher in his cosmology – the wisest except for the emu. The law man read in that government crest a story of two kangaroos. These kangaroos fought each other because they believed they were enemies, but after they had been fighting for a while, they realised they were merely different, came to respect each other, and then travelled together through Country to share the law.

The court case began. The law man's lawyer told him to stand when the magistrate came in, that he was not to speak and that she would talk for him. When the magistrate entered, he noticed the magistrate's separate entrance. He felt the court room change when the ceremony began. Everyone stood.

The law man felt the elevation and the barrier of the bench, and the magistrate become the locus of authority.

The magistrate read a report written about the law man. He heard the police prosecutor and the lawyer talk. Then the magistrate spoke. He denounced the law man's conduct and sentenced him – *leniently*, thinks the criminal lawyer inside me, *a sentence that could not be appealed: the magistrate had denounced the defendant – stressing the aggravating details of the prosecution case, as well as carefully noting the mitigating features. Because he spoke so forcefully about the aggravating features and set out all the relevant detail carefully, this allowed him to order a disposition at the lower end of the range and minimised the risk that the prosecution would appeal it as the sentence would be unlikely to be overturned.*

But this is how the law man remembered it:

> *He's saying to me, 'Stuff your law. I'm going to charge you with this law.' He says, 'Your law doesn't matter.'*
>
> *But I think, 'Hang on! That's confusing me!' – because I see all that painting around those walls and I see that crest that says to me: 'No, I'm still in [the] law'. I felt like, 'I'm still here – I know I'm still in this Country – but this has nothing to do with [the] law.'*
>
> *[He said he wants to] charge me with that law book, [that . . .] he studied, [with] what he learnt. And I'm seeing another law book – in those paintings on the wall and also in that crest . . . [but] he doesn't see this other book. He's only staring at his law book . . .*

The law man was dissatisfied with the ceremony, the way the process was conducted, and the values that were expressed. It was at odds with the place, Country – *ngurra* –, in which it was conducted. He had expected the ceremony to transform him and restore balance, and he expected to be punished if necessary to achieve that. Instead, he had played no part in this meaningless ritual. He left the courtroom with nothing more than a piece of paper with a date to see a community corrections officer.

Colonising-state law was not what he thought it would be. It was not that he thought it should have no power over him, not at all. The power it exercised was hollow and did not deliver a legitimate outcome. It did not restore balance or harmony. It was not lawful.

. . .

This story is about incomprehension – not of this law man, nor of the First Peoples of this continent. First Peoples understand coloniser-settler law, although not in the way that coloniser-settlers see it. This story is about incomprehension of coloniser-settler lawyers and those enraptured by systems of law transplanted and since transformed through colonisation. This is not about whether First Law is legible or lawful. It is. The law man's story has been shared to show the implications of asking the wrong question about 'First Law'. I am offering a provocation about how we – those of us who have been trained in, teach and practice – understand the state legal system and the idea of 'law' itself.

. . .

A Simple Provocation?

The editors of this volume initially asked me to write about the legal history of 'Indigenous criminal law'. It was a compelling provocation, all the more so in the context of contributing to a canon, part of a series that reproduces aspects of English traditions of law to be distributed around the planet by an editing house from a European centre of legal imperialism, the motherland of colonial Australia. This request was out of the ordinary, a turn against *terra nullius* and the colonial denial of the law since the British have always been within this *terra plenus* – our *ngurra*, our home, our being. In that invitation is a recognition that First Peoples exist and so too does First Law. That invitation, I welcomed.

But I could not do what I had been asked. I could not – cannot – write about 'Indigenous criminal law'. The reasons are layered.

The law across this continent is so vast and complex that it is impossible for one person to comprehend it all and the diverse ways that it is realised. Let us imagine that, somehow, I could overcome my limitations as a little human and it were possible for me to have all that knowledge. It would still not be possible for me to share it, because the law of all those places is not mine to tell. I am not a 'boss nor a director', neither *kirda* nor *kurdungurlu*.

While I can share basic precepts and I may be permitted or even obliged to share some law from some places, to share more than this without authority or authorisation would be unlawful. Let us imagine, though, that I transgressed that law. There would be little to be gained in my attempting to share that law with you if you were not in the place of that law. While we can learn from a person with authority, such a teacher offers only a fraction of what law is there to learn from Country.

But none of these is the fundamental reason I cannot write about 'Indigenous criminal law'. I cannot write of it because there is no such thing.

The editors' response to my counter-provocation has been curious, open and generous. Reconciliatory. I understand it led them to reflect on the framing of this volume. They made more than space for us within the canonical compartments of law; they revisited the structure and nature of those compartments and reimagined the possibilities of law in this Country beyond state law.

While it is possible for me to share basic precepts of First Law, will you recognise this as law and that the basic precepts found diverse laws across the continent? Recognising First Law can be difficult not merely because of difference, but because colonisation reaches into every part of our lives including how we understand law and what we think law is. We need to reflect before we can recognise law from this place. Let us first return to the law man's story.

The story is an incomplete account from a criminal lawyer's point of view. Have I left out the most important parts? (*But what did he* do?)

The law man and I have spoken about this story several times. Each time he has wanted me to share this story. Perhaps you think I am trying to protect him by giving you this parsed account? Those of us who have been at the interface of colonising-state law with First Peoples' communities and seen the devastation wrought by coloniser-settler constructions of criminality – what it can do to defendants, those close to them, to their community – understand reasons for holding back part of this story, even after many years. Protecting him would be pragmatic, and also patronising and disrespectful. I parsed the story – left out the 'most important parts' – to serve another purpose: to leave the reader unsatisfied, to draw out questions – especially, I expect, from other criminal lawyers. Instead of answers, I have questions for you about your reading of his story.

What is it that you want to know? What is that you think is important in this story?

Do you want to help him to understand, to see the logic of colonising-state law?

What assumptions did you make about the events that brought him before the court?

What did you assume about the legal process – what have you been taught about colonising-state law?

When you talk about First Law, what words do you use and have you heard used?

What terminology do you know for what is possibly the oldest continuing legal system in the world, for his law?

What judgments have you made? Have you already decided that what he did was 'wrong' or 'right'?

What judgments do you feel entitled to make? Why do you think 'judgment' is relevant to legal process?

What do you think you already know about this story?

Do you feel that we need to do something about his actions? Do you want to save him from his law – law that required him to perform an act that colonising-state law criminalised?

Do you want to save him from his barbarism? Do you want to civilise him? Or do you just want punishment and retribution?

Engaging in This 'Terrain'

Some may interpret the way that I am engaging with this provocation as an act of 'refusal'.[1] It is refusal in that I resist the framing of the provocation.[2] I am attempting – in a long history of attempts by First Peoples – to engage, to communicate. (This is being lawful.) In this chapter, I engage because I have seen and experienced desert law men and women engaging repeatedly, and because I have an obligation to them and to my family far from the desert in sandstone Country.

I am mindful of the possibilities and limits of engaging in this 'terrain', this publication. Knowledge about First Law cannot be consumed through reading – even a heavy, hardcover canon. 'In communicating the law, it is not simply a process of telling a story.'[3] While one may want knowledge, what one needs first is sensibility, insight – not into First Peoples, rather into oneself and one's context. When the 'strange' starts to become familiar, then one begins to realise that what is 'normal' is – in reality – 'strange', and can see what has always been there. The compartments of state law are neither natural nor inevitable; one might even consider them 'strange' (I do).

Creating space in this history is helpful, but not if that space is between administrative law and contracts or a 'special' sub-category created for us, for example, under criminal law or family law. Forcing First Law into such compartments diminishes First Law and impedes the naïve reader's capacity to understand it. Ambelin Kwaymullina and Blaze Kwaymullina described colonising-state law as reflecting a 'reductionist worldview': where 'the whole is never more than the sum of its measurable parts' and this 'results in compartmentalised disciplines of knowledge'.[4] Irene Watson suggests that

1 See e.g. Audra Simpson, 'On Ethnographic Refusal: Indigeneity, "Voice" and Colonial Citizenship' *Junctures* 9 (2007): 67.

2 See e.g. Audra Simpson, 'Consent's Revenge' *Cultural Anthropology* 31, no. 3 (2016): 326–33.

3 Irene Watson, 'Power of the Muldarbi: The Road to its Demise' *Australian Feminist Law Journal* 11, no. 1 (1998): 28, 36.

4 Ambelin Kwaymullina and Blaze Kwaymullina, 'Learning to Read the Signs: Law in an Indigenous Reality' *Journal of Australian Studies* 34, no. 2 (2010): 195, 197.

colonisation has reduced transplanted common law to mere rules and regulations.[5] Such reductionism either splits the inherent holism of First Law or requires it to transform to fit a compartment. If I had been asked to participate in this way, then I would have had to refuse.[6]

This 'terrain' of 'compartmentalised disciplines of knowledge' is not the only way to imagine law. The phenomenon of law is more mutable, less stable and less cohesive than this represents.[7] Despite the promulgation of a 'centralist model of law', law is not monopolised by the nation state.[8]

It is impossible to explain First Law within a coloniser-settler account of Australian law: 'the rewriting needs to be done from "another space", outside the jurisdiction of the Australian common law and the sovereignty of the Australian state'.[9] Colonising-state law is inherently 'jurispathic'[10] of First Law. Our ancestors and senior law men and women who have shared their law with coloniser-settlers did not hope for their law that it would be absorbed within coloniser-settler law. Rather, the hope was and still is that the newcomers might recognise the reality of this place and its inherent laws. So let us continue towards that.

In being oppositional, my purpose is to be generative. In engaging in this canon, I am conscious that I am entering a legal field of the colonising-state where there have been 'unequal and uneven forces of cultural representation involved in the contest for political and social authority'.[11] I do so specifically

5 While Kwaymullina and Kwaymullina describe coloniser-settler law as 'positivist' and 'reductionist', they note that there are also more complex traditions in western thought: Ibid, 197.

6 Cf Irene Watson and Kathy Bowrey, 'Can Australian Legal Feminism See Aboriginal Country?' Paper presented at the Australian Feminist Judgments Project Symposium University of Queensland St Lucia on 2 December 2014 in which Professor Watson explained why she could not participate in that project, specifically in the rewriting of *Kartinyeri*.

7 Robert M. Cover, 'Foreword: Nomos and Narrative' *Harvard Law Review* 97 (1983): 4. See also Desmond Manderson, 'Beyond the Provincial: Space, Aesthetics, and Modernist Legal Theory' *Melbourne University Law Review* 20 (1995–1996): 1048, 1052.

8 Margaret Davies, 'The Ethos of Pluralism' *Sydney Law Review* 27 (2005): 87, 91 at footnote 16; Margaret Davies, 'Legal Pluralism', in Peter Cane and Herbert M Kritzer (eds), *The Oxford Handbook of Empirical Legal Research* (Oxford: Oxford University Press, 2010); Sally Engle Merry, 'Legal Pluralism' *Law and Society Review* 22, no. 5 (1988): 869.

9 Irene Watson, 'First Nation Stories, Grandmother's Law', in H. Douglas, F. Bartlett, T. Luker and R. Heather (eds), *Australian Feminist Judgments: Righting and Rewriting Law* (Oxford: Hart Publishing, 2014; 2015), 46, 53.

10 Robert Cover, writing about the United States Supreme Court, observed: '[J]udges of the state are jurispathic – they kill the diverse legal traditions that compete with the State.' Cover, 'Foreword: Nomos and Narrative', 40ff.

11 Homi K. Bhabha (1992) 'Freedom's Basis in the Indeterminate', *October* 61 (Summer, 1992): 46–57, 46.

to contest deficit accounts and counter 'the occlusion or demeaning representations'[12] of First Law and First Nations peoples' way of being by the colonising-state. To begin, I return to the provocation originally suggested by the editors to unpick presumptions within it.

What's in a Question?

My reaction to the request to write about 'Indigenous criminal law' has been questions and then more questions. Many matters I cannot treat as 'common sense', assumed or obvious. In this cross-examination I hold myself to account as much as other lawyers; I am still disentangling my state legal education/practice/enculturation from what else I know and who else I am, sifting what is useful from what is not, and still wrangle with my participation in the criminalisation system.

> *By 'criminal law', what do you mean? What do you imagine already about what I understand by 'Indigenous criminal law'? (It is fair to say that you must at least imagine that I think there is such a thing as 'Indigenous criminal law'.)*
>
> *So, I have to ask: what do you imagine is 'Indigenous criminal law'? What might that tell me about what you imagine First Law is? Or about how you imagine what 'law' is? I wonder if you have thought about what else 'law' might be? (I think you must have, otherwise you could not have asked it.)*
>
> *What does your question do? What effect does it have? (Questions have agency, after all.) What knowledge does this provocation instantly create before I've even drawn breath to respond – as I ground myself and prepare to walk across that burning bridge again.*

Inherent in the provocation is that Indigenous law exists. For First Peoples of this place and after what we have experienced, to exist in any form is a relief. I worry that this recognition is precarious and may be lip service – but, I do not dismiss this: 'lip service' is words. Our state law schools have trained us to weaponise words. Words are powerful. They are the drops of water that can eventually crack a boulder.

While English language cannot capture what First Law is, I am grateful that we have moved on from terms that suggest that it is not real law. First Law is, thankfully, less-and-less referred to by state lawyers as 'lore' (that can evoke taletelling) or 'customary' law (that evokes a sense that it is 'lite' law). Within our field, we are even beginning to distinguish colonising-state law

12 Christine Regan and Jakelin Troy, 'BlackWords and "reciprocal recognitions"' *Australian Aboriginal Studies* 1 (2014): 1, 119.

from other types of law within a place. In my experience in law schools, discussions only ever used to reference 'The Law'; I have observed in recent conversations at my law school, some colleagues now refer more precisely to 'state law' or 'coloniser-settler law' in distinction from – while acknowledging – other forms of law in the social field.[13]

So, yes, there is Indigenous law. But 'Indigenous *criminal* law'?

Inherent in the complete provocation is that there exists Indigenous *criminal* law. This is discomforting. 'Indigenous criminal law' presupposes that First Peoples would have a version of the colonising-state criminal law and that I refute.

Change the Frame

Pause for a moment and reflect on First People's experience of 'criminal law' and its systems and what our perspectives might be. Do you realise this system has been and is devastating to many in our communities?

In the experience of many in our communities, First Peoples are the objects of criminal law, of law enforcement, not the subjects who experience its purported benefits. Coloniser claims about the 'rule of law' ring hollow and the label 'criminal justice' would be ludicrous if it were not so tragic. More precisely described as a criminalisation system, it captures up to thirty times more First Nations people than any other population.

Imagine – somehow serendipitously – we had law that replicated coloniser-settler criminal law. If we did that to ourselves, we would not still be peoples. We would not have continued as long as we did. We would not still be here to contend with that 'muldarbi',[14] *colonisation.*

'Criminal law' is not something that we would develop for ourselves, for our peoples to flourish. ***'In a world composed of relationships, the ultimate value of a law must be determined by how well it sustains, maintains and renews the connections between all life.'***[15] *This is something that the criminal law has not done for us. Instead, what it has brought us is death, pain, disruption and dislocation, and this continues to exacerbate.*

This is not law – this is a 'muldarbi'.[16]

It would be impossible for us to have 'criminal law' and the system that supports it.

13 For example, 'Gendering the Rule of Law? An Informal Discussion' convened by Anne McDuff, Margaret Thornton, Kate Ogg and others on 16 March 2021 (ANU College of Law, Canberra).

14 Meaning 'demon spirit': Watson, 'Power of the Muldarbi', 28, or 'beast': Irene Watson, 'First Nations, Indigenous Peoples: Our Laws Have Always Been Here', in Irene Watson (ed.), *Indigenous Peoples as Subjects of International Law* (London: Taylor & Francis Group, 2017), 96.

15 Kwaymullina and Kwaymullina, 'Learning to Read the Signs', 206.

16 Watson, 'Power of the Muldarbi'.

Another Perspective

When you say 'criminal law', do you really mean to ask, 'How do we respond to socially destructive behaviour?' One answer is: 'It depends' – it depends on what happened, on their character or nature, on the context, on – I can't tell you because it has not happened yet. I can say that the purpose is ultimately the restoration of balance.

Or

Do you want us to tell you how – not whether – we make an individual responsible so we can blame that person, so they can be guilty, convicted – forever? It is possible that one person can be held to account for one thing – but we can only understand this destructive behaviour if we consider the larger context and how others played their part in it. 'Guilt' is a strange idea – and then to leave a person alone with that guilt – that is not law, that is a curse.

Or

Is what you really want to know: 'what does someone have to do to be subjected to the sort of violence that you dispense in the state criminalisation system?' – the assault and kidnapping by the police, the separation from home and kin, the uncertainty and pressure of an experience over which we have no control and of a process in which we are muted, the sealing up of a human being – even sealed from the earth and the sky – alone in a cold cement box, the contempt of prison guards, removal into others' Country for weeks, months, years.

We are not that cruel. If we did that, then everyone is suffering. Better to die and go back into the ground and the air.

But then I forget – maybe you don't know. How can you see it, feel it? This system was not designed to touch you, for you to feel its effect. You live with a fantasy that criminal law is sanitised, cool and bloodless. 'Reasonable'. 'Lawful.'

You even call it a 'criminal justice system'.

Can you see how violent colonising-state law and its systems are? Can you see that it is not just ideology, morality, and principles – it is physical. I know you already know that colonisation has damaged and changed our law and attacked everything else that is part of us, especially those who have had contact for longest.

Have you wondered, though,

what has colonisation done to the law that the colonisers transplanted here? How has colonisation affected you? – how you make sense of the world? How has it affected how you see First Peoples and our law?

. . .

Irrecognition and Commensurability

Some state lawyers have recognised the existence of First Law and attempted to incorporate it into colonising-state law. This assumes that First Law is commensurable with state law.

In the 1980s and 1990s, Law Reform Commissions and committees inquired into state law recognition of 'Aboriginal Customary Law'. These reports imagined ways Aboriginal laws could be added to legislative provisions, used to interpret principle or relied upon as evidence. Aboriginal law was examined through the prism of colonising-state law and slotted into its compartments. The Australian Law Reform Commission (ALRC), for example, described a case where Aboriginal defendants succeeded in a defence of 'claim of right' in answer to a dishonesty charge, having removed from a gallery 'traditional Aboriginal bark paintings'.[17] Rather than recognition, the success of this defence relies on a legal finding that the defendants – although they believed they had a legal or moral right or a duty to take the paintings – in reality did not, as they were not the 'true owner'. This case reinscribed what Aileen Moreton-Robinson called coloniser-settler 'possessive logic',[18] which this case (and the ALRC) left 'omnipresent, but invisible, unnamed and unmarked'. The case study does not critique whether the paintings were originally appropriated from Aboriginal people, nor whether – more compellingly – they might not be able to be possessed or that, for example, the object may itself have had agency. A case that concerns First Law and that treats 'possession' and 'who can possess' as common sense ought to be regarded sceptically, interrogated and disrupted.

In the 1990s and 2000s, ill-conceived attempts by judicial officers and lawyers to recognise Aboriginal law were instead damaging. Notoriously, in cases concerning serious gender violence, defence lawyers led evidence without resistance from prosecutors and successfully persuaded judicial officers that the acts of the defendant were lawful under Aboriginal law[19] and so mitigated the seriousness of the conduct. The worst of these cases were factually wrong about kinship and other laws: for example, those which

17 ALRC 1986, *Recognition of Aboriginal Customary Law* (1986), 'Chapter 18: Aboriginal Customary Laws and Substantive Criminal Liability' [434], 310–11; *R v Craigie and Patten* [Unreported, November 1980); see ACL RP 6A, 67–9 cited in ALRC, ibid, [435] 311, footnote 100.

18 Aileen Moreton-Robinson 'The Possessive Logic of Patriarchal White Sovereignty: The High Court and the Yorta Yorta Decision' *Borderlands E-journal* 3, no. 2 (2004): [12].

19 See the commentary on Jackie Pascoe, GJ, Wunungmurra – and reflect on all the other women whose cases could never come to a colonising-state court because of these cases, and radically disrupted gender power relations in our communities.

relied on a perverted concept of 'marriage' (a concept that is arguably not a tradition of at least some First Peoples) to explain grossly unlawful personal transgressions, such as aggravated sexual assault against a child.[20] This ignorance and miscognition of Aboriginal law was the basis for prosecuting charges that mischaracterized the criminality and mitigated sentences. The irrecognition of Aboriginal law perpetuated myths about Aboriginal masculinity and played to racist tropes of Aboriginal men as violent and Aboriginal women as subordinated to men.[21] Aboriginal women decried this misrepresentation of Aboriginal law as 'bullsh*t law'.[22]

Attempts by legislators to address this failed. Realising that Aboriginal law was being misrepresented, but determined that it should be properly recognised in 2004, the Attorney General of Northern Territory of Australia created a system that was supposed to encourage lawyers to critically engage with and to educate judges about Aboriginal law. It failed because the scheme relied on a level of cultural competence that state-trained lawyers did not have and was inserted into a system of law that obscured and veiled that system's biases.[23]

These powerful legal deficit accounts[24] have been used to justify higher levels of state intervention, control and criminalisation.[25] Meanwhile the criminal law and its system has not restored balance with respect to the terrible violence unleashed on young women. For many in our communities, the criminal law is lawless.[26] It brings lawlessness, not peace. Many in First

20 E.g. *Hales v Jamilmira* ('Jackie Pascoe case') [2002] (Unreported, Maningrida Court of Summary Jurisdiction, 30 April 2002); cf *Hales v Jamilmira* [2003] NTCA 9, where the appeal court could correct only the error regarding mitigation.

21 Shino Konishi, 'Representing Aboriginal Masculinity in Howard's Australia', in Ronald Jackson and Murali Balaji (eds), *Global Masculinities and Manhood* (Chicago, IL: University of Illinois Press, 2011).

22 See e.g. A. Bolger, *Aboriginal Women and Violence* (Australian National University, North Australia Research Unit, 1991). See also Judy Atkinson, 'To Do Nothing is Tantamount to Genocide' *Indigenous Law Bulletin* 6, no. 20 (2006): 20; K. Cripps and S. C. Taylor, 'White Man's Law, Traditional Law, Bullshit Law: Customary Marriage Revisited' *BALAYI: Culture, Law and Colonialism* 10 (Nov 2009): 59–72.

23 M. S. Williams, 'Innervating Colonialism: Exploring the Retraction of Indigenous Rights through Two Sentencing Provisions' *Australian Feminist Law Journal* 44, no. 2 (2018): 203–20.

24 Cressida Fforde, Lawrence Bamblett, Ray Lovett, Scott Gorringe and Bill Fogarty, 'Discourse, Deficit and Identity: Aboriginality, the Race Paradigm and the Language of Representation in Contemporary Australia' *Media International Australia Incorporating Culture and Policy* 149, no. 1 (2013): 162.

25 M. Hinkson, 'In the Name of the Child', in J. Hinkson and M. Hinkson (eds), *Coercive Reconciliation: Stabilise, Normalise, Exit Aboriginal Australia* (North Carlton, Vic.: Arena, 2007).

26 [Kwem. Joe Jabananga James], Jerry Jangala Patrick, Henry Jakamarra Cook, personal communication (various dates, September–November 2011; October–November 2012).

Peoples' communities see state law as a law-killer, as jurispathic. The attempted recognition of First Law such as that of the ALRC and even the experiments in the criminal courts may be best understood as part of the process of coloniser-settlers creating the possibility for their own personal and structural decolonisation. These attempts cannot be understood as recognising the First Law nor respecting its continuing and foundational authority.

More recently, more First Peoples have become adept in navigating the 'two laws', and have negotiated agreements or successfully lobbied for legislative and policy reform that support First Peoples' ways of being. Examples include the recent recognition of parentage in the Torres Strait[27] or the Yamatji Nation Native Title Settlement.[28] This is vital work and the skills and tenacity of those who achieved these reforms cannot be understated, but such activism and agency may be easily misconstrued. The bureaucratic and legal processes and the legal meaning of these outcomes do not reflect First Law practices or principles. Piecemeal success does not represent substantive recognition of First Law. It demonstrates the limits of what is possible within existing systemic constraints and the need to revise legal foundations and structures, as fundamentally the colonising-state systems, laws and structural biases remain unaltered.

First People have been saying for a long time, there is a problem with the way that state legal actors see and represent First Law, and how state legal actors assess their own law and its structures. More than two decades ago Irene Watson set herself the task of recentring the First Law, working out how to free the 'raw law' that was 'buried alive'.[29] One pathway to this, she argued, is to help coloniser-settlers to see how their own law is not serving them either, not in the long run. She observed that '[w]hat the greater

Lajamanu – in the context of discussing the failed police repression of a Yapa dispute resolution through criminalisation that instead exacerbated social disruption.

27 H. Loban, K. E. Van Doore and Z. Rathus, 'Parentage not Parenthood: Ending Discriminatory Laws and Policies Regarding the Legal Recognition of Torres Strait Islander Traditional Adoption' *Australian Journal of Family Law* 31, no. 3 (2018): 135.

28 This was a complex and vast land use agreement in a densely settled part of south-west Western Australia achieved despite the state law that contemplates that native title is capable of being extinguished. See, for example, the documents relating to the Yamatji Nation Agreement available at: www.wa.gov.au/organisation/department-of-planning-lands-and-heritage/yamatji-nation-agreement-land-component and www.wa.gov.au/government/document-collections/yamatji-nation-indigenous-land-use-agreement-documents, accessed 10 December 2021.

29 E.g. an early article: Irene Watson, 'Buried Alive' *Law and Critique* 13, no. 3 (2002): 253–69. See also Irene Watson, *Aboriginal Peoples, Colonialism and International Law: Raw Law* (Abingdon: Routledge, 2014).

humanity have come to know as law is a complex maze of rules and regulations . . . ' and suggested that these threaten entrapment rather than liberation. She sees colonising-state law as a part of a larger concern that globally the earth is suffering from the effects of Western civilisation and colonisation.[30] If state lawyers can develop insight into how First Peoples see coloniser-settler law, then it may be possible to understand what First Peoples consider lawful.

Indigenous teachers share a little, wait for understanding, then share a little more. Only when a child can digest *nyanya*, can they have *mangarri* and *kuyu*. Even then, they will not be forced to eat; autonomy is highly valued and respected, even in children. Similarly, First Peoples have been and are waiting for coloniser-settlers to understand. Our ancestors waited and watched newcomers who entered their Country – Jerry Jangala Patrick has talked about how, before the colonisers came, they would wait, hidden, and watch the newcomer until they showed they understood how to behave in Country and were not dangerous.[31] Only then would they come out to show the newcomer how to be in that Country safely, and there was ceremony – a celebration of their relationship with their *ngurrajinta*, their Countrymen – a celebration of the ancient and deep relationship of people who may never have met before. Like our ancestors, First Peoples are waiting and watching until you show you understand what has already been shared, so that then we can share more. It is important not to mistake our 'waiting' for 'refusal'.

As I have been writing, I have been waiting. To see First Law, we must start and continue to decolonise ourselves. To decolonise ourselves, at the same time we need to decolonise the social structures that continue to influence our ways of thinking and being, and that hold us in this unhealthy relationship with each other and this place. These systems are outmoded and do not serve our aspirations nor our spiritual needs; they threaten if not our existence then certainly our children's. We cannot live without Country, like a drop of blood cannot live outside the body. Country can live without us, but – as Anne Poelina, Clinton Schultz and others have shared – Country will be lonely without us.[32]

30 For the purpose of elucidation, Kwaymullina and Kwaymullina describe coloniser-settler law as positivist and reductionist, but note that there are also more complex traditions in Western thought. Kwaymullina and Kwaymullina, 'Learning to Read the Signs', 197.

31 Jerry Jangala Patrick, personal communication (Lultju, Northern Territory of Australia, 20 November 2011).

32 Anne Poelina, Rooted Messages, at https://rootedmessages.com/anne-poelina/ [2 minutes 59 seconds], accessed 10 December 2021. See also N. Redvers, A Poelina, C. Schultz,

I now share the 'basic precepts', as Mary Graham described them and which she shared across the continent. Will you be able to see past the interfering glosses of what you think you know? Will you dismiss its simplicity or allow yourself to reflect and realise its depth? What follows is a recitation of what has been shared before but rarely heard. Perhaps the uncomfortable questions I have asked of you may create the conditions for reorientation, and you may understand now what many have already shared for so long.

Basic Precepts: Country, Relationality and Respecting Autonomy

The foundation of all First Peoples' philosophy, law, sociality and being is Country. From Country spring all other basic precepts: that law is from Country and that we are inherently related to each other and all other beings. This is what underlies the astoundingly diverse local laws, interrelated as we are by the same earth and sky. If fully appreciated, these basic precepts offer a way to disrupt the misperception that it is impossible to decolonise law.

Every account must start with Country, to remind ourselves who we are, our place in the existence, and with whom we are in relationship.[33] We are 'connected' to Country, but it is more than this: we are of Country. We become human out of Country, and when the human life ends, we return to Country, and life continues. Country is the whole, the existence. It is not only land, so we do not stand on it nor are we above it. Country is every living being, the land and the sky are not separated; the cosmos is not another realm. If you start with this basic precept, then it is impossible to believe that you are above land, that you could control it. Understanding the nature of Country and one's relationship with it engenders responsibility and obligations to Country in all its aspects, including to other humans. Everyone has their own unique role to play in this matrix of responsibilities. Through mutual obligation we – Country – thrive. The unique responsibility of each person and our most fundamental relationship with Country means that we respect the autonomy of others. This can be described as 'relational

D. M. Kobei, C. Githaiga, M. Perdrisat, D. Prince and B. S. Blondin, 'Indigenous Natural and First Law in Planetary Health' *Challenges* 11, no. 2 (2020): 29.

33 M. S. Williams and W. S. J. Patrick, 'Thoughts on the "Law of the Land": The Persistence of Aboriginal Law in Australia', in J. Hendry, M. L. Tatum, M. Jorgensen and D. Howard-Wagner (eds), *Indigenous Justice* (Basingstoke: Palgrave Macmillan, 2018), 143–57.

autonomy' and it is from this that we derive our authority as First Peoples, both collectively and individually.

If you understand yourself as part of a whole, then you could not imagine 'owning' it.

> *Is there anything – anyone – you lay your eyes on without imagining 'who possesses that?' Imagine being free of that.*

If you understand that your being is only in Country temporarily and you will one day leave it (either to another realm or you will simply cease to be) then it becomes possible to treat Country as disposable, to feel entitled to extract from Country whatever you choose to satisfy your wants. It is possible to be reckless and ignore the First Law that plainly forbids this.[34] One's attitude to Country and one's understanding of what is lawful is very different if one understands oneself as continually part of Country. On the other hand, if one understands the world as centred around the human being – if religion, for example, has taught you or your forebears that this existence was created for you – then it is likely your laws will revolve around the relations between people and deprioritise other beings or perhaps not even recognise them as beings.

Law Is from Country

Country is fundamental to everything,[35] and so Country must inform every account of law. When Irene Watson talks of Country, she uses her people's language for 'land' – 'ruwi'; perhaps as you read you can hear the sound of her Country when she calls First Law – the law of the *ruwi* – 'raw law'.[36] In every account of First Law shared, First Peoples are careful to state that knowledge and law is local to a place. As diverse as the Country is across this continent and its islands, so too are the laws; the law of each place arises from the particularity of that place. That particularity concerns its plants, rocks and other living beings local to that place. Human beings are as important as other living beings. When First Peoples talk of Country, it is important to understand that Country has a macro and micro aspect: while it is a particular place for which certain people are responsible,[37] simultaneously Country is

34 For a discussion about Warlpiri language and how it rejects any sentiment of anthropocentrism, see ibid.

35 E.g. Christine Black, *The Land is the Source of the Law: A Dialogic Encounter with Indigenous Jurisprudence* (London: Routledge-Cavendish, 2010).

36 Watson, 'Buried Alive', 254.

37 Within the limitations of English a place which in reality 'owns' or 'cares for' us can be described as 'my' or 'our' Country meaning a particular area.

the whole continent and the whole existence, endlessly interconnected, interconnecting and reproducing or recreating.[38] Even the stars go into the ground.[39]

Across the continent, the law interconnects stories, family groups, clans and tribes, trading routes, and life forces. There is commonality, and there is also distinctiveness. Kwaymullina and Kwaymullina explained the implications of this for law in this way:

> [L]aw cannot exist in isolation from the connections between all life. Law both sustains and reflects the nexus of relationships, the pattern of creation that is the world. Law is part of a larger way of knowing the world, one which is formed by a living landscape . . .[40]

Watson tells us that 'Law came to us in a song, it was sung with the rising of the sun, law was sung in the walking of the mother earth, law inhered in all things, law is alive, it lives in all things . . . .'[41] While there is Country there is law, and it only needs to be uncovered. This is an astounding counter-narrative to the ongoing colonising discourse of dispossessed land and deficient people. This counter-narrative to the dominance and jurispathy of colonising-state law is sensible: how can people – even those with machines and a fantastic belief that they are above and separate from the earth, and who treat the earth like a 'magic pudding'[42] – ever conquer Country? A corollary of this is that First Law cannot be eliminated, because the law is of Country.

Bill Neidjie said, 'The white man's law is always changing, but Aboriginal Law never changes . . . .'[43] I have heard many desert people echo these words.

38 This is why desert ladies sit down with me and say, 'we are all Yapa – all the same, just different'.

39 Warlpiri law men and women have shared with me stories about the stars going into the ground – e.g., the constellation known as the Southern Cross goes below the horizon when the yams are ready to be dug up and eaten.

40 Kwaymullina and Kwaymullina, 'Learning to Read', 198.

41 Irene Watson, 'Kaldowinyeri-Munaintya: In the Beginning' *The Flinders Journal of Law Reform* 4 (2000): 3, 4. See also: Irene Watson, 'Naked People's Rules and Regulations' *Law Text Culture* 4 (1998): 1 and Irene Watson, 'Indigenous People's Law Ways: Survival against the Colonial State' *Australian Feminist Law Journal* 8 (1997): 39.

42 The magic pudding was a grumpy character in an early twentieth-century Australian children's book that remain popular for a century. Other characters would eat part of the pudding, which would later magically restore itself. Norman Lindsay and Walter Syer, *The Magic Pudding: Being the Adventures of Bunyip Bluegum and His Friends Bill Barnacle and Sam Sawnoff* (Sydney: Angus & Robertson, 1918).

43 Mr Bill Neidjie, 'Kakadu Man' quoted in Mary Graham, 'Some Thoughts about the Philosophical Underpinnings of Aboriginal Worldviews' *Australian Humanities Review* 45 (2008): 181.

That is because legislators always change their law, and the application of the law usually makes no sense of the problem, delivers a disproportionate response, and leaves the community in a worse situation than they were in before. They see no constants in state law, nothing like the rhythms of the earth and the sky. The constant to which Bill Neidjie referred was Country on a long temporal scale. Country is alive and changes like all the living beings of which it is constituted. Life-changes follow patterns. When one knows Country, one knows how to respond well so that all can thrive. The law requires people to respond to Country – as all beings must, but only in the same way that all beings respond as interrelated elements of the existence: seasons change, stars and shadows move across the sky, tides move in and out as the moon rises and goes back into the earth, trees bend with the wind. These changes are seasonal, geological but knowable to anyone who will learn from Country.

Diverse kinship laws express and facilitate the astounding complexity of relationship and philosophy. These kinship systems underlie the success and longevity of First Peoples societies over millennia. Such complex systems of kinship are not necessary to achieve reproduction or avoid incest. Kinship expresses and enables participation of people in processes far more profound, the revelation of which becomes increasingly complex and esoteric as one learns more.[44] These laws express First Peoples' continuing participation in *tjukurrpa*,[45] the stories that reflect the continuous creation of Country.

Relationality/relatedness is a 'basic precept' of First Law across this continent.[46] If you are in this Country, then we are in relationship with each other – or we ought to be. This is so even where it is not immediately apparent. This value of relationality is expressed in many ways, most obviously through kinship practices. Everyone, every 'thing' is connected. In the societies of the First Peoples on this continent, as Mary Graham says, 'You are not alone in the world'.[47] ('Wiyarrpa' – *'poor thing', I can hear the desert ladies say about the* kardiya *who sleeps alone.*) Everyone has their place; it ought to be impossible to be exiled.

44 Personal communication Musharbash January 2021.

45 Pintupi, Warlpiri and other desert languages evoking laws, ceremonies, songs, etc. that tend to concern the ongoing creation of Country for which identified groups of knowledge holders are responsible and whose performance of ceremonies, etc. ensures the ongoing creation of Country. Often translated to 'dreaming', in English. There is no adequate translation of *tjukurrpa*.

46 Graham, 'Some Thoughts about the Philosophical Underpinnings of Aboriginal Worldviews', 105.

47 Ibid.

Outsiders tend to see only the legal relationships between people, not the larger context of those relationships or what other relationships there might be. These relationships are expressed in meetings, in ceremonies, in dispute resolutions, in everyday encounters. I have observed a senior law man walking between two young women having a jealous argument, on the verge of a physical fight. As he did so, he called out to them and said to each of them their skin name and reminded them how that connected them. The young women – both teenagers – quietened, and he continued more quietly, reminding them of their kin and their clans, and how they were part of larger connections. He gestured to the places where they were each from, where their close kin were, across language groups and landscapes. He reminded them of stories and ceremonies for which they were responsible and the interrelationships of those stories, how that drew people together across place and time. The sentiment was so strong that it held them still, reflective for moments, and then tearful, they held each other and said sorry. *Mala mala*. Balance was restored for the time being. It was an ordinary, everyday sort of event.

In a more formal context, I have observed law men and women of the Yuendumu Kurduju Committee participating in the visiting magistrate's community court do something similar. They did not merely admonish ('growl') the troublemakers before the court, they exhorted them to remember who they were by reminding them to whom they were connected and where, and the importance of the obligations and responsibilities that came with those connections. Remembering and reiterating those connections can bring into perspective the smallness of a dispute between individuals, selfishness or self-destructiveness.

First Peoples look for the ways that we are connected. I have seen this in different forms across the continent. When meeting someone for the first time, Warlpiri usually call them *ngurrajinta* – Countryman (not 'stranger'). This is the same word used to refer to the closest family members.[48] Restoration of relationships micro and macro is highly valued. Lawful relationality extends beyond humans. Peoples are connected to animals, plants and things by different kin arrangements. For example, in Central Australia there are skin-names, in the north-east of the continent and western New South Wales, there are totems. Everybody has a place in the existence; no one should be homeless.[49]

48 See Patrick and Williams, 'Thoughts on the "Law of the Land"'.

49 Irene Watson, various Yapa, my father's teachers – all follow the logic of this and contemplate the possibility of 'the many non-Indigenous need to become Aboriginal again'. This does not necessarily mean to this place – but to their place on the planet.

Relationality goes beyond just webs of connections. It is about identity. Moreton-Robinson observed this:

> Indigenous people are the human manifestations of the land and creator beings, they carry title to the land through and on their bodies . . . The relationship between people and their Country is synonymous and symbiotic. This is why the connection to land is never broken.[50]

If First Peoples are of Country, then even if we are away from our Country, we are not severable, as Country is not severable – it is always whole. Moreton-Robinson argues that this explains coloniser-settler insecurity.[51] The dispossession strategy of forcibly removing a person from Country – as violent as it is – or creating conditions that require a person to move away from their Country is not enough to 'sever' a person from their Country.[52] Yapa, Yamatji, Koori, Anangu, Pama[53] and more – the people – are also Country. The challenge for an Indigenous person is to resist the influence of colonial discourse and misrepresentation of our identity, defining us as 'raced', and to reject the implications that this has for our identity. In other words, the challenge for First Nations people is to refuse to be 'raced' and to remain as Country, a *ngurrajinta* – a 'Countryman' – unseverable from Country. This is key to understanding what it is to be Indigenous to this place – not skin colour, not disadvantage. The First Peoples are part of Country, and from this flows our authority. That authority is not exercised as power or dominion. Some call this authority 'sovereignty' – but that word is adequate and polluted by its association with hierarchies and possessiveness. Our authority is responsibility, our obligation to fulfil our role as part in the vast network of relations that constitutes our home.

Within webs of interconnectedness, we are responsible for each other's well-being. In human terms, this manifests as obligations to specific kin,[54] and

'The many non-Indigenous need to become Aboriginal again. But to become Aboriginal in their place and in their culture not ours. To copy Aboriginality of us would perpetuate the rape and appropriation.' Watson, 'Power of the Muldarbi', 35.

50 Moreton-Robinson, 'The Possessive Logic', [12]. She made this observation in the context of the problematic Court ruling that the Yorta Yorta people could not establish a continuing connection to the land (cf Country) they attempted to claim under native title.

51 Aileen Moreton-Robinson, 'I Still Call Australia Home: Indigenous Belonging and Place in a White Postcolonizing Society', in S. Ahmed, M. Sheller, A.-M. Fortier and C. Castada (eds), *Uprootings/Regroundings: Questions of Home and Migration* (Abingdon: Routledge, 2020), 23–40.

52 Tony Spiers (my father), personal communication (Ourimbah, various dates).

53 These are all words in first languages for 'people/person'.

54 For example, this can manifest as 'demand sharing', where one has a relationship of obligation with another and can ask for someone to do or give something. I have

has been critical to First Peoples' survival. When considered in isolation, it may seem oppressive. The reality, however, is that obligation born of relationality is balanced with the need for individuals to exercise autonomy. We respect this autonomy – of a person, a clan, a people – because autonomy allows us to learn directly from Country – from our environment and from our life. Our primary relationship is one with Country. Ultimately, everything returns to and comes from Country.

Interrelatedness means that the laws of one place may be able to be shared with the people of another place. Peoples have traded not only material objects, but also law, ceremonies, and stories.[55] This occurred because there was normative order across Country, between peoples and clans – inter–'Nation' relationships.[56] In some instances, it appears that the knowledge/law/ceremonies shared related to segments of a shared *tjukurrpa*. However, even though we are all *ngurrajinta* (Countryman) and closely connected with each other, not all laws brought from one place to another within the continent will necessarily transplant well. For this reason, we heed closely those with authority, those who have responsibility for a place and its laws.

Relationships are within and beyond this place. First Peoples have exchanged and formed close connections not only across the continent but also beyond it and with those who have come to us.[57] (*Not every relationship has to be one of unequals.*) First Peoples of this place have maintained

observed and experienced this in desert communities in central Australia and Gamilaraay Country in north-west New South Wales. On 'demand sharing', see N. Peterson, 'On the Persistence of Sharing: Personhood, Asymmetrical Reciprocity, and Demand Sharing in the Indigenous Australian Domestic Moral Economy' *The Australian Journal of Anthropology* 24, no. 2 (2013): 166.

55 E.g. Yuendumu Warlpiri people passed on the Kurduju ceremony to the Willowra Warlpiri peoples in exchange for blankets and money: Francoise Dussart, *Warlpiri Women's Yawulyu Ceremonies: A Forum for Socialization and Innovation* (PhD Thesis, ANU, 1988), 124–5. Wanta Jampajimpa Patrick, e.g., told me that the Pintupi people gave the jardiwanpa ceremony to the Warlpiri: personal communication (2011; 2012); and Dussart reports that in return the Warlpiri gave blankets and money: Dussart, ibid, 125.

56 Ambellin Kwaymullina has shared her perspectives on the ancient legal traditions between of Aboriginal Peoples: 'Aboriginal Nations, the Australian Nation-state and Indigenous International Legal Traditions', in Irene Watson (ed.), *Indigenous Peoples as Subjects of International Law* (London: Taylor & Francis, 2017). (I am averse to using the term 'nation' as it evokes the Westphalian nation state, diminishing and misrepresenting First Peoples' polities, especially their ontological basis. Nonetheless, I respect, appreciate and will defend others' use of the term 'First Nations' for our Peoples.)

57 E.g. the Macassans and Afghan traders in northern and central Australia: R. Ganter, 'Muslim Australians: The Deep Histories of Contact' *Journal of Australian Studies* 32, no. 4 (2008): 481–92.

relationships with Islander neighbours, and today are part of a global movement of Indigenous peoples, advancing First Nations and other Indigenous peoples' rights. Learning about each other's laws and experiences can help us to make sense of contemporary challenges. Some ceremonies and philosophies resonate with our Country, but not all. Almost all other First Peoples have been colonised by Europeans longer than we, and their continuities of culture may not be as ancient as our own. While there is richness and inspiration in exchange, we must reflect on its commensurability. If we are to remember the centrality of Country while we and other Indigenous peoples are still being colonised, we need to reflect on whether the laws of First Nations peoples beyond this continent really are commensurable with our First Law. Such laws can share traits that are more like coloniser-settler law, governance and ways of being, and less like those of our own.

. . .

Conclusion: Recentring First Law and Decolonising Settler Law

Irene Watson asked more than twenty years ago: 'But does my voice communicate? And how will an academic terrain receive it? . . . [will these ideas] be received or even understood?'[58] These questions have preoccupied me in reciting this knowledge already shared by others about First Law. Since colonisation has begun, First Peoples have shared so much. The history of our encounters – our own accounts as well as coloniser versions – is littered with instances of our ancestors' attempts to engage the coloniser in lawful conduct, to share lawfully and to show how to behave lawfully in this place: trading routes, resources, information about Country and its beings, language and philosophy. What was shared was typically squandered, and the possibility of relationship was refused. Worse, coloniser-settlers have taken and still take more than they need, and have even wiped out life that cannot return – animals, plants, rivers and other things colonisers do not consider living.

Some First Peoples have taken up the coloniser-settlers' promise of legal rights and legislative provisions, and have been persuaded that this was a means of enabling their people to pursue their way of being,[59] including

58 Watson, 'Power of the Muldarbi', 28.

59 E.g. *Coe v Commonwealth (No. 2)* (1993) 214 CLR 422 (where the High Court of Australia rejected the application that Wiradjuri people are a sovereign nation or alternatively are a domestic dependent nation entitled to self-government and rights over their traditional land); *Walker v NSW* (1994) 182 CLR 45 (where the High Court of Australia

being allowed to practice law or use colonising-state law to protect law places.[60] Despite the 'means' (colonising-state law) being radically dissimilar to First Law, the 'ends' have justified engaging with it. Others had no choice but to respond to litigation or had no standing as a victim.[61] Others who engage find themselves required to give evidence of First Law[62] – transformed into evidence, *kardiya* judges interpret it, despite their illiteracy and incompetence in First Law. It has been said that Indigenous people's participation in any colonising legal process effectively subordinates the Indigenous law to the colonisers', strengthening the coloniser-settler legal order as it swallows the law of those colonised.[63] First Peoples and others have written about the disregard of, and damage done to, First Law by state lawyers and court hearings.[64] But, as I hope is clear by now, this is impossible unless Country itself is annihilated.

The continued hostility and violence of colonising law means that First Law still finds its strongest expression outside the state legal field. First Law has been left to the social sciences and creative arts – mainstream Australian society now permits our knowledge-holders, social justice advocates, and law men and women to be recognised as artists, performers, commentators or

held that the laws of New South Wales applied equally to all people in that jurisdiction, and that under a repugnancy principle that NSW law applies where any other law is inconsistent); *Cubillo & Gunner v The Commonwealth* [2000] FCA 1084 (where the Full Court of the Federal Court dismissed an appeal by the Aboriginal claimants seeking damages for, *inter alia*, their removal from their families and detention at certain state-run institutions for Aboriginal children).

60 E.g. *Kartinyeri v Commonwealth* (1998) 195 CLR 337 (where the High Court did not settle the question of whether the Commonwealth can pass a law that is detrimental to a racial group under the race power in the Commonwealth Constitution 1901 s 51(xxvi) and Racial Discrimination Act 1975 (Cth)).

61 E.g. Munda's silent victim: *Munda v Western Australia* (2013) 302 ALR 207.

62 E.g. while Wik extended the rights recognised in the Torres Strait under *Mabo*, it was the impetus for the Commonwealth government to restrict further the Native Title Act 1993. Members of the Yorta Yorta Aboriginal Community v Victoria (2002) 214 CLR 422, in which the court found that Yorta Yorta could establish that they had continually observed without substantial modification laws and customs that have a connection to the land or waters such that it can still be characterised as 'traditional', and thus were denied native title.

63 E.g. Sally Falk Moore, *Social Facts and Fabrications: 'Customary' Law on Kilimanjaro, 1880–1980* (Cambridge: Cambridge University Press, 1986), 11; Sally Engle Merry, 'Law and Colonialism' *Law and Society Review* 25, no. 4 (1991): 889–922.

64 E.g. 'Survival inside the belly of the Muldarbi compels Nungas to go before the state's native title processes where native title applicants are required to prove the extent to which their nativeness has survived genocide': Irene Watson, 'Buried Alive', 263. See also: Moreton-Robinson, 'The Possessive Logic of Patriarchal White Sovereignty', 1–9; Marcia Langton, 'The Hindmarsh Island Bridge Affair: How Aboriginal Women's Religion became an Administerable Affair' *Australian Feminist Studies* 11, no. 24 (1996): 211–17; or Judy Atkinson, 'Traditional Violence and Bullsh*t Law' *newmatilda.com* (2006).

just 'Aboriginal people' performing arcane practices. While First Nations peoples are permitted into state law schools (in fact, there is a hard push for enrolments), mainstream Australia still does not recognise the First Law as *law*. Colonising law, its structures, and culture until now seem unable to recognise Indigenous peoples' law without fundamentally altering or damaging, if not destroying, it, not only here but everywhere the Europeans invaded. From First Peoples' perspectives, the colonising law is a *muldarbi* and jurispathic.

We have not come far enough in our relationship; it should not be like this. This is why First Peoples continue to share the law for which we are responsible with the state, its settlers and each other: it is existential to us – and it should be to you. Our forebears and senior law men and women now – who still patiently sit down with yet another four-wheel-drive full of Akubra-hat-wearing *kardiya* from the capital – believe in the possibility of decentring colonising-state law, and even recentring First Law. It is time to reflect on what it means to be lawful, and recognise what is possible while it is still possible.

'Two Laws under One Law'

In 2011, I worked with the Lajamanu Law and Justice Committee[65] as the men reworked a ground (sand) painting for a *kurdiji* – a shield – and the women made a corresponding canvas painting. This petition, seeking recognition of the First Law, was given to a magistrate, a representative and embodiment of state law. The image related to the Kurduju ceremony and depicted what, until then, they called 'Yapa law'[66] – Yapa law was symbolised as an arc curving around the top of the shield and enfolding the other images. During our discussions and sharing about Yapa law and the nature of coloniser-settler law, the men discussed the translation of the image to the shield, and spontaneously decided to change this ancient depiction of law. (This flexibility is an example of the wisdom in their understanding of law: law requires us to respond to what is in Country – and in this case, what is in Country is both *kardiya* law and Yapa law.) Under the arc, they now placed two new symbols – one for Yapa (Warlpiri people) and one for *kardiya* (settlers). This more nuanced sense of law they

65 This included Jerry Patrick, Henry Cook, [Kwem, Joe James], Peter Jigili, Molly Tasman, [Kwem Rosie Tasman], [Kwem Lily Hargreaves], Agnes Donnelly, Robin Lawson, Elaine Johnson and others.

66 Yapa n. person/human being (Warlpiri).

expressed simply in Aboriginal English: 'Two laws under one law'. The sense they were attempting to impart was that there is one law, as there is one Country and this cares for all of us, we are all within Country – it is impossible not to be. Of course, we are subject to its laws – this is reality and not to listen is insane. This is why Bill Neidjie could say: 'Aboriginal law . . . is valid for all people.'[67]

The magistrate accepted the shield and the painting graciously. He took it back to Darwin. Sent off into the world, its message has had no public life. I was told that the shield sits in the magistrate's chambers in Darwin. Its message remains dormant, waiting to be heard.

67 Bill Neidjie, 'Kakadu Man' quoted in Graham, 'Some Thoughts about the Philosophical Underpinnings'.

II

⋆

PUBLIC AUTHORITY

5
Colonial Settlement to Colony

BRUCE KERCHER

First Charter of Justice

When the First Fleet arrived in Sydney Cove in 1788, it was accompanied by the ambiguous baggage of English law. New South Wales was to be a penal colony, a place for the cast-off criminals of Britain and Ireland after the loss of the North American colonies, which had received convicts for over a century.

On the face of it, the new penal colony was subject to military law and administration. The governors were military or naval officers. The judge had the military title of Judge Advocate and the criminal court consisted of him plus six naval or military officers. The Judge Advocate was also the judge in the civil court. Most of those holding this position were not military or naval officers but, until the arrival of the first barrister as Judge Advocate at the end of 1809, their commissions required each of them to obey the governors according to the 'rules and disciplines of war'.[1]

The new colony's legal structure was autocratic, with the governor at its centre. There was no colonial council, legislature or court of original jurisdiction until 1824. In the meantime, the governors alone made local laws, called orders or proclamations. In the absence of an Executive Council the governors were also in complete control of colonial administration, and they controlled the courts. They called the criminal and civil courts into session and, in civil matters, they sat alone in the colony's Court of Appeal. In addition, they had the Crown's power of pardon of criminal sentences. A few pardon matters were sent to London and a very few civil appeals reached the appeals committee of the Privy Council. The governors made regular administrative reports to London, the courts very much less so. The distance from England, physically and legally, added to the governors' high degree of legal autonomy in the new colony.

1 Alex Castles, *An Australian Legal History* (Sydney: Law Book Company, 1982), 48.

One other characteristic of early New South Wales law was its amateurism. The first judges had no legal training, and there were no official lawyers to advise the governors. This was common across the Empire in the early nineteenth century. Even the appeals committee of the Privy Council included some members without legal qualifications; so, there should be no surprise that Sydney saw the brief appearance of only one legally qualified judge before 1809.

A Transitional Constitution

From the beginning, New South Wales was a Crown Colony, in that its governors were appointed directly by the Crown. This was so in part because New South Wales was founded as a convict colony with a tiny free population. But it also reflected a broader, empire-wide shift in colonial government. The loss of the American colonies (all of which had elected legislatures) led to the imposition of direct Crown rule in colonies conquered or settled after 1782. New South Wales was the first of these new colonies, followed by Trinidad.[2]

Even in the context of this shift, New South Wales was unusual among Crown Colonies for its complete lack of what later came to be called the 'separation of powers'. As the first governors ruled without Council and had power to dominate the courts, judicial, administrative and legislative powers all rested in his hands. Step by step, the colony moved towards separation, through the introduction of legally qualified judges from 1810, the establishment of an Executive Council and, most importantly, the commencement of a legislature (both in 1824). Even with these changes, power remained in the hands of people appointed by the British Crown: it was merely spread among more officials.

The other Australian colonies were less quirky. Van Diemen's Land was formally part of New South Wales until its establishment as a separate penal colony in 1825. Until then, officials shared the amateurism and autocracy of law and governance in Sydney. However, from 1825, the independent colony was established with a court, Legislative Council and Executive Council, mirroring the new institutions in New South Wales.[3] Western Australia,

2 Lauren Benton and Lisa Ford, *Rage for Order: The British Legal Order and the Original of International Law 1800–1850* (Cambridge: Cambridge University Press, 2016), 42–3.

3 Alex Castles, *Lawless Harvests or God Save the Judges* (Melbourne: Australian Scholarly Publishing, 2007); Alex Castles, 'The Vandemonian Spirit and the Law' *Papers and Proceedings of the Tasmanian Research Association* 38, Nos 3 and 4 (1991): 105.

founded in 1829 as a free colony, without convicts for its first twenty-one years, also received an appointed council and legislature. It had trial by jury almost from the beginning, an institution of English law deemed unsuitable for the convict colonies. However, Western Australia started with simple courts, similar to those of New South Wales before 1824, but these were staffed by legally qualified judges from the start. These simple courts slowly became more sophisticated in their approach, aided by the colony's legal profession. A similar pattern applied in the Court of Quarter Sessions, the criminal court.[4] South Australia was not a penal colony at any time after its foundation in 1836. After an initial period with a hybrid constitution, it operated under what was by then becoming a more conventional model, with an appointed Legislative Council and Executive Council.[5] The South Australian Supreme Court was established in 1837, with trial by jury, but with a court of appeals consisting of the Executive Council. The Supreme Court was legally professional from the start. Its first long-term judge, Charles Cooper, was attached to English forms and practices. One of his colleagues from 1853, Benjamin Boothby, shared this attachment to an absurd degree, acting with what Castles and Harris described as 'paranoiac zeal'.[6] There could not have been a greater contrast with the autocratic government, legal pluralism and legal amateurism of New South Wales' first twenty years. By the 1840s the Australian colonies had institutions similar to other Crown colonies in the Empire and, at least ostensibly, were 'ruled by law'.

This chapter explores the gradual and halting unfolding of 'rule by law' in early New South Wales amidst evolving tensions about how best to balance justice, English law and local circumstances in a penal colony. It does this by exploring legal contests about the apparent influence of the military on the courts; the legal and social rights of convicts; land law; the enforcement of debts; the reception of English statutes; and whether Aboriginal people were bound by British law.

4 (1829) 10 Geo. IV c 22; Supreme Court Ordinance 1861 (WA); Court of Civil Judicature Act 1832 (WA), 2 Will. IV No. 1. See John Bennett and Alex Castles (eds), *A Source Book of Australian Legal History* (Sydney: Law Book Co, 1979) 209–15; Castles, *Australian Legal History*, chapter 12; Enid Russell, *History of Law in Western Australia* (Nedlands: University of Western Australia Press, 1980) chapters 2–4, 7–15.

5 Alex Castles and Michael Harris, *Lawmakers and Wayward Whigs: Government and Law in South Australia, 1836–1986* (Adelaide: Wakefield Press, 1987); Castles, *Australian Legal History*, 310–25; John Bennett, *Sir Charles Cooper* (Annandale: The Federation Press, 2002); John McLaren, *Dewigged, Bothered and Bewildered: British Colonial Judges on Trial, 1800–1900* (Toronto: University of Toronto Press, 2011), chapter 8.

6 Castles and Harris, *Lawmakers and Wayward Whigs*, 127.

Amateur and professional judges took different approaches to each of these issues. There are at least two different ways of understanding such differences. One is to see them as disputes over what English law, correctly understood, technically required. Another approach – and the one adopted here – is to see the different views as attempts to apply and, if necessary, adapt English law to local conditions. This latter approach takes account, not only of the letter of the English law that the colonists brought with them but also of the social, economic and political conditions of the colony and ways in which they differed from conditions in England. It may be called 'pluralistic' in the sense that it allows of the possibility that while English law was simply 'applied' in some circumstances, in others it was adapted or modified to suit local circumstances, forming a second 'settler' strand in the law of the colonies.

Amateurism and Pluralism in Early New South Wales, 1788–1814

The first Judge Advocate of New South Wales, David Collins, proclaimed the commencement of the courts on 7 February 1788. He immediately faced the problem of adapting and creating law to fit novel circumstances.

The colony's Court of Criminal Judicature remained in existence from 1788 until 1824, when its jurisdiction was passed to the permanent Supreme Court. Unlike the colony's Court of Civil Jurisdiction, the establishment of the first criminal court was authorised by statute.[7] Both courts were established by the First Charter of Justice, Letters Patent of 2 April 1787.[8] The charter authorised the imposition of capital or corporal punishment. Criminal procedure was required to be more summary than in England. There was no provision for grand juries or indictments. The Judge Advocate drew up the charges, ran the trial and voted on the verdict along with the other members of the court.[9] Decisions were to be by majority rather than unanimity, five votes out of seven being required for capital sentences.

The law of England was explicitly to be applied in criminal cases. The charter stated that the criminal court 'shall have all such powers as by the Laws of England are incident and belonging to a Court of Record'. It went on

7 (1787) 27 Geo. 3, c. 2.

8 Available at www.foundingdocs.gov.au/resources/transcripts/nsw3ii_doc_1787.pdf, accessed 14 May 2019; and Bennett and Castles, *A Source Book of Australian Legal History*, 19–22.

9 Castles, *Australian Legal History*, 48.

to say that 'such punishment so to be inflicted being according to the Laws of ... England as nearly as may be considering and allowing for the Circumstances and Situation of the place ... and the Inhabitants thereof'. This allowed some legal flexibility, which was soon used. On the first day of criminal trials, Collins's court may have gone beyond its formal powers when it sentenced Thomas Hill, a convict, to confinement in irons on a small rocky island adjacent to Sydney Cove for stealing food.[10] Was this merely corporal punishment as explicitly authorised, or did Hill's banishment go beyond that? Already, on the court's first sitting day, the major issue of the reception of English law had arisen.

David Collins was a serving officer of the Marines. He was not a lawyer. Nor was his successor Richard Atkins, a retired military officer whom Governor Bligh later called 'a disgrace to human jurisprudence'.[11] An attorney, Richard Dore, held the office between 1798 and 1800, after which Atkins returned until the military coup against Governor Bligh. After a year in which a succession of military officers held the acting position of Judge Advocate, Atkins returned again in 1809 until the arrival of the barrister, Ellis Bent, as the permanent replacement at the end of that year. The legal amateurs Collins and Atkins showed marked willingness to depart from some of the laws of England, as the civil cases, especially, show. Even the lawyers, Dore and Ellis Bent, did the same in different situations.[12] Pragmatic adoption and rejection of English law, and even invention of new law, were characteristic of the early judges.

Judge Advocate Dore's legal fluidity was shown when he presided over the peculiar criminal trial of several Europeans who had been charged with killing Aborigines, *R v Powell and others*.[13] Despite being convicted of deliberately killing them, the defendants were not hanged. A majority of the court wanted to send the case to London for final decision on the sentencing, while three others favoured corporal punishment only. At this time, it was not accepted, even by the colonial court, that the wilful killing of Indigenous people was the same as the murder of colonists.[14]

10 *R v Hill* [1788] NSWSupC 2.

11 Quoted by John Bennett, 'Richard Atkins – An Amateur Judge Jeffreys?' *Journal of the Royal Australian Historical Society* 52 (1966): 261, 282 from Banks's papers.

12 On the Judge Advocates, see John Nagle, *Collins, the Courts and the Colony* (Sydney: UNSW Press, 1996); Bennett, 'Richard Atkins'; Alan Atkinson, 'Richard Atkins: the Woman's Judge' *Journal of Colonial History* 1 (1999): 115; John Currey, *David Collins, a Colonial Life* (Melbourne: Melbourne University Press, 2000); Charles Curry, *The Brothers Bent* (Sydney: Sydney University Press, 1968); Bruce Kercher, *Debt, Seduction and other Disasters* (Annandale: Federation Press, 1996), chapter 2.

13 [1799] NSWSupC 7.

14 Lisa Ford, *Settler Sovereignty* (Cambridge, MA: Harvard University Press, 2010), 97–9.

The Court of Civil Jurisdiction departed even more markedly from English law. In regard to the civil court, unlike the criminal court, there was no explicit reference to the application of English law, nor allowance for that law's adaptation to colonial circumstances. The charter required the court 'to give Judgment and Sentence according to Justice and Right'. It is in the looseness of that phrase that the pluralism of early New South Wales law became most evident. From the civil court, there was a right of appeal to the governor. In cases where the claim exceeded £300, there was a right of further appeal from the governor to the Privy Council. In claims under £300, the civil law was thus entirely in the hands of the Judge Advocate and the governor. Even above that amount, the possibility of appeals to the Privy Council was used much more as a threat than as a practical way to resolve contested issues of law. An ex-convict merchant, Simeon Lord, lodged or threatened to lodge numerous appeals to London, but only one case was heard by the appeals committee of the Privy Council before 1814, and it ran for many years.[15] According to Ellis Bent JA, the practical difficulty of appealing to London meant that colonial debts above £300 were unenforceable.[16]

The very first case decided by the civil court in July 1788 demonstrated that flexibility. In *Cable v Sinclair*,[17] Henry Cable and his wife Susannah Holmes sued Duncan Sinclair, the master of one of the ships of the First Fleet for the loss of their baggage on the voyage out. Both plaintiffs were convicts who had been sentenced to death for felony and subsequently transported instead of being executed. Under English law, their death sentences meant that they were attainted, unable to hold property, give evidence or sue in court. Judge Advocate Collins ignored that law and found for the convict plaintiffs. In doing so, he allowed convicts a greater degree of autonomy in the colony than they would have had in England. By giving convicts legal standing, the civil court laid the groundwork for transported convicts to find their own housing in New South Wales and earn their own money after their official work day for the government or assigned masters had finished. This should not have been allowed under English law. The legal position of transported convicts was the subject of conflict for decades to come. An amateur judge ignored English law on the topic in order to do justice, but what would

15 *Lord v Palmer* [1803] NSWSupC 3; *Lord, attorney of Mechan v Palmer, administrator of estate of Stogdell*, 1809, at www.law.mq.edu.au/research/colonial_case_law/privy_council_decisions/cases/case_index/lord_v_palmer_1809/, accessed 15 May 2019.

16 Kercher, *Debt, Seduction*, 16–17; Bruce Kercher, 'Unreported Privy Council Appeals from the Australian Colonies before 1850' *Australian Law Journal* 77 (2003): 309.

17 [1788] NSWSupC 7.

happen when lawyers took judicial office? The question was as much political as legal, being at the heart of the colony's conflicts until the abolition of convict transportation.

Justice and English law were not always in tension in New South Wales. In the civil case of *Boston v Laycock*,[18] for instance, a free settler successfully sued soldiers for assault even though the defendant soldiers argued that their special role in keeping the peace in New South Wales should exempt them from liability. Governor Hunter affirmed the decision in the Court of Appeal, declaring that soldiers were subject to the ordinary law. Military juries would continue in criminal matters until 1840, but the same civil law applied to everyone, dispelling the notion that the early colony's government and law were merely military. As in *Cable v Sinclair*, what we would now call the 'rule of law' was applied in *Boston v Laycock*. However, the orthodox version of English law was applied in the latter case.[19]

A pragmatically pluralist approach to the reception of English law was often evident in the Court of Civil Jurisdiction's debt recovery decisions.[20] When a litigant failed to pay a judgment debt, the Charter allowed only seizure and sale of goods, followed by imprisonment for debt if there were insufficient goods and chattels to meet the debt. The Charter contained no provision for relief through insolvency. At the end of the eighteenth century, insolvency laws were regularly passed in England which allowed debtors to be released from prison in return for the assignment of all of their property to the benefit of their creditors. Those laws did not apply in the colony, leading to the possibility that debtors would be imprisoned perpetually. As fledgling colonies ran on credit and returns could be uncertain, this could have operated harshly against business people in New South Wales, endangering property and liberty. Some, like Judge Advocate Dore, favoured the officer-traders by allowing them to imprison debtors and seize their goods.

Others, including Judge Advocates Collins and Atkins, softened these rules, going well beyond English law and the requirements of the Charter of Justice in doing so. Collins protected farmers by allowing them to conditionally assign their growing crops to creditors so they could avoid prison for late payment. Atkins went further, by ordering extensions of time for

18 [1796] NSWSupC 6.

19 Victor Windeyer, '"A Birthright and Inheritance": The Establishment of the Rule of Law in Australia' *Tasmania University Law Review* 1 (1961): 635, 662; Rae Else-Mitchell, 'The Foundation of New South Wales and the Inheritance of the Common Law' *Journal of the Royal Australian Historical Society* 49 (1963): 1, 6.

20 Kercher, *Debt, Seduction*, chapter 8.

payment and payment by instalments.[21] He also acted to protect debtors against fluctuations in the value of their crops when they were offered as security. In the controversial case of *Macarthur v Thompson*, after disastrous local floods that caused wheat prices to skyrocket, Atkins allowed repayments of a debt in currency equivalent to the ordinary (rather than inflated) value of grain.[22]

Such adaptations of law played into volatile local politics, the most important of which were emerging tensions between officer-traders and emancipated-convict farmers and merchants. The Atkins court, in particular, appeared to prefer the rights of emancipist farmers to soldier-creditors. From 1806, such resentments were overlaid by perceptions that the court was corrupt and influenced unduly by the infamously abrasive Governor Bligh. Since his arrival, Bligh had tried to crack down on rum distillation and had forcibly resumed land in Sydney most of which had been informally occupied, but some of which was leased. The perceived complicity of the court in Bligh's tyranny was supposedly confirmed when, in late 1807, Atkins had John Macarthur arrested for failure to appear in court about a ship bond, and then charged Macarthur with contempt when he impugned the sobriety and ethics of the judge in open court.[23] The legal crisis reached a peak on 26 January 1808, when the military arrested Governor Bligh and deposed him. The coup leader, Lieutenant Colonel Johnston, appointed himself acting governor. Johnston acted quickly to dismiss Atkins as Judge Advocate and stacked the interim court with military officers. These military judges set about tyrannising Bligh's supporters and, like Dore before them, wound back Atkins's modifications of debt law and expanded imprisonment for debt in favour of officer-creditors.[24]

Meanwhile, the Rum Rebellion demonstrated the sensitivity of the Empire to allegations of tyranny and injustice. Johnston was eventually recalled to London to face a court martial. His allegation there was that Bligh had been a tyrant: in deposing Bligh, Johnston claimed, he was upholding law and justice, not opposing it. Though the coup was treasonous, Johnston was sentenced to a mild punishment, being cashiered.[25]

21 Kercher, *Debt, Seduction*, 193–7.
22 *Macarthur v Thompson* [1806] NSWKR 3; [1806] NSWSupC 3.
23 'Copy of the Protest against Judge Advocate Atkins, read by Mr. John McArthur, to the Members Composing the Criminal Court Assembled the 25th of January 1808', in John Ritchie (ed.), *A Charge of Mutiny: The Court Martial of Lieutenant Colonel George Johnston for Deposing Governor William Bligh in the Rebellion of 26 January 1808* (Canberra: National Library of Australia, 1988), 466–7.
24 Kercher, *Debt, Seduction*, 41–2.
25 H. V. Evatt, *Rum Rebellion* (Sydney: Angus & Robertson, 1938); Benton and Ford, *Rage for Order*, chapter 3.

The British government made no structural changes as a result of the coup. Claims of tyranny were met by the continuation of autocracy. However, the power of allegations of maladministration of justice did have some effect. They resulted in the appointment of a barrister, Ellis Bent, as the new Judge Advocate. He travelled to Sydney with Bligh's replacement, Governor Macquarie. Bent brought greater order to the decisions of the courts and their record keeping. His law followed a similar pattern, formality beginning to replace informality: in the great majority of his civil court decisions, he followed English law; but sometimes he was pressured not to do so. On his voyage to New South Wales he wrote that 'lest I should lose any of my Law (which God knows I can little spare) I read some every day'.[26] Again, debt illustrates Bent's departure nicely. He also favoured creditors, but not for political reasons. From his arrival at the end of 1809, Ellis Bent adopted the English approach under which creditors controlled the process of debt enforcement. This approach did not favour imprisonment, but it offered more efficient means for the liquidation and distribution of debtor property for the benefit of creditors.[27]

Like convict rights and debt recovery law, land law was subject to conflicts in early New South Wales. Governors were authorised to make Crown grants of land, and colonists were free to buy or sell those grants. Both the grants and conveyances of land should have followed formalities, but as late as 1814 much of the colony's land was held under informal customary arrangements. As noted, Bligh's refusal to honour such arrangements had contributed significantly to the rebellion in 1808. Informal land grants came under close scrutiny in Bent's decision in *Sanders v Jones*.[28] This is one of the occasions when Bent departed significantly from English law. He upheld an entirely informal conveyance which did not meet the standards of English conveyancing law, nor the requirements of a governor's order. Land titles in the colony were held by colonial custom, and in this case the popular custom was elevated into what passed for formal law in the colony.

This was not the only time that Bent failed to enforce the governor's orders. He did the same in cases concerning the governor's attempts to regulate the issue of promissory notes. In the absence of sufficient sterling for the colony's growing commerce, local people issued promissory notes as payment. These were negotiable, passing from person to person as if they were cash. The governors tried to prohibit the issue of hand-written notes, as

26 Ellis Bent, Journal, 1 September 1809, in Bent Papers 1802–41, National Library of Australia, MS 195. See Kercher, *Debt, Seduction*, 44–5.

27 Kercher, *Debt, Seduction*, 197.

28 [1814] NSWSupC 5.

well as those drawn in 'currency' rather than sterling, and those made by serving convicts. Bent ignored these regulations. Governor Macquarie accused him of doing so because he profited by trading in the promissory notes himself. Once again, the customs of the colony were elevated into the colony's judge-made law above the orders of the governors.[29] Bent's resistance to the governor's orders illustrated nascent judicial independence in New South Wales.

Ellis Bent also lobbied for the reform of the civil court system. The Court of Civil Jurisdiction had suited small debt and contract cases, he said, but the increase in sophisticated commercial and litigious transactions required its replacement. What began as an entirely convict-focused colony had changed into a place of significant commerce among free settlers and influential emancipists. He also said that there was a need for professionally qualified attorneys to plead before a new civil court.[30] The only legal representation before 1814 was provided by several convicts who had been attorneys in England or Ireland before they were transported, usually for one of the lawyers' crimes of fraud, perjury or forgery. One of them, George Crossley, was Governor Bligh's principal legal adviser. So, the founders of the Australian legal profession were criminals. The Court of Civil Jurisdiction permitted them to practise as law agents in the absence of any alternative.[31] These recommendations led to crisis in the next period of New South Wales legal history.

Formalisation of the Law: Second Charter of Justice, 1814–23

The Second Charter of Justice in 1814 created a new Supreme Court for New South Wales which lasted until 1824.[32] The new court had civil jurisdiction only over matters worth £50 and above. The charter made no change to the criminal court, which retained the military appearance it had had since 1788 and continued to be headed by the Judge Advocate. The Supreme Court of Civil Jurisdiction was headed by a judge who sat with two lay magistrates.

29 Kercher, *Debt, Seduction*, 133–6; and see Bruce Kercher, 'Resistance to Law under Autocracy' *Modern Law Review* 60 (2003): 779.

30 Bent to Under-Secretary Cooke, 7 May 1810, in Bennett and Castles, *Source Book of Australian Legal History*, 27–9.

31 David Neal, *The Rule of Law in a Penal Colony* (Cambridge: Cambridge University Press, 1991), 99–102; Kercher, *Debt, Seduction*, 60–3; Castles, *Australian Legal History*, 106–7.

32 Letters Patent, 4 February 1814, in Bennett and Castles, *Source Book of Australian Legal History*, 31–8.

There was no longer an appearance of military influence over large commercial matters. The new court was also given jurisdiction over equity matters, one of the most sophisticated areas of law. It had not been clear whether the previous Court of Civil Jurisdiction had equity jurisdiction. The Supreme Court was also more formal than its predecessor had been. Procedure was no longer to be summary: the court was to operate more like the courts in England. Enforcement of judgments remained the same, however. Appeals to the governor were continued, now for cases of £300 and above and, following Ellis Bent's recommendation, appeals to the Privy Council were only allowed in matters of £3,000 and above.[33] As in the previous period of the Court of Civil Jurisdiction, appeals were very rarely decided by the Privy Council in London.

The new charter also created two lower-level civil courts for matters up to £50, a Governor's Court in Sydney and a Lieutenant Governor's Court in the island of Van Diemen's Land. These minor courts consisted of the Judge Advocate and two fit and proper persons, as had the previous Court of Civil Jurisdiction. This is where the previous court's informality would continue, but only for smaller cases.

The Second Charter made few changes to the governors' autocracy. There was still no Executive Council or Legislative Council. All that was achieved was a winding-back of judicial informality. The new Judge of the Supreme Court was Ellis Bent's brother Jeffery Bent. He arrived in Sydney. The two attorneys, who were supposed to be sent by the British government to appear before his court, did not arrive. Jeffery Bent refused to allow his court to sit while the only available legal advocates were convict attorneys who had previously been practising as law agents in the Court of Civil Jurisdiction. Their assistance had been valuable to Richard Atkins and even Governor Bligh, but not to the new judge, Jeffery Bent. Judge Bent refused to admit the convicts to practice and boycotted his own new Supreme Court until proper lawyers arrived. He was eventually removed from office. The dispute over emancipist rights had its first judicial victim. The court remained closed until the arrival of his successor, Barron Field, in February 1817.[34]

Like Ellis and Jeffery Bent, Field J was a barrister. His judgments in the Supreme Court were based on sophisticated legal language and close textual analysis. Ellis Bent had shown no such inclination, rarely offering detailed

33 Kercher, *Debt, Seduction*, 17; Kercher, 'Unreported'.

34 *Admission of Convict Attorneys* [1815] NSWSupC 1. See Neal, *The Rule of Law*, 102–4; Castles, *Australian Legal History*, 107–8. On his amoval, see McLaren, *Dewigged, Bothered and Bewildered*, 130–42.

reasons for his decisions. In *Marsden v Howe*, for instance,[35] Field J gave a close reading of the Second Charter of Justice in drawing the jurisdictional boundaries between the Governor's Court and the Supreme Court. This language and his heavy reliance on decided cases was new to the colony, as was his reliance on Latin. In large cases, the time of amateur informality had passed.

Increased formality did not answer all of the fundamental questions raised by the colony's convict status. In *Doe dem Jenkins v Pearce and Wife*,[36] Field J revisited the most delicate political question in the colony, the impact of attainder on transported convicts. Attainder applied to those whose sentence of death had been commuted to convict transportation. While under sentence, English law held that these people were unable to exercise the ordinary rights of daily life: holding property, suing in court to assert their rights, and even giving evidence in court. Judge Advocate Collins had ignored this law in 1788, but that course was not open to a legally qualified judge. Field avoided crisis by demanding strict proof of attaint before imposing its restrictions. Only the original court transcript in England or Ireland could show whether a person had been sentenced to death. Other sentences of transportation did not carry attaint. Departing from the 1788 decision of *Cable v Sinclair*, Field found that attaint did operate in the colony, but he nullified its impact by demanding that the original record be sent for from the other side of the world. Strict attention to the law allowed a continuation of the local, relative, legal freedom of convicts.

Field protected convict litigants only until it threatened his personal interests. The issue was back before the courts in *Eagar v Field*,[37] a decision of Wylde JA in the Governor's Court. (Wylde had replaced Ellis Bent after the latter's death in 1815.) In this case, Field was a litigant who now argued in his personal capacity against convict rights. The plaintiff Eagar was an emancipated attorney who sued Field for defamation and over the allegedly illegal fees Field had charged as judge in the Supreme Court. Eagar had been pardoned by the governor, but Field argued that this local pardon was informal and, as a result, even after his pardon Eagar was still unable to take legal action because he continued to be attainted. The English decision in *Bullock v Dodds*[38] had held that a pardon was valid only through the Great Seal of England. This time, Field successfully argued for a twelve-month adjournment of the action while proof of Eagar's status as an attainted person was obtained from Ireland. This central question of the rights of convicts

35 [1818] NSWSupC 2. 36 [1818] NSWSupC 4. 37 [1820] NSWSupC 3.
38 (1819) 2 Barn and Ald 258, 106 ER 361.

remained unsettled until the next stage of the colony's constitutional development.

Van Diemen's Land

The island of Van Diemen's Land was part of the colony of New South Wales until 1825, when it acquired separate colonial status. First occupied by the British in 1803, it fell within the jurisdiction of New South Wales civil and criminal courts until 1825. It had its own magistrates' courts and, later, a local civil court for minor matters. For major cases, people had to wait until a visit by a Sydney judge, or litigants or defendants had to travel to Sydney. The island had a lieutenant governor who made similar orders to those made by the governors in Sydney.[39] If Sydney's legal system was remote from supervision, Hobart's was doubly so, resulting in what Alex Castles called an independent quality to the island's law, which matched the independent, cynical character of its colonists.[40]

The physical separation from Sydney courts became a serious obstacle to the enforcement of the island's criminal law. As early as 1805, some of those charged with crimes were sent to Sydney for trial, but this was expensive. The absence of an effective criminal court to deal with bushranging played some role in the imposition of martial law in 1814. In 1816, Governor Macquarie declared that convicts in Van Diemen's Land charged with the commission of local crimes should be tried by the colony's magistrates in all cases except murder. When tried before the magistrates, convicts were subject to flogging or removal to penal settlements in matters which English law would have declared capital. This confirmed an established local practice, which freed some convicts from the possibility of capital punishment. The island's magistrates were not always careful about legal rights and obligations. When well-connected free people on the island were accused of crimes, they were granted liberty on entering into a bond not to offend again. Free people should have been sent to Sydney for trial where they, unlike the island's convicts, would be liable to capital punishment for offences short of murder. The Court of Criminal Judicature did not visit Van Diemen's Land until 1821.[41]

39 Castles, *Lawless Harvests*, 23–4. 40 Alex Castles, 'Vandemonian Spirit'.

41 *R v Franklin* [1821] NSWSupC 1; see Castles, *Lawless Harvests*, 28–9, 49–54, 84–9; Bruce Kercher and Brent Salter (eds), *Kercher Reports: Decisions of the New South Wales Superior Courts, 1788–1827* (Sydney: Francis Forbes Society, 2007), 585.

Civil matters were also dealt with more informally in Van Diemen's Land than in Sydney. The island's magistrates took on civil as well as criminal trials. That was the only civil litigation on the island until the Second Charter of Justice established a Lieutenant Governor's Court with jurisdiction up to £50, presided over by Van Diemen's Land's own Deputy Judge Advocate. It sat for the first time in 1816 and remained in operation until it was abolished in 1824. Some litigants learned to split claims into batches of £50 to save the expense of travelling to the Supreme Court in Sydney. The island's civil court was soon hearing hundreds of cases a year, as informally as the Court of Civil Jurisdiction had done in Sydney. Like Atkins's court in Sydney, the Lieutenant Governor's Court's adopted flexible judgment practices, allowed married women to sue, and let convict attorneys act as 'agents' of litigants. It went one important step further than Atkins. The court's flexibility regarding female litigants went much further than Sydney's in at least one case. In both Sydney and Hobart, some wives appeared before the courts as agents for their absent husbands. However, in Hobart, Margaret Whiteman acted as a recognised agent for other men in cases before the Lieutenant Governor's Court. Free (male) lawyers finally arrived in Van Diemen's Land in 1820. At last, there was conventional active legal practice in Hobart. Field visited Hobart to constitute a civil court in circuit for the first time in 1819.[42]

The Slow Decline of Autocracy

In 1819, the British government appointed a conservative barrister and former Chief Justice of Trinidad, Thomas Bigge, to inquire into the governing institutions of New South Wales and what soon became the separate colony of Van Diemen's Land. This was one of numerous inquiries into the management and constitutions of British colonies across the world.[43] When Bigge arrived in Sydney, it was riven by disputes over the appointment of emancipated convicts to official positions, and the suitability to penal colonies of liberal institutions such as jury trial. The British government had sent Bigge out to recommend ways to increase the deterrent effect of convict transportation to the colony. Bigge recommended changes to the convict system and to land distribution, but not to the colony's fundamental institutions. Autocracy should continue.[44]

42 *Barker v Jemott* [1819] NSWSupC 1; see Castles, *Lawless Harvests*, 21–2, 50, 56, 63–73.
43 Benton and Ford, *Rage for Order*, chapter 3.
44 Ibid; Castles, *Lawless Harvests*, 97–8; Castles, *Australian Legal History*, 128–9.

His recommendations about the constitution were not followed. Rather the British government favoured more radical changes recommended by Edward Eagar, the emancipist attorney who had clashed with Barron Field. In particular, Eagar complained about the extent of the governor's law-making power in the absence of a Legislative Council or Executive Council. The result, he said, was 'a pure and simple despotism'.[45] The 1823 New South Wales Act[46] provided for the creation of Van Diemen's Land as a separate colony (from 1825) and gave both colonies a constitution that more closely resembled colonial governments established in all new colonies after 1790. Together with new Charters of Justice, Parliament created appointed Legislative Councils and new Supreme Courts in both colonies. The creation of Legislative Councils remedied claims, first voiced by Jeremy Bentham in 1803, but repeated by John Macarthur in 1805 and Ellis Bent in 1815, that the governor of New South Wales had always lacked power to legislate and had been acting illegally since 1788.[47] Under the new judicial system, trial by jury would remain very limited.[48] Executive Councils were created in 1825.[49] The new arrangements, according to Benton and Ford, were not a strict copy of English structures, but 'a coherent formula of tempered autocracy, legal pluralism, and a procedurally constructed rule of law'.[50] Elected legislatures, responsible government and ordinary jury trial were still in the distant future.

Legislation and Repugnancy

The Legislative Councils for New South Wales and Van Diemen's Land established after 1823 did more than legitimate the governors' law-making powers, which had been on shaky foundations since 1788. The Council was a fairly weak institution. Only the governors could introduce legislation and, in limited circumstances, legislation could pass with only minority support in the Legislative Council, of which the Chief Justice was a member.[51]

The main obstacle to the governors' legislative powers was placed in the hands of the colonies' judges. Before a proposed new law could be put to the Legislative Council, the Act required the Chief Justice of the colony to certify that the bill was not repugnant to the laws of England and that it was consistent with such laws so far as the colony's circumstances admitted

45 Quoted in Benton and Ford, *Rage for Order*, 64.

46 (1823) 4 Geo. 4 c 96.

47 Castles, *Australian Legal History*, 36–8.

48 Bennett and Castles, *Source Book of Australian Legal History*, 53, 116.

49 Castles, *Australian Legal History*, 132.

50 Benton and Ford, *Rage for Order*, 84.

51 Castles, *Australian Legal History*, 130.

(Section 29). This vaguely worded provision gave the Chief Justice the power of veto.

When judges exercised their power of veto over legislation, they were refusing to allow colonial law to deviate from the standards of English law. This power was sometimes used to defend liberties. When, in the late 1820s, Governor Darling attempted to control a hostile press by imposing a stamp duty on the newspapers and introducing a licensing statute, the liberal-minded Forbes CJ vetoed the bill. He argued that, even in New South Wales, freedom of the press was part of the constitutional birthright of English people and concluded that the proposals were repugnant. His counterpart in Van Diemen's Land, Pedder CJ, reached the opposite conclusion. Forbes's view was confirmed by the Crown law officers in London.[52]

The position was reversed in the *Bushranging Acts* controversy in 1834.[53] By this time a new repugnancy provision had been introduced.[54] The Australian Courts Act of 1828 removed the veto power of the Chief Justice, instead empowering any judge of the Supreme Court to declare that a newly passed law was repugnant. However, this declaration operated merely as a warning, requiring the governor and Legislative Council only to review the Bill. The legislature could stick with its law and send it on to London for final assent. The Bushranging Act allowed the detention of any person suspected of being a bushranger, or who could not prove that they were free. On this occasion, the usually conservative Burton J was alone in declaring the repressive Bushranging Act repugnant, and thus upholding the liberties of English people. The usually more liberal Chief Justice Forbes and Dowling J found that the law was justified, due to the extreme circumstances of the colony. Pluralism, in this case, was illiberal.

Such disputes about the repugnancy of colonial legislation were sent to the Colonial Office, and particularly to James Stephen Junior, its principal legal officer from 1813 onwards. His view was that English law should not be an inflexible model for all colonial legislation. Though he closely scrutinised legislation from the slave colonies, Stephen was a colonial pluralist. He advised that

> Whatever is tyrannical or very foolish you may safely call 'repugnant' &c. But whatever is necessary for the comfort of good government of the colony you may very safely assume to be in perfect harmony with English law . . .

52 *Newspaper Acts Opinion* [1827] NSWSupC 23. See B. Edgeworth, 'Defamation Law and the Emergence of a Critical Press in Colonial New South Wales (1824–1831)' *Australian Journal of Law and Society* 6 (1990): 50.

53 See *R v Elliot* [1834] NSWSupC 11.

54 (1828) Geo. 4 c 83, s 22.

> Take a new code, wherever the old one won't suit you. Keep up the family resemblance between your law and ours as well as you can, and never think it worthwhile to go mad over a difficulty which an act of his Excellency in Council can grind into powder with a blow.[55]

The introduction of greater formality and professionalism in colonial law was not the end of pluralism. Colonial law could still deviate markedly from that of England.

The Reception of English Law in the New Supreme Courts

A key part of the conversation about repugnancy rested on a long debate about which English statutes applied in New South Wales and Van Diemen's Land. The Australian colonies were assumed to be settled colonies even in the face of obvious Indigenous occupation of the land. The common law position of 'settled' colonies was that they received the laws of England insofar as they were applicable to the colony's circumstances.[56] This left some room for colonies to pick and choose which English legislation applied (except, of course, where legislation was explicitly declared to apply to the colonies). The date on which laws were received was very important. After the date of reception, colonial legislation could pass divergent legislation in order to meet local needs (subject to deeper questions about whether such laws violated fundamental principles of the imperial constitution). In general, settled colonies were understood to receive English law on the date of their foundation. However, this was not clear in New South Wales, in part because early governors never received formal legislative powers.

The date of reception mattered enormously in the 1820s in New South Wales because English law – particularly criminal law – changed radically between 1788 and 1823. Capital punishment was removed from relatively minor crimes through a series of statutes. As shown by the Van Diemen's Land case of *R v Madden*,[57] the principal question was whether the statutory changes which had been made in England since 1788 were automatically part of colonial law. If not, the penal colonies would retain capital punishment for

55 Roger Therry, *Reminiscences of Thirty Years' Residence in New South Wales and Victoria* (1863, reprinted Sydney University Press, 1974) 318. See Paul Knaplund, *James Stephen and the British Colonial System 1813–1847* (Madison, WI: University of Wisconsin Press, 1953), 232–3; Benton and Ford, *Rage for Order*, chapter 3.

56 William Blackstone, *Commentaries on the Laws of England* (9th edition, 1783, reprinted 1978), 1: 108.

57 [1829] TASSupC 9.

offences which were no longer capital in England. These were questions of life and death.

Led by Forbes CJ, in 1828 the New South Wales Supreme Court judges advised the governor that English statutes passed up to the date of establishment of the colony's Legislative Council in 1823 were automatically received as part of New South Wales law. This covered the criminal reform statutes passed before then, but it did not seem to help colonial prisoners sentenced to death after the 1827 passage of further English statutes repealing capital punishment that were not formally adopted by the colonial legislatures. Despite that, the New South Wales judges managed to save these prisoners from execution too. These pragmatic but unconventional opinions allowed the colony to avoid the potentially scandalous embarrassment of executing colonists for crimes that were no longer capital in England. In these cases, pragmatism led to the adoption of English law in the colony even when, technically, that should not have happened.[58]

The Australian Courts Act,[59] Section 24 resolved uncertainty (and justified the Court's caution) by declaring 25 July 1828 as the new date of reception. It also reworded the repugnancy test, stating that

> all laws and statutes in force within the Realm of England at the time of the passing of this Act . . . shall be applied in the administration of justice in the courts of New South Wales and Van Diemen's Land respectively, so far as the same can be applied within the said colonies.[60]

Did the statutory words 'so far as the same can be applied' have the same meaning as the old common law test of 'applicable to the colony's circumstances'? Was the new test quite different, requiring merely that it be possible to apply the law in a colony rather than inquiring, more broadly, whether the law was generally applicable to its conditions? These questions were in issue in the most absorbing of the reception cases, *MacDonald v Levy*.[61] In this case, the Supreme Court of New South Wales was required to decide whether English usury laws that placed a statutory cap on interest rates were in force in the colony. The court split two to one. In dissent, Burton J said that he had only to decide whether the English statute 'can' be applied. He held that it

58 *Applicability of Criminal Laws Opinion* [1828] NSWSupC 22. See Lisa Ford and David Roberts, '"Mr Peel's Amendments" in New South Wales: Imperial Criminal Reform in a Distant Penal Colony' *Journal of Legal History* 37 (2016): 198–214.

59 9 Geo. 4 c 83.

60 See Alex Castles, 'The Reception and Status of English Law in Australia' *Adelaide Law Review* 2 (1963): 1.

61 [1833] NSWSupC 47.

could be; and, so, the law was applicable. The fact that the colony had always had much higher interest rates than those in England did not mean that there was a colonial custom allowing higher rates. In majority, Forbes CJ (with whom Dowling J concurred) held that what the statutory test required was to judge the suitability of the English law in question to the colony's situation. Forbes argued that there was nothing worse than to be ruled by unsuitable laws. Usury laws were local to England. The fact that they had never been applied in the colony showed that there was a universal assumption that this English statute had never been adopted.[62]

The permanent Supreme Court also had to revisit the question of convict attaint, which had been in issue since 1788. The Court of Civil Jurisdiction had ignored the issue, and the first Supreme Court had avoided it by requiring that the original record of conviction be obtained from the other side of the world. Even the permanent Supreme Court retained some of the flexibility which had been evident since 1788. In *R v Farrell, Dingle and Woodward*,[63] the defence argued that the principal witness in a case of bank robbery was a convict attaint who could not testify before the court. The witness had been convicted of a capital felony in the colony and there was no need to send to England or Ireland for a record of his conviction to settle the point of attainder. According to Forbes CJ, the unavoidable question for the full court was whether such evidence would be admitted 'in this colony'. Forbes was in a minority in holding that the law of felony attaint applied in New South Wales as it undoubtedly did in England. 'We must look to the spirit of the law of England' he said, and only in a case of extreme necessity would such a fundamental law not be followed in the colony. The majority (Dowling and Stephen JJ) disagreed. Long usage had allowed convict evidence to be admitted in the colony. Given the nature of its population, they held, necessity required that result.[64]

Ultimately, Forbes's view of the declaratory nature of test of the statutory reception of law came to be accepted in Australia; but even on this broader approach to the legislation, the common law of the Australian colonies and States eventually came closely to resemble that of England. Burton's attitude, if not his test, came to be accepted. Judicial pluralism declined with the departure of Forbes in 1836, partly as a result of the Privy Council hearing more appeals and being more willing to state binding principles for the

62 See also *R v Maloney* [1836] NSWSupC 24. 63 [1831] NSWSupC 44.

64 On this and other cases, see Bruce Kercher, 'Perish or Prosper: the Law and Convict Transportation in the British Empire, 1700–1850' *Law and History Review* 21 (2003): 527–84.

colonies. In 1879, the Privy Council declared that it was 'of the utmost importance that in all parts of the empire where English law prevails, the interpretation of that law should be as nearly as possible the same'.[65]

Indigenous Law

Pluralism was not restricted to colonial innovations on inherited English law. For centuries, European law struggled with the recognition of Aboriginal law, sovereignty and titles to land.[66] Prior to the High Court's decision in *Mabo v Queensland (No. 2)*,[67] the Australian courts had refused recognition of native title and sovereignty under a doctrine which became known as *terra nullius*. That judicial refusal initially came from the decision of the Supreme Court of New South Wales in *R v Murrell* in 1836.[68] The case was reported retrospectively in the 1890s and adopted generally as the only early reported decision.[69] With the concurrence of Forbes CJ and Dowling J, Burton J held that there was only one law in the colony, the law of England. Aborigines were bound and protected by that law, even in cases of violent clashes among themselves. Aborigines were too primitive to have laws or sovereignty of their own, Burton said. This well-known decision was a reversal of a much less known decision of Forbes CJ and Dowling J only seven years earlier. In *R v Ballard*[70] the court reached quite the opposite decision on whether the colonial court had jurisdiction when one Aboriginal person killed another. Forbes held then that the wisest course was to do what had been done in North America and to refrain from interfering with transactions of any kind among Indigenous people. They 'make laws for themselves, which are preserved inviolate, & are rigidly acted upon'.

65 *Trimble v Hill* (1879) 5 App Was 342, 345 quoted in Bruce McPherson, *The Reception of English Law Abroad* (Brisbane: The Supreme Court of Queensland Library, 2007), 27; and Paul Finn, *Law and Colonial Government in Colonial Australia* (Oxford: Oxford University Press, 1987), 166.

66 See Lauren Benton, *Law and Colonial Cultures: Legal Regimes in World History, 1400–1900* (Cambridge: Cambridge University Press, 2002); Stuart Banner, *Possessing the Pacific: Land, Settlers and Indigenous People from Australia to Alaska* (Cambridge, MA: Harvard University Press, 2007). See chapters 14 and 15 in this volume.

67 (1992) 175 CLR 1. 68 (1836) 1 Legge 72.

69 The unanimous judgment was written by Burton J and was only briefly reported in Legge's Reports. The fullest account of his views is in an archived manuscript transcribed at www.law.mq.edu.au/research/colonial_case_law/nsw/other_features/correspondence/documents/document_47/, accessed 30 November 2021; and see *R v Murrell and Bummaree* [1836] NSWSupC 35.

70 [1829] NSWSupC 26.

The position of Indigenous people established in *Ballard*, half inside English law and half outside, was also evident in the Western Australian courts before their formal restructuring into the Supreme Court. The same applied in South Australia where, as late as 1851, Cooper J was reluctant to try Indigenous people for conduct among themselves.[71] Nor was *R v Murrell* the final word even in New South Wales. In the Port Phillip District decision of *R v Bonjon*,[72] Willis J found that Aborigines could not be tried for conduct *inter se*. Ultimately, however, it was the view of Burton J which came to prevail until *Mabo*. According to the best-known case, *R v Murrell*, there was only one law in physical area of the Australian colonies, that of England. Sovereignty rested solely in British hands.

Contrasting Approaches to the Reception of English Law

In the half-century after the foundation of New South Wales in 1788, its law and constitutional structures changed from being suitable for the simple requirements of a small convict settlement to matching the more complex needs of the much larger towns across the Australian colonies. From autocratic and legally amateur beginnings, the British government moved step by step towards the kinds of structures familiar across the post-revolutionary British Empire. It established Legislative Councils for the Australian colonies, appointed professional judges without military titles, and eventually dropped the requirement of military juries in criminal cases. So far as the substance of the law is concerned, the approach taken here has emphasised legal pluralism. Pluralism characterised the approach to the administration of justice from the very beginnings of the settlement in 1788. Nor did the arrival of professional judges bring it to an end.[73] However, it is important not to fall into the trap of over-emphasising colonial innovation in finding examples of pluralism. The great majority of colonial law showed a strong affinity to the law of England, and many of the changes were made with British approval. Yet some were not, and that was important. We have also seen that the judges, amateur and professional, appeared attached to deciding cases according to the law as they conceived it, though law's meaning varied from one person to the next.

71 Ann Hunter, *A Different Kind of 'Subject': Colonial Law in Aboriginal-European Relations in Nineteenth-century Western Australia 1829–61* (North Melbourne: Australian Scholarly Press, 2012); Castles, *Australian Legal History*, 529–31.

72 [1841] NSWSupC 92.

73 Kercher and Salter, *Kercher Reports*, xxv–xxvi.

6

Colonial Self-government

ANN CURTHOYS AND JESSIE MITCHELL

Colonial self-government was a relatively brief phase in Australia's history, operating for around forty-five years in five of the six colonies, and in one, Western Australia, for only ten. In this chapter we explore how and why it replaced previous systems of British rule and how, once in place, it worked as a system of government in six very different colonial settings. In exploring the origins, workings and consequences of colonial self-government we focus on its implications for Aboriginal people, who, throughout its operation, experienced continuing dispossession, loss of self-determination and population decline. In the first section, we consider how self-government came to be sought, avoided, rejected and eventually granted, while in the second section we outline what self-government meant in practice for settlers and Aboriginal people. In both sections we consider the long history of Aboriginal assertions of rights against a political system that systematically failed to recognise their sovereignty, give them a parliamentary voice, or acknowledge the fact and consequences of their violent dispossession.

Towards Self-government: 1835–56

From the mid-1830s, as the wealth of the colonies and size of the free population grew, settlers campaigned for greater political representation and control over government decisions. While they would triumph in gaining political representation in the 1840s and ultimately self-government in the 1850s, they did not do so easily. Not only did they encounter continuing resistance to their very presence from Aboriginal societies, but the British government was at first reluctant to accede to their demands. Furthermore,

This chapter is based on research funded by the Australian Research Council, Discovery grant DP0770332.

those who gained self-government in the 1850s would be much more diverse socially, economically, and politically than the squatters and gentlemen of the 1830s who first sought representation, so that the struggle for self-government also became a contest for power within settler society itself.

At the time when demands for political representation first emerged in earnest, New South Wales was a Crown Colony. After the American Revolution, there had been a reassertion of Crown authority over British colonies to such an extent that around the empire, local settlers and their representative bodies had little power over the executive government. In New South Wales, established initially as a series of penal and strategic outposts with land granted to military officers and government officials, settlers had even less power than their counterparts in other settler colonies such as Upper and Lower Canada. The governor, appointed by and answerable to the British government, was limited mainly by British policy and, to a degree from 1823, by the advice of an appointed Legislative Council, whose members were nominated by the Crown in consultation with the governor.[1] Other limits on gubernatorial power in the 1820s and 1830s included, under the Act of 1823, institutions such as non-government newspapers, trial by jury for civil cases, a Supreme Court and an office of the Chief Justice. However, there were no elected representatives until 1843.

By the middle 1830s, changes in the nature of the settler colonies led to challenges to Crown power. There was a growing enthusiasm in Britain for settler-colonialism, drawing on earlier European utopian visions of new colonists in new worlds. Edward Gibbon Wakefield's proposal that governments should fund emigration to the colonies from the revenue derived from the sale of land had a significant influence on the new Whig government elected in 1830. As New South Wales grew in wealth and population, as pastoralism spread and as migration increased, the settlers wanted more control over how they were governed. An Australian Patriotic Association, formed in May 1835, held large public meetings and gathered 5,000 signatures for a petition to Governor Bourke for a Council in which three-quarters of members would be elected.[2] Significantly, a more conservative petition by the wealthy 'exclusive' faction, urging that representation be delayed until free immigration had overwhelmed the convict and ex-convict population,

1 Parliament of New South Wales, '1822–1842 – The First Legislature', www.parliament.nsw.gov.au/about/Pages/1822-to-1842-The-First-Legislature.aspx, accessed 24 November 2021.

2 Andrew Tink, *William Charles Wentworth: Australia's Greatest Native Son* (Sydney: Allen & Unwin, 2009), 139.

attracted only 398 signatures.[3] Governor Bourke supported the larger petition, modifying it to suggest that the new Constitution Act allow for a Council that was two-thirds, rather than three-quarters, elected.[4] The British government, however, wary of representation in a convict colony, decided to postpone any decision until a Select Committee on Transportation, under the chairmanship of William Molesworth, had reported.[5]

While settlers were pushing for a greater voice and decision-making in their own colonial society, through their actions they were simultaneously removing these capacities from Aboriginal societies by dispossession and exploitation. Suffering from the social disruption, violence and introduced disease, Aboriginal societies sought either to expel the British from their lands or to negotiate new arrangements. From the beginning, they recognised the governor as the key figure in the new system, hoping that kinship-like bonds would help them survive. From Arthur Phillip's arrival in 1788, each governor had met them personally with gestures of goodwill and conciliation.[6] These were extended from 1814, when Governor Macquarie instituted an annual feast and distribution of blankets and supplies, attracting hundreds of Aboriginal people and huge crowds of white observers.[7] Governors' relationships with Aboriginal people were complex: while some knew the governor personally and fostered relationships with him, many Aboriginal people also knew that he was ultimately responsible for punitive operations against them.

These hopes and conflicts are best known to us now in the example of Van Diemen's Land, where Aboriginal peoples' mix of resistance to and negotiation with government were extensively documented. Hoping to end the frontier violence between settlers, military and Aboriginal groups,

3 A. C. V. Melbourne, *Early Constitutional Development in Australia: New South Wales 1788–1856; Queensland 1859–1922, with Notes to 1963* (St Lucia: University of Queensland Press, 1963), 210–1; John M. Ward, *James Macarthur, Colonial Conservative, 1798–1867* (Sydney: Sydney University Press, 1981), 60–1.

4 *Historical Record of Australia (HRA)* Series I, Volume 18 (Melbourne: Library Committee of the Commonwealth Parliament, 1914–1925), 391, 456; Zoe Laidlaw, 'Richard Bourke: Irish liberalism Tempered by Empire', in David Lambert and Alan Lester (eds), *Colonial Lives across the British Empire: Imperial Careering in the Long Nineteenth Century* (Cambridge: Cambridge University Press, 2006), 131ff.

5 John M. Ward, *Colonial Self-Government: The British Experience 1759–1856* (London: Macmillan, 1976), 154.

6 Shino Konishi, 'The Father Governor: The British Administration of Aboriginal People at Port Jackson, 1788–1792', in Matthew McCormack (ed.), *Public Men: Masculinity and Politics in Modern Britain* (London: Palgrave Macmillan, 2007), 54–72.

7 R. H. W. Reece, 'Feasts and Blankets: The History of Some Early Attempts to Establish Relations with the Aborigines of New South Wales, 1814–1846' *Archaeology and Physical Anthropology in Oceania* II, no. 3 (October 1867): 193–5.

Lieutenant Governor Arthur appointed George Augustus Robinson to travel around the colony with some surviving members of the South-east people to persuade Aboriginal peoples to relocate away from the settlers and thus away from their own land. As Henry Reynolds and Lyndall Ryan have noted, on these journeys, Robinson was dependent on Aboriginal knowledge and diplomacy.[8] Robinson secured an agreement that if the surviving Aboriginal people relocated away from the Van Diemen's Land mainland, the governor would provide them with peace, protection, material goods and the right to keep visiting their homelands. Arthur then sent them to Flinders Island, where government officers gathered them into an institutional environment with rigid daily routines, poor living conditions and endemic illness, leading to a tragic population decline.

If Aboriginal people were rapidly losing their lands, livelihood and self-determination under British imperial rule, a transfer of political control to the settlers posed a new threat to their survival. At the same time as settler demands for representation began in the mid-1830s, the violent seizure of Aboriginal lands in New South Wales entered a particularly intense phase, as settlers surged ever more deeply into Aboriginal areas seeking new pastures. As a major financial asset for whoever governed the colonies, land was one resource over which Britain wanted to retain control. Britain wished, too, to maintain imperial control of Aboriginal policy, which was becoming a matter of concern as evangelical and humanitarian figures who had successfully sought the end of slavery in the British Empire in the Slavery Abolition Act of 1833 turned their attention to the destruction of Aboriginal lives throughout the Empire. Humanitarians were now influential in the House of Commons which, in March 1835 on the motion of Thomas Fowell Buxton, established a Select Committee on the Aboriginal Tribes (British Settlements) to investigate and suggest solutions.[9] At the same time, the new British government, which formed the following month, was marked by stronger evangelical influence than ever before, and Lord Glenelg, as Secretary of State for the Colonies, stressed Aboriginal protection more strongly than his predecessors had done.[10] The Select Committee's final report in July 1837 confirmed that Aboriginal

8 Henry Reynolds, *Fate of a Free People* (Camberwell: Penguin, 2004), 137–50; Lyndall Ryan, *Aboriginal Tasmanians* (St Leonards: Allen & Unwin, 1996), 102, 129–55.

9 Henry Reynolds, *Law of the Land* (Ringwood: Penguin, 1987), 84; Zoe Laidlaw, '"Aunt Anna's Report": The Buxton Women and the Aborigines Select Committee, 1835–1837' *The Journal of Imperial and Commonwealth History* 32, no. 2 (2004): 4.

10 Alan Mark Thornton, *The Philosophical Radicals: Their Influence on Emigration and the Evolution of Responsible Government for the Colonies* (Claremont, CA: Pomona College, 1975), 75.

peoples everywhere were being degraded and destroyed by settler violence, alcohol and introduced diseases, and suggested that colonisation could be conducted with less bloodshed and loss of livelihood if the British imperial government took a stronger role in managing things.[11] Only the Crown, it argued, should have the power to purchase or acquire Aboriginal peoples' land, and governments should use the revenue raised to provide protection and religious instruction to Aboriginal people.[12] The imperial government should appoint protectors under the authority of the governor as mediators between settlers and Aboriginal people; and colonial legislatures should not be trusted with Aboriginal policy matters. The Report commented, 'Whatever may be the legislative system of any Colony, we therefore advise that, as far as possible, the Aborigines be withdrawn from its control.'[13]

When Australian colonial governments attempted to follow the new British policy by establishing protectorates in New South Wales, South Australia and Western Australia, by funding missions and rationing systems, and by sometimes prosecuting white men for frontier violence, settlers opposed them and used the issue to argue for their own right to representation. Matters came to a head in New South Wales when eleven white men were arrested for murder following the massacre of around thirty Aboriginal people at Myall Creek in June 1838. Arguing that it was they, not Aboriginal people, who needed government protection, settlers attacked the imperial government as distant, authoritarian and ignorant of their situation. The *Sydney Herald* recommended 'passive resistance through the jury box' (meaning acquittal of white men accused of murdering Aboriginal people), since colonists had no direct means of rejecting laws and policies imposed upon them.[14] The conviction and hanging of seven of the men after a second trial provoked outrage and hostility towards Aboriginal protection, linked rhetorically to settlers' lack of adequate representation.[15] In 1840, the *Port Phillip*

11 House of Commons, 'Report of the Select Committee on Aborigines (British Settlements)' *British Parliamentary Papers, 1837*, Volume 7: 3–87; Alan Lester and Fae Dussart, *Colonization and the Origins of Humanitarian Governance* (Cambridge: Cambridge University Press, 2014), 85.

12 'Report of the Select Committee on Aborigines', 79; Richard Cole Harris, *Making Native Space: Colonialism, Resistance, and Reserves in British Columbia* (Vancouver: University of British Columbia Press, 2002), 10.

13 'Report of the Select Committee on Aborigines', 77.

14 *Sydney Herald*, 15 October 1838, 2. Rebecca Wood, 'Frontier Violence and the Bush Legend: The Sydney Herald's Response to the Myall Creek Massacre Trials and the Creation of Colonial Identity' *History Australia* 6, no. 3 (2009): 67.7.

15 *The Australian*, 27 December 1838; Terry Irving, *The Southern Tree of Liberty: the Democratic Movement in New South Wales before 1856* (Annandale: Federation Press, 2006), 17.

Herald blasted the protectors' attempts to prosecute white men for frontier violence as a 'subversion of the principles of the British constitution' and, in 1842, described such attempts as 'calculated to arouse the indignation of a free, and, besides, a British people'.[16] When missions floundered and closed, it became accepted among settlers that such ventures were doomed, along with Aboriginal people themselves.[17]

Largely as a consequence of events in Britain's colonies in North America, imperial authorities were more responsive to settler demands when the New South Wales Constitution Act again came under review in 1842. The British government was especially concerned by armed rebellions in Upper and Lower Canada in 1837–8 and sent Lord Durham to take control and investigate. Responsive to demands by colonial politicians, Durham recommended that Britain grant a larger measure of self-government to the colonists as a way of maintaining the North American colonies within the Empire: a system which came to be known as 'responsible government', whereby governments were answerable not to Britain via the governor, but to the local legislature.[18] For several years, while British governments pondered the proposal apprehensively, demands for responsible government in the Canadian colonies intensified.

For colonists in New South Wales, there was rising anger that in contrast to the Canadian colonies they did not even have representation in the form of elected members of the Legislative Council, let alone responsible government. While sharply divided by class and politics, during the 1840s colonists were increasingly united by a belief in their right to have a role in governing themselves on the basis that they were descended from a people with long traditions of liberty, independence and good government – a heritage described variously as English, British or Anglo-Saxon.[19] Spokesmen claimed rights of representation also on the basis that they were *settlers* who had displaced and replaced Aboriginal peoples, portraying themselves as conquerors of a 'savage' landscape. For example, at a meeting in Sydney in February 1842 in favour of representative government, one of the speakers, Captain Maurice O'Connell, said settlers had proved their mettle by the

16 *Port Phillip Herald*, 8 December 1840 and 21 May 1841.

17 Jessie Mitchell, *In Good Faith? Governing Aboriginal Australia through God, Charity and Empire, 1825–1855* (Canberra: ANU Press, 2011), 177–8.

18 House of Commons, 'Report on the Affairs of British North America from the Earl of Durham with Appendices' *British Parliamentary Papers, 1839*, Volume 2, Irish University Press Series, Colonies: Canada (Dublin: Irish University Press, 1968), 23.

19 John Hirst, *Australia's Democracy: A Short History* (Sydney: Allen & Unwin, 2002), 26; Irving, *The Southern Tree of Liberty*, especially 17–53, 200–4.

profits they had made here, building civilisation in this 'dreary worthless waste' where 'some fifty years ago not an echo awoke the dead stillness of the forest, but the wild shout of the savage, or the tuneful note of its feathered inhabitants'.[20]

Rarely, if ever, did settlers seeking political representation consider that Aboriginal people could possess the same rights, or indeed any political rights at all. Rather, they made rhetorical jokes about Aboriginal 'savages' as the opposite of what an enfranchised British subject should be. When the conservative pastoralist James Macarthur gave a speech in 1842 to the New South Wales Legislative Council, in which he argued that political power must be restricted to men of property to avoid anarchy and '*vile democracy*', he contrasted their rights as Britons to the dangerously democratic notion of 'the abstract rights of man' which, if followed to their logical conclusion, 'would justify the Cannibalism of the natives of New Zealand, and even admit the savages of this Colony to a share in the Government'.[21] This was a conservative land-owner speaking, but radicals and liberals were no more able to envisage Aboriginal political participation. Even the radical Catholic, E. J. Hawksley who, in the *Australasian Chronicle* criticised Macarthur's opposition to democracy and called for political representation for working-class male colonists, agreed that the rights sought by settlers could not extend to Aboriginal people; settlers were, he said 'asking for civil rights – rights which man in a state of nature, never had and never can have'.[22]

This time, agitation for representation was successful and, in July 1842, Britain amended the Constitution Act to allow that the Legislative Council be two-thirds elected. It also increased the Council's financial powers, but excluded it from control over the distribution and management of land.[23] Crown lands and land revenue would remain under imperial control; and under the accompanying Australian Sale of Waste Land Act 1842, Crown land would be sold at a minimum price of twenty shillings per acre.[24] A bitter

20 *Sydney Gazette and New South Wales Advertiser*, 1 March 1842, 2.
21 *Colonial Observer*, 9 March 1842, Volume 1, no. 23. See also discussion in Irving, *The Southern Tree of Liberty*, 77.
22 *Australasian Chronicle*, 3 March 1842, 2.
23 The Australian Constitutions Act (No. 1), 5 and 6 Vic. c 76. Long title: An Act for the Government of New South Wales and Van Diemen's Land; Ward, *Colonial Self-government*, 168–9; J. B. Hirst, *The Strange Birth of a Colonial Democracy: New South Wales 1848–1884* (Sydney: Allen & Unwin, 1988), 17.
24 An Act for regulating the Sale of Waste Land belonging to the Crown in the Australian Colonies, 22 June 1842, 5 and 6 Victoria, c.36. Ward, *Colonial Self-government*, 170; A. G. L. Shaw, 'British Attitudes to the Colonies, c.1820–1850' *Journal of British Studies* 1, no. 9 (1969): 89–90.

political conflict over the control of land ensued and this time the pastoralists, who were determined to retain their hold on vast acres of land at little or no cost, dominated the Council after the first elections in New South Wales in 1843.[25] When, in April 1844, Gipps decided, in line with British policy, to raise significantly the cost of land, the Legislative Council opposed him and squatters organised vociferous opposition in public meetings and in local and British newspapers. Wealthy land holders spoke freely of their constitutional rights, while the *Sydney Morning Herald* declared in May 1844 that the colonists of New South Wales should be ruled 'like free British subjects and not like so many felons or slaves'.[26] By 1846, the squatters had been able to muster such substantial support in England that Gipps was outmanoeuvred and forced to concede squatters the cheap leases which he had previously opposed.[27]

Meanwhile, by the mid-1840s, self-government was becoming a real prospect for many British colonies. Afraid of risking Britain's hold on the Canadian colonies and unnerved by the unrest engulfing mainland Europe, which showed the need to keep taxes (and therefore the cost of colonisation) low, Earl Grey as Secretary of State for the Colonies had, between 1846 and 1848, instituted responsible government in Nova Scotia and the Province of Canada.[28] Self-government provided an opportunity to pass administrative costs to the colonists themselves.

While settlers were slowly but successfully extending their rights to govern themselves and the land they had seized, Aboriginal people were losing their own autonomy and control over the landscape; they must fight for what little was left. It was in the place where Aboriginal dispossession had been most acute, Van Diemen's Land, that a new assertion of Aboriginal rights emerged. The people of Flinders Island began, as Leonie Stevens and others have shown, to challenge the authority of the commandant sent to govern them, through letters, newspapers and petitions.[29] Addressing Lieutenant Governor Denison as 'Father', gesturing both towards imperial paternalism and to Aboriginal people's own traditions of kinship, they asserted that they were a free people

25 Stephen Roberts, *The Squatting Age in Australia 1835–1847* (Melbourne: Melbourne University Press, 1970 [1935]), 220.

26 *Sydney Morning Herald*, 2 May 1844. Quoted in Mark McKenna, *The Captive Republic: A History of Republicanism in Australia 1788–1996* (Cambridge: Cambridge University Press, 1996), 31.

27 Roberts, *The Squatting Age*, 252.

28 Miles Taylor, 'The 1848 Revolutions and the British Empire' *Past and Present* 166, no. 1 (2000): 146–80.

29 Leonie Stevens, *'Me Write Myself': The Free Aboriginal Inhabitants of Van Diemen's Land at Wybalenna, 1832–47* (Clayton, Vic.: Monash University Press, 2017).

who had withdrawn peacefully from their land and were therefore entitled to be protected from tyranny and enjoy the rights of white men.[30] Their campaign against the domineering and aggressive Superintendent Henry Jeanneret reached a peak in February 1846, when they worked with their catechist, Robert Clark, to draw up the first petition to a reigning monarch from Australian Aboriginal people.[31] Addressed to Queen Victoria, this document had both a specific objective – to exclude Jeanneret – and a wider view. Using language that evoked both equality and paternalism, it assured the Queen: 'we are your free children . . . we were not taken prisoners but freely gave up our country to Colonel Arthur then the Governor after defending ourselves'.[32] Denison dismissed Jeanneret, closed the institution whose population had shrunk to a shocking low of forty-seven people, and removed survivors to the Tasmanian mainland.[33]

By asserting their rights as a free people, the Aboriginal people of Van Diemen's Land were also referencing another issue that presented a dilemma for colonial governance: the persistence of convict transportation. After the highly critical report to Parliament in August 1838 by the Molesworth Committee on Transportation, the British government had reorganised transportation to Van Diemen's Land so as to increase its control over convict labour and place greater emphasis on the reformation of convicts. The matter came to a head when, with British prisons continuing to fill in the context of economic disruption and social distress, Earl Grey decided in 1847 to continue transportation to Van Diemen's Land, resume it to New South Wales (where transportation had been suspended in 1840), and introduce it to the Cape Colony. He had, however, seriously under-estimated the political and social changes in the Australian colonies. His proposals met with massive protest meetings and petitions in New South Wales and Van Diemen's Land.[34] Even employers, who appreciated cheap convict labour, began to oppose transportation as deleterious to the development of a free and virtuous society.[35] In Sydney, on 11 June 1849, when the *Hashemy*, bringing convicts, arrived in port,

30 Walter George Arthur to G. W. Walker, 30 December 1845; Mary Ann Arthur to Colonial Secretary of Van Diemen's Land, 30 December 1845; Walter George Arthur to Colonial Secretary of V.D.L., 15 June 1846, in Bain Attwood and Andrew Markus (eds), *Struggle for Aboriginal Rights* (St Leonards: Allen & Unwin, 1999), 38–41; Reynolds, *Fate of a Free People*, 12, 25.

31 See Ryan, *Aboriginal Tasmanians*, 265–76; Reynolds, *Fate of a Free People*, 12.

32 Ibid, 7–8.

33 Ibid, 7–15; Ryan, *Aboriginal Tasmanians*, 203–5.

34 L. L. Robson, *A History of Tasmania: Volume 1: Van Diemen's Land from the Earliest Times to 1855* (Melbourne: Oxford University Press, 1983), 484–6, 513.

35 Chris Holdridge, 'The Pageantry of the Anti-Convict Cause' *History Australia* 12, no. 1 (2015): 141–64.

5–6,000 people turned out to protest.[36] The anti-transportation campaign proved successful; in November 1849 Grey agreed to abandon plans to resume transportation to New South Wales, though it would be another three and a half years before transportation to Van Diemen's Land ended. At the same time, Britain gained a new outlet for its convicts in labour-starved Western Australia, to which it transported convicts from 1850 until 1868, which meant both representative and responsible government were delayed.[37]

By the end of the decade, the obstacles to self-government for the Australian colonies (other than Western Australia) were rapidly disappearing. Colonial populations had grown, especially in South Australia, which Britain had earlier considered to have too few settlers to warrant representative government, and support for self-government now came from a variety of social classes. Britain had already largely lost control over land policy in the battle between Gipps and the pastoralists in 1846. Accordingly, the British government demonstrated its gradual turn towards self-government in the Australian Colonies Government Act in 1850. Although the Act did not grant self-government, as some colonial politicians hoped, it did move in that direction. It increased the powers and representativeness of the Legislative Councils in each colony, separated the restive Port Phillip District into a new colony named Victoria, and provided a mechanism for colonies to propose new constitutions embodying the principles of self-government.[38]

Aboriginal policy was no longer a sticking point in considerations of transferring powers to the colonists. By 1850, British governments and commentators had withdrawn support from the protectionist policies of a decade earlier, having concluded that they had failed, as signified by Governor Fitzroy's closure of the Port Phillip protectorate in December 1849. As a result, the 1850 Act made no reference to the rights or protection of Aboriginal people. When the London-based Aboriginal Protection Society protested and urged some form of constitutional protection, the government response was that since Aboriginal people were fully recognised as British subjects, nothing further needed to be done.[39] The

36 A. G. L. Shaw, *A History of the Port Phillip District: Victoria before Separation* (Melbourne: Melbourne University Press, 2003), 153, 177–8.

37 Melbourne, *Early Constitutional Development*, 364.

38 Peter Cochrane, *Colonial Ambition: Foundations of Australian Democracy* (Melbourne: Melbourne University Press, 2006), 256–7.

39 Ann Curthoys, '"The Lying Name of Government": Empire, Mobility and Political Rights', in Jane Carey and Jane Lydon (eds), *Indigenous Networks: Mobility, Connections and Exchange* (New York: Routledge, 2014), 78.

policies of protection, civilisation and amalgamation were being publicly abandoned.

Under the provisions of the Australian Colonies Government Act, politicians in the four colonies during the early 1850s proposed new constitutions and British governments amended them. The process was accelerated by the gold rushes, which began in New South Wales in 1851 and spread to the much richer gold fields of Victoria. In making the colonies attractive destinations with high levels of free immigration, the gold rush undermined the deterrent powers of transportation. Transportation to Van Diemen's Land ended in December 1853.

Aboriginal issues played little role in these constitutional debates, and after 1850 the Aborigines Protection Society played no discernible part. British authorities did retain some qualms about transferring control of Aboriginal policy to settler governments, who might pass legislation that was, in the words of one official in the Colonial Office, 'palpably immoral, especially in relation to the unrepresented aborigines or immigrants of colour'.[40] However, despite these concerns, the British government was withdrawing from responsibility for Aboriginal governance, a position most clearly expressed by Herman Merivale of the Colonial Office in a comment on a dispatch of 5 August 1854, that 'The Executive here has, I think, now done what it can: the duty and responsibility will rest with the legislatures of Australia.'[41]

After a series of proposals and counter-proposals, the agreed colonial constitutions gave the colonial governments extensive powers, limited only by continuing British control over matters of imperial interest and Britain's (rarely exercised) power of veto over legislation. With the fundamental issues settled, Britain approved the colonial constitutions in sequence – that of Van Diemen's Land on 1 November 1854, those of New South Wales and Victoria (and an Order in Council changing the name of Van Diemen's Land to Tasmania) on 16 July 1855, and finally that of South Australia on 4 January 1856. The constitutions of New South Wales and Victoria granted the colonial governments control over land, while a concurrent Repeal of Waste Lands (Australia) Act[42] explicitly handed control over land to all four

40 Report from Sir Frederick Rogers to the Secretary of State for the Colonies on the Australian Constitutional Acts, 6 September 1854, CO 881/1, VII, clause 20.

41 Merivale, comment dated 5 August 1854, written on Fitzroy to Newcastle, 23 December 1853, No. 163, CO 201/467, New South Wales, 1853, Volume 5, November–December.

42 18 & 19 Vic. c 61.

colonies.[43] The process of breaking New South Wales into smaller, more manageable, colonies continued. In 1859 the British government agreed with separationist demands in the colony's northern districts and carved them off to form the new colony of Queensland. Owing to the small size of the settler population, less than 9,000 in 1855, and the introduction of convict transportation in 1850, Western Australia was excluded from the transition to self-government and was expressly excluded from the provisions concerning the transfer of power over land to colonial governments. It would be another thirty-five years before it, too, acquired self-government.

The Self-governing Colonies

When the self-government era began in 1856, the total recorded population of Australia was a little under 900,000. In 1900, the last year before the Federation on 1 January 1901, it had increased more than four-fold to just under 4 million.[44] This rapid expansion had occurred unevenly as did the economic fortunes of the colonies. While Victoria, New South Wales, Queensland and South Australia experienced a long economic boom and dramatic population growth from 1860 to 1890, followed by a severe economic depression in the 1890s, Western Australia boomed in the 1880s and 1890s; Tasmania was in economic recession for most of the period. Pastoral, agricultural, maritime and mining industries flourished around the country but the mix of industries varied: Queensland and South Australia were heavily dependent on pastoralism while New South Wales and Victoria were developing more diversified economies including, especially in Victoria, the emergence of a manufacturing sector.

Colonial governments had thus a variety of challenges before them. Under their constitutions, they were generally free to legislate as they wished unless Britain's wider interests were seen to be threatened, a situation clarified by the imperial Colonial Laws Validity Act 1865, which removed the requirement of consistency with English law.[45] Commentators at the time and since have often represented the period of self-government as a democratic milestone in Australian history; and, from the settler point of view, there are good

43 Ann Curthoys and Jessie Mitchell, *Taking Liberty: Indigenous Rights and Settler Self-Government in Colonial Australia, 1830–1890* (Cambridge: Cambridge University Press, 2018), 237.

44 Australian Bureau of Statistics, Historical Population, www.abs.gov.au/statistics/people/population/historical-population/latest-release accessed 24 November 2021.

45 Bruce Kercher, Chapter 5 in this volume.

reasons to do so. These new governments introduced manhood suffrage very early in world terms, much earlier than in Britain. South Australia, which had included it in the constitution, came first, followed quickly by two colonies that made the change through electoral legislation – Victoria in 1857 and New South Wales in 1858. Queensland was slower, introducing it in 1872, followed by Western Australia in 1893 and Tasmania last in 1900.[46] As Judith Brett shows, the self-governing colonies also became innovators in the administration of democracy, first, in the introduction of the secret ballot and second, in the development, initially in South Australia, of the first permanent electoral administration in the world.[47] Towards the end of the period of self-government, the colonies passed a range of reforms, including payment for members of parliament, and the abolition of plural voting. In world terms, South Australia became a very early example of enacting women's suffrage in 1894, and Western Australia followed suit in 1898. In the last decade of self-government, the colonies became leaders in enacting a new kind of democracy in which the state took a direct role in industrial relations. A key development occurred in 1896 when Victoria introduced legislation for the establishment of wages boards and establishing minimum wage rates, though most of the examples of what some called 'state socialism' came after Federation.[48]

There were other areas, too, in which some of the self-governing colonies passed legislation that was relatively progressive. The colonies were enabled to pass their own divorce legislation after Britain passed a Matrimonial Causes Act in 1857, which enabled courts to grant divorce and judicial separation. At first, in a series of Acts from 1858 to 1873, they followed the British legislation in allowing divorce for husbands on the grounds of adultery alone, but for wives only if there were additional grounds such as desertion or cruelty. There was, however, a push to extend the grounds of divorce to include desertion, drunkenness and assault, which succeeded in Victoria in the Divorce Act 1889 and New South Wales in the Divorce Amendment and Extension Act 1892. Throughout the self-government period, the cost of divorce fell, women rose as a proportion of those seeking

46 Henry Reynolds, *A History of Tasmania* (Cambridge: Cambridge University Press, 2011), 225.

47 Judith Brett, *From Secret Ballot to Democracy Sausage: How Australia Got Compulsory Voting* (Melbourne: Text Publishing, 2019), 37.

48 Marilyn Lake, 'Challenging the "Slave-Driving Employers": Understanding Victoria's 1896 Minimum Wage through a World-History Approach' *Australian Historical Studies* 45, no. 1 (2014): 87–102.

divorce, and petitioners for divorce came from a wide range of economic backgrounds.[49]

While developments such as these would help the colonies gain a reputation as progressive in matters of labour relations and women's rights, self-government was not a blessing for everyone. For Aboriginal people it often brought not more, but less, control over their own lives. One negative consequence of self-government was a significant loss of Aboriginal peoples' direct connection to the governor. Where earlier governors had sometimes been anxious to negotiate or conciliate as seemed necessary to ensure Aboriginal acceptance of settler presence, now, under self-government, governors had little direct power over Aboriginal policy, though they retained some social and ceremonial importance. From an Aboriginal perspective, colonial chief secretaries and premiers were no substitute. They rarely considered Aboriginal people as political subjects with whom they needed to negotiate, lacked any sense of kinship obligations and had little ceremonial or symbolic presence. There was no attempt in any of the colonies to provide an Aboriginal voice in parliament along the lines of the New Zealand Māori Representation Act of 1867. Aboriginal groups who had once undertaken performances to cement relations with a governor did not continue the practice for the new colonial premiers. When Aboriginal people did meet governors in the era of self-government, such as Governor Gore Browne in Tasmania or Governor Daly in South Australia, the meetings did not carry the diplomatic weight of earlier conversations, although at times some behind-the-scenes gubernatorial pressure seems to have been placed on government officials.[50] On one important occasion, in 1863, Kulin in Victoria used the governor's levée to communicate directly with royalty, presenting a loyal address and gifts for the royal family on the occasion of Queen Victoria's birthday and her marriage to Prince Albert.[51] Contact with royalty could at times be more direct, with Aboriginal people in most colonies meeting with Prince Alfred, the Duke of Edinburgh, during his tours in 1867 and 1868.[52]

49 Hilary Golder and Diane Kirkby, 'Marriage and Divorce Law before the Family Law Act 1975', in Diane Kirkby (ed.), *Sex, Power, and Justice: Historical Perspectives on Law in Australia* (Melbourne: Oxford University Press, 1995), 158–61.

50 Curthoys and Mitchell, *Taking Liberty*, 258–9; *South Australian Advertiser*, 28 February 1863, 3.

51 Diane Barwick, *Rebellion at Coranderrk* (Canberra: Aboriginal History Inc, 1988), 66.

52 Jessie Mitchell, '"It will enlarge the ideas of the natives": Indigenous Australians and the Tour of Prince Alfred, Duke of Edinburgh' *Aboriginal History* 34 (2010): 197–216.

Though Aboriginal men in some colonies had the right to vote, colonists had granted that right unwittingly, and over time it would be eroded. The colonial constitutions had envisaged a franchise limited by property which effectively meant that Aboriginal people could not vote; but when colonial electoral acts introduced universal manhood suffrage, thus removing property qualifications, suddenly Aboriginal men could, and some did. Colonial politicians in New South Wales, Victoria and South Australia, who had not foreseen this consequence of their new electoral laws, were surprised and concerned to see them voting.[53] In Victoria, the chances of Aboriginal men voting were subsequently reduced by a provision in the Electoral Act of 1865 that expressly excluded from voting anyone in receipt of charitable relief, which included those living on missions and reserves. Queensland went further in 1885 by passing legislation to disenfranchise all Aboriginal men that would not be rescinded until eighty years later.[54] When Western Australia introduced manhood suffrage in 1893, it effectively excluded most Aboriginal men (enfranchising only those who had owned freehold estate valued at £50 for at least six months), and they would not be enfranchised until 1962.[55]

Western Australia and South Australia had introduced legislation to admit Aboriginal evidence in court in the years before self-government, but in 1849 the pastoralist-dominated Legislative Council in New South Wales had refused to do so. Soon after achieving status as a separate colony, Victoria passed legislation admitting Aboriginal evidence in 1854, but New South Wales would take another two decades to do the same.[56] In 1860, Attorney General Hargraves authorised courts to accept evidence from Aboriginal people who were regarded as competent to testify, commenting that 'if an aboriginal witness be competent in other respects to give evidence, his being an aboriginal is not ground to reject his testimony if

53 See Naomi Gabrielle Parkinson, 'Impersonating a Voter: Constructions of Race, and Conceptions of Subjecthood in the Franchise of Colonial New South Wales, c. 1850–1865' *The Journal of Imperial and Commonwealth History* 47, no. 4 (2019): 652–75.

54 John Chesterman and Brian Galligan, *Citizens without Rights: Aborigines and Australian Citizenship* (Cambridge: Cambridge University Press, 1997), 224, fn 11, citing Electoral Act 1865 (Vic), s 20. The New South Wales Electoral Act of 1880, 44 Vic. No. 13, clause 12, page 155 had a similar clause, but as there were few missions at the time, few Aboriginal men were affected. Patricia Grimshaw, Shurlee Swain, Julie Evans and David Phillips, *Equal Subjects, Unequal Rights: Aboriginal Peoples in British Settler Colonies, 1830–1910* (Manchester: Manchester University Press, 2003), 137–8.

55 Anna Haebich, *For their Own Good: Aborigines and Government in the Southwest of Western Australia, 1900–1940* (Nedlands: UWA Publishing, 1988), 51.

56 Re Victoria, see 17 Vic. No. XI, ss vii–xi, Law of Evidence Further Amendment Act, 14 March 1854,

given on oath'.[57] It seems, however, that in practice, courts rarely heard or accepted Aboriginal people's evidence: its acceptance in April 1875 in Sydney's Central Criminal Court attracted wide public comment.[58] Finally, after considerable confusion, the *Evidence Further Amendment Act*, admitting Aboriginal evidence, became law on 14 August 1876, though some judges continued to rule Aboriginal evidence inadmissible. Queensland did not admit Aboriginal evidence until it, too, finally passed enabling legislation in 1884.[59]

The consequences of self-government for Aboriginal people varied from colony to colony. In some, the processes of land-taking, frontier violence and dispossession were over (Tasmania) or nearly so (New South Wales and Victoria), while in others (Queensland, South Australia and Western Australia) it continued for several decades. There were also differences in the colonies' policy-making for Aboriginal people once violent conflict had ended. Some, such as Victoria and South Australia, adopted protectionist policies reminiscent of earlier British rule, while others, such as New South Wales, were more laissez faire, assuming that Aboriginal populations would soon disappear. These differences arose partly from the varying class relations and political ideologies within settler society, partly from the very different responses and political cultures of Aboriginal peoples, and partly from the fact that some colonies were in a better position than others to use and exploit Aboriginal labour. The Aboriginal policies developed in various colonies reveal their broader, respective characters.

In Tasmania, for example, we see an especially stark version of the more general desire in the self-governing colonies to forget the sometimes-shameful past and focus on the future. This active 'forgetting' could apply both to the convict past and frontier violence. Colonial governments assumed that they would soon have no Aboriginal population to control, manage or support, and for several decades introduced no new policies or practices. The declining community at Oyster Cove, popularly seen as representing the 'end of their race', attracted a morbid interest in its members' impending and, then, actual deaths and, after that, in their remains, leading to grave robbing and dismemberment in the name of science.

57 Attorney General Memo, 8 May 1860, attached to letter from Police Office, Bombala to Colonial Secretary, 21 April 1860, Colonial Secretary In Letters, No. 59/1787, NSW Archives Office, 4/3422.

58 *Sydney Morning Herald*, 11 May 1875.

59 Oaths Act Amendment Act, Qld, 1884; Chesterman and Galligan, *Citizens without Rights*, 36.

Colonists saw the death in 1876 of Truganini, thought to be the last Tasmanian Aboriginal person of full descent, as signifying the extinction of Tasmanian Aboriginal people since, at the time, settlers assumed that mixed-race descendants did not 'count' as constituting their survival. At the same time, colonial governments generally denied the Aboriginality of the growing community of mixed descent on the Furneaux islands in Bass Strait, though in parliament there were moments of recognition that they had obligations to the islanders as descendants of Aboriginal people.[60] In the last three decades of the century the Islanders, under strong leaders including Lucy Beedon and George Everett, found support from two main sources – the Anglican Church and Governor Du Cane – in their ultimately successful campaigns for a schoolteacher for their children and for land to be reserved for their own use. The Tasmanian government set aside land on Cape Barren Island in 1872 and again in 1881, forming the Cape Barren Island Reserve.[61]

Across Bass Strait, Victoria, with its huge influx of a free and generally middle-class immigrants during the gold rushes and afterwards, became the most striking example of a colony in which most of the settler population had no direct experience and little knowledge of the frontier violence that had occurred across the colony. It also became the site of a more state-interventionist form of government both in economic and Aboriginal policy.[62] As Amanda Nettelbeck outlines in her chapter in this volume, Victoria became the first self-governing colony to introduce its own legislation to manage its Aboriginal population and developed systems of institutionalisation and surveillance that would be adopted in most of the colonies as the nineteenth century progressed. Significantly, the Act to Provide for the Protection and Management of the Aboriginal Natives of Victoria in 1869 gave the Aboriginal Protection Board extensive powers over the movement, lives and livelihood of Aboriginal people in Victoria.[63] There were other areas, too, in which Victoria led the way in passing legislation specifically directed at Aboriginal people. Prompted by concerns about public order in country towns and maintaining a supply of Aboriginal rural labour it was, for

60 Curthoys and Mitchell, *Taking Liberty*, 262, 264.

61 Ryan, *Aboriginal Tasmanians*, 281; Kristyn Harman, 'Protecting Tasmanian Aborigines: American and Queensland Influences on the Cape Barren Island Reserve Act, 1912' *The Journal of Imperial and Commonwealth History* 41, no. 5 (2013): 749.

62 Marian Sawer, *The Ethical State? Social Liberalism in Australia* (Melbourne: Melbourne University Press, 2003); Marilyn Lake, *Progressive New World* (Cambridge, MA: Harvard University Press, 2019).

63 Richard Broome, *Aboriginal Victorians: A History since 1800* (Crows Nest: Allen & Unwin, 2005), 130.

example, the first colony during the period of self-government to pass legislation prohibiting the sale of alcohol to Aboriginal people. Its 1864 legislation was followed by similar legislation in New South Wales in 1868, South Australia in 1869, Western Australia in 1880, Queensland in 1885 and Tasmania in 1908.[64]

There was a very different situation in Queensland, which, when it became a self-governing colony on 6 June 1859, still had vast regions which Aboriginal people occupied and controlled. The Queensland government diverged from its predecessor governments in New South Wales and Britain in the systematic nature of its seizure of land; where the former had been inconsistent, shifting between various policies of conciliation, dispersal and suppression, Queensland pursued a consistent policy of suppression through the state-sanctioned Native Mounted Police. From the 1860s to the 1890s, it became one of the bloodiest frontiers of all, as successive colonial governments, from the 1850s onwards, used the Native Mounted Police widely to 'disperse' Aboriginal people resisting colonial settlement, dispersal being a euphemism for forcible relocation and more often direct killing. Government policy shifted in the 1880s towards establishing reserves and missions and managing Aboriginal labour, the latter in the Native Labourers' Protection Act of 1884 and the Pearl-Shell and Beche-de-Mer Fishery Act of 1886.[65] The extension of government surveillance was ultimately enshrined in the Aboriginals Protection and Restriction of the Sale of Opium Act of 1897. It covered all Aboriginal people in the colony and consolidated the government's power to move people onto and off reserves against their will; forcible removals became increasingly common.[66] The government set out to enforce the drawing up of written contracts and to control and manage interracial sexual relations, and residence on or off reserves.[67] Such powers would be extended further within the newly federated Australia in the twentieth century.

New South Wales was different again. The older and more populous colony had retained a considerable and visible Aboriginal population and,

64 Victoria: Licensing Act 1864; New South Wales: Publicans Act 1868; South Australia: Licensed Victuallers Amendment Act 1869–1870, No. 16, s 65; Queensland: Licensing Act 1885, s 67(c).

65 Chesterman and Galligan, *Citizens without Rights*, 34.

66 Chesterman and Galligan, *Citizens without Rights*, 37; Raymond Evans, *A History of Queensland* (Port Melbourne: Cambridge University Press), 139.

67 Dawn May, *Aboriginal Labour and the Cattle Industry: Queensland from White Settlement to the Present* (Cambridge: Cambridge University Press, 1994), 58–66; Chesterman and Galligan, *Citizens without Rights*, 43–53.

as a self-governing colony, experienced little frontier violence once it lost its northern districts to form Queensland in 1859. Lacking the Victorian desire to control until the early 1880s, its main government policy for the first twenty-five years of self-government was the annual blanket distribution which also served as a way to keep track of the Aboriginal population. One reason for this laissez faire approach was the character of colonial liberalism in New South Wales; here, unlike in Victoria, the liberals did not diverge from their conservative and pastoralist opponents on matters of Aboriginal policy. They were not humanitarians in relation to Aboriginal people and did not advocate in Parliament for the need to assist, educate or manage Aboriginal people. Pressure for government assistance came rather from both Aboriginal people themselves and from missionaries and their supporters. From the 1860s, there were many petitions from Aboriginal people for boats for fishing, some of which succeeded.[68] Over the next decade, there were successful campaigns for the establishment of reserves and missions resembling those in Victoria. In 1874, a private missionary, Daniel Matthews, established a mission for Yorta Yorta and other Aboriginal peoples on his own land along the Murray River and in 1878, in a bid to gain government funding, established an Aborigines Protection Association in Sydney to campaign for a reserve system similar to that in Victoria. After considerable pressure, including the presentation of a petition in 1881 from the men at Maloga for their own land, adjoining the mission,[69] the government established an Aborigines Protection Board in 1883, though it lacked the legislation granting it the powers of its Victorian counterpart. For the last decade and a half of self-government, the New South Wales government set aside many reserves for Aboriginal use, including the land the Maloga petitioners had requested.[70]

South Australia combined elements of the other colonies. There was a strong humanitarian tradition of government support and especially provision of rations to people whose food sources colonisation had disrupted. At the same time, the colony's frontier was expanding as pastoralists spread into new lands and sought to contain Aboriginal resistance and use cheap

68 Thomas Grieve, Senior Constable, Nowra, to Officer-in-Charge-of-Police, 23 June 1876, Colonial Secretary's In Letters, No. 76/4523, encl. with No. 76/4876, State Records NSW, 1/2335.

69 Barwick, *Rebellion at Coranderrk*, 302; Bain Attwood, *Rights for Aborigines* (Crows Nest: Allen & Unwin, 2003), 27. See entry for 19 April 1879, Matthews Diaries, quoted in Nancy Cato, *Mister Maloga: Daniel Matthews and His Mission, Murray River, 1864–1902* (St Lucia: University of Queensland Press, 1976), 121.

70 Heather Goodall, *Invasion to Embassy: Land in Aboriginal Politics in New South Wales, 1770–1972* (Sydney: Allen and Unwin, 1996), 93.

Aboriginal pastoral labour. The result was that while some aspects of South Australia's missionary tradition survived, they operated alongside a harsh punishment regime aiming to control Aboriginal people and ensure their availability as workers. The colony's mix of desires for Aboriginal protection, education and employment was evident in the report of a Legislative Council Select Committee on Aboriginal policy in 1860, which recognised that Aboriginal people had 'an equitable title to the lands they occupied, and of which they are virtually all dispossessed' and called for a new protectorate and wider rationing systems,[71] but also wanted land reserved for Aboriginal use to be leased to settlers, and urged a policy of child removal.[72] After the report, the government re-established the office of Chief Protector (which had been abolished in 1856) and of two part-time sub-protectors, granted reserves of land for Moravian and Lutheran missions in the north, and expanded the number of ration depots in an effort to reduce Aboriginal attacks on pastoral stations in search of food, and to maintain an Aboriginal labour force in pastoral districts.[73]

The legal status of Aboriginal people, often uncertain in the colonies during the self-government period, was especially contested in South Australia. Although the principle, that British law should prevail even in internal Aboriginal disputes, had been established (though not necessarily observed) from settlement in 1836, the police commissioner from 1853 to 1867, Major Peter Warburton, was strongly of the view that they ought not to arrest Aboriginal people for crimes committed against each other. While the South Australian government never officially adopted his approach, it may well have influenced what happened on the ground. As Amanda Nettelbeck and Robert Foster point out, the police tended, though somewhat inconsistently, to leave traditional law in place as long as it did not harm settler interests.[74] When Aboriginal

71 On the idea of compensation in humanitarian discourse in the Australian colonies, see Anne O'Brien, 'Humanitarianism and Reparation in Colonial Australia' *Journal of Colonialism and Colonial History* 12, no. 2 (2011).

72 'Report of the Select Committee of the Legislative Council upon "The Aborigines", printed 16 October 1860', in *Proceedings of the Parliament of South Australia: 1860*, Volume 3 (Adelaide: Government Printer, 1860), 2.

73 Robert Foster, 'Rations, Coexistence, and the Colonisation of Aboriginal Labour in the South Australian Pastoral Industry, 1860–1911' *Aboriginal History* 24 (2000): 5; Amanda Nettelbeck, Russell Smandych, Louis A. Knafla and Robert Foster, *Fragile Settlements: Aboriginal Peoples, Law, and Resistance in South-West Australia and Prairie Canada* (Vancouver: UBC Press, 2016), 109; Christine Stevens, *White Man's Dreaming: Killalpaninna Mission, 1866–1915* (Melbourne: Oxford University Press, 1994); *South Australian Register*, 30 April 1864, 2; 19 May 1865, 2; 9 November 1865, 2; 23 November 1865, 2; 13 December 1865, 2; 30 December 1865, 2.

74 A. Nettelbeck and R. Foster, 'Reading the Elusive Letter of the Law: Policing the South Australian Frontier' *Australian Historical Studies* 38, no. 130 (2007): 296–311, 302, 305.

actions did harm settler interests, on the other hand, punishment could be harsh. Accused Aboriginal men were forced to walk long distances, chained by the neck, to the nearest court for trial, a practice also adopted in Western Australia. In both colonies, furthermore, there was a high rate of Aboriginal death in prison.[75] For a brief period in South Australia, public executions, which had long been abandoned, were resumed, for Aboriginal people specifically, after four Aboriginal men were found guilty of the murder in March 1861 of a pregnant woman, Mary Ann Rainbird, and her two children.[76] Under the Act to Regulate the Execution of Criminals (1861), Aboriginal convicted men could be hanged publicly, as near the scene of their crimes as possible, the aim being to deter further Aboriginal attacks on settlers.[77] However, after several public executions in the early 1860s, the law fell into disuse, and the government removed it from the statute books in 1876.[78]

For Western Australia, colonial self-government would be a brief period indeed. Its late introduction, compared to the other colonies, meant that when the first self-governing Parliament met, a country-wide Federation movement had already begun and was gathering pace. The delay in self-government had come originally as a result of the colony's small settler population; it was mainly with the discovery of gold in the 1880s and subsequent economic development, that the settler population expanded to a size making self-government feasible. By the time there was a genuine colonial campaign seeking self-government in Western Australia in the mid-1880s, however, the British government had seen colonial self-government in action for thirty years around the Empire and had been concerned by the extensive frontier violence in Queensland. Furthermore, under its own watch in Western Australia, settlers in the pearling and pastoral industries had treated Aboriginal people with extreme violence, subjecting them to forced labour, which observers increasingly described as a form of slavery. The huge land mass involved was also a concern; they were being asked to hand over a large territory to relatively few settlers. After considerable debate in the late 1880s, the solution sought was to grant self-government but include in the constitution a section which retained British control of Aboriginal policy. The Aborigines Protection Board would report not to

75 Nettelbeck et al., *Fragile Settlements*, 130.

76 Peter Lindy, *The Rainbird Murders* (Norwood: Peacock Publications, 1993).

77 Alex C. Castles and Michael C. Harris, *Lawmakers and Wayward Whigs: Government and Law in South Australia 1836–1986* (Adelaide: Wakefield Press, 1987), 22.

78 John Maguire, 'Judicial Violence and the Civilising Process' *Australian Historical Studies* 2, no. 111 (1998): 187–209, see 201.

the premier but directly to the governor, and its operations would be funded directly from the colony's revenue to the amount of £5,000 a year or 1 per cent of internal revenue when it exceeded £500,000.

With the coming of self-government, Western Australia entered on an especially deadly phase in Aboriginal-settler relations. The strongly pro-pastoralist government, headed by John Forrest, whose ministry in 1891 consisted of four cabinet ministers all of whom owned pastoral property, passed a series of punitive measures designed to assist the pastoral industry by bringing Aboriginal people, and especially their labour, under control. These included expanding the use of flogging (including by passing legislation in 1892 prescribing the conditions under which magistrates could order the flogging of Aboriginal people convicted of cattle stealing and other crimes) and, in the Aboriginal Offenders Act Amendment in 1893, increasing the severity of punishment for cattle killing.[79] Despite its guaranteed funding, the Aborigines Protection Board was severely hampered by having to operate alongside an uncooperative colonial government.[80] There was such hostility to the Board and the constitutional clause that protected it and ensured its funding that after a sustained campaign led by John Forrest, in 1897 the British government repealed the clause. This meant that the colonial government finally gained complete control over Aboriginal affairs; one of its first actions was to replace the Board with a much smaller, less independent, and more parsimoniously funded, Aborigines Department.[81] Three years later, the six colonies federated to form the Commonwealth of Australia, and Western Australia's brief phase of colonial self-government had ended.

Conclusion

Historians of the moves towards Federation draw attention to the similarities between the colonies and the consequent emergence of a new national

79 K . Forrest, *The Challenge and the Chance: The Colonisation and Settlement of North West Australia 1861–1914* (Carlisle, WA: Hesperian Press, 1996), 208; Mark Finnane and John Maguire, 'The Uses of Punishment and Exile: Aborigines in Colonial Australia' *Punishment and Society* 3, no. 2 (2001): 284–5; Chris Owen, *'Every Mother's Son is Guilty': Policing the Kimberley Frontier of Western Australia 1882–1905* (Crawley: University of Western Australia Press, 2016), 269, 273.

80 Paul Hasluck, *Black Australians: A Survey of Native Policy in Western Australia 1829–1897* (Melbourne: Melbourne University Press, 1970 [1942]), 119; Peter Johnston, 'The Repeals of Section 70 of the Western Australian Constitution Act 1889: Aborigines and Governmental Breach of Trust' *UWA Law Review* 19 (1989): 326–7; Peter Biskup, *Not Slaves, Not Citizens: The Aboriginal Problem in Western Australia 1898–1954* (St Lucia: University of Queensland Press, 1973), 25.

81 Owen, *'Every Mother's Son is Guilty'*, 267.

feeling and identity, as well as to their differences, which shaped the years of negotiation that led up to Federation itself. Through the lens of government Aboriginal policies, we can see how the six colonies had, over more than four decades, diverged and yet retained enough similarity to form a viable federation and national entity. The differences were many – in the role of the justice system in managing frontier conflict, the role of the state in supporting poverty-stricken Aboriginal groups and individuals, the extent to which indentured and Aboriginal labour was needed and used, and the degree of government intervention into Aboriginal lives. These differences would continue in the twentieth century, when the Commonwealth government would play little role in Aboriginal policy until after the change to the Constitution in 1967 authorising Commonwealth involvement. Yet this list of differences in the colonial era also hints at some fundamental similarities – the assertion of control over land and the expectation that Aboriginal people would be governed but never govern. While settlers, at times, expressed a sense of obligation to those whose lands they had usurped and a recognition, as they sometimes put it, that Aboriginal people were the original owners of the soil, settler political consciousness was founded on an assumption of Aboriginal inferiority and the inevitability (and in many minds the desirability) of their disappearance as a people.[82]

In this bleak context, Aboriginal people all over the continent continued to experience a deep and continuing sense of loss and betrayal. At the same time, they maintained families and cultural traditions, keenly aware of both their own laws and values and those of the dominant society. They also laid the foundations for the political activism that would flourish in the twentieth century and now, the twenty-first. The tradition of petitioning we have discussed here, for example, continued, with well-known twentieth century examples including the petition from the Aboriginal Advancement League to King George VI in 1937, the Yirrkala bark petition to the Commonwealth Parliament in 1963, and the Larrakia petition of 1972 to Queen Elizabeth II seeking land rights, a treaty, and political representation. Aboriginal people have not forgotten these petitions, a group in January 2010 presenting the visiting Prince William with a copy of the petition to King George VI, which the Australian government of the time had failed to forward.[83] The Uluru

82 Richard Broome, '"There were vegetables every year Mr Green was here": Right Behaviour and the Struggle for Autonomy at Coranderrk Aboriginal Reserve' *History Australia* 3, no.2 (2006): 43.4.

83 Louise Hall and Jessica Mahar, 'How Willie Wombat Charmed the Block' *Sydney Morning Herald*, 20 January 2010.

Statement of 19 June 2017, encapsulated in the slogan, 'Voice, Treaty, Truth', and drawn up by Aboriginal representatives after an extensive period of consultation and negotiation, builds on these traditions but also departs from them. It is not a petition but rather an offer to non-Aboriginal Australians to join with Aboriginal people in creating a new constitution, reaching treaties and agreements, and acknowledging the past as a basis for a new more egalitarian and respectful future.

7

Federation

BRENDAN LIM

Introduction

Histories of Australian Federation are histories of an idea. The framers of the 1901 Constitution did not only establish a practical, workable machinery of federal government for their time. They also called forth and gave shape to a constitutive idea that would sustain that machinery long beyond their own lives. The idea was pithily expressed by the young Robert Garran, writing in 1897 for 'every citizen [who] will soon be asked to give a responsible vote' on the adoption of the new federal constitution.[1] The 'fundamental idea', Garran said, 'is always that of a twofold sovereignty – the sovereignty of the national government for national purposes; the sovereignty of the provincial or "state" governments for provincial purposes'. Federation, therefore, 'is essentially a compromise . . . between the opposing forces of centralization on the one hand, of local independence on the other'.[2] Negotiating that 'essential compromise' requires a federal political community to articulate its legal and political understanding of 'sovereignty' (which may be more or less complete) and also to distinguish between national and provincial purposes. They are inevitably ongoing processes of constitution-making for successive generations of a political community bound to the idea of federation. Compromise and flexibility continue to define the Australian federal political community, which the High Court maintains to be of

I thank the editors, and also Professor Rosalind Dixon, Stephen Free SC and Dr Zsofia Korosy, for reading earlier drafts of the chapter and providing helpful comments and suggestions. Errors and omissions are mine alone.

1 R. Garran, *The Coming Commonwealth* (Sydney: Angus and Robertson, 1897), Preface.
2 Ibid, 15.

a 'dualist kind'[3] while simultaneously denying any notion of 'distinct and dual sovereignty'.[4]

In his history of Federation, which has been cited repeatedly by the High Court in the nearly fifty years since its publication,[5] John La Nauze observed that Australians before 1890 'were not concerned to define federation much more closely than as a system of government' having a dualist character.[6] To implement Federation practically, as La Nauze said, is a 'more intricate business'. Under the broad umbrella of Federation as a dualist form of government, there is significant room for choice about the character of the institutions and the adjustment or balance of the concurrent centres of power. Nonetheless, that intricate business of choice and implementation should not be mistaken for an exercise of 'defining' Federation. No such 'definition' was settled even when the framers of the Constitution, in the 1890s, came to spell out the detail and entrench for subsequent generations certain institutions, rules and principles. Compromise, which Garran perceived to be the essence of Federation, presupposes a framework for politics: reasonable clarity and agreement about what is and what is not negotiable, and the capacity for adjustment to changed circumstances. As Aroney put it in his historical analysis of Australian Federation, federal systems exhibit not so much a division of power as a sharing of power 'within the context of an ever-shifting set of parameters shaped by processes of negotiation, compromise and, at times, cooperation'.[7]

The idea of Federation can therefore never be fully or finally defined. This idea is simultaneously less and more than the set of institutions, rules or principles that implement it at any given time. It is a malleable concept, capable of instantiation in a variety of different conceptions,[8] and capable of accommodating different views or interpretations of the concept's best form.

3 See e.g. *Australian Securities and Investments Commission v Edensor Nominees Pty Ltd* (2001) 204 CLR 559, [12] (Gleeson CJ, Gaudron and Gummow JJ), citing C. Saunders, 'Administrative Law and Relations between Governments: Australia and Europe Compared' *Federal Law Review* 28, no. 2 (2000): 263–90, 290. See also *O'Donoghue v Ireland* (2008) 234 CLR 599, [150] (Kirby J dissenting).

4 *Betfair Pty Ltd v Western Australia* (2008) 234 CLR 418, [97] (Gleeson CJ, Gummow, Kirby, Hayne, Crennan and Kiefel JJ).

5 See e.g. *Commonwealth v Queensland* (1975) 134 CLR 298, 331 (Murphy J); *Williams v Commonwealth* (2012) 248 CLR 156, [43], [44], [48] (French CJ); *Alqudsi v The Queen* (2016) 258 CLR 203, [108] (Kiefel, Bell and Keane JJ); and many cases in between.

6 J. A. La Nauze, *The Making of the Australian Constitution* (Melbourne: Melbourne University Press, 1972), 4.

7 See N. Aroney, *The Constitution of a Federal Commonwealth: The Making and Meaning of the Australian Constitution* (Cambridge: Cambridge University Press, 2009), 18.

8 See e.g. W. B. Gallie, 'Essentially Contested Concepts' *Proceedings of the Aristotelian Society* 56 (1955–1956): 167–98; J. Rawls, *A Theory of Justice* (Cambridge, MA: Harvard

This is not a philosophical or definitional argument about the meaning of Federation. The ongoing processes of working out, and revising from time to time, applicable conceptions of Federation are processes that constitute the political community. The possibility that Federation may be claimed for different ends is not a failure of constitution-making but rather part of its success. To understand the history of Federation as the history of an idea is to understand that invocations of that history, and claims that are made upon it, are points of opening rather than closing for a discourse, or ongoing compromise, of constitutional law.

In this chapter, I explore this fundamental point through some reflections upon Federation's origins in the mid-nineteenth century, its outcomes in the productive decade of constitution-making from 1891 to 1901, some of its outworkings since 1901, and the omission and opportunity in respect of the constitutional position of Australia's First Peoples, as perceived from a contemporary perspective. I follow this course with the simultaneous objective of summarising some important aspects of the standard legal-historical account of Australian Federation.

Origins (1847–90)

Australian Federation was achieved only after some 'sixty years of spasmodic official effort and fluctuating public interest to bring the Commonwealth into being'.[9] Standard accounts identify the origins of the federal movement in the failed plans of Earl Grey, the Colonial Secretary in Lord John Russell's first government.[10] On 31 July 1847, Earl Grey dispatched to New South Wales the imperial government's proposal for a new constitution and for a separate colony of Victoria, which until 1851 was part of New South Wales. The proposal was 'greeted … with a storm of indignation',[11] partly because there had been no local consultation and partly because the changes themselves were unacceptable, providing, for example, for merely indirect election of the Houses of Assembly. One aspect of Earl Grey's proposal was to

University Press, 1971), 5; R. Dworkin, *Taking Rights Seriously* (London: Bloomsbury, first published 1977, 1997 edition), 167–9.

9 L. F. Crisp, *Australian National Government* (Melbourne: Longman Cheshire, 1983, 5th edition), 1.

10 See especially J. Quick and R. R. Garran, *The Annotated Constitution of the Australian Commonwealth* (Sydney: Butterworths, first published 1901, 2002 edition), 81; La Nauze, *Making of the Australian Constitution*, 1. See also S. Crennan, 'Federation', in C. Saunders and A. Stone (eds), *The Oxford Handbook of the Australian Constitution* (Oxford: Oxford University Press, 2018), 78–95, 83.

11 Quick and Garran, *Annotated Constitution*, 82.

establish a General Assembly for the Australian colonies with powers in relation to matters of common concern. Import and export duties, roads and railways, and the postal service were identified as subject matters appropriate to be dealt with at a level of responsibility above the municipal level but below the imperial level. This was itself perceived to be 'unobjectionable, and possibly even useful'[12] but, as well as becoming a somewhat accidental casualty of the vigorous opposition to the plan as a whole, was probably also premature. The colonies were 'at the time … striving for power to manage [their] own affairs', such that 'the importance of union was rather future than present'.[13] The British government ultimately abandoned its plans to impose Federation, acknowledging the strength of local opposition.

The episode illustrates that, from an early stage, the idea of Federation in Australia was destined to be an Australian idea, not one to be imposed by imperial powers. Political union and distinctive Australian identity would go hand-in-hand. Earl Grey's failures presaged the imagination of a political community that would be something more than 'just the overseas relations of the British'.[14] This is not to say, however, that imperial thought did not exert significant influence on Federation in Australia. The second half of the nineteenth century saw major developments in colonial constitutional law that would eventually shape the Australian conception of Federation.

La Nauze deals quite shortly with the period extending from the late 1850s to the beginning of the 1880s, as a time when the people were 'less concerned with an abstraction like federation than with opportunities and conflicts within their own societies'.[15] During this period, several select committees examined the question of federal union, but '[i]n no colony was there any general enthusiasm, or even interest, in the subject'.[16] The period has been described as one of 'some talk … and little action'.[17] But if there was a lack of practical action towards union in this period, the same cannot be said of the development of the ideas that would eventually sustain Federation. Australian Federation is now often characterised as an American idea accommodated to a British polity. While the framers of the Constitution were, eventually, heavily influenced by the United States model – and also looked further afield to Canada, Switzerland and elsewhere for inspiration – they

12 Ibid. 13 Ibid, 89.
14 H. Irving, *To Constitute a Nation: A Cultural History of Australia's Constitution* (Cambridge: Cambridge University Press, 1999), 28.
15 La Nauze, *Making of the Australian Constitution*, 2.
16 Quick and Garran, *Annotated Constitution*, 92–100. 17 Crennan, 'Federation', 83.

became acclimatised to federal ideas worked out and expressed in colonial legal structures around the time of this supposedly inactive phase of the movement.

Self-government having been attained,[18] the colonies became practiced in determining for themselves many matters of local concern. They 'reproduced in miniature' the institutions and practices 'familiar in the sovereign polities of the great world'.[19] Local legislative initiatives even shaped constitutional arrangements in the colonies, providing among other things for the secret ballot, adult male suffrage in the legislative assemblies, female suffrage, and payment of members of Parliament.[20] Sir Samuel Griffith later claimed in 1890, with some overstatement, that the colonies were 'accustomed for so long to self-government' that they had 'become practically almost sovereign states'.[21]

'Practically almost' was an important qualification. It glossed not only the imperial power to revoke the colonial constitutions, but also the more immediate experience of Westminster enacting laws for the colonies. Such laws prevailed over inconsistent local laws by a doctrine of repugnancy, eventually clarified and re-expressed in the Colonial Laws Validity Act 1865.[22] In this way, any local government was undoubtedly subordinate to imperial sovereignty. At the same time, however, the superior imperial authority observed certain practical or conventional limitations. As Garran put it in 1897, it was 'pretty well understood how far [the imperial powers] are likely to be exercised'.[23] Sir Owen Dixon later said of this period that the British Parliament 'so sparingly exercised its residual authority that, in practice, the restraint ... was seldom encountered'.[24]

By the time of Federation, people perceived 'a division ... effected between colonial and Imperial functions which has a semi-federal appearance'.[25] As a result, Federation 'involve[d] few ideas altogether strange'.[26] The colonies were familiar with uniformly applicable laws made at Westminster. They were familiar with the idea and practice of limited

18 See Curthoys and Mitchell, Chapter 6 in this volume.
19 La Nauze, *Making of the Australian Constitution*, 2.
20 See G. Carney, *The Constitutional Systems of the Australian States and Territories* (Cambridge: Cambridge University Press, 2006), 47.
21 Official Record of the Debates of the Australasian Federal Convention, Melbourne, 10 February 1890, 10.
22 28 & 29 Vic. c 63.
23 Garran, *Coming Commonwealth*, 110.
24 O. Dixon, 'The Statute of Westminster, 1931', in S. Crennan and W. Gummow (eds), *Jesting Pilate and Other Papers and Addresses by the Right Honourable Sir Owen Dixon* (Annandale: Federation Press, 2019, 3rd edition), 188–202, 189.
25 Garran, *Coming Commonwealth*, 110–11.
26 Ibid.

sovereign legislative powers of their own. Importantly, they were familiar also with the resulting doctrine of repugnancy or inconsistency. By what would be enacted in 1900 as Section 109 of the Constitution, dealing with inconsistency between Commonwealth and State laws, the States are 'in effect . . . treated in relation to the federal Parliament as the colonies were treated in relation to the imperial Parliament'.[27]

There was familiarity also with a conception of judicial power to review local legislation for transgressions of constitutional limits. The doctrine of repugnancy pre-dated responsible government. The Legislative Council of New South Wales, established in 1823, was expressly denied power to make laws or ordinances that were 'repugnant' to imperial laws.[28] This followed an imperial precedent dating back to the Second Virginia Charter of 1609.[29] That limit on legislative power could be enforced by the imperial government exercising a bureaucratic power of disallowance.[30] In the Australian colonies, the courts were also involved in advising or opining on the validity of laws and ordinances, albeit in a role that was more political than judicial.[31] Furthermore, 'repugnancy' was not a clearly defined legal standard, but rather one of 'utter flexibility'[32] capable of reflecting normative opinion of 'constitutional propriety' or policy views about topics regarded as appropriate for 'imperial legal conformity'.[33]

The doctrine of repugnancy was re-expressed in the Colonial Laws Validity Act 1865 as one concerned only with those imperial laws intended to apply in the colonies by paramount force (and not with the laws of England generally). The role of the courts in determining repugnancy was confirmed as a properly judicial role, exercised in justiciable disputes, rather than a political or advisory role as it had been at an earlier time. As local law-making expanded under self-government, the Privy Council developed a line of authority to the effect that colonial legislatures were, 'within [express] limits, . . . intended to have plenary powers of legislation' and that the

27 La Nauze, *Making of the Australian Constitution*, 58.

28 See New South Wales Act 1823 (4 Geo. IV c 96); Australian Courts Act 1828 (9 Geo. IV c 83).

29 See E. Campbell, 'Colonial Legislation and the Laws of England' *University of Tasmania Law Review* 3 (1965): 148–75, 149.

30 Ibid, 171; D. Ward, 'Legislation, Repugnancy and the Disallowance of Colonial Laws: The Legal Structure of Empire and Lloyd's case (1844)' *Victoria University of Wellington Law Review* 41 (2010): 381–402.

31 See Campbell, 'Colonial Legislation', 155–61.

32 B. Kercher, 'Why the History of Australian Law is Not English' *Flinders Journal of Law Reform* 7, no. 2 (2004): 177–204, 178.

33 Ward, 'Legislation, Repugnancy and Disallowance', 389.

'established Courts of Justice, when a question arises whether the prescribed limits have been exceeded, must of necessity determine that question . . . by looking to the terms of the instrument by which, affirmatively, the legislative powers were created, and by which, negatively, they are restricted'.[34] That could be a more or less accurate description, even today, of the High Court's basic constitutional function in relation to adjudicating the validity of legislation.

By the 1880s, the Australian colonies started to take more active steps towards union. Growing discontent with the economic dislocation caused by conflicting tariffs and duties was a significant motivation for attempts to achieve greater economic union.[35] So too was defence: concerns about the expansion of European colonial powers into the Pacific have been described as 'the real motive power' and 'emergency' that drove efforts in this period.[36] It was feared that Germany would annex New Guinea, and France the New Hebrides and New Caledonia, the latter as a penal colony for recidivists. Moreover, it was perceived that the imperial government's own interests in connection with foreign affairs might not align with the regional interests of the Australian colonies. For example, the imperial government disavowed Queensland's bold attempt to take possession of New Guinea in the Queen's name.[37]

At the urging of the Victorian premier, James Service, representatives of the seven colonies, together with Fiji, convened in Sydney on 28 November 1883. Service's proposal for a 'Federal Union' did not find favour. Instead, the Convention resolved to create the Federal Australasian Council, a legislative body with authority to deal with specified matters of common interest, although lacking any means to raise revenue or enforce its laws.[38] The Federal Council was duly created by an imperial enactment in 1885. New South Wales, despite its initial support for the resolution (the idea seems to have been suggested in 1880 by its premier, Henry Parkes), did not participate. The Federal Council passed some laws – on statutory interpretation, evidence, service and execution of process, and regulation of fisheries – but generally 'did little to justify its existence'.[39]

34 *R v Burah* (1878) 3 App Cas 889, 904–5 (Lord Selborne). See also *Powell v Apollo Candle Company* (1885) 10 App Cas 282 (on appeal from the Supreme Court of New South Wales).

35 Quick and Garran, *Annotated Constitution*, 100–9; Aroney, *Constitution of a Federal Commonwealth*, 145.

36 Quick and Garran, *Annotated Constitution*, 110. See also La Nauze, *Making of the Australian Constitution*, 2; Crennan, 'Federation', 83–4.

37 Quick and Garran, *Annotated Constitution*, 110.

38 Ibid, 110–11.

39 Ibid, 115.

Meanwhile, Parkes pursued a yet more ambitious initiative for Federation. In 1889, an imperial review of the defences of the Australian colonies recommended the federation of the armed forces and various reforms of the defence system to achieve, effectively, 'national' coordination.[40] Seizing the opportunity that this recommendation presented, Parkes renewed his call for the creation of a national government in a speech at Tenterfield on 24 October 1889 (an event that is famous now but does not seem to have been regarded as particularly significant at the time).[41] The Federal Council, Parkes argued, was inadequate for the task because it lacked any executive power and was not directly representative of or responsible to the people. To pursue his vision of a truly federal government, Parkes advocated for 'a Convention of leading men from all the colonies' to be appointed as delegates by their respective legislatures.[42]

In February 1890 in Melbourne, representatives of the colonies (including New Zealand) met in a conference, which unanimously recognised the insufficiency of the Federal Council and resolved to pursue more formal union by a National Australasian Convention of delegates of each legislature 'empowered to consider and report upon an adequate scheme for a Federal Constitution'.[43] The Melbourne Conference also canvassed important debates about the character of Australian federation.

Notably, it established that 'there would be no simple adoption of the most obvious model' of Canadian federalism.[44] While Sir Samuel Griffith spoke at length about the British North America Act 1867, Andrew Inglis Clark introduced the American model as a preferred alternative. The American and Canadian precedents represented a large and important divide in federal models. American federalism confers limited powers on the central government, thereby preserving the greater sovereignty of its constituent states. Canadian federalism confers limited powers on the constituent provinces, with the greater residue left to the central government. Inglis Clark who, on one view, became the 'primary architect' of the Constitution,[45] was perhaps the most well-informed of Australia's constitutional framers, especially on matters of American law. As a Tasmanian, he also represented the interests of a smaller colony, which was concerned not to allow a new centralised

40 Ibid, 117.
41 See J. Williams, 'The Emergence of the Commonwealth Constitution', in H. P. Lee and G. Winterton (eds), *Australian Constitutional Landmarks* (Cambridge: Cambridge University Press, 2003), 1–33, 12.
42 Quick and Garran, *Annotated Constitution*, 118.
43 Ibid, 119–21.
44 La Nauze, *Making of the Australian Constitution*, 17.
45 *Theophanous v Herald & Weekly Times Ltd* (1994) 182 CLR 104, 172 (Deane J).

government to be dominated by the more populous colonies. In an early example of claiming the very word, 'Federation', for what was, at best, one conception of the idea, Inglis Clark persuaded many that the Canadian precedent was 'an instance of amalgamation rather than of federation'.[46] From this point, the Canadian model was 'no longer considered appropriate in design for the Australian situation'.[47]

Outcomes (1891–1901)

Each colony followed through on the agreement reached in Melbourne by giving parliamentary concurrence to the resolution to convene a National Australasian Convention and by appointing delegates to attend. The Convention met in Sydney over the course of a month in March 1891. It produced a complete draft Constitution which remained influential in the subsequent Convention of 1897–8 and formed the basis for much of the Constitution as enacted.[48] The draft was in truth prepared by a small sub-committee of Griffith, Inglis Clark and Charles Cameron Kingston. Before the committee got to the drafting, however, the delegates debated over eleven sitting days a series of resolutions proposed by Parkes and intended to guide the drafting process.[49] The resolutions reflected the broad contours of the emerging idea of Federation and recorded the significant issues and debates that would shape it.

Parkes' first resolution, consistent with the preference ascertained at the Melbourne Conference for an American rather than Canadian style of Federation, embodied the practical consensus around an idea of Federation committed to 'the reservation of provincial rights in provincial matters':[50]

> That the powers and privileges and territorial rights of the several existing colonies shall remain intact, except in respect to such surrenders as may be agreed upon as necessary and incidental to the power and authority of the National Federal Government.

The next three resolutions concerned the other large, conceptual commitments of the Convention: 'absolutely free' interstate trade and intercourse, a federal tariff, and a single national defence. Other resolutions sought to outline the basic character of a 'complete national government, with

46 Official Record of the Debates of the Australasian Federal Convention, Melbourne, 12 February 1890, 57.

47 Williams, 'Emergence', 14.

48 La Nauze, *Making of the Australian Constitution*, 78.

49 These are recorded in Quick and Garran, *Annotated Constitution*, 125.

50 Ibid, 126.

Figure 7.1: C.W. Readett, 'The Federal Works' [1898?], National Library of Australia, nla.obj-135578526. This cartoon depicts Edmund Barton and George Reid, of New South Wales, and the Braddon Block, a reference to the insistence by Edward Braddon, of Tasmania, on substantial redistribution of Commonwealth revenue to the States.

legislative, judicial, and executive departments'.[51] Parliament was to be bicameral, one chamber representing the states, the other the nation, and the Executive was to be responsible to Parliament. The judiciary was to consist of a federal Supreme Court, with appellate jurisdiction for all of Australia.

Although Parkes' resolutions, with some amendments, were ultimately adopted unanimously, they left open significant areas of disagreement that were exposed and elaborated further in debate. The problem of how to apportion surplus national revenue to the States, upon the transfer of the exclusive power to raise customs duties, emerged as a major difficulty (see Figure 7.1). So too the compromise between large and small states. Equal representation of the states in the Senate was virtually axiomatic, being

51 Ibid.

'conceded from the outset'.[52] But just how great a concession that would be depended entirely on the extent of the Senate's powers, something that became 'among the most divisive issues at the Conventions'.[53] The 1891 draft was 'less definite and less elaborate in its treatment of some of the vexed problems'.[54] Nonetheless, it contained 'the whole foundation and framework' of the Constitution that would eventually be enacted in 1900.[55]

After the 1891 Convention, the federal movement stalled again. The colonial Parliaments 'wait[ed] for New South Wales',[56] whose commitment was essential to the enterprise. Meanwhile, domestic politics in New South Wales saw Parkes forced to an election by elements of his own party who opposed Federation because it seemed to them that protectionists would dominate a federal Parliament and control national economic policy to the colony's detriment. And although the Parkes government was returned, an emerging Labour Party held the balance of power, causing focus to turn to its domestic agenda. Labour considered that federation would 'do nothing' to solve pressing social and industrial problems.[57] This coincided with drought, industrial unrest and severe economic depression.[58]

The Depression, however, also 'served to draw popular attention to the potential benefits of federation',[59] especially the economic benefits of greater cooperation and coordination. The years between the conventions saw '[t]he idea of federation ... kept alive by individuals and organizations outside parliament'.[60] Leagues and associations supporting the federal cause gradually built popular support for renewed efforts to federate. In 1893, a conference of the Australasian Federal League held in the border town of Corowa, New South Wales, resolved that the colonies should legislate for a process towards Federation. The resolution contemplated a 'statutory convention or congress' attended by elected representatives, which would adopt a bill for a federal constitution and submit it 'by some process of referendum to the verdict of each colony'.[61] New South Wales, now led by George Reid, whose opposition to Parkes had stalled the 1891 draft, soon

52 Ibid, 131.
53 C. Howard and C. Saunders, 'The Blocking of the Budget and Dismissal of the Government', in G. Evans (ed.), *Labor and the Constitution 1972–1975: Essays and Commentaries on the Constitutional Controversies of the Whitlam Years in Australian Government* (Melbourne: Heinemann, 1977), 251–87, 253.
54 Quick and Garran, *Annotated Constitution*, 135. 55 Ibid.
56 La Nauze, *Making of the Australian Constitution*, 89.
57 Quick and Garran, *Annotated Constitution*, 150. 58 Williams, 'Emergence', 16–17.
59 Crennan, 'Federation', 93. 60 La Nauze, *Making of the Australian Constitution*, 90.
61 Quick and Garran, *Annotated Constitution*, 153.

supported the idea of a second convention and between 1894 and 1896 the colonies other than Queensland enacted the requisite legislation.[62]

The second Convention met three times in Adelaide (March–April 1897), Sydney (September 1897) and Melbourne (January–March 1898). There was a lively debate at the outset about whether the 1891 draft should serve as a starting point for deliberations. The Convention formally decided to start afresh. Leading delegates including Barton and Deakin – despite being among the seventeen of fifty delegates who had also participated in the first Convention – supported 'a fresh commencement with fresh resolutions, maintaining that either method would lead to the same result but that this manner of reaching it was much more in accordance with the independent elective character of this Convention'.[63] However, in practice the new draft came to incorporate much of the 1891 draft.

The 'fresh resolutions' of 1897, which Barton drafted, closely tracked those of Parkes adopted at the 1891 Convention, including the first resolution affirming the preservation of states' rights subject only to 'such surrenders as may be agreed upon'. But Barton now prefaced them with a new rhetoric, which claimed the purpose of creating a federal government to be 'to enlarge the powers of self-government of the people of Australia'.[64] At the Convention, Barton drew particular attention to this re-statement of the federal objective, which he thought was 'often lost sight of amid talk of the surrender of powers'.[65] Barton's rhetoric captured a somewhat novel philosophical conception of federalism. Pre-existing American political philosophy (familiarity with which is apparent in Inglis Clark's personal papers) held that 'by dividing power and creating "two citizenships" federalism acted as a check on absolutism'.[66] In contrast, Barton's re-expression of the Australian federal objective perceived the political exercise not as one of ensuring division of power, but instead 'as a means of empowering self-government by the people of Australia' and translating that power 'to a higher and more beneficial plane'.[67]

62 La Nauze, *Making of the Australian Constitution*, 90–1.

63 A. Deakin, *The Federal Story* (1944), quoted in J. M. Williams, *The Australian Constitution: A Documentary History* (Melbourne: Melbourne University Press, 2005), 476. See also La Nauze, *Making of the Australian Constitution*, 108.

64 See La Nauze, *Making of the Australian Constitution*, 112; Williams, *Documentary History*, 479.

65 La Nauze, *Making of the Australian Constitution*, 113.

66 J. M. Williams, 'Introduction to the 1997 Reprint', in A. Inglis Clark (ed.), *Studies in Australian Constitutional Law* (Melbourne: Charles F. Maxwell, first published 1901, 1997 reprint, St Leonards: Legal Books), iii–xxxix, x–xi.

67 See S. Gageler, 'Beyond the Text: A Vision of the Structure and Function of the Constitution' *Bar News* (Winter, 2009): 30–41, 33–4.

The emphasis on self-government was consistent with the popular movement that had reinvigorated the federal cause, and which found expression in the 'elective character' of the second Convention and the intention that the new Constitution be ratified in referendums. It was also consistent with the emerging sense of nationhood. Democratic commitments of the time were 'far from ideal by today's standards',[68] but the few substantial departures from the 1891 draft reflected a 'rise in democratic sentiment'[69] and a national vision of the political community. Senators were to be chosen by the people, not by state legislatures. Constitutional amendments were to be approved by a referendum, by contrast with the American model, which requires ratification by state legislatures or conventions, and even more unlike the British North America Act 1867, which contained no general provision for its own amendment. Definition of the franchise was not to be left to the states but was brought within the uniform control of the Commonwealth Parliament. A democratically inspired deadlock provision allowed persistent disagreement between the Houses of Parliament to be resolved by a double dissolution election and, if necessary, a joint sitting of both Houses.[70]

Thus, while the draft Constitution that emerged from the 1897–8 Convention closely resembled the 1891 draft, which remained recognisable in 'almost every clause',[71] that essential continuity should not be misinterpreted to discount the importance of the deliberations, debates and disagreements of the second Convention. Indeed, those deliberations played out not only inside the Convention, but also outside. After the Adelaide sitting, colonial Parliaments debated the draft Bill and presented many amendments for consideration at the Sydney sitting.[72] The draft was also shared with the Colonial Office, which discreetly conveyed its views through the New South Wales premier, George Reid.[73] Griffith and Inglis Clark, who had written the 1891 draft but were not at the second Convention, provided input privately.[74] Significant debates continued around the financial settlement, and the powers and composition of the Senate, as they did around questions concerning railway rates (which seem almost quaint more than a century later,

68 H. Irving, 'The People and their Conventions', in M. Coper and G. Williams (eds), *Power, Parliament and the People* (Annandale: Federation Press, 1997), 113–25, 122.
69 Williams, 'Emergence', 19.
70 See generally Quick and Garran, *Annotated Constitution*, 135–6; Williams, 'Emergence', 19–20; Crennan, 'Federation', 94–5.
71 La Nauze, *Making of the Australian Constitution*, 136.
72 Ibid, 161–8; Aroney, *Constitution of a Federal Commonwealth*, 174–5.
73 La Nauze, *Making of the Australian Constitution*, 170–6.
74 Ibid, 168–70.

and exemplify the need for Federation, as an idea, to respond to new problems over time).[75]

Although equal representation of the states in the Senate had been 'conceded from the outset' in 1891, there was a renewed objection from some New South Wales delegates. They perceived unfairness in the less populous states having disproportionate voting power in the Senate (see Figure 7.2). On the other hand, those less populous states perceived a risk that their interests would potentially be swamped by those of the more populous states. Ultimately, equal representation remained widely accepted, but not as a result of any commitment to it as a normative axiom of federalism. Rather, it was recognised as a point of practical compromise necessary to secure the assent of the smaller colonies.[76] Thus, the Constitution guarantees equal representation only to 'Original States',[77] and not to states that might later be admitted or established. Acceptance of equal representation by the larger colonies also went hand-in-hand with an assumption that there would be a mechanism for resolving deadlock between the Houses that would prioritise a conception of the national interest over sectional state interests.[78]

Quite how to protect the national interest when the Houses disagreed was contentious and it was the subject of the 'longest and most important debate of the Sydney sitting'.[79] One suggestion was a national referendum, resolving deadlock by a simple majority of those voting. This would provide finality, but 'ignored the individual States' because voters in less populous states could be outnumbered by those in more populous states. Another suggestion was the dissolution and re-election of both Houses, simultaneously or consecutively. This would 'safeguard[] State interests', because the Senate's power would not be diluted; but it would not ensure a resolution of the deadlock in the new Parliament.[80] Following much debate on these mechanisms and several variations, Joseph Carruthers suggested a joint sitting of both Houses, following a double dissolution. Members of the House of Representatives (who would outnumber the Senators by two to one) would have a numerical advantage in a joint sitting, the magnitude of that advantage depending on the voting rules adopted. Carruthers proposed that a supermajority of three-fifths should be required to carry a deadlocked measure; but the Convention ultimately agreed on a simple or 'absolute majority' (in the words of Section 57). This mechanism also did not reflect any deep commitment to a perceived essential incident of

75 See Quick and Garran, *Annotated Constitution*, 187–206. 76 Ibid, 189.
77 Commonwealth Constitution, s 7. 78 See now, Commonwealth Constitution, s 57.
79 Quick and Garran, *Annotated Constitution*, 189. 80 Ibid, 190.

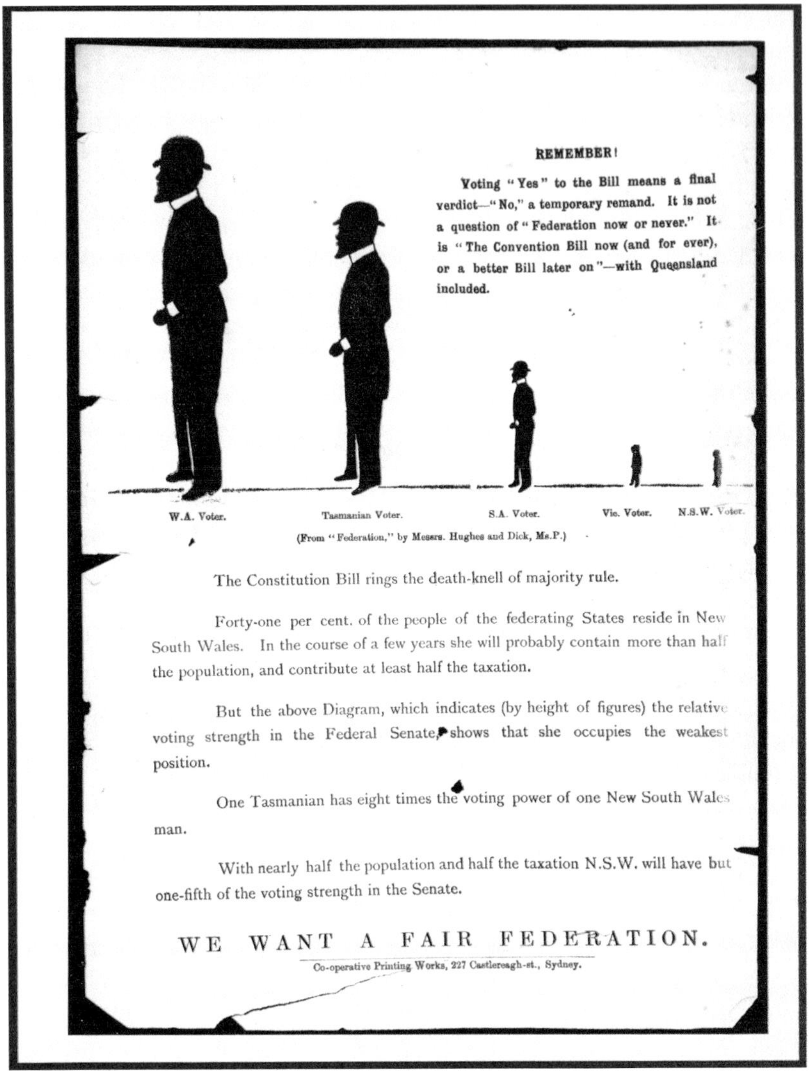

Figure 7.2: Australian Federation poster, 1901 [1989], National Library of Australia, nla.obj-136366161. This NSW poster protests unequal state representation in the Senate.

federation: 'no one waxed enthusiastic over the joint sitting for its own sake'; but 'it was supported as being on the whole the best compromise that the Convention would agree to'.[81]

81 Ibid, 192.

The Convention thus recognised the imperfections in its practical accommodation of state and national interests. The potential conflict between a powerful Senate, having veto powers over government bills (including financial bills), and the principle of responsible government was clearly perceived. The framers' experience with British constitutional law taught them, however, that the Constitution in practice would be sufficiently 'elastic' to allow the problem to be worked out later. Griffith proposed 'to leave to the future the avoiding of these difficulties, and . . . not make difficulties in advance'.[82] Barton, also expressing a thoroughly British political ethos, was confident that '[h]owever we may err in allotting too much or too little power to this or that body, we still have the good sense of an English-born race to carry us through'.[83] A political instinct and practical willingness to leave some problems unsolved is part and parcel of any compromise. But it has particular significance in relation to the 'essential idea' of Federation. As the constitutional conventions illustrate, just as any agreement between polities to federate will inevitably be incomplete, so any workable idea of Federation must also be incomplete. Areas of contestability left open are therefore not gaps in the realisation of Federation but rather necessary and essential elements of it. It is often asserted, following Dicey, that Federation requires a rigid constitution.[84] It should not be thought, however, that there is absolute rigidity or that the interpretation of a federal constitution involves a search for eternally 'true' incidents of the federal structure. Federation, as an idea, establishes frameworks for the ongoing negotiation of compromised positions and, in that sense, is flexible rather than rigid.

Following the Melbourne sessions of the second Convention, the proposed Constitution was presented in referendums in each colony. The franchise at this time excluded most women and many Indigenous Australians and other racial minorities, and only about 60 per cent of eligible electors participated.[85] Nevertheless, by the standards of the day, there was an authentic popular movement involving real 'participation . . . in which public debate, petitions, letters to the press, and scrutiny of official processes

82 Official Record of the Debates of the Australasian Federal Convention, Sydney, 5 March 1891, 48.

83 Official Record of the Debates of the Australasian Federal Convention, Sydney, 17 March 1891, 410.

84 A. V. Dicey, *Introduction to the Study of the Law of the Constitution* (London: Macmillan, first published 1885, 10th edition 1959), 146.

85 G. Lindell, 'Why is Australia's Constitution Binding? – The Reasons in 1900 and Now, and the Effect of Independence' *Federal Law Review* 16 (1986): 29–49, 30.

were not only accepted, [but] central'.[86] Equally, it was accepted that it was legally necessary to secure the passage of the Constitution by imperial legislation. This was achieved, although not before the Colonial Office, concerned to protect British commercial interests, insisted on a widening of the class of cases in which appeals could be brought to the Privy Council.[87]

Outworkings (1901–the Present)

As the history of Federation shows, the compromise between national and provincial manifestations of the political community was expressed not in an entirely rigid constitutional settlement, but primarily in a framework for politics. Constitutional law not only constrains the exercise of political power but also enables it.[88] Federation is therefore an ongoing project of coordination and negotiation. The evolution of the Australian Federation since 1901 has generally been in the direction of centralisation, not just as a matter of legal or political ideology but, more fundamentally, as a reflection of the growth in fact of a truly national political, social and economic community. Both reflecting and reinforcing that fact, there has been a gradual expansion of Commonwealth legislative and financial power, coupled with different forms of cooperation between the two levels of government.

The centralisation of power has not been uncontested. Ever since the enactment of the Constitution, the idea of Federation has been claimed in support of very different conceptions of government.[89] This is, of course, entirely consistent with Federation understood as a framework for ongoing negotiation and compromise.

The first Justices of the High Court – Chief Justice Griffith and Justices Barton and O'Connor, who had all played leading roles in the drafting of the Constitution – conceived of Federation as a political compact in which the Commonwealth and the states were sovereign in their respective fields and, moreover, in which the Commonwealth's field was narrowly confined. That conception recalled the opening resolution at each of the 1891 and 1897

86 Irving, 'The People and their Conventions', 122.
87 La Nauze, *Making of the Australian Constitution*, 248–69.
88 See further, B. Lim, 'An Australian Reads Living Originalism' *Sydney Law Review* 34 (2012): 809–28.
89 The most dramatic example of conflict between competing conceptions of Federation played out during the years of Gough Whitlam's Labor government (1972–5), culminating in the constitutional crisis of 1975 and the vice-regal dismissal of the government. Space does not permit that episode to be recounted here, but see further B. Lim, *Australia's Constitution after Whitlam* (Cambridge: Cambridge University Press, 2017).

Conventions, which, as mentioned above, declared the powers and privileges of the colonies to 'remain intact . . . except in respect to such surrenders as may be agreed upon'. The Court gave effect to this conception of Federation by approaching the interpretation of the Constitution on a premise that there were certain domestic matters reserved to the states and upon which federal power would not readily be construed to intrude.

Sometimes, the perceived reservation of power in relation to 'domestic affairs' was based on little more than an asserted 'spirit of the Constitution', as in *Peterswald v Bartley*, which concerned the question whether the power to impose licence fees on the manufacture of beer or spirits had been 'withdrawn' from the states by the conferral of exclusive Commonwealth power to levy excise duties (Section 90).[90] At other times, some textual justification was advanced for the claim. For example, where Section 51(i) of the Constitution allocated to the Commonwealth Parliament power to make laws with respect to 'trade and commerce with other countries, and among the States', the Court perceived an implied reservation of power in respect of the unmentioned intrastate trade and commerce. Other legislative powers were thereby subjected to that implicit reservation, even where the language would otherwise be more naturally read with broader effect. Thus, in *R v Barger*, a law imposing taxation except on manufacturers paying fair and reasonable wages, despite being a law with respect to taxation, was seen to intrude upon the internal regulation of trade in the states and therefore to be beyond power.[91] The conception of dual sovereignty also came to be reflected in a doctrine of implied intergovernmental immunities, which guarded against legislative interference by either state or Commonwealth with the sovereignty of the other. States were held to lack power to tax Commonwealth public servants,[92] and the Commonwealth was held to lack power to regulate labour disputes between state railways and their employees.[93]

This early vision of Federation, so different from that which prevails today, was not simply the product of different normative preferences. It rested on the lived political experience of the time: in many areas of regulation, each of

90 (1904) 1 CLR 497, 507; see also J. Stellios (ed.), *Zines's The High Court and the Constitution* (Annandale: Federation Press, first published 1981, 6th edition 2015), 7.

91 See e.g. *R v Barger* (1908) 6 CLR 41, 54. See also, e.g., *Huddart, Parker & Co Pty Ltd v Moorehead* (1909) 8 CLR 330 in relation to Section 51(xx), which confers power to make laws with respect to foreign, trading or financial corporations.

92 *D'Emden v Pedder* (1904) 1 CLR 91; *Deakin v Webb* (1904) 1 CLR 585.

93 *Federated Amalgamated Government Railway and Tramway Service Association v New South Wales Railway Traffic Employees Association* (1906) 4 CLR 488.

the pre-Federation colonies had been 'a foreign country to the other'.[94] This tended to weigh against construing the Constitution to alter too radically the relations between the federating states. But it did not follow that federal relations could or should remain for all time on that particular footing. As a shared sense of nationhood emerged, and as the experience of relating as foreign countries receded, a different conception of Federation would be required.

The early doctrines were overruled in 1920 in the Engineers' case.[95] That case raised a question whether certain Commonwealth industrial laws applied to sawmills operated by the Western Australian government. Prevailing doctrine required the legal argument to be that the law applied because the sawmills were trading entities rather than government entities (of course, they were both). But the parties were given leave to challenge the earlier cases. Griffith, Barton and O'Connor were no longer members of the Court. A new generation of judges reasoned that the Constitution should be interpreted 'according to its own terms, finding the intention from the words of the compact, and upholding it throughout precisely as framed'.[96] This legal technique was deployed to disavow the Court's earlier reasoning as reflecting a 'vague, individual conception of the spirit of the compact'.[97] This was, of course, a disavowal only of one particular idea of Federation, not of the necessity for having an idea of Federation. The new interpretive approach, astutely described as somewhat 'self-contradictory',[98] simply reflected a different idea of Federation. Where the Griffith Court saw a constitutional role for the judiciary in confining each of the dual sovereigns within its own sphere, the Court in 1920 saw the Federation built around a Commonwealth with broader powers, the exercise of which would be policed primarily by the 'constituencies' – that is, the people – controlling 'by ordinary constitutional means any attempt on the part of the national Parliament to misuse its powers'.[99] This recalled Barton's prefatory words to the fresh resolutions of 1897 (although he might not have imagined those words to have this import), which stated the federal objective in terms of enlarging the powers of self-government.[100]

Constitutional law today does not explain the different conceptions of Federation which prevailed before and after the landmark Engineers' case in

94 See *Huddart, Parker & Co Pty Ltd v Moorehead* (1909) 8 CLR 330, 372 (O'Connor J).
95 *Amalgamated Society of Engineers v Adelaide Steamship Co Ltd* (1920) 28 CLR 129. See also Stellios, *Zines's The High Court*, 1–11.
96 (1920) 28 CLR 129, 142. 97 Ibid, 145.
98 R. T. E. Latham, 'The Law and the Commonwealth', in W. K. Hancock (ed.), *Survey of British Commonwealth Affairs: Problems of Nationality 1918–1936* (Oxford: Oxford University Press, 1937), I: 510–615, 563–4.
99 (1920) 28 CLR 129, 151. 100 See also Gageler, 'Beyond the Text'.

terms of one being correct and the other wrong.[101] To do so would raise the embarrassing prospect that the nation laboured under an erroneous construction of its fundamental law for twenty years, misled by judges who had been intimately involved in the initial drafting of the Constitution. Consistent with the history of Federation as the history of an idea, constitutional law today follows Sir Victor Windeyer, who explained the Engineers' case in 1971 in these terms:

> I have never thought it right to regard the discarding of the doctrine of the implied immunity of States and other results of the Engineers' case as the correction of antecedent errors or as the uprooting of heresy . . . [I]n 1920 the Constitution was read in a new light, a light that reflected from events that had, over 20 years, led to a growing realisation that Australians were now one people and Australia one country and that national laws might meet national needs . . . [R]eading the instrument in this light does not to my mind mean that the original judges of the High Court were wrong in their understanding of what, at the time of federation, was believed to be the effect of the Constitution and in reading it accordingly. As I see it the Engineers' case, looked at as an event in legal and constitutional history, was a consequence of developments that had occurred outside the law courts as well as a cause of further developments there.[102]

Garran, as recalled by Geoffrey Sawer, also appears to have thought that the framers 'often saw problems in totally different light from that of later years'.[103] But to speak of a 'different light' in which the Constitution was read in 1920 might mislead one to think that there was some inevitability about the change in direction, or some sense in which it was 'correct' to change course in 1920. It might also mislead one to think that the post-*Engineers* vision was only perceived in 1920 when, in fact, it was articulated as a competing view of Federation well before that.

In truth, the very idea of Federation is inherently incomplete and has been both accommodated to and exploited for evolving political conceptions of self-government. Constitutional interpretation is not a discipline that necessarily responds to 'the taxonomy of "truth" and "error"'.[104] Instead, it admits the possibility that a constructional choice might be made for good reasons at

101 But see J. Goldsworthy, 'Justice Windeyer on the Engineers' Case' *Federal Law Review* 37 (2009): 363–74; Lim, 'Living Originalism', 821–3.

102 *Payroll Tax Case* (1971) 122 CLR 353, 396–7, cited in *Work Choices Case* (2006) 229 CLR 1, [193] (Gleeson CJ, Gummow, Hayne, Heydon and Crennan JJ). See also Gageler, 'Beyond the Text', 32, citing '*The Armistice*' (1918) 25 CLR v.

103 G. Sawer, 'Foreword', in Quick and Garran, *Annotated Constitution*, v–vi, vi.

104 *Wurridjal v Commonwealth* (2009) 237 CLR 309, 353 (French CJ).

one point in time, and yet later be shown to be 'incompatible with the ongoing development of constitutional jurisprudence' or 'weakened by subsequent decisions or in the light of experience'.[105]

The expansion of Commonwealth power after the Engineers' case was gradual and depended on the political branches actually asserting broader powers. By way of illustration, the pre-Engineers' case interpretation of the corporations power was not formally overruled until 1971, when the Court determined a challenge to the Trade Practices Act 1965 (Cth), the validity of which depended on the Commonwealth's power to regulate the trading activities of trading corporations whether or not in interstate trade.[106]

Among the more significant expansions of the Commonwealth's power since the Engineers' case was its establishment of an effective monopoly over income tax through laws imposing taxation at a rate that left no practical room for the states to continue their own imposts.[107] In upholding the Commonwealth scheme, the Court, as in the Engineers' case, emphasised that adjustments of the relationship between the Commonwealth and the states were constrained primarily by political rather than legal processes, the 'remedy for alleged abuse of power . . . [being] found in the political arena and not in the courts'.[108] The financial dominance thus achieved allowed the Commonwealth to exert influence outside of its traditional spheres by making financial grants to the states under Section 96 of the Constitution for specific purposes or on conditions, even in ways that 'reach a long way into the internal procedures of State governments or the relationship between State governments and the State community'.[109]

The Commonwealth's financial dominance also established certain practical conditions for an expansion of its legislative responsibilities. While many argued that the solution to vertical fiscal imbalance lay in the Commonwealth returning a greater share of its revenues to the states,[110] the Whitlam government pioneered the position (now adopted as orthodox

105 Ibid.
106 *Strickland v Rocla Concrete Pipes Ltd* (1971) 124 CLR 468, overruling *Huddart, Parker & Co Pty Ltd v Moorehead* (1909) 8 CLR 330.
107 See *South Australia v Commonwealth* (1942) 65 CLR 373; *Victoria v Commonwealth* (1957) 99 CLR 575. See also C. Saunders, 'The Uniform Income Tax Cases', in Lee and Winterton (eds), *Australian Constitutional Landmarks*, 62–84.
108 *South Australia v Commonwealth* (1942) 65 CLR 373, 429 (Latham CJ).
109 C. Saunders, 'Towards a Theory for Section 96: Part 2' *Melbourne University Law Review* 16 (1988): 699–724, 705.
110 See e.g. R. Menzies, *Central Power in the Australian Commonwealth: An Examination of the Growth of Commonwealth Power in the Australian Federation* (Melbourne: Cassell, 1968), 89; P. H. Lane, 'Economic Federalism, Excise Duty and Receipt Duty' *Australian Law Journal* 43 (1969): 614–23, 623.

by both major political parties at the Commonwealth level) that the requisite realignment was not a distribution of greater revenues to the states, but instead an expansion of the Commonwealth's responsibilities to match its financial capabilities.[111]

The expansion of legislative power has not occurred with complete freedom from legal limitations based on normative conceptions of the federal structure. For example, the Court still approaches characterisation – the issue of whether a Commonwealth law has sufficient connection with a constitutional head of power – as raising what was recently described in *Spence v Queensland* as 'questions of degree'.[112] In that case, a Commonwealth law, which expressly permitted political donations to be made to state political parties or campaigners (notwithstanding state law prohibitions) so long as those donations might be used for federal electoral purposes, was held to be beyond power. The law was perceived to have only a slight impact on federal elections, and a much more substantial impact on non-federal matters, including state elections. The Court's evaluative judgment, reflecting a conception of the federal structure and the subject matter of state elections as being 'within the heartland of State legislative power',[113] characterised the law as lacking sufficient connection with the Commonwealth's limited legislative powers.[114]

Similarly, the Court has recently discerned legal limits which may come to constrain the practical significance of the Commonwealth's financial dominance. The Court held that parliamentary authorisation beyond a mere appropriation of funds is required for many kinds of expenditure, perceiving that otherwise the Commonwealth's ability to spend may permit it to bypass the state consent required in relation to Section 96 grants or, indeed, bypass the Senate which, in theory, represents state interests.[115]

Perhaps most fundamentally, it is recognised that any flexible idea of federation, in which federal-state relations can be worked out through the political process, presupposes the continuing capacity of the different polities to engage in that political process. In this respect, legal constraints have an important role to play. In 1947, the early doctrine of implied intergovernmental immunities found re-expression in this attenuated form, when the Latham Court struck down the Commonwealth's attempt to prohibit the banks,

111 Lim, *Australia's Constitution after Whitlam*, 65–6, 74–5.

112 *Spence v Queensland* (2019) 268 CLR 355, [59] (Kiefel CJ, Bell, Gageler and Keane JJ).

113 Ibid, [80]. 114 Ibid, [51]–[84].

115 *Williams v Commonwealth* (2012) 248 CLR 156, [60] (French CJ), [148] (Gummow and Bell JJ), [248] (Hayne J), [503] (Crennan J).

without permission from the Commonwealth, conducting business with the states, thereby requiring the states to bank with the Commonwealth Bank.[116] Dixon J, whose reasoning has remained most influential, perceived that the Constitution was founded on a 'conception of a central government and a number of State governments separately organized' and 'predicates their continued existence as independent entities'.[117]

While it could not plausibly have been suggested, consistently with the Engineers' case, that states enjoyed a general immunity from any interference, burden or hindrance, they were seen still to be immune from laws that were 'aimed at the restriction or control of a State in the exercise of its executive authority'.[118] Anticipating objections similar to those recorded in the Engineers' case about recourse to 'political rather than legal considerations', Dixon responded: 'The Constitution is a political instrument. It deals with government and government powers ... It is not a question whether the considerations are political, for nearly every consideration arising from the Constitution can be so described, but whether they are compelling.'[119] For Dixon, like Griffith and Isaacs before him, 'Federation' was a necessarily political idea, to be revised and renegotiated within the inherently flexible framework afforded by the Constitution; but this conception carried with it a certain minimum legal constraint protecting the baseline conditions required to enable that political process. Articulating the categories of law that impermissibly impair the ability of a state to function as a body politic and distinguishing them from laws that merely regulate within constitutionally acceptable boundaries, continues to be a practical exercise in federalism worked out over time, drawing on the values and experience of the time.[120]

Within the flexible framework inherent in the idea of Federation, the Australian political community has continued to debate and shape its own federal relations and has generally been able to adapt them to the needs of the time. This was dramatically illustrated during the peculiar time in which this chapter was written in 2020 and early 2021. Australia's response to the COVID-19 pandemic saw the rapid formation by intergovernmental agreement of a 'National Cabinet', comprised of the prime minister and the premiers and chief ministers of the states and territories. Subsequently, this

116 *Melbourne Corporation v Commonwealth* (1947) 74 CLR 31. 117 Ibid, 82. 118 Ibid.
119 Ibid.
120 See e.g. *Austin v Commonwealth* (2003) 215 CLR 185; *Clarke v Federal Commissioner of Taxation* (2009) 240 CLR 272; *Fortescue Metals Group Ltd v Commonwealth* (2013) 250 CLR 548, 609–11.

new institution formally replaced the Council of Australian Governments.[121] Meanwhile, state and territory governments took a visibly leading role in the internal response to the public health emergency, with resulting variation throughout Australia in health and quarantine requirements and risk tolerances. Many state borders closed, testing the limits of the constitutionally guaranteed freedom of interstate trade, commerce and intercourse.[122]

The idea of Federation may accommodate multiple dimensions at the same time. For example, in some respects a 'competitive' conception of Federation is accepted, recognising the benefits that may flow from regional innovation and comparison of diverse policy experiments.[123] In other respects, federal and state governments pursue common goals through a 'cooperative' conception of Federation given expression in intergovernmental agreements or arrangements.[124] Such cooperative action may 'deal with matters that lie beyond the powers of any single legislature'[125] or with matters over which the Commonwealth might well have power but chooses, instead, to deal with cooperatively (see Figure 7.3). Political theory has developed since the 1890s, and the idea of Federation can be richer today as a result. Faith is kept with constitutional history by recognising that the constitutional concept of Federation is inherently flexible and was always intended to accommodate practical adjustment to contemporary experience.

Omission and Opportunity (the Present–the Future)

It is not a purpose of this chapter to offer an appraisal of Federation. But it would be an incomplete history not to reflect – albeit briefly and

121 See C. Saunders, 'A New Federalism? The Role and Future of the National Cabinet', Melbourne School of Government, Policy Brief No. 2, 1 July 2020; T. Tulich, B. Reilly and S. Murray, 'The National Cabinet: Presidentialised Politics, Power-sharing and a Deficit in Transparency' on AUSPUBLAW (23 October 2020) https://auspublaw.org, accessed 14 December 2021.

122 *Palmer v Western Australia (No. 4)* [2020] FCA 1221; *Palmer v Western Australia* [2021] HCA 5.

123 G. Appleby and B. Lim, 'Democratic Experimentalism', in R. Dixon (ed.), *Australian Constitutional Values* (Oxford: Hart Publishing, 2018), 221–42.

124 R. French, 'Co-operative Federalism', in Saunders and Stone (eds), *The Oxford Handbook*, 807–29.

125 *R v Duncan; Ex parte Australian Iron and Steel Pty Ltd* (1983) 158 CLR 535, 560 (Mason J) (regarding a Coal Industry Tribunal established by Commonwealth and New South Wales laws).

Figure 7.3: Livingstone Hopkins, 'Federation, Australia, approximately 1898' National Library of Australia, nla.obj-452465790. This cartoon references the Convention debates over the regulation of Australia's cross-border river systems.

inadequately – upon the conspicuous exclusion from the constitutional settlement of Australia's First Peoples.

First Peoples were, until a referendum in 1967, expressly excepted from the scope of the Commonwealth legislative power to make laws with respect to 'the people of any race for whom it is deemed necessary to make special laws' (Section 51(xxvi)). Until that same referendum, they were not counted in the

Commonwealth census (Section 127). These two references to First Peoples 'both seemed to say that they were of no intrinsic national importance'.[126] Indeed, examination of the drafting history of those clauses reveals that even they were not centrally concerned with the position of the First Peoples. Section 51(xxvi) was included so that the Commonwealth Parliament could legislate with respect to 'Polynesian labourers' or 'Indian coolies'. The carve-out, inserted at the request of a New Zealand delegate in 1891, was initially for 'the Maori race of New Zealand'. Only later was it adjusted to 'make clear, what was in fact the case, that [the power] had not been intended to apply to the affairs of the Australian Aborigines, the control of which was to be retained by the States' (which variously had differing economic relationships with the Indigenous populations, especially in relation to labour).[127] Similarly, Section 127 was incidental to the financial settlement, which would allocate surplus revenue according to population.[128] In respect of First Peoples, there was a distinct 'lack of engagement on the part of the framers'.[129]

The substantial exclusion of First Peoples is a large and still unresolved constitutional issue.[130] That exclusion reflects a significant omission from our idea of Federation. When white Australians started to develop lists of subject matters that they considered appropriate to be dealt with by a national government, the relationship between the state and the First Peoples was not among them. Although it was an issue in some of the colonies more than others, '"native administration" was a matter of scant concern in building the Australian nation'.[131] One of the New Zealand delegates to the 1890 Melbourne Conference remarked that the proposed federal Parliament would be an institution 'that cares nothing and knows nothing about native administration'.[132]

But the idea of Federation, as I have sought to demonstrate in this chapter, has proven itself to be remarkably flexible. It may be in an iteration of that idea that an ongoing constitutional settlement and relation with the First

126 S. Brennan and M. Davis, 'First Peoples', in Saunders and Stone (eds), *The Oxford Handbook*, 29–55.

127 La Nauze, *Making of the Australian Constitution*, 67. 128 Ibid, 67–8.

129 J. Williams and J. Bradsen, 'The Perils of Inclusion: The Constitution and the Race Power' *Adelaide Law Review* 19 (1997): 95–142, 110.

130 See especially The Uluru Statement from the Heart reproduced in Referendum Council, Final Report of the Referendum Council (Commonwealth of Australia, 2017), i. See also Brennan and Davis, 'First Peoples', 27.

131 Irving, *To Constitute a Nation*, 113.

132 Ibid, 112. Official Record of the Debates of the Australasian Federal Convention, Melbourne, 11 February 1890, 42.

Nations is achieved. If the idea of Federation is understood broadly, as a means of compromising the co-existence of distinct but related political communities, then as Wiradjuri scholar and co-editor of this volume, Mark McMillan, has proposed, it may 'offer something new to the discussion regarding sovereign relationships in the constitutional recognition debate'.[133] Suggestions, that the continuing 'sovereignty' of First Nations would necessarily be incompatible with the Constitution, give insufficient weight to the different, and qualified, ways in which the 'sovereignty' of the states has been conceived and re-conceived as the idea of Federation has evolved to meet changing circumstances, or indeed as self-government has been conferred by legislation on new territories.

The Uluru Statement from the Heart, delivered in 2017, was the outcome of wide consultation with, and deliberation within, Aboriginal and Torres Strait Islander communities (First Nations Regional Dialogues) culminating in a gathering of 250 delegates at Uluru (National Constitutional Convention).[134] It calls for constitutional recognition through a Voice, conceived as a constitutionally recognised body with responsibility to provide advice and consultation on the exercise of legislative and executive power on certain matters of significance to First Peoples. It also calls for a Makarrata Commission to oversee truth-telling and treaty-making with Aboriginal and Torres Strait Islander peoples.[135] As Dylan Lino has recently explained, these forms of recognition could be 'understood as federal arrangements between Aboriginal and Torres Strait Islander and settler peoples'.[136] There are structural parallels between the sub-national representation that could be achieved through the proposed Voice and the sectional representation of states sought to be achieved in the Senate (although the advisory powers of the Voice would be markedly different from the veto powers of the Senate). Similarly, inherent in a conception of making treaties with First Peoples is a commitment to negotiating self-rule and shared rule.[137] Federalism, Lino argues, can thus provide 'a way of conceptualising and justifying the

133 M. McMillan, 'Is Federalism Being Undermined in the Current Surge to "Recognise" Indigenous Australians in (and into) the Commonwealth Constitution?' *Indigenous Law Bulletin* 8, no. 25 (2016): 15–19, 16.

134 Referendum Council, *Final Report of the Referendum Council* (Commonwealth of Australia, 2017).

135 Ibid, i.

136 D. Lino, *Constitutional Recognition: First Peoples and the Australian Settler State* (Annandale: Federation Press, 2018), 217.

137 Ibid, 233–40.

recognition of Indigenous peoplehood that mediates settler and Indigenous traditions'.[138]

The idea of Federation, as a constitutional framework for recognising Australia's First Peoples, may even find sympathetic resonance within Indigenous traditions. These too appear to have combined forms of self-rule and shared rule.[139] It may therefore be an idea that not only justifies a framework for Indigenous recognition but also finds expression in the precise form of recognition. For example, there appears to be support for a form of Voice which incorporates local and regional voices, with the 'design of the local voices [to] reflect the varying practices of different Aboriginal and Torres Strait Islander communities'.[140]

Australians' own experience with Federation and overseas experience of settler Federations like the United States and Canada, to which Australia might look again for constitutional inspiration, illustrate that there already exist the basic constitutional resources to negotiate the 'essential compromise' between distinct political communities integrated within one nation. Distinct 'sovereignties' can be accommodated because our conception of what 'sovereignty' might entail continues to be capable of ongoing adjustment. Similarly, the precise representative character of a Voice, and the identification of the particular matters on which it would be empowered to provide advice, remain to be worked out.[141] But as the history of Federation shows, they are obstacles of a kind that have been overcome before.

Conclusion

Federation in the nineteenth century was a remarkable achievement of political determination, creativity and, above all, compromise. Compromise, as Garran perceived, was the 'fundamental idea' of Federation. In the twentieth and twenty-first centuries and beyond, Australian Federation has not been, is

138 Ibid, 218.

139 McMillan, 'Is Federalism Being Undermined', 15; C. Morris, 'Constitutional Dreaming', in C. Sampford and T. Round (eds), *Beyond the Republic: Meeting the Global Challenges to Constitutionalism* (Annandale: Federation Press, 2001), 290–9, 294; Lino, *Constitutional Recognition*, 247.

140 Commonwealth of Australia, Joint Select Committee on Constitutional Recognition relating to Aboriginal and Torres Strait Islander Peoples, Final Report (November 2018), [2.19]; see also [2.302], [2.306] and [3.57], [3.58], [3.63]–[3.66] (discussing submissions of Professors Anne Twomey, George Williams and Rosalind Dixon).

141 See Commonwealth of Australia, National Indigenous Australians Agency, Indigenous Voice Co-Design Process: Interim Report to the Australian Government (October 2020).

not, and will not be merely an inherited artefact of history. What was really inherited was the 'fundamental idea', coupled with the responsibility of self-government to sustain that idea. The idea – the compromise – must, of course, be worked out within the bounds of the constitutional framework, which itself requires fidelity to the breadth, generality and intended application of the idea to 'the varying conditions which the development of our community must involve'.[142] The history of Federation, both before and after 1901, is an illustration of that constitutional truth, as its future also surely will be.

142 *Jumbunna Coal Mine NL v Victorian Coal Miners' Association* (1908) 6 CLR 309, 367–8 (O'Connor J).

8

Constitutionalism in Australia

CHERYL SAUNDERS

Concepts of Constitutionalism

Constitutionalism is a term with no fixed meaning. Both its scope and what may be described as its properties vary with context.[1] The evolution and operation of constitutional arrangements in Australia demonstrate the challenge of defining constitutionalism in a way that is both sufficiently concrete to be meaningful and sufficiently flexible to allow for differences between states that, instinctively, merit association with constitutionalism.

Constitutionalism has obvious links to the concept of a constitution. In its most narrow formulation, it implies no more than compliance with the constitution. Used in this way, the terms effectively are interchangeable.[2] Usually constitutionalism is taken to mean more than that; to make greater demands on the substance of the constitution to which it gives effect.[3] Constitutions themselves vary, however, in their ambition, in the matters for which they provide and in the manner in which they do so.[4] Too prescriptive an understanding of the substantive requirements for a constitution also risks unduly narrowing the idea of constitutionalism for

1 Compare, for example, the formulations canvassed and offered in Dieter Grimm, 'The Achievement of Constitutionalism and its Prospects in a Changed World', in Petra Dobner and Martin Loughlin (eds), *The Twilight of Constitutionalism* (Oxford: Oxford University Press, 2010), 3, and David Feldman, '"Which in Your Case You Have Not Got": Constitutionalism at Home and Abroad' *Current Legal Problems* 64 (2011): 117.

2 Arguably, this is the way the term is used by A. V. Dicey in 1899, contemporaneously with the making of the Commonwealth Constitution: A. V. Dicey, 'Will the Form of Parliamentary Government Be Permanent?' *Harvard Law Review* 13 (1899): 67.

3 Writing in the immediate aftermath of World War II, this distinction was made in one of the early contributions to the modern conception of constitutionalism by Charles Howard McIlwain, *Constitutionalism Ancient and Modern* (Ithaca, NY: Cornell University Press, 1947), 1.

4 Joseph Raz, 'On the Authority and Interpretation of Constitutions: Some Preliminaries', in L. Alexander (ed.), *Constitutionalism: Philosophical Foundations* (Cambridge: Cambridge University Press, 1998), 152.

the purposes of comparison. This chapter adopts a middle ground, which requires constitutional norms and practices to meet certain general standards for the purposes of constitutionalism. At their most general, these standards call for a system of government by and for the people and the organisation of public power in ways that preclude its arbitrary exercise.[5] By these means, indirectly if not directly, constitutionalism also offers some protection for individual rights.

Constitutionalism also requires consideration of the properties of a constitution. These include both the status of the constitution, as the set of fundamental norms with which any exercise of public power is expected to comply and the authority for the constitution, on which its legitimacy draws and which is generally attributed to the people, inclusively defined.[6] A major fault line for these purposes lies between constitutional systems in which there is a designated codified or written constitution and those in which there is not. The latter, of which the United Kingdom and New Zealand are paradigmatic cases, accept that the legislature may override constitutional norms as a matter of law and that decisions of the legislature are not controlled by judicial review. The characteristically evolutionary character of an uncodified constitution also obscures the source of authority for the constitution, attenuating its attribution to the people.[7] Formulations of constitutionalism respond to these difficulties in different ways. Some exclude uncodified constitutional arrangements altogether.[8] Others include them, by emphasising the relevance of process and dialogue irrespective of legal status,[9] by relying on sub-categories of political and legal constitutionalism,[10] or by distinguishing between legal and political sovereignty.

Drawing these two dimensions of constitutionalism together, four features emerge that are widely shared and, collectively, offer a yardstick for evaluation. First and most obviously, there must be a constitution, comprising norms and practices that are regarded as important, whether codified as fundamental law or not. Secondly, the constitution should be conceived as

5 For McIlwain, this required a balance to be struck between jurisdiction and gubernaculum: McIlwain, *Constitutionalism Ancient and Modern*, 143–6.
6 Grimm, 'The Achievement of Constitutionalism'.
7 A. V. Dicey, *The Law of the Constitution, edited by* J. W. F. Allison (Oxford: Oxford University Press, 2013), Part 1: 43.
8 By implication, Grimm, 'The Achievement of Constitutionalism'.
9 Feldman, 'Which in Your Case You Have Not Got'.
10 Marco Goldoni and Chris McCorkindale, 'Three Waves of Political Constitutionalism' *King's Law Journal* 30 (2019): 74.

deriving its authority from the people, actively in consequence of the manner of its making, or more passively, as acquiescence at the outset and over time.[11] Third, the constitution should provide a framework for government of and by the people in a form that structures public power so as both to empower and limit the institutions of the state. Finally, the constitution should be effective, in the sense that compliance is the norm, departure from which can be sanctioned in some way.

Australian constitutionalism fits within these parameters, albeit with some distinctive characteristics of its own, to be explained in the pages that follow. It centres on a codified constitution that is thin in comparative terms and operates within a constitutional culture influenced by attitudes derived from an uncodified constitutional context. The authority on which the binding quality of the constitution rests initially was ambiguous but by now is firmly attributed to the people. The identity of the constitutional people, in turn, has evolved and continues to do so. The constitution structures power, between levels of government, between institutions and between people and the state, but provides little entrenched protection for individual rights. The constitution is construed and applied by courts with substantial independence. Compliance with judicial decisions, including decisions on constitutional questions, is regarded as an imperative of the rule of law.[12]

The foundations of Australian constitutionalism were influenced by ideas and experiences drawn from other jurisdictions, shaped by the distinctively Australian context into which they were received and in which Australian constitutionalism developed over time. Australian constitutionalism has remained open to external ideas throughout its long history. However, the manner and extent of their influence was progressively constrained as local constitutional arrangements consolidated and developed an organic character of their own, in conditions of considerable political stability. The next section identifies the principal sources of external influence on Australian constitutionalism and key contextual factors that deserve note. The remainder of the chapter explores each of the four features of constitutionalism as they have evolved in Australia, demonstrating how the various influences have combined to shape Australian constitutionalism today.

11 Russell Hardin, 'Why a Constitution?', in Denis J. Galligan and Mila Versteeg (eds), *Social and Political Foundations of Constitutions* (Cambridge: Cambridge University Press, 2013), 51.

12 Kenneth Hayne, 'Rule of Law', in Cheryl Saunders and Adrienne Stone (eds), *The Oxford Handbook of the Australian Constitution* (Oxford: Oxford University Press, 2018), 167, 181–6.

Influences

Sources

The original influence on Australian constitutionalism, which is ongoing, was the United Kingdom. As the then imperial power, Great Britain established what ultimately became six Australian colonies from 1788. A convenient categorisation of the status of these colonies, drawn from Blackstone, identified them as 'settled', rather than ceded or conquered, justifying a wholesale reception of English law to provide the foundations of colonial law, to the extent that it was applicable.[13] In this way, some of the staples of British constitutional arrangements fed into Australian constitutionalism as well. These comprise both statutes and case law and include aspects of Magna Carta, the Bill of Rights 1688, the Act of Settlement 1701, the Case of Proclamations,[14] the Case of Prohibitions[15] and *Entick v Carrington*.[16]

In time, Australian institutions, both legislatures and courts, determined what law had been received and what would be retained.[17] For the most part, however, principles of these kinds, reflecting the values of due process, representative government, judicial independence and limitations on arbitrary power, which became characteristic of common law constitutionalism more generally, remained in place. Moreover, as the colonies developed their own institutions it was both natural and, during imperial times inevitable, that the Australian institutions of government would be modelled on those in the United Kingdom. Institutions particularly relevant for present purposes included parliamentary government broadly along Westminster lines and generalist courts that, consistently with common law practice, dealt with legal challenges to government action as well as litigation between private parties.

British influence on the early development of Australian constitutionalism was framed by the conditions of the nineteenth century. Ministerial responsibility to the Westminster Parliament was well established by the 1850s.[18] The discretionary authority of the Crown had diminished to the point where Walter Bagehot, channelling earlier writers, characterised the monarchy in 1867 in terms of a 'dignified' rather than 'efficient' aspect of the constitution.[19] Long overdue reform and expansion of the franchise in 1832, 1867 and 1884

13 William Blackstone, *Commentaries on the Laws of England* (4 volumes, Oxford: Clarendon Press, 1765), I: 104–5.

14 [1610] EWHC KB J22.

15 [1607] EWHC KB J23.

16 [1765] EWHC KB J98.

17 See, for example, the Imperial Acts Application Acts of each of the states.

18 William Selinger, *Parliamentarism* (Cambridge: Cambridge University Press, 2019), 171.

19 Ibid, 175.

had made the House of Commons more representative, progressively reduced patronage through the Crown and weakened the authority of the House of Lords.[20] By the 1870s, the movement for women's suffrage was underway.[21] Positivism overcame natural law as the dominant approach to legal thinking, exemplified by the writings of Jeremy Bentham and John Austin, coinciding with other complementary developments including new appreciation of the reform potential of legislation and consolidation of the doctrine of *stare decisis*.[22] In the latter part of the century, the influential work of A. V. Dicey characterised and rationalised parliamentary sovereignty, reconciled it with a particular version of the rule of law and extolled the virtues of the British Constitution.[23]

These ideas, institutions and attitudes infused the early development of constitutional government in Australia, including the constitutions adopted by each of the colonies between 1855 and 1890.[24] They remained influential, through habit and willing emulation, long after imperial constraints were gone. The movement to unite the colonies in a Federation, which eventually succeeded in 1901, required something more, nevertheless. The new level of government, the Commonwealth, which Federation would require, would have institutions broadly along British lines, building on the experiences of government in the Australian colonies, which now would become states. For the federal model itself, the Australians turned to the United States, which became the second, major source of external influence on the foundations of Australian constitutionalism.

The United States was a convenient fit for a federating Australia: a common law country, a Federation formed by aggregation, as Australia would also be, with a codified and entrenched constitution, written in English, through which the federal compact was protected. Several of the key participants in the Federation movement were familiar with the Constitution of the United States, including Andrew Inglis Clark, who developed a draft Constitution for the Australian Federation on which the first constitutional convention drew.[25] Conveniently, James Bryce published

20 Reform Act 1832; Reform Act 1867; Representation of the People Act 1884.

21 Clare Wright, *You Daughters of Freedom* (Melbourne: Text Publishing, 2018), 92.

22 Neil Duxbury, *The Nature and Authority of Precedent* (Cambridge: Cambridge University Press, 2008), chapter 2.

23 Dicey, *The Law of the Constitution*. Allison's useful edition prints the original lectures of 1885 and traces the changes in subsequent editions authored by Dicey himself.

24 J. Quick and R. R. Garran, *The Annotated Constitution of the Australian Commonwealth* (Sydney: Legal Books, 1995), 35–78.

25 Susan Crennan, 'Federation', in Cheryl Saunders and Adrienne Stone (eds), *The Oxford Handbook of the Australian Constitution* (Oxford: Oxford University Press, 2018), 78, 90.

his influential work, *The American Commonwealth*, in 1888, just before the later Federation movement began, and it became a regular work of reference for the framers of the Australian Constitution.[26] The style of Bryce's work may have enhanced its appeal in Australia as well: detailed, relatively non-prescriptive, emphasising the continuities, as well as the disjunctions, between America and Britain. Bryce's portrayal of the US Constitution as 'not revolutionary but post-revolutionary', as Stephen Gageler puts it, further eased acceptance of the relevance of US experience to a constitutional system already showing signs of the evolutionary character that would become one of its most distinctive traits.[27]

There were other formative external influences on Australian constitutionalism as well. These included Canada, where Federation (also within the British Empire) had been achieved as recently as 1867,[28] and the two European confederations of Germany and Switzerland.[29] Both the range and depth of Australian engagement with external sources for the design and conceptualisation of the federal constitution can be gleaned from the references in the contemporary annotation of the new Constitution by Quick and Garran.[30] Nor has the influence of external sources been confined to the foundational period of Australian constitutionalism. As might be expected, those jurisdictions that exercised influence at the time of the founding continued to do so subsequently through scholarship, law reform, judicial decisions and in myriad other ways. Australian constitutionalism typically has been open to consideration of new ideas, whether or not they are adopted for use.[31]

Context

The context in which any constitutional system is established and operates has a determinative effect on the form and substance of constitutionalism. Context for this purpose potentially comprises many aspects of national life at

26 J. A. La Nauze, *The Making of the Australian Constitution* (Melbourne: Melbourne University Press, 1972), 273.

27 Stephen Gageler, 'James Bryce and the Australian Constitution' *Federal Law Review* 43 (2015): 177 at 184.

28 British North America Act 1867 (UK).

29 Nicholas Aroney, 'The Influence of German State-theory on the Design of the Australian Constitution' *International and Comparative Law Quarterly* 59 (2010): 669.

30 Quick and Garran, *The Annotated Constitution*.

31 In relation to use by courts, see Cheryl Saunders and Adrienne Stone, 'Reference to Foreign Precedents by the Australian High Court: A Matter of Method', in Tania Groppi and Marie-Claire Ponthoreau (eds), *The Use of Foreign Precedents by Constitutional Judges* (Oxford: Hart Publishing, 2013), 14.

the founding and over time: geography, demography, politics, social and economic conditions, geopolitics. It is not possible to canvass the entire field here, although the general point should be noted. Rather, this section focuses on selected aspects of context that have had significant effects on Australian constitutionalism.

First, and importantly, the lands that became Australia had been inhabited by Indigenous peoples for more than 60,000 years when the British government established the Australian colonies. The culture of the Indigenous peoples, their ways of life and their languages were entirely unfamiliar to the new arrivals. The response of the colonists, encouraged by Western theories of colonisation and civilisation, was to ignore the possibility that Indigenous peoples might have pre-existing rights, including property rights, in a land that was treated as 'practically unoccupied'.[32] One consequence, to which reference has already been made, was the absorption of British law into the colonies as the foundations of the new legal systems. After some ambivalence that lasted decades, it became accepted that the new law applied to disputes between Indigenous people as well.[33]

Indigenous Australians were 'subjects', but assumptions about their cultural and civilisational inferiority left them marginalised and were used to justify depriving them of even the most basic civil and political rights.[34] This structural inequality in the constitutional system persisted for much of the twentieth century and, while it began to be rectified in the latter part of the century, instances of systemic discrimination continue to occur.[35] The assumptions on which the settled status of the colonies was based were finally overturned in 1992, in *Mabo v Queensland (No. 2)*, but without providing an alternative explanation for the claims of British sovereignty.[36] This gap, still unfilled, remains a pressing constitutional question,[37] which in the second decade of the twenty-first century is actively being pursued through treaties, constitutional recognition, or both.[38] It has potential to surface in unexpected

32 John Waugh, 'Settlement', in Saunders and Stone (eds), *The Oxford Handbook of the Australian Constitution*, 56, 64.
33 Ibid, 69–73.
34 P. G. McHugh, *Aboriginal Societies and the Common Law* (Oxford: Oxford University Press, 2014), 201.
35 Sean Brennan and Megan Davis, 'First Peoples', in Saunders and Stone (eds), *The Oxford Handbook of the Australian Constitution*, 27, 51–2.
36 *Mabo v Queensland (No. 2)* (1992) 175 CLR 1.
37 It surfaced again, in a new guise, in *Love v Commonwealth* (2020) 94 ALJR 198, when the High Court held, by majority, that Indigenous Australians who did not hold Australian citizenship nevertheless were not aliens within the meaning of Commonwealth constitutional power.
38 Brennan and Davis, 'First Peoples'.

ways; as in *Love*; *Thoms*, where the High Court held that individuals recognised as Indigenous Australians but who lacked formal citizenship nevertheless were not 'aliens' within the reach of Commonwealth constitutional power and could not be deported from Australia.[39]

The characterisation of the Australian colonies as 'settled' also encouraged the assumptions and practices of monolegalism, which remains a defining feature of Australian legal and constitutional arrangements. In consequence, even as aspects of Indigenous law were recognised in the latter part of the twentieth century, they were formally given effect by incorporation through the common law or statute, rather than as sources of law in their own right.[40]

A second contextual factor which pervaded the evolution of Australian constitutionalism is the impact of Australian colonial status. Its influence continued, in increasingly attenuated form, well into the twentieth century. Because the first settlement, in New South Wales in 1788, was a convict colony, the reception of relevant British law and the establishment of even the most basic representative institutions was delayed until the 1820s, as the colony assumed a more civic character.[41] Even then, as David Neal has shown, the earliest experiences of constitutionalism, in the form of elements of the rule of law, took place in courts, which necessarily had been established for the exigencies of a convict colony, rather than in representative institutions.[42] Over time, the large eastern colony of New South Wales fragmented, with the separate establishment of what became Tasmania, Victoria and Queensland, and new settlements took place in South Australia and Western Australia. While each of these six colonies had an early story of constitutionalisation of its own, they shared similar characteristics for present purposes.

For all of them, ultimate authority lay with the institutions of the imperial power in London. No colonial Parliament ever held 'sovereignty' in the absolute form in which Dicey described it and no colonial government could rely on non-intervention by the personal representative of the Crown to the extent assumed by the principles of 'responsible' government. Doubts about the relationship between colonial law and general British law in the immediate aftermath of self-government ultimately were resolved

39 *Love v Commonwealth* (2020) 94 ALJR 198.

40 For a similar point in relation to New Zealand, see Claire Charters, 'Recognition of Tikanga Māori and the Constitutional Myth of Monolegalism: Reinterpreting Case Law', in R. Joseph and R. Benton (eds), *Māori Governance* (Auckland: Thomson Reuters, 2019).

41 Quick and Garran, *The Annotated Constitution*, 36–7.

42 David Neal, *The Rule of Law in a Penal Colony* (Cambridge: Cambridge University Press, 1991).

through the imperial Colonial Laws Validity Act 1865, in favour of a relatively limited version of the doctrine of repugnancy. Almost in passing, however, that Act also explicitly authorised the colonies to entrench some, but not all, parts of their constitutions in terms that continue to plague state constitutions today.[43] The colonies were familiar with judicial review of the validity of legislation and decisions of the colonial courts were subject to final appeal by the Privy Council in London.

Even on Federation in 1901, the new Commonwealth level of government was subject to restrictions of broadly similar kinds, within the framework of a new Constitution, itself an enactment of the imperial Parliament. Full independence came gradually, managed for a while through Dominion status. Independence was achieved at various different times by various institutions and levels of government, through an extended evolutionary process that avoided any significant break in legal continuity.[44] The process was not complete until the enactment of the Australia Acts in 1986 by both the Commonwealth and the United Kingdom. From this relatively late date, therefore, the development of Australian constitutionalism finally was formally under Australian control at both levels of government, even though de facto control had been achieved long before.[45]

The composition of the population in the period when the foundations of constitutionalism were laid may also have influenced the distinctively democratic character of the constitutional arrangements that emerged, although cause and effect necessarily are speculative. Penal settlement brought to Australia more than 160,000 convicts, primarily of English or Irish background, many of whom were poor and had been sentenced for relatively minor theft and some of whom had been sentenced for political offences. Free settlement tended to attract people who lacked opportunity at home and had a sufficient sense of adventure to travel a very long distance with highly uncertain prospects. The discovery of gold, from 1851, brought a further influx of a heterogeneous population, primarily from Britain and Ireland, other parts of Europe, China and the United States.[46] These patterns of immigration provided a springboard

43 Colonial Laws Validity Act 1865, s 5.

44 Susan Kenny, 'Colonies to Dominion, Dominion to Nation', in J. T. Gleeson, J. A. Watson and R. C. A. Higgins (eds), *Historical Foundations of Australian Law* (2 volumes, Annandale: Federation Press, 2013), I: 245.

45 Anne Twomey, 'Independence' in Saunders and Stone (eds), *The Oxford Handbook of the Australian Constitution*, 96.

46 Migration Heritage Centre, 'Australia's Migration History', www.migrationheritage.nsw.gov.au/belongings-home/about-belongings/australias-migration-history/index.html, accessed 20 March 2021.

for a distinctive commitment to electoral democracy, which became a hallmark of Australian constitutionalism as it developed in the latter half of the nineteenth century. Property qualifications, at least for lower Houses of the colonial Parliaments, were abolished and upper Houses were, typically at least, elected.[47] The secret ballot was introduced.[48] The movement for women's suffrage took hold and achieved success well before its counterpart in England.[49] These attitudes infused the drafting of all the Australian Constitutions and continued into the twentieth century with, for example, the introduction of compulsory voting. Writing in 1902, Harrison Moore described the 'predominant feature' of the new Commonwealth Constitution as 'the prevalence of the democratic principle, in its most modern guise'.[50]

Australian constitutionalism is more than the sum of its parts. The combination of British institutions with United States federalism, together with influences from Canada, Switzerland and elsewhere, was unique. All adopted features were adapted in some way to Australian conditions, instinctively or by design. They were complemented by others that were Australian innovations, of which those linked to electoral democracy are examples. Over time, the components of the Australian constitutional system developed organically as working constitutional arrangements. New trajectories typically are triggered by issues of concern in or to Australia, to which the system responds. Some of these issues, and the constitutional responses to them, are identified in the sections that follow.

Constitutions

Australian constitutionalism centres around a written, deeply entrenched Constitution, but bears traces of the unwritten constitutional culture from which it originated.

Each of the Australian states also has its own written Constitution, now recognised by Section 106 of the Commonwealth Constitution. These instruments originated as the Constitutions of the several colonies in the second half of the nineteenth century. All were made under the authority of the British Parliament and within the constraints it prescribed. British legislation authorised both the making and amendment of colonial constitutions,

47 Judith Brett, *From Secret Ballot to Democracy Sausage* (Melbourne: Text Publishing, 2019), 8.
48 Ibid, 8–9. 49 Wright, *You Daughters of Freedom*.
50 Quoted in Joo-Cheong Tham, 'Political Participation', in Saunders and Stone (eds), *The Oxford Handbook of the Australian Constitution*, 979, 984.

subject to the need to comply with any 'manner and form' requirement laid down for the enactment of laws 'respecting the Constitution, Powers and Procedure' of the colonial legislature.[51] Absent this obligation to respect a limited range of manner and form requirements, there may have been doubt about whether the principle of parliamentary sovereignty allowed alteration of the ordinary law-making procedure at all, even for the purpose of making or changing a constitution. These early Constitutions were drawn up by the colonial Parliaments and thereafter amended by them or re-enacted as a whole. Many parts of the Constitutions could be amended without compliance with special manner and form requirements and so had the status of ordinary law that could readily be overridden by ordinary legislation. Had Australia not federated, it is likely that the form of constitutionalism in each of the Australian polities would have developed within an uncodified constitutional tradition, as subsequently happened in New Zealand.

The limited power to entrench parts of their Constitutions that was given to the colonies in 1865 was reaffirmed for the states by Section 6 of the Australia Acts in 1986.[52] In 1865, it had been welcome confirmation of the ability of the colonies to protect any parts of their Constitutions at all, in a constitutional tradition that typically assumed that a Parliament could not bind its successors. In modern times, however, it manifests as an anachronism, which potentially constrains states from entrenching their Constitutions as a whole. A limited power to entrench has its roots in colonial law and practice and reflects the narrow range of matters with which colonial constitutions typically dealt. It is hard to square with the contemporary conception of the idea of a written constitution as fundamental law in an independent Australia. It is also hard to justify a manner and form requirement only for laws affecting the 'constitution, powers and procedures of the legislature' in constitutions that deal with such a wide range of other matters, including courts, local government, independent institutions and preambular recognition of Indigenous peoples.

In fact, over the course of the twentieth century, the states used their power to prescribe manner and form requirements more adventurously, in relation to both procedure and substance. A wider range of procedures have been used including, in some cases, requirements for a referendum, entrenching selected parts of state Constitutions more deeply. The relative ease with

51 Colonial Laws Validity Act 1865, s 5.

52 For elaboration on the matters in this paragraph generally see Gerard Carney, 'State Constitutions', in Saunders and Stone (eds), *The Oxford Handbook of the Australian Constitution*, 277.

which such requirements can be imposed has sometimes led to their use for politically contested arrangements, to protect them against a change of government. Examples have included the abolition or preservation of state upper Houses in Queensland and New South Wales respectively and protection of the position of the governor in Queensland and Western Australia.[53] Laws of these kinds might be categorised as concerning the 'constitution, powers and procedure of the legislature', thus falling within the original colonial limitations in terms of substance. More adventurously still, however, some states have also stipulated manner and form requirements for other substantive parts of their Constitutions including, for example, the Supreme Court.[54] State Parliaments themselves treat such provisions as effective and, so far, there has been no final resolution of these complex legal questions.

Despite expansion of the scope of state Constitutions, none provides protection for rights.[55] The omission typically is justified, in Diceyan fashion, by reference to the political and legal safeguards offered by Parliaments and independent courts. From the early years of the twentieth century, nevertheless, the self-governing Australian Capital Territory and the states of Victoria and Queensland enacted statutory rights protection, drawing broadly on the model of the Human Rights Act 1998 (UK), adapted to the context of sub-national levels of government and to the constraints of the codified constitutions.[56] These charters have had a modest, but notable, impact on law and political practice, offering encouragement to other states and territories to follow suit.

In most of these respects, the experience with the Constitution for the Commonwealth of Australia was quite different, for reasons attributable to its original purpose of providing a federal framework within which the six colonies would unite.[57] The Constitution was drafted in two conventions, the second of which comprised delegates directly elected by voters in four of the five participating colonies.[58] It became law through enactment by the

53 Ibid. 54 Constitution Act 1975 (Vic).

55 Constitution Act 1934 (Tas), s 46, which provides a guarantee of religious freedom, is an exception.

56 Human Rights Act 2004 (ACT); Charter of Human Rights and Responsibilities Act 2006 (Vic); Human Rights Act 2019 (Qld). Some of the challenges of accommodating such legislation to a codified constitutional context were revealed in *Momcilovic v The Queen* (2011) 254 CLR 1.

57 The term 'Commonwealth' is used in different senses in the Constitution and the Imperial Act through which it is made law: to refer to the political entity of Australia and to the level of central government. See Quick and Garran, *The Annotated Constitution*, 366.

58 Queensland did not send a delegation to the Australasian Federal Convention of 1897–8; the Western Australian delegation was chosen by the Parliament, rather than direct election.

British Parliament, as the only then accepted means of giving it paramount legal status within Australia and avoiding conflict with other imperial law. The Constitution, given effect by Section 9 of the Imperial Act, was deeply entrenched by a mechanism modelled loosely on the use of referendums in Switzerland. This required bills that amended the Constitution and had been passed by the Commonwealth Parliament to be approved by a national majority of voters and by a majority of voters in a majority of states.[59] At the time, this mechanism was expected to make the Constitution relatively flexible, although it has not turned out to be so in practice.[60]

Federation came at a turning point in the evolution of Australian statehood. Lack of independence was reflected in the manner in which the Constitution became law and in many of its provisions, including the contested continuation of appeals to the Privy Council.[61] On the other hand, unlike the Constitution of Canada, the Australian Constitution contained its own procedure for change and several other provisions foreshadowed the possibility of the future exercise within Australia of imperial powers relating to Australia.[62] Within six years after federation, Australia became one of a group of countries classified as Dominions within the British Empire; by 1926, Dominion status had evolved to refer to 'autonomous Communities within the British Empire ... in no way subordinate to one another ... associated as members of the British Commonwealth of Nations'.[63] As a result of these developments, the Commonwealth level of government became responsible for Australia's external affairs and both the Monarch and the Governor General acted on Commonwealth government advice in relation to Commonwealth affairs. The Statute of Westminster 1931 (Imp) enabled the Commonwealth to free itself from the paramountcy of imperial law (while preserving the status of the Constitution) and to assume full extraterritorial powers. This option was not taken until 1942, when it was backdated to 1939.[64] A residual British power to legislate for Commonwealth matters on request was finally removed by the Australia Acts 1986 (UK and Aust), which also preserved the status of the Constitution.[65] All these and

59 Commonwealth Constitution, s 128.
60 Cheryl Saunders, 'The Parliament as Partner: A Century of Constitutional Review', in G. Lindell and R. Bennett (eds), *Parliament: The Vision in Hindsight* (Annandale: Federation Press, 2001), 454.
61 Commonwealth Constitution, s 74.
62 Commonwealth Constitution, ss 128, 51(xxxviii) and 74; arguably also s 2.
63 Balfour Declaration by the Imperial Conference of 1926; quoted in Kenny, 'Colonies to Dominion', 258.
64 Statute of Westminster Adoption Act 1942 (Cth).
65 Australia Acts 1986, ss 1, 5.

related steps, by which Australia acquired independence, were achieved without alteration of the Constitution, rendering much of its meaning and operation opaque and leaving to the courts the responsibility of adjusting the meaning of the Constitution to these new circumstances when appropriate cases arose.[66]

The Commonwealth Constitution is thin in terms of substance. Its primary purposes were to establish the Commonwealth as a new level of central government and to provide the framework for the relationship between the Commonwealth and the states. The manner in which these provisions evolved over time is explored more closely under the heading of 'Power' below. Like the constitutions of the states, the Commonwealth Constitution makes almost no provision for rights, although a few scattered sections have played a rights-type role[67] and some protection for interests in the nature of rights has been implied from the institutional arrangements for which the Constitution provides.[68] Otherwise, again as at the state level, rights protection is left to political action, political restraint or the general law, all now influenced to some degree by Australia's international human rights commitments.[69] The possibility of a legislative bill of rights for the Commonwealth was considered in 2008 but effectively rejected.[70]

In these circumstances, there is a case for arguing that the Australian constitutions are not fully codified, even in the sense of comprising norms of the most fundamental kind. The continuing, but extraconstitutional, legal effect of statutes by which independence was secured, including the Australia Acts, provide one basis for such a claim. Laws securing important rights, including Indigenous rights, of which the Racial Discrimination Act 1975 and the Native Title Act 1993 are key examples at the Commonwealth level, provide others. Measures of these kinds are significant for the purposes of understanding the modalities of Australian arrangements. As a generalisation, nevertheless, the codified constitutions dominate

66 For example, the decision that the United Kingdom is a 'foreign power' for the purposes of s 44(i) in *Sue v Hill* (1999) 199 CLR 462.

67 Section 51(xxxi) (compensation for acquisition of property); s 80 (trial by jury); s 116 (aspects of religious freedom); s 117 (discrimination on the grounds of state residence).

68 *Australian Capital Television v Commonwealth* (1992) 177 CLR 106; *Roach v Electoral Commissioner* (2007) 233 CLR 162; *Chu Kheng Lim v Minister for Immigration, Local Government and Ethnic Affairs* (1992) 176 CLR 1.

69 Scott Stephenson, 'Rights Protection in Australia', in Saunders and Stone (eds), *The Oxford Handbook of the Australian Constitution*, 905.

70 National Human Rights Consultation, Report (2009) http://library.bsl.org.au/jspui/bitstream/1/1320/1/NHRC_Report.pdf, accessed 20 March 2021; Human Rights (Parliamentary Scrutiny) Act 2011 (Cth).

Australian constitutional imagination, in terms of political practice, popular understanding and, inevitably, judicial review.

Authority

The idea that constitutionalism requires the Constitution to draw its authority from the people can be understood in several ways. It may refer to the authority for a written Constitution, which typically is ascribed to the people, at least virtually and usually more practically, on the basis of the manner in which the Constitution is made. Alternatively, or in addition, it may refer to the people as political sovereign, underpinning the legitimacy of governing institutions, at least some of which are chosen by the people through elections and ultimately held to account by the people. Both understandings have a role in the evolution of Australian constitutionalism.

At best, the people are only indirect authority for the constitutions of the Australian states, given the manner of their making and the dominant role of state Parliaments in amendment and re-enactment. Constitutionalism at the state level thus relies on the democratic role of the people as electors. At the Commonwealth level, however, the position is different. The process of constitution-making in the 1890s was unusually inclusive for its time, involving both a directly elected Convention and approval of the draft by referendums. The preamble to the Constitution Act refers to the agreement of the 'people' of the several colonies and the Constitution can be changed only with the agreement of the electors, in the manner described in Section 128. On the other hand, initially at least, the legal status of the Constitution as fundamental law depended on its enactment by the British Parliament, which also had some influence on content. Even when the last vestiges of British authority to legislate for Australia were removed by the Australia Acts in 1986, the status of the Constitution was saved.[71] These alternative explanations of the authority for the Commonwealth Constitution co-existed in tandem for much of the twentieth century. The more palatable view, nevertheless, always has been that authority lies with the Australian people. This view has been reflected in decisions of the High Court as the logical consequence of the end of British authority to legislate for Australia and there can be no doubt that it now prevails.[72]

71 Australia Acts 1986, s 5.

72 *Australian Capital Television Pty Ltd v Commonwealth* (1992) 177 CLR 106, 137 (Mason CJ); see also *Clubb v Edwards* (2019) 267 CLR 171, 191 [29], 196 [51], 198 [60] (Kiefel CJ, Bell and Keane JJ).

Thus, the centrality of the people, in the abstract, is a firmly established feature of the Australian constitutional system. The identity of the people, however, in the practical sense of those holding full political rights, entitled to exercise political sovereignty, has varied over time. By a long evolutionary process, the concept of the people, in this sense, has not only become more inclusive but also achieved a measure of constitutional protection.

The Commonwealth Constitution describes the composition of the House of Representatives by reference to 'the people of the Commonwealth'.[73] Australia's relationship with Britain at the time of Federation, however, meant that the Constitution did not provide for a status of Australian citizen to frame the contours of 'the people'. The category of belonging then in use, on which the Constitution relied, was British subjecthood nuanced, when the need arose, by a 'substantial connection' with Australia.[74] The Constitution, accordingly, provided protection against discrimination on the grounds of state residence to any 'subject of the Queen';[75] conferred on the Commonwealth Parliament express power to make laws with respect to 'aliens', rather than 'citizens';[76] and disqualified those with 'allegiance . . . to a foreign power' from election to the Commonwealth Parliament in terms that were relatively unproblematic at a time when British subject status was so widespread.[77]

It was not until 1948 that Australian citizenship was established, under the Nationality and Citizenship Act 1948 (Cth). Consistently with decisions of the Commonwealth (of Nations) Conference on Nationality and Citizenship 1947, the Australian legislation created its own rules for citizenship but preserved the status of British subject.[78] The reference to subjecthood remained in Australian citizenship legislation until the time of the Australia Acts, and British subjects enrolled before 26 January 1984 are still not only entitled but required to vote in Commonwealth elections.[79] Decisions of the High Court played a significant role in managing the constitutional transition from subject to citizen, but there are limits to which this can be done without formal constitutional change.[80]

73 Commonwealth Constitution, s 24.
74 Elisa Arcioni, 'Citizenship', in Saunders and Stone (eds), *The Oxford Handbook of the Australian Constitution*, 339, 344.
75 Commonwealth Constitution, s 117.
76 Commonwealth Constitution, s 51 (xix); the power also extends to 'naturalisation'.
77 Commonwealth Constitution, s 44(i).
78 Jatinder Mann, 'The Evolution of Commonwealth citizenship, 1945–1948 in Canada, Britain and Australia' *Commonwealth and Comparative Politics* 50 (2012): 293.
79 Arcioni, 'Citizenship', 342. The legislation was the Australian Citizenship Amendment Act 1984 (Cth), which came into effect on 1 May 1987.
80 See e.g. *Street v Queensland Bar Association* (1989) 168 CLR 461; *Sue v Hill* (1999) 199 CLR 462; *Singh v Commonwealth* (2004) 222 CLR 322.

In Australia, as elsewhere, the original democratic aspiration was male suffrage. The first battleground was property qualifications. As noted in the second section of this chapter, these began to be removed for voting for the lower Houses of the colonial Parliaments from 1856, although they remained for upper Houses somewhat longer.[81] There were no property qualifications for voters under the first Commonwealth Franchise Act, in 1902. By the time of Federation, the contest was over the next issue, of female suffrage. Women already were enfranchised in South Australia and Western Australia and the remaining states would follow suit soon after, Victoria being the last, in 1908. The struggle over female franchise is reflected in the Commonwealth Constitution, which provided for the Commonwealth to use state voting laws until Commonwealth legislation could be enacted. Section 41 protected the rights of voters already enfranchised by state law.[82] Section 128 anticipated the possibility that states with female franchise might have an advantage in a referendum by requiring the votes cast in those states to be halved. Not surprisingly in these circumstances, the first Commonwealth franchise empowered women both to vote and stand for federal election, excluding 'natives' unless otherwise qualified to vote in a state.

The enfranchisement of Indigenous Australians took much longer. Indigenous people were expressly excluded from the franchise in some colonies and, later, states until, in the case of the last state, Queensland, 1965. Indigenous peoples were also expressly excluded from the Commonwealth franchise in 1902 subject to the guarantee, such as it was, for existing voters in Section 41. Section 127 of the Constitution, removed by referendum in 1967, also provided that they should 'not be counted' in 'reckoning the number of people of the Commonwealth' including, presumably, for the purposes of calculating the distribution of seats between states in Section 24. After incremental changes over the preceding decades, the federal franchise was finally extended to Indigenous Australians in 1962, although they were not subject to the requirements to enrol and vote that applied to other Australians until 1983.[83]

This gradual broadening of the 'people' for the purposes of Australian constitutionalism took place through legislation that interacted only tangentially with provisions of the Constitution. From 1975, however, the

81 Carney, 'State Constitutions', 282.

82 It did not otherwise have prospective operation, however: *R v Jones* (1972) 128 CLR 221; *R v Pearson; ex parte Sipka* (1983) 152 CLR 254.

83 Brett, *From Secret Ballot to Democracy Sausage*, chapter 5.

constitutional references to the Houses of the Commonwealth Parliament being 'directly chosen by the people' began to be given substance by the High Court, in ways that further structured the power of the Parliament to make laws about elections.[84] By these means, the Constitution has been interpreted in ways that effectively entrench a right to vote, subject to reasonable restrictions.[85] It is clear from these cases that it now would not be constitutionally possible to return to a time when any adult Australian citizen was denied the vote on the grounds of sex or Indigeneity. Controversy over the ambit of 'the people' has moved on, to prisoner voting, as in *Roach*, and the inflexible administration of voting rules, as in *Rowe*, with the High Court now as final arbiter.

In these decisions, in essence, the High Court has accepted that the identity of the people has evolved over time, in ways to which constitutional requirements respond.[86] A similar development can be observed in relation to the constitutional protection of trial by jury, which has been held now to require the inclusion in juries of women as well as men, whatever the position may have been in 1901.[87] These developments undoubtedly correspond broadly with Australian expectations. They are also consistent with the weight that Australian constitutionalism places on electoral democracy.

Power

The substance of Australian constitutionalism depends largely on the organisation of public power between levels and arms of government, within the framework of the Commonwealth Constitution. These arrangements both empower and impose limitations on institutions in ways that have evolved over time.

The Constitution provides a framework for Australian federalism. A federal system divides legislative and other powers between two levels of government and, thus, by definition limits the power of each. On its face, the Constitution leaves considerable power with the states including, relevantly for present purposes, human rights and the general criminal law. A federal division of power alone can contribute to constitutionalism; the inability of the Commonwealth Parliament to ban the Communist Party in Australia in the 1950s, for lack of relevant legislative power, illustrates the point.[88]

84 Tham, 'Political Participation', 979.

85 *Roach v Electoral Commissioner* (2007) 233 CLR 162; *Rowe v Electoral Commissioner* (2010) 243 CLR 1.

86 Tham, 'Political Participation', 1007.

87 *Cheatle v The Queen* (1993) 177 CLR 541.

88 *Australian Communist Party v Commonwealth* (1951) 83 CLR 1.

Over the course of the twentieth century, the Commonwealth became the more powerful level of government through expansive interpretation of Commonwealth power by the High Court, the accretion of Commonwealth control over the most lucrative revenue sources and Commonwealth dominance of intergovernmental relations. Key moments in this process include a more literal approach to the interpretation and application of heads of Commonwealth legislative power by the High Court from 1920, after World War I;[89] Commonwealth acquisition of monopoly control over income taxation from 1942, during World War II;[90] and the increasing formalisation of intergovernmental arrangements after the establishment of the Council of Australian Governments in 1992.

Some of these developments detrimentally affected constitutionalism, by providing incentives for the Commonwealth to achieve outcomes through spending and intergovernmental action in ways that avoid Parliament, lack transparency, and make accountability more difficult to secure. Other aspects of the growth of federal power have been positive for constitutionalism. The decision of the High Court that Commonwealth legislative power with respect to 'external affairs' empowered Parliament to enact laws to give domestic effect to treaties to which Australia is a party, including human rights treaties, is an example.[91] The direction of development has not been all one way. The courts remain active in enforcing the federal division of powers. Noteworthy decisions in this regard, in the early part of the twenty-first century, include a requirement for many Commonwealth executive spending programs to be supported by legislation, enabling their validity to be tested more effectively,[92] and restrictions on the use of intergovernmental schemes to circumvent constitutional limits on power.[93] Despite the relative shift in the federal balance of power, moreover, the states retain significant capacity for innovation and experimentation in ways that further constitutionalism. Examples include the legislative bills of rights enacted in the Australian Capital Territory, Victoria and Queensland; the state-based Indigenous treaty processes underway from 2018; and the Victorian Voluntary Assisted Dying Act 2017 (Vic).

89 *Amalgamated Society of Engineers v Adelaide Steamship Co* (1920) 28 CLR 129.
90 *South Australia v Commonwealth* (1942) 65 CLR 373.
91 *Koowarta v Bjelke Petersen* (1982) 153 CLR 168; *Commonwealth v Tasmania* (1983) 158 CLR 1.
92 *Williams v Commonwealth* (2012) 248 CLR 156; *Williams v Commonwealth (No. 2)* (2014) 252 CLR 416.
93 *ICM Agriculture Pty Ltd v Commonwealth* (2009) 240 CLR 140.

As the limits on power derived from Federation weakened, those associated with the relationship between institutions within each level of government strengthened. These take several different forms.

First, under both the Commonwealth and state Constitutions the personal representative of the Crown possesses some 'reserve' powers that can be exercised without or against government advice. To that extent, they provide a check on political power that arguably offers a necessary backstop where the government no longer has the support of a majority in the lower House of a Parliament. The dynamics of the exercise of these powers changed over the course of the twentieth century as it was confirmed that the Governor General and, later, the state governors, were required to act on the advice of Australian, rather than British ministers, in 1926 and 1986 respectively.[94] The ambiguity of the Constitution in relation to powers of this kind was exposed in 1975, when the Governor General dismissed a prime minister who retained the confidence of the House of Representatives but was unable to secure supply from the Senate.[95] The constitutionality of the Governor General's actions were contested and they remain divisive, complicating agreement on a model for an Australian republic, which would need either to deliberately preserve the current ambiguity or to resolve the point of disagreement in some way.

Bicameralism is another significant dimension of the institutional division of public power in Australia. The Commonwealth and all state Parliaments except Queensland have legislatures with two chambers, the former as an accoutrement of federalism and the latter originating in colonial times. Their contribution to constitutionalism is complicated, both by the anti-democratic origins of the colonial second chambers and by the extent to which, even now, second chambers counter or at least delay decisions of a majority in the other House. All Australian second chambers now are elected, however, albeit through a variety of electoral arrangements. The greater deliberation that they bring to the legislative process has become valued in a political culture in which party discipline typically dictates outcomes in the lower House. As matters presently stand, all second chambers have considerable authority in relation to legislation and scrutiny of executive government.[96] The High Court has upheld the powers of upper Houses to hold governments to account, modifying the principles of responsible government in

94 Kenny, 'Colonies to Dominion'.

95 Commonwealth Parliament, *House of Representatives Practice* (7th edition, 2018), chapter 1.

96 Carney, 'State Constitutions', 284.

Australia to that extent.[97] One effect of these developments has been to strengthen legislatures as institutions in their own right, and to give them a degree of independence from executive control.

A third and most significant form of allocating powers between institutions comes under the rubric of separation of powers. The influence of the Constitution of the United States on the drafting of the Commonwealth Constitution caused the structure of the first three chapters of the latter, dealing respectively with the Parliament, the Executive government and the Judicature, to be modelled on the first three Articles of the Constitution of the United States. Despite differences in the relationship between the legislature and the executive in the two countries, within the first three decades after Federation it was held that the Constitution established a three-way separation of powers at the Commonwealth level.[98] This holding has some salience even between the legislature and the executive, despite the interdependence necessitated by Westminster-style parliamentary government.[99] It has had particular application, however, in relation to the judiciary. By the midpoint of the twentieth century, the separation of judicial power had evolved to a point where it precluded institutions other than courts from exercising federal judicial power and precluded Federal Courts from exercising other forms of power.[100] The focus on the Judicature chapter of the Constitution that the reasoning in this line of cases encouraged ultimately led to confirmation that Section 75 entrenches the original jurisdiction of the High Court to deal with unlawful action by Commonwealth officers.[101] As the further consequences of separation of judicial power were explored by a more rights-conscious Court at the turn of the twenty-first century, it became clear that the doctrine could provide some protection for due process and for personal liberty, at least of citizens.[102] However, it had no impact on the position of non-citizens detained by the government under statutory authority for very considerable periods of time, ostensibly while their refugee claims were processed or alternative arrangements for their future were made.[103]

97 *Egan v Willis* (1998) 195 CLR 424.

98 *Victorian Stevedoring and General Contracting Co Pty Ltd v Dignan* (1931) 46 CLR 73.

99 Cheryl Saunders, 'Separation of Legislative and Executive Power', in Saunders and Stone (eds), *The Oxford Handbook of the Australian Constitution*, 617.

100 *R v Kirby; ex parte Boilermakers' Society of Australia* (1956) 94 CLR 254.

101 *Plaintiff S157/2002 v Commonwealth* (2003) 211 CLR 476. The ground had been laid much earlier, however, in 1945: *R v Hickman* (1945) 70 CLR 598.

102 Fiona Wheeler, 'Due Process, Judicial Power and Chapter III in the New High Court' *Federal Law Review* 32 (2004): 205.

103 *Al-Kateb v Godwin* (2004) 219 CLR 562; *M68/2015 v Minister for Immigration and Border Protection* (2016) 257 CLR 42.

The different structure of the state constitutions means that there is no formal, legally entrenched three-way separation of powers at the state level. However, the relationship between the legislative and executive branches is much the same for the states as for the Commonwealth and also is affected in five states by the bicameral structure of the Parliament. In 1996, moreover, it became apparent that the separation of judicial power under the Commonwealth Constitution had some effect at the state level as well, at least to the extent of protecting the integrity of the state courts that could be empowered to exercise federal jurisdiction and were, for this reason, part of an 'integrated' court system.[104] In a separate but conceptually related development, in 2010 the High Court held that state Supreme Courts cannot constitutionally be deprived of their inherent jurisdiction to determine the lawfulness of state government action.[105] This decision was based in an interpretation of the reference to Supreme Courts in Section 73 of the Commonwealth Constitution, which confers appellate jurisdiction on the High Court. It brought the doctrine applicable to the Supreme Courts in line with that applicable to the High Court. It is part of an observable trend to submit state constitutional arrangements to the Commonwealth Constitution to a greater degree, thus protecting them against easy amendment.

The point was made earlier that, unusually in comparative terms, Australian constitutionalism does not make express provision for the protection of rights. Over the latter part of the twentieth century, nevertheless, the new emphasis on rights that began to characterise constitutionalism in other parts of the world had effects in Australia as well, some of which have been noted earlier, but which are conveniently collated here. The High Court adopted a less formalist approach to the few rights-type provisions already in the Constitution.[106] Judicial interpretation of constitutional provisions establishing the Parliament and the courts began to offer limited but significant protection for some political rights and aspects of due process. At the turn of the century, the legislative bills of rights described in previous sections were enacted in three sub-national jurisdictions and considered in others. More generally, Australian judicial doctrine and method also developed approaches to both statutory interpretation and understanding of the requirements of common law principle that tended to be more rights-protecting.

104 *Kable v Director of Public Prosecutions (NSW)* (1996) 189 CLR 51.
105 *Kirk v Industrial Court of New South Wales* (2010) 239 CLR 531.
106 Stephenson, 'Rights Protection'.

Compliance

Compliance with the Constitution and the law is a core aspect of the rule of law in Australia and historically has been a strength of Australian constitutionalism.

Even before Federation, judicial review of the validity of both legislation and government action was familiar in Australia, although the primary yardstick was imperial law and the ultimate arbiter was the Privy Council. Federation was the catalyst for the effective entrenchment of judicial review in a codified Constitution, reinforced by consideration of the precedent of the US Supreme Court in *Marbury v Madison*, of which the framers of the Australian Constitution were aware.[107] Consistently with the common law tradition, Australia adopted a system of diffuse review in which all courts potentially could deal with questions arising under the Australian Constitution subject to the jurisdiction of the High Court as the final court of appeal (once appeals to the Privy Council ended).[108] Moreover, despite continued adherence to the traditional imperial practice of appointment of judges by the executive alone, Australian courts generally have been accepted as independent and impartial. It is testament to the confidence in judicial independence in Australia that the states accept the High Court as both arbiter of the federalism provisions of the Constitution and final interpreter of state legislation, even though they have a minimal role in High Court appointments.[109]

The High Court claims for itself the ultimate authority to interpret the Constitution and to resolve constitutional disputes.[110] Initially, the claim was justified by reference to the requirements of federalism but, since 1951 at the latest, it has been described as 'axiomatic'.[111] Ready acceptance of the claim on the part of the political branches may be assisted by the thin substance of the Constitution and the High Court's own relatively narrow understanding of the scope of judicial power. Since the reformation of Commonwealth administrative law from the 1970s, judicial power to review the 'legality' of government action has been distinguished from non-judicial power, exercised by 'tribunals',

107 *Marbury v Madison* 5 US (1 Cranch) 137 (1803); F. M. Neasey and L. J. Neasey, *Andrew Inglis Clark* (Hobart: University of Tasmania Law Press, 2001), 194–5.

108 Commonwealth Constitution, s 74; Privy Council (Limitation of Appeals) Act 1968 (Cth); Privy Council (Appeals from the High Court) Act 1975 (Cth); Australia Acts 1986, s 11.

109 Under Section 6 of the High Court of Australia Act 1979 (Cth) State Attorneys-General are required to be 'consulted' on appointments.

110 Hayne, 'Rule of Law', 173.

111 *Australian Communist Party v Commonwealth* (1951) 83 CLR 1, 262 (Fullagar J).

not courts, to review its 'merits'.[112] Any temptation on the part of the political branches to oust the jurisdiction of the Court in constitutional and other public law cases is discouraged both by the status of the Constitution and by the conferral on the High Court, by Section 75 of the Constitution, of original jurisdiction to review administrative action by Commonwealth 'officers', which now has been interpreted to invalidate all but the least effectual ousters.

Compliance by the executive branches of government with the decisions of courts is an aspect of the rule of law that, generally, can be taken for granted in Australia. It is put to the test whenever a court decides a case against a government, particularly when the issues at stake involve high-ranking officials or go to the heart of the policy position of government as, for example, in the *Communist Party* case.[113] Usually the test is passed easily enough, even if the court confines itself to the remedy of a declaration.

Nevertheless, there is no room for complacency. Tensions with the executive branch over the meaning and application of immigration legislation in the early decades of the twenty-first century sometimes causes more peremptory remedies to be used.[114] Continued Commonwealth spending without legislation in areas with no obvious link to Commonwealth heads of legislative power suggests that the executive branch is directly flouting the decisions in the *Williams* cases about the scope of inherent executive power. The perfunctory response of the Commonwealth to the first *Williams* case, to provide legislative backing for vulnerable programs through loosely worded delegated legislative instruments, points to another characteristic but worrying feature of Australian constitutionalism: a willingness on the part of both the legislature and the executive to comply with the letter, but not the spirit, of the law.[115]

Conclusions

Australian constitutionalism is the product of a history in which influences from constitutional systems elsewhere blended and were adapted to local conditions over time. To this extent it is not an unusual story. Most constitutional systems develop in this way, although differences in aspirations, comparative models and context typically lead to outcomes that are distinctive in many respects, notwithstanding global interdependence.

Particularly distinctive features of Australian constitutional arrangements include its emphasis on electoral democracy, its dependence on the integrity

112 *Attorney-General (NSW) v Quin* (1990) 170 CLR 1, 35–6 (Brennan J).
113 *Australian Communist Party v Commonwealth* (1951) 83 CLR 1.
114 Hayne, 'Rule of Law', 185. 115 Ibid, 182–3.

of public institutions, and the absence of express, entrenched protection of rights. These features make Australia an interesting case study in a form of political constitutionalism under an entrenched constitution. This approach has been effective enough to establish Australia as a state that can appropriately be described in terms of constitutionalism. It has weaknesses as well, however, which already have prompted moves towards rights protection that is both more deliberate and more secure. Further change is likely to be necessary to maintain the benefits of constitutionalism in the future.

Australian constitutional development is unusual also in maintaining unbroken legal continuity for a period of almost 250 years. Continuity has persisted, despite three major shifts in the nature of the Australian state: erosion of the basis for the original British claim of sovereignty; the aggregation of six separate polities into a single federated state; and the transition from colonial status to independence. The preservation of continuity in these circumstances may be attributed both to Australian stability and to Australian pragmatism. In the third decade of the twenty-first century, however, it is possible to see that it has left some problems in its wake that will require resolution in due course by a more deliberate steering of Australian constitutionalism.

9

Indigenous Governance

9.1 Mparntwe/Alice Springs: Towards a History of Indigenous and Settler Jurisdictions

TIM ROWSE AND JENNIFER GREEN

> The town grew up dancing and still the dancing is there under the town. Subdivisions spread, but we still keep going. We still have the culture, still sing the song . . . It's the same story we have from the old people, from the beginning here in the Centre.[1]

Indigenous law remains consequential within Australia's colonised places where, in towns such as Mparntwe/Alice Springs, it continues to exist in the same territory as colonial law.[2] The quote from the late Wenten Rubuntja AM that begins this chapter alludes to this persistence of Indigenous culture, custom and law in the town, as does the image illustrated in Figure 9.1.[3] Two traditions of landscape painting provide a powerful visual metaphor for the co-existence of systems of law, reflecting an aspiration 'for the mutual recognition and respect of mainstream law and traditional Indigenous laws in Australia'.[4]

We thank Jason Gibson, Joel Liddle, Russell Goldflam and the participants in the Australia and New Zealand Law and History Conference 2019 and a School of History seminar at the Australian National University in 2020 for their comments on earlier drafts of this chapter.

1 Wenten Rubuntja AM cited in C. Ruff, J. Rhodes and D. Brooks, *Site Seeing*. Exhibition catalogue. (Alice Springs: Institute for Aboriginal Development 1991). See also W. Rubuntja and J. Green, *The Town Grew Up Dancing: The Life and Art of Wenten Rubuntja* (Alice Springs: Jukurrpa Press, 2002), 1.

2 The term Mparntwe refers to one of the Arrernte 'Countries' or 'estates' that lie partially within the administrative boundaries of Alice Springs. It is sometimes spelt as Mbantua.

3 The word *atnengkerre* is translated as 'law' in this image, but the term has a range of other meanings including 'Dreaming (totem)', 'Dreaming story' and 'dream'. See J. Green, 'The Altyerre Story – "Suffering Badly by Translation"' *The Australian Journal of Anthropology* 23 (2012): 158–78.

4 R. Goldflam, 'The (non-)Role of Aboriginal Customary Law in Sentencing in the Northern Territory' *Australian Indigenous Law Review* 17(2013): 71–80, 71.

Figure 9.1: (COLOUR CENTREPIECE) Atnengkerre Atherre Akwete – Two Laws Together. Artwork Wenten Rubuntja and Chips Mackinolty. Reproduced with permission of Chips Mackinolty and the Aboriginal Artists Agency Ltd. (For the colour version, please refer to the plate section)

Australia's colonial history has given rise to many 'recognition spaces' where colonial authority has been confronted with evidence of the continuing existence of Indigenous customary law.[5] Adapting Noel Pearson's concept 'recognition space' from his discussions of 'native title' (a concept deployed by the High Court of Australia in 1992 and legislated by the Australian Parliament in 1993) we acknowledge that settler-colonial 'recognition' is not necessarily sympathetic, and it may only be episodically evident. The colonist's gaze may be admiring, hostile or dismissive. Such inconsistent or unreliable recognition has sometimes been described as 'muted'.[6]

This chapter presents episodes of recognition in Mparntwe / Alice Springs that have arisen from the overlapping of two systems of law in a space inhabited by both Arrernte and non-Arrernte people.[7] Although the colonisation of Arrernte Country forced the Arrernte to alter some embodied practices of their law, it did not extinguish that law. For Arrernte people, the town area continues to be a sacred and sentient landscape, which has existed since 'time immemorial'.

Observing the Arrernte in Alice Springs

The town of Alice Springs was built as a result of the construction of a telegraph line across the Australian continent. The technology of telegraphy required repeater stations at intervals of two hundred miles, and in 1872 the South Australian government built one near a water source on the Todd River. In 1888 the town of 'Stuart' was proclaimed on the western bank of the Todd, and in 1933 'Alice Springs', the name of the repeater station, became the official name of the town.

Francis Gillen was appointed as Alice Springs' post and telegraph station master in 1892. A sympathetic observer of the Arrernte people on whose land he lived, in 1894 he commenced a collaboration with the anthropologist Walter Baldwin Spencer that yielded detailed descriptions of ceremonies in

5 'Native title is . . . the space between the two systems of law, where there is recognition.' N. Pearson, *Up from the Mission* (Melbourne: Black Inc, 2009), 44.

6 H. Douglas and M. Finnane, *Indigenous Crime and Settler Law: White Sovereignty after Empire* (Basingstoke: Palgrave Macmillan, 2012), 125.

7 In this chapter we use the spelling 'Arrernte' for the language associated with Alice Springs. See J. Henderson and V. Dobson, *Eastern and Central Arrernte to English Dictionary* (Alice Springs: IAD Press, 1994). Other spellings that appear in some sources include Arunta and Aranda.

which the Arrernte enacted their law. Gillen's duties included special magistrate and sub-protector of Aboriginals, but he knew that his was not the only law enforced in Central Australia. In his diary in 1901 he recorded how an Arrernte 'deputation' had explained the recent killing of a 'helpless old man'.

> [T]he old man's son had recently come to this locality in the form of Kurdaitja [a magically empowered assassin] & had pointed the bone at the wife of the [avenging] party, causing her great suffering and death. The old man knew of his sons [sic] malicious intentions & did not try to prevent him carrying them out, he [the old man] was therefore slaughtered.[8]

Gillen's diary entry conveys no censure, and nor did he call for this killing to be investigated and prosecuted. He simply noted that this was the Arrernte way. Although he did not refer to his informants' explanation of the killing as an exposition of Arrernte jurisdiction, we as historians interpret it in such terms. Like other colonial officials, Gillen accepted that, at this time and in this place, there were limits to colonial jurisdiction. Although all Aboriginal people were 'British subjects', such killings *inter se* (Aboriginal killer and victim) exercised the customary prerogative to take life in response to another's transgression.

Although the ambition of colonial law was to subject all violence *inter se* to criminal jurisdiction, judges in the Northern Territory pragmatically acknowledged that Aboriginal customary law was also in force at the outer edges of colonial rule. In 1900 Justice Charles Dashwood took the continuing relevance of Aboriginal customary law into account when he sentenced an Aboriginal killer to three months in prison with hard labour for manslaughter; the jury had recommended mercy on the ground that the offence was also the administration of tribal punishment and that the deceased had provoked the assault. Dashwood's leniency was 'the first known case in the Northern Territory jurisdiction where tribal custom was deemed relevant to considering both the motive of the offender and the sentence imposed'.[9]

Colonial administration, including criminal law, suppressed customs deemed offensive to colonists. Indeed, colonists understood their own authority and way of life as fatal to *all* aspects of Arrernte custom, and it was widely believed that in Central Australia Aboriginal people were (in

8 F. Gillen, *Gillen's Modest Record: His Journal of the Spencer-Gillen Anthropological Expedition across Australia, 1901–1902, edited by* Philip Jones (Adelaide: Friends of the State Library of South Australia, 2017), 104.

9 Goldflam, 'The (non-)Role', 71; D. Mildren, *Big Boss Fella All Same Judge* (Annandale: The Federation Press, 2011), 26.

Spencer's words) 'rapidly degenerating and disappearing'.[10] Their 'disappearance' was not necessarily physical; it referred to marked and rapid cultural changes. Colonists were sure that Aboriginal peoples were 'detribalising'. Dr Cecil Cook, the Northern Territory's Chief Protector of Aboriginals from 1927 to 1939, described the 'typical course' of detribalisation when briefing the Minister for the Interior in 1935.

> Young men are displaced from their normal status in the tribe by being placed in employment. In the course of this employment they may be required to visit places in their own country which under the laws of their own social organization, they must not visit under penalty perhaps of death. On the other hand, the appeal of the white man's food and particularly of horsemanship tend to alienate the youth's sympathy from his elders in favour of the new employment whilst the attractions of the new mode of life may render the elders tolerant of these heresies. Gradually the elders lose control and the young men reach maturity unfamiliar with and uninterested in the details of tribal ritual, knowledge of which dies with the old men. In the course of time those ceremonies and sanctions which held the tribe together are lost and the individual becomes an isolated unit without social background either European or native.[11]

Casual observation reinforced such generalisations. The psychologist Stanley Porteous, who had read Spencer and Gillen's accounts of the Arrernte from the 1890s, described them, after visiting Central Australia in 1929, as 'hardly [to be] recognised as the same tribe. Their social organisation has broken down, their traditions are forgotten . . . .'[12] Although anthropologists who worked in Central Australia were finding Aboriginal peoples, including Arrernte, keen to explain their customs as a living tradition, the widely accepted view was that significant changes in economy and belief were extinguishing Aboriginal customary law.[13]

Nonetheless, colonial authorities continued to take 'custom' into account as a determinant of Aboriginal behaviour in the Northern Territory. In 1932 Acting Justice William Henry Sharwood began to review the Northern Territory's legal system. He received a petition from twenty jurors suggesting that an Aboriginal person charged with killing another Aboriginal person

10 W. B. Spencer, *Wanderings in Wild Australia* (London: Macmillan and Co. 1928), 1: xvi.
11 C. E. Cook to Administrator, 7 October 1935, National Archives of Australia CRS A1 1937/70.
12 S. D. Porteous, *The Psychology of a Primitive People* (London: Edward Arnold, 1931), 131.
13 J. Gibson (2019) '"Factotum and friend": Anthropologists, Informants and Ethnographic Exchange in Central Australia' *History and Anthropology* doi=10.1080/02757206.2019.1580706.

be tried in a special tribunal with expertise in Aboriginal custom.[14] Though no such tribunal was ever established, the Crimes Ordinance 1934 (Cth) conceded discretion to judges in their sentencing of Aboriginal people convicted of murder: 'the judge shall not be obliged to pronounce sentence of death, but, in lieu thereof, may impose such penalty as, having regard to the circumstances of the case, appears to the court to be just and proper'. In considering such a sentence the court should take into account 'any relevant native law or custom and its application to the facts of the case and any evidence which may be tendered in mitigation of penalty'.[15] The judges' discretion applied, whether or not the victim was an Aboriginal person. In a further official concession to the enduring force of customary law, in 1936 the Commonwealth government appointed an anthropologist, T. G. H. Strehlow, as the Territory's first Patrol Officer. It was understood that his knowledge of Aboriginal law would guide his summary punishment of minor offences by Aboriginal people.[16] By such concessions to the persistence of Indigenous jurisdiction colonial law sought to include 'Aboriginal natives' as 'British subjects'.

Legislating Control

Belief that 'detribalisation' would be rapid and inevitable – albeit unpredictable in its duration – gave colonial authorities 'humane' reasons to manage the lives of Aboriginal people: to mitigate their supposed demoralisation and to steer them towards conformity with non-Aboriginal ways of living. South Australia legislated the Northern Territory Aborigines Act 1910 (SA). This was followed by the Aboriginals Ordinance of 1911 (Cth), which was passed by the Commonwealth government after it took control of the Northern Territory. The Commonwealth repealed the 1911 law in 1918, but continued its powers, defining the category of persons who could be regulated as 'Aboriginal' in respect of their place of living, employment, associations and rights to hold property (including money). The Chief Protector became the 'guardian' of Aboriginal children. He could declare areas prohibited to Aboriginal people, remove Aboriginal camps from town areas and regulate employment and movement to and from reserves or institutions. It became illegal for a non-

14 Mildren, *Big Boss Fella*, 87.
15 Crimes Ordinance 1934 (*Commonwealth Gazette* 26, 3 May 1934). These provisions continued in the Criminal Law Amendment Ordinance 1939.
16 T. Rowse, 'Strehlow's Strap: Functionalism and Historicism in a Colonial Ethnography' *Journal of Australian Studies* 16, no. 35(1992): 88–103.

Aboriginal person to 'habitually consort' with an Aboriginal woman and for Aboriginal people to drink alcohol. An amendment of the Ordinance in 1936 allowed exemption of selected individuals, and in 1953 a further amendment exempted all Aboriginal people known as 'half-castes' from the controls set out in the Aboriginals Ordinance 1918–53 (Cth). Subsequent legislation – the Welfare Ordinance and the Wards' Employment Ordinance and others – applied these controls to 'wards', effectively all people classified as 'full blood' Aboriginal in the Northern Territory. In 1964 the Ordinances were amended so that there were no longer offences against or by persons classed as 'wards' – effectively the end of the legal abridgement of Aboriginal people's rights of citizenship.[17] From 1959 Aboriginal people were increasingly able to receive pensions (aged, widow, invalid) in the form of cash, and in December 1968 male Aboriginal pastoral workers were eligible for award wages.

For much of the period in which such legal restrictions applied, people known to be of mixed Euro-Australian and Aboriginal descent were subject to especially intensive management because of their supposed genetic potential to adopt non-Aboriginal ways of life and because they were assumed to be less able to conform to what remained of the traditional ('tribal') way of life. From 1914 to 1942 the Northern Territory Administration institutionalised 'half-caste' children from Central Australia in 'the Bungalow', which occupied a series of sites in and around Alice Springs. The Bungalow housed children who were 'detribalised', as one local put it: 'to keep them going towards the whites and give them their future chance'.[18] Many of the children were related to local Aboriginal men and women, but Aboriginal adults who saw the children as theirs to help raise according to local traditions were excluded by the matron (Mrs Ida Standley) and by the police. Here we see the beginnings of one contest faced by an Indigenous jurisdiction: whether the 'half-caste' child would be raised within the Aboriginal domain.

As Alice Springs grew to be a service and employment centre, other Aboriginal people from the wider region were attracted to it. In 1927, the white population of the town numbered a mere forty, while in the whole of Central Australia in 1930 there were only some 590 whites compared with about 5,500 Aboriginal people (not including the 260 people counted as 'half-

17 The crucial Ordinances were the Social Welfare Ordinance 1964 (No. 31 of 1964) the Licensing Ordinance 1964 (No. 35 of 1964) and the Licensing Ordinance (No. 2) 1964 (No. 1 of 1965).

18 Geo T. Ballingall to Minister for Home Affairs, [undated] 1932, National Archives of Australia (NT) F1/42/70a 'Half-caste institution, Alice Springs'.

castes').[19] The attractiveness of Alice Springs to the region's Aboriginal people put pressure on the custodians of the land in and around Mparntwe to accommodate not only non-Aboriginal aliens (such as Chinese and Euro-Australians) but also Indigenous 'outsiders' such as the Luritja, Pitjantjatjara, Warlpiri and Anmatyerr. Colonists who sought to manage town-camping became aware of intra-Aboriginal diplomacy. In 1931 George Ballingall warned the administration that because 'tribes' with a presence in Alice Springs had long fought 'in settlement of boundaries', Aboriginal people employed around the town tended to keep to their different camps.[20] One official, Dr W. B. Kirkland, disputed Ballingall: Aboriginal people working and camping in Alice Springs 'have been so long in close contact with the Whites that tribal customs have long ceased to play a great part in their lives'; they had modified their customs 'to conform with the new environment' and there were now 'four different tribes living in the aboriginal camp' where the administration was issuing rations in 1931. Dr Kirkland was confident that a single authorised camp, three miles north of the town, would be at peace.[21] Whether intra-Aboriginal relationships were competitive or cooperative, friendly or hostile, these abiding distinctions of Country/person identity were manifestations of something fundamental to Indigenous jurisdiction: that persons and networks of persons were consubstantial with their 'Country'.

When Arrernte jurisdiction was enacted as ceremonies on Arrernte Country, close to the township of Alice Springs, settler authorities had to adopt some policy towards them. Frank McGarry, a Catholic lay missionary with the Little Flower Mission, established in 1935 on Charles Creek, just to the north of the township, illustrates the flexibility such events required on both sides. Mission residents approached McGarry, inviting him to witness an initiation ceremony that took place in low hills within walking distance of the township. Senior Arrernte men showed McGarry more ceremonies and took him to a secret storehouse of *tjuringa* (*tywerrenge*) north of the town. McGarry persuaded these ceremonial leaders not to conduct a ceremony that he considered brutal. He learned the limits of his influence when he tried to abbreviate an initiation that, in his view, went on too long: 'The mob had

19 P. Donovan, *Alice Springs: Its History and the People Who Made It* (Alice Springs: Alice Springs Town Council, 1988), 140. The state, at this time, had little capacity to enumerate Aboriginal people across the administrative unit of 'Central Australia', so any figure must be treated with caution.

20 Geo T. Ballingall to Minister for Home Affairs and Territories, 2 April 1931, National Archives of Australia (NT) F1 42/70(a).

21 Dr W. B. Kirkland to Administrator, 1 May 1931, National Archives of Australia (NT) F1/42/70a 'Half-caste Institution, Alice Springs'.

Figure 9.2: First communion at the Little Flower Mission, Charles Creek, Alice Springs. Image courtesy of Catholic Church, Alice Springs.

their way, and me a lesson.'[22] The Little Flower Mission was also conducting baptisms at this time (Figure 9.2). Thus, we can infer that in 1937 the Arrernte were seeking a *modus vivendi* between two spiritualities and two ways of socialising children: the Arrernte way and the Irish-Australian Catholic way. That interface continued: oral histories confirm that while missionaries forbade children from speaking Indigenous languages, children still had contact with Arrernte senior men and women and participated surreptitiously in the rich ceremonial life of the townspeople. When the Arrernte claimed native title to land in and around Alice Springs in 1996 the claimants included some surviving senior people who had been members of the 1938 'confirmation class' at the Little Flower Mission at Charles Creek as well as their descendants brought up in Arrernte law.

After World War II: A 'Mainly Aboriginal Life'

The Bungalow's physical and legal sequestration of 'half-castes' formed them as a self-consciously distinct segment of the Aboriginal population, but this did not assure the 'detribalisation' of people of mixed descent. In 1953, the participation of two 'three-quarter caste Aboriginal men' in an initiation ceremony 'in an

22 F. O'Grady, *Francis of Central Australia* (Sydney: Wentworth Books, 1977), 65.

area adjacent to the sanitary camp south of Alice Springs township' was explained by surprised officials as proof of their moral failure: they were allegedly 'poor types and heavy drinkers'.[23] To distinguish them in this way helped to maintain the official view that, generally, mixed-descent Aboriginal people around Alice Springs *were* detribalising and assimilating. However, such incidents demonstrated instead that officials had underestimated the robustness of Aboriginal customary law among all Aboriginal people – of whatever genetic admixture – living in or near Alice Springs. Officials who based their administration of Aboriginal lives on the detribalisation thesis were sometimes puzzled and horrified by evidence that a distinctly Indigenous way of life was continuing. For example, in 1958 one public servant wrote that mixed-descent households 'pick the eyes out of two cultures without acknowledging responsibility to either'.[24] This is another episode of the recognition of continuing Aboriginal jurisdiction in Mparntwe, however dismissive or begrudging.

Although convinced of 'the low degree of intelligence of the average aborigine', Justice Martin Kriewaldt, the sole judge of the Northern Territory Supreme Court 1951–60, conceded that, because of the persistence of an Aboriginal milieu, his administration of the criminal law must take Aboriginal customary law into account.[25] Kriewaldt was acting under the discretion afforded to judges by the Criminal Law Amendment Ordinance 1939 (Cth).[26] Reviewing his trials just before his death, Kriewaldt found that 'the majority of Aborigines I have tried have had a good deal of such contact [with "white civilisation"] but lived a mainly "aboriginal" life'.[27] Satisfied that the law was protecting Aboriginal people from harm by non-Aboriginal people, Kriewaldt argued that colonial authorities should take more notice of what Aboriginal people considered to be provocative behaviour by other Aboriginal people. If more were done to regulate Aboriginal behaviour according to Aboriginal norms of conduct, there would be fewer acts of violence among Aboriginal people, he speculated, for 'in nearly every case the actions of the accused were regarded as wrong by the aborigines most nearly concerned'.[28]

23 McCoy to McCaffery (District Superintendent), 18 March 1953, National Archives of Australia (NT) Fl 53/417 'Inspection Reports, Gap Settlement, Alice Springs'.
24 E. C. Evans to Director of Welfare, 3 October 1958, National Archives of Australia (NT) F1 58/1539 'Control of Wards in Alice Springs Area'.
25 Justice M. Kriewaldt, 'The Application of the Criminal Law to the Aborigines of the Northern Territory of Australia' *The University of Western Australia Law Review* 1 (1960): 1–50, 33.
26 Douglas and Finnane, *Indigenous Crime*, 131.
27 Kriewaldt, 'The Application', 25.
28 Ibid, 25–6.

Government officials had to admit that 'detribalisation' was not proceeding as fast as the designers of assimilation policy had anticipated. Generalising about the wider Aboriginal population, the Welfare Branch Annual Report of 1968–9 concluded that:

> Detribalisation in the sense of surrender of their basic social organisation and social arrangements has not . . . gone very far, and traditional institutions such as marriage patterns, and traditional attachment to particular geographical areas are still greatly respected.[29]

Within a few years the Commonwealth government had announced a new policy of 'self-determination'. On 6 April 1973 Prime Minister Gough Whitlam stated that 'the basic object' of the policy 'is to restore to the Aboriginal people of Australia their lost power of self-determination in economic, social and political affairs'. Beckett has suggested 'welfare colonialism' as a label for the ensuing practices of government – characterised by a realisation that Aboriginal 'cultural values and modes, whether originating before conquest or formed under conditions of colonial exclusion, cannot be cancelled by decree'. In this revised colonial project, 'political incorporation of the Indigenous minority within the nation-state can be effected only through special structures, which institutionalise colonial distinctions, while creating a political constituency which has simultaneously to be maintained and controlled'.[30]

In Mparntwe/Alice Springs these special structures include town camps (the position of seventeen such camps in 2020 is shown in Map 9.1). When town campers organised under the name Tangatjira (later Tangentyere) Council in February 1974, they chose an Arrernte word that means 'working together' or 'cooperating'.[31] The town campers began to formalise their status, not only by seeking special purpose leases, but also by negotiating with each other. The location of these leases within the town area was based in part on the totemic geography of the land and on the complex networks of social relationships between its Indigenous residents. Heppell and Wigley reported in 1978 that the Arrernte traditional land owners recognised that other Aboriginal groups needed the security of tenure afforded by the special purpose leases that the Northern Territory Administration was now prepared

29 Northern Territory Administration Welfare Branch Annual Report 1968–9 (24 February 1970), 25.

30 J. Beckett, 'Aboriginality, Citizenship and the Nation-state' *Social Analysis* 24 Special Issue Aborigines and the *State* in Australia (1988): 3–18, 14.

31 Henderson and Dobson, *Eastern and Central Arrernte*, 273.

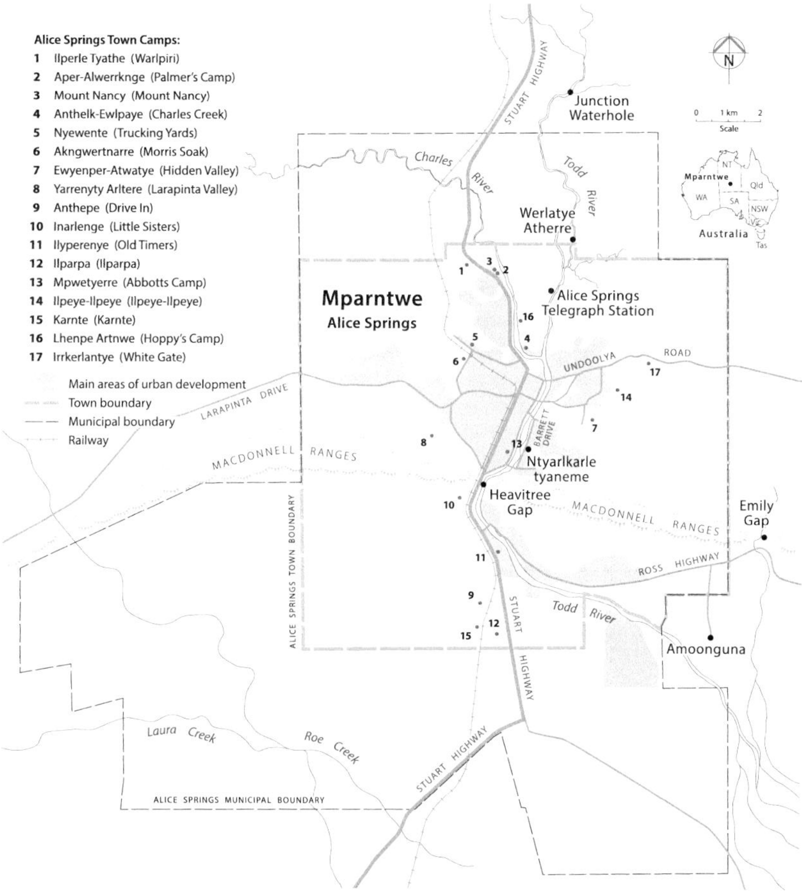

Map 9.1: Map of Alice Springs showing the location of town and municipal boundaries, the main areas of urban development, and the locations of the town camps. Cartographer: Brenda Thornley.

to grant.[32] In granting special purpose leases, the Northern Territory Administration was acknowledging that Arrernte and other Aboriginal people were part of the resident town population, entitled – at the very least – to houses and ablution blocks managed by Tangentyere Council.

The Arrernte aspired to stronger tenure. In 1975, when the Whitlam government's Aboriginal Land Rights bill was before the Australian Parliament, they

32 M. Heppell and J. Wigley, *Black Out in Alice: A History of the Establishment and Development of Town Camps in Alice Springs* (Canberra: The Australian National University, 1981), 55.

made submissions to the Interim Aboriginal Land Commissioner, Justice Dick Ward. Before Ward could complete his report the bill lapsed. Under the next government the Aboriginal Land Rights (Northern Territory) Act 1976 (Cth) (henceforth ALRA) was passed, in amended form, in December 1976. However, the Act differed from the bill in not allowing land claims based on need, such as those within the town area. While the Act converted reserve land to Aboriginal freehold, this did not benefit the Alice Springs Arrernte, as the only reserve in their Country – the Bungalow – had ceased to be a reserve in 1963. Reviewing the ALRA after seven years, Mr Justice Toohey noted 'the position of the Aranda people living in Alice Springs . . . whose traditional land lies very much in and around that town'.[33]

Contested Sites

In Section 73 of the ALRA, the Fraser government gave the Northern Territory government power to pass legislation protecting sacred sites. In 1978 the Northern Territory government passed the Aboriginal Sacred Sites Act 1978 (NT) and established the Aboriginal Sacred Sites Protection Authority.[34] Like other Aboriginal people in the Territory, the Arrernte revealed the position and significance of sacred sites so that they could be registered under the Act and thus protected. In doing so, the Arrernte have publicly attested their ongoing jurisdiction. However, two controversies from the 1980s epitomised the tension between site protection and urban development.

Northern Territory governments – opposed to land rights in the 1980s – were ambivalent protectors of sacred sites. On Boxing Day in December 1982 they ordered the bulldozing of part of a site called Ntyarlkarle tyaneme (lit. 'where the elephant grub lies across') to provide improved road access to the Alice Springs casino (see Figure 9.3). This was despite written assurances that work would not proceed on the site until the issue of the road's alignment had been resolved with custodians, and in spite of the fact that the site was registered under the Northern Territory government's own Aboriginal Sacred Sites Act. As Wenten Rubuntja AM put it:

> Now it's Marshall Perron – the man who never stops. He never listens for one bit. At Barrett Drive we put up a sign: '$1,000 fine for somebody doing

33 Justice J. Toohey, *Seven Years On* (Canberra: Australian Government Publishing Service, 1984), 12, 13.

34 In 1989, the Northern Territory government passed the Northern Territory Aboriginal Sacred Sites Act (NT) 1989, which continues the work of site protection under the Aboriginal Areas Protection Authority.

Figure 9.3: Barrett Drive where it dissects Ntyarlkarle tyaneme, the caterpillar site. Photo: J Green.

> the wrong thing' ... He never think one bit of it. He just cut off that caterpillar tail.[35]

The custodians were given no warning of the desecration. They were profoundly upset by the Northern Territory government's refusal to live by its own laws, as well as by the perceived consequences of the desecration in the form of increased rates of local illness and misfortune. One traditional owner, Thomas Stevens Peltharre lamented that, '[t]his Ntyarlke caterpillar belonging to this site was still alive before this road went through'.[36] Another, Doris Stuart Kngwarreye, said: 'we call it Broken Promise Drive – that's where the government couldn't go and prosecute itself. It was their law that said that sites shouldn't be damaged.'[37]

35 Cited in P. McEvoy and P. Lyon, *The Land Is Always Alive – The Story of the Central Land Council* (Alice Springs: Central Land Council, 1994), 35.
36 T. Stevens, *Altyerre Ipenhe Anwernekenhe Akurneleke Kerte: Damaging Our Dreaming Land* (Alice Springs: Yipirinya School Council, 1984).
37 Cited in *Every Hill Got a Story, edited by* Margaret Bowman (Melbourne: Hardie Grant Books and Central Land Council, 2015), 225.

The other example of the Northern Territory government contesting Arrernte custodianship of their land is the series of disputes over proposals to dam the Todd River. In 1979, the Northern Territory government and many town residents welcomed the proposal to construct a recreation lake near Alice Springs. The Sites Authority responded by identifying the Arrernte custodians of the area that would be inundated. In March 1983, following a major flood, Chief Minister Paul Everingham announced that a dam would be built near the Alice Springs Telegraph station. Custodians protested that this would flood several sites and ceremonial grounds, including Werlatye Atherre (lit. 'two breasts'), an area of traditional significance to women and an important part of the Two-Women Dreaming. This Dreaming links Arrernte women to other groups, including Pitjantjatjara women of the Western Desert to the south and southwest of Alice Springs. Traditional owners maintained a protest camp near the site for six months.

Following the Easter floods of 1988, in which three Aboriginal lives were lost in the town, plans for a flood mitigation dam were renewed. The Northern Territory government began investigating another potential site at Junction waterhole, about nine kilometres north of Alice Springs, and, in Arrernte terms, closely related to the Werlatye Atherre site. In 1991 construction began. An application was made to halt the project on behalf of the traditional owners and in 1992 Robert Tickner, the Minister for Aboriginal Affairs, issued an emergency declaration under the Aboriginal and Torres Strait Islander Heritage Protection Act 1984 (Cth) to stop work. Following an inquiry conducted by retired judge Hal Wootten, in May 1992 Tickner issued a declaration under Section 10 of the Act to protect the sacred sites for twenty years. Director of the Central Land Council, David Ross, declared the decision a turning point:

> Too often in the past the development of Alice Springs has been at the expense of the Aboriginal people. Sacred sites have been destroyed and desecrated and the protests of Aboriginal people have been rubbished and ignored. Now at last we have seen some justice.[38]

Native Title

After the High Court of Australia's decision in *Mabo v Queensland (No. 2) 1992* overturned the founding fiction of *terra nullius*, the Australian

38 David Ross, as cited in McEvoy and Lyon, *The Land Is Always Alive*, 109.

Parliament passed the Native Title Act 1993 (Cth), recognising the rights of Australian Aboriginal peoples to own Country according to traditional laws and customs. In 1996, a native title claim by Arrernte families whose 'estates' or Country lies in and around Alice Springs was referred to the Federal Court. In 2000 the Federal Court of Australia determined that:

> The persons who hold the common or group rights comprising the native title (the common law holders) are those Aboriginals who are descended (by birth or by adoption) from the original Arrernte inhabitants of the Mparntwe, Antulye and Irlpme estates who are recognised by the respective *apmereke-artweye* and *kwertengerle* of those estates under the traditional laws acknowledged and the traditional customs observed by them as having communal, group or individual rights and interests in relation to such estates.[39]

The rights recognised amounted to an Indigenous jurisdiction – rights to occupation, use and enjoyment of the land and waters of the determination area and its natural resources, rights to be acknowledged as traditional Aboriginal owners, to make decisions, protect the land, and to safeguard the cultural knowledge associated with it.

As custodian Doris Stuart Kngwarreye commented, 'it was the first town that had native title found to exist all over the Alice Springs municipal boundary ... And that was because we could still prove connection to country, because our sites were still here.'[40] Evidence of the strength and continuity of the Arrernte language formed part of the argument for the native title claim. Although all Australian Indigenous languages are endangered, Arrernte remains 'relatively strong' and one of the few where there is intergenerational transmission.[41] In 2019 a 'recognition space' for Arrernte was created in the town's pedestrian mall, in the heart of Mparntwe with the launch of an on-line Arrernte word-list celebrated at a public event at Apmere Angkentye-kenhe 'the Place for Language'.[42]

39 *Hayes v Northern Territory of Australia* [2000] FCA 671, 3. The Arrernte terms *apmerekeartweye* and *kwertengerle* refer to complementary roles held by custodians in relation to land and ceremonies. *Apmereke-artweye* are sometimes glossed as 'owners' and *kwertengerle* as 'managers', although this is a simplification of the Arrernte concepts. See Henderson and Dobson, *Eastern and Central Arrernte*, 287, 455.

40 Cited in *Every Hill Got a Story*, 225.

41 Department of Infrastructure, Transport, Regional Development and Communications (DoITRDC), Australian Institute for Aboriginal and Torres Strait Islander Studies (AIATSIS) and Australian National University (ANU), *National Indigenous Languages Report* (Canberra: Australian Government, 2020), 49.

42 https://arrernte-angkentye.online/, accessed 7 January 2020.

Criminal Law – Recognition Curtailed

Laws recognising 'sacred sites' and 'native title' are 'recognition spaces' in which a version of Aboriginal law is codified and given legal consequence. Recognition spaces have encouraged people to assert Arrernte jurisdiction, to make it visible to a divided non-Indigenous public. In the Northern Territory's codification of the criminal law, the possibility of recognition was reduced when the Criminal Code Act 1983 (NT) repealed the Criminal Law Amendment Ordinance 1939 (Cth) that had conferred power to sentence Aboriginal people convicted of murder to a penalty at the discretion of the judge. Instead, the Code required judges to impose a single mandatory penalty of life imprisonment without parole. While the 1983 Criminal Code fixed maximum (and in the case of murder, mandatory minimum) sentences for the offences it established, it did not otherwise regulate the exercise of sentencing powers until the Sentencing Act 1995 (NT). In the opinion of one observer, the common law recognition of customary law in the 1980s and 1990s continued but was 'cautious, halting and equivocal'.[43] When deciding whether to bail an accused or what sentence to impose for a conviction, magistrates and judges heard testimony, in some cases, that the accused/convicted Aboriginal person was due for punishment under customary law. Judges differed in their responses. There was no settled view about whether the imminence of a customary penalty should affect the court's bail decision or sentence. Even when magistrates and judges did recognise that an accused or convicted Aboriginal person was liable to customary punishment, their recognition fell short of authorising such action. In a 1992 judgment (*R v Minor* (1992) NTLR 183), Justice Mildren said that while spearing a thigh might not be unlawful, 'it would be quite wrong for a sentencing judge to so structure his sentence as to actually facilitate an unlawful act'.[44] This case was subsequently cited in support of bail applications or sentencing submissions in which the defendant sought to enlist the support, or at least the permission, of the court to undergo violent punishment.

However, in Sections 90 and 91 in the Northern Territory National Emergency Response Act 2007 (Cth) the Australian government, as part of its 'Northern Territory Intervention', all but extinguished Territory judges' discretion to recognise customary law in sentencing. These provisions were continued in Section 16AA of the amended Crimes Act 1914 (Cth) in 2012. A sentencing court is not permitted to have regard to cultural practice or

43 Goldflam, 'The (non-)Role', 73. 44 Quoted in ibid, 74.

traditional law for the purpose of assessing the seriousness of criminal behaviour. By 2007, presentations involving Aboriginal traditional law to judges sentencing in the Northern Territory Supreme Court had dwindled to a trickle. In Goldflam's summary:

> from 1994 to September 2006, of 1798 Aboriginal offenders sentenced by the Court, only 13 submitted that their offending was mitigated by a circumstance involving customary law: five cases in which the offence was committed as punishment for a breach of customary law; four in which the offender was provoked by a breach of customary law; two in which the victim was a promised bride; and two in which the offender was acting in accord with customary law. Some of these submissions were accepted, and others were not.[45]

Perhaps by forbidding judges to take Aboriginal law into account, the Australian government in 2007 and 2012 was making a point of colonial principle: that Australia has the sovereign right to choose in which domains of life any vestige of Aboriginal jurisdiction can be tolerated or encouraged.

Conclusion

The persistence of Indigenous jurisdiction in Arrernte Country since its first settler occupation in 1872 suggests the need to move beyond the recognition of 'native title' in *Mabo* to tell a history of Australian jurisdiction that highlights continuing Indigenous law. We can study episodes in which the interactions of Indigenous and non-Indigenous people produce representations of 'custom', of culture, of law. However, just as colonial law cannot 'know' Indigenous customary law except through contingent and imperfect representations of it, so, as non-Indigenous historians of Mparntwe/Alice Springs, we can write the history of Arrernte jurisdiction only by giving accounts of episodes in which – for various reasons – Arrernte jurisdiction became visible and entered the settler-colonial archive as a representation of (what we are choosing to call) Arrernte jurisdiction. Our assumption is that Arrernte jurisdiction is an ongoing reality that lies beyond any particular way of seeing it, representing it, or narrating it. Any history cannot avoid being episodic, each episode a moment of incomplete 'recognition'. What is inside

45 Ibid, 75, citing M. Warbrooke 'To What Extent is Customary Law Raised as a Mitigating Factor in Criminal Cases in the Northern Territory?' (LLB Research Paper, Charles Darwin University, 2006), 34.

the recognition space is only a representation of customary law created to meet the needs of a revised legal architecture of colonial government, though it may be highly valued by the colonised as a concession to their interests. Customary law continues to exist outside the recognition space, beyond the representation that native title legislation and jurisprudence offers. Arrernte jurisdiction remains potent in the lives of Arrernte people; it is what continues to give Arrernte people themselves an answer to the question: what is it to act lawfully?

. . .

9.2 Gunditjmara and Ngarrindjeri: Case Studies of Indigenous Self-government

DARYLE RIGNEY, DENIS ROSE, ALISON VIVIAN, MIRIAM JORGENSEN, STEVE HEMMING AND SHAUN BERG

Introduction

The reality of 'persistent pluralisms, where Indigenous aspirations, collectivities and laws have continued and even structured the interaction of Indigenous peoples with settler governments',[46] makes Australia's assertion of a single, indivisible sovereignty conceptually untenable. Relations among the Australian state and Aboriginal and Torres Strait Islander peoples[47] are

We pay our respects to the Aboriginal and Torres Strait Islander peoples of Australia and acknowledge the challenges they face in asserting their sovereignty, exercising their rights to self-determination and fulfilling their obligations as custodians of Country. We pay our respects to the Gunditjmara People and the Ngarrindjeri Nation, with which we collaborate as citizens, Indigenous nation-building practitioners, educators and theorists. We acknowledge their efforts to self-govern and to consistently challenge the status quo. We appreciate the patience and guidance from the editors and thank Anthea Compton and Amy Della-Sale for their much-needed assistance. Our Indigenous nation-building collaboration among the Gunditjmara People, the Ngarrindjeri Nation, Jumbunna Institute for Indigenous Education and Research and the Native Nations Institute at the University of Arizona has been supported by two ARC-funded projects: DP1092654 and LP140100376. Further research into Ngarrindjeri nation-building was supported by ARC-funded projects: LP13010013 and DP1094869. The views expressed herein are those of the authors and are not necessarily those of the Australian Government or Australian Research Council.

46 L. Ford, 'Locating Indigenous Self-determination in the Margins of Settler Sovereignty' in L. Ford and T. Rowse (eds), *Between Indigenous and Settler Governance* (Abingdon: Routledge, 2013), 1–2.

47 We note that Aboriginal and Torres Strait Islander political collectives use a variety of terms to describe themselves, for example, nation, clan, people, society, community, polity etc. For the purposes of this chapter, we use the term 'people', since it is the term

conducted in an environment of contested sovereignty. On the one hand, Australia's legal and political institutions hold that Aboriginal and Torres Strait Islander sovereignty was superseded at the time of invasion which, they further hold, establishes legal centralism[48] and precludes parallel law-making.[49] On the other hand, settler-colonial governments simultaneously enter into myriad agreements with Aboriginal and Torres Strait Islander peoples that assume the existence of collectives with self-governing capacities and negotiating authority.[50] In recent decades some Australian Indigenous peoples have seized the opportunity inherent in this disconnect; by putting their status claims on the table in negotiations with the settler-colonial state and by demanding de facto *intergovernmental* relationships, they have generated incremental change to Indigenous/non-Indigenous relations.

While reframing the status quo has been slow, current debates about recognition of Aboriginal and Torres Strait Islander peoples in the Australian Constitution, the possibility of treaties negotiated between state governments and Indigenous peoples, and the emergence of policies with the stated intention to facilitate Indigenous self-determination[51] and create representative bodies for Aboriginal nations[52] illustrate an enormous transition in relations during the last fifty to seventy years. Until the 1950s, settler-colonial government policy was predicated on the assimilation of Indigenous people and disappearance of Aboriginal and Torres Strait Islander collectives (a policy that clearly failed). By contrast, today's most pressing policy debates grapple with the question of what appropriate relations among Indigenous peoples and the Australian Federation might entail. While not ignoring the

used in the United Nations *Declaration on the Rights of Indigenous Peoples* to describe Indigenous collectives with the right to self-determination. We also use the terms 'Aboriginal and Torres Strait Islander' and 'Indigenous' interchangeably.

48 Griffiths contrasts the reality of 'legal pluralism' (the coexistence of a social group of legal orders which do not belong to a single 'system') to the ideology of 'legal centralism' (law is and should be the law of the state, uniform for all persons, exclusive of all other law, and administered by a single set of state institutions), describing the former as 'fact' and the latter as 'myth, an ideal, a claim, an illusion'. See J. Griffiths, 'What is Legal Pluralism?' *Journal of Legal Pluralism* 18 (1986): 4.

49 *Members of the Yorta Yorta Aboriginal Community v Victoria* (2002) 214 CLR 422, 443 [44] (Gleeson CJ, Gummow and Hayne JJ).

50 A. Reilly, 'A Constitutional Framework for Indigenous Governance' *Sydney Law Review* 28 (2006): 403–19.

51 See State of Victoria, *Victorian Aboriginal Affairs Framework 2018–2023* (2018), www.aboriginalvictoria.vic.gov.au/victorian-aboriginal-affairs-framework-2018-2023, accessed 20 August 2020; State of Victoria, *Treaty in Victoria* (2018), www.aboriginalvictoria.vic.gov.au/treaty, accessed 3 September 2020.

52 See State Aboriginal Affairs, *Aboriginal Regional Authorities: A Regional Approach to Governance in South Australia*, Consultation Paper (Adelaide: Government of South Australia, February–March 2015).

challenges to, and vulnerability of, Indigenous self-governing, both Indigenous nations' progress and the evolved focus of policy conversations cause us to anticipate a future in which settler-colonial governments must accommodate Indigenous sovereignty and self-government.

Indigenous peoples' quest for self-government in Australia and internationally is not symbolic. Instead, it demonstrates an evidence-based approach to community development. As Australian and North American research demonstrates, self-government gives Indigenous nations increased capability to achieve sustained community well-being. For example, the North American evidence illustrates that Indigenous governments clearly outperform settler-colonial governments that attempt to act on their behalf.[53] Aboriginal and Torres Strait Islander nations in Australia do not have the same political, constitutional and legal status as North American Indigenous nations, and empirical evidence regarding socio-economic circumstances and well-being is not collected at the Indigenous nation level in Australia to enable direct comparison. However, evidence of self-identified Aboriginal and Torres Strait Islander nations similarly improving community well-being suggests parallel findings.[54]

Two Aboriginal nations asserting their status as distinct peoples and, in so doing, demonstrating capacity to achieve their community development goals are the Gunditjmara People[55] and the Ngarrindjeri Nation. While their self-governing efforts have not yet produced institutions that settler-colonial eyes might identify as governments,[56] their intention to self-govern according to Gunditjmara and Ngarrindjeri norms is indisputable.

53 See, for example, M. Jorgensen (ed.), *Rebuilding Native Nations: Strategies for Governance and Development* (Tucson, AZ: University of Arizona Press, 2007); W. Nikolakis, S. Cornell and H. W. Nelson (eds), *Reclaiming Indigenous Governance: Reflections and Insights from Australia, Canada, New Zealand, and the United States* (Tucson, AZ: University of Arizona Press, 2019).

54 See, for example, A. Vivian, M. Jorgensen, A. Reilly, M. McMillan, C. McRae and J. McMinn, 'Indigenous Self-Government in the Australian Federation' *Australian Indigenous Law Review* 20 (2018): 215–42; A. Vivian, M. Jorgensen, D. Bell, D. Rigney, S. Cornell and S. Hemming, 'Implementing a Project within an Indigenous Research Paradigm: The Example of Nation Building Research' *Ngiya: Talk the Law* 5 (2016): 47–74; J. Hunt and D. Smith, 'Understanding and Engaging with Indigenous Governance: Research Evidence and Possibilities for Engaging with Australian Governments' *Journal of Australian Indigenous Issues* 14 (2011): 30–53.

55 'The Gunditjmara People' is the name chosen for the political and social collective of Gunditjmara clans in what is now southwest Victoria. This chapter will also refer to 'Gunditjmara people', being Gunditjmara individuals who we have formally or informally interviewed or who we heard speaking at Gunditjmara Full Group meetings or other meetings.

56 We note elsewhere that we prefer to use the term 'Indigenous government' because we wish to draw attention to the institutions and mechanisms that Indigenous peoples

We are a group of Indigenous nation-building practitioners and theorists who have been working with the Ngarrindjeri Nation and Gunditjmara People towards self-government in a variety of capacities – as citizens, as advisers and as researchers. We present two case studies that describe significant successes, namely the Gunditjmara People achieving World Heritage status for the Budj Bim Cultural Landscape and the Ngarrindjeri Nation entering into treaty negotiations with the South Australian government. We argue that effective and culturally legitimate community decision-making structures and processes – in other words, self-government – made these outcomes possible. At the time of writing in early 2021, both nations are in the process of transforming their institutions of self-governance. In this chapter, we describe what the nations were able to achieve with former iterations of their institutions.

The Gunditjmara People: UNESCO World Heritage Status for the Budj Bim Cultural Landscape

In July 2019, 14 Gunditjmara People travelled to Baku, Azerbaijan to hear that their almost forty-year campaign to have the Budj Bim Cultural Landscape (BBCL) inscribed on the World Heritage List by the United Nations Educational, Scientific and Cultural Organization (UNESCO) had succeeded.[57] The pride and satisfaction felt by the Gunditjmara community in its own achievements and those of its ancestors cannot be overstated: this was a high point for the Gunditjmara People as a nation. But the landmark success also should be acknowledged for what it illustrates about the impact of self-government on the Gunditjmara People's capacity to achieve its aspirations. The success of the campaign exemplifies the Gunditjmara People's commitment to self-determination and to asserting its collective rights; its clear vision and statement of identity as a community of traditional

are using to self-govern: See Vivian et al., 'Indigenous Self-Government in the Australian Federation', 223.

57 The UNESCO World Heritage Committee inscribed the Budj Bim Cultural Landscape on the World Heritage List on 6 July 2019. The BBCL was deemed to have outstanding universal value under criteria (iii) 'to bear a unique or at least exceptional testimony to a cultural tradition or to a civilization which is living or which has disappeared' and (v) 'to be an outstanding example of a traditional human settlement, land-use, or sea-use which is representative of a culture (or cultures), or human interaction with the environment especially when it has become vulnerable under the impact of irreversible change'. See UNESCO, Budj Bim Cultural Landscape, https://whc.unesco.org/en/list/1577/, accessed 28 January 2021.

owners; and its creation of effective decision-making structures that reflect Gunditjmara values. Combined, these attributes magnify the community's capacity to identify, plan and implement highly meaningful projects that can be commenced by one generation and completed by another. In other words, the success of the World Heritage campaign demonstrates that the Gunditjmara People are governing comprehensively *in their own right* rather than exercising responsibility solely within siloed programs developed and approved by settler-colonial governments.

Gunditjmara Country is located in the fertile and resource-abundant coastal region now known as south-western Victoria and south-eastern South Australia. Prior to colonisation, a significant population of Gunditjmara people built numerous stone house villages and a vast *kooyang* (short finned eel) aquaculture systems, which they developed and maintained for over 6,600 years. Engineered from volcanic rock produced when an ancestral creation being revealed himself in the centre of this landscape as the volcano Budj Bim (formerly Mt Eccles), the aquaculture complex consists of an interconnected series of ponds, channels, fish traps, weirs and wetlands that could operate at various water levels, ensuring food security through all but the very worst droughts.[58]

Known as the 'fighting Gunditjmara', the nation fiercely resisted settler-colonialism, waging guerrilla warfare against 'settler' pastoralists in the Eumarella Wars of the 1840s and, during the opening decades of the 1900s, repeatedly refusing relocation away from Gunditjmara Country by the Aborigines Protection Board. In the 1980s, the Gunditjmara People's unrelenting resistance and advocacy bore fruit as the Gunditjmara People began to regain control of Gunditjmara Country. Aluminium producer Alcoa's decision to locate a smelter on culturally significant Gunditjmara lands was pivotal. Led by two Gunditjmara women, Sandra Onus and Christina Frankland, the campaign against the Portland aluminium smelter generated the first High Court holding (the decision in *Onus v Alcoa*) that collective rights of Aboriginal and Torres Strait Islander peoples, founded in their own law, were potentially enforceable in settler-colonial courts.[59] The ruling

58 The Gunditjmara People with G. Wettenhall, *The People of Budj Bim: Engineers of Aquaculture, Builders of Stone House Settlements and Warriors Defending Country* (Empress Publishing for the Gunditj Mirring Traditional Owners Aboriginal Corporation, 2010), 18–23.

59 Ten years before the *Mabo (No. 2)* decision, the High Court had acknowledged that the Gunditjmara People had specific custodianship obligations determined by its own laws and customs that could be enforced by a settler-state court. See *Onus v Alcoa of Australia Ltd* (1981) 149 CLR 27.

triggered a 1982 out-of-court settlement with the Victorian Government that returned several culturally significant properties to Gunditjmara ownership (including Lake Condah Mission lands), provided an additional land compensation package, and guaranteed resources to study the feasibility of reconstructing a portion of the aquaculture complex.[60] Over the subsequent decades, the Gunditjmara People has used Indigenous Land and Sea Corporation grants and native title co-management arrangements to systematically create the substantial 10,000 hectare landholding that it cares for today.

At the time of the *Onus v Alcoa* settlement, the Gunditjmara People recognised that regaining responsibility for Country required management and development planning. The Kerrup-Jmara Elders Aboriginal Corporation (Kerrup-Jmara EAC), established to manage the settlement land and financial resources, commenced operation with a twenty-seven person board representing all Gunditjmara families. Yet after a time, Kerrup-Jmara EAC was advised that such a management structure was unwieldy and impractical and that a small corporate-style board would be more efficient. Ultimately, managerial inexperience produced serious setbacks, including the need to sell some parcels of settlement land to pay debt and the loss of direct control over several significant cultural sites (which were put in trust by the Victorian Government), and Kerrup-Jmara EAC was liquidated. Some senior Gunditjmara people are adamant that operating according to corporate rules prevented the Kerrup-Jmara EAC from being a community-driven body on Country and influenced its demise. Their sense is that when only a small number of people, who did not meet on Country, made decisions on behalf of the entire community, transparency and accountability were difficult to achieve. In particular, the revised Kerrup-Jmara EAC management structures made it difficult for community members to remain informed of the latest developments and to provide input that could affect decision-making.

At about the same time, the Lake Condah and District Cooperative, which was responsible for service delivery to Aboriginal and Torres Strait Islander people in the region, also experienced financial difficulties. Its closure left the Gunditjmara community without an Aboriginal controlled organisation

60 The return of Country was accompanied by a compensation package and resources for feasibility studies for reconstruction of the Tae Rak (Lake Condah) cultural weir and reconstruction of fish traps, stone houses and interpretive facilities at Tyrendarra. See J. K. Weir, *The Gunditjmara Land Justice Story* (Canberra: Australian Institute of Aboriginal and Torres Strait Islander Studies, 2009), 14.

providing needed health and other services. Nonetheless, using forums such as the Heywood Local Aboriginal Education Consultative Group, Gunditjmara people continued to meet. An Aboriginal and Torres Strait Islander Commission (ATSIC) grant for a table and chairs allowed a small group of community volunteers to meet about health issues, a collaboration which since has grown into a major enterprise delivering services to the Indigenous community in the region, the Winda-Mara Aboriginal Corporation (WMAC).[61]

The impetus to create a new Gunditjmara decision-making body arose when the Gunditjmara People decided to lodge an application for native title in 1996. In the wake of Kerrup-Jmara EAC's collapse and painful loss of land, the Gunditjmara People could have been torn apart, but was not. Instead, community leaders looked to the lessons from Kerrup-Jmara EAC's successes and failures to guide the next iteration of collective decision-making. The native title claimants concluded that both substantive decisions *and* the decision-making process itself should accord with Gunditjmara values and aspirations. In short, collective decision-making processes should be able to engage with and receive input from the entire Gunditjmara People, with a strong preference for consensus and an understanding that leadership is not an individual enterprise. While certain individuals have been pivotal to Gunditjmara success, they speak for Country and community because they have community authorisation.

The processes and structure that the native title applicants created became the 'Gunditjmara Full Group' (the Full Group), a monthly community meeting organised under the auspices of Gunditj Mirring Traditional Owners Aboriginal Corporation (GMTOAC), the Gunditjmara People's Prescribed Body Corporate and Registered Aboriginal Party established in 2005. The Full Group was never incorporated but made community decisions that GMTOAC implemented. Initially created to generate instructions for the Gunditjmara People's native title lawyers, over time the Full Group evolved into a sophisticated forum for deliberation and decision-making on all issues affecting the Gunditjmara People, ranging from statutory obligations under native title and cultural heritage legislation through to language use,

61 With no specific organisation to take care of Traditional Owner business, after the demise of Kerrup-Jmara EAC and before the Gunditjmara People's native title determination by consent WMAC effectively acted as a vehicle for community decision-making for the Gunditjmara Traditional Owners. For example, WMAC was pivotal in articulating the community's vision in the Lake Condah Sustainable Development Project, lobbying for the declaration of the Budj Bim National Heritage Landscape, holding title to and managing the Tyrendarra Indigenous Protected Area and managing significant Gunditjmara land and facilities held in trust by the Victorian Government.

engagement with researchers and project proponents, economic development and regional development.

The Full Group's rules and processes were designed to embody transparency, accountability and full, prior and informed consent, which it attained to an extraordinary degree. Rules included that:

- *all* Gunditjmara people were entitled to attend meetings and speak on all issues whether they were GMTOAC members or not, although only GMTOAC members could vote on GMTOAC matters;
- meetings were to be held on Country on the same day every month on a set schedule;
- decisions required 75 per cent support of attendees to attempt to emulate broad community acceptance;
- a resolution could not be voted upon until it had been sent to members to consider (i.e., a resolution could not be moved and passed on the same day);
- the agenda, proposed resolutions and *all* associated materials were to be sent to all attendees before the meeting; and
- the agenda for every meeting had to have the same structure.

Gunditjmara people and those who wished to engage with them were expected to abide by these rules and comply with the Full Group's deliberative processes. Meetings, which, in practice, constituted monthly Special General Meetings under GMTOAC's constitution, were notable for robust discussion and their intentional inclusivity: all Gunditjmara people were encouraged to participate, including young people. Elders' advice was sought based on their cultural knowledge and lived experience but they did not have a distinctive or definitive decision-making role.

Taken together, the rules meant that the Full Group did not accept requests to review decisions. Once a decision was made, it was not revisited unless changed circumstances made it impossible to implement (for example, when government funding or policy changed) or when such a great length of time had passed that the prevailing environment itself had changed and the decision was no longer fit for purpose. This generated a high degree of stability and confidence in resultant decisions.

Nonetheless, a reality faced by all representative institutions, whether Indigenous or non-Indigenous, is that governing processes are not perfect. For the Full Group, the high standards set for participation and inclusion inadvertently created challenges that increased over time. Creating systems to enable free, prior and informed consent required serious commitment from community-based decision-makers. First, to enable access to *all* background information, a large amount of material was posted each month, which became a burden for both GMTOAC and attendees. GMTOAC experienced considerable expense and impact on productivity associated with staff writing extensive monthly reports and compiling the reports, financial statements, correspondence, and any proposals with accompanying diagrams and documentation. Similarly, some attendees found it difficult to be across all relevant information, and for an escalating number, the increasingly technical decisions facing the Full Group were particularly taxing. Second, free, prior and informed consent sometimes created protracted discussion even about small decisions. Difficult decisions were particularly fraught: in one instance, debate about a highly sensitive cultural matter took years to resolve. Full Group meetings were conducted from early morning until evening on a weekday, meaning that not all Gunditjmara people could attend and that those who could were exhausted. Finally, the question arose of how to truly engage the entire nation, including considerations of how decision-making authority might be shared (how jurisdiction could be allocated) between community members living on Country and those elsewhere, and of how the Full Group could determine who had authority to make decisions.

By 2015, a number of Gunditjmara people began to discuss options for the next stages of Gunditjmara governing, but these conversations were overtaken by events: opposition to a Full Group decision about where to build a Gunditjmara Keeping Place and the repatriation of Gunditjmara ancestors divided the community. Disagreement with the Keeping Place decision eventually led to challenges to the Full Group decision-making process itself and whether it represented the most appropriate form of governing. Ultimately, the Full Group came to a stalemate, and even uncontroversial decisions could not be made. To the great shame of some Elders and community members, for a short time GMTOAC was put into special administration by the Office of the Registrar of Indigenous Corporations.

The Registrar of Indigenous Corporations stated that the Gunditjmara governance model contributed to disputes and led to deadlock, yet was silent on how alternative decision-making models could have satisfactorily resolved such complex and culturally sensitive issues. Together with the Full Group, the special administrator wrote a new constitution and installed an eight-member board. At the time of writing, the Gunditjmara People is developing the next iteration of community decision-making and is seeking community input about the basis for representation and preferences for structure.

Despite the demise of the Full Group, the numerous successes and accolades during its fifteen-year operation demonstrate the Gunditjmara People's wisdom in creating a community-wide decision-making forum. Rebuilding their ancestors' weir to re-flood Tae Rak (Lake Condah), achieving a native title determination by consent and becoming a leading contributor to regional planning for Indigenous and non-Indigenous people all required stable, effective governance strategies delivered by the Full Group. Attaining UNESCO World Heritage listing for the BBCL, a goal conceived in the 1980s and realised in 2019, is perhaps the most high-profile among all the nation's achievements and the one that most clearly illustrates the Gunditjmara People's deep commitment to self-determination and to regaining control over Gunditjmara Country.

Certain clear strategies are apparent in the accomplishment. The first and most significant is that, although nominations to UNESCO's World Heritage Committee are made by states parties,[62] the Gunditjmara People controlled the nomination process. Gaining World Heritage status was a Gunditjmara initiative and Gunditjmara people drove the process, determined the shape and scope of the nomination, collected the necessary data and conducted necessary analysis; this was an exercise of self-determination and not a negotiated role. In fact, when it appeared that the federal government might not nominate the BBCL, the Gunditjmara People was prepared to assert its status as a distinct and sovereign Indigenous nation and nominate the BBCL itself. Ultimately, the Gunditjmara People did not have to test UNESCO's admission boundaries. The Australian government lodged the nomination in February 2018, the BBCL was inscribed on the World Heritage List in July 2019, and the rest, as they say, is history.

The Ngarrindjeri Nation: From Regional Authority to Treaty Negotiations with the State of South Australia

In July 2007 Ngarrindjeri leaders and Elders met at Pomberuk (Murray Bridge) on the Lower River Murray in South Australia to sign-off on the establishment of the Ngarrindjeri Regional Authority (NRA). The NRA was instituted by Ngarrindjeri to represent the Ngarrindjeri Nation in

62 Through the State Party Tentative List, states parties identify properties which they consider to be cultural and/or natural heritage of outstanding universal value and therefore suitable for inscription on the World Heritage List.

negotiations and engagements with external parties and most importantly, to strengthen self-determination and self-governance. With the authority of a peak nation body, the Ngarrindjeri Nation signed its first treaty in August 2007 with other First Nations. Identifying, organising, and acting as a nation,[63] Ngarrindjeri became a founding signatory to the United League of Indigenous Nations Treaty 2007 signed on Lummi Nation Country (USA).[64] After a decade of sustained political negotiation, Ngarrindjeri governance and partnership development, Ngarrindjeri led the successful call for historic treaty negotiations with the South Australian Labor government led by Premier Jay Weatherill. In 2017 Ngarrindjeri signed a formal agreement with the Crown in the Right of the State of South Australia to enter into a treaty with the Ngarrindjeri Nation.[65] Treaty negotiations stalled at this point and were discontinued by the subsequent South Australian Liberal government, elected in March 2018. This abrupt end to such important negotiations was deeply traumatic for Elders and leaders, who carried the weight of responsibility for generations of Ngarrindjeri who had survived British invasion and ongoing colonisation.

Non-Indigenous invasions of Ngarrindjeri lands and waters (Yarluwar-Ruwe) along the Murray River and in the South-east of South Australia began in the early 1800s with whalers, sealers and explorers such as Captain Charles Sturt. These interventions intensified with the establishment of the colony of South Australia in 1834 and the arrival of the first settlers in 1836, bringing an ever-increasing flow of non-Indigenous people, interests, institutions, laws, customs and ideas. By the 1980s, former South Australian Aboriginal missions were transitioning towards self-managing communities with Indigenous-run boards working together to produce better lives and futures for their people.[66] From the late 1970s emerging Ngarrindjeri leaders supported Elders in the establishment of broader regional community organisations such as the Lower Murray Nungas Club, the Ngarrindjeri

63 Stephen Cornell first argued that identifying, organising and acting are common features of Indigenous self-government reclamation in CANZUS countries. See S. Cornell, 'Processes of Native Nationhood: Indigenous Politics of Self-Government' *International Indigenous Policy Journal* 6 (2015): 4.

64 See United League of Indigenous Nations, *United League of Indigenous Nations Treaty 2007*, www.indigenousnationstreaty.org/, accessed 24 January 2021.

65 See D. Rigney, S. Bignall, S. Hemming, A. Vivian and S. Berg, 'Treating Treaty as a Technology for Indigenous Nation Building', in D. Smith, A. Wighton, S. Cornell and A. V. Delaney (eds), *Developing Governance and Governing Development International Case Studies of Indigenous Futures* (London and New York: Rowman and Littlefield International, in press).

66 See S. Hemming, P. G. Jones and P. A. Clarke, *Ngurunderi: An Aboriginal Dreaming* (Adelaide: South Australian Museum, 1989).

Land and Progress Association and the Mannum Aboriginal Progress Association.[67]

Ngarrindjeri resistance and post 1967 Referendum self-management prepared the way for later expressions of self-determination and Indigenous nation (re) building.[68] In 1987 the internationally famous Camp Coorong: Race Relations and Education Centre began running sovereign educational and political programs promoting an understanding of the traumas of colonisation, the strength of Ngarrindjeri resistance and the importance of Ngarrindjeri knowledges. That initiative coincided with the re-establishment of the Ngarrindjeri Tendi. The Tendi is a 'traditional' form of Ngarrindjeri governance with decision-making overseen by the Rupelli (Head).[69] The missionary George Taplin wrote the following about the Tendi in the early 1870s:

> I am rather sorry that the Tendi is not so potent as it used to be among the natives. It is still resorted to as an excellent means of discussing and disposing of difficulties, but its penalties cannot always be carried out. I have no doubt that men of the Narrinyeri have suffered imprisonment at the hands of the whites for carrying out the sentence of the Tendi in cases where it awarded substantial justice against offenders.[70]

The Ngarrindjeri Tendi was formally reconstituted in the mid-1980s, as an incorporated body, with support from large community meetings. It was entirely a Ngarrindjeri decision to reinstate the Tendi with nation-wide objectives that continue to follow Ngarrindjeri cultural principles and pursue Ngarrindjeri justice and sovereignty. Ngarrindjeri leaders made this clear in the Ngarrindjeri Yarluwar-Ruwe Plan, stipulating that the 'Tendi, our formal governing council, ensured and will continue to ensure our stable and sustainable society, which

67 See S. Hemming, D. Rigney, S. Berg, C. Rigney, G. Rigney and L. Trevorrow, 'Speaking as Country: A Ngarrindjeri Methodology of Transformative Engagement' *Ngiya: Talk the Law* 5 (2016): 22–46; S. Hemming, D. Rigney and S. Berg, 'Ngarrindjeri Nation Building: Securing a Future as Ngarrindjeri Ruwe/Ruwar (Lands, Waters and All Living Things)', in W. Nikolakis, S. Cornell and H. Nelson (eds), *Reclaiming Indigenous Governance: Reflections and Insights from Australia, Canada, New Zealand, and the United States* (Tucson, AZ: University of Arizona Press, 2019), 71–104.

68 Ngarrindjeri leaders viewed the 1967 Referendum as a landmark event that signalled wider Australian support for Indigenous people. For Ngarrindjeri this marked an important shift towards justice and led to the development of policies and programmes that supported self-determination.

69 See Ngarrindjeri Nation, *Ngarrindjeri Nation Yarluwar-Ruwe Plan: Caring for Sea Country and Culture* (Adelaide: Ngarrindjeri Tendi, Ngarrindjeri Heritage Committee, Ngarrindjeri Native Title Management Committee, 2006), 5.

70 G. Taplin, 'The Narrinyeri', reprinted in J. D. Woods (ed.), *The Native Tribes of South Australia* (Adelaide: E. S. Wigg and Son, 1879), 36.

maintains our obligations to Sea Country'.[71] This political move had no link to non-Indigenous programs and pre-dated native title, ATSIC, and Aboriginal heritage legislation.[72] This body went on to form a crucial collaboration with the new Ngarrindjeri Heritage and Native Title Management Committees. With the support of the Ngarrindjeri Land and Progress Association this collaboration was a vital element in Ngarrindjeri Nation (re)building, leading to the establishment of the NRA and a successful decade of Ngarrindjeri government.

In 2006 the new Tendi oversaw the Ngarrindjeri Nation meeting to elect an interim Ngarrindjeri Governance Working Party (NGWP) to develop a proposal for a new peak Ngarrindjeri governance body incorporating traditional forms of law and governance with contemporary forms of representation. The newly formed NRA governing board consisted of the chairpersons of various Ngarrindjeri community organisations, Ngarrindjeri representative committees and the Tendi, and included four elected community positions. The NRA holds annual elections to elect new Ngarrindjeri community members to sit on the Board and to select the NRA Chair, Vice-Chair and other executive positions. The NRA constitution aligns with elements of the older Tendi constitution and includes the Ngarrindjeri native title claim group description as a method for determining NRA membership.[73] The foundational NRA jurisdiction was delineated in the following aims:

- to develop strategic planning and policy for the Ngarrindjeri region;
- to develop long-term, representative and skilled governance for the Ngarrindjeri Nation;
- to respect existing Ngarrindjeri governance and organisational expertise;
- to build economic self-sustainability;
- to care for Ngarrindjeri lands and waters;
- to ensure a future for Ngarrindjeri people on Ngarrindjeri Ruwe; and
- to develop partnerships with Indigenous and non-Indigenous people and organisations to achieve these goals.[74]

71 Ngarrindjeri Nation, *Ngarrindjeri Nation Yarluwar-Ruwe Plan*, 5, 11.

72 Southern South Australia has never had a regime of Aboriginal land rights.

73 The Tendi constitution includes the following 'Objects': To work for the protection of the welfare, legal and human rights of Ngarrindjeri people and to advocate on their behalf; To work towards the attainment of land rights, for Ngarrindjeri people and to make claims for formal recognition of land rights by the appropriate authorities; To promote recognition and protection of the cultural heritage of Ngarrindjeri people and in particular matters relating to land and protection of sites and burial grounds that are of significance to Ngarrindjeri people; and To do all such things as may be incidental to the attainment of such objects. See S. Hemming and D. Rigney, 'Ngarrindjeri Governance Power point presentation', unpublished (2006).

74 See ibid.

During the development of the NRA proposal the NGWP acted as an interim Ngarrindjeri government body working with other key Ngarrindjeri organisations and committees to develop the foundational *Ngarrindjeri Nation Yarluwar-Ruwe Plan: Caring for Sea Country and Culture*.[75] It features a Ngarrindjeri Vision for Country that makes clear the essential interconnection between the well-being of the Ngarrindjeri Nation and a lawful responsibility to care for/as Ngarrindjeri lands and waters.[76] The Yarluwar-Ruwe Plan gave the newly established NRA a constitutional document with which to radically challenge dominant non-Indigenous representations of Ngarrindjeri as culturally extinct, unauthentic 'fringe-dwellers', with only past-oriented 'archaeological' relationships with Ngarrindjeri Yarluwar-Ruwe (Country).[77] It is a First Nation plan and includes a political statement of sovereignty in the form of the 2003 Ngarrindjeri Proclamation of Dominion, and promotes the ground-breaking Ngarrindjeri Kungun Ngarrindjeri Yunnan agreement (Listen to Ngarrindjeri speaking – KNYA) strategy for engaging with non-Indigenous governments and other external parties.[78]

Ngarrindjeri leaders and supporters first developed the KNYA strategy in 2002 to negotiate with the Alexandrina Council over a cultural heritage and development issue.[79] This new contract law strategy aimed to avoid a repeat of the traumatic Ngarrindjeri experience of the Hindmarsh Island Bridge Royal Commission and associated court cases and enquiries.[80] These legal

75 Ngarrindjeri Nation, *Ngarrindjeri Nation Yarluwar-Ruwe Plan*. 76 ibid, 5.

77 See S. Hemming and D. Rigney, 'Decentring the New Protectors: Transforming Aboriginal Heritage in South Australia' *International Journal of Heritage Studies* 16 (2010): 90–106.

78 See S. Hemming, D. Rigney and S. Berg, 'Ngarrindjeri Futures: Negotiation, Governance and Environmental Management', in S. Maddison and M. Brigg (eds), *Unsettling the Settler State: Creativity and Resistance in Indigenous Settler-State Governance* (Sydney: Federations Press, 2011), 98–113; and S. Hemming, D. Rigney and S. Berg, 'Researching on Ngarrindjeri Ruwe/Ruwar: Research Methodologies for Positive Transformation' *Australian Aboriginal Studies* 2 (2010): 92–106.

79 See S. Hemming and T. Trevorrow, 'Kungun Ngarrindjeri Yunnan: Archaeology, Colonialism and Re-claiming the Future', in C. Smith and H. M. Wobst (eds), *Indigenous Archaeologies: Decolonising Theory and Practice* (London: Routledge, 2005), 243–61.

80 The Hindmarsh Island Bridge 'controversy' began with Ngarrindjeri Elders attempting to use Aboriginal heritage legislation to protect culturally significant places on Ngarrindjeri Country. This led to investigations of culture and tradition in multiple court cases (including in the High Court) and a Royal Commission. The Royal Commission famously found that Ngarrindjeri and supporters had fabricated 'women's business' to stop development. This finding was contradicted in 2001 in the Federal Court vindicating the Ngarrindjeri Nation. See D. Bell, *Ngarrindjeri Wurruwarrin: A World That Is, Was, and Will Be* (Melbourne: Spinifex, 1998); and M. Simons, *The Meeting of the Waters: The Hindmarsh Island Affair* (Sydney: Hodder Headline, 2003).

settings had provided deep experience of a meeting place of laws that only facilitated the imposition of non-Indigenous sovereignty over Ngarrindjeri law and ways of being.[81] Rather than using non-Indigenous legislation to engage with settler authorities in relation to issues associated with Ngarrindjeri Yarluwar-Ruwe, Ngarrindjeri leaders therefore decided to engage through formal negotiations producing legal contract agreements. As Steve Hemming, Daryle Rigney and Shaun Berg have argued, 'KNY agreements rely on contract law to allow parties to agree upon basically whatever they want, and they offer the capacity to create a relationship that counters past wrongs and inscriptions of powers'.[82] By 2009 this characteristic, sovereign approach to engagement produced a whole-of-government KNYA with the Crown in the Right of South Australia, incorporating formal recognition of the Ngarrindjeri Nation, the NRA as the peak Ngarrindjeri government body, and Ngarrindjeri 'traditional' responsibility for Ngarrindjeri Yarluwar-Ruwe (lands and waters).[83] The 2009 KNYA includes the following recitals:

> D. The Ministers have expressed a desire for a new relationship between the State of South Australia and Ngarrindjeri based upon mutual respect and trust acknowledging that Ngarrindjeri consider protection and maintenance of culture and cultural sites upon its land and water central in every respect to Ngarrindjeri community well being and existence.
>
> E. By this Agreement the Ministers wish to provide support and resources to the Ngarrindjeri Regional Authority Inc and enter into negotiations and consultations with the Ngarrindjeri about the maintenance and protection of Ngarrindjeri culture and cultural sites and the natural resources of the Land [defined as lands and waters].[84]

This methodology informed the later Ngarrindjeri treaty negotiations and can be understood as a relational strategy of self-determination or sovereignty.[85]

81 For a related discussion of the Australian legal system's interaction with Indigenous law in the native title context, see: S. Dorsett and S. McVeigh, 'Conduct of Laws: Native Title, Responsibility, and Some Limits of Jurisdictional Thinking' *University of Melbourne Law Review* 36 (2012): 470–93.

82 Hemming, Rigney and Berg, 'Ngarrindjeri Futures: Negotiation, Governance and Environmental Management', 105.

83 See ibid.

84 See ibid, 110.

85 See, for example, S. Hemming, D. Rigney, S. Bignall and G. Rigney, 'Indigenous Nation Building for Environmental Futures: *Murrundi* Flows through Ngarrindjeri Country' *Australasian Journal of Environmental Management* 26 (2019): 216–35; J. Boron and S. Marke, 'Exerting Sovereignty through Relational Self-Determination: A Case Study of Mineral Development in Stk'emlupsemc te Secwépemc Territory' *The Journal of Rural and Community Development* 15 (2020): 151–74.

During the period 2009–17 the NRA was supported by a Research Policy and Planning Unit, an employment and contracting company called Ngarrindjeri Ruwe Contracting (NRC) and an overarching business entity called Ngarrindjeri Enterprises Pty Ltd. NRC managed the contracts secured by the NRA, employed the staff supporting NRA programs and partnered with other Ngarrindjeri family businesses such as Ngopamuldi Aboriginal Corporation.[86] These partnerships produced long-term business and employment opportunities for Ngarrindjeri and supported community organisations such as Raukkan Council. At the time of writing in late 2021, the NRA Board continued to meet monthly, to partner in major Australian Research Council funded projects and to act as the peak body representing the Ngarrindjeri Nation in negotiations with outside parties. Member organisations and committees bring issues to the NRA Board for consideration and major issues impacting the Ngarrindjeri Nation are taken to large community meetings.

Until the Liberal Party won the 2018 South Australian election, the NRA leadership had regular meetings with South Australian government ministers in a formal Leader-to-Leader arrangement, and all government programs operating on Ngarrindjeri Yarluwar-Ruwe, or proposed projects and programs, were taken to monthly KNYA Taskforce meetings for discussion and negotiation. South Australian government departments, Natural Resource Management Boards, Local Councils and other government agencies had seats on this Taskforce, which was co-convened by the NRA and the South Australian Department of Environment, Water and Natural Resources.[87] The NRA also played a leadership role in advocating for the establishment of the Moorundi Aboriginal Community Controlled Health Service, and influenced the South Australian government to develop a state-wide Aboriginal Regional Authorities policy.[88]

The NRA also played an important role in leading environmental initiatives. As a response to the Murray-Darling Basin's Millennium Drought (2001–9) the NRA negotiated and partnered in a major federally funded environmental program known as the South Australian Murray Futures Program (2009–17). Through the 2009 Whole-of-Government KNYA the NRA negotiated significant resources for the administration of the NRA's programs aimed at restoring well-being to the Ngarrindjeri Nation and to

86 See S. Hemming and D. Rigney, *Restoring Murray Futures: Incorporating Indigenous Knowledge, Values and Interests into Environmental Water Planning in the Coorong and Lakes Alexandrina and Albert Ramsar Wetland*, Goyder Institute for Water Research Technical Report Series No. 16/8 (Adelaide: Goyder Institute, 2016).

87 Ibid. 88 State Aboriginal Affairs, *Aboriginal Regional Authorities*.

Ngarrindjeri Yarluwar-Ruwe. This successful collaborative program was recognised in 2015 when a Ngarrindjeri-led team won the Australian River *prize* for best practice in river management.[89] Importantly, the NRA's negotiation and engagement frameworks are first and foremost underpinned by the Ngarrindjeri's clear political positioning as a sovereign First Nation. This positioning is strongly expressed in the following statement regarding a priori rights to 'water' in the NRA submission to the Murray-Darling Basin Authority (MDBA):

> Ngarrindjeri consider they have the first right, a right attached to the exercise of their cultural rights, interests and responsibilities, that precedes all other rights including but not limited to the legislative function of the MDBA to allocate water for particular uses. The rights and interests of the Ngarrindjeri require that water flows into, through, and from, their country from up river. This is a right a priori to all others and the MDBA should commence their consideration of allocations without interference or diminishment of these rights.[90]

In 2010 George Trevorrow (Rupelli of the Ngarrindjeri Tendi and founding Chair of the NRA), Matthew Rigney and Tom Trevorrow (all deceased), as leaders of the Ngarrindjeri Nation, reflected on the trauma and oppression of colonisation and the failure to honour original promises to protect the rights of Indigenous people contained in the South Australian Letters Patent, 1836:

> Our Old People, our Elders, and our families have been subjected to oppressive laws for a long time. These laws have denied our Elders equal human status; they have taken our land; they have imprisoned some of us on Reserves and Missions; they have placed us in gaols; they have wrecked our communities and our economy. For all of us we need to understand why the laws have failed to protect our rights to land. It makes no sense to us why our native rights to our lands and waters were protected in the Letters Patent but not in reality.[91]

These reflections indicate the depth of feeling underpinning the powerful political pressure the Ngarrindjeri Nation brought to the question of a just settlement through the negotiation of a potential treaty or treaties. [92]

89 Hemming et al., 'Indigenous Nation Building for Environmental Futures'.

90 See Ngarrindjeri Regional Authority (NRA), 'NRA Submission to Murray-Darling Basin Authority for and on Behalf of the Ngarrindjeri People in Relation to the Proposed Basin Plan', 16 April 2012, Berg Lawyers, Adelaide.

91 See G. Trevorrow, T. Trevorrow and M. Rigney, 'Preface', in S. Berg (ed.), *Coming to Terms: Aboriginal Title in South Australia* (Adelaide: Wakefield Press, 2010), vii.

92 See D. Rigney, S. Hemming and S. Berg, 'Letters Patent, Native Title and the Crown in South Australia', in E. Johnston, M. Hinton and D. Rigney (eds), *Indigenous Australians and the Law* (London and New York: Routledge-Cavendish, 2008, 2nd edn), 161–78.

Different Nations but Similar Approaches and Challenges

Ideally, Aboriginal and Torres Strait Islander governments in Australia would be recognised within the Federation, enabling government-to-government relations with all levels of Australian government (municipal, state and federal) and nation-to-nation relations with the Commonwealth. Ideally, each Indigenous nation also would possess well understood jurisdiction, mutually recognised by both Indigenous and settler-colonial governments, over all lands, waters, people and issues for which they have responsibilities – even if, in some cases, that jurisdiction overlapped or was shared with other governments. An even more ideal situation would be one in which appropriate financial resources were available to Indigenous nations through a mixture of public finance options, broadly including both intergovernmental revenue sharing and Indigenous nations' own revenue generation. In sum, three R's – recognition, responsibility and resources – would be hallmarks of a best-case scenario for Indigenous public government in Australia.

As the case studies show, when compared against this ideal, the Gunditjmara People and Ngarrindjeri Nation have made great strides towards the creation of autonomous Indigenous national governments; but they remain vulnerable. Both have been able to create, use and substantially sustain true institutions of public government. Even in the absence of recognition, these nations have demonstrated capacity to create and use governing institutions that support community decision-making, harness administrative and financial resources available for governance activities, and enable collective action.

The Gunditjmara People and Ngarrindjeri Nation arrived at this destination in similar ways. Both understood that settler-colonial institutions consistently have rejected the concept of Indigenous self-government within the Federation and, as a result, neither sought settler-colonial permission for, or validation of, their self-determined nation-level decision-making institutions. Both determined that nation-level decision-making structures were necessary as a result of crises (the failure of the Kerrup-Jmara EAC and the Kumarangk (Hindmarsh Island) Bridge crisis) – and each determined that to emerge from crisis, its community needed to find a way to speak with a common voice and to manage its identity as 'a people' rather than as a group of 'Aboriginal individuals'. Both exploited opportunities presented by settler-colonial policies to achieve their own ends including native title and Regional Partnership schemes, regardless of settler-colonial governments' intentions for those policies. Both used a series of community meetings to garner broad-based support for their governance work and to create transparency about purposes and goals. Ultimately, both established governing systems that suited their specific values and aspirations and that reflected the internal and external political environments of the time – and which in turn are reasons why the two nations' recent governing forms differ (an 'organisation of organisations' at Ngarrindjeri and a 'legislature of the whole' at Gunditjmara) and have changed over time.

The Gunditjmara People and Ngarrindjeri Nation also face similar and serious ongoing challenges in maintaining and developing their governance systems. First and foremost, they wrestle with the fact that Australian settler-colonial governments have neither the will nor a conceptual framework to engage constructively with self-governing Indigenous nations. Engagement errors are of omission and commission. For example, the Gunditjmara People's experience is that state and federal governments have viewed – and have engaged with – the Gunditjmara governing apparatus in a piecemeal fashion, failing to accommodate or appreciate the representative role of the overarching and integrated system that is in place. By contrast, the Ngarrindjeri Nation suffered from the assumption that because the NRA existed, their governing structure had capacity parallel to that of the local or state governments, resulting in unmanageable demands for response and performance.

Relatedly, both nations struggle to acquire or raise resources to support their self-governance missions. The Ngarrindjeri Nation, for example, was able to access 'start up' funding for the NRA but unable to acquire funds or raise revenue for adequate follow-on organisational consolidation and capacity enhancement. Thus, while the NRA was able to make agreements and win contracts that allowed the Ngarrindjeri Nation to gain a measure of jurisdictional authority and to exercise Ngarrindjeri responsibilities on Country, it lacked the resources to fully develop and maintain necessary 'wrap around' governance infrastructure. Similarly, while the Gunditjmara People have secured funding from the government of Victoria and the Commonwealth of Australia through a range of policies and programs, much of their broadly focused government development has depended on their ability to make do with less, use funds for multiple purposes, and challenge settler-colonial administrators when they attempt to place restrictions on transferred resources (which might be appropriate for organisations serving 'disadvantaged populations' but are less appropriate when engaging with the governing body of a self-governing Indigenous nation). In sum, there is a pressing need for both Indigenous nations to have access to funding streams for their public sectors that are separate from the funds required to fulfil programmatic responsibilities and, instead, are available for investment in government-strengthening, according to self-determined national need.

In fact, a key government-strengthening investment that the Gunditjmara People and Ngarrindjeri Nation each need – and which, based on recent experience, they may want to consider – is in mechanisms for dispute resolution. In particular, each nation is in want of mechanisms for the resolution of disputes between citizens of the nation and their government, and between actors representing the various parts of the Indigenous nation's governing system. In the absence of such mechanisms, settler-colonial institutions are the fallback when these disputes arise. This is problematic. Settler-colonial judicial mechanisms are not animated by the same values as Indigenous dispute resolution systems would be, and are not necessarily informed about the processes and aims of Indigenous governance. As a result, there is great scope for settler-colonial courts and judges to make decisions that harm Indigenous nations and their nation-building efforts. And yet, it is not enough for Indigenous nations themselves to develop internal dispute resolution mechanisms. Australian settler-colonial governments also must recognise and defer to these Indigenous institutions. If the federal, state and local governments of Australia do not take this step, they undermine the intents and purposes of Indigenous government. As an example, individuals who may be unhappy with a decision made collectively by their community – even if made according to cultural *and* settler-colonial protocols – can often bring actions in settler-colonial courts challenging the decision. While the issue may then be 'resolved' according to settler-colonial law, it is rare that it is seen as resolved by the community.

This discussion points to a larger phenomenon that pervades the development of Indigenous government in Australia: the fact that settler-colonial governments can delay or force the deferral of Indigenous nations' self-governing activities through dismissal, inattention, capricious decision-making and bad faith. To some extent, both the Gunditjmara People and Ngarrindjeri Nation are struggling with exactly these problems in their current efforts to reform, strengthen and expand their governing systems. They are not alone in this struggle.

Conclusion

Aboriginal and Torres Strait Islander self-government is a reality in Australia, albeit one that is vulnerable within settler-colonial institutions that shape

Indigenous/non-Indigenous relations. While Aboriginal and Torres Strait Islander peoples and settler-colonial governments face significant challenges in establishing Indigenous self-governing systems and accommodating them within the Australian federation, the potential for immense social, cultural, economic and, in particular, healing benefits mean that Indigenous self-government should be an urgent priority. Today's ad hoc and incremental movement towards Indigenous self-governing should be transformed into systematic and systemic development.

III

*

PUBLIC AUTHORITIES IN ENCOUNTER

10

The Challenge of Indigenous Polities

KIRSTY GOVER AND EDDIE CUBILLO

Introduction

Any history of Australia's settler-colonial legal system and its constitutional politics must include some account through time of its relationship with Aboriginal and Torres Strait Islander peoples as polities. The settler legal system installed itself on the edge of a continent where Aboriginal political societies had long been organised as sovereign peoples exercising their own inherent law-making authority. In this chapter we look at how the Australian settler-colonial constitutional order has received and responded to Aboriginal and Torres Strait Islander peoples as political communities, since the 1960s. Throughout this period, as before it, the reticence and unease of Australia's settler legal system in encounter is striking.

In Australia's settler law, the presence of Indigenous law and legal authority is denoted (reductively) as 'traditional ownership'.[1] The overlay of settler law has suppressed the vitality of some traditional legal orders but the roots of Indigenous authority remain intact. As will be shown, while many traditional owner communities have managed to maintain their inherent

Aboriginal and Torres Strait Islander people should be aware that this chapter mentions the names of deceased persons. Kirsty is a first generation New Zealander who grew up on Kāti Māmoe-Ngāi Tahu land and has lived on Wurundjeri land since 2009. Eddie is an Aboriginal man with strong family links in both the urban and rural areas throughout the Northern Territory. He is of Larrakia/Wadjigan and Central Arrernte descent. Eddie has served on ATSIC's Yilli Rreung Regional Council, including as Council Chair, chaired the North Australian Aboriginal Justice Agency (NAAJA) and the Aboriginal Justice Advisory Committee, served as Anti-Discrimination Commissioner of the Northern Territory, and was as an Executive Officer with National Aboriginal and Torres Strait Islander Legal Service (NATSILS). The authors thank Paul McHugh, Fiona Hussin, Aurora Milroy, Amanda Porter and Geoff Richardson for thoughtful comments on earlier drafts, as well as our editors Peter Cane and Lisa Ford. Thanks to the Melbourne Law School Academic Research Service, and especially to Ken Zhunwye Kiat (MLS JD '20), for excellent editorial assistance.

1 The phrase has its legal origins in the Northern Territory's Aboriginal Land Rights Act 1976 (ALRA). See e.g. Aboriginal Land Rights (Northern Territory) Act 1976 (Cth), s 3.

authority *in situ* and to self-govern in the interstices of the institutions and legal regimes imposed on them, in settler law those communities are largely characterised as racial groups, not polities. This remains the settler legal position even for traditional owner communities holding recognised communal native title or land rights.[2] Notwithstanding the footholds that Indigenous self-governance has gained in settler law, especially in property and cultural heritage regimes,[3] in general the recognition of traditional owners as property-holders has been accompanied by a consistently emphatic judicial disavowal of Indigenous sovereignty, law-making authority and distinctive constitutional identity. As will be shown, courts routinely deflect Indigenous sovereignty claims, refusing to countenance the possibility that Aboriginal and Torres Strait Islander peoples hold 'even . . . a limited kind' of sovereignty as nations,[4] or that their law has independent authority.[5] Settler officials have likewise strategically and publicly suggested that Indigenous representative institutions are incompatible with principles of equality and non-discrimination. This idea, that rights predicated on distinctive Indigenous political identities effect racial preferences and discriminate against non-Indigenous Australians, has dogged efforts to defend Aboriginal and Torres Strait Islander land and people from settler government over-reach. It is a distinctively Australian premise. Other settler states have recognised that Indigenous traditional owner groups are political groupings with inherent, constitutional or treaty-based rights to self-govern (in Canada and the United States) or are historic political groupings whose rights and property are inherently theirs, and do not compromise the human rights of non-members (Aotearoa New Zealand).[6]

In what follows we trace developments in the recognition of traditional ownership, and (in glimpses) of traditional law and custom, in Australian law. It follows several threads of Indigenous advocacy, beginning with Yolngu political and legal claims-making in the 1960s. We consider the rise and demise of the Aboriginal and Torres Strait Islander Commission (ATSIC), address the governance space opened (and then partially closed) by native title jurisprudence and legislation, and finish with the work currently in play: contemporary

2 *Gerhardy v Brown* (1985) 159 CLR 70, p. 118 (Brennan J).
3 See Kearney, Chapter 15 and Rowse and Green, Chapter 9.1 in this volume.
4 *Coe v Commonwealth* (1979) 53 ALJR 403, 405.
5 *Members of the Yorta Yorta Aboriginal Community v Victoria* (2002) 214 CLR 422, 444 [44] (Gleeson CJ, Gummow and Hayne JJ).
6 This chapter does not delve into the comparative jurisprudence on Indigeneity and racial discrimination. For a discussion of the key cases and approaches taken by other CANZUS states see Kirsty Gover, 'The Treaty and Human Rights in New Zealand Law: Can We Add the Declaration and Stir?', in A. Erueti (ed.), *International Indigenous Rights in Aotearoa* (Auckland: Upstart, 2017), 41, 53–7.

calls for constitutional recognition and a 'Voice to Parliament'. The story is largely one of settler resistance to Indigenous legal and political authority, in the face of sustained intergenerational Indigenous advocacy. To some traditional owner communities of course, the settler legal system is remote, their lives and law continuing much as they always have. But where the independent authority of Indigenous polities has become *too* visible, or where there is too little settler access and control, settler law-makers have doubled down. The abolition of ATSIC takes this form, as does the Northern Territory Intervention, and arguably, on a more technocratic register, settler judicial review of Indigenous law-making. The 2020 High Court case of *Love v Commonwealth of Australia* ('*Love-Thoms*')[7] takes its place here too, essentially coupling a modest concession to traditional law and custom with an insistence that Indigenous peoples are not 'peoples' in any other legal sense.

This chapter records some of the recent history of the interface between settler and Indigenous law-making polities in Australia – the former arriving suddenly and from mid-air, insisting on its absolute singularity, the latter spread across Australia, anchored in the ground, and stabilised by an intricate web of legal relationships. When the two orders touch, things often go wrong. We write this chapter in the shadow of settler sovereignty dogma, and in the knowledge that the settler sovereign's claim to exhaustive authority over Indigenous land is legally suspect, even on its own terms.

Competing Visions of the Australian Body Politic

Writing in 2008, Gumatj elder Galarrwuy Yunupingu made it clear that the sovereign Yolngu political order to which he belongs is independent of settler government:

> The clans of east Arnhem Land join me in acknowledging no king, no queen, no church and no state. Our allegiance is to each other, to our land and to the ceremonies that define us.[8]

The Australian High Court's view of the Australian polity could not be more different. In *Love-Thoms* the court was asked to decide whether non-citizen Indigenous persons could be deported as 'aliens'.[9] Justice Gordon was one of

7 (2020) 94 ALJR 198.

8 Galarrwuy Yunupingu, 'Tradition, Truth & Tomorrow', *The Monthly*, December 2008–January 2009.

9 At the time of writing, the Commonwealth government was pursuing a reversal of the *Love-Thoms* result in the High Court, in the apparent hope that the retirement of two of the majority judges (Nettle and Bell JJ) would enable the Court to overturn its previous

the four majority judges who held that Indigenous people could never be aliens, regardless of their citizenship, because of the strength of their connection to Australian land and waters. In some parts of the majority judgments this connection to *land* also entails the incorporation of Indigenous peoples into the Australian settler body politic. On one reading, the *Love-Thoms* 'win' for Indigenous peoples is premised on the denial of their peoplehood:

> The roots of Federation in popular sovereignty (and the dominant force of that idea today as the legitimating force of the *Constitution*) are consistent with the conclusion that the 'people of Australia' *necessarily* includes Indigenous peoples.[10]

Accordingly, in Gordon J's view, it was settler 'recognition' that extinguished the possibility of political Indigenous sovereignty, while non-justiciability preserved juridical settler sovereignty intact. On this account 'recognition' is an act of almost magical unilateralism, conjuring a unified Australian people without any reference to Indigenous consent or agency:

> Recognition of Indigenous peoples as a part of the 'people of Australia' is directly contrary to accepting any notion of Indigenous sovereignty persisting after the assertion of sovereignty by the British Crown. Recognition of Indigenous peoples as part of the 'people of Australia' denies that Indigenous peoples retained, or can now maintain, a sovereignty that is distinct or separate from any other part of the 'people'.[11]

The common law conception of popular sovereignty articulated in this account therefore further entrenches the settler denial of Indigenous peoples' juridical sovereignty by linking it to an express rejection of the status of Indigenous peoples as polities, or 'distinct political societies'.[12] The contrast between the High Court's vision of an undifferentiated Australian body politic as 'the people of Australia' and Yunupingu's conception of Yolngu sovereignty as vested in an independent, interconnected confederacy of clans, is illustrative of a deep, long-standing and constitutive tension in Australian law and politics. Settler sovereignty demands a single people, so the state's origin story, enacted every day by settler officials, requires that Indigenous

decision. See *Minister for Immigration, Citizenship, Migrant Services and Multicultural Affairs & Anor v Montgomery* (S192/2021).

10 *Love v Commonwealth of Australia* (2020) 94 ALJR 198, 267 [353] (Gordon J) (emphasis in original).

11 Ibid, 268 [356] (Gordon J).

12 Ibid, 223 [102] (Gageler J).

peoples not be *peoples* at all. Instead, Australian Indigenous peoples have been assiduously characterised in politics and law as members of a 'particular race' (helped by terminology supplied by the Constitution's 'race power' and the federal Racial Discrimination Act 1975).[13]

Even in their capacity as 'traditional owners' internally governed by 'traditional law and custom', Indigenous polities have been described as racial communities. In the High Court's view, for example, traditional ownership itself is 'a criterion based on race',[14] so that in the worst case, '[r]ecourse to the notion of traditional ownership may readily be had to effect the most obnoxious discrimination'.[15] As will be shown, ATSIC was characterised by settler officials as a racially constituted organisation in ways that facilitated its abolition, and likewise ministerial responses to the proposed 'Voice to Parliament' have emphasised the possibility that it discriminates against non-Indigenous voters. This strategic correlation, subsuming Indigenous political organisations and communities within the flattening horizon of 'race', provides a legal justification for denying the authority and legitimacy of Indigenous law and legal institutions. Most treacherously, it has made all Indigenous rights protections precarious, by making it legally possible to challenge them as forms of racial preference.[16]

Land Rights in Politics and Court

As the reality of racial inequality became politicised around the world in the 1960s, Yolngu leadership spear-headed Aboriginal political and legal claims-making in Australia. Their 1963 *Yirrkala Bark Petitions*, presented to the House of Representatives and Senate, protested the government's decision to grant part of their reserved traditional territory to the Nabalco Corporation for bauxite mining.[17] Then fifteen years old, Galarrwuy Yunupingu helped his father, Mungurrawuy, draft and translate the petition's text. The Parliamentary Committee they asked for was established. It recommended that sacred sites within the excised land be protected and that housing and

13 Australian Constitution, s 51(xxvi); Racial Discrimination Act 1975 (Cth), ss 9 and 10.
14 *Gerhardy v Brown* (1985) 159 CLR 70, 118 (Brennan J).
15 Ibid, 84 (Gibbs CJ). The distinction between native title holders and persons not holding native title rights is likewise framed as a racial distinction, not a political or even proprietary one: *Mabo v Queensland (No. 1)* (1988) 166 CLR 186, 243; *Western Australia v Ward* (2002) 213 CLR 1, 104 [117]; *Western Australia v Commonwealth (Native Title Act Case)* (1995) 183 CLR 373, 438.
16 See *Maloney v The Queen* (2013) 252 CLR 168.
17 AIATSIS, 'Yirrkala Bark Petitions 1963', www.abc.net.au/news/2013-07-10/yirrkala-bark-petitions-50-years-on/4809610, accessed 13 December 2021.

other benefits in the mining town be reserved to the Yirrkala people, but did not counsel against the land grant itself.[18] Even these modest recommendations were not accepted by the Commonwealth government and the mining lease was finalised in 1968.[19] (A pattern of appointing and ignoring Committees and Commissions has become a core part of Australian statecraft in its dealings with Indigenous peoples.[20]) In response, the Yirrkala clans took their claims out of the political arena and into the Northern Territory Supreme Court, asserting their 'communal native title' over the mine site. It was Australia's first judicial consideration of native title. The clans lost.

In what has become known as the 'Gove Land Rights Case' (*Milirrpum v Nabalco Pty Ltd*),[21] Daymbalipu Mununggurr, Roy Dadaynga Marika, Mungurrawuy Yunupingu and Milirrpum Marika (all assisted by the teenage Galarrwuy as translator) explained the intricacies of the law laid down by their great spirit ancestors who, in the course of setting out the law, also created the clans as peoples and secured their indelible connection to country.[22] In many respects, Justice Blackburn's decision is an enlightened one, less dogmatic on the link between sovereignty and law than the High Court would later be in its native title findings.[23] Blackburn J recorded his scepticism about 'Austinian analys[es] of the nature of law', refusing the Commonwealth's insistence that a recognisable 'sovereign' was necessary, instead recognising the Yirrkala-based Gumatj and Rirratjingu clans as a 'definable community' governed by what was undoubtedly law:

> In my opinion, the arguments put to me do not justify the refusal to recognize the system proved by the plaintiffs in evidence as a system of law. Great as they are, the differences between that system and our system are, for the purposes in hand, differences of degree. I hold that I must recognize the system revealed by the evidence as a system of law.[24]

18 Commonwealth, 'Report from the Select Committee on the Grievances of the Yirrkala Aborigines, Arnhem Land Reserve' (29 October 1963), 12.

19 Mining (Gove Peninsula Nabalco Agreement) Ordinance 1968 (NT).

20 For an examination of this practice in Australian government responses to systemic racism in the criminal justice sector, see Eddie Cubillo, 'What Does "Self-Determination" Mean in the Context of Legal Service Provision for Aboriginal and Torres Strait Islander Legal Services (ATSILS)?' (PhD manuscript 2021, on file with author). See also M. Davis, 'Chained to the Past: The Psychological Terra Nullius of Australia's Public Institutions', in A. D. Stone, J. P. Goldsworthy and T. D. P. Campbell (eds), *Protecting Rights without a Bill of Rights: Institutional Performance and Reform in Australia* (Farnham: Ashgate, 2006), 175, 175–6.

21 *Milirrpum v Nabalco Pty Ltd* (1971) 17 FLR 141.

22 Ibid, 147, 166, 183.

23 See Dorsett, Chapter 2 in this volume.

24 *Milirrpum v Nabalco Pty Ltd* (1971) 17 FLR 141, 268.

While Yolngu law was markedly 'subtle and elaborate',[25] the Judge held, the peoples' relationship to land was not a proprietary one.[26] There was, accordingly, nothing in that system for the common law to extract and protect as a property right or interest. In the result *Milirrpum v Nabalco* entrenched the long-standing orthodoxy of *terra nullius*. A spark of promise was, however, discernible: Blackburn J made it clear that while the land claimed and granted by the Crown was 'no one's', the Yirrkala were their own people, and not for the taking. The decision in *Love-Thoms*, however, decided nearly fifty years later, *does* come close to suggesting this, because all judges accept as a premise that Indigenous people had and have no independent constitutional identity as polities, but rather were simply submerged within the incoming settler body politic.

The possibility of a Yolngu appeal from their Supreme Court loss, which might have yielded a '*Mabo (No. 2)*' twenty years before that case was actually heard, was headed off by the incoming Whitlam government's election promise to legislate for Aboriginal land rights, a commitment that was picked up and implemented by Prime Minister Malcolm Fraser following Whitlam's 1975 dismissal. Exercising its constitutional power to legislate for the Northern Territory, the Commonwealth initiated Australia's first grand experiment in traditional owner recognition, by establishing the Northern and Central Land Councils as the institutional face of the Northern Territory Aboriginal Land Rights Act 1976 (ALRA). The ALRA converted former Aboriginal reserves to Aboriginal freehold title, complete with rights of exclusive possession, protected by a statutory 'permit system' (requiring outsiders to obtain consent before entering Aboriginal land).[27] The Act also enabled traditional owners to receive freehold grants of their traditional land on the recommendation of the Aboriginal Land Commissioner.[28] The central criterion for their recognition as traditional owners was that their 'spiritual affiliations' placed them under a 'primary spiritual responsibility' for the land

25 Ibid, 273.

26 'I do not find myself much impressed by this line of argument. The inadequacy of the Austinian analysis of the nature of law is well known. I do not believe that there is utility in attempting to provide a definition of law which will be valid for all purposes and answer all questions. If a definition of law must be produced, I prefer "a system of rules of conduct which is felt as obligatory upon them by the members of a definable group of people" to "the command of a sovereign", but I do not think that the solution to this problem is to be found in postulating a meaning for the word "law". I prefer a more pragmatic approach.' Ibid, 274.

27 Aboriginal Land Rights (Northern Territory) Act 1976 (Cth), ss 70, 73.

28 Ibid, ss 5, 10–12. See also the explanation by Brennan J in *R v Toohey* (1982) 158 CLR 327, 354–5.

in question.[29] Thereafter, they would be represented by Land Trusts, who act on the instruction of the Land Councils, at least once removed from traditional owners, in a relationship often (and controversially) mediated by settler anthropologists. That said, the Act is arguably the high-water mark of recognised traditional owner self-government in Australia, and its framework has survived largely intact through successive ideological swings in settler law and policy. While their capacity to properly represent traditional owners has at times been questioned, the Land Councils (including those later established under the ALRA[30] and land rights legislation in New South Wales and South Australia[31]) remain the most enduring and powerful, and best-resourced, instantiation of Indigenous political representation in Australia.

Once up and running, the Land Councils did not restrict their leadership to local matters. The Yolngu people's push for treaty in the 1980s, for example, was in part directed through Council leadership. In 1988, Galarrwuy Yunupingu, then part-way through his twenty-year tenure as Chair of the Northern Land Council, and Wenten Rubuntja, Chair of the Central Land Council, presented the Barunga Statement to Prime Minister Bob Hawke on behalf of the 'Indigenous owners and occupiers of Australia'. The authors of the statement called on 'the Commonwealth Parliament to negotiate with us a Treaty recognising our prior ownership, continued occupation and sovereignty and affirming our human rights and freedom'.[32] The statement was presented at the Barunga Sports and Cultural Festival, an annual event held in a small remote town in the Northern Territory (now called 'the Barunga Festival'). In TV footage of the presentation, Prime Minister Hawke is visibly moved.[33] He promised a treaty 'between the Aboriginal people and the Government on behalf of all the people of Australia' by 1990.[34] The crowd at Barunga, comprised mostly of traditional owners, understood the significance of the moment, and the feeling of optimism was palpable to everyone

29 Aboriginal Land Rights (Northern Territory) Act 1976 (Cth), s 3.

30 The Tiwi Land Council of the Tiwi Islands was established in 1978, and the Anindilyakwa Land Council of the Groote Archipelago was established in 1991.

31 Anangu Pitjantjatjara Yankunytjatjara Land Rights Act 1981 (SA); Aboriginal Land Rights Act 1983 (NSW).

32 'The Barunga Statement', https://aiatsis.gov.au/explore/barunga-statement, accessed 13 December 2021.

33 ABC archived footage: www.facebook.com/ABCDarwin/videos/flashback-friday-barunga-festival-1988/10156573372809873/, accessed 13 December 2021.

34 Prime Minister, 'Transcript of Speech at Barunga Sports and Cultural Festival, Northern Territory: 12 June 1988', https://pmtranscripts.pmc.gov.au/release/transcript-7334, accessed 13 December 2021.

there.[35] They had gotten the prime minister of Australia on board. But the treaty never happened. Hawke ultimately failed to persuade his government to follow through. It was, and is, a deeply disappointing missed opportunity to embed the status of Indigenous peoples as polities in a national agreement. Even today, while treaty processes are underway in Victoria, the Northern Territory and Queensland, the possibility of a Commonwealth treaty, or even for Commonwealth involvement in state and territory treaty-making, remains remote.

Throughout this period, litigation continued alongside political advocacy, again with an emphasis on treaty. On the crest of the 1970s land rights movement, in 1979 Paul Coe brought Aboriginal sovereignty to the High Court on behalf of his Wiradjuri Nation and the broader 'Aboriginal community'. Coe sought a declaration that the common law entitled 'the [A]boriginal people to the continuation of the proprietary and/or possessory and other rights which they had prior to 1770 unless these are taken away by bilateral treaty, lawful compensation and/or lawful international intervention'.[36] The claim, said the High Court, was 'quite absurd and so clearly vexatious as to amount to an abuse of the process of the Court'.[37] The judgments in *Coe v the Commonwealth* (1979) mark the nadir of modern Australian judicial conceptions of settler-Indigenous relations and history. As the Court would insist in successive judgments (including *Love-Thoms*), no parallel could be drawn between 'the Aboriginal people', notably described in the racialised singular, and North American Indigenous nations:

> [I]t is not possible to say, as was said ... of the Cherokee Nation, that the Aboriginal people of Australia are organised as a 'distinct political society separated from others' ... they have no legislative, executive or judicial organs by which sovereignty might be exercised ... The contention that there is in Australia an Aboriginal nation exercising sovereignty, even of a limited kind, is quite impossible in law to maintain.[38]

Meanwhile, in the Torres Strait, the traditional owners of the islands of Mer, Erub and Ugar were embarking on their legal campaign against the state of Queensland. Eddie Koiki Mabo, Reverend David Passi, Celuia Mapo Salee, Sam Passi and James Rice claimed native title over their traditional territories, stating a case to the High Court in 1982. The case was sent to the Queensland Supreme Court, and re-emerged ten years later from the High Court as *Mabo*

35 Eddie Cubillo, personal correspondence with Kirsty Gover, on file with authors. Eddie was present at the Barunga festival in 1988.

36 *Coe v Commonwealth* (1979) 53 ALJR 403, 405. 37 Ibid, 407. 38 Ibid, 408.

(No. 2), confirming that native title appears in the common law as a set of rights *in rem*, enforceable against the world at large. Because of this judgment, for the first time the existence (although not the authority) of Indigenous law was confirmed. Once recognised, native title rights and interests become 'tips of icebergs', a tiny, but visible, part of the vast complexity of Indigenous law beneath the surface of the settler overlay.

Mabo (No. 2) engendered a renewed optimism among Indigenous political leaders. The Wiradjuri Nation again asserted its sovereignty in the High Court, this time in a 1993 challenge lead by Isobel Coe, Paul Coe's sister. Again the Court refused to endorse an analogy to the sovereignty held by recognised tribes in US federal common law, repeating again that any contention that Aboriginal peoples in Australia are 'dependent domestic nation[s], entitled to self-government and full rights over their tribal lands, is but another way of putting the sovereignty claim'.[39] In the intervening years since 1993, and notwithstanding the common law recognition of Indigenous 'societies' and their 'traditional law and custom' in *Mabo (No. 2)*, the High Court has not budged on its refusal to countenance the distinctive political and law-making authority of Indigenous peoples. *Mabo (No. 2)* confirmed that 'at sovereignty'[40] traditional owners governed themselves in accordance with their traditional law and custom, but that the 'change in sovereignty' prevented those communities from thereafter generating enforceable law. The 2020 *Love-Thoms* decision, mentioned above, confirms this status quo, extending common law recognition to the 'connection' that Aboriginal peoples have with land, but admitting of no substantive common law *rights* flowing from that connection. In the view of the majority judges, reference to a body of traditional law and custom could establish the fact of a person's membership in an Aboriginal community (applying Brennan J's 'membership test' in *Mabo (No. 2)*)[41] but the authority of traditional owners to make and adapt membership law, let alone their right to self-govern, remains unrecognised.

39 *Coe v Commonwealth (The Wiradjuri Claim)* (1993) 118 ALJR 193, 200.

40 See e.g. *Members of the Yorta Yorta Aboriginal Community v Victoria* (2002) 214 CLR 422, 454 [77] (Gleeson CJ, Gummow and Hayne JJ). Meaning the year at which British sovereignty was asserted over the traditional land in question. For the land comprising the former colony of New South Wales, this was 1788. For the islands of Mer, Erub and Ugar it was 100 years later, in 1879.

41 *Mabo v Queensland (No. 2)* (1992) 175 CLR 1, 70 (Brennan J).

Traditional Law and Custom in Native Title Law

In what follows, we trace some of the threads of promise in the recognition of 'traditional law and custom' in native title governance. The native title law and governance framework houses two types of officially recognised Indigenous law. On the one hand, bodies of law and custom that are substantially unchanged 'since sovereignty' and on the other, the lived, day-to-day application and development of Indigenous law in the governance of native title by traditional owners. As the following discussion shows, in the latter it is possible to see, in the relationship between native title holders and their corporate representative structures, a body of traditional law and custom that is current, alive and endorsed by settler legislation. It is this body of law and custom that governs the decision-making processes of the common law, native-title-holding community, including the granting or withholding of consent to proposals put to them by their corporate representatives. This body of law and custom seems not subject to the continuity requirements that pertain when a group is describing its traditional law and custom as evidence of their connection to country, or the content of native title rights and interests. This autonomous body of law is referenced by settler law in the Native Title Act and its regulations.[42] Because its existence is acknowledged by, but not constituted by, these references, it approaches something like the 'parallel system of law-making' deemed impermissible by the High Court in *Members of the Yorta Yorta Aboriginal Community v Victoria* (2002).[43] By the lights of settler law, it is implicit that this body of law does not run afoul of the prohibition against 'sovereignty adverse to that of the Crown'.[44] The governance of native title rights and interests in accordance with traditional law and custom 'as currently acknowledged and observed'[45] is a narrow and uneven laneway running between and across two bodies of law. But the space provided for its operation in native title legislation offers to outsiders a rare glimpse of traditional law and custom in action *alongside and within* settler law. It also exposes that body of law to judicial review, in ways that are problematic. The section that follows considers the scope and import

42 Native Title (Prescribed Bodies Corporate) Regulations 1999 (Cth), reg. 4; Corporations (Aboriginal and Torres Strait Islander) Act 2006, s 661–1(2).

43 *Members of the Yorta Yorta Aboriginal Community v Victoria* (2002) 214 CLR 422, 444 [44] (Gleeson CJ, Gummow and Hayne JJ).

44 *Coe v Commonwealth (The Wiradjuri Claim)* (1993) 118 ALJR 193, 115. See also Dorsett, Chapter 2 in this volume.

45 *Mabo v Queensland (No. 2)* (1992) 175 CLR 1, 61 (Brennan J).

of this glimpse, as a 'crack in the door' of settler sovereignty's self-proclaimed comprehensivity.

In a litigated native title claim, the burden of proof falls on the traditional owners. The evidentiary requirements imposed on native title claimants are prohibitively onerous, obliging them to show that they have maintained a connection to their land and waters as a society united in its observation of traditional laws, in a manner 'substantially uninterrupted since sovereignty'.[46] For Indigenous groups on the eastern mainland, 'sovereignty' happened in 1788. Traditional owners must produce evidence to show that they have maintained continuous connection to their Country in the face of colonial encroachment, while the role of state and Commonwealth litigants is to emphasise that those encroachments succeeded in separating people from country. As Wayne Atkinson, a Yorta Yorta elder and lead claimant in the Yorta Yorta people's native title claim, has explained, '[t]he native title process is emotionally and physically draining', and takes place against a backdrop of 'community hostility and antipathy towards Indigenous rights'.[47] The euphemistic 'tide of history', which the *Mabo (No. 2)* court held could 'wash away'[48] the observance of traditional law and custom, contains within it violence, including coercive dispossession and massacre.[49] The test also denies title to peoples that have managed to stay alive together on their land if their generation-to-generation observation of traditional law and custom has been interrupted.[50] In Australian common law, any government land grant over or acquisition of the traditional territory in question since the assertion of British sovereignty 'extinguishes' native title rights to the extent of the inconsistency between the two sets of rights. This 'inconsistency of incidents'[51] extinguishment rule further ensures that many successful native title determinations recognise only a limited set of rights and interests that fall far short of exclusive possession.[52] Those peoples that emerge intact from the stormy passage between what Justice Brennan in *Mabo (No. 2)* called the 'Scylla' of sovereignty

46 *Members of the Yorta Yorta Aboriginal Community v Victoria* (2002) 214 CLR 422, 456 [87].

47 Wayne Atkinson, '"Not One Iota" of Land Justice: Reflections on the Yorta Yorta Native Title Claim 1994–2001' *Indigenous Law Bulletin* 5, no. 6 (2001): 19, 20.

48 *Mabo v Queensland (No. 2)* (1992) 175 CLR 1, 60 (Brennan J).

49 As Wayne Atkinson points out '[i]t is ironic in the extreme, many might say obscene, that the crimes against humanity, which constitute this "tide", can be invoked by those seeking to deny Indigenous groups their rights to land'. Atkinson, 'Not One Iota', 20.

50 Ibid. See also *Members of the Yorta Yorta Aboriginal Community v Victoria* (2002) 214 CLR 422, 444 [46] (Gleeson CJ, Gummow and Hayne JJ).

51 *Western Australia v Ward* (2002) 213 CLR 1, 91.

52 Of the total land mass over which native title has been determined to exist, 66.4 per cent is covered by non-exclusive native title rights and interests (such as rights to enter the land for traditional hunting, fishing or ceremonial purposes): National Native Title

and the 'Charybdis' of extinguishment, are then compelled by settler law to adopt a corporate structure, called a Native Title Registered Body Corporate (NTRBC).[53] The first NTRBC was registered in 1997. At the time of writing, there were 234 NTRBCs in Australia, each representing a common law native-title-holding community.[54] The number of NTRBCs has steadily increased by an average of ten new NTRBCs every year.

As one might expect, given the relatively short history of NTRBC governance in Australia, the roles and functions of NTRBCs are in flux, and their legal responsibilities (in settler law) are sometimes imprecisely defined. Nearly half of NTRBCs have no reported income.[55] Despite this disability, the proximity of NTRBCs to traditional owners means that they take on other 'non-native title related' representative, cultural and service delivery roles on behalf of their communities.[56] In a familiar tension between settler and Indigenous legal obligations, attention by Indigenous representatives to community norms and relationships may 'conflict with normal corporation and directors duties'.[57] Researchers at the Australian Institute of Aboriginal and Torres Strait Islander Studies (AIATSIS) give an example:

> [A] director may have very specific exchange; ritual; kin and other obligations towards for example their mother's brother. By upholding those obligations they will be maintaining a system of authority and law that supports effective corporate governance and their particular responsibilities to their kin group. The particular director may submit that in upholding Indigenous law they are acting in accordance with their fiduciary obligations. However this may appear to be in direct conflict with the related party

Tribunal, 'Native Title Determinations: As at 1 July 2020', www.nntt.gov.au/Maps/Determinations_map.pdf, accessed 13 December 2021.

53 *Mabo v Queensland (No. 2)* (1992) 175 CLR 1, 63 (Brennan J).

54 Prescribed Bodies Corporate, 'PBC National Snapshot', www.nativetitle.org.au/learn/role-and-function-pbc/pbc-national-snapshot, accessed 13 December 2021.

55 See Office of the Registrar of Indigenous Corporations, 'Registered Native Title Bodies Corporate', www.oric.gov.au/top-500/2015–16/RNTBCs, accessed 13 December 2021. In the 2015–16 financial year, 44.7 per cent of NTRBCs reported nil income or were exempt from providing income data.

56 See e.g. Geoff Buchanan, 'Gender and Generation in Native Title: Director Demographics and the Future of Prescribed Bodies Corporate' *Land, Rights, Laws: Issues of Native Title* 6 (2015): 1. See also Office of the Registrar of Indigenous Corporations, *A Guide to Writing Good Governance Rules: For Registered Bodies Corporate and Registered Native Title Bodies Corporate* (2011), 5, www.oric.gov.au/sites/default/files/documents/06_2013/ORIC-PBCs-guide_May11.pdf, accessed 13 December 2021.

57 Lisa Strelein, Cedric Hassing and Belinda Burbidge, 'AIATSIS Response to Office of the Registrar of Indigenous Corporations (ORIC) Technical Review of the Corporations (Aboriginal and Torres Strait Islander Act) 2006' (31 October 2017), 5.

> provisions of corporations law models and the requirement to act in the 'best interests' of the corporation . . . [58]

More broadly, it is the common law native title holders, via their NTRBC, who determine the internal allocation and regulation of particular rights and interests within the community, in accordance with their law. Native title rights and interests can be defended against third parties by the equitable and common law proprietary remedies available to all holders of property rights,[59] as well as by the protections in the Native Title Act.[60] However, since they are typically *communal* property rights, held by groups whose members have multiple traditional legal responsibilities to one another, there remains considerable uncertainty about whether and when a settler court can intervene in disputes between members of the title-holding community. *Mabo (No. 2)* made it clear that the 'incidents' of native title including inheritance, succession, marital property, the acquisition or transferal of rights between members of the community, and the identification of sub-group rights-holders, are 'matters to be determined by the laws and customs of the [I]ndigenous inhabitants'.[61]

The Native Title Act and regulations[62] render some of this law visible to outsider by requiring NTRBCs to have written and publicly accessible constitutions. The connection between the corporate body's constitution and traditional laws and customs is most acutely at stake in matters concerning the legal relationships between NTRBC representatives and the traditional owner community. Settler law regulates the conduct of this relationship through the Native Title Act (Prescribed Bodies Corporate) regulations. These specify that a NTRBC must 'consult with, and obtain the consent of, the common law [native title] holders . . . before making' certain decisions pertaining to the use of native title rights; and traditional law can be called on to govern this process:[63]

> If there is a particular process of decision-making that, under the Aboriginal or Torres Strait Islander traditional laws and customs of the common law

58 Ibid, 24–5. 59 *Mabo v Queensland (No. 2)* (1992) 175 CLR 1, 61 (Brennan J).
60 Native Title Act 1993 (Cth), div. 3.
61 *Mabo v Queensland (No. 2)* (1992) 175 CLR 1, 61 (Brennan J).
62 Native Title (Prescribed Bodies Corporate) Regulations 1999 (Cth), reg. 4; Corporations (Aboriginal and Torres Strait Islander) Act 2006, s 661–1(2).
63 Native Title (Prescribed Bodies Corporate) Regulations 1999 (Cth), reg. 8. These are decisions affecting native title rights and interests, decisions to enter into agreements with third parties with respect to native title rights and interests, decisions to allow non-native title holders to become members of the NTRBC, and decisions to include reference to a consultation process in the constitution of the NTRBC.

> holders, must be followed in relation to the giving of the consent ... the consent must be given in accordance with that process.[64]

Further, some NTRBC constitutions make express reference to the governing authority of Indigenous law by requiring that the resolution of internal disputes, membership decisions or consultation be done in accordance with traditional laws and customs.[65] In these circumstances, traditional law and custom may fall to be interpreted by settler judges, if a dispute about its content finds its way to court. Disputes turning on NTRBC constitutions can and have been reviewed in the Federal Court.[66]

To summarise, as settler law currently stands, intra-group disputes about the content of traditional law and custom fall, in the first instance, to be resolved by the NTRBC (in consultation with, and with the consent of, the common law native title holders) in accordance with that group's written constitution. If not resolved, these disputes may be subjected to judicial determination in a settler court. Examples of judicial intervention are few, speaking to the enduring authority of traditional law and custom in Indigenous communities. However, the legislative requirement that native-title-holding communities adopt corporate representative bodies can pull Indigenous law out of the wings and onto the stage in settler-style litigation. The power of a settler court to dissect and decide matters of traditional law is seen by some to be an encroachment on Indigenous self-governance, even when the dispute is brought to the court by traditional owners. In this view, judicial intervention seeks to solve a problem engendered by previous settler interventions, and the only sound approach is to defer to Indigenous self-governance and dispute resolution. Exactly how this is to be done and in what circumstances, as well as the ways in which costs and benefits are distributed by outcomes, will likely become more pressing questions in the future.

As noted, so far instances of settler judicial intervention on the content of traditional law and custom (after a native title determination has been issued) have been few and far between. The High Court's decision in *Love-Thoms* suggests there may be more on the horizon, because a person claiming non-

64 Native Title (Prescribed Bodies Corporate) Regulations 1999 (Cth), reg. 8(3).

65 See e.g. Gunggandji – Mandingalbay Yidinji Peoples PBC Aboriginal Corporation RNTBC Constitution (Rule Book) 2017, sch. 1(b); Butchulla Aboriginal Corporation RNTBC Rule Book 2017, sch. 7.13(a); The Rule Book of Gunggandji Aboriginal Corporation RNTBC 2019, ss. 3.4, 6.14, 14.8.

66 See, for a recent example, *Stevens v Wintawari Guruma Aboriginal Corporation NTRBC* [2016] FCA 149, concerning constitutional rules on the revocation of membership for 'misbehaviour'.

alien status on the basis of their Aboriginality must show that they are recognised as a member of a particular people, 'by the elders or other persons enjoying traditional authority among those people'.[67] This can require a court to investigate the basis of a supporting elder's traditional authority and the traditional law and custom that vests decision-making power in that person.[68] These are examples in which Indigenous law 'breaches the surface' of Australian settler law, in a way that makes Indigenous law (for better or for worse) cognisable to judges *as law*, rather than as fact. It is as close as settler law comes to recognising the status of traditional owners and communities as self-governing, law-making polities. For the time being it is the extent of 'strong legal pluralism' in Australia. It poses a formidable challenge for settler judges,[69] but also offers opportunities for truly transformative jurisprudence.

The Rise and Fall of ATSIC

From 1990 to 2005 the local property-based governance spaces provided by land rights and native title legislation were complemented by the regional and national Indigenous representative structures of ATSIC, with its broad mandate for decision-making in Indigenous affairs. Having failed to generate a national treaty, ATSIC was the Hawke government's centrepiece manifestation of its 'self-determination policy'. It remains widely regarded as the most significant institutional development in state-Indigenous relations in Australia's history.[70] At its inception, ATSIC was heralded as a 'bold and unique experiment' in Indigenous governance, 'melding grassroots representation with culturally responsive service delivery'.[71] As a legislatively

67 *Mabo v Queensland (No. 2)* (1992) 175 CLR 1, 70 (Brennan J), cited in *Love-Thoms* at [76] (Bell J).

68 *Webster v Minister for Immigration, Citizenship, Migrant Services and Multicultural Affairs* [2020] FCA 702. For an elaboration on this point, see Michelle Foster and Kirsty Gover, 'Determining Membership: Aboriginality and Alienage in the Australian High Court' *Public Law Review* 31 (2020): 35.

69 See e.g. the experience of federal court judge Hon. Justice Debbie Mortimer, in judicial review cases involving statutory requirements for traditional owner consent: Debbie Mortimer, 'Coming to Terms with Communal, Land-Related Decision-Making by Aboriginal and/or Torres Strait Islander Peoples in a Public Law Context', in Jason N. E. Varuhas and Shona Wilson Stark (eds), *The Frontiers of Public Law* (Oxford: Hart Publishing, 2020), 177, n. 4.

70 Larissa Behrendt, 'The Abolition of ATSIC: Implications for Democracy' (November 2005) *Democratic Audit of Australia*, www.library.bsl.org.au/jspui/bitstream/1/679/1/200511_behrendt_atsic.pdf, accessed 13 December 2021.

71 Geoff Richardson (Meriam, Kuku Yalanji, Djabugay), formerly Executive Officer to the Chairperson (SES Band 1), ATSIC. Personal correspondence with Eddie Cubillo, on file with authors.

mandated national body led by Indigenous elected officials, for whom only Aboriginal and Torres Strait Islanders could vote, ATSIC was a focal point of Indigenous advocacy and leadership. Its summary dissolution by the Howard government in 2005 came after fifteen difficult years, during which the Commission struggled to meet the competing expectations of its Indigenous constituencies, the settler public, and responsible federal ministers. The trials and triumphs of ATSIC have been well-documented elsewhere, and the detail will not be traversed here.[72] Whatever else might be said, ATSIC was a powerful and influential organisation, albeit one with limited discretions and a varying degree of legitimacy in the eyes of traditional owners.

ATSIC was comprised of two separate institutional arms, an elected arm representing Aboriginal and Torres Strait Islanders in thirty-six regions (originally sixty), that made decisions on the allocation of loans, grants and service delivery funding, and an administrative arm tasked with implementing those decisions (reconstituted in 2003 as the Aboriginal and Torres Strait Islander Services (ATSIS)). Each of the thirty-six Regional Councils was comprised of ten to twenty councillors elected for three-year terms, amounting to a collective cohort of approximately 400 culturally mandated Indigenous representatives.[73] The eighteen National Commissioners were elected by Regional Councils, grouped in sixteen zones, with an additional councillor for the Torres Strait Region, and a National Chairperson elected by Commissioners from among their own number (an Eighteenth Commissioner was elected by the relevant zone to fill the spot left by the Chairperson).

As Larissa Behrendt has explained, because ATSIC was obliged by its mandating legislation to perform both representative and administrative functions, its work required a 'delicate balancing act'.[74] Its functions were wide-ranging. It was to formulate, implement and monitor programs for Indigenous people, develop policy proposals for state and national governments meeting Indigenous priorities, assist and advise both Indigenous

72 See e.g. Behrendt, 'The Abolition of ATSIC'; Will Sanders, 'ATSIC Elections and Democracy: Administration, Self-Identification, Participation and Representation' (July 2003), https://apo.org.au/sites/default/files/resource-files/2003-07/apo-nid7263.pdf, accessed 13 December 2021. For a recent contribution, see Harry Hobbs, 'Public Law, Legitimacy and Indigenous Aspirations', in Jason N. E. Varuhas and Shona Wilson Stark (eds), *The Frontiers of Public Law* (Oxford: Hart Publishing, 2020).

73 Geoff Richardson (Meriam, Kuku Yalanji, Djabugay), formerly Executive Officer to the Chairperson (SES Band 1), ATSIC. Personal correspondence with Eddie Cubillo, on file with authors.

74 Behrendt, 'The Abolition of ATSIC'.

communities and the responsible minister, protect Indigenous cultural knowledge, collect and publish statistical information, conduct research, acquire and make grants of property, and make loans and grants of money.[75] Despite the breadth of its mandate, ATSIC's remit was not comprehensive. It did not extend to health and education, and the Commission had limited funding authority in the critical areas of 'domestic violence, languages, heritage protection and housing'.[76] The federal government required a large portion of its funding to be devoted to particular government programs, especially the Community Development Employment Projects scheme and the Community Housing and Infrastructure Program, together by far the largest programs administered by ATSIC. Further, its policy-making and monitoring mandate was often difficult to fulfil in the face of governmental inertia.[77] These and other restraints on ATSIC's real power were not well understood by communities and the broader public, and delays in service delivery (for example in resolving the Indigenous housing backlog) were often attributed to ATSIC, rather than to the responsible government ministry.[78] As Larissa Behrendt has pointed out:

> These misconceptions about ATSIC's role directed attention away from government departments (federal and state and territory) with the actual responsibility for Indigenous policy and service delivery.[79]

In an additional layer of complexity, the responsibilities of Regional Councillors to local kin and political groupings, were strongly felt at the local level, as expressions of foundational principles of traditional cultural obligation.[80] The public perception of regional nepotism and pork-barrelling in the allocation of grants and other interests was difficult to manage. As Lowitja O'Donoghue explained, ATSIC representatives were caught in the middle between competing structures of accountability:

> For us it means adopting two identities – one for at home and one that's for the office . . . That is the flip side to the 'nepotism' – the conflict of interest in serving two masters.[81]

75 Aboriginal and Torres Strait Islander Commission Act 1989, ss. 3, 7(1).
76 Behrendt, 'The Abolition of ATSIC', 4. 77 Ibid, 3.
78 Geoff Richardson (Meriam, Kuku Yalanji, Djabugay), formerly Executive Officer to the Chairperson (SES Band 1), ATSIC. Personal correspondence with Eddie Cubillo, on file with authors.
79 Behrendt, 'The Abolition of ATSIC', 4.
80 Geoff Richardson (Meriam, Kuku Yalanji, Djabugay), formerly Executive Officer to the Chairperson (SES Band 1), ATSIC. Personal correspondence with Eddie Cubillo, on file with authors.
81 Lowitja O'Donoghue, 'Lowitja Reflects on ATSIC' *ATSIC News*, June 2004, 13.

The portrayal of ATSIC and its leadership in Australian media was not sympathetic to these dilemmas. The level of scrutiny directed to allegations of mismanagement in ATSIC is widely regarded by affiliates as disproportionate to the scale of the purported wrong-doing,[82] and is probably reflective of racism.[83] The election of the Howard government in 1996 ensured that a deeper and more structural ideological battle would be fought in the media and in political debate about the role of ATSIC.

Prior to 1999 the ATSIC Chairperson was a government appointee. The shift to a process for electing Chairs, and the selection of a Tjapwurrong man Geoff Clark to that role in 1999, is widely and credibly reported to mark the advent of determined rights-based advocacy by ATSIC.[84] The Commission's assertion of independence in this period, and its unapologetic pursuit of social change and justice, is believed by ATSIC affiliates to have galvanised the Howard government's hostility towards it.[85] Clark was a forceful advocate for Indigenous rights, widely regarded in settler circles as a 'radical', and his 1999 election to Chair by a national Indigenous constituency signalled the Board's support for the 'rights agenda' he pursued before and after joining the Commission.[86] The beginning of Clark's tenure coincided with the election of liberal-right Prime Minister John Howard, bringing the Liberal Coalition to power after thirteen years of Labor Party rule.[87] The Howard government began instantiating a new Indigenous affairs policy premised on a 'whole-of-government' approach involving the 'mainstreaming' of Indigenous policy-making. This entailed distributing responsibility and resources for Indigenous policy among central government agencies. The underlying ethos is widely regarded as assimilationist in intent.[88] The resultant difference between ATSIC's focus on self-determination and the Howard government's policy of 'practical reconciliation', could hardly have been more stark. This clash of values would lead ultimately to ATSIC's abolition. The final decision to

82 Geoff Richardson (Meriam, Kuku Yalanji, Djabugay), formerly Executive Officer to the Chairperson (SES Band 1), ATSIC. Personal correspondence with Eddie Cubillo, on file with authors.
83 Lauren Heinritz, '"The Ship Has Gone Down with the Captain": A Study of the Framing of Aboriginal and Torres Strait Islander Commission (ATSIC) Chairman Geoff Clark in The Australian' (2005), 5, https://ro.ecu.edu.au/cgi/viewcontent.cgi?article=2262&context=theses_hons, accessed 13 December 2021.
84 Eddie Cubillo, personal communication with Kirsty Gover, on file with authors.
85 Eddie Cubillo, personal communication with Kirsty Gover, on file with authors.
86 Heinritz, 'The Ship Has Gone Down', 5. See also ATSIC's final Annual Report 2003–4, including a review from Geoff Clark as Chair: at 2–4.
87 Heinritz, 'The Ship Has Gone Down', 5.
88 Select Committee on the Administration of Indigenous Affairs, 'After ATSIC: Life in the Mainstream?' (March 2005), Preface, xvi, 1, 1.23.

disband ATSIC was so marked in its haste and unilateralism that it was later described by the Senate Committee as evidencing the government's 'crash-through' approach to reform in Indigenous affairs, deploying 'surprise and momentum' to disable and ignore Indigenous opposition to government proposals.[89]

In the lead-up to the abolition, it became clear that Prime Minister Howard could not accept ATSIC's rights-based focus nor its focus on representing the political ambitions of Indigenous polities. He accused ATSIC (and its Commissioners) of improperly aspiring to be 'a separate body which has a separate political existence and [is] more preoccupied with symbolic issues and rights issues than it does of [sic] the advancement of the cause of the people who have elected them'.[90] The opposition Labor Party supported the government's decision to abolish ATSIC, albeit with the caveat that it should be replaced by a differently constituted national Indigenous representative body.[91] In these debates Indigenous democracy was presented as a trivial distraction from the more important task of implementing social policy. As the prime minister explained, abolishing ATSIC showed that the government's intention to provide better services to Indigenous peoples, was 'more important to [him] and to members of the Government than arguing about who represents who'.[92] The Minister for Indigenous Affairs, Amanda Vanstone, likewise suggested that efforts to address Indigenous disadvantage required governments to 'put Indigenous politics aside' and ignore 'people talking about who's going to get a job, who's going to have the opportunity to say this or that'.[93] The representative functions of ATSIC were accordingly deemed irrelevant to Indigenous policy-making.

The legal and ethical obligations of ATSIC representatives were formidably complex. ATSIC Commissioners and Councillors were legislatively accountable both to the Commonwealth government and to their own Indigenous electorates. The latter set of obligations encompassed a range

89 Even before the legislation was passed, the government began the transfer of $1 billion worth of ATSIC programs to government agencies: Select Committee on the Administration of Indigenous Affairs, 'After ATSIC', 3 [1.9].

90 Department of the Prime Minister and Cabinet, 'Interview with John Laws Radio 2UE', 16 April 2004, https://pmtranscripts.pmc.gov.au/release/transcript-21207, accessed 13 December 2021.

91 Latham to scrap 'incapable' ATSIC. See also Select Committee on the Administration of Indigenous Affairs, 'After ATSIC', 1.32.

92 John Howard, 'Joint Press Conference with Senator Amanda Vanstone Parliament House, Canberra' (2004), https://pmtranscripts.pmc.gov.au/release/transcript-21205, accessed 13 December 2021.

93 Ibid.

of duties set out in Indigenous law, down to the most local expression of family commitment. This tension was emphasised in the 2003 review of ATSIC, commissioned by Howard and led by Indigenous elder and academic Jackie Huggins. The Review panel recommended that ATSIC be re-configured to be more responsive to local communities and traditional owners, noting that the 'regional councils are the foundation of ATSIC' and recommending 'a package of reforms which gives greater control of ATSIC to Aboriginal and Torres Strait Islander people at a regional level'.[94] The Review Report was submitted to government in November 2003. By April 2004 the government had resolved to disestablish ATSIC and, in a little over a year, the abolition bill passed with bipartisan support, bringing an end to ATSIC on 24 March 2005. The Regional Councils received three months' grace before they, too, were disestablished on 1 July 2005.[95]

Perhaps the most striking aspect of the abolition process was the government's failure to take into account the views of the people most affected by it. Indigenous community members and leaders, including ATSIC Councillors and Commissioners, for the most part welcomed the government's commissioned Review and participated in the process of re-envisioning how the institution should look and work.[96] The government's refusal to entertain or respond to the recommendations contained in the 2003 Review Report was a further indicator of the strength of its ideological opposition to Indigenous self-determination. The 2004 ATSIC Senate Inquiry put it this way:

> [A] major source of resentment for many in the Indigenous community, is the fact that having commissioned the ATSIC Review, which presented the Government with a model to reform ATSIC based on extensive consultation, the Government suddenly announced the complete abolition of ATSIC. This was done with limited explanation and no discussion. A large number of people, organisations and communities participated in this review in good faith, with a commitment to a process of honest critique and reform. Abolition of ATSIC was never mentioned: rather, there was a legitimate expectation that the Government would proceed with at least the general direction of the Review's findings.[97]

In the absence of Indigenous viewpoints, a large part of the responsibility for ATSIC's demise lies with the settler majority, who failed to hold their elected

94 Aboriginal and Torres Strait Islander Commission, 'In the Hands of the Regions: A New ATSIC', Report (November 2003), 5.
95 Aboriginal and Torres Strait Islander Commission Amendment Bill 2004.
96 Eddie Cubillo, personal correspondence with Kirsty Gover, on file with authors.
97 Select Committee on the Administration of Indigenous Affairs, 'After ATSIC', 1.19.

representatives to account. Megan Davis has reflected on the complacency of the settler public during the abolition process, evidenced by their failure to question or critique the image of ATSIC presented by government, and the striking absence of scholarly and public acknowledgment of the Indigenous perspectives on ATSIC's value. She explains:

> [t]he Australian polity (this does not include Indigenous peoples) has proven incredibly trusting and unquestioning of the government's rejection of the value of Aboriginal participation in decision-making. Self-determination has been conflated with ATSIC. Mind you, there is next to no academic analysis or evidence base of what ATSIC achieved and did not achieve and whether it actually failed. It is mostly anecdote. Importantly, there is virtually no interrogation of whether ATSIC, in the minds of Indigenous Australians, was self-determination.[98]

Huggins has in turn reflected on Indigenous Australians' 'shock about the total devastation and the quickness of the response from the government',[99] explaining that her acceptance of the invitation to serve on the 2003 Review Panel had proved to be 'a poisoned chalice' that made it clear to her that '[t]he government of the day uses you in whatever fashion they see fit'.[100] Former Chair of ATSIC, Gatjil Djerrkura, crystallised a widely held Indigenous view when he argued that unstated goal of the process was assimilation, and the core problem was that '[t]he Prime Minister has long refused to accept the fundamental difference of Aboriginal people in our community'.[101]

Once again, in the abolition of ATSIC, the settler government's line on the composition of the Australian body politic was forcibly imposed on Indigenous peoples. As ever, for Indigenous peoples their political difference is undeniable and inevitable, and persists even if the blanket of settler law denies it formal recognition at the surface. In any case, it is doubtful that even a deferential ATSIC would have survived the hostility of Howard's government, given his insistence that Indigenous people were collectively members of a particular race and not members of polities. His opposition to ATSIC was evident at its inception in 1989 when he spoke in parliament against the establishing legislation put forward by the incumbent Labor government:

> I take the opportunity of saying again that if the Government wants to divide Australian against Australian, if it wants to create a black nation within the

98 Megan Davis, 'Listening but Not Hearing' *Griffith Review* 51 (2016).
99 ABC Local Radio, 'ATSIC Bowled Out' (18 April 2004), www.kooriweb.org/foley/resources/politics/abc18apr04.html, accessed 13 December 2021.
100 L. Scott, 'Indigenous Campaigner Jackie Huggins Has Been Fighting for Aboriginal Rights for Half a Century and She's Not Done Yet', *The Courier Mail*, 14 April 2018.
101 Ibid.

> Australian nation, it should go ahead with [ATSIC] legislation ... [which] strikes at the heart of the unity of the Australian people. In the name of righting the wrongs done against [A]boriginal people, the legislation adopts the misguided notion of believing that if one creates a parliament within the Australian community for [A]boriginal people, one will solve and meet all of those problems.[102]

The abolition of ATSIC, then, results from the long-standing preoccupation in Australian law and politics with an idealised, politically undifferentiated Australian body politic, 'the Australian people', within which Indigenous peoples are represented, if they are at all, as racial minorities with no other relevant constitutional or political status.

Predictably, perhaps, ATSIC's replacement was to be a government-appointed advisory expert body, the National Indigenous Council (NIC). Importantly, in the minds of settler parliamentarians, NIC was 'not meant to be a representative body. It [was] a group of respected individuals with practical experience and expertise.'[103] In the words of the responsible minister, the NIC would 'serve the Australian community and the Indigenous community far more effectively [because] they are not dependent on the votes of a few', adding that 'because of their own experience, their own skills and their own expertise [its members] are not answerable to a particular group.'[104] Years later Vanstone would admit that abolishing ATSIC's Regional Councils 'might have been a mistake'.[105] Certainly the loss of the Regional Councils was particularly strongly felt by Indigenous peoples, as was evident in testimonies before the Senate Committee assessing the ATSIC abolition bill. Former ATSIC Regional Councillor Martin Sibosado (Kullarri Regional Council) offered a vision of ATSIC as a regionally driven institution, with the security of a legislative framework, that could be populated to reflect the traditional boundaries and structures of peoples in the regions. Inter-group relations would be managed by reference to the 'common law' shared by traditional owner communities. He described to a Senate Committee how

102 Commonwealth, *Administration of Aboriginal Affairs*, House of Representatives, 11 April 1989, 1328 (John Howard).

103 Commonwealth, *Aboriginal and Torres Strait Islander Commission Amendment Bill 2004*, Senate, 1 December 2004, 1–2 (Chris Ellison).

104 Commonwealth, *Questions without Notice: Indigenous Affairs*, Senate, 7 December 2004, 29 (Amanda Vanstone).

105 'I didn't have as negative a view of the ATSIC regional structures as of the central one, but if something's going to go, you really have to make a clean job of it ... In hindsight, that might have been a mistake.' Amanda Vanstone in S. Fitzpatrick, 'Dismantling ATSIC Probably a Mistake, Says Amanda Vanstone', *The Australian*, 1 August 2018.

his regional council had worked with community to designate traditional owner constituencies as 'wards', adapting the legislative frame to their own law:

> It was our hope that, if ATSIC had survived, the regional council would be drawn from the ward representatives and their plans would be captured in the regional plans. We would just take the plans of those ward councils and that would form the Kullarri Regional Council. However, without a legislative base, that is going to prove difficult for us. . . . While we have given [the wards] generic names – north, middle, town and south – it gets back to that cultural ruling or, if you like, common law. If you are town people, Yawuru people, you cannot tell Bardi people what to do. That is understood . . .
>
> Whether you are articulate, educated, traditional or cultural, if you are an Aboriginal person, it would be greatly disrespectful – and it is common law – to attempt to override or speak on behalf of an area to which you have no ties. We are really going back to a cultural base and, as I said, as a regional council we are trying to find the balance between contemporary Australian governance, our Aboriginal cultural common law protocols and the way we do things . . .
>
> We believe there is one law for everyone, but when I say that I mean that we are attempting to marry up our Aboriginal law with Australian common law. We believe that can be done. I believe we have the confidence of our elders who have put us in these positions to be able to do that.[106]

As Sibosado pinpoints, 'without a legislative base' traditional governance remains below the settler radar, relatively undetectable, but still subject to the vagaries of settler governance. There is no successor to ATSIC. Some of its functions have been picked up by other national-level independent Indigenous advocacy bodies, such as the National Native Title Council, established to provide the national voice in native title matters that was once offered by ATSIC.[107] The National Congress of First Peoples was established in 2009, and incorporated as a public company to ensure its independence from government, representing nearly 180 Indigenous organisations across the country. Federal government funding for the Congress, provided by the then Labor government, was withdrawn by the Liberal/National Coalition government following its election in 2013, and the Congress quickly ran into financial difficulties. It was finally dissolved in 2019.[108] Even without a national meeting

106 Select Committee on the Administration of Indigenous Affairs, *Administration of Indigenous Affairs*, Hansard, 22 July 2004, 12 (Martin Sibosado).

107 www.nntc.com.au/about/, accessed 13 December 2021.

108 Cassandra Morgan, 'National Congress of Australia's First Peoples' Closure a Step Back for Aboriginal People: Rod Little', *The Canberra Times*, 27 October 2019.

place, the old order of traditional ownership and law persists; but in the absence of formal recognition that could deter settler opportunism, officials are enabled to pick and choose among Indigenous leaders according to the designs of the day. It is undeniably true that the loss of ATSIC in 2005 heralded a phase of Commonwealth extremism in the Northern Territory in 2007. This is the subject of the next section.

Inhumanitarian Intervention in the Northern Territory

Two years after the abolition of ATSIC, Indigenous aspirations for local self-governance were further undermined by the Commonwealth government, this time when it enacted a suite of legislation to effect the Northern Territory National Emergency Response in 2007. Ostensibly to address violence and child abuse in remote Aboriginal communities, the legislative package ran to 500 pages, passed by both houses of the Commonwealth legislature in less than a week. The measures removed the capacity of communities to control entry onto their land by doing away with the 'permit system',[109] quarantined the social welfare income of community members, and enabled the federal government to compulsorily acquire five-year leases on the Aboriginal freehold land that had been secured by the ALRA thirty years prior.[110]

'The Intervention', as it has come to be known, was expressly coercive and discriminatory. It could not be effected consistently with the Racial Discrimination Act (RDA) 1975, the application of which was accordingly suspended by the Intervention's enacting legislation. The Land Councils were not consulted on the proposed measures, and neither were the traditional owners subjected to them.[111] Aboriginal communities living on their own land were characterised as 'failed societ[ies]'[112] with 'no natural social order of production and distribution'.[113] The logic put to the public via the Commonwealth legislature was that autonomy and isolation had engendered

109 The ALRA prohibits entry onto Aboriginal land held by an Aboriginal Land Trust without a permit issued by the Aboriginal Land Council for the area: Aboriginal Land Rights (Northern Territory) Act 1976 (Cth), ss 70, 73.

110 Northern Territory National Emergency Response Act 2007 (Cth), s 31.

111 Central Land Council, 'Submission to Senate Standing Committee on Legal and Constitutional Affairs: Inquiry into Commonwealth Emergency Response Bills' (10 August 2007), 1, on file with authors.

112 Commonwealth, *Parliamentary Debates*, House of Representatives, 7 August 2007, 10 (Mal Brough).

113 Ibid, 11 (Mal Brough).

dysfunction in Aboriginal communities, and that greater exposure to settler scrutiny and influence was the remedy.[114] Most of the measures continue today in modified legislative form, now designated as 'special measures' (broadly, and paradoxically, 'affirmative action' measures) under the RDA, impliedly designed to protect Indigenous peoples 'in the equal enjoyment of human rights and fundamental freedoms' by addressing their disadvantage.[115] The lack of common law consultation requirements, the lack of a treaty, the failure of the RDA to generate consultation obligations as a condition of 'special measures',[116] and the expansive nature of constitutional Commonwealth legislative power in the Northern Territory[117] all enabled the Intervention. These deficits in Australian settler law have further motivated Indigenous advocacy for constitutional recognition, discussed below.

Contemporary Indigenous Advocacy in the Political Arena: Voice, Treaty, Truth

In 2019, seventy-two-year-old Galarrwuy Yunupingu reflected on his dealings with eight Australian Prime Ministers, ahead of a meeting with his ninth:

> This time we are saying enough is enough for the Yolngu people. There have been many times that we have gone to the government [saying] what they must do to help Aboriginal people – they haven't done it. If they don't come to us with an answer, we will tell you what we, the Yolngu people are going to do. We will dismiss the constitution, and [say] not to worry about it because we'll have thrown it out of Australia into the saltwater.[118]

Yunupingu was speaking in reference to the government's refusal to accept the proposed 'Voice to Parliament' contained in the 2017 Uluru Statement from the Heart. The statement was endorsed by more than 250 Indigenous leaders at a constitutional convention at Uluru, on Anangu land in the Central Australian Desert. It explains that 'the ancient sovereignty' of

114 'Closed towns mean less public scrutiny, so the situation has been allowed to get worse and worse. Normally, where situations come to light which are as terrible as the child abuse occurring in the Northern Territory, solutions are pursued relentlessly by the media. But, closed towns have made it easier for abuse and dysfunction to stay hidden.': Commonwealth, *Parliamentary Debates*, House of Representatives, 7 August 2007, 12 (Mal Brough).

115 Stronger Futures in the Northern Territory Act 2012 (Cth). See e.g. ss. 7, 33, 37.

116 See *Maloney v The Queen* (2013) 252 CLR 168, 185–6 [24]–[25] (French CJ).

117 See *Wurridjal v The Commonwealth* (2009) 237 CLR 309, 423 [302] (Kirby J).

118 Galarrwuy Yunupingu, Garma festival, Friday 3 August 2019 (author's notes). See P. Taylor, 'Fix It or We'll Throw Constitution into Sea: Galarrwuy Yunupingu', *The Australian*, 3 August 2019.

Aboriginal and Torres Strait Islanders 'is a spiritual notion' that has persisted for some 60,000 years and 'co-exists with the sovereignty of the Crown'. The authors of the Statement 'seek constitutional reforms to empower our people and take a rightful place in our own country', calling for 'a First Nations Voice enshrined in the Constitution' and a 'Makarrata Commission to supervise a process of agreement-making between governments and First Nations and truth-telling about our history'. These three proposals have come to be known by the short-form: 'Voice, Treaty, Truth'. This chapter concludes by addressing constitutional recognition claims as the latest assertion of the distinctive sovereign identities of Indigenous peoples as nations and polities. We cast a critical eye on the Commonwealth's responses (and lack thereof).

Given that the High Court's insistence that it cannot 'determine the consequences'[119] of settler sovereignty in ways that imply Indigenous political agency and authority, the 'sovereignty' question in Australia, whether framed as law-making authority or self-governance, seems amenable (for now) only to political remedies, not judicial ones. The Uluru Statement from the Heart picks up the baton handed to Indigenous leaders by the authors of the Barunga Statement and the Yirrkala Bark Petitions. It proposes a way forward that appeals directly to 'the people' of Australia, and not to settler officials. Megan Davis, a centrally important figure in the development and defence of the Uluru Statement, explains the significance of this strategy:

> The Uluru Statement from the Heart was tactically issued to the Australian people, not Australian politicians. It is the people who can unlock the Australian Constitution for Aboriginal people, as they did in 1967, and the descendants of the ancient polities can unlock what is sorely lacking in this country, a fuller expression of Australia's nationhood.[120]

As Davis points out, the lack of settler political leadership on progress towards constitutional recognition of First Peoples seems to necessitate a face-to-face encounter, between those peoples and their settler counterparts, through the vehicle of a referendum. Elsewhere, she has explained that for many Aboriginal and Torres Strait Islanders, 'reconciliation is the

119 'Although the question whether a territory has been acquired by the Crown is not justiciable before municipal courts, those courts have jurisdiction to determine the consequences of an acquisition under municipal law.' *Mabo v Queensland (No. 2)* (1992) 175 CLR 1, 32 (Brennan J).

120 Megan Davis, 'The Long Road to Uluru: Walking Together' *Griffith Review* 60 (2018): 13–32, 13.

wrong concept', because 'it means to restore friendly relations. And we, as First Nations and Australians, have never even met each other. There was never any pre-existing relationship.'[121] These insights are a salient caution against borrowing concepts from other settler states in which inter-people relationships have historic grounding in national constitutions and treaties. They provide a crucial backdrop for the proposed 'Voice to Parliament', and the efforts of traditional owners to conclude treaties with the states and territories. For Australian Indigenous peoples as an 'extreme minority'[122] the referendum path to recognition is difficult and precarious. Amendments to Australia's Constitution require a majority of voters in each state and a majority of voters nation-wide to vote affirmatively in a referendum.[123] To take their 'rightful place' in Australia's constitutional order as the Uluru Statement proposes, Indigenous peoples must convince a 'double majority' of Australian voters that this is what justice requires. Because of the constitutional framework imposed on Indigenous polities, in this democratic exercise, as in all others, Aboriginal and Torres Strait Islander voters will be outnumbered thirty-five to one by their settler counterparts.[124]

As noted above, the proposals' prospects of success at a referendum have been hampered by the response of settler political leaders.[125] The Statement takes its place within a convoluted institutional history. For brevity, this history is addressed here only in outline, with the aim of characterising the hurdles that have been overcome to date and identifying those which remain to be faced. The possibility of constitutional recognition for Indigenous peoples was first officially raised in 2010 by the Labor government Prime Minister, Julia

121 Megan Davis, 'A one-syllable change to the anthem is hardly something to celebrate' *Canberra Times*, 1 January 2021. See also Gregory Phillips, Can We Breathe? *IndigenousX*, 31 December 2020. https://indigenousx.com.au/can-we-breathe/, accessed 13 December 2021. 'Internationally, the concept of reconciliation presumes there was peace between two equal parties, then a conflict, and then a need to talk, atone, forgive and rebuild. In the Australia context, this was always fundamentally a lie.'

122 Noel Pearson, 'A Rightful Place: Race, Recognition and a More Complete Commonwealth', *Quarterly Essay* 55 (September 2014), www.quarterlyessay.com.au/essay/2014/09/a-rightful-place, accessed 13 December 2021.

123 Australian Constitution, s 128.

124 The Australian Bureau of Statistics, Aboriginal and Torres Strait Islander Population 2016 census data summary shows that Aboriginal and Torres Strait Islander peoples represented 2.8 per cent of the national population: '2016 Census Shows Growing Aboriginal and Torres Strait Islander Population' (27 June 2017).

125 For an account of this recalcitrance and Indigenous proposals for forward movement, see Davis, 'The Long Road to Uluru'; Megan Davis, 'No Time for the Meek: Keeping Faith with the Uluru Reforms', *The Monthly*, October 2019, www.themonthly.com.au/issue/2019/october/1569370776/megan-davis/no-time-meek#mtr accessed 13 December 2021.

Gillard.[126] Since then, the Commonwealth has heard from its Expert Panel on Constitutional Recognition of Indigenous Australians, which reported in 2012,[127] a Joint Select Committee on Constitutional Recognition of Aboriginal and Torres Strait Islander Peoples, which reported in mid-2015,[128] followed by the sixteen-member Referendum Council's report in 2017 (in which the Uluru Statement was embraced), and the report of the second Joint Select Committee in 2018 (again taking up the Uluru Statement).[129] The Referendum Council's dialogues with Indigenous peoples were the most inclusive Indigenous consultative process ever undertaken in Australia, comprised of thirteen regional meetings that culminated in the 250-strong gathering of leaders at Uluru. Consultation continues, now under the direction of Australia's first Aboriginal Minister for Indigenous Australians, the Hon Ken Wyatt, albeit with the prospect of constitutional entrenchment seemingly off the table.[130] This is a major divergence from the aims of the Uluru Statement. The government's model re-envisions the Voice to Parliament as a legislative body that advises the Executive Branch, rather than a constitutionally enshrined body that communicates directly with the federal Parliament. Of course the memory of the ATSIC abolition looms large in the minds of Indigenous peoples.

As noted above, the Referendum Council's 2017 report envisaged that the Voice to Parliament would be enshrined in the Constitution, and that its functions would be specified in legislation. The Commonwealth government rejected this proposal within months of hearing it, seeding concern by publicly describing the body as a 'third chamber' of Parliament. Prime Minister Malcolm Turnbull, along with the Attorney General and Minister for Indigenous Australians, issued a statement

126 K. Lazzaro, 'Julia Gillard wants Indigenous People Recognised in Constitution', ABC Radio National, 8 November 2010.

127 Expert Panel on Constitutional Recognition of Indigenous Australians, 'Recognising Aboriginal and Torres Strait Islander Peoples in the Constitution' (Final Report, 15 January 2012): recommending that the race power be replaced with a provision enabling laws to be made for Aboriginal and Torres Strait Islanders, and adding a provision prohibiting racial discrimination.

128 Joint Select Committee on Constitutional Recognition of Aboriginal and Torres Strait Islander Peoples, 'Final Report' (June 2015).

129 Referendum Council, 'Final Report of the Referendum Council' (30 June 2017), viii.

130 'I want to be very clear. The question we put to the Australian people will not result in what some desire, and that is an enshrined voice to the parliament . . . these two matters, whilst related, need to be treated separately.': P. Taylor, 'Wyatt Rules Out Indigenous Voice in People Poll', *The Australian*, 17 August 2019. See also *Indigenous Voice Co-Design Process, Interim Report to the Australian Government* (October 2020), https://voice.niaa.gov.au/sites/default/files/2021-01/indigenous-voice-codesign-process-interim-report-2020.pdf, accessed 8 April 2022.

asserting that '[the Voice] is contrary to the principles of equality of citizenship in Australia',[131] and incompatible with Australian democratic values:

> Our democracy is built on the foundation of all Australian citizens having equal civic rights . . . A constitutionally enshrined additional representative assembly for which only Indigenous Australians could vote for or serve in is inconsistent with this fundamental principle.[132]

Against the cold face of monolithic settler sovereignty, Indigenous expressions of their status as interconnected peoples and polities endure, in the Uluru Statement from the Heart, in the treaty-making processes, in the ways that communities live their sovereignty on their land,[133] and in the vision advanced by Indigenous leadership. In 2018, Djawa Yunupingu (brother of Galarrwuy) spoke about Yolngu sovereignty at the Garma Festival, an annual Yolngu cultural gathering that has become the site (and theatre) of high-level Indigenous-settler political engagement:

> [O]ur sovereignty is not a hard and brutal sovereignty, it does not take from others – it does not exclude or steal. Our sovereignty is welcoming, just like you see and feel here at *Garma*, which is a public ceremony . . . the Truth is that we are not United in this country – we are not Comfortable – and we remain uncertain and troubled by this Truth. Because we live side by side – Two People – Two Laws – One Country.[134]

Conclusion

As the foregoing illustrates, the long history of encounter between Indigenous and settler leaders reveals profoundly different visions of 'the Australian people'. In the model promoted and imposed by settler officials, the Australian public comprises a single 'people' exercising popular sovereignty, from whom the legitimacy of the state derives and to whom public institutions are ultimately accountable. This Australian 'polity' is thought to be united in Federation by the Commonwealth Constitution; and within this

131 Malcolm Turnbull, 'Press Conference with the Right Honourable Jacinda Ardern, Prime Minister of New Zealand' (5 November 2017).

132 Department of Prime Minister and Cabinet, 'Response to Referendum Council's Report on Constitutional Recognition' (26 October 2017).

133 'Mob on country exercise sovereignty by getting on with it. They couldn't care less about the constitution.' Eddie Cubillo, personal correspondence with Kirsty Gover, on file with authors.

134 Yothu Yindi Foundation, 'Djawa Yunupingu: Speech 4 August 2018', www.yyf.com.au/news/detail.aspx?SubjectID=1&ArticleID=155, accessed 13 December 2021.

constitutionalised people, the states are understood to be 'bodies politic', 'whose existence and nature are independent of the powers allocated to them'.[135] The status of Indigenous peoples is not recognised in this way. They appear in this order as a racial population with no constitutional status other than as the passive object of the Commonwealth's power to make special laws for the 'people of any race'.[136] This foundational mistake sustains a pervasive settler scepticism about Indigenous assertions of political difference and suspicion of Indigenous representative bodies. Because the status of Indigenous peoples as polities is readily denied as a matter of settler law, claims premised on Indigenous sovereignty and self-determination, including advocacy for differentiated representative bodies for Indigenous constituencies, are made vulnerable to claims that they instantiate forms of racial privilege. Aboriginal and Torres Strait Islander polities have challenged this constitutive error since the earliest days of colonial state-making. Settler Australians have been slow to take up the challenge or to hold their elected officials to account. The work of critique and advocacy and the burden of governmental failures falls overwhelmingly on a community that makes up just 3 per cent of Australia's national population. It is undoubtedly time that settlers themselves accepted a fair share of this labour. The material and human resources of Indigenous communities are stretched thin, but their persistence as sovereign peoples with inherent law-making authority is one that discomforts settler officials as much in the twenty-first century as in the time of the First Fleet.

135 *Melbourne Corporation v The Commonwealth* (1947) 74 CLR 31, 82, per Dixon J.
136 Australian Constitution, s 51 (xxvi).

11

Australia as Empire

MIRANDA JOHNSON AND CAIT STORR

Introduction: Australia as Product and Agent of Empire

Australia is both a product of the British Empire and an agent of empire. Through much of the twentieth century, the country was an imperial power in the South Pacific, the Southern Ocean, and even the proximate Indian ocean. However, the rights and responsibilities that flow from empire are commonly ignored or forgotten by Australian citizens today. Indeed, there are few scholarly considerations of the *legal* history of Australian empire.[1]

Telling a story of Australian empire troubles conventional narratives of nationhood premised on an expansion outwards to the natural limits of the continent, by tracing Australia's multidirectional imperial interests in its contiguous seas.[2] The establishment of Australia as a new power in the Pacific region, in particular, throws light on the imperial dimensions of Australia's self-realisation as a sovereign state, a fact that is often obscured when the making of the country is considered primarily in terms of its vertical relationships to Britain or the United States.

The colony of New South Wales was involved in complex – if later obscured – diplomatic and legal relationships that extended far beyond the continent's shores. As the Australian colonies grew in population and wealth, the balance of regional power shifted markedly. At the end of the nineteenth

1 Antony Anghie, 'Race, Self-Determination and Australian Empire' *Melbourne Journal of International Law* 19, no. 2 (2018): 423–61. Marilyn Lake, 'The Australian Dream of an Island Empire: Race, Reputation and Resistance' *Australian Historical Studies* 46 (2015): 410–24.

2 Howitt argues that Federation-era Australians bore a 'remarkably oceanic understanding of space'. Rohan Howitt, *Ideological Origins of the Australian Antarctic, 1839–1933* (PhD thesis, Department of History, University of Sydney, 2019), 327. On Oceania as an interconnected space of Indigenous life, thought, and action, see Epeli Hau'ofa, Vijay Naidu and Eric Waddell (eds), *A New Oceania: Rediscovering Our Sea of Islands* (Suva: University of the South Pacific, 1993).

century, federation manifested a shared colonial ambition to secure Australia's regional supremacy against the perceived incursions of competing European empires. This ambition was realised through the acquisition of extensive territory in Papua and later New Guinea, in the destructive exploitation of resources and labour in Nauru, as well as in claims to Antarctica and islands in the Southern Ocean.

Foregrounding Australian imperialism therefore subverts the dominant narrative of twentieth century Australian legal history as a gradual deconstruction of a (British) imperial project, or 'dedominionisation'.[3] Instead, we propose that 'Australia' is a phenomenon constructed and maintained through ongoing assertions of the authority to define place and person, across a region that exceeds territorial and racial borders. The consolidation of this imperial project has long been concerned with the making and maintaining of whiteness, white space and white entitlement. This racialisation continues to evolve, rename and re-assert itself in new ways in a wide range of legislative and administrative techniques for constructing territories and persons.

The legal tools of Australian empire have included direct assertions of territorial jurisdiction; shifting constructions of territorial inclusion and exclusion, such as the territorial sea and the maritime migration zone; assertions and protections of rights in natural resources, both within and beyond 'sovereign' borders (for example in the Greater Sunrise Basin, and in relation to Australian mining interests in Papua New Guinea and Nauru); the implementation of differential citizenship rules, specific labour migration regimes and visa programs; and constantly shifting constructions of Indigeneity. Though often destructive, Australian empire has not been totalising. Indigenous laws have challenged imperial jurisdiction, and their recognition and institutionalisation became a matter of critical debate in the independence constitutions of the later twentieth century.

Colony, Empire, and the Pacific in the Nineteenth Century

From its beginnings, the colony of New South Wales was entangled in webs of interdependency with Pacific peoples and resources (see Map 11.1). The early nineteenth-century 'salt-pork trade' with Tahiti, for instance, entailed

3 Kosmas Tsokhas, 'Dedominionization: The Anglo-Australian Experience, 1939–1945' *The Historical Journal* 37, no. 4 (1994): 861–83.

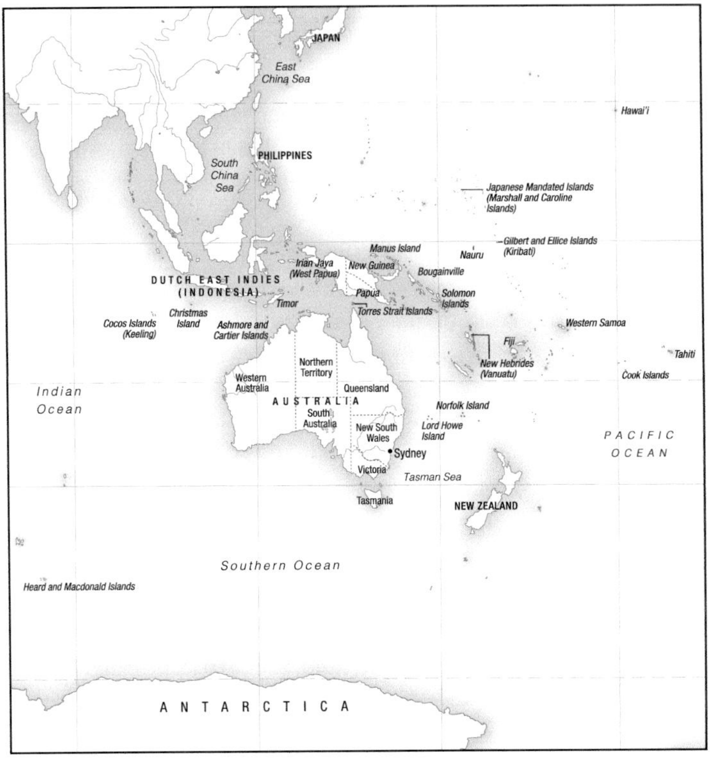

Map 11.1: Australasia and the Western Pacific

varying and fluid negotiations of laws and the recognition of Indigenous sovereignty.[4] Even by the end of the nineteenth century, as colonies asserted their power and dominance in the region, colonial Queensland's sugar plantations were dependent on cheap, indentured labour of Pacific Islanders for achieving considerable profits.[5] The initial dependency of the tiny convict settlement on the edge of a vast continent was not, however, admitted in founding documents that extended British authority over 'all the Islands adjacent in the Pacific'. In his 1787 commission as governor-in-chief of

4 Alecia Simmonds, 'Cross-Cultural Friendship and Legal Pluralities in the Early Pacific Salt-Pork Trade' *Journal of World History* 28, no. 2 (2017): 219–48; Vanessa Smith, *Intimate Strangers: Friendship, Exchange and Pacific Encounters* (Cambridge: Cambridge University Press, 2010).

5 Kay Saunders, 'The Workers' Paradox: Indentured Labor in the Queensland Sugar Industry to 1920', in Kay Saunders (ed.), *Indentured Labour in the British Empire, 1834–1920* (London: Croom Helm, 1984), 213–59.

New South Wales, Arthur Phillip was enjoined to establish as quickly as possible a settlement at Norfolk Island 'and prevent its being occupied by the subjects of any other European Power'.[6] What the historian J. M. Ward later called the 'adjunct policy' did not, in fact, have immediate effect but the instructions did establish that the new convict colony's future was as much, if not more, oriented sea-wards as it was towards the vast interior, as yet unexplored and uncharted by Europeans.[7]

Australian elites would come to see themselves as 'masters of the Pacific'.[8] However, there was nothing inevitable about the transformation of colonies of convict and, later, free white settlers into a regional imperial power. The pre-history of formal Australian empire is littered with thwarted plans and stymied political desires. Furthermore, unlike the independent United States on whom Australian imperialists at times modelled themselves, the Australian colonies could not engage in foreign diplomacy or annex territory in their own name.

The piecemeal incorporation of the Torres Strait Islands into Queensland's jurisdiction required imperial approval. The most proximate of these islands (those lying within a three-mile limit from the continent's shores), including Thursday Island where a magistrate was stationed, were incorporated under Queensland's jurisdiction through an argument for 'adjacency' based on the opinion of imperial law officers in 1863. In 1872 that limit was extended to sixty miles offshore and, in 1879, all islands of the Torres Strait were annexed to Queensland by Letters Patent and confirmed by colonial legislation.[9] Notably, official discourse asserted the 'urgent need' to protect island inhabitants from white traders and others. Those living within the sixty-mile limit automatically became 'natives of Queensland'. Yet, at this time, no specific legislation regulated Indigenous peoples on the mainland; according to one historian, the 'least influential' motivation for annexation of the islands was protection of Torres Strait Islanders.[10]

6 Arthur Phillip's Second and Permanent Commission, 2 April 1787, *Historical Records of Australia*, 1st series, Volume 1, 2.

7 J. M. Ward, *British Policy in the South Pacific: 1786–1893* (Sydney: Australasian Publishing Co, 1948).

8 Alfred Deakin quoted in Geoffrey Serle, 'The Victorian Government's Campaign for Federation, 1883–1889', in A. W. Martin (ed.), *Essays in Australian Federation* (Melbourne: Melbourne University Publishing, 1969), 31.

9 R. D. Lumb, 'The Torres Strait Islands: Some Questions Relating to their Annexation and Status' *Federal Law Review* 19 (1990): 154–68.

10 Steve Mullins, 'Queensland's Quest for Torres Strait: The Delusion of Inevitability' *Journal of Pacific History* 27, no. 2 (1992): 165–80.

In the late 1860s, some Sydney colonists began to articulate an expansionist policy in the Pacific, notably in relation to Fiji where new cotton plantations were booming. Arch imperialists commonly invoked an 'Australasian Monroe Doctrine' to assert British rights in the South Pacific, in competition with French and, later, German imperial expansion.[11] But whereas the 1823 Monroe Doctrine declared US economic and diplomatic primacy in Latin America to the exclusion of all other imperial and colonial interests, Australian Monroeism was consistent with Australia's membership of the British Empire. It gave rise to experimental formulations of sub-empire, or *imperium in imperio*, as political ideology and as constitutional structure.[12] The limits of sub-imperial power were strikingly demonstrated by Queensland's attempted annexation of the eastern half of the island of New Guinea on 4 April 1883, purportedly in response to a German newspaper report of impending takeover. The British imperial government refused to recognise Queensland's claim on the ground that the added expense was unnecessary, as there was 'no reason for supposing that the German government contemplates any scheme of colonisation'.[13] The colonies reacted strongly to the imperial government's refusal, and the 'Australasian Convention on the Annexation of Adjacent Islands and the Federation of Australasia', later known as the first Federation Convention, was held in Sydney in November and December 1883 to formulate a collective response. In an attempt to placate the colonies, the Colonial Secretary, the Earl of Derby, promised to extend the consular jurisdiction of the British High Commission of the Western Pacific over British subjects in New Guinea.[14]

The 'New Guinea crisis' highlighted two major factors in the development of Australian statehood: first, that the 'self-governing' Australasian colonies had no legal control over their 'external sovereignty', nor capacity to enter into treaties of commerce and defence; and second, that the colonial perception of their own strategic interests in the Pacific region was beginning to diverge from that of the imperial government. The formation of an 'Australian' state required articulation not only of the legal bases on which the colonies would federate, but also of the relationship of that Federation to

11 Roger C. Thompson, *Australian Imperialism in the Pacific: The Expansionist Era, 1820–1920* (Melbourne: Melbourne University Press, 1980).

12 Cait Storr, '"*Imperium in Imperio*": Sub-Imperialism and the Formation of Australia as a Subject of International Law' *Melbourne Journal of International Law* 19, no. 1 (2018): 335–68.

13 J. L. Whitaker, N. G. Gash, J. F. Hookey and R. J. Lacey (eds), *Documents and Readings in New Guinea History: Pre-History to 1899* (Milton, Qld: Jacaranda Press, 1975), 478.

14 Thompson, *Australian Imperialism*, 51.

the British Empire. Over the 1880s and 1890s, the Federation conventions provided an intercolonial forum for negotiation of the former; and the Colonial Conferences, held between the imperial government and the self-governing Dominions, an intra-imperial forum for the latter. These debates repeatedly returned to the issue of establishing a legal basis for Australian annexation of islands in its own right.

The imperial government was largely receptive to internal Federation of the self-governing colonies but continued to insist that in a context of increasing global tensions, its retention of external affairs powers was vital to the integrity of the British Empire. In 1884, following German corporate expansion into northern New Guinea, Britain and Germany agreed to the establishment of the protectorate of British New Guinea over the southeast of the island, and the protectorate of German New Guinea over the north-east. There was also a struggle with the French for supremacy over the New Hebrides (now Vanuatu), a significant labour-recruiting ground for European trading firms in the Pacific. In scientific expeditions, Australians sought to extend their influence in the Southern Ocean and over Antarctica.[15] At the same time, at the Federation Conference in 1890, the colonies of New Zealand and Fiji (the latter by then a British protectorate) were formally invited to join an 'Australasian' federation.[16] Both ultimately declined, though the Commonwealth Constitution of 1901 held open the possibility that New Zealand might one day enter the federation.

After a century of engagement between the colonies, adjacent islands and those farther away, the Constitution provided the federal Parliament the power to determine Australia's relations with 'Pacific islands' (Section 51(xxx)). This was distinguished from external affairs powers more generally, as the first prime minister of Australia Edmund Barton explained in aspirational terms, on the ground that the Australian Commonwealth would play a particular role in 'regulating' the islands, as 'part of the British Empire'.[17] As it turned out, the federal Parliament rarely if ever invoked this head of power to regulate the Pacific islands. Nevertheless, law was a critical tool, and sometimes weapon, in the regulation of islanders within Australia and in Australia's offshore territories. The Pacific Island Labourers

15 See Howitt, *Ideological Origins*.
16 Nicholas Aroney, 'New Zealand, Australasia and Federation' *Canterbury Law Review* 16 (2010): 31–46.
17 *Official Record of the Debates of the Australasian Federal Convention. Third Session. Melbourne, 20th January to 17th March 1898* (2 volumes, Melbourne: Robert S. Brain, Government Printer, 1898), 1: 30.

Act of 1901 forcibly repatriated many islanders who had been brought to work in Australia, mainly in Queensland (over 60,000 worked there between 1863 and 1904).[18] The legislation was introduced in the first tranche of Commonwealth legislation that, along with the Immigration Restriction Act, formally inaugurated the White Australia policy. Like Indigenous peoples in Australia, Pacific Islanders who remained within Australia were excluded from citizenship status. Māori in Australia, however, could vote at the federal level and be naturalised as citizens, though they were excluded from old age pension provisions. This notable exception for a racial minority was a concession to New Zealand in case that country decided to join the Federation.[19]

Soon after Federation, the protectorate of British New Guinea was placed under the authority of the Australian Commonwealth. The Papua Act of 1905 incorporated the Territory of Papua within the Commonwealth, created the position of Lieutenant Governor, and a six-member Executive Council, all appointed by the Governor General. The act also provided for the creation of a Legislative Council, which included non-official members, usually drawn from the white resident population of the territory, as well as the aforementioned officers.[20] No provision was made for Indigenous representation.

The early period of colonial administration in the Territory focused on controlling a labour pool for white-owned plantations and establishing the terms of land leases to white settlers. Land could only be purchased by the colonial administration, which also restricted Indigenous entrepreneurialism, and policed liquor licensing and inter-racial sexual relationships.[21] The administration was concerned neither with securing the consent of the (Indigenous) governed, nor with the development or progress of Indigenous peoples towards self-rule in colonial Papua. Yet law was central to the imposition and maintenance of colonial rule in Papua. Drawing largely on English common law, as well as specific Queensland statutes introduced after 1889, colonial law made no specific mention of the continuity or otherwise of 'native custom' in the Papua Act, although this was later recognised in the New Guinea Laws Repeal and Adopting Ordinance of 1921.[22] Instead,

18 Tracey Banivanua Mar, *Violence and Colonial Dialogue: The Australian-Pacific Indentured Labor Trade* (Honolulu: University of Hawai'i Press, 2007).

19 Paul Hamer, *From Federation to the "50s": Māori Inclusion and Exclusion in Australia since 1901* (unpublished PhD thesis, Monash University, 2018), 21.

20 Papua Act 1905 (Cth).

21 Edward P. Wolfers, *Race Relations and Colonial Rule in Papua New Guinea* (Sydney: Australia and New Zealand Book Co, 1975).

22 J. R. Mattes, 'Sources of Law in Papua and New Guinea' *The Australian Law Journal* 37 (September 1963): 148–53. Papua Act 1905 (Cth), s 21(5).

exceptional law was created for dealing with Indigenous peoples' disputes *inter se*. Native Regulations determined hygiene matters and curfews, and established a Court of Native Matters, which was preoccupied with punishing 'sorcery', inadequately defined and understood.[23] So, while the Court preserved certain aspects of 'custom' as 'cultural fact', judges subordinated Indigenous law to colonial objectives.[24] Traditional dispute settlement practices endured and even flourished during the period; yet the attempt to subordinate Indigenous law as customary law would come to haunt the reformist agendas of the post-war period and the plans of the architects of decolonisation.

War, Australia's Legal Status and Mandate Rule in New Guinea and Nauru

The occupation of German New Guinea and Nauru was the first military action taken by the new Commonwealth in World War I in October 1914, at the behest of the imperial government.[25] The legal nature of Australia's continued occupation of New Guinea and Nauru was to become an issue of diplomatic and scholarly contention over the following decades. The official history of Australian involvement in World War I focuses on the galvanising of a national identity through shared adversity, culminating in Australia's accession to sovereign independence with the passage of the Statute of Westminster in 1931, incorporated into Australian legislation in 1942.[26] However, this account underplays how directly Australia's war experience was informed by the pursuit of old colonial ambitions for Pacific supremacy. Those ambitions came to focus on the German Pacific territories, which in 1914 comprised German New Guinea and Nauru; German Samoa (later Western Samoa); and the Marshall and Caroline Islands north of the equator.[27]

23 Peter Fitzpatrick, *Law and State in Papua New Guinea* (London: Academic Press, 1980); Michael Goddard, 'The Snake Bone Case: Law, Custom, and Justice in a Papua New Guinea Village Court' *Oceania* 67, no. 1 (1996): 50–63. On exceptional law more generally, see Shaunnagh Dorsett, *Juridical Encounters: Māori and the Colonial Courts, 1840–1852* (Auckland: Auckland University Press, 2017).

24 Sinclair Dinnen, 'Sentencing, Custom and the Rule of Law in Papua New Guinea' *The Journal of Legal Pluralism and Unofficial Law* 20 (1988): 19–54, 26.

25 C. E. W. Bean, 'Australia's Position at the Outbreak', in Bean (ed.), *Official History of Australia in the War 1914–1918* (Sydney: Angus & Robertson, 1941, 11th edition), 1: 1, 13.

26 Statute of Westminster 1931 (Imp); Statute of Westminster Adoption Act 1942 (Cth).

27 W. M. Roger Louis, *Great Britain and Germany's Lost Colonies 1914–1919* (Oxford: Clarendon Press, 1967).

Contention over the nature of Australia's occupation of German New Guinea and Nauru was directly related to uncertainties about Australia's own legal status, both within the British Empire and the international order. In the intra-imperial arena, the war had made plain that the growing ambitions of the self-governing Dominions of Australia, New Zealand, South Africa and Canada to pursue regional interests in their own right were irreconcilable with the imperial government's insistence on maintaining control over external affairs. Prior to the war, imperial control over external affairs meant that the Dominions were regarded as having 'no international standing whatever'.[28] Imperial Conferences established in the late nineteenth century had provided an outlet for ventilation of growing Dominion demands for greater autonomy. The imperial government developed a compromise solution, devolving 'internal' heads of power to colonial governments while maintaining direct control over entry into treaties of defence.[29] That distribution of constitutional powers showed strain as war became more likely in the early decades of the twentieth century. Australia was particularly aggrieved at being bound by the 1886 Anglo-German Demarcation Agreement and, later, by the 1907 Anglo-Japanese Alliance, criticised in the media as a threat to the White Australia policy.[30]

For Australia, then, sovereign independence was a goal to be realised through the assumption of control over its own Pacific territories as much as through control over domestic affairs. Regional supremacy was held out as a measure of political 'maturity' as readily as was sovereignty itself. For Prime Minister W. M. Hughes, an Australian sub-empire in the Pacific was a corollary of the White Australia policy, and Australia's military occupation of German New Guinea and Nauru provided an opportunity to realise it.[31] The question of how to convert military occupation into permanent territorial acquisition was openly discussed in federal Parliament and in the media as a means of realising Australia's 'Pacific Ocean destiny'.[32] Key strategies included merging the military administration of occupied German New Guinea with the civil administration of the Territory of Papua, and securing

28 Lassa Oppenheim, *International Law: A Treatise* (London: Longmans, Green and Co, 1905), 1: 102–3.

29 H. Duncan Hall, *The British Commonwealth of Nations: A Study of its Past and Future Developments* (London: Methuen & Co, 1920), 3.

30 'Congested Japan: The Danger to Australia – Why White Immigration is Imperative', *The Daily Telegraph* (Sydney), 5 July 1907, 7.

31 W. M. Hughes, *The Splendid Adventure: A Review of Empire Relations within and without the Commonwealth of Britannic Nations* (London: Ernest Benn, 1929), 99–102.

32 'Melbourne, Wednesday, 12th August 1914', *The Age* (Melbourne), 12 August 1914, 8.

Australian control over the lucrative Nauruan phosphate operation, established under German control by the British-owned Pacific Phosphate Company. Even pre-Federation ambitions to annex the New Hebrides, which from 1906 had been administered as a dual condominium of France and Britain, were revived.[33] Australia's wartime aspirations in New Guinea and Nauru were mirrored in South Africa's occupation of German South West Africa, and New Zealand's occupation of German Samoa.

But the Dominions' expansionist ambitions during World War I were at odds not only with the imperial government, but with the growing consensus at the international level against territorial aggrandisement in the war settlement.[34] In 1917, both US President Woodrow Wilson and British Prime Minister David Lloyd George declared their support for internationalised administration of the occupied territories as an alternative to post-war division among the Allied powers of the 'spoils of war'. By 1918, the concept of 'internationalised administration' had coalesced around two basic principles: 'open door' trade, and 'self-government' of subject populations – meaning, in Lloyd George's framing, 'government by the consent of the governed'.[35] Both principles were vigorously contested by Australia, which continued to insist on exclusive 'ownership' of 'German properties, interests and territories captured in the Pacific Islands' as 'paying back the cost of the war'.[36] South African General Jan Smuts' proposal for a mandate system, whereby individual powers would administer occupied German and Ottoman territories under the oversight of a new League of Nations, gathered momentum as the preferred compromise for post-war internationalisation.[37] Notably, Smuts maintained that German South West Africa and the German Pacific should be exempted from the mandate regime because they were 'inhabited by barbarians, who not only cannot possibly govern themselves, but to whom it would be impracticable to apply any ideas of political self-determination in the European sense'.[38]

33 Roger C. Thompson, 'The Labor Party and Australian Imperialism in the Pacific, 1901–1919' *Labour History* 23 (1972): 27–37, 28.
34 J. A. Hobson, *Towards International Government* (London: George Allen & Unwin, 1915); W. E. B. Du Bois, 'Manifesto of the Second Pan African Congress' *The Crisis* 23, no. 1 (1921): 5–10.
35 Prime Minister Lloyd George, speech delivered to Trades Union Congress, Caxton Hall, London, 5 January 1918.
36 'The Riches of Nauru', *Daily Post* (Hobart), 19 May 1917.
37 J. C. Smuts, *A League of Nations: A Practical Suggestion* (London: Hodder and Stoughton, 1918).
38 Ibid, 15.

In the months before the Paris Peace Conference, the irreconcilability of British with Australian plans for the occupied German Pacific territories fed Prime Minister Hughes's determination that Australia represent itself in peace settlement negotiations. In international law, Australia's self-representation at the Paris Conference marked its accession to sovereign independence, years before the 1926 Balfour Declaration, which is often identified in constitutional history as marking the 'independence' of Australia from Britain. At Versailles, Hughes doggedly pursued Australia's 'Pacific Ocean destiny', not only prosecuting the case for outright annexation of New Guinea and Nauru, but vigorously contesting Japan's proposal that the covenant of the new League include a statement of racial equality.[39] The Australian delegation also contested Japan's insistence that League Members be free to trade on equal terms in all internationalised territories. Conflict between Australia and Japan over regulation of post-war Pacific trade was more than academic. The Marshall and Caroline Islands, former German territories north of the equator, were earmarked for Japanese mandatory control, effectively creating a de facto border between territory controlled respectively by Australia and Japan. The diplomatic battle over the racial equality clause and open door trade in the former German Pacific, therefore, reflected deeper tensions over the construction of 'the Pacific' itself as a historical, geopolitical and anthropological space in the aftermath of world war.[40]

The compromise reached over post-war administration of the occupied territories was awkward.[41] The Covenant of the League of Nations provided for a tiered system of A, B, and C Mandates to be overseen by a new Permanent Mandates Commission, comprised primarily of ex-colonial and imperial administrators.[42] The A Mandates comprised the former Ottoman territories in the Middle East, and the B Mandates, most of the former German territories in Africa. The C Mandates comprised South West Africa and the German Pacific territories, including German New Guinea, Nauru, Western Samoa, and the Marshall and Caroline Islands. This tripartite classification was justified on the basis of a linear teleology of civilisational

39 Naoko Shimazu, *Japan, Race and Equality: The Racial Equality Proposal of 1919* (London and New York: Routledge, 1998).
40 Alison Bashford, 'The Pacific Ocean', in David Armitage, Alison Bashford and Sujit Sivasundaram (eds), *Oceanic Histories* (Cambridge: Cambridge University Press, 2018), 63–4.
41 Covenant of the League of Nations, Article 22.
42 Susan Pedersen, *The Guardians: The League of Nations and the Crisis of Empire* (Oxford: Oxford University Press, 2015).

development, but clearly reflected a pragmatic bargain struck between negotiating powers. According to the Covenant of the League, Mandatory Powers of C Mandates were obliged to carry out a 'sacred trust of civilisation' by furthering the 'well-being and development' of 'native populations'. This paternalist principle provided scant guarantee for advancement of local self-determination.[43] C Mandates were 'to be administered as part of the territory of the Mandatory Power' and exempted from open door trade requirements, which left Mandatory Powers with significant latitude to exercise executive control and economic monopolisation, with little basis for legal contest.[44]

The C Mandates of New Guinea and Nauru were conferred on the British Empire and, in 1920, Australia was appointed as administering authority of both. However, the imperial government and New Zealand resisted Australia's attempt to monopolise Nauruan phosphate. As the mandate system was negotiated in Paris, Britain, Australia and New Zealand secretly brokered the Nauru Island Agreement, instituting a tripartite monopoly over Nauruan phosphate, to be overseen by the new British Phosphate Commission (BPC).[45] The BPC acquired all of the Pacific Phosphate Company's assets, including its phosphate operation on Ocean Island, or Banaba, in the British protectorate of the Gilbert and Ellice Islands.[46] The BPC, which consisted of three commissioners appointed by the British, Australian and New Zealand governments, was granted exclusive control over all matters pertaining to the Nauruan phosphate operation, leaving the Australian administrator of Nauru to govern the local population.

The Commonwealth developed a professional bureaucracy of territorial administration in the interwar period. This growing field of public sector expertise drew on both the 'science of colonial administration' taught in British universities, and Australia's own experience with the Aborigines Protection Boards.[47] As Australia developed its mandatory administration of Nauru and New Guinea, which included annual reporting to the League of

43 Gerrit W. Gong, *The Standard of 'Civilization' in International Society* (Oxford: Clarendon Press, 1984); Ntina Tzouvala, 'Civilization', in Jean d'Aspremont and Sahib Singh (eds), *Concepts for International Law: Contributions to Disciplinary Thought* (Cheltenham: Edward Elgar, 2018), 83–104.

44 Luther Harris Evans, 'Are "C" Mandates Veiled Annexations?' *Southwestern Political and Social Science Quarterly* 7 (1927): 381–400.

45 Nauru Island Agreement Act 1919 (Cth).

46 Maslyn Williams and Barrie Macdonald, *The Phosphateers: A History of the British Phosphate Commissioners* (Melbourne: Melbourne University Press, 1985); Katerina Martina Teaiwa, *Consuming Ocean Island: Stories of People and Phosphate from Banaba* (Bloomington, IN: Indiana University Press, 2014).

47 J. D. Legge, *Australian Colonial Policy: A Survey of Native Administration and European Development in Papua* (Sydney: Angus and Robertson, 1956).

Nations, the bureaucracy of the Australian Territory of Papua was significantly expanded, with a view to the eventual merging of Papua with mandatory New Guinea.[48] Sir Hubert Murray, the long-serving Lieutenant Governor and Chief Judicial Officer of Papua, exercised sweeping executive powers within the territory and advocated a paternalist, anthropology-led approach to the 'inevitable' extinction of native custom and culture.[49]

The question of native status was a central theme in the law of territorial administration. The Commonwealth adopted different approaches in the mandates awarded by the League of Nations and in territories already annexed to Australia. In New Guinea and Nauru, the existence of international mandatory obligations with respect to native well-being and development required the formalisation of 'native' status, which had been unevenly defined under German protectorate law.[50] In stark contrast to the legal position within Australian sovereign territory, prior native land ownership was recognised in the Mandates of New Guinea and Nauru, as had been the practice under German rule. But beyond this basic foundation, Australian administrators exercised almost total executive power to define the rights and freedoms of Indigenous peoples in New Guinea and Nauru, from health, education, immigration and labour regulation to land leasing and quarantining of royalties in trust. The territory of Papua retained its own pre-war regime of native law. Although Papua was formally regarded as Australian territory and Papuans as British subjects, the Australian administration retained regulations that had been introduced by the former British protectorate to restrict Papuan movement, primarily as a labour control measure.[51]

As Australia, Japan and New Zealand joined the European empires in assuming control over external territories, a patchwork of colonial, imperial and international jurisdictions produced a volatile cartography of imperial tensions across the region. The Dutch colony of Irian Jaya bordered the Australian territory of Papua and the New Guinea Mandate. The Nauru Mandate bordered Britain's continued administration of the Gilbert and

48 Patricia O'Brien, 'Remaking Australia's Colonial Culture? White Australia and its Papuan Frontier 1901–1940' *Australian Historical Studies* 40 (2009): 96–112.

49 Sir Hubert Murray, *Papua of Today, Or, An Australian Colony in the Making* (London: P. S. King & Son Ltd, 1925), 210–51.

50 Stewart Firth, 'Colonial Administration and the Invention of the Native', in Donald Denoon with Stewart Firth, Jocelyn Linnekin and Karen Nero (eds), *Cambridge History of the Pacific Islanders* (Cambridge: Cambridge University Press, 2008), 254–88.

51 Pacific Island Labourers Act 1906 (Cth). Peter M. McDermott, 'Australian Citizenship and the Independence of Papua New Guinea' *University of New South Wales Law Journal* 32, no. 1 (2009): 50–74.

Ellice Islands (now Kiribati) as a colonial protectorate.[52] To the north of the equator, Japan's assumption of the Pacific Islands Mandate produced a border between Japan and Hawai'i, the latter annexed by the United States in 1898. Imperial Japan's discontent with Australia's rejection of racial equality and open door trade requirements in the C Mandates continued to escalate. Within Australia, older Monroeist sentiment took on an anti-Japanese inflection, which escalated after Japan's withdrawal from the League in 1933.[53]

The Australian Mandates of New Guinea and Nauru and the Japanese Pacific Islands Mandate proved critical to the geography of conflict in the Pacific during World War II; and as Bashford notes, it 'was the Pacific War that globalised the second "world" war'.[54] Japan attacked Rabaul in New Guinea in 1941 and Nauru in 1942, following a German raid on Nauru in 1941. Australian civil administrators withdrew from both mandated territories in 1942.[55] Because of its central Pacific location, Nauru became an important strategic point in Japan's regional offensive. By 1944, Japanese soldiers outnumbered Nauruans on the island, and over half the Nauruan population was interned on Chuuk Atoll in the Marshall Islands, under extreme conditions of starvation and deprivation, many never to return.[56] Between 1942 and 1944, New Guinea became a front in the Pacific war, disrupting an already uneven landscape of colonial administration. Japan established its military base on Manus Island, in the Admiralty Islands in northern New Guinea. The Australia New Guinea Administrative Unit (ANGAU) was established in Port Moresby to coordinate Australian activity in Papua and New Guinea, including native policing and labour recruiting, effectively erasing the distinction between New Guinea as an international mandate and Papua as an annexed territory.[57] Across both regions, ANGAU co-ordinated indentured Indigenous labour to serve the ANZAC forces. According to anthropologist W. E. H. Stanner, the 'natives . . . rendered the Allied cause most excellent war service' despite 'severe' 'turnover of labour' and 'sickness and disease'.[58]

52 Doug Munro and Stewart Firth, 'Towards Colonial Protectorates: The Case of the Gilbert and Ellice Islands' *Australian Journal of Politics and History* 32 (1986): 63–71.
53 Merze Tate, 'Australasian Monroe Doctrine' *Political Science Quarterly* 76 (1961): 264–84.
54 Bashford, 'The Pacific Ocean', 82.
55 Stewart Firth, 'The War in the Pacific', in Denoon et al. (eds), *Cambridge History of the Pacific Islanders*, 294–5.
56 Yuki Tanaka, 'Japanese Atrocities on Nauru during the Pacific War: The Murder of Australians, The Massacre of Lepers and the Ethnocide of Nauruans' *The Asia-Pacific Journal* 4 (2010): 1–19.
57 W. E. H. Stanner, 'New Guinea under War Conditions' *International Affairs* 20, no. 4 (1944): 481–94.
58 Ibid, 488.

From Post-war Trusteeship to Political Independence and Neo-imperialism

World War II precipitated decolonisation in much of Asia and Africa, beginning with the Proclamation of Indonesian Independence in 1945. The global decolonisation movements placed new pressures on Australia's Pacific empire, conflicting directly with Australia's post-war foreign policy of 'exert[ing] dominant political influence in the area with a view to maintaining Australian security behind a peripheral screen of islands'.[59] Australia retained administrative control of Nauru and New Guinea under the new United Nations trusteeship system, but the UN Charter identified 'self-government or independence' as a goal of trusteeship, conflicting directly with Australia's paternalist attitudes towards Indigenous peoples.[60] It also expanded on the legal obligations owed by 'trustees' with respect to political and economic preparation of local populations for independence, and increased the capacity of New Guinean and Nauruan peoples to make direct representations to the UN Trusteeship Council, which included a growing cohort of decolonising and anti-imperial states.

The Commonwealth had anticipated the weakening of its executive powers in New Guinea and Nauru during the war by creating the new Department of External Territories in 1941. The new department amalgamated Australia's administration of Papua and Norfolk Island with that of New Guinea and Nauru. H. V. Evatt, then Minister for External Affairs and an active participant in negotiations over the structure of the new United Nations, was instrumental in reframing Australia's regional ambitions as consonant with international post-war norms.[61] He promoted a major role for Australia in Pacific reconstruction, and his ideas informed the Australia–New Zealand Agreement (or 'Canberra Pact') of 1944.[62] Against the emergence of US dominance, the Canberra Pact 'demanded an ANZAC voice in peace in the Pacific' and declared a defensive zone from the Cocos to the Cook Islands.[63] Australian administrators forestalled the question of

59 David Goldsworthy, 'British Territories and Australian Mini-imperialism in the 1950s' *Australian Journal of Politics and History* 41 (1995): 356–72.

60 Norman Harper and David Sissons, *Australia and the United Nations* (New York: Manhattan Publishing Co, 1959), 180–215.

61 Jon Piccini, *Human Rights in Twentieth-century Australia* (Cambridge: Cambridge University Press, 2019).

62 Australia–New Zealand Agreement, Canberra, 21 January 1944.

63 W. David McIntyre, 'Australia, New Zealand, and the Pacific Islands', in Judith Brown (ed.), *The Oxford History of the British Empire,* Volume IV: the Twentieth Century (Oxford: Oxford University Press, 1999), 667–92.

decolonisation of Australia's external territories by shifting from outright denial of independence, as had been routine during the mandate period, towards asserting the slow pace of native 'development'. The UN Trusteeship Council itself accepted Australia's arguments that independence was 'unsuitable' for the people of Papua New Guinea and Nauru well into the early 1960s, citing an 'absence' of Indigenous political organisation, and 'low' levels of 'political advancement' towards the European model of sovereign statehood.[64]

On this basis, Australia consolidated its law and practice of territorial administration as a key dimension of Australian post-war statecraft and public sector expertise.[65] The Australian School of Pacific Administration (ASOPA) was formed in 1945, with a curriculum designed in conjunction with the Anthropology Department at the University of Sydney.[66] John Kerr, a prominent barrister and judge who later served as Governor General, was appointed as the school's first Principal, training public servants for service not only in Papua, New Guinea and Nauru, but also in the Northern Territory. The Papua and New Guinea Act 1949 provided for joint administration of the two territories, but significant legal distinctions remained. Australia's trusteeship obligations – including the obligation to promote political independence – applied only to New Guinea. Under the Australian Nationality and Citizenship Act 1948, Papuans were considered Australian citizens, while New Guineans – and Nauruans – were not.[67] As Charles Rowley, Principal of ASOPA from 1950–64, observed: by the mid-1960s a 'sixth of the people who owe allegiance to the Commonwealth of Australia are native-born inhabitants of the Territory of Papua and New Guinea'.[68] But Papuans' Australian citizenship remained heavily qualified: they had to seek special permission to visit the continent and could stay for a maximum of three months.[69]

64 United Nations Visiting Mission to Trust Territories in the Pacific, *Report on New Guinea*, Trusteeship Council Official Records: Twelfth Session, 1953, Supplement 4, 4–5; United Nations Visiting Mission to Trust Territories in the Pacific, *Report on Nauru*, UN Trusteeship Council Official Records, 12th session, UN Doc T/1054 (26 May 1953), 2.

65 Harper and Sissons, *Australia and the United Nations*, 180–215.

66 H. I. Hogbin and C. Wedgwood, 'Local Groupings in Melanesia' *Oceania* XXIII (1953). I. C. Campbell, 'The ASOPA Controversy: A Pivot of Australian Policy for Papua and New Guinea, 1945–49' *Journal of Pacific History* 35 (2000): 83–100.

67 McDermott, 'Australian Citizenship'.

68 C. D. Rowley, *The New Guinean Villager: A Retrospect from 1964* (Melbourne: Cheshire Publishing, 1972), 11.

69 Donald Denoon, *A Trial Separation: Australia and the Decolonisation of Papua New Guinea* (Canberra: ANU E-Press, 2012), 9.

In 1951, the Department of External Territories was amalgamated with the Department of the Interior, forming the new Department of Territories under Director Paul Hasluck. Hasluck's 'positive Australianism' served the commitments of the 1944 Canberra Pact, while claiming to meet legal responsibilities of trusteeship.[70] As Australia repositioned itself as the agent of modernisation in the Pacific, strong ideological convergences emerged over the 1950s between the Commonwealth's assimilationist policies regarding Aboriginal and Torres Strait Islander peoples and its developmentalist policies regarding 'native populations' in New Guinea and Nauru.[71] The professionalisation of territorial administration occurred in close relationship with the promotion of Australian commercial investment in the territories, largely in natural resource exploitation and primary industry. Hasluck emphasised agrarian development as a first step in political development, protecting the rights of small land holders and supporting the growth of a coffee industry in the Papua New Guinean Highlands, while opposing the expansion of European-run large-scale plantations. Development projects in villages were undertaken, he claimed, always with the 'friendly co-operation of the local people'.[72]

Yet there was a concealed violence in this liberal developmentalist vision. The '*taim kiap*', or extension of liberal imperial rule in the 1950s and 1960s through the appointment of patrol officers in the Western Province, entailed the supplanting of local legal orders and suppression of Indigenous violence, such as regional warfare and cannibalism, by colonial state law. At times entire villages were punished for continuing their own practices. As one Faiwolmin man from the Western Province recalled, when 'the Europeans came . . . they were really rough. We were frightened of them. They came with a gun and they shot a pig and . . . they destroyed our garden'.[73] But perhaps most effective was the placement of some children in district boarding schools where they were taught English, enabling these students to access roles in the administration while severing their ties to their mothers and the transmission of cultural knowledge in their own communities.

70 Scott MacWilliam, 'Anti-Conservatism: Paul Hasluck and Liberal Development in Papua New Guinea' *Australian Journal of Politics and History* 65, no. 1 (2019): 83–99.

71 Jane Landman, 'Visualising the Subject of Development: 1950s Government Film-making in the Territories of Papua and New Guinea' *Journal of Pacific History* 45 (2010): 71–88.

72 Paul Hasluck, *A Time for Building: Australian Administration in Papua and New Guinea 1951–1963* (Melbourne: Melbourne University Press, 1976), 79.

73 Quoted in Nicole Polier, '"When Australia was the Big Name for Papua New Guinea": The Colonial Constitution of Fiaiwolmin Subjects' *Journal of Historical Sociology* 8 (1995): 257–77.

The post-war shift towards developmentalist justifications for prolonged Australian control of its trust territories was met with growing Indigenous resistance. In parts of Papua New Guinea, the war had impressed on local people a new sense of the world and of their place in it, fostering expectations of racial and civic equality. As Peter Simongun of Wewak in the East Sepik pointed out, 'Yes, we have helped you in this war, now we are like cousins, like brothers. We too have won the war. Now whatever knowledge, whatever ideas you have, you can give them to us. Before all the things we did, you gaoled us, and you fined us all the time. But now. What now?'[74] On Manus Island, reclaimed by Australia after Japanese abandonment of the military base, activist Paliau Maloat sought political self-determination. The Paliau movement resisted colonial government and reformed village life by removing social divisions and insisting that all money should be pooled and land held in common.[75] In the early 1960s, Paliau visited the United States under the sponsorship of the United Nations, and was elected to the first House of Assembly in 1964 representing Manus. A co-founder of the Papua and New Guinea Union ('Pangu') Parti, he continued to hold political power into the 1970s.

The Department of Territories responded to the Paliau movement by implementing 'native' government structures, designed by Australian administration and overwhelmingly advisory in nature. The Department of Territories introduced local councils in Papua and New Guinea, and in Nauru.[76] The Papua and New Guinea Act 1949 created a single Legislative Council for both territories, with 'three elected European members and three executive-nominated native members'.[77] It also created 'Advisory Councils for Native Matters', appointed directly by the Australian Administrator and with no legislative or executive powers.[78] In Nauru, the ad hoc 'Council of Chiefs', initially created under German rule in the late nineteenth century, was renamed the Nauru Local Government Council in 1951, but granted no executive power.[79]

74 Simongun quoted in John Dademo Waiko, *A Short History of Papua New Guinea* (Melbourne: Oxford University Press, 1993), 124.
75 Ton Otto, 'The Paliau Movement in Manus and the Objectification of Tradition' *History and Anthropology* 5 (1992): 427–54.
76 Hasluck, *A Time for Building*, chapter 15.
77 Papua and New Guinea Act 1949 (Cth), ss 35–53; Ian Grosart, 'Native Members in the Legislative Council of the Territory of Papua and New Guinea 1951–1963' *Journal of Pacific History* 1 (1966): 147–64.
78 Papua and New Guinea Act 1949 (Cth), ss 25–9.
79 Nauru Local Government Council Ordinance No. 2 of 1951.

Over the 1950s and 1960s, as self-determination evolved from a rhetorical ideal of international relations towards a legally definable right in international law, Australia's strategy of deferring independence became increasingly untenable.[80] Encouraged by global decolonisation movements, New Guinean and Nauruan advocates made increasing use of native council structures as sites of local organisation and as avenues onto the international platform provided by the UN Trusteeship Council. In the 1950s, under the leadership of Head Chief Hammer DeRoburt, the Nauru Local Government Council (NLGC) contested Australia's justifications for continued legal and political authority in Nauru, including the BPC's monopolisation of Nauruan phosphate and the calculation of phosphate royalties on a paternalist 'needs-based' calculation.[81] Following the UN General Assembly's 1960 Declaration on the Granting of Independence to Colonial peoples, the Trusteeship Council changed its position on Nauru and Papua New Guinea, and Soviet and African delegates on the Council pressured Australia to hasten plans for independence.[82] As Australia's long-desired dream of a formal empire in the South Pacific dissolved in the political upheavals of the 1960s, the Department of Territories changed its rhetorical strategy again, away from using development as a means of deferring independence and towards entrenching 'informal' modes of economic and cultural dominance that could be retained as formal administrative control was ceded.[83]

Nauru's transition to political independence was negotiated between 1965 and 1968 in the 'Nauru Talks' between the Department of Territories and the NLGC. By 1965, the BPC had strip-mined one-third of Nauru's land mass, feeding cost-price superphosphate into the agricultural sectors of Australia, New Zealand and the United Kingdom. The Nauru Talks focused on two main issues in the transition to independence: ownership of the phosphate operation, which the BPC sought to retain; and liability for rehabilitation of mined-out land, which Australia sought to resist.[84] The Department of Territories, led by Charles Barnes, attempted to solve both problems by proposing that the entire Nauruan population be resettled on an island within

80 U. O. Umozurike, *Self-Determination in International Law* (Hamden, CT: Archon Books, 1972).

81 Letter from the Nauru Local Government Council to the British Phosphate Commissioners dated 30 May 1957, reproduced in Barrie Macdonald, *In Pursuit of the Sacred Trust: Trusteeship and Independence in Nauru* (New Zealand: New Zealand Institute of International Affairs, 1988), 40.

82 *Declaration on the Granting of Independence to Colonial Countries and Peoples*, UN Doc A/RES/1514(XV) (14 December 1960).

83 Goldsworthy, 'British Territories and Australian Mini-imperialism'.

84 Nancy Viviani, *Nauru: Phosphate and Political Progress* (Canberra: ANU Press, 1970).

Queensland's territorial waters under an attenuated form of 'self-government' as a municipal council, leaving the island itself to the BPC.[85] The Nauruan delegation, led by Hammer DeRoburt, rejected Australia's resettlement proposal.

The parties eventually agreed that the Nauruan people would form a republic on Nauru, but would be required to buy out the BPC's assets, and guarantee continued phosphate supply to the tripartite governments.[86] The UN Trusteeship Council approved the proposed independence agreement in 1967. Australia argued that the agreement included an implied indemnity against any Nauruan claims for compensation for environmental and economic exploitation during the mandate and trusteeship periods.[87] Hammer DeRoburt rejected that claim, but insisted that the liability issue should not delay independence.[88] The Republic of Nauru gained independence in January 1968.[89] The Constitution of the new republic was drafted by Professor James Wight Davidson, a New Zealand-born, Cambridge-trained colonial historian appointed as inaugural Professor of Pacific History at the Australian National University in 1950.[90]

By contrast, the independence of Papua New Guinea remained uncertain into the late 1960s. Over the 1950s and 1960s, numerous proposals for continued Australian control circulated, including a proposition from a Papua New Guinean delegation that the eastern half of the island become the 'seventh state' of the Commonwealth. This was unthinkable to those in the Australian government who held firm to the ideology of a White Australia.[91] In 1958, Sir John Kerr had even proposed that if direct annexation of Papua and New Guinea was not possible, Australia should campaign for a new Dominion of its own – the 'Federation of Melanesia', incorporating Papua, New Guinea and Dutch New Guinea.[92] That proposal was not supported by Hasluck, as it implied acceptance of an enforceable right of self-determination in international law, a position Australia had actively sought to

85 Ibid, 143–7. 86 Nauru Independence Act 1967 (Cth).

87 United Nations Trusteeship Council, Official Records, 13th special session, 1323rd meeting (22 November 1967), 4.

88 Nancy Viviani, 'Nauru Phosphate Negotiations' *Journal of Pacific History* 3 (1968): 151–4.

89 J. W. Davidson, 'The Republic of Nauru' *Journal of Pacific History* 3 (1968): 145–50.

90 J. W. Davidson, 'The Decolonisation of Oceania' *Journal of Pacific History* 6 (1971): 133–50, 134; J. W. Davidson, 'Understanding Pacific History: The Participant as Historian', in Peter Munz (ed.), *The Feel of Truth: Essays in New Zealand and Pacific History* (Wellington: A. H. & A. W. Reed, 1969), 25–40.

91 Denoon, *A Trial Separation*, 4.

92 Hank Nelson, 'Liberation: the End of Australian Rule in Papua New Guinea' *Journal of Pacific History* 35 (2000): 269–80, 271.

resist.[93] It also risked alienating Indonesia, which regarded itself both as an exemplar of anti-imperialism and the rightful successor to Dutch rule, including in West Papua. Throughout the 1960s and 1970s, the protection of Australian mining and agricultural interests in Papua New Guinea remained paramount in the approaches of the Department of Territories and the Department of External Affairs. This meant ignoring the desires of a growing independence movement in Bougainville, the site of the Panguna copper mine, leading to a bitter decade-long civil war after Papua New Guinea achieved independence in 1975 and took control of the island.[94] As with Nauru, pressure from the UN Trusteeship Council accelerated the trajectory of New Guinean independence, as did the staunch anti-imperial views of then Labor leader, Gough Whitlam, who proclaimed that 'Australia was never truly free until Papua New Guinea became free'.[95] Whitlam's visit to Papua New Guinea in 1969 helped reverse the Hasluckian policy of prioritising 'leisurely' economic development over political independence. Following Nauruan independence, the Department of Territories focused on preparing a roadmap for speeding up independence in Papua New Guinea.

When Whitlam's Labor Party formed government in 1972, it upended the policy landscape of the Department of Territories, seeking Aboriginal land rights in the Northern Territory and decolonisation for Papua New Guinea. Michael Somare, then leader of the Pangu Parti, insisted that Papua New Guinean priorities lead the process, and emphasised the need to consult communities first. Somare and his team, suspicious that 'Australia would make all its constitutional decisions for it and continue to set the pace', wanted a 'home grown' Papua New Guinean Constitution, as opposed to an Australian-drafted version.[96] A constitutional Planning Committee was appointed to lead the consultation process across the country and, in 1975, a Law Reform Commission (LRC) was also created.[97] Of central concern to many New Guineans was the question of dual citizenship, which the

93 Victor Kattan, '"There Was an Elephant in the Court Room": Reflections on the Role of Judge Sir Percy Spender (1897–1985) in the South West Africa Cases (1960–1966) after Half a Century' *Leiden Journal of International Law* 31 (2018): 147–70.

94 Donald Denoon, *Getting under the Skin: The Bougainville Copper Agreement and the Creation of the Panguna Mine* (Melbourne: Melbourne University Press, 2000).

95 Denoon, *A Trial Separation*, 1.

96 Michael Somare quoted in Jonathan Ritchie, 'From the Grassroots: Bernard Narokobi and the Making of Papua New Guinea's Constitution' *The Journal of Pacific History* 55 (2020): 235–54, 237. See also Bernard Narokobi, *The Melanesian Way* (Boroko, Papua New Guinea: Institute of Papua New Guinea Studies; Suva, Fiji: Institute of Pacific Studies, University of the South Pacific, 1983).

97 Denoon, *A Trial Separation*, 112–13.

Constitution ultimately disallowed, in large part because of the second-class Australian citizenship previously awarded to colonial subjects. The LRC, headed by Bernard Narokobi, a recent graduate of the University of Sydney's law faculty, was tasked with not only consolidating but also decolonising the Papua New Guinean legal code, which included overturning colonial codes and their assumptions regarding sorcery and sexuality, particularly adultery.[98] However, as critics pointed out at the time, no women were appointed to decision-making roles in either organisation.[99]

Conclusion: The Legacies and Continuities of Australia as Empire

The history of Australian empire in the Pacific has produced complex relations of political, economic and cultural domination and resistance that defy contemporary distinctions of territory and citizenship. Statist accounts of Australian legal history have been significantly enriched by scholarship tracing the shifting dynamics of legal and political power within the British Empire, the shifting articulations of Australia's attempts at regional self-assertion, and most importantly, the histories of Indigenous and Islander engagement and resistance to European presumptions to rule.[100] This scholarship suggests that, far from being alternative modes of hierarchical global ordering, the imperial, the international and the national are intersecting projects that require ongoing renewal against the existence of other modes of community, and other modes of history.

Through constructions of territory and citizenship, and through the authorisation and regulation of movement across those foundational jurisdictional thresholds, law has been an indispensable tool of Australian empire, and continues to be so. The legacies of Australia's imperial aspirations remain clear, even as the vocabulary and techniques of empire continue to shift. The old imperial presumptions – to a regional 'screen of islands', to racial and cultural superiority, and to resource dominance – continue to find new expression. Contemporary examples include Australia's use of Nauru,

98 Alex Golub, 'Legislating the Melanesian Way: Bernard Narokobi and the Law Reform Commission of Papua New Guinea' *The Journal of Pacific History* 55 (2020): 255–73.

99 Ibid, 266–7.

100 Tracey Banivanua Mar, *Decolonisation and the Pacific: Indigenous Globalisation and the Ends of Empire* (Cambridge: Cambridge University Press, 2016); Miranda Johnson, *The Land Is Our History: Indigeneity, Law and the Settler State* (New York: Oxford University Press, 2016).

Manus Island and Christmas Island as sites for the offshore detention of asylum seekers; and its aggressive pursuit of oil and gas resources in the Timor Sea.[101] At the same time, Australia's tradition of territorial administration continues through the Commonwealth's involvement in governance and development throughout the Pacific, in public service secondments, technical assistance, and aid programs, in Papua New Guinea and Nauru, and as well as in Timor Leste, the Solomon Islands and Vanuatu.

The old imaginary of 'adjacent islands' also continues to shift and evolve, as does the formal cartography of administered territories, internal and external to Australian sovereign jurisdiction. Australian-administered islands now include Norfolk Island, Ashmore and Cartier Islands, Christmas Island and the Cocos (Keeling) Islands, the Coral Sea Islands (off the Great Barrier Reef) and Heard and Macdonald Islands. Territories include the Australian Antarctic Territory, as well as the Australian Capital Territory and Northern Territory, the latter two now classed as 'self-governing' with the Commonwealth providing strategic governance advice. Legacies of imperial rule continue to define these spaces, and the political imaginations that construct and resist them. Considering Australia's legal history as both product and agent of empire complicates the nationalising impulse, and entangles the country in its region – where, of course, it has always been.

101 Anthea Vogl, 'Over the Borderline: A Critical Inquiry into the Geography of Territorial Excision and the Securitisation of the Australian Border' *UNSW Law Journal* 38 (2015): 114–45; Katerina Teaiwa, 'Ruining Pacific Islands: Australia's Phosphate Imperialism' *Australian Historical Studies* 46 (2015): 374–91; *Arbitration under the Timor Sea Treaty (Timor-Leste v Australia)* (Permanent Court of Arbitration, Case 2015–42); *Timor-Leste v Australia (Questions Relating to the Seizure and Detention of Certain Documents and Data)*, International Court of Justice, Summary of Judgments and Orders (2014); Cait Storr, *International Status in the Shadow of Empire: Nauru and the Histories of International Law* (Cambridge: Cambridge University Press, 2020).

12

Australia and the World

COEL KIRKBY

The state we now call Australia emerged through successive worlds. The old worlds did not disappear, but persist to this day. From time to time their unresolved legal contradictions burst into the present to pose radical challenges to the dominant legal order in the continent. Older legal histories tell the story of Australia and the world as a coming-of-age tale, as a penal colony grew into a self-governing dominion and finally a sovereign state. But beginning this story 60,000 years earlier unsettles the unspoken assumptions of the settler state's natal narrative. The First Fleet invaded a continent of nations bound by a thick web of international legal relations. The British colonies and their successor never resolved their relationship with these First Nations. This unfinished business of the past continues to shape the legal relationships between Australia and a world that now consists of a great multiplicity of nations, states and international bodies within and beyond its jurisdiction.

Reflecting on the country's relationship with international law, James Crawford, Australia's most prominent international lawyer, wrote that 'Australia has always, despite the historical remoteness from international affairs, manifested its support for a global rules-based order'.[1] Yet a historical turn in international legal scholarship has recovered the origins of this global order in the expansion and domination of European empires.[2] Indigenous

1 J. Crawford and R. Cameron, 'International Law in Australia Revisited' *Adelaide Law Review* 40 (2019): 199.

2 A. Anghie, *Imperialism, Sovereignty, and the Making of International Law* (Cambridge: Cambridge University Press, 2007); L. Benton, *Law and Colonial Cultures: Legal Regimes in World History, 1400–1900* (Cambridge: Cambridge University Press, 2002); M. Koskenniemi, *The Gentle Civilizer of Nations: The Rise and Fall of International Law, 1870–1960* (Cambridge: Cambridge University Press, 2002). The international turn might be traced even earlier to the work of the Lumbee scholar, R. A. Williams, *The American Indian in Western Legal Thought: The Discourses of Conquest* (Oxford: Oxford University Press, 1990).

scholars also remind us that First Nations' legal orders governed international relations for millennia before this hegemonic imposition.[3] This chapter takes up this new scholarship to retell the legal history of Australia through three successive worlds. The first world is the ancient history and unfinished business of international relationships between First Nations, and between them and the settler state. The second world is the British Empire, a global state that aimed to impose a single legal order over its imperial jurisdictions. The third world is the international system of sovereign states that covers the globe today. If Australians have pursued a 'rules-based order', this pursuit has always reflected their own conflicting desires for the liberation and domination of neighbouring peoples, lands and seas.

Dreaming the International

The first humans alighted on this island continent at least 60,000 years ago. They did not arrive as individuals, but as peoples of one kind or another. Soon these peoples would occupy the entire continent from its tropical shores to its Antarctic coasts. These many millennia have a deep history of relations among human polities governed by what we might call an 'international' law. First Nations' international laws governed the movement of people through country, marriage between people, trade and sharing resources, and interpersonal violence. This history is not merely of antiquarian or archaeological interest: these laws survive in the present promising a radical alternative for a legal structure of just relations between the different nations occupying the continent.

Our historical knowledge of international law comes from three main sources, often complimentary though sometimes conflicting. The first source is the *Nura* (Dharug), *Daramoolen* (Ngunnawal), *Ngarrankarni* (Gija), *Tjukurpa* (Pitjantjatjara) and other 'Dreamings' (as evocatively, if misleadingly, translated into the English language). Dreamings connect deep time and the present, and establish lawful relationships through oral stories as well as songs, dances, painting and other practices. Christine Black, a Kombumerri and Munaljahalai scholar, reminds us that the laws extended not only beyond the borders of territory, but also beyond those of life and death.[4] One vital function of these

3 C. Black, *The Land Is the Source of the Law: A Dialogic Encounter with Indigenous Jurisprudence* (London: Routledge, 2011); C. Jones, *New Treaty, New Tradition: Reconciling New Zealand and Maori Law* (Vancouver: UBC Press, 2016); J. Borrows, *Freedom and Indigenous Constitutionalism* (Toronto: University of Toronto Press, 2016).

4 Black, *The Land*; C. Black, *A Mosaic of Indigenous Legal Thought: Legendary Tales and Other Writings* (London: Routledge, 2016).

laws was to delimit the nature and boundaries of belonging, and to regulate and contest right relations with those beyond one's own people. The laws also created certain relationships between individuals or groups and specific sites or species on country. Dreamings thus wove a thick web of lawful relations – the 'songlines' that criss-crossed the continent – binding people to each other and their country.[5]

The second source for the deep history of international relations on the continent comes from the modern scientific disciplines of archaeology, anthropology and linguistics.[6] Whereas Dreamings bound the present to the past and future, new scientific discourses of geological and evolutionary time generate a much longer and differentiated temporal scale for planetary and human history. Not only were First Nations present in the continent tens of thousands of years earlier than settler scientists had presumed, but these nations evolved into a great diversity of political forms. The archaeological evidence of these international relationships survives in the artefacts of material goods, such as stone and seeds, that were traded along extensive and extended routes connecting the continent and its peoples. Anthropological evidence also shows how these great chains of sharing between nations transmitted intellectual knowledge like songs, dances and stories. Far from a static world without history – as early British settlers had assumed – the island continent was humming with international exchanges that transformed the land and its people over tens of thousands of years.

The third source for international relations is the written records showing how First Nations tapped into global trading networks from China and Europe. By 1720 (and perhaps up to a century earlier) Makassan fishermen from Sulawesi arrived on the northern shores of the continent in search of *trepang* or sea cucumber.[7] They negotiated relationships of trade and seasonal production with First Nations as part of a larger trade network extending to the main *trepang* market in China. At the same time Portuguese, Dutch,

5 Gay'wu Group of Women, *Song Spirals: Sharing Women's Wisdom of Country through Songlines* (Crows Nest: Allen & Unwin, 2019).

6 B. Griffiths, *Deep Time Dreaming: Uncovering Ancient Australia* (Melbourne: Black Inc, 2018); A. McGrath and M. A. Jebb (eds), *Long History, Deep Time: Deeping Histories of Place* (Canberra: ANU Press, 2015); P. Veth and S. O'Connor, 'The Past 50,000 Years: An Archaeological View', in A. Bashford and S. Macintyre (eds), *The Cambridge History of Australia: Indigenous and Colonial Australia* (Cambridge: Cambridge University Press, 2013), 1: 17–42.

7 C. Macknight, '"The View from Marege": Australian Knowledge of Makassar and the Impact of the Trepang Industry Across Two Centuries' *Aboriginal History* 35 (2011): 121–43; C. Macknight, *The Voyage to Marege: Macassan Trepangers in Northern Australia* (Melbourne: Melbourne University Press, 1976).

French and British ships began to arrive on the continental coast. Like the Makassan trepangers, most aimed to trade with the First Nations they encountered. Unlike the Makassans, however, the British would soon come to stay.

Invasion, Empire, Dominion

The First Fleet invaded the lands of the Eora nation in 1788. The British arrived with the intention of establishing a new penal colony and pre-empting rival European claims to the continent. Yet the most remarkable event was one that did not happen. Saliha Belmessous reminds us that the British had made contemporary treaties with local peoples across the globe from Western Africa to Malaysia, and Madagascar to North America.[8] The glaring exception would be Port Jackson. While European powers claimed sovereignty by the rights of discovery, cession or conquest, their claims to property rights were secured from purchase through treaty. First Nations were deemed exceptional since in (most) British eyes they did not display any of the fundamental characteristics of European nations: commerce, cultivation or politics. The new settlement was thus an invasion without conquest, an ambivalent claim to dominion over a coast and, soon, a continent that ignored its ancient laws of international relations.

The unilateral British assertion of sovereignty imposed an imperial legal order on a continent.[9] Each new colony was ruled autocratically under a governor representing the Crown. Free men had some say in government through Legislative Councils, while convicts and women had no say at all. Australia's relations with the world were conducted exclusively by the governors, in regional matters, and the British government globally. The only real access to justice beyond the continent was through legal appeals to the United Kingdom. Lord Brougham championed the reform of colonial justice by creating the Judicial Committee of the Privy Council to hear the myriad forms of colonial appeals that had long been heard by various British courts and offices.[10] He aimed to solve the twin challenges

8 S. Belmessous, 'The Tradition of Treaty-Making in Australian History', in S. Belmessous (ed.), *Empire by Treaty: Negotiating European Expansion, 1600–1900* (Cambridge: Cambridge University Press, 2014), 186–213.

9 D. M. Schreuder, 'Empire: Australia and "Greater Britain", 1788–1901', in A. Bashford and S. Macintyre (eds), *The Cambridge History of Australia: Indigenous and Colonial Australia* (Cambridge: Cambridge University Press, 2013), 1: 511–34.

10 Judicial Committee Act 1833, 3 & 4 Will. 4 c 41; Judicial Committee Act 1844, 7 & 8 Vic. c 69.

of the rapidly expanding global empire, namely the difficulties of distance and difference. The difficulty of distance was whether British judges were capable of understanding and applying the many distinct legal jurisdictions within the overarching imperial legal order.[11] The difficulty of difference was the specific problem of how these judges could interpret and rule on the application of alien legal orders from Hindu law to African custom (importantly, no British judge ever applied or interpreted First Nations' laws).[12]

British domination was imperfect; and in its cracks grew new forms of non-state international legal relations. Lauren Benton and Lisa Ford show how the British imperial 'rage for order' in the early nineteenth century was driven in large part by local actors at the margins of empire.[13] In New South Wales, for instance, a 'coup' against Governor William Bligh in 1808 helped to establish constitutional limits on autocratic governance in British colonies.[14] New subaltern international relations also grew across imperial networks. Some First Nations moved from armed resistance to written petitions to assert their claims to country.[15] These petitions were often targeted to local colonial officials, but some addressed the imperial Crown directly. In 1846, for instance, the Flinders Island residents addressed Queen Victoria in a letter asserting their rights as subjects, specifically the right to remove any officials who treated them as 'slaves'.[16] Mission stations and reserves also became international sites composed of survivors from many different nations. Coranderrk grew into a nexus connecting and sustaining the Kulin nation and neighbouring nations across the colony and beyond.[17] The Pacific Islander peoples indentured on plantations and the 'lascar' crews on ships also created new connections to the Pacific and South Asia, as well as with

11 P. Mitchell, 'The Privy Council and the Difficulty of Distance' *Oxford Journal of Legal Studies* 36 (2016): 26–57.
12 B. Ibhawoh, *Imperial Justice: Africans in Empire's Court* (Oxford: Oxford University Press, 2013), 29–32.
13 L. Benton and L. Ford, *Rage for Order: The British Empire and the Origins of International Law, 1800–1850* (Cambridge: Cambridge University Press, 2016).
14 Ibid, 31–43.
15 A. Curthoys and J. Mitchell, '"Bring This Paper to the Good Governor": Aboriginal Petitioning in Britain's Australian Colonies', in S. Belmessous (ed.), *Native Claims: Indigenous Law Against Empire, 1500–1920* (Oxford: Oxford University Press 2012), 182–203; K. O'Brien, *Petitioning for Land: The Petitions of First Peoples of Modern British Colonies* (London: Bloomsbury Academic, 2019).
16 Curthoys and Mitchell, 'Bring This Paper', 186–7.
17 G. Nanni and A. James, *Coranderrk: We Will Show the Country* (Canberra: Aboriginal Studies Press, 2013); D. E. Barwick, *Rebellion at Coranderrk* (Canberra: Aboriginal History Inc, 1998).

local First Nations.[18] These subaltern networks mobilised bodies and ideas that would develop new challenges to the racial hegemony imposed first by the British legal order and then succeeding international legal orders.

The Imperial International

The Australian colonies burst across the continent through a series of booms and busts in the second half of the nineteenth century.[19] The accompanying demographic and territorial expansion that followed created a global 'Anglo-World' across the continent and, indeed, the world. While the Eureka Rebellion (among others) provoked British grants of responsible government for the colonial legislatures, most Australian settlers still saw themselves and their political future as British above all else.[20] Australian politicians began to imagine new ways to constitute their relations between themselves, the British Empire and the world. Yet they never imagined a future polity independent of global empire. This is obscured in later nationalist histories that retell this period as the now familiar story of visionary 'fathers' leading the fractured colonial Parliaments towards Federation in a single and ultimately independent nation. Here, the Whiggish drama is driven by a contrast between the new antipodean nationalists and the old colonial imperialists. Yet the reality was complicated by the fact that these men were always fervent imperialists who saw themselves as British above all else.[21]

In 1890 Henry Parkes, then premier of New South Wales, opened the Melbourne confederation conference of 1890 with a racialised declaration of imperial loyalty. 'The crimson thread of kinship', Parkes declared, 'runs through us all.'[22] All Australians, he continued, were 'Britons' who 'represent a race for the purposes of settling new colonies'. For Parkes and others, the union of the Australian colonies was thus only a step towards the ultimate

18 T. Banivanua Mar, 'Belonging to Country: Racialising Space and Resistance on Queensland's Transnational Margins, 1880–1900' *Australian Historical Studies* 43 (2012): 174–90; D. I. Salesa, *Racial Crossings: Race, Intermarriage, and the Victorian British Empire* (Oxford: Oxford University Press, 2011).

19 J. Belich, *Replenishing the Earth: The Settler Revolution and the Rise of the Anglo-World, 1783–1939* (Oxford: Oxford University Press, 2009).

20 A. Curthoys and J. Mitchell, 'The Advent of Self-Government, 1840s–90', in A. Bashford and S. Macintyre (eds), *The Cambridge History of Australia: Indigenous and Colonial Australia* (Cambridge: Cambridge University Press, 2013), I: 149–69.

21 H. Irving, *To Constitute a Nation: A Cultural History of Australia's Constitution* (Cambridge: Cambridge University Press, 1998); H. Irving, 'Making the Federal Commonwealth, 1890–1901', in A. Bashford and S. Macintyre (eds), *The Cambridge History of Australia: Indigenous and Colonial Australia* (Cambridge: Cambridge University Press, 2013), I: 242–66.

22 H. Parkes, *The Federal Government of Australasia: Speeches Delivered on Various Occasions (November, 1889–May, 1890)* (Sydney: Turner and Henderson, 1890), 75.

end of a British world state ruled by a single race united by the 'crimson thread' of their blood. In this new imperial discourse of 'Greater Britain', as Duncan Bell reminds us, 'the colonial empire was seen anew as a space for transformative moral and political action, for the shaping of a patriotic imperial citizenry, and for the salvation of the endangered "mother country"'.[23]

In these years the future Australian federation was not seen as a nascent nation so much as a growing part of an organic imperial whole. The pressing question was how the antipodean British were to take their place within an international legal order. Three years before Parkes's speech, delegates from the self-governing settler colonies arrived in London for the Golden Jubilee celebrating the fifty-year reign of Victoria – now self-consciously an imperial monarch recently styled the Queen of the United Kingdom of Great Britain and Ireland and Empress of India. The Jubilee was an 'imperial' spectacle that aimed to project an image to Britain and the world of its status as a global state and universal ideal. Not only did the British rule several hundred million subjects across the world, but they did so in the name of liberty and civilisation. The tension between this boastful vision and its brutal reality would drive legal developments in Australia and elsewhere well into the next century.

After the Jubilee the premiers met with Sir Henry Holland, Secretary of State for the Colonies, at the inaugural Colonial Conference to discuss the reconstitution of intra-imperial relations. After Queen Victoria's Diamond Jubilee a decade later, the new Colonial Secretary, Joseph Chamberlain, welcomed back the premiers with a vision of the imperial state as a maturing family. 'We are looking to the colonies as still children, but rapidly approaching manhood.'[24] This intra-imperial meeting became the Colonial (later imperial) Conference, a kind of imperial cabinet composed of the Colonial Secretary and the colonial premiers. These men had competing ideas about the Conference: some hoped it would be the first step in the constitution of a supra-national parliament to govern the British Empire and dominate the world.

But neither Chamberlain nor the Australian premiers saw the move towards colonial 'manhood' as inconsistent with greater imperial integration. Indeed, some imperial federalists believed that uniting the antipodean settler

23 D. Bell, *The Idea of Greater Britain: Empire and the Future of World Order, 1860–1900* (Princeton, NJ: Princeton University Press, 2007), 9.

24 Quoted in J. C. Mitcham, *Race and Imperial Defence in the British World, 1870–1914* (Cambridge: Cambridge University Press, 2016), 64.

colonies would accelerate their capacity to assist the 'Mother' Parliament in Westminster to govern their global empire through the informal institution of the Colonial Conference and, perhaps, even a future imperial parliament. These proposals ranged from an 'extra-parliamentary' federation where leading officials gave advice on imperial affairs, to 'supra-parliamentary federalism' with a new sovereign legislature composed of representatives from Britain and the settler colonies. This imperial parliament would have exclusive power to legislate on imperial matters and international affairs – especially the declaration of war and deciding on an equitable sharing of defence costs.

Despite the allure of imperial federation, the Australian colonial governments and their Commonwealth successor all insisted on asserting one legislative power against the wishes of the British government: immigration. In the later nineteenth century, colonial legislatures elected by white male suffrage began to exercise their law-making authority over migration to expel non-white residents and exclude future ones – a set of policies later known as 'White Australia'. The laws were largely aimed at 'Asiatics', especially Chinese and Japanese men and women. The British government did not necessarily disagree with the sentiment, but found it awkward to defend Australian racial restrictions – especially those affecting their Indian subjects, whose subjection they justified with the promise of equal legal status as British subjects. But the Australian governments persisted with their racist immigration policies in the face of British, Japanese and other critics. By the turn of the century the new Australian Federation would lead the world in drawing what W. E. B. Du Bois called the 'color line' of municipal and international laws segregating white nations from 'darker' nations.[25]

The Empire and the League

If Gallipoli was the birthplace of Australia's national identity, Paris was the origin of its own imperial aspirations and international legal personality. In 1914 Australia automatically followed the United Kingdom to war against Germany and its allies. But after the war Australia would press its claim to speak for itself in post-war peace-making and the nascent League of Nations. At the Paris Peace Conference in 1919, Prime Minister Billy Hughes insisted on separate representation for the self-governing Dominions in these

25 M. Lake and H. Reynolds, *Drawing the Global Colour Line: White Men's Countries and the International Challenge of Racial Equality* (Cambridge: Cambridge University Press, 2008); V. Prashad, *The Darker Nations: A People's History of the Third World* (London: New Press, 2007).

negotiations and distinct status as a national member in the League. He also signed up Australia to the Permanent Court of International Justice, though it was never a party to proceedings during the court's brief existence.[26] Most importantly, Hughes won three important concessions in the League of Nations negotiations that protected Australia's new imperial ambitions to extend 'White Australia' into Oceania.[27]

Hughes first insisted on full indemnity by Germany for the cost of war, not just for direct damages, as the Americans proposed. This related to Hughes's second demand that Germany give up its colonial possessions. Australia insisted on annexing German New Guinea under a form of colonial rule free from the burdens, demanded by the League of Nations, to govern for its inhabitants' benefit as a 'sacred trust of civilisation'. Hughes only agreed to the proposed mandate system after the League delegates agreed to create a special 'C' class mandate for Australia that permitted it to exclude foreigners. This concession was intended to extend the 'White Australia' policy in the new colonies and was vociferously protested by the Japanese delegates. Finally, Hughes rejected any formulation of the 'racial equality' clause demanded by the Japanese delegates. His parochial aim was to preserve Australia's ability to impose its 'White Australia' policy by restricting non-white – and especially Asian – immigration. Australia's imperial ambitions expanded further when it inherited the British government's contested claim over a large part of the Antarctic in 1933.[28]

Despite these nationalist assertions, during the interwar years Australian governments always made their claims within a larger imperial international order. In fact they actively resisted opportunities for greater independence in the international order. The British and settler premiers agree on the Balfour Declaration (1926) that affirmed that the United Kingdom and the white-ruled Dominions were 'autonomous Communities within the British Empire, equal in status, in no way subordinate one to another in any aspect of their domestic or external affairs'. The Declaration and the subsequent Statute of Westminster (1932) are usually taken as a (or even *the*) start of Australia's legislative independence from the United Kingdom.[29] But this statute was not

26 J. Crawford, '"Dreamers of the Day": Australia and the International Court of Justice' *Melbourne Journal of International Law* 14 (2013): 2–3.

27 S. Pedersen, *The Guardians: The League of Nations and the Crisis of Empire* (Oxford: Oxford University Press, 2015); A. Pert, *Australia as a Good International Citizen* (Sydney: Federation Press, 2014), chapter 2.

28 United Kingdom, Order in Council, 7 February 1933; Australian Antarctic Territory Acceptance Act 1933 (Cth).

29 A. Pert, 'The Development of Australia's International Legal Personality' *Australian Yearbook of International Law* 34 (2016): 149–89.

implemented by Commonwealth legislation for a decade.[30] As late as the Commonwealth Prime Ministers Conference of 1944, John Curtin would make a call (ultimately rejected) for a permanent imperial secretariat composed of delegates from the white-ruled Dominions.[31] Australia remained a reluctant state actor in international affairs until it was prised from the British Empire by the cataclysmic consequences of World War II.

New World Orders

Australia left an old world of empires behind in 1939 and emerged into a new world of states by 1945. The war in the Pacific drew Australian fighting forces into the American offensive against the Japanese, as the British concentrated on Europe. Never had the distance from the United Kingdom seemed so great as when bombs fell on Darwin in 1942. This changing reality forced Australian governments to reckon with managing its apparent isolation – in part self-imposed through its 'White Australia' policy – in a new post-imperial world characterised by international institutions and regional treaties. Australian governments also had to reconcile calls for decolonisation with their own aspirations for regional hegemony, control over natural resources beyond Australia's continental shores and the denial of equal international relations to First Nations. The evolving answers to these questions would shape Australia's place in the world while also closing off other possible legal futures.

Birthing the United Nations

Australia only began to speak in its own voice to other nations during the 1940s. The Lyons and first Menzies governments had set up legations to the United States, China and Japan, as well as a High Commission in Canada.[32] But it was the Chifley and Curtin governments that created a foreign affairs ministry with a global system of diplomatic missions in all continents. Australia also pressed its new vision of the future international order at the United Nations Conference on International Organization (1945). Herbert Vere Evatt, Australia's dazzling delegate, emerged as the champion of the small and middle powers. He succeeded in twenty-six of his thirty-eight

30 Statute of Westminster Adoption Act 1942 (Cth).
31 J. Curran, *Curtin's Empire* (Cambridge: Cambridge University Press, 2012), chapter 4.
32 C. Bridge, 'Australia, Britain and the British Commonwealth', in A. Bashford and S. Macintyre (eds), *The Cambridge History of Australia: The Commonwealth of Australia* (Cambridge: Cambridge University Press, 2013), 2: 529.

proposed amendments to the UN Charter.[33] Evatt failed to limit the Security Council's permanent members' veto to Chapter VII peace and aggression questions. But he did secure Article 2(7), which effectively shielded Australia's 'White Australia' policy, of imposing legal controls on non-white immigration, from challenge in international law.[34] Only after safely securing that exception did Evatt press for a global court, the new International Court of Justice (ICJ), to pursue 'justice and the rule of law' with compulsory jurisdiction in interstate disputes.[35]

A year earlier Australia had joined the Allied states at the UN Monetary and Financial Conference (better known as 'Bretton Woods') to create a new global infrastructure for investment finance, monetary policy and trade. The International Bank for Reconstruction and Development (which later grew into the World Bank) would grant loans to low-income countries in exchange for policy reforms. The International Monetary Fund (IMF) aimed to provide international financial stability, mainly by managing exchange rates and making short-term liquidity loans in extreme cases. However, Australian politicians were divided by the American-led, new, international economic order. Some supported Keynes' even more ambitious model of the IMF as an international central bank with the additional function of promoting full employment.[36] But one Labor minister denounced Bretton Woods as a 'hitlerite dream' that would surrender Australia's 'very sovereignty' to international financiers and force 'open its doors to a flood of coloured labour'.[37]

Chifley defended the stability offered by the proposed international system and his Labor government would sign the Bretton Woods agreement in 1947, as well as the General Agreement on Trade and Tariffs (GATT) that aimed to reduce or eliminate tariffs on a range of products. Australia also played a leading role in establishing new international legal regimes to manage resources beyond national territorial jurisdiction. The most successful – and controversial – was the International Convention on the Regulation of Whaling, established with the conflicting aims of conserving whale stocks and developing the whaling industry.[38] These many treaties would construct

33 Pert, 'The Development', 80.

34 J. Piccini, *Human Rights in Twentieth-century Australia* (Cambridge: Cambridge University Press, 2019), 42–3.

35 Crawford, 'Dreamers of the Day', 523.

36 S. Cornish, 'Sir Leslie Melville: Keynesian or Pragmatist?' *History of Economics Review* 30 (1999): 126–50.

37 J. Suares, *JB Chifley: An Ardent Internationalist* (Melbourne: Melbourne University Press, 2019), chapter 4.

38 International Convention on the Regulation of Whaling, opened for signature 2 December 1946, 161 UNTS 72 (entered into force 10 November 1948).

a complicated and multi-centric international legal order that facilitated, regulated and intensified the financing and exploitation of natural resources within and beyond state territorial jurisdictions.

Australia's outsized role in creating a new international legal order had a more ambivalent outcome for the question of decolonisation. While President of the General Assembly (1948–9), Evatt pursued an active agenda that focused on social democracy over national liberation. He helped draft the United Nations Universal Declaration of Human Rights (1948), which did not include a right to self-determination, and convinced Australia to join the International Refugee Organization. Evatt also intervened directly in decolonisation controversies. In 1947, in response to the Netherlands' 'police action' in Indonesia, Australia and India made the first call for a member to be expelled from the UN.[39] Australia also led the push to end the British mandate in Palestine, which resulted in a controversial partition creating the state of Israel and a stateless Arab population.[40] (The nascent Israeli state would count Julius Stone, the pre-eminent Australian jurist, as its staunchest defender in international law.[41]) Despite its interventions in the UN, Australian governments never questioned their own regional empire in Nauru and Papua New Guinea or the continued denial of international relations to First Nations.

Australia's Cold War

As the Cold War slowly settled across the globe, Australia oscillated between the UN global order, and its old British and American allies. The emergence of Japan, then the 'Asian tigers' and, finally, China forced the Australian government to reconsider its role in the region and the world. Australia's long-standing 'White Australia' policy was never acceptable to its new trading partners nor any longer to many of its own citizens. Human rights provided a useful discourse to champion Australia's belief in its distinctive national character without unduly undermining its aggressive international acts both to secure its borders from undesirable immigrants and to conserve or exploit marine resources from oil to whales. The slow and contested

39 D. Fettling, 'J.B. Chifley and the Indonesian Revolution, 1945–1949' *Australian Journal of Politics and History* 59 (2013): 517–31.

40 D. Mandel, *H. V. Evatt and the Establishment of Israel: The Undercover Zionist* (London: Frank Cass, 2004).

41 B. Saul, 'Julius Stone and the Question of Palestine in International Law', in H. Irving, J. Mowbray and K. Walton (eds), *Julius Stone: A Study in Influence* (Sydney: Federation Press, 2010), 238–61.

decolonisation of the Pacific did not subdue but renewed Australia's economic interests in its now independent neighbours' undersea resources.

Australia's ambivalent relationship with the UN system was reflected in its continued reliance on its old alliances with the English-speaking British and American states against the apparent threat of the Soviet Union and emerging Asian economic powers. The Menzies government chose to stand almost alone with Britain during its illegal invasion of Egypt in the Suez Crisis of 1956. But acts of imperial nostalgia were increasingly tempered by a regional realism that recognised America's post-war domination of the Pacific and the perceived threat of Chinese-led communism. The Australia, New Zealand, United States Security Treaty (1951) created a collective security pact against regional military threats.[42] Australia also joined the South East Asia Treaty Organization (1954–77), a multilateral defence treaty aimed at containing China, composed of the United States, United Kingdom, France, New Zealand, Pakistan, Philippines and Thailand. These moves opened up a new horizon for collective international military action beyond the UN's multilateral and technocratic mechanisms. Alleged violations of these treaties would also provide an alibi for Australia's ill-fated military invasion in Vietnam.

While reinforcing its older ties to the Anglo-American world, Australia also engaged and evaded international courts and treaty systems for the legal resolution of interstate disputes. In the early 1950s the Menzies government worried that Japan would contest Australia's claim to the continental shelf and its exclusion of Japanese pearl fishers. At first it agreed with Japan to refer the dispute to the ICJ; but in 1954 Australia revised the terms of its acceptance of the compulsory jurisdiction under Article 36(2) of the ICJ Statute to exclude maritime delimitation cases. The two parties eventually resolved their dispute with the Australia–Japan Commerce Treaty (1957).

Australia was a key advocate of international law of the sea treaties to protect its national interests as an island continent. This required a fine balancing between its freedom to navigate the seas while restricting the entry of other nations into its own sovereign waters. Australia was one of the first states to sign the Geneva Conventions on the Law of the Sea (1958), which later included the recognition and protection of its enormous Exclusive Economic Zone – the world's third largest. Australia also agreed to suspend (but not renounce) its territorial claims to the polar south when it

42 T. K. Robb and David James Gill, 'The ANZUS Treaty During the Cold War: A Reinterpretation of U.S. Diplomacy in the Southwest Pacific' *Journal of Cold War Studies* 17 (2016): 109–57.

signed the Antarctic Treaty (1961) that established the Antarctic Treaty System for the peaceful management of the continent's land and seas.

By the 1960s, Australia relented to growing internal and external pressure to end its dominion over Indigenous and UN trustee peoples. In 1967, the Holt government had responded to the First Nations' campaign for equal rights by holding a successful referendum to grant the federal government power to make laws for the 'Aboriginal race' – though the Commonwealth government still refused to make international treaties. A year later Australia accepted Nauru's independence by ending its UN trusteeship, jointly administered with the United Kingdom and New Zealand. The election of a Labor government under Gough Whitlam accelerated the region's decolonisation.[43] In 1975 it granted independence to Papua New Guinea but failed to pass the ambitious Aboriginal Land Rights (Northern Territory) Bill, before falling that same year.

The winds of change also blew through the cosy club of British and colonial premiers. In 1971, the first Commonwealth Heads of Government Meeting (CHOGM) was held in Singapore. Its members included the settler colonies of the old Imperial Conference, though it was now dominated by the anti-colonialist leaders of the newly independent African, Asian and Pacific states. The CHOGM provided a high-profile international forum to press for the decolonisation of the white settler states – especially the apartheid regimes in Rhodesia and South Africa. Australia fell further away from its mother country when the United Kingdom joined the European Economic Community in 1973. This shock exacerbated the longer trend of Australia's declining trade with the United Kingdom relative to its regional partners, especially Japan and the United States. It also intensified a growing tension between the manufacturing and agricultural sectors, which pushed for more and less protectionist trade measures respectively. Since the GATT rules favoured the former, industrial-scale Australian agriculturalists began building a powerful lobby group that would play an outsized role in reforming international trade rules two decades later.

In the shadow of global decolonisation, ancient relationships were renewed and new alliances formed between First Nations, their Pasifika neighbours and anti-colonial internationalists. Tracey Banivanua Mar traces the emergence of a new global political consciousness that connected Aboriginal claims to country with Pasifika nationalism and radical Black thought in the United States, United Kingdom and Africa.[44] In

43 M. Kirby, 'Whitlam as Internationalist: A Centenary Reflection' *Melbourne University Law Review* 39 (2016): 850–94.

44 T. Banivanua Mar, *Decolonisation and the Pacific: Indigenous Globalisation and the Ends of Empire* (Cambridge: Cambridge University Press, 2016).

these decades First Nations also made new political connections with self-consciously 'Indigenous' peoples in the settler states of Canada, New Zealand and the United States.[45] After the 1967 referendum, old languages of civil rights superseded those of sovereignty to make stronger claims to self-rule within and against the settler state. They also helped to build an international 'Indigenous' movement that recognised and built on the common historical experiences of European colonisation. In 1982 the global 'Indigenous' movement would gain a toehold at the UN when the Economic and Social Council formed a minor subcommission, the Working Group on Indigenous Populations, to inquire into their rights in international law.[46] The result would be a new language of international rights to press long-standing First Nations' claims to sovereignty over country.

Engaging the World

In the 1970s and 1980s successive Australian governments re-engaged with the world during the culmination of the Cold War. The Whitlam government began to reorient Australia from the UK and USA to the UN. It signed, ratified and implemented several key international treaties on human rights and decolonisation. In 1975 it ratified the International Covenant on Economic, Social and Cultural Rights (ICESCR) and implemented the UN Convention for the Elimination of All Forms of Racial Discrimination through the Racial Discrimination Act 1975. Despite its commitment to international human rights, the Whitlam government did recognise the Soviet Union's controversial claim to sovereignty over the Baltic states and declined to support the East Timorese pro-independence movement. The Fraser government ratified several important international human rights instruments, including the ICESCR in 1975 (by the preceding caretaker government), the International Covenant on Civil and Political Rights (ICCPR) in 1980 (with major reservations and declarations demanded by certain states) and the UN Convention on the Elimination of Discrimination against Women in 1983.

In the 1980s, Labor governments continued to implement a number of international human rights treaties (or parts thereof) through Commonwealth

45 M. Johnson, *The Land Is Our History: Indigeneity, Law, and the Settler State* (Oxford: Oxford University Press, 2016); D. Lino, *Constitutional Recognition: First Peoples and the Australian Settler State* (Sydney: Federation Press, 2018).

46 M. Davis, 'To Bind or Not to Bind: The United Nations Declaration on the Rights of Indigenous Peoples Five Years On' *Australian International Law Journal* 19 (2012): 20–3.

laws.[47] They withdrew most reservations to the ICCPR in 1984, and then acceded to optional protocols for the ICCPR and other human rights treaties that allowed individuals to complain of violations. The complaint mechanism was taken up in the *Toonen* case, which challenged a Tasmanian law criminalising homosexual acts.[48] The Keating government eventually legislated to override Tasmania's criminal law after the UN Human Rights Committee found it violated ICCPR, Article 17.[49] Labor's turn to human rights affirmed its vision of Australia as a lonely beacon of humane liberalism in the isolated antipodean oceans.

The Whitlam government also reoriented Australia's relationship to British and international courts and commissions. It ended all remaining federal appeals to the Privy Council in 1975, while returning to neglected international courts to pursue foreign policy ends.[50] In 1973 Australia (and, separately, New Zealand) proceeded against France in the ICJ for the latter's proposed nuclear testing in the South Pacific. However, the Court declined to rule in the proceedings on the grounds that France had renounced any nuclear testing after 1974.[51] Nevertheless, the high-profile case emphasised the Australian government's renewed commitment to internationalist legal solutions to serious political disagreements. Australia continued to pursue its foreign policy interests, such as living marine resources, through international organisations. By the mid-1970s Australia's whaling industry faced collapse after over a century of exponential overfishing ended in the near extinction of several whale species. The Fraser government adopted the recommendations of an independent inquiry to ban whaling altogether – a move that coincided with its aim to exclude Japanese whaling ships from its maritime claims in the Antarctic seas. In 1982 Australia reversed its long-standing support for whaling by voting in the International Whaling Commission for a legally binding moratorium on commercial whaling.

With the dismissal of Whitlam and the election of Malcolm Fraser, Australia briefly shifted its energies from UN-focused internationalism to

47 Sex Discrimination Act 1984 (Cth); Privacy Act 1988 (Cth); Crimes (Torture) Act 1988 (Cth); Disability Discrimination Act 1992 (Cth); Human Rights (Sexual Conduct) Act 1994 (Cth); Racial Hatred Act 1995 (Cth).

48 Human Rights Committee, Communication No. 488/1992, UN Doc CCPR/C/50/D/488/1992 (31 March 1994).

49 K. Gelber, 'Treaties and Intergovernmental Relations in Australia: Political Implications of the Toonen Case' *Australian Journal of Politics and History* 45 (1999): 330–46.

50 Privy Council (Appeals from the High Court) Act 1975 (Cth).

51 *Nuclear Tests (Australia v France)* (Judgment) [1974] ICJ Rep 253.

its older alliances with the United Kingdom and the United States. Fraser's 'New Federalism' granted states greater autonomy in certain domestic matters, as well as allowing states to include representatives in the Commonwealth delegations for international treaty-making.[52] This new policy also provided a convenient alibi for non-implementation of some international obligations whenever a state refused. Australia's last constitutional ties with the UK were finally severed by the new Labor government under Hawke, including the formal abolition of all appeals to British courts. In 1986 the British and Australian legislatures passed respective Australia Acts, which Anne Twomey calls the country's 'statutes of independence'.[53] The Commonwealth version declared Australia 'a sovereign, independent and federal nation', though this did not alter Australia's long-standing status as an independent state in international law.

The Fraser and Hawke governments had moderated, without renouncing, Whitlam's decolonising agenda. The Fraser government had pursued two small steps in regional decolonisation. First, it created a new legal category of 'temporary refugee' aimed primarily at protecting Vietnamese 'boat people', who did not fall under the narrower definition of 'refugee' in the UN Refugee Convention. Over 100,000 Vietnamese refugees eventually resettled in Australia. Second, at the 1977 CHOGM Fraser personally denounced racial segregation in Rhodesia and South Africa. He later helped secure a transition to democratic, non-racial government in Zimbabwe. However, his government did not pursue Whitlam's more radical land rights legislation for First Nations. Instead, it only enacted a watered-down version limited to the Northern Territory.[54] The Hawke government – unlike the Canadian government four years earlier – did not take the opportunity of the 1986 constitutional repatriation to respond to Indigenous demands, in the Barunga Statement, for an international treaty 'recognising our prior ownership, continued occupation and sovereignty and affirming our human rights and freedoms'. The Australian state remained a single sovereign nation that refused to recognise First Nations as equals through treaty.

52 B. Lim, *Australia's Constitution after Whitlam* (Cambridge: Cambridge University Press, 2017), 70–2; C. Saunders and K. Wiltshire, 'Fraser's New Federalism: An Evaluation' *Australian Journal of Politics and History* 26 (1980): 355–71.

53 A. Twomey, *The Australia Acts 1986: Australia's Statutes of Independence* (Sydney: Federation Press, 2010).

54 Aboriginal Land Rights (Northern Territory) Act 1976 (Cth).

After the Cold War

After the end of the Cold War the unfinished business of the past continued to unsettle Australia's place in a globalising world. To some, the apparent victory of the 'West' confirmed the dominance of capitalist, liberal democracy. But the history of Australia's colonial past returned to challenge this triumphant story. How would Australia pursue its economic and strategic interests in a region increasingly dominated by China? How should it relate to its independent neighbours, former colonies with new claims to maritime resources and historical reparations? How might Australia regulate immigration without reviving the past racial restrictions of 'White Australia'? And how could it respond to First Nations whose members were granted formal equality yet condemned to material inequality?

The end of the Cold War was followed by many smaller conflicts that Labor and Liberal governments joined as part of UN peacekeeping operations and UN-sanctioned military interventions. Australia sent warships to support the American invasion of Iraq (1990–1). The next year over a thousand Australian military personnel joined UNITAF in Somalia (1992–3). Closer to home, Australia contributed to security forces in Cambodia, Bougainville, Fiji, Solomon Islands and East Timor. The latter became Australia's largest military venture since the American War in Vietnam. The Howard government first sent some personnel to assist UNAMET (1999), a UN peacekeeping mission to monitor the East Timorese independence referendum, and then led INTERFRET (1999–2000), a UN-sanctioned peacekeeping mission to restore security in the violent aftermath of that vote.

Australia's intervention in East Timor was also part of an aggressive assertion of sovereign claims to territory (and its natural resources) beyond the continent. After helping to secure East Timorese independence, Australia followed up with an attempt to coerce the new nation into an inequitable deal to share the revenues of its offshore gas deposits. In 1995 Portugal had launched proceedings against Australia in the ICJ on the grounds that Australia, by treating with Indonesia rather than Portugal regarding maritime delimitation in the Timor Gap treaty (1989), had violated the East Timorese right to self-determination under international law. But the ICJ held that Portugal's claim was inadmissible since the real issue was a preliminary one of whether Indonesia's occupation of East Timor was legal.[55]

55 *East Timor (Portugal v Australia)* (Judgment) [1995] ICJ Rep 90.

Australia repeated its belligerent international action in cases of colonial reparations and freedom of the high seas. In 1991, Nauru had began proceedings against Australia in the ICJ for breaching its duties regarding UN trusteeship obligations, thus infringing Nauru's right to self-determination and sovereignty over natural resources.[56] Australia also initially resisted, though eventually agreed to settle the claim by paying Nauru $103 million in compensation. East Timorese independence again raised the question of unjust maritime boundary making. The new government declined to accede to the Timor Gap treaty and, instead, negotiated two new treaties on maritime boundaries and resource sharing. But in 2002, East Timor asserted its maritime rights in the ICJ. Just as it had three decades earlier, Australia preemptively modified its declaration under Article 36(2) UNCLOS to exclude maritime delimitation from the ICJ's compulsory jurisdiction. Two years later, East Timor abrogated the existing treaty after Australia spied on it during negotiations.[57]

Australia continued to press its claims to neighbouring maritime resources through new interpretations and revised rules for the international law of the sea. In 1994, it ratified the United Nations Convention on the Law of the Sea (1982) and, a decade later, laid claim to an extended continental shelf, resulting in associated claims to an expanded Exclusive Economic Zone and corresponding rights to maritime resources. The Australian government used these new rules to renew its claim to oil and gas deposits off East Timor's coast. However, East Timor instigated a conciliation process under the UN Convention on the Law of the Sea (UNCLOS) at the Permanent Court of Arbitration, which led to a new treaty recognising its stronger claims in international law of the sea.[58] Australia itself used similar UNCLOS provisions to challenge Japanese fishing of southern Bluefin tuna.[59] Propelled by popular demand, Australia next lodged and won a case against the Japanese government's support of whaling in the Southern Ocean

56 *Certain Phosphate Lands in Nauru (Nauru v Australia)* (Judgment) [1992] ICJ Rep 240; C. Storr, *International Status in the Shadow of Empire: Nauru and the Histories of International Law* (Cambridge: Cambridge University Press, 2020).

57 *Questions relating to the Seizure and Detention of Certain Documents and Data (Timor-Leste v Australia)* (Discontinuance) [2014] ICJ Rep 572.

58 P. Tzeng, 'The Peaceful Non-Settlement of Disputes: Article 4 of CMATS in Timor-Leste v Australia' *Melbourne Journal of International Law* 18 (2017): 349–73.

59 *Southern Bluefin Tuna Cases (New Zealand v Japan; Australia v Japan)* (Award on Jurisdiction and Admissibility) (International Tribunal for the Law of the Sea, Case Nos 3 & 4, 4 August 2000). See also B. Campbell, 'International Dispute Resolution: Australian Perspectives and Approaches' *Australian Yearbook of International Law* 35 (2018): 1–15.

Sanctuary, which overlapped with the Australian Whale Sanctuary that incorporated the Exclusive Economic Zone of the Australian Antarctic Territory (a territorial claim supported by only four states).[60] However, Australia's apparent victory ended with Japan withdrawing from the International Whaling Convention to resume whaling freed from the legal restrictions of the treaty.

Australia's recent attempts to evade its international human rights and refugee law obligations ironically mirrored Japan's whaling strategy.[61] In the late 1980s, a trickle of Cambodian 'boat people' provided a bipartisan alibi for the return of 'White Australia' policies. The Keating government responded to this new refugee influx with restrictions on migration including, in 1992, mandatory detention for all unauthorised arrivals. Cambodian asylum seekers successfully appealed to the UN Human Rights Committee on the ground that their arbitrary detention violated ICCPR, Article 9.[62] The Howard government – with Labor support – took the policy a step further with the 'Pacific solution', which aimed to intercept all unauthorised maritime arrivals at sea and detain them on Nauru and in Papua New Guinea. Under the motto of 'stopping the boats', Australia has created a population of indefinitely imprisoned people seeking asylum under the UN Refugee Convention.[63] In 1998, the Howard government also signed the Rome Statute for the International Criminal Court, but made a controversial declaration (of doubtful legal effect in international law) to limit the Court's jurisdiction by requiring the effective approval of the Australian government for any prosecution of its citizens. The Australian dilemma is how to support 'a global rules-based order' while exempting themselves from its central coercive mechanisms.

Australia has similarly struggled to reconcile its aims of greater international free trade with its sovereign right to regulate the economy to achieve health, environmental and other goals. The Hawke and Keating governments drove a long transformation of the Australian economy that included the revision and expansion of bilateral and multilateral trade

60 *Whaling in the Antarctic (Australia v Japan: New Zealand Intervening)* (Judgment) [2014] ICJ Rep 226; see M. Fitzmaurice and D. Tamada (eds), *Whaling in the Antarctic: Significance and Implications of the ICJ Judgment* (Leiden: Brill, 2016).

61 C. Higgins, *Asylum by Boat: Origins of Australia's Refugee Policy* (Sydney: NewSouth Publishing, 2017).

62 Human Rights Committee, Communication No. 560/1993, UN Doc CCPR/C/59/D/560/1993 (30 April 1997).

63 J. McAdam and K. Purcell, 'Refugee Protection in the Howard Years: Obstructing the Right to Seek Asylum' *Australian Yearbook of International Law* 87 (2008): 92–113.

agreements. Bilateral treaties allowed Australia to evade some of the problems of negotiating complex multi-party treaties, but also exposed them to challenges to domestic legislation by foreign corporations under the arbitration rules of the United Nations Commission on International Trade Law (UNCITRAL). The Australian government did win one important investor-state dispute before the Permanent Court of Arbitration in 2015. The Court agreed with Australia that it had no jurisdiction to hear Philip Morris's challenge to 'plain packaging' legislation under a bilateral treaty between Australia and Hong Kong.[64] However, this formal victory has belied the reality of significant informal resolutions in favour of foreign corporations.

Australia also pursued its economic interests in ambitious multilateral free trade agreements. In the 1980s, Australia had joined the Cairns Group of countries that exported agricultural products, to reduce trade restrictions on these commodities. In 1995, they succeeded in revising the GATT (now the World Trade Organization) to lower barriers to agricultural trade. While this led to significant new and profitable agricultural markets, manufacturing lost some protection from international competition. In 1989, Australia joined the Asia-Pacific Economic Cooperation, to promote freer trade and economic integration in the region; and, five years later, adopted the Bogor Goals, aimed at a free trade agreement. Australia has also pursued a free trade agreement, the Trans-Pacific Partnership Agreement, with the region's developed economies. When the United States withdrew from the agreement in 2017 shortly after it came into force, Australia and several other states agreed on the new Comprehensive and Progressive Agreement for Trans-Pacific Partnership in 2018.

The last of Australia's unfinished business is the oldest. Since the 1992 High Court decision in *Mabo (No. 2)*[65] affirming the existence of native title, successive Australian governments have granted and then withdrawn legal rights for First Nations to control country. In 2007, Australia voted against the UN Declaration on the Right of Indigenous Peoples, though the new Labor government would endorse it two years later. The Declaration remains unimplemented in domestic law and subsequent First Nations' proposals for constitutional recognition and reconciliation have gone unanswered. In 2017, delegates to the Aboriginal and Torres Strait Islander Referendum

64 *Philip Morris Asia Limited v The Commonwealth of Australia* (UNCITRAL, PCA Case No. 2012–12); see also S. Chesterman, 'Asia's Ambivalence about International Law and Institutions: Past, Present and Futures' *European Journal of International Law* 27 (2016): 945–78.

65 (1992) 175 CLR 1.

Convention issued the 'Uluru Statement from the Heart' calling for a two-stage process to address the legacy of racialised exclusion. The first step would create a constitutional 'First Nations Voice' to allow First Nations to scrutinise Commonwealth legislation affecting their interests. The second step would create a 'Makarrata Commission' to make agreements – the long-denied international treaties – between First Nations and the Australian state. This business is still the unfinished past in our unfolding present.

IV

*

LAND AND ENVIRONMENT

13

Settlement and Dispossession

LISA FORD AND DAVID ANDREW ROBERTS

This chapter explores the legal history of dispossession in the nineteenth century. It does so first by considering the law and politics of omitting to treat with Aboriginal peoples for land in Australia. This was not a neat act of dispossession: there was no declaration of '*terra nullius*' in 1788, whatever late twentieth-century commentators might say.[1] The failure to treat was a deeply significant move nonetheless, though its ramifications changed over time. The chapter then explores dispossession through the mixture of legality and lawlessness that fed the pastoral boom in Australia and dispossessed Aboriginal peoples of control and use of Country on a vast scale after 1820. With the advent of self-government, dispossession shifted in tempo. Australian versions of the Homestead Acts passed by various colonies after 1861 and expanded by soldier settlement schemes after World War I transformed many pastoral runs into small, fee simple farms which were largely closed to Indigenous Australians. This long and varied process of dispossession by tenure was fed by acts and omissions of jurisdiction. The failure to prosecute or to convict settler murderers and rapists aided dispossession by withholding jurisdiction – an omission veiled by decades of prevarication about the status of Indigenous Australians in law. However, as other chapters in this volume show, when Aboriginal people were finally declared to be British subjects from the 1830s, law's 'protection' was delivered through the erasure of Indigenous law and sovereignty; and it provided cover for genocidal violence. British law was the handmaiden of dispossession.

1 D. Ritter, 'The "rejection of terra nullius" in Mabo. A Critical Analysis' *Sydney Law Review* 18, no. 1 (1996): 5–33; Andrew Fitzmaurice, 'The Genealogy of Terra Nullius' *Australian Historical Studies* 38, no. 129 (2007): 1–15; Bain Attwood, '"The Law of the Land": History, Law and Narrative in a Settler Society' *History Compass* 2 (2004): 1–30. On the origins and adoption of the notion of *terra nullius* more broadly, see L. Benton and B. Straumann, 'Acquiring Empire by Law: From Roman Doctrine to Early Modern European Practice' *Law and History Review* 28, no. 1 (2010): 1–38.

Dispossession by Settlement without Treaty

As Coel Kirkby pointed out in his chapter on international law, the first and, arguably, the most enduring dispossession of Indigenous people in Australia was the failure to make treaties. Though not everyone agrees about their character and import, treaty-like agreements between European colonists and Indigenous peoples formed an essential part of the geopolitics of North American settlement as soon as European competition for colonies began.[2] French, English and Spanish emissaries plied Indigenous peoples with weapons in return for furs and favours. Indigenous peoples, meanwhile, quickly learned to play European polities off against each other for better deals. Treaty was the most appropriate basis to manage relationships in such a context, though they were often signed with the wrong parties, provided grossly inadequate compensation for land purchases and were increasingly honoured in their breach.[3] Such negotiations even took on a standard form, developed in the hinterlands of New France and New England and exported throughout the continent, wampum beads and all.[4] Treaties also followed settlers to the nineteenth-century Pacific and Africa, bolstered by the 'contagion of sovereignty' set off by the American Revolution and by the shift to indirect rule after the Indian Rebellion.[5] Why then was no treaty signed in 1788, when the British arrived in New South Wales?

Governor Arthur Phillip's reasons for not treating with Indigenous Australians are undocumented.[6] Most likely it was an omission reflecting uncertainty and expediency.[7] Scant information about New South Wales before settlement suggested that it was 'very thinly peopled'. When asked, in 1785, whether some site might 'be obtained by cession or purchase', Joseph

2 For the importance of treaty-making in all European expansion, see the essays in S. Belmessous (ed.), *Empire by Treaty: Negotiating European Expansion, 1600–1900* (Oxford: Oxford University Press, 2015).

3 Stuart Banner, *How the Indians Lost Their Land: Law and Power on the Frontier* (Cambridge, MA: Harvard University Press, 2009).

4 Richard White, *The Middle Ground: Indians, Empires, and Republics in the Great Lakes Region, 1600–1815* (Cambridge: Cambridge University Press, 1991); Daniel Richter, *Facing East from Indian Country: A Native History of Early America* (Cambridge, MA: Harvard University Press, 2001).

5 David Armitage, 'The Contagion of Sovereignty: Declarations of Independence since 1776' *South African Historical Journal* 52, no. 1 (2005): 1–18.

6 With the exception of E. Scott, 'Taking Possession of Australia: The Doctrine of "Terra Nullius" (No-Man's Land)', *Journal of the Royal Australian Historical Society* 26, no. 1 (1940): 1–19, Australian historians were extraordinarily slow to consider this question. But see Bain Attwood's recent contribution: Bain Attwood, *Empire and the Making of Native Title: Sovereignty, Property and Indigenous People* (Cambridge: Cambridge University Press, 2020), 14–42.

7 Ibid, 35–8.

Banks simply noted that 'there was nothing we could offer that they [Indigenous Australians] would take'.[8] So, Phillip was merely instructed to 'live in amity and kindness with them', although he was also expected to report back on how 'these people' could be 'turned to the advantage' of the colony, suggesting that some sort of agreement was not entirely off the table.[9] As it turned out, the colony struggled and relations with local Aboriginal people did not go well. After an early phase of 'unabated animosity' and 'petty warfare', local Eora peoples assiduously avoided the settlement. They were then devastated by 'an extraordinary calamity', a smallpox epidemic that halved their population in April–May 1789.[10] When the Eora did come back to town in 1790, as Grace Karskens has shown, they stayed in the governor's house, frequented its shanties and worksites, plied its shorelines and trod its dirt tracks as if (indeed because) they owned the place.[11] Intercultural relations, like the colony itself, remained informal, 'mundane', reactive and 'edgy'.[12]

By the late eighteenth century, European ideas of statehood were narrowing at the same time as science and industrialism were magnifying the ambitions of empire. What Cook and Banks observed from the decks of the *Endeavour* as they sailed the coast of New South Wales in 1770 and hoisted a British flag at Possession Island was a 'wandering' and 'pusillanimous' people, strangely introverted and uniquely uninterested in 'the superfluous materials of a civilised culture'. Though they 'seemed inclined to hostilities' they 'did not appear at-all to be feared'.[13] Over a decade later, the architects and first inhabitants of the new colony did not speculate explicitly about the rights of these people to land, self-governance and livelihood; but intellectual tools for doing so abounded. By then, Enlightenment chauvinism was crystallising into a denial of Indigenous rights – particularly of non-sedentary

8 Joseph Banks, cited in Robert J. Miller, Jacinta Ruru, Larissa Behrendt and Tracey Lindberg, *Discovering Indigenous Lands: The Doctrine of Discovery in the English Colonies* (Oxford: Oxford University Press, 2010), 185.

9 Merete Falck Borch, *Conciliation – Compulsion – Conversion: British Attitudes towards Indigenous Peoples, 1763–1814* (Amsterdam / New York: Rodopi, 2004).

10 Judy Campbell, *Invisible Invaders: Smallpox and Other Diseases in Aboriginal Australia 1780–1880* (Melbourne: Melbourne University Press, 2002).

11 Grace Karskens, *The Colony: A History of Early Sydney* (Crows Nest, NSW: Allen & Unwin, 2009).

12 Grace Karskens, 'Phillip and the Eora: Governing Race Relations in the Colony of New South Wales' *Sydney Journal* 5, no. 1 (2017): 41; Shino Konishi, *The Aboriginal Male in the Enlightenment World* (Abingdon: Pickering and Chatto, 2012), 1; and see Konishi throughout for examples of the inconsistent lens Enlightenment chauvinism brought to European encounters with Indigenous peoples in Australia.

13 Joseph Banks, cited in R. Stanfield, *Race and Identity in the Tasman World, 1769–1840* (London / New York: Routledge, 2015), 64.

peoples. This had important ramifications for law. John Locke, expanding on Hobbes's meditations on savagery and civility, had espoused a very seductive philosophy of civil society.[14] In the beginning, said Locke, 'natural men' (whom he compared to Native Americans) lived as equals, free of the yoke of the state. However, when men began taming and tilling the earth, they acquired property which needed protection. Vulnerable property-holders traded their natural liberty to a king in return for his protection (law).[15]

Locke did not explicitly advocate for, or justify, Indigenous dispossession, though some scholars have argued that his interest in the South Carolina colony suggests that he had exactly this in mind.[16] Regardless, notions of a fast link between sedentary farming, property and sovereignty did no good for Indigenous peoples. The Swiss philosopher and jurist Emer de Vattel adopted Locke's principles in his monumental *The Law of Nations* (1758), arguing that hunter-gatherer societies were not states, and that the inefficiencies of their land use undercut any claim to tenure and justified their confinement within 'closer limits'.[17] Such maxims were not widely advocated in 1788, but they opened the prospect that uncompensated occupation of 'waste' land might be lawful.[18] While this Eurocentric law of nations was invoked by some Native Americans to assert their own claims to nationhood, by the 1830s settler elites were using it to underpin much larger dispossessions.[19] Vattel's footnotes were cited in an epochal NSW Supreme

14 Pat Maloney, 'Hobbes, Savagery, and International Anarchy' *American Political Science Review* 105, no. 1 (2011): 189–204.

15 Karl Olivecrona, 'Appropriation in the State of Nature: Locke on the Origin of Property' *Journal of the History of Ideas* 35, no. 2 (1974): 211–30.

16 David Armitage, 'John Locke, Carolina, and the Two Treatises of Government' *Political Theory* 32, no. 5 (2004): 602–27; David Armitage, 'John Locke, Theorist of Empire?', in Sankar Muthu (ed.), *Empire and Modern Political Thought* (Cambridge: Cambridge University Press, 2012), 84–111; James Tully, 'Aboriginal Property and Western Theory: Recovering a Middle Ground' *Social Philosophy and Policy* 11, no. 2 (1994): 153–80. Compare recent critiques by Holly Brewer, 'Slavery, Sovereignty, and "Inheritable Blood": Reconsidering John Locke and the Origins of American Slavery' *American Historical Review* 122, no. 4 (2017): 1038–78; William Uzgalis, 'John Locke, Racism, Slavery, and Indian Lands', in Ed Naomi Zack (ed.), *The Oxford Handbook of Philosophy and Race* (New York: Oxford University Press, 2016), chapter 1.

17 S. Beaulac, 'Emer de Vattel and the Externalization of Sovereignty' *Journal of the History of International Law* 5 (2003): 237–92.

18 Stuart Banner, *Possessing the Pacific: Land, Settlers, and Indigenous People from Australia to Alaska* (Cambridge, MA: Harvard University Press, 2007); David Boucher, 'The Law of Nations and the Doctrine of Terra Nullius' in Olaf Asbach and Peter Schröder (eds), *War, the State and International Law in Seventeenth-century Europe* (Farnham: Ashgate, 2010), chapter 4.

19 Gregory Ablavsky, 'Species of Sovereignty: Native Nationhood, the United States, and International Law, 1783–1795' *Journal of American History* 106, no. 3 (2019): 591–613.

Court case in 1836 (*R v Murrell*[20]) that held that Indigenous Australians had no sovereignty, land rights or law. Instead, they were at the mercy of the British Crown, not quite equal subjects but nevertheless subjected to British jurisdiction. Moreover, all of the land in New South Wales belonged to the Crown.[21]

If this story sounds simple and linear, it was not so. The *Murrell* decision settled Aboriginal legal status in New South Wales uneasily, as Heather Douglas and Mark Finnane have so powerfully shown.[22] Moreover, throughout the early nineteenth century, the imperial centre (as opposed to colonial courts) failed to take a definitive and enduring approach to Aboriginal sovereignty or land title. The fate of Indigenous peoples in settler colonies occupied parliamentary committees and, after 1820, prompted wildly divergent instructions to colonial governments. The legal status of Aboriginal people in Australia was also seriously debated by colonial courts and executives throughout the 1830s. The aforementioned *Murrell* decision in 1836, declaring that Aboriginal people had no sovereignty and were subject to British law for crimes *inter se*, was just one of several contradictory legal milestones in this decade. Notably, it was questioned in *R v Bonjon*, decided in Port Phillip in 1841, and elsewhere.[23] Aboriginal title to land was also inconsistently mooted at home and in the Australian colonies. In 1835, John Batman signed a private treaty for land with the Kulin peoples in Port Phillip (it is unclear how the Kulin understood that arrangement), flustering authorities until the deal was nullified by the Crown.[24] At the same time, the South Australia Company took fright when Sir George Grey suggested that the proposed boundaries of the colony 'might embrace in its range numerous Tribes of Peoples, whose Proprietary Title to the Soil, we have not the slightest grounds for disputing'[25] while the first governor, John Hindmarsh, was instructed to ensure that Aboriginal people were protected 'in their persons and in the

20 *R v Murrell and Brummaree* [1836] NSWSupC 35.

21 B. Kercher, 'Native Title in the Shadows: The Origins of the Myth of Terra Nullius in Early New South Wales Courts', in Gregory Blue, Martin Bunton and Ralph C. Croizier (eds), *Colonialism and the Modern World: Selected Studies* (Armonk: M. E. Sharpe, 2002), 100–19.

22 Heather Douglas and Mark Finnane, *Indigenous Crime and Settler Law: White Sovereignty after Empire* (Houndmills: Palgrave Macmillan, 2012).

23 [1841] NSWSupC 92.

24 Bain Attwood, *Possession: Batman's Treaty and the Matter of History* (Carlton: Miegunyah Press, 2009); James Boyce, *1835: The Founding of Melbourne and the Conquest of Australia* (Collingwood: Black Inc, 2013).

25 Glenelg, quoted in Shaun Berg, *Coming to Terms: Aboriginal Title in South Australia* (Kent Town: Wakefield Press, 2010), 70.

free enjoyment of their possessions'.[26] This last injunction was side-stepped neatly by local officials, who asserted that Aboriginal South Australians 'occupy no lands in the especial manner contemplated by this instruction'. The Colonial Office soon lost interest in the outcome: Crown-appointed protectors received no instructions respecting Aboriginal land rights.[27] In any case, as Hannah Robert has shown, discussions of Aboriginal rights became mired in the chauvinism of protection. Even the most radical 'rights-talk' threatened to collapse into regimes of moral improvement, policing and control.[28]

While there is no easy explanation for the failure to sign a treaty in the early years of settlement, the legacy of this absence has been devastating. No matter how disingenuous and dishonoured, treaties between settler colonies and Indigenous peoples made a difference. They carried within them acknowledgments of land title and sovereignty that, in the twentieth century, underpinned important claims to resources and self-governance. It is for this reason that, though its legal meaning hardened and shifted over time, the failure to treat with Indigenous peoples in 1788 in New South Wales, and in 1836 in Port Phillip and South Australia, were arguably the most important acts of dispossession by law effected by the British Crown.

Dispossession by Land Grants

The physical dispossession of Indigenous peoples in nineteenth-century Australia was realised through a combination of violence and grants of tenure. We will tell the tenure story first, though the two are inextricable. Initially, the impact of granting land to settlers on Indigenous landholdings seemed negligible – small acreages were given to former convicts, to select civil and military officials and to free settlers in an attempt to reverse the fortunes of a starving settlement. Throughout the hinterlands of the Cumberland Plains, especially around Parramatta and along the

26 Instruction to Governor Hindmarsh, 12 July 1836, quoted in Attwood, *Empire and the Making of Native Title*, 91.

27 A useful summary with quotations can be found in Amanda Nettelbeck, *Indigenous Rights and Colonial Subjecthood: Protection and Reform in the Nineteenth-Century British Empire* (Cambridge: Cambridge University Press, 2019), 92–4. For subsequent developments in South Australia, see D. Ward, 'Constructing British Authority in Australasia: Charles Cooper and the Legal Status of Aborigines in the South Australian Supreme Court, c. 1840–60' *Journal of Imperial and Commonwealth History* 34, no. 4 (2006): 483–504. Compare Attwood, *Empire and the Making of Native Title*, 65–95.

28 Hannah Robert, *Paved with Good Intentions: Terra Nullius, Aboriginal Land Rights and Settler-Colonial Law* (Ultimo: Halstead Press, 2016).

Hawkesbury and its tributaries, small farming communities sprouted. From the mid-1810s, following the marking of a path along the ridges of the Great Dividing Range west of Sydney, the first remote communities were established in the central west around Bathurst. However, at the beginning of the 1820s, the colony's population, its cultivated land and its livestock remained almost exclusively within a seventy-kilometre radius of Sydney.[29]

In both New South Wales and Van Diemen's Land, dispossession through tenure accelerated dramatically as a result of critical policy changes in the aftermath of an 1819–21 commission of inquiry. Following the counsel of ambitious local graziers and their British financiers, Commissioner John Thomas Bigge recommended that expansive land grants and a large proportion of the convict workforce be made over to a better sort of capitalist settler. Hundreds of thousands of acres were granted in fee simple, supplemented by 'tickets of occupation' for remote and unsurveyed grazing runs. In Van Diemen's Land, by the mid-1820s, almost all arable land had been occupied by settlers.[30] In New South Wales, this policy shift resulted in the sudden settlement of the Hunter Valley to the north, Bathurst in the west, and the Illawarra and south-western districts. By the late 1820s, the geographical reach of the mainland colony was exploding, with vast swathes of land, thousands of head of stock and the bulk of the colony's growing labour force falling into the hands of less than 8 per cent of the colony's population, most of them free settlers.[31]

This phenomenal growth, which wended through the second quarter of the nineteenth century, was driven by markets and followed by law. Stimulated by a reduction of British tariffs, wool production in New South Wales surged dramatically in the 1820s. But on a dry continent even the largesse of free grants and occupation tickets could not keep pace with the aggressive demand for pasture. So, graziers, both established and aspiring, 'squatted' wherever they could, tramping inland down creeks and through mountain passes in all directions. Settlers sent armed convicts and millions of sheep into the vast interior, spilling with startling rapidity onto land that was

29 Lisa Ford and David Andrew Roberts, 'Expansion, 1820–1850', in Alison Bashford and Stuart McIntyre (eds), *Cambridge History of Australia* (Port Melbourne: Cambridge University Press, 2013), 1: 121–48; T. M. Perry, *Australia's First Frontier: The Spread of Settlement in New South Wales, 1788–1829* (Melbourne: Melbourne University Press, 1963), 130–2.

30 Sharon Morgan, *Land Settlement in Early Tasmania: Creating an Antipodean England* (Melbourne: Cambridge University Press, 2003).

31 E. Higginbotham, 'The 1828 Census and the Analysis of Rural Settlement in New South Wales' *Australasian Historical Archaeology* 11 (1993): 52–75.

not granted by the state. They entered new and unvisited places, immediately competing for life-giving water and pastures carefully cultivated by Aboriginal people to attract native animals. This was a catastrophic invasion that everywhere created conflict. The early phases of this dispossession were also illegal.[32]

In New South Wales, Governor Ralph Darling tried to arrest expansion by drawing a frontier line around nineteen counties. These 'limits of location' marked the only regions in the colony in which land could be granted, purchased or leased.[33] His successor, Richard Bourke, followed up with the Crown Lands Encroachment Act of 1833,[34] which declared that no one occupying land outside the limits could claim any sort of tenure, even through adverse possession. To keep some measure of order beyond the boundaries, the office of Commissioner of Crown Lands was established to check 'encroachment, intrusion and trespass'.[35] Despite complaints that it was 'a bill for breaking the heads of squatters', the Act did not make squatting a crime.[36] As a result, it was totally ineffective. Withholding tenure provided no disincentive: the money made from wool justified the risk of improving land without it. In fact, informal local markets developed in which squatters sold and purchased runs extra-legally.[37] There followed a so-called 'Heroic Age' of Australian squatting that drove pastoralism into far-western New South Wales and through the New England highlands into what is now southern Queensland. In the far south, Vandemonian settlers crossed Bass Strait to reach Port Phillip and Portland Bay (Victoria), converging with 'overlanders' from New South Wales moving south from the Murrumbidgee River.[38]

A series of failed attempts to bring squatters within the law ensued. The imperial 1831 'Ripon regulations' ended the free land grant system throughout

32 John C. Weaver, 'Beyond the Fatal Shore: Pastoral Squatting and the Occupation of Australia, 1826 to 1852' *American Historical Review* 101, no. 4 (1996): 981–1007.

33 June Phillip, 'Wakefieldian Influence and NSW, 1830–1832' *Historical Studies: Australia and New Zealand* 9, no. 34 (1960): 173–80; D. N. Jeans, 'Territorial Divisions and the Location of Towns in New South Wales, 1826–1842' *Australian Geographer* 10 (1967): 243–55.

34 NSW 4 Wm 4 No. 10.

35 4 Will. 4 No. 11a. The powers of the Commissioners were substantially increased in 1839 when a new Act allowed them to evict unlicensed squatters (2 Vic. No. 27).

36 *The Australian*, 13 September 1833, 3.

37 This informal economy won important recognition in the courts by the end of the 1830s, including (in 1839) the right to sue in trespass against any person except the Crown. *Scott v Dight* [1839] NSWSupC 16.

38 Stephen H. Roberts, *The Squatting Age in Australia, 1835–1847* (Melbourne: Melbourne University Press, 1935).

the empire, offering cheap, surveyed land closer to settlements in an effort to tempt settlers back towards Sydney. This system, of course, had no attractions for pastoralists. By the mid-1830s it was clear that the only way to bring squatters within the law was to compromise by allowing them a 'permissive occupancy' through licensing. Legislation in New South Wales allowed squatters to licence runs in 'Border Districts' around the fringes of the colony. Commissioners of Crown land were appointed to collect revenue, issue fines and seize stock, mediate boundary disputes and monitor the composition and movement of regional populations.[39] The Panic and Depression of the 1840s brought further concessions: from 1842, local regulations allowed squatters to purchase small portions of a run after five years occupancy. Still, squatters and their trading partners wanted a greater stake in their runs.[40]

Mobilising with increasing efficiency, the squatters finally convinced the British Parliament to recognise the legality of pastoralism by converting licences to leases. The Australian Colonies Waste Lands Act 1846[41] (an amendment of the 1842 Act), was implemented by Order in Council of 9 March 1847.[42] Henceforth, pastoral leases could be obtained for any term not exceeding fourteen years, with rents determined by stock capacity, at a minimum price of £10 per annum. Leaseholders held a pre-emptive right to purchase portions of their runs in freehold – not more than 160 acres at no less than £1 per acre – although the Crown retained the right to grant or sell any portion for 'public purposes', including 'for the use or benefit of the Aboriginal inhabitants of the country'. These developments reflected a stark reality: weak colonial government, weak imperial will and overwhelming profits made settler and imperial legislation uncomfortable collaborators in the dispossession of Indigenous Australians.

This legislation applied to the whole of Australia, even in South Australia and the Swan River colony where pastoral booms had scarcely begun and where different legal responses to pastoral expansion pertained. In 1842 South Australia established a licensing system similar to that in New South Wales, in order both to check encroachment on the colony's wastelands and to curb the expectation that squatting might platform legal title. The Act

39 Crown Land Unauthorised Occupation Act of 1836 (7 Wm IV. No. 4); Act to 'further . . . restrain the unauthorised occupation of Crown Lands' (2 Vic. No. 27). In 1842, Parliament's Crown Lands Sale Act 'for regulating the sale of waste lands belonging to the Crown in the Australian colonies' (5 & 6 Vic. c 36) protected licensees from sale by the Crown, although land could still not be obtained freehold.

40 Phillip McMichael, *Settlers and the Agrarian Question: Foundations of Capitalism in Colonial Australia* (Cambridge: Cambridge University Press, 1984), 142–4.

41 9 & 10 Vic. c 104. 42 *The Australian*, 3 August 1847, 2–3.

distinguished between 'depasturing licences', purely for the running of stock, and 'occupation licences', which permitted some cultivation and building, and established an annual levy based on assessments of stock numbers. It gave the governor or the Resident Colonisation Commissioner power to issue and adjust regulations, and established Commissioners of Crown Lands in line with the New South Wales model. The powers of this office were increased in 1846 before local legislation was brought into line with imperial legislation in 1848.[43] This shift was well in time for pastoral expansion into South Australia's arid north, which awaited the breeding of new, drought-hardy sheep, beginning with the Peppin Merino in the 1860s. New desert breeds dramatically increased wool and lamb production throughout the continent, and helped South Australia to produce 9.4 per cent of Australia's wool by 1890.[44]

Disastrous and extensive land grants early in Western Australia's settlement had placed much proximate, arable land (and a good deal of indifferent land) in the hands of a very few owners: by 1850 just 7,419 acres of land were in cultivation. Squatting in the west grew around and in tension with these landholdings. By 1850, Western Australia had over 128,000 sheep and it was clear that wool and beef, not wheat, would underpin its nascent economy.[45] In 1841, the Swan River administration allowed pastoralists who purchased 160 acres to run their flocks and herds over adjacent Crown lands, until these rules were disallowed by the Colonial Office on the ground that a minimum of 320 acres had to be purchased. In August 1842, the colony legislated to permit licensed occupation on payment of (a controversially large) £20 per 4,000 acres, admitting 'to a certain extent' some pre-emptive rights and compensation for improvements when a licence was not renewed. This Act was disallowed because it was repugnant to the 1842 Imperial Act.[46] Another Squatting Act in 1844 was mostly concerned with the removal and prosecution of illegal occupants, but was followed by regulations that reduced the price of licences. In 1850, a new law opened up fresh territory

43 An Act for Protecting the Waste Lands of the Crown in South Australia from encroachment intrusion and trespass, 6 Vic. No. 8, 1842; An Act to regulate the Occupation of Crown Lands in South Australia, 10 Vic. No. 11, 1846; Act to Regulate the Occupation of Crown Lands in South Australia, 11 & 12. Vic. No. 10, 1848.

44 Michael Pearson and Jane Lennon, *Pastoral Australia: Fortunes, Failures & Hard Yakka: A Historical Overview* (Collingwood: CSIRO Publishing, 2010), 71, 129.

45 Stephen H. Roberts, *History of Australian Land Settlement, 1788–1920* (Melbourne: Macmillan & Co, 1924), 65–7, 217–18.

46 Act to Regulate the Temporary Occupation of Crown Lands in the Colony of Western Australia, 7 Vic. No. 14, 1844; Government Regulations, 17 October 1844, in *Perth Gazette*, 26 October 1844, 4.

by offering eight-year leases of suitable grazing land and one-year leases of land suitable for agriculture. Still, by 1865, Western Australia had only 260,000 sheep grazing 15 million acres of land. As in South Australia, Western Australia's pastoral explosion came later. By 1885, there were 1.5 million sheep grazing 152 million acres of land, but that was still just 2.5 per cent of all the sheep in Australia. However, by 1921, after the Peppin Merino and refrigerated shipping facilitated the explosion of sheep and cow production in arid regions and across Australia's North, the acreage given over to pastoral leases in Western Australia reached 259 million acres.[47]

Pastoral leases, like occupation licences before them, were varied. It was unclear what rights they were intended to provide to their holders. A normal lease provides exclusive possession to the leaseholder but, as Reynolds and Dalziel argued in the context of land rights litigation in the 1990s, pastoral leases granted under imperial legislation were never intended to prevent Aboriginal access to land.[48] Actually, policy under this head was very inconsistent. Henry Grey (Secretary of State for War and the Colonies from 1846–52) felt strongly that pastoral tenures were 'not intended to deprive the natives of their former right to hunt'.[49] Although the 1846 Waste Lands Act offered no basis for it, a June 1849 Order in Council issued under that Act authorised the governor to insert conditions in pastoral leases that ensured Aboriginal access to pastoral runs. Reynolds and Dalziel argue that even pastoral leases granted under separate, local legislation after self-government should be read in the light of imperial efforts to protect Indigenous people around the Empire. Others disagree, suggesting that humanitarian impulses in this period were contradictory, more often concerned with tempering frontier violence than with strong recognition of Indigenous land rights.[50]

47 Pearson and Lennon, *Pastoral Australia*, 80.

48 Henry Reynolds and Jamie Dalziel, 'Aborigines and Pastoral Leases – Imperial and Colonial Policy, 1826–1855' *UNSW Law Journal* 19 (1996): 315. See also Ann Curthoys and Jessie Mitchell, *Taking Liberty: Indigenous Rights and Settler Self-Government in Colonial Australia, 1830–1890* (Cambridge: Cambridge University Press, 2018), 188.

49 Earl Grey to Governor Fitzroy, 11 February 1848, quoted in Robert Foster and Amanda Nettelbeck *Out of the Silence: The History and Memory of South Australia* (Kent Town: Wakefield Press, 2012), 95.

50 Bain Attwood, 'Introduction: the Past as Future: Aborigines, Australia and the (dis)course of History', in B. Attwood (ed.), *In the Age of Mabo: History, Aborigines and Australia* (St Leonards: Allen & Unwin, 1996), vii–xxxviii; Johnathon Fulcher, 'The Wik Judgment, Pastoral Leases and Colonial Office Policy and Intention in NSW in the 1840s' *Australian Journal of Legal History* 4, no. 1 (1998): 33–56; David Andrew Roberts, '"They would speedily abandon the country to the new comers": The Denial of Aboriginal Rights', in Martin Crotty and David Andrew Roberts (eds), *The Great Mistakes of Australian History* (Sydney: University of New South Wales Press, 2006), 14–31.

Nevertheless, the notion that pastoral leases did not concede exclusive possession underpinned the High Court's *Wik* judgment of 1996, which found that such leases did not extinguish native title.

More importantly, and despite the violence that accompanied all pastoral expansion, running a few sheep or cattle in a vast arid wilderness without fences or adequate supervision did not effectively exclude Aboriginal people from their traditional land (see Figure 13.1). Indeed, access to pastoral runs was guaranteed for a time by the end of penal transportation (and, with it, of cheap convict labour). Pastoralists found themselves reliant on Aboriginal labour.[51] So began what McGrath and others have described as a period of co-existence – short-lived in much of New South Wales and Victoria, but which characterised pastoral enterprises in Australia's northern regions (stretching across Western Australia, the Northern Territory and Queensland) until the civil rights era,

Figure 13.1: (COLOUR CENTREPIECE) Augustus Earle (~1826), A native family of New South Wales sitting down on an English settlers farm. National Library of Australia, nla.obj-134500174. Grace Karskens points out that this family is solid, while the station and settlers fade into the background. (For the colour version, please refer to the plate section)

51 H. Goodall, *Invasion to Embassy: Land in Aboriginal Politics in New South Wales, 1770–1972* (St Leonards: Allen and Unwin, 1996), 57–8.

when pastoralists were required to pay equal wages to Aboriginal workers. Where Aboriginal labour was integral to the pastoral industry, kinship groups maintained ties with Country. Indeed, the seasonal migrations of Aboriginal people determined pastoral work patterns in the Northern Territory into the 1960s.[52] Of course, these employment relationships were grossly unequal. Aboriginal people, including children (often abducted and taken from their traditional homes and kin) were frequently paid with inferior food and poor accommodation and were subject, at times, to brutal discipline and sexual exploitation.[53] This détente recognised Aboriginal ownership of land only informally. Colonial law combined with greed to ensure that 'native title' to land was not recognised in Australian law until the 1990s.

Dispossession by Closer Settlement

The second wave of dispossession by law was less geographically expansive but more complete. As Australian colonies obtained self-government, and as their legislatures became more democratic, Aboriginal Australians were even more marginalised. Their dispossession came to be understood as a mark of settler progress and their supposed 'savagery', the antithesis of the modern settler-citizen.[54] But this hardening chauvinism did not cause the second dispossession; democracy and land hunger did. New legislatures (everywhere except Western Australia) were voted in by poor and middling men who had flocked to the Australian colonies during the 1850s gold rush. Their immediate focus was not Aboriginal people, but squatters whose leases encompassed most arable parts of the colonies. New voters wanted cheap land and needed more food. As a result, squatters became the target of very potent critiques from democrats and demagogues.[55] They were empowered to act from 1855,

52 Ann McGrath, *Born in the Cattle: Aborigines in Cattle Country* (Sydney: Allen & Unwin, 1987); P. Brock, 'Pastoral Stations and Reserves in South and Central Australia, 1850s–1950s' *Labour History* 69 (1995): 102–14; K. Booth and L. Ford, 'Ross v Chambers: Assimilation law and policy in the Northern Territory' *Aboriginal History* 40 (2016): 3–25.

53 T. Rowse, *White Flour, White Power: From Rations to Citizenship in Central Australia* (Cambridge: Cambridge University Press, 2002). On the employment of children in the colonial period, see Shirleene Robinson, 'Queensland Settlers and the Creation of the First 'Stolen Generations': The Unofficial Removal of Aboriginal Children in Queensland, 1842–1897' *Journal of Australian Colonial History* 4, no. 1 (2002): 1–16.

54 J. Mitchell, '"The Galling Yoke of Slavery": Race and Separation in Colonial Port Phillip' *Journal of Australian Studies* 33, no. 2 (2009): 125–37; Leigh Boucher, 'Race, Rights and the Re-forming Settler Polity in Mid-Nineteenth Century Victoria' *Journal of Australian Colonial History* 15 (2013): 83–104.

55 Peter Cochrane, *Colonial Ambition: Foundations of Australian Democracy* (Carlton: Melbourne University Publishing, 2006).

when the British Parliament's new Australian Waste Lands Act repealed the 1840s statutes and paved the way for newly self-governing Australian colonies to legislate for the disposal of their own lands.[56]

In 1861, the New South Wales Parliament passed two Crown Lands Acts (the Robertson Acts), which allowed would-be farmers to select and purchase blocks of Crown land (40 to 320 acres) on a modest deposit of five shillings per acre. The old nineteen counties and limits of location were done away with.[57] The Acts were passed a year before the first 'homestead' legislation in the United States and a decade ahead of Canada's Dominion Lands Act. Comparable (though more closely supervised) policies were enacted in Queensland in 1860, supplemented by an innovative 'grazing farmers' scheme of 1868, as the new colony sought closer settlement and economic diversification in the wake of its separation from New South Wales.[58] Victoria, after a number of failed attempts, passed a similar act in 1865 to open land for purchase and leasing.[59] South Australia eventually followed suit, a decade after it gained responsibility for Crown lands in 1859, legislating the so-called 'Strangways Act' in 1869 against the powerful opposition of pastoralists.[60] In the first years of the Robertson Acts in New South Wales, 445,000 acres were occupied by 17,000 people and the amount of cultivated land increased by 54 per cent. By 1883, 16,354,000 acres of land had been occupied under the scheme, and 'nearly three million acres . . . taken by other means'.[61] In Victoria, almost 15 million acres of Crown land had been alienated under its Crown Lands Alienation Act by 1879, with another 7 million acres sold through auction.[62] Nor did such 'closer settlement' schemes abate, becoming more sophisticated and sustained from the last decades of the nineteenth century, reaching Western Australia by 1910, and expanding again, after World War I, as rewards for returned soldiers.[63]

56 Australian Waste Lands Act, 18 & 19 Vic. c 56.

57 Crown Lands Alienation Act 1861 No. 26a; Crown Lands Occupation Act 1861 No. 27a.

58 Roberts, *History of Australian Land Settlement*, 277–9.

59 Crown Lands Alienation Act 1860 24 Vic. No. 15; Amending Land Act, 1865 29 Vic. No. 237.

60 Waste Lands Amendment Act (1868–9 32 Vic. No. 14).

61 Roberts, *History of Australian Land Settlement*, 255; Sylvia Morrissey, *Squatters and Selectors: A Social and Economic History* (Melbourne: Oxford University Press Australia, 1983).

62 Department of Lands and Agriculture, *Report of Proceedings Taken under the Provisions of the Land Act* (Melbourne: Victorian Parliament, 1880), 3.

63 Roberts, *History of Australian Land Settlement*, 299–308; 338–9; Marilyn Lake, *The Limits of Hope: Soldier Settlement in Victoria, 1915–1938* (Melbourne: Oxford University Press, 1987); Melanie Oppenheimer and Bruce Scates, *The Last Battle: Soldier Settlement in Australia, 1916–1938* (Melbourne: Cambridge University Press, 2016).

This process marked a new and decisive phase of dispossession. Pastoralism had long been viewed as an unworthy and wasteful form of land use, hardly more legitimate than hunting and gathering.[64] The imperial and most colonial governments had long wanted closer settlement but had despaired of it in the golden age of squatting. The closer settlement Acts did more than ideological work, however. They changed the relationship of many Australian colonists with the land. As noted, some pastoral leases and many lessees permitted Aboriginal access. In contrast, small farms were not intended to be shared space. Closer settlement grants promised exclusive possession in fee simple – a final and inexorable extinguishment of Aboriginal tenure that not even recent moves to recognise native title can unpick. As a practical matter, the shift from looser modes of land use to freehold agriculture closed off access to Country, disrupting Aboriginal life patterns and work opportunities in the southeast.

Aborigines in Victoria and New South Wales fought to maintain access to their Country under the selection acts. They also fought for dedicated Aboriginal reserves.[65] At the same time, settler governments moved to make reserve lands places of confinement and control. This process unfolded most fully in Victoria, where an Aboriginal Protection Board administered reserves from the late 1860s.[66] Things moved more slowly in New South Wales. The first thirty-five reserves created in 1850 had been of little interest or use to Aboriginal people, because pastoralism allowed them to live new lives on Country. This changed under the pressures of closer settlement. Largely in response to Aboriginal demand for reserve lands, thirty-two reserves were created in New South Wales from 1861–84, and more still after the establishment of the Aboriginal Protection Board in 1883. Sometimes these reserves were successfully farmed by Aborigines, although these efforts were frequently undone by the intense and sustained opposition of white settlers who coveted the land for themselves – prompting what Goodall described as a 'second dispossession' during the early 1900s.[67] From the time of the NSW Board's creation, it fought to turn reserves into places where Indigenous people could be encouraged to gather by making them exclusive

64 R. Waterhouse, 'The Yeoman Ideal and Australian Experience, 1860–1960', in K. Darian-Smith, P. Grimshaw, K. Lindsey and S. McIntyre (eds), *Exploring the British World: Identity, Cultural Production, Institutions* (Melbourne: RMIT Publishing, 2004), 440–59.

65 Heather Goodall, 'Land in Our Own Country: The Aboriginal Land Rights Movement in South-Eastern Australia, 1860–1914' *Aboriginal History* 14 (1990): 1–24.

66 Curthoys and Mitchell, *Taking Liberty*, 274–7.

67 Goodall, *Invasion to Embassy*, 163.

sites of ration distribution. The NSW board was not given powers to coerce Aboriginal people onto reserves until the twentieth century.

In South Australia, where Aboriginal protection began with the colony's founding, reserves were established from the 1840s, but many were sold off and all were kept deliberately small so as to encourage Aboriginal South Australians to use land more intensively or, increasingly, to serve as sites of ration distribution.[68] Reserves served a mix of functions in Western Australia. Though 21 million acres had been reserved in vast pastoral regions by 1921 (some set up as cattle stations), closer settlement and mining schemes led to enormous pressure to reduce Aboriginal land holdings soon after.[69] In Queensland, reserves were largely resisted until the infamous Aboriginals Protection and Restriction of the Sale of Opium Act in 1897 allowed the state to force Aboriginal and Torres Strait Islander people onto reserves against their will. Some 7,000 people were confined under the Act over the next four decades.[70] The threat of removal from reserves became a key means of keeping Aboriginal communities passive and subordinate, while the state and missionary establishments themselves served the purpose of gathering and policing Aboriginal and Torres Strait Islander people. Such places helped to corral Aboriginal and Torres Strait Islander workers into exploitative and often unpaid agricultural, pastoral and domestic service (see Map 13.1).[71]

The key legal tool here was Aboriginal protection legislation. From the 1860s in Victoria and at the turn of the century in Western Australia (1886), Queensland (1897), New South Wales (1909) and South Australia (1911), a spate of protection legislation assisted Aboriginal dispossession by restricting Aboriginal rights to move from reserves and missions, stealing their children and banishing their mixed-race family members to towns and cities. In Tasmania, where land was set aside on Cape Barren Island in 1881 for the use of the descendants of Aboriginal women and European sealers, a Reserve Act in 1912 attempted to force residents to build houses and cultivate land under threat

68 Judith Raftery, *Not Part of the Public: Non-Indigenous Policies and Practices and the Health of Indigenous South Australians, 1836–1973* (Kent Town, SA: Wakefield Press, 2006), 91.

69 Peter Biskup, *Not Slaves, Not Citizens: The Aboriginal Problem in Western Australia, 1898–1954* (St Lucia: University of Queensland Press, 1973), 101–6.

70 Thom Blake, 'Deported . . . at the Sweet Will of the Government: The Removal of Aborigines to Reserves in Queensland 1897–1939' *Aboriginal History* 22 (1988): 51–61.

71 Nettelbeck, *Indigenous Rights and Colonial Subjecthood*, 190–1; Jackie Huggins, 'White Aprons, Black Hands: Aboriginal Women Domestic Servants in Queensland' *Labour History* 69 (1995): 188–95; Raymond Evans and Joanne Scott, '"Fallen among Thieves": Aboriginal Labour and State Control in Inter-War Queensland' *Labour History* 69 (1995): 115–30; Robert Castle and Jim Hagan, 'Regulation of Aboriginal Labour in Queensland: Protectors, Agreements and Trust Accounts 1897–1965' *Labour History* 72 (1997): 66–76.

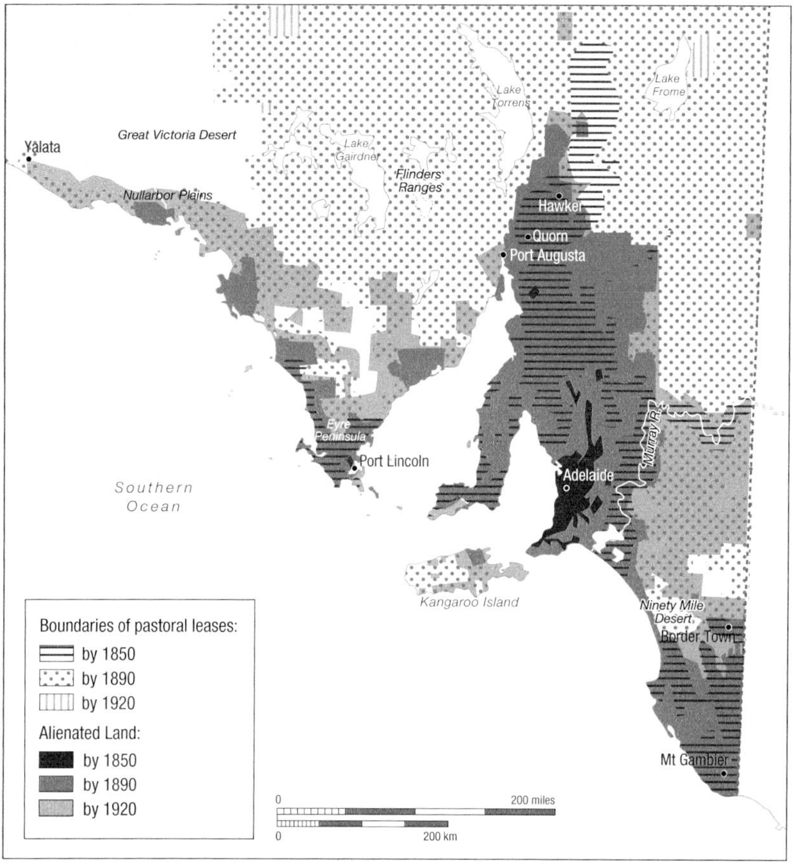

Map 13.1: Dispossession in South Australia

of expulsion.[72] These were regimes largely implemented by the colonial (then state and territory) police though, in many places, missionary establishments also played a significant role. However, where they endured, missions and reserves have supported successful common law and statutory claims since the 1970s.[73]

72 Kristyn Harman, 'Protecting Tasmanian Aborigines: American and Queensland Influences on the Cape Barren Island Reserve Act, 1912' *Journal of Imperial and Commonwealth History* 41, no. 5 (2015): 744–64.

73 The best overview of protection legislation and its ramifications remains Anna Haebich, *Broken Circles: Fragmenting Indigenous Families, 1800–2000* (Freemantle: Freemantle Arts Centre Press, 2000).

Violence as Dispossession

Protection regimes effected intimate violence against Indigenous peoples. They succeeded and co-existed with ubiquitous, state-sponsored and private-vigilante violence in the service of dispossession. Every mode of expansion by grant, squatting, license, leasehold and purchase was, in varying degrees, murderous. Though, as the best scholarship on Indigenous–settler encounter has demonstrated, accommodation and co-existence occurred constantly in Australian history, it is also true that every expansion of settlement in the Australian colonies was resisted by Aboriginal people or bolstered by violence against them.[74]

In New South Wales, between 1792 and 1801, Aboriginal raids on remote farms threatened the very security of the colony, inviting military reprisals and settler vigilantism. The two combined when, in 1801, a sympathetic but increasingly anxious Governor King issued a government order permitting the fatal capture of 'Pemulwuy'.[75] Thereafter, the government repeatedly authorised settlers to kill Aborigines in times of trouble.[76] Such delegations of state power to kill reached an early peak in 1816 when Governor Lachlan Macquarie defended expanding agriculture on the Cumberland Plains by issuing a series of proclamations that forbade Aboriginal people from approaching settlements in groups of more than six, offered rewards for the detention or destruction of certain individuals identified as 'open and avowed Enemies to the Peace' and authorised settlers to 'repel . . . Attacks or Incursions by Force of Arms'.[77]

Such delegations followed two strands of thinking about Aboriginal legal status. In the early years of settlement, as Mark Finnane outlines in this volume, the status of Indigenous people vis-à-vis the Crown was unclear. Into the 1820s, some judges in New South Wales argued that Indigenous Australians could not understand legal proceedings against them so could not be tried in settler courts (and, thus, were not protected by British law).

74 Ann McGrath, *Illicit Love* (Lincoln, NE: University of Nebraska Press, 2018); Lisa Ford and Tim Rowse (eds), *Between Indigenous and Settler Governance* (Abingdon: Routledge, 2011).

75 E. Willmot, *Pemulwuy: The Rainbow Warrior* (Sydney: Bantam, 1988); Lyndall Ryan, 'Untangling Aboriginal Resistance and the Settler Punitive Expedition: The Hawkesbury River Frontier in New South Wales, 1794–1810' *Journal of Genocide Research* 15, no. 2 (2013): 219–32.

76 Lisa Ford, *Settler Sovereignty: Jurisdiction and Indigenous People in America and Australia, 1788–1836* (Cambridge, MA: Harvard University Press, 2010), 45–6.

77 Stephen Gapps, *The Sydney Wars: Conflict in the Early Colony, 1788–1817* (Sydney: NewSouth Publishing, 2018).

Accordingly, it is probable that the first Indigenous person was tried and convicted of a crime (rape) in 1816, nearly thirty years after first settlement, because he had been raised in Sydney.[78] Another strand of legal reasoning held that Aboriginal people were not bound by British law, and so could not be punished or protected by it. In 1827, the barrister defending a mounted police officer charged with murdering an Aboriginal prisoner in the Hunter Region argued that Aboriginal Australians could be killed with impunity by settlers because they had not been conquered or treated with and, so, were not subjects of the king.[79] This argument was rejected in the case of settler-Indigenous crime. However, a similar argument was accepted by the Supreme Court in *R v Ballard* in 1829. In that case, the court informed the Attorney General that it had no jurisdiction to try crimes between Aboriginal people because they owed no allegiance to the Crown and had laws of their own.[80]

The shift towards exercising jurisdiction over Aboriginal people for frontier violence had ramifications for the way violence was dispensed by the state in greater New South Wales. After 1820, formal delegations of the power to kill Indigenous people became rare.[81] Governor Macquarie's successor, Thomas Brisbane, sought to regularise decentralised violence by placing the western frontier under martial law in 1824, suspending ordinary law to allow the military to restore order by whatever means. Brisbane's new Attorney General (and, later, activist for Indigenous protection), Saxe Bannister, saw martial law as the only way to legitimately use violence against Aboriginal people. However, the experiment was not repeated in New South Wales. Notoriously, Bannister could not convince Governor Ralph Darling to declare martial law in the Hunter Region in 1826. Darling argued that martial law was not required to justify the killing of 'a few naked Savages, who, however treacherous, would not face a Corporal's Guard'.[82] However, in Van Diemen's Land, self-proclaimed humanitarian George

78 *R v Mow-watty* [1816] NSWKR 2; [1816] NSWSupC 2; L. Ford and B. Salter, 'From Pluralism to Territorial Sovereignty: The 1816 Trial of Mow-watty in the Superior Court of New South Wales' *Indigenous Law Journal* 7 (2008): 67–86.

79 *R v Lowe* [1827] NSWKR 4; [1827] NSWSupC 32; Kelly K. Chaves, '"A solemn judicial farce, the mere mockery of a trial": The Acquittal of Lieutenant Lowe, 1827' *Aboriginal History* 31 (2007): 122–40.

80 *R v Ballard* [1829] NSWSupC 26; B. Salter, 'For Want of Evidence: Initial Impressions of Indigenous Exchanges with the First Colonial Superior Courts of Australia' *University of Tasmania Law Review* 27, no. 2 (2008): 145–60.

81 John Connor, *The Australian Frontier Wars, 1788–1838* (Sydney: UNSW Press, 2002).

82 B. H. Fletcher, *Ralph Darling: A Governor Maligned* (Melbourne: Oxford University Press, 1984), 186.

Arthur declared martial law for three years from 1828 to quell Aboriginal resistance. There, bounties were offered for the capture of Aboriginal people and a 'Black Line' of 2000 soldiers and citizens was formed to drive remnant populations onto the remote Tasman Peninsula. The crux of the problem, according to the Vandemonian authorities, was that the Aboriginal tendency to 'wander over extensive tracts of Country without cultivating or permanently occupying any portion of it' was 'utterly inconsistent with the peaceable pursuits of a civilised society'.[83] Ethnic cleansing was the chosen solution.

From the mid-1820s, the shifting rhetoric surrounding Aboriginal legal status meant that state-sponsored violence against Indigenous people was less likely to be cast as a military matter, and was referred to increasingly as a matter of policing. Armed and mounted police forces (at first comprised of men seconded from the military) were dispatched to violent frontiers – sometimes under instructions that looked like war but were increasingly described as efforts to keep the King's Peace.[84] As Amanda Nettelbeck shows in this volume and elsewhere,[85] armed policemen throughout the Australian colonies arrested, harassed, and even massacred Aboriginal people to defend land grants and pastoral leases or to enforce labour contracts, all in the name of law. Policing violence was most brutal in what became Queensland where, from until the late 1840s, a police force composed of Aboriginal people recruited from the south were ordered to treat Indigenous people in groups of more than three as enemies of the state who could be dispersed (or killed) at will.[86] South Australian police officer William Willshire's campaign against Aboriginal people in Central Australia in the 1880s and 1890s provides another notorious example of policing by massacre.[87] Aboriginal peoples were also

83 Julie Evans and Tessa Fluence, 'Securing the Settler Polity: Martial Law and the Aboriginal Peoples of Van Diemen's Land' *Journal of Australian Colonial History* 15 (2013): 1–22; Graeme Calder, 'Routing a Rebellion or Crushing a Crime Wave: Proclaiming Martial Law and a Call-To-Arms in Van Diemen's Land, 1828–1830' *Legal History* 12 (2008): 127–50; Jacqueline Fox, 'Criminalising Frontier Conflict in Van Diemen's Land: Indigenous Prosecutions during the Black War' *Journal of Australian Colonial History* 17 (2015): 65–82.

84 Lisa Ford, 'Protecting the Peace on the Edges of Empire: Commissioners of Crown Lands in New South Wales', in Bain Attwood, Lauren Benton and Adam Clulow (eds), *Protection and Empire: A Global History* (New York: Cambridge University Press, 2017), 175–93.

85 Nettelbeck, Chapter 20 in this volume; Amanda Nettelbeck and Lyndall Ryan, 'Salutary Lessons: Native Police and the "Civilising" Role of Legalised Violence in Colonial Australia' *The Journal of Imperial and Commonwealth History* 46, no. 1 (2018): 47–68.

86 Jonathan Richards, *The Secret War: A True History of Queensland's Native Police* (St Lucia: University of Queensland Press, 2008).

87 Amanda Nettelbeck and Robert Foster, *In the Name of the Law: William Willshire and the Policing of the Australian Frontier* (Kent Town, SA: Wakefield Press, 2007).

increasingly punished by operation of law. South Australia, where Aboriginal people were declared to be subjects of the king from the outset, were more likely to be executed than in any other Australian colony.[88] In Western Australia, local police had the support of magistrates armed, from 1849, with extensive summary jurisdiction to punish Aboriginal offenders with two dozen lashes and six months in prison. This jurisdiction was used most often to punish Aboriginal labourers.[89]

At the same time, everywhere, British law failed to protect Aboriginal Australians against settler exploitation and violence, both because the criminal justice system was simply unable to effectively investigate and prosecute far-flung violence, and because it helped settlers get away with murder.[90] From the outset in New South Wales, settlers were very seldom tried for killing or injuring Aboriginal people and even fewer were convicted. Five convicts tried in 1799 for 'wantonly killing two natives' (adolescent boys, well known to the community) were found guilty, but the reservations of some members of the quasi-military court meant that they were neither hanged nor imprisoned for their crime.[91] Much more typical was the fate of Lieutenant Lowe. While his barrister failed to convince the court that his victim was not protected by British law, and despite clear evidence against him, Lowe was acquitted to public applause.[92] At Myall Creek in 1838, pastoral labourers slaughtered at least twenty-eight Aboriginal people and burned their bodies, but it took two trials by a determined colonial government to have them hanged. At the same time, two infamous massacres

88 Amanda Nettelbeck and Robert Foster, 'Colonial Judiciaries, Aboriginal Protection and South Australia's Policy of Punishing "with Exemplary Severity"', *Australian Historical Studies* 41, no. 3 (2010): 319–36; Alan Richard Pope, *One Law for All? Aboriginal People and Criminal Law in Early South Australia* (Canberra: Aboriginal Studies Press, 2011), 135–56.

89 Amanda Nettelbeck, '"Keep the Magistrates Straight": Magistrates and Aboriginal "Management" on Australia's North-west Frontiers, 1883–1905' *Aboriginal History* 38 (2014): 19–37. See also A. Hunter, *A Different Kind of 'Subject': Colonial Law in Aboriginal-European Relations in Nineteenth-century Western Australia, 1829–61* (North Melbourne: Australian Scholarly Press, 2012).

90 Amanda Nettelbeck, '"Equals of the White Man": Prosecution of Settlers for Violence against Aboriginal Subjects of the Crown in Colonial Western Australia' *Law and History Review* 31, no. 2 (2013): 355–90; Susanne Davies, 'Aborigines, Murder and the Criminal Law in Early Port Phillip, 1841–1851' *Australian Historical Studies* 22, no. 88 (1987): 313–35; Mark Finnane and Fiona Paisley, 'Police Violence and the Limits of Law on a Late Colonial Frontier: the "Borroloola case" in 1930s Australia', *Law and History Review* 28, no. 1 (2010): 141–71.

91 Criminal Court, Minutes of Proceedings, 16 October 1799, State Records NSW, X905, 323, 329–62.

92 *R v Lowe* [1827] NSWKR 4; [1827] NSWSupC 32; Chaves, 'A solemn judicial farce, the mere mockery of a trial'.

undertaken by forces led by Majors Mitchell (1836) and Nunn (1837–8) were much discussed but never brought to trial.[93] Similar patterns existed in almost every other colony, aided, as Mark Finnane points out, by the long-standing refusal to accept (and later to give credit to) Aboriginal evidence. Western Australia is the sole (and partial) exception: it tried twenty-nine colonists (and acquitted only eight) for crimes against Aboriginal people in the first fifty years of settlement.[94] Throughout the continent, the legal system fed these appalling failures to protect Aboriginal people from dispossession by violence and murder.

Law facilitated dispossession by both deploying and failing to police violence against Aboriginal people. Both were practical as well as ideological evils. Nascent mechanisms of state were incapable of protecting anyone in the vast expanses of the Australian interior. In New South Wales, Van Diemen's Land and what would become Victoria, the violence between settlers and Aboriginal people spread and escalated from the late 1820s. In South Australia, Western Australia, Queensland and the Northern Territory, informal violence combined with violent policing lasted a century, as pastoralism spread northwards and into remote inland deserts. The spread and scale of violence (and the failure of the colonial state to stop it) is captured viscerally in massacre maps assembled by Lyndall Ryan.[95] For the most part, violent dispossession was effected out of sight of the state. To this day, communities tell stories about what their ancestors did to dispossess Indigenous people in order to grow crops and raise sheep and cows on Aboriginal land.[96]

Conclusion

The failure to treat with Indigenous people grew, over time, into the doctrine of *terra nullius* – an epistemic dispossession that shaped Australian jurisprudence from the late 1830s until the *Mabo* decision in 1992. Though pastoral leases left open formal and informal access for Aboriginal people to Country, early land grants and the opening of more and more land to purchase in fee simple over the course of the nineteenth and early twentieth centuries

93 Roger Milliss, *Waterloo Creek: The Australia Day Massacre of 1838, George Gipps and the British Conquest of New South Wales* (Ringwood: McPhee Gribble, 1992).
94 Nettelbeck, 'Equals of the White Man', 356–7.
95 https://c21ch.newcastle.edu.au/colonialmassacres/, accessed 1 December 2021.
96 D. Roberts, 'Bells Falls massacre and Bathurst's History of Violence: Local Tradition and Australian Historiography' *Australian Historical Studies* 26, no. 105 (1995): 615–33.

formally and practically dispossessed Indigenous people. However, as so many of the chapters in this volume show, Aboriginal dispossession was an irregular and often unsuccessful project. There are myriad examples of persistent (often heroic) Aboriginal access to Country. Even in Van Diemen's Land, where the Arthur administration tried to physically remove Aboriginal people from the island, some remained on or near Country. As Paul Irish has shown, Indigenous people tenaciously demanded and negotiated access even to the new suburbs of Sydney in the late nineteenth century.[97] Jenny Green and Tim Rowse show in this volume how formal refusals to recognise Aboriginal tenure in Alice Springs have not stopped their participation in land management, particularly through heritage legislation passed in the late twentieth century.[98]

In other places, the coincidence of missions and reserves with ancient claims to Country, combined with dogged maintenance of even partial access to traditional sites, has been rewarded with some species of Aboriginal land title. A series of land title acts granted by states since the 1970s gave usually remote, lightly used or mission land to some Aboriginal peoples in fee simple. Meanwhile, the epochal *Mabo* decision in 1992 rewarded the success of some communities in maintaining 'continuing connections' with their land with 'native title', rejecting the doctrine of *terra nullius* embraced from the 1830s. Informal negotiations, particularly by mining companies with potential claimants, has created a new, informal tenure in the shadow of *Mabo*. The combination led Jon Altman to suggest some years ago that 20 per cent of Indigenous Australians met the 'legal tests of customary ownership' and exercised some control over 20 per cent of the continent.[99] However, much of that land brings only slight profit and only to a tiny proportion of Aboriginal and Torres Strait Islander people. Most Indigenous Australians live in cities where they remain triply dispossessed: uncompensated for their dispossession; reaping none of the paltry benefits of modern legal recognition of title; and not sharing equally in the economic bounties of settler citizenship.

97 Paul Irish, *Hidden in Plain View, The Aboriginal People of Coastal Sydney* (Sydney: NewSouth Publishing, 2017).
98 Rowse and Green, Chapter 9.1 in this volume.
99 Jon Altman, 'Land Rights and Development in Australia: Caring for, Benefiting from, Governing the Indigenous Estate', in Lisa Ford and Tim Rowse (eds), *Between Indigenous and Settler Government*, 126, 133.

14

Australian Land Law

MAUREEN TEHAN

Introduction

Australian land law is as old as human occupation of the Australian land mass. First Nations'[1] oral histories and post-colonisation recordings of those histories detail complex systems of law and relationships with land, involving duties for, and reciprocity with, land and revealing a metaphysical and physical world governing obligation, entitlement, kinship, succession and identity among other things.[2] Colonisation brought the English common law involving an entirely different relationship to and with land, resulting in a complex of power of external origin in charge of a new geopolitical 'unsettled space'.[3] Following colonisation, there were two systems and ideas of land law and relations, operating 'simultaneously, in ignorance of each other or in open conflict, and sometimes in uneasy tension and fragile co-existence'.[4] New meanings, unrelated to First Nations' epistemology, became engraved upon the landscape and in its peoples' consciousness[5] both inside the frontier and beyond.[6] The new property system was central

1 First Nation/s is used to describe the original inhabitants of Australia unless the context otherwise requires.

2 Bill Neidjii, *Story About Feeling* (Broome: Magabala Books, 1989); Irene Watson, 'Indigenous Peoples' Law-ways: Survival against the Colonial State' *Australian Feminist Law Journal* 8, no. 1 (1997): 39; Kearney, Chapter 15 in this volume.

3 Irene Watson, 'Settled and Unsettled Spaces: Are We Free to Roam?', in Aileen Moreton-Robinson (ed.), *Sovereign Subjects: Indigenous Sovereignty Matters* (Sydney: Allen & Unwin, 2007); Nicholas Blomley, *Unsettling the City; Urban Land and the Politics of Property* (Abingdon: Routledge, 2004), 14 cited in Sarah Keenan, *Subversive Property: Law and the Production of Spaces of Belonging* (Abingdon: Routledge, 2015), 94.

4 Heather Goodall, *Invasion to Embassy: Land in Aboriginal Politics in New South Wales 1770–1972* (Sydney: Allen & Unwin, 1996), 23.

5 Cole Harris, *The Resettlement of British Columbia: Essays on Colonialism and Geographical Change* (Vancouver: UBC Press, 1997), xii; Maureen Tehan, 'A Hope Disillusioned an Opportunity Lost? Reflections on Common Law Native Title and Ten Years of the Native Title Act' *Melbourne University Law Review* 27, no. 2 (2003): 523–71, 523.

6 Blomley, *Unsettling the City*, 124.

both to the process of colonisation and to reshaping of the space it inhabited.[7] Seeing this conflict in terms of jurisdiction, Dorsett suggests that colonisers at best, attempted to contain Indigenous jurisdictions and, at worst, simply denied their existence and force.[8] As a result of this conjunction, land has been a central preoccupation of post-colonisation Australian history[9] marking a discordant and legally endorsed relationship of power and dispossession common in all settler societies.[10]

The English common law became the 'law' of the colony when sovereignty was claimed in 1788. By the mid-nineteenth century it was clear that each of the colonies was developing its own unique approaches to land law,[11] which reflected the particular social, economic and geographical environment of the colonies.[12] In spite of these unique developments and departures from the English common law and feudal principles, the baggage of the common law remained the fundamental underlying principle for colonial land law.

Mabo v Queensland (No. 2) ('*Mabo*') required a reassessment of Australian land law as understood in 1992.[13] Consideration of a 'peculiarly Australian'[14] land law required the reframing of the history of Australian land law, which arguably entailed the 'doctrinal revision of the entire conceptual basis of Australian property law'.[15] It required a reaching back to 1788 and a rethinking of the history of Australian land law. In doing this the Court found that pre-colonisation land interests could be recognised and protected by the Australian common law. The rights recognised are described as native title.[16] Expanding the conceptual shift in *Mabo*, *Wik v Queensland*

7 Keenan, *Subversive Property*, 122.
8 Dorsett, Chapter 2 in this volume.
9 Henry Reynolds and Jamie Dalziel, 'Aborigines and Pastoral Leases – Imperial and Colonial Policy 1826–1855' *UNSW Law Journal* 19, no. 2 (1996): 315–77, 316.
10 Harris, *The Resettlement of British Columbia*.
11 Alex Castles, *An Australian Legal History* (Sydney: Law Book Company, 1982), 456; Andrew Buck, 'Property Law and the Origins of Australian Egalitarianism' *Australian Journal of Legal History* 1 (1995): 145–66, 158–61; see generally Andrew Buck, *The Making of Australian Property Law* (Sydney: Federation Press, 2006).
12 Castles, *An Australian Legal History*, 456; Buck, 'Property Law and the Origins of Australian Egalitarianism', 158–61; see generally Buck, *The Making of Australian Property Law*; *Wik Peoples v Queensland* (1996) 187 CLR 1, 182 ('*Wik*'), 122, 129–30 (Toohey J).
13 *Mabo v Queensland* (1992) 175 CLR 1 ('*Mabo*'), 29 (Brennan J); *Wik*, 182 (Gummow J).
14 Adrian Bradbrook, Susan MacCallum, Anthony Moore and Scott Grattan, *Australian Real Property Law* (Sydney: Law Book Co, 2011, 5th edition), 3.
15 Brendan Edgeworth, 'The Mabo "Vibe" and its many Resonances in Australian Property Law', in Sean Brennan, Megan Davis, Brendan Edgeworth and Leon Terrill (eds), *Native Title from Mabo to Akiba: A Vehicle for Change and Empowerment* (Sydney: Federation Press, 2015), 75–98, 76.
16 See Behrendt and Brennan, Chapter 16 in this volume.

('*Wik*'),[17] in its consideration of the effect of pastoral leases on native title, grafted native title onto colonial era, statutory departures from common law tenures. Writing land law history can now only be done through the prism of *Mabo* (and *Wik*). Thus, using *Mabo* as its framework, this chapter identifies the legal and conceptual underpinning of the Crown's powers over land as well as some of the uniquely Australian elements of the colonising land law in the nineteenth century. It suggests that *Mabo* was crucial in freeing Australian land law from some of its common law feudal origins, particularly by redefining the nature of Crown title. Paradoxically though, *Mabo* also reinstated the prominence of the fundamental doctrines of the common law – the doctrines of tenure and estates – in asserting the immovability of the 'skeleton of principle' that those doctrines represent.[18]

English Land Law in Australia: The Doctrines of Tenure and Estates

In 1788 the Australian continent was occupied by multiple First Nations living in accordance with their laws.[19] Yet as a matter of the coloniser's law, the colony of New South Wales was treated as empty, practically uninhabited or *terra nullius*.[20] Into this space Governor Phillip brought 'the ambiguous baggage of English law'.[21] In the early years, it was unclear how much English law became the law of the colony[22] but that question was and remains foundational to land law in Australia: it determined what law applied to settlers in relation to land and the effect of that law on First Nations' relationships with and enjoyment of their land and law. What appeared clear to the colonisers is that the imperial 'baggage' included the land law doctrines of tenure and estates; and it is these doctrines that have most significantly impacted on First Nations' land laws and possession. Although various cases confirmed that the doctrine of tenure was the law of the colonies,[23] the legal

17 (1996) 187 CLR 1. 18 *Mabo*, 29 (Brennan J).

19 See Irene Watson, 'Aboriginal Recognition: Treaties and Colonial Constitutions, "We Have Been Here Forever"' *Bond Law Review* 30, no. 1 (2018).

20 Ibid; *Cooper v Stuart* 14 App Cas 14, 291; *Milurrpum v Nabalco Pty Ltd* (1971) 17 FLR 141.

21 Kercher, Chapter 5 in this volume; Curthoys and Mitchell, Chapter 6 in this volume; see generally Henry Reynolds, *The Law of the Land* (Ringwood: Penguin, 1987); Peter Russell *Recognising Aboriginal title: the Mabo case and Indigenous Resistance to English-settler Colonialism* (Sydney: University of New South Wales Press, 2006).

22 Castles, *An Australian Legal History*, 378–99.

23 *Attorney-General v Brown* (1847) 1 Legge 312; *Cooper v Stuart* (1889) 14 App Cas 286; *Williams v Attorney-General (NSW)* (1913) 16 CLR 404; *Randwick Corporation v Rutledge* (1959) 102 CLR 54; *New South Wales v Commonwealth (the Seas and Submerged Lands Case)* (1975) 135 CLR 337.

effect of these English doctrines on First Nations' land laws was not fully explored until *Mabo*. Even then, questions in relation to conflicting views of sovereignty and First Nations' jurisdiction remain unresolved.[24]

The doctrine of tenure derives from the English feudal landholding system that William the Conqueror established in 1066. It was fundamental to land law in England.[25] The doctrine stemmed largely from the theory (often described as a fiction) that all land was *owned* by the sovereign who, in that capacity, granted land to his loyal lords.[26] The sovereign had *plenum dominium* (absolute ownership) in the land and, from that, carved out rights which were granted to others. The Crown retained the underlying title as absolute owner of the land and its 'tenants' held a beneficial title, or a right to use and possess the land, based on a feudal relationship established as a result of the grant. Land was given in return for the performance of obligations. There were various tenures (or ways of holding the land) reflecting the nature of the obligations owed by the tenant, such as payment of money or provision of services (including knight or spiritual or agricultural services) and, in the case of socage tenure, rent.[27] Over time, this feudal system, with its multiple tenures[28] and the services and obligations attached to them, disappeared leaving only socage tenure, which ultimately became the fee simple title.[29]

Alongside the doctrine of tenure, the other main element of the transplanted English land law was the doctrine of estates. An estate in land has been described as an 'abstract entity' which defines the quality and duration of a title to land. The estates known to the common law are freehold and leasehold (which is a lesser interest than freehold). The central characteristic of both freehold and leasehold estates is a right of exclusive possession of the land. This is a corollary of the doctrine of tenure, according to which: while the holder of a freehold estate might be described colloquially as 'owner', in fact they hold 'an estate in the land', and that estate is 'held of the Crown'. Hepburn has noted that the doctrine of estates rather than the doctrine of tenure was the preoccupation of the nineteenth century as it deals with 'how' land is held rather than 'why'.[30] The doctrine of estates remains central to

24 Watson, 'Aboriginal Recognition'; Watson, 'Aboriginal Laws and Colonial Foundation' *Griffith Law Review* 26, no. 4 (2018): 469–79; see Dorsett, Chapter 2 in this volume.
25 Bradbrook et al., *Australian Real Property Law*, 42.
26 William Blackstone, *Commentaries on the Laws of England* (1803), II: 50–1, cited in *Mabo*, 16. (Brennan J); *Case of Tanistry* (1608) Davis, 28; Edgeworth, 'The Mabo "Vibe"', 80; *Wik*, 175 (Gummow J); Samantha Hepburn, 'Feudal Tenure and Native Title: Revising an Enduring Fiction' *Sydney Law Review* 27, no. 1 (2005): 49–86, 69ff.
27 Bradbrook et al., *Australian Real Property Law*, 42–5.
28 Ibid.
29 Ibid; Statute of Quia Emptores 1290; Tenures Abolition Act 1660; Statute of Wills 1540.
30 Hepburn, 'Feudal Tenure', 73–4.

many parts of Australian land law and has had a major impact on the contemporary recognition of First Nations' land interests by the dominant colonising legal system.

A number of key land law principles are explicable in terms of the feudal origins of the law. Technically, the Crown holds an underlying title in all land. As a result, a distinction is drawn between ownership and possession (and the right to possession of land). Various significant legal rights attach to possession of and the right to possess land. Under the doctrine of estates, several people may simultaneously have proprietary interests (including estates) in the same piece of land.

These basic principles of English law developed in distinctive ways in Australia. This chapter now considers some of these developments.

Land Law in Early Colonial Settlements

Fundamental to the development of Australian land law was that as a matter of the coloniser's law, the colony was 'practically uninhabited' or '*terra nullius*' and, therefore, a 'settled' colony,[31] a notion only partially disrupted in *Mabo*.[32] This view relied predominantly on the work of Blackstone: 'it hath been held, that if an uninhabited country be discovered and planted by English subjects, all the English laws then in being, ... are immediately there in force'[33] but 'only so much of the English law as is applicable to their own situation and condition of an infant colony'.[34] Disputes arose as to precisely which English laws applied in the colony and how variations could be made,[35] at least until 1828 when the Australian Courts Act[36] provided that all 'laws and statutes' then in force in England were to be applied 'so far as the same can be applied within the said Colonies'.[37] What was clear was that, as in England, the Crown, represented by the governors, had power under English law to make grants of land to settlers without regard for any land interests or relationships of First Nations.

31 Castles, *An Australian Legal History*, 20, 379–80, 383–6, 389, 393; but see also Kercher, Chapter 5, Finnane, Chapter 27 and Ford and Roberts, Chapter 13 in this volume.

32 Gerry Simpson, 'Mabo, International Law, Terra Nullius and the Stories of Settlement: An Unresolved Jurisprudence' *Melbourne University Law Review* 19, no. 1 (1993): 195–210; David Ritter, 'The "rejection of terra nullius" in Mabo: A Critical Analysis' *Sydney Law Review* 18, no. 1 (1996): 5–33.

33 Blackstone, *Commentaries on the Law of England*, 1: chapters 4 and 6.

34 Ibid.

35 Castles, *An Australian Legal History*, 11, 493–507; Bruce Kercher, *Debt, Seduction and Other Disasters* (Sydney: Federation Press, 1996), 2–3.

36 9 Geo. IV c 83, B and C.

37 Castles, *An Australian Legal History*, 387.

While many have noted the incongruity of the doctrine of tenure for the colony,[38] any doubts about the application of the principle in the colony were largely removed by *Attorney-General of NSW v Brown* ('*Brown*')[39] and finally and decisively by the Privy Council in *Cooper v Stuart*,[40] confirming the view that all interests in land in the colonies must derive directly from a grant from the Crown. By implication the corollary was that First Nations' pre-colonisation interests in land were unrecognised. In *Brown*, Stephen CJ said 'the waste lands of this colony are, and ever have been, from the time of first settlement in 1788, ... in the Sovereign's possession; and ... as his or her property, they have been and may now be effectually granted to subjects of the Crown'.[41] Thus all lands were the property of the Crown because 'there is no other owner'[42] and all third-party rights in land must be held 'mediately or immediately from the Crown',[43] that is must be traced to an original grant from the Crown.

The twin notions of 'practically' empty lands 'peacefully annexed' and absolute Crown ownership, because 'there is no other owner', combined to deprive First Nations of their land or any title to land recognised by the colonisers: notions described in *Mabo* as both fictions[44] and not in accord with the 'facts as we know them'.[45] This thinking about the effect of the act of colonisation and the operation of the colonisers' land law remained relevant well into the twentieth century.[46] Importantly, it was the basis of the decision in *Milurrpum v Nabalco Pty Ltd* ('*Milirrpum*')[47] the first case to directly confront these issues in relation to surviving First Nations' rights in land. The claim by the Yolgnu that they had a right to their land based upon their pre-colonisation occupation was unsuccessful.[48] This disjunction of prior occupation and colonising land laws was a direct result of the reasoning in *Cooper v Stuart* and the doctrine of tenure. The application of the principles, as Brennan J put it, resulted in First Nations being 'dispossessed of their land parcel by parcel'[49] as the Crown, as absolute beneficial owner, granted land to third parties or reserved land for its own use. Although the manner and form

38 *Mabo*, 47 (Brennan J); *Wik*, 186–7 (Gummow J quoting Jenks, *A History of the Australasian Colonies* (1896), 59); *Wik*, 215 (Kirby J); Bradbrook et al., *Australian Real Property Law*, 45.

39 (1847) 1 Legge 312.

40 (1889) 14 AC 286.

41 *Brown*, 316 (Stephen J). 'Waste lands' in this context means land that the Crown has not yet alienated to third parties or reserved to itself.

42 Ibid, 317–8.

43 Ibid, 319.

44 *Mabo*, 42 (Brennan J).

45 *Mabo*, 39 (Brennan J).

46 *Williams v A-G (NSW)* (1913) 16 CLR 404; *Randwick Municipal Council v Rutledge* (1959) 102 CLR 54; *New South Wales v Commonwealth* (1975) 135 CLR 337.

47 (1971) 17 FLR 141.

48 *Milirrpum*, 262 (Blackburn J); Behrendt and Brennan, Chapter 16 in this volume.

49 *Mabo*, 69 (Brennan J).

of the Crown's exercise of power varied over time (see below), its power to grant interests in land, unaffected by the prior occupation of First Nations, endured until *Mabo* reconsidered the basis of the Crown's absolute title to land, its power to grant land and the impacts on First Nations' land interests. Given the legal proposition that the Crown held absolute beneficial ownership of land at the time of colonisation, it followed that various governors could exercise prerogative power to deal with and grant the *waste lands* of the Crown, that is land that had not yet been alienated to a third-party. These powers were exercised without regard to any First Nations' land law or interests, and this was the process that effectively dispossessed First Nations of their land 'parcel by parcel'.[50] However, in reality, as Goodall says, the 'differing systems of ideas about land came to operate simultaneously, in ignorance of each other or in open conflict and sometimes in uneasy tension and fragile co-existence',[51] reflecting Dorsett's notion of jurisdictional plurality.[52]

In the early years of the colony the administration of justice, including land law, was chaotic[53] and uncertain. There were disputes about which English laws were applicable and about the governors' powers, including the power to vary English legislation.[54] Land administration was haphazard and disorderly[55] with informal systems of land dealing, little attention to the Statute of Frauds (which required certain formalities in land dealings) and scant regard for the registration of Crown grants.[56] Similarly chaotic and 'haphazard' land administration existed in Van Diemen's Land.[57] The Australian Courts Act[58] resolved the issue of applicability of English law at least.[59]

The Emergence of Unique Australian Land Titles: Crown Land, Statutory Titles and Reserves

The only feudal tenure to arrive in New South Wales was common socage, which very soon took the form of freehold grants (usually a fee simple title) most often with a condition for a perpetual annual payment to the Crown,[60]

50 *Mabo*, 66 (Brennan J). 51 Goodall, *Invasion to Embassy*, 23.
52 Dorsett, Chapter 2 in this volume.
53 Kercher, *Debt, Seduction*, 123–47; Kercher, Chapter 5 in this volume.
54 Castles, *An Australian Legal History*, 378–99. 55 Kercher, *Debt, Seduction*, 122–31.
56 Ibid, 122–7; Kercher, Chapter 5 in this volume.
57 Castles, *An Australian Legal History*, 289–90.
58 The Australian Courts Act 1828, 9 Geo. IV c 83.
59 Section 24; Castles, *An Australian Legal History*, 397.
60 Enid Campbell, 'The Quit Rent System in Colonial New South Wales' *Monash University Law Review* 35, no. 1 (2009): 33–44, 33–4.

known as a quit rent.[61] This form of title was eventually 'converted into a new form, purchase by instalments',[62] and land was ultimately freed from quit rents.[63] In the early years most land was granted by the Crown, but by the 1830s the Crown was alienating most land 'by sale'.[64] Farming land was generally granted as freehold, subject to conditions such as living on the land and cultivating it,[65] whereas town land was at first leased and later granted as freehold.[66] Forms of occupancy rights[67] were also common. The Sale of Waste Lands Act 1842,[68] brought the disposition of Crown land under statutory control for the first time[69] and made sale the only method of alienation of Crown land.[70] It also represented the beginning of new forms of title that were different from the feudal or common law tenures. The early informal system of colonial innovations concerning inherited English law has been described as a form of legal pluralism.[71]

In 1829 the New South Wales settlement was limited to nineteen counties, covering 34,000 square miles; settlement beyond these counties was prohibited.[72] Settlers began moving beyond these limits to pasture stock, and governors were powerless to prevent the movement. Recognising this reality, in 1836 Governor Bourke introduced a system of annual licences of ten pounds per run regardless of size.[73] Outside the nineteen counties, it was unlawful to operate without a licence, and a land-owner within the nineteen counties required a lease.[74] Orders in Council 1847 made pursuant to the Sale of Waste Lands Act Amendment Act 1846,[75] were 'the first step ... along a road which led to the subsequent invention of a multitude of Australian tenures of new types'.[76] The colony was divided into three areas: the settled district (the original nineteen counties), the intermediate district, and the unsettled district which was the rest of the colony.[77] For the first time land could be leased for up to fourteen years for

61 Kercher, *Debt, Seduction,* 130; Bradbrook et al., *Australian Real Property Law,* 45; Andrew Lang, *Crown Land in New South Wales* (Sydney: Butterworths, 1973), 1.

62 Kercher, *Debt, Seduction,* 131.

63 Peter Butt, *Land Law* (Sydney: Lawbook Co, 2010, 6th edition), 84.

64 Campbell, 'The Quit Rent System', 35.

65 Kercher, *Debt, Seduction,* 128.

66 Lang, *Crown Land,* 2–3.

67 Kercher, *Debt, Seduction,* 127.

68 The Sale of Waste Lands Act 1842, 5 & 6 Vic. c 36.

69 *Wik,* 109 (Toohey J).

70 Butt, *Land Law,* 918.

71 Kercher, Chapter 5 in this volume; Dorsett, Chapter 2 in this volume.

72 Lang, *Crown Land,* 3.

73 Ibid, 3–4; Butt, *Land Law,* 918.

74 Lang, *Crown Land,* 4.

75 Sale of Waste Lands Act Amendment Act 1846, 9 & 10 Vic. c 104.

76 Thomas Fry, 'Land Tenures in Australia' *Res Judicatae* 3 (1946–1947): 158–70, 160–1, quoted in *Wik,* 109 (Toohey J).

77 Lang, *Crown Land,* 6.

pastoral purposes in the unsettled district and eight years in the intermediate district.[78]

With the establishment of responsible government in the 1850s, control of land passed from the executive to colonial legislatures.[79] From this point on, 'management and disposal of Crown lands was vested in'[80] colonial legislatures and executive power in relation to land had to be exercised pursuant to legislative authority rather than the Crown's prerogative power. As a result of these arrangements, a major portion of Crown lands passed into private hands and 'introduced a system of Crown leasehold tenures which led to the whole of Australia being transformed in subsequent decades into a patchwork quilt of freeholdings, Crown lease-holdings, and Crown "reserves"'.[81] Further, the incidents of these tenures or types of land holding titles were more likely to be found in the legislation under which the rights were granted than in common law.[82] These significant departures from English land law were in part out of 'simple necessity'[83] associated with the particular geographical and social elements in the colonies.[84] The development of the system of Crown reserves, the regulation of mining by way of leases and licences distinct from the common law and, in part, flowing from the discovery of gold,[85] and the creation of the unique title by registration scheme by Robert Torrens, are all examples of a distinct Australian property or land law emerging by the 1860s.[86]

Around this same period, 'Imperial and colonial governments . . . recognised that Aboriginal people were entitled to protection from violence, to receive education, religious instruction and other benefits of civilisation and to continue to occupy and use their traditional lands as they had at the time of settlement, subject to the rights of the Crown'.[87] Both the reservations in pastoral leases that enabled First Nations to access and use land for hunting and ceremonial activity, and the setting aside of land for the use and benefit of First Nations, known as reserves, were partial responses to these objectives.[88]

78 Ibid; *Wik*, 109 (Toohey J).
79 Lang, *Crown Land*, 8; Curthoys and Mitchell, Chapter 6 in this volume.
80 *Wik*, 110 (Toohey J).
81 Fry, 'Land Tenures in Australia', 160–1, quoted in *Wik*, 110 (Toohey J).
82 *Wik*, 112 (Toohey J).
83 Castles, *An Australian Legal History*, 456.
84 *Wik*, 122 (Toohey J).
85 Castles, *An Australian Legal History*, 456.
86 Buck, 'Property Law and the Origins of Australian Egalitarianism', 158–61.
87 Reynolds and Dalziel, 'Aborigines and Pastoral Leases', 325.
88 Ibid, 334; Goodall, *Invasion to Embassy*, 57–61.

The Pastoral Lease

Pastoral leases mark a major divergence between common law estates and interests in land and the unique forms of landholding developed in the colonies. The relationship between these leases and First Nations' rights in relation to land fell squarely for determination in *Wik*, in which the Court was asked to determine whether a pastoral lease necessarily extinguished native title. The argument was that pastoral leases involved the grant of an estate in land, that is, a grant of exclusive possession that resulted in the complete extinguishment of native title. The case is central to understanding the extent to which Australia developed its own land law and the diminishing role of the common law tenures in that development. While some of these developments paid scant regard to First Nations' land interests, in the contemporary native title world some of these developments have paradoxically preserved First Nations' land interests from the major legal effects of Crown actions.

'The pastoral lease had its origins in the Sale of Waste Lands Act Amendment Act 1846 (Imp) and an Imperial Order in Council of 9 March 1847.[89] Self-government transferred the Crown's power in relation to land to the legislature meaning that from that time 'any authority of the Crown in that respect had to derive from statute'.[90] Gummow J observed that '[t]here followed the enactment ... of statutes designed to provide for conditions unknown in England and to meet local wants in a fashion unprovided for in England'.[91] Similarly, Toohey J noted that 'a concept of feudal tenure [was] brought to Australia but subjected to change through a complex system of rights and obligations adapted to the physical, social and economic conditions of the new colony ...'.[92] This shift in political decision-making about land[93] drove a wedge between the common law estates and the forms of landholding titles that might now be created.

As Ford and Roberts note in this volume,[94] the 1830s and 1840s saw support, for ensuring that First Nations' enjoyment of land was not disrupted too severely, in the form of moves to preserve Indigenous access to pastoral lands[95] in New South Wales, South Australia[96] and later Western

89 Reynolds and Dalziel, 'Aborigines and Pastoral Leases', 321.
90 *Wik*, 174 (Gummow J).
91 Ibid. 92 *Wik*, 122 (Toohey J). 93 Curthoys and Mitchell, Chapter 6 in this volume.
94 Ford and Roberts, Chapter 13 in this volume.
95 Reynolds and Dalziel, 'Aborigines and Pastoral Leases', 325.
96 Ibid, 323–8; *Wik*, 109 (Toohey J); Robert Foster, 'Coexistence and Colonisation on Pastoral Leaseholds in South Australia 1851–99', in John McLaren, Andrew Buck and Nancy Wright (eds), *Despotic Dominion: Property Rights in British Settler Societies* (Vancouver: UBC Press,

Australia.[97] In New South Wales, the form of the provision inserted in pastoral leases reserved to the 'Aboriginal Inhabitants of the Colony': 'such free access to the said Run or Parcel of Land, hereby demised or any part thereof, and to the trees and water thereon as will enable them to procure the Animals, Birds, Fish and other food on which they subsist'.[98]

The statutory tenures or landholding titles were many and varied.[99] In Queensland, Toohey J noted that 'at least at the time Dr Fry was writing, there were approximately seventy different kinds of Crown leasehold and Crown perpetual leasehold tenures'[100] with 'minute differences between various forms of tenure'.[101] 'These tenures, including pastoral leases . . . are the creature of statute and the rights and obligations that accompany them derive from statute.'[102] As a result, 'the terms "lease" and "licence" applied in a new and generic sense'.[103] Thus a pastoral lease was described as 'a qualified grant of an interest in land being a statutory interest in Crown land created to meet the requirements of Australian conditions'.[104]

Some leases included a right of pre-emption (right to purchase) while others included no right to purchase and were for a specified term only.[105] Even though land was held under lease for pastoral purposes, 'the Crown . . . retained control over land in these districts'.[106] These land provisions were revised in New South Wales in 1861[107] providing for further sale and leasing of Crown land. The land classifications were changed and, within each area, land could be selected as freehold and could be purchased under a conditional purchase, the conditions including taking up residence and completing various improvements.[108] Pastoral leases were also permitted subject to

2005), 248–65; Shaun Berg. 'A Fractured Landscape: The Effect of Aboriginal Title to Land by the Establishment of the Province of South Australia', in Shaun Berg (ed.), *Coming to Terms: Aboriginal Title in South Australia* (Adelaide: Wakefield Press, 2010), 1–24, 20; Paul Havemann, 'The Rule of Law, Betrayal and Reparation', in Berg (ed.), *Coming to Terms*, 122–47, 133; Ford and Roberts, Chapter 13 in this volume.

97 Reynolds and Dalziel, 'Aborigines and Pastoral Leases', 321, footnote 35; see *Western Australia v Ward* (2002) 213 CLR 1 paras [157]–[196] especially [169] (Gleeson CJ, Gaudron, Gummow and Hayne JJ); see Ford and Roberts, Chapter 13 in this volume.

98 Reynolds and Dalziel, 'Aborigines and Pastoral Leases', 367.

99 Bradbrook et al., *Australian Real Property Law*, 342.

100 Fry, 'Land Tenures in Australia', 158, quoted in *Wik*, 112 (Toohey J).

101 Bradbrook et al., *Australian Real Property Law*, 341.

102 *Wik*, 112 (Toohey J).

103 *Wik*, 174 (Gummow J).

104 *North Ganalanja Aboriginal Corporation and Another v State of Queensland and Another* (1995) 132 ALR 565 at 586 (Lee J) quoted in Reynolds and Dalziel, 'Aborigines and Pastoral Leases', 319.

105 Butt, *Land Law*, 340.

106 Reynolds and Dalziel, 'Aborigines and Pastoral Leases', 330.

107 Crown Lands Alienation Act 1861 and Crown Lands Occupation Act 1861.

108 Lang, *Crown Land*, 8–9.

location and size.[109] Conflict, disruption, dispute, and fraudulent and speculative land dealings, arose[110] and the Crown Lands Act 1884 (NSW) sought to address these with significant amendment of the legislation. The Act redrew the boundaries of land divisions and established the size or area of land grants in each division. The Act provides an example of the range of forms of landholding created by legislation. Similar forms were created in other jurisdictions. These included conditional purchase leases, pastoral leases, occupation licences for grazing and homestead leases, as well as leases for activities such as wharves and jetties, quarries, sawmills and the like.[111] Perpetual leases were also among the landholding forms[112] and provide a very clear example of the divergence between the statute and the common law, which recognised no such title. The endurance of the statutory lease can be gauged by the fact that in 1992, 70 per cent of land in Queensland, predominantly in pastoral areas, was still leased.[113] Statutory leases were also a feature of residential land in both the Northern Territory and the Australian Capital Territory, where much residential land is still held on ninety-nine-year leases.[114]

The conundrum that is the relationship between the common law tenures and statutory landholding forms was revived in the wake of *Mabo*.[115] *Wik* turned on the shift from the common law land system to one of statute-based titles and rights that occurred in the nineteenth century. *Wik* considered whether certain pastoral leases under the Land Act 1910 (Qld) necessarily extinguished native title because they granted exclusive possession to the lessees. The case made clear that the rights granted under a statutory title were to be found in the statute (and the document granting the title), not the common law.[116] As Gaudron J noted 'grant of perpetual leases which . . . were expressed to be "leases in perpetuity" . . . were unknown to the common law and . . . cannot possibly take its meaning from it'.[117] Therefore a grant of a right of exclusive possession is to be determined by an examination of the language of statutes and grants rather than the common law of leases (although the methodology is similar). In finding exclusive possession was

109 Ibid, 9.
110 Butt, *Land Law*, 919; Lang, *Crown Land*, 9–10; Ford and Roberts, Chapter 13 in this volume.
111 Lang, *Crown Land*, 11; Castles, *An Australian Legal History*, 464–5.
112 *Wik*, 112 (Toohey J); *Wilson v Anderson* (2002) 213 CLR 431.
113 Bradbrook et al., *Australian Real Property Law*, 341.
114 Ibid, 338–9.
115 Behrendt and Brennan, Chapter 16 in this volume.
116 *Wik*, 112 (Toohey J), 152 (Gaudron J), 188–9 (Gummow J), 243 (Kirby J).
117 *Wik*, 153 (Gaudron J), 201 (Gummow J).

not granted, the *Wik* judgments considered the variety of statutory titles and the distinction between them and the common law. Thus, although they are commonly called 'leases', pastoral leases may not be 'leases' in the common law sense, reflecting the development of statutory land titles in Australia.

Subsequent cases have revived confusion between statutory leases and common law tenures. The nature of a lease in perpetuity under Section 23 of the Western Lands Act 1901 (NSW) and (its effect on native title) was the subject of the High Court decision in *Wilson v Anderson*.[118] Less than six years after *Wik*, the High Court took a different approach to this relationship, Gleeson CJ saying '[t]here is nothing surprising or novel about a conclusion that the incidents of a statutory lease are not exhaustively defined by statute, and may include the incidents of a lease as provided by the common law'.[119] The plurality in that case referred to Dr Helmore's comment that '[a] "perpetual lease" is a contradiction of terms and the conditions to which these tenures are subject are in no way inconsistent with the incidents of a fee simple upon condition'.[120] Notwithstanding that the perpetual lease was unknown to the common law and effectively a unique tenure, the Court retreated to the common law to give meaning to the perpetual lease to which various conditions were attached. It noted that 'these conditions and obligations, whether imposed directly by the *Western Lands Act* or permitted by the statute to be attached to the grant, were not inconsistent with the incidents of a grant of a determinable fee simple'.[121] Rather than focus on the unique nature of the rights granted, the court appeared to find comfort in reverting to the old common law titles of the fee simple, whether, absolute, 'determinable' or 'upon condition'.[122] As a result, the Court held that the perpetual lease Douglas Wilson held over his property under the Act extinguished native title.

Reserves for the Benefit of First Nations

In the mid-nineteenth century, a partial response to continued conflict and violence at the frontier was the creation of reserves for the use and benefit of First Nations.[123] Crown reserves and Crown land reserved for particular

118 (2002) 213 CLR 431. 119 *Wilson v Anderson*, 421 [19] (Gleeson CJ).
120 *Wilson v Anderson*, 443 [88] (Gaudron, Gummow and Hayne JJ).
121 *Wilson v Anderson*, 451 [115] (Gaudron, Gummow and Hayne JJ).
122 *Wilson v Anderson*, 443 [113] (Gaudron, Gummow and Hayne JJ, quoting Basil Helmore, *The Law of Real Property in New South Wales* (1966, 2nd edition), 66–7).
123 Goodall, *Invasion to Embassy*, 46–8; Reynolds and Dalziel, 'Aborigines and Pastoral Leases', 323–9; Ford and Roberts, Chapter 13 in this volume.

purposes became a feature of land titling arrangements and a further departure from common law. They were and remain a central element of the relationship between First Nations, their land law and the colonising system of law, emerging in the land rights and native title eras as important areas for First Nations' rights and control of their lands.

The terms 'reserve', 'reserved' and 'reservation' have different meanings in the context of Australian land law and, as Lang observed, the terms 'reserve' and 'reserved' 'are applied for more than one purpose'.[124] Land can be reserved *from* a particular action, for example from sale or lease, and land can be reserved *for* a particular purpose such as 'the use and benefit of Aboriginal inhabitants'.[125] In addition, the rights reserved in pastoral leases for First Nations to undertake certain activities on pastoral lands are carved out of the grant of rights to the pastoralist. From inception, land reserved from sale remained Crown land.[126] However, once reserved for a purpose, land would eventually be dedicated or vested, usually in trustees,[127] setting out the rights associated with the land and its management.[128]

The Sale of Waste Lands Act 1842,[129] was the first statutory recognition of the power of the Crown to reserve land in all the 'Australian colonies'.[130] Section III of the Act established a process that involved, first, reserving land from sale or grant and, then, authorising the Crown to either reserve the land 'to Her Majesty ... or [dispose] of it in such other manner as for the public interest ... as may be required for ...' a range of purposes. There then follows a long list of purposes including 'the use or benefit of the aboriginal inhabitants of the Country'. The 1842 Act provided the legal basis for the provision of land for First Nations in the form of reserves. Reserves varied in size and location but, at least in the pastoral areas, were generally contiguous with a particular First Nation's Country. Following a long and conflicted process, thirty-five reserves were created in 1850 in the pastoral lands area in New South Wales. These were small – mostly a square mile – but efforts were made to encourage First Nations to see them as their own pieces of land;[131] and in some cases, for example the Brewarrina fisheries,

124 Lang, *Crown Land,* 77. 125 Sale of Waste Lands Act 1842, 5 & 6 Vic. c 36, s III.
126 Ibid; *Randwick Municipal Council v Rutledge* (1959) ALJR 367, 371–5 (Windeyer J).
127 Bradbrook et al., *Australian Real Property Law,* 354.
128 Ibid, 356–7; Lang, *Crown Land,* 78; and see *Randwick Municipal Council v Rutledge* (1959) ALJR 367.
129 Sale of Waste Lands Act 1842, 5 & 6 Vic. c 36.
130 Sale of Waste Lands Act 1842, 5 & 6 Vic. c 36, s XXII; Reynolds and Dalziel, 'Aborigines and Pastoral Leases', 330; Berg (ed.), *Coming to Terms,* 14.
131 Goodall, *Invasion to Embassy,* 55.

they protected land of particular importance to First Nations.[132] Access to pastoral land for hunting, fishing and cultural activities was more important for First Nations, so reserves contiguous to these lands were highly valued.[133]

In South Australia, forty-two reserves for the use and benefit of Aboriginal people were created between 1836 and 1860.[134] Reserves were also created over time in Western Australia and in Victoria and Queensland. The size, scale and location of these reserves varied but they were, at least initially in the country of the relevant First Nation.[135] From the latter part of the nineteenth century, reserves, together with the creation of Protection Boards, became a sinister tool for dispossession and control of First Nations.[136] This remained the case until well into the twentieth century.

Though the Crown claimed title over reserves, the act of reservation of land for the use and benefit of Aboriginal people generally protected the land from further alienation for private or Crown use. As a result, land was available to satisfy political claims for land rights made in the latter part of the twentieth century. The first example of this was in 1966, when the South Australian government created the Aboriginal Lands Trust, which was empowered to acquire a fee simple title to reserves and lease them to their First Nations inhabitants.[137] The Trust, a central body which controlled all reserves, could include up to twelve First Nations people; and although no sub-surface or mineral rights were included, legislation required the payment of some royalties to the Trust arising from mining on Trust lands. The handover of reserves to First Nations inhabitants or traditional owners then became a common technique in the growing land rights movements. For example, all reserves within the claimable land areas in the Northern Territory were included in Schedule 1 of the Aboriginal Land Rights (Northern Territory) Act 1976 (Cth) and became Aboriginal inalienable freehold land under that Act. Approximately half of the land handed back to traditional owners under the Pitjantjatjara Land Rights Act 1981 (SA)[138] was reserve land.[139]

132 Ibid, 55–6. 133 Ibid, 57–60; Reynolds and Dalziel, 'Aborigines and Pastoral Leases', 334.
134 Havemann, 'The Rule of Law, Betrayal and Reparation', 133.
135 Reynolds and Dalziel, 'Aborigines and Pastoral Leases', 330.
136 For example, see Goodall, *Invasion to Embassy,* chapter 7; Nettelbeck, Chapter 20 in this volume.
137 Aboriginal Land Trust Act 1966 (SA).
138 Now known as the Anangu Pitjantjatjara Yankunytjatjara Land Rights Act.
139 Pitjantjatjara Land Rights Act 1981 (SA), First Schedule (a).

In the native title era, reserves have continued to play a crucial role in making land available for claim and protecting it for the use and benefit of Aboriginal peoples from acts that might otherwise extinguish native title.[140] Even where extinguishment may have occurred as a result of the legal effect of vesting reserves or for some other reason, the provisions of Section 47A of the Native Title Act 1993 (Cth) allow such extinguishment to be disregarded in relation to reserves for the benefit of Aboriginal inhabitants, among other reasons.[141]

Sub-surface Rights, Mining Leases and Licences

At common law, ownership of land included the sub-soil. Although the depth of this ownership might have been a 'matter of conjecture',[142] it extended sufficiently to include minerals and the right to extract them.[143] Only gold and silver, known as the royal minerals, were held by the Crown by royal prerogative.[144] Initially in the new colony, mining was permitted by grant of a fee simple but, as with other land policy and management, the treatment of sub-surface rights and minerals developed a peculiarly Australian tone. Gummow J in *Wik* noted that '[i]n 1891, it was said that "the whole of our mining law is founded on statutes for which no precedent existed in any other country"'.[145] First by reservations in grants of land and ultimately by statute, minerals became the property of the Crown.

The pattern of reserving resources for the Crown appeared in some of the earliest land grants, which reserved timber for the Crown for 'the public purpose of maintaining a naval fleet'.[146] Minerals were not included in the reservations.[147] By 1828 land grants started to include reservations of gold and silver (although as they were royal minerals this was not strictly necessary) and, in 1831, coal was added to the reservations in land grants[148] as well as

140 Behrendt and Brennan, Chapter 16 in this volume. 141 Ibid.

142 Butt, *Land Law*, 14 referencing Adrian Bradbrook, 'The Relevance of the *Cujus Est Solum* Doctrine to the Landowner's Claim to Natural Resources Located above and beneath the Land' *Adelaide Law Review* 11 (1988): 462.

143 Butt, *Land Law*, 15; Bradbrook et al., *Australian Real Property Law*, 795.

144 Ase of Mines (1568) 1 Plow 310; 75 ER 472 (KB); Butt, *Land Law*, 15; Bradbrook et al., *Australian Real Property Law*, 795.

145 *Wik*, 174, footnote (636) quoting Armstrong, *A Treatise on the Law of Gold-Mining in Australia and New Zealand* (1901, 2nd edition), vi, from the Preface to the first edition (1891) (Gummow J).

146 Sharon Christensen, Pam O'Connor, William Duncan and Ross Ashcroft, 'Early Land Grants and Reservations: Any Lessons from the Queensland Experience for the Sustainability Challenge to Land Ownership' *James Cook University Law Review* 15 (2008): 42–66, 51.

147 Butt, *Land Law*, 16. 148 Ibid; Christensen et al., 'Early Land Grants', 53.

other resources such as gravel and stone.[149] Generally, between 1850 and 1861 minerals were not reserved in Crown grants.[150] In New South Wales, from 1861, conditional purchases were required to contain reservation of minerals and from 1885 all grants were required to contain such reservations.[151] In Queensland after 1861, reservations of minerals could occur; but in the absence of reservations the minerals ran with the fee simple grant.[152] From late nineteenth century all colonies/States claimed ownership of minerals either through reservations or specific legislation.[153] For example, in Queensland the Mining on Private Land Act 1909 (Qld) provided that all grants of land after 1909 were subject to reservations of minerals whether or not made expressly in the grant.[154] The pattern was similar in other jurisdictions.[155] Recent examples of specific legislation vesting some or all minerals in the Crown include the Coal Acquisition Act 1981 (NSW,) Section 5 of which vests all coal in the state,[156] the Mineral Resources Development Act 1990 (Vic), Section 9 and the Mining Act 1971 (SA), Section 16.

Statute rather than the common law became the mechanism for regulating mining; and the Victorian Mining Act 1865 was something of a model for other jurisdictions.[157] The Act defined key terms such as 'earth' being 'rock, stone, quartz, clay, sand, soil and minerals'. Using definitions in this way became commonplace in mining statutes, a shift from the common law. The 1865 Act established a scheme of miners' rights: a claims register (Sections 4–8), mining leases (Sections 24–30) and licences to search (Section 35). This scheme became the predominant method of regulating mining activity, and developed 'principles and practices which were often indigenous in character'.[158] A mining lease could be granted on or below 'Crown land not demised' for the 'purposes of mining' (Section 24). Licences to search for metals, other than gold, could also be granted (Section 35). In Queensland, from 1860, grants of fee simple title for mining purposes could be made;[159] but after 1882 land could only be leased for mining purposes.[160] Licences, leases and grants of mining rights expanded. For example, in Western Australia in 1978 there were 'thirty nine different types of titles provided in the' Mining

149 Ibid, 52. 150 Butt, *Land Law*, 16. 151 Ibid.

152 Christensen et al., 'Early Land Grants', 57–8.

153 Crown Lands Act 1884 (NSW), s 7; Land Act 1891 (Vic), s 12; Mines Act 1891 (No. 2) (Vic), s 3; The Mining on Private Land Act 1909 (Qld), ss 6, 21; Crown Lands Act 1888 (SA), s 9; Mining Act 1904 (WA), s 117; The Crown Lands Act 1905 (Tas), s 27.

154 Christensen et al., 'Early Land Grants', 65.

155 Bradbrook et al., *Australian Real Property Law*, 796. 156 Ibid; Butt, *Land Law*, 17.

157 Castles, *An Australian Legal History*, 468. 158 Ibid.

159 Crown Lands Alienation Act 1860 (Qld), 24 Vic. No. 15.

160 Mineral Lands Act 1882 (Qld).

Act 1904 (WA).[161] The Mining Act 1978 (WA) reduced these to three specific titles – prospecting licence, exploration licence and mining lease, with 'two general titles (general purpose lease and miscellaneous licence)'.[162]

Initially mining was only permitted on Crown land; but ultimately, access by third parties to private land for mining was permitted, even though the minerals were largely the property of the Crown. In Victoria the Mining on Private Property Act 1884 (Vic) provided for access to private land for mining.[163] The Mining on Private Land Act 1909 (Qld) (Section 6(2)) included a reservation for 'access for the purpose of searching for or working on any mines of gold or minerals in part of the land'.[164] Similar provisions were included in various forms across jurisdictions and compensation provisions were included.[165]

As with regulation of pastoral lands, the language of 'lease' and 'licence' was used but did not necessarily accord with the common law meanings of these terms or result in a grant of exclusive possession.[166] These words took their meaning from statute not common law, reinforcing the emergence of a unique Australia land law[167] and emphasising the tangential relationship with its common law antecedents. As occurred in *Wik* in relation to the divergence of common law and statutory uses of the term 'lease' and 'demise', a similar approach was taken to the meaning and effect of 'lease' and 'demise' under the Mining Act 1904 (WA) and the Iron Ore (Mount Goldsworthy) Agreement Act 1964 (WA). In *Western Australia v Brown*,[168] the High Court found that the right granted by a mining lease was not 'the unqualified right to exclude any and everyone from access to the land, for any reason or no reason',[169] that is, not a right of exclusive possession.

These schemes for regulating title to minerals and mining activity made no reference to First Nations' use of land on which mining might occur nor to their use of resources that mining might disrupt. As if to reinforce the parallel systems of law across the Australian continent, this silence meant there was no protection for '[t]he spirits, beings and ideas about land that inhabited and animated the country prior to colonisation [which] gave the land and people

161 Michael Hunt, 'The Mining Act 1978 of Western Australia' *Australian Mining and Petroleum Law Journal* 2, no. 1 (1979): 1–23, 8.
162 Ibid, 9. 163 Castles, *An Australian Legal History*, 467.
164 Christensen et al., 'Early Land Grants', 65.
165 For example Mining Act 1906 (NSW), s 60; Mining (Amendment) Act 1918 (NSW) amending s 64.
166 *Wik*, 117 (Toohey J). 167 *Wik*, 174 (Gummow J). 168 (2014) 253 CLR 507.
169 *Western Australia v Brown* (2014) 253 CLR 507, 525 (French CJ, Hayne, Kiefel, Gageler and Keane JJ).

meanings [and] had nothing to do with the imaginings and meanings of the coloniser',[170] or for First Nations' control and use of resources. In 1974 Woodward noted that 'to deny Aborigines the right to prevent mining on their land is to deny the reality of their land rights'.[171] Emerging land title schemes for First Nations reflected this need for control of access to their land for mining, for example, in the Aboriginal Land Rights (Northern Territory) Act 1976 (Cth). However, recognition of both cultural and economic rights associated with resources themselves did not occur until recently, when rights to resources have been recognised in some native title cases.[172] Limited protection of culturally significant sites and cultural landscapes from disruptive mining activity did not occur until the 1970s and varies across jurisdictions. Even now, the protection provides only procedural rights rather than property rights in heritage,[173] and frequently fails to adequately protect heritage sites.[174]

Land Title by Registration: The Torrens Land Registration System

The old English system of land title conveyancing came to Australia with English law in 1788. The administration of land and land law in the early colonies was chaotic, and the conveyancing system aggravated the situation.[175] The major problem was the requirement that the seller prove they had a valid title to deal with the land. This meant that a documentary chain of title was required necessitating that the title be traced back to its original Crown grant plus all and any transactions that had occurred since the grant.[176] In some circumstances such a search would not or could not reveal all the dealings that may have resulted in a person other than the seller having an interest in the land. The complex set of rules governing priorities of interests in the system together with the common law doctrine of notice

170 Tehan, 'A Hope Disillusioned', 523; see also Goodall, *Invasion to Embassy*, 1–19.

171 Sir Edward Woodward, *Aboriginal Land Rights Commission: Second Report* (Canberra: Australian Government Publishing Service, 1974), 108.

172 *Western Australia v Willis* (2015) 239 FCR 175, paras 44, 114, 215; *BP (Deceased) on behalf of the Birriliburu People v Western Australia* [2014] FCA 715; Behrendt and Brennan, Chapter 16 in this volume.

173 *Chapman v Minister for Aboriginal and Torres Strait Islander Affairs and Ors* (1995) 133 ALR 74, 79; Maureen Tehan, '"To Be or Not To Be (Property)": Anglo-Australian Law and the Search for Protection of Indigenous Cultural Heritage' *University of Tasmania Law Review* 15, no. 2 (1996): 267–305.

174 Calla Wahlquist, 'Rio Tinto blasts 46,000-year-old Aboriginal site to expand iron ore mine', *The Guardian*, 26 May 2020.

175 Castles, *An Australian Legal History*, 458.

176 Bradbrook et al., *Australian Real Property Law*, 183.

meant that the purchaser often acquired an inferior title, possibly subject to other interests,[177] or (because of forgery or fraud in a prior transaction rendering the transaction void) no title at all.[178] Searching was lengthy, costly and often ineffective.[179] The purchaser's 'inability to discover and verify in a certain and simple manner the preceding dealings relating to the land'[180] was the heart of the problem.

Deeds registration systems were introduced early on in all colonial jurisdictions[181] but did not overcome these problems. It was the Deed evidencing the transaction rather than the title that was registered.[182] Registration 'did not cure defects'[183] in the seller's title deriving from an invalid transaction in the chain[184] nor guarantee that boundaries were accurate.[185] Other attempts to address these problems included legislation in New South Wales to validate previous transactions[186] and establishing the Caveat Board in Van Diemen's Land;[187] but difficulties in providing proof of a valid and enforceable title to land remained.[188]

The administration of land titles was even more chaotic in South Australia than in other colonies, at least in part because of the colony's origins. Wakefield's ideas of systematic colonisation funded by sale of land in the colony to aspiring immigrants[189] meant that land was sold in England even before the first colonisers departed; and many land transactions continued to occur in England.[190] This led to considerable land speculation in South Australian land: English purchasers often had no intention of taking up the land in South Australia.[191] Compounding the problem was the lack of evidence of Crown grants, often 'little more than receipts issued by the Commissioner of Public Lands and the Colonial Treasurer'[192] with little detail of size, location or boundaries. There was competition for land and priority disputes between those who purchased unsurveyed blocks abroad

177 Ibid, 183–4; Butt, *Land Law*, 698–700, 743.
178 Bradbrook et al., *Australian Real Property Law*, 184. 179 Ibid. 180 Ibid.
181 Registration of Deeds Act 1825, 6 Geo. IV No. 22 (NSW); Registration of Deeds Act 1827, 8 Geo. IV No. 5 (Van Diemen's Land); Registration of Deeds Act 1842, 5 Vic. No. 8 (SA).
182 Castles, *An Australian Legal History*, 459. 183 Butt, *Land Law*, 743. 184 Ibid.
185 Castles, *An Australian Legal History*, 459.
186 Ibid, 458, footnote 51; Crown Lands (Grants) Act 1836, 6 Will. IV No. 16.
187 Castles, *An Australian Legal History*, 458. 188 Butt, *Land Law*, 743. 189 Ibid, 170.
190 Ian Robertson 'The Rise and Rise of Aboriginal Title to Land: The Effect on Predecessor Title to Aboriginal Land under the Torrens System', in Berg (ed.), *Coming to Terms*, 206, 208.
191 Douglas Pike, 'Introduction of the Real Property Act in South Australia' *Adelaide Law Review* 1 (1960): 169, 171; Robertson, 'The Rise and Rise', 208; Castles, *An Australian Legal History*, 458.
192 Pike, 'Introduction', 173.

and those who purchased government surveyed land in the colony.[193] Conveyancing and the requirements of establishing 'good title' were major problems. Pike noted that '[i]n 1857 there were said to be 40,000 titles to land in the colony; of these three-quarters of the original deeds were lost, one-third were owned by absentees, some of whom could not be traced, and at least 5,000 were seriously complicated, if not defective'.[194]

Against this background Robert Torrens devised his system of 'title by registration', which came into operation in South Australia on 2 July 1858.[195] From that date, all land alienated by the Crown would be governed by the Act, with provision made for conversion of existing general law (or old law) land titles to Torrens titles.[196] The system was a dramatic change from the English common law conveyancing system and was controversial, particularly with the legal profession and the courts.[197] Significantly, it was a legislative scheme, mirroring the development of other statutorily defined land laws fashioned for and by the emerging colonies.[198] At the heart of the system was the creation of a register on which were recorded, in a Folio, all relevant particulars in relation to a defined parcel of land, including the identity of the proprietor and any other person holding an interest in the land, any encumbrances, and a description of the land and its boundaries. The owner was given a copy of the title details (the duplicate Certificate of Title), mirroring the contents of the corresponding Folio, and became an integral part of the purchase / sale transaction. All future dealings were then recorded on the Folio and the duplicate Certificate of Title. The purchaser acquired the legal title *upon* registration: thus, the descriptor 'title by registration'.[199] Once the transaction was registered, the register provided conclusive evidence of title, including the identity of the registered proprietor. Registration cured any defects that might have arisen in the transaction (or in the title if it had been created under the old system) including defects that might otherwise have rendered the transaction void. Thus, it was not necessary to inquire into previous dealings. Subject to certain exceptions (generally set out in the legislation) including fraud, the registered proprietor acquired an

193 Ibid, 172. 194 Ibid.

195 *Real Property Act 1858* 21 Vic. c 15 (SA); Pike, 'Introduction', 182; see generally Douglas Whalan, *The Torrens system in Australia* (Sydney: Law Book Company, 1982) and *Adelaide Law Review, Special Issue: 150th Anniversary of the Torrens Title System* 2 (2009).

196 Pike, 'Introduction', 182; Castles, *An Australian Legal History*, 460.

197 Pike, 'Introduction', 181–4; Bradbrook et al., *Australian Real Property Law*, 186–7; Butt, *Land Law*, 744–5; Castles, *An Australian Legal History*, 460.

198 *Wik*, 174 (Gummow J).

199 *Breskvar v Wall* (1971) 126 CLR 376, 384 (Barwick CJ), 399 (Windeyer J).

'indefeasible' title, that is, one that could not be questioned. The State 'assumed the responsibility for the validity of titles'.[200] An Assurance Fund was established to compensate those who might have lost their title or interest as a result of the operation of the system.[201] The system, which became known as the Torrens system, was simple, cheap, efficient and effective. Nevertheless, it built on the fundamental principles of English land law by adopting the doctrine of estates and other common law land interests such as easements.[202]

This unique South Australian scheme was quickly adopted by all the colonies[203] with some variations not relevant here.[204] The wide variety of new tenures created by colonial statutes were treated distinctively in the Torrens system in each colony. For example, some colonies provided for the registration or recording of Crown leases while others did not.[205] The Torrens system was also adopted by New Zealand[206] and a number of other countries.[207] In the *Wik* case, the Torrens system was cited by Gummow J as the first example of 'statutes designed to provide for conditions unknown in England and to meet local wants . . .'.[208] Among those conditions were 'the vast sparsely populated territory'[209] and the lack of a 'landed class for whose benefit much of English land law had evolved'.[210]

First Nations' entitlements to and interests in land based on prior and continuing occupation had been largely disregarded when the colony of South Australia was established, notwithstanding that the Letters Patent seemed to indicate clearly that nothing should affect 'the rights of any Aboriginal natives . . . to the actual occupation or enjoyment in their own Persons or in the Persons of their Descendants of any Lands therein now actually occupied or enjoyed by such Natives . . .'.[211] As we now know, First Nations' rights were seriously and adversely affected.[212] In this respect, South Australia followed the pattern set in other colonies.

200 Pike, 'Introduction', 181–2. 201 Ibid.
202 Bradbrook et al., *Australian Real Property Law*, 6, 185.
203 Ibid, 187; Real Property Act 1861 (Qld); Transfer of Land Act 1862 (Vic); Real Property Act 1862 (Tas); Real Property Act 1862 (NSW); Transfer of Land Act 1875 (WA).
204 Bradbrook et al., *Australian Real Property Law*, 187. 205 Ibid, 352.
206 Land Registry Act 1860 (NZ). 207 Butt, *Land Law*, 746.
208 *Wik*, 174 (Gummow J).
209 Butt, *Land Law*, 743. 210 Ibid.
211 Letters Patent Establishing the Province of South Australia (19 February 1836) in Berg (ed.), *Coming to Terms*; *Fejo v Northern Territory* (1998) 195 CLR 96, 129 [50] (Gleeson CJ, Gaudron, McHugh, Gummow, Hayne and Callinan JJ).
212 Sean Brennan, 'The Disregard for Legal Protections of Aboriginal Land Rights in Early South Australia', in Berg (ed.), *Coming to Terms,* 90–121; Behrendt and Brennan, Chapter 16 in this volume, especially on extinguishment of native title.

The extent to which the Torrens system contributed to such adverse effects is unclear. It was the act of the Crown's alienation of land that had an extinguishing impact on First Nations' land interests, whereas the Torrens system regulated and ordered land administration after alienation. It has been suggested that bringing old law land under the Real Property Act in South Australia may have had an impact on native title, perhaps giving rise to a claim against the Assurance Fund established under the Act.[213] The impact of the indefeasibility provisions of the system and the curing of defects in transactions upon registration, as well as the relationship of the provisions of Torrens statutes and the Native Title Act 1992 (Cth) are also uncertain.[214] Once a determination of native title is made under the Native Title Act 1993 (Cth)[215] it is recorded in the National Native Title Register.[216] There is provision in the Act for the Registrar to notify the relevant Land Registry of the determination;[217] but the native title interest is not 'registered' within the meaning of the Torrens legislation. Issues in relation to interaction of the registers have not yet been explored or litigated.[218]

On the other hand, land granted under land rights legislation such as the Anangu Pitjantjatjara Yankunytjatjara Land Rights Act 1981 (SA) and the Aboriginal Land Rights (Northern Territory) Act 1976 (Cth), is granted as an inalienable fee simple title which is registered in the Torrens register in the relevant jurisdiction.[219]

Mabo and *Wik*: Reimagining Australian Land Law

First Nations' systems of land holding and relationships, and the knowledges, laws and cultures that give them their form and substance, endured after

213 Robertson, 'The Rise and Rise', 211–26; Real Property Act 1886 (SA) Part 18.

214 Ulla Secher, 'Native Title – An Exception to Indefeasibility and a Ground for Invoking the Deferred Indefeasibility Theory' *James Cook University Law Review* 17, no. 73 (2000); *Hayes v Northern Territory* [1999] FCA 1248, para 90(iv).

215 Behrendt and Brennan, Chapter 16 in this volume.

216 Native Title Act 1993 (Cth), s 192.

217 Native Title Act 1993 (Cth), s 199.

218 Margaret Stephenson and Maureen Tehan, 'The Recording and Management of Indigenous Lands and Title: Is Reform Required?' *Australian Property Law Journal* 24 (2015): 235–255; Jennifer Jude, *The Registration, Recording or Noting of Native Title* (PhD Thesis, University of Queensland, 2018).

219 For example, see also Aboriginal Land Rights Act 1983 (NSW); Ed Wensing, 'Land Justice for Indigenous Australians: Dealings in Native Title Lands and Statutory Aboriginal Land Rights Regimes in Australia and Why Land Tenure Reform Is Critical for the Social Reconstruction of Aboriginal People and Communities' A Seminar on Development on Aboriginal Freehold Land, 2014, James Cook University, Cairns, https://openresearch-repository.anu.edu.au/bitstream/1885/25031/14/01_Wensing_Land_Justice_for_Indigenous_2014.pdf, accessed 13 December 2021.

colonisation,[220] albeit unrecognised by the colonising legal system. The *Mabo* plaintiffs sought a reckoning of these two systems of land law from the High Court. What emerged was a form of recognition of prior occupation of land by First Nations in accordance with their laws, but ultimately subjugated to the colonising system of law.[221] *Mabo* required a reconsideration of the fundamental principles underpinning the acquisition of sovereignty; and, as a result, the Court reached back to 1788 (and beyond) to reconsider the historical record and the extent to which it supported the doctrinal basis of Australia's colonisation and its land laws, especially the doctrine of tenure. The Court provided a new way of viewing both the historical and legal records resulting in 'a doctrinal revision of the entire conceptual basis of Australian property law'.[222] Thus the history of colonising land law must be read in the light of *Mabo*.

Brennan J identified the twin fictions underlying the colonising land law – that the colony was practically unoccupied and peacefully annexed and that the Crown acquired absolute beneficial title to all land. However, he found that 'this Court is not free to adopt rules that accord with contemporary notions of justice and human rights if their adoption would fracture the skeleton of principle which gives the body of our law its shape and internal consistency'.[223] He said that the doctrine of tenure 'is a doctrine which could not be overturned without *fracturing the skeleton* which gives our land law its shape and consistency'.[224] As a result, the Court would not disrupt the earlier finding that New South Wales was a settled colony. Thus, from the outset, these two propositions that had been so significant in the dispossession of First Nations and the disruption of their systems of law and governance, were removed from the reconsideration of Australia's system of governance and land law.

However, according to Brennan J it was possible for the Court 'to determine the *consequences* of an acquisition (of sovereignty) under municipal law'.[225] The *Mabo* Court proceeded on the basis that the colony was an inhabited but settled colony.[226] In that context it was necessary that the

220 Watson, 'Indigenous Peoples' Law-ways'; Neidjii, *Story about Feeling*; Goodall, *Invasion to Embassy*; Dorsett, Chapter 2, and Behrendt and Brennan, Chapter 16 in this volume.

221 Behrendt and Brennan, Chapter 16 in this volume; see generally Ulla Secher, *Aboriginal Customary Law: A Source of Common Law Title to Land* (Oxford: Hart Publishing, 2014); Peter Butt, Robert Eagleson and Patricia Lane, *Mabo, Wik & Native Title* (Sydney: Federation Press, 2001).

222 Edgeworth, 'The Mabo "Vibe"', 76.

223 *Mabo*, 29 (Brennan J).

224 *Mabo*, 45 (Brennan J) (emphasis added).

225 *Mabo*, 32 (Brennan J) (emphasis added).

226 Simpson, 'Mabo, International Law'; Ritter, 'The "rejection of terra nullius"'.

Court find a way of accommodating the existence of those inhabitants and their laws at the time sovereignty was acquired, without disrupting the allocation of rights and interests in land accrued under 200 years of colonial land law; a process described by Bartlett as a 'pragmatic compromise'.[227] In one sense the Court unpacked the fictions that underlay the long-held legal view about land law in Australia. First, the court accepted that the colony was inhabited.[228] In reconsidering the consequences of that fact, the court classified Crown powers as being either *imperium* or *dominium*.[229] In other words, the court separated the Crown's sovereign, constitutional power (*imperium*) from the proposition that the Crown was the absolute beneficial owner of land (*dominium*), describing the previous conflation of the two as 'the fallacy of equating sovereignty and beneficial ownership of land'.[230] The Crown acquired only 'a radical title to land and a sovereign political power over land',[231] which was 'merely a logical postulate required to support the doctrine of tenure'[232] when the Crown exercised its power to either grant an interest in land or appropriate ownership of land to itself.[233] 'The radical title ... acquired with the acquisition of sovereignty cannot ... confer an absolute beneficial title to occupied land.'[234] The distinction between the Crown's power to grant title and its ownership of land created a space within which the court could extend a form of recognition to the laws and land interests of First Nations that existed at the time the Crown acquired sovereignty. The rights recognised are known as 'native title rights'.

In doing this, the Court 'recast the entire landscape so as to produce a dualistic rather than a monistic structure of property law'.[235] It recognised what had in fact been the case since 1788 – the existence of continuing First Nations' systems of laws determining interests in land – confirming the existence of two systems of land law in Australia and bringing the systems into relation with each other in a new way. Significant limitations were placed on the full enjoyment of First Nations' law as recognition could not be at the expense of the operation of the doctrine of tenure over the previous 200 years:

> Crown grants should be seen as the foundation of the doctrine of tenure which is an essential principle of our land law. It is far too late in the day to contemplate an allodial or other system of land ownership. Land in Australia

227 Richard Bartlett, '*Mabo*: Another Triumph for the Common Law' *Sydney Law Review* 15 (1993): 178–186, 185.

228 *Mabo*, 39 (Brennan J). 229 *Mabo*, 44 (Brennan J). 230 *Mabo*, 51 (Brennan J).

231 *Mabo*, 52 (Brennan J). 232 *Mabo*, 50 (Brennan J). 233 Ibid.

234 *Mabo*, 48 (Brennan J). 235 Edgeworth, 'The Mabo "Vibe"', 90.

> which has been granted by the Crown is held on a tenure of some kind and the titles acquired under the accepted land law cannot be disturbed.[236]

First Nations property rights were then subject to grants made by the Crown since 1788 and liable to extinguishment.[237]

While it was long thought that the doctrine of tenure had fallen into irrelevancy,[238] *Mabo* revived and reinstated it to a central position as the conceptual underpinning of Australian land law. This is so notwithstanding the reimagining of the doctrine's application in an occupied settled colony and that the Crown had a radical title rather than beneficial ownership of land. The doctrine's feudal origins of 'mutual rights and obligations' no longer has relevance in Australia;[239] but Bradbrook et al. now suggest that the doctrine 'still provides a basic structure to Australian real property law'.[240] The tenor of the *Wik* decision also suggests 'a shift from the "strictures of feudal tenure"';[241] but the fundamental doctrine remains in place.

Conclusion

As a matter of the coloniser's law, the English common law became the 'land law' of the colony when the colony of New South Wales was established in 1788. By the mid-nineteenth century it was clear that the colonies were developing their own unique land laws more appropriate for the circumstances of the colonies. It was also clear that First Nations' land laws endured the impacts of colonising land laws, including the doctrines of tenure and estates. While *Mabo* reset the land law system by recognising First Nations' land laws, it did so by reinstating the significance of these doctrines as providing the 'skeleton of principle' of the colonising land law system. These doctrines, particularly tenure, had hung silently like a shadow over Australian land law but, now revived, they remain a fundamental impediment to a truly Australian land law encompassing equal recognition and enjoyment of First Nations' land laws.

236 *Mabo*, 47 (Brennan J).
237 *Mabo*, 69–70 (Brennan J), 89, 110 (Deane and Gaudron JJ), 195 (Toohey J); Behrendt and Brennan, Chapter 16 in this volume.
238 Hepburn, 'Feudal Tenure', 73–4.
239 Bradbrook et al., *Australian Real Property Law*, 49.
240 Ibid.
241 Samantha Hepburn, 'Disinterested Truths: Legitimation of the Doctrine of Tenure Post-Mabo' *Melbourne University Law Review* 29 (2005): 1–38, 30 quoted in Bradbrook et al., *Australian Real Property Law*, 55.

15

Aboriginal Land Rights, Subjection and the Law

AMANDA KEARNEY

The law has changed, and you can get some of your land back . . .[1]

Introduction

Matters of long-term land rights have been of utmost concern for Indigenous peoples internationally, with global resonance found across settler-colonial spaces including Australia, Canada, the United States and New Zealand.[2] The restitutionary politics that underscore legislative land rights reveals a settler-colonial history of attempting to come to terms with historical possession of lands and water, and the ongoing tensions that exist in countries where Indigenous laws and settler legal systems come into tense relation. This is certainly the case in Australia, where the Aboriginal Land Rights (Northern Territory) Act 1976 (ALRA), introduced in 1976, remains the country's most enduring form of legislative land rights. So, too, it maps across federal efforts at land restitution, dealt with through the Native Title Act 1993.[3]

Born of a critical moment in Australia's social and political history, the ALRA, is a vestige of earlier attempts to grapple with Aboriginal rights and restitution. The Act has led to the restitution of large stretches of land and coastal areas in the Northern Territory and has a history of implementation in a relatively consistent policy setting. For many Aboriginal groups, the era

1 Ted Laurie QC, speaking to traditional owners in the Borroloola District, quoted in *Traditional Owners Borroloola District* (film), Tapes 1–11, Australian Institute of Aboriginal Studies (AIAS) Film Unit, 1977.

2 Christa Scholtz, *Negotiating Claims: The Emergence of Indigenous Land Claim Negotiations in Australia, Canada, New Zealand and the United States* (New York: Routledge, 2006).

3 L. Kelly and L. Behrendt, 'Creating Conflict: Case Studies in the Tension between Native Title Claims and Land Rights Claims' *Journal of Indigenous Policy*, Special Issue 8 (2007): 73–93; N. Laing, 'Distinguishing Native Title and Land Rights: Not an Easy Path to Rights OR Recognition' *Journal of Indigenous Policy*, Special Issue 8 (2007): 50–72.

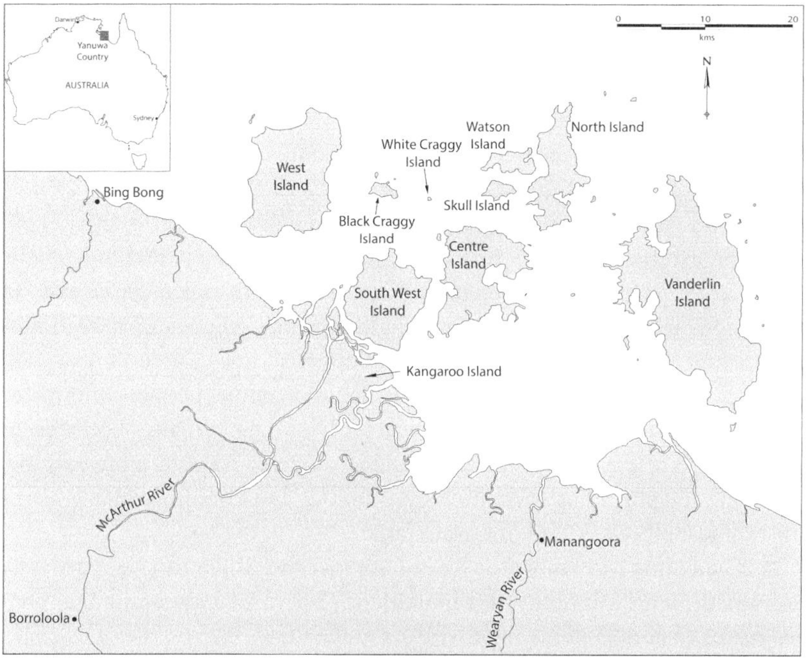

Map 15.1: Yanyuwa Country

of seeking rights under the ALRA has now transformed into one of self-management of Country and the seeking of economic and cultural futures for younger generations of Aboriginal land-owners.[4] Behind every hand-back of land there is a story. For the first group to lodge a claim under the Act in 1976, the Yanyuwa (and including Binbingka, Garrwa and Mara claimants) in the southwest Gulf of Carpentaria, their story now stretches over four decades (see Map 15.1). This is a key chapter in Australia's political, legal and social history, one that continues to shape Aboriginal lives in the present and influence the nation's future.

4 'Country' is a term used by many Indigenous Australian language groups to refer to their homelands as made up of land, sea, bodies of water, kin and resources. It is a holistic term; see J. Bradley and A. Kearney, '"You Whitefellas pull everything apart": Epistemic Learnings in Exploring Landscape', in M. Atha (ed.), *The Routledge Companion to Landscape Studies* (Abingdon: Routledge, 2018, 2nd Edition), 288–98. For a detailed Yanyuwa-centric view of Country in the South-west Gulf of Carpentaria, see J. Bradley with Yanyuwa Families and N. Cameron, *'Forget About Flinders': An Indigenous Atlas of the Southwest Gulf of Carpentaria* (Brisbane: J. M. McGregor Ltd, 2003).

The Yanyuwa story is central to this chapter, in which I present an exploration of Aboriginal peoples' experiences with legislative land rights, under the ALRA, and the process of subjection that 'makes a claimant' and leads to Indigenous complexity and knowledge production. 'Indigenous complexity' is an expression used here to denote an intricacy and capacity for high-level negotiation of change and cultural shift. This is a vision of Indigenous cultures as highly adept at accommodating, resisting and negotiating the external pressures that distinguish settler-colonial and Indigenous relations. It maintains a long-standing critique of nostalgic views of Indigenous relationships to culture and land which propagates reductionist readings of 'former' tradition and 'contemporary' loss. These do not fully account for the many varied ways in which Indigenous people continue to relate to their culture and lands/waters. This chapter also operates to centralise Aboriginal law, and in particular Yanyuwa Law, as a pre-existing, surviving and prevailing epistemology, ontology and axiology which governs life in the south-west Gulf of Carpentaria.

It is by coming to know Yanyuwa Law that the ALRA can be more fully examined for its strengths and limitations. Yanyuwa Law maintains both resistance to and entanglement with Australian law. There exists a complex relationship between the two, which leads me to contend, throughout this chapter, that legislative land rights are not simply law imposed from above but have seduced people to live by their rules. For some, abiding by the demands of legal restitution has opened up avenues of enablement and has brought restitution. It remains, however, that when navigating the legal pursuit of Aboriginal land rights there is always the risk of reducing Indigenous 'history and tradition [to] mere opinion, blown by political winds'.[5] This is because land rights ultimately rest upon evidence: a statement of the past, which directly effects the present and future. In such statements, the past, present and future are made political, contentious, conflicting and concessionary.

By aligning this chapter's account of land rights with one community and locating the fight for restitution in one Aboriginal Country, both before and after British invasion, I maintain an anthropological commitment to ethnographically grounding legal history in the double perspective which encompasses the local, familial and personal, along with the general conditions of the national, historical and human.[6] As an anthropologist drawn to

5 T. O'Regan, *New Myths and Old Politics* (Wellington, NZ: Bridget Williams Books, 2014).
6 M. Jackson, *Lifeworlds: Essays in Existential Anthropology* (Chicago, IL: University of Chicago Press, 2013), xvi.

phenomenological framings of human life, and drawing on my earlier writings on the paradoxical nature of legislative land rights in a settler polity,[7] I seek to highlight the plurality and ambiguity that is intersubjective life, as set within the arena of legislative land rights and Indigenous law, as pertaining to lands and waters.[8] Addressing the role of legislative land rights in driving the pursuit of rights and in compelling social transformation through evidentiary demands upon Aboriginal claimants, it becomes apparent that in a settler polity, although we exist as singular beings and participants in wider fields of being that encompass other people, material presences (lands/waters) and abstractions (the law), our relations are 'uncertain, constantly changing and subject to endless negotiation'.[9] This is vividly cast in the to-and-fro of oppositional politics concerning Indigenous rights broadly and land rights specifically. The making and unmaking of Aboriginal land claimants has a complex history reflected in the evolution of statutory declarations, and legislative instruments themselves. These complexities are also evident in the juridical interpretations and applications of the law and the shifting nature of evidentiary demands, the scrutinising of evidence, the receipt of Indigenous testimonies and the subjecting of Aboriginal claimants to cross-examination on their identity and existence.

There have always been different laws in Australia. Before British settlement, these mapped onto over 500 distinct Aboriginal languages, homelands and laws. 'Being in relation' is the very nature of any law. Law operates to organise the self in relation to the collective, defined broadly as other people, other presences, the state or ancestral beings, and decides on outcomes for those who contravene expectations. These defining aspects link Indigenous laws and Western law in many respects. How healthy the relation is, and on what terms the relations are decided and governed, are questions which sit at the centre of this chapter. Drawing briefly on land rights legislation, in the specific form of the ALRA, as an interstitial space in which two laws meet, challenge one another, and converge in some ways, this chapter strives to ground the praxis of law as it relates to the lands and waters of Indigenous Australians. Examining 'land rights' in this dual legal sense, within the interstitial, I consider the principle

7 A. Kearney, 'Returning to That Which Was Never Lost: Indigenous Australian Saltwater Identities, a History of Australian Land Claims and the Paradox of Return' *History and Anthropology* 29, no. 2 (2018): 184–203.

8 Jackson, *Lifeworlds: Essays in Existential Anthropology*, 9.

9 Ibid, 9.

of 'subjection',[10] that is the official promulgation of social classifications through which individuals are to be known, by themselves, by other individuals and by the officials, and allowed to act. Legislative land rights illuminate one official context in which the powerful construct those spaces in which Indigenous Australians have been enabled to participate in the social life, body politic, economics and politics of the nation.

Background to Australian Land Rights and the Aboriginal Land Rights (Northern Territory) Act 1976

In Australia, the land claim process has always been intensely political. In 1972, launching his party's election campaign, Labor leader Gough Whitlam announced that: 'We will legislate to give Aborigines land rights – not just because their case is beyond argument, but because all of us as Australians are diminished while the aborigines are denied their rightful place in this nation'. However, rather than pursue a national land rights law, Whitlam chose to establish a precedent in the Commonwealth-controlled Northern Territory. In 1973 and 1974 Justice Woodward headed a Royal Commission into Aboriginal land rights in the Northern Territory.[11] He reported that two aims of land rights were 'the doing of simple justice to a people who have been deprived of their land without their consent and without compensation' and 'the preservation, where possible, of the spiritual link with his own land which gives each Aboriginal his sense of identity'.[12] Additional aims of land rights were noted as follows:

> 3. ii. The promotion of social harmony and stability within the wider Australian community by removing, as far as possible, the legitimate causes of complaint of an important minority group within that community.
>
> iii. The provision of land holdings as a first essential for people who are economically depressed and who have at present no real opportunity of achieving a normal Australian standard of living . . .

10 M. Foucault, 'The Subject and Power', in L. Hubert Dreyfus and P. Rabinow (eds), *Michel Foucault: Beyond Structuralism and Hermeneutics* (Chicago, IL: University of Chicago Press, 1983), 208–26; M. Foucault, *Discipline and Punish: The Birth of the Prison*, translated by Alan Sheridan (New York: Vintage Books, 1979); see T. Biolsi, 'The Birth of the Reservation: Making the Modern Individual among the Lakota' *American Ethnologist* 22, no. 1 (1995): 28–53 for an application of subjection to an analysis of federal Indian law and native rights.

11 A. E. Woodward, *Aboriginal Land Rights Commission: Report 1* (Canberra: Australian Government Printer, 1974); A. E. Woodward, *Aboriginal Land Rights Commission: Report 2* (Canberra: Australian Government Printer, 1974).

12 Woodward, *Aboriginal Land Rights Commission: Report 2*, 2.

v. The maintenance and, perhaps, improvement of Australia's standing among the nations of the world by demonstrably fair treatment of an ethnic minority.[13]

Justice Woodward reported, as paramount, a commitment to '[e]nsuring that none of these interests or rights are further whittled away without consent, except in those cases where the national interest positively demands it – and then only on terms of just compensation'.[14] The Aboriginal Land (Northern Territory) Bill was introduced to Parliament in October 1975, but the Whitlam government was dismissed before the legislation could pass the Senate, in the constitutional crisis of November 1975.[15] In its original form the legislation allowed Crown land to be granted to Aboriginal people in the Northern Territory if they could demonstrate their traditional connections to that land. Lands granted were to be held by Land Trusts as an inalienable freehold title. The Act also gave Indigenous communities the right to control mining exploration on Aboriginal lands and created an obligation for mining companies to consult with Indigenous people before beginning mineral exploration. The protection of Aboriginal sacred sites was also enforced by this legislation. The incoming government of Liberal prime minister Malcolm Fraser buckled to pressure from mining and pastoral industry groups and conservative politicians in the Northern Territory and drafted a new bill from which many of the more progressive advancements were absent including, in particular, 'needs-based claims' and 'historical residency'; and the Whitlam government's proposed Commonwealth provision for the protection of sacred sites was handed over to the Northern Territory government.[16] After a series of politically sanctioned amendments, the ALRA came into force on 26 January 1977.[17]

As a legal undertaking, the ALRA requires that documentary evidence and a claimant connection report be submitted, outlining a vast body of cultural insight and competency on behalf of all, if not most, claimants. Aboriginal claimants are subject to cross-examination in the context of a hearing where documentary and testimonial evidence is matched up against statutory

13 Ibid, 2. 14 Ibid.

15 Central Land Council (CLC). 'History of the Land Rights Act' (n. d.) www.clc.org.au/articles/info/history-of-the-land-rights-act/, accessed 13 November 2019.

16 The vesting of control over Aboriginal sacred sites to the Northern Territory government continues to be a cause for concern for Aboriginal people. Breaking away sacred site protection from the rights of Aboriginal owners, under the ALRA, ignores the ontological premise on which people assert and maintain relationships to Country.

17 Central Land Council (CLC). 'History of the Land Rights Act'.

definitions of Aboriginality.[18] A local descent group must be identified, which fits the definition of a 'Traditional Aboriginal Owner'. For the purposes of the Act, a 'traditional Aboriginal owner' is defined as follows:

> ***traditional Aboriginal owners***, in relation to land, means a local descent group of Aboriginals who:
> (a) have common spiritual affiliations to a site on the land, being affiliations that place the group under a primary spiritual responsibility for that site and for the land; and
> (b) are entitled by Aboriginal tradition to forage as of right over that land.[19]

Spiritual affiliations and ancestral knowledge must be communicated and performed by individuals and collectives, and spiritual responsibilities must also be proven, along with a capacity to transmit knowledge across the claimant group generationally. Responsibilities and rights to forage must be evidenced along with strength of attachment to the land under claim. In order for a land claim to proceed, the Land Commissioner must be satisfied that the claimants are the right traditional owners according to Aboriginal law. In order to determine this, bush courts and proofing sessions often take place on Country, putting the Land Commissioner and other legal representatives into close relationship with the Aboriginal claimant group members. The land claim is then heard and the Land Commissioner makes a recommendation to the Minister for Aboriginal Affairs. The Land Commissioner also considers, and must hear, any detriment to others that may occur in the event of land title being granted to the claimant group. As a result of an amendment to the ALRA by the Hawke government, no more land claims could be lodged after 30 June 1997. There remain, however, some claims still outstanding, and sixteen land claims recommended for grant by the Land Commissioner from 1981 to 2004 have not been finalised.[20] The current Land Commissioner, Hon J. R. Mansfield, is yet to report his findings on a detriment review in relation to these sixteen claims, one of which relates to parts of Yanyuwa Country.[21] In sum, the era of land rights under the ALRA is not

18 R. Martin and D. Trigger. '"Nothing never change": Mapping Land, Water and Aboriginal Identity in the Changing Environments of Northern Australia's Gulf Country' *Settler Colonial Studies* 5, no. 3 (2015): 320, 324; E. Povinelli, *The Empire of Love: Toward a Theory of Intimacy, Genealogy and Carnality* (Durham, NC: Duke University Press, 2006).

19 Aboriginal Land Rights (Northern Territory) Act 1976, No. 191, Part 1, 3 Interpretation.

20 Australian Government, National Indigenous Australians Agency, *Detriment Review 2017–2018*, www.niaa.gov.au/indigenous-affairs/land-and-housing/aboriginal-land-commissioner/detriment-review-2017-2018, accessed 13 November 2019.

21 J. Olney, *McArthur River Region Land Claim (Claim No. 184)* (Canberra: Australian Government Publishing, 2002).

over, despite the fact that it has not been possible to lodge claims for land since 1997.

To date, a number of scholars have addressed the legal framework of the ALRA, government responses to the Act, the role of anthropologists and the Act's limitations.[22] The 1980s and early 1990s was a fertile time for Indigenous writing on the ALRA and land rights, more broadly articulating both positive and negative responses to the Act.[23] Others have attended to the specific details of precursor cases, including *Milirrpum v Nabalco Pty Ltd*,[24] while Altman,[25] Altman and Pollack[26] and Peterson[27] have investigated the economic ramifications of land rights in the Northern Territory, and the Act's role in facilitating Indigenous socio-economic advancement.[28] Prevailing interest in the ALRA remains focused on how it informs contemporary land use and management programs on Indigenous lands; for example, Jackson et al.[29] have discussed the implications of land rights for river

22 C. Fletcher, *Grounds for Agreement: Evaluating Responses of Northern Territory Governments to the Aboriginal Land Rights (NT) Act 1976. Report No. 7/1998* (North Australian Research Unit/ANU, 1998); M. Gumbert, *Neither Justice Nor Reason* (St Lucia: University of Queensland Press, 1984); J. Reeves, *Building on Land Rights for the Next Generation: Report of the review of the Aboriginal Land Rights (Northern Territory) Act 1976* (Aboriginal and Torres Strait Islander Commission, 1998); D. B. Rose, *Women and Land Claims* (Canberra: Native Titles Research Unit, Australian Institute of Aboriginal and Torres Strait Islander Studies, 1995), 6, 1–8.

23 F. Gale (ed.), *We are Bosses Ourselves: The Status and Role of Aboriginal Women Today* (Australian Institute of Aboriginal Studies, 1983); N. Peterson and M. Langton, *Aborigines, Land and Land Rights* (Australian Institute of Aboriginal Studies, 1983); G. Yunupingu (ed.), *Our Land is Our Life: Land Rights Past, Present and Future* (St Lucia: University of Queensland Press, 1997).

24 B. Hocking, 'Aboriginal Law Does Now Run in Australia: Reflections on the *Mabo* Case: From *Cooper v Stuart* through *Milirrpum* to *Mabo*' *Sydney Law Review* 15 (1993): 187–205; R. Van Krieken, 'From Milirrpum to Mabo: The High Court, *Terra Nullius* and moral entrepreneurship' *UNSW Law Journal* 23(2000): 63–77; N. Williams, 'Stanner, Milirrpum and the Woodward Royal Commission', in M. Hinkson and J. Beckett (eds), *An Appreciation of Difference: WEH Stanner and Aboriginal Australia* (Canberra: Aboriginal Studies Press, 2008), 198–216.

25 J. Altman, *Sustainable Development Options on Aboriginal Land* (Canberra: Centre for Aboriginal Economic Policy Research, 2001).

26 J. Altman and D. Pollack, *Financial Aspects of Aboriginal Land Rights in the NT* (Canberra: Centre for Aboriginal Economic Policy Research, 1998).

27 N. Peterson, 'Capitalism, Culture and Land Rights: Aborigines and the State in the Northern Territory' *Social Analysis* 18 (1985): 85–101.

28 J. Altman, F. Morphy and T. Rowse (eds), *Land Rights at Risk? Evaluations of the Reeves Report* (Canberra: Centre for Aboriginal Economic Policy Research, 1999).

29 S. Jackson, M. Storrs and J. Morrison, 'Recognition of Aboriginal Rights, Interests and Values in River Research and Management' *Ecological Management and Restoration* 6, no. 2 (2005): 105–10.

management, while Yunupingu and Muller,[30] and Marshall[31] contend with the Act's limited provisions for freshwater and sea rights. Norman has explored the comparative case of Aboriginal land rights, making clear that there are distinctions between other parts of the country and Northern Territory experiences.[32]

There Was and Is Always Law

Since they lodged their first claim under the ALRA in 1976, Yanyuwa have put their Law on the line by fighting for their unceded lands and waters under a white legal system. In doing so, they made their own Law vulnerable to cross-examination; yet this commitment has also rallied and galvanised their community throughout a sustained period of struggle. Since this original claim, the Borroloola Aboriginal community, and more specifically Yanyuwa families, have launched a fresh claim in 1992 for lands not returned in 1976,[33] and an additional claim under the ALRA in 2000 for their sea grass beds and the riverbanks of their Country.[34] They have, in more recent years (in 2015), utilised the Native Title Act to seek further acknowledgment of their traditional ownership, thus rounding out their options for legal restitution, all the while being in unwavering possession of their own Law for Country.

In fighting for their Country, Yanyuwa are asserting their exclusive and ancestrally based right to lands and waters that culturally delimit their language, their old people, their ancestors, and present generations of Yanyuwa living in and around this region. Yanyuwa Country was created by ancestral beings as they walked, crawled, slithered, climbed, flew and stopped on Country, some leaving their mark, others leaving their story, their body or remnants of their activity, and all leaving their Law.[35] This is, in the first instance, a process of physical becoming and an enlivening of the world. It also contains vital knowledge and information, referred to

30 G. Yunupingu and S. Muller, 'Cross-Cultural Challenges for Indigenous Sea Country Management in Australia' *Australasian Journal of Environmental Management* 16, no. 3 (2009): 158–67.

31 V. Marshall, *Overturning Aqua Nullius: Securing Aboriginal Water Rights* (Canberra: Australian Studies Press, 2017).

32 H. Norman, *'What do we want?': A Political History of Aboriginal Land Rights in NSW* (Canberra: Aboriginal Studies Press, 2015).

33 J. Bradley, *Warnarrwarnarr-Barranyi Land Claim* (Darwin: Northern Land Council, 1992).

34 J. Bradley, *Yanyuwa Sea Country Claim* (Darwin: Northern Land Council, 2000).

35 D. B. Rose, *Dingo Makes Us Human: Life and Land in Australian Aboriginal Culture* (Cambridge University Press, 2000), 104.

by Yanyuwa as *narnu yuwa* – 'Law', that is a governing system of how things are sustained and thrive through relations.

Yanyuwa are saltwater people: that is they are *li-Anthawirriyarra*, people whose essence and Law comes from the sea. Describing this more fully, Yanyuwa woman, Dinah Norman a-Marngawi, explains:

> Let me tell you something, the sea, the saltwater, the waves, they are my mother, the sea is my mother, it is my mother's ancestor. I have known this since I was small. Further I will tell you the sea has names, many names, names for the reefs, names for the sea grass beds, names for the sand bars, and the sea has boundaries, we know these boundaries, they did not come here recently. From the time of the ancestral beings and our human ancestors they have been here. Our songs and ceremony are also in the sea, they are running through the sea, both along the bottom of the sea and they also rise and travel on the surface of the sea. White people think the sea is empty that it has no law, but the law and the ceremony is there in the salt water, in the fish, in the sea birds, the dugong and the turtle, it is there and we knowledgeable people are holding it.[36]

As Battiste and Youngblood Henderson remark in the opening pages of their work *Protecting Indigenous Knowledge and Heritage*, 'from the beginning, the forces of the ecologies in which we live have taught Indigenous peoples a proper kinship order and have taught us how to have nourishing relationships with our ecosystems . . . These ecologies do not surround Indigenous peoples; we are an integral part of them and we inherently belong to them'.[37] Povinelli writes of this as genealogy: social construction of the human is through relations; and the subject is bound by various kinds of inheritances.[38] Salmón writes of it as kincentricity, or a kincentric ecology, as one in which all is in relation.[39] This is distinct from the organising principle of autology, where the human being is an autonomous, self-determining subject, in whom sovereignty is vested.[40] Autological and genealogical discourses respectively differentiate kinds of people, societies and civilisational orders. These distinctions are in turn often central to law and legal apprehensions of individual and collective rights and responsibilities. They underscore aspects of the ALRA, whereby 'genealogical' connections for a claimant group must

36 From Bradley's ethnographic fieldnotes, in Bradley and Kearney, 'You Whitefellas pull everything apart', 297.

37 M. Battiste and J. Youngblood Henderson, *Protecting Indigenous Knowledge and Heritage: A Global Challenge* (Saskatoon: Purich Publishing, 2000), 9.

38 E. Povinelli, 'What's Love Got to Do with It? The Race of Freedom and the Drag of Descent' *Social Analysis: The International Journal of Anthropology* 49, no. 2 (2005): 173–81.

39 E. Salmón, 'Kincentric ecology' *Ecological Applications* 10, no. 5 (2000): 1327–32.

40 Povinelli, 'What's Love Got to Do with It?'; Povinelli, *The Empire of Love*.

be proven in front of an audience of judges, lawyers and those who claim detriment (for example, local white residents, commercial fishing operations, white tourism enterprises). This audience is likely to be culturally conditioned to value the autological principle of 'a human right' and are likely to find the principle of being in kinship relation with a non-human species, place or ancestral beings a challenging proposition. The translative tension in this encounter is witnessed in every Aboriginal land claim, diffused only by the nuanced understanding and epistemic mobility of land commissioners, judges, lawyers and other key decision-makers in this process.

There is specificity to Yanyuwa Law which holds people and their Country in relation through elaborate kinship and genealogy. This specificity exists because of *narnu yuwa*, the law that governs Yanyuwa Country and life. *Narnu yuwa* comes from the *yijan*, a time when the ancestors travelled across the land and sea, imbuing the world with order, identity and potency.[41] Often referred to as the Dreaming, for Yanyuwa, the *yijan* is beyond the temporal limits of 'past and present', it is always. *Yijan* is more expansive than an 'ancestral time', and also contains the bodies of knowledge which inform understandings of the reality of Country, that is the ecological order, as made up of non-human species, elements, geology and geography. *Narnu yuwa* – Law, can be called upon in a moment to determine and govern human action and decision-making. It can also act upon human and non-human life, reflected at times as ill health of Country, linked to alien presences that now move across Indigenous countries throughout Australia, in often destructive and dismissive manners. These new elements in Country vary from context to context; but in the case of a Yanyuwa experience, they have included early settlers who acted without regard for the law, tourists who disregard the law for Country and move throughout the region without restraint, non-human species like cane toads which have poisoned Country, and mining companies that disrupt places of importance in ways that are often irreversible. Yanyuwa have publicly declared their fear of damage to Country and of disrespect for their Law, describing their position in such ways, 'Our generation and our grandfathers been fighting for this Country to keep it together, now they've come and destroyed this Country.'[42] Jerry Brown put it more pointedly:

41 Bradley, *Warnarrwarnarr-Barranyi Land Claim*; J. Bradley and Yanyuwa Families, *Wuka nya-nganunga li-Yanyuwa li-Anthawirriyarra – Language for Us, the Yanyuwa Saltwater People* Volume I (Melbourne: Australian Scholarly Publishers, Volume 1, 2016; Volume 2, 2017).

42 J. Bardon, 'McArthur River Mine's Burning Waste Rock Pile Sparks Health, Environmental Concerns among Gulf of Carpentaria Aboriginal Groups' *ABC News*,

> Ah dear me, I am crying. I have tears in my eyes, I am rubbing my eyes. I grew up with the old men for this Country, they gave me eyes to see the Law for this Country. Listen to me! I am standing here alone, the old men have all died. I am here do not pretend not to know me! Listen to me! You are my kin, your essence is the same as me, do not pretend not to know me. This Country is blocked, it is shut up, you have entangled yourself, what has happened here? I am blind in this Country, you are shutting up, closing in, where is the open Country, when I was young I could see a long way, from here to the sea. Oh you poor thing, the old people have all died . . . no fucking good altogether.[43]

According to Yanyuwa Law, the individuated self does not exist, rather a person exists in a deeply relational sense that involves a genealogical casting of a person in relation to other aspects of life. As a first orientation, and among Elders in the Yanyuwa community, a person's identity is established through their clan membership. Yanyuwa are organised through a semi-moiety system of four clan groups, Rrumburriya, Mambaliya, Wuyaliya and Wurdaliya, whereby descent is traced through the paternal and maternal lines, with one's parents belonging to opposite and aligned clans. Identity is forged through a person's *ardirri* – their spirit child. Spirit children were placed into the land by ancestral beings. A spirit child enters the body of a woman in anticipation of pregnancy, often coming from the ancestral Country of the father and awaits birth in the form of a human child. A person's spirit child determines one's place in the world through their father's Country and is said to inhabit the body of a living person throughout their lifetime, residing deep within their bones.[44]

Adding to the parameters by which identity is set and asserted by Yanyuwa, are references to 'bush names'. These names are given to children by senior kin, and are often names shared with someone of their grandparent's generation and often are actual place names, for example *a-Mananku\-rmara* – a feminine bush name which directly references the place of Manankurra, to the east of Yanyuwa Country; or *a-Muluwamara* for the place of Muluwa, the ancestral Wave Dreaming. Bush names may also be the names of non-human species, for example, *a-Badjamalanja* – a feminine bush name which links a person with the Wood Swallow as kin within their clan group; or *Rijirrngu*, that is, a masculine bush name that is the fin of the Groper when she arrived on a part of Country called Alawuyawiji, where her

27 July 2014 www.abc.net.au/news/2014-07-27/mcarthur-riverminegulf-of-carpentaria-anger-smoke-plume/5625484, accessed 1 December 2019.

43 Jerry Brown Ngarnawakajarra, 2000, recorded in John Bradley's ethnographic fieldnotes and quoted in A. Kearney, *Violence in Place* (Abingdon: Routledge, 2017), 60.

44 Bradley and Yanyuwa Families, *Wuka nya-nganunga li-Yanyuwa li-Anthawirriyarra*, 1: 399, 408.

body now rests. A highly sophisticated system of linking people closely to Country, their clan and other kin, bush names, language proficiency, ceremonial ownership and responsibility, place knowledge and ancestral linkages, determine identity for Yanyuwa.[45]

For middle and younger generations, some but not necessarily all of these determinants of relational orientation are called upon for the assertion of identity. This reflects processes of change within this community. Not all forms of Yanyuwa knowledge have been maintained, a sad and real consequence of the impact of coloniality on Yanyuwa life, through loss of access to Country, Western education, premature deaths and a breakdown in the sharing of traditional knowledge forms across generations. Each generation has found its way amidst these conditions and identified the guiding aspects of Law for affirmation and enactment of identity.[46] For younger Yanyuwa, identity is often asserted through family lines, where family names speak to ancestry and lineages of land-owning groups, clan membership, bush names (increasingly), and linkages to the current generation of community leaders and Elders. Language and ceremony play a lesser role. This should not be read as cultural decline, but rather generational responses to changing conditions of everyday life. Irrespective of the shifts in dependence on ceremonial ownership and responsibility, and perhaps place knowledge, Yanyuwa continue to map their place in the world in relation to one another and Country. This is the cornerstone of their Law.

A distinguishing feature of many Indigenous Australian cultures and heritages is that they are grounded in the importance of Country, that is the lands, seas, and waters which hold the ancestral Law for Indigenous language groups. The land and sea form a canvas on and through which ancestral activity is always moving and present. Rose writes of Indigenous homelands as Country, that is a 'nourishing terrain', 'a place that gives and receives life. Not just imagined or represented, it is lived in and lived with.'[47] People talk about Country in the same way they talk about a person: they speak to Country, sing to Country, visit Country, worry about Country, feel

45 See M. Garde, 'Person Reference, Proper Names and Circumspection in Bininj Kunwok Conversation', in I. Mushin and B. Baker (eds), *Discourse and Grammar in Australian Languages* (Amsterdam: John Benjamin Publishing, 2008), 208, for one of the few detailed discussions of Aboriginal bush names.

46 A. Kearney, *Cultural Wounding, Healing and Emerging Ethnicities* (Basingstoke: Palgrave Macmillan, 2014); P. Adgemis, *We Are Yanyuwa, No Matter What* (PhD Thesis, Monash University, 2017).

47 D. B. Rose, *Nourishing Terrains: Australian Aboriginal Views of Landscape and Wilderness* (Canberra: Australian Heritage Commission, 1996), 2.

sorry for Country, and long for Country. People say that Country knows, hears, smells, takes notice, takes care, and is sorry or happy. Country is not a generalised or undifferentiated type of place. It is fathomed in equal parts through an understanding of tangible and intangible cultural expressions. Yet there can be no separation of these two forms, for Country is at once: kin; language; Law, human and non-human. Ethical imperatives run through a kincentric ecology such as this, ensuring that the world is one of 'familiarity'.[48] By extension a kincentric ecology entails action, obligation and presence. That this obligation of caring for Country should extend to the imperative to fight for the right to stolen waters and lands is evident across the last forty-four years of Yanyuwa engagements with the ALRA.

Under the Mango Tree: A Community Meets to Discuss Land Rights

At the back of the present-day Yanyuwa camp, in the township of Borroloola there stands a group of large mango trees (see Figure 15.1). They offer some of

Figure 15.1: Mango trees at the back of the Yanyuwa camp, long-time meeting and ceremony place

48 Salmón, 'Kincentric ecology', 1329.

the lushest foliage, and coolest of shade in an otherwise dry and hot place. Although the trees are an introduced species, they have become an important feature in the Yanyuwa camp. This grove of trees has also been the site of young boys' initiation ceremonies (*a-Marndiwa*), a place for the singing of *kujika* (songlines) and a place to meet with government officials for community meetings.[49]

On 6 and 7 September 1977 a group of Aboriginal people sat under a large mango tree in Borroloola to discuss the future of their ancestral lands and waters. About 200 people attended this meeting, including Aboriginal people living in Borroloola, mostly members of the Yanyuwa language group, but also Garrwa and Mara. Also in attendance that day were relatives brought from Doomadgee in Queensland, and Numbulwar in the Northern Territory.[50] This event marked three weeks before the Borroloola land claim hearing, which would take place in Darwin to decide the future of Yanyuwa people's Country. The Northern Land Council had lodged the Borroloola land claim with the Aboriginal Land Commissioner in June 1977. John Avery, the anthropologist who gave evidence for the Northern Land Council and Traditional Owner claimants, gives a snapshot of this meeting, 'The people waited quietly for their turn to explain their connections to the various countries as set out in the land claim book.'[51] He concludes his recollection as follows; 'In retrospect, the Borroloola people were unlucky to have their claim run first before the standards, methods and procedures that would guide later claims were settled.'[52]

This event was momentous for many reasons, not the least being that it marked the beginning of a long and protracted fight for land rights, but also that it brought about the realisation that Yanyuwa actually had to fight for their lands and waters. According to Avery, the nature of dispossession had not yet dawned on Yanyuwa, who considered their lands and waters their own.[53] Avery recalls that Yanyuwa, in the time leading up to the first claim 'did not speak as if their land had been taken away from them'.[54] Most of their lands were vacant except for a few white hermits; thus, initially the need to fight for the return of lands may not have seemed so pressing and urgent.[55]

49 P. Memmott, 'Reviving Culture on Mornington Island', in M. Moran (ed.), *Serious Whitefella Stuff: When Solutions became the Problem in Australian Indigenous Affairs* (Melbourne: Melbourne University Press, 2016), 73–101. For a detailed discussion of *kujika* – Yanyuwa songlines, see J. Bradley and Yanyuwa Families. *Singing Saltwater Country* (Sydney: Allen & Unwin, 2010).

50 J. Avery, 'Borroloola: The First Land Claim' *Land Rights News* (July 2016): 20–3, www.nlc.org.au/uploads/pdfs/LRN_July-2016_Web.pdf, accessed 12 November 2019.

51 Ibid, 23. 52 Ibid. 53 Ibid, 22. 54 Ibid. 55 Ibid.

Presiding over the case was Justice Toohey, the Land Commissioner, and the Minister for Aboriginal Affairs. Justice Toohey attended the meeting under the mango tree, which was a lead-up to the hearing (later held in Darwin). The mango tree meeting was filmed, photographed and audio recorded. In each of these documentations, one sees a group of Aboriginal men gathered in discussion and being spoken to by white representatives of the Northern Land Council. What is not immediately apparent from the photographs and filmed recordings of the event is that to the right of the camera, off screen, sits a group of Aboriginal women, Yanyuwa, Mara and Garrwa, of all ages. These women sit on calico blankets in the shade of an adjoining tree with their children and dogs. They are not immediately present in the conversation and only appear in a short snippet of recorded footage with muted sound. In this moment, they are seen consulting with the anthropologist, John Avery, on matters of women's hunting patterns and locations across Country. Transcripts from this event make clear that the conversation which took place almost exclusively involved the men of the region.

The mango tree meeting was co-ordinated as an event in which traditional owners were identified and verified in the company of the claimant group. The gathering's purpose, then, was to establish the proper people to claim certain parts of their Country, and to document named individuals as the traditional owners of the land under claim. That this aligning of 'proper people to Country' would take place with the almost total exclusion of women as land-owners and claimants would later become clear. The people formally documented and submitted as claimants and Aboriginal land-owners at this meeting would later be called upon to give evidence in a court of law as to their 'true identity' and links to Country. Ted Laurie QC states at the meeting '[i]f your claim is a true claim, then everybody else will say it is true'.[56] Peer-based verification was demanded under the legislative land rights process, itself an artefact of a long-held habit of scrutinising Aboriginal people and their claims to Indigeneity.[57] As one Yanyuwa man, Graham Friday, remarked, over three decades after the first Borroloola land claim, 'land claims are just like the welfare days, where everyone's name gets written down, and everyone has to prove who they are'.[58]

The footage captured on the eleven film reels of the mango tree meeting bears the hallmarks of a stilted, cross-cultural exchange between Aboriginal

56 AIAS, *Traditional Owners Borroloola District* (film), Tapes 1–11.
57 Rose, 'Land Rights and Deep Colonising'.
58 A. Kearney, author's ethnographic fieldnotes (2017).

people, and white linguists, administrators, bureaucrats and lawyers.[59] What is impressive about this event, and what is captured on film, is the fact that people who are gathered are willing to subject themselves and their Law to the scrutiny of another legal system. Avery writes that news of the possibility to claim land came in June 1975, when John Wilders and others from the Northern Land Corporation (the interim Northern Land Council) flew to Borroloola to meet with local Aboriginal people and other residents of Borroloola (including the police officer, the manager of the Welfare Depot, and cattle station owners), to tell the audience that 'the government would *allow* Aboriginal people to claim back their traditional Country in the Pellew Islands and on the town common'.[60]

The Yanyuwa Land Claim Story

The first Yanyuwa claim (Borroloola 1 Claim) was, in many ways, a test case which resulted in only a partial grant of land. Accounting for the strain of Aboriginal people's cross-examination, Avery reflects that, the 'Aboriginal evidence was over in a miserable, gut-wrenching, heartbreaking two days'.[61] The 1977 claim resulted in Yanyuwa being acknowledged as the Aboriginal owners, and being granted freehold title to part of the land under claim: 'all of Vanderlin Island and West Island and the unalienated Crown land on the Town Common (excepting small areas of special purpose lease)'.[62] Aboriginal land title was not recognised, nor recommended for grant over Southwest Island, Centre Island, North Island and significant smaller islands and islets in the Edward Pellew Group of Islands. Justice Toohey 'did not make recommendations that these areas be granted along with Vanderlin and West Islands because . . . [t]here was, in his view, insufficient evidence of visitation and of the desire to live or use these areas'.[63] This was a devastating outcome for Yanyuwa, who would rally and lodge a reclaim in 1979, which would eventually be heard in 1992.

At the time of the first Borroloola land claim, mining interests operated in the region, and had identified infrastructure requirements across Yanyuwa Country to support expansion. According to Avery the 'land claim was shaping up as a fight with the mining company over its plans to run a pipeline and roads over bridges straddling islands to a port on Centre Island'.[64] This involved a proposal for an offshore port facility on Centre Island, a central island under claim in the first land claim. As a result, the 1977 land claim took place against a backdrop of

59 AIAS, *Traditional Owners Borroloola District*, Tapes 1–11.
60 Avery, 'Borroloola', 21 (emphasis added). 61 Ibid, 22. 62 Ibid, 23. 63 Ibid, 22.
64 Ibid.

political lobbying. Aboriginal lands, in this instance, were enmeshed in the projection of mining development in the region. Those portions of land denied through the claim process were central to the proposed plans being tabled and discussed by Mount Isa Mines. Further factors influencing the outcome of the land claim, political by nature, were the exclusion of women and the matter of Aboriginal people of white parentage. This would also fall beyond the scope of the 1977 claim, and was only addressed in the 1992 reclaim, after which time amendments would be made to the Act in regard to the inclusion of people of mixed descent, and fuller recognition for matrilineal descent lines in Yanyuwa. In February 1992, the Federal Court ruled that persons of matrilineal descent could satisfy the term 'Traditional Aboriginal Owners' as defined in the Act. In the case of Yanyuwa Country this meant the inclusion, for the first time, of people who identified as traditional owners through their mothers, despite having non-Aboriginal fathers. These people had been denied their place previously, though some of them included people who had been raised Yanyuwa and had lived their entire lives moving through and living on Yanyuwa Country.

The weight of identity politics, racism and the dismissal of women (who were not called upon to give evidence – and nor was maternal descent considered a pathway towards land holding rights) in the first claim, combined with the political lobbying around the safeguarding of future mining interests in the region, had detrimental effects on Yanyuwa in their pursuit of 'legal' rights to Country. The outcomes reflect the tensions inherent in a Western legal process operating to determine the legitimacy of Aboriginal claims to land, when such claims are steeped in another (Yanyuwa) legal discourse.[65] In 1996 a decision was reached on the 1992 reclaim case, overwhelmingly determining Yanyuwa as the Aboriginal owners of the more extensive lands claimed. In 2006, after ten years of negotiation, the second Yanyuwa land grant, determined in 1996, was handed back, with the matter fully resolved in 2015. During this protracted period of resolution, Yanyuwa also launched what might have become one of the most radical moves to restore sea country in recent Australian settler-colonial history. The Yanyuwa Sea Beds and Banks Claim, lodged in 2000, sought title over 120 kilometres of the littoral (intertidal) zone and river banks. This was the first claim ever made to the intertidal zone (predating the Blue Mud Bay decision of 2008) and the sea grass beds and banks of a river. It was a powerful display of Yanyuwa communal agency and saltwater identity.

65 Kearney, 'Returning to That Which Was Never Lost'.

Although the Land Commissioner, Justice Olney, determined, without reservation, that Aboriginal freehold title exists and should be recognised, it was not and has never subsequently been granted. This case remains one of the sixteen unresolved outcomes before the current Land Commissioner.

Yanyuwa contexts expose the social and legal shifts which occurred in order to deliver the actuality of land rights, as illustrated through fierce opposition and lengthy court challenges.[66] There is, however, no denying that benefits have come from legislative land rights, with decisions often being reached by extremely empathic and informed land commissioners, supported by good lawyers, and anthropologists. Yet the measure of success can only fully be gauged when juxtaposed with the denial of rights that demanded restitution in the first place. Aboriginal people never ceded their lands and waters and yet have had no choice but to operate within a structurally white legal system to redress their situation of loss. In which case, the benefits must also be measured against the significant costs that have been exacted for many claimants. Emotional fatigue from fighting for lands and waters is apparent among Yanyuwa. Requiring close examination are the cultural shifts that have come with asserting 'Aboriginality' in accordance with non-Indigenous law, and the requirement to conform to a discourse of authenticity, and challenges faced in securing economic futures across restored lands. Land rights is a process of social transformation.

Making Yanyuwa Claimants – Subjection and Laws

In the context of a land claim, 'claimants' face huge evidentiary burdens. One of the key actors in the sequence of Yanyuwa land claims, elder Pyro Dirdiyalma, conveyed his frustration at the discrepancies in claim experiences and outcomes when, in 2002, he remarked, 'with some places that land claim boss is a bit hard for you, he's a bit hard for that land, he can't understand much, he's got no Law in his head, so he makes it a bit hard for you, you know'.[67] Of the land claim process, he elaborated,

> We teach that judge all day long. I been callin him all those names . . . All the sea side, that sea all got name for Country. I learn all these names traveling in

66 J. Avery and D. McLaughlin, *Submission by Northern Land Council to the Aboriginal Land Commissioner on the Borroloola Region Land Claim* (Darwin: Northern Land Council, 1977); Bradley, *Warnarrwarnarr-Barranyi Land Claim*; Bradley, *Yanyuwa Sea Country Claim*; P. Gray, *Warnarrwarnarr-Barranyi Land Claim* (Canberra: Australian Government Publishing, 1997); Olney, *McArthur River Region Land Claim*; Justice Toohey, *Borroloola Land Claim* (Canberra: Australian Government Publishing, 1979).

67 Kearney, author's ethnographic fieldnotes (2002).

> dugout canoe, taught all this by my father, my grandfather, my great grandfather – all the old fellas. He [judge] know I got bush names for all this Country, all the way from that sea to Manankurra. We straighten up the law for that Country like a boundary, a Country sense. These are boundary from the beginning. They all know me and like me those judges. I been schooled by the old people I tell them lawyers. My whole life I been going to school that way. When I told them, I tell im lawyers too. I gonna give you a lot of word, a lot of Aboriginal Law, because I have to talk straight longa him so you take him and show him. He [whitefellas] call that name thinkin its him Country, but my Country himself, never even have a yarn or a talk. He don't know big boss, Aboriginal people are big boss.[68]

Despite the arduous demands on Indigenous claimants to satisfy criteria steeped in notions of tradition within a context of deep colonising, Yanyuwa have cultivated an urgent patience in their approach to restitution. 'Urgent patience', is taken from Gordon's work on social death and hauntings.[69] This form of 'holding' and 'waiting' is 'a way of being in the ongoing work of emancipation, a work never measured by legalistic pronouncements, a work that inevitably must take place while you're still confined'.[70] Gordon reflects that, for those living with suffering, living in poverty or alongside structural violence, or for those living with the effects of other impoverishment, social death is rendered and narrated by others.[71] This social death is written into the colonial administrations' historical declaration of rights over Indigenous lands and waters, the violence of alienation and dispossession and, ultimately, the imperative to fight within a structurally white system of land rights for piecemeal returns. The Yanyuwa fight for rights to their sea country as something that was never ceded is the act of 'something-to-be-done', a response to 'a situation that requires immediate attention'.[72] It is approached with an 'urgency that's autonomous and self-directed towards ends and aims not wholly given and certainly not given permission by the system's logics or crises but rather invented elsewhere and otherwise'.[73] Emotional fatigue is apparent for Yanyuwa, and tensions have emerged over time, in the wake of successful land claim outcomes. At present, these are: communal disagreement about how to manage Country, the capacity to include and provide rights to non-Indigenous spouses of Yanyuwa land

68 Kearney, author's ethnographic fieldnotes (2002).
69 A. Gordon, *Ghostly Matters: Haunting and the Sociological Imagination* (Minneapolis, MN: University of Minnesota Press, 2008); A. Gordon, 'Some Thoughts on Haunting and Futurity' *Borderlands* 10, no. 2 (2011): 16.
70 Ibid.
71 Gordon, *Ghostly Matters*; Gordon, 'Some Thoughts on Haunting and Futurity'.
72 Ibid, 8. 73 Ibid, 8.

holders, the distribution of royalty monies forthcoming from the region's mining industry, and access rights to parts of island Country subject to restrictions based on gendered and generational distinctions.

The specific design of legislative land rights, the mobilising of legal and statutory definitions of Aboriginality, traditional ownerships, ongoing connection, and the evidentiary demands placed upon Aboriginal people are what 'make a claimant'. These are processes that construct and hold in place fundamental social classifications through which individuals are known by officials, and potentially, over the long term, themselves. These become the conditions which determine how people are allowed to act and potentially how they choose to act. Elsewhere, Biolsi has applied the principle of subjection to better understand Indigenous and settler relations through Law.[74] He writes of the birth of Indian federal law and reservations in the United States, and the making of 'reservation individuals' among the Lakota. Subjection is a useful analytical device in this case, to examine the process of social transformation that Lakota reservation dwellers and Aboriginal 'claimants' undergo in the pursuit of rights. For the latter, it is the seduction of legislative land rights, set against a scene of alienation and lack of land security, which opens up avenues of enablement; people see potential in white structures to redress the loss. While concessionary, there is still agency in this choice and ingenuity expressed through the realisation of 'a need to act' and representation of Yanyuwa identity to maintain Yanyuwa Law, and responsibilities to Country and ancestors through the form of a land right.

Biolsi reflects on the 'everyday ness' of living within the settler-colonial polity as a reality that partly determines people's lives, but does not exhaust the everyday worlds of Indigenous people.[75] Living within the settler polity is attributable to the 'density' which defines people's lives, that is a 'complexity and a politics not reducible to a single subject position'.[76] Biolsi describes this as more than intersectionality, where life is a composite of political struggle and everydayness; it is a life composed of many actions, fighting, dancing, teaching, thinking, loving.[77] Density reveals an 'infinitely less schematic livedness', which, in this case, is taken to signify Indigenous complexity,

74 Biolsi, 'The Birth of the Reservation'.

75 T. Biolsi, 'Racism, Popular Culture and Rosebud Reservation' *Native American and Indigenous Studies* 6, no. 1 (2019): 77–110.

76 Ibid; C. Anderson, 'Critical Indigenous Studies: From Difference to Density' *Cultural Studies Review* 15, no. 2 (2009): 82–100.

77 Biolsi, 'Racism, Popular Culture and Rosebud Reservation'; Anderson, 'Critical Indigenous Studies', 92, inspired by R. Kelley, 'On the Density of Black Being', in C. Kim (ed.), *Scratch* (New York: Studio Museum of Harlem, 2005), 9–10.

decision-making, choices and compulsion to act.[78] This is a compelling frame through which to view the Yanyuwa experience of land claims over the last forty-three years and their decision repeatedly to seek restitution utilising the instruments of the colonial state. Those who seek land rights are cast as the 'minority', Indigenous laws are peripheralised, and the person is recast as a claimant, or member of a claimant group, thus making them 'legible', 'readable' and 'available' to the political and economic calculation that determines legislative and legal land rights.[79] Yet through the process of legal restitution, people have the opportunity to give evidence of their Law, compel others to witness it and, in doing so, to act fully in their own communal interests. They are not transformed into radically new subjects, because the principle of obligation and responsibility for Country underscores the need to fight for land rights.

Throughout this chapter I have attempted to account for existing Indigenous laws in relation to lands and waters in Australia. These laws co-exist with white Australian law and may find themselves entangled in the context of an Aboriginal land claim. They do not come together easily and the greater demand for concession often lies on the side of Indigenous law. That said, Yanyuwa culture and Law have not been obliterated by legislative land rights nor the legal fight it entails. In fact, many aspects of Law and culture have been assured through the act of generational knowledge transfer that is demanded as an evidentiary mandate and by the intense scrutiny of the knowledge that must be displayed during the process of land claim hearings. Public declarations of knowledge, kinship and identity have now been shared by and witnessed among four generations of Yanyuwa. The youngest members of this community recall, through social memory, what their old people had to prove; and they are often reminded of the need to continually 'prove' who they are, in case everything is taken away once again. While evidencing a deep anxiety about the threat of loss, this subjection has also manifested as a site of complex ongoing knowledge production about Indigeneity in the present, practised as a generationally shared reminder of the need to know the terms of Country, Law and kinship. There are numerous subject positions available to Yanyuwa as they move through the space of restitutionary politics, much more so than is commonly recognised. The complexity is evidenced by how well Aboriginal people have read the demands of white law, how well they have enacted the role of claimant, how well they have

78 See Biolsi, 'The Birth of the Reservation'; Biolsi, 'Racism, Popular Culture and Rosebud Reservation'; Anderson, 'Critical Indigenous Studies'.
79 Biolsi, 'Racism, Popular Culture and Rosebud Reservation', 29.

navigated the white system of legislative land rights, all the while maintaining their own Law. This echoes Anderson's principle of density and highlights Indigenous complexity.[80] Could the same be said for white law, were it faced with a formidable and threatening presence which denied its authority and legitimacy?

80 Anderson, 'Critical Indigenous Studies'.

16

Land Justice

JASON BEHRENDT AND SEAN BRENNAN

Introduction

This chapter explores the extent to which statutory land rights and native title contribute to land justice for Indigenous people. Both land rights and native title provide for limited 'repossession'[1] in the face of nearly 200 years of uncompensated dispossession. The long period of frontier violence, the oppressive policies of 'Protectionism' and then 'Assimilation' that operated from the late nineteenth century deep into the twentieth century, and the grant of countless land titles by the Crown since 1788, all shape the way land rights and native title work in the present day. The emergence of these two legal regimes in the last quarter of the twentieth century also attests to First Nations peoples' resistance to dispossession, their cultural resilience, and their organised use of political processes and courts to recover rights over territory.

Despite some overlap, the two legal regimes differ markedly from each other in terms of process and outcome. Further, while the centrepiece of native title regulation is a national law – the Native Title Act 1993 (Cth) – statutory land rights emerged jurisdiction-by-jurisdiction at the state and territory level. This chapter provides an overview of three state and territory land rights regimes, which demonstrate different approaches to the policy challenges of restoring Indigenous land ownership in response to the distinctive circumstances and Indigenous political demands of their regions. The chapter then considers the recognition and development of native title rights and interests.

1 J. Altman and F. Markham, 'Burgeoning Indigenous Land Ownership: Diverse Values and Strategic Potentialities', in S. Brennan, M. Davis, B. Edgeworth and L. Terrill (eds), *Native Title From Mabo to Akiba: A Vehicle for Change and Empowerment?* (Sydney: Federation Press, 2015), 126.

Land Rights Legislation

Historical Context

By the mid-twentieth century circumstances varied widely for Indigenous people. While many had been pushed to the fringes of towns and cities, some were able to remain on Country in camps on pastoral properties, where they were a convenient source of labour. Other families resided on reserves, the rationale of which was as much the regulation and control of Indigenous people as providing a living space.

From the 1920s, Aboriginal people increasingly asserted the need for more independence and for land justice. These calls were led by political organisations, such as the Australian Aboriginal Progressive Association in the 1920s and Aborigines Progressive Association in the 1930s.[2] Momentum continued to build as political movements mobilised around the Yirrkala Bark Petition to Parliament in 1963, the Wave Hill walk off by pastoral workers and their families in 1966, the 1967 Referendum, and the establishment of the Aboriginal Tent Embassy in Canberra in 1972.

In response, government policy in a number of states slowly shifted towards providing more secure tenure for a very few Aboriginal communities, in some cases giving them a level of control through the establishment of lands trusts for Aboriginal reserves. These schemes included those established under the Aboriginal Lands Trust Act 1966 (SA), Aboriginal Lands Act 1970 (Vic), Aboriginal Affairs Planning Authority Act 1972 (WA) and Aborigines (Amendment) Act 1973 (NSW).

The establishment of reserves and, subsequently, trusts occurred without any legal recognition of pre-existing property rights. As a matter of historical fact, Australia was not *terra nullius* (the land of no one); and Indigenous societies had maintained territorial rights and responsibilities under their own laws and customs since time immemorial. But, the British saw the common law as arriving in 1788 and, from 1836, the Australian courts, after a period of ambiguity, insisted that the laws of the colonies applied to all, including Indigenous people.[3]

These contradictions were brought to court in *Milirrpum v Nabalco Pty Ltd* (the 'Gove Land Rights Case') which involved a claim by the Yolngu people for recognition of their traditional rights and interests. Justice Blackburn's lengthy decision in 1971 recorded the detailed system of law and custom maintained by the Yolngu people; but ultimately held that those rights were

2 J. Maynard, *Fight for Liberty and Freedom. The Origins of Australian Aboriginal Activism* (Canberra: Aboriginal Studies Press, 2007), 5–6.

3 *R v Murrell* [1836] NSWSupC 35.

not recognised under Australian law.[4] The decision stood in contrast to decisions in Canada[5] and the United States.[6] Indigenous property rights had also been recognised in Papua New Guinea[7] and by the Privy Council.[8]

The newly elected Whitlam Labor government responded to the Gove Land Rights Case by establishing the Woodward Royal Commission, which, in 1974, recommended the introduction of Aboriginal land rights legislation.[9] The subsequent enactment of the Aboriginal Land Rights (Northern Territory) Act 1976 (Cth) (the ALR (NT) Act) represents a high-water mark for Commonwealth intervention in the cause of land justice for Aboriginal people prior to the recognition of native title. The Commonwealth subsequently enacted the Aboriginal Land Grant (Jervis Bay Territory) Act 1986 (Cth) to transfer land to the Aboriginal community at Wreck Bay, and the Aboriginal Land (Lake Condah and Framlingham Forest) Act 1987 (Cth), which (at the request of the Victorian Government) provided for the transfer of certain reserve lands, at Framlingham Forests and Lake Condah, to Aboriginal corporations.

The federal enactment of the ALR (NT) Act coincided with moves by some state governments also to provide a more substantive land base for Indigenous people. Over two decades, statutory schemes were enacted in South Australia, New South Wales, Queensland and Tasmania.[10] Western Australia was the only state which took no steps to enact land rights legislation.

In introducing these schemes, governments placed varying emphasis on the importance of providing Aboriginal people with land justice, recognising traditional relationships to land, and establishing a land base which might contribute to greater economic independence. However, these measures also reflected the limits of political will of each government to meet the

4 (1971) 17 FLR 141.
5 *St Catherine's Milling and Lumber Company v The Queen* (1888) 14 App Cas 46.
6 *Johnson v McIntosh*, 21 US (Wheat) 543 (1823).
7 *Administration of Papua and New Guinea v Daera Guba* (1973) 130 CLR 353, 397 (Barwick CJ).
8 *Amodu Tijani v Secretary, Southern Nigeria* [1921] 2 AC 399.
9 Aboriginal Land Rights Commission, Second Report (Canberra: AGPS, 1974).
10 Anangu Pitjantjatjara Yankunytjatjara Lands Rights Act 1981 (SA); Aboriginal Land Rights Act 1983 (NSW); Maralinga Tjarutja Land Rights Act 1984 (SA); Aboriginal Land Act 1991 (Qld); Torres Strait Islander Land Act 1991 (Qld) and Aboriginal Lands Act 1995 (Tas). More limited legislation to transfer specific parcels of land to Aboriginal control included the Land Administration Act 1997 (WA), s 83; Aboriginal Land (Northcote Land) Act 1989 (Vic); Aboriginal Lands Act 1991 (Vic) and Aboriginal Land (Manatunga Land) Act 1992 (Vic). In addition there was legislation for the ownership and management of National Parks: for example, National Parks and Wildlife Amendment (Aboriginal Ownership) Act 1996 (NSW); Statute Amendment (Co-Managed Parks) Act 2004 (SA); Parks and Reserves (Framework for the Future) Act 2003 (NT) and Cape York Peninsula Heritage Act 2007 (Qld).

aspirations of Indigenous people when faced with industry lobbying and political opposition.[11] As a result, the nature and scope of the statutory schemes vary considerably.

Some of the issues with which these schemes have grappled include determining what land is made available for return to Aboriginal people and whether it will occur by direct transfer, or by a claim procedure, or both. If by claim, is that claim based on traditional ownership, or compensation and accommodation for dispossession and displacement? Should land be held on trust; what organisational structure for land holding is needed; and how are those organisations to be resourced so they can operate effectively? Once restored to Aboriginal hands, how can the land be dealt with? Is it inalienable? Or can it be leased, mortgaged and sold, and if so, under what conditions? Finally, does the transfer of land include ownership of minerals and, if not, what are the circumstances under which mining might occur on those lands? All these questions affect the capacity of statutory land rights to deliver land justice and the degree to which they explicitly address the intersection of culturally distinct legal orders.

The three examples that follow highlight the different approaches which have been adopted to answering these questions.

Aboriginal Land Rights (Northern Territory) Act 1976 (Cth)

The ALR (NT) Act is Commonwealth legislation that applies only in the Northern Territory and creates an explicit legal interface between Aboriginal and settler law. The relevant Minister can establish Aboriginal land trusts to hold land for the benefit of Aboriginal people 'entitled by Aboriginal tradition to the use or occupation of the land concerned'.

Upon its enactment, former missions and reserves listed in Schedule 1 of the ALR (NT) Act were transferred directly to Aboriginal land trusts and, from time to time, negotiations have led to the addition of more areas to the schedule for administrative transfer. The Act also established a process for *claims* to unalienated land to be made on behalf of people identifying as 'traditional Aboriginal owners', defined as 'a local descent group of Aboriginals who: (a) have common spiritual affiliations to a site on the land, being affiliations that place the group under a primary spiritual

11 It is also important to appreciate that many of these schemes have not been stagnant but have undergone a variety of reviews and amendments either to limit or enhance their provisions.

responsibility for that site and for the land; and (b) are entitled by Aboriginal tradition to forage as of right over that land'.[12]

Amendments made in 1987 inserted a sunset clause that prevented fresh land claims after June 1997. By then 249 land claims had been made to Aboriginal Land Commissioners under the Act, of which eighty-four involved inquiries into whether the claimants were traditional Aboriginal owners. In almost every case, the minister was satisfied that inalienable fee simple title to the land should be granted. Nearly 50 per cent of the Northern Territory has been restored to traditional owners under this legislation.

The ALR (NT) Act also established Aboriginal Land Councils to represent, and negotiate on behalf of, Aboriginal people living in their area, to protect the interests of traditional owners and other Aboriginal people, to assist people to make land claims, and to provide support to Aboriginal land trusts.

The ALR (NT) Act provides a number of protections for land granted under the Act ('Aboriginal land'). Access to Aboriginal land generally requires a permit. The land can be compulsorily acquired only by the Commonwealth and not by the Northern Territory government. The grant of a mining interest on Aboriginal land is prohibited without an agreement between the intending miner and the Aboriginal Land Council for the area. A Land Council cannot enter an agreement about mining unless it has consulted with the traditional owners and is satisfied that they understand the agreement and have given informed consent. This rule anticipated the principle of 'free, prior and informed consent' over development on Indigenous land that was later enshrined by the United Nations in 2007 in its Declaration on the Rights of Indigenous People.

The Commonwealth has used mining income to resource the system. Sums equivalent to the royalties paid to the Crown for mining on Aboriginal land are transferred into the Aboriginals Benefit Account ($391.4 million in 2021–22). Some of that money is returned to people affected by the mining activities, some is used to fund the operations of the Land Councils, and the balance is available for lease administration and project funding through a periodic application process.

Aboriginal Land Rights Act 1983 (NSW)

In New South Wales, the first substantive legislative move towards land rights was the Aborigines Act 1969 (NSW), which repealed the Protectionist-era Aborigines Protection Act 1909 and established a Director of Aboriginal

12 Aboriginal Land Rights (Northern Territory) Act, s 3.

Welfare and an appointed Aboriginal Advisory Council (AAC). The legislation allowed for leases to be awarded to Aboriginal people over Aboriginal reserves. The minister's Second Reading Speech noted that the '[e]mphasis in the new legislation has changed from welfare to a fostering of self-reliance and independence for the Aboriginal people'.[13] Amendments in 1973 vested the former reserve land in an Aboriginal land trust, and provided that the AAC be elected, not appointed.

Meanwhile, Aboriginal mobilisation created political momentum for a broader remedy for Aboriginal dispossession.[14] In 1978, the Legislative Assembly appointed a Select Committee chaired by Maurie Keane MP to investigate the causes of Aboriginal disadvantage in New South Wales and to inquire into land rights. The resulting Keane Report in 1980 recommended the enactment of land rights legislation but noted that models from jurisdictions like the Northern Territory would not be suitable in New South Wales. Following further complicated political manoeuvring,[15] state Parliament passed the Aboriginal Land Rights Act 1983 (NSW) ('ALRA (NSW)'). Though the Minister for Aboriginal Affairs, Frank Walker, noted that some lands granted under the scheme 'will retain a cultural and a spiritual significance', the need to provide Aboriginal people with economic independence as well as compensation for past injustice was central to the policy underlying the ALRA (NSW).[16]

The ALRA (NSW) established 119 Local Aboriginal Land Councils (LALCs), thirteen Regional Councils and one state-wide body, being the New South Wales Aboriginal Land Council (NSWALC). Regional councils were subsequently removed from the scheme.[17] Membership of a LALC is not limited to people who might be regarded as traditional owners. It is open to adult Aboriginal people who are accepted by the council as residing in the area or having a sufficient association with the area. The ALRA (NSW) established a fund to support Aboriginal Land Councils and to provide a means of purchasing land. For fifteen years, 7.5 per cent of land tax was paid into the fund (effectively by the present-day beneficiaries of dispossession), providing a capital base ($676 million in 2021) that has given the Land Council system independence from government and the budgetary cycle.

13 New South Wales, *Parliamentary Debates*, Legislative Council, 26 February 1969, 3963.

14 See generally, H. Goodall, *Invasion to Embassy: Land in Aboriginal Politics in New South Wales, 1770–1972* (Sydney: Sydney University Press, 1996), chapter 24.

15 H. Norman, *'What Do We Want?' A Political History of Aboriginal Land Rights in New South Wales* (Canberra: Aboriginal Studies Press, 2015).

16 New South Wales, *Parliamentary Debates*, Legislative Assembly, 24 March 1983, 5089.

17 Norman, *What Do We Want?*, 170–3.

The ALRA (NSW) allowed for the transfer of areas from the lands trust established in 1973 to the relevant LALC. It also created an *administrative* process for claiming land, without reference to traditional connections. On application, the Minister determines whether the area claimed is 'claimable Crown lands'. That definition applies to land able to be sold, leased, reserved or dedicated under Crown lands legislation; not lawfully used or occupied; not needed or likely to be needed for an essential public purpose; not, in the opinion of the Minister, needed or likely to be needed as residential lands; and not the subject of a registered native title claim or determination. The Minister has no discretion not to transfer 'claimable Crown lands' and any refusal to do so can be appealed to the Land and Environment Court. Generally speaking, land is transferred as alienable freehold and includes ownership of minerals (other than gold, silver, coal, petroleum and uranium). Land vested in a Land Council cannot be compulsorily acquired except through a special Act of Parliament. Since November 1994 the transfer of land is subject to any native title rights and interests that exist in the land.

Outside native title, New South Wales has the only claims process in Australia that still operates to return additional land to Aboriginal hands. Its efficacy has been limited by delay: there is a huge backlog of unprocessed claims (36,769 at June 2020). Nevertheless, land councils have won a steady stream of victories in litigation over what is claimable land. While land councils hold less than 1 per cent of land in New South Wales and a similar fraction of the national Indigenous estate,[18] many of the 6,000 parcels are in built-up areas with a high commercial value. That potential for economic empowerment differentiates this system from most others, where land holdings are overwhelmingly located in remote parts of Australia.

That commercial value is increased by the fact that land councils in New South Wales have broad powers to 'deal with land'.[19] A LALC, however, cannot (for example) sell land without an approval from the NSWALC. There are also procedural safeguards in the Act (notification, supermajority requirements at a meeting of members etc.) aimed at preserving the purposes and integrity of the land rights system.

18 Productivity Commission, *Overcoming Indigenous Disadvantage: Key Indicators 2020* (Canberra: Australian Government, 2020), Table 9A.2.1.

19 The phrase 'deal with land' is defined broadly: Aboriginal Land Rights Act 1983 (NSW), s 40(1).

Aboriginal Land Act 1991 (Qld)

The reserve system in Queensland survived largely unchanged into the 1980s, with about 20 per cent of the Aboriginal and Torres Strait Islander population living in these discrete regional and remote communities without secure communal tenure.[20] The trustees of the reserves were church or public officials, and unilateral government action could dramatically reduce reserve boundaries.[21]

Rising pressure for recognition of Aboriginal land rights met a generally hostile response from the state government led by Premier Joh Bjelke-Petersen (1968–87).[22] When the Commonwealth offered greater self-management to residents of Queensland reserves in 1978,[23] Bjelke-Petersen responded by de-gazetting Aurukun and Mornington Island reserves and re-constituting them as shires under local government legislation. As part of Bjelke-Petersen's manoeuvre, the shire councils, with councillors elected from the local Aboriginal population, were granted fifty-year renewable leases over the previous reserves. The council had some ability to negotiate access by miners, and there were some Aboriginal rights to subsistence hunting and use of forest products and quarry material, but strong ministerial control was retained over the sale or lease of land.[24]

The state responded to renewed pressure to legislate land rights in the 1980s with the creation of deeds of grant in trust (DOGIT), which conferred freehold title for a public purpose over other former reserves. To distance the scheme from an Aboriginal land rights agenda, these tenure changes were included in the mainstream Land Act. In substance, DOGITs skirted the question of traditional ownership by enabling a form of freehold over former reserves to be vested in Aboriginal Councils, elected by residents – an echo of the 'local government' approach to land rights taken in 1978.[25] The consultation process on these tenure changes was described as 'virtually non-existent'.[26]

20 Australian Bureau of Statistics, *Census 86 – Aboriginal and Torres Strait Islander People in Queensland* (Canberra: ABS, 1989), 7.
21 F. Brennan, *Land Rights Queensland Style: The Struggle for Aboriginal Self-Management* (St Lucia: University of Queensland Press, 1982), 86–8.
22 Queensland, *Parliamentary Debates*, Legislative Assembly, 1 April 1982, 5467–76.
23 Aboriginal and Torres Strait Islanders (Queensland Reserves and Communities Self-Management) Act 1978 (Cth).
24 Local Government (Aboriginal Lands) Act 1978 (Qld), particularly s 6 and Schedule.
25 Community Services (Aborigines) Act 1984 (Qld). Parallel provisions were made for former Torres Strait Islander reserves under the Community Services (Torres Strait) Act 1984 (Qld).
26 N. Pearson, 'The Deed of Grant in Trust and Hope Vale Aboriginal Community, North Queensland' *Aboriginal Law Bulletin* 2, no. 38 (1989): 12.

These 1980s' reforms surrendered some government control over land. A DOGIT could be revoked only by an Act of Parliament.[27] The grant also included the existing Aboriginal housing stock.[28] The government, however, retained ownership of minerals, timber and like resources, and the right to take back some land for public purposes. Councils later gained a land holder's right to object to mining, and Aboriginal residents had some legal entitlement to take natural resources. Councils could grant leases on DOGIT land, but it was not common under provisions which were 'complicated and restrictive'.[29]

In February 1991, Labor premier, Wayne Goss (1989–96), activated an election promise to implement Aboriginal land rights,[30] though this move was also compromised by rushed consultation and secret negotiations with vested interests. Passage of the Aboriginal Land Act 1991 (Qld) four months later sparked disenchantment and protest from Aboriginal campaigners.[31] This was a limited scheme largely superimposed on the existing DOGIT and reserve system, with some potential to expand the existing 'Indigenous estate' so that, for example, National Parks and unallocated land became 'Aboriginal land'. The Act essentially reproduced the rules from DOGITs about taking natural resources and responding to mining activity.

Land could either be the subject of a claim by Aboriginal groups to a Land Tribunal on the basis of 'traditional affiliation' or 'historical association', or it could be administratively transferred. But there were a variety of legal and practical constraints. A proposal for a land acquisition account based on the New South Wales capital fund model was rejected. There was no statutory recognition of land councils and no obvious way to finance land claims. A sunset clause meant that all claims had to be lodged within fifteen years.[32] The Act limited 'claimable land' to Crown land outside of a city or town in which no third-party had an interest. Importantly, the executive government retained control over the claims process at both ends. An individual area that met these statutory criteria remained beyond reach unless a minister also

27 Land Act 1962 (Qld), ss 342 and 352A. Note, however, Queensland has a unicameral Parliament, typically under government control.

28 Brennan, *Land Rights Queensland Style*, 88.

29 L. Terrill, 'Converting Aboriginal and Torres Strait Islander Land in Queensland into Ordinary Freehold' *Sydney Law Review* 37 (2015): 525.

30 Queensland, *Parliamentary Debates*, Legislative Assembly, 20 February 1991, 6208.

31 B. Miller, 'Clayton's Land Rights: The Queensland Aboriginal Land Act – An Aboriginal Coordinating Council Perspective' *Aboriginal Law Bulletin* 2, no. 52 (1991): 9; Brennan, *Land Rights Queensland Style*, 124–55, 169. Parallel legislation for the Torres Strait passed the following day.

32 Aboriginal Land Act 1991 (Qld), s 4.05. The deadline was fixed at 21 December 2006.

declared it to be 'claimable' in the Government Gazette, and no claim was granted until the minister accepted a Land Tribunal recommendation.

Of the sixty claims made to the Land Tribunal before the deadline in 2006, half related to National Parks and most of the rest to parcels of unallocated state land. Claims were highly concentrated in Cape York Peninsula. Just over 50 per cent of claims resulted in a positive recommendation that Aboriginal freehold title be granted, which the minister adopted in all but two cases.[33]

The system was significantly improved by the Cape York Peninsula Heritage Act 2007 (Qld). Previously, many handbacks of National Parks had been long delayed because joint management arrangements were unacceptable to the Aboriginal groups involved.[34] Under the new regional tenure resolution strategy, traditional owners could become freehold owners of National Parks in Cape York without a leaseback to the Crown in perpetuity, provided they agreed to the area being jointly managed as a National Park. By late 2021, there were thirty-two of these Aboriginal-owned parks in the Cape, covering more than 2 million hectares.[35] With its transfer mechanism, the 1991 Act allows land to be added to the Indigenous estate by agreement and executive action, bypassing the claims process. As a result, negotiations under the tenure resolution strategy in Cape York also delivered 1.5 million hectares of 'unfettered Aboriginal freehold' outside National Parks by 2018.[36] Importantly, this transfer option under the Act is not time-limited by the sunset clause. Obtaining Aboriginal freehold by agreement with the government is an attractive option for many native title claimants; so, the transfer mechanism under this land rights legislation has also assisted in the negotiated resolution of several native title claims in Queensland.[37]

With such strong executive control at both ends, the land claims process has made an extremely small dent on dispossession in Queensland. On the other hand, the ability to declare areas as transferable land and then hand

33 Aboriginal Land Tribunal, *Report on the Operations of the Land Tribunal Established under the Aboriginal Land Act 1991 for the Year Ended 30 June 2016* (2016), 3–9 and Annexure A. See also the like report for the year ended 30 June 2018 and *Queensland Government Gazettes* 2016–2020 and *Dempsey v Queensland* (2014) 317 ALR 432, 495.

34 Queensland Parks and Wildlife Service, *Indigenous Partnerships in Management of Protected Areas* (2011), 3.

35 Nature Conservation (Protected Areas) Regulation 1994, schedule 4.

36 Evidence to Economics and Governance Committee, Queensland Parliament, Brisbane, 24 July 2018, 86 (Ms Trad).

37 Queensland Department of Natural Resources, *Mines and Energy, Tenure Based Options for Unallocated State Land in Native Title Claims and Indigenous Land Use Agreements* (2020).

them back as freehold title to traditional owners has proved useful in addressing demands for land justice in negotiated settlements, both inside and outside the native title system. Benefits have skewed very much towards Cape York Peninsula, where it has contributed to a significant long-term reconstruction of the tenure map. Queensland is a very large state and outside its Far North, the system of statutory land rights has delivered a tiny fraction of the land once owned by Aboriginal people.[38]

Native Title

Introduction

The enactment of some land rights legislation, after the mid-1970s, did not prevent people pressing for the recognition of traditional laws and customs relating to land through the courts, culminating in the landmark High Court decision in *Mabo v Queensland (No. 2)* ('*Mabo (No. 2)*').[39] The extent to which this common law recognition of native title has provided land justice for Indigenous people remains an open question. Many groups are still pursuing court determinations recognising their legal rights. Others, having achieved formal legal recognition, are navigating the challenges of managing their communal interests and dealing with third parties who want access to their country. Because of strict legal rules about continuity and extinguishment, there are many for whom the system offers nothing, or only disappointment and defeat. In addition, by the 2020s the courts had only begun to clarify the compensation regime for the loss of native title as a result of past extinguishment, including what amounts to 'just terms' for dispossession.

Here we focus on two institutional factors that have proved highly influential for the question of land justice. First, the shifting judicial interpretation of native title law in the courts; and second, the posture taken by governments as respondents to native title claims, and as architects of the policy and legislative frameworks in which native title rights are pursued. Throughout, a third decisive factor has also been in play, that is, the way that Aboriginal and Torres Strait Islander people and their organisations have responded and adapted to legal constructions of native title.

38 Entities holding Aboriginal and Torres Strait Islander land under the Aboriginal Land Act 1991 and the Torres Strait Islander Land Act 1991 (map) www.qld.gov.au/firstnations/environment-land-use-native-title/land-trusts, accessed 17 December 2021.

39 (1992) 175 CLR 1.

The Legal Foundations of Native Title

In 1982 plaintiffs from Mer (Murray Island) in the Torres Strait commenced a claim in the High Court for recognition of their traditional rights over land. The High Court judgment on the key legal issues in *Mabo (No. 2)* included the following findings, which also applied to the Australian mainland:

(1) The validity of the Crown's assertion of sovereignty over the Murray Islands in 1879 is not justiciable in Australian courts.
(2) The original inhabitants' rights and interests in land and waters survived the acquisition of sovereignty and are recognised and protected by the common law as native title rights and interests.
(3) As sovereign, the Crown has legal power to extinguish native title by legislation or the creation of inconsistent interests. Once extinguished the rights cannot be revived.
(4) Native title rights and interests vary depending on the nature of the traditional laws and customs, and may include usufructuary rights, such as rights to hunt, fish and gather, or more comprehensive rights of ownership which are often expressed as a right to possession, occupation, use and enjoyment as against the whole world.
(5) Native title rights and interests will no longer exist where the original inhabitants have ceased to acknowledge and observe those laws and customs.

In 1985, to pre-empt the Mabo litigation, the Queensland government had attempted to retroactively extinguish any traditional rights and interests that may have existed in Torres Strait.[40] In *Mabo v Queensland* ('*Mabo (No. 1)*')[41] a High Court majority held that the state legislation breached Section 10(1) of the federal Racial Discrimination Act 1975 (Cth) (RDA) because it extinguished the claimed property rights in a racially discriminatory manner.

This finding also assumed great significance in the wake of the High Court decision in *Mabo (No. 2)*, as the Commonwealth weighed a legislative response. The protection afforded to native title by the RDA cast doubt over the validity of official acts affecting native title after 1975. This included mining leases underpinning huge resource projects, as well as thousands of land grants made by governments to mainly non-Indigenous Australians. Miners and the states pressed for the retrospective validation of their interests by the Commonwealth. The salience of mining interests in this area of law was also demonstrated by the enactment, in the resource-rich state of

40 Queensland Coast Islands Declaratory Act 1985 (Qld). 41 (1989) 166 CLR 186.

Western Australia, of the Land (Titles and Traditional Usage) Act 1993 (WA), which sought to abolish all native title, without compensation, and replace it with weaker statutory rights of traditional usage.

Shortly after, the Commonwealth enacted the Native Title Act 1993 (Cth) (NTA). The key features of the NTA were as follows:

(1) It validated 'past acts' which may have been invalid due to the RDA.
(2) It recognised native title, protected it against inconsistent state legislation, and confirmed rights to compensation when native title is affected by the validation of other interests or by acts done after 1993.
(3) It created a right to negotiate in relation to mining activities and compulsory acquisitions, to allow affected people the opportunity to secure community benefits and protections for their land.
(4) It created a system for making and resolving native title claims. A National Native Title Tribunal (NNTT) was established to process and mediate claims, with matters being referred to the Federal Court if they could not be resolved.
(5) Native title representative bodies could assist groups to make native title claims and, if they were successful, a body corporate was required to be established to hold the native title on trust, or act as agent for the native title holders.

The Act was to be complemented by two other federal government initiatives: a fund to support market purchases of land and a 'social justice package'. The fund (now the Indigenous Land and Sea Future Fund) was established in 1995 along with a body to administer it (now the Indigenous Land and Sea Corporation). The social justice package never eventuated.

The Western Australian government challenged the constitutional validity of the NTA and Aboriginal groups from the Kimberley and Western Desert cross-challenged the Land (Titles and Traditional Usage) Act 1993 (WA) on the basis that it was inconsistent with the NTA and the RDA. In 1995, the High Court upheld the federal NTA and found the state Act invalid.[42] Following the enactment of the NTA, each state (including eventually Western Australia) passed complementary legislation to give effect to the federal scheme and to validate interests in their state.

While *Mabo (No. 2)* confirmed that the Australian common law could recognise native title, it left uncertain what acts would be effective to extinguish it. In *Wik Peoples v Queensland* (*Wik*) the High Court held that

42 *Western Australia v Commonwealth* (1995) 183 CLR 373.

pastoral leases in Cape York were interests created by statute rather than common law 'leases', and not wholly inconsistent with all native title rights and interests.[43] This meant that native title could legally co-exist with a pastoral lease, and potentially other non-exclusive interests granted by the Crown. However, in any conflict between native title and a Crown grant, the latter prevails.[44] This priority for the Crown has sweeping application, well beyond pastoral leases, to any official action since 1788 regarded as legally valid.

Despite the outcome in *Wik* being an obvious possibility beforehand,[45] states had recklessly granted interests as if it were certain native title was totally extinguished by pastoral leases. Following *Wik*, pressure was again brought on the Commonwealth to validate interests, this time those granted with disregard for the NTA. Mining and other industry sectors pushed to curb other effects from *Wik* and improve their legal position under the NTA. Some in the pastoral industry went as far as calling for the wholesale extinguishment of native title on all pastoral leases. The Keating Labor government, which sponsored the original NTA, had lost power at the March 1996 election, and these commercial interests found a more receptive ear in the new Liberal Prime Minister John Howard, who said that 'the *Wik* decision pushed the pendulum too far in the Aboriginal direction'.[46] His Deputy Tim Fischer, from the rural-based National Party, infamously promised 'bucketfulls of extinguishment'.[47]

The Howard government baulked at wholesale extinguishment, at least in part because of the huge compensation costs associated with Section 51(xxxi) of the Constitution, which guaranteed 'just terms' for the acquisition of property. But it developed a '10 Point Plan' to amend the NTA. After a protracted public and parliamentary battle, most of the plan was implemented through the Native Title Amendment Act 1998 (Cth). The Act confirmed extinguishment by a broad range of historical interests, pre-empting the testing of such issues in the courts, and retroactively validated the latest round of unlawful state grants. The rules governing development on native title land were rewritten to allow developers to pursue a wider range of activities without having to engage with Indigenous groups under the 'right to negotiate'. Addressing concerns that some of the NNTT's functions were an unlawful exercise of judicial power,[48] the Act now required

43 (1996) 187 CLR 1. See Tehan, Chapter 14 in this volume. 44 (1996) 187 CLR 1, 133.
45 *North Ganalanja Aboriginal Corporation v Queensland* (1996) 135 ALR 225.
46 John Howard, 'Amended Wik 10 Point Plan', *Media Release*, 8 May 1997.
47 ABC Radio, Interview with Tim Fischer, *PM*, 16 May 1997.
48 *Brandy v Human Rights and Equal Opportunity Commission* (1995) 183 CLR 24.

native title claims to be commenced in the Federal Court at the outset. More stringent requirements applied to the making of claims, in order to reduce unrepresentative or overlapping applications. The Act also gave greater support to negotiated outcomes by providing for Indigenous Land Use Agreements; and, in one concession to native title holders, it became possible for courts to disregard extinguishment in certain circumstances.[49]

Two Key Influences on Subsequent Developments

Judicial Development of Native Title Case Law

It might have been expected that the highly prescriptive Howard amendments to the NTA would minimise the role of judges in the development of native title law. In truth, however, the NTA refrained from answering some core questions prompted by *Mabo (No. 2)*, including whether a range of tenures and other official actions extinguish native title, what legal content to give 'native title' as a property right, what is it that groups need to prove to satisfy a court that they are native title holders for particular territory, and what constitutes 'just terms' compensation for native title extinguishment.

Since 1992, judicial decisions on issues of extinguishment, title, proof and compensation have placed major limits on land justice for Indigenous people while, nevertheless, opening some opportunities.

Extinguishment

The *Wik* majority did not decide what would happen after a pastoral lease expired. Would native title revive (on the basis it had been merely 'regulated' in the meantime), or had the grant of the pastoral lease permanently destroyed some part of it? It was a very significant question given that perhaps half of the Australian continent was at some point subject to a pastoral lease.

In 2002, in *Western Australia v Ward* ('*Ward*'),[50] the High Court decided that the effect of pastoral leases was permanent 'partial extinguishment' of the native title rights and interests to the extent of any inconsistency between the native title rights and the rights that had been conferred by the lease.

The High Court moderated the severity of extinguishment law in subsequent cases. In *Western Australia v Brown*, for example, the Court emphasised that extinguishment occurs only where conferral of rights by a grant or other official act '*necessarily* implies the non-existence' of the native title rights.[51] Further, the *exercise* of native title rights can be significantly limited without

49 Native Title Act 1993 (Cth) (NTA), ss 47A and 47B.
50 (2002) 213 CLR 1.
51 *Western Australia v Brown* (2014) 253 CLR 507, 523 (emphasis added).

extinguishing the rights themselves.[52] For several judges, this perspective was reinforced by a principle of statutory interpretation through which the English common law had, for centuries, protected property rights against abrogation: the requirement for a *clear and plain intention* to extinguish attributable to the Crown or Parliament.[53]

Although, by 2015, the High Court appeared better disposed to the less destructive idea of 'regulation', partial extinguishment by pastoral leases was already baked into Australian native title law. *Ward*'s legacy was a diminished property right across vast areas that might otherwise have been *exclusive* native title zones.

Title

The *Ward* decision was also significant in characterising native title as a property right and fleshing out its legal content.[54] There, the High Court showed its preference for a piecemeal 'bundle of rights' view rather than a more holistic 'title' or ownership conception. This spawned native title determinations around Australia that listed specific rights, in general by reference to activities carried out on the land.[55] Native title is frequently described as the non-exclusive right to hunt and fish on the land and water, to camp, to conduct ceremonies and so on.

A shift away from such 'definitional over-specificity',[56] towards a more generalised and holistic notion of connection with Country came in the *Akiba* case in 2010.[57] This was a claim by the united communities of the Torres Strait for recognition of their native title rights over Sea Country, including their right to take marine resources for commercial purposes. On appeal, the High Court downplayed the need for 'sectioning of the native title right into lesser rights or "incidents" defined by the various purposes for which it might be exercised'.[58] Instead, a native title right or interest 'defines a relationship between the native title holders and the land or waters to which the right or interest relates. The right is one thing; the exercise of it for a particular purpose is another.'[59]

52 *Akiba v Commonwealth* (2013) 250 CLR 209, 229.
53 *Queensland v Congoo* (2015) 256 CLR 239, 264, 301.
54 It is characteristic of Australian native title law that extinguishment doctrine has played a central role in defining what native title is: Lisa Strelein, 'Conceptualising Native Title' *Sydney Law Review* 23 (2001): 95, 108.
55 *Western Australia v Ward* (2002) 213 CLR 1, 83, 95.
56 S. Young, *The Trouble with Tradition: Native Title and Cultural Change* (Sydney: Federation Press, 2008), 291.
57 *Akiba v Commonwealth (No. 3)* (2010) 204 FCR 1.
58 *Akiba v Commonwealth* (2013) 250 CLR 209, 224.
59 Ibid, 225.

A by-product of this approach has been an increasing willingness to recognise that native title rights can have a commercial character because a right to *trade* resources can be encompassed within a broader and more generally expressed right to take resources and use them.[60]

Proof

According to *Mabo (No. 2)*, to prove native title, claimants must show they have substantially maintained their connection to country by the observance of traditional law and custom.[61]

In 2002, in the *Yorta Yorta* case, the High Court fixed the word 'traditional' with layers of additional meaning, raising the evidentiary threshold that *Mabo (No. 2)* had appeared to set.[62] Specifically, groups seeking native title recognition had to show *continuity* since the Crown asserted sovereignty and in three different dimensions: in the 'society' from which a group derives its laws and customs, in the observance of laws and customs themselves, and in the rights and interests over land and waters to which those laws give rise.

As a result, a government respondent has a good chance of defeating a native title claim if it can show that the myriad impacts of two centuries of colonisation – including frontier warfare and the paternalistic, often oppressive policies of the 'Protection' and 'Assimilation' eras – have significantly interrupted any one of the three dimensions of 'tradition' (society, laws or rights).

Risk v Northern Territory (2006) illustrates the difficulties created. The Larrakia have been repeatedly recognised by Northern Territory and Commonwealth governments, outside the court room, as the traditional owners for the area around what is now known as Darwin. The Federal Court judge hearing their claim for recognition in 2005 called them 'a strong, vibrant and dynamic society'.[63] Yet the Larrakia failed in their legal quest for native title recognition because the multiple pressures on their society (not of their own making) caused the observance of traditional law to break down for a few decades in the mid-twentieth century. Groups seeking native title recognition continue to fail due to the application of *Yorta Yorta* continuity requirements.[64]

60 S. Brennan, 'The Significance of the Akiba Torres Strait Regional Sea Claim Case', in S. Brennan et al. (eds), *From Mabo to Akiba*, 37. See, for example, *Western Australia v Willis* (2015) 239 FCR 175 and *Rrumburriya Borroloola Clam Group v Northern Territory* (2016) 255 FCR 228.

61 *Mabo v Queensland (No. 2)* (1992) 175 CLR 1, 59–60, 70. See also NTA, s 223.

62 *Members of the Yorta Yorta Aboriginal Community v Victoria* (2002) 214 CLR 422.

63 *Risk v Northern Territory* [2006] FCA 404.

64 See for example *Bodney v Bennell* (2008) 167 FCR 84; *Starkey v South Australia* (2018) 261 FCR 183. The moderation of judicial attitudes in other areas of the law raises questions for the rather literal approach to continuity taken in *Yorta Yorta*: see S. Young, 'The

Compensation

By narrow majority in *Mabo (No. 2)*, the High Court said extinguishment was not compensable at common law.[65] The NTA then introduced a scheme for recovery of 'just terms' for future acts that adversely affect native title and for a limited category of past extinguishing acts.[66] But the substantial barriers to recovery (including very high litigation costs) deterred most groups. When eventually tested by a case from Timber Creek, a remote Northern Territory township, the High Court confirmed in 2019 that the freehold price for land would be the proxy measure for *economic* loss of exclusive possession native title, with substantial reductions where the extinguished rights were non-exclusive.[67] Over strenuous Commonwealth and territory objections, the Court upheld the trial finding of $1.3 million for *non-economic*, or cultural, loss over a one square kilometre area – a warning sign that all governments would need to take seriously their liabilities for past dispossession.

The Posture Adopted by Governments

As respondents to native title claims, as policy-setters, and as authors of the legislative framework within which the history of native title has unfolded so far, the legislative and executive branches of government at Commonwealth, state and territory levels have powerfully influenced the potential for native title law to provide greater land justice.

Respondents

In Australia's Federation, the sub-national governments are primarily responsible for land management and are necessarily the primary respondents to native title claims.[68] The Commonwealth is most likely to get involved in areas where it has a direct jurisdictional interest, such as the offshore zone.

Where native title has been recognised, it has been mostly through a consent determination, where the state or territory informs the Federal Court it agrees to recognise native title on the basis it has negotiated with the claimants. But that fact can disguise the power relations at work in a system where governments are repeat players in court, with deep pockets and little to lose from the status quo (that being the non-recognition of native title). Though the NTA system provides processes of mediation and the Federal

Increments of Justice: Exploring the Outer Reach of *Akiba*'s Edge Towards Native Title "Ownership"' *UNSW Law Journal* 42 (2019): 825.

65 *Mabo v Queensland (No. 2)* (1992) 175 CLR 1, 15–16. 66 NTA, s 51.

67 *Griffiths v Northern Territory* [2019] HCA 7, [3]. 68 NTA, s 84(4).

Figure 9.1: (COLOUR CENTREPIECE) Atnengkerre Atherre Akwete – Two Laws Together. Artwork Wenten Rubuntja and Chips Mackinolty. Reproduced with permission of Chips Mackinolty and the Aboriginal Artists Agency Ltd.

Figure 13.1: (COLOUR CENTREPIECE) Augustus Earle (~1826), A native family of New South Wales sitting down on an English settlers farm. National Library of Australia, nla.obj-134500174. Grace Karskens points out that this family is solid, while the station and settlers fade into the background.

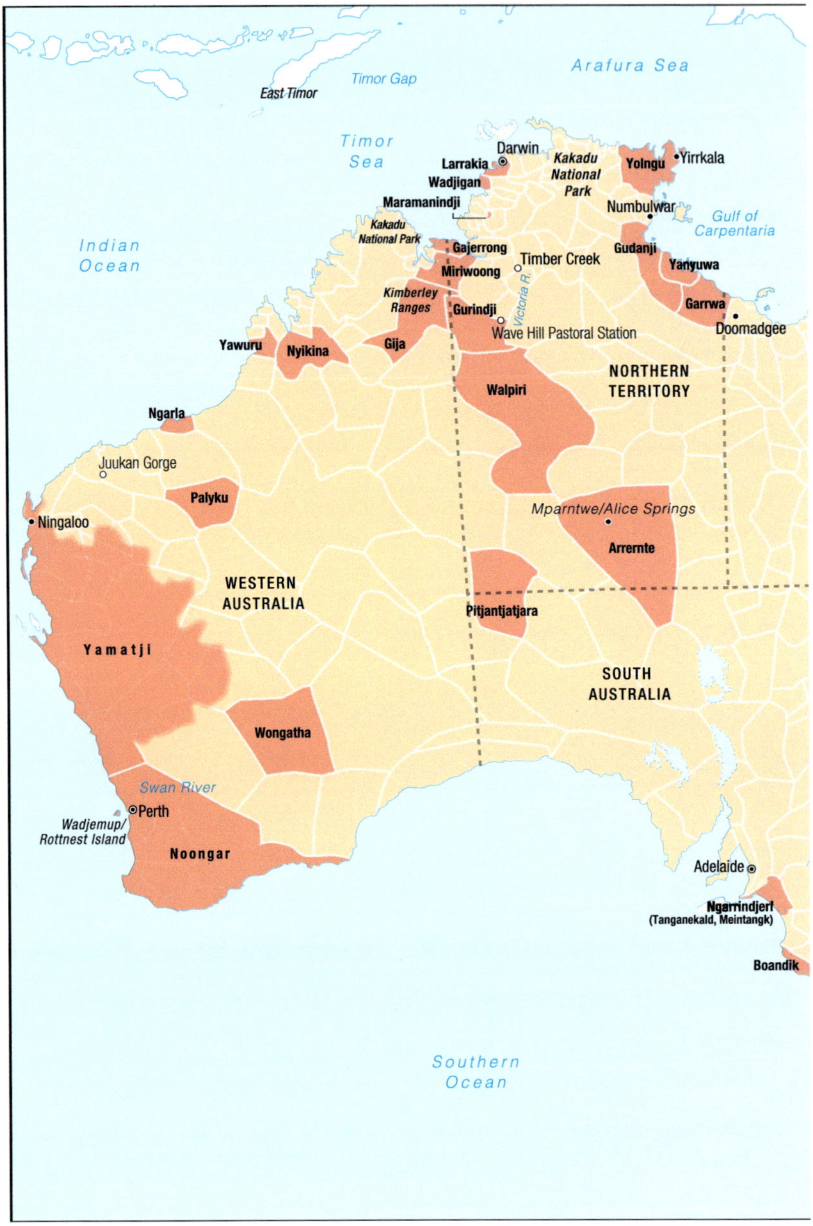

Map 0.1: Australia – Place and Peoples Mentioned

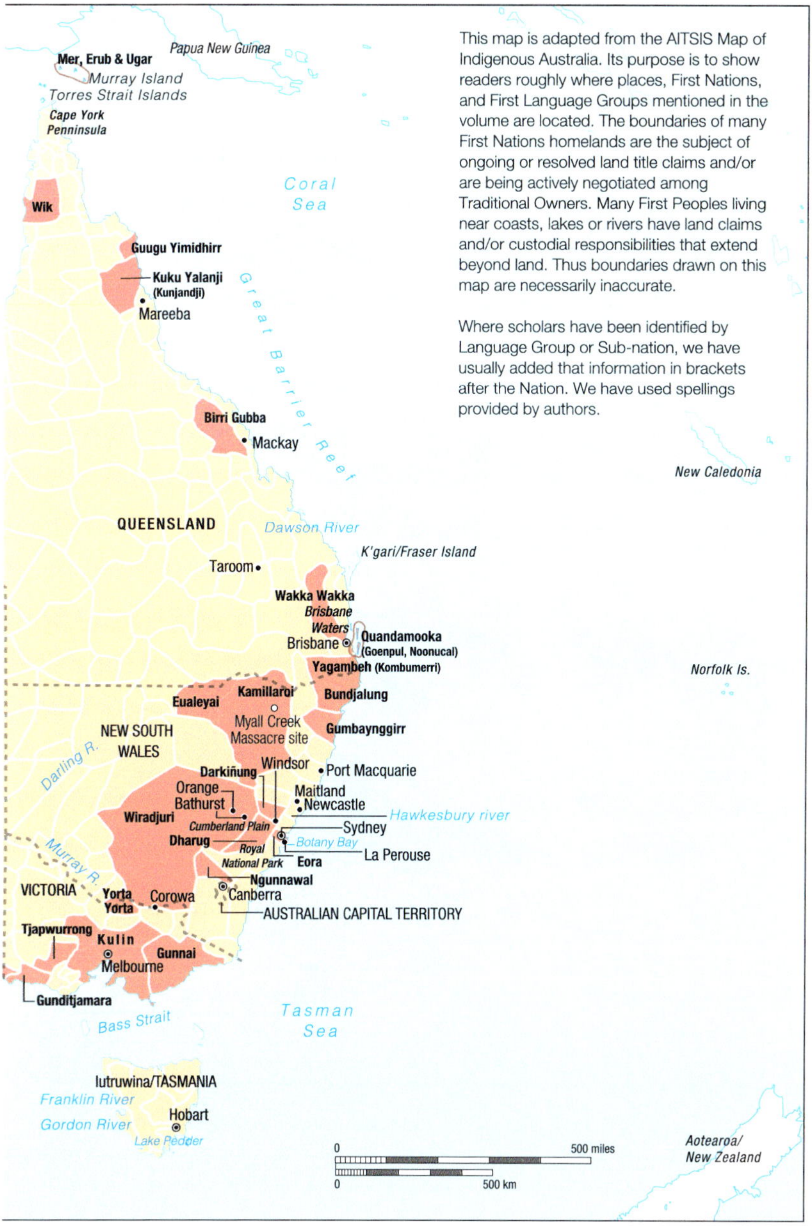
This map is adapted from the AITSIS Map of Indigenous Australia. Its purpose is to show readers roughly where places, First Nations, and First Language Groups mentioned in the volume are located. The boundaries of many First Nations homelands are the subject of ongoing or resolved land title claims and/or are being actively negotiated among Traditional Owners. Many First Peoples living near coasts, lakes or rivers have land claims and/or custodial responsibilities that extend beyond land. Thus boundaries drawn on this map are necessarily inaccurate.
Where scholars have been identified by Language Group or Sub-nation, we have usually added that information in brackets after the Nation. We have used spellings provided by authors.
Papua New Guinea
Mer, Erub & Ugar
Murray Island
Torres Strait Islands
Cape York Penninsula
Coral Sea
Wik
Guugu Yimidhirr
Kuku Yalanji (Kunjandji)
Mareeba
Great Barrier Reef
Birri Gubba
Mackay
New Caledonia
QUEENSLAND
Dawson River
K'gari/Fraser Island
Taroom
Wakka Wakka
Brisbane Waters
Brisbane
Quandamooka (Goenpul, Noonucal)
Yagambeh (Kombumerri)
Norfolk Is.
Kamillaroi
Eualeyai
Bundjalung
Myall Creek Massacre site
Gumbaynggirr
NEW SOUTH WALES
Darling R.
Darkiñung
Windsor
Port Macquarie
Orange
Bathurst
Maitland
Newcastle
Hawkesbury river
Wiradjuri
Cumberland Plain
Sydney
Dharug
Botany Bay
Royal National Park
Eora
La Perouse
Murray R.
Ngunnawal
VICTORIA
Yorta Yorta
Corowa
Canberra
AUSTRALIAN CAPITAL TERRITORY
Tjapwurrong
Kulin
Gunnai
Melbourne
Gunditjamara
Bass Strait
Tasman Sea
lutruwina/TASMANIA
Franklin River
Gordon River
Hobart
Lake Pedder
0
500 miles
0
500 km
Aotearoa/ New Zealand

Map 0.1: (cont.)

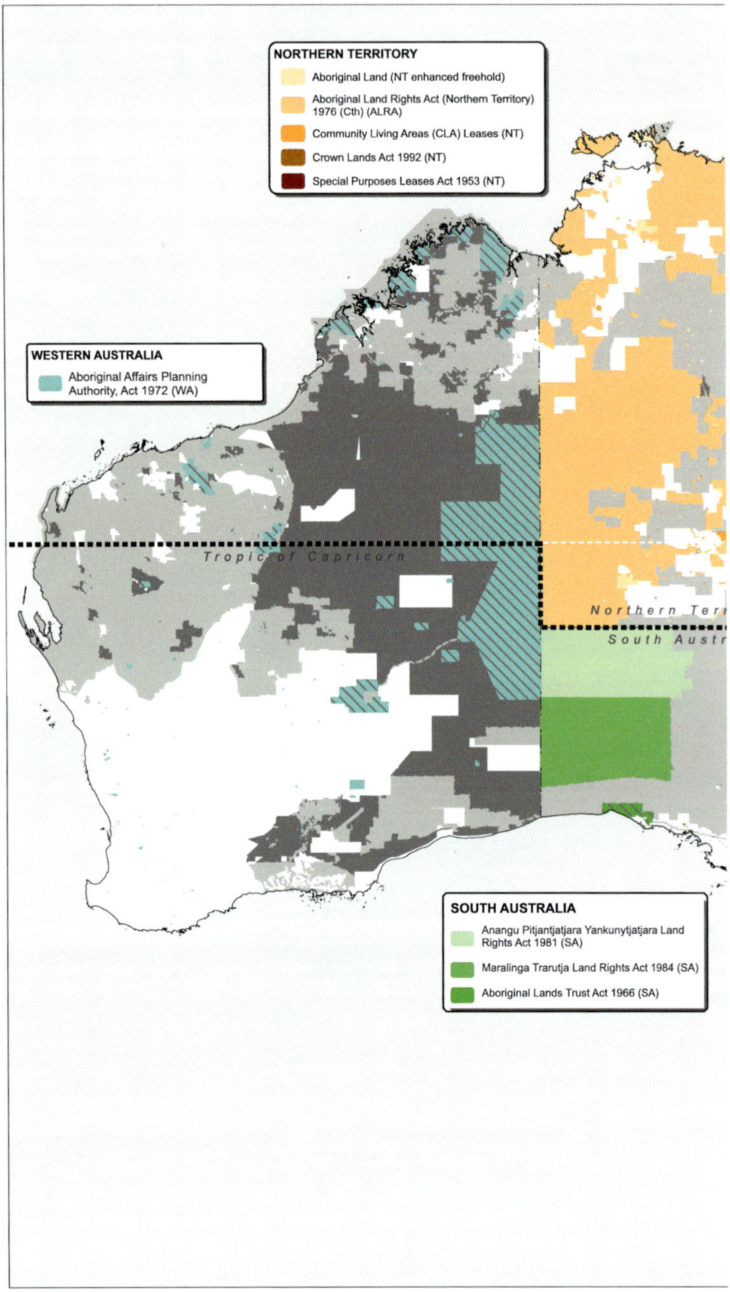

Map 1.1: Indigenous Estates as at 1 January 2021

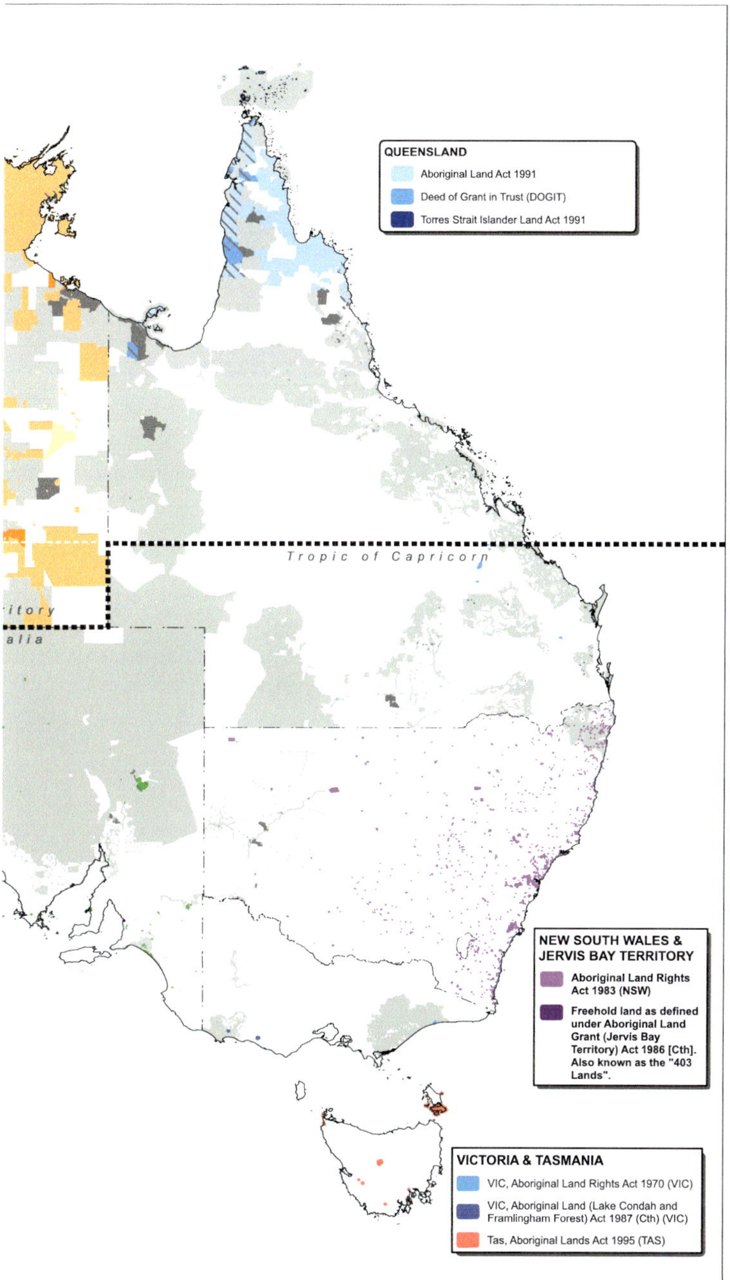
QUEENSLAND
Aboriginal Land Act 1991
Deed of Grant in Trust (DOGIT)
Torres Strait Islander Land Act 1991
Tropic of Capricorn
itory
alia
NEW SOUTH WALES & JERVIS BAY TERRITORY
Aboriginal Land Rights Act 1983 (NSW)
Freehold land as defined under Aboriginal Land Grant (Jervis Bay Territory) Act 1986 [Cth]. Also known as the "403 Lands".
VICTORIA & TASMANIA
VIC, Aboriginal Land Rights Act 1970 (VIC)
VIC, Aboriginal Land (Lake Condah and Framlingham Forest) Act 1987 (Cth) (VIC)
Tas, Aboriginal Lands Act 1995 (TAS)

Map 1.1: (cont.)

National
Native Title
Tribunal

Indigenous Estates

Land granted under specified indigenous land granted instruments

As at 1 January 2021

Indigenous estates only represents those indigenous land areas granted under the following jurisdictional land grant instruments:
Aboriginal Land (NT enhanced freehold), Aboriginal Land Rights Act (NT) 1976 (Cth) (ALRA), Community Living Areas (CLA) Leases under the Associations Act 2012 (NT), Crown Lands Act 1992 (NT), Special Purposes Leases Act 1953 (NT), Aboriginal Land Act 1991 (Qld), Torres Strait Islander Land Act 1991(Qld), Aboriginal and Torres Strait Islander Land Holding Act 2013 (Qld), Corporations (Aboriginal and Torres Strait Islander) Act 2006 (Cth), Aboriginal Affairs Planning Authority Act 1972 (WA), Aboriginal Lands Trust Act 1966 (SA), Anangu Pitjantjatjara Yankunytjatjara Land Rights Act 1981 (SA), Maralinga Tjarutja Land Rights Act 1984 (SA), Aboriginal Land Rights Act 1983 (NSW), Aboriginal Lands Act 1970 (Vic), Aboriginal Land (Lake Condah and Framlingham Forest) Act 1987(Cth) (Vic), Aboriginal Lands Act 1995 (Tas) and Aboriginal Land Grant (Jervis Bay Territory) Act 1986.

Spatial data sourced from and used with permission of:
Dept of Aboriginal Affairs (WA), Landgate (WA), Dept of Resources (QLD) © The State of Queensland, Dept of Customer Service (NSW), Dept of Infrastructure, Planning & Logistics (NT), Dept of Planning, Transport & Infrastructure (SA), Dept of Infrastructure, Planning & Logistics (NT), Dept of Environment, Land, Water & Planning (VIC), and Geoscience Australia, Australian Government. Reference to ACT also includes Jervis Bay Territory. © Commonwealth of Australia.

Determinations where native title exists

Determined Outcome

Native title exists (exclusive)

Native title exists (non-exclusive)

* Overlaps may exist between determined areas and granted indigenous estates

Prepared by:
Geospatial Services, National Native Title Tribunal 4/02/2021

Some or parts of some determinations may not yet be in effect or on the National Native Title Register (NNTR). The court may decide that the determination of native title will take effect conditional upon some future event occurring, for example, the registration of an Indigenous Land Use Agreement or the establishment and registration of a prescribed body corporate (PBC). In these cases the determination, or relevant part, will not be registered on the NNTR until the condition has been met.

Map 1.1: (cont.)

Court requires mediation in good faith,[69] governments showed little willingness to engage in the negotiated resolution of native title matters until the key test cases on extinguishment, title and proof of connection were resolved, substantially in their favour, by *Ward* and *Yorta Yorta*. Though later judicial approaches moderated the severity of native title law, governments were still prone to prolong settlement discussions and litigation. On countless occasions, Elders, whose evidence was central to a group's claim, have not survived to see their native title rights eventually recognised.

Even decades on from *Mabo (No. 2)*, problems persist. In recognising the native title rights of Western Bundjalung People in 2017, Justice Jagot of the Federal Court rebuked New South Wales for dragging its feet. Jagot J said that the state's failings were 'systemic' and necessitated a change of approach, particularly for 'claims which are *prima facie* cogent and thus call for a timely, fair and sensible resolution by agreement'. She challenged the traditional rationale for putting native title claims to the test on sundry legal and factual issues: that the state is a guardian for the community's interest. The claimants 'are also part of the community', she said, and it should not be assumed 'that the "interests of the community" are somehow in opposition to the recognition of native title rights and interests'.[70]

Policy-setters

Justice Jagot's comments draw attention to the wider policy context in which governments conduct native title litigation. Since the inception of the NTA, states and territories have faced two recurrent policy questions in calibrating the 'interests of the community'.

First, a state or territory must decide what evidence to require, in a 'connection report', from a native title group that seeks a consent determination. How close should it be to what a court would demand if every issue was put in contest? In his 2009 Native Title Report, the Social Justice Commissioner described evidentiary thresholds set by states and territories as 'onerous' and said that the 'unfettered ability of states and territories to impose and unilaterally alter these requirements creates an inequality of bargaining power'.[71]

69 See NTA, ss 86A–E and Federal Court Act 1977 (Cth), ss 37M and 37N. See also NTA, ss 94E(5) and 94P, and *Widjabul Wia-Bal v Attorney General of New South Wales* [2020] FCAFC 34, [34]–[36].

70 *Western Bundjalung People v Attorney General of New South Wales* [2017] FCA 992, [62]–[70].

71 Aboriginal and Torres Strait Islander Social Justice Commissioner, *Native Title Report 2009* (Sydney: Australian Human Rights Commission, 2009), 90. See also Justice North's comments in *Hunter v Western Australia* [2009] FCA 654, [22].

Nearly a decade on, a key research body reported that some states continued to apply an 'extraordinary burden of proof and high "trade-offs" to secure consent determinations'.[72]

Secondly, how should the state or territory respond to demands, from a native title claim group, for a broader settlement that transcends technical questions of native title recognition and addresses wider aspirations for empowerment and recognition? Nationally, governments have rebuffed or ignored good faith attempts by Indigenous people to call for a broader structural reform agenda, even when governments have invited such claims.[73]

At a local or regional level, in responding to native title claims, states have sometimes been prepared to give effect to broader policy commitments on reconciliation and empowerment. In the wet tropics rainforests, for example, Queensland eventually settled the Eastern Kuku Yalanji native title claim in 2007 by signing fifteen Indigenous Land Use Agreements. These, and the associated consent determination, recognised native title over a substantial area, granted inalienable and alienable freehold to Yalanji, and established joint management of conservation areas by the traditional owners and government, with potential employment opportunities.[74]

Agreements have made it possible to adapt to local post-contact history, as well as the varying aspirations and circumstances of the relevant Indigenous group. The Traditional Owner Settlement Act 2010 (Vic) (TOSA) departed from a strict native title approach. In a state where the stern test of continuity in *Yorta Yorta* and the prevalence of extinguishment make it difficult to achieve a native title determination in court, Victoria created an alternative process for agreeing to recognise Aboriginal groups as traditional owners. TOSA agreements potentially cover access to natural resources, economic development opportunities and the restoration of some ownership and management rights over land.

The most comprehensive agreement to emerge out of the native title system is the South West Native Title Settlement over Noongar country in Western Australia, that cleared its final legal hurdle in January 2021.[75] It

72 Australian Institute of Aboriginal and Torres Strait Islander Studies, *AIATSIS Submission – Reforms to the Native Title Act 1993 (Cth) Options Paper* (2018), 4.

73 See, for example, the reports on consultations for a Social Justice Package produced in the mid-1990s by the Aboriginal and Torres Strait Islander Commission and the Social Justice Commissioner, and in 2017 the Uluru Statement from the Heart on constitutional recognition and structural reform.

74 'Eastern Kuku Yalanji Agreements' *Australian Indigenous Law Review* 11 (2007): 112.

75 South West Aboriginal Land and Sea Council, *About the Settlement Agreement* www.noongar.org.au/about-settlement-agreement, accessed 17 December 2021.

displaced native title recognition in favour of a package focused on economic, social and cultural empowerment plus freehold ownership of, and leasehold over, land. The settlement, which was said to be worth $1.3 billion, related to 200,000 square kilometres and 30,000 Noongar, who were recognised as traditional owners by the state.

It is difficult to identify what has motivated these sporadic efforts by the states across two decades to take matters out of the hands of its litigators. In 2008–9 the Commonwealth government consciously adopted policies to encourage broader settlements across the Federation and sponsored amendments to the NTA to support such efforts. But there has been little sign of sustained Commonwealth leadership or a commitment by all governments to overcome the disconnect between general Indigenous affairs policies and their response to native title claims.

Legislators

The NTA, enacted during the Keating government and heavily amended in the Howard era, underwent little substantive change in the first two decades of the twenty-first century.

Reforms in 2009 gave the Federal Court greater control over management of native title claims, making it harder for states and territories to string out 'connection report' negotiations. But, overall, there has been little government enthusiasm for improving the prospects of land justice for First Nations groups through statutory amendment of the NTA.

This was not for want of suggestions. In 2008, the soon-to-be Chief Justice of the High Court, Robert French, put forward modest proposals to ease the difficulties of proving native title.[76] A Native Title Amendment (Reform) Bill 2011, introduced by cross-bench Senator Rachel Siewert, 'languishe[d] friendless' in the Parliament.[77] In 2015, the Australian Law Reform Commission recommended changes to the definition of native title that would better recognise the fact that traditional law evolves over time, particularly under conditions of colonisation, and mitigate the strict standard of continuity applied in *Yorta Yorta*.[78] None of those proposals made it into law.

76 Justice R. French, 'Lifting the Burden of Native Title: Some Modest Proposals for Improvement' *Federal Judicial Scholarship* (2008): 18.

77 P. Finn, 'Mabo into the Future: Native Title Jurisprudence' *Indigenous Law Bulletin* 8, no. 2 (2012): 6.

78 Australian Law Reform Commission, *Connection to Country: Review of the Native Title Act 1993 (Cth): Final Report* (Canberra: Commonwealth of Australia, 2015) 18–22.

Governments have left similarly undisturbed the rules set out in the NTA for third-party access to and development of native title land – the 'future act regime'. Its keystone, the 'right to negotiate' mechanism, was supposed to empower native title parties. Their bargaining power was premised on mining companies wishing to avoid the costs of delay and the risk of adverse arbitration findings, by seeking instead to negotiate an agreement about a proposed resource project.

However, these assumptions proved to be seriously flawed. The mining industry holds great power in Australia, especially in Western Australia, where it dominates the state economy and where the 'right to negotiate' matters most. It is perhaps unsurprising, then, that the NNTT has almost never ruled against the development of a mine when an application has proceeded beyond the negotiating period to arbitration. The Act also forbids the NNTT, as an arbitral body, from imposing a condition on a mining approval that would give native title holders a royalty or share of profits in the mine. The statutory 'delay' of six months for negotiation with native title parties is rarely a challenge for resource companies that typically face far longer timelines for environmental, financing and other approvals. In other words, the Act does too little to redress the power imbalance between miners and Aboriginal groups, who cannot legally say no to a mine. The national outcry over the destruction of sacred caves in Juukan Gorge in 2020 by the mining company Rio Tinto reflected not only the weakness of heritage protection laws but also the limited bargaining power of native title parties.[79]

Traditional owner groups in minerally prospective areas have concluded beneficial agreements that would have been inconceivable in Australia prior to *Mabo (No. 2)*.[80] But with no substantive amendments to the 'right to negotiate', the Act has not kept pace with expectations that traditional owners should obtain greater economic advantage from Indigenous property regimes.

Conclusion

The Achievement of Land Justice?

In assessing the contribution of statutory land rights and native title to land justice for First Nations people, the raw statistics tell part of the story. In 1966

79 W. Bergmann and C. O'Faircheallaigh, 'Time for Law Reform in Light of Rio Tinto's Choice to Destroy Juukan Gorge', 16 June 2020 https://nit.com.au/time-for-law-reform-in-light-of-rio-tintos-choice-to-destroy-juukan-gorge, accessed 17 December 2021.

80 See for example, the Argyle Diamonds Indigenous Land Use Agreement of 2005 www.atns.net.au/agreement?EntityID=2591, accessed 17 December 2021.

'no person owned land in Australia by virtue of being Aboriginal'.[81] In 2020 about 15 per cent of the Australian landmass was Indigenous owned or controlled under various statutory schemes, and native title was recognised over approximately 38 per cent – with some overlap, due to both legal regimes applying in some areas.[82]

Recovering Land

Achieving native title recognition has generally proved expensive, time-consuming and arduous for the groups involved. The internal challenges of unifying and organising to sustain a successful claim can be a factor but judicial choices in key test cases, as well as government behaviour, have also impeded progress. The comparative experience with statutory land rights has depended partly on the legal process adopted in each jurisdiction. Direct negotiations can deliver vast areas by legislative transfer, as in South Australia decades ago.[83] Claims processes have restored a lot of land, but governments have often fought to stymie claims, sometimes under legislation they took credit for introducing. Even when the law says that a transfer should happen automatically in relation to areas that are 'claimable land', there are no guarantees against bureaucratic and political delay, as the backlog in New South Wales demonstrates.

Adding New Land

With no sunset clause, only the ALRA (NSW) and the national native title system offer claims processes that might yet increase the size of the Indigenous estate. The other main possibility rests in government willingness, in Queensland and the Northern Territory, for example, to transfer administratively areas of land. But such outcomes require Indigenous groups to find the leverage to compel such agreements. Virtually all land held under native title or land rights is in areas classified as remote or very remote where, according to the 2016 census, only 19 per cent of the Indigenous population lives. Unless governments devise new regimes (such as TOSA in Victoria), many groups will miss out altogether on recovering rights over land and waters.

81 Royal Commission into Aboriginal Deaths in Custody, *National Report* (Canberra: Commonwealth of Australia, 1991), 2: 19.2.2.
82 Productivity Commission, *Overcoming Indigenous Disadvantage*, Tables 9A.2.1, 9A.2.3.
83 Anangu Pitjantjatjara Yankunytjatjara Lands Rights Act 1981 (SA), Maralinga Tjarutja Land Rights Act 1984 (SA).

Rights and Resourcing

Statutory land rights regimes tend to deliver secure property rights (often freehold) and a strong say over mining and development – though the local detail always matters. Innovative funding approaches in New South Wales and the Northern Territory built long-term foundations for their land rights systems, creating space for independent Aboriginal decision-making. By contrast, native title is twice as likely, so far, to be recognised as a bundle of non-exclusive rights, rather than as strong-form exclusive possession;[84] and, at their highest, the NTA rules about development provide limited leverage via the 'right to negotiate'. A lack of strategic government thinking about post-claim support leaves many native title corporations in a financially vulnerable position.[85]

Juridification

Under both systems, success – whether by claim, negotiation or obligatory transfer – almost always results in the creation of a new corporate body to hold and manage land. Land trusts, Land Councils and native title corporations are subject to a complex web of Western legal duties and responsibilities, overlaid upon Indigenous decision-making processes.[86] This juridification of Indigenous social relations is a feature of the land justice story in Australia.[87] Apart from the heavy administrative burden for organisations, it raises difficult but inescapable questions of accountability. At worst, it risks alienating the individuals involved from a more immediate and practical experience of 'landedness'.

The Future

Land rights and native title recognition also confer unequal but real negotiating power. That is reflected, for example, in the 1370 Indigenous Land Use Agreements made over one-third of Australia by January 2021, some without a formal native title determination. As remote areas are often simultaneously

84 National Native Title Tribunal, Determinations of Native Title www.nntt.gov.au/assistance/Geospatial/Pages/Maps.aspx, accessed 17 March 2021.

85 Productivity Commission, *Resources Sector Regulation* (Canberra; Commonwealth of Australia, 2020), 334–5.

86 M. Langton, 'Maximising the Potential for Empowerment: The Sustainability of Indigenous Native Title Corporations', in S. Brennan et al. (eds), *From Mabo to Akiba*, 171–83.

87 D. Martin, *Rethinking the Design of Indigenous Organisations: The Need for Strategic Engagement* (Canberra: CAEPR, 2003), 10.

rich in both minerals and biodiversity, economist and anthropologist, Jon Altman, suggests land holders have new opportunities to leverage the finite bargaining power associated with land rights and native title, but also face difficult choices between commerce and conservation.[88]

Land justice is an omnibus term. It captures a mix of motivations for pursuing legal rights over land that vary from group to group. Success in regaining territory can satisfy the quest of Aboriginal and Torres Strait Islanders for formal recognition by the Australian state as rightful owners of the land. It can improve the chances of protecting important places or spending time with family pursuing cultural activities on country. Where people also have ambitions to create new economic opportunities, land justice in a more enduring sense will always rely on the resourcefulness, resilience and unity of purpose of title-holding communities. It will also depend very importantly on law, policy and government behaviour. Over more than half a century, Australia has developed law and systems for native title and land rights that have focused heavily on the process for recovering land and for regulating or facilitating access to Indigenous land by third parties. To better fulfil the promise of land justice, much more attention will need to be devoted to practical support from government as First Nations groups, exercising self-determination, seek to build better lives on their part of the Indigenous estate.[89]

88 J. Altman, 'Land Rights and Development in Australia', in L. Ford and T. Rowse (eds), *Between Settler and Indigenous Governance* (Abingdon: Routledge, 2012).

89 B. Burbidge, M. Barber, T. M. Kong and T. Donovan, *Report of the 2019 Survey of Prescribed Bodies Corporate (PBCs)* (Canberra: AIATSIS, 2021); Senior Officers Working Group, *Report – COAG Investigation into Indigenous Land Administration and Use* (Canberra: Commonwealth of Australia, 2015).

17

Environment

RUTH A. MORGAN AND JUDITH S. JONES

Since 1788 settler law has provided a means either to prevent or progress certain forms of environmental change, according to the values and needs of the settler state. These exploitative interests of the settler state are in sharp contrast to the approach of First Nations' law, of caring for country, as reflected in the ancient and continuing culture of Indigenous peoples.[1] The historical record suggests a reactionary pattern of environmental exploitation (or lack thereof) giving rise to settler environmental anxieties that stimulate legislative intervention. Despite the promise of the wave of environmental legislation of the 1970s and 1980s, the gulf between 'the letter of legislation and its implementation' has only widened since.[2] The latest State of the Environment Report bears out the consequences of this shortfall: the main drivers of environmental problems – land use change, habitat destruction, invasive species, and climate change – are broadly the same as those listed in the first report in 1996, while the continent's biodiversity continues to decline.[3]

That Australia's 'grab bag' of environmental laws have fallen short of effectively enabling the protection, conservation and management of the continent's natural heritage is not surprising. After all, Australian environmental law has followed the pattern of wider environmental policy-making, which policy analyst Stephen Dovers characterises as 'episodic, lurching, ahistorical, myopic *ad hocery*', often in response to political or biophysical

Research for this chapter was generously funded by the Australian Research Council (DE160101125, DP180100807, Morgan).

1 See for example, I. Watson, *Aboriginal Peoples, Colonialism and International Law: Raw Law* (New York: Routledge, 2015), 29–54.

2 T. Bonyhady, 'The Disappointment of the Law', in S. R. Dovers and S. Wild River (eds), *Managing Australia's Environment* (Annandale: The Federation Press, 2003), 463–71.

3 W. J. Jackson et al., *Australia State of the Environment 2016: Overview* (Canberra: Department of the Environment and Energy, 2017).

crises.[4] There is no single source of Australian environmental law; instead, environmental law comprises statutes, regulations, codes and policies across the Commonwealth and state and territory levels.

Given the fragmentary nature of environmental law and its incremental evolution, it is not possible to provide an exhaustive record of its development since 1788. Instead, we examine the shifting nature and focus of environmental law across the three historical eras of Australian environmental policy-making identified by forester and historian Kevin Frawley. We commence with the exploitative pioneering phase of the late eighteenth and nineteenth centuries; then turn to the national development and wise use of resources that followed Federation; and conclude with the rise of modern environmentalism from the 1960s.[5] Although what constitutes the 'environment' is unstable and diverse across these phases, constant throughout are the opposing paradigms of regulation and policy, of exploitative legislation that guides resource development and specific projects, and protective legislation that guides (or attempts to guide) conservation.[6] Such broader and longer understandings of environmental law in settler Australia reveal how the legislative responses to modern environmental concerns both perpetuated and differed from the much earlier history of settler efforts to protect nature and natural resources, whether for aesthetic, moral or utilitarian concerns, as well as to the legislative efforts to utilise natural resources. Situating environmental law in a broader and longer history counters the tendency to frame environmental concerns and policy as 'fully modern', and reveals both continuity and change in the ways settler Australians have understood the 'environment' since 1788.[7]

Exploitation, 1788–1901

The first phase of European occupation of the Australian continent may be characterised as a period dominated by the Crown dispossessing Indigenous peoples of their land, water and sea country, and then, over time, allocating property rights in land, and any associated natural resources, to private

4 S. R. Dovers, 'On the Contribution of Environmental History to Current Debate and Policy' *Environment and History* 6 (2000): 140 (emphasis original).

5 K. Frawley, 'Evolving Visions: Environmental Management and Nature Conservation in Australia', in S. R. Dovers (ed.), *Australian Environmental History: Essays and Cases* (Melbourne: Oxford University Press, 1994), 55–78.

6 Ibid.

7 S. R. Dovers, 'The Australian Environmental Policy Agenda', *Australian Journal of Public Administration* 72 (2013): 114–28.

interests for their exploitation. From the earliest decades of the British colony of New South Wales, settler law prioritised the exploitation of land and water resources in order to advance the interests of pastoralism, mineral extraction and closer settlement. These laws encouraged and facilitated colonial improvement, while occasionally intervening either to arrest excesses that might endanger the colonial project, or to curtail the power of land holders. Although exploitation dominated, sporadic measures for environmental protection also emerged, first in governor's orders relevant to colonial settlements, and then, subsequently, through colonial parliamentary regulations that attempted to manage the 'great land rush' and specific environmental problems that emerged as a result.[8] These early local regulations stealthily began the process of modifying received English law – those ancient English common law property rights to use and take flora and fauna associated with the land and waterways, and riparian rights to the water itself.[9]

Colonial authorities quickly implemented measures to conserve natural resources around the earliest settlements. For instance, Governor Phillip used executive orders to attempt to prevent the erosion and pollution of the Tank Stream, the primary source of water supplies for the Sydney township.[10] Along the Hawkesbury River, meanwhile, Governor King issued orders that forbade timber cutting to prevent erosion of the riverbanks.[11] In the Pacific, King had earlier imposed restrictions on the cutting of plantain or banana trees on Norfolk Island in order to ensure the outpost's food supplies. Other attempts to limit the exploitation of the island's petrels and the felling of Norfolk pines were less successful.[12] The mixed successes of these conservation initiatives suggest that, while some authorities sought to realise a long-term vision of conservation, others believed in what historian Grace Karskens describes as the 'seeming boundlessness' of the colony's natural resources.[13]

As these early attempts to protect natural resources suggest, there were limits to the law. Whether pertaining to wildlife or riparian rights, in this 'new situation and the condition of [the] infant colony', the English common law principles with which settlers were familiar were likely contestable and

8 J. C. Weaver, *The Great Land Rush and the Making of the Modern World, 1650–1900* (Montreal: McGill-Queen's University Press, 2003).
9 T. Bonyhady, *The Law of the Countryside: The Rights of the Public* (Abingdon: Professional Books, 1987), 191–3, 215–33.
10 D. Collins, *An Account of the English Colony in New South Wales: From Its First Settlement in January 1788 to August 1801* (London: A. Strahan, 1804), 25.
11 T. Bonyhady, *The Colonial Earth* (Carlton: Miegunyah Press, 2000), 6–7.
12 Ibid, 5.
13 G. Karskens, *The Colony: A History of Early Sydney* (Crows Nest: Allen and Unwin, 2009), 384.

open to settler adaptation and colonial judicial reinterpretation.[14] Irrespective of any presumed or even locally confirmed legal principle, lawlessness was rife.[15] Unable to curtail the land rush fuelled by growing demand and high prices for Australian wool from the 1820s, the New South Wales government granted squatters temporary tickets of occupation, which gave way in 1826 to a revenue-generating system of one-year leases.[16] As the squatters' footprint grew beyond the alienated lands closest to the coast, the colonial authorities attempted to oversee them with the introduction of annual depasturing licences 'beyond the Limits' in 1836.[17] The introduction of Crown leases followed in 1847, the squatters having exerted pressure to have licensed lands transformed into leasehold.[18] Legislative efforts by the self-governing colonies to curtail the squatters' growing power through the Free Selection Acts in Victoria (1860) and New South Wales (1861) did little to loosen their grip, as they used their wealth and knowledge to ensure they retained the most fertile and well-watered lands.[19]

With the attainment of settler self-government in the Australian colonies from 1855 came the right to legislate over their own affairs, including land policy. In South Australia, for instance, the Scrub Lands Act 1866 required lessees to clear one-twentieth of the land of mallee each year, for twenty years, until all arable land was cleared. Colonial Parliaments also now began to legislate to address specific environmental problems that had emerged and might threaten the colonial project. Obstacles to pastoral expansion were found in what colonists described as 'pests' and 'weeds', for which they demanded legislative intervention to accelerate their control. One of the first acts of the self-governing parliament of South Australia was to legislate, in 1862, for the prevention of the further spread of the Scotch thistle, just one of the escapee garden plants that were propagating voraciously at the

14 A. Castles, *An Australian Legal History* (Sydney: Law Book Co, 1982); B. Kercher, *An Unruly Child: A History of Law in Australia* (St Leonards: Allen & Unwin, 1995).

15 A. R. Buck, *The Making of Australian Property Law* (Annandale: Federation Press, 2006); H. Reynolds, *The Law of the Land* (Ringwood: Penguin, 1987).

16 J. C. Weaver, 'Beyond the Fatal Shore: Pastoral Squatting and the Occupation of Australia, 1826 to 1852' *American Historical Review* 101 (1996): 981–1007.

17 Crown Lands unauthorised Occupation Act 1836, 7 Will. No. IV; Crown Lands unauthorised Occupation Act 1839, 2 Vic. No. XXVII.

18 Buck, *The Making of Australian Property Law*; Reynolds, *The Law of the Land*.

19 C. Lloyd, *Either Drought or Plenty: Water Development and Management in New South Wales* (Sydney: Dept. of Water Resources, 1988), 52; E. O'Gorman, *Flood Country: An Environmental History of the Murray-Darling Basin* (Collingwood: CSIRO Publishing, 2012), 71–2. For consideration of associated natural resource exploitation, see P. Karsten, *Between Law and Custom: High and Low Legal Cultures in the Lands of the British Diaspora – The United States, Canada, Australia and New Zealand, 1600–1900* (New York: Cambridge University Press, 2002), 141–5, 183–6.

expense of the colony's native grasses.[20] Later, in New South Wales, pastoralists complained that kangaroos were competing with their stock for pasture. Their alarm led to the passage of the Pastures and Stock Protection Act 1880 (NSW), under which kangaroos and wallabies were declared vermin, and bounties were offered for their destruction.[21] This act also pertained to rabbits, chief among those introduced species that had brought unexpected and unwanted consequences.[22] These developments were at odds with the nascent conservation movement, which had campaigned for legislation such as the Game Act 1867 (Vic) and the Animals Protection Act 1879 (NSW), to conserve native game and imported species (including birds), at least in part to ensure the sustainability of hunting and the fur trade.[23] Despite protective legislation, native mammal populations plummeted and imported species defied law and industrial technologies, as they thrived on the changes to the land wrought by the settler economy.[24]

By the 1870s, the practice of ringbarking trees had accelerated across the pastoral lands to encourage pasture growth and thus increase carrying capacity for livestock.[25] With tree clearing already the topic of the 'first sustained critique of the settlers' impact on their environment', as Tim Bonyhady has argued, some critics decried the practice as wasteful, while others cautioned of the possibility of climate deterioration as a result.[26]

20 P. M. Kloot, 'Dr Richard Schomburgk's "Naturalised Weeds" (1879)' *Journal of the Adelaide Botanic Gardens* 2 (1980): 195–220. The Thistle and Bur Act of 1862 repealed an earlier act of 1851, which had been similarly directed at the control of the Scotch thistle.

21 K. Boom, D. Ben-Ami, D. B. Croft et al., '"Pest" and Resource: A Legal History of Australia's Kangaroos' *Animal Studies Journal* 1 (2012): 17–40.

22 S. White, 'British Colonialism, Australian Nationalism and the Law: Hierarchies of Wild Animal Protection' *Monash University Law Review* 39 (2012): 452–72; P. Minard, *All Things Harmless, Useful, and Ornamental: Environmental Transformation through Species Acclimatization, from Colonial Australia to the World* (Chapel Hill, NC: University of North Carolina Press, 2019).

23 Boom et al., 'Pest', 17–40; B. Stubbs, 'From "Useless Brutes" to National Treasures: A Century of Evolving Attitudes toward Native Fauna in New South Wales, 1860s to 1960s' *Environment and History* 7 (2001): 23–56.

24 T. Dunlap, *Nature and the English Diaspora: Environment and History in the United States, Canada, Australia, and New Zealand* (Cambridge: Cambridge University Press, 1999), 81–2. Australia has the worst record for the loss of mammals of any continent, with some thirty endemic mammals lost since 1788; see J. C. Z. Woinarski, A. A. Burbridge and P. L. Harrison, 'Ongoing Unravelling of a Continental Fauna: Decline and Extinction of Australian Mammals Since European Settlement' *PNAS* 112 (2015): 4531–40.

25 K. Douglas, '"For the sake of a little grass": A Comparative History of Settler Science and Environmental Limits in South Australia and the Great Plains', in J. Beattie, E. O'Gorman and M. Henry (eds), *Climate, Science and Colonisation: Histories from Australia and New Zealand* (Basingstoke: Palgrave Macmillan, 2014), 99–117.

26 Bonyhady, *The Colonial Earth*, 85; T. Griffiths, 'How Many Trees Make a Forest? Cultural Debates about Vegetation Change in Australia' *Australian Journal of Botany* 50 (2002): 375–89.

Consequently, ringbarking was controlled by the New South Wales Land Acts Amendment Act 1875, which stipulated that ringbarking on Crown lands by pastoral lessees required special permission from the minister. Within a decade, however, ringbarking was legalised again, and recognised as an 'improvement' for which compensation could now be sought under the provisions of the Lands Acts Further Amendment Act 1880. Critics feared that pastoral tenants would proceed to ringbark with the aim of preventing free selection on their runs, leading to the introduction of new controls in the Ringbarking on Crown Lands Regulation Act 1881.[27] Although the 1881 Act was repealed in 1885 and penalties were introduced under the Crowns Land Act 1884 for those who undertook ringbarking without permission, the practice continued well into the twentieth century.[28]

In the colony of Victoria, meanwhile, legislators intervened to clarify the access to water on the gold fields. Conflicts quickly arose as miners competed for the abundant and reliable water supplies necessary for alluvial mining in the dry conditions of the colony's inland.[29] In response, colonial officials fashioned local laws out of the English common law of 'riparian access' and the American legal doctrine of 'prior appropriation', with which many miners who had rushed from the Californian and Colorado gold fields were already familiar.[30] The Mining Statute 1865 (Vic), for instance, clarified water rights in detail, and recognised licences and water infrastructure as chattel goods that could be bought and sold.[31] Through these efforts to adjudicate disputes over access and rights, the state asserted an increasing authority over the distribution of water, which established the foundations for the effective public ownership of water rights by the 1880s.[32]

Legislative efforts to improve the sanitary conditions of the colonial cities similarly borrowed from regulatory examples devised elsewhere. By the mid-nineteenth century in the Australian colonies, as in Britain, Western Europe and North America, crowded urban spaces had become associated with social and physiological ills. Among the grim conditions facing the urban working

27 B. Stubbs, 'Land Improvement or Institutionalised Destruction? The Ringbarking Controversy, 1879–1884, and the Emergence of a Conservation Ethic in New South Wales' *Environment and History* 4 (1998): 145–65.

28 Ibid.

29 P. Davies and S. Lawrence, 'A "mere thread of land": Water Races, Gold Mining and Water Law in Colonial Victoria' *Journal of Australian Colonial History* 16 (2014): 165–84.

30 Ibid.

31 S. Lawrence, P. Davies and J. Turnbull, 'The Archaeology of Water on the Victorian Goldfields' *International Journal of Historical Archaeology* 21 (2017): 49–65.

32 Davies and Lawrence, 'A "mere thread of land"', 167.

classes were polluted water supplies, outbreaks of typhoid and high infant mortality rates.[33] Yet colonial governments were slow to introduce the kinds of health legislation that had been introduced in Britain as a result of the Chadwickian movement for sanitary reform, instead leaving the responsibility for sanitation and public health to municipalities.[34] Worsening conditions and public outcry finally led to specific legislation to address water contamination and public health, such as the Water Pollution Prevention Act 1875 (NSW) and the Public Health Act 1889 (Vic).[35]

The reservation of parks also served progressive efforts to ameliorate urban ills. In New South Wales, for example, Sir John Robertson sought to bequeath to the people 'a national domain for rest and recreation'.[36] By early 1879, the colonial government had reserved 18,000 acres of land (doubled the following year to 36,300 acres) south of Sydney for 'the use of the public forever as a national park'.[37] Other colonies soon followed with their own 'national parks'; Victoria reserved a small area at Ferntree Gully in 1881, and South Australia created its first park in 1891.[38] Although Sydney's (Royal) National Park was the first legislated national park in the world, political expediency during the World Centennial of National Parks in 1972 led to the rewriting of this history to celebrate, instead, the establishment of Yellowstone in the United States.[39] In contrast to remote Yellowstone, which sought to protect 'wilderness' from the advancing frontier, Australian parks more closely resembled the emerging British model of

33 M. Lewis and R. Macleod, 'A Workingman's Paradise? Reflections on Urban Mortality in Colonial Australia 1860–1900' *Medical History* 31 (1987): 387–402.

34 S. Fisher, 'The Pastoral Interest and Sydney's Public Health' *Australian Historical Studies* 20 (1982): 73–89; R. A. Morgan, *Running Out? Water in Western Australia* (Perth: UWA Publishing, 2015), 24–7, 33–7.

35 Fisher, 'The Pastoral Interest', 73–89; Peter Christoff, 'Regulating the Urban Environment', in P. Troy (ed.), *Serving the City* (Sydney: Pluto Press, 2006), 34–59.

36 T. D. Elwell, *An Official Guide to the National Park of New South Wales* (Sydney: Government Printer, 1893), 7; M. Harper and R. White, 'How National Were the First National Parks? Comparative Perspectives from the British Settler Societies', in B. Gissibl, S. Höhler and P. Kupper (eds), *Civilizing Nature: National Parks in Global Historical Perspective* (New York: Berghahn Books, 2012), 58.

37 Elwell, *An Official Guide*, 7.

38 W. Frost and J. Laing, 'From Yellowstone to Australia and New Zealand: National Parks 2.0' *Global Environment* 12 (2013): 72. On Fern Gully, see Bonyhady, *The Colonial Earth*, 102–25.

39 L. Robin, 'Being First: Why the Americans Needed It, and Why Royal National Park Didn't Stand in Their Way' *Australian Zoologist* 36 (2013): 321–31. Yellowstone was established as a 'public park', with the first use of 'national park' in US legislation occurring only in 1899 with the act that created 'Mount Rainier National Park'. Sydney's National Park was renamed Royal National Park in 1955 after Queen Elizabeth II, who passed the park during her royal tour of Australia the previous year.

ornamental and recreational spaces for urban residents.[40] Established in close proximity to the colonial cities and accessible by rail, they served as 'additional city lungs' for the physical and moral betterment of 'the people'.[41]

Meanwhile, in the two decades since Sir John Robertson had sought to deliver closer settlement with the Selection Acts in New South Wales, the 'outside country' of the colony had been transformed by sheep and cattle. This period of rapid pastoral expansion had coincided with a series of seasons of above-average rainfall and, by the 1880s, the western leases were consolidated in the hands of the wealthier pastoralists.[42] Yet drought and rabbits soon began to exact their toll, and officials slowly realised that their vision of western agricultural progression would not materialise.[43] By the 1890s further legislative efforts to break the monopoly of large pastoral interests had resulted in a crisis, as falling wool prices and economic depression added to the woes of indebted pastoralists and new settlers on the eve of the Federation Drought.[44] A Royal Commission into their condition recognised the environmental devastation wrought by just forty years of pastoral occupation.[45] Although the Commission's report suggested a new awareness of the limited carrying capacity of the land in the state's west, the subsequent Western Lands Act 1901 did not effectively alleviate the causes of land degradation.[46] The Act made little provision for overstocking and substantially eased rents for pastoralists, effectively ensuring the continuation of pastoralism in the marginal lands of the west.[47]

National Development and Wise Use, 1901 to the 1960s

Federation in 1901 did little to upset the role of the erstwhile colonies in fostering the utilisation of the continent's natural resources. Deriving initially

40 Robin, 'Being First', 321–31; Harper and White, 'How National Were the First National Parks?', 59.
41 Robin, 'Being First', 321–31; Harper and White, 'How National Were the First National Parks?', 50–67.
42 T. Griffiths, 'One Hundred Years of Environmental Crisis' *Rangeland Journal* 23 (2001): 8.
43 Ibid, 9.
44 M. Quinn, 'Committed to Conserve: The Western Lands Act, 1901, and the Management of the Public Estate of the Western Division of New South Wales' *Australian Geographical Studies* 35 (1997): 183–94.
45 Bonyhady, 'The Disappointment of the Law', 463–4.
46 Quinn, 'Committed to Conserve', 183–94; Griffiths, 'One Hundred Years', 5–14.
47 Bonyhady, 'The Disappointment of the Law', 464; Quinn, 'Committed to Conserve', 183–94.

from 'exploitative' resource legislation, the states pursued sectoral approaches to the development of particular natural resources, such as timber, minerals, water, urban land and agricultural land.[48] The framers of the Constitution understood these pursuits as pertaining to static resources; consequently, most resource development, land use and natural resource regulation continued from 1901 as matters for state and territory law, rather than federal law.[49] Only navigable rivers were explicitly addressed in the Constitution under Section 100, because of the contest between New South Wales and South Australia over the 'reasonable use of waters of rivers for conservation or irrigation'.[50] The developmentalist ethos persisted long after 1901, now guided by a utilitarian approach that counselled the efficient and rational utilisation of the continent's resources to ensure the unhindered progress of the new nation.[51]

The Federation Drought (1895–1903) framed not only the inauguration of a new nation and its Constitution, but also ongoing discussions about the waters of the Murray River. Since the 1880s, South Australia, New South Wales and Victoria had wrestled over questions of navigation on, and irrigation from, the river that crossed their borders. With the end of the drought in 1903, negotiations faltered; but eventually a Victorian Royal Commission in 1910 established the importance of a permanent inter-jurisdictional board or commission to oversee the river's management.[52] Finally, in late 1915, the Murray River Waters Agreement was incorporated into legislation and passed by each of the four Parliaments – New South Wales, Victoria, South Australia and the Commonwealth. The agreement outlined a program of engineering works with cost-sharing; specified the nature of water-sharing rules that would provide a defined monthly flow to South Australia; and established a commission of four members, representing the four governments.[53] Although tensions lingered between the parties, major works were soon underway, including projects such as the

48 M. D. Farrier, 'Fragmented Law in Fragmented Landscapes: The Slow Evolution of Integrated Natural Resource Management Legislation in New South Wales' *Environment and Planning Law Journal* 19 (2002): 89–108; Frawley, 'Evolving Visions', 67.

49 J. Crawford, 'The Constitution', in T. Bonyhady (ed.), *Environmental Protection and Legal Change* (Annandale: Federation Press, 1992), 4.

50 Australian Constitution; see also, J. Williams and A. Webster, 'Section 100 and State Water Rights' *Public Law Review* 21 (2010): 267–74.

51 See, J. M. Powell, *An Historical Geography of Modern Australia: The Restive Fringe* (Melbourne: Cambridge University Press, 1988), 150–89.

52 D. Connell, *Water Politics in the Murray-Darling Basin* (Annandale: Federation Press, 2007), 91–2.

53 Ibid, 95.

construction of the Hume Dam upstream from Albury, and a series of weirs along the Murray, Murrumbidgee and Darling rivers to support navigation.[54] The Commonwealth made its funding contribution to the enlargement of the Hume Dam in 1945 conditional on the states making plans to reduce silt build up and to improve the land and water management of the irrigators who would use this additional water. Historian Daniel Connell suspects this was the first example of the use of financial pressure by the Commonwealth to achieve environmental objectives in the Murray-Darling Basin.[55]

As the first suburban nation bloomed along the coast, settler Australians inherited British concerns about the nature of the built environment. The rise of the modern town planning movement sought to coordinate urban improvement with land use zoning, such as residential, commercial and industrial, to ensure residents' health and productivity.[56] A guiding principle of the state-based town and country planning legislation that followed was 'amenity', which had been fundamental to the garden-city movement at the turn of the twentieth century.[57] The South Australian Town Planning and Development Act 1920, for instance, regulated subdivisions with 'conservation of any natural beauties or amenities'.[58] Yet, as Murray Wilcox (then a solicitor) observed in 1967, powers to control development remained weak, as '[e]conomic factors were decisive, outweighing considerations for living amenity, the availability of transport and public services, traffic problems, and the preservation of natural beauty'.[59]

Beyond the suburbs, the state Crown took an interest in exploiting all forms of natural resources as 'property' whether in the public or the private estate. To facilitate their wise use, resources in the public estate, such as Crown forests reserves, were formally brought under state-based management controls, such as the Forestry Act 1909 (NSW) and the Forestry Act 1916 (NSW).[60] Meanwhile, land holder resources in the private estate, which had been largely unfettered prior to Federation, were now progressively subject to legislative encroachment by the state Crown. Importantly, these resumptions by the Crown did

54 Ibid, 98. 55 Ibid, 99.

56 R. Freestone, 'Australian Environmental Planning: Origins and Theories', in J. Byrne, N. Sipe and J. Dodson (eds), *Australian Environmental Planning: Challenges and Future Prospects* (Abingdon: Routledge, 2014), 21–35.

57 A. Kelly, 'Securing Urban Amenity: Does It Coincide with Biodiversity Conservation at the Local Government Level?' *Australasian Journal of Environmental Management* 13 (2006): 243–53.

58 Cited in Freestone, 'Australian Environmental Planning', 24.

59 M. R. Wilcox, *The Law of Land Development in New South Wales* (Sydney: Law Book Co, 1967), 188.

60 See L. T. Carron, *A History of Forestry in Australia* (Canberra: ANU Press, 1985).

not wholly acquire private landholdings. If they had, the state would certainly have been legally obliged to pay compensation to land holders. Rather, the state Crowns passed legislation that gradually eroded land holders' possession of certain rights that had traditionally formed part of the 'bundle of rights' associated with private land. Early on, this process included the severance and resumption of rights to minerals (commencing in New South Wales, for instance, in 1884),[61] as well as the legislative modification of access rights to water, such as the Water Rights Act 1896 (NSW), which abolished common law rights to water in New South Wales.[62] The Crown's renewed ownership of, or controls over access to, minerals and water was frequently uncompensated acquisition of property for two reasons. First, the state Crown was not constitutionally obliged to pay compensation, although it might voluntarily have offered some form of structural adjustment payment in some circumstances; and second, Australia did not have the kind of 'regulatory takings' doctrine that had developed in the United States, which would otherwise have required the Commonwealth to pay compensation to private land holders wherever the legislation effectively 'sterilised' their interest in the land.[63] Once successfully resumed by the Crown, these rights could then become available for exploitation, licensed and regulated by the states under relevant water, irrigation or mining Acts.

As private land holders were encouraged to heedlessly increase production through land clearing and intensive cropping, growing environmental anxieties about soil degradation during the interwar period prompted the further erosion of land holders' 'bundle of rights'. Across the nation, state legislation created land remediation obligations, or imposed environmental protections and land use restrictions, broadly based on US legislation.[64] Through state-based subsidies, and with the objective of a productivity win-win for the state and land holders alike, legislation such as the Soil Conservation Act 1938 (NSW) and the Soil and Land Conservation Act 1945 (WA), created positive obligations and encouraged land holders to 'voluntarily' remediate agriculturally valuable soils. Other state legislation, such as the Native Plants

61 T. Bonyhady, 'Property Rights', in T. Bonyhady (ed.), *Environmental Protection and Legal Change* (Annandale: Federation Press, 1992), 74.

62 Ibid, 41–78; Williams and Webster, 'Section 100 and State Water Rights', 267–74.

63 *Newcrest Mining (WA) Ltd v Commonwealth* (1997) 190 CLR 513; *ICM Agriculture Pty Ltd v Commonwealth* (2009) 240 CLR 140.

64 This legislation was to some extent modelled on the US example; see L. Robin, *Defending the Little Desert: The Rise of Ecological Consciousness in Australia* (Carlton: Melbourne University Press, 1998), 29; S. Sauter, 'Lessons from the US: Australia's Response to Wind Erosion (1935–1945)' *Global Environment* 8 (2015): 293–319.

Protection Act 1930 (Qld), required specific protections that modified common law land holder rights to 'take flora and fauna'. States further extended these restrictions by imposing limits on the removal of 'flora', 'native vegetation' and 'biodiversity' on private land.[65] Although land holders welcomed state-based subsidies for land remediation,[66] many continued into the twenty-first century to criticise the states' failure to compensate them for such restrictions on their land use.[67] Nevertheless, some commentators recognise that progress towards environmental protection would 'grind to a halt' if every regulatory act affecting private property provoked an entitlement for compensation.[68]

Modern Environmentalism, 1960s to 2020

Heralded by the 1962 publication of Rachel Carson's *Silent Spring*, the ecological awakening of the 1960s reflected a growing international concern for the environment and the toll human activity was taking upon it. At home, the environmental costs of Australia's post-war economic growth came under closer scrutiny, raising questions about the nation's long-established faith in developmentalism. Although the continent's unique flora and fauna had long captured the attention of nature enthusiasts, this modern environmental movement recognised that such species belonged to an interdependent system of life that required conservation and protection as a whole.[69] Preventing the destruction of these areas became the focus of the growing Australian conservation movement, as it campaigned to place the environment on the political agenda and politically legitimise its concerns.[70] Both in Australia and overseas, even more significant than the protests themselves, were the nature of subsequent political, institutional and legal responses. As

65 Bonyhady, 'Property Rights', 43.

66 J. Jones, 'Emergence of the Soil Conservation Act 1938 (NSW): The Origins of a Co-operative and Voluntary Regulatory Approach to Landcare on Private Land, 1884–1938' *Environmental and Planning Law Journal* 35 (2018): 5–25.

67 J. Bradsen, 'Land Degradation: Current and Proposed Legal Controls' *Environmental and Planning Law Journal* 4 (1987): 113–33; R. J. Fowler, 'Vegetation Clearance Controls in South Australia: A Change of Course' *Environmental and Planning Law Journal* 3 (1986): 48–66; D. Farrier, 'Vegetation Conservation: The Planning System as a Vehicle for the Regulation of Broadacre Agricultural Land Clearing' *Melbourne University Law Review* 18 (1991): 26–59; J. Kehoe, 'Land Clearing in Queensland' *Environmental and Planning Law Journal* 23 (2006): 148–57.

68 K. Gray, 'Can Environmental Regulation Constitute a Taking of Property at Common Law?' *Environmental and Planning Law Journal* 24 (2007): 164.

69 Bonyhady, *The Colonial Earth*.

70 T. Bonyhady, *Places Worth Keeping: Conservationists, Politics, and Law* (Sydney: Allen and Unwin, 1993).

we show, crafting these responses was all the more complicated in a federated nation where the states had always had relatively free rein to 'develop' Crown resources.[71]

It was the states that responded first to the growing ecological and human-health concerns about pollution. They did so with what came to be known as the 'command and control' approach of air, noise and water pollution regulatory regimes, such as the Clean Air Act 1957 (Vic), Clean Air Act 1964 (WA) and the Noise Control Act 1975 (NSW). Henry Bolte's Liberal-Country Party government of Victoria introduced the nation's first Environment Protection Act in 1970. State legislation, such as the National Parks and Wildlife Act 1972 (SA), began to recognise natural and cultural heritage, and set aside more areas for wildlife. Doing so not only created areas of parkland and reserves, but also established statutory protections for listed species of threatened flora and fauna. Vacant lands under Crown ownership, much of which had been historically deemed unsuitable for agriculture, soon dominated these reserves, to which the states added lands that appeared to have few alternative uses. Political pragmatism aside, the strategy was ecologically fraught, as it had resulted in a fragmented and geographically biased system of 'leftovers', rather than 'crown jewels'.[72] Consequently, as an employee of the NSW National Parks and Wildlife Service conceded in 1990, the 'reserve system is not representative and does not adequately conserve the plants and animals native to New South Wales'.[73] This pattern could be found across the nation, leading conservation biologist Harry Recher to respond, '[w]e need to manage wildlife on all lands regardless of tenure, but this requires significant changes in community and political attitudes to land ownership and the social responsibilities of land owners'.[74]

Modest as the results of these initiatives have since been, even this emerging wave of ecological and natural heritage protectionism did not seize all state governments, carrying, as it did, a threat to their unfettered use and development of natural resources. Contrary to the environmentalism of the decade, the Tasmanian state government revoked the status of

71 P. Warde, L. Robin and S. Sörlin, *The Environment: A History of the Idea* (Baltimore, MD: Johns Hopkins University Press, 2018), 252.

72 R. L. Pressey, 'Conservation Reserves in NSW: Crown Jewels or Leftovers' *Search* 26 (1995): 47–51.

73 P. Reed, 'An Historical Perspective On: Conserving What? The Basis for Nature Conservation Reserves in New South Wales, 1967–1989' *Australian Zoologist* 26 (1990): 87.

74 H. F. Recher, 'Wildlife Conservation in Australia: Prophesies of Doom' *Australian Zoologist* 26 (1990): 69.

Lake Pedder as a national park in 1967 and cleared the way politically for its subsequent inundation.[75] The earlier phases of environmental governance also persisted: jurist David Grinlinton found that while the majority (60 per cent) of conservation and environmental protection and planning legislation had been enacted since 1970, a similar proportion (59 per cent) of resource allocation and development legislation in force in 1987 was enacted prior to the mid-1960s.[76]

After the federal election of 1972 brought an end to nearly three decades of conservative power, the Whitlam Labor government initiated a bold wave of federal ecological and heritage reform. In what appeared to signal a new era of national environmental regulation, these reforms included a set of relatively benign ecological and heritage protections in the National Parks and Wildlife Conservation Act 1975, the Great Barrier Reef Marine Park Act 1975 and the Australian Heritage Commission Act 1975.[77] Potentially more disruptive, however, were the Whitlam government's novel legislative procedures contained in the Environment Protection (Impact of Proposals) Act 1974 (EPIPA). This legislation established a new suite of environmental studies and assessments, following the US example. Signalling some legal tentativeness (and perhaps political circumspection) about an over-reach of Commonwealth legislative power, this legislation was limited to assessing projects or policies in which Commonwealth agencies were involved, and expressly included state-based projects that required Commonwealth export or foreign investment approval.

It was the subsequent Fraser Coalition government that tested the reach of the Commonwealth's power to rely on this legislation, which it used to intervene in the development approval processes of the Queensland state government. Under EPIPA the Commonwealth initiated environmental studies into sand mining on Fraser Island, which local conservationists had campaigned to stop since the early 1970s. This move represented a clear

75 D. Hutton and L. Connors, *A History of the Australian Environment Movement* (Melbourne: Cambridge University Press, 1999), 119–21.

76 D. Grinlinton, 'The Environmental Era and the Emergence of "Environmental Law" in Australia – A Survey of Environmental Legislation and Litigation, 1967–1987' *Environmental and Planning Law Journal* 7 (1990): 74–105.

77 P. Christoff, 'EPAs: Orphan Agencies of Environmental Protection', in S. R. Dovers and S. Wild Rivers (eds), *Managing Australia's Environment* (Annandale: Federation Press, 2003), 302–17; A. Kellow, 'Thinking Globally and Acting Federally: Intergovernmental Relations and Environmental Protection in Australia', in K. M. Holland, F. L. Morton and B. Galligan (eds), *Federalism and the Environment: Environmental Policymaking in Australia, Canada and the United States* (London: Greenwood Press, 1996), 135–56.

Commonwealth intrusion into an area of resource development that had traditionally been a state responsibility.[78] The intervention also seemed at odds with the Fraser government's overall commitment to reversing Whitlam's centralisation of power in Canberra.[79] The sandmining company in question, Murphyores, challenged the Commonwealth's power to conduct these environmental investigations under EPIPA, but lost in the High Court. The court upheld the Commonwealth's power to enact the procedures for environmental assessment on the basis of an expansive interpretation of the overseas trade and commerce powers under Section 51 of the Australian Constitution.[80] As a result, the Fraser government was the first federal government to halt a resource development project in one of the states on environmental grounds and was the first to provide compensation to those affected by its intervention.[81]

Meanwhile, state legislation such as Victoria's Environment Effects Act 1978 and the Environmental Planning and Assessment Act 1979 (EPAA) in New South Wales imposed increased control over planning and development law by local authorities and required environmental impact assessment of major state projects and activities. Under Section 123 of the EPAA, citizens were granted open standing, such that 'any person' could access the newly created Land and Environment Court to seek judicial review of state government decisions pertaining to environmental governance.[82] Having observed the restrictions on the public's legal standing to challenge environmental decisions at the Commonwealth level, conservationists made the most of these expanded rights for public participation in New South Wales.[83] During the 1980s, for instance, they won a series of cases against the state's Forestry Commission, which had disregarded its statutory obligations to undertake environmental impact assessment obligations under the EPAA.[84] In response to these legal victories for conservationists, the New South Wales government amended the environmental legislation to alleviate the environmental assessment burden on the Commission.[85]

78 J. Formby, 'The Australian Government's Experience with Environmental Impact Assessment' *Environmental Impact Assessment Review* 7 (1987): 207–26.
79 Bonyhady, *Places Worth Keeping*, 15.
80 *Murphyores Inc. Pty. Ltd v The Commonwealth* (1976) 136 CLR 1.
81 Bonyhady, *Places Worth Keeping*, 16.
82 J. S. Cripps, 'Administrative law', in T. Bonyhady (ed.), *Environmental Protection and Legal Change* (Annandale: Federation Press, 1992), 29.
83 See *ACF v Commonwealth* (1980) 146 CLR 493, 537–8; *Onus v Alcoa (Aust) Ltd* (1981) 149 CLR 27, 66.
84 *Prineas v Forestry Commission of NSW* (1984) 53 LGRA 160; *Kivi v Forestry Commission of NSW* (1982) 47 LGRA 38; *Jarasius v Forestry Commission of NSW* (1988) 71 LGRA 79.
85 Bonyhady, *Places Worth Keeping*, 82–103.

In their struggle to protect not only places, but also associated habitats and species 'worth keeping',[86] conservationists used the courts to contest federal environmental protection powers to limit the state governments' historic autonomy over natural resource development. Among those places was the Franklin River in south-west Tasmania, which the Hydro-Electric Commission proposed to dam in 1979. Galvanised by the defeat of the earlier campaign to save Lake Pedder, conservationists had already taken a new strategic direction. They now emphasised the river's aesthetic value, while questioning the economic credibility of the development proposal.[87] With the support of the Australian Conservation Foundation, the Tasmanian Wilderness Society commenced the Franklin Blockade in December 1982 on the very day the state's south-west was proclaimed a World Heritage Area on the grounds of its natural and cultural values. The blockade lasted until March 1983, when Bob Hawke's Labor Party won the federal election and the new Prime Minister declared he would honour his election promise to save the Franklin.[88]

In the Tasmanian Dam case that followed the election, the High Court upheld the validity of Commonwealth legislation preventing the construction of the Gordon-below-Franklin Dam.[89] Specifically, the Court upheld the Commonwealth's ability to use both the corporations power and the external affairs power under Section 51 of the Constitution. The decision also had implications for the ways in which federal law could facilitate the aspirations of Aboriginal peoples' protection of Indigenous cultural heritage.[90] In the search for cave sites of natural significance in the late 1970s, conservationists had rediscovered Kutikina and confirmed that south-west Tasmania had a deep human history of some 20,000 years.[91] The High Court accepted that a sacred site of special significance to Aboriginal peoples in Tasmania could also be of universal value, consistent with the Commonwealth's 1975 listing of the Tasmanian Wilderness as a site of World Heritage.

86 Ibid.

87 K. Crowley, 'Saving the Franklin: A People's Rebellion in a Distant Forest' *Island Magazine* 93/94 (2003): 34–43.

88 Ibid, 40–1. 89 *Commonwealth v Tasmania* (1983) 158 CLR 1.

90 Just the previous year, *Koowarta v Bjelke-Petersen* (1982) 153 CLR 168 had established that the external affairs power (s 51(xxix)) was wide enough to vest jurisdiction in the Commonwealth Parliament to make valid domestic laws that gave effect to treaties and Conventions to which Australia was a signatory, such as the World Heritage Convention, 1975. See A. Genovese, 'Critical Decision 1983: Remembering *Commonwealth v Tasmania*' *Griffith Law Review* 24 (2015): 1–15.

91 B. Griffiths, *Deep Time Dreaming: Uncovering Ancient Australia* (Melbourne: Black Inc, 2018).

At home and abroad then, environmental activism and a growing ecological consciousness were effecting policy and legislative changes. Underlying these changes was a reorientation in the understanding of environmental issues underway since the 1960s: during the 1980s, discrete and short-term approaches to particular problems gave way to a 'whole problem' outlook encapsulated in the concept of 'sustainability'.[92] This perspective increasingly understood sustainability and economic growth as compatible and interdependent, rather than mutually exclusive, policy options. This relationship was framed in terms of 'sustainable development', as defined by the World Commission on Environment and Development in 1987.[93] These changes culminated in the Rio Declaration produced at the 1992 United Nations Conference on Environment and Development, which asserted that 'environmental protection shall constitute an integral part of the development process and cannot be considered in isolation from it'.[94]

By this time, the Hawke federal Labor government had commenced a policy process to develop a national strategy for ecologically sustainable development (ESD). As a signatory to the United Nations Convention on Biological Diversity (1992), and the United Nations Framework Convention on Climate Change (1992) Australia had international obligations to implement ESD in domestic affairs. Broadly, the concept of ESD required the effective integration of economic and environmental considerations in decision-making processes through the implementation of the precautionary principle; intergenerational equity; conservation of biological diversity and ecological integrity; and improved valuation, pricing and incentive mechanisms for resource use.[95] But any national, perhaps 'Australian' version of ESD, as represented in the national strategy for ESD, was merely hortatory. It was quickly realised that since the states and territories held most of the power over planning and natural resource management, implementation of national obligations of ESD would rely on the amendment of existing state and territory legislation. All jurisdictions rapidly incorporated ESD into at least some environmental legislation, regulations and planning instruments.[96]

92 L. Robin, *How a Continent Created a Nation* (Sydney: UNSW Press, 2007), 176–7.
93 G. H. Brundtland, *Our Common Future* (Oxford: Oxford University Press, 1987).
94 United Nations, Annex 1: Rio Declaration on Environment and Development, A/CONF.151/26 (Vol. 1) (Geneva: UN, 1992).
95 G. Bates, 'Legal Perspectives', in S. R. Dovers and S. Wild River (eds), *Managing Australia's Environment* (Sydney: Federation Press, 2003), 255–301.
96 C. Barton, 'The Status of the Precautionary Principle in Australia: Its Emergence in Legislation and as a Common Law Doctrine' *Harvard Environmental Law Review* 22 (1998): 516–17.

By the end of the 1990s ESD could be expressly found in over 120 pieces of state, territory and federal legislation.[97] But the uptake was far from uniform or comprehensive. Despite this legislative proliferation, there was sectoral and jurisdictional fragmentation in the policy and legislative response. Referring to the division of legislative power between the Commonwealth and the states, for instance, jurist James Crawford observed in 1992:

> The 'message' of environmental groups over the past two decades has been, above all, an emphasis on the wholeness of the environment, and on the need for coherent strategies to overcome problems of environmental impact or deterioration – in the words of Schedule 1 to the Resource Assessment Commission Act 1989 (Cth), 'an integrated approach to conservation . . . and development'. Australia is further away from unitary management of the environment than it ever was.[98]

The Hawke government's adoption of a sectoral approach to ESD served only to reinforce the very fragmentation that sustainable development sought to overcome, a view that both environmental and industry advocates shared.[99]

As a result of this sectoral and jurisdictional fragmentation of ESD across federal, state and territory legislation, there was a lack of consistency of legal principles in the process of its implementation. More often than not, the adopted wording was merely slotted into pre-existing legislation in each state or territory jurisdiction wherever it would fit. ESD became an additional, sometimes contradictory, legislative objective to which unspecified weight was assigned. Alternatively, ESD was included in non-binding guidance or policy documents as an aspirational statement.[100] In light of these developments, policy scholars were sceptical of both federal and state government commitments to political consensus: in state-based approvals regimes, less tangible, overarching issues of an environmental and social nature, such as biodiversity and the greenhouse effect, were separated from the more economically focused factors.[101]

97 Robin, *How a Continent Created a Nation*, 176.

98 Crawford, 'The Constitution', 7. The short-lived Resource Assessment Commission (RAC) was established in 1989 in an attempt to resolve growing conflict between development and environmental interests both within and outside the government.

99 B. Jolly and E. McCoy, 'Ecologically Sustainable Development and the Fragmentation of Policy: A Critical Review' *Policy, Organisation and Society* 7 (1994): 34–9.

100 Robin, *How a Continent Created a Nation*, 176. Less commonly, substantive provisions of statutes were amended to expressly or impliedly include ESD as one of a number of competing considerations in administrative decision-making, such as for environmental approvals, e.g. *Minister for Planning v Walker* (2008) 161 LGERA 423.

101 See Jolly and McCoy, 'Ecologically Sustainable Development', 34–9.

The critics were right to be sceptical. Implementation of ESD through these statutory mechanisms provided plenty of room for interpretation and discretionary administrative decisions that could accommodate a variety of political purposes and development-oriented outcomes. With the reform and re-enactment of statutory regimes since the 1990s, the concept of ESD has become uncoupled from earlier formulations, while recent state and territory legislation has incorporated ESD in a more nuanced manner.[102] These changes have only added to the diversity of formulations of ESD and interpretations 'in context'. In terms of doctrinal development at least, the legacy of separate jurisdictions and the multiplicity of statute-specific formulations and interpretations have resulted in a lack of any common national jurisprudence. Nevertheless, the decisions of Chief Justice Preston of the Land and Environment Court of New South Wales remain highly influential and legally persuasive in the interpretation of the notion of ESD in the courts of all Australian jurisdictions.[103]

Among the components of ESD was the precautionary principle, a decision-making approach in the absence of scientific certainty that has had a lively legal history in Australia. As part of ESD, precaution needed to be widely implemented in federal, state and territory legislation. But in the early 1990s the principle's precise legal meaning was highly contested. Consequently, Parliaments were considerably circumspect about expressly creating precautionary decision-making obligations, even though legislative regimes may have referred to the principle of precaution. In 1993, however, Justice Paul Stein of the NSW Land and Environment Court – in a bold judicial move that might be characterised as the development of a common law principle – held that the precautionary principle was relevant to a decision to issue a licence to 'take or kill' endangered fauna (even though the principle was not an express consideration) and he applied it as a 'statement of common sense' in *Leatch v National Parks and Wildlife Service and Shoalhaven City Council* ('*Leatch*').[104] In circumstances 'where uncertainty or ignorance exists concerning the nature or scope of environmental harm', he stated, 'decision-makers should be cautious'.[105] Later reflecting on the rise

102 For example, the Planning Act 2016 (Qld), s 3(2); Sustainable Forests (Timber) Act 2004 (Vic), s 5.

103 See further B. Preston, 'The Judicial Development of Ecologically Sustainable Development', in D. Fisher (ed.), *Research Handbook on Fundamental Concepts of Environmental Law* (Cheltenham: Edward Elgar Publishing, 2016), 475–524.

104 (1993) 81 LGERA 270; see also P. L. Stein, 'Are Decision-makers Too Cautious with the Precautionary Principle?' *Environmental and Planning Law Journal* 17 (2000): 3–23.

105 *Leatch* (1993) 81 LGERA 270, 282.

of the precautionary principle during the 1990s, Stein argued for its legal significance in having changed 'the underlying assumption from freedom of exploitation to one of conservation'.[106]

Although Stein's interpretation had limited formal legal authority beyond New South Wales, it was nevertheless a thought-provoking decision that received international notoriety and other Australian judges subsequently endorsed his 'cautious' approach.[107] Yet, debate about the precautionary principle's interpretation, and its importance to environmental administration, continued to swirl in the early 2000s.[108] In *Telstra Corporation v Hornsby Shire Council* ('*Telstra*'), however, a new risk-based threshold test for precautionary decision-making was specified. In this 2006 case before the NSW Land and Environment Court, the telecommunications company challenged a refusal by the local council of the company's application to install a suburban mobile phone tower.[109] In the course of his interpretation of the principle in the context of the state's statutory planning law,[110] Chief Justice Brian Preston comprehensively summarised themes in the international and Australian case law and academic commentary, before expounding a new interpretative approach that separated the serious threat and scientific uncertainty assessments in the application of the principle.[111] Although this decision is technically not binding on decision-makers in other statutory contexts, and is merely persuasive for judges in other Australian jurisdictions, the *Telstra* decision has been highly influential in the subsequent shaping of Australian environmental law jurisprudence on precaution.

In the meantime, against the backdrop of ESD considerations, a more cooperative relationship regarding environmental issues had emerged between the federal government and the states, which was formalised in

106 P. L. Stein, 'A Cautious Application of the Precautionary Principle' *Environmental Law Review* 2 (2000): 1–10.

107 *Greenpeace Australia v Redbank Power Company* (1994) 86 LGERA 143 (Pearlman CJ); *Tuna Boat Owners Association of SA v Development Assessment Commission & Anor* 110 LGERA 1.

108 E. Fisher, J. Jones and R. von Schomberg, 'Implementing the Precautionary Principle: Perspectives and Prospects', in E. Fisher, J. Jones and R. von Schomberg (eds), *Implementing the Precautionary Principle* (Cheltenham: Edward Elgar Publishing, 2006), 1–18.

109 [2006] NSWLEC 133.

110 Protection of the Environment Administration Act 1991 (NSW), s 6(2)(a); Environmental Planning and Assessment Act 1979 (NSW), ss 4(1), 79C(1)(e).

111 This decision has been criticised by J. Peel, 'When (Scientific) Rationality Rules: (Mis)Application of the Precautionary Principle in Australian Mobile Phone Tower Cases' *Journal of Environmental Law* 19 (2007): 103–20.

the 1992 Intergovernmental Agreement on the Environment (IGAE). During the 1980s, the increasing recourse of the environmental movement to the Commonwealth to challenge state decisions had proven a successful tactic, leading to Commonwealth intervention to protect from resource use significant areas, such as Coronation Hill in Kakadu National Park.[112] Intergovernmental relations, however, were strained by these manoeuvres. Matters came to a head in the Wesley Vale pulp mill dispute in Tasmania (1987–9), which laid bare the need for a more robust and transparent conceptual and legislative framework for environmental decision-making at the state and the Commonwealth levels.[113] The subsequent development of the framework of the IGAE clarified state and federal roles and responsibilities according to the subsidiarity principle and sought to align decision-making at all levels with ESD.[114]

Accordingly, a spirit of cooperative federalism imbued the 1992 National Forest Policy Statement (NFPS). The NFPS established a framework for the formulation of regional forest agreements (RFAs) that was intended to provide the chief mechanism by which the Commonwealth could extract itself from oversight of forest management, a politically divisive issue since the 1970s. As a result, the primary responsibility for ecologically sustainable forest management, to ensure that commercial uses of old growth forests were both appropriate and desirable, rested with the states.[115] The escalation of a forestry dispute in 1994 underlined the need for a policy response such as the RFA mechanism. The federal Keating Labor government had approved increases in woodchip exports against the advice of its own Environment Minister. In addition to public rallies and a loggers' blockade of Capital Hill in Canberra, the Tasmanian Conservation Trust successfully mounted a test case against the Minister for Resources, who had issued a woodchip export licence to Tasmanian timber company, Gunns Ltd.[116] The Federal Court held

112 M. B. Lane, 'Regional Forest Agreements: Resolving Resource Conflicts or Managing Resource Politics' *Australian Geographical Studies* 37 (1999): 142–53.

113 N. M. Economou, 'Australian Environmental Policy Making in Transition: The Rise and Fall of the Resource Assessment Commission' *Australian Journal of Public Administration* 55 (1996): 12–22; G. Curran and R. Hollander, 'A Tale of Two Pulp Mills: Realising Ecologically Sustainable Development in Australia' *Australian Journal of Public Administration* 67 (2008): 483–97.

114 T. Buehrs and G. Alpin, 'Pathways Towards Sustainability: The Australian Approach' *Journal of Environmental Planning and Management* 42 (1999): 315–40.

115 J. McDonald, 'Regional Forest (Dis)Agreements: The RFA Process and Sustainable Forest Management' *Bond Law Review* 11 (1999): 295–342.

116 P. Christoff, 'Progress up a Tree: The ALP's Woodchip Debacle' *Arena Magazine* 16 (1995): 22–4. See *Tasmanian Conservation Trust Inc v Minister for Resources* (1995) 127 ALR 580.

that the Minister for Resources had failed to observe Commonwealth environmental impact assessment requirements in reaching his decision. Nevertheless, as its endorsement of the IGAE had signalled, the environmental ascendancy of the Hawke era was now over as environmental issues became increasingly marginal under the economic rationalist approach of the subsequent Keating Labor government.[117]

Meanwhile, conservationists held out hope that successive federal governments would exploit the full extent of the Commonwealth's constitutional power to show national leadership in matters of environmental protection. But the cooperative federalist approach continued after the election of the Howard Coalition government in 1996, signalling an ongoing reluctance to intervene in the developmentalism of the states.[118] The subsequent enactment of the Environment Protection and Biodiversity Act 1999 (Cth) (EPBC), by which the government sought to reduce the duplication of environmental assessment, demonstrated the Coalition's desire for an even narrower role in environmental protection. Bilateral arrangements associated with the Act allowed for state and territory assessment processes to be accredited by the Commonwealth as having satisfied the Commonwealth's legal obligations. For its part, the Commonwealth confined its focus to the protection of those aspects of the environment that were 'matters of national environmental significance'. In addition to actions on Commonwealth lands, and actions undertaken by the Commonwealth and Commonwealth agencies, these matters pertain to World Heritage properties, National Heritage places, wetlands of international importance (under the Ramsar Convention on Wetlands, 1971), nationally listed threatened species and ecological communities, internationally listed migratory species, 'nuclear actions' (such as uranium mining), and the Commonwealth marine environment, many of which reflect Australia's obligations under international environmental treaties.[119] In line with the Coalition's reticence to address anthropogenic climate change, the Act did not include a federal requirement to assess projects with climate impacts (a 'greenhouse trigger'), and it excluded forestry operations carried out in accordance with the RFAs. Meanwhile, the

117 N. M. Economou, 'Backwards into the Future: National Policy Making, Devolution and the Rise and Fall of the Environment', in K. Walker and K. Crowley (eds), *Australian Environmental Policy 2: Studies in Decline and Devolution* (Sydney: UNSW Press, 1999), 65–80.

118 P. Toyne, *The Reluctant Nation: Environment, Law and Politics in Australia* (Crows Nest: ABC Books, 1994).

119 L. Godden and J. Peel, 'The Environment Protection and Biodiversity Conservation Act 1999 (Cth): Dark Sides of Virtue' *Melbourne University Law Review* 31 (2007): 106–45.

states and territories retained the bulk of power to impose detailed controls on land use and natural resource management.[120]

The 1999 Act may have been the most significant development in federal environmental law since the early 1970s, but critics argued that it was a missed opportunity to expand Commonwealth involvement in environmental regulation and conservation. Consequently, the overall mood towards the practice of environmental law turned pessimistic. As Stephen Dovers and conservation biologist David Lindenmayer had already observed in 1997, '[d]espite strong messages from the scientific and policy literature and from national and international policy, instructing us to do far more than before, governments are, in at least some cases, actually doing less'.[121] The 1999 Act was more a symptom than the cause of this retreat. During the 1990s, both state and federal governments had increasingly opted for deregulation and economic instruments with the aim of removing impediments to development and freeing up markets.[122] This 'enduring developmentalist ethos of government', as Tim Bonyhady argued in 1999, was serving to erode the environmental protections that both state and federal legislation had enacted since the 1970s. In New South Wales and elsewhere, the commitment to ESD, legislative or otherwise, had quickly become more rhetorical than real.[123]

Although the Coalition had sought to devolve its environmental obligations to the states, the courts soon found that it had failed to do so. In 2001, the Federal Court in *Booth v Bosworth* established the potential for more expansive environmental impact assessment at the Commonwealth level, extending beyond the site-specific impacts of proposals to impacts which took effect beyond the area of the activity.[124] This case concerned the effects of the operation of an electrified grid – installed on a lychee farm to protect the fruit from the flying fox – on the populations of flying foxes inhabiting the nearby Wet Tropics World Heritage Area in Queensland.[125] In 2004, in the *Nathan Dam Case*, the Full Court of the Federal Court of Australia further expanded the potential for the 1999 Act to extend to the indirect impacts of development proposals on 'matters of national

120 C. McGrath, 'One Stop Shop for Environmental Approvals A Messy Backward Step for Australia' *Environmental and Planning Law Journal* 31 (2014): 164–91.

121 S. R. Dovers and D. Lindenmayer, 'Managing the Environment: Rhetoric, Policy and Reality' *Australian Journal of Public Administration* 56 (1997): 66.

122 E. Papadakis and R. Grant, 'The Politics of "light handed regulation": New Environmental Policy Instruments in Australia' *Environmental Politics* 12 (2003): 25–50; Bonyhady, 'The Disappointment of the Law', 468–9.

123 Ibid, 468. 124 [2001] FCA 1453 (17 October 2001) (Branson J).

125 Godden and Peel, 'The Environment Protection and Biodiversity Conservation Act', 126.

environmental significance'.[126] Concerned that a dam near Taroom, on the Dawson River in central Queensland, could impact downstream 'matters of national environmental significance', such as the Great Barrier Reef World Heritage Area, the Queensland Conservation Council challenged the decision of the Commonwealth Environment Minister that any such impacts fell outside the scope of the provisions of the Act. The Full Federal Court rejected the minister's narrow construction of relevant impacts and held that the notion of 'impact' could include indirect consequences reasonably within the proponent's knowledge, such as (in this case) farmers' use of the dam's water for irrigation.[127]

In response to this broadening scope of environmental impact assessment required under the Act as interpreted by the courts, the Coalition government proposed a raft of amendments to streamline the EPBC Act. Environmental law scholars Lee Godden and Jacqueline Peel interpreted these 2006 amendments as the product of the government's 'overriding concern that the EPBC Act ought to be more developer-friendly'.[128] Whether too friendly or not, as Chris McGrath has pointed out, it is in state and territory planning, mining and petroleum laws that the bulk of controls on land use and natural resource management reside. In 2008–9 alone, he noted, the EPBC Act referrals represented less than 0.2 per cent of the number of development applications under state and territory planning laws.[129] Nevertheless, the rise of the coal seam gas industry and concerns about its potential impact on agricultural lands and local groundwater systems prompted federal intervention and the expansion of the EPBC Act.[130] The Gillard Labor government amended the EPBC Act in 2013, adding the 'water trigger', which requires that coal seam gas proposals likely to impact significantly on water resources be referred to the Commonwealth for environmental approval.[131]

With the return of the Coalition to federal government came a renewed effort to restrict the capacity of environmental groups to challenge major developments under the Act. This move was a response to what the government described as 'green lawfare', such as the successful appeal against the

126 *Minister for the Environment and Heritage v Queensland Conservation Council Inc* [2004] FCAFC 190 (30 July 2004) (Black CJ, Ryan and Finn JJ).

127 Ibid, 126–7. 128 Ibid, 122. 129 McGrath, 'One Stop Shop', 165.

130 M. Roarty, *The Development of Australia's Coal Seam Gas Resources* (Canberra: Department of Parliamentary Services, 2011).

131 J. Gray, 'Trans-jurisdictional Water Law and Governance in the Context of Unconventional Gas Mining: The Australian Experience', in J. Gray, C. Holley and R. Rayfuse (eds), *Trans-jurisdictional Water Law and Governance* (New York: Routledge, 2016), 218.

approval of the new Carmichael Coal Mine in Queensland.[132] In January 2015 the Mackay Conservation Group had appealed to the Federal Court against the federal Environment Minister's decision to approve the mine. During the proceedings, the parties found that the minister had failed to follow the conservation advice for matters of national environmental significance in relation to two listed threatened species, the yakka skink and the ornamental snake.[133] Despite subsequent judicial reviews (again in 2015 and then in 2019), both the state and federal governments have given the controversial coal mine environmental approval to proceed.[134] Indeed, the vast majority of activities referred for federal environmental impact assessment are ultimately approved, frequently relying on the controversial mechanism of 'biodiversity offsets' to counter anticipated losses.[135]

Entirely separate to the EPBC Act, the Commonwealth has come to play a significantly greater role in the nation's water management law, and policy, again prompted by prevailing environmental conditions. As the Millennium Drought (1996–2010) continued to exact a severe socio-economic and ecological toll on the Murray-Darling Basin in the south-east of the continent, the Howard Coalition government undertook to address the management of water resources in the region. With its Water Act 2007, the federal government built on nearly two decades of intergovernmental attempts to address problems such as salinity, over-allocation of water resources, and environmental degradation in the Basin, while protecting the priorities of the states.[136] The Act set out

132 R. Pepper, 'Ms Onus and Mr Neal: Agitators in an Age of "green lawfare"' *AIAL Forum* 90 (2017): 52–64; C. Clark, 'The Politics of Public Interest Environmental Litigation: Lawfare in Australia' *Australian Environment Review* 31 (2016): 258–62; C. McGrath, 'Myth Drives Australian Government Attack on Standing and Environmental "Lawfare"' *Environmental and Planning Law Journal* 33 (2016): 3–20.

133 A. McIntosh, H. Roberts and A. Constable, 'An Empirical Evaluation of Environmental Citizen Suits under the Environment Protection and Biodiversity Conservation Act 1999 (Cth)' *Sydney Law Review* 39 (2017): 85–121.

134 *Australian Conservation Foundation Incorporated v Minister for the Environment* [2016] FCA 1042 (29 August 2016) (Griffiths J); *Australian Conservation Foundation Incorporated v Minister for the Environment and Energy* [2017] FCAFC 124 (25 August 2017) (Dowsett, McKerracher and Robertson JJ).

135 M. S. Ward, J. S. Simmonds, A. E. Reside et al., 'Lots of Loss with Little Scrutiny: the Attrition of Habitat Critical for Threatened Species in Australia' *Conservation Science and Practice* 1 (2019): e117; K. Miller, J. Trezise, S. Kraus, K. Dripps and M. Evans, 'The Development of the Australian Environmental Offsets Policy: From Theory to Practice' *Environmental Conservation* 42 (2015): 306–14.

136 P. Kildea and G. Williams, 'The Constitution and the Management of Water in Australia's Rivers' *Sydney Law Review* 32 (2010): 595–616; D. Connell, 'The Role of the Commonwealth Environmental Holder', in D. Connell and R. Q. Grafton (eds), *Basin Futures: Water Reform in the Murray-Darling Basin* (Canberra: ANU Press, 2011), 327–38.

a detailed regime for the use and management of water resources, and required the development of a 'Basin Plan' that would include sustainable diversion limits, a management plan as to water quality and salinity, and specific Basin-wide water trading rules to secure a uniform approach to the trading of water rights.[137] The Murray-Darling Basin Authority was created the following year to assume responsibility for the Basin's water management.

The basis for water trading in the Basin, the nation's largest river system, rests on the de-coupling of entitlements to water from entitlements in land. This process, of state-directed 'unbundling' had been one of the key tenets of the 1994 Council of Australian Governments (COAG) Water Directive Framework, which had brought together the neoliberal principles of competitive neutrality and user pays with ESD.[138] The COAG National Water Initiative of 2004 refined this framework: the Commonwealth offered financial incentive payments to states and territories to unbundle water rights and introduced new legislation to help facilitate trade in an attempt to move water to places where it was most highly valued.[139] This water 'market' is regulated at the state level, and functions as a licensed cap-and-trade system, whereby a specified volume of water can be extracted or diverted and allocated, on an annual basis, while still leaving enough water set aside for the environment.[140]

Critics of this approach to regulatory design, however, have argued that these kinds of structural reforms to water management to address water scarcity have focused less on sustainability than on economic instruments, such as property rights and water markets.[141] Others, too, question the extent to which the 2004 National Water Initiative facilitates the participation of Indigenous Australians in water planning, particularly in regions such as New South Wales where there is fierce competition for water.[142] The Initiative provides that Indigenous access is to be achieved principally through

137 Kildea and Williams, 'The Constitution and the Management of Water', 595–616.

138 D. Connell, S. R. Dovers and R. Q. Grafton, 'A Critical Analysis of the National Water Initiative' *Australasian Journal of Natural Resources Law and Policy* 10 (2005): 82–107. Land and water were first 'unbundled' in 1983 when South Australia created a limited water market system. See J. McKay, 'The Theory and Practice of Australian Institutional Reforms to Incorporate Water Markets in Integrated Water Resources Management', in J. Maestu (ed.), *Water Trading and Global Water Scarcity: International Experiences* (New York: Routledge, 2013), 259.

139 Gray, 'Trans-jurisdictional Water Law', 219.

140 J. Horne and R. Q. Grafton, 'The Australian Water Markets Story: Incremental Transformation', in J. Luetjens, M. Mintrom and P. 't Hart (eds), *Successful Public Policy: Lessons from Australia and New Zealand* (Canberra: ANU Press, 2019), 165–90.

141 Connell et al., 'A Critical Analysis', 81.

142 P-L. Tan and S. Jackson, 'Impossible Dreaming: Does Australia's Water Law and Policy Fulfil Indigenous Aspirations?' *Environmental and Planning Law Journal* 30 (2013): 132–49; L. Hartwig, S. Jackson and N. Osborne, 'Trends in Aboriginal Water

planning processes that take into account the possible existence of native title rights to water in the catchment or aquifer area, as well as for any water allocated to Indigenous people for 'traditional cultural purposes'.[143] However, the slow pace of native title determination and the limited nature of consultation between state agencies and Indigenous peoples on matters of water planning, have proven to be among the issues that have hindered specific allocations to Indigenous Australians.[144] Despite the Native Title Act 1993, which established a form of native title where traditional lands are occupied in accordance with traditional laws and customs, in the Murray-Darling Basin, as elsewhere, native title rights have not been extended to water, and any grants of access to water for cultural purposes remain limited.[145]

Conclusion

At the time of writing, the nation's environmental legislation is under renewed scrutiny. The interim report on the EPBC Act, published in June 2020, was damning. Independent Reviewer Graeme Samuel declared in this report, '[t]he operation of the Act is dated and inefficient, and it is not fit to manage current or future environmental challenges, particularly in light of climate change'.[146] Moreover, he surmised, '[t]he EPBC Act does not position the Commonwealth to protect the environment and Australia's iconic places in the national interest'.[147] Further still, the report found, the Act has failed properly to include the knowledge and practices of Indigenous peoples in environmental management. Samuel's interim report recommended wholesale reform of the national environmental law, with legally binding and enforceable National Environmental Standards that articulate clearly defined and specific rules for decision-making. The extent to which the Morrison Coalition Government attends to these recommendations and arrests the 'overall state of decline' of Australia's natural environment remains to be seen.[148]

Meanwhile, in the wake of drought, algal blooms, fish kills, problematic Commonwealth buy-backs and the exposure of water theft, the management of the Murray-Darling Basin has also been subject to intensive review. An

Ownership in New South Wales, Australia: The Continuities between Colonial and Neoliberal Forms of Dispossession' *Land Use Policy* 99 (2020): 104869.

143 Tan and Jackson, 'Impossible Dreaming', 134. 144 Ibid, 137–9. 145 Ibid, 140.

146 G. Samuel, *Independent Review of the EPBC Act: Interim Report* (Canberra: Dept. of Agriculture, Water and the Environment, 2020), iii.

147 Ibid. 148 Ibid, 3.

independent assessment of social and economic conditions in the Basin called for the pace of water recovery to slow so that local communities could better cope with changes. In addition, the independent panel sought urgent change to improve the socio-economic circumstances of the Basin's First Nations peoples, with policy reform and additional resources to support their access to water for cultural, environmental and economic uses.[149] Just as this independent panel released its final report in early September 2020, the Wentworth Group of Concerned Scientists presented its own worrying findings. The Group found that since 2012, 20 per cent of the water expected each year under the Murray-Darling Basin Plan did not flow past key sites, such as Ramsar wetlands. Poor enforcement, inadequate modelling and more efficient irrigation infrastructure numbered among the possible reasons for this shortfall.[150] These findings alone point to the ways in which the implementation of the Murray-Darling Basin Plan, a legislatively mandated tool of the Water Act 2007, has proved 'little short of catastrophic'.[151]

After the Savage Summer of 2019/20, during which fires burned an unprecedented area of land across New South Wales, Victoria, Queensland, South Australia, the Australian Capital Territory and Western Australia, both state and federal governments have undertaken inquiries into bushfire management. In August 2020, the Berejiklian Liberal government accepted all seventy-six recommendations of the independent inquiry in New South Wales, which included compulsory land clearing, water bombing and hazard-reduction burning.[152] Since then, the Royal Commission into National Natural Disaster Arrangements (known as the Commonwealth 'Bushfires Royal Commission') has published its own interim observations. Improving the consistency and clarity of the plethora of Commonwealth, state and territory legislation pertaining to critical infrastructure was just one of over a 100 observations relating to disaster-preparedness as Australia 'increasingly faces cascading, concurrent and compounding natural disasters'.[153]

149 R. Sefton et al., *Final Report: Independent Assessment of Social and Economic Conditions in the Murray-Darling Basin* (Melbourne: Panel for Independent Assessment of Social and Economic Conditions in the Murray-Darling Basin, 2020), 11.

150 M. Colloff et al., *Assessment of River Flows in the Murray-Darling Basin: Observed Versus Expected Flows under the Basin Plan, 2012–2019* (Sydney: Wentworth Group of Concerned Scientists, 2020).

151 J. Gray, '"Thieves, shady deals and murder": Water Theft, Buy Backs and Fish Kills in the Murray Darling Basin of Australia', in L. Westra, K. Bosselmann and M. Fermeglia (eds), *Ecological Integrity in Science and Law* (Cham: Springer, 2020), 38.

152 D. Owens and M. O'Kane, *Final Report of the NSW Bushfire Inquiry, 31 July 2020* (Sydney: Dept. of Premier and Cabinet, 2020).

153 Royal Commission into National Natural Disaster Arrangements, *Interim Observations, 31 August 2020* (Canberra: Royal Commission, 2020), 14.

As the Australian economy continues to remain vulnerable to global instability and insecurity, and the prospect of recession, it is timely to reflect on Tim Bonyhady's assessment of environmental protection in the wake of the Global Financial Crisis of 2008. Back then he observed, 'governments sacrifice the environment when the economy is in decline'. 'Recessions', he added, 'lead not just to financial collapse but environmental races to the bottom'.[154] Hindered by political expediency, a fragmented system of environmental protection, an enduring ethos of developmentalism, and endemic short-sightedness, as this chapter has shown, Australia's state, territory and federal environmental law has proven to be relatively weak in restraining this reckless pattern. As long as there are spoils for the spoilers, it seems, Australia's lands and waters, its flora and fauna, its minerals and airs are ripe for the taking.

154 T. Bonyhady, 'Introduction', in T. Bonyhady and A. Macintosh (eds), *Mills, Mines and Other Controversies* (Sydney: Federation Press, 2010), 2.

V

SOCIAL ORGANISATION

18

Colonial Law and its Control of Aboriginal and Torres Strait Islander Families

TERRI LIBESMAN, KATHERINE ELLINGHAUS AND PAUL GRAY

My last memory of her for many years was her waving pathetically, as we waved back and called out goodbye to her, but we were too far away for her to hear us. I heard years later how after watching us go out of her life, she wandered away from the police station three miles along the road leading out of the town to Moonahculla. She was worn out, with no food or money, her apron still on. She wandered off the road to rest in the long grass under a tree. That is where old Uncle and Aunt found her the next day ... They found our mother still moaning and crying. They heard the sounds and thought it was an animal in pain.[1]

This chapter summarises the relentless efforts of settler law-makers in Australia to undermine Aboriginal and Torres Strait Islander families from the early nineteenth century to the present day. Disrupting Aboriginal and Torres Strait Islander families was a goal that was not (at first) directly articulated by the British. Nevertheless, the attack on Aboriginal and Torres Strait Islander families by settler law was a constant feature of Australian settler-colonialism from the point of invasion, underpinned by pervasive notions of white supremacy and an all-encompassing lack of understanding, knowledge and respect for Aboriginal and Torres Strait Islander humanity, kinship and culture. This chapter addresses how, through the eras of protection, assimilation, integration, self-determination, and in recent policies of privatisation and 'permanency', settler law has been both peculiarly focused on and destructive of Aboriginal and Torres Strait Islander families. Through these laws, the settler state has made the disappearance of Aboriginal and Torres Strait Islander peoples a cornerstone of establishing

[1] Margaret Tucker, *If Everyone Cared: Autobiography of Margaret Tucker M.B.E.* (Sydney: Ure Smith 1977), 94.

their settler nation on Indigenous land.[2] We argue that child removal has been the most destructive and enduring function of settler law since colonisation.

The written archive and the body of settler law outlines a chilling record of the many complex ways in which Australian colonies, territories and governments dismembered Aboriginal and Torres Strait Islander families. It is important to note, however, that the actions of the state are only one aspect of this story. This chapter cannot fully describe the lived experiences of Aboriginal and Torres Strait Islander families, such as the pain of Yorta Yorta activist Margaret Tucker's mother quoted at the beginning. Aboriginal and Torres Strait Islander people continue to share their stories in many forums, including the National Inquiry into the Separation of Aboriginal and Torres Strait Islander Children from their Families, and public education programs led by Aboriginal and Torres Strait Islander communities.[3] We do aim, however, to convey the laws that authorised such pain. We also endeavour to outline how these laws both reflect and reinforce racist assumptions that imagine Aboriginal and Torres Strait Islander families to be inferior or inherently harmful, and their children in need of 'rescue' by settler society and culture. Despite these harmful laws enacted over numerous generations, Aboriginal and Torres Strait Islander communities have survived, strengthened by enduring bonds to community, Country and culture, and continue to resist settler control and intervention in their families and communities.[4] We begin this chapter by acknowledging the pain, courage and resistance of Aboriginal and Torres Strait Islander families that have been a constant feature of the Australian story since 1788.

Early Child Removal (1788 to the 1860s)

Settler attacks on Aboriginal and Torres Strait Islander families pre-dated settler laws that would later enable child removal and family separation.[5] Historian Anna Haebich has noted the first recorded removal of an

[2] Eve Tuck and K. Wayne Yang, 'Decolonization Is Not a Metaphor' *Decolonization: Indigeneity, Education and Society* 1, no. 1 (2012): 1–40; Sana Nakata, 'The Re-Making of Nation and Indigenous Australian Children' *Australian Journal of Public Administration* 76, no. 4 (2017): 397–9.

[3] See, for example, the Mobile Education Centre developed by Kinchela Boys Home Aboriginal Corporation, https://kinchelaboyshome.org.au/what-we-do/education-program/, accessed 9 December 2021.

[4] Sally Babidge, Pamela J. Stewart and Andrew Strathern, *Aboriginal Family and the State: The Conditions of History* (Abingdon and New York: Routledge, 2016), 67.

[5] 'Bringing Them Home', *Report of the National Inquiry into the Separation of Aboriginal and Torres Strait Islander Children from Their Families Report*, 1997 www.humanrights.gov.au/sites/default/files/content/pdf/social_justice/bringing_them_home_report.pdf, accessed 28 December 2019, part 2, page 2.

Aboriginal or Torres Strait Islander child, by the Government Surgeon Dr Jacob Mountgarrett, who removed a two-year-old boy (as well as several bodies for dissection) following an 1804 massacre of Moomairremener people.[6] Evident in these early instances of removal, Haebich argues 'was the denial of Aboriginal humanity in the presumption of the colonists prerogative to take and keep the children and to recast their identities to fit the culture of their new masters'.[7] Haebich also shows the baser drives behind this removal, noting for example that the presence of an Aboriginal or Torres Strait Islander child companion 'created an illusion of the status conferred on wealthy slave owners and European aristocracy by their "sable valets" and "body servants", popular in eighteenth-century Europe'. In return the children cost the colonists little to obtain and to keep: being 'part of the family' generally meant cheap clothes, little food and no pay.[8] In this early period there were no controls over how abducted children were treated. Children were exploited for sex or labour; and there was little possibility of their captors being taken to court for physical or sexual abuse. Extra-legal child removal by soldiers, convicts and private citizens, sanctioned by neither the colony nor the metropole, continued with impunity throughout the eighteenth and nineteenth centuries and well into the twentieth century.[9]

The phenomenon of British colonists abducting Aboriginal and Torres Strait Islander children took place in the context of the harsh treatment of impoverished and neglected children across the British Empire in the belief that their removal from perceived negative influences gave them a chance to reform. This rescue narrative, along with notions of racial superiority, resulted in an intense focus on intervening in the lives of Aboriginal and Torres Strait Islander children. As early as 1814, missionary William Shelley persuaded Governor Macquarie to open a Native Institution in Port Jackson. Established in 1815, it set the 'Australian template of Aboriginal education' by separating children from their families on the expectation that, as historian Peter Read described it, 'the Aboriginal infant mind, removed from the contaminating influence of its own society, was to become the blackboard upon which the European secrets were to be written'.[10] The 1837 Report of the Parliamentary Select Committee

[6] Anna Haebich, *Broken Circles: Fragmenting Indigenous Families, 1800–2000* (Fremantle: Fremantle Arts Centre Press, 2000), 65–6.

[7] Ibid. [8] Ibid, 79.

[9] Kath (Apma) Travis Penangke, *Minnie, Mum and Me: The Black Headed Snake* (Melbourne: Self-Published, 2019).

[10] Peter Read, 'Shelley's Mistake: The Parramatta Native Institution and the Stolen Generations', in Martin Crotty and David Roberts (eds), *The Great Mistakes of Australian History* (Sydney: University of New South Wales Press, 2006), 33.

on Aboriginal Tribes (British settlements) echoed this focus on children, proposing that 'the education of the young will of course be among the foremost of the cares of the missionaries'.[11] In early New South Wales, 'Missions and early government institutions provided incentives, in the form of food supplies, blankets and other European goods, for families struggling with the impact of colonisation to leave their children in school'.[12] Before any legislation targeted Aboriginal and Torres Strait Islander peoples explicitly, settler law permitted the removal of Indigenous children through Children's Welfare Acts whereby 'neglected' or 'criminal' children could be placed in service or in industrial or reformatory schools – tools to which modern Australian states have reverted.[13] Meanwhile, settler violence, particularly by European men, split families through murder, rape and abduction. Because missionaries focused on children as the easiest converts, missions could be devastating for Aboriginal families. Missions were places where children were at risk of removal and where families were sometimes physically separated from each other in separate dormitories. Some missionaries kidnapped children, including the Church Missionary Society mission to the Wiradjuri in Wellington Valley, New South Wales, in the 1830s and 1840s.[14]

Protection and Families (1860s to the 1960s)

In the nineteenth century and well into the twentieth, a discourse of 'protection' justified settler law-makers' attacks on the integrity of Aboriginal and Torres Strait Islander families. The ideology of protection traversed colonial sites from the Caribbean, to New Zealand, the Cape Colony and eventually Australia, beginning with the arrival of specially appointed 'protectors' in the Port Phillip District (later Victoria) in 1839.[15] In Victoria the efforts of these early protectors caused limited damage to Aboriginal family groups. These

[11] Report of the Parliamentary Select Committee on Aboriginal Tribes (British settlements). Reprinted, with Comments, by the 'Aborigines Protection Society', 1837, 127; Andrew Armitage, *Comparing the Policy of Aboriginal Assimilation: Australia, Canada and New Zealand* (Vancouver: UBC Press, 1995), 204.

[12] Ibid, 42.

[13] See, for example, Neglected and Criminal Children's Act 1864 (Vic). For a comprehensive list of state, territory and colonial legislation enabling Aboriginal and Torres Strait Islander children see https://aiatsis.gov.au/collections/collections-online/digitised-collections/remove-and-protect, accessed 9 December 2021.

[14] Laura Rademaker, *Found in Translation: Many Meanings on a North Australian Mission* (Honolulu: University of Hawai'i Press, 2018), 22.

[15] Alan Lester and Fae Dussart, 'Trajectories of Protection: Protectorates of Aborigines in Early Nineteenth-century Australia and Aotearoa New Zealand' *New Zealand Geographer* 64 (2008): 205–20.

men were unable to curtail family mobility and were forced in some cases to travel with them and observe rather than engage in disruption and regulation of their lifestyle. For this (and other) reasons, as Rachel Standfield has shown, these early experiments were seen as failures.[16] Elsewhere, though, they were more impactful.[17]

At the turn of the century, colonial Australian governments began to enact legislative mechanisms to continue their surveillance and control of Aboriginal and Torres Strait Islander people. These Acts almost all had the word 'Protect' in their title. Protection meant safeguarding Indigenous peoples from settler violence, but the Acts did much broader work. While the powers delegated to Chief Protectors, protectors, police and (later) welfare officers varied significantly, they broadly conferred significant powers to intervene in the lives of Aboriginal and Torres Strait Islander families.[18] As Amanda Nettelbeck has shown, as settlers increasingly depended on Aboriginal labour, protection legislation also increasingly focused on stringently controlling regulations between colonial employers and their Aboriginal workers.[19] Protection Acts ignored the wider relationships that defined Aboriginal and Torres Strait Islander families and actively severed the continuity between generations by separating family members. They specifically undermined the ability of Aboriginal and Torres Strait Islander families to stay together in three ways; by giving administrators powers to remove children, controlling relationships and defining Aboriginality in ways that physically divided families.

A number of motivations caused colonial governments to exercise ever-increasing powers to strike at the heart of the Aboriginal and Torres Strait Islander family: children.[20] These included: the sense that children were assimilable and better off away from their families; the idea that children were somehow 'neglected' or abandoned; and assumptions that removing children would promote biological absorption and assimilation once they grew up and formed bonds outside their communities.[21] In Victoria, the First Report of the Central Board Appointed to Watch over the Interests of the

[16] Rachel Standfield, '"The Vacillating Manners and Sentiments of These People": Mobility, Civilisation and Dispossession in the Work of William Thomas with the Port Phillip Aboriginal Protectorate' *Law, Text, Culture* 15 (2011): 162–84.

[17] Samuel Furphy and Amanda Nettelbeck (eds), *Aboriginal Protection and Its Intermediaries in Britain's Antipodean Colonies* (Abingdon: Routledge, 2019).

[18] Haebich, *Broken Circles*, 148.

[19] Nettelbeck, Chapter 20 in this volume; Amanda Nettelbeck, *Indigenous Rights and Colonial Subjecthood: Protection and Reform in the Nineteenth-century British Empire* (Cambridge: Cambridge University Press, 2019), 171.

[20] Nakata, 'The Re-Making' 397–9.

[21] See 'Bringing Them Home'.

Aborigines in the Colony declared that there were 'many neglected black and half-caste children throughout the Colony, who are utterly uncared for, and in all probability, if steps be not taken to rescue them, they will become as idle and as depraved as the worst examples among the white population'.[22] In his affidavit written in support of Lorna Cubillo and Peter Gunner, Aboriginal plaintiffs who were suing the federal government for their forced removal from their families and communities, Peter Read found in the Northern Territory legislation 'some thirty justifications for separating part-Aboriginal children . . . These included the stated need for domestic labour, to "breed out the colour", to prevent "half-caste" boys menacing society and girls from becoming prostitutes, to make them fit for absorption, and to fulfill their national destiny of institutionalisation and absorption.'[23]

While each state/colony had different policies, there were common themes. The first Protection Act, passed in Victoria in 1869, allowed the governor to make regulations and orders '[f]or the care, custody and education of the children of Aborigines'.[24] The 1886 'Half-Caste' Act extended this, allowing the governor to make orders '[f]or the transfer of any half-caste child being an orphan to the care of the Department for neglected children or any institutions within the said colony for orphan children'.[25] A review of letters from Aboriginal women in Victoria to missionaries and government officials from the 1860s to the 1920s noted that one of the greatest concerns raised was the well-being of their children and families, testifying to the extensive separation of Aboriginal families in this period of history.[26]

The first Protection Act passed in New South Wales in 1909 conferred on the Board the duty 'to provide for the custody, maintenance, and education of the children of aborigines' and gave it the power to apprentice Aboriginal children (aged over fourteen and under twenty-one).[27] Peter Read argued that in New South Wales the Board drove the legislation, rather than the other way around. Soon after the 1909 Act was passed, the Board complained

[22] *First Report of the Central Board Appointed to Watch over the Interests of the Aborigines in the Colony* (Melbourne: Government Printer, 1861), 11.

[23] Peter Read, 'The Stolen Generations, the Historian, and the Court Room' *Aboriginal History* 26 (2002): 54.

[24] An Act to Provide for the Protection and Management of the Aboriginal Natives of Victoria 1869 (Vic), clause 2.

[25] An Act to amend an Act entitled 'An Act to Provide for the Protection and Management of the Aboriginal Natives of Victoria' 1886 (Vic), clause 8.

[26] Elizabeth Nelson, Sandra Smith and Patricia Grimshaw (eds), *Letters from Aboriginal Women of Victoria, 1867–1926* (Parkville: History Department, University of Melbourne, 2002), 25.

[27] Aborigines Protection Act 1909 (NSW), clauses 7 and 11.

that their powers to remove children were inadequate. In 1915 the government 'rewarded' the Board with an amendment that permitted the removal of Aboriginal children without parental consent, if the Board considered it to be in the interest of the child's 'moral or physical welfare'. This invested significant powers in officials, without judicial oversight. Read noted that the 'racial intention was obvious enough for all prepared to see, and some managers cut a long story short when they came to that part of the committal notice, "Reason for Board taking control of the child". They simply wrote, "being Aboriginal".'[28]

In Queensland the earliest Act giving the state the power to remove 'neglected' children or those convicted of a criminal offence to an industrial or reformatory school gave seven reasons why a child might be deemed neglected – the seventh being that they were 'born of an aboriginal or half-caste mother'.[29] The Act, passed in 1897, gave the governor the power to provide 'for the transfer of any half-caste child, being an orphan, or deserted by its parents, to an orphanage' and to prescribe the 'conditions on which any aboriginal or half-caste children may be apprenticed to, or placed in service with, suitable persons'.[30] Queensland was arguably the most extreme in its drive to permanently segregate Aboriginal families and only began to relinquish control with great reluctance from the 1970s.[31] In 1886, the first protection legislation passed in Western Australia established a Board to advise the governor of 'proposals or suggestions relating to the care, custody, or education of the children of Aboriginals' and allowed magistrates to apprentice children for a period of indenture until they turned twenty-one years.[32] An 1897 Act established an Aborigines Department, which had, as one of its duties, the 'custody, maintenance, and education of the children of Aborigines'.[33] A 1905 Act enabled the governor to detain any child in an institution or orphanage or place them into service.[34]

[28] Aborigines Protection Amending Act 1915 (NSW); Peter Read, *A Rape of the Soul So Profound: The Return of the Stolen Generations* (St Leonards: Allen & Unwin, 1999), 54.

[29] An Act to provide for the establishment of Industrial and Reformatory Schools 1865 (Qld), clause 6.

[30] Aboriginals Protection and Restriction of the Sale of Opium Act, 1897 (Qld), clause 31.

[31] Haebich, *Broken Circles*, 173.

[32] An Act to provide for the better protection and management of the Aboriginal Natives of Western Australia, and to amend the Law relating to certain Contracts with such Aboriginal Natives, 1886 (WA), clauses 6 and 36.

[33] An Act to further amend the Constitution Act of 1889, and for the better Protection of the Aboriginal Race of Western Australia, 1897 (WA), clause 7.

[34] An Act to make provision for the better protection and care of the Aboriginal inhabitants of Western Australia, 1905 (WA), clause 60.

In South Australia an 1844 Act allowed two justices to indenture any 'Aboriginal or half-caste child' as an apprentice without the consent of parents and made the Protector of the Aborigines of South Australia the legal guardian of 'every half-caste and other unprotected Aboriginal child'.[35] The Aborigines Act of 1911 made the Chief Protector the legal guardian of 'every aboriginal and every half-caste child, notwithstanding that any such child has a parent or other relative living, until such child attains the age of twenty-one years' and conferred extraordinary powers to decide where Aboriginal people may live and to move them around the state.[36] The Northern Territory was under South Australia's jurisdiction until 1911, when an Ordinance of that year set up its own regime of child removals. This Ordinance gave the Chief Protector wide-ranging powers 'to undertake the care, custody, or control of any aboriginal or half-caste if in his opinion it is necessary or desirable in the interests of the aboriginal or half-caste for him to do so'.[37] In 1953 a new Ordinance gave the Director of Welfare extensive powers to move (and to authorise others to move) people defined as 'wards' around the Territory and beyond it, but tried to limit those powers if it would mean the separation of children under the age of fourteen from their parents.[38] Finally, in Tasmania a series of laws giving powers over destitute children were passed from 1867, but because of the official fiction that there were no Aboriginal people in that state, there were no targeted Acts except for the Cape Barren Island Reserve Act 1912, which made no particular mention of children.[39]

In addition to the removal of children, protection legislation also actively disrupted Aboriginal and Torres Strait Islander families through the definitions of Aboriginality they imposed. Ideas about descent and blood quantum were applied by self-interested colonisers in a failed attempt to define out of existence populations whose ongoing presence challenged the legitimacy of the settler state and to whom they had an obligation to give financial support.[40]

[35] An Ordinance to provide for the Protection, Maintenance, and Up-bringing of Orphans and other Destitute Children of the Aborigines, 1844 (SA), clauses 1 and 5.

[36] An Act to make provision for the better Protection and Control of the Aboriginal and Half-caste In-habitants of the State of South Australia, 1911, clauses 10 and 17.

[37] Aboriginals Ordinance, 1911 (NT), clause 3.

[38] An Ordinance to Provide for the Care and Assistance of Certain Persons, 1953 (NT), clause 21.

[39] Although see for example, An Act to provide for the Establishment in Tasmania of Institutions for the Industrial Training and Benefit of Vagrant Children and Youthful Offenders, 1867 (Tasmania).

[40] Katherine Ellinghaus, *Blood Will Tell: Native Americans and Assimilation Policy* (Lincoln, NE: University of Nebraska Press, 2017).

These definitions also worked as a way of splitting families. The 'caste' system ('full blood', 'half-caste', 'quadroon', 'octoroon') divided families across generations, defining some generations as Aboriginal (and therefore 'under the Act') and some not. Such classifications determined whether Aboriginal people were eligible to live on government-controlled reserves or stations. In New South Wales, for example, Heather Goodall recounts how the 1909 Act allowed the Board to 'turn those judged not to be "Aboriginal enough" off reserves' where their families resided.[41]

Some protection legislation removed the right of Aboriginal and Torres Strait Islander people to choose their own spouses. Queensland, Western Australia and the Northern Territory at times made the marriage of an Aboriginal woman to a non-Aboriginal man dependent on the permission of a government official. In the Northern Territory and Western Australia in the 1920s and 1930s, Chief Protectors Cecil E. Cook and Augustus O. Neville, enthusiastically used these clauses to encourage biological absorption.[42] South Australia, New South Wales and Victoria never included clauses making the marriages of Aboriginal women dependent on the approval of a protector. Nevertheless, government officials were able to control marriages in these states through their powers to remove people from missions and stations and deny them rations. In Victoria, managers of the various stations and reserves wrote to the Chief Protector asking permission for particular marriages to take place. Indeed, by 1910 it had become the 'custom of the Managers to inform the Board when Aborigines intend to be married, and to ask whether it will consent, as well as allow the couple to live at the station'.[43]

The case of Elsie Barrett shows how deeply protection legislation allowed government officials to control Aboriginal women's sexuality and their choices of partners. In 1914, sixteen year-old Elsie Barrett was removed from Lake Tyers mission, by a policeman and a 'female attendant' to a Salvation Army Home in West Brunswick, Melbourne. The Victorian Board for the Protection of Aborigines kept Elsie in the home for seven years, despite the efforts of her mother and grandfather to convince them to release her. Elsie had been removed because she had formed a relationship

[41] Heather Goodall, *Rivers and Resilience: Aboriginal People on Sydney's Georges River* (Sydney: University of NSW Press, 2008), 136.

[42] Katherine Ellinghaus, 'Absorbing the Aboriginal Problem: Controlling Marriage in Australia in the Late Nineteenth and Early Twentieth Century' *Aboriginal History* 27 (2003): 185–209.

[43] Memo to H. P. Keogh, 14 March 1910, Item 8, B329, Central Board for the Protection of Aborigines Correspondence Files, NAAV.

with a man who was labelled a 'half-caste' and was thus seen as ineligible to live at the mission. Jessica Horton argues that Elsie was not removed because of neglect or assimilation; rather, 'Elsie was removed and segregated for disciplinary reasons, including the desire to discipline her family and the mission community at large' for non-compliance with white mission standards of sexual propriety.[44]

Finally, some protection legislation created a legal identity – 'exemption' – which also had a profound impact on Aboriginal and Torres Strait Islander families. Protection legislation in Queensland (1897), Western Australia (1905), Northern Territory (1936), South Australia (1939) and New South Wales (1943) offered some Aboriginal and Torres Strait Islander people 'exemption' from the various controls over their lives imposed by protection legislation. These policies were operational until the shift of the responsibility for Aboriginal affairs from state governments to the federal government in the 1960s.[45] As Sally Babidge has argued, exemption introduced a 'hegemony of the ideal Aboriginal Australian, the state produced good types of Aboriginal persons at the same time as it was attempting to eliminate less desirable "types."'[46] Successful applicants had to demonstrate assimilative behaviour, including living in nuclear families, and standards of dress, hygiene and behaviour deemed acceptable by settler society. Exemption presented Aboriginal people with improved opportunities to escape stringent government control and improve their prosperity, including employment and education, the right to drink in hotels, and greater freedom to marry and to rear their own children. However, this was tempered by the requirement that exempted people live away from reserves and missions, and seek permission to visit or even cease contact with family, friends and community who were not exempt. This resulted in exemptees and their families experiencing varying levels of separation and dislocation from their communities across generations.[47]

[44] Jessica Horton 'The Case of Elsie Barrett: Aboriginal Women, Sexuality and the Victorian Board for the Protection of Aborigines' *Journal of Australian Studies* 34, no. 1 (2010): 3. See also Nelson et al. (eds), *Letters from Aboriginal Women of Victoria*, 70–82.

[45] Aboriginals Protection and Restriction of the Sale of Opium Act, 1897 (Qld), clause 33; An Act to make provision for the better protection and care of the Aboriginal inhabitants of Western Australia, No. 14 of 1905 (WA), clause 63; An Ordinance to Amend the Aboriginals Ordinance, 1936 (NT), clause 2; Aborigines Act Amendment Act 1939 (SA), clause 11a; New South Wales Aborigines Act (Amendment) Act, 1943, clause 18c. A new regime of exemption known as Citizenship Rights was introduced by the Natives (Citizenship Rights) Act 1944 (WA).

[46] Sally Babidge, *Aboriginal Family and the State: The Conditions of History* (Brookfield: Ashgate Publishing, 2013), 230.

[47] See Lucinda Aberdeen and Jennifer Jones *(eds), Black, White and Exempt: Aboriginal and Torres Strait Islander Lives Under Exemption* (Canberra: Aboriginal Studies Press, 2021);

Assimilation and Families (1950s to the 1960s)

The Protection era reflected settler assumptions, grounded in social Darwinism, that the Aboriginal and Torres Strait Islander population was 'inevitably doomed', and settler society should 'smooth the dying pillow' of Aboriginal and Torres Strait Islander peoples.[48] However as settler governments became aware that the Aboriginal and Torres Strait Islander population was increasing, particularly of those it described as being of mixed descent, they intensified efforts to force Aboriginal and Torres Strait Islander children into settler society under a policy of assimilation. A combination of factors led to the acceleration of Aboriginal child removal in the 1950s and 1960s, including assimilation policy, intergenerational poverty, entrenched racism within child welfare departments, a shortage of white children for adoption, a racist failure to recognise the existence, let alone value, of Aboriginal communal and extended family relations, together with a paternalistic belief that Aboriginal children should be saved from their 'wretched and un savable' Aboriginal parents.[49] These ideological beliefs and policies were both generated by and generated child welfare policy which continued a legacy of intervention in Aboriginal and Torres Strait Islander families and communities.

In 1940, New South Wales was first to implement the assimilationist welfare model. The other states followed, Queensland being the last in 1965.[50] Despite the repeal of explicitly discriminatory child welfare laws, discriminatory practices continued under state and territory welfare departments. Many senior bureaucrats and child welfare practitioners, bolstered by national assimilation policy, believed in their entitlement to remove Aboriginal and Torres Strait Islander children. Officials moved seamlessly from Aboriginal Protection Boards to child welfare departments,[51] bringing with them a culture of intervention in Aboriginal and Torres Strait Islander

Judi Wickes, '"Never Really Heard of It": The Certificate of Exemption and Lost Identity', in Peter Read, Frances Peters-Little and Anna Haebich (eds), *Indigenous Biography and Autobiography* (Canberra: ANU Press, 2008), 73–91.

48 'Bringing Them Home', 23.

49 Anna Haebich, *Spinning the Dream: Assimilation in Australia 1950–1970* (Fremantle Press, 2008), 248.

50 Aborigines Protection (Amendment) Act 1940 (NSW); Aboriginal and Torres Strait Islander Affairs Act 1965 (Qld); 'Bringing Them Home'; Robert Van Krieken, 'Rethinking Cultural Genocide: Aboriginal Child Removal and Settler Colonial State Formation' *Oceania* 75, no. 2 (2004): 125–51.

51 Andrew Armitage, *Comparing the Policy of Aboriginal Assimilation: Australia, Canada, and New Zealand* (Vancouver: University of British Columbia Press, 1995), 67; 'Bringing Them Home', 27.

families. Thus, formal legal equality provided little protection for Aboriginal families. Aboriginal and Torres Strait Islander families rarely had legal representation or any way of understanding child welfare proceedings brought before the court.[52] This made the power imbalance between departmental officers and parents all but insurmountable.

Since the 1950s, neglect – which is closely associated with poverty – has been the predominant reason for removal of Aboriginal and Torres Strait Islander children.[53] The foundations of poverty were laid with the dispossession of Aboriginal and Torres Strait Islander peoples from their lands and traditional economies, and exacerbated by the immediate and ongoing legacy of formal discrimination[54] including the exclusion of Aboriginal and Torres Strait Islander people from government supports intended to build the wealth and security of communities, particularly following World War II.[55] The failure of the state and its child welfare departments to acknowledge responsibility for systemic and structural barriers driving poverty, and therefore neglect, is reinforced by an individualised focus that facilitates the blaming of parents, in particular mothers. This culture of blame is reinforced by long-standing racial prejudices against Aboriginal and Torres Strait Islander families and communities.

While government social supports were designed to strengthen white nuclear families, the 'welfare' which Aboriginal and Torres Strait Islander people received was designed to undermine and surveil families. Mechanisms of control permeated the minutia of daily living. Heather Goodall describes housing which was 'pepper potted' within white neighbourhoods and built for nuclear rather than extended families. This served the dual purpose of surveillance by white neighbours and undermined responsibilities to fulfil kinship obligations to accommodate extended family.[56] A punitive and judgmental response to hospitality to extended family remains a contentious ground for intervention in contemporary Aboriginal family life.

52 Anna Haebich, 'Neoliberalism, Settler Colonialism and the History of Child Removal' *AILR* 19, no. 1 (2015/2016): 2.

53 Australian Institute of Health and Welfare 2001, *Australia's Welfare 2001* Canberra: Australian Government, 2001); T. Libesman and K. Cripps, 'Aboriginal and Torres Strait Islander Children's Welfare and Well-being', in L. Young, M. A. Kenny and G. Monahan (eds), *Children and the Law in Australia* (Chatswood: LexisNexis Australia, 2016), 307–36.

54 L. Behrendt, C. Cunneen, T. Libesman and N. Watson, *Aboriginal and Torres Strait Islander Legal Relations* (Oxford: Oxford University Press, 2019).

55 Haebich, *Spinning the Dream*.

56 Heather Goodall, *Invasion to Embassy: Land in Aboriginal Politics in New South Wales, 1770–1972* (Sydney: Allen and Unwin, 1996), 318.

Government decisions, to exclude Aboriginal and Torres Strait Islander peoples from social supports available to other Australians, spanned from support for home ownership[57] to maternity allowances[58] and child endowments to assist in keeping families together.[59] Inclusion of Aboriginal and Torres Strait Islander people in such social benefits was incremental; entitlement to social security benefits was finally attained in 1966.[60] Ironically however, these benefits were paid to reserve and mission managers rather than parents, supporting the institutions which separated Aboriginal and Torres Strait Islander children from their families rather than families themselves.[61]

A shift, in the late 1950s and 1960s, away from the institutionalisation of children removed from their families was influenced by contemporaneous child development theory, in particular Bowlby's theory of attachment.[62] Attachment theory emphasises the importance of stable bonds with a primary caregiver in providing the foundations for social and emotional development, with an early focus on the mother-child relationship that reflected Western perspectives and failed to grapple adequately with the implications of cultural diversity in child rearing practices, – a challenge that persists.[63] Paradoxically this shift did not reduce forced and unjustified removals of Aboriginal and Torres Strait Islander children from their families. Rather it shifted their destination to white foster and adoptive homes. Deinstitutionalisation of out-of-home care was not only driven by child development theories but also by the high cost of running children's homes, and the poor outcomes for children.[64] Aboriginal welfare boards,

57 Haebich, *Spinning the Dream*, 242–3; Rod Little, 'Two Generations of Housing in the South and Mid-west, Western Australia, 1960–95', in Peter Read (ed.), *Settlement: A History of Australian Indigenous Housing* (Canberra: Aboriginal Studies Press, 2000), 167–76.

58 M. Lake, 'A Revolution in the Family: The Challenge and Contradictions of Maternal Citizenship in Australia', in S. Koven and S. Michel (eds), *Mothers of a New World. Maternalist Politics and the Origins of Welfare States* (New York: Routledge, 1993).

59 P. Brock, 'Aboriginal Families and the Law in the Era of Segregation and Assimilation, 1890s–1950s', in D. Kirkby (ed.), *Sex, Power and Justice. Historical Perspectives of Law in Australia* (Melbourne: Oxford University Press, 1995), 133–49.

60 A. Markus, 'Legislating White Australia, 1900–1970', in D. Kirkby (ed.), *Sex, Power and Justice. Historical Perspectives of Law in Australia* (Melbourne: Oxford University Press, 1995), 237–51.

61 Haebich, *Broken Circles*, 451; H. Goodall, 'Assimilation Begins in the Home: the State and Aboriginal Women's Work as Mothers in New South Wales, 1900s to 1960s', in A. McGrath and K. Saunders (eds), *Aboriginal Workers. Special Issues of Labour History*, no. 69 (November 1995).

62 J. Bowlby, *Maternal Care and Mental Health* (Geneva: World Health Organization, 1951).

63 H. Keller, 'Attachment and Culture' *Journal of Cross-Cultural Psychology* 44, no. 2 (2013): 175–94.

64 A. Markiewicz, 'The Child Welfare System in Victoria' *Children Australia* 21, no. 3 (1996): 32–41.

which did not have sufficient resources to look after the children in their 'care', advocated for adoption, which provided a cheap and theoretically permanent solution.[65]

As a result, Australia had one of the highest rates of adoption in the world in the 1960s.[66] High rates of Indigenous adoption were supported by a popular belief in the right of suburban white married families to adopt a child to complete their family.[67] The link between adoption, white superiority and child rescue pervaded popular media, particularly in the 1950s and 1960s. Advertisements offering Aboriginal children for adoption were placed in newspapers. Debates took place in magazines, such as *Woman's Day*; adoption of Aboriginal children being portrayed in a similar manner to the adoption of stray animals.[68] It was simultaneously paternalistic, racist and fashionable to have 'little black children playing in the yard'. As welfare policies reduced the number of non-Indigenous children made available for adoption, continued demand for adoptions drove the forced adoption of Aboriginal children in an era when adoptions were closed, secretive, and generally denied – to as great an extent as possible – the existence of biological parents. Adopting Aboriginal children was easier than adopting other children, involved less, if any, scrutiny of the adopting family's home or suitability, and there was no waiting period.[69]

Despite the ease with which Aboriginal children could be fostered and adopted through child welfare legislation, child welfare departments routinely removed Aboriginal children illegally. There are also accounts of white women offering Aboriginal women things like second-hand clothes in exchange for 'informal adoption' of their baby.[70] Some settlers spoke out against such practices. In 1968, the Victorian Director of Aboriginal Affairs expressed concern about a trade in Black babies,[71] while the *Canberra Times* reported 300 Aboriginal children had been illegally adopted in Victoria.[72] Some individuals wrote letters to newspapers and magazines advocating for

[65] 'Bringing Them Home', 69.
[66] Marian Quartly and Shurlee Swain, 'The Market in Children: Analysing the Language of Adoption in Australia' *History Australia* 9, no. 2 (2012): 69–89, 81.
[67] Juliet Harper, 'Reflections on Entitlement to a Child in Australian Women's Journals,1947–1987' *Children Australia* 15, no. 4 (1990): 8–12.
[68] 'Should She Adopt an Aboriginal?', *Australian Women's Weekly*, 16 November 1960, 2; 'Their Foster Son Is an Aboriginal', *Australian Women's Weekly*, 28 August 1963, 4.
[69] Shurlee Swain, *'Homes Are Sought for These Children'*: Locating Adoption within the Australian Stolen Generations Narrative' *American Indian Quarterly* 27, nos 1–2 (2013).
[70] 'Clothes Offered for Aboriginal Baby' *Canberra Times*, 28 June 1968.
[71] Haebich, *Spinning the Dream*; Haebich, *Broken Circles*, 576.
[72] 'Aboriginal Children "Better with Parents"', *Canberra Times*, 26 June 1968.

Aboriginal parents, or raising issues with respect to the inappropriateness of inter-racial adoption.[73]

While child welfare departments flaunted unabashed exercises of power over Aboriginal and Torres Strait Islander families, Aboriginal and Torres Strait Islander parents contested and resisted removal however they could. Parents wrote to welfare departments requesting information and the return of their children. These letters were often not answered or replied to with perfunctory dismissal or lies by departmental officers. The extraordinary effort that it took for often illiterate and poverty-stricken families to pursue powerful departments is testimony to their love for their children and their determination to bring them home. While in rare cases this was successful, usually it was not.

The callous illegality of the system in this period is demonstrated by the experience of Thora Karpaney and Joe Trevorrow. Their son, Bruce Trevorrow, was removed from his family at thirteen months by stealth. On Christmas day 1957 Bruce's parents were concerned as he experienced a bad case of diarrhoea. They secured the help of a neighbour, who was able to drive Bruce to the Royal Adelaide hospital.[74] After Bruce's admission, Thora and Joe, Bruce's parents, phoned the hospital repeatedly to find out when they could bring Bruce home. They were told he was doing well but that he was not ready to come home. Thora wrote to the Aboriginal Protection Board (APB) in July 1958, 'I am writing to ask if you will let me know how baby Bruce is and how long before I can have him home as I have not forgot I got a baby in there and I would like something defenat [sic] about him this time, trust you will let me know as soon as possible'.[75] The Secretary of the APB replied that Bruce was 'making good progress but as yet the doctor does not consider him fit to go home'.[76] Bruce, after recovering quickly, had in fact been fostered to a white family more than six months earlier, on 6 January 1958.

Mrs Davis had responded to a newspaper advertisement offering Aboriginal children for adoption. The APB never assessed the Davis's suitability as foster carers and failed to check on Bruce's progress.[77] When Bruce's parents tried to find him, they experienced veiled threats from authorities

[73] Quartly and Swain, 'The Market in Children'; F. Paisley, 'Policies of Child Removal', in A. Burton (ed.), *Gender, Sexuality and Colonial Modernities* (London: Routledge, 1999); Judith Bessant, 'History and Australian Indigenous Child Welfare Policies' *Policy Studies* 34, no. 3 (2013): 310–25.

[74] *Trevorrow v State of South Australia (No. 5)* (2007) 98 SASR 136, para 108.

[75] Ibid, para 125.

[76] Ibid, para 126.

[77] Ibid, para 117.

about the removal of their other children.[78] Joe, who passed away, never saw Bruce again.[79] Thora did not see her son until nine years later, when Bruce was sent 'home' for a holiday in 1966. Mrs Davis, who could not cope with Bruce, posted his toys and belongings after a second 'holiday' in 1967. Neither Bruce nor his family were prepared for or supported to successfully manage this reunion. It did not go well and Bruce spent the next eight years in state institutions. He exited state care battling alcohol addiction and lived a precarious life thereafter.

Bruce Trevorrow was the first successful Stolen Generations litigant. The courts failed to provide justice for prior Stolen Generation litigants *Kruger v Commonwealth*,[80] *Cubillo v Commonwealth*,[81] and *Williams v Minister of Aboriginal Land Rights Act and State of NSW (No. 3)*,[82] with technical and narrow decisions. These decisions have been widely critiqued for their complicity in harms and for the lost opportunity to provide a jurisprudence of regret.[83] The documentary evidence tendered in Bruce's litigation suggested that at least 300 Aboriginal children had in the same period been removed illegally in South Australia.[84] The Court at First Instance made the finding, upheld on appeal, that authorities knew at the time Bruce was taken that his removal would likely cause harm.[85]

Human Rights Advocacy (Late 1960s to Early 1980s)

From the late 1960s human rights advocacy influenced both the understanding of the nexus between poverty and child welfare, and the framing of

[78] Kirsten Gray and Terri Libesman, 'Commentary and Judgment: State of South Australia v Lampard-Trevorrow [2010] SASC 56', in Nicole Watson and Heather Douglas (eds), *Indigenous Legal Judgments – Bringing Indigenous Voices into Judicial Decision Makings* (London: Routledge, 2021); *Lampard-Trevorrow* (2010) 106 SASR 33, 384 [246], 45.

[79] *Trevorrow v State of South Australia (No. 5)*, para 4.

[80] (1997) 190 CLR 1.

[81] (2001) 112 FCR 455.

[82] (2000) Aust Torts Reports, 81–578.

[83] See for example, Antonia Buti, 'Kruger and Bray and the Common Law' *University of New South Wales Law Journal* 21, no. 1 (1998): 232; Jennifer Clark, 'Cubillo v Commonwealth Case Note' *Melbourne University Law Review* 25, no. 1 (2001): 218; Robert van Krieken, 'Is Assimilation Justiciable? Lorna Cubillo and Peter Gunner v Commonwealth' *Sydney Law Review* 23 (2001): 239; Chris Cunneen and Julia Grix, 'The Limitations of Litigation in Stolen Generations Cases' (Research Discussion Paper No. 15, Australian Institute of Aboriginal and Torres Strait Islander Studies, 2004); Trish Luker, 'Intention and Iterability in *Cubillo v Commonwealth*' *Journal of Australian Studies* 28, no. 84 (2005): 35; Ann Curthoys, Ann Genovese and Alexander Reilly, *Rights and Redemption: History, Law and Indigenous People* (Sydney: University of New South Wales Press, 2008); Ann Genovese, 'Metaphor of Redemption, Myths of State: Historical Accountability in Luhrmann's Australia and Trevorrow v South Australia' *Griffith Law Review* 20 (2011): 67.

[84] *Trevorrow v State of South Australia (No. 5)*, 74.

[85] Ibid, para 885.

Indigenous and children's rights nationally and internationally. This was also a period of reform with respect to women's rights in the family. The introduction of a 'single parents' pension in 1976, gave impoverished mothers some capacity to resist the removal of their children. At the same time, Aboriginal and Torres Strait Islander communities and organisations increasingly called for the right to make decisions about their own children.[86] These broader trends influenced child welfare for Aboriginal and Torres Strait Islander children by focusing policy on non-discrimination and recognising (at least in theory) the importance of understanding and respecting the cultural particularity of Aboriginal and Torres Strait Islander families. There was a temporary and incomplete shift from a deficit understanding of Aboriginal and Torres Strait Islander families to one which engaged with the broader social and historical factors which underpin abuse and neglect and recognised the cultural rights of Aboriginal and Torres Strait Islander children. However, this shift was short-lived, abandoned in a new turn to individual responsibility and privatisation in the 1990s.

In this interim period, local, state and national Aboriginal children's agencies were formed,[87] as part of a broader move from more local advocacy to the formation of centralised and service-oriented Aboriginal and Torres Strait Islander organisations. At the pivotal First National Adoption Conference in 1976, Sommerlad presented the results of a survey which articulated the experience of Aboriginal and Torres Strait Islander families of the removal of their children to white families.[88] Aboriginal delegates to the conference resolved to form Aboriginal child care agencies.[89]

Aboriginal Legal Services likewise drew attention to the relationship between young Aboriginal people removed from their families into white homes and their contact with the juvenile justice system.[90] Aboriginal advocates, including Molly Dwyer and Graham Atkinson in Victoria, were inspired by the approaches of Indigenous peoples in North America responding to child welfare on reserves,[91] as well as the potential within the landmark Indian Child Welfare Act 1978 (US), which provided for extensive tribal

[86] Terri Libesman, *Decolonising Indigenous Child Welfare – Comparative Perspectives* (London: Routledge, 2014), chapter 2.

[87] Linda Briskman, *The Black Grapevine: Aboriginal Activism and the Stolen Generations* (Annandale: The Federation Press, 2003), chapter 5.

[88] Elizabeth Sommerlad, 'Homes for Blacks: Aboriginal Community and Adoption', in C. Picton (ed.), *Proceedings of First Australian Conference on Adoption* (Sydney: The Committee of the First Australian Conference on Adoption, 1976).

[89] Briskman, *The Black Grapevine,* chapter 5.

[90] Haebich, 'Neoliberalism', 27.

[91] Briskman, *The Black Grapevine,* 44.

control of child welfare affecting their children.[92] They highlighted the urgent need to form an organisation to respond to harms being caused by child welfare systems in Australia, and to provide Aboriginal children with community and culturally based support and care.[93]

The first Aboriginal children's agency, the Victorian Aboriginal Child Care Agency, was established in Victoria in 1976. Its charter was to reduce loss of children from their community, support the retention of their Aboriginal identity, affirm the role of Aboriginal extended family, involve Aboriginal adults and young people in traditional helping roles, and recognise and identify problems experienced by youth leading to encounters with juvenile justice and imprisonment. Aboriginal and Torres Strait Islander children's organisations articulated that their survival as distinct peoples relied on community care for their children,[94] reflecting ongoing debates about Aboriginal self-determination and self-management. They also brought public and political attention to the damage which removal of their children through adoption and fostering to non-Aboriginal families continued to cause.[95] In 1981 a national advocacy organisation, the Secretariat of National Aboriginal and Islander Child Care (SNAICC) was established.[96]

Aboriginal and Torres Strait Islander advocates were involved in the development of the International Convention on the Rights of the Child in the decade 1979 to 1989 and lobbied the government to ratify this treaty.[97] In subsequent decades they have engaged extensively with international human rights bodies, utilised the Declaration on the Rights of Indigenous Peoples (2007) as an advocacy tool, and exchanged ideas and support with First Nations children's advocacy organisations both nationally and internationally, particularly in the United States, Canada and New Zealand.[98]

Aboriginal and Islander Child Care Agencies advocated effectively for the establishment of the Aboriginal and Torres Strait Islander child placement principle (ATSICPP). The ATSICPP has five interrelated elements;

92 Libesman, *Decolonising Indigenous Child Welfare,* chapter 5; Briskman, *The Black Grapevine,* chapter 5.

93 Ibid. 94 Ibid, chapter 6.

95 Nigel D'Souza, 'Forum – The Stolen Generation: From Removal to Reconciliation: Authors of Our Own History' *UNSW Law Journal* 21 (1998): 204–7, 205.

96 Briskman, *The Black Grapevine,* 63.

97 Libesman, *Decolonising Indigenous Child Welfare,* 41.

98 Cindy Blackstock, Muriel Bamblett and Carla Black, 'Indigenous Ontology, International Law and Application of the Convention to the Over Representation of Indigenous Children in Out of Home Care in Canada and Australia' *Child Abuse and Neglect* 110 (2020): 1–11.

prevention, partnership, placement, participation and connection, and recognises the importance, for Aboriginal and Torres Strait Islander children, of connections to family, community, culture and Country.[99] Although incorporated into legislation in the Northern Territory in 1983, followed by other jurisdictions over the next two decades, and, finally, Western Australia in 2006,[100] these provisions largely focused on prioritising family and community placements in out-of-home care rather than keeping families together and fulfilling the broader intent of the principle. Indeed, the ATSICPP is often misunderstood as being narrowly focused on this placement element, rather than recognising its broader intent of upholding Aboriginal and Torres Strait Islander children's rights to family, community, culture and identity.[101] Legislation also requires that relevant Aboriginal or Torres Strait Islander organisations and, in some jurisdictions, extended family, be consulted about the child's placement. In each jurisdiction, children who are placed with non-Indigenous carers are to be assisted to remain connected with their family, language and culture, and, in most jurisdictions there is a stated aim to reunite children placed in non-Indigenous care with their families and communities. An ongoing problem, noted repeatedly by the United Nations Committee on the Rights of the Child and National Inquiries, has been the failure to implement the principle in practice.[102]

The 1990s Turn from Rights to Individual Responsibility

Following the 1993 Royal Commission into Aboriginal Deaths in Custody, which found that half of those whose deaths they investigated had been removed as children from their families, the peak Aboriginal and Torres Strait Islander children's organisation, the Secretariat of National Aboriginal

[99] SNAICC – National Voice for our Children, *Understanding and applying the Aboriginal and Torres Strait Islander Child Placement Principle: A Resource for Legislation, Policy and Program Development* (2017).

[100] Australian Human Rights Commission, *Historical Context – The Stolen Generations*, https://bth.humanrights.gov.au/significance/historical-context-the-stolen-generations, accessed 15 December 2021.

[101] Fiona Arney, Marie Iannos, Alwin Chong, Stewart McDougall and Samantha Parkinson, 'Enhancing the Implementation of the Aboriginal and Torres Strait Islander Child Placement Principle: Policy and Practice Considerations', CFCA Paper No. 34 (2015).

[102] Libesman and Cripps, 'Aboriginal and Torres Strait Islander Children's Welfare and Well-being', 307–36.

and Islander Child Care (SNAICC) advocated for a National Inquiry into the Separation of Aboriginal and Torres Strait Islander Children from their families. The national inquiry both popularised and polarised debates about the history of forced and unjustified removals of Aboriginal and Torres Strait Islander children from their families, contemporary responsibility for redress, and the national identity. Recommendations emphasised the importance of self-determination in contemporary child welfare, empowering Aboriginal and Torres Strait Islander communities to exercise jurisdiction over child protection systems and other social systems.[103] It noted that, despite some child welfare departments' intentions to transform, their entrenched colonial culture had prevented this from happening.[104]

However, the election of the Howard government in 1996 saw a retreat from rights-based policy and the hardening of the 1980s turn away from communal care and responsibility towards heightened individual responsibility. It was accompanied by a push to privatise child welfare services, together with a disavowal of state responsibility for the intergenerational harms, ongoing socio-economic disadvantage, and inappropriate and ineffective child protection systems that contributed to the growing over-representation of Aboriginal and Torres Strait Islander children in child welfare systems. Discriminatory social welfare policies again increased control and surveillance of Aboriginal families. In 2007 the Commonwealth government's 'Northern Territory Emergency Response' imposed, among other restrictions, cashless welfare benefits on seventy-three Aboriginal communities in Northern Territory.[105] Similar provisions have subsequently been rolled out to select communities, disproportionately impacting Aboriginal and Torres Strait Islander families.[106] Similarly, racist beliefs about the harmful or neglectful nature of Aboriginal and Torres Strait Islander families remain part of public discourse. In 2018, the Sunrise program broadcast a segment calling for the increased adoption of Aboriginal children by white families, making broad generalisations about abuse and neglect in Indigenous families and proposing a repeat of the Stolen Generations

[103] 'Bringing Them Home', chapter 26, Recommendation 43.

[104] 'Bringing Them Home', chapter 21.

[105] N. Watson, 'From the Northern Territory Emergency Response to Stronger Futures: Where is the Evidence that Australian Aboriginal Women are Leading Self-Determining Lives?', in Suvendrini Perera and Sherene H. Razack (eds), *At the Limits of Justice: Women of Colour on Terror* (Toronto: University of Toronto Press, 2014), 335–55; J. Altman and M. Hinkson (eds) *Coercive Reconciliation: Stabilise, Normalise, Exit Aboriginal Australia* (Melbourne: Arena Publications, 2007).

[106] S. Bielefeld, 'Income Management and Indigenous Women: A New Chapter of Patriarchal Colonial Governance?' *UNSW Law Journal* 39, no. 2 (2016): 843–78.

policy.[107] The segment was later found to have breached broadcasting standards.[108]

The rejection of historical responsibility was amplified by the refusal of the Howard government to apologise to the Stolen Generations. While a historic national apology followed in February 2008, it offered no reparations, nor necessary systemic reform of contemporary child protection. Despite the apology, the deeper lack of recognition of the harms caused is evident in the ongoing framing of contemporary child welfare as a problem of individual deficits within families.

Meanwhile, the growing number of children receiving child protection services has led to numerous state/territory and national reviews since 1990.[109] These reviews have consistently found that child protection systems are ineffective, unsustainable and disproportionately impact Aboriginal and Torres Strait Islander families. They urge systemic reform including greater focus on prevention and early intervention.[110] The recent Family Is Culture review, commissioned in response to Aboriginal communities', and particularly grandmothers', demands for justice and accountability regarding contemporary removals of Aboriginal children, noted the 'historical continuity' of intrusive and oppressive child welfare systems targeting Aboriginal and Torres Strait Islander families. However, these recommendations often remain unimplemented,[111] or are partially implemented in ways that preserve or extend authority to intervene in Aboriginal and Torres Strait Islander families while minimising state responsibility or accountability. This is inconsistent with principles of the rule of law and the legitimate exercise of power, which require relationships of trust between those who exercise powers and those subject to it.[112]

107 Amanda Meade, 'Sunrise Segment on Indigenous Adoptions Lands Seven in More Hot Water', *The Guardian*, 14 June 2019, www.theguardian.com/media/2019/jun/14/sunrise-segment-on-indigenous-adoption-lands-seven-in-more-hot-water, accessed 15 December 2021.

108 Ibid.

109 Royal Commission into Institutional Responses to Child Sexual Abuse, Final Report, Volume 12, Contemporary Out-of-home Care (Canberra: Commonwealth of Australia, 2017).

110 URBIS, *Reviews of the NSW Child Protection System 2008–2019: An Analysis of Key Findings and Degree of Implementation* (NSW Family Services Inc, 2020); Megan Davis, *Family Is Culture Review Report: Independent Review of Aboriginal Children in OOHC Family Is Culture* (Sydney, 2019).

111 URBIS, *Reviews of the NSW Child Protection System.*

112 Libesman, Decolonising Indigenous Child Welfare, 83–105.

Just as rising costs and poor outcomes in institutional care contributed to the period of forced adoptions in the mid-twentieth century, governments have responded to ineffective and unsustainable out-of-home care systems by turning to reforms that minimise transparency, accountability and ultimately responsibility for children removed from their families. In addition to privatising service delivery and delegating responsibilities to non-government organisations, recent reforms have also focused on streamlining 'permanency' through legal orders that transfer parental responsibility to third parties, either permanently or until the age of eighteen. Permanency reforms across all Australian jurisdictions have set short time frames, usually two years, for children either to be restored to their families or transitioned to permanent third-party orders. Once again, such provisions enable governments to limit their responsibility by permanently 'exiting' large numbers of children from government supervision into private out-of-home care, third-party orders or adoption. Aboriginal and Torres Strait Islander children are disproportionately affected, despite the ongoing opposition of Aboriginal and Torres Strait Islander communities. They are often placed in non-Aboriginal placements, and with non-Aboriginal agencies.[113] The national apologies to the 'Stolen Generations' and the 'Forgotten Australians' for the lifelong harms inflicted by earlier policies of forced adoptions are a distant memory for legislators and there is little guarantee that these practices will not be repeated.

Conclusion

While Aboriginal and Torres Strait Islander child welfare policies have changed from the overt discrimination of protectionism, through assimilation and integration, then briefly to self-determination and subsequently to privatisation, the characterisation of Aboriginal and Torres Strait Islander families as deficient, in need of saving and a burden on the state have remained consistent. More recent reforms have sought to minimise this 'burden' of the state's responsibility for their extensive intervention in the lives of Aboriginal and Torres Strait Islander children and families, while continuing to emphasise settler-colonial authority over Aboriginal and Torres Strait Islander peoples, particularly children. Despite persistent modern rhetoric purporting to place the welfare and well-being of Aboriginal and Torres Strait Islander children at the centre of welfare regimes, 'benevolent'

[113] SNAICC – National Voice for our Children, *Family Matters Report 2020* (2020).

state intervention has consistently harmed and achieved poor outcomes for 'rescued' children. Rather, the surveillance and control of Aboriginal and Torres Strait Islander children and families has been driven by colonial aspirations and dominant Anglo understandings of family and childhood to do the work of 'building and sustaining the white imaginary of the Australian nation. As long as these children ceased to exist, as long as they either died or could be successfully assimilated, the legitimacy of the new white Australian nation-state could remain intact.'[114]

[114] Sana Nakata, 'The *Infantalisation* of Indigenous Australians: *A Problem* for *Democracy*', in Sandra Phillips and Julianne Shultz (eds), *Griffith Review 60: First Things First* (Text Publishing, 2018), 104–16.

19

The Legal History of Non-Indigenous Marriage

ALECIA SIMMONDS

Marriage, we are told, is about love, that exquisitely private and ineffable emotion which resides far from the province of law. Marriage is what happens when two people come together before family and friends to pledge their commitment to each other; to make their most intimate feelings public; to present a foundation of words and vows from which to project a life together into the future. What this future may look like is up to them. Marriage is a shared project of romantic imagination: there are as many different versions of marriage as there are married people.

But if marriage is such a personal affair, why did homosexual couples have to wait until 2017 to marry?[1] And why is polygamy not legally possible in Australia?[2] As this chapter will demonstrate, marriage is also a public act; an 'artefact of government',[3] an entirely legal creation whose threads spin out beyond spouses, weaving themselves into the fabric of empires, nations and states, as well as populations, economies and social relations.[4] Marriage excludes certain people, privileges others, imposes obligations and structures emotions, sexuality, gender and ethnicity. When two people in an official wedding ceremony say 'I do' they awaken a formidable machinery of power.

A story of the legal regulation of marriage could be written in triumphalist tones. We might begin with the British settlers wading ashore at Botany Bay carrying the patriarchal traditions of the English common law with them,

1 Marriage Act 1961 (Cth), s 2A, amended by Marriage Amendment (Definition and Religious Freedoms) Bill 2017 (Cth).

2 Marriage Act 1961 (Cth), s 23B(1)(a). Note that this is criticised in Belinda Fehlberg et al., *Australian Family Law: The Contemporary Context* (Melbourne: Oxford University Press Australia, 2014, 2nd edition), 125–6.

3 Nan Hunter, 'Marriage, Law and Gender: A Feminist Inquiry', in Lisa Duggan and Nan Hunter (eds), *Sex Wars: Sexual Dissent and Political Culture* (Abingdon: Routledge, 1995), 110, cited in Heather Brook, *Conjugal Rites: Marriage and Marriage-like Relationships before the Law* (Basingstoke: Palgrave Macmillan, 2007), 32–3.

4 Nancy Cott, *Public Vows* (Cambridge, MA: Harvard University Press, 2000); see also Brook, *Conjugal Rites*, 5.

then proceed to the nineteenth-century property and divorce reforms, continuing past the sexual revolutions of the 1960s and 1970s until we arrive at marriage equality today. But the relationship of intimacy to the state is more complicated than progress narratives suggest. While marriage rates may be declining,[5] marriage continues to have unparalleled cultural symbolic power and to occupy the most privileged relationship status in law: marriage is the norm against which all other conjugal relationships are measured; a status whose existence the law presumes; and an institution which the Family Law Act commits to protecting.[6] Unhappy spouses may no longer have to prove moral fault when seeking to dissolve a marriage, but judicial determinations of custody and property in Family Court hearings will often see the imposition of moral values and gender norms.[7] To this extent, the history of marriage is also a history of divorce because the shifting rules of marriage are made legible by the state at the moment of the marriage's disintegration. When courts declare what broke the marriage contract, they articulate what terms ought to have composed it.[8]

If marriage transforms the social and legal status of its subjects, turning men into husbands and women into wives,[9] then marriage itself has also been a site of transformation. Those who seek to 'defend' traditional marriage will, upon closer study, find themselves shielding a moving target; an institution that has been capable of extraordinary change. How do we imagine this institution over more than two centuries? We might think of marriage spatially, as a kind of territory in a larger map of conjugality whose borders are policed by the state at the moment of entrance and exit, and which has decreased in size and significance over time.[10] Or we could think of it as a species of governance, where we witness, as Heather Brook (invoking Foucault) has argued, a shift from sovereign power or rules-based conjugality

5 Australian Institute of Family Studies, 'Marriage Rates in Australia', https://aifs.gov.au/facts-and-figures/marriage-rates-australia, accessed 10 January 2022.

6 Family Law Act 1975 (Cth), s 43(1)(a). See also Fehlberg et al., *Australian Family Law*, 116–17.

7 See Jocelynne Scutt and Di Graham, *For Richer, for Poorer: Money, Marriage and Property Rights* (Ringwood: Penguin Books, 1984), 98; Leonore Weitzman, *The Divorce Revolution* (New York: The Free Press, 1985). See also Carol Smart, *The Ties That Bind* (London: Routledge and Kegan Paul, 1984), ix, who argues that divorce is the moment when the private family becomes public and that marriage creates a legal status with certain privileges and sustains women's economic dependence within marriage and the family; Alecia Simmonds, 'Domesticating Violence', in Camilla Nelson and Rachel Robertson (eds), *Dangerous Ideas about Mothers* (Crawley: University of Western Australia Publishing, 2018), 35–48.

8 Brook, *Conjugal Rites*, 120.

9 Cott, *Public Vows*, 3.

10 Brook describes conjugality as a 'territory' and I am indebted to her spatial imaginings here: Brook, *Conjugal Rites*, 199–200.

to norms; from external-regulation to self-regulation.[11] We may think of it as the pinnacle of a conjugal hierarchy, 'heterosexuality's central institution',[12] or we could draw out its precise meanings in a settler-colonial nation where it has been a site of legal change and continuity;[13] departing from its British common law roots while maintaining its association with social stability, gender norms and purportedly ennobled forms of affection. It could also be seen as the site of a grand conflict between liberal individualism and male headship in the family.[14] Keeping these large conceptual strands in our grasp, this chapter will proceed via the minutiae, through a series of case studies each of which represents a pivotal moment in the legal history of marriage: the shift from cohabitation to official state-sanctioned marriage in the colonial period; a tilting of the balance away from male headship to liberal individualism in the interwar period; and the gradual deinstitutionalisation of marriage in the early twenty-first century. This chapter will keep the personal and the political in sight at all times, illuminating the governance of conjugality and its crises over the long arc of legal modernity.

Marriage during the Colonial Period

The Marital Contract

In the late eighteenth and nineteenth centuries, marriage functioned as an institution, a lived reality and a political metaphor for the relationship between citizens and state: protection on one side was met by obedience on the other and the ties could not be dissolved. Jean-Jacques Rousseau described the family as 'the little commonwealth',[15] where people marry 'in order to fulfil the duties of civil society jointly, to govern the house prudently, to rear their children well'.[16] This vision of marriage as a site of governance that radiates outward to ensure the stability of state governance was indebted to a Western liberal

11 Brook, *Conjugal Rites*, 13–40 and 144–51.

12 Stevi Jackson and Sue Scott, *Feminism and Sexuality: A Reader* (New York: Columbia University Press, 1996), 24.

13 Hilary Golder and Diane Kirkby, 'Marriage and Divorce Law before the Family Law Act 1975', in Diane Kirkby (ed.), *Sex, Power and Justice: Historical Perspectives of Law in Australia* (Melbourne: Oxford University Press, 1995), 150–67.

14 Norma Basch, 'Marriage and Domestic Relations', in Michael Grossberg and Christopher Tomlins (eds), *The Cambridge History of Law in America* (Cambridge: Cambridge University Press, 2008), 247.

15 Carole Pateman, *The Disorder of Women: Democracy, Feminism and Political Theory* (Cambridge: Polity Press, 1989), 24.

16 Jean-Jacques Rousseau, *La Nouvelle Heloise*, translated by J. H. McDowell (University Park, PA: Pennsylvania State University Press, 1968), 261–2, as cited in Pateman, *The Disorder of Women*, 27.

philosophical tradition, particularly social contract theory, that premised its theory of civil society on a public/private distinction. Social order, it was thought, depended upon a separation between the public and private spheres which mirrored the presumed innate differences between women and men, and regulated women's 'disorderly' sexuality. Women, governed by feeling, were the natural inhabitants of the private world of family whereas men, governed by reason, inhabited the public world of statecraft. If the private sphere was bound by moral laws and the natural ties of love and affection then the public sphere was bound by objective, universal laws accessible through reason.[17] Philosophers' presumptions about women's incapacity for civil or political reason and their fears of women's sexuality meant that they advocated for women to be kept away from matters of state and, given women's irrationality, to be governed by men within the private sphere. Conversely, white men's capacity for self-governance through reason and headship of a family qualified them to be participant members of the state.[18]

This allocation of each sex to their respective sphere was effected through the legal apparatus of coverture, which was premised upon a sacramental view of marital unity held by the medieval church,[19] and encapsulated in the words of William Blackstone: 'the very being or legal existence of the woman is suspended during the marriage, or at least is incorporated and consolidated into that of the husband; under whose wing, protection, and *cover*, she performs everything'.[20] Men, upon becoming husbands, obtained full civil and political status, and became the representative and protector of their wives and children. Women, upon becoming wives, became the dependents

17 Carole Pateman, *The Sexual Contract* (Palo Alto, CA: Stanford University Press, 1988). See also Moira Gatens, *Imaginary Bodies: Ethics, Power and Corporeality* (Hove: Psychology Press, 1996), 51, cited in Brook, *Conjugal Rites*, 35; Nancy Fraser, 'Rethinking the Public Sphere: A Contribution to the Critique of Actually Existing Democracy' *Social Text* 25/26 (1990): 56–80; Nicola Lacey, 'Theory into Practice? Pornography and the Public/Private Dichotomy' *Journal of Law and Society* 20, no. 1 (1993): 93–113; Susan Moller Okin, 'Gender, the Public and the Private' *Revista Estudos Feministas* 16, no. 2 (2008): 305–32; Susan Moller Okin, 'The Public/Private Dichotomy', in Colin Farrelly (ed.), *Contemporary Political Theory: A Reader* (Thousand Oaks, CA: Sage Publications, 2004), chapter 17.

18 Basch, 'Marriage and Domestic Relations', 245–79.

19 Note that the sacramental origins of coverture are still a source of some academic contestation. See Lee Holcombe, *Wives and Property* (Oxford: Martin Robertson, 1983), 18.

20 Emphasis added. The definitive statement on coverture is found in William Blackstone, *Commentaries on the Laws of England* (Oxford: Clarendon Press, 1765), 1: 442–5. See also Basch, 'Marriage and Domestic Relations', 245–6; Cott, *Public Vows*; Regina Graycar and Jenny Morgan, *The Hidden Gender of Law* (Canberra: Canberra Federation Press, 1990); Brook, *Conjugal Rites*.

of men, with their legal identity extinguished, and an obligation to respond to masculine protection with obedience. Any personal property that the wife brought to the marriage was claimed by her husband, who also managed her real property. She was to have no separate legal identity, which meant that she could not sue or be sued except in the joint names of herself and her husband, and could only contract to secure 'necessaries' for the household.[21] As his 'chattel', or property, she could also not be raped by her husband for he could not trespass upon that which he already owned.[22] He could rewrite her will. The wife's legal disabilities were met by the husband's responsibilities: the husband was responsible for the wife's debts, including those that she brought to the marriage; and because the wife acted as her husband's agent, Blackstone gave husbands the right to beat women, or in his words, the 'power of correction ... within reasonable grounds'.[23] As men assumed governance of the private sphere, the family was envisaged as self-regulating, quarantined from state laws and from public discourses of justice and commerce.[24]

As Carol Pateman has argued, the marriage contract was the means by which women were incorporated into civil society; and calling it a contract disguised the reality of subordination through a language of equality, consent and choice. Yet marriage was not about contract so much as status: once the couple had consented to the original contract they had no capacity to dissolve it nor to alter its terms as set by the state.[25] These ideas were crucial to the development of marriage law in Australia, although they did not arrive fully formed. Government policy consolidated the marital family as the foundation of civil society in the shift from the early colonial period (1788–1830) to, approximately, the Victorian era (1837–1901), when widespread cohabitation ceded its place to state-sanctioned marriage. It is a shift encapsulated in the case of *Cox v Payne*.[26]

Cox v Payne: *From Cohabitation to Legally Sanctioned Marriage*

In 1825 Sarah Cox, the eighteen-year-old daughter of unmarried, convict parents, sought 'reparation for her wounded feelings' from her duplicitous

21 See Blackstone, *Commentaries on the Laws of England*, 442–5 and Holcombe, *Wives and Property*, 29–30.

22 Sir Matthew Hale, *The History of the Pleas of the Crown Volume 1* (E and R Nutt, 1736), 629. For scholarship on rape in marriage, see Wendy Larcombe and Mary Heath, 'Developing the Common Law and Rewriting the History of Rape in Marriage in Australia: PGA v The Queen' *Sydney Law Review* 34, no. 4 (2012): 785–809; Jill Elaine Hasday, 'Contest and Consent: A Legal History of Marital Rape' *California Law Review* 88 (2000): 1373–506.

23 Blackstone, *Commentaries on the Laws of England*, 286.

24 Susan Moller Okin, *Justice, Gender, and the Family* (New York: Basic Books, 1989), 3–4.

25 Pateman, *The Sexual Contract*.

26 *Cox v Payne* (1825) NRS 13471 [9/5198].

lover, Captain Payne, in the New South Wales Supreme Court. It was the first time the action for breach of promise of marriage had been brought before a jury in the colony. Like many working-class women during this time, Cox met Payne while residing at her employer's house, where she worked as an apprentice seamstress. 'Love letters passed between them couched in terms of the strongest affection', and one year later Payne announced to Cox's sister his intentions of marriage, vowing that 'his eyes might drop out of his head if he did not fulfil his promise'. Yet for all his effusive declarations of love, Payne was fickle with his affections. He commenced a series of clandestine courtships with other women, eventually leading to his marriage to a wealthy widow. Upon learning of his perfidy, Cox released a volley of letters, bursting with invective, at her 'ungrateful wretch' of a lover. Her mother and close friend, Mrs Beckett, also confronted Captain Payne demanding an explanation for his deception, to which Captain Payne remarked, nonplussed, that 'promises and pie-crusts were made to be broke'. The jury did not agree and awarded Sarah Cox the substantial sum of 100 pounds damages.[27]

Cox v Payne demonstrates that the history of marriage does not begin at the altar but rather with a promise of marriage: courtship created contract and enlivened legal obligation. But precisely when legal force should be attached to romantic words was contested in the colony. On one side we have Payne representing a moment in the late eighteenth and early nineteenth centuries when cohabitation and serial monogamy were favoured over marriage.[28] On the other side we have Cox marking a new era when marriage and orderly families were to be the foundation of the social order, and where a woman's respectability, as much as that of the colony, depended upon men keeping their promises of marriage.[29]

27 Ibid. See also reports of the case in the newspapers: *The Australian*, 19 May 1825; *Sydney Gazette*, 19 May 1825. See also Alecia Simmonds, '"Promises and pie-Crusts were made to be broke": Breach of Promise of Marriage and the Regulation of Courtship in Early Colonial Australia' *Australian Feminist Law Journal* 23 (2005): 99–120.

28 For America, see Cott, *Public Vows*, 32; for Australia see Patricia Grimshaw et al., *Creating a Nation: 1788–1990* (Carlton: McPhee Gribble, 1994), 49–50; Bruce Kercher, *An Unruly Child: A History of Law in Australia* (Sydney: Allen & Unwin, 1995), 50–1. See also the female register of Reverend Samuel Marsden, which concluded that of the 1,430 women in the colony, about two-thirds were 'unmarried and concubine': Samuel Marsden, 'A Statement of the Married and Unmarried Women with the Number of Their Children in New South Wales' in *Series 40.071: Letter received by Banks from William Bligh* (Unpublished, 1806–7).

29 See Penny Russell, *Savage or Civilised?: Manners in Colonial Australia* (Sydney: UNSW Press, 2010); Kirsten McKenzie, *Scandal in the Colonies: Sydney and Cape Town, 1820–1850* (Melbourne: Melbourne University Press, 2004).

Marriage was encouraged through government policy, such as sending women of marriageable age to the colonies or permitting female convicts to obtain freedom upon marrying a free settler or a convict with a ticket of leave. Yet, most of the early colony's residents opted for cohabitation. Informal marriages or 'living tally' were common among the poor in early nineteenth-century England, Australia and America, primarily because they allowed people to move freely in and out of relationships. Divorce may have been virtually impossible until the mid-nineteenth century, but self-divorce was popular and could be effected through placing an advertisement in the paper stating that the couple had parted by 'mutual consent'.[30] Colonial elites also commonly cohabited with convicts. In New South Wales, the civil court accepted and protected popular preferences for cohabitation through extending legal protections to de facto wives. For instance, if a de facto wife's partner died intestate, the Court would award her the assets and control of the man's estate.[31] They also extended these privileges to unwed women whose partners had gone back to England.[32]

In the years that yawned between the first settlement at Sydney Cove and Sarah Cox's breach of promise action in 1825, the colony changed; it stumbled out from a long night of frolicsome cohabitation and blinked in the glare of a new moral puritanism. Queen Victoria was not yet on the throne, but preparations were in train. First came Governor Macquarie, prim and indefatigable. In an 1810 proclamation entitled 'Illicit Intercourse, evils arising therefrom' he lamented 'the scandalous and promiscuous custom so generally and shamelessly adopted, throughout the Colony of Persons of different sexes cohabiting and living together unsanctioned by the legal ties of matrimony'.[33] He noted that unwed women were successfully making claims on wills and inheritances in the courts based on the fact that they had lived for some years with a man. This, he declared, would end. If cohabiting without marriage was a 'scandal to Religion, to Decency and to all good Government',[34] then marriage was essential to 'Morality and Decorum' and would also save unmarried women and their children from the 'calamity' of social scorn and a lack of provision.[35] He would 'Encourage Lawful marriage by every possible Means.'[36] Macquarie went further than any

30 For America see Cott, *Public Vows*, 35.

31 Bruce Kercher, *Debt, Seduction and Other Disasters* (Sydney: Federation Press, 1996), 79.

32 Kercher, *An Unruly Child*, 50–1.

33 Lachlan Macquarie, 'Illicit Intercourse, Evils Arising Therefrom', in *NRS 1043 Colonial Secretary: Digest of Proclamations and General Orders, 1791–1821*, SZ756, Reel 6039 (25 February 1810), 579.

34 Ibid, 579. 35 Ibid, 580. 36 Ibid.

previous governor in enforcing marriage: he offered incentives such as property and financial benefits for convicts if they married, and then took away inheritance rights from the unwed.[37] His proclamation established that the 'mere circumstances of illegal cohabitation, for whatever length of time' would not confer valid title to property on unmarried women. The civil courts had to abide by this law.[38] This shift towards a more rigid moral order was mirrored in other colonies throughout empire and is thought to be a product of the growth of evangelicalism, increasing numbers of white women in the colonies, and the rise of the middle classes, whose claims to political power rested upon their perceived 'moral superiority'.[39] By the 1830s and 1840s, an ideology of family based on official, monogamous marriage had firmly taken hold. Marriage would now be the fate of most white colonial women; a product of both government policy and law, aided by a severe demographic imbalance between the sexes in which men outnumbered women for most of the nineteenth century.[40]

Government efforts to encourage marriage in the colony were assisted by a lax juridical approach to the formal requirements of marriage laws. In British common law, marriage was valid with 'the consent of two persons, able to contract, expressed in words of present mutual acceptance ... without the intervention of a priest'.[41] But the statutory requirement, specifically Lord Hardwicke's Marriage Act 1754 was stringent. In an effort to prevent clandestine marriage, the Act stipulated parental consent, public notice through the posting of banns and a public ceremony in the Anglican Church, as components of marriage.[42] Judicial opinion in colonial Australia held that Lord Hardwicke's Marriage Act and the subsequent Marriage Act 1823 did not apply because of the denominational diversity in the colony and because marriages, whatever form they took, should have legal recognition so as to discourage 'licentiousness and debauchery'.[43] To this extent, the

37 Hilary Golder, *Divorce in Nineteenth-century New South Wales* (Sydney: UNSW Press, 1985), 26; Grimshaw et al., *Creating a Nation*, 56–7.
38 Macquarie, 'Illicit Intercourse, Evils Arising Therefrom', 580–1.
39 Deborah Cohen, *Family Secrets: Shame and Privacy in Modern Britain* (Oxford: Oxford University Press, 2017), 45.
40 In 1861, there were '138 white men for every 100 white women'; by 1891 that number had lowered to 119: Grimshaw et al., *Creating a Nation*, 116. See also Golder and Kirkby, 'Marriage and Divorce Law before the Family Law Act 1975', 152.
41 Ibid, 152–3.
42 An Act for the Better Preventing of Clandestine Marriage 1753, 26 Geo. II c 33 ('Lord Hardwicke's Marriage Act').
43 Golder and Kirkby, 'Marriage and Divorce Law before the Family Law Act 1975', 153. Note also that the Australian Courts Act 1828 (Imp), s 24 provided that all laws and statutes that are in force in England are to be applied 'so far as the same can be applied'

first statute regulating marriage in the colony, the Marriage Act 1834 in force until the Marriage Act 1961,[44] was framed broadly, legitimating all prior and subsequent Catholic or Presbyterian marriages. Subsequent legislation (the Marriage Act 1855)[45] provided for the recognition of all marriages in the colony to date, regardless of religious denomination, and validated civil marriages with no clergy. These statutes were consistent with English law, insofar as they required marriage to be formalised in the appropriate manner, but their tolerance of religious diversity was a colonial innovation, reflective of the heterogeneous population and the absence of a state religion, as much as a bourgeois belief in marriage as a great civiliser. They also show that marriage in Australia has always been a civil, not a religious, institution.

Returning to the case of *Cox v Payne*, we can now understand its wider political and social resonances. Sarah won her case, in part, because promises of marriage needed to be taken seriously in a colony that was beginning to base its claims to respectability on the moral foundation of orderly marital families. She also won because she successfully proved her own chastity; evidence of sexual promiscuity would have justified Captain Payne's breach of promise. Yet Sarah, unbeknownst to the jury, was pregnant at the time of her trial to her barrister, William Charles Wentworth; and following her trial she bore two children out of wedlock to him.[46] Where illegitimacy would barely have been remarked upon for her parents, who arrived in the colony in 1807, Sarah suffered a life of social scorn, excluded from Society events and prohibited by her eldest daughter's husband from contacting her eldest daughter. Sarah may have exercised her civil and political rights in court and won, but when she gave birth to two illegitimate children, she lost all social rights and status. The case reminds us that understanding the legal regulation of marriage means going beyond the law to the informal machinery of power wielded by communities to maintain moral and social order. Her case also warns us against progressivist narratives of marriage: colonial Australia began not with official marriage but with the loose and dissoluble bonds of cohabitation, closer to the forms of conjugality we have today than our stiff caricatures of eighteenth- and nineteenth-century romance.

thus allowing for local conditions and colonial divergence. In this case Lord Hardwicke's Marriage Act explicitly stated that it only had force in England and Wales.

44 Marriage Act 1961 (Cth). 45 Marriage Act 1855 (NSW).

46 See Carol Liston, *Sarah Wentworth, Mistress of Vaucluse* (Glebe: Historic Houses Trust of New South Wales, 1988).

Marriage Post-Federation

Adkins v Adkins: *Property, Desire and Divorce*

Thomas Adkins sat in the Hobart offices of his wife's solicitors and signed a contract outlining the terms upon which his wife, Thelma Adkins, would return home.[47] It was December 1944 and Thelma and her children had left Thomas two months earlier with a catalogue of grievances, including Thelma's unwanted pregnancies. The contract is a remarkable document that reveals Thelma's bid for autonomy in an institution that curtailed her freedom in accordance with her status as a wife. It provided, *inter alia*:

> 3. THAT Mr Adkins agrees
>
> a) That his wife immediately takes a holiday extending over a period of one month.
>
> b) That his wife takes an annual holiday of 14 days.
>
> c) That such holidays be taken by Mrs Adkins alone or with her children. Mr Adkins not to accompany her.
>
> . . .
>
> e) That Mr Adkins allows and pays his wife the same amount of money for housekeeping and personal expenses as he paid to her before she left her home.
>
> . . .
>
> 5. That Mrs Adkins not be required to live with her husband as his wife.[48]

In spite of the contract, Thomas continued to ask Thelma for sex. When she refused, he petitioned for divorce on the grounds of desertion, claiming that clause 5 of the contract was void because it was against public policy. The 'wilful and unjustifiable refusal of sexual intercourse', he argued, was the 'equivalent to desertion'. His argument was based on Section 7 of the Matrimonial Causes Act (Tas) 1860, which defined desertion as, *inter alia*, 'the wilful or non-justifiable refusal to permit marital intercourse'. The Tasmanian Supreme Court and the High Court on appeal upheld the contract and dismissed Mr Adkins's divorce petition.[49] On the question of public policy, it was held that it was 'in the interests of the children that they should agree to come together even without sexual intercourse' rather than 'break up the home'. The principle of contractual freedom was also affirmed by Justice Morris: 'There is nothing to prevent Mrs Adkins laying down

47 *Adkins v Adkins* [1946] TASStRp 1; *Adkins v Adkins* (1948) 76 CLR 623.

48 *Adkins v Adkins* [1946] TASStRp 1, 2, cited in Marilyn Lake, 'Marriage as Bondage: The Anomaly of the Citizen Wife' *Australian Historical Studies* 30, no. 112 (1999): 116 as the case of Wilson.

49 *Adkins v Adkins* [1946] TASStRp 1; *Adkins v Adkins* (1948) 76 CLR 623, 627.

conditions for her return.'[50] If Mr Adkins accepts them 'she may in all justice insist upon adherence to the terms he has accepted'.[51]

Historian Marilyn Lake has analysed the case of Adkins through the lens of citizenship. The status of wife, she argues, was an 'anomaly in a modern democracy. In rendering personal and sexual service to her husband in return for keep, in being locked into a contract that required her to place her body at the husband's disposal and in performing work without pay, the wife lacks the citizen's rights of property in her person and in her labour.'[52] By the twentieth century, white women had gained substantial civil and political freedoms when compared to women like Sarah Cox. They could vote, run for Parliament, own property, engage in litigation, work in offices or factories, move unchaperoned through the streets and have sex, without the same level of moral opprobrium as suffered by their counterparts in the nineteenth century. And, like Thelma Adkins, white feminist activists were now importing public notions of economic and bodily autonomy to the private sphere of marriage and family. While Thelma Adkins's case was typical of feminist contestations over the meaning of marriage, as a woman she was atypical in her capacity to negotiate her way out of the marital contract. The idea that the terms of marriage were externally imposed by the state and that a husband could not divest himself contractually of this power, including that of his conjugal rights to the wife's body, remained settled in Australia until no-fault divorce in 1975 and state legislation outlawing rape in marriage in the 1980s and 1990s.[53] To this extent, the case stands at a juncture in the legal history of marriage: highlighting both its history in the laws of coverture and its future as a (largely) individually negotiated contract or set of norms. It could be seen as representing a gradual shift away from status towards autonomy, or a reconfiguration of the family away from a model of male headship to that of liberal individualism.[54]

50 *Adkins v Adkins* [1946] TASStRp 1, 4. 51 Ibid. 52 Lake, 'Marriage as Bondage', 121.

53 Criminal Law Consolidation Act Amendment Act 1976 (SA), s 73; Crimes (Sexual Assault) Amendment Act 1981 (NSW), s 61A(4); Criminal Code Act 1983 (NT), s 192(1); Acts Amendment (Sexual Assaults) Act 1985 (WA), s 325; Crimes (Amendment) Act 1985 (Vic), s 62(2); Crimes (Amendment) Ordinance (No. 5) 1985 (ACT), s 92R; Criminal Code Amendment (Sexual Offences) Act 1987 (Tas), s 185(1); Criminal Code, Evidence Act and other Acts Amendment Act 1989 (Qld), s 31. See also *R v L* [1991] HCA 48; H. A. Finlay and Alastair Bissett-Johnson, 'The Legal Effect of Marriage', in H. Finlay and A. Bissett-Johnson (eds), *Family Law in Australia* (Melbourne: Butterworths, 1972), 133–56; Wendy Larcombe and Mary Heath, 'Case Note: Developing the Common Law and Rewriting the History of Rape in Marriage in Australia: *PGA v The Queen*' *Sydney Law Review* 34 (2012): 785–807.

54 Basch, 'Marriage and Domestic Relations'.

That Thelma Adkins was even able to conceive of herself as having contractual rights within marriage was a product of two major legal innovations in the late nineteenth century. The first was the right for married women to own property, and the second was the right to divorce. The former was enabled through the passage of the Married Women's Property Act, which was passed by the British Parliament in 1870 and adopted by most Australian colonies between the 1870s and 1890s.[55] This gave women the right to own property separate from their husbands, to have their earnings and investments protected, and to sue and be sued.[56] Legislation granting the right to divorce was enacted in all Australian colonies by 1873.[57] These two innovations began the long process of eroding the doctrine of coverture through asserting a basic, yet radical idea: husbands and wives do not necessarily share a commonality of interest.

The Married Women's Property Act was an American innovation that was argued for by liberal women's rights advocates through a language of rights to life, liberty and property.[58] As Norma Basch has argued, if property was the problem, insofar as coverture made wives the property of men, then property could also be the solution if wives were invested with the 'same self-ownership and independence society had granted to free, white men'.[59] But the Married Women's Property Acts only partly eroded the laws of coverture. Women were still unable to sue their spouses, a restriction that was only abolished by the Family Law Act in 1975; and, as the Adkins case reveals, men still controlled the family income and wives still lacked rights to bodily and sexual integrity in marriage. Furthermore, the right of a wife to ensure that her husband had provided adequate property for her and her children in his will was defeated by the perceived greater right of male testamentary freedom. The Testator's Family Maintenance Legislation, passed in 1916, introduced the court as an intercessory party between the husband and wife, but did not alter the moral framework under which, as Bruce Kercher

55 Married Women's Property Act 1879, 42 Vic. No. 11 (NSW); Married Women's Property Act 1870, 34 Vic. No. 384 (Vic); Married Women's Property Act 1890, 54 Vic. No. 9 (Qld); Married Women's Property Act 1884, 46 & 47 Vic. No. 300 (SA); Married Women's Property Act 1935, 26 Geo. V No. 90 (Tas); Married Women's Property Act 1892, 55 Vic. No. 20 (WA).

56 See Holcombe, *Wives and Property*.

57 Matrimonial Causes Act 1858 (SA); Matrimonial Causes Act 1860 (TAS); Divorce and Matrimonial Causes Act 1861 (Vic); Divorce and Matrimonial Causes Act 1863 (WA); Matrimonial Causes Jurisdiction Act 1864 (Qld); Matrimonial Causes Act 1873 (NSW); Golder, *Divorce in Nineteenth-Century New South Wales*, 179–88.

58 Basch, 'Marriage and Domestic Relations', 259. 59 Ibid, 259.

has argued, 'only deserving women had a right to family property'.[60] As we will see in cases involving custody disputes, a wife's rights in law were determined by her perceived virtue: she would be rewarded if the judge perceived her to be a 'good' wife and punished if not.

A similar moral framework can be seen in divorce legislation. Australia inherited its divorce laws from Britain, where there was a deep connection between law, the state religion and the interests of the propertied classes.[61] As a sacrament administered by the church and governed by the ecclesiastical courts, marriage was envisioned as an indissoluble lifelong commitment. The only way out was through a judicial separation in the ecclesiastical courts (where the couple would stay married but be permitted to live apart) or divorce through an Act of Parliament (which was so rare as to make this option more a theoretical than an actual possibility). Judicial separation and divorce were procedures that had been devised in the seventeenth century to protect the propertied upper classes from the risk posed by adulterous wives and illegitimate heirs to the transmission of property through an untainted line of succession.

At the time of the foundation of the Australian colonies, the courts were given no matrimonial jurisdiction; and ecclesiastical courts were never established in Australia. This meant that divorce by court order was not a legal possibility in Australia until the British Matrimonial Causes Act of 1857.[62] This Act transferred the jurisdiction over marriage from the ecclesiastical courts to the civil courts and established a new court with the power to grant divorce and judicial separation. Judicial separation afforded petitioners the same rights as divorce to separate and keep their own earnings, but meant that the couple were still recorded as legally married, which did not offend Catholic Church edicts prohibiting divorce.[63] It was an adversarial fault-based system of divorce[64] based on a sexual double standard: a husband merely had to show adultery, but his wife had to prove adultery and a further ground, such as desertion, cruelty or the commission of certain crimes.[65]

60 Kercher, *An Unruly Child*, 143–4.

61 Henry Finlay, *To Have But Not to Hold: A History of Attitudes to Marriage and Divorce in Australia 1858–1975* (Annandale: The Federation Press, 2005), 74.

62 Matrimonial Causes Act 1857 (UK) 20 & 21 Vic. c 85. For histories of divorce in England see Lawrence Stone, *Road to Divorce: England 1530–1987* (Oxford: Oxford University Press, 1990); Lawrence Stone, *Broken Lives: Separation and Divorce in England, 1660–1857* (Oxford: Oxford University Press, 1993); S. M. Waddams, 'English Matrimonial Law on the Eve of Reform (1828–57)' *Journal of Legal History* 21, no. 2 (2000): 59–82. For further information on the Matrimonial Causes Act 1857, see Stephen Cretney, *Family Law in the Twentieth Century: A History* (Oxford: Oxford University Press, 2005), 161–95.

63 Golder, *Divorce in Nineteenth-century New South Wales*, 206–7.

64 Brook, *Conjugal Rites*, 71.

65 Matrimonial Causes Act 1873 (NSW), s 22.

The Matrimonial Causes Act was the model for Australian divorce legislation, and it involved a protracted struggle between the Colonial Office and various Australian colonial governments. Those in favour of divorce reform wanted to adopt the British legislation, but without the sexual double standard and with greater protection for deserted wives. In Australia, they argued, the legislation was needed *not* to protect aristocratic property from false heirs – which was the basis of the sexual double standard – but rather to protect destitute wives and children whose deserting husbands, under the laws of coverture, would often return to claim the wife's independent earnings.[66] Legislation in the 1840s and 1850s aimed to protect deserted women by enabling them to sue their prodigal husbands for maintenance, and indeed magistrates had awarded deserted women maintenance prior to the passage of the Act, albeit without being granted power by the legislature to do so.[67] But maintenance was difficult to enforce if the husband could not be found, slipped across colonial borders, or simply did not have money.

After decades of resistance from the imperial office (who sought to impose standardised legislation across the Empire) divorce legislation was finally enacted. All colonies accepted the British model of divorce law by 1873,[68] and by 1892, following reforms in the 1880s, New South Wales and Victoria had abolished the double standard and now had the most liberal divorce laws in the British Empire: women could divorce on a range of grounds including desertion, assault, habitual drunkenness and cruelty.[69] By 1928, all Australian states had legalised divorce for desertion and adultery, and most of them also accepted drunkenness, imprisonment, assault and insanity as grounds for the dissolution of marriage.[70] The extension of the grounds for divorce were intended to affirm the institution of marriage. State parliaments wanted women to 'rescue themselves and relieve the state by finding new husbands

66 Golder, *Divorce in Nineteenth-century New South Wales*; Finlay, *To Have But Not to Hold*.

67 See e.g., Deserted Wives and Children Act 1840 (NSW). See also Christina Twomey, *Deserted and Destitute: Motherhood, Wife Desertion and Colonial Warfare* (Melbourne: Australian Scholarly Publishing, 2005).

68 Golder, *Divorce in Nineteenth-century New South Wales*, 179–88.

69 Kercher, *An Unruly Child*, 140. See Matrimonial Causes Act Amendment Act 1881 (NSW); Divorce Act 1889 (Vic); Divorce Amendment and Extension Act 1892 (NSW), s 1(b) and (d).

70 Matrimonial Causes Amendment Act 1881 (NSW); Divorce Act 1889 (Vic); Divorce Amendment and Extension Act 1892 (NSW), s 1(b) and (d); Matrimonial Causes Act 1899 (NSW), s 14; Divorce Amendment Act 1911 (WA) (No. 7 of 1912), s 23; Matrimonial Causes Act Amendment Act 1918 (SA); also Marriage Act 1928 (Vic), s 77; Matrimonial Causes Ordinance 1932 (ACT), s 3(2).

to support them'.[71] Divorce meant easier remarriage and a privatisation of the responsibility for the costs of family.

The rates of divorce were never as high in Australia as in America or Britain, although there were three moments when they rose considerably. First, during a 'divorce boom' in the 1890s as a result of the divorce extension laws; second, during the two world wars, primarily because of adultery during periods of separation and the psychological damage caused by war; and then finally, during the 1960s as serial monogamy became more widely accepted.[72] As reflected in the parliamentary debate around the first piece of federal uniform legislation on marriage (the Matrimonial Causes Act 1959), which permitted divorce after five years separation and made 'habitual cruelty' a sufficient ground for the dissolution of marriage,[73] people in the mid-twentieth century began to place different expectations upon marriage: the desire for happiness chafed against earlier ideas of duty. Marriage was still a sign of civility and civilisation, a mark of citizenship, but it was also associated with personal fulfilment – an absence of which increasingly justified leaving its bonds. These cultural shifts were fiercely contested at the time, with divorcees labelled as 'intolerant, selfish, mean and immoral' by one Australian politician in 1959.[74] Similar criticisms were directed towards feminists; and, indeed, divorce reform and women's liberation were interrelated: shifts in perceptions of marriage were driven largely by the changing economic, social and political status of women, whose independence and workforce participation increased throughout the twentieth century, reducing the significance of marriage as their erstwhile primary vocation.

The final important change to divorce came with the 1975 Family Law Act, that set aside the Matrimonial Causes Act and introduced no-fault divorce.[75]

71 Golder and Kirkby, 'Marriage and Divorce Law before the Family Law Act 1975', 160.

72 Brook, *Conjugal Rites*, 148–9.

73 Note that in the Matrimonial Causes Act 1959 (Cth), s 28(d), one party had to be found to have 'during a period of not less than one year, habitually been guilty of cruelty to the petitioner'. Thus the legislation sanctioned violence at the same time as it purportedly curtailed it.

74 Commonwealth, *Parliamentary Debates*, House of Representatives, 12 November 1959, 2709 (Frank Stewart), cited in Brook, *Conjugal Rites*, 125.

75 See generally, Frank Bates, 'A Family Court in Australia – Its Implications for Lawyers and Legal Education' *The Law Teacher* 9, no. 1 (1975): 18–22; Kep Enderby, 'The Family Law Act: Background to the Legislation' *UNSW Law Journal* 1 (1975): 10–30; Margaret Lusink, 'The Family Law Act 1975–77 – Australia' *Conciliation Courts Review* 16 (1978): 39–44; Neville Turner, 'The Commonwealth Family Law Act: The First Challenge' *Children Australia* 1, no. 3 (1976): 51–6; Helen Rhoades and Shurlee Swain, 'A Bold Experiment? Reflections on the Early History of the Family Court' *Australian Family Lawyer* 22, no. 1 (2011): 11–15; Helen Rhoades, 'The Family Court of Australia: Examining Australia's First Therapeutic Jurisdiction' *Journal of Judicial Administration* 20

There was now one single ground for the dissolution of the marriage – 'irretrievable breakdown'[76] – rather than the fourteen grounds for divorce which existed in 1970;[77] and divorce was permitted after a one-year waiting time, rather than five years. In its focus on individual will over family lineage, the Act, in Golder and Kirkby's words, 'marked a final break with the aristocratic origins of divorce'[78] and it also signified a shift in popular and legal understandings of marriage. Marriage was no longer an institution with a set of rules prescribed by the state that might be transgressed by 'guilty parties',[79] but rather a self-regulating system based on a model of 'consortium vitae' or 'living together' that would end when one or both spouses decided that it no longer met their expectations. As a judge in 1976 explained:

> What comprises the marital relationship for each couple will vary. Marriage involves many elements some or all of which may be present in a particular marriage – elements such as dwelling under the same roof, sexual intercourse, mutual society and protection, recognition of the existence of the marriage by both spouses in public and private relationships.[80]

By allowing the marriage to be unilaterally challenged by either spouse at any time, no-fault divorce fatally undermined the principle of conjugal unity underpinning coverture. Following no-fault divorce, Heather Brooks argues, the court's interest in marriage shifted from questions of morality to the management of property. In an adversarial, fault-based system, women were punished if they did not live up to an ideal of wifely femininity and motherhood, as determined by an all-male courtroom; today, the court's major concern is with 'economic disposal and management'.[81] Part of this judicial management involves determinations of child custody where, it could be argued in the alternative, moral judgment for perceived transgressions of gender norms continues.

(2010): 67; John Fogarty, 'Establishment of the Family Court of Australia and its Early Years' *Family Matters* 60 (2001): 90.

76 Brook, *Conjugal Rites*, 139.

77 According to the Australian Bureau of Statistics, the most popular were desertion, cruelty, drunkenness and separation: Australian Bureau of Statistics, *Annual Publications on Marriage and Divorce* (ABS: 1967–1974), cited in Brook, *Conjugal Rites*, 124.

78 Golder and Kirkby, 'Marriage and Divorce Law before the Family Law Act 1975', 167.

79 Katter describes fault-based divorce as a 'quasi criminal approach whereby conduct is seen as breaching a code of behaviour and for which . . . [the] offender ought to be punished': Norman A. Katter, *Conduct, Fault and Family Law* (Sydney: Law Book Company, 1987), 5.

80 *Todd (No. 2)* (1976) FLC 90–008, cited in Brook, *Conjugal Rites*, 145.

81 Brook, *Conjugal Rites*, 150.

When situated in this historical context, the ruling in *Adkins v Adkins* appears less as a final judgment than a jostling of voices; a contestation between a past that looked to traditions of coverture and a future based on contractual freedom, where the status of wife and husband was not solely fixed by the state but rather negotiated between two individuals. Mr Adkins was not wrong to assume that his wife owed him sex. This was enshrined in law insofar as the absence of sex 'without reasonable excuse' constituted desertion. The rationale for this was found in ideas of coverture; the notion that the wife was the property of the husband and that her consent to this status on the day of her marriage – the moment she said 'I do' – constituted consent to all aspects of the marital contract for the duration of the marriage. As marriage was the only legitimate site for the procreation of children, 'conjugal rights' had the backing of law. It was, indeed, a question of public policy. On the other hand, Mrs Adkins was also able to negotiate her way out of the marital contract in a manner that her predecessors for most of the nineteenth century could not have done. This was because the Married Women's Property Acts gave her the capacity to make a contract, and because divorce laws shattered the myth of conjugal unity. The family was still crucial to public policy, but there was a shift in focus from the nineteenth to the twentieth centuries: the emphasis was less on the institution of the family as the moral foundation for the social order than the rights of the child to a nuclear family unit.

Child Custody

The Court refused Mr Adkins's divorce petition because any alleged 'marital offence' was trumped by the emerging principle of the 'best interests of the child'. This ruling reflects the growing status of the child as a rights-bearing subject in mid-twentieth century Australia, and the porous boundaries between divorce and child custody. It was not simply that divorce often involved disputes over who would rear the children, but that in an adversarial, fault-based system, the outcome of a divorce trial would determine a spouse's rights to the child. A finding of guilt would usually involve relinquishing custody rights. Over the course of Australian history, judges were guided by legislative frameworks that increasingly limited the common law's presumption of paternal rights to the child, and by shifting socio-cultural ideas on gender, sexuality and childhood. If the history of divorce shows a shift from a model of marital unity under male headship to liberal individualism, then much the same can be said of the history of child custody.

From the penal colony to today, we witness the state playing the role of an intercessory party between husband, wife and children, limiting patriarchal rights within the family at the moment of its breakdown and enlarging its own authority. Constance Backhouse usefully groups the statutory framework governing child custody into three main stages of reform: (1) minimal intrusion on paternal rights; (2) parental equalisation; and (3) paramountcy of infant welfare.[82] To this we could add a fourth that emerged in the 1990s: shared parenting.

The first major challenge to paternal custody rights came with the colonial adoption of Lord Talfourd's Act 1839.[83] The Act gave married women standing to petition for access to their children under the age of seven and, in so doing, curtailed the early common law presumption that fathers were the 'natural guardians' of their legitimate children. Like the later custody provisions of the Matrimonial Causes Act, Lord Talfourd's Act enshrined a sexual double standard in law: evidence of 'adultery, intemperance, or any misconduct' on the part of the mother would disentitle her to custody rights, and indeed any rights to have contact with her children at all. The enactment of legislation aimed at parental equalisation (the second phase of reform), in all colonies and states between 1887–1935,[84] eradicated explicit reference to the sexual double standard but conferred ample judicial discretion to take into account 'the conduct of the parents' and, thus, to continue the punishment of adulterous mothers. This legislation incorporated equitable principles concerning the 'welfare of the infant' and was extended in New South Wales to include, in certain circumstances, a maternal preference in cases where the 'tender age of the child or its state of health' made it expedient to do so.[85] It was the product of fierce feminist campaigning around egalitarian child custody, emerging theories of child development and popular beliefs in the sanctity of motherhood and its role in the creation of a new white nation.

82 Constance Backhouse, 'Mother Factor in Australian Child Custody Law, 1900–1950' *Australian Journal of Legal History* 6 (2000): 51–111.

83 This was adopted in Australia in WA, NSW and Qld: An Act for Adopting Certain Acts of Parliament 1844 (WA) adopted the imperial statute titled An Act to Amend the Law Relating to the Custody of Infants 1839 (UK) 2 & 3 Vic. c 54; in NSW, the imperial statute was adopted in the Infants' Custody Act 1854 (NSW). See also *In re Harris* (1936) 37 SR (NSW) 17, 22; Equity Act 1867 (Qld), ss 148, 150.

84 Guardianship of Infants Act 1887 (Tas), s 6; Guardianship of Infants Act 1887 (SA), s 7; Custody of Infants Act 1912 (Vic), s 6; Guardianship of Infants Act 1920 (WA), s 5; Guardianship of Infants Act 1934 (NSW), s 2. See Backhouse, 'Mother Factor in Australian Child Custody Law, 1900–1950', 67–9.

85 Custody of Children and Children's Settlement Act of 1894 (NSW), s 1.

Notions of the 'welfare of the infant' came to the fore in the third phase of reform and continue to be significant today. Any lingering common law presumptions of a father's paternal rights were buried under a new doctrine pronouncing the paramountcy of child welfare and 'equality in law between the sexes', which was enshrined in Australian legislation modelled upon an English Act of 1925.[86] While this resulted in custody being awarded to women in the majority of cases, the precise numbers, according to Backhouse, were not as overwhelming as historians have suggested. In her study of custody decisions in the first half of the twentieth century, Backhouse found that in two-thirds of the reported cases, judges awarded to mothers and, in one-third, to fathers. This child-focused model of decision-making continued with the 1975 Family Law Act, which introduced a new legal framework for resolving disputes about child care arrangements and established a dedicated family court with an in-house counselling section. Whereas, under the fault-based system, decisions made about children tended to be influenced by the judge's finding on the divorce petition, now judges drew upon the expertise of psychologists and counsellors.

The final stage of child custody reform was a political reaction to the Family Court's frequent custody rulings in favour of mothers post-1975. Having been burdened with the labour of care prior to divorce, the best interests of the child were logically seen to reside in the mother's hands. Following pressure from the Men's Rights Lobby, the idea that shared parenting was constitutive of the best interests of the child was introduced in the 2005 Family Law Amendment (Shared Parental Responsibility) Act,[87] under which the primary consideration for the judge was the 'benefit to the child of having a meaningful relationship with both parents' and a secondary consideration was the 'need to protect the child from harm caused by violence, abuse or neglect'. Changes to the Family Law Act were enacted in 2012 after sufficient evidence amassed by judges and scholars had demonstrated that shared parenting amendments were failing to protect women and children from domestic violence. The 'friendly parent' provisions were removed, the definition of domestic violence was broadened, and protecting children from physical and psychological

86 The English law was An Act to Amend the Law with Respect to the Guardianship, Custody and Marriage of Infants 1925 (UK) 15 & 16 Geo. 5 c 45, s 1. This was enshrined in Guardianship of Infants Act 1926 (WA), s 2; Guardianship and Custody of Infants Act 1928 (Qld); Marriage Act 1928 (Vic), ss 15 and 16; Guardianship of Infants Act 1934 (NSW), s 3; Guardianship of Infants Act (SA), s 11(1). See Backhouse, 'Mother Factor in Australian Child Custody Law, 1900–1950', 69–72.

87 Family Law Amendment (Shared Parental Responsibility) Act 2006 (Cth).

harm was prioritised.[88] Despite these changes, it is argued that our family law regime remains wedded to the idea that contact with the non-residential parent is crucial to the child's well-being. Stories of violence against women and children persist.[89]

De Facto Relationships and Marriage Equality

Kevin and Jennifer were elated. It was February 2003 and the Full Bench of the Family Court had just ruled that their marriage was valid; Kevin, a transgender man, was considered to be a 'man' in the everyday sense and for the purposes of the Marriage Act.[90] This was the second time they had appeared in court defending their right to marry. Kevin was registered as female at birth in 1965 but had always identified as male and was accepted as such by family and friends. In 1995, he underwent gender realignment surgery although elected not to have further surgery for the construction of a penis. He and Jennifer lived as a de facto couple with their children and had a marriage certificate issued by a celebrant in 1999, which followed a commitment ceremony two years prior. Although Kevin had been given a new birth certificate recognising him as male, the Attorney General disputed the validity of their wedding on the grounds that Kevin was not a man at the time of the wedding. The Family Court disagreed.[91]

In the leading judgment, for the first time in Australian legal history, Justice Chisholm held that a post-operative transgender person is to be treated according to their reassigned gender.[92] He made this decision by drawing upon medical evidence and evidence of social acceptance of Kevin's gender identity. Further, and marking a break with prior decisions, he held that genital reassignment surgery was not a threshold requirement; that is, it

88 Julie Stubbs and Jane Wangmann, 'Competing Conceptions of Victims of Domestic Violence within Legal Processes', in Dean Wilson and Stuart Ross (eds), *Crime, Victims and Policy: International Contexts, Local Experiences* (London: Palgrave Macmillan, 2015), 115. See also Samantha Jeffries et al., 'Good Evidence, Safe Outcomes in Parenting Matters Involving Domestic Violence? Understanding Family Report Writing Practice from the Perspective of Professionals Working in the Family Law System' *University of New South Wales Law Journal* 39, no. 4 (2016): 1355–88; Helen Rhoades, 'The Dangers of Shared Care Legislation: Why Australia Needs (Yet More) Family Law Reform' *Federal Law Review* 36, no. 3 (2008): 279–99.

89 See Jeffries et al., 'Good Evidence, Safe Outcomes'; Jess Hill, 'Suffer the Children: Trouble in the Family Court' *The Monthly*, November 2015, 36–45.

90 Marriage Act 1961 (Cth).

91 *The Attorney-General for the Commonwealth v 'Kevin and Jennifer' and Human Rights and Equal Opportunity Commission* [2003] FamCA 94 (*'Kevin and Jennifer'*).

92 *In Re Kevin (Validity of Marriage of Transsexual)* [2001] FamCA 1074, [19] (Chisholm J).

did not matter that Kevin had not undertaken phalloplasty procedures. In so declaring, the case was a significant moment in transgender jurisprudence as well as in the history of marriage. It rejected the man/penis and woman/vagina distinction traditionally specified in the law of marriage and its corollary, argued by the Attorney General, that 'procreation is one of the essential purposes of marriage'.[93] Marriage, the Full Bench recognised, was an historically contingent institution that today had more to do with companionship than the accomplishment of particular sex acts. Marriage, they held, should not be 'frozen in time',[94] and ought to be uncoupled from sexual morality: '[W]e think it strongly arguable that marriage is now a secularised institution in our society . . . its historical Christian origins are not relevant or helpful.'[95]

Like the other cases examined in this chapter, *In Re Kevin* represents a pivotal moment in the legal history of marriage. The Court did not decide upon the question of the validity of same-sex marriage because it was accepted by all parties that for a marriage to be valid it must be between a man and a woman. The case looked backwards, legitimating marriage as a heterosexual union, as well as forward, acknowledging the historical contingency of marriage, the flexibility of its meaning as determined by spouses rather than the state, and detaching it from its historical associations with child rearing or its original underpinnings as the only lawful site for the procreation of children. In fact, the case suggested that the question of procreation was no longer foundational to marriage. If we are to imagine marriage as a territory, then we would say that *In Re Kevin* represents a time when its borders were beginning to open, the laws governing the territory were more flexible and the territory itself was expanding to (eventually) encompass queer conjugal arrangements.

The fact that Kevin and Jennifer were not content with their de facto status and were willing to go to court twice to defend their right to marry, suggests much about the superior cultural and legal status of marriage compared to other forms of conjugality in our society. In the 1990s, when they first sought to formalise their union with a commitment ceremony and then with a marriage certificate, de facto heterosexual couples had most of the same legal rights as married heterosexual couples. Non-marital relationships had been regulated by state law since the enactment of the De Facto Relationships Act 1984 (NSW).[96]

93 '*Kevin and Jennifer*', [152]. 94 Ibid, [87].
95 Ibid, [151]; see also Brook, *Conjugal Rites*, 60, 62, 64–5.
96 Fehlberg et al., *Australian Family Law*, 136; De Facto Relationships Act 1984 (NSW). For background reading on de facto relationships in Australia, see generally Hilary Astor and John Nothdurft, 'Report of the New South Wales Law Reform Commission on De Facto Relationships' *The Modern Law Review* 48, no. 1 (1985): 61–72; Siew-Ean Khoo,

Initially the law only recognised heterosexual de facto relationships, but this was expanded throughout the 1990s to homosexual relationships. By 2004 significant legislative change had brought same-sex couples close to legal equality with de facto heterosexual couples in most jurisdictions, although a 2007 Human Rights and Equal Opportunity Commission (HREOC) inquiry into discrimination against same-sex couples found fifty-eight discriminatory laws, all of which were amended in 2008.[97] In that year the states also referred their powers to the Commonwealth, and the Family Law Act was amended to provide that the legal effects of breakdown for marital and de facto relationships were the same. These legal changes reflect broader shifts throughout the twentieth century, as the cultural significance of marriage diminished. Yet it would be incorrect to suggest equivalence between the legal status of married and de facto couples. Marriage is registered while cohabitation is not, which in legal terms means that marriage is a status from which legal consequences immediately flow, whereas non-marital relationships need to be proved based on a set of criteria modelled on those of marriage: for instance, a common residence, financial dependence or interdependence, and ownership or property.[98] Kevin and Jennifer may have been influenced by the legal privileges that continue to attach to marriage, but they also probably wanted to marry because of its symbolic importance in the community, and the associations it carries of privacy, respectability and stability.

Kevin and Jennifer's victory in 2003 came one year before the conservative Liberal government introduced a bill to amend the Marriage Act 1961 to specify that marriage was between a man and a woman.[99] It was introduced as part of an effort to prevent the recognition of same-sex marriages that had been conducted overseas. From Federation until 1961, each state and territory was responsible for regulating people's entrance and exit from marriage. This changed in 1961 when the Australian Parliament, using its power to legislate with respect to marriage under Section 51(21) of the Constitution, passed the

'Living Together as Married: A Profile of De Facto Couples in Australia' *Journal of Marriage and Family* 49, no. 1 (1987): 185–91; Jenni Millbank, 'The De Facto Relationships Amendment Bill 1998 (NSW): The Rationale for Law Reform' *Australasian Gay & Lesbian Law Journal* 8 (1999): 1–26; Jenni Millbank, 'The Changing Meaning of "De Facto" Relationships' *Current Family Law* 1 (2006): 1–11.

97 Human Rights and Equal Opportunity Commission, *Same-Sex: Same Entitlements: National Inquiry into Discrimination against people in Same-Sex Relationships* (HREOC, 2007), 10.

98 Family Law Act 1975 (Cth), s 4AA. See also Brook, *Conjugal Rites*, 154 and Stephen Parker, Patrick Parkinson and Juliet Behrens, *Australian Family Law in Context: Commentary and Materials* (Sydney: Law Book Company, 1994), 299.

99 Marriage Amendment Bill 2004 (Cth).

Marriage Act 1961 to regulate marriage law uniformly across the country. At the time of promulgation, Section 5 of the Marriage Act did not contain a definition of marriage because, as Senator Gorton argued in the 1970s, 'marriage, of course, can mean a number of things',[100] and there was a deliberate effort not to limit its scope. Although Section 46 of the Marriage Act required authorised celebrants to say that 'marriage, according to law in Australia, is the union of a man and woman to the exclusion of all others',[101] Gorton was clear that Section 46 would not have the force of law to define a marriage.[102] The 2005 legislation amended Section 5 to define marriage as 'the union of a man and a woman to the exclusion of all others, voluntarily entered into for life'. It also provided that homosexual unions solemnised in foreign countries would not be recognised in Australia. Family Court judge Alistair Nicholson described the Act as 'one of the most unfortunate pieces of legislation that has ever been passed by the Australian Parliament'.[103] Where state governments had recognised same-sex relationships through measures including legislation enabling the registration of same-sex and other domestic relationships, it was accepted that it would be constitutionally invalid for them to enact laws enabling same-sex marriage. Marriage equality legislation was left to the Commonwealth, which unequivocally opposed it.

Between 2005 and the passing of marriage equality legislation in 2017, a grassroots movement for marriage equality evolved using a range of techniques from public rallies, mock weddings and social media, to advertising campaigns, public opinion polls and parliamentary activism. Over the fourteen years of the campaign there were twenty-three bills and four Senate inquiries in Parliament attempting to challenge the laws. The most significant of the bills were those that sought to eliminate exclusionary references to sexual orientation and gender in the Marriage Act but which, in each instance, were defeated in the Senate.[104] The marriage equality movement argued, in accordance with traditional liberal notions of formal equality, that the state should recognise and protect individual choice and freedom, and

100 Commonwealth, *Parliamentary Debates*, Senate, 18 April 1961, 544 (John Gorton).
101 Marriage Act 1961 (Cth), s 46(1), amended by Marriage Amendment (Definition and Religious Freedoms) Act 2017 (Cth).
102 Commonwealth, *Parliamentary Debates*, Senate, 18 April 1961, 544 (John Gorton).
103 Alastair Nicholson, 'The Legal Regulation of Marriage' *Melbourne University Law Review* 17 (2005): 556–68, cited in Fehlberg et al., *Australian Family Law*, chapter 5.
104 Marriage Equality Amendment Bill 2009 (Cth); Marriage Equality Amendment Bill 2010 (Cth); Marriage Amendment Bill 2012 (Cth); Barbara Baird, 'Twenty-first Century LGBTI Activism in Australia: The Limits of Equality' *Australian Historical Studies* 49, no. 4 (2018): 475–92, 485.

promote equality in society. Marriage law was clearly out of step with anti-discrimination law and with a state that, since no-fault divorce, purportedly regulated people's intimacies according to law rather than morals. In dictating that homosexual people could not marry, the state drew an exclusionary line within the citizenry and enshrined heterosexual dominance in law.

Marriage equality was opposed on traditional religious grounds – that marriage was a sacred union between a man and a woman designed for procreation. There was also opposition within the gay and lesbian movement, where people argued that the institution of marriage was beyond reform, that marriage equality would simply incorporate gays and lesbians into a heterosexist and sexist institution, and would render suspect those who refused its bonds.[105] Marriage signalled a conservative break from the utopian politics that had always characterised gay and lesbian activism – a belief in more liberationist ways of conducting intimacy.[106] Those in favour of marriage equality argued that same-sex relationships had the same legitimacy and value as heterosexual relationships. They also argued that although almost all legal rights that were attached to marriage were now attached to de facto gay relationships, that the label 'marriage' mattered, and that marriage offered homosexual people the same privacy and decency that had always been the exclusive preserve of heterosexuals. With Australia increasingly out of step with the rest of the Western world, the Liberal government in 2017 conducted a public ballot on marriage equality through the post and, in November 2017, it was announced that 79.5 per cent of Australians voted in the ballot: 61 per cent in favour and 38 per cent against. A Marriage Equality Bill was introduced shortly after, passing through both Houses of Parliament with little opposition.[107] Marriage equality activists declared that love had finally conquered.

Returning to *In Re Kevin*, we can see how the case represented a shift in judicial thinking about marriage which was later reflected in arguments for marriage equality. The law granted equal treatment to a transgender couple because it could recognise similar standards of conjugality; the question was one of likeness to a heterosexual norm. This kind of reasoning was indebted to legal developments that we can trace from the late twentieth to the early twenty-first centuries: from no-fault divorce, which transformed marriage

105 Paula Ettelbrick, 'Since When Is Marriage a Path to Liberation?', in Andrew Sullivan (ed.), *Same-Sex Marriage: Pro and Con – A Reader* (New York: Vintage Books, 1997, 2004), 118–25, cited in Brook, *Conjugal Rites*, 30.
106 See Baird, 'Twenty-first Century LGBTI Activism in Australia'.
107 Marriage Amendment (Definition and Religious Freedoms) Bill 2017 (Cth).

into a set of normative performances rather than rules and offences; to the rise in cohabitation where the law of marriage was extended to 'marriage-like' conjugal arrangements; to marriage equality. The question as to whether marriage equality results in a 'norming' of same-sex relationships or a radicalising of marriage remains open to debate.[108]

Conclusion

Concluding a legal history of marriage in Australia with gay marriage may incline us towards linear, progressivist view of the past: that we have shaken off the stiff oppressive carapace that once cloaked marriage and are now dancing under a shower of rainbow confetti. While the institution of marriage has become less exclusionary and rule-bound, we need to remember that our current preference for cohabitation has much in common with the late eighteenth and early nineteenth centuries where serial monogamy was the norm. We would also do well to remember that while marriage may now be just one territory in a wider map of conjugality, it is larger and more dominant than all others. The borders of marriage are still policed, with polygamous relationships not permitted into its province, and it continues to have unparalleled cultural, symbolic significance, being associated more than any other conjugal form with social respectability. Marriage is enshrined as a social good within the Family Law Act while cohabitation, civil partnerships and caring relationships are not. Yet, when we think about Blackstone's definition of marriage, legal innovation and liberalisation are undeniable. Over three centuries we have seen a shift from coverture to cohabitation, from female subjugation enshrined in marriage law to formal (albeit not substantive) gender equality; and from an idea of marriage as externally prescribed status to that of an individually negotiated contract, blind to racial,

108 See for example, Baird, 'Twenty-first Century LGBTI Activism in Australia'; Louise Richardson-Self, 'Questioning the Goal of Same-Sex Marriage' *Australian Feminist Studies* 27, no. 72 (2012): 205–19; Paula Ettelbrick, 'Since When Is Marriage a Path to Liberation?', in Robert M. Baird and Stuart E. Rosenbaum (eds), *Same-sex Marriage: The Moral and Legal Debate* (Amherst, NY: Prometheus, 1997); Paula Ettelbrick, 'Domestic Partnerships, Civil Unions, or Marriage: One Size Does Not Fit All' *Albany Law Review* 64, no. 3 (2001): 905–15; Cheshire Calhoun, *Feminism, the Family, and the Politics of the Closet: Lesbian and Gay Displacement* (Oxford: Oxford University Press, 2000); Cheshire Calhoun, 'Who's Afraid of Polygamous Marriage – Lessons for Same-sex Marriage Advocacy from the History of Polygamy' *San Diego Law Review* 42 (2005): 1023–42; William N. Eskridge Jr., *Equality Practice: Civil Unions and the Future of Gay Rights* (Abingdon: Routledge, 2002); Jennifer M. Lehmann (ed.), *The Gay & Lesbian Marriage & Family Reader: Analyses of Problems and Prospects for the 21st Century* (New York: Richard Altschuler & Associates, Inc, 2001).

sexual and gender difference. While Christian morality pervaded the language of mid-nineteenth-century politicians, lawyers and judges, mid-twentieth-century discourse saw a shift towards the promotion of individual liberty, happiness and freedom. Compared with the nineteenth century, today marriage is one option among many – freely entered into and relatively easily dissolved – as we prioritise not duty and forbearance but self-fulfilment and love.

20

Protection Regimes

AMANDA NETTELBECK

On 26 May 1997, the *Report of the National Inquiry into the Separation of Aboriginal and Torres Strait Islander Children from their Families* – the 'Bringing Them Home' report – was tabled in federal Parliament. It contained searing accounts of loss, suffering and survival experienced by people whose lives were dictated by the Aboriginal Protection or Welfare Boards that operated around Australia's states and territories until the late 1960s. More than a decade after the report's release, the then Prime Minister Kevin Rudd delivered a national apology to the Stolen Generations who were systematically alienated from their families, Country and culture in the name of protection. In Australia today, the term 'protection' is perhaps most closely associated with these practices and institutions of assimilation imposed upon Indigenous people through much of the twentieth century. They were authorised by laws that granted state governments wide-ranging powers of control over Indigenous lives, purportedly for their own good. The human and cultural costs of Australia's protection laws have been multigenerational, and their impacts continue to resonate for Indigenous communities.[1]

Yet apart from the legal regime of assimilation that defined Indigenous policy through the mid-twentieth century, protection has a longer and more complex history in Australia, as it does globally.[2] This chapter will trace some of the different ways in which government programs of protection were conceived and applied to Indigenous Australians, from the appointment of

Research towards this chapter was supported by an ARC Discovery grant DP140103049.

[1] Commonwealth of Australia, *Bringing Them Home: Report of the National Inquiry into the Separation of Aboriginal and Torres Strait Islander Children from Their Families Report* (Canberra: Human Rights and Equal Opportunity Commission, 1997); Anna Haebich, *Broken Circles: Fragmenting Indigenous Families, 1800–2000* (Fremantle: Fremantle Arts Centre Press, 2000).

[2] Lauren Benton, Adam Clulow and Bain Attwood (eds), *Protection and Empire: A Global History* (Cambridge: Cambridge University Press, 2018).

nineteenth-century protectors to the repeal of Protection Acts. Other chapters in this volume identify some of the consequences of protection policy in fracturing Indigenous families and perpetuating a system of minimal government welfare.[3] Complementing those points of focus, this chapter considers how protection evolved from a plan to extend the law's benefits to Indigenous people as 'new' British subjects to a regime of state governance that circumscribed their mobility, managed the distribution and earnings of their labour, and surveilled most aspects of their daily life.

Notably, as protection transformed over time into an ever more complex system of governance, its legal powers also grew more robust. The history of protection, then, is a history of state encroachment into Indigenous lives through incremental degrees of legal authority. But this history of state power also dovetails with the history of Indigenous political action. For as long as the project of protection has existed in Australia, Indigenous people have responded to it in strategic ways. From the earliest iteration of protection as an aspirational colonial project to 'improve' Indigenous people through rights of British subjecthood, through to its later expression as a legal program of state surveillance, Indigenous people have engaged with protection by petitioning for the return of land, calling for equal civil rights as British subjects and protesting the inequalities of exceptional laws.[4]

Early Protection Policy in the Australian Colonies

The application of protection policies to Indigenous Australians dates to the mid-1830s, when the imperial government determined to clarify their status as British subjects due the same legal entitlements as were due to settler subjects. The Colonial Office confirmed this position in 1834, emphasising that the rights of the king's Aboriginal subjects must be upheld by the law.[5] Before this moment, colonial governors had dealt with Indigenous people with mixed strategies of conciliation and military force. Nothing in their instructions clarified how they were to understand Indigenous people's legal status or how they were to deal with the problems of frontier violence that were endemic to Australia's pastoral frontiers. The legal fiction that the continent was settled without conquest was constantly undermined by the

[3] See Libesman, Ellinghaus and Gray, Chapter 18, and O'Brien, Chapter 21, in this volume.
[4] See Foley and McKinnon, Chapter 22 in this volume.
[5] Secretary of State to Governor Bourke, 1 August 1834, *Historical Records of Australia*, Series 1 (Sydney: Library Committee, Commonwealth Parliament, 1922), 17: 491.

ubiquity of frontier conflict wherever settlers took up land. Indeed, many settlers considered themselves to be openly at war with Indigenous people.[6]

Australian colonial authorities were hardly alone in finding that frontier violence accompanied colonial settlement wherever it spread. By the mid-1830s, widespread conflicts over land, including renewed hostilities on the eastern Cape frontier, persuaded imperial observers that Indigenous people in all British settlements must be compensated for their dispossession with clearly defined rights that could be defended in law.[7] But although Indigenous rights became an empire-wide concern, conditions in the Australian colonies appeared to demand an especially urgent response.[8] Escalating settler migration and pastoral expansion there was matched by intensifying frontier conflict, which the governors of New South Wales and Van Diemen's Land had tried to check during the 1820s with declarations of martial law. Yet such government tactics only had short-term effects; neither force nor diplomacy seemed to have enduring capacity to regulate the violence of Australia's unruly frontiers. In this fraught environment, the clarified status of Indigenous people as the king's subjects was meant to reinforce the Crown's jurisdiction in Australia's colonies and bolster the rule of law, ultimately replacing bloodshed with peace. By the late 1830s, it was a matter of policy that the law's protections extended to Indigenous and settler subjects alike.

The Colonial Office put this policy into action by appointing Protectors of Aborigines as officials who would monitor the rights and responsibilities of Indigenous people as British subjects. By the end of 1839, protectors had been dispatched to three Australian jurisdictions where pastoral investment was on an upward trajectory: the Port Phillip District of New South Wales (Victoria), and the newer colonies of Western Australia and South Australia. This placed protection agents in each of the existing Australian colonies except Van Diemen's Land, where a protection office was not seen to have practical relevance in the wake of the 'Black Wars' and the removal of Aboriginal survivors to Flinders Island. These colonial protectors were granted magisterial powers so that they could uphold the Crown's jurisdiction on disputed frontiers. Their legal duties included a responsibility to investigate acts of unlawful violence, activate prosecutions, arrange defence counsel for Indigenous people who came before the courts, and otherwise

[6] For instance, Henry Reynolds, *Forgotten War* (Sydney: NewSouth, 2013).
[7] British Parliamentary Papers (BPP), *Report from the Select Committee on Aborigines (British Settlements)*, No. 425 (1837), 82–4.
[8] Ibid.

educate them in codes of British justice. This last responsibility included a role to develop a 'provisional code' of rules that could serve 'for the regulation of the Aborigines' while they transitioned into meaningful life as British subjects.[9]

Beyond their magisterial powers, protectors had a more aspirational set of duties to build Indigenous people's practical British subjecthood by inducting them into all the 'arts' of settler society.[10] The imperial philosophy of humanitarian governance that underpinned protectors' duties was grounded in the idea that Indigenous people's fuller subjecthood would emerge from a combination of guaranteed legal rights, education and training. This was a philosophy that British abolitionists had already applied to slaves, but it was not only driven by an impulse to improve material conditions for exploited peoples. As Alan Lester and Fae Dussart write, the principles of humanitarian governance were also focused on achieving 'the more effective ordering and regulation of enslaved people' whose exploitation had become a moral problem of empire but who were not 'considered ready for an experiment in individual freedom'.[11] In a parallel way, Indigenous people were seen as needing development towards actualisation as British subjects, and Protectors of Aborigines were the agents who would oversee this process.

As the institutional vehicles of humanitarian governance, protection offices had numerous applications in the British Empire beyond the Australian colonies. From the mid-1820s until just after abolition, Protectors of Slaves operated in several British slave colonies to adjudicate master-slave disputes and (at least in appearance) uphold the new amelioration laws that were meant to mitigate the worst exploitations of the slavery system.[12] These protectors provided the model for Protectors of Immigrants, the government agents who represented legal oversight of the empire's post-abolition indentured labour system. Protectors were also appointed in New Zealand when it became a Crown Colony via treaty in 1840. Styled 'Protectors of Aborigines' as in the Australian colonies, the role of New Zealand's protectors was to mediate the transition from Māori to British sovereignty. Well before the British Empire, too, earlier empires pursued

[9] Ibid, 83–4.

[10] Lord Glenelg to Governor Gipps, 31 January 1838, BPP, *Aborigines (Australian Colonies)*, 34, No. 627 (1844), 166–7.

[11] Alan Lester and Fae Dussart, *Colonization and the Origins of Humanitarian Governance* (Cambridge: Cambridge University Press, 2014), 56.

[12] Trevor Burnard, 'A Voice for Slaves: The Office of the Fiscal in Berbice and the Beginning of Protection in the British Empire, 1819–1834' *Pacific Historical Review* 87, no. 1 (2018): 30–53.

similar protection arrangements to manage the behaviour of their mobile subjects, to consolidate their jurisdiction abroad, or to assert their centralising authority in times of political flux.[13] In effect, Australia's early Protectors of Aborigines fitted within a much wider global network of imperial protection agencies that existed to govern colonial relationships.[14]

But although Australia's Protectors of Aborigines adapted an existing office, their roles developed in distinctly local ways. Port Phillip's was the most robustly staffed of Australia's protection departments, reflecting the fact that, by the late 1830s, voracious settler occupation had already caused extensive Indigenous dispossession and upheaval in the district. The system of Aboriginal protection that emerged in Port Phillip through the 1840s was one in which protectors attempted to gather fractured Indigenous communities onto dedicated government stations where they might live as Christian farmers, sheltered from further settler interference. Rather than interpreting their role as one of legal reform, labour placement and social training, Port Phillip's protectors were largely motivated by missionary aspirations. This quickly isolated them from other colonial officials, who expected them to be more forceful in enlisting their magisterial powers to pacify troubled frontiers.

Such disconnection between protectors and the colonial administration was exceptional. Protectors in the newer colonies of South Australia and Western Australia fitted more seamlessly into the business of humanitarian governance, as that was interpreted by local governors. In South Australia, the work of protection was directed into practical efforts to integrate Indigenous people into colonial society through schemes of labour, education and settlement, and to adapt them to codes of British justice. Western Australia's system of protection was more distinctive for its alignment with policing. There, protectors exercised their magisterial powers more regularly to police and prosecute Indigenous crime, reasoning that demonstrations of lawful punishment would teach Indigenous people to obey the law and thereby deter settlers from illegal acts of retaliatory violence against them.[15]

13 Lauren Benton and Lisa Ford, *Rage for Order: The British Empire and the Origins of International Law, 1800–1850* (Cambridge, MA: Harvard University Press, 2016), 85–116; Lauren Benton and Adam Clulow, 'Introduction: The Long, Strange History of Protection', in Benton et al. (eds), *Protection and Empire*, 1–9.

14 Amanda Nettelbeck, *Indigenous Rights and Colonial Subjecthood: Protection and Reform in the Nineteenth-century British Empire* (Cambridge: Cambridge University Press), 19–29.

15 Amanda Nettelbeck, '"A Halo of Protection": Colonial Protectors and the Policy of Aboriginal Protection as Punishment' *Australian Historical Studies* 43, no. 3 (2012): 396–411.

However, regardless of local variations, none of these early protection offices enjoyed much success in systematically reducing frontier violence, influencing Indigenous people's reform, or upholding their rights and responsibilities as British subjects. Despite their magisterial powers, protectors had limited practical leverage: they were few in number and their authority as government officials was unequal to the weight of pastoral interests. But just as importantly, their magisterial powers were weakened by the limitations of colonial legal culture itself. Even when acts of frontier violence were investigated, conditions of vast distance, limited policing resources and settler secrecy obstructed the collection of evidence for prosecutions. When sufficient evidence did allow cases to be prosecuted, the criminal justice system proved ill-equipped to treat Indigenous people as legal equals. The inadmissibility of Indigenous evidence in courts, the prejudice of settler juries when it did become admissible, the protracted dearth of suitable interpreters, and the variety of ways settler violence could be mitigated, all created obstacles to the possibility of legal redress.

On the other hand, once Indigenous people had been claimed as subjects of the Crown, their supposed equality before the law made them more regularly subject to prosecution, incarceration and execution for attacks on settlers and their property. New South Wales's governor George Gipps expressed this neatly in 1841 when he assured the Colonial Office that his government would treat Indigenous people with impartiality, as amenable to the law's defences and penalties as any other British subjects.[16] This position, that Indigenous people received the law's protections as British subjects, was not only unrealised in practice; it also blocked any official avenue for recognising Indigenous jurisdiction.[17] Colonial judges and juries often expressed doubt about whether the court's jurisdiction applied in a meaningful way to Indigenous defendants who had little or no experience with colonial society; but, at least formally, Indigenous jurisdiction was considered extinguished by Britain's assertion of sovereignty.[18] Practices of traditional law that openly clashed with codes of British justice rendered Indigenous people even more susceptible to criminalisation. The promise of Indigenous equality before the law might have carried strong utopian appeal

16 Governor Gipps to Lord Russell, 7 April 1841, BPP, *Aborigines (Australian Colonies)*, No. 627 (1844), 105.

17 See Finnane, Chapter 27 in this volume.

18 Judgment of Justice Burton, 4 February 1836, Document 47, 'Original Documents on Aborigines and Law', 1797–1840, Macquarie University, www.law.mq.edu.au/research/colonial_case_law/nsw/other_features/correspondence/documents/, accessed 15 January 2020.

for reformers in Britain, but the principle that one law prevailed for all proved a distinctive disadvantage to Indigenous people.

The idea that Indigenous protection would arise from enforcement of the Crown's uniform jurisdiction did not hold in the same way for New Zealand. The 1840 Treaty of Waitangi stamped Māori as British subjects, as was already true for Indigenous Australians. But in contrast to the Australian colonies, where Indigenous sovereignty was never officially recognised, Māori sovereignty had been formally recognised in 1835, and this laid a stepped pathway to British jurisdiction there.[19] While Britain's claim to sovereignty subjected Indigenous Australians by default to settler law, the Colonial Office was willing to accept that Māori could continue to 'live under Native Law and Native Custom' in matters between themselves (except where they conflicted with 'universal Laws of morality') until they transitioned to settler law.[20] As mediators of this transition, New Zealand's protectors were given powers of summary jurisdiction and were asked to 'make themselves conversant' with Māori laws, on an understanding that they would arbitrate between settler and Māori modes of justice while Māori accommodated themselves to British customs.[21]

No such familiarity with Indigenous laws was expected of Protectors of Aborigines in the Australian colonies, where the Crown's sole jurisdiction outwardly prevailed. Nonetheless, Indigenous people continued to practice their own laws, and – at least during the 1840s when terms of colonial interaction were relatively fluid – systems of protection offered a point of cross-cultural contact through which Indigenous people could assert their own expectations of lawful behaviour. Historians have suggested that Indigenous people imparted expectations of lawful or 'right behaviour' in their interactions with protectors and missionaries in order to safeguard interests in land.[22] In addition, their relationship to protectors could provide Indigenous people with an avenue to shore up resources, negotiate future

[19] Shaunnagh Dorsett, *Juridical Encounters: Māori and the Colonial Courts, 1840–1852* (Auckland: Auckland University Press, 2017).

[20] James Stephen to Mr Hope, 19 May [1843], CO 209/16, folio 455, National Archives, UK (NA).

[21] Lord Russell to Captain Hobson, 9 December 1840, CO 209/8, NA.

[22] Richard Broome, '"There Were Vegetables Every Year Mr Green Was Here": Right Behaviour and the Struggle for Autonomy at Coranderrk Aboriginal Reserve' *History Australia* 3, no. 2 (2006): 43.1–43.16; Joanna Cruikshank and Mark McMillan, 'Lawful Conduct, Aboriginal Protection and Land in Victoria, 1859–1869', in S. Furphy and A. Nettelbeck (eds), *Aboriginal Protection and its Intermediaries in Britain's Antipodean Colonies* (London: Routledge, 2020).

security, or remind colonial officials of reciprocal obligations.[23] At least some protectors were alert to the practice of Indigenous laws and, while not necessarily conceding to those laws, attempted to accommodate Indigenous expectations of lawful behaviour through acts of diplomacy.[24]

A shift in the politics of protection occurred through the 1850s when all the Australasian colonies except Western Australia became self-governing, and responsibility for Indigenous policy transferred from the Colonial Office to settler governments. By this time, earlier government objectives to build Indigenous colonial citizenship through a combination of legal rights and cultural training were widely perceived to have failed and, between 1849 and 1857, the original offices of Aboriginal protection were abolished or allowed to lapse. The system of protection as a set of dedicated magisterial offices appointed to build and uphold the rights and capacities of British subjecthood no longer existed. However, as Indigenous people became increasingly relegated to the fringes of settler society, vestiges of protection remained visible in distributions of government rations and blankets as a form of residual welfare.[25]

Settlers tended to regard these distributions dismissively as a dole to the destitute. In contrast, historians have suggested that Indigenous people received them as a form of 'right behaviour' from colonial authorities, and government blankets in particular became an important part of an adapted Indigenous economy.[26] As scholars have argued, protection arrangements also became privatised in this mid-century period as the pastoral sector became increasingly reliant upon Indigenous labour, effectively turning the pastoralist into an informal kind of protector, responsible for providing Indigenous workers with rations and other forms of material security.[27] This arrangement had some advantages in enabling Indigenous people to remain on their own country, although it was also inherently exploitative and left workers unpredictably dependent upon the temperament of their employer. Ann McGrath's landmark study of Indigenous workers in the cattle industry shows how much settler violence, or the threat of it, was

[23] For instance, Rachel Standfield, 'Protection, Settler Politics and Indigenous Politics in the Work of William Thomas' *Journal of Colonialism and Colonial History* 13, no. 1 (2012).

[24] For instance, William Thomas to George Augustus Robinson, 13 February 1844, VPRS 11, Item 8, File 1844/869, Public Record Office of Victoria.

[25] See O'Brien, Chapter 21 in this volume.

[26] Michael Smithson, 'A Misunderstood Gift: The Annual Issue of Blankets to Aborigines in New South Wales, 1826–48' *Push* 30 (1991): 75.

[27] Ann McGrath, *Born in the Cattle: Aborigines in Cattle Country* (Sydney: Allen and Unwin, 1997), 100; Tim Rowse, 'A Short and Simple Provisional Code: The Pastoralist as "Protector"' in Furphy and Nettelbeck (eds), *Aboriginal Protection and its Intermediaries.*

interwoven with mutual dependency in pastoral labour relationships.[28] In these ambivalent ways, a semblance of protection vested in residual government welfare and private employment arrangements continued after the closure of the first Aboriginal protection offices.

Even in this fallow period of policy neglect, however, the official position that Indigenous people enjoyed the Crown's protection continued to provide them with strategic scope to assert their political concerns through petitions or personal addresses to authorities as high as the Queen herself.[29] On a famous occasion in 1863, a Kulin delegation gave Victoria's governor Barkly, at his Queen's Birthday reception, gifts and a message for the sovereign. Historians have widely understood this approach as a diplomatic strategy by the Kulin to protect their stake in the land that became Coranderrk station.[30] The Kulin's ongoing political agency in protecting their future at Coranderrk is particularly well known, but there were many other occasions in the history of Australia when Indigenous people leveraged the idea of the Crown's protection to call upon authorities for the rights of citizenship and equality that were due to them as British subjects.[31] The strength of Indigenous petitioning over time, in Australia as in other settler nations, charts the way that Indigenous communities continued to respond to the impositions of settler law and governance to challenge the loss of their lands, to question new policy agendas, and to call the attention of authorities to their unmet rights.[32]

By the end of the 1860s, the governmental conception of Aboriginal protection had fundamentally shifted from a transformative (and still unfulfilled) promise of legal equality to an uneven dissemination of government welfare, supplemented by employer paternalism. As Ann Curthoys and Jessie Mitchell argue, the emerging model of colonial democracy in this era of settler self-government was one that explicitly marginalised Indigenous

[28] McGrath, *Born in the Cattle*.

[29] Sarah Carter and Maria Nugent (eds), *Mistress of Everything: Queen Victoria in Indigenous Worlds* (Manchester: Manchester University Press, 2016).

[30] For instance, Maria Nugent, '"The Queen Gave Us the Land": Aboriginal People, Queen Victoria and Historical Remembrance' *History Australia* 9, no. 2 (2012): 182–200.

[31] Bain Attwood and Andrew Markus, *Thinking Black: William Cooper and the Australian Aborigines' League* (Canberra: Aboriginal Studies Press, 2004); Ann Curthoys and Jessie Mitchell, '"Bring This Paper to the Good Governor": Aboriginal Petitioning in Britain's Australian Colonies', in Saliha Belmessous (ed.), *Native Claims: Indigenous Law Against Empire, 1500–1920* (Oxford: Oxford University Press, 2011).

[32] Ravi de Costa, 'Identity, Authority and the Moral Worlds of Indigenous Petitions' *Comparative Studies in Society and History* 48, no. 3 (2006): 669–98; Karen O'Brien, *Petitioning for Land: The Petitions of First Peoples of Modern British Colonies* (London: Bloomsbury, 2019).

rights.[33] However, arguably the most significant shift in the politics of protection took place between 1869 and 1912, as settler states consolidated their sense of entitlement to political independence and economic growth. In this window of time, the introduction of protection statutes across Australia incrementally created a more uniform and institutionalised protection regime; and, in contrast to the earlier nineteenth century, it was now supported by significant legal powers. Colony by colony and state by state, protection statutes gave protectors or their proxies a new level of authority to manage the place of Indigenous people within the white settler state, enabling them to direct the movement of individuals on and off reserves, to control marriages and family finances, and to set the terms of employment.[34]

The Evolution of Protection Statutes

The passage of Victoria's *Aborigines Protection Act 1869* marked the beginning of protection as a legally empowered project in Australia, and it recalibrated the terms of Aboriginal protection around a mixed agenda of segregation, labour management and child custody.[35] Victoria had been an independent colony since 1851, and its early adoption of protection legislation was precipitated by the sheer impact of Indigenous dispossession since the region's pastoral occupation in the mid-1830s as the Port Phillip District. Victoria was many times smaller than Australia's other mainland colonies and it offered more uniformly fertile land for grazing stock. As a result, pastoral takeover there was swift, within the space of two decades creating conditions for a closer model of Indigenous management than was yet possible in the other, much larger mainland Australian colonies. A decade before Victoria introduced this first Protection Act, its local government undertook a commission of inquiry to investigate future needs for Indigenous policy. A key recommendation of the Inquiry's 1859 report was for the government to establish a network of reserves, where 'remnant' Aboriginal tribes could live out their lives protected from 'abject want and misery'.[36] Following this recommendation, Victoria created Australia's first reserve system overseen

[33] Ann Curthoys and Jessie Mitchell, *Taking Liberty: Indigenous Rights and Settler Self-Government in Colonial Australia, 1830–1890* (Cambridge: Cambridge University Press, 2018).

[34] See also Kirkby, Chapter 29 in this volume.

[35] Aborigines Protection Act (33 Vic. No. 3[49]) 1869 (Victoria).

[36] Government of Victoria, *Report of the Select Committee of the Legislative Council on the Aborigines* (Melbourne: Government Printer, 1859), iv.

by a Central Board, although in its first decade the Board was not backed by statutory authority.[37]

But with Victoria's introduction of the Aborigines Protection Act 1869, an Australian colonial government for the first time granted itself wide-ranging legal authority to determine the place of Indigenous people's residence, to manage the terms of their employment contracts, to apportion their earnings, and to decide arrangements for the custody of their children. In this new era of protection as a program of legal governance, the conditions of Indigenous life became considerably more constrained. Even so, Indigenous people in Victoria continued to adapt to the changing political landscape by petitioning for rights, developing new forms of economic and cultural sustainability in agricultural reserve communities, and arguing for state protections to expand their limited holdings in reserved land.[38]

In the mid-1880s, conditions in colonial Victoria transitioned again. At an immediate level, the expense of government-funded reserves prompted concerns about how to reduce costs; but, more broadly, settler-colonial theories of racial classification by bloodline were becoming consolidated in law in ways that supported a philosophy of assimilation for Indigenous people of mixed descent.[39] Known as the 'Half-Caste Act', the Aborigines Protection Act 1886 replaced Victoria's 1869 Act and forced people of mixed descent to find work outside the government stations, where Indigenous communities had rebuilt themselves, leaving so-called 'full blood' Indigenous people confined to reserves and, in the process, undermining family coherence.[40]

Beyond Victoria, however, neither a reserve-based model of segregation nor a legally monitored program of assimilation had yet emerged as viable policy. By the 1880s, Indigenous people everywhere were incorporated as workers into colonial industries, especially pastoralism. This encouraged the expansion of the privatised model of 'protection' grounded in employer paternalism, diminishing the pressure on governments to take greater responsibility for Indigenous welfare. South Australia and New South

[37] Jessie Mitchell and Ann Curthoys, 'How Different was Victoria? Aboriginal "Protection" in a Comparative Context', in L. Boucher and L. Russell (eds), *Settler Colonial Governance in Nineteenth-century Victoria* (Canberra: ANU Press/Aboriginal History, 2015), 183–201.

[38] Boucher and Russell (eds), *Settler Colonial Governance in Nineteenth-century Victoria*.

[39] Mark McMillan and Cosima McRae, 'Law, Identity and Dispossession: The Half-Caste Act of 1886 and Contemporary Legal Definitions of Indigeneity in Australia', in Z. Laidlaw and A. Lester (eds), *Indigenous Communities and Settler Colonialism* (London: Palgrave Macmillan, 2015), 233–44.

[40] Aborigines Protection Act Amendment (50 Vic. No. 912) 1886 (Victoria).

Wales had reintroduced a position of Protector of Aborigines in 1860 and 1880 respectively, and New South Wales established an Aborigines Protection Board in 1883, but these measures were not supported by any centralised policy or legislation. Also important in delaying a centralised policy in the mainland colonies outside Victoria was their sheer territorial scale. Western Australia alone was eleven times the size of Victoria. Its vast northern and interior hinterlands, and those of Queensland and the South Australian-administered Northern Territory, were still opening to new economic development, exposing more Indigenous populations to new waves of colonial occupation and the violence of dispossession. These combined factors did not encourage local governments to adopt Victoria's model of protection as a program of close legal management. Instead, the responsibility for ensuring that Indigenous people received the ordinary protections of the law remained nominally embodied in police and magistrates, the same legal officers who aggressively policed and prosecuted them.

Although protection legislation was slower to arrive in jurisdictions outside Victoria, Australian colonial governments nonetheless sought to limit Indigenous people's access to urban settler spaces while still facilitating their place as workers in colonial economies. Notions of protection played a role in this process. In South Australia, the protector worked through the 1880s and 1890s to regulate Indigenous mobility and employment by asking police to arrest the unemployed as vagrants if they lingered in town, while simultaneously using the rations scheme to encourage employment.[41] In Western Australia, police sometimes arrested unemployed Indigenous people as vagrants on grounds that this kept them away from pastoral runs and protected employed Indigenous workers from disruptive influences.[42] Victoria's Central Board for the Protection of Aborigines also considered the threat of arrest on vagrancy charges potentially useful in containing Indigenous people to the protective safety of government stations.[43]

Western Australia was the first colony to follow Victoria, with its Aborigines Protection Act 1886. The Act created an Aborigines Protection Board, although it was politically unpopular and carried little influence with

[41] Protector Edward Hamilton, January 1880–February 1908, Protector's Letterbook, GRG 52/7, State Records of South Australia.

[42] Constable Duffy to Sergeant Houlahan, 8 December 1899, Acc 430, File 1900/320, State Records Office of Western Australia (SROWA).

[43] *Report of the Commissioners Appointed to Inquire into the Present Condition of the Aborigines of this Colony, and to Advise as to the Best Means of Caring for and dealing with them in the Future* (Melbourne: Government Printer, 1877), 50–66.

the pastoralist-backed legislature.[44] The more notable feature of Western Australia's new protection legislation was its detailed focus on managing the conditions of Indigenous labour. This reflected the fact that, thanks to a slow-growing settler population and a thin supply of European labour, economic growth in Western Australia had relied heavily upon Indigenous labour from the colony's earliest years. The limited supply of free labour was temporarily boosted by the importation of convict labour through the 1850s and 1860s; but, with the cessation of penal transportation in the late 1860s, this unfree labour supply was relatively short-lived. Instead, settlers depended upon Indigenous workers to meet their labour needs, particularly from the 1860s, as the colony's northern frontiers expanded with investment in pastoralism, pearling and mining.

Western Australia's introduction of a Protection Act focused on regulating Indigenous labour followed years of reported and rumoured abuse against Indigenous workers in these northern economies. A well-known problem was the kidnapping and enforced indenture of Indigenous people to supply labour on lucrative pearling and pastoral frontiers. By 1886 when Western Australia's Protection Act came into effect, allegations of Aboriginal abduction and other widespread abuses had already generated several magisterial investigations and brought scandal on the colony in accusations that it tolerated a system of slavery.[45] The Aborigines Protection Act 1886 was supposed to end these practices of abuse by girding all labour arrangements with 'every possible precaution'.[46] It reinstated the position of Protectors of Aborigines – an office that had lapsed some three decades earlier – and focused their duties on managing Indigenous contracts with settler employers.

Yet, although the provisions of the Act were designed to ensure the consent and rights of Indigenous workers, they created much greater legal authority to determine the supply and conditions of Indigenous indenture. Protectors or their proxies (including honorary justices of the peace, who were usually local pastoralists and employers of Aboriginal workers) could now set the terms of Indigenous people's labour agreements with settlers. The Act required that employers supply payment in rations, clothing and blankets, although it did not mandate wages. It allowed local magistrates to

[44] 'The Aborigines Protection Board: Official Correspondence', *The West Australian*, 25 September 1893; 'Aborigines' Protection Board: Discussion in the Assembly', *The Inquirer and Commercial News*, 23 October 1896.

[45] *Legislative Council Papers Respecting the Treatment of Aboriginal Natives* (Perth: Government Printer, 1886); J. B. Gribble, *Dark Deeds in a Sunny Land, or Blacks and Whites in North-West Australia* (Perth: Stirling Bros, 1886).

[46] Governor Broome to the Secretary of State, 12 and 13 July 1886, CO 881/8/3, NA, 85, 91.

'bind by indenture' any Aboriginal or 'half-caste' child to the age of 21, and granted the government powers to requisition Aboriginal prisoners as unpaid labourers to work on public building projects. Finally, it carried over the provisions of master and servant legislation to punish breaches of contract.[47]

In theory, these provisions placed legal checks on abusive masters, but in practice, they proved most useful in punishing indentured Indigenous workers who absconded from their employment or refused to work.[48] A review of the labour protection system in 1900 indicated that pastoral employers valued its capacity to secure their Aboriginal labour force against labour poaching or desertion; only two dissenting voices suggested that the system supported 'a form of slavery'.[49] In many ways, then, Western Australia's system of Aboriginal labour protection mirrored the system of legal supervision over indentured workers that operated elsewhere around the British Empire more to manage labour supply than to protect labourers' rights.[50]

The legal powers of Australia's evolving protection regime expanded again at the end of the nineteenth century with the introduction of Queensland's Aboriginals Protection and Restriction of the Sale of Opium Act 1897. Queensland's Act established a much stronger legal framework for the management of Indigenous people than was available in Victoria's and Western Australia's existing protection legislation. It provided for the re-appointment of Protectors of Aborigines and reserve superintendents who held far-reaching powers to direct Indigenous people to live on or off reserves, to approve or to revoke their employment permits, to apportion the outcomes of their labour, to supervise the movements and personal relationships of 'half-caste' women, and to determine the custody and apprenticeship of Indigenous children.[51]

The provisions of Queensland's 1897 Act to govern Indigenous lives with near-comprehensive authority created the template for similarly comprehensive acts passed over the next decade or so in the other Australian colonies or states: Western Australia's Aborigines Act 1905, New South Wales's Aborigines Protection Act 1909, the Northern Territory Aboriginals Act 1910 and South Australia's Aborigines Act 1911. In Tasmania, Indigenous people were widely presumed to have 'died out'; but even so, the spread of protection legislation

47 Aborigines Protection Act (50 Vic. No. 25) 1886 (WA).

48 For instance, Resident Magistrate (Roebourne) to the Bishop of Perth, 27 May 1889, State Library of Western Australia, MN2216.

49 William Harris to the Chief Protector, 20 April 1900, and Resident Magistrate (Roebourne) to the Chief Protector, 24 January 1901, Acc 255, 51/1900, SROWA.

50 James McNeill and Chimman Lal, *Report on the Conditions of Indian Immigrants*, CO 323/717, fol. 219–342, NA.

51 Aboriginals Protection & Sale of Opium Act (61 Vic. No. 17) 1897 (Qld).

influenced the introduction of Tasmania's Cape Barren Island Reserve Act 1912, which established specific conditions on which so-called 'half-caste' Aboriginal Tasmanians could continue to live on the island.[52] By the onset of World War I, a legal regime of protection grounded in principles of state surveillance and guardianship was in place across the country.

Protection policy had always been shaped at the level of local colonial or state governments, even though many of its features were shared or adapted across jurisdictions. In 1937, the Australian Commonwealth for the first time initiated a national debate on 'Aboriginal welfare'. Although protection policy would continue to be state directed, the 1937 conference – attended by Chief Protectors of Aborigines and other government representatives from most states – was significant in triggering a nation-wide review of Indigenous policy. Eased by decades of culturally assimilationist practices and persuaded by the theory of biological absorption championed by Western Australia's Chief Protector of Aborigines, A. O. Neville, the conference delegates endorsed a nation-wide plan to assimilate people of mixed descent into white Australian society. In contrast, so-called 'full blood' people would remain segregated on reserves.[53] This mixed vision of assimilation and segregation based on degrees of bloodline was supported by each state's existing legal powers of protection, which already authorised practices of child removal and reserve management. Queensland's long-standing Chief Protector of Aborigines, John Bleakley, identified the nature of protection in this interwar period when he emphasised to his fellow delegates the need to maintain 'benevolent supervision' over Indigenous people and the requisite government authority to exercise it.[54] Notably, the government officers tasked as protectors in this twentieth-century era were often local police officers.

Protection and Stolen Wages

A point raised by Chief Protector Bleakley at the 1937 conference was that Indigenous workers in Queensland were employed on a wage 'considerably

[52] The Cape Barren Island Reserve Act (3 Geo. V. No. 16) 1912 (Tas); Kristyn Harman, 'Protecting Tasmanian Aborigines: American and Queensland Influences on the Cape Barren Island Reserve Act, 1912' *Journal of Imperial and Commonwealth History* 41, no. 5 (2013): 744–64.

[53] Commonwealth of Australia, *Aboriginal Welfare: Initial Conference of Commonwealth and State Aboriginal Authorities* (Canberra: Commonwealth Government Printer, 1937), 3.

[54] Commonwealth of Australia, *Aboriginal Welfare*, 6; John Chesterman and Brian Galligan, *Citizens without Rights: Aborigines and Australian Citizenship* (Melbourne: Cambridge University Press, 1997), 151–2.

lower' than that of white workers, and he suggested that the delegation consider an Aboriginal 'minimum living wage' for nation-wide application. Chief Protector Neville countered that in Western Australia 'we have no fixed wages or awards for the natives', and he argued that there was little point discussing 'a scheme which involves heavy expenditure'.[55] In its summary of advice on future policy, the delegation recommended that the Commonwealth provide the states with financial assistance to support 'the care, protection and education of the natives', but made no comment on wages.

As discussion at the national conference indicated, the sections of state protection statutes that related to labour were never concerned with establishing wage parity for Indigenous workers. In fact, the protection regime had itself helped to invest Indigenous labour into Australia's economic growth for virtually no financial reward to the workers themselves. Rather than being concerned with wage security, the legal provisions for protecting Indigenous workers conceived of labour as a vehicle for Indigenous training. These provisions included that employers be morally upright and be able to supply a sufficiency of rations, clothing and medical care. While superficially appearing to guarantee minimum entitlements for workers, then, protection provisions helped to prop up a labour system that functioned on a feudal model of indenture.[56]

At the same time as they placed contractual limits on the movement and freedoms of Indigenous workers, protection statutes also specified restrictions on women of mixed descent as part of wider government efforts to stamp out miscegenation or 'komboism'. The provisions of Queensland's 1897 Act, mirrored in other states and territories, established that the employment of every 'aboriginal or female half-caste' was conditional upon approval of a protector, Justice of the Peace or police officer; that every employed 'aboriginal or female half-caste' must remain under the supervision of a protection officer; and that it was an offence to accommodate or move any 'aboriginal or female half-caste' without permission.[57] Protection policy thereby enabled a particularly gendered form of state intervention into labour relations. As Victoria Haskins has argued, state policy directed Indigenous women into domestic work within white households and placed

55 Commonwealth of Australia, *Aboriginal Welfare*, 12, 20.
56 Thalia Anthony, 'Postcolonial Feudal Hauntings of Northern Australian Cattle Stations' *Law, Text, Culture* 7 (2003): 277.
57 Aboriginals Protection Act 1897 (Qld), ss 14–17.

white women employers in charge of them as representatives of its own 'civilising authority'.[58]

Queensland established a minimum Indigenous wage relatively early, but the bar was set low. A 1901 amendment to the 1897 Act specified a minimum Aboriginal wage of five shillings per month, or ten shillings per month for seamen, with wages to be held in trust by the protector or a police representative, who could expend it on behalf of the workers. Updated regulations over time reset Queensland's Indigenous minimum wage, but Rosalind Kidd notes that it only ever rose to two-thirds of the standard wage for non-Indigenous workers. Moreover, her research shows that misuse and poor book-keeping of Aboriginal trust accounts were widespread, that such accounting inadequacies were officially tolerated despite periodic scrutiny, and that workers had no rights of appeal about the questionable handling of their accounts.[59] The protection legislation of jurisdictions other than Queensland did not mandate a cash wage for Indigenous workers outside urban areas, but, where cash wages were provided, the law similarly allowed that they be paid into a trust account and acquitted under supervision of a protection officer. Withheld earnings were even used to pay for Indigenous 'welfare' services that were properly the responsibility of state governments.[60]

The building momentum of the Aboriginal rights movement through the 1930s and a series of Aboriginal strikes over the coming years brought a new degree of national attention to the inadequacy of Indigenous wages in the mid-twentieth century, and to the wider structures of racial inequality they reflected.[61] Nonetheless, pastoralists continued to exploit their Indigenous workers with little risk of prosecution, and where Indigenous workers were paid, their wages continued to be held in trust by state officers or Protection

[58] Victoria Haskins, '& So We are "Slave owners!": Employers and the NSW Aborigines Protection Board Trust Funds' *Labour History* 88 (2005): 147–64; Victoria Haskins, 'Domesticating Colonizers: Domesticity, Indigenous Domestic Labor, and the Modern Settler Colonial Nation' *American Historical Review* 124, no. 4 (2019): 1290–301.

[59] Rosalind Kidd, *Trustees on Trial: Recovering the Stolen Wages* (Canberra: Aboriginal Studies Press, 2006), 61–7.

[60] Rosalind Kidd, 'Taken on Trust', submission 49 to the Senate Legal and Constitutional References Committee Inquiry into Stolen Wages (July 2006), 3, www.aph.gov.au/Parliamentary_Business/Committees/Senate/Legal_and_Constitutional_Affairs/Completed_inquiries/2004-07/stolen_wages/submissions/sublist, accessed 18 January 2020; Thalia Anthony, 'Unmapped Territory: Wage Compensation for Indigenous Cattle Station Workers' *Australian Indigenous Law Review* 11, no. 1 (2007): 8.

[61] For instance, Bain Attwood and Andrew Markus, *The Struggle for Aboriginal Rights: A Documentary History* (Sydney: Allen and Unwin, 1999); Anne Scrimgeour, '"We Only Want Our Rights and Freedom": The Pilbara Pastoral Workers Strike, 1946–1949' *History Australia* 11, no. 2 (2014): 101–24.

Boards, leaving them powerless to invest or to spend their own earnings.[62] A critical change came in 1966, when the Northern Territory moved to include Indigenous workers within the pastoral award. However, while this appeared to promise the prospect of wage equality, it was highly qualified as a civil rights success. The provision of a 'slow worker' clause allowed pastoralists to pay less than the standard award, and the clarified award made Indigenous workers newly vulnerable to losing their long-standing place in the pastoral economy.[63]

In 2006, the federal government undertook a national inquiry into wages unpaid or withheld under the umbrella of past protection policies. The inquiry highlighted the entangled relationship between stolen wages and the Stolen Generations, whereby protection policies forced Indigenous workers into employment schemes that took them away from their families or took their children into state custody.[64] The report arising from the inquiry recommended that the Commonwealth and each state government provide Indigenous people with unhindered access to their records, undertake a process of Indigenous consultation to document experiences of stolen wages, and establish appropriate compensation schemes to redress unpaid entitlements.[65]

Commenting at the close of the national inquiry, Senator Andrew Bartlett emphasised the urgency of this process of redress. He noted that the 'exploitation of thousands of Indigenous people over decades was a building block of the prosperity which Australia as a nation enjoys today', a prosperity that has left 'many Indigenous people in poverty'.[66] Several years before the national inquiry, Queensland established a compensation scheme in restitution for stolen wages, followed by New South Wales and Western Australia. All these schemes, however, faced criticism that they were limited in their scope and inadequate in their restitution. In 2019, more than a decade after the national inquiry, a successful class action brought against the Queensland government signalled an advance in stolen wages reparation. Nonetheless, the issue of Indigenous stolen wages remains in many ways 'unfinished business' in Australia today.[67]

[62] Kidd, 'Taken on Trust', 33.
[63] *Re Cattle Station Industry* (Northern Territory) Award (1966) 113 Commonwealth Arbitration Reports 651; Thalia Anthony, 'Reconciliation and Conciliation: The Irreconcilable Dilemma of the 1965 "Equal" Wage Case for Aboriginal Station Workers' *Labour History* 93 (2007): 15–34.
[64] Senate Standing Committee on Legal and Constitutional Affairs, 'Unfinished Business: Indigenous Stolen Wages' (Canberra: Department of the Senate, December 2006), 60–1.
[65] Ibid, 7, xiii–xiv. [66] Ibid, 130. See Watson, Chapter 31 in this volume.
[67] Thalia Anthony, 'The New Mabo? $190 Million Stolen Wages Settlement is Unprecedented, but Still Limited', *The Conversation*, 10 July 2019.

Protection's Afterlives

Having been envisaged in the 1830s as a magisterial office that would build a place for Indigenous people within the growing settler world, protection by the late nineteenth century had become a policy tool that cemented their marginalisation from it. Rather than endowing Indigenous people with legal equality, originally conceived as the 'gift' of British subjecthood, protection finally subjected them to an ever more complex set of exceptional laws. This shift in the politics of protection was not a radical change, however, but a cumulative transition as early imperial faith in racial 'improvement' through legal entitlements and training became replaced with belief in a fixed racial hierarchy underpinned by legislation.[68]

But even in the mid-twentieth-century heyday of protection as a legal regime, state guardianship over Indigenous lives was neither complete nor unambiguous. Katharine Booth and Lisa Ford trace how the state's protective authority was challenged in the 1955 case of *Ross v Chambers*, a civil suit brought by the Northern Territory Administration on behalf of Indigenous pastoral workers against their abusive employers. In this case, the judge repudiated the assumed authority of the welfare agency to sue on behalf of its Aboriginal 'wards', determining – against long-standing practice – that Aboriginal adults held legal subjecthood to sue on their own behalf. The civil suit collapsed in face of this check on a government's power 'to protect as well as to infringe' the rights of Indigenous workers. But having brought the suit as a 'public performance of Aboriginal protection', the Northern Territory Administration then scrambled to limit Indigenous legal agency by amending the existing legislation to better secure the state's authority over its Aboriginal wards.[69] Regardless of the outcome, this case exposed the fragilities of protective governance and the ambiguity of the state's legal powers, in a decade when they appeared to be most comprehensive.

Over the 1960s and early 1970s, protection laws and welfare boards were gradually phased out around Australia as the civil rights era influenced a shift in policy away from a philosophy of state guardianship towards one of self-determination.[70] During their lifespan, protection's exceptional laws

68 Russell McGregor, *Imagined Destinies: Aboriginal Australians and the Doomed Race Theory, 1880–1939* (Carlton: Melbourne University Press, 1997).

69 Katharine Booth and Lisa Ford, 'Ross v Chambers: Assimilation Law and Policy in the Northern Territory' *Aboriginal History* 40 (2016): 13, 22.

70 For a timeline of state protection laws and their repeal, see AIATSIS, 'To Remove and Protect', https://aiatsis.gov.au/collections/collections-online/digitised-collections/remove-and-protect, accessed 20 January 2020.

had worked to constrain almost every aspect of Indigenous independence, but they did not extinguish Indigenous cultural identity or silence Indigenous protest against the state's discriminatory powers. A 1923 petition by Ngarrindjeri people of South Australia's Point Macleay mission is notable for its moral authority in calling out the state's contradictory claims to protect Indigenous children by removing them from their own homes against their parents' wishes.[71] William Cooper's 1933–7 petition to the king, although not forwarded by the Australian government, is especially well known for its powerful reminder of the Crown's original promise of Indigenous rights and its demands for recognition of those rights in the form of political representation.[72]

The Indigenous legal scholar Irene Watson (Tanganekald, Meintangk Boandik) has argued that although Aboriginal protection policies and statutes have formally ended in Australia, their legacies continue to be felt in various forms of government paternalism and in assimilative vocabularies that echo with the foundational terms of colonialism. She makes the point that the ideological traces of protection – with its underpinnings in the assumption of settler jurisdiction and state guardianship – persist today in the continuing disinclination of Australian federal governments to acknowledge Aboriginal sovereignty.[73] Her comments serve as a reminder that protection regimes have a history that has not ended, but that has ongoing repercussions for Indigenous people's relationship to the Australian state.

[71] 'Give Us Our Children: The Aborigines' Plea', *The Observer*, 29 December 1923.

[72] 'Petition of the Aboriginal Inhabitants of Australia to His Majesty, King George V' in Attwood and Markus, *Thinking Black*, 35–6.

[73] Irene Watson, 'Aboriginality and the Violence of Colonialism' *Borderlands e-Journal* 8, no. 1 (2009): 1–8.

21

Economic and Social Welfare

ANNE O'BRIEN

How can we begin to interpret the laws underpinning English, settler and Indigenous welfare systems as they intersected across different ecologies and polities over time? The attempt seems almost foolhardy. It does, however, offer the chance to pare back the meanings of basic concepts and to focus on connections and disconnections between these systems. To note, for example, that in modern liberal states, 'welfare' was a distinct domain that managed the casualties of a hierarchical social order when the market or the family failed; and that welfare was reinforced by 'the law' in maintaining and defending that order. To recognise that within Indigenous societies individual welfare was ensured by family and kin groupings – 'everybody was responsible for each other' – and that these groupings were governed by holistic laws, which integrated ontology and materiality.[1] These differences are foundational to this chapter, but so too are connections. Settler welfare was a tool of Indigenous dispossession, 'a way of denying sovereign rights to Indigenous people', as Maramanindji scholar Darryl Cronin has put it.[2] More than that, it was financed by the sale of Indigenous land. In each new post-invasion site, however, Indigenous communities maintained and adapted customary law, and deployed aspects of settler welfare to advance their own well-being.

A number of scholars have argued that Australian settler welfare is distinctive. Esping-Andersen's influential typology saw Australia and the other Anglophone countries as liberal regimes distinguished by targeted, residual welfare.[3] Including state-based wage determination as welfare, Francis

1 B. Randall, *Songman: the Story of an Aboriginal Elder of Uluru* (Sydney: ABC Books, 2003), 12.
2 D. Cronin, 'Welfare Dependency and Mutual Obligation: Negating Indigenous Sovereignty', in A. Moreton Robinson (ed.), *Sovereign Subjects: Indigenous Sovereignty Matters* (Sydney: Allen & Unwin, 2007), 179.
3 G. Esping-Andersen, *The Three Worlds of Welfare Capitalism* (Princeton, NJ: Princeton University Press, 1990).

Castles argued that Australia (and New Zealand) stood apart from the Anglophones: the early entry of labour into parliament drove the push for industrial arbitration; and Australia can best be seen as a 'wage-earner's welfare state'.[4] Later studies accepted the framework but argued that 'white, male, wage-earner's welfare state' is more accurate.[5] Extending the parameters further, Chris Deeming and Paul Smyth argued that in contrast to Britain, Europe or the United States, the state in late nineteenth-century Australia aimed for more than the social protection of wages-earners: it provided the capital infrastructure and utilities for growth. Australia was a 'social investment state' a century before the term was taken up by British New Labour in the early 1990s.[6]

While these models do not address the settler-colonial context they provide a framework that helps explain the centrality of that context. This chapter seeks to demonstrate the racialised and gendered nature of the wage-earner's welfare state and to extend Deeming and Smyth's social investment thesis back to 1788. It argues that while social investment worked to advance settler prosperity, it was the motor of Indigenous dispossession. Further, while social protection could demean settlers – women were particularly vulnerable to surveillance and control – it was skewed against the First Nations. As subjects of governance without the rights of citizenship, they experienced targeted welfare at its most residual and destructive.[7] Very little welfare history includes Indigenous peoples as subjects; even less considers them as agents. And yet their experience is crucial in understanding the role of welfare in the broader history of settler-colonialism.

Deep Time Economies Survive

While the legal justification of colonisation was based on the erroneous assumption that Indigenous peoples lived in abject poverty, the first journal keepers provided evidence to the contrary. First Fleet officer Watkin Tench commented that the Eora were 'nimble, sprightly and vigorous', which

[4] F. G. Castles, *The Working Class and Welfare: Reflections on the Political Development of the Welfare State in Australia and New Zealand, 1890–1980* (Sydney: Allen & Unwin, 1985).

[5] S. Macintyre, 'The Short History of Social Democracy in Australia' *Thesis Eleven* 15 (1986): 3–14; A. O'Brien, *Philanthropy and Settler Colonialism* (Basingstoke: Palgrave Macmillan, 2015), chapter 4.

[6] C. Deeming and P. Smyth, 'Social Investment after Neoliberalism: Policy Paradigms and Political Platforms' *Journal of Social Policy* 44 (2015): 297–318.

[7] J. Chesterman and B. Galligan, *Citizens without Rights: Aborigines and Australian Citizenship* (Cambridge: Cambridge University Press, 1997).

suggests their health was probably better than that of most Londoners in the 'years of scarcity', as the 1790s were known.[8] Over the last thirty years, a considerable body of research has supported Tench's observation, revising the assumption that Aboriginal peoples lived at the mercy of the elements.[9] In the last decade, the idea that Aboriginal economies were sophisticated, complex and diverse has started to penetrate mainstream narratives.[10]

Oral histories and autobiographies have shown how the law governing this careful management derives from the ontological and spiritual significance of 'country' over 'deep time'. Country could be land, sky or sea; it bore the imprint of ancestral beings whose stories were the source of 'legitimate law' without legislation.[11] In the words of Yankunytjatjara elder Bob Randall, Tjukurrpa (philosophy of life) gave a very strong sense of Karinya (connectedness), passed on by epic song cycles that conveyed deep truth.[12] Randall was born in the Central Desert, the last region to feel the effects of colonisation and one of the driest: mobility and knowledge of the land's sources of water and food were essential for survival.[13] Country was part of Randall's 'intimate family' – he lived in 'a home without walls' where bush food was plentiful.[14] Anangu woman Ninu Ward learned from her grandmother's law 'the proper protocols for a good life'; she grew up 'healthy and strong' – 'we hunted and were always full of good food'. She was taught how to find water and how to get moisture from Mingkulpa (native tobacco) in time of drought.[15]

Recent histories have shown how survivors of the east coast invasions navigated 'new, dynamic, dangerous, hybrid' worlds.[16] Eora who survived

8 Cited in T. Flannery, *1788* (Melbourne: Text publishing, 1996), 51; L. Patriquin, *Agrarian Capitalism and Poor Relief in England, 1500–1860* (Basingstoke: Palgrave Macmillan, 2007).

9 For key authors see T. Griffiths, 'Reading Bruce Pascoe', *Inside Story*, 26 November 2019.

10 B Gammage, *The Biggest Estate on Earth: How Aborigines Made Australia* (Sydney: Allen & Unwin, 2012); B. Pascoe, *Dark Emu: Aboriginal Australia and the Birth of Agriculture* (Broome: Magabala Books, 2014); Ian J. McNiven, 'Farmers or Hunter-Gatherers? The Dark Emu Debate' *Australian Historical Studies* 52, no. 4 (2021): 641–4.

11 D. Bird Rose, *Nourishing Terrains: Australian Aboriginal Views of Landscape and Wilderness* (Canberra: Australian Heritage Commission, 1996); Ian Keen, *Aboriginal Economy and Society: Australia at the Threshold of Colonisation* (Melbourne: Oxford University Press, 2004), 244.

12 B. Randall, *Songman: The Story of an Aboriginal Elder of Uluru* (Sydney: ABC books, 2003), 3, 12, 7.

13 D. James, 'Tjukurpa Time', in A. McGrath and M. A. Jebb (eds), *Long History, Deep Time* (Canberra: ANU Press, 2015), 34.

14 Randall, *Songman*, 3.

15 N. Nugalka Ward, *Ninu: Grandmother's Law* (Broome: Magabala Books, 2018), 132, 56.

16 G. Karskens, 'Nah Doongh's Song', *Australian Book Review*, August 2019, 31–7.

the violence, disease and economic disruption in the Sydney area drew individual settlers into networks of reciprocity by working for them, supplying them with food, passing on traditional knowledge, hunting and fishing with them.[17] The Kulin came to early Melbourne to 'barter, buy munitions, exchange their labour and sell goods such as skins and lyrebird feathers'.[18] Misconstrued as 'beggars', they sought 'a kind of reciprocity for what they had lost'.[19]

Aboriginal owners interacted with expanding settler economies in the nineteenth century. During the 1850s gold rushes in New South Wales, they used the exodus of labour to combine working as shepherds for relatively decent wages with moving across country to maintain traditional ceremonies.[20] In Victoria they acted as guides and sometimes dug for gold – but objected to paying the licence fee for 'the country belonged to them'.[21] By the 1860s, they were negotiating for land on which they could maintain communities, deploying the language and practices of the selection acts to claim a 'small portion of a vast territory that is ours by Divine Right'. Over the next twenty years thirty-two reserves were created in New South Wales, twenty-seven of which were created through Aboriginal demand.[22]

By the turn of the century, modernity and coercive paternalism had pushed communities to the margins of the major cities, but they continued to adapt customary economies. Aboriginal people at La Perouse, in Sydney, fished and sold their catch to the markets, rented out their boats; and, after Botany Bay became a tourist destination in the early twentieth century, they sold shell work and curios and provided boomerang demonstrations.[23] In the south-western suburbs of Sydney, Aboriginal communities camped on land around Salt Pan Creek, members travelling to strengthen community ties and attachment to places. Since it was not reserved land, it offered some sanctuary from the surveillance of the NSW Aborigines Protection Board,

[17] P. Irish, *Hidden in Plain View: The Aboriginal People of Coastal Sydney* (Sydney: UNSW Press, 2017), 99.

[18] P. Edmonds, *Urbanising Frontiers: Indigenous Peoples and Settlers in 19th Century Pacific Rim Cities* (Vancouver: UBC Press, 2010), 125, 138.

[19] L. Russell, '"Tickpen", "Boro Boro": Aboriginal Economic Engagements in Early Melbourne', in Leigh Boucher and L Russell (eds), *Settler Governance in Nineteenth Century Victoria* (Canberra: ANU Press, 2015), 27.

[20] H. Goodall, *Invasion to Embassy: Land in Aboriginal Politics in NSW* (Sydney: Allen & Unwin, 1996).

[21] F. Cahir and I. D. Clark, '"Why Should They Pay Money to the Queen?": Aboriginal Miners and Land Claims' *Journal of Australian Colonial History* 10, no. 1 (2008): 115–28.

[22] Goodall, *Invasion to Embassy*, 78, 87.

[23] M. Nugent, *Botany Bay: Where Histories Meet* (Sydney: Allen & Unwin, 2005).

whose legal authority to remove children was significantly increased in the early twentieth century.[24]

Poor Laws

In nineteenth-century Australia, social investment provided the infrastructure for the expansion of British imperialism. Colonial Parliaments assisted immigrants from the 1830s and introduced Aboriginal protection regimes around the same time. They legislated to control land settlement from the 1840s, funded railways and telegraphs in 'the long boom' of 1860–90, and paid for public education from the 1870s. By the turn of the century, the new nation was pioneering welfare initiatives celebrated by a visiting French sociologist as 'socialism without doctrines'.[25] This expanding field of investment built on the legacy of the convict era, when the state had provided for the sick, the young and 'objects of charity'.

Welfare as protection bore the imprint of the English poor law, though no such law was passed in Australia. Its absence was largely due to the dominance of the state in providing for the convict poor, but this was not the whole story. A poor law might have been introduced in the late 1840s, when the imperial government was no longer paying for the support of convicts to New South Wales. But it was not: to potential tax-payers the poor law was a gross imposition, to potential inmates it was anathema, particularly after the 'reforms' of 1834. These were based on the principle of 'less eligibility', which mandated that the able-bodied enter a workhouse where conditions would be harsher than those of the poorest labourer outside.[26] The poor law undermined the immigrant dream. Settlers wanted work, not sustenance; and over the next decades, at moments of recession, the unemployed petitioned colonial governments to provide it.[27] Poorly conceived as well as targeted on the poor, the reforms of 1834 drew poverty – long seen as the natural lot of the labouring classes – into the realm of crime.[28]

[24] H. Goodall and A. Cadzow, *Rivers and Resilience: Aboriginal People on Sydney's George's River* (Sydney: UNSW Press, 2009).

[25] N. G. Butlin, *Investment in Australian Economic Development, 1861–1900* (Cambridge: Cambridge University Press, 1964); B. Kingston, *The Oxford History of Australia* (Melbourne: Oxford University Press, 1988), 3: 98.

[26] J. R. Poynter, *Society and Pauperism: English Ideas on Poor Relief* (Melbourne: Melbourne University Press, 1969).

[27] J. B. Hirst, 'Keeping Colonial History Colonial: The Hartz Thesis Revisited' *Historical Studies* 21 (1984): 85–104.

[28] H. Stretton, *Poor Laws of 1834 and 1996* (Melbourne: Brotherhood of St Laurence, 1996); G. Himmelfarb, *The Idea of Poverty: England in the Early Industrial Age* (New York: Vintage Books, 1985).

The absence of the English poor law had complex ramifications. For all the horrors of its reform, the poor law enshrined the right to assistance. Without it, there was no statutory protection against poverty. In most situations, voluntary charity filled the vacuum; but there were times and places when it did not. In Van Diemen's Land in the depressed 1840s, for example, there were not enough wealthy settlers willing to support a benevolent society, and the colonial government would not support the children of convicts. Those refused help have left no trace; but, without recourse in law to assistance, their vulnerability is clear.[29]

Elsewhere the absence of the poor law strengthened charity, which became the main provider of 'outdoor relief' – rations, relief in kind and occasionally rent assistance – and over the next century women predominated among its recipients and its workforce.[30] Paradoxically, public revenue was crucial for charity's financial viability, even in post-gold-rush Victoria, where Benevolent Societies arose in almost every suburb. The preferred subsidy was pound for pound, though it was sometimes more. Governments also ran 'asylums' for the aged and infirm in all the colonies and, in South Australia and Western Australia, were responsible for providing rations. However, while the apparatus of the poor law was not transferred, the ethos of 1834 – less eligibility and the deserving/undeserving dichotomy – infused colonial institutions. Indeed, it may have been stronger as immigrants sought to distance themselves from undeserving convicts. In colonies that began as places of secondary punishment, asylums were arguably as bad as British workhouses. Strands of collectivism and fraternity, on the other hand, can be discerned in the practice and rhetoric of some of Victoria's gold fields asylums.[31]

The main source of funding for welfare in the nineteenth century was Indigenous land. In the first few decades funding came indirectly from wool exports that enabled the flourishing of British industry; from the 1830s it came directly from the sale and leasing of land. Indeed, the first schemes of assisted immigration in New South Wales were funded by the sale of land; the colony of South Australia was established through the sale of land. Land distribution was a central issue in settler politics; and the relatively early granting of male suffrage in the mid-1850s swelled agitation

[29] J. Brown, *'Poverty is Not a crime': The Development of Social Services in Tasmania, 1803–1900* (Hobart: Tasmanian Historical Research Association, 1972).

[30] P. Harris, 'Penny-pinching Activities: Managing Poverty under the Eye of Welfare', in K. Saunders and R. Evans (eds), *Gender Relations in Australia: Domination and Negotiation* (Sydney: Harcourt, Brace, Jovanovich, 1992), 287–301.

[31] O'Brien, *Philanthropy*, chapter 3.

among the gold rush immigrants for a stake in the land. Laws were passed in the 1860s enabling them to purchase it. By the 1870s, public works were funded from various sources; the most important was revenue from the sale or leasing of Indigenous land.[32]

Stolen land paid for welfare, and welfare was introduced to appease, cajole and control Indigenous peoples as they fought to defend their land. Welfare did not, however, work as the early governors anticipated. The Native Institution was founded during the war on the Cumberland Plain in 1815 in an attempt to assimilate the young; it failed once parents realised that they lost all access to their children.[33] The first missions in New South Wales had formally closed by 1841 because Aboriginal peoples did not take to them.[34] Blankets distributed from the mid-1820s came to be seen by Aboriginal peoples as a form of reciprocity, compensating them for their losses; efforts to cease distribution failed, at least in part because Aboriginal mentors tutored settlers in 'right behaviour'.[35] By the late 1830s, some humanitarians were aware of the enormity of the losses sustained: one compared giving Aboriginal people blankets to 'robbing a man of £100 and giving him a shilling'.[36]

Children under Law

If nineteenth-century colonists were content with subsidised voluntarism to provide sustenance for the poor, they drew on the authority of the law to deal with problem children. Indeed, protection's proclivity to protecting society rather than the individual is nowhere clearer than in the field of child welfare: its focus was on the citizen of the future rather than 'the child in the present'.[37] By the mid-nineteenth century, orphaned or neglected children came to be seen as a threat, and child rescuers called for the state to intervene to break the transmission of culture. In Australia they did so in both Indigenous and non-Indigenous families, but in the former parental

32 Kingston, *The Oxford History*, 38–41.

33 J. Brooke and J. L. Kohen, *The Parramatta Native Institution and the Black Town* (Sydney: NSW University Press, 1991), 65.

34 J. Mitchell, *In Good Faith: Governing Indigenous Australia through God, Charity and Empire, 1825–1855* (Canberra: ANU Press, 2011).

35 M. Smithson, 'A Misunderstood Gift: The Annual Issue of Blankets to Aborigines in New South Wales 1826–48' *Push* 30 (1992): 73–108; Irish, *Hidden in Plain View*, 61.

36 Cited in O'Brien, *Philanthropy*, 34.

37 S. Swain, 'Enshrined in Law: Legislative Justifications for the Removal of Indigenous and Non-indigenous Children in Colonial and Post-colonial Australia' *Australian Historical Studies* 47, no. 2 (2016): 191–208.

insufficiency was assumed to derive from race rather than neglect or misfortune. The older expectation of the English Poor Law – that poor children should work to support themselves rather than be supported by the state – carried over, and child labour remained fundamental to colonial child welfare.[38]

Child removal was one field where laws for Indigenous peoples pre-dated those for settlers. The first laws enabling the removal and apprenticeship of children, enacted in South Australia and Western Australia in 1844, were directed towards Aboriginal children, in contexts that suggest the importance of colonists' desire for their labour.[39] In the case of settler children, on the other hand, the first legislation was impelled by a sense of threat. Following a Select Committee report in New South Wales in 1859 that found children 'infesting' the streets in 'a darkening mass of physical and moral disease', an Industrial Schools Act was passed in 1866 that gave police wide powers to arrest children 'exposed to moral danger'.[40] Similar laws were passed in the other colonies around this time.[41] Even when the family was seen as unfortunate rather than negligent, legal responses reflected the intention to punish parents for their perceived failures.[42]

The child-as-threat was dominant within child rescue until the 1950s.[43] Over that time, however, signs of the modern idea of 'the best interests of the child' emerged in theory if not in practice. In the 1870s critics campaigned against the impersonal nature of large institutions, and fostering or 'cottage homes' became preferred options. Periodic scandals showed that fostered children were also liable to abuse and exploitation and large institutions remained widespread, stimulated in large part by religious sectarianism. Whatever form out-of-home care took, children were exposed to neglect and danger, despite a swag of legislation and regulation put in place from the 1890s to specify dietary and accommodation requirements, inspect boarding out, and regulate work and punishment.[44] No system was sufficiently resourced because destitution made these children seem 'somehow lesser than other children'.[45]

[38] Ibid. [39] Ibid, 196. [40] O'Brien, *Philanthropy*, 73.

[41] S. Swain, *History of Child Protection Legislation* (Commonwealth of Australia: Royal Commission into Institutional Responses to Child Sexual Abuse, 2014), 7.

[42] Ibid, 13.

[43] N. Musgrove and S. Swain, 'The Best Interests of the Child: Historical Perspectives' *Children Australia* 35, no. 2 (2010): 35–7.

[44] Swain, *History of Child Protection*, 8.

[45] S. Swain, 'Gender-based Violence in Out-of-home Care', in Alana Piper and Ana Stevenson (eds), *Gender Violence in Australia: Historical Perspectives* (Melbourne: Monash University Publishing, 2019), 144.

The major acts that removed Indigenous children were associated with the policy of protection, which, by the 1860s, had become a means of segregation and labour management.[46] The Victorian Protection Act of 1869, the first to mandate that Aboriginal communities should live on reserves, did not focus on children; but it enabled the practice, which became widespread, of children living separately from their parents in boarding houses.[47] By the turn of the century, Protection Acts were passed in the north, where Indigenous peoples were still numerous. As they related to children, these laws worked differently in different jurisdictions: in Queensland, children were more likely to be in dormitories, separated from their parents but having some contact with them; in Western Australia, children were more likely to be fully separated.[48] Light-skinned children were particularly vulnerable to removal. Many Indigenous parents wanted education for their children and, as Anna Haebich argues, by the post-war period in Western Australia there were some improvements in that state's 'appalling record in Aboriginal education'.[49] It came at great personal cost – to kin and communities as well as individuals – as oral history and autobiography show.[50] Ninu Ward remembers that her grandmother would 'cuddle me in her arms and tell me great stories, especially women's stories and women's Law'.[51] Bob Randall felt safety and 'total freedom' as a child because there were 'plenty of adult eyes' on him.[52]

The post-World War II years saw a rising volume of professional criticism directed at out-of-home care following the Curtis report of 1946, which exposed the detrimental effects of evacuation on English children during the war.[53] In the 1950s, legislation began to reflect the idea that 'the best interests of the child' should take precedence over 'the best interests of the state', though it rarely translated into the lived experience of children.[54] In the late twentieth century, the combined efforts of activist groups, state officials and public intellectuals drew the historical deficiencies of child welfare to

46 See Nettelbeck, Chapter 20 in this volume.
47 B. Attwood, *The Making of the Aborigines* (Sydney: Allen & Unwin, 1989), 17–18.
48 T. Rowse, *Indigenous and Other Australians since 1900* (Sydney: UNSW Press, 2018), 107–9.
49 A. Haebich, 'Nuclear, Suburban and Black: Middleton's Vision of Assimilation for Nyungar Families', in T. Rowse, *Contesting Assimilation* (Perth: API Network, 2005).
50 D. Mellor and A. Haebich, *Many Voices: Reflections on Experiences of Indigenous Child Separation* (Canberra: National Library of Australia, 2002), 61.
51 Ward, *Ninu*, 56. 52 Randall, *Songman*, 12.
53 S. Swain, 'Beyond Child Migration: Inquiries, Apologies and the Implications for the Writing of a Transnational Child Welfare History' *History Australia* 13, no. 1 (2016): 139–52.
54 Swain, *A History of Child Protection*, 9.

public attention. Major inquiries were established into the removals of Indigenous children (1997), child migrants (2002), care leavers (2004, 2005) and forced adoptions (2012).[55] The report into the removal of Indigenous children, known as the 'Bringing Them Home' Report, struck a chord with mainstream Australia: 'sorry books' gained thousands of signatories and several thousand people walked in solidarity with Aboriginal and Torres Strait Islander peoples across the Sydney Harbour Bridge. The report provided strong evidence that the mental health implications of removing Aboriginal and Torres Strait Islander children were very high but those children are still more likely to be removed than any other group, despite the work of activist organisations such as Gunnedah's Grandmothers against Removals.[56]

The State, Activists and a Great Divergence

From 1901 to the 1970s, the Commonwealth government legislated across an increasingly broad range of welfare fields. This program improved the material lives of many working class people but also created new social divisions. Government activity occurred in two bursts – in the Federation decade and the 1940s. The first was funded by overseas borrowing; government enterprises such as the post office, telegraph and railways; and indirect taxes such as customs and excise, as well as the continued sale and leasing of Indigenous land.[57] The second was funded largely by increasing the number of people who paid income tax.

From the 1870s to World War I, the state drove economic growth through investment in railways and other public works. Australian public expenditure as a proportion of gross domestic product was twice that of Britain and the US.[58] Laws were passed to protect workers in factories and mines, to provide workers compensation, to provide pensions to the aged and invalid, to assist women in childbirth and, following bitter and protracted strikes in the early 1890s, to arbitrate in industrial disputes. Feminists campaigned for reform of the law regarding married women's property, divorce, conditions of work and the suffrage, seeking to create what Marilyn Lake has called

[55] Swain, 'Beyond Child Migration'.
[56] N. Musgrove and D. Michell, *Foster Care in Australia: Just Like a Family?* (Basingstoke: Palgrave Macmillan, 2018), 302.
[57] Kingston, *The Oxford History*, 38.
[58] A. Capling and B. Galligan, *Beyond the Protective State: The Political Economy of Australia's Manufacturing Industry Policy* (Cambridge: Cambridge University Press, 1992), 27.

a 'maternalist welfare state'.[59] These interventions were informed by British philosopher T. H. Green's 'new liberalism' as it interacted with international feminism and the new Australian Labor Party's desire to 'civilise capitalism' and restrict Asian immigration.[60] One of the first political parties of working men to enter Parliament, the Labor Party held the balance of power in the New South Wales government during the 1890s, and held office federally between 1910 and 1913, the first labour-based party in national government.[61]

In many ways, the interventions of these years were significant departures. Following the establishment of the Commonwealth Arbitration Court in 1904, a landmark ruling three years later – the 'Harvester' judgment' – introduced the radical principle of a minimum wage, declaring that any company that could not pay its workers a wage that was 'fair and reasonable' for a man to support his wife and three children should not be in business. Old age and invalid pensions, introduced in 1908, were premised on a new principle: the pension was a 'right' not 'a pauper dole'.[62] The Maternity Allowance broke new ground in making a grant of £5, for medical care, to women – including unmarried women – on the birth of a 'viable child'. These interventions were skewed, however, by gendered assumptions and racial exclusions. In defining women as dependent, the Harvester judgment led the way in entrenching women's unequal wages.[63] Deeming 'Aboriginal natives', Asians and 'aliens' ineligible for pensions and allowances excluded them from the benefits of citizenship.[64]

After the war, conservative governments maintained the state's role in investment but not in protection. Under Prime Minister S. M. Bruce the Commonwealth government rejected the two major innovations in the 1920s – child endowment and national insurance – despite Royal Commissions recommending them, and despite the adoption of national insurance in many countries of European origin.[65] Historians have debated the extent to which Australia was 'left behind' in this period, after 'leading the

59 M. Lake, *Getting Equal: The History of Australian Feminism* (Sydney: Allen & Unwin, 1999).
60 Marian Sawyer, *The Ethical State? Social Liberalism in Australia* (Melbourne: Melbourne University Press, 2003).
61 Macintyre, 'The Short History of Social Democracy'.
62 John Murphy, *A Decent Provision: Australian Welfare Policy 1870–1949* (Farnham: Ashgate, 2011).
63 P. Grimshaw, M. Lake, A. McGrath and M. Quartly, *Creating a Nation* (Ringwood: Penguin, 1994).
64 Chesterman and Galligan, *Citizens without Rights*.
65 Murphy, *A Decent Provision*, chapter 6.

world' in the previous thirty years.[66] Using path-dependency theory, John Murphy argues that the two periods were closely connected by the depth of attachment to industrial arbitration.[67] Herein lay the opposition to both child endowment and national insurance. Men in the labour movement saw child endowment as a threat to the minimum wage, and national insurance as cutting across the right to work; but insurance was also opposed by employers, who resisted the cost, and friendly societies and charities, who saw it as a threat.[68] It is significant, however, that widows' pensions (1926) and child endowment (1927) were both introduced in New South Wales where women in the labour movement were well organised.[69] Taking veteran welfare into account also forces a rethink of this period: returned services organisations became a powerful force in Australian politics and veterans were seen as having the right to support. Repatriation benefits were relatively generous by international standards and more egalitarian across rank, though proving eligibility was a site of ongoing contest. Funded from consolidated revenue, they reduced the funding available for civilian welfare.[70]

Impelled by the need for wartime consensus and bitter memories of the depression, the 1940s saw an escalation of investment and protection in a scheme Stuart Macintyre has described as 'Australia's boldest experiment'. Keynesian macro-economic steering would provide full employment supported by a safety net – child endowment, civilian widows' pensions, new maternity allowances and funeral benefits, unemployment, sickness and special dependency benefits, free hospital treatment for low-income earners and free pharmaceuticals. These benefits were funded by the extension of federal income tax, first introduced in a limited way in 1915 to finance the war effort.[71]

Women gained little structural support from welfare in this period. Interwar feminists campaigned for child endowment and widows' pensions but their main ambition was equal pay, a cause that made little headway. Paid to the mother, child endowment provided her with a modicum of independence but, in substituting the state for the breadwinner, it ultimately

66 J. Roe, *Social Policy in Australia: Some Perspectives* (Sydney: Cassell, 1976).

67 Murphy, *A Decent Provision.*

68 S. Macintyre, *Winners and Losers: The Pursuit of Social Justice in Australia* (Sydney: Allen & Unwin, 1985).

69 K. Deverall, 'They Did Not Know Their Place: The Politics of Annie Golding and Kate Dwyer' *Labour History* 87 (2004).

70 S. Garton, *The Cost of War: Australians Return* (Melbourne: Oxford University Press, 1996).

71 S. Macintyre, *Australia's Boldest Experiment: War and Reconstruction in the 1940s* (Sydney: NewSouth Publishing, 2015).

reinforced women's economic dependence.[72] Indeed, welfare ranged white women on a hierarchy of deservedness according to their partners' status: women married to men in work were at the top; war widows' benefits were higher than those of civilian widows; unmarried mothers were liable to have their babies removed. The mothering work of Aboriginal women was not recognised by child endowment nor their widowhood by a pension, and all were vulnerable to having their children taken.

During the 1950s and 1960s, the conservative Menzies government retained social security benefits but expanded welfare to the middle class: it reduced the means test on old age pensions, extended child endowment and introduced tax deductions. It also provided funding to voluntary organisations to expand their facilities for the aged and disabled. By the 1960s the system lacked coherence. Many of the regulations governing benefits were based on out-moded or ill-informed assumptions: deserted wives, for example, were not eligible to apply for benefits until six months after their husband left even though most were 'almost destitute' straight away.[73] Despite its flaws, the investment and protection program in place from the 1940s to the 1970s reduced inequality.[74]

Throughout this period the experience of Aboriginal communities was shaped by policies of protection and assimilation, which remained a responsibility of the states. The laws of the early twentieth century were represented as protecting Indigenous peoples against unscrupulous employers, but they controlled their movements, intruded into their personal lives and took their wages, while systemising their exclusion from citizenship. They became more coercive in the 1930s, when it became clear that Aboriginal people were not 'dying out'.[75] Despite their assimilationist intent, the reserves and missions created umbrella structures that enabled resistance and, ultimately, survival.[76] It is important to note that while historians date assimilation as government policy from the late 1930s to the early 1970s, most Indigenous people see the experience of assimilation stemming back to 1788.[77]

[72] Grimshaw et al., *Creating a Nation*; C. Baldock and B. Cass, *Women, Social Welfare and the State in Australia* (Sydney: Allen & Unwin, 1983).
[73] J. Stubbs, *The Hidden People* (Melbourne: Cheshire Lansdowne, 1966), 136–8.
[74] A. Leigh, *Battlers and Billionaires: The Story of Inequality in Australia* (Melbourne: Black Inc, 2013), 37.
[75] Chesterman and Galligan, *Citizens without Rights.*
[76] P. Brock, *Outback Ghettos: Aborigines, Institutionalisation and Survival* (Cambridge: Cambridge University Press, 1993); Rowse, *Indigenous and Other Australians.*
[77] Rowse, *Contesting Assimilation*, 1.

The letter of settler law, and the ideas behind it, started to change in the 1940s. Rather than white welfare being withheld from Indigenous Australians, it was proffered as an incentive to become 'white'. All Aboriginal people who were 'non-nomadic' were conditionally eligible for all Commonwealth benefits introduced in the 1940s. To qualify, however, they had to have a certificate of exemption contingent on whether they were 'living according to European standards', had 'cut ties' with those on reserves and showed sufficient 'character' and 'development'.[78] A lexical shift from protection to welfare reflected assimilation's modernising aspiration: protectors were renamed welfare officers and protection authorities were renamed welfare authorities.[79]

Throughout the period, Indigenous activists felt acutely the injustice of being subjected to the heavy hand of inept and sometimes corrupt bureaucracies. They wrote letters, made deputations and, from the 1920s, formed organisations: the Australian Aborigines Progressive Association was formed in 1924 to agitate for an inquiry into the Aborigines Protection Board; its leaders were hounded by the police and they were threatened with their children being removed.[80] Aboriginal people felt the injustice of being excluded from welfare benefits they saw as their due. Veterans of World War I, for example, rarely received the war gratuity, and far from being helped towards 'independence', their lands were resumed for white soldier settlers.[81] In the Depression, Aboriginal people at La Perouse were given rations while white families received the dole.[82] Under the terms of the Act, Aboriginal women in New South Wales were entitled to child endowment. Rather than being paid to the women themselves, however, it was paid to the managers of reserves and missions to cover the shortfall from cuts imposed in the Depression.

Activists repeatedly sought to shame politicians, accusing them of abusing the ethical intent of the law they claimed to uphold. In a letter to the prime minister in 1939, Yorta Yorta leader William Cooper pointed out that excluding Aboriginal people from pensions and maternity allowances was not

[78] J. Murphy, ' Conditional Inclusion: Aborigines and Welfare Rights in Australia, 1900–47' *Australian Historical Studies* 44, no. 2 (2013): 206–26, 223.

[79] J. C. Altman and W. Sanders, *From Exclusion to Dependence: Aborigines and the Welfare State in Australia* (Canberra: ANU Press, 1991), 2.

[80] J. Maynard, *Fight for Liberty and Freedom: The Origins of Australian Indigenous Activism* (Canberra: Aboriginal Studies Press, 2007).

[81] Garton, *The Cost of War*; T. C. Winegard, *Indigenous Peoples of the British Dominions and the First World War* (New York: Cambridge University Press, 2011), 248–9.

[82] H. Goodall, 'Pearl Gibbs: Some Memories' *Aboriginal History* 7, no. 1 (1983): 20–2.

consistent with British justice.[83] Joe Anderson told the audience of a 'Cinesound' newsreel in 1933, that 'one of the greatest laws among Aboriginals was to love one another, and he always kept to this law'. He wanted due rights, not charity. 'The black man owned Australia' Anderson declared, 'and he now demands more than charity.'[84] According to Douglas Nicholls, founder of the Victorian Aborigines Advancement League, 'the atmosphere charity' had 'clouded Aboriginal welfare for 173 years'. White Australians had 'a debt to pay'.[85]

The Whitlam Moment

The Whitlam government came to power in 1972 towards the end of the 'golden age' of post-war prosperity, and following twenty years of conservative government. A product of 1960s radicalism, when the intelligentsia in the West called for alternatives to capitalism, it has been described as 'a shining aberration' – and it came closer to Esping-Andersen's social democracies than had any previous Australian government.[86] It sought to promote 'positive equality' and social participation. Among its innovations were the Australian Assistance Plan, which was based on empowering local communities, and the Department of Urban and Regional Development, which saw planning as essential for maximising equalities.[87]

Whitlam sought to move away from the 'charity-governed' model of welfare to a universal model. His introduction of a universal health care system, abolition of the means test on the old age pension, and scrapping of University fees, were all universal measures. He combined these with selective benefits that provided social protection for a wider range of groups including disabled children and supporting mothers. Indeed, while Australian feminists had long seen the state as the way to greater equality, it was under Whitlam that feminism gained an institutional presence.[88] His government funded women's refuges and community child care, extended the minimum wage to women, reopened the equal pay case and introduced accessible

[83] Murphy, 'Conditional Inclusion'.
[84] Goodall and Cadzow, *Rivers and Resilience*, 155, xiii.
[85] Leaflet, '"We have a debt to pay", Northcote Hostel for Aboriginal Boys & Girls', Museum of Victoria, https://collections.museumvictoria.com.au/items/1591651, accessed 27 March 2020.
[86] G. Bolton, *Oxford History of Australia* (Melbourne: Oxford University Press, 1986), Volume V.
[87] J. Hocking (ed.), *Making Modern Australia: The Whitlam Government's Twenty-first Century* (Melbourne: Monash University Publishing, 2017).
[88] Lake, *Getting Equal*, 253.

no-fault divorce.[89] Whitlam created a new federal Department of Aboriginal Affairs (DAA) in Canberra in 1972, which had a policy of recruiting Aboriginal people; and services for Aboriginal and Torres Strait Islander people were established in other government departments.[90]

Embrace of Black Power by Aboriginal activists in the 1970s drove the push for new community organisations that would be controlled by Aboriginal people. Legal services, health services, women and children's services and housing co-operatives were established in Fitzroy, Redfern and Brisbane, responses to endemic health problems, malnutrition and police brutality. However, funding for Indigenous organisations came through government departments, pointing up the contradictions in self-determination operating within boundaries set by the settler state. Activists saw government funding as compensation and wanted control over its use.[91]

Whitlam's vision was confounded by the end of prosperity. Following the oil crisis of 1973, unemployment rose and Australia experienced 'stagflation' – unemployment and inflation concurrently – a pairing that Keynes had declared impossible. The rise in unemployment was accompanied by an ongoing campaign by right-wing think-tanks and the tabloid press to demonise the unemployed as 'dole bludgers'.[92] The Fraser government cut spending. Like Menzies, Fraser maintained benefits for those whom he considered 'deserving' – the aged, disabled, parents and the young unemployed – but he cut programs that sought to empower the poor and reshape institutions.[93]

The Neoliberal Turn

The global shifts of the 1970s irrevocably altered the labour market, the welfare terrain and the relationship between them. The decline of manufacturing in the West made under-employment endemic and stagflation brought Keynesian economics into disrepute. Under the energetic advocacy of long-time free marketeers, Milton Friedman and Friedrich von Hayek, neoliberalism became orthodoxy. While this term has been criticised as too broad to be useful, its very expansiveness marks out major change: faith in

89 Susan Ryan, *Revisiting the Revolution: Whitlam and Women* (Sydney: Whitlam Institute, 2020), 8.

90 Altman and Sanders, *From Exclusion*, 313.

91 G. Foley, 'Whiteness and Blackness in the Koori Struggle for Self-determination' *Just Policy: Journal of Australian Social Policy* 19/20 (2000): 74–88.

92 V. Archer, 'Dole Bludgers, Taxpayers and the New Right: Constructing Discourses of Welfare in the 1970s' *Labour History* 96, May (2009): 177–90.

93 F. Crowley, *Tough Times: Australia in the Seventies* (Melbourne: Heinemann, 1986), 375–7.

the 'free' market as driver of economic and social progress, out-sourcing of service delivery and renewed fear that welfare without conditions leads to moral and social decay.[94] Neoliberalism meant different, not necessarily less, governance. In Australia it entailed a retreat from social investment and the imposition of more rigid conditions on protection. Underlying the shifts were the real challenges of dealing with economic stagnation in the face of globalisation and significant increases in public sector spending: welfare spending in Australia went from 17.7 per cent of the Commonwealth Budget in 1971 to 27.3 per cent in 1981.[95] The welfare wars, however, were waged more on ideological than economic grounds, particularly after the fall of communism in Europe in 1989, which strengthened the belief that public spending was an unhealthy restraint on capitalism. Comparative research produced in the early 1990s showed that economic growth was not impeded by the size of welfare spending and that the economic crisis of the past decades could not be blamed on the growth of welfare.[96]

One of the major shifts of this period was the formal dismantling of the national system of wage determination that had been in place since Federation. Reflecting the extent of bipartisan support for market-oriented reform, Paul Keating's Labor government began this process with the introduction of enterprise bargaining in 1993. In 1997 the Howard government strengthened the hand of employers by introducing individual contracts, outlawing compulsory unionism and restricting lawful industrial action. It was the 2005 policy known as 'Work Choices' that gave 'unprecedented' support to employers. It removed protections against unfair dismissal, imposed greater penalties on industrial action, reduced the powers of independent tribunals and state jurisdictions, and allowed individual contracts that ignored minimum penalty rates and overtime shifts.[97] It was instrumental in the Coalition's defeat in the 2007 election.

While Labor governments dispensed with the idea of universal welfare, their in-principle commitment to social justice went some way towards keeping neoliberal ideology in check. The Hawke government's 'social wage' and 'Family Assistance Package' mitigated some of the worst effects of economic transformation and, under the first feminist Cabinet Minister,

94 D. Rodgers, 'The Uses and Abuses of "Neoliberalim"', *Dissent Magazine*, Winter, 2018.

95 P. Mendes, *Empowerment and Control in the Australian Welfare State* (New York: Routledge, 2018).

96 P. Saunders, *Welfare and Inequality: National and International Perspectives on the Australian Welfare State* (Cambridge: Cambridge University Press, 1994), 137.

97 M. Goot, 'The New Millennium', in A. Bashford and S. Macintyre (eds), *The Cambridge History of Australia* (Cambridge: Cambridge University Press), Volume 2.

Susan Ryan, feminists in the government made some gains in child care, equal pay and Sex Discrimination Law.[98] The Howard government embraced neoliberalism more fully: it tightened the criteria for unemployment benefits and reduced their level, toughened the 'activity test' and associated penalties for non-compliance, reduced rent assistance, and cut services including the Commonwealth Dental Health Program.[99] A new term – 'welfare dependency' – emerged. Implying a pathology that was systemic not just individual, it was used to disparage the previous government's policies and gain support for radical change.[100] Indeed, the ensuing shifts were radical to the point of undermining democratic norms. The out-sourcing of employment services side-stepped Parliament: when the Senate blocked the Reform of Employment Service Bill in 1996 the government went ahead anyway, using its constitutional power to enter into contracts.[101] These contracts contained 'commercial in-confidence' clauses that protected tenders from public scrutiny and ensured that successful tenderers would refrain from public comment, a process that enabled governments to avoid accountability and was found by a series of parliamentary inquiries to be highly inefficient.[102] Out-sourcing gave renewed prominence to voluntary organisations – now elevated by a discourse of 'partnership' – even as they were treated as 'a shunting yard' that enabled the state to avoid the political risks of failure.[103]

The Global Financial Crisis of 2009 (GFC) went some way towards reviving Australia's tradition of social investment. The Rudd Labor government followed Keynesian logic to stimulate the economy through an immediate boost to household income and spending on national infrastructure. It rescinded some of the most extreme features of the previous government's policies, such as 'Work Choices' and the 'gagging clauses' on non-profits, and

98 Mendes, *Empowerment and Control*; Eva Cox, 'A Feminist Proposal for a Fair Universal Social Dividend' *Hecate* 45, no. 1-2 (2020): 247–66.

99 Mendes, *Empowerment and Control*.

100 B. Engels, 'Old Problem, New Label: Reconstructing the Problem of Welfare Dependency in Australian Social Policy Discourse' *Just Policy: A Journal of Australian Social Policy* 5 (2006).

101 R. Harris, 'Avoiding the Worst of All Worlds: Government Accountability for Outsourced Employment Services' *AIAL Forum* 54 (2007).

102 A. D. Barton, 'Public Sector Accountability and Commercial-in-confidence Outsourcing Contracts' *Accounting, Auditing & Accountability Journal* 19, no. 2 (2006): 256–71.

103 S. Wright, G. Marston and C. McDonald, 'The Role of Non-profit Organisations in the Mixed Economy of Welfare-to-work in the UK and Australia' *Social Policy and Administration* 45, no. 3 (2011): 299–318.

it introduced a Fair Work Act.[104] Inequality, however, continued to grow.[105] The Labor government did not raise unemployment benefits. On the contrary, they went from being 33 per cent of the average wage in 2003 to 23 per cent in 2011. Under Julia Gillard, Labor improved the wages of low-paid workers, most of whom were women, but it pursued welfare-to-work policies that disadvantaged single parents, who were also predominantly women.[106] The stereotype of 'passive welfare' was enflamed by the tabloid press even as a study of 150 people on income security payments published in 2011 showed that most were actively engaged in local activities, one-third were employed part-time work; most agreed with the trend in welfare policy at the same time as suffering its stigma, frequently experiencing Centrelink as a place of humiliation.[107]

In the field of Indigenous policy, the Howard government's reversals undermined Indigenous sovereignty.[108] It abolished the Aboriginal and Torres Strait Islander Commission (ATSIC), rejected 'self-determination' and, setting up a dichotomy between the symbolic and the practical, pursued a policy of 'mainstreaming' despite a plethora of reports that found mainstream services less effective.[109] From the late 1990s, Noel Pearson became the highest profile Indigenous commentator on welfare, given precedence by Newscorp's *The Australian*, which dominated the news agenda on Indigenous affairs between 1988 and 2008.[110] Pearson's argument that Aboriginal people wanted 'a foothold in the economy not passive welfare' was similar in many ways to previous calls from Indigenous leaders.[111] Some remote communities in the 1970s called for an alternative to 'sit down' money, which led to the introduction of the Community

[104] Deeming and Smyth, 'Social Investment', 302; Wright et al., 'The Role of Non-profit Organisations', 309.

[105] Leigh, *Battlers and Billionaires.*

[106] Carol Johnson, *Social Democracy and the Crisis of Equality: Australian Social Democracy in a Changing World* (Singapore: Springer, 2019).

[107] J. Murphy, S. Murray, J. Chambers, S. Martin and G. Marston, *Half a Citizen: Life on Welfare in Australia* (Sydney: Allen & Unwin, 2011).

[108] Moreton Robinson, *Sovereign Subjects.*

[109] A. Gunstone, 'These Blokes are Re-inventing the 19th Century: The Howard Government's Record on Indigenous Affairs, 1996–2006' *The Journal of Indigenous Policy* 7 (2007); see for example, B. Fredericks, '"There is nothing that identifies me to that place": Indigenous Women's Perceptions of Health Spaces and Places' *Cultural Studies Review* 15, no. 2 (2009): 29–44.

[110] K. McCallum and L. Waller, 'Media Stars and Neoliberal News Agendas in Indigenous Policymaking', in Will Sanders (ed.), *Engaging Indigenous Economy: Debating Diverse Approaches* (Canberra: ANU Press, 2016).

[111] N. Pearson, 'The Light on the Hill', Ben Chifley Memorial Lecture, 12 August 2000.

Development Employment Program (CDEP) in 1977.[112] In a context where neoliberalism's default position was a narrative of blame, however, the main point – that marginalisation enforced welfare dependency rather than the other way round – was lost in public discourse.[113]

The Howard government's Northern Territory Emergency Response in 2007 opened another more radical chapter in the long history of welfare colonialism.[114] It abolished CDEP (which had created 35,000 jobs and facilitated 'a degree of community self-management') and introduced Compulsory Income Management (CIM).[115] Intended as a short-term measure, CIM was retained and extended to non-Indigenous communities under Labor as well as Coalition governments despite the fact that there was 'no robust evidence' to suggest that it was meeting its intended objectives.[116] On the contrary, it eroded Indigenous peoples' rights while providing hefty profits for the financial services provider, Indue Ltd. It did nothing to address the structural constraints on employment in rural areas where the disparity in employment rates of Indigenous and non-Indigenous people had increased since 'closing the gap' became the mantra of policy.[117]

Despite this context, Indigenous health professionals and social workers have worked hard to disseminate Indigenous ideas of well-being.[118] And despite the media's preoccupation with 'dysfunction', research shows collective work for well-being paying off. The 'mixed mob' in urban Newcastle, first mobilised in the 1970s, has developed an Aboriginal 'social infrastructure' that has enabled 'better than average' opportunities for work

112 L. O'Donohue, 'In Indigenous Affairs Nothing is New, Just Forgotten', Annual Spann Oration, *Australian Journal of Public Administration* 56, no. 4 (1997): 5–10.

113 M. Walter, 'Indigenous Sovereignty and the Australian State', in Moreton Robinson, *Sovereign Subjects*, 162.

114 See Foley and McKinnon, Chapter 22 in this volume.

115 K. Jordan and J. Altman, 'From Welfare to Work or Work to Welfare?', in K. Jordan (ed.), *Better than Welfare? Work and Livelihoods for Indigenous Australians after CDEP* (Canberra: ANU Press, 2016), 1–23.

116 M. Gray and R. Bray, 'ANU Centre for Social Methods and Research Submission into Social Security' (Administration) Amendment (Income Management and Cashless Welfare) Bill 2019 (Submission No. 7).

117 S. Bielefeld, 'Indigenous Peoples, Neoliberalism and the State: A Retreat from Rights to "Responsibilisation" via the Cashless Welfare Card', in D. Howard-Wagner, M. Bargh and I. Altamirano-Jimenez (eds), *The Neoliberal State, Recognition and Indigenous Rights* (Canberra: ANU Press, 2018), 147–65; Jordan and Altman, 'From Welfare to Work', 3–7.

118 B. Bennett, S. Green, S. Gilbert and D. Bessarab, *Our Voices: Aboriginal and Torres Strait Islander Social Work* (Melbourne: Palgrave Macmillan, 2013); S. Lohoar, N. Butera and E. Kennedy, *Strengths of Australian Aboriginal Cultural Practices in Family Life and Child Rearing* (Canberra: Australian Institute of Family Studies, 2014).

and education.[119] Since gaining native title in 2010, the Yaruwu in Broome have established Nyamba Buru Yawuru, a not-for-profit organisation that manages 3,000 hectares of land, a technology consultancy and a construction joint venture, based on the holistic idea of 'Mabu liyan' or living well.[120] It is no coincidence that many of those honoured by the National Aboriginal and Islanders Day Observance Committee (NAIDOC) awards are women and men who have contributed in significant ways to the well-being of their communities.[121] Such achievements are particularly impressive in light of the resurgence of welfare as a weapon.

Conclusion

The history of Indigenous well-being is one of survival and loss, adaptability and struggle, achievement and pain. Indigenous land was used to fund settler welfare and Indigenous peoples experienced that welfare at its most meagre and controlling. Settlers experienced welfare as social investment geared towards economic growth and the immigrant dream was grounded in the promise of work and independence. This history has heightened the marginalisation of women's caring labour and given rise to a particularly entrenched fear of what is disparaged as 'the welfare habit': it blames the unemployed, downplays the conditions with which they deal, and stymies public discussion of social policy – despite the recurring pattern showing that unemployment increases when social investment declines. Indeed, the last decade has seen Australia at the forefront of Anglophone countries in installing regimes of welfare conditionality.[122] And yet, Australia's long history of social investment has not been altogether extinguished – it was revived during the GFC and was deployed to combat COVID-19 – nor have Indigenous ways of well-being been lost. Understanding the intersecting histories of these malleable, enduring strands provides some clarity on how we might approach what some have seen as impending automation and a 'post-work' future.[123]

[119] D. Howard-Wagner, *Successful Urban Aboriginal-driven Community Development: A Place-based Study of Newcastle* (Canberra: ANU Press, 2017).

[120] M. Yap and E. Yu, 'Expressions of Indigenous Rights and Self-determination from the Ground Up: A Yaruwu Example', in Howard-Wagner et al. (eds), *The Neoliberal State*, 93–109.

[121] https://www.naidoc.org.au/awards/winner-profiles, accessed 23 December 2021.

[122] P. Mendes, G. Marston and Ilan Katz, 'Introduction' for Special Issue on Income Management, *The Australian Journal of Social Issues* 61, no. 4 (2016): 393–7.

[123] E. Klein, J. Mays and T. Dunlop (eds), *Implementing a Basic Income in Australia: Pathways Forward* (Basingstoke: Palgrave Macmillan, 2019).

22

Civil Rights and Indigenous People

GARY FOLEY AND CRYSTAL MCKINNON

Indigenous nations and individuals across what we now call Australia have been in an ongoing fight for their lands, lives and kin since first contacts with colonial forces. People have utilised a variety of means for this fight, including warfare, petitions, marches, boycotts, art, music and the courts. Indigenous people have been subject to racialised legislation and practice across all jurisdictions. These have included laws that limited people's ability to choose where they could live and work, who they could marry or associate with, whether people received equal pay or any pay at all, the right to vote, the food and drink they consumed, the shops and establishments they were allowed to enter, and where and whether they were allowed to travel. These restrictive laws and practices can be understood as a denial of 'civil rights'. Like political theorist John Chesterman, we are using the term civil rights here to mean 'the shared legal, political and social rights of [all] citizens that are provided for by Commonwealth and state laws', not the distinct group rights of Indigenous peoples.[1]

As Indigenous people, our separate rights originate from our sovereignty, which we derive from our ontological relationship to our land and to our territory.[2] This sovereignty is embodied, thus all of the battles and protests we undertake as sovereign Indigenous people can be understood to arise from our connection to our lands.[3] So though we maintain that all political resistance can be understood to be about land and sovereignty, we focus, in this chapter, on battles to change restrictive and racist Commonwealth and state law.

We position these efforts for civil rights within a dynamic matrix of protest and resistance efforts undertaken by Indigenous people – all of which occur in

[1] J. Chesterman, *Civil Rights: How Indigenous Australians Won Formal Equality* (St Lucia: University of Queensland Press, 2005), 3.

[2] Aileen Moreton-Robinson, *The White Possessive: Property, Power, and Indigenous Sovereignty* (Minneapolis, MN: University of Minnesota Press, 2015), 11.

[3] Crystal McKinnon, *Expressing Indigenous Sovereignty: The Production of Embodied Texts in Social Protest and the Arts* (unpublished PhD thesis, La Trobe University, 2018), 108.

relation to each other and which are mutually constitutive. Indigenous people can march in the streets on 26 January to commemorate Invasion Day or enter into negotiations with the state for contemporary treaties because of those Aboriginal parents who petitioned mission managers for their children, those Aboriginal authors who put their stories in novels, and those warriors who fought guerrilla warfare on the invasion frontiers. Given the sheer number of ways Indigenous people have organised and protested and resisted, it is difficult to pinpoint a single time or even a few events to begin a chapter on Indigenous people and our fight for civil rights.

For the purposes of our contribution to this collection, we begin by focusing on the period between 1923 and the 1967 Referendum, a time which captures some of what we consider to be nationally significant battles for civil rights undertaken by Indigenous people and organisations. We end with a discussion of the evolution of the Black Power movement, which marked a significant change in methods undertaken by Aboriginal people in the fight for justice and rights. As will become clear, these events are all connected and as we consider them together in this section, we will show how they have been a generative movement for Indigenous civil rights in Australia.

In the twentieth century organised Aboriginal political resistance began with the formation of the Marcus Garvey-inspired Australian Aboriginal Progressive Association (AAPA) in 1923. Founded and led by Fred Maynard, the radical platform and activities of the AAPA, which established numerous branches throughout northern New South Wales, were too much for the NSW Police and Aborigines Protection Board: they moved to supress the AAPA by 1927.[4] In the 1930s another two significant Aboriginal organisations were established. The first, formed early in 1936, was the Australian Aborigines League (AAL), which was established by William Cooper, Doug Nicholls, Bill and Eric Onus, and others in Melbourne.[5] Membership of the AAL was open to all Aboriginal people and its aims were 'to gain for Aboriginal people those civil and human rights denied since occupation'.[6] A year later in 1937, the second organisation was formed in Dubbo, New South Wales, by Bill Ferguson and Jack Patten, and called the Aborigines

[4] J. Maynard, *Fight for Liberty and Freedom: The Origins of Australian Aboriginal Activism* (Canberra: Aboriginal Studies Press, 2007), 186.

[5] A. Markus, *Blood from a Stone* (Clayton: Monash Publications in History, 1986), 10.

[6] VAAL, *Victims or Victors?: The Story of the Victorian Aborigines Advancement League* (Melbourne: Hyland House, 1985), 27.

Progressive Association (APA).[7] Ferguson was the APA's Secretary, and Patten was the President.

On 12 November 1937, the same year the APA was founded, it joined forces with the AAL to hold a meeting to discuss the upcoming occasion of the Sesquicentenary of the First Fleet. Attending the November meeting were the APA's Patten, Ferguson and Pearl Gibbs, along with the AAL's Marge Tucker, Nicholls and Cooper, and a few other Aboriginal activists. The AAL's president Cooper had proposed that 'the 150th anniversary of the landing of the first fleet of European invaders, to be celebrated on 26th January 1938, should instead be held by Aborigines as a Day of Mourning'.[8]

This meeting initiated what would become one of the most significant protests with an ongoing legacy for Indigenous people in Australia. In its wake, preparations began to hold a protest to counter the notion that the arrival of the First Fleet was something to celebrate. This idea was described by historian Heather Goodall as a 'brilliantly symbolic plan . . . recognised as a turning point in capturing white attention'.[9] Organisers strategically planned their campaign platforms, messaging, logistics, speakers, and how to publicise the event for both Indigenous and non-Indigenous people. Activists at the meeting prepared an announcement for the protest and their plans were reported on the front page of the *Argus* newspaper the next day, 13 November 1937. It told readers that along with being 'in mourning' for all that they had lost, they hoped that their protest 'would direct the attention of the people of Australia to the desire of the [A]borigines for full rights of citizenship'.[10]

Building upon this initial messaging, Ferguson and Patten together wrote a manifesto entitled *Aborigines Claim Citizen Rights!*[11] In this document, Patten and Ferguson comprehensively examined the contemporary situation of Aboriginal communities and people, including criticism of government policies and treatment of Aboriginal people. The manifesto asked for 'justice, citizenship rights and freedom from the constraints of the Acts'.[12] The first page of the manifesto began with a paragraph pointing out that the 150th

[7] See H. Goodall, *Invasion to Embassy: Land in Aboriginal Politics in New South Wales, 1770–1972* (St Leonards: Allen and Unwin, 1996).

[8] R. Broome, *Aboriginal Australians: Black Responses to White Dominance 1788–1994* (St Leonards: Allen and Unwin, 1994), 167.

[9] Goodall, *Invasion to Embassy,* 230.

[10] 'Aborigines' Day of Mourning: Plan for 150th Anniversary', *The Argus*, 13 November 1937, 1.

[11] J. Patten and W. Ferguson, *Aborigines Claim Citizen Rights! A Statement of the Case for the Aborigines Progressive Association* (Sydney: The Publicist, 1938).

[12] Broome, *Aboriginal Australians,* 167.

anniversary of the First Fleet's arrival is 'not a day of rejoicing for Australia's Aborigines; it is a day of mourning'.[13] Patten and Ferguson detailed the history of the 'Aborigines Protection Acts', with a section specifically entitled 'What "Protection" means.'[14] After this national discussion, they used New South Wales as a case study and showed the manner in which the state's Aborigines Protection Act 1909–36 and the Board for Protection of Aborigines that the Act established, defined who was 'Aboriginal' and then segregated individuals by judging what percentage of their blood was 'Aboriginal'.[15] They meticulously and convincingly demonstrated that protection legislation was a civil rights issue, by analysing at length the means by which racist discourses of blood quotas had been used by the state to name and control people they determined were 'Aborigines'. Many things that Patten and Ferguson detailed, such as 'exploitation of Aboriginal labour', and not wanting to be 'studied' as scientific or anthropological curiosities, are issues that Indigenous people in Australia still grapple with today.[16]

In early January 1938 *Aborigines Claim Citizen Rights!* was published as a pamphlet in order to get news of the event and the organising collective's platform circulating in the community, both Aboriginal and non-Aboriginal. On the last page of the manifesto was a full-page invitation to attend the 'Australian Aborigines Conference, Sesqui-Centenary Day of Mourning & Protest, to be held in the Australian Hall, Sydney on Wednesday, 26 January, 1938 (Australia Day)'.[17] The invitation stated explicitly that 'Aborigines and Persons of Aboriginal Blood only are invited to attend'.[18] This call to all Aboriginal people from different countries across Australia was a momentous occurrence. Its significance has been understated by historians, as it shows the emergence of a nation-wide Aboriginal political consciousness accompanied with strategic organising across jurisdictions and state borders.

Along with the pamphlet, the activists produced both posters and handbills for the event, which were 'sent west, north and south to as many pockets of Aboriginal people as possible'.[19] Patten himself travelled into the countryside to hand deliver invitations to Aboriginal people on government policed reserves.[20] It is important to remember that this was an incredibly difficult era for Aboriginal political organisers because of the range of restrictive and

[13] Patten and Ferguson, *Aborigines Claim Citizen Rights!*, 3. [14] Ibid, 5–6. [15] Ibid, 6–8.
[16] Ibid, 9–10. [17] Ibid, 12. [18] Ibid.
[19] S. Gilbert, 'Pearl Gibbs (Gambanyi) Never Forgotten', in A. Cole, V. Haskins and F. Paisley (eds), *Uncommon Ground: White Women in Aboriginal History* (Canberra: Australian Institute of Aboriginal Studies, 2005), 107–26.
[20] Ibid, 110.

Figure 22.1: A blackboard displayed outside the hall proclaims, 'Day of mourning', Courtesy of the State Library of New South Wales, Q 059 / 9 Mitchell Library (Printed Books Collection).

discriminatory state laws that controlled the movement of Indigenous people.

So, when the 26 January arrived, while non-Indigenous people were celebrating the re-enactment of the First Fleet at Sydney Cove, on the other side of Sydney Aboriginal people gathered in protest at Australian Hall (see Figure 22.1). *Aborigines Claim Citizen Rights!* was distributed among the 100-strong crowd of people, which included Cooper, Gibbs, Tucker, Nicholls, Ferguson, Patten and Jack Johnson.[21] Patten read the resolution proposed on the back page of the manifesto to the conference attendees. It was as follows:

> We, representing the Aborigines of Australia, assembled in conference at the Australian Hall, Sydney, on the 26th day of January, 1938, this being the 150th Anniversary of the Whiteman's seizure of our country, hereby make protest against the callous treatment of our people by the whitemen during the past 150 years, and we appeal to the Australian nation of today to make new laws for the education and care of Aborigines, we ask for a new policy which will raise our people to full citizen status and equality within the community.[22]

[21] *The Australian Abo Call*, No. 1, April 1938, 2. [22] Ibid.

This resolution was passed unanimously. The proceedings of the meeting were recorded and later published in the April edition of *The Abo Call*, the first Aboriginal political newspaper, founded by Patten in 1938.[23] It reported that Aboriginal people across Australia, including Western Australia, Queensland and North Australia expressed support with large numbers of telegrams and letters.[24] The number and vast reach of these responses highlight that while nations of Aboriginal people are different, we share common struggles.

Following the conference, a delegation of conference attendees, including Cooper, Ferguson and Patten, met with the Prime Minister Joseph Lyons and presented him with their proposal for a national policy for Aboriginal people. This was rejected, perhaps in part because the federal government could not legislate on behalf of Aboriginal people under Section 51(xxvi) of the Constitution. This would not change until the 1967 referendum, when an overwhelming majority of the Australian people voted to alter the Constitution to give the Commonwealth power to legislate for Aboriginal people living in the states.

In 1956 the early foundations for the campaign for the Yes vote were created when Day of Mourning organiser Pearl Gibbs, who by then was also the former Secretary of the APA, co-founded the Australian Aboriginal Fellowship (AAF) in Sydney with Faith Bandler. Faith Bandler was a woman of South-sea Islander descent whose father had been kidnapped and brought to Australia as a slave to work on the Queensland sugar fields. The AAF proved to be an important organisation in the 1950s and was a vehicle for the political education and organising abilities of a new generation of activists. The organisation's main purpose was to create a forum for a partnership between Aboriginal and non-Aboriginal people in New South Wales. It would use that partnership to campaign against state government policies of assimilation and strive towards educating the wider community about issues affecting Aboriginal people.[25]

The AAF's first public meeting on 29 April 1957 attracted a crowd of around 1,500 people, with hundreds of Aboriginal people including La Perouse residents who arrived by bus.[26] Other attendees included organisers of the Day of Mourning, Gibbs and Nicholls, Aboriginal opera singers Nancy Ellis and Harold Blair, Aboriginal activists Bert Groves and Bill Onus, an organiser of the Pilbara Aboriginal Workers Strike Don McLeod, Les Haylen who was

[23] Ibid. [24] Ibid.

[25] F. Bandler and L. Fox (eds), *The Time Was Ripe: The Story of the Aboriginal-Australian Fellowship 1956–1969* (Sydney: Alternative Publishing Co-operative Ltd, 1983).

[26] M. Lake, *Faith: Faith Bandler, Gentle Activist* (Crows Nest: Allen and Unwin, 2002), 71.

the Labor member of the House of Representatives for Parkes, and feminist writers and poets Dame Mary Gilmore and Dorothy Hewitt.[27] This was the biggest meeting about Aboriginal civil rights since the Day of Mourning some 19 years earlier. The bill posters advertising the meeting stated they sought a 'New Deal for Aborigines' and an opportunity to 'discuss ways and means of raising the living standards of Aborigines and their integration into the Australian community'.[28] As historian Marilyn Lake wrote, at this meeting the AAF had adopted the specific goal 'to bring about a referendum to delete the "discriminatory clauses" from the Commonwealth Constitution'.[29]

Following the successful launch and first meeting of the AAF, the organisation became affiliated with numerous trade unions, as well as the Australian Union of Women. One of the most significant developments from the work of the AAF was the formulation and distribution of a petition for constitutional amendments to enable the federal government to take responsibility for Aboriginal affairs.[30] This petition had been developed by non-Aboriginal feminist, Jessie Street, in conjunction with Bandler and Gibbs, and their campaign underpinned the successful 1967 Referendum. Street argued, 'there is every reason to suppose that . . . similar improvements in their standards of living would follow if Aborigines were given civil and political rights and social benefits'.[31] The AAF also called for land rights and the improvement of living conditions for Aboriginal communities in New South Wales, as well as conducting a successful campaign in 1962 to repeal certain sections of the NSW Aborigines Protection Act 1909. The AAF also played an important role in conceiving of and advocating for a national body to represent the interests of Aboriginal peoples.

As a result of the AAF's coalition-building efforts, in February 1958 the first national Indigenous political organisation, the Federal Council for Aboriginal Advancement (FCAA), was formed, presenting itself as a national voice for Aboriginal people. Its first meeting took place in Adelaide, where only four of the twenty-five people who attended were Aboriginal. They were Groves, Nicholls, Onus and Jeff Barnes.

The AAF delegate, Groves, critiqued government policies for assimilation at this meeting. The paper he delivered questioned what the government policies of 'assimilation' would mean for Aboriginal people, and implored organisations not to adopt the term in their constitutions. He told the group that the AAF had discussed the use of the term, and that though it implies

27 Ibid, 70. 28 See copy of handbill in Bandler and Fox, *The Time Was Ripe*, 16.
29 Lake, *Faith: Faith Bandler, Gentle Activist*, 70. 30 Ibid, 65.
31 Jessie Street, *Report on Aborigines in Australia* (Sydney: Self-published, 1957), 3.

'citizenship and equal status', which were good, it also meant the 'disappearance of the Aborigines as a separate cultural group and ultimately their physical absorption by the European part of the population'.[32] He called for the use of 'integration' instead – a goal which would ensure Aboriginal people would continue to exist as a distinct group. The shaping of the FCAA through the advocacy of Groves and the AAF set the course of the organisation's campaign for a referendum for constitutional change over the next decade. This was not its only goal, however. Along with the necessity of a constitutional amendment, its professed aims focused on ending discriminatory laws and legislation and the gaining of civil rights, such as basic citizenship entitlements and housing, equal wages, and access to education. As the organisation grew, the dominance of non-Indigenous people on its governing committee became entrenched, and even as it changed its name to Federal Council for the Advancement of Aboriginal and Torres Strait Islanders (FCAATSI) at its Easter conference in 1964, there were rumblings of Aboriginal discontent at the lack of Indigenous control.

In 1962, Aboriginal peoples' voting rights had been ensured through legislation at Commonwealth level, following a Commonwealth inquiry by a *Parliamentary Select Committee on Voting Rights of Aborigines*. For state elections, voting rights had been established at varying times. Queensland was the last state to grant voting rights to Aboriginal people in 1965. While many racial laws were being wound back in the 1960s, 'formal and informal segregation and local restrictive by-laws and regulations remained firmly in place in many parts of the country'.[33] In February 1965, this was exposed by the 'Freedom Ride' through western and northern New South Wales. Charlie Perkins led thirty non-Indigenous students from the 'Student Action for Aborigines (SAFA)' through some of New South Wales's most notoriously racist country towns, such as Moree, Walgett and Bowraville, where discriminatory race-based council restrictions and by-laws were rife. A not uncommon example of local council restrictions is seen in the minutes of the Moree Municipal Council of December 1955, which read as follows:

> 3. Patronage of Baths and Memorial Hall. That no person, being a full-blooded or half-caste aboriginal of Australia, or being a person apparently having an admixture of aboriginal blood, shall use or occupy or be present in or upon, or be allowed or permitted or invited to use or occupy or be present

[32] Groves quoted in Lake, *Faith: Faith Bandler, Gentle Activist*, 80.

[33] T. Banivanua Mar, *Decolonisation and the Pacific: Indigenous Globalisation and the Ends of Empire* (Cambridge: Cambridge University Press, 2016), 189.

> in or upon, the premises of the Council known as the Memorial Hall or in or upon any of the buildings or places ancillary thereto, including the Supper Room, Kitchen, Servery, Toilets and Passages AND THAT no such person as aforesaid shall use or occupy or be present in or upon, or be allowed or permitted to use or occupy or be present in or upon, the Premises of the Council known as the Bore Baths or in or upon any of the buildings or places there with.[34]

Freedom riders were pelted with eggs and tomatoes by a crowd of several hundred angry local white people when they defied this by-law and tried to desegregate the Moree swimming pool. The crowd 'was extremely abusive and violent . . . some students were punched' and after meeting with the Mayor, who agreed to propose desegregation at the town meeting, riders had to leave town under police escort.[35] But the resultant publicity resounded around the world and exposed the vicious nature of Australian racism in an unprecedented way. Freedom Ride participant and historian Ann Curthoys perhaps best described the result: 'In the ensuing public debate, urban public knowledge of racial discrimination grew, some soul-searching went on in the country towns, racial segregation was challenged and in some cases ended, and alternative ideas of inclusion, equality, and full citizenship rights were much debated.'[36] As Adam Shoemaker described it, the Freedom Ride was an

> internationally inspired . . . product of cooperation between whites and blacks committed to the same ideals, confrontationist but non-violent, the Freedom Ride was a consciousness-raising exercise that was very effective. Awakening media interest in Aboriginal affairs was, for the first time, marshalled in favour of the Black Australian cause, to the severe embarrassment of many white townspeople in rural New South Wales. All of these elements foreshadowed a pattern of protest that was to continue and expand in the 1970s and 1980s.[37]

The increased exposure of segregation and racism added to the groundswell of non-Indigenous support for the FCAATSI campaign for constitutional change. Most importantly, for Aboriginal people, as Gary Foley states, 'it

[34] Minute of the Moree Municipal Council, December 1955, quoted in G. W. Ford, 'The Student Bus' *Outlook* 9, no. 2 (1965).

[35] A. Curthoys, 'The Freedom Ride and the Tent Embassy', in G. Foley, A. Schaap and E. Howell (eds), *The Aboriginal Tent Embassy: Sovereignty, Black Power, Land Rights and the State* (Abingdon: Routledge, 2014), 98–113, 109.

[36] A. Curthoys, *The Freedom Ride – Its Significance Today* (National Museum of Australia: National Institute of the Humanities Forum, 2002), 12.

[37] A. Shoemaker, *Black Words White Page: Aboriginal Literature 1929–1988* (St Lucia: University of Queensland Press, 1989), 107.

was an enormous influence on my generation; we were inspired by that moment. it had a powerful effect on my generation, the young generation'.[38]

Since the 1950s, FCAATSI framed their campaign to 'change the Constitution as a question of civil rights, and particularly, whether or not Aborigines and Torres Strait Islanders should have rights that were equal to all Australians.'[39] Bandler, who earlier co-founded the AAF, became one of the most prominent campaigners for the 1967 Referendum.[40] Her work and the work of countless others led to success after some 10 years of campaigning. The campaign used many different methods, including producing leaflets, writing to newspapers, speaking on radio shows, and door knocking to make their case to the voters.

The referendum sought to change the following two sections of the Australian Constitution:

> Section 51. The Parliament shall, subject to this Constitution, have power to make laws for the peace, order, and good government of the Commonwealth with respect to: . . .
>
> (xxvi) the people of any race, other than the aboriginal race in any State, for whom it is deemed necessary to make special laws: . . .
>
> Section 127. In reckoning the numbers of the people of the Commonwealth, or of a State or other part of the Commonwealth, aboriginal natives shall not be counted.[41]

The referendum asked voters to amend Section 51(xxvi) by removing 'other than the aboriginal race in any State', and to remove Section 127 entirely.

In 1967, more than 90 per cent of Australians voted 'Yes' in this referendum. Some see the referendum's importance as overstated in the fight for civil rights. For instance, Chesterman has written that 'its limited legal significance renders it unable to be seen as the principal defining moment'.[42] However, such arguments miss the significance of the referendum for that generation of Aboriginal rights campaigners and for many Aboriginal people generally – to them, it has enormous significance as a symbol of success in the campaign for Aboriginal rights. To many it represented the end of government discrimination (much of which had been dispensed by the states) and offered the hope of social and political reform. The importance of the referendum was impressed

38 G. Foley, 'Black Power, Land Rights and Academic History' *Griffith Law Review* 20, no. 3 (2011): 608–18, 612.

39 Banivanua Mar, *Decolonisation and the Pacific*, 187.

40 Lake, *Faith: Faith Bandler, Gentle Activist*.

41 J. Chesterman and B. Galligan, *Defining Australian Citizenship: Selected Documents* (Carlton: Melbourne University Press, 1999), 173.

42 Chesterman, *Civil Rights*, 9–10.

on the increasingly impatient younger generation of Aboriginal activists by the leaders of FCAATSI. These young people were told to assist in the campaign for a 'Yes' vote as that would be the answer to Indigenous people's ongoing oppression and marginalisation.[43]

Though some declared the battle won, many Aboriginal people did not experience change in their everyday lives. For example, in New South Wales things got significantly worse as the state government disestablished its Aborigines Welfare Board and withdrew administration from the forty-five reserves around the state, effectively abandoning more than 20,000 Aboriginal people.[44] As Oodgeroo Noonuccal put it at the time, the referendum 'did not benefit the black Australians though it eased the guilty conscience of white Australians in this country and overseas'.[45] This perceived failure of the referendum to improve the lives of Aboriginal people led to disillusionment and discontent on the part of the younger Aboriginal generation. The hope that the referendum and its promise of civil rights equality would change the lives of Aboriginal people was not realised, and the next generation of activists looked for different ways to create social change. As Foley said, the failures of this campaign:

> led to a radicalisation of the young generation, who had been politicised by seeing Charlie Perkins' Freedom Ride. My generation, in seeing the referendum fail, believed that the tactics and strategies of the older generation were now discredited. It wasn't really the older generation's fault, but we believed that their tactics had failed, so we sought other ways.[46]

Out of the growing discontent and the search for new ways to achieve rights and justice, the Australian Black Power Movement was born. It began to emerge in the late 1960s when there was global circulation of a new ideology of Black Power, and increased engagements between American Black Power leaders and Indigenous leaders in Australia.[47] A key moment in galvanising the Black Power movement in Australia occurred in 1969, when the Aborigines Advancement League under the leadership of Bruce McGuinness and Bob Maza, invited Caribbean activist, academic and civil rights leader, Roosevelt Brown, to give a talk on 'Black Power' in Melbourne.

[43] See G. Foley, 'Black Power in Redfern 1968–1972' 5 October 2001, www.kooriweb.org/foley/essays/essay_1.html, accessed 1 February 2018.
[44] S. Bennett, 'The 1967 Referendum', *Australian Aboriginal Studies* (2) (1985): 26–31.
[45] K. Walker, 'Black-White Coalition Can Work', *Origin*, 18 September 1969.
[46] Foley, 'Black Power, Land Rights and Academic History', 612–3.
[47] A. Stastny and R. Orr, 'The Influence of the US Black Panthers on Indigenous Activism in Australia and New Zealand from 1969 Onwards' *Australian Aboriginal Studies* (2014): 60–74, 61.

There, Brown called for Indigenous people to develop forms of self-governance and encouraged Black empowerment.[48] In Sydney the movement was stimulated by contact between Aboriginal activists and African American soldiers from the Vietnam war. These soldiers would visit Redfern and bring African American political literature, which was difficult to obtain in Australia.[49]

One of the issues which most affected Aboriginal people, and continues to do so, is policing and police brutality. In Sydney, 'because of the degree of daily confrontation with police in Redfern, it should be of no surprise that the young radicals came to decide that the issue of police harassment and intimidation should be tackled'.[50] Adopting methods used by the American Black Panther Party, in 1969 Aboriginal activists in Redfern including Paul Coe, Gary Williams, Foley, Billy and Lyn Craigie, began observing and collecting information on the police. Foley writes that 'within a matter of months Aboriginal activists collected extensive evidence of arbitrary arrests, beatings, wrongful imprisonment and other serious allegations'.[51] It was from this work that the Redfern Aboriginal Legal Service was created in 1970. This was the first of its kind in Australia, and soon after it opened, the Aboriginal Medical Service was established in 1971 in Redfern; and together, they put into practice the Aboriginal community control ethos of Black Power captured in the words of Aboriginal leader, Chicka Dixon: 'When we were talking about black power, we were talking about blacks having the power to control their destiny.'[52] The Black Power movement stood for land rights, Self-Determination and economic and political independence for all the Aboriginal peoples of Australia.

In 1971, increasingly frequent demonstrations strengthened the Black Power movement, including the Anti-Vietnam Moratorium rallies and protests against the tour of South African Springboks rugby team. Aboriginal activists from across Australia were travelling and assisting each other in local rallies, protests and movement building. In his Australia Day speech in 1972, delivered on what Indigenous people call Invasion Day, Prime Minister Billy McMahon rejected land rights for Aboriginal communities. This speech was heard by a group of Indigenous activists in Sydney, four of whom

48 See ibid, 67 and Foley, 'Black Power, Land Rights and Academic History', 613.

49 Ibid, 613–14; and G. Foley, 'Black Power in Redfern 1968–1972' in Z. Begg, and K. De Souza, and You Are Here and Performance Space (eds), *There Goes the Neighbourhood: Redfern and the Politics of Urban Space* (Sydney: Performance Space, 2009), 12–21, 15.

50 Foley, 'Black Power in Redfern 1968–1972', 15. 51 Ibid, 15.

52 C. Dixon, 'The History of the Struggle for Aboriginal Rights', First in Line, *ABC Radio*, 22 August 1989, in Foley et al. (eds), *The Aboriginal Tent Embassy*, 122.

volunteered to go to Canberra and establish an Aboriginal Embassy, because McMahon's statement 'demonstrated that Indigenous peoples in Australia were effectively aliens in their own land'.[53] At 1.30 a.m. on 27 January Aboriginal activists Michael Anderson, Tony Coorey, Bert Williams and Billie Craigie erected a beach umbrella on the lawns of Parliament House in Canberra, with signs reading 'Aboriginal Embassy', 'Land Now Not Lease Tomorrow' and 'Land Rights Now or Else!'[54]

This was to become one of the most significant political protest actions of the twentieth century in Australia. That day 'evolved into a six-month political stand-off between radical Aboriginal activists and a conservative Australian government'.[55] It resulted in increased international awareness of Indigenous struggles for justice and 'forced an end to the notorious national government policy of Assimilation and for the first time put Aboriginal issues firmly onto the national political agenda'.[56] In the following decades, the fight for justice and for the actualisation of civil rights for Aboriginal people continued to be at the forefront of the Aboriginal political movement.

As we have discussed, various forms of race-based restrictions and laws were in place across the jurisdictions throughout most of the nineteenth and twentieth century. The fights against these by Aboriginal people have been consistent and widespread. Progress towards gaining civil rights gathered momentum in the 1960s, which resulted in many of those race-based restrictions and laws being dismantled. Though the winding-back of these laws saw the civil rights battle largely won, racism against Indigenous people was part of the social fabric of Australia. For many Aboriginal peoples, the gaining of civil rights failed to result in equity and equality in their lives. The Embassy still stands in Canberra as a stark reminder to all that the struggle for Aboriginal rights continues, despite the many gains made by Aboriginal activists over the nineteenth and twentieth centuries.

[53] G. Foley, A. Schaap and E. Howell, 'Introduction' in Foley et al. (eds), *The Aboriginal Tent Embassy*, xxv–xxx, xxv

[54] M. Anderson, 'Founding of the Embassy' [interview with Brenda Gifford, recorded at the National Film and Sound Archive, 17 June 2011] in Foley et al. (eds), *The Aboriginal Tent Embassy*, 117–22, 122.

[55] Foley et al., 'Introduction', xxv. [56] Ibid, xxv.

23

Rights

FRANK BONGIORNO

Modern Australian political discourse about rights is often framed by a sense of absence: that Australia is, in global terms, unusual and deficient in lacking a bill of rights. This absence does matter, for it means that many of the rights backed by constitutional protections in other jurisdictions depend in Australia on the operation of the common law, on legislative enactment, or on the discovery by High Court judges of implied rights in the federal Constitution. Certain rights – such as freedom of speech and freedom of the press – are more poorly protected than in the United States of America, a natural point of comparison given the indebtedness of Australia's federal Constitution to that of the United States. The concept of 'equal protection' – a basis for civil rights claims that was embodied in the US Constitution's Fourteenth Amendment, adopted soon after the Civil War – has no explicit place in the Australian Constitution.[1] Indeed, the latter does not even define citizenship, let alone set out citizenship rights.

The definition of the powers of the Commonwealth in the Constitution does, however, provide some basic rights, such as Section 51(xxxi)'s stipulation that property must be acquired from an individual 'on just terms', trial by jury in federal courts (Section 80), and Section 116's prohibitions against laws interfering with the free exercise of any religion, establishing any religion, or imposing religious observance or tests for public office. These rights were expressed as limitations on Commonwealth power rather than as conferring rights on individuals or citizens, and they have no application to the relationship between the states and their residents.

Still, for most of Australia's European history since the eighteenth century, there was no powerful sense of an absence of rights that would be remedied

[1] Peter Cane, *Controlling Administrative Power: An Historical Comparison* (Cambridge: Cambridge University Press, 2016), 141.

by a bill of rights or similar instrument. With the occasional exception, Australia's founding fathers accepted A. V. Dicey's opinion that the common law and the courts could adequately protect people's rights without the assistance of a formal bill of rights.[2] Until about the 1960s, Australia's British legal and constitutional heritage in combination with its own local customs and traditions were seen as guarantors of such rights. The quest for the recognition of rights was often understood in terms of the need to make Australia more, rather than less, like Britain. It is only from around the 1960s, the point at which British Australia started to unravel, and when the global 'rights revolution' gathered momentum, that the sense of an absence became more salient.[3]

Rights Beginnings

The process by which Aboriginal people were constituted as British subjects who, in theory, had the same rights at other British subjects in Australia, was protracted, their status being determined 'slowly and hesitantly'.[4] Legal historians have drawn attention to how early colonial settlement assumed multiple sovereignties, including those of Aboriginal nations, so that Indigenous people were only gradually brought within the status of 'British subject'.[5] Officials assumed Aboriginal sovereignty had survived the arrival of the British in January 1788. From about 1815, however, as settlement in New South Wales and Van Diemen's Land (Tasmania) expanded inland, there was a trend towards a more modern form of territorial sovereignty that would soon come to treat Indigenous people as British subjects with certain basic rights rather than as people of another nation with its own laws.[6] Even then, they were not, in practice, treated in the same manner as settlers; their rights being circumscribed not least because most whites perceived them as unfit to participate in the legal system, as they could not swear a Christian oath. Moreover, as the colonies embraced more representative forms of politics,

2 Ibid, 142–3.

3 Jon Piccini, *Transnational Protest, Australia and the 1960s: Global Radicals* (London: Palgrave Macmillan, 2016).

4 Bruce Kercher, *An Unruly Child: A History of Law in Australia* (St Leonards: Allen & Unwin, 1995), 5.

5 Lisa Ford and Tim Rowse (eds), *Between Indigenous and Settler Governance* (Abingdon: Routledge, 2013).

6 Lisa Ford, *Settler Sovereignty: Jurisdiction and Indigenous People in America and Australia, 1788–1836* (Cambridge, MA: Harvard University Press, 2010).

Indigenous people would be seen as unqualified for involvement in self-government as well.[7]

Indigenous people took for granted an ancient right to the soil, based on Dreaming stories that assumed the oneness of the land and all that lived on it. The new settlers equally believed that they had a right to enjoy the fruits of the land – its water, its food supply and its soils – based on their occupation of a domain that they defined as public, nature's bounty, a gift of God. In making such claims, they were supported by the most influential theorists, such as John Locke, who defined the right to property in terms of the application of labour to nature. These competing claims would be the basis of contention between settlers and Indigenous people, and would fuel much violence as settlement expanded.

Such contrasting understandings rested, in large part, on different rights regimes, each rooted in distinctive sets of beliefs. The settlers did, quite often, recognise that the assertion of their own apparent rights had resulted in an infringement on the rights of Indigenous people. As one colonist in Van Diemen's Land wrote to a newspaper in 1824,

> We ought to feel that we have invaded a domain from which our invasion has expelled those who were born, bred, and providentially supplied in it; that we have driven by our usurpation, families from their birth-place, and then completed our cruelty by destroying in sport, and consuming for profit, the principal means of their subsistence.[8]

Australia was founded as a penal colony, a kind of open-air prison, but the convicts were convinced that they possessed rights that had not been eliminated by transportation. While the idea of the equality of all British subjects before the law was a myth, it was a powerful one that could shape the behaviour of both felon and free.[9] On the one hand, convicts and emancipists believed in the existence of an ancient English constitution that bestowed certain rights. And while such claims might be denied by the authorities as 'absurd', they could still motivate resistance to arbitrary punishment at the hands of either government or master; and claims for rights such as trial by jury that would come to occupy a central place in emancipist campaigns. But

[7] See Curthoys and Mitchell, Chapter 6 in this volume; Ann Curthoys and Jessie Mitchell, *Taking Liberty: Indigenous Rights and Settler Self-Government in Colonial Australia, 1830–1890* (Cambridge: Cambridge University Press, 2018).

[8] *Hobart Town Gazette*, 23 July 1824, quoted in Henry Reynolds, *This Whispering in our Hearts* (St Leonards: Allen & Unwin, 1998), 7.

[9] Douglas Hay et al., *Albion's Fatal Tree: Crime and Society in Eighteenth-century England* (London: A. Lane, 1975).

convicts also brought with them a 'plebeian moral economy' that formed the basis of claims such as a right to a basic level of material provision at the expense of government, and the right not to have to engage in excessive labour.[10]

While appeals to the rights of freeborn Britons or to a moral economy depended to a great extent on real or imagined precedent, the writings of Tom Paine, and the idea of inalienable rights associated with the revolutionary tradition, were also found among convicts, emancipists, soldiers, officers and free settlers.[11] Irish convicts, some of whom had been engaged in rebellion at home, contributed to a rich discourse of rights in a place whose status as a penal colony and an autocracy might have seemed unpromising in this respect. Early rebellions in the colony, such as of Irish convicts at Castle Hill in 1804, or of the officers against Governor William Bligh in 1808, drew to some extent on this discourse of rights. In the latter case, there was widespread dismay about the governor's arbitrary use of his power – which included the demolition of homes – against those who believed they had, by their occupation, established a right to certain property in Sydney.[12]

At the heart of emancipist agitation in the 1820s and 1830s was the claim that the rights of former convicts and their offspring should not be inferior to those of free settlers and, moreover, that the rights enjoyed in the colonies should be similar to those enjoyed by the king's subjects at home. While New South Wales in 1823, and then Van Diemen's Land in 1825, had each been granted Legislative Councils, these did not represent a major step towards representative government or the recognition of individual political rights. The councils were appointed by the governor and met in camera, and the governor retained great discretionary authority over the lives of colonists, but especially over convicts and Indigenous people. The reforms of 1823 did, however, provide one check on the power of the governor that would soon prove itself as a practical source of rights for ordinary subjects. It established a Supreme Court and, most importantly, gave the Chief Justice the role of

10 Alan Atkinson, 'Four Patterns of Convict Protest' *Labour History*, 37 (1979): 28–51; Stuart Macintyre, *Winners and Losers: The Pursuit of Social Justice in Australian History* (Sydney: Allen & Unwin, 1985), 12–13.

11 T. G. Parsons, 'Was John Boston's Pig a Political Martyr? The Reaction to Popular Radicalism in Early New South Wales' *Journal of the Royal Australian Historical Society* 71, no. 3 (1985): 163–76; Alan Atkinson, 'The Little Revolution in New South Wales, 1808' *International History Review* 12, no. 1 (1990): 65–75; Noel McLachlan, *Waiting for the Revolution: A History of Australian Nationalism* (Ringwood: Penguin, 1989), 26–49.

12 Grace Karskens and Richard Waterhouse, '"Too sacred to be taken away": Property, Liberty, Tyranny and the "Rum Rebellion"' *Journal of Australian Colonial History* 12 (2010): 1–22.

ensuring that any legislation approved by the governor was consistent with English law as far as the circumstances of the colony admitted. When Governor Ralph Darling sought to control the press, the Chief Justice, Francis Forbes, refused to certify some of the relevant legislation. While this was a victory for freedom of the press, Darling nevertheless subsequently imprisoned the editor of the *Monitor*, E. S. Hall, under a law that punished editors guilty of seditious or blasphemous libel.[13]

Trial by jury, including the right of former convicts to sit on juries, was also central to the settlers' understanding of the rights of Englishmen. While emancipists had clashed with Darling, in the 1830s they gained a more sympathetic governor in Richard Bourke. Under his rule, a jury system that permitted emancipists to sit would be established in 1833, in spite of the opposition of the Exclusive faction.[14] Calls for representative government also gathered momentum in the 1830s and, in the wake of rebellion in Canada in 1837–8, New South Wales and Van Diemen's Land each had a partly elected Legislative Council after 1842.[15] Advocates of representative institutions from the landed gentry of the colonies did not argue in terms of advancing democracy; rather, they tied the vote, and the right to sit for Parliament, to the possession of property, and thought in terms of 'interests' being adequately represented.[16] Yet at the same time, more radically democratic claims for political rights were articulated in an emerging urban plebeian culture.[17]

In many instances, free migrants of the later 1830s and 1840s had come from a British society in which political hierarchies were being challenged by the working-class Chartist movement. Chartist politics had its resonance in mid-nineteenth-century Australia even before the massive gold rush wave of immigration in the 1850s, via figures such as Henry Parkes, formerly a Birmingham Chartist and later famous as the 'Father of Federation', and Edward Hawksley, editor of the *People's Advocate*.[18] People such as these were democrats: in line with the demands of the People's Charter, they advocated

[13] Erin Ihde, *A Manifesto for New South Wales: Edward Smith Hall and the Sydney Monitor, 1826–1840* (Melbourne: Australian Scholarly Publishing, 2004).

[14] Richard Bourke to E. G. Stanley, 2 October 1833, *Historical Records of Australia*, 1, 17: 236–8; Hazel King, *Richard Bourke* (Melbourne; Oxford University Press, 1971), 158–60.

[15] See Curthoys and Mitchell, Chapter 6 in this volume.

[16] J. B. Hirst, *The Strange Birth of Colonial Democracy: New South Wales 1848–1884* (Sydney: Allen & Unwin, 1988), Preface.

[17] Terry Irving, *The Southern Tree of Liberty: The Democratic Movement in New South Wales before 1856* (Leichhardt and Annandale: The Federation Press, 2006).

[18] Andrew Messner, 'Contesting Chartism from Afar: Edward Hawksley and the *People's Advocate*' *Journal of Australian Colonial History* 1, no.1 (1999): 62–94.

the right of all men to vote and to stand for Parliament, alongside a range of other democratic reforms such as the secret ballot and the abolition of property qualifications for parliamentarians.

Democratic Rights

The gold rushes are usually understood as advancing the cause of democratic rights in Australia. While undoubtedly true, this did not occur before bloodshed on the Ballarat gold fields in December 1854. Moreover, the most significant right that migrants demanded in the early 1850s was to dig for gold without excessive interference on the part of government. Growing resentment of the licence fee would lead to demands for 'no taxation without representation', but the more fundamental right being claimed at first was that of the individual digger against any claims that the Crown might assert over the wealth beneath the soil.[19] Moreover, the limited size of claims – at about two-and-a-half square metres – implied a democratic approach to such matters, in which no one would be permitted to lock up too large a claim for themselves and, thereby, limit the rights of others.

After the Eureka uprising, the possession of a Miner's Right, as it was called, included the right to vote in elections for the Victorian Legislative Council (Port Phillip District having separated from New South Wales on the eve of the gold rush to become the colony of Victoria). And once miners had been enfranchised, it was difficult to argue that other men should be deprived of the right to vote. The land reform or 'selection' movement, especially in Victoria, asserted the right of the settler to 'a vote, a rifle and a farm'. The right to bear arms did not, in Australia, gain constitutional protection on US lines but the idea of an armed male citizenry was popular and, indeed, the basis of national defence for decades in the absence of a large professional army.[20] Meanwhile the right to vote increasingly became aligned with 'manhood' rather than 'property', at least in elections for the lower house of the bicameral Parliaments that emerged with responsible government after 1855.

The Australian colonies were among the most precocious in the world in their recognition of political rights – of men at first, and then of women. The

[19] David Goodman, 'Gold and the Public in the Nineteenth-century Gold Rushes', in Benjamin Mountford and Stephen Tuffnell (eds), *A Global History of the Gold Rushes* (Oakland, CA: University of California Press, 2018), 65–87.

[20] Craig Wilcox, 'Did Australia Sustain an Armed Citizenry? Graeme Davison and the Gun Debate' *Australian Historical Studies* 31, no. 115 (2000): 331–4.

British People's Charter had six points: annual Parliaments, male suffrage, voting by ballot, no property qualifications for parliamentarians, pay for parliamentarians and equal electoral districts. In Australia, several points of the Charter were fully or partly implemented in the early decades of responsible government. By 1860, manhood suffrage was accepted in three of the six colonies – Victoria, New South Wales and South Australia[21] – and property qualifications were abolished for those standing in lower-house elections. The secret ballot was so commonly associated with the democratic innovation of the colonies that it became known internationally as 'the Australian Ballot'. Equal electoral districts proved harder to implement, especially in the states during the twentieth century, with rural electorates often having much smaller numbers than those in the city, thereby magnifying the electoral power of the countryside. Payment of members of Parliament appeared in each of the colonies from 1870, beginning on a temporary basis in Victoria; and annual Parliaments, while never implemented, did find expression in relatively short parliamentary terms compared with Britain's (The House of Commons had seven-year terms until 1911). Following New Zealand in 1893, women would be progressively enfranchised, beginning with South Australia in 1894. Unlike New Zealand, South Australia also allowed women to stand for Parliament from the outset. In other Australian colonies/states, women's right to vote sometimes came many years before their right to stand for election, but when the Commonwealth was established, the two came together for the national Parliament in 1902.[22]

The political rights that white men were willing to extend to women in response to the demands of the women's suffrage movement would not be enjoyed by Indigenous people. While they did sometimes vote in colonial elections, they were increasingly deprived of voting rights.[23] For settlers in the age of White Australia, political rights were understood in racial terms. White men, and increasingly white women, were deemed sufficiently civilised to fulfil the civic responsibilities that were seen to attach to democratic political rights. Indigenous men and women were not. And as the years passed, at least some Aboriginal people worried that gaining the most basic

[21] Note that Queensland, once separated from New South Wales in 1859, did not have full manhood suffrage until 1872: Mark Lauchs, 'The Return of Manhood Suffrage to Queensland, 1863–1872' *Journal of Australian Colonial History* 12 (2010): 119–42.

[22] Judith Brett, *From Secret Ballot to Democracy Sausage: How Australia Got Compulsory Voting* (Melbourne: Text Publishing, 2019); Clare Wright, *You Daughters of Freedom: The Australians Who Won the Vote and Inspired the World* (Melbourne: Text, 2018), 17–160.

[23] See Curthoys and Mitchell, Chapter 6 in this volume.

of political rights, the right to vote, might imply that they would have to surrender certain valued aspects of their cultural difference.[24] Others – usually of mixed European and Indigenous background – would come to argue that their possession of a vote should be seen as evidence of a fitness to enjoy a range of other rights that were increasingly being marked out in the years around the turn of the century. The veteran Yorta Yorta activist William Cooper, in arguing for an extension of political rights in the 1930s, appealed to Magna Carta and British justice. As Tim Rowse has argued, for Cooper the term 'British' was 'a non-racial category, a civilizational universal' that was potentially 'inclusive' and 'respectful' of Aboriginal people.[25]

The idea of social rights – if not the terminology – was hardly new in Australia in the late nineteenth century. The claim to such rights harked back to the moral economy asserted by convicts, and it had been continued in demands for state interventions to ensure working men's access to land and jobs.[26] But from about 1880, there was an expansion of the claim to social rights.[27] This was largely the result of an increasingly ambitious union movement, an emergent Labor Party, and a working class that thought the state had a duty to modify market outcomes to ensure economic justice.[28] Socialism was an ingredient, but it was also the work of progressive liberals such as Alfred Deakin in Victoria and Bernhard Ringrose Wise in New South Wales, who were influenced by the new liberalism in Britain and progressivism in the United States.[29]

By the early years of the twentieth century, a wide range of social rights had been registered on the political agenda and were being implemented by legislative and judicial means.[30] Francis Castles has called the outcome

[24] Tim Rowse, *Indigenous and Other Australians since 1901* (Sydney: University of New South Wales Press, 2017), 237.

[25] John Maynard, *Fight for Liberty and Freedom: The Origins of Australian Aboriginal Activism* (Canberra: Aboriginal Studies Press, 2007), 91; William Cooper to Thomas Paterson, 16 June 1937 and William Cooper to Joseph Lyons, 26 October 1937 in Bain Attwood and Andrew Markus, *Thinking Black: William Cooper and the Australian Aborigines' League* (Canberra: Aboriginal Studies Press, 2004), 73, 81; Tim Rowse, 'The Identity of Indigenous Political Thought', in Ford and Rowse (eds), *Between Indigenous and Settler Governance*, 105, 107.

[26] Macintyre, *Winners and Losers*, chapters 2 and 4.

[27] T. H. Marshall, *Citizenship and Social Class, and Other Essays* (Cambridge: Cambridge University Press, 1950).

[28] Stuart Macintyre, *The Labour Experiment* (Melbourne: McPhee Gribble, 1989).

[29] Marilyn Lake, *Progressive New World: How Settler Colonialism and Transpacific Exchange Shaped American Reform* (Cambridge, MA: Harvard University Press, 2019).

[30] Marian Sawer, *The Ethical State: Social Liberalism in Australia* (Carlton: Melbourne University Press, 2003), esp. chapters 1 to 4.

a 'wage-earners' welfare state'.[31] It was, in some respects, parsimonious – especially in relation to social security – but more generous in its support of the family through the male breadwinner. The right of the male breadwinner to a living wage was also understood as upholding the rights of women and children in families to live in 'frugal comfort'. Justice Henry Bournes Higgins's decision to award a basic wage of forty-two shillings in the Harvester judgment of 1907[32] was the critical moment in the recognition of such rights, but it would be many years before they would be enjoyed by male wage-earners in general. Women who were workers were not seen to have the right to a living wage, for they were deemed to lack family responsibilities. The Harvester judgment thereby registered a certain kind of male right, one that would ideally be enjoyed by all adult men, and would provide the basis for the right to form a family: in essence, upholding what feminist philosophers have understood as male sexual rights.[33]

Most Australians of 1901 regarded their British heritage as the surest foundation of their rights. Nonetheless, there was discussion in the 1890s of the possibility of incorporating a US-style bill of rights in a new federal constitution. The main advocate was a Tasmanian Federation father, Andrew Inglis Clark, a lawyer with republican sympathies. But, as Hilary Charlesworth points out, there was a view that the kinds of rights embodied in the US bill of rights had already been secured in Australia through 'representative and responsible government' and, more seriously, that a bill of rights would detract from states' autonomy. Opponents of a bill of rights were especially concerned that it might undermine the ability of state governments to practice racial discrimination.[34]

From British to Human Rights

The idea that the ancient English constitution and Magna Carta guaranteed the rights of British people endured, remaining powerful in Australia until the 1950s, and vestiges of it survive today. Nonetheless, the World War II period

[31] Francis G. Castles, *The Working Class and Welfare: Reflections on the Political Development of the Welfare State in Australia and New Zealand, 1890–1980* (Wellington and Sydney: Allen & Unwin in association with Port Nicholson Press, 1985).

[32] *Ex Parte H. V. McKay* (1907) 2 CAR 1.

[33] Carole Pateman, *The Sexual Contract* (Cambridge: Polity Press, 1988).

[34] Hilary Charlesworth, *Writing in Rights: Australia and the Protection of Human Rights* (Sydney: University of New South Wales, 2002), 20–5; Andrew Byrnes, Hilary Charlesworth and Gabrielle McKinnon, *Bills of Rights in Australia: History, Politics and Law* (Sydney: University of New South Wales Press, 2009), 25.

revived interest in the explicit protection of rights through the constitution. Under new powers the federal Labor government proposed in 1942, the Parliament would be able to make any law that, in its declared opinion, would lead to 'economic security and social justice'. The government also favoured a de facto bill of rights, seeking to incorporate Franklin Delano Roosevelt's 'four freedoms' (freedom of speech and expression, and worship, and freedom from want and fear) into the Australian Constitution.[35] The failed referendum proposal of 1944 contained provisions that would have provided bill of rights-style protections to freedom of speech and religion.

The appeal to British justice as the foundation of Australian liberty was integral to the case made in the 1951 referendum by Herbert Vere Evatt, wartime Attorney General and, by this time, Leader of the Opposition, against amendment of the constitution to ban the Communist Party.[36] Notably, Evatt had also appeared before the High Court (of which he had previously been a justice) to argue that the Menzies government's legislation to ban the Communist Party was unconstitutional, leading to a 6–1 decision in favour of the challenge. That decision had indicated that even the most conservative of courts could offer a practical protection of the right to association in the absence of a declaratory bill of rights – not through the explicit recognition of the individual rights of the citizen but, in this instance, by preventing the encroachment of the executive on functions properly exercised by the judiciary.[37] However, the appeal to British justice and the English common law as a source of rights decreased with the decline of the British Empire itself in the 1950s and 1960s. Evatt had, as president of the United Nations General Assembly (1948–9), contributed to the emergence of a different international human rights system founded on 'respect for human dignity' and embodied in the Universal Declaration of Human Rights.[38] Jon Piccini has suggested that the Declaration was sometimes understood as building on British conceptions of constitutional rights, belonging to a lineage that stretched back to Magna Carta and the Glorious Revolution.[39] Nonetheless, the development of international human rights instruments

[35] *Post-war Reconstruction: A Case for Greater Commonwealth Powers* (Canberra: L. F. Johnston, Commonwealth Government Printer, 1942), 108, 77–8, 107, 120.
[36] Frank Bongiorno, 'Herbert Vere Evatt and British Justice: The Communist Party Referendum of 1951' *Australian Historical Studies* 44, no. 1 (2013): 54–70.
[37] George Williams, 'The Suppression of Communism by Force of Law: Australia in the Early 1950s' *Australian Journal of Politics and History*, 42, no. 2 (1996): 233.
[38] Geoffrey Robertson, *Statute of Liberty: How Australians Can Take Back Their Rights* (North Sydney: Vintage Books, 2009), 29.
[39] Jon Piccini, *Human Rights in Twentieth-century Australia* (Cambridge: Cambridge University Press, 2019), 68.

through the United Nations and its agencies, decolonisation of the European empires, and the activities of the anti-apartheid and US civil rights movements, all contributed to internationalising the protection of human rights in Australia.

The impact of this process has been both profound and contested. Indigenous people had been demanding equal rights for decades, but as late as the 1950s, they remained without political, legal and social rights taken for granted by other Australians. Based on their circumstances – judged according to white conceptions of their advancement to civilisation – many still lacked the vote, social security, freedom of movement, equal pay, control over their wages and the right to drink alcohol. Almost all of the more than 15,000 so-called 'full bloods' in the Northern Territory were formally designated as 'wards', not 'citizens'.[40] Across the country, Indigenous people were excluded from public spaces by local – sometimes municipal – regulations, policies and practices.[41] The assimilation policy of the federal government, as pursued by the influential Minister for Territories, Paul Hasluck, sought to bring Aboriginal people within the civic community of the nation, so that they would 'eventually . . . attain the same manner of living as other Australians and . . . live as members of a single Australian community enjoying the same rights and privileges, accepting the same responsibilities, observing the same customs and influenced by the same beliefs, hopes and loyalties as other Australians'.[42] Hasluck's assimilationist push was indebted to social liberalism's concern with economic justice; but in its failure to pay due regard to Aboriginal heritage, culture and identity, it would prove 'incapable of resolving the problems of Australia's Indigenous minority' and it attracted a growing chorus of Black and white critics.[43] Still, in the 1950s assimilation had gained both Indigenous and non-Indigenous supporters, who saw it as a pathway to equal rights.[44]

There was another approach to rights, however, pursued not so much as an alternative to but as an adjunct to the claims for equal rights. From the early 1960s, the Federal Council for the Advancement of Aboriginal and Torres Strait Islanders (FCAATSI) sought to use the International Labour Organization's (ILO's) Convention 107 (1957) to advance the special rights of

[40] Russell McGregor, *Indifferent Inclusion: Aboriginal People and the Australian Nation* (Canberra: Aboriginal Studies Press, 2011), 85.

[41] Ann Curthoys, *Freedom Ride: A Freedom Rider Remembers* (Crows Nest: Allen & Unwin, 2002).

[42] Paul Hasluck, quoted in McGregor, *Indifferent Inclusion*, 77. [43] Ibid, 81.

[44] Ibid, 107–18; Bain Attwood, *Rights for Aborigines* (Crows Nest: Allen & Unwin, 2003), 144–6.

Indigenous people. This Convention asserted: 'So long as the social, economic and cultural conditions of the populations concerned prevent them from enjoying the benefits of the general laws of the country to which they belong, special measures shall be adopted for the protection of the institutions, persons, property and labour of these populations.' This approach did not imply that the struggle for rights taken for granted by other Australians should cease, but rather that there were rights to be enjoyed by Indigenous people that could not be advanced merely by asserting their formal equality.[45]

Modern Rights

The period since the late 1960s has seen the development of legislation and case law that has, at least in theory, strengthened the rights of citizens. The 'new' administrative law of the 1970s, which saw the establishment of the Administrative Appeals Tribunal (1975) and the Commonwealth Ombudsman (1976), enhanced the right to gain a review of the merit of decisions made by government. Freedom of Information legislation was Whitlam Labor government policy, influenced by US legislation of 1966, but not coming to fruition until 1982 under the Fraser Coalition government. It provided for greater scrutiny of some government decision-making but with wide exemptions for cabinet processes – a reminder of the continuing force of Westminster doctrine in conditioning citizens' rights.[46] The Archives Act 1983 established a thirty-year rule (now twenty years) – again with some exemptions – for access to most government documents, including cabinet records. The expansion of this 'right to know' was accompanied by a growing recognition of the right to privacy, embodied in the federal Privacy Act 1988. The development of ever more sophisticated surveillance technologies, deployed by large multinational corporations for profit and by government agencies on the justification that they are essential to law enforcement, have ensured that the issue remains contentious and the right to privacy precarious.

Efforts to introduce an Australian bill of rights have been unsuccessful. It was on the Whitlam government's agenda, as part of Attorney General Senator Lionel Murphy's ambitious program of legal and constitutional

[45] Ibid, 169–70.

[46] Peter Cane, 'The Making of Australian Administrative Law', in Peter Cane (ed.), *Centenary Essays for the High Court of Australia* (Sydney: LexisNexis Butterworths, 2004), 314–32; Cane, *Controlling Administrative Power*, 134, 197, 199, 426–30.

reform. But his Human Rights Bill of 1973 came under fierce attack and lapsed when Parliament was dissolved in 1974. From 1983, when the Hawke government came to power, the idea of a legislated bill of rights was revived by its young Attorney General, Gareth Evans, who had been involved in drafting the Murphy bill. His proposals, too, went nowhere in the face of considerable opposition, not even making it to Parliament before his removal as Attorney General late in 1984. An Australian bill of rights introduced by his successor Lionel Bowen, while less ambitious than Murphy's or Evans's proposals, was also to be abandoned late in 1986.[47]

A subsequent attempt at constitutional amendment via a referendum in 1988 failed miserably, being rejected overwhelmingly by voters. It included a mini bill of rights covering fair elections (for both federal and state / territory contests), the extension of the right to trial by jury to certain cases at the state / territory level, freedom of religion, and fair terms when property was acquired by any government, not only by the Commonwealth. Church schools feared that the freedom of religion provision might endanger government funding, and the Catholic Church campaigned against the referendum proposals.[48] More generally, the government failed to achieve the bipartisan support generally considered essential to a successful result.

Many groups in Australian society that had traditionally suffered discrimination – Indigenous people, migrants, the unemployed, the poor, women, gays and lesbians, the young, the elderly, the mentally ill and the disabled – often asserted their rights by appealing to international standards, and sometimes directly referencing international conventions, covenants and agreements. A vigorous women's movement gained momentum after 1965, when Brisbane women protested their exclusion from male social rituals by chaining themselves to the public bar of the Regatta Hotel. At this time, women were excluded from jury service in some Australian states and territories, from employment in occupations deemed to constitute male work, and from continuing in the Commonwealth Public Service after marriage. From late in 1969, Women's Liberation articulated an agenda that gave increasing emphasis to women's legal, economic and sexual rights. The long-running campaign for women's right to equal pay, and an end to employment discrimination based on gender could, from the 1950s, appeal to a range of ILO and UN conventions. But there was only limited progress

[47] Gareth Evans, *Incorrigible Optimist: A Political Memoir* (Carlton: Melbourne University Press, 2017), 9–11. For 'A short history of Australian bills of rights', see Byrnes et al., *Bills of Rights in Australia*, chapter 2.

[48] *Canberra Times*, 17 August 1988, 2; *Sydney Morning Herald*, 29 August 1988, 2.

before the arrival of the Whitlam government in 1972. The marriage bar was removed from the Commonwealth Public Service in 1966 under the Holt Coalition government, and the Arbitration Commission granted equal pay of limited scope in 1969. After intervention by the Whitlam government late in 1972, the Arbitration Commission extended the adult minimum wage to women in 1974, thereby formally ending a system that, since the early years of the century, had upheld the rights of men to a living wage while confining women to a permanent state of inferiority.[49] In all of these developments, the central role of the executive and Parliament in defining rights has been foremost; but Australia's unusual system of industrial arbitration – which has played a central role in shaping the sexual division of labour and therefore in conditioning women's right to work and a fair wage – has also been influential.[50] In 1984 the Hawke Labor government piloted the Sex Discrimination Act through Parliament. It outlawed discrimination against women in the workplace as well as in relation to consumer services, such as housing and credit, but it also gave wide exemption to religious organisations, including church schools.[51]

Regardless of political colour, federal governments have developed an architecture for the recognition of human rights in government and administration. The Fraser government established the Human Rights Commission in 1981 as a statutory authority, a journey towards recognition of human rights in Australian federal law that the Hawke government continued through the Human Rights and Equal Opportunity Commission Act 1986. That has not prevented fierce attacks on commissioners by subsequent conservative governments and other culture warriors who resent their independence from government and insistence on Australia's obligation to observe international human rights.

Australia's federal system had been one of the reasons for the rejection of a bill of rights in the 1890s, and it remains a complex terrain. Outside its own jurisdiction of the Australian Capital Territory (the Northern Territory gained self-government in 1978, the Australian Capital Territory would not do so until 1989), the federal government did little to advance a range of rights

[49] Gisela Kaplan, *The Meagre Harvest: The Australian Women's Movement 1950s–1990s* (St Leonards: Allen & Unwin, 1996); Marilyn Lake, *Getting Equal: The History of Australian Feminism* (St Leonards: Allen & Unwin, 1999), chapters 7 to 11; Gough Whitlam, *The Whitlam Government 1972–1975* (Ringwood: Viking, 1985), 511–16.

[50] Edna Ryan and Anne Conlon, *Gentle Invaders: Australian Women at Work 1788–1974* (Melbourne: Thomas Nelson, 1975).

[51] Frank Bongiorno, *The Eighties: The Decade That Transformed Australia* (Collingwood: Black Inc, 2015), 56–7.

bearing on sexuality that remained largely within the realm of the criminal law. The rights of gay men – mainly focused on the right to have sex between consenting adults in private – were fought out at the state level, with South Australia first achieving full decriminalisation in 1975 and Tasmania the last, in 1997. The latter resulted from a successful appeal by gay activists to the United Nations Human Rights Committee and the subsequent passage of federal legislation implementing Australia's international obligations concerning sexual privacy.[52]

Many feminists of the 1970s wanted the right to abortion on demand but, like sodomy laws before it, the matter lay within the realm of state criminal law. Reform most commonly resulted from court decisions widening the scope for lawful termination, as occurred in Victoria in 1969 and New South Wales in 1971. Legislation in South Australia in 1969 was an exception; Victoria did not remove abortion from the criminal law until 2008, while New South Wales waited until 2019 and South Australia until 2021.

Land Rights

The referendum of 1967, which achieved a 'Yes' vote of about 90 per cent, symbolically – and paradoxically – recognised the full inclusion of Indigenous people in the polity on something like equal terms with other Australians at the same time as it empowered the Commonwealth to make special laws for 'the aboriginal race'. The paradox, in many ways a reflection of the ambiguities of the efforts of the settler-colonial state itself to erase difference while discriminating against First Peoples, survives to perplex. Following the 1967 referendum, Aboriginal and Torres Strait Islander people increasingly took on leadership roles in organisations fighting for their rights and 'land rights' became central to their claims on the settler state. This was a different kind of claim from earlier agitation by Aboriginal organisations for the return of

[52] Malcolm Cowan and Tim Reeves, 'The "Gay Rights" Movement and the Decriminalisation Debate in South Australia, 1973–1975', in Robert Aldrich and Gary Wotherspoon (eds), *Gay and Lesbian Perspectives IV: Studies in Australian Culture* (Sydney: Department of Economic History and the Australian Centre for Lesbian and Gay Research, University of Sydney, 1998), 164–93; Alan Berman, 'The Repeal of the Sodomy Laws in Tasmania in 1997 and the Status of Homophobia in Contemporary Australia', in Shirleene Robinson (ed.), *Homophobia: An Australian History* (Annandale: The Federation Press, 2008), 236–53. See also Graham Willett, *Living Out Loud: A History of Gay and Lesbian Activism in Australia* (St Leonards: Allen & Unwin, 2000).

agricultural land that had been taken from Indigenous peoples and distributed to white farmers in the years between the 1880s and the 1920s. The modern claim for land rights rested on new forms of archaeological, anthropological and historical knowledge, and depended on both a local sense of belonging and historical memory – as in the case of Gurindji claims to Wattie Creek in the Northern Territory in 1966 – and on a sense of pan-Aboriginality that transcended the local and particular.[53]

A claim for recognition of their ownership of the land via native title by the Yolngu people of the Gove Peninsula would be rejected in *Milirrpum v Nabalco Pty Ltd*[54] (also known as the Gove Land Rights Case), but Richard Blackburn's judgment took seriously the implications for the settler state of Aboriginal peoples' intense belonging to their country. He recommended political action in favour of the plaintiffs; federal land rights legislation for the Northern Territory followed in 1976. The machinery it established provided opportunities for Indigenous people to articulate, within a legal context, their deep belonging to country and would contribute to an expanding Indigenous estate; but, conceived as 'a return of rights or a return to country', the legislation also contained many limitations.[55]

It was the Racial Discrimination Act 1975, passed in the dying days of the Whitlam government, that would ultimately prove indispensable to the recognition of native title when it eventually came in 1992. That Act, as interpreted in *Mabo v Queensland (No. 1)*,[56] prevented the conservative Queensland government from lawfully extinguishing the native title rights of the litigants, a group of traditional owners from the Murray Islands in the Torres Strait. The recognition of native title in *Mabo v Queensland (No. 2)*[57] signalled a revolution in Indigenous land rights and Australian property law. Yet it also depended on many of the same threads that had recast rights claims more generally in Australia since the 1960s, such as international conventions and standards; in this case, as incorporated into Australian law by the federal Racial Discrimination Act.

[53] Attwood, *Rights for Aborigines*, chapters 10 to 13.

[54] *Milirrpum v Nabalco Pty Ltd* (1971) 17 FLR 141.

[55] Deborah Bird Rose, 'Histories and Rituals: Land Claims in the Territories', in Bain Attwood (ed.), *In the Age of Mabo: history, Aborigines and Australia* (St Leonards, NSW: Allen & Unwin, 1996), 35–53; Amanda Kearney, 'Returning to That Which Was Never Lost: Indigenous Saltwater Identities, A History of Land Claims and the Paradox of Return' *History and Anthropology* 29, no. 2 (2019): 198.

[56] *Mabo v Queensland (No. 1)* [1988] HCA 69, (1988) 166 CLR 186.

[57] *Mabo v Queensland (No. 2)* [1992] HCA 23, (1992) 175 CLR 1.

Rights Now

The interest in a bill of rights has been resilient, despite the absence of federal legislation implementing key international treaties such as the International Covenant on Civil and Political Rights and the International Covenant on Economic, Social and Cultural Rights. Following the United Kingdom's Human Rights Act 1998, there have been legislative developments at the sub-national level. The Australian Capital Territory moved first, with its own human rights legislation in 2004, followed by Victoria's Charter of Human Rights and Responsibilities in 2006 and Queensland's Human Rights Act in 2019. While there are differences between the systems, the basic requirement is that public authorities act in accordance with human rights. In the Victorian legislation, there is provision for the Parliament to override the charter in exceptional cases. The Supreme Court can declare a law inconsistent with human rights, but it cannot override it.[58]

At the federal level, the idea of a legislated bill or charter of rights has attracted some interest. In 2008, the Rudd Labor government appointed lawyer and Jesuit priest, Frank Brennan, to undertake a consultation. The following year, having received over 35,000 written submissions and expressing concern about the need to mend Australia's 'patchwork quilt of protections', Brennan's committee called for a national Human Rights Act.[59] The government did not implement this recommendation, but instead released a human rights framework that included provision for a Parliamentary Joint Committee on Human Rights and a requirement for legislative statements of compatibility. Legislation to this effect eventually passed the Parliament in 2011. The Law Council of Australia called for a federal Human Rights Act in November 2020, but conservative parties have consistently opposed bills of rights, either constitutional or legislative, increasing the potential political cost for any federal Labor government inclined to try introducing one. It may be considered doubtful whether this inclination is very strong even on the Labor side of politics.

One manifestation of the transition from British justice to 'an Australian idiom of human rights' is the call by some lawyers for a bill of rights that would 'be indelibly Australian'; that is, based on the rights that Australians

[58] Victorian Equal Opportunity & Human Rights Commission, 'Victoria's Charter of Human Rights and Responsibilities', www.humanrights.vic.gov.au/legal-and-policy/victorias-human-rights-laws/the-charter, accessed 21 December 2021; Byrnes et al., *Bill of Rights in Australia*, chapters 4 and 5.

[59] Brenda Tronson, 'The National Human Rights Consultation Report in Outline', *Bar News* (Summer 2009–2010), 33–5.

in particular 'have struggled to achieve'. The appeal to British justice was based on a common culture, identity and popular historiography. But, as Charlesworth has pointed out, the international human rights system is more vulnerable in Australia to the criticism that the standards it seeks to impose are foreign and illegitimate.[60] By way of contrast, the appeal to Britishness was an appeal to a strongly felt sense of history and identity. This contrast is somewhat ironic in view of the indebtedness of the Universal Declaration of Human Rights and, later, the European Convention on Human Rights, to British influence, and the assumption that these instruments would extend to other rights already largely enjoyed by Anglophone communities.

Certainly, the 1990s's judicial trend towards finding implied rights in the Constitution – such as an implied right to political communication recognised by the Court in 1992 – has seemed to some critics a fairly flimsy approach to rights protection. *Comcare v Michaela Banerji*[61] – a case involving the anonymous use of social media – demonstrated the limits of the implied freedom of political communication in the case of a public servant.[62] On the other hand, in *Roach v Electoral Commissioner*,[63] the High Court found that amendments to federal electoral law preventing prisoners (serving a sentence of three years or less) from voting were inconsistent with Australia's democratic system.

The absence of a bill of rights has had no appreciable effect on the prevalence of rights discourse in Australia. Much political debate in Australia is conducted in terms of 'rights' that fail to receive adequate protection. Both the right and left play this game. So, the Australian Council of Trade Unions called its campaign (2005–7) against the Howard Coalition government's anti-union *WorkChoices* industrial relations legislation 'Your Rights At Work'. The Abbott Coalition government, with the support of right-wing think tanks and columnists, sought to amend Section 18(c) of the Racial Discrimination Act, which places restrictions on the right of a person 'to offend, insult, humiliate or intimidate another person or a group of people' on the basis of 'race, colour or national or ethnic origin'. The government proposal was to remove 'offend', 'insult' and 'humiliate', but leave 'intimidate'. The federal Attorney General George Brandis, in seeking to defend the

[60] Ravi de Costa, *A Higher Authority: Indigenous Transnationalism and Australia* (Sydney: University of New South Wales Press, 2006), 7; Charlesworth, *Writing in Rights*, 62–5; Robertson, *Statute of Liberty*, 150.

[61] *Comcare v Banerji* [2019] HCA 23.

[62] Kieran Pender, '*Comcare v Banerji*: Public Servants and Political Communication' *Sydney Law Review* 41, no. 1 (2019): 131–47.

[63] [2007] 233 CLR 162.

watering down of this provision from attacks by the Labor Party in the Senate, invented the 'right to be a bigot', hitherto unknown in Australian law.[64] The Turnbull government responded to the achievement of marriage equality in 2017 by initiating an inquiry into religious freedom, which conservatives claimed had been undermined by allowing same-sex marriage, and the Morrison Coalition government subsequently moved to draft a bill providing greater protections against religious discrimination. On the other side of the debate, marriage equality itself was represented by its proponents as a matter of equal rights, and a wide range of other social, political and economic claims are now couched in terms of the language of 'rights', often 'human rights': health care, food, clothing, water, shelter, protection from violence and a basic income. Arguments about education, including the cost of tertiary education, are often presented within a rights framework: 'education is a right, not a privilege'. Here and in other contexts, Australian discourse has been shaped by the proliferation of international conventions and transnational rights-talk.

In 1997, the popular Australian film *The Castle* turned Section 51(xxxi) into the best-known clause in the Australian Constitution. The working-class family featured in the film, the Kerrigans, face being turned out of their home because of a proposal to extend the airport adjacent to their house.[65] In an unlikely High Court victory, the Kerrigans and their neighbours – with the help of a pro bono QC – triumph over the forces of faceless government and corporate darkness. In upholding the adage that 'a man's home is his castle', and with some passing reference to the Indigenous experience and the *Mabo* judgment along the way, the 'vibe' of the Australian Constitution proves sufficient to keep the predators at bay. The film nevertheless attests to the prevalence of rights discourse in Australia. If the Constitution did not really provide protection for the Kerrigans, *The Castle* seems to suggest, a properly democratic constitution that enshrined the people's rights would do so.

In reality, there remain significant frailties in Australia's rights regime, which are accompanied by a lack of consensus on the best way of dealing with them. Claims to a range of freedoms that most Australians take for

[64] *The Guardian*, 24 March 2014, www.theguardian.com/world/2014/mar/24/george-brandis-people-have-the-right-to-be-bigots, accessed 21 December 2021.

[65] The brutality of the process depicted fictionally in *The Castle* has had a more recent echo at the New South Wales State Government level in the real treatment of residents whose homes stood in the way of Sydney's WestConnex Motorway Project. See Matt O'Sullivan, '"Absolute insult" for St Peters residents turfed out of homes for WestConnex', *Sydney Morning Herald*, 18 October 2016, www.smh.com.au/national/nsw/absolute-insult-for-st-peters-residents-turfed-out-of-homes-for-westconnex-20161018-gs4xbk.html, accessed 21 December 2021.

granted are often based on a 'vibe', without there being either constitutional or legislative guarantees, or a body of case law that can be relied on to offer support. The COVID-19 pandemic of 2020 underlined some of these weaknesses. Australian citizens who might have assumed that their passports guaranteed them the right to re-enter their country found themselves prevented from doing so, as a result of a lack of quarantine spaces. The right to move across state boundaries was severely circumscribed by state governments for the first time – for non-Indigenous people – since the Spanish Influenza pandemic of 1919. State governments imposed severe restrictions on the activities of their citizens for extended periods.

There were protests – and even occasional appeals by disgruntled citizens to the Universal Declaration of Human Rights – but most citizens seem to have pragmatically accepted the temporary curtailment of their rights.[66] This may well provide confirmation of the reputedly utilitarian or Benthamite strain that commentators have sometimes viewed as influential in Australian society, the notion that rights are created by government and laws rather than trumping them.[67] To this extent, the influence of a modern rights discourse in Australia might have been moderated by the burden of the alternative history explored in this chapter.

[66] David Estcourt, 'Do You Have a Right To Not Wear a Mask?', *Age*, 27 July 2020, www.theage.com.au/national/victoria/do-you-have-a-right-to-not-wear-a-mask-20200727-p55fqb.html, accessed 21 December 2021.

[67] Hugh Collins, 'Political Ideology in Australia: The Distinctiveness of a Benthamite Society' *Daedalus* 114, no. 1 (1985): 147–69; Brett, *From Secret Ballot to Democracy Sausage*.

24

Citizenship and Immigration

RAYNER THWAITES

Introduction

This chapter focuses on the nature and operation of the relevant membership statuses in the period since Federation.[1] In that time, Australian citizenship law has passed through a number of successive eras, each marking moves away from the centrality of membership in the British Empire and towards a more distinct and self-sufficient national citizenship.[2] This trajectory occurs in the wider context of 65,000 years of continuing First Nations' settlement in Australia.[3] The history of immigration to, and citizenship in, Australia is also a history of colonisation, with profound effects on First Nations.[4]

This historical trajectory overlaps with another; the operation and long, slow, demise of the White Australia policy, a 'complex set of legislative and administrative measures aimed at severely restricting non-European [and particularly Asian] immigration', with the objective of creating a white British nation state.[5] These transformations and the accompanying legislative and constitutional shifts are the central subjects of this chapter. In closing,

Research for this chapter has been supported by an Australian Research Council Discovery Early Career Researcher Award, 'Conditional citizenship? Revocation's implications for Australians' (DE160101123). Thanks to all the participants at the workshop on this volume in December 2019, in particular my commentator, Frank Bongiorno, to Helen Irving, Coel Kirkby and the editors Lisa Ford and Peter Cane for comments.

1 In its focus on the definition and incidents of citizenship status it is distinct from the body of work on the history of migrants and refugees to Australia. For an overview of the latter see Ruth Balint and Zora Simic, 'Status of the Field Review Essay: Histories of Migrants and Refugees in Australia' *Australian Historical Studies* 49 (2018): 378.

2 The division between eras employed in this chapter is indebted to Patrick Brazil, 'Australian Nationality and Immigration', in K. W. Ryan (ed.), *International Law in Australia* (Sydney: Law Book Co, 1984, 2nd edition), 210–27.

3 Stephanie Mawson, 'Historiographical Review: The Deep Past of Pre-colonial Australia' *The Historical Journal* 64, no. 5 (2021): 1477–99.

4 Ann Curthoys, 'Immigration and Colonisation: New Histories' *UTS Review* 7, no. 1 (2001): 170.

5 Gwenda Tavan, *The Long, Slow Death of White Australia* (Melbourne: Scribe Publications, 2005), 1.

I look at some pervasive assumptions that are currently being undermined or challenged: that an Australian's citizenship is secure once granted; that (constitutional) alien and (statutory) citizen are antonyms; and that Australia is a country of settlement.

As a legal status, citizenship is centrally about 'home', the residential security marked by a right to enter, and reside in, Australia.[6] So understood, citizenship sets boundaries on the immigration power.[7]

Introduction to the Constitutional Framework

Australia came into existence as a legal entity on New Year's Day 1901, through the federation of six British colonies under the Commonwealth of Australia Constitution Act 1900, an Act of the British Parliament giving effect to the Constitution Bill. The text of the Constitution had, with small exceptions, been settled in a series of constitutional conventions in the 1890s attended by mostly elected delegates of the various colonies that went on to become states. This text was adopted by voters in those colonies in referendums held in the period 1898–1900. Under the Constitution, the six colonies were transformed into states and a federal government established on the Westminster 'responsible government' model. The new government was largely sovereign in domestic matters, but in terms of its foreign relations, Australia, in common with the other Dominions, had limited independence within the British Empire.

Delegates to the conventions debated whether 'Australian citizenship' should be included in the Constitution.[8] In the result, the concept of Australian citizenship did not appear in the constitutional text. This was, in part, a reflection of the 'political realities of that time', namely Australian reliance on the supra-national concept of British nationality.[9] Section 51, which enumerates the subject matters on which the federal Parliament can legislate, contains no explicit power to legislate on citizenship.[10] In the

6 The right to enter and reside in Australia evidently does not speak to all the ways one can be homeless *within* Australia, from lack of a house to loss of land.

7 Though there are contrary instances, for example the Australian citizenship conferred on those born in Papua New Guinea.

8 Kim Rubenstein, *Australian Citizenship Law* (Sydney: Law Book Co, 2017, 2nd edition), chapter 2, 35–62. See also Helen Irving, *To Constitute a Nation: A Cultural History of Australia's Constitution* (Cambridge: Cambridge University Press, 1999), chapter 9, 156–70.

9 *Re Patterson; ex parte Taylor* [2001] HCA 51, (2001) 207 CLR 391, [267] per Kirby J ('*Re Patterson*').

10 The heads of power in Section 51 of the Constitution are concurrent powers. The states can still legislate on these subject matters until the Commonwealth chooses to do so. When the Commonwealth does choose to legislate on these matters, the

absence of explicit authority to enact citizenship legislation, we have to look elsewhere for authority to legislate. The most relevant heads of federal legislative power are Sections 51(xix) 'Naturalization and aliens' and 51(xxvii) 'Immigration and emigration'. In common usage these powers are referred to as the 'aliens power' and 'immigration power' respectively.

Until the 1980s federal legislation on citizenship and immigration was grounded in the immigration power. Thereafter, it relied instead on the aliens power. The reasons for and the consequences of this shift are addressed below.

The Colonial Period, 1901–20

The relevant 'citizenship' status ascribed to the Australian population at Federation was that of 'British subject'. The status of 'British subject' was shared throughout the British Empire, subject to qualifications in respect of 'local' naturalisation noted below. The law relating to acquisition and loss of British subject status was a matter of common law until 1920.[11]

Notwithstanding the existence of a 'common status' of British subject, Australia distinguished for immigration purposes between British subjects in general and British subjects whom it regarded as being members of its own community. The relevant legal questions for those challenging the application of immigration laws to them was not whether or not they were British subjects but, in addition to birth in Australia, whether or not they were returning home,[12] or had made their permanent homes in Australia and hence had become part of the Australian community.[13]

Immigration restrictions that cut across the possession of British subject status were a necessary component of the racially discriminatory 'White

corresponding state laws are invalid to the extent of the inconsistency: Australian Constitution, s 109. Until 1920, immigration policy was primarily dealt with at the state level: see Geoffrey Sherington, 'Settlement 1881–1914', in James Jupp (ed.), *The Australian People: An Encyclopedia of the Nation, Its People, and Their Origins* (Melbourne: Cambridge University Press, 2001, 2nd edition), 49–53.

11 In that year Australian legislation was introduced to adopt the British Empire's 'common code', the model for which was contained in the British Parliament's British Nationality and Status of Aliens Act, 1914 (see under The 'Common Code', 1920–49 below). There is a complication as to timing. There is a question of whether the British Nationality and Status of Aliens Act 1914 (Imp) applied in the Dominions, which would move the date for change from common law to statute earlier. There is also the exception constituted by legislation on naturalisation and naturalised citizens.

12 *Potter v Minahan* [1908] HCA 63, (1908) 7 CLR 277. See Kate Bagnell, 'Potter v Minahan: Chinese Australians, the Law and Belonging in White Australia' *History Australia* 15 (2018): 458.

13 *Ex Parte Walsh and Johnson; In re Yates* [1925] HCA 53, (1925) 37 CLR 36.

Australia' policy that shaped immigration policy for generations after Federation.[14] British subject status was held by many across the Empire who did not meet the racially discriminatory strictures of the Australian policy and accordingly were denied entry.[15] The immigration restrictions constituted what has aptly been termed a 'de facto administrative Australian citizenship' which distinguished between those British subjects who could be denied entry and deported, and those who could not.[16] The main mechanism of this de facto administrative citizenship was the dictation test. The test, set out in the Immigration Restriction Act 1901, provided that persons would be prohibited from landing, or deported, if they failed to write out a passage of fifty words in a European language as dictated by an officer.[17] A concise account of the dictation test was offered by the High Court in 1936: 'It was merely a convenient and polite device . . . for the purpose of enabling the Executive Government of Australia to prevent the immigration of persons deemed unsuitable because of their Asiatic or non-European race.'[18] In its pursuit of a 'White Australia', the country exemplified Clive Parry's observation that the shared legal status concealed 'very great discrimination between British subjects by means of immigration regulations'.[19]

As noted, the ability to make immigration distinctions between Australian British subjects and other British subjects was first grounded in the immigration power in Section 51(xxvii). It was the lack of alignment between British subjecthood and the desired membership of the Australian community that drove reliance on this power in preference to the aliens power. Those whom the government wished to exclude or remove under immigration law included both aliens *and* (some) British subjects (those from India and Hong Kong, for example, falling in the latter category). The immigration

14 Tavan, *The Long, Slow Death*.

15 The right to enter Australia could also be denied to British subjects for other reasons, for example requirements as to 'character'.

16 David Dutton, *Citizenship in Australia: A Guide to Commonwealth Government Records* (Canberra: National Archives of Australia, 1999), 13, www.naa.gov.au/help-your-research/research-guides/citizenship-australia-guide-commonwealth-government-records, accessed 22 December 2021.

17 On the dictation test's application see David Dutton, *One of Us? A Century of Australian Citizenship* (Sydney: UNSW Press, 2002), 34–9. The dictation test was abolished by the Migration Act 1958. The White Australia policy continued to be implemented in the absence of this particular statutory mechanism, only being unequivocally abolished in the early 1970s.

18 *R v Davey, ex parte Freer* [1936] HCA 58, (1936) 56 CLR 381 per Evatt J for the Court. In addition to its use as a tool of racial exclusion, the test was also applied to persons considered politically undesirable.

19 Clive Parry, *Nationality and Citizenship Laws of the Commonwealth and Ireland* (London: Stevens & Sons, 1957), xv–xvi.

power enabled immigration control with respect to persons in both categories.[20]

It was the High Court of Australia, the nation's highest appellate court, that came to define who was an 'immigrant'; a person to whom immigration powers applied. In so doing, it also defined who was immune to these powers of exclusion and removal. In the early decades of the Commonwealth of Australia, it did this with reference to the concept of 'community': 'the ultimate fact to be reached as a test whether a person is an immigrant or not is whether he is or is not at that time a member of the Australian community'.[21] The concept of 'membership of the Australian community' lacked the legal specificity of connecting factors such as domicile, residence, personal presence or citizenship, though it drew on these concepts, with the balance between them shifting over time. This lack of specificity was part of the concept's appeal. For its intelligibility, the concept of 'community' relied on certain widespread assumptions concerning the habits and mores, and particularly the ethnic composition (presumed to be British or European), of the Australian population.[22] The immigration power was read as subject to an 'absorption' doctrine. A person could become a non-immigrant through absorption into the Australian community, thereby moving beyond the scope of the government's powers of exclusion and removal.

The only Australian legislation on 'citizenship' status in this period concerned naturalisation. The 'convenient and polite device' of the dictation test in immigration deflected confrontation over racial discrimination through use of administrative discretion. In contrast, racial discrimination was apparent on the face of the naturalisation legislation, written into the terms of

20 See for example *R v MacFarlane; Ex parte O'Flanagan and O'Kelly* [1923] HCA 39, (1923) 32 CLR 518, 556 per Isaacs J.

21 *Potter v Minahan*, [1908] HCA 63, (1908) 7 CLR 277, 308 per Isaacs J. Isaacs J was in dissent over what constituted membership, but at one with the majority in holding that the limits of the immigration power were determined by who was, and who was not, a member of the community. Between the two world wars there was a shift marked by growing legal endorsement of a broader scope for exclusionary powers, often racialized. On this interwar shift, see Dutton, *One of Us?*.

22 In addition to legal exclusion of British subjects on the grounds that they were 'immigrants' and not part of the Australian community, discrimination also took the form of extra-legal indifference as to whether non-whites *were* British subjects, ascribing alienage as matter of race, instead of place of birth: see Peter Prince, *Aliens in Their Own Land: 'Alien' and the Rule of Law in Colonial and Post-Federation Australia* (PhD thesis, ANU, 2015); Peter Prince, 'The "Chinese" always belonged' *History Australia* 15 (2018): 475.

Naturalization Act 1903.[23] As with immigration regulation, naturalisation in the early, post-Federation landscape sits awkwardly with the idea of a common subject status across the British Empire. Under the 1903 statute, naturalisation became a matter exclusively for the federal government to determine (with reciprocal recognition of earlier colonial/state grants of naturalisation secured across Australia).[24] But an Australian certificate of naturalisation was initially only 'local' in effect. It conferred the status of British subject on the recipient within Australia but, in contrast to British imperial naturalisation (adopted in 1914), it was generally regarded as ineffective elsewhere in the Empire.[25] A person naturalised as a British subject in Australia (or other colony or Dominion) held a 'limping status: they were subjects in the territory in which they were naturalised and while abroad, but not elsewhere in British territory'.[26]

The 'Common Code', 1920–49

In 1914, the British Parliament enacted the British Nationality and Status of Aliens Act. The 1914 Act set out to codify the rules relating to acquisition and loss of British nationality, previously a matter of common law. It was intended to preserve a common status of nationality throughout the British Empire, based on a common code.

The existence of this 'common code' was compatible with the autonomy of the different Dominions that were to adopt it. This was manifest in the manner of the code's implementation. The promoters of the code relied not on the sovereign authority of the imperial (British) Parliament to impose it, but on parallel action by the various Dominions. Australia adopted the common code in its Nationality Act of 1920. The 1920 Act constituted the first general Australian legislation on nationality, as opposed to on specific matters of local naturalisation.

The 1920 Act addressed a prominent contemporary concern by providing for reciprocal recognition of naturalisation certificates issued by the United Kingdom, Australia and the other Dominions. In contrast with the 1903 Act, the 1920 Act did not expressly deny persons the ability to apply for

23 Naturalization Act 1903 (Cth), s 5. On the parliamentary history leading to an expressly discriminatory naturalisation provision see A. C. Palfreeman, *The Administration of the White Australia Policy* (Melbourne: Melbourne University Press, 1967), 104–5.

24 Naturalization Act 1903 (Cth), ss 13 and 4 respectively.

25 See for example, *Markwald v Attorney-General* [1920] 1 Ch 348, referenced more recently in *Re Patterson*, [296] per Kirby J.

26 See further Parry, *Nationality and Citizenship Laws*, 6, 80–1 and 445–9.

naturalisation on grounds of race. In its place, it conferred 'absolute discretion' on the Governor General to give or withhold a naturalisation certificate without providing a reason, giving the government scope to apply any policy on naturalisation of non-Europeans it thought fit. Under this provision, only forty-five persons characterised by the Australian government as being of an Asian ethnicity were naturalised between 1904 and 1953.[27]

The 1920 Act, following the British template, contained statements stressing that the status of *naturalised* British subject was 'to all intents and purposes the status of a natural-born British subject'.[28] A large hole in this claim was constituted by the provisions relating to loss of British subject status. The 1920 legislation made extensive provision for revocation of British subject status acquired through naturalisation.[29] Under the 1920 Act, a certificate of naturalisation could be revoked where the person granted the certificate had shown him or herself 'by act or speech to be disaffected or disloyal to His Majesty', or had been ordinarily resident 'out of his Majesty's dominions' (other than in certain circumstances), among other reasons.[30] British subject status acquired through naturalisation was accordingly a more conditional and vulnerable status than birthright citizenship (acquired by conditional descent in addition to birthplace). The proposition that vulnerability to loss of status was limited to naturalised citizens was qualified by gender.[31] Under the 1920 Act, upon marriage to an alien man, a woman who was an Australian born British subject automatically lost her British nationality (a long-standing practice that was also followed in Britain, as in most of the world).[32] Marital denaturalisation ended with the 1948 Act that introduced statutory Australian citizenship. The other grounds for revocation continued until they were finally repealed (with one exception) in 1958.[33]

27 Dutton, *One of Us?*, 43.
28 Nationality Act 1920 (Cth), s 11, in the terms of the British Nationality and Status of Aliens Act 1914, s 3(1).
29 The 1920 Act was not the first time an expansive discretion to revoke the citizenship of naturalized citizens, unrelated to fraud, was legislated. Amendments made to the 1903 Act in 1917 conferred a sweeping discretion on the Governor General to revoke the citizenship of naturalized citizens. The 1920 Act constrained this discretion, albeit by substituting broad grounds for denaturalisation.
30 Nationality Act 1920, s 12, adopting the terms of the British Nationality and Status of Aliens Act 1914, s 7.
31 And also by the prohibition on Australians acquiring another citizenship: see under 'Dual Citizenship' below.
32 On the history of marital denaturalisation see Helen Irving, *Citizenship, Alienage and the Modern Constitutional State: A Gendered History* (Cambridge: Cambridge University Press, 2016).
33 See under 'The Demise of Long-standing Discriminations and Distinctions among Citizens' below.

The Introduction of Statutory Australian Citizenship (and the Continuance of British Subject Status), 1949–87

The Continued but Diminishing Salience of British Subject Status

Australian citizenship came into existence in 1949, with the entry into force of the Nationality and Citizenship Act 1948 (renamed the Australian Citizenship Act in 1973).

Internal and external factors contributed to Australia's adoption of statutory citizenship: the development of local nationalism, Australia's increasing desire and capacity to act independently on the international plane, and the breakdown of the common code, the last most prominent in Canada's creation of a distinct 'Canadian citizenship' in 1946.[34] The 1948 Act implemented the policy determined by the Conference of Nationality Experts of the British Commonwealth in 1947. The Australian form of the 'common clause', the central tenet of the new Commonwealth arrangement, was contained in Section 7 of the 1948 Act which provided: 'A person who, under this Act, is an Australian citizen . . . shall, by virtue of that citizenship be a British subject.'[35] This formula inverted the logic of the preceding 'common code' on British nationality. The acquisition of national citizenship became primary, and British subjecthood a secondary and derivative status. Their priority thus inverted, these statuses co-existed for several decades.

British nationals who were not Australian citizens (by birth, descent or naturalisation) were still not aliens; indeed the statute defined 'alien' as a person who was not a British subject.[36] In effect, a tripartite regime was established composed of: (1) Australian citizens (who were simultaneously British subjects); (2) British subjects who were not Australian citizens; and (3) aliens. The racial distinctions of the White Australia policy cut across the subject–alien distinction, further complicating the landscape.

The new status of Australian citizenship was predominantly acquired by birth in Australia. Citizenship by descent was available to those born outside

34 The weighting of these internal and external factors is a matter of ongoing debate; see for example, Jatinder Mann, 'The Evolution of Commonwealth Citizenship, 1945–1948 in Canada, Britain and Australia' *Commonwealth & Comparative Politics* 50 (2012): 293.

35 Nationality and Citizenship Act 1948 (Cth), s 7.

36 In full the definition read; '"alien" means a person who is not a British subject, an Irish citizen or a protected person': ibid, s 5.

Australia to an Australian father.[37] Other avenues for acquisition of Australian citizenship distinguished between British subjects and aliens. British subjects who were not Australian citizens could become Australian citizens by registration,[38] a process distinct from the naturalisation available to non-British subjects (aliens). Registration largely tracked naturalisation, but eased or omitted a number of its restrictions. Registration, in contrast to naturalisation, did not require any declaration of an intention to apply, required a shorter period of residence and did not require an oath of allegiance.[39]

The preferential treatment of non-citizens who were British subjects came to an end in 1973.[40] From that point onwards, Australian citizenship law did not distinguish between acquisition of citizenship by non-citizen British subjects and other non-citizens.

A massive demographic shift accompanied Australia's growing independence from the United Kingdom. Australia's population has more than tripled since World War II, from about 7 million in October 1945 to 24 million in February 2016.[41] Large-scale migration also led to a radical expansion in the diversity of national origins of the Australian citizenry. Eric Richards breaks the post-war demographic shift into two phases. The first, 'Europeanisation' between 1947 and 1972 shifted Australia from predominant dependence on migrants from the British Isles.[42] Over this first phase, there was a steady geographic expansion in the European (and neighbouring) countries looked to as a source of immigration, broadly south and east, driven by demographic

37 'or, in the case of a person born out of wedlock, his mother was an Australian citizen . . . ': Nationality and Citizenship Act 1948 (Cth)(as enacted), s 11.

38 The registration process was limited to countries specified in the legislation, namely: 'the United Kingdom and Colonies, Canada, New Zealand, the Union of South Africa, Newfoundland, India, Pakistan, Southern Rhodesia and Ceylon' (s 7) or Irish citizen (ss 8 and 12).

39 Nationality and Citizenship Act 1948 (Cth), ss 12–13 (registration) cf ss 14–16 (naturalisation). The continued salience of the distinction between British subjects and aliens following the introduction of statutory citizenship also affected vulnerability to deportation. Aliens could be deported after committing an offence of violence to the person or extortion carrying a sentence of a year or longer. In contrast, non-citizen British subjects could only be deported for such an offence within five years of arrival: See Migration Act 1958 (as first enacted) (Cth), ss 12 and 13.

40 Australian Citizenship Act 1973 (Cth).

41 Australian Bureau of Statistics, '3101.0 – Australian Demographic Statistics', June 2015, Released 15 February 2016, www.abs.gov.au/ausstats/abs@.nsf/lookup/3101.0Media%20Release3June%202015, accessed 22 December 2021.

42 Eric Richards, *Destination Australia: Migration to Australia since 1901* (Sydney: UNSW Press, 2008), x–xi. In the twenty-four years from 1947 to 1971, '2.5 million people from all over Europe were persuaded, assisted and conveyed to Australia': ibid, 204. As suggested by the quote, government assisted immigration was a key feature of this phase.

concerns.[43] The second phase, after the formal end of the White Australia policy, saw a shift from dependence on migrants from Europe.[44] While the formal ending of the White Australia policy did not immediately register in changed patterns of migration to Australia, over time the balance of immigration has shifted to a diverse range of Asian countries.[45]

The Demise of Long-standing Discriminations and Distinctions among Citizens

Since the Naturalization Act 1920, the White Australia policy as applied to citizenship had been implemented through the use of administrative discretion. The established policy was that non-Europeans should not be granted the right of permanent residence (which was a prerequisite for naturalisation). In 1957 there was a change in cabinet policy, making non-Europeans eligible for naturalisation if they had lived in Australia for fifteen years after being lawfully admitted.[46] Remaining distinctions between Europeans and non-Europeans with respect to visas and naturalisation and other 'final overt vestiges of discrimination against non-Europeans' were formally abolished under the Whitlam Labor government (1972–5).[47]

Over the same period, distinctions between naturalised and birthright citizenship were dismantled. The 1948 Act, as enacted, maintained a marked distinction between those who had acquired their membership status by birth on the one hand and those who had acquired it by naturalisation or registration on the other. As noted under 'The Common Code, 1920–49', above, extensive grounds for revocation and deprivation of citizenship were confined to those who had acquired Australian citizenship by naturalisation (and post-1949, registration). These distinctions did not, however, last more than a decade into the new era.

All the grounds of revocation confined to naturalised or registered citizens, with the exception of fraud in the naturalisation or registration process, were repealed in 1958. On introducing the amending legislation to Parliament, the responsible minister stated that it had as one of its 'principal

43 Richards, *Destination Australia*, chapters 7 and 8.   44 Ibid, x–xi.

45 James Jupp, 'Changes in Immigration Patterns since 1972', in Jupp (ed.), *The Australian People*, 75–8. And see, for example, the statistics on citizenship conferrals by nationality in David Smith, Janice Wykes, Sanuki Jayarajah and Taya Fabijanic, *Citizenship in Australia* (Department of Immigration and Citizenship, 2011), www.homeaffairs.gov.au/research-and-stats/files/citizenship-in-australia-2011.pdf, accessed 22 December 2021.

46 Tavan, *The Long, Slow Death*, 97–103. In 1966 the period after which a non-European could apply for resident status and Australian citizenship was dropped to five years: ibid, 156–66.

47 Tavan, *The Long, Slow Death*, 199.

objectives . . . eras[ing] from the Nationality and Citizenship Act every discrimination, except one [the fraud ground], between naturalized Australians and people born in Australia'.[48] In commending these repeals to Parliament, the minister gave as the government's motivation 'a desire to welcome our new citizens with speed, sincerity and warmth into our national life'.[49]

1987 to the Present

The Departure of British Subject Status from Australian Law and Constitutional Re-alignments

In 1982, the long-standing doctrinal assumption that a British subject could not be a (constitutional) alien was rejected. Writing in *Pochi v McPhee*, Chief Justice Gibbs of the High Court stated that the assumption that 'a person who is a British subject under the law of the United Kingdom cannot be an alien within s 51(xix) [The aliens power]' is 'incorrect'.[50] In support of this statement Gibbs referenced changes indicating the independence of Australia and the severing of imperial ties. A consequence of this conclusion was that the aliens power could now be used to regulate the admission and removal of non-citizen British subjects from Australia. There was no longer a need to rely on the immigration power to achieve that objective.

Pochi also made clear that the aliens power was not subject to an absorption doctrine such as that which had been applied to the immigration power.[51] Length of residence or other means of demonstrating an individual's absorption into the Australian community were irrelevant to the operation of the aliens power. Determination of who was a statutory citizen determined, for practical purposes, who was a constitutional non-alien.

Enabled by this confirmation of changed constitutional assumptions, in the 1980s references to 'British subject' and equivalent terms were removed from the Migration Act 1958 and the Australian Citizenship Act 1948, the primary pieces of Australian legislation regulating immigration and citizenship respectively (the Citizenship Act amendments coming into force in 1987). Statutory expungement of the status was symptomatic of wider shifts in Australian law at the time that consolidated and finalised the formal independence of Australian law from the United Kingdom.[52]

48 Commonwealth, *Parliamentary Debates*, House of Representatives, 26 August 1958, 711 (Mr Alexander Downer, Minister for Immigration).

49 Ibid. 50 *Pochi v McPhee* [1982] HCA 60, (1982) 151 CLR 101, 109 [9]. 51 Ibid, 111 [12].

52 The High Court declared the United Kingdom to have been a 'foreign power' 'at least since 1986' in *Sue v Hill* [1999] HCA 30, (1999) 199 CLR 462. See also Anne Twomey, *The*

These 1980s amendments defined 'alienage' in terms of the absence of Australian (statutory) citizenship – a binary distinction. The question of whether constitutional doctrine would follow this shift, defining constitutional membership with reference to statutory citizenship, was the subject of a series of subsequent cases in the High Court of Australia. At issue was a class of persons occupying a grey area in the transition from the old to the new membership status, namely British subjects who had come to Australia in the window between the advent of Australian citizenship and Britain's unequivocally becoming a foreign power, and never registered or naturalised as Australian citizens.[53]

The cases: *Nolan* (1988), *Patterson* (2001) and *Shaw* (2003) all concerned challenges to deportation orders against non-citizen British subjects.[54] Each of the litigants had made their life in Australia for decades after arriving as British subjects. They resisted deportation on the basis that the legislation relied on was not constitutionally valid in its application to them. They argued that, as British subjects in the relevant period, they could not be aliens. In effect, they argued that by way of their British origins, coupled with their prolonged residence, they had a deeper connection with Australia than any alien. Underlying the cases was the question – do Australian citizenship's origins in British nationality law still have a constitutional role to play in determining the connection of such British subjects to Australia? The cases hinged on the relevance of British nationality for questions of Australian membership status.

The litigants in the three cases challenged the idea that citizen and alien were antonyms, such that the only options were to be a citizen non-alien or a non-citizen alien. The litigants' claim was that persons who arrived and lived in Australia as British subjects before the 1984 statutory changes enjoyed a special, privileged status as non-alien, non-citizen members of the Australian constitutional community. The High Court's response to an argument of this form fluctuated: a majority rejected the argument in *Nolan* (1988), accepted it in *Re Patterson; Ex parte Taylor* (2001), and ultimately

Australia Acts 1986: Australia's Statutes of Independence (Sydney: Federation Press, 2010), chapters 1 and 2.

53 Jordens notes that from the late 1960s and early 1970s only 5 per cent of roughly 1 million eligible British subjects had applied for Australian citizenship: see Ann-Mari Jordens, *Redefining Australians* (Alexandria: Hale & Iremonger, 1995), 154 and chapter 9, fn 4.

54 *Nolan v Minister for Immigration & Ethnic Affairs* [1988] HCA 45, (1988) 165 CLR 178; *Re Patterson*; *Shaw v Minister for Immigration and Multicultural Affairs* [2003] HCA 72, (2003) 218 CLR 28.

rejected it in *Shaw* (2003). The position the High Court arrived at in *Shaw* was that British subjecthood was now constitutionally irrelevant.[55]

Shaw (2003) rejected the existence of a category of non-citizen non-aliens constituted by British subjects who came to Australia in the transitional period.[56] *Shaw* inaugurated a period in which citizen and alien were understood as antonyms. If a person was not a (statutory) citizen, he or she was a (constitutional) alien. This binary understanding was unsettled seventeen years later in the *Love and Thoms* decision (discussed below under 'Aboriginal Non-citizens: Outside Statutory Membership but inside Constitutional Membership'), with reference to a different category of persons.

Dual Citizenship

One of the most consequential changes in citizenship since Federation, not only in Australia but worldwide, has been a sea change in attitudes to dual citizenship, from antipathy to acceptance. From 1870[57] to 2003, statute provided that an Australian who, by some voluntary and formal act, acquired the citizenship of another country (other than through marriage)[58] automatically ceased to be an Australian citizen.[59] This denial of an Australian's ability to acquire additional citizenship(s) without loss of Australian citizenship did not amount to an outright prohibition on dual citizenship. The bar to dual citizenship only went 'one way'. It did not preclude a person becoming a dual

55 *Shaw* established that British subjecthood was constitutionally irrelevant to rights to enter and remain. It remains relevant to the statutory right to vote. Until 1984 citizenship was not a prerequisite for the franchise, what was required was subjecthood plus residence. Even after the introduction of citizenship as a prerequisite for voting, by virtue of grandfathering provisions British subjects who were on the electoral roll immediately before Australia Day 1984 do not have to become Australian citizens to continue voting. Australian Electoral Commission figures from 2009 showed 160,000 persons in this category on the electoral roll: see Graeme Orr, *The Law of Politics: Elections, Parties and Money in Australia* (Sydney: Federation Press, 2019, 2nd edition), 54–6.

56 See text accompanying note 53, above. In *Shaw* the High Court held that the aliens power extended at least to British subjects who entered Australia after the introduction of Australian statutory citizenship in 1949. In *Chetcuti v Commonwealth* [2021] HCA 26, a majority of the High Court pushed the relevant date back further, holding that a British subject who arrived in Australia in 1948, but had never obtained statutory citizenship, was an alien.

57 British Naturalization Act 1870. The application of this Act in the colonies produced considerable confusion: see Irving, *Citizenship, Alienage and the Modern Constitutional State*, 58.

58 For the period from 1949 on. See text accompanying note 32 above.

59 Australian Citizenship Act 1948 (Cth), s 17, as amended by Australian Citizenship Amendment Act 1984 (Cth). Citizenship is used generally here to include the status of British subject.

citizen by acquiring Australian citizenship by naturalisation while retaining her or his original nationality.[60]

Amendments entering into force in 2003 repealed the relevant provision, Section 17, so allowing an Australian to acquire another citizenship without losing her or his Australian citizenship.[61] The repeal of Section 17 had been recommended in 1994 by the parliamentary Joint Standing Committee on Migration (JSCM).[62] In making the recommendation, the JSCM stated:

> The Committee rejects the argument that one cannot owe allegiance or commitment to more than one country. It is estimated that three million Australians currently possess dual citizenship. There is no evidence to suggest that these persons are disloyal or lack a commitment to Australia simply because they have chosen not to relinquish their former ties and heritage.[63]

The jealous view of allegiance rejected by the JSCM re-emerged as a matter of national discussion in 2017, in response to the sudden, prominent, and effective use of the parliamentary disqualification provision contained in Section 44(i) of the Constitution. The relevant portion of Section 44(i) provides that any person who is the subject or citizen of a foreign power is incapable of being chosen for, or sitting in, the federal Parliament. The provision had been largely quiescent since Federation, though warnings about its potential damaging effects in modern demographic conditions had been sounded since at least the mid-1970s.[64] Roaring into life in 2017, Section 44(i) resulted in the disqualification or

60 The Australian Citizenship Council, reporting in 2000, characterised s 17 as a 'major anomaly in that some Australian Citizens, estimated to be around 4.4 million, are able to lawfully possess more than one Citizenship, while those who start from the base of having Australian Citizenship and acquire another Citizenship lose their Australian Citizenship': Australian Citizenship Council, *Australian Citizenship for a New Century* (Canberra: Commonwealth of Australia, 2000), 60–1.

61 Australian Citizenship Legislation Amendment Act 2002 (Cth).

62 See Joint Standing Committee on Migration, *The Parliament of the Commonwealth of Australia, Australians All: Enhancing Australian Citizenship* (Canberra: Australian Government Printing Service, 1994), recommendation 55. The JSCM recommendation was endorsed by Australian Citizenship Council in 2000 (see Australian Citizenship Council, *Australian Citizenship for a New Century*, 65), with the 2002 legislation repealing Section 17 of the Citizenship Act being responsive to the report of the Australian Citizenship Council.

63 Joint Standing Committee on Migration, *The Parliament of the Commonwealth of Australia*, para 6.92.

64 See the Appendices in the Report of the Commonwealth Joint Standing Committee on Electoral Matters, *Excluded: The Impact of Section 44 on Australian Democracy* (Canberra: Commonwealth of Australia, May 2018) for past discussions, in constitutional conventions and parliamentary reports, of the problems posed by s 44.

resignation of fifteen members of the 45th Parliament (the Parliament elected in 2016). The High Court of Australia has interpreted the relevant limb of Section 44(i) as disqualifying dual citizens from nominating for, or sitting, in the Australian Parliament.[65]

As currently interpreted, Section 44(i) reflects an antipathy to dual citizenship that was widely shared at the time the Constitution was drafted and that characterised much of the twentieth century, but is disconsonant with the law, demography and social context of twenty-first century Australia. A dramatic increase in the prevalence of dual citizenship among the Australian citizenry means that the restrictions imposed by Section 44(i) on nominating for, or sitting in, federal Parliament currently act as a barrier to participation for a sizeable proportion of the Australian population, with a disproportionate effect on those of more recent migrant background.[66] The response that the barrier is readily surmountable – that it can be addressed through a person's renunciation of their 'non-Australian' citizenship – underestimates the complexities of foreign citizenship law, both in ascertaining whether one has a foreign citizenship, and how one can divest oneself of it.[67] The current adverse effects of Section 44(i) point to the potential dangers of making detailed constitutional provision for matters of citizenship given the changeability of the concept.

Disallegient Conduct and a More Substantive Citizenship, Easier to Lose

It is legally accepted that there are limits on the ability of statutory citizenship to determine constitutional non-alienage, 'Everyone agrees that the term "aliens" does not mean whatever Parliament wants it to mean.'[68] What is not clear is what these limits are. Legal issues emerging in the second half of the

65 Subject to an implied 'constitutional imperative' that has never been successfully invoked: *Re Canavan* [2017] HCA 45, (2017) 263 CLR 284.

66 This was a central theme of the 2018 report of Parliamentary Joint Committee on Electoral Matters: *Excluded: The Impact of Section 44 on Australian Democracy*. It was also a discernible theme of the 2019 federal election; see for example, Jeremy Gans, 'Second Class Surnames', *Inside Story*, 26 April 2019, https://insidestory.org.au/second-class-surnames, accessed 22 December 2021.

67 On these complexities see Rayner Thwaites and Helen Irving, 'Allegiance, Foreign Citizenship and the Constitutional Right to Stand for Parliament' *Federal Law Review* 48 (2020): 299.

68 *Singh v Commonwealth* [2004] HCA 43, (2004) 222 CLR 322, [5] per Gleeson CJ.

2010s have raised, and in one case placed, limits on Parliament's ability to create, deport and exclude non-citizens.

In December 2015, new and expansive powers of citizenship deprivation were enacted.[69] Introduced into Parliament as laws 'address[ing] the challenges posed by dual citizens who betray Australia by participating in terrorism related activities',[70] the laws were putatively aimed at excluding 'foreign' fighters, but applied to Australians who held a second nationality (a second nationality being required so as not to render the person stateless in contravention of Australia's international law obligations). The animating assumption was that only citizens have a right to enter and remain.[71] Deprived of that status erstwhile citizens can be excluded or deported.

The powers raise new and distinct questions about the nature and limits of the aliens power and Australian citizenship. Prior to use of the powers introduced in 2015, Australia had not, at least since the advent of statutory citizenship in 1949, exercised a power of unilateral deprivation of citizenship for 'disallegient conduct'.[72]

The wider potential implications of these new powers of citizenship deprivation centre on the legal theory the government relied on to support the powers.[73] At the centre of that theory is a shift from a formal to a substantive conception of allegiance. Allegiance was central to the common law on British subjecthood and from there became part of Australian constitutional doctrine on the aliens power. A formal concept of allegiance had

69 The deprivation provisions were introduced by the Australian Citizenship Amendment (Allegiance to Australia) Act 2015, which amended the Australian Citizenship Act 2007 (Cth). The scope of key deprivation powers enacted in 2015 were expanded in late 2020: see the Australian Citizenship Amendment (Citizenship Cessation) Act 2020 (Cth).

70 Commonwealth, *Parliamentary Debates*, House of Representatives, 24 June 2015, 7369 (second reading speech).

71 This assumption has been challenged by new powers to issue temporary exclusion orders: See Counter-Terrorism (Temporary Exclusion Orders) Act 2019 (Cth). See Helen Irving, 'Can We Come Home Now?: *Temporary Exclusion Orders Act* Raises Serious Constitutional Concerns' *LSJ Law Society of NSW Journal* 59 (2019): 68.

72 A section providing for deprivation of citizenship if a person 'serves in the armed forces of a country at war with Australia' was inserted into Australian citizenship legislation as enacted in 1948, remaining in the statute till amended in 2015, but it has never been used: Elbritt Karlsen, 'Cancellation of Australian Citizenship Built on Shaky Foundations?' *Flagpost: Blog of the Parliamentary Library*, 21 July 2015: www.aph.gov.au/About_Parliament/Parliamentary_Departments/Parliamentary_Library/FlagPost/2015/July/citizenship, accessed 22 December 2021. On the introduction of citizenship deprivation provisions in 1917 (and 1920) and their repeal in 1958, see respectively the text accompanying notes 30 and 48 above.

73 The discussion of the deprivation powers draws on Helen Irving and Rayner Thwaites, 'Comment: Australian Citizenship Amendment (Allegiance to Australia) Bill 2015 (Cth)' *Public Law Review* 26 (2015): 143.

been upheld in the 2006 decision of *Koroitamana*.[74] In that case, when the High Court ruled that 'an alien is a person who does not owe allegiance to Australia',[75] it meant simply that an alien is not a citizen, as defined under the Australian Citizenship Act. On this formal conception, allegiance is signified by the possession of statutory citizenship. This formal conception of allegiance is not sufficient to support the 2015 deprivation powers.

The deprivation powers rely instead on the theory that duties of allegiance underpin statutory citizenship. In the words of the relevant minister, the citizen's duty of allegiance 'was not created by the Citizenship Act, but . . . is recognised by it'.[76] More particularly, the powers are predicated on the view that:

> Australian citizenship is a common bond . . . [and] citizens may, through certain conduct incompatible with the shared values of the Australian community, demonstrate that they have severed that bond and repudiated their allegiance to Australia.[77]

Under the 2015 amendments, certain forms of conduct were defined as 'inconsistent with allegiance' to Australia and therefore triggering deprivation. Determination of whether a person is a citizen under the act is now a two-stage test: first, is the person a citizen under the formal rules found in the current legislation; and second, if formally eligible, is he or she otherwise disqualified for having committed prescribed conduct?[78] On this theory nonalienage is defined with reference to a *substantive* concept of allegiance, and citizenship is conditional on not engaging in prescribed conduct. In this 'thick' conception, citizenship status is a privilege that can be withdrawn.

The deprivation powers in the 2015 Act, and the concepts of allegiance and constitutional membership on which they rely, have yet to be tested in the courts.[79]

74 *Koroitamana v Commonwealth* [2006] HCA 28, (2006) 227 CLR 31.
75 As accurately summarised in the Minister's second reading speech: Commonwealth, *Parliamentary Debates*, House of Representatives, 24 June 2015, 7369.
76 Ibid.
77 Australian Citizenship Amendment (Allegiance to Australia) Act 2015 (Cth), s 4, 'Purpose of this Act'.
78 The mechanisms for deprivation of citizenship were amended in 2020, expanding the powers and in one case substituting a ministerial deprivation decision for 'automatic' deprivation of citizenship by operation of the statute: see Australian Citizenship Amendment (Citizenship Cessation) Act 2020 (Cth).
79 By early 2019, the powers had been used twelve times: see the Minister for Home Affairs – Media Release, 'Prakash citizenship', 2 January 2019, https://minister.homeaffairs.gov.au/peterdutton/Pages/prakash-citizenship.aspx, accessed 22 December 2021. The legislation allows for three years between a deprivation decision and notification to the person affected. A legal challenge to the deprivation powers is due to be heard by the High

Aboriginal Non-citizens: Outside Statutory Membership but Inside Constitutional Membership

In *Love and Thoms* (2020) the High Court of Australia placed constitutional limits on the Parliament's power to deport (one category of) non-citizens. In that decision, a majority of the High Court held that Aboriginal Australians were not aliens and so not vulnerable to deportation.[80] It was the first time that the relevance of Aboriginality for the aliens power had been litigated.

The two plaintiffs were born outside of Australia – Love in the Independent State of Papua New Guinea, Thoms in New Zealand. Each had an Australian citizen parent of Aboriginal descent. Each was born with the citizenship of the country of their birth and not Australian citizenship. Both had moved to Australia as young children and resided permanently there for several decades.[81] Love identified as Kamilaroi and was recognised as such by an Elder of that Aboriginal community. Thoms identified as Gungarri and was accepted by members of the Gungarri people as such. He was also a native title holder. As adults they were each convicted of crimes to which were attached sentences of twelve and eighteen months respectively. That led to an automatic cancellation of their visas, pursuant to a legislative provision that makes a sentence of imprisonment of twelve months or more a breach of the 'character test'.

The question for the High Court was whether, by reason of their Aboriginality, the plaintiffs were members of the Australian constitutional community and so not vulnerable to deportation. The majority held that 'Aboriginal Australians are not within the reach of the "aliens" power conferred by s 51(xix) of the Constitution'.[82] In so ruling, they rejected the proposition that constitutional status is determined by statutory citizenship, such that alien is the antonym of citizen. They held that the relationship between statutory and constitutional membership is looser – one can be both a non-citizen and a non-alien; i.e. outside statutory membership but inside constitutional membership. More particularly, they held that Aboriginal Australians belong to

Court in 2022: see *Alexander v Commonwealth of Australia*, High Court of Australia, file number S103/2021.

80 *Love v Commonwealth of Australia; Thoms v Commonwealth of Australia* [2020] HCA 3 ('*Love and Thoms*'). This account of the case draws on Elisa Arcioni and Rayner Thwaites, 'Indigeneity as a Basis for Constitutional Membership – Recent Developments in Australia' *Juridikum* 4 (2020): 425.

81 Mr Love from December 1984 (when he was aged five); Mr Thoms from November 1994 (when he was aged six).

82 'I am authorised by the other members of the majority to say that although we express our reasoning differently, we agree that Aboriginal Australians . . . are not within the reach of the "aliens" power . . . ': *Love and Thoms*, [81] per Bell J.

Australia in a way that demands and has constitutional recognition; that precludes their being aliens and therefore precludes deportation.[83]

The four majority judges reasoned from the common law's recognition of rights and interests drawn from traditional Aboriginal law and custom, as established in *Mabo (No. 2)* (1992).[84] The majority held that recognition of these rights and interests was premised on the common law's recognition of the Aboriginal societies that held and generated Aboriginal law and custom, including law and custom as to membership. Common law recognition of those societies had constitutional significance, informing the interpretation of the relevant constitutional term, alien.

Who is an Aboriginal Australian? The majority agreed this was to be determined, in the context of the case, in accordance with the tripartite test from *Mabo (No. 2)*. The test's three elements are: self-identification; recognition by the relevant Aboriginal community; and descent.[85] In the context of a long and difficult history of the law seeking to identify Aboriginal people – often for non-beneficial purposes – any attempt to crystallise one definition of Aboriginality is problematic.[86] What is clear from *Love and Thoms* is that the question of whether a person is an Aboriginal Australian is justiciable.[87]

The majority made clear that the ruling that Aboriginal Australians were non-aliens did not, in and of itself, confer statutory citizenship upon them. As non-aliens Aboriginal Australians were not vulnerable to removal and exclusion from Australia. But that was not to say that Aboriginal Australians in the

83 The Australian government indicated it intends to challenge this decision in *Montgomery v Minister for Immigration*, High Court of Australia, file number S173/2021, then S192/2021: see [2021] HCATrans 188 (8 November 2021).

84 *Mabo v Queensland (No. 2)* [1992] HCA 23, (1992) 175 CLR 1. The majority in *Love and Thoms* was comprised of Bell, Nettle, Gordon and Edelman JJ. The minority was Kiefel CJ, Gageler and Keane JJ.

85 A tripartite test with these elements has had a life preceding, and alongside, the *Mabo* judgment. It was adopted by Federal Cabinet in 1978, has been incorporated into some legislation (for example the Aboriginal Land Rights Act 1983 (NSW)) and has been referred to in other cases (for example, *Commonwealth v Tasmania* [1983] HCA 21, (1983) 158 CLR 1, 274). Between the various usages, there are significant differences as to the content of the three elements: see Michelle Foster and Kirsty Gover, 'Comment: Determining Membership: Aboriginality and Alienage in the Australian High Court' *Public Law Review* 31 (2020): 105, 109–12.

86 For an introduction to criticisms of the test, see for example the Australian Law Reform Commission, 'Legal definitions of Aboriginality': *Essentially Yours: The Protection of Human Genetic Information in Australia* (ALRC Report 96, 2010) [36.11]–[36.40].

87 With regard to the plaintiffs, the government accepted that Thoms was Aboriginal and within hours of the decision being handed down he was released from immigration detention where he had been held pending removal. The High Court left the position of the other plaintiff, Love, unsettled, remitting the factual question of his Aboriginality to the Federal Court. The proceedings were stayed pending judgment in matters including *Montgomery* (see above n 83): see file number QUD223/2020.

position of the plaintiffs were citizens. Aboriginality did not equate with citizenship. Citizenship was a status determined by statute and, unless and until there was a change to the relevant statutory provisions, the plaintiffs remained non-citizens.[88] The continuing non-citizenship of the plaintiffs opens up the possibility that, outside of their rights to enter and remain in Australia (rights integral to non-alienage), they might be subject to other disabilities of non-citizens, and conversely not be subject to certain obligations of citizenship.

A Country of Citizens?

This chapter has focused on citizenship as a determinant of who can enter and remain in Australia. There is another set of issues about access, namely whether those who are here, and in particular those who have been lawfully resident for a prolonged period, have a pathway to Australian citizenship.

For much of Australia's history, this issue has been of secondary importance. Immigration has functioned as the primary means of exclusion. Once here, immigrants have been placed on the pathway to citizenship. The assumption has been that today's immigrants are future citizens and the parents of future citizens.[89] The factual foundations for this assumption have been softening since the mid-2000s. There has been a shift from permanent to temporary visas, in a context in which permanent residence is a prerequisite for naturalisation. The number of temporary residents present in Australia more than doubled in the seven years from 2006 to 2013, from around 350,000 to 800,000.[90] In April 2020, the number was almost 1.3 million.[91]

88 No challenge was made to the validity of the governing statutes for immigration and citizenship – the Migration Act 1958 and the Australian Citizenship Act 2007 respectively. The question before the Court was whether the deportation provisions of the Migration Act applied to the plaintiffs. The majority held they did not.

89 This national self-understanding rests on a degree of historical selectivity, overlooking the operation of the White Australia policy. See for example, the deportation of those of Pacific Island ethnicity from Queensland in the early twentieth century: Peter Prince, 'Australia's Most Inhumane Mass Deportation Abuse? Robtelmes v Brenan and the Expulsion of Alien Islanders' *Law & History* 5 (2018): 117.

90 Peter Mares, *Not Quite Australian: How Temporary Migration is Changing the Nation* (Melbourne: Text Publishing, 2016), 56. This number does not include the largest category of temporary visa holders; New Zealanders who entered Australia after 26 February 2001. Persons in this category combine indefinite leave to remain in Australia with a highly circumscribed pathway to permanent residence. For an overview, see Susan Love and Michael Klapdor, 'New Zealanders in Australia: A Quick Guide' Parliament of Australia, Parliamentary Library, Research Paper Series, 2019-20 (13 February 2020), www.aph.gov.au/About_Parliament/Parliamentary_Departments/Parliamentary_Library/pubs/rp/rp1920/Quick_Guides/NewZealandersInAustralia, accessed 22 December 2021.

91 For the statistics see David Coleman MP, Former Minister for Citizenship, 'Coronavirus and Temporary Visa Holders', 4 April 2020: https://minister.homeaffairs.gov.au/davidcoleman/Pages/Coronavirus-and-Temporary-Visa-holders.aspx, accessed 22 December 2021.

The increasing proportion of those on temporary, as opposed to permanent, visas has led to the phenomenon of the long-term temporary; long-term residents in Australia moving from one temporary visa to another.[92] This has in turn affected the nature of permanent migration to Australia, which is increasingly a two-step process, with those characterised as '"new" settlers' often having spent considerable time in Australia as temporary migrants.[93] '[P]ermanent settlement continues, but it is now part of a hybrid system, intricately and intimately entwined with a much larger program of temporary entry, which serves as the primary gateway to establishing a life in Australia.'[94]

An increase in the proportion of residents who are 'long term temporary' raises the prospect of a two-tiered society, with an increasingly large proportion of residents lacking the security of citizenship status. The exclusion in 2020 of those without citizenship or permanent residence from key government support responding to the COVID-19 pandemic, an exclusion affecting well over a million people, has underscored the divide.[95]

The increasing reliance on temporary migrants lacking a clear path to citizenship has been accompanied by a change in the language of government, from talk of 'settlement' to talk of border and immigration policies as a 'filter'. In a speech looking forward to the seventieth anniversary of the creation of an Australian Department of Immigration in June 2015, the Secretary of the government department responsible for citizenship policy stated that the department should declare 'the original mission of 1945 – to build the population base – to have been accomplished'. In an age of 'globalised travel, investment and labour mobility', the focus on permanent residence was largely displaced by the need for 'a strategy and plan for attracting those in the ready-made global pool of travellers, students, skilled workers and business-people, the latter with money to invest and ideas to commercialise'.[96] Little was said about citizenship policy, settlement or

The number in the text for April 2020 is arrived at by taking the 672,000 New Zealanders and 203,000 visitor visas away from the total of 2.17 million temporary visa holders.

92 Mares, *Not Quite Australian*. On difficulties of obtaining data on this phenomenon see ibid, 56–64.

93 Ibid, 7. Shanti Robertson, *Transnational Student-Migrants and the State: The Education-Migration Nexus* (Basingstoke: Palgrave Macmillan, 2013).

94 Mares, *Not Quite Australian*, 36.

95 With the exception of New Zealanders, temporary visa holders were excluded from the Jobkeeper and Jobseeker programs: See David Coleman MP, 'Coronavirus and Temporary Visa Holders'.

96 Michael Pezzullo (Secretary of the Department of Immigration and Border Protection), 'Sovereignty in an Age of Global Interdependency: The Role of Borders' (speech at the Australian Strategic Policy Institute, 4 December 2014) www.aspi.org.au/index.php/event/sovereignty-and-australian-border, accessed 22 December 2021.

integration and how these might fit with the transactional approach outlined in the speech.

Conclusion

The years since Federation have seen marked shifts in the legal concepts and categories that determine the nature of citizenship status, reflecting shifts in Australia's understanding of its place in the world and of the meaning of citizenship. There is little sign that change is slowing. Legal issues and challenges implicating citizenship and constitutional membership have arisen with regularity over the last five years: powers of citizenship deprivation, parliamentary disqualification, the relevance of Aboriginality to deportation. The social context for citizenship is shifting, for example in the implications of reliance on temporary visas, the incidence and consequences of dual citizenship and Australia's changing relationship with its First Nations.

The hope is that the ongoing change reinforces rather than undermines the basic securities citizenship status can provide, both to the person who holds it and to the country of which they are a part: a country to call home and a long-term resident population that holds, or is eligible for, citizenship.

VI

SOCIAL ORDERING

25

Criminal Law and the Administration of Justice in Early New South Wales and Van Diemen's Land

DAVID ANDREW ROBERTS

In the House of Commons in March 1819, during debate on controversies arising from the distant penal colony of New South Wales, the long-serving Under-Secretary of State for War and the Colonies remarked that the 'materials of which that colony was composed were so extremely combustible' as to require 'a strong compressive force to prevent them from bursting into flames'.[1] Henry Goulburn was here evoking a pervasive notion that the convict colony's singular purpose and unusual population demanded more coercive systems of government and law than might be acceptable elsewhere. That more coercive system included an autocratic governor with immense executive powers, a military-style court and a magistracy wielding a wide-ranging authority that, as one governor put it, 'would certainly be out of place in any but a Slave Code'.[2] To critics like Jeremy Bentham, these were the ingredients of a 'vast conservatory of military law', offensive 'to the sense of every Briton'.[3]

Nevertheless, most scholars broadly agree with Gregory D. Woods's assessment that the rule of law functioned adequately if imperfectly in early Australia, producing a strong degree of social stability in rather remarkable circumstances.[4] Certainly these colonies were places where the law was

This research is funded by an Australian Research Council Discovery Project Grant, Inquiring into Empire: Remaking the British Empire after 1815 (DP180100537).

1 *Parliamentary Debates*, Volume 32, 23 March 1819 (London: Hansard, 1819): 1234.

2 Bourke to Stanley, 15 January 1834, *Historical Record of Australia (HRA) 1*, 17: 323.

3 'Panopticon versus New South Wales', 1802, in *The Works of Jeremy Bentham: Now First Collected* (London: W. Tait, 1838), Part 3, 211; T. Causer, '"The evacuation of that scene of wickedness and wretchedness": Jeremy Bentham, the Panopticon and New South Wales, 1802–1803' *Journal of Australian Colonial History* 21 (2019): 1–24.

4 Gregory D. Woods, *A History of Criminal Law in New South Wales: The Colonial Period, 1788–1900* (Annandale: Federation Press, 2002); J. Braithwaite, 'Crime in a Convict Republic' *The Modern Law Review* 64, no. 1 (2001): 11–50, is rather more effusive, seeing

shaped by multiple forces and conversations, and where attendant notions of fairness and freedom were acutely felt and constantly debated.[5] However, the challenge of applying criminal law in the convict colonies evoked modification and confusion. This chapter provides an overview of the administration of criminal justice in the early settlements of New South Wales and Van Diemen's Land over forty years from 1788, showing how the desire to apply English law in a simple and coercive form created vital tensions in the local legal order, as the authorities sought to deal with both free and unfree citizens, and faced the challenge of applying English law to a population already under sentence of the law.

The Court of Criminal Jurisdiction

There was a fundamental tension in the foundation of the colony's legal order. While the rights of all citizens in New South Wales, including convicts, were safeguarded by the wholesale introduction of English law, that protection was diluted by a desire to administer law in the most simple and effective form. The preference, in fact, had been to place the colony under the annual Articles of War, allowing for both the expeditious trial of felonies and misdemeanours and also the summary treatment of lower-level 'immoralities, misbehaviour, or neglect of duty'. Instead, lawyers advising the Home Office determined that convicted civilians could not normally be governed like soldiers, although special allowances might be made for the '*particular circumstances* that attend this settlement'.[6] What emerged, then, was a strange compromise, crafted for a particular population for whom neither military law nor trial by jury seemed permissible. As the New South Wales Charter of Justice put it, English criminal law would be applied in the convict colony 'as nearly as can be considering and allowing for the circumstances and situation of the place . . . and the inhabitants'.[7]

This civil–military tension was ingrained in the colony's Court of Criminal Jurisdiction, which was designed to apply English law 'in a more summary way'. The Court was convened by the governor and presided over by

a legal order that transformed 'powerless criminals into productive law-abiding citizens' who 'pioneered a low-crime future'.

5 Paula Jane Byrne, *Criminal Law and Colonial Subject* (Cambridge: Cambridge University Press, 2003); David Neal, *The Rule of Law in a Penal Colony: Law and Practice in Early New South Wales* (Sydney: Cambridge University Press, 1991), 85–113.

6 Nepean to Hamilton, 24 October 1786, in A. Frost, *The First Fleet: The Real Story* (Melbourne: Black Inc, 2011), 35 (emphasis in original).

7 New South Wales Charter of Justice, 2 April 1787.

a Deputy Judge Advocate who prosecuted for the Crown and voted in judgments, alongside six naval or military officers sworn in the same manner as an English jury but not subject to challenge by defendants. Hybridity was further evident in the Court's sentencing powers, for while it was broadly permitted to punish 'according to the Laws of ... England' (including sentence of death, which required the concurrence of at least five of the seven members), the court was also directed to consider treating capital offences with corporal punishment whenever a death sentence was not warranted. Further, in non-capital cases, the court could award 'corporal punishment not extending to life or limb'. These specifications were notable, first, for omitting transportation as a punishment option, probably because there was nowhere else for these convict colonists to be transported to. As explained below, transportation law was adopted in the colony anyway, inviting modification and guaranteeing confusion. Second, the language of corporal punishment evoked the so-called 'Devil's Article' of the Mutiny Act, which gave military tribunals extraordinary latitude to define and punish disciplinary offences.[8] As one observer noted, this Court was something 'altogether new in the British annals', although it was not necessarily offensive given 'the necessity of the case'.[9]

Over the next thirty years, the Criminal Court became the key apparatus for the rough application of England's 'Bloody Code' to a struggling and belligerent colonial outpost. The Court dealt mostly with larcenies, of food and clothes especially, as well as varieties of house robbery and thefts from the Crown. Later, as the colony dispersed into the hinterland, horse and stock theft became more common, as did offences against the person. These crimes were typically punished with ferocious floggings – 2,000 lashes for stealing biscuits worth a little over six shillings, for example, at a time when the Court's workload was clearly fuelled by hunger. The Court also issued sentences of confinement, which initially meant being kept on 'the small, white, rocky island, adjacent to the cove' known as Pinchgut Island.[10] Other punishment options included work in irons, ration reductions, time in the pillory, and the chaining together of offenders. These cruder forms of corporal

8 G. A. Steppler, 'British Military Law, Discipline, and the Conduct of Regimental Courts-Martial in the Later Eighteenth Century' *English Historical Review* 102, no. 405 (1987): 859–86.

9 W. Tench, *A Narrative of the Expedition to Botany Bay: With an Account of New South Wales* (London: Bailey, Lemoine and Parsons, 1789), 69, 71.

10 George Barrington, *An Account of a Voyage to New South Wales* (London: M. Jones, 1810), 1: 472.

punishments remained a feature of court sentencing until the 1810s, when they receded in favour of solitary confinement, and transportation.

If sometimes the Court's sentences seemed shockingly harsh, it is notable that they were frequently ordered for offences that could warrant greater punishments under English law, including capital punishment. As one Judge Advocate noted, when criticised for awarding dangerously protracted sentences of solitary confinement, such punishments were conceivably an 'extension of mercy' when issued for atrocious crimes which could have one 'doomed to death'.[11] It is likely that the innovation and ferocity of New South Wales' sentences reflected the lack of alternatives to the death penalty, given that prisoners could not be sent away under sentence of transportation. Certainly, there was some restraint in the application of the death penalty in early New South Wales.[12] Statistically, the Court in its first ten years was three times more likely to acquit or return no verdict (in all cases, capital and non-capital) than it was to award sentence of death. Further, the governors (to whom the royal prerogative of mercy was devolved) reprieved over half of the capital convictions issued by the Court. It was the mitigation of death sentences which invited some of the most innovative sentencing outcomes, which were fashioned by very local and current circumstances. For example, one man was 'pardoned on condition of being the common executioner', meaning, as a contemporary put it, that he was to 'either Hang or be Hanged'.[13] A more problematic scenario was posed by reprieving the condemned 'on condition of their residing in some one or other of the Islands dependent on this territory', a peculiar form of transportation, perhaps. That was both practically and legally awkward, because although the governor could presumably reprieve a death sentence on any terms he chose, transportation was, as noted, not a sentencing option explicitly contemplated by the Charter of Justice.

It was therefore an early and bold deviation when, in late 1788, the first Deputy Judge Advocate, David Collins, sentenced a thief to 'be transported' for seven years. That sentence presented a conundrum, for the man was already transported for seven years under the sentence of an English court.

11 Anon [Nicholas Bayley to Henry Edward Bunbury], enclosed in Bathurst to Macquarie, 24 January 1817, *HRA 1*, 9: 197–200; Macquarie to Bathurst, 4 December 1817, *HRA 1*, 9: 505–7; Darling to Macquarie, 2 December 1817, *HRA 1*, 9: 513–15.

12 The colony's gory 'heyday of capital punishment' came some decades later. Tim Castle, 'Constructing Death: Newspaper Reports of Executions in Colonial New South Wales, 1826–1837' *Journal of Australian Colonial History* 9 (2007): 51–68.

13 George Bouchier Worgan, cited in J. Cobley, *Sydney Cove 1788* (London: Hodder and Stoughton, 1963), 92.

Somewhat dubiously, the local Court interpreted its own sentence as a compounding punishment, ordering that the man 'remain in the country for life'. He was subsequently freed and became a farmer. It was the last time, for many years, that sentence of transportation was issued by the colonial Court. Meanwhile, the establishment of the isolated settlement on Norfolk Island allowed individuals to be sent away for their crimes, across the seas but within the jurisdiction of the colony. For over a decade individuals were sent from Sydney to Norfolk Island under sentences labelled 'hard labour' but described by some as 'confinement', 'banishment', 'exile' or a 'second transportation'. Such punishments acquired their own local meanings and outcomes in colonial New South Wales, but the chaotic terminology reflected a degree of informality and uncertainty in local sentencing.[14]

Transportation, as a distinct and standard punishment, made its firm appearance in Court sentencing in 1797 during a turbulent period of bushranging on the edges of the hinterland. Here, vagrancy laws were evoked (against the instincts of a governor who wanted certain troublemakers executed without trial) which prescribed transportation as the punishment for breaking out of custody or being at large while under sentence. Sentence of 'transportation' was soon after ordered for other non-capital crimes, issued in hundreds of cases over the next decade, to convicts and emancipists mostly but also sometimes to free arrivals, the locally born, and soldiers and sailors. Again, there were attempts to articulate the local sentence in relation to an 'original' sentence of transportation, ordering the local sentence be served 'in addition to and to be completed from', or 'computed from', or 'commence at' the 'expiration of' the British sentence, for example.[15] This was a significant local modification, almost thirty years before England's Criminal Law Act of 1827 expressly allowed the aggregate term of two sentences to exceed the punishment awardable for either conviction.[16]

The simplest way to mimic transportation was to remove individuals to remote sites on the fringes of the colony, beginning with the 'Coal River' settlement at Newcastle north of Sydney. Newcastle emerged in the 1810s as a particularly unpleasant station for stock thieves, burglars and receivers, where convicts not only endured a relative form of banishment and

14 David Andrew Roberts, 'Exile in a Land of Exiles: The Early History of Criminal Transportation Law in New South Wales, 1788–1809' *Australian Historical Studies* 48, no. 4 (2017): 1–16.

15 Court of Criminal Jurisdiction, Minutes of Proceedings, January 1801–December 1808, SANSW 5/1149.

16 Criminal Law Act, 7 & 8 Geo. 4 c 28, 21 June 1827.

confinement but were subjected to extra-punitive work conditions that seemed to befit the doubly convicted. The point was reinforced by unusual caveats in Court sentencing – having convicts flogged as well as transported, and/or insisting that transportation involve being 'kept to hard labour' or be served 'in irons' for part or the entirety of the term. Governors also sent hundreds of men to penal settlements in commutation of death sentences, usually for 'life' and often stipulating 'hard labour' or 'labour in double irons'. These sentences included clear breaks from English norms which treated transportation and hard labour as legally discrete punishments. By the early-1820s, as transportation to penal stations emerged as one of the most important pillars of local punishment, these extra-punishment zones became exemplars of the type of terror so desired by the British government. But they simultaneously became a great source of legal confusion and contestation.[17] However, responsibility for that lay not so much with the Court as with the colony's other and more controversial tier of justice – the magistracy.

The Magistrates

As noted, the instinct of the colony's founders was to have the settlement placed under the Articles of War. That, among other things, would have allowed the local authorities, through a type of lower-level regimental courts martial, to punish a vast substratum of minor offences and disciplinary matters loosely defined as 'immoralities, misbehaviour or neglect of duty'. It transpired, instead, that this business fell to the colonial magistrates who assumed sweeping and increasing responsibilities in the management of convict life and labour. Their vital role in the administration of local justice, however, was complicated and controversial for a number of reasons. First, the authority of the colonial magistrates was poorly defined. The 1787 Charter of Justice provided for the colony's three most senior administrators – the governor, lieutenant governor and the Deputy Judge Advocate – to be justices of the peace. Further, Governor Arthur Phillip's (second) commission of April 1787 empowered him to appoint other officers to the magistracy, which he did, although initially there were few able or willing to act in that capacity. The only guidelines provided, at that stage, was that the magistrates 'shall have the same power . . . as Justices of the Peace have within that part of the Great Britain called England'. Second, the magistrates subsequently

17 Lisa Ford and David Andrew Roberts, 'New South Wales Penal Settlements and the Transformation of Secondary Punishment in the Nineteenth-century British Empire' *Journal of Colonialism and Colonial History* 15 (2014): n. p.

developed expansive local powers over many decades before their authority was formally defined – powers that were often legally questionable and proved difficult to correct. Third, they acted in a challenging and complicated space wherein they dealt with non-capital crimes committed by convicts, as well as convict disciplinary offences, the distinctions between those classes of offence being too easily blurred. As explained below, attempts to clarify and formalise their proceedings created legal chaos.

The architects of the colony did not explicitly establish a lower-tier court for the maintenance of convict discipline. Nevertheless, only eight days after the first sitting of the Criminal Court in February 1788, the Deputy Judge Advocate and other notables gathered to 'examine all offences committed by the convicts, and determine on and punish such as were not of sufficient importance for trial by the criminal court'.[18] This, the so-called Judge Advocate's bench, proved to be a very busy entity, meeting on at least 160 occasions in its first three years from 1789 to 1791. The bench survived a brief interregnum in 1792 when all legal and disciplinary responsibilities were assumed by the military, and another in 1814 when Judge Advocate Ellis Bent dramatically refused to sit with an emancipist magistrate, Simeon Lord.[19] As settlements sprouted across the hinterland, more civil officers were made magistrates, especially at Sydney and Parramatta, and later at Hawkesbury when it seemed necessary to check the 'licentiousness of the settlers' there.[20] Magistrates were also appointed in the remote settlements of Norfolk Island and Van Diemen's Land, where they were the sole authority for treating every crime short of murder. Magistrates quickly became vital to almost every aspect of the colony's administration, tasked with conducting all manner of inquiries and investigations, with monitoring the demography, industry and infrastructure of remote settlements, issuing licences for the sale of alcohol, administering the constabulary and, of course, monitoring the allocation, movement and behaviour of convicts.

In terms of the administration of justice in early New South Wales and Van Diemen's Land, the greatest business of the magistrates involved the treatment of 'complaints' involving convicts – especially drunkenness, indecent language, gambling, disobedience of orders and absence from work – sometimes called 'convict offences'. However, that workload was interspersed with more serious matters that could have been treated as

18 David Collins, *An Account of the English Colony in New South Wales*, edited by Brian H. Fletcher (Sydney: A. H. & A. W. Reed, 1975), 1: 10.
19 C. H. Currey, *The Brothers Bent* (Sydney: Sydney University Press, 1968).
20 King to Portland, 28 September 1800, *HRA 1*, 2: 657.

capital felonies, especially compounded forms of larceny (burglary and robbery) and malicious forms of assault. Although these cases were sometimes referred to the superior jurisdiction, generally the magistrates served to ease the workload of the superior Court by treating serious crimes with simpler and lesser punishments.[21] These responsibilities rendered magisterial proceedings both busy and severe. At Parramatta for example, in the three years 1818 to 1820, twelve gentlemen, sitting alone or in small combinations, adjudicated cases involving just under 1,500 individuals, 85 per cent of them prisoners in servitude. For offences ranging from larceny to swearing they issued sentences of confinement, punitive labour and time in the stocks, occasionally ordering individuals to be chained together or to wear a log. But the staple of the magistrates was flogging. Over 60 per cent of male convicts brought before the Parramatta bench in these years were flogged, with more than 32,000 lashes ordered at an average of forty-six strokes per person.[22] Increasingly, magistrates also took to sending the worst convicts away, to Van Diemen's Land or to the burgeoning penal settlement at Newcastle, where they joined the colony's most serious offenders ordered there under Court sentences or the governor's commutation warrants. Thus, at Newcastle, and later at Port Macquarie, convicts sentenced by magistrates for absconding and neglect of duty could suffer the same extreme deprivations inflicted on burglars and stock thieves.[23]

This central role in the administration of convict discipline and criminal justice involving convicts made magistrates the most powerful figures in the business and politics of the colony. It also made them exceedingly unpopular. In the southern settlements of Van Diemen's Land, their arbitrary behaviour and maladministration generated such simmering resentment and lawlessness among the lower orders as to goad the lieutenant governor into an illegal declaration of martial law.[24] Nevertheless, in the 1810s, Governor

21 Judge Advocate's Bench, Minutes of Proceedings, 1788–1821, SANSW NRS-3397; David Neal, 'Law and Authority: The Magistracy in New South Wales, 1788–1840' *Law in Context* 3 (1985): 45–74.

22 Returns of Punishment at Parramatta, January 1818 to September 1820, Appendices to the Commission of Inquiry, 311–57. For context, see Matthew Allen, 'The Myth of the Flogging Parson: Samuel Marsden and Severity of Punishment in the Age of Reform' *Australian Historical Studies*, 48, no. 4 (2017): 486–501.

23 David Andrew Roberts, 'Colonial Gulag: The Populating of the Port Macquarie Penal Settlement, 1821–1832' *History Australia* 14, no. 4 (2017): 588–606.

24 Alex Castles and Stephan Petrow, *Lawless Harvests or God Save the Judges: Van Diemen's Land, 1803–55, a Legal History* (Melbourne: Australian Scholarly Publishing, 2007); A. C. Castles, 'The Vandemonian Spirit and the Law' *Tasmanian Historical Research Association Papers and Proceedings* 38 (1991): 105–18; James Boyce, *Van Diemen's Land* (Melbourne: Black Inc., 2008), chapter 6.

Macquarie increased the authority of the magistrates, at the same time as he zealously asserted his power to decide whom he would appoint, leading to complaints about gubernatorial interference in the administration of justice and the lingering military 'cast' of colonial law.[25] Macquarie's insistence on appointing emancipists to the magistracy became one of the defining controversies of his reign, followed closely by his exercising of power to dismiss magistrates who opposed him politically. It was the magistrates themselves, however, who shone the worst light on the institution, their brutality combining with ineptitude, infighting and illegality to create 'a train of embarrassments', as one governor described it. That culminated in a sensational scandal in the mid-1820s when it was revealed that the Parramatta bench was engaging in practices 'repugnant to the clearest maxims both of law and moral justice', including flogging to exact confessions.[26]

A kinder interpretation of the predicament was that the magistrates were struggling not only with the great multitude of matters brought under their cognizance, but also with the unique duty of applying an informal and makeshift disciplinary code to convicts.[27] From the 1820s, the executive sought restraints on the power and autonomy of the landowner-magistrates, especially through the appointment of stipendiary officers, sometimes called 'Police' or 'Resident' magistrates.[28] Although they may have been viewed sceptically by remote elites who treasured their local autonomy, and by convicts and other labourers who probably saw little difference and much collusion between magistrates of all descriptions, stipendiaries would play an increasingly important role in policing both the population centres and the frontiers of settlement.[29] That these were often military officers further aroused suspicions about state power. New South Wales set a precedent with a string of Commandants ruling the penal settlements and convict work stations. In Van Diemen's Land, Lieutenant Governor Arthur faced

25 Bent to Bathurst, 1 July 1815, *HRA 4*, 1: 130.

26 Brisbane to Bathurst, 28 September 1825, *HRA 1*, 11: 851; Byrne, *Criminal Law and Colonial Subject*; L. Benton and L. Ford, 'Magistrates in Empire: Convicts, Slaves, and the Remaking of the Plural Legal Order in the British Empire', in L. Benton and R. J. Ross (eds), *Legal Pluralism and Empires, 1500–1850* (New York: New York University Press, 2013), 173–97.

27 Paula J. Byrne, '"The Public Good": Competing Visions of Freedom in Early Colonial New South Wales' *Labour History* 58 (1990): 76–83.

28 Hilary Golder, 'The Making of the Modern Magistracy' *Journal of the Royal Australian Historical Society* 77 (1991): 30–40.

29 John Hirst and David Neal describe the appointment of stipendiary magistrates as an important shift of power away from the honorary magistrates towards central government. J. B. Hirst, *Convict Society and Its Enemies: A History of Early New South Wales* (Sydney: Allen & Unwin, 1983), 145, 149; Neal, *The Rule of Law*, 124–6, 158–63.

enormous opposition to his creation of a centralised policing system that relied heavily on military officers, although the Colonial Office ultimately approved of the 'evil', the disordered state of the island requiring a 'temporary sacrifice of many principles of law, which, under other circumstances, can hardly be too scrupulously maintained'.[30] Yet again, it seemed necessary, given the colony's purpose and population, for law and order to be maintained through more coercive measures than might be acceptable elsewhere. That thinking would come under increasing attack during the early nineteenth century.

Trouble and Changes

In the 1810s, the glaring imperfections in the administration of local justice were very publicly revealed in the operation of the Criminal Court. A stream of messy proceedings and dubious outcomes did little to improve the Court's reputation.[31] For example, sensational libel cases exposed the Court's vulnerability and incapacity in complex matters involving prominent and powerful citizens (such as the Colonial Secretary and the colony's most eminent chaplain).[32] In other matters too the court continually managed to disappoint, issuing death sentences to individuals who were later proved innocent, and exonerating others in cases that aroused enormous public surprise and indignation.[33] There were quiet injustices too; prisoners being sent to the colonial gulags at Newcastle and Port Macquarie, for example, even after they had been acquitted in trials.[34] In the growing repugnance for this relic of

30 Goderich to Arthur, 17 July 1827, *HRA 3*, 6: 110–11; Stefan Petrow, 'Policing in a Penal Colony: Governor Arthur's Police System in Van Diemen's Land, 1826–1836' *Law and History Review* 18, no. 2 (2000): 351–95.

31 Campbell to Lawson, 23 January 1810, SANSW 4/3490A; Herbert Vere Evatt, *Rum Rebellion: A Study of the Overthrow of Governor Bligh by John Macarthur and the New South Wales Corps* (Sydney: Angus and Robertson, 1939); Grace Karskens and Richard Waterhouse, '"Too Sacred to Be Taken Away": Property, Liberty, Tyranny and the "Rum Rebellion"' *Journal of Australian Colonial History* 12 (2010): 1–22.

32 *R v Campbell* [1817] NSWKR 5; See J. M. Bennett, 'The Day of Retribution – Commissioner Bigge's Inquiries in Colonial New South Wales' *American Journal of Legal History* 15, no. 2 (1971): 85–106.

33 Repeated for example, in *Sydney Gazette*, 11 October 1817, 18 October 1817, and 4 April 1818; Eager to Bathurst, 3 April 1823, *HRA 4*, 1: 441–76; Macquarie to Bathurst, 31 July 1813, *HRA 1*, 8: 7; *Sydney Gazette*, 17 July 1813, 2–4; J. T. Bigge, *Report of the Commissioner of Inquiry, on the Judicial Establishments of New South Wales, and Van Diemen's Land* (London: House of Commons, 1823), 33.

34 Lisa Ford and David Andrew Roberts, 'Legal Change, Convict Activism and the Reform of Penal Relocation in Colonial New South Wales: The Port Macquarie Penal Settlement, 1822–26' *Australian Historical Studies* 46, no. 2 (2015): 174–90.

the past there were some key and constant refrains, especially concerning the Court's independence and integrity. As the young Judge Advocate Ellis Bent reported in 1811 (his words became a mantra) the Court's military appearance and flavour, and especially the absence of juries comprised of free citizens, meant that it could not 'command that veneration, awe, or respect, which ought ever to attend upon a Court of Justice'.[35]

These criticisms of the colony's superior court were reiterated persistently over the next decade, without effect. After they were aired prominently in George Eden's House of Commons Select Committee on Transportation in 1812, Secretary of State Earl Bathurst acknowledged the 'incompetence' and 'inconveniences' of the colony's judicial system, although to him the problems seemed 'at present not very severely felt'. The sticking point was trial by jury in criminal cases. Bathurst thought it a 'worthy' question, but surely a step too far given 'the peculiar constitution of that society'.[36] On that fundamental concern, above all others, the reform of the colony's criminal jurisdiction hinged and stalled, more-or-less completely, for another decade. It was accepted that the colony's developing commercial activities demanded an immediate overhaul of the civil jurisdiction, so a new Charter of Justice in 1814 established a Supreme Court with jurisdiction extending to Van Diemen's Land. But for the time being, the 'Criminal Department' remained completely unaltered.

Some change was presaged by two critical House of Commons Select Committees in 1819. First, the Select Committee on the State of Gaols featured lengthy evidence on New South Wales, some of it relating to the 'considerable improvement' required in the local administration of justice.[37] Second, James Mackintosh's monumental Select Committee on the Criminal Law as Relates to Capital Punishment in Felonies foreshadowed changes to the draconian 'Bloody Code' – reforms that would bear heavily on the criminal laws responsible for populating New South Wales, being also the laws in force in the colony itself, at this time, as explained below.[38] Renewed pleas for change also came from the colony, a long and impassioned petition

35 Bent to Liverpool, 19 October 1811, *HRA* 1, 7: 816. See David Neal, 'Law and Authority: The Campaign for Trial by Jury in New South Wales' *Journal of Legal History* 8, no. 2 (1987): 107–28.

36 *Report from the Select Committee on Transportation* (London: House of Commons, 1812); Bathurst to Macquarie, 23 November 1812, *HRA* 1, 7: 674.

37 *Report from the Select Committee on the State of Gaols, etc.* (London: House of Commons, 1819).

38 Phil Handler, 'Forging the Agenda: The 1819 Select Committee on the Criminal Laws Revisited', *Journal of Legal History* 25, no. 3 (2004): 249–68.

to the Prince Regent from 'the gentlemen, clergy, settler, merchants, land-holders and other free inhabitants' fully exposing the court's failure to meet the rising interests and expectations of the population. In particular, the petition prayed for trial by jury, lest the colony be 'suffered to remain the solitary exception within the wide range of British Rule and Dominion'.[39] The Honourable Henry Grey Bennet concurred, his observations as a member of the Select Committee on Prisons convincing him that the colony's Court was an institution 'revolting to a free-born Englishman', although he could not accuse it of 'unreasonable severity' given its apparent leniency in the treatment of capital offences.[40] These mounting concerns played a key role in shaping a commission of inquiry which would, finally, provide the catalyst for some change.

Unsurprisingly, the arrival of Commissioner John Thomas Bigge in New South Wales attracted an outpouring of grievance and agitation. Although most complaints concerned the civil jurisdiction, there were some thorough critiques of the Criminal Court, the arguments now mostly old and well-rehearsed. The sum of it all, in the words of Judge Advocate John Wylde, was that the 'system of summary and simple procedure' established in 1787, when justice 'upon the spur of the occasion, seemed requisite for the intimidation and due restraint' of several hundred convicts, was no longer appropriate thirty-five years later, now that 'the numerous sons of the first settlers' were coming of age.[41] Yet ultimately, Commissioner Bigge muffled all this agitation. The changes he proposed in his Report on the Judicial Establishments were minimal. He recommended the 'immediate and entire separation of the criminal jurisdictions of New South Wales and Van Diemen's Land', giving the latter its own court, both to be headed by a judge and assisted by an Attorney General. Bigge further suggested the courts be reserved for the trial of capital offences committed by free people, with all business involving convicts going before benches of three or more magistrates. But he utterly rejected concerns about the use of military juries. Indeed, he thought them even more effective than the civilian juries of England. He recommended an increase to seven military or naval officers (six votes should be required to award sentence of death), with the judge having no vote in the verdict but exclusive responsibility for nominating punishments. But on the critical

39 Petition of the Free Inhabitants of New South Wales, *HRA 1*, 10: 55–65,
40 Henry Grey Bennet, *A Letter to Earl Bathurst, Secretary of State for the Colonial Department* (London: James Ridgway, 1820).
41 Wylde to Bigge, 16 July 1821, *HRA 1*, 4: 353–89.

matter of trial by civilian jury, Bigge and his backers remained adamant that the time was still not right.[42]

Nevertheless, in the wake of the Bigge inquiry, indeed before the commissioner's Report on the Judicial Establishments was printed, high-level forces set out to reconstitute the colony's legal apparatus. What was presented to Parliament and passed on 19 July 1823 was the Act for the Better Administration of Justice in New South Wales and Van Diemen's Land, referred to as the New South Wales Act. This allowed for the establishment of Supreme Courts and the appointment of Chief Justices in both New South Wales and Van Diemen's Land. As per the commissioner's recommendations, civilian juries were still disallowed, although the military members, now expanded to seven officers, were 'liable to be challenged or objected to upon the special Ground of direct Interest or Affection'.[43] The Court would continue to hear all capital cases, including those involving convicts in servitude. And further, although Bigge barely touched on the magistracy in his reports, the Act formalised a lower-tier criminal jurisdiction by establishing English-style Courts of Quarter and General Sessions. These lower-level courts were given a summary jurisdiction over the two classes of offence committed by convicts – non-capital offences, on the one hand, as defined in law, for which magistrates could now formally issue short sentences of transportation or 'removal', or extend an original British sentence; and on the other, the vast array of convict disciplinary offences, now legally defined for the first time as 'Drunkenness, Disobedience of Orders, Neglect of work, Absconding or Desertion, abusive Language to . . . Employers or Overseers, Insubordination or other turbulent or disorderly Conduct'. As explained below, the transformation of the colony's legal system produced mixed results. In short, the reforms to the superior court were small. The reforms to the lower courts were disastrous.

Justice Upended

Pursuant to the New South Wales Act, the New South Wales Supreme Court was created by a Third Charter of Justice dated 14 October 1823, which also appointed Francis Forbes as Chief Justice. The Court in Van Diemen's Land was established slightly earlier, by warrant dated 18 August 1823, with John Lewes Pedder appointed Chief Justice. Commissions were issued to Saxe

42 Bigge, *Report of the Commissioner of Inquiry*.
43 New South Wales Act, 4 Geo. IV c. 96, 1823.

Bannister and Joseph Tice Gellibrand to serve in the new officers of Attorney General in New South Wales and Van Diemen's Land respectively. The old Criminal Court ended on 19 February 1824, its last session distinguished by the fact that no one was capitally convicted.[44] Both of the new charters were promulgated in May 1824 and the two Supreme Courts commenced immediately – in Hobart on 24 May, and in Sydney on 6 June. If these changes were swift, they were also restrained. As Judge Advocate Wylde put it, local legal procedures seemed to 'be so little altered'.[45] Certainly, there was little change in the business of the Court, or in its sentencing practices. In his first sittings across June to September 1824, Chief Justice Forbes tried just under 100 people, mostly for the colony's quintessential crimes of housebreaking and stock theft, sentencing thirty people to death. In Van Diemen's Land, Pedder was even busier, trying over 200 people in 1824 and passing sixty-two death sentences. Much like the days of the old Criminal Court, these sittings heralded spates of executions and a flood of sentences of transportation, either mandated by the Court or required as a condition of the governor's mercy, channelling prisoners into the new penal settlements at Port Macquarie, and later Moreton Bay, and Macquarie Harbour in Van Diemen's Land.[46]

It was the formalisation and expansion of the use of transportation law in the colony that caused the most significant problems. In 1826, after an Imperial Act allowed colonial governors to appoint destinations for convicts transported from their own jurisdictions,[47] Governor Darling formally proclaimed Port Macquarie, Moreton Bay and Norfolk Island as sites for the reception of convicts sentenced to transportation in New South Wales. A local Transportation to Penal Settlements Act[48] formalised those settlements as discrete and special zones – 'insulated by law, and separated from the other parts of the Colony'[49] – for convicts and emancipists reconvicted in the colony (those who came free to or were born in the colony were henceforth exonerated from serving at penal settlements for a first conviction). Van Diemen's Land followed suit in September 1827 with a Transportation Act and a subsequent proclamation appointing Norfolk

44 Reports of Prisoners tried in the Court of Criminal Jurisdiction, 1820–1824, SANSW X820, 125–21.

45 Wylde to Goulburn, 5 January 1824, *HRA* 4, 1: 529–31.

46 Returns of Prisoners tried at the New South Wales Supreme Court, 1824–1825, SANSW X727; Supreme Court of Van Diemen's Land, Reports of Prisoners Tried, 1824–1831, Mitchell Library, DL ADD554.

47 Transported Offenders Punishment Act, 6 Geo. 4 c 69, 1825.

48 7 Geo. IV No. 5.

49 *R v Flanagan et al.* (1827), reported in *Sydney Gazette*, 24 February 1827, 3 (Forbes CJ).

Island as the destination for offenders locally sentenced to transportation.[50] A raft of questions ensued, particularly in New South Wales. Who nominated the destination of a prisoner locally sentenced to transportation? Could individuals be removed from or moved between penal stations on the orders of the executive? Could 'ordinary' convicts be sent to a penal station, without a local conviction, providing they were 'kept separate and distinct' from other prisoners? What laws and regulations were one subjected to at a penal settlement, and what powers could be vested in the local commandant/magistrate? Was escaping from a penal settlement a capital offence, in the manner of returning from transportation? Further confusions arose after 1824 when secretaries of state were empowered to order prisoners to penal settlements without a colonial conviction.[51]

These dilemmas seemed insignificant, however, or were far more easily settled in law and legislation, when compared to those arising from the jurisdiction of the magistrates after 1823. As noted, the New South Wales Act provided for the establishment of Courts of Quarter and General Sessions, intended to try non-capital crimes and misdemeanours, and also to deal with lower-level misbehaviours committed by convicts. But if the intention of the Act was to legitimise customary proceedings that were now critical to the maintenance of discipline in the colony, while drawing local criminal jurisdiction closer to metropolitan practice, the reform effort failed. Almost immediately, fundamental and disruptive questions emerged concerning the legal status of pre-existing sentences. After executive contemplation of that question in 1825, hundreds of convicts were withdrawn from the gulag at Port Macquarie in quiet acknowledgment of their having been illegally sentenced 'for want of Jurisdiction in the Magistrates before the [1823] Act'.[52] Simultaneously, it was quietly noted that the New South Wales Act did not provide for magistrates operating outside of Sessions, including magistrates sitting alone. That was a serious oversight in a colony with disorderly and expanding borders. Legislative attempts to fix this were ad hoc and contradictory. Parliament allowed remotely situated magistrates to exercise the same powers as were vested in a Sessions Court, even when sitting alone, while the New South Wales Governor in Council restricted

50 Act for the Transportation of Offenders from Van Diemen's Land (8 Geo. 4 No. 4).

51 They acquired that power under Section 13 of the 1824 Transportation Act, 5 Geo. 4 c 84.

52 Executive Council Minutes, 3 June 1826, cited in Ford and Roberts, 'Legal Change, Convict Activism', 219.

single and remote magistrates to issuing less severe punishments than the Sessions.[53]

From the mid-1820s, earnest law officers and provocative defence attorneys noticed a raft of anomalies and illegalities, as customary practices collided with new rules. They noted that magistrates were inflicting multiple punishments for a single offence, and that they were sentencing on suspicion and laying inexact charges. Sometimes, in some places, there was evidence of sustained and excessive severity, especially on the penal settlements where 'very frequent sentences of corporal punishment' might, only at a stretch, be regarded as necessary for the management of 'the desperate class of characters' sent there.[54] Mostly, magistrates struggled with the legalities of some of their new sentencing powers. They could now, for example, sentence convicts to transportation, 'remove' them to remote parts of the colony, or extend an original British sentence. In both colonies, questions emerged about the differences between transportation and 'removal', and about the conditions under which an extended sentence was to be served. Were local sentences 'superadded' to or served concurrently with a sentence from the United Kingdom? How did transportation, removal and extension sit in relation both to one another and to other punishments such as flogging and hard labour? Very quickly the *Phoenix* prison hulk in Sydney Harbour, and the penal settlements themselves, became hotbeds of talk about unlawful detention. A rapid accumulation of claims against magistrates and other civil officers caused the Colonial Office in 1830 to refuse financial responsibility for 'any acts . . . which may not be in strict conformity with the law'.[55]

The confusion in magisterial jurisdiction was only exacerbated by a string of peculiar exigencies in the late 1820s. In both colonies, in 1828, delays in re-legislating the Sessions Courts nearly deprived the magistrates of their summary jurisdiction over convicts. Then, in 1830, it was feared that magistrates only had summary jurisdiction over convicts serving under British sentences, and not those locally convicted by the Supreme Courts.[56] There were doubts about how many magistrates were required to constitute a Sessions Court, and about whether multiple courts could operate at one and the same time. The onslaught of meticulous legal quibbling left Lieutenant Governor Arthur feeling that 'every species of restraint over the

53 Act for Punishing Offences Committed by Transports in the Colonies, 6 Geo. IV c 69, 22 June 1825; Summary Punishment Act, 6 Geo. IV No. 5, 8 February 1825.

54 Moore to McLeay, 31 January 1827, SANSW, 27/1203, 4/1921.

55 Murray to Darling, 16 July 1830, *HRA* 1, 15: 587.

56 11 Geo. IV No. 13.

Convicts . . . [was] regarded as a doubtful exercise of power'.[57] When his Chief Justice declared the local Sessions Act repugnant to English law because it potentially impinged on the liberties of free people, Arthur boldly ignored the opinion and had the legislation passed anyway.[58] Perhaps the most extraordinary crisis occurred in 1831, when the Vandemonian administration imagined that the death of King George IV had left the colony 'without any legal government' whatsoever.[59] The authorities feared 'a state of general anarchy' should doubts about the power of magistrates become 'known to the convicts'.[60]

But mostly, the magistrates were confused about their dual role as dispensers of convict discipline and arbiters of lower-level crime. It hardly mattered that the 1823 Act was clear about the distinctions between the two classes of offences assigned to their jurisdiction. Magistrates remained shockingly ignorant of the difference between the non-capital crimes which warranted punishments such as transportation, and those lesser 'convict offences' which did not. Frequent opinions from the law officers, numerous published notices and a clear determination by the Supreme Court in New South Wales in 1829 did little to correct the customary behaviours of the magistrates.[61] Eventually, in Van Diemen's Land, a combination of 'wholly illegal and exceedingly inconsistent' actions by remote magistrates led to an 1830 Act that carefully circumscribed the offences and punishments that lay within the jurisdiction of magistrates.[62] New South Wales did the same thing, at the same time, but with contradictory outcomes. The authority of single magistrates to adjudicate non-capital crimes was removed but the number of lashes which magistrates could award for lower-level misbehaviours was tripled.[63] Governors Darling and Arthur were a world apart on the efficacy and ethics of flogging. In New South Wales Governor Richard Bourke finally provided the clarification needed, his celebrated Convict Punishment and Summary Jurisdiction Act of 1832 serving finally to settle long-contested legal issues surrounding the summary jurisdiction of colonial magistrates and the local

57 Arthur to Murray, 25 May 1839, *HRA 3*, 8: 367–74.
58 Executive Council Minutes, 4 February 1830, EC4-1-1, Tasmanian Archives: 511–12.
59 Montagu and Stephen to Arthur, 1 January 1831, CSO1 904–19169, Tasmanian Archives: 231–8.
60 Minutes of the Executive Council, 30 April 1829, *HRA 3*, 8: 433–5.
61 Transportation Opinion [1829] NSWSupC 5.
62 Quarter Sessions and Summary Jurisdiction Act, 10 Geo. 4 No. 2, February 1829.
63 Punishment and Transportation Act, 11 Geo. IV No. 12; Act to Amend the 1829 Quarter Sessions Act, 11 Geo. IV No. 13, May 1830.

application of English transportation law.[64] There was intense opposition to the reforms, led by elite landowner-magistrates on the fringes of the colony, who resented the diminution of their powers to terrorise local workforces.[65] But there was no mass conflagration or disorder, and New South Wales magistrates no longer sent convicts to colonial gulags for petty theft, running away or for being 'incorrigible'.

Changing Law

What was really changing, at this time, was the criminal law itself. First, the role of the Australian settlements as receptacles for transported offenders was re-cemented. A renewed and revised Transportation Act in 1824 sought, in the words of Home Secretary Robert Peel, 'to make transportation a much more severe mode of punishment than it had generally been hitherto'.[66] A year later, an Act For Punishing Offences Committed by Transports paved the way for convicts to be sent directly to Australia from all of His Majesty's foreign possessions.[67] Second, Parliament was simultaneously abolishing the death penalty for many crimes in preference for sentences of transportation, while also improving the efficiency of legal procedures and policing.[68] These reforms, ramped up in the late 1820s, not only resulted in more convicts being sent to Australia, they also impacted those spheres of criminal law, especially larceny, burglary, cattle stealing, property destruction and highway robbery, that constituted the core criminal business of the new courts in New South Wales and Van Diemen's Land. In New South Wales especially, this produced a number of legal and political exigencies, involving questions about

64 Punishment and Summary Jurisdiction Act, 3 Wm IV No. 3, August 1832; David Andrew Roberts, 'The "illegal sentences which magistrates were daily passing"': The Backstory to Governor Richard Bourke's 1832 Punishment and Summary Jurisdiction Act in Convict New South Wales' *The Journal of Legal History* 38, no. 3 (2017): 231–53.

65 Lisa Ford and David Andrew Roberts, 'The Convict Peace: The Imperial Context of the 1833 Convict Revolt at Castle Forbes' *Journal of Imperial and Commonwealth History* 49, no. 1 (2021): 1–21.

66 Act for the Transportation of Offenders from Great Britain, 5 Geo. 4 c 84; *Parliamentary Debates: New Series*, Volume 11, 4 June 1824 (London: Hansard, 1825), 1092.

67 Act for Punishing Offences Committed by Transports in the Colonies and for regulating Powers of JPs in New South Wales (6 Geo. 4 c 69).

68 Michael A. Rustigan, 'A Reinterpretation of Criminal Law Reform in Nineteenth-century England' *Journal of Criminal Justice* 8, no. 4 (1980): 205–19; Andrew Todd Harris, *Policing the City: Crime and Legal Authority in London, 1780–1840* (Columbus, OH: Ohio State University Press, 2004); Galen Broeker, *Rural Disorder and Police Reform in Ireland, 1812–36* (London: Routledge and Kegan Paul, 1970); John McGowan, *Policing the Metropolis of Scotland: A History of the Police and Systems of Police in Edinburgh & Edinburghshire, 1770–1833* (Musselburgh: Turlough, 2010).

the reception of new statutes and, more quietly, the status of vital laws that were repealed by the distant Parliament. Those questions were largely settled when Parliament's Australian Courts Act 1828 asserted that all reforms to England's criminal law (up to 25 July 1828) would be in force in both New South Wales and Van Diemen's Land from 1 March 1829, as far as they 'could then be reasonably applied'.[69]

Thereafter, local unelected legislatures, established in both colonies after the 1823 New South Act (and increased by the Australian Courts Act 1828) became fairly consistent in importing Parliament's latest criminal law reforms, although Van Diemen's Land, with its surly history of lawlessness, proved somewhat resistant to 'the opinion entertained by many philanthropic persons'.[70] The southern colony was, for example, slower than New South Wales to fully accept the abolition of the death penalty for stock theft and stealing from a dwelling house.[71] Similarly, the swathe of alterations introduced by Home Secretary Lord John Russell in 1837 – reforms which left only a small handful of crimes subject to capital punishment (such as treason and murder) – were speedily and wholly embraced in New South Wales in August 1838,[72] although in Van Diemen's Land they were introduced more slowly and sometimes only with local modifications.[73] Both colonies were remarkably slower to adopt metropolitan reforms that removed the death penalty for rape, such were the gnawing anxieties of a society built on conquest and convictism.[74] Further, there were local Acts crafted specifically for local conditions, most notably the infamous

69 Lisa Ford and David Andrew Roberts, '"Mr Peel's Amendments" in New South Wales: Imperial Criminal Reform in a Distant Penal Colony' *The Journal of Legal History* 37, no. 2 (2016): 198–214.

70 Arthur to Attorney General, 24 November 1835, Letterbook of Lieutenant Governor's Correspondence Addressed to Crown Law Officers, TAHO, GO55: 424–5.

71 An Act to Extend to Van Diemen's Land Certain Statutes Passed in England, 5 Will. IV No. 6. The Act only extended the recent English statute (6 Will. IV No. 17) as far as it related to stealing in dwelling house up to five pounds or more, stealing a horse or killing cattle. A number of other English statutes from 1833 and 1834 were eventually adopted in Van Diemen's Land in 1837, removing the death penalty for house-breaking (3 & 4 Will. 4 c 44), and for letter stealing and sacrilege (5&6 Will. 4 c 81). Act for Extending to This Colony Sundry Statutes Passed for the Amendment of the Criminal Law (8 Will. IV No. 1).

72 2 Vic. No. 10, 28 August 1838.

73 An Act for Extending to This Colony Sundry Statutes Passed for the Amendment of the Criminal Law in Cases of Forgery and Piracy (2 Vic. No. 18); An Act to Amend the Laws of This Colony Relating to Burglary and Stealing in a Dwelling-House (2 Vic No. 21); An Act to Amend the Laws of This Colony Relating to Robbery and Stealing from Vessels in Distress or Wrecked (2 Vic. No. 28).

74 Amanda Kaladelfos, 'The Politics of Punishment: Rape and the Death Penalty in Colonial Australia, 1841–1901' *History Australia* 9, no. 1, 155–75.

Bushranging Acts from 1830 which gave extraordinary powers to every individual to detain another citizen on suspicion of being an absconded convict. The Chief Justice, who reluctantly allowed the legislation, thought it 'armed the government with larger powers, than are known to any other portion of His Majesty's dominions'.[75]

In the several years following the 1838 Imperial Acts Adoption Act, the number of convictions in the Supreme Court in New South Wales declined markedly. Naturally there were fewer executions. In New South Wales, it was usually only rapists, murderers (including in 1838 seven men who murdered an Aboriginal child at Myall Creek), those who abetted murder, and occasionally some (notably convicts still in servitude) convicted of particularly violent burglaries, who were liable to be executed. There were also ameliorative laws in Van Diemen's Land, despite the ongoing influx of convicts from around the British globe. These reduced the sentences of transportation which could be awarded by magistrates, for example, and repealed older laws which made escape from a penal settlement a capital offence, the latter considered 'a blot in the legislation of this colony'.[76] In New South Wales, for years after the cessation of transportation from the United Kingdom, transportation remained a strong and consistent feature of local court sentencing, accounting for around 40 to 50 per cent of sentences issued by the court into the mid-1840s. Despite growing opposition to the practice, not least from the New South Wales judges, horse and cattle thieves, forgers, robbers and receivers, were still being sentenced to transportation and sent to Norfolk Island, some marked 'not to be returned', or to Van Diemen's Land or the new penal settlement at Cockatoo Island in Sydney Harbour.[77] The practice declined markedly in 1847, when a local act addressed 'impediments' to the execution of sentences by substituting transportation with 'hard labour on the roads or other public works'.[78] For many,

75 11 Geo. IV No. 10, 21 April 1830; Forbes to Murray, 19 July 1830, *HRA 1*, 15: 664–69.

76 Act to Amend the Law in Respect to the Constitution of Courts of General Quarter Sessions and the Punishment and Control of Transported and Other Offenders (7 Vic. No. 17), 9 January 1844; Eardley-Wilmott to Stanley, 15 February 1844, Governor's Dispatches, Tasmanian Archives, GO33-1–47, 411–12.

77 Supreme Court Sydney, Returns of Prisoners Tried and Sentenced, 1838–1841, SANSW X43, 1842–1845, SANSW X44. A proclamation by Governor George Gipps dated 16 August 1841 established Van Diemen's Land as the destination for prisoners sentenced to transportation in New South Wales. See *New South Wales Government Gazette*, No. 67, 20 August 1841, 1101.

78 Act to Substitute other Punishments for Transportation beyond the Seas, 11 Vic. No. 34 (2 October 1847). Among the last known recipients of a local sentence of transportation was William Wildman, for forgery, in March 1848. Supreme Court returns, 1846–1849, SANSW X47, 45.

that meant being sent to Newcastle, to work on the breakwater commenced by an earlier generation of convicts, thirty years before.

Trial by Jury

As noted, the reordering of law and justice in New South Wales and Van Diemen's Land stalled and stumbled on the question of trial by jury. The slow and tormented path to resolving that issue revealed much about the mood for compromise and modification of law that seemed required for a society built on convictism. While the New South Wales Act of 1823 allowed for the limited use of juries in civil actions, no provision was made for them in criminal matters, although Section 8 of the Act *did* authorise the King in Council to introduce criminal trial by civilian jury, if desired at some later time. As noted above, the strong advice of a succession of governors and Judge Advocates, and also the pleas of an increasingly vocal colonial public for trial by jury, were derailed by the commission of inquiry. Commissioner Bigge in fact dedicated much time and ink to making the case against it. But such obduracy merely turned the issue into the colony's most heated and poignant political dispute over the next twenty years. The controversy was propelled by a landmark ruling in October 1824 in which Chief Justice Forbes, answering confusion among the magistrates as well as disagreement between the colony's senior law officers, allowed the use of civilian juries in the new courts of Quarter Sessions. There being no 'express language' in the New South Wales Act to prescribe otherwise, Forbes ruled that the new courts must 'proceed in like manner, as Courts of Sessions proceed in England'.[79] That included the use of juries in trials and grand juries to determine when criminal charges should be brought to trial.

A local Act in March 1825[80] ensured that juries were only empanelled in matters involving free citizens, and so the summary jurisdiction intended for convicts continued. Early evidence suggested a great improvement in the administration of justice, a view supported by the colony's magistrates themselves, who saw great 'public advantage' in extending the experiment further.[81] In Van Diemen's Land, however, there was no doubt convicts could be tried without indictment or jury.[82] Courts of Sessions were held at Hobart from January 1825, and in Launceston from June 1825, before the jury

79 *R v the Magistrates of Sydney* [1824] NSWKR 3; [1824] NSWSupC 20; A. C. Castles, *An Australian Legal History* (Sydney: Law Book Co, 1982), 185–6.

80 6 Geo. 4 No. 9. 81 Brisbane to Bathurst, 23 October 1823, *HRA 1*, 11: 892–4.

82 Gellibrand to Bathurst, September 1825, *HRA 3*, 5: 238–9.

question came to the new Supreme Court.[83] Then, Chief Justice Pedder reached the opposite conclusion – there could be no trial by jury in Quarter Sessions without a king's Order in Council.[84] These determinations placed 'many impediments in the way of cheap and substantial justice' in Van Diemen's Land.[85] There, the Quarter Sessions would deal only with convicts under summary jurisdiction, while all and even the most 'trifling cases' involving free people went to the Supreme Court, keeping the Court very busy and ensuring the gaols were consistently full of prisoners awaiting trial.[86]

The momentum towards trial by jury was stalled by the 1828 Australian Courts Act, which explicitly put the proceedings of the lower courts on the same footing as that of the higher Supreme Court (that is, neither could empanel a jury), ending the brief experiment with civilian juries in the Sessions. However, the 1828 Act did authorise the King in Council to devolve the power to establish jury trial in criminal cases to the governors and their Legislative Councils. That was subsequently done by an Order in Council dated 28 June 1830, although neither Governor Darling in New South Wales nor Lieutenant Governor Arthur in Van Diemen's Land was inclined to champion the cause. In New South Wales in February 1832 Governor Richard Bourke persuaded his Council to pass a Jury Trials Act,[87] which defined a jury (when required or allowed) as consisting of twelve civil inhabitants, bound by the rules and procedures of the Courts of Record at Westminster. Importantly, that Act also allowed for civilian juries in criminal cases in (very) limited circumstances, notably whenever the governor or senior colonial or military officials had 'some personal interest' in a prosecution. The same measure was enacted in Van Diemen's Land two years later, Attorney General Alfred Stephen prevailing in the face of Lieutenant Governor Arthur's extreme apprehension.[88]

From 1833, trial by jury was allowed in New South Wales whenever any 'person or persons shall be desirous of having' it, in both the Supreme Court and Courts of Sessions, and some disqualifications were relaxed to allow

83 Alphabetical List of persons Tried before the Quarter Sessions, May 1825–September 1839, TAHO, LC 219, TAHO.

84 *R v Magistrates of Hobart Town* [1825], in Hobart Town Gazette, 16 July 1825; A. C. Castles, 'The Judiciary and Political Questions: The First Australian Experience' *Adelaide Law Review* 5, no. 3 (1975): 294–318.

85 Arthur to Hay, 15 November 1826, *HRA* 3, 5: 421–33.

86 Arthur to Bathurst, 24 March 1827, *HRA* 3, 5: 698.

87 2 Will. 4 No. 3.

88 An Act for the Extension of Trial by Jury – And to Regulate the Constitution of Juries (5 Will. IV No. 11); J. M. Bennett, *Sir Alfred Stephen: Third Chief Justice of New South Wales 1844–1873* (Annandale: Federation Press, 2009), 71–9.

more emancipists to act as jurors. Magistrates in the lower courts still proceeded summarily against convicts in non-capital criminal cases, but in the Supreme Court men and women in servitude could opt to be tried by a jury of twelve inhabitants.[89] Nevertheless, there remained some preference for military juries. As late as 1838, when just over half the individuals sentenced by the Court were convicts still in servitude, and most the rest were emancipists, ninety-five of the 172 convictions (55 per cent) issued involved a military jury.[90] Attempts to entrench the use of civil juries further stalled in the face of more obstructionism from colonial elites and prevarication in the Colonial Office. Finally, in September 1839 New South Wales required full civilian juries for the Supreme Court and Sessions in all cases excepting those that were still subject to summary jurisdiction.[91] In 1840 military juries were also abolished in Van Diemen's Land (effective from 1 January 1841).[92] At last, it seemed that the legal system in both colonies was approaching the standard expected in England.

Conclusion

This chapter has traced some of the tensions and confusions at the heart of the administration of justice in colonial New South Wales and Van Diemen's Land. Criminal law in the early Australian settlements was shaped constitutionally, institutionally and practically by the need to control convict populations, for fear of them 'bursting into flames'. This required a simplified and more coercive system of law, inviting a myriad of compromises and peculiarities. Although there was from the outset a sense that law and justice needed to be strictly and fairly applied, in practice modification and innovation was required. These included a peculiar and messy application of English transportation law and the establishment of extra-penal settlements, as well as the assumption of vast responsibilities and powers by magistrates whose administration of justice and convict discipline was at times highly informal, chaotic and brutal.

This chapter has also considered some of the developing pressures for reform and formalisation which were, however, stalled by resistance to the

89 Jury Trials Act, 4 Will. 4 No. 12, 23 August 1833.

90 Supreme Court Sydney, Returns of Prisoners Tried and Sentenced, 1838–1841, SANSW X43.

91 Act to Make Further Regulation with Respect to Trial by Jury in Criminal Issues, 3 Vic. No. 11, 20 September 1839.

92 Act to Regulate Trial by Jury, 4 Vic. No. 33, 20 November 1840, 5 November 1840.

use of civilian juries in the superior court and generated immense confusion and crises throughout the system. Although there was a broad shift towards the Anglicisation of the system, the imperial and local governments remained willing to deviate from metropolitan law and were slow to correct informalities and injustices. Ultimately, the end of convict transportation in New South Wales and the shift towards a carceral model in Van Diemen's Land alleviated much of this perceived pressure to adapt law to local circumstances. As is noted in the next chapter, all that remained by 1900 were unusually well-developed systems of criminal record keeping and deep fears that Australian society had crime in its genes.

26

Criminal Justice after the Convicts: A History of the Long Twentieth Century

ANDY KALADELFOS AND ALANA PIPER

Introduction

This chapter outlines the socio-legal history of Australian criminal justice in the twentieth century, a period that has received little scholarly attention compared to its colonial counterpart.[1] Our history examines the interactions between justice institutions – police, courts and prisons – and offenders on the one hand, whose liberty depended upon the day-to-day application of developing legal principles, and victims on the other, who continued to seek a justice response from a system that took little account of their interests. Using new databases and archives available through digitisation,[2] we take a socio-legal approach to the history of the criminal law, examining how social groups navigated increasingly complex criminal justice institutions. Our history places widespread institutional change and social action in longitudinal perspective, showing the vast use of criminal justice institutions, agents, laws and policies to regulate social behaviour, and their effect on social and legal understandings of crime, criminality and victimisation.

The Twentieth Century

Contemporary legal scholars such as Arlie Loughnan have rightly sought to revitalise scholarly interest in twentieth-century Australian criminal

1 Mark Finnane, 'After the Convicts: Towards a History of Imprisonment in Australia' *Australian and New Zealand Journal of Criminology* 24, no. 2 (1991): 105–17; Mark Finnane, 'The ABC of Criminology: Anita Muhl, J. V. Barry, Norval Morris and the Making of a Discipline in Australia' *British Journal of Criminology* 46, no 3 (2006): 399–422.

2 Both authors are founding members of the collaborative research team, *The Prosecution Project*, which documents the history of the Australian criminal trial, 1788–1960. Mark Finnane, Andy Kaladelfos, Alana Piper, Yorick Smaal, Robyn Blewer, Lisa Durnian. *The Prosecution Project Database*, version 2, 2020 https://app.prosecutionproject.griffith.edu.au/, accessed 2 December 2021.

law. Far from a period that merely 'consolidated' the grand legal changes of the past two centuries – such as the development of the adversarial criminal trial – the twentieth century defined legal and social constructions of individuals and their relationship to the state.[3] Specifically, Loughnan shows that notions of criminal responsibility – a major theoretical foundation of the criminal law – developed in Australia in the mid-twentieth century. From a doctrinal, legal perspective, this period gave birth to Australian criminal law as a legal practice and a jurisprudential tradition distinct from the British, in which the origins of modern ideas about criminal responsibility and criminalisation is typically traced back to the nineteenth century.[4]

The development of Australian legal traditions occurred side by side with growing statutory apparatus and an expanding criminal court system. From the late nineteenth century onwards, each state adopted an amalgamated criminal law statute or a criminal code that streamlined dozens of previous acts into a single document.[5] Many states debated the introduction of a criminal code, and those that adopted one implemented the code created by Queensland's Justice Samuel Griffith with minor state-based modifications. The turn of the twentieth century witnessed the development, in the High Court of Australia, of a national appellate court system; and the remits of state appellate courts were expanded to hear, for the first time, appeals on matters of fact (New South Wales, 1912; Queensland, 1913; Victoria, 1914; South Australia, 1924; Tasmania, 1924; Western Australia, 1935).[6] All states introduced specialist courts in the early twentieth century to complement the existing three tiers that operated in most jurisdictions: magistrates courts (formerly petty sessions), district courts (formerly Quarter Sessions) and Supreme Courts – the last two hearing indictable offences. Between 1895 and 1907, influenced by international reforms in child protection, Children's Courts appeared in all states, some having power to try offences committed

3 Arlie Loughnan, *Self, Others and the State: Relations of Criminal Responsibility* (Cambridge: Cambridge University Press, 2020).

4 Nicola Lacey, *In Search of Criminal Responsibility: Ideas, Interests, and Institutions* (Oxford: Oxford University Press, 2016); Lindsay Farmer, *Making the Modern Criminal Law: Criminalization and Civil Order* (Oxford: Oxford University Press, 2016).

5 Criminal Law Act 1876 (SA); Criminal Law Amendment Act 1883 (NSW); Crimes Act 1890 (Vic); Criminal Code Act 1899 (Qld); Criminal Code Act 1902 (WA); Criminal Code Act 1924 (Tas).

6 Criminal Appeal Act 1912 (NSW); Criminal Code Amendment Act 1913 (Qld); Criminal Appeal Act 1914 (Vic); Criminal Appeals Act 1924 (SA); Criminal Code Act 1924 (Tas); Supreme Court Act 1935 (WA).

by and against children.[7] In Western Australia, the Court of Native Affairs sat from 1936 to 1954 hearing offences between Indigenous people.[8]

Histories of the twentieth century emphasise the centrality of institution-building to the creation of Australia's modern vision of itself.[9] Like the criminal law, criminal justice institutions were not merely 'consolidated' but used to bring to fruition the state's vision for a regulated population. State-based policing and prosecution became the chief means to regulate groups who were considered socially undesirable on the basis of their social status, criminal status, age or racial background. Child protection and immigration regulations were just two areas that relied upon the criminal law in the twentieth century to enact their power, using policing and prosecution of juveniles, and regulatory offences to control groups perceived by society as being problematic independent of the particular offences of which they were convicted.

Criminal justice infrastructure, first designed for use in a nineteenth-century penal colony, was strengthened in the twentieth. In the nineteenth century, criminal justice institutions, such as the mounted police and paramilitary forces, had played the dominant role in mass killing of Indigenous people across the continent.[10] By the twentieth century the criminal law was a constant companion to dispossession, increasingly used to regulate relations between Aboriginal people in frontier areas and to bring Indigenous people under the control and regulation of the British legal system.[11] Colonial technologies of convict identification and management were equally important, ensuring that criminal identification and extensive documentation of criminal history became pillars of twentieth-century policing.

In twentieth-century Australia, criminal justice and criminal law were enmeshed in many major areas of state policy, including education, labour,

7 Chris Cunneen and Rob White, *Juvenile Justice: Youth and Crime in Australia* (Melbourne: Oxford University Press, 2007).

8 Native Administration Act 1936 (WA).

9 Stuart Macintyre, *Australia's Boldest Experiment: War and Reconstruction in the 1940s* (Sydney: NewSouth Publishing, 2005); Judith Allen, *Sex and Secrets: Crimes Involving Australian Women since 1880* (Melbourne: Oxford University Press, 1990); Stephen Garton, *Out of Luck: Poor Australian and Social Welfare, 1788–1988* (Sydney: Allen and Unwin, 1990); Dorothy Scott and Shurlee Swain, *Confronting Cruelty: Historical Perspectives on Child Abuse* (Carlton: Melbourne University Press, 2002); Mark Finnane, *Punishment in Australian Society* (Melbourne: Oxford University Press, 1997).

10 Lyndall Ryan et al., 'Preliminary Findings: Colonial Frontier Massacres, 1788–1930' https://c21ch.newcastle.edu.au/colonialmassacres/introduction.php#findings, accessed 2 December 2021.

11 Heather Douglas and Mark Finnane, *Indigenous Crime and Settler Law: White Sovereignty after Empire* (Basingstoke: Palgrave Macmillan, 2012).

immigration, the welfare state and 'protection' of Indigenous people. These policies were developed through overlapping systems of regulation in what the American sociologist, David Garland, famously characterised as the 'penal-welfare' state.[12] Large-scale institutional, governmental, economic, social and cultural systems formulated and responded to the regulatory desires of national and state governments. Overall, the twentieth century was a period of tremendous change in criminal justice institutions and in legal practice; but the pace of change was often slow, unfolding incrementally and in different ways in the various states.

Defining the Criminal

Defining what constitutes a crime and who are considered criminals are core tasks of the criminal law. Public conceptions and theories shifted in the course of the twentieth century, as the result of growing focus on 'criminality' as a definable, and therefore manageable, identity. Theories of criminality were posited by various professional bodies engaged in the criminal justice process: police, penologists, sociologists, welfare administrators, doctors and others. But in some respects, there were overarching continuities with nineteenth-century views. Firstly, offending was not considered synonymous with criminality in the public mind; that is, the public drinker or reckless driver, or even the first-time serious offender, was not considered a 'criminal' in the same way as the thief or repeat offender.[13] Secondly, the 'criminal' was typically perceived to be an individual who belonged to a larger subculture in which such offending was normalised. In the nineteenth century, this was termed the 'criminal class'; in the twentieth century, other descriptors developed, such as underworld, underclass, wasters, social residuum or the 'bludging class'.[14] Crime continued to be considered not just something people do, but a statement about who they are. Such an understanding continues to severely impact individuals' abilities to move out of the criminal justice system once brought within its remit.

Nineteenth-century views continued to influence the concerns that twentieth-century administrators had about national criminality. Although

12 David Garland, *The Culture of Control: Crime and Social Order in Contemporary Society* (Oxford: Oxford University Press, 2002).

13 Alana Piper, 'Digital Crowdsourcing and Public Understandings of the Past: Citizen Historians Meet Criminal Characters' *History Australia* 17, no. 3 (2020).

14 Chris McConville, 'From "Criminal Class" to "Underworld"', in Graeme Davison, David Dunstan and Chris McConville (eds) *The Outcasts of Melbourne: Essays in Social History* (Sydney: Allen & Unwin, 1985), 69–90.

penal transportation to Australia had ended in 1868, the effect on the growing populace of bringing approximately 164,000 convicts to the colonies worried policymakers into the twentieth century. Theories about those 'born' criminal, touted by international theorists such as Cesare Lombroso, proved influential in Australia. Indeed, Lombroso thought the Australian criminal type was worthy of study, writing to prison authorities at the turn of the century requesting photographs of unique national types such as the 'bushranger' and the 'larrikin' (an Australian term meaning a member of a youthful, urban gang).[15] Populist eugenic theories of crime continued to appear in Australian discourse until the mid-twentieth century and influenced debates in criminal justice policy about classifying dangerous criminals and imposing punishments such as segregation, castration or sterilisation.[16]

Simultaneously, biological views about crime jostled with more popular environmentalist discourses, among Australian prison authorities, that stressed offenders' upbringings.[17] Captain Frederick Neitenstein, the Comptroller General of NSW Prisons, argued that the 'pest' of the Australian larrikin would not be reduced without targeted efforts to change the environment, behaviour and values of young men: 'larrikinism is a product of defective social conditions', he explained, 'chiefly brought about by the neglect of parents to rear their children properly'.[18] Neitenstein thought criminality was less inevitable than did Lombroso and his followers, but his solutions were just as punitive. He advocated strict disciplinary rehabilitation and training for young offenders, such as military service. Neitenstein had been an administrator of NSW juvenile justice and, so, in his view, criminal justice went hand-in-hand with so-called child protection. He felt that the state would best ensure that poor children would become diligent workers by melding the child protection and punishment systems.

Throughout the twentieth century, allegations of increases in crime, more often than not fuelled by sensationalism or political purposes, were rebutted by crime statistics. In 1906, for example, statistician Timothy Coghlan rejected claims that Australia's education system was leading to more

15 Amanda Kaladelfos, *Crime and Outrage: Sexual Villains and Sexual Violence in New South Wales, 1870–1930* (PhD thesis, University of Sydney, 2010).
16 Emily Wilson, *Prevention Is Better Than Cure: Eugenics in Queensland 1900–1950* (North Melbourne: Australian Scholarly Publishing, 2010).
17 Stephen Garton, 'Frederick William Neitenstein: Juvenile Reformatory and Prison Reform in New South Wales, 1878–1909' *Journal of Royal Australian Historical Society* 75, no. 1 (June 1989): 51–64.
18 'The Sydney Larrikin', *Evening News*, 8 January 1908, 6.

crime, stating that the figures showed that the 'Australian native-born are far less driven to crime' than those born elsewhere. Here Coghlan was referring to white native-born people, implicitly refuting the convict legacy. Further into the twentieth century, against the backdrop of the White Australia policy, concern about crime focused not on the effect of convict origins, but on the influx of immigrants of different racial backgrounds and cultural beliefs. During the mass immigration after World War II, politicians and the press fuelled investigations into the criminal propensity of immigrants, despite wide-ranging statistical evidence, collated by police and the immigration department, that the alleged propensity had little basis in fact.[19] Unspoken in any of these twentieth-century debates over national criminality was the impact of settler and state-led violence towards Indigenous people that itself continued well into the twentieth century alongside nation-wide child removal policies. Indeed, criminal justice institutions and child protection systems themselves were complicit in violence towards Indigenous people.

Policing Crime

In the twentieth century, the day-to-day work of the police and courts continued to be dominated by traditional crime categories. Peter King's observation that property crime lies at the heart of the criminal law's workings holds true in Australian higher courts.[20] In Australia, rates of theft prosecutions went up and down with social and economic pressures, increasing at times of social disruption. The gold rush in the nineteenth century and the 1890s depression saw very high rates of theft prosecutions.[21] Similarly, after World War I, prosecutions for theft rose again, constituting 81 per cent of the cases that came before the courts during the Great Depression.[22] Prosecutions for serious property offences, such as breaking and entering, rose from a quarter of prosecutions at the turn of the century to almost half by the 1950s. These increases were likely spurred, in part, by advances in policing technologies such as fingerprinting, as well as increased rates of

19 Andy Kaladelfos and Mark Finnane, 'Immigration and Criminality: Australia's Post-War Inquiries' *Australian Journal of Politics and History* 64, no. 1 (2018): 48–64.

20 Peter King, *Crime and Law in England, 1750–1840: Remaking Justice from the Margins* (Cambridge: Cambridge University Press, 2006).

21 Alana Piper and Lisa Durnian, 'Theft on Trial: Prosecution, Conviction and Sentencing Patterns in Colonial Victoria and Western Australia' *Australian and New Zealand Journal of Criminology* 50, no. 1 (2017): 5–22.

22 Prosecution Project Data, *Victorian Supreme Court Register 1900–1960*.

reporting resulting from the rise of burglary insurance.[23] The lower courts remained dominated by minor offences usually resulting in fines, but the character of those offences changed greatly across the century. Public drunkenness preponderated lower courts at the start of the century and traffic offences at its close, following the advent of the motor car and associated regulation.[24] The temptations and dangers presented by motor vehicles led to new understandings of traditional theft and homicide, as well as a widening array of traffic offences such as speeding and driving under the influence of alcohol.[25]

Changing social attitudes likewise influenced the types of crime that received public and official attention, leading to the creation of new offence categories and the disappearance of others. Studies of the rise of gang activity during the interwar period have often focused on the social history of infamous figures, like Squizzy Taylor and Kate Leigh, who held sway over teeming criminal underworlds in Melbourne and Sydney.[26] However, such gangs also had a deep impact on criminal law, spawning new offences such as criminal consorting, and new institutions including the increased regulation of firearms and drugs, and the development of the vice squad in urban policing.[27] Responses to interpersonal violence, particularly sexual assault and domestic violence, varied in their intensity across the century. Although domestic violence is frequently referred to as an issue that has long been 'silenced', concern about violence within the home periodically attracted the attention of police, courts and the media across the twentieth century. World War I produced concerns that the violence men had experienced during wartime would be translated into violence within the family home.[28] Child

23 Eloise Moss, 'Burglary Insurance and the Culture of Fear in Britain, 1889–1939' *The Historical Journal* 54, no. 4 (2011): 1039–64.

24 Satyanshu K. Mukherjee, Evelyn N. Jacobsen and John R. Walker, *Source Book of Australian Criminal and Social Statistics 1804–1988* (Canberra: Australian Institute of Criminology, 1989).

25 Graeme Davison and Sheryl Yelland, *Car Wars: How the Car Won Our Hearts and Conquered Our Cities* (Crows Nest: Allen & Unwin, 2004); Kerry King, *A Lesser Species of Homicide: Drivers, Death and the Law* (Crawley, WA: UWA Publishing, 2020).

26 Larry Writer, *Razor: A True Story of Slashers, Gangsters, Prostitutes and Sly Grog* (Sydney: Pan, 2002, 2nd edition); Leigh Straw, *The Worst Woman in Sydney: The Life and Crimes of Kate Leigh* (Sydney: NewSouth, 2016).

27 Mark Finnane, 'Gun Control in a Strong State: The Legal Regulation of Firearms in Australia' *Law & History* 1, no. 1 (2014): 56–76; Alfred W. McCoy, *Drug Traffic: Narcotics and Organized Crime in Australia* (Sydney: Harper & Row 1980); Arlie Loughnan, 'Consorting, Then and Now: Changing Regulations of Responsibility for Crime' *University of Western Australia Law Review* 45, no. 2 (2019): 8–36.

28 Elizabeth Nelson, *Homefront Hostilities: The First World War and Domestic Violence* (North Melbourne: Australian Scholarly, 2014).

sexual abuse, when it came to notice of the court, was understood as a serious crime, but the vulnerabilities of victims to reputational ruin in reporting these offences limited the effectiveness of law.[29] Second-wave feminism brought increased attention to the issue of violence against women and children, including recognition of violence that had not previously been considered a criminal act, such as spousal rape, which was gradually criminalised across Australian jurisdictions from 1976 to 1994.[30] The very slow pace of modernisation of the criminal law is likewise revealed by the long retention of many so-called 'moral' offences. Among the acts only decriminalised in the last decades of the twentieth century – or in some jurisdictions the early twenty-first century – were abortion, sex work, fortune-telling and sex between men.[31]

While the broad crime categories may have remained the same, rates of reported crime fluctuated significantly across the twentieth century. For all serious indictable offences, the first decade of the twentieth century generated the highest reported crime rates of the first half of the century. Despite panics about the growth of criminal underworlds, arrests and prosecutions actually decreased through the interwar period, although it was marked with significant social disruption.[32] Prosecutions of property offences did increase during the Great Depression, and again after the mid-1950s, along with offences against the person. However, these substantial post-war increases were not uniform across all categories of crime, reflecting policing and prosecution priorities. For example, prosecutions for sexual offences against adolescent girls increased by 450 per cent throughout the 1950s while prosecutions of rape, primarily involving adult women, saw no increase. The lack of rape prosecutions reflected the continued practice of only prosecuting sexual assaults of adult women where they fitted 'real rape' myths (offences

29 Lisa Featherstone and Amanda Kaladelfos, *Sex Crimes in the Fifties* (Carlton: Melbourne University Publishing, 2016).

30 Lisa Featherstone, '"That's What Being a Woman Is For": Opposition to Marital Rape Law Reform in Late Twentieth-Century Australia' *Gender & History* 29, no. 1 (2017): 87–103.

31 Barbara Baird, 'Decriminalization and Women's Access to Abortion in Australia' *Health and Human Rights Journal* 19, no. 1 (2017): 197–208; Raelene Frances, *Selling Sex: A Hidden History of Prostitution* (Sydney: University of New South Wales Press, 2007); Alana Piper, '"A Menace and an Evil": Fortune-Telling in Australia, 1900–1918' *History Australia* 11, no. 3 (2014): 53–73; Yorick Smaal, 'Flappers and Felons: Rethinking the Criminal Law and Homosex in Interwar Australia, 1920–1939', in Sean Brady and Mark Seymour (eds), *From Sodomy Laws to Same-Sex Marriage: International Perspectives since 1989* (London: Bloomsbury Academic, 2019), 83–93.

32 Satyanshu K. Mukerjee, *Crime Trends in Twentieth-century Australia* (Sydney: Australian Institute of Criminology, 1981), 43–4.

in public, involving strangers, with physical violence) and the reticence to charge rape offences while capital punishment was still in use.[33]

The increasing use of technology and information sharing in policing was a significant twentieth-century change. These shifts built on Australia's convict origins and its wide-ranging systems of identification of criminals.[34] From the nineteenth century, instruments of policing, such as the state-based police gazettes, allowed tracking of criminals by both customs and police agencies, and over state lines, by publicising warrants for arrests accompanied by physical descriptions. Criminal conduct in the early to mid-twentieth century was increasingly monitored by professionalised policing institutions that linked with other state-run agencies such as customs, mental health, and child protection. These systems worked together to ensure the running of state and national regulatory systems, such as the Immigration Restriction Act 1901, which enacted the racialised 'White Australia Policy' and identified criminal conduct and mental 'defectiveness' as two of the exclusionary criteria for entry to the country and deportation upon serious conviction.[35]

Older technologies like the convict register systems were aided by new technologies in tracking individuals. Photographing offenders had become routine by the 1920s, and a visual image of the offender was regularly included alongside character information about them in police reports. Fingerprint records were likewise gradually added to these files. State fingerprint bureaus were introduced across Australia in the early 1900s, but their use in detection accelerated when a centralised fingerprint bureau was established in Sydney in 1941. This development greatly increased the ability of police to track repeat offenders within and beyond jurisdictional boundaries.[36]

By the interwar period, criminal identification systems, such as the police gazettes, had advanced to include 'modus operandi' reports, in line with modern thinking about criminal propensity and character. These reports included short narrations of a criminal's past and their fit within medico-legal

33 Featherstone and Kaladelfos, *Sex Crimes*.

34 Mark Finnane, 'Controlling the "alien" in Mid-twentieth-century Australia: The Origins and Fate of a Policing Role' *Policing and Society: An International Journal of Research and Policy* 19, no. 4 (2009): 442–67.

35 Mark Finnane and Andy Kaladelfos, 'Australia's Long History of Immigration, Policing and the Criminal Law', in Peter Billings (ed.), *Crimmigration in Australia: Law, Politics and Society* (Singapore: Springer, 2019), 19–37; Glenn Nicholls, *Deported: A History of Forced Departures from Australia* (Sydney: UNSW Press, 2007).

36 Dean Wilson and Mark Finnane, 'From Sleuths and Technicians? Changing Images of the Detective in Victoria', in Clive Emsley and Haia Shpayer-Makov (eds), *Police Detectives in History, 1750–1950* (Aldershot: Ashgate, 2006), 135–56.

and socio-legal determinations of the officers writing them. These reports were developed alongside the professionalisation of detection in the Criminal Investigation Branches around the country. A 1938 police gazette, for example, reported on the criminal history of prisoner number 131. Including a full-length and two facial photographs, the police recorded Leslie Thomas Tarrant's three aliases, place of birth, height and details on his physical appearance. Accompanying these personal details was a brief criminal history of his offences and movement across state borders between Queensland and New South Wales. The report then made detailed comments on his criminal behaviour: he was a 'cat burglar', entering homes at night when women were alone. He was a 'daring and fearless criminal', the gazette pronounced, who frequented the city with other known criminal associates, themselves linked by police report.[37] Such classification not only affected policing but also filtered into attitudes to court testimony, sentencing outcomes and prison classifications of offenders by their degrees of dangerousness.[38] The production of police and character reports was part of the larger shift from interest in the facts of a crime to a focus on criminals and their lives, and would pave the way in the mid-century for the introduction of reintegration services such as the parole board, which completed the pre- and post-conviction reports on felons that remain standard today.[39] The extraordinarily detailed documentation of the personal lives of hundreds of thousands of individual offenders demonstrates the extent and suggests the impact of modern police surveillance and intelligence gathering in Australia.

Prosecuting Offenders

The adversarial trial process described by premier British historian John Langbein as emerging in England during the eighteenth century and being cemented by the early nineteenth century arguably did not become the norm in criminal trials in Australia *or* England until the twentieth century.[40] While the heart of the adversarial trial was a confrontation between two qualified

37 NSW Police, *NSW Police Gazette: NSW Police Criminal Register*, '131. Leslie Thomas Tarrant', 28 March 1938.
38 John Pratt, 'Governing the Dangerous: An Historical Overview of Dangerous Offender Legislation' *Social and Legal Studies* 5 (1996): 21–36.
39 Alana Jayne Piper, 'To Judge a Thief: How the Background of Thieves became Central to Dispensing Justice, Western Australia, 1921–1951' *Law & History* 4 (2017): 113–44; Featherstone and Kaladelfos, *Sex Crimes*.
40 John Langbein, *The Origins of Adversary Criminal Trial* (Oxford: Oxford University Press, 2003).

legal opponents, until the late nineteenth century almost half of the defendants before Victoria's Supreme Court were undefended at trial.[41] During the nineteenth century, public provision of defence counsel had only been extended to those charged with capital crimes or Indigenous defendants; but from the early twentieth century, legislation began to emerge enabling impoverished criminal defendants to be assigned defence counsel.[42] However, by the time modern legal aid structures began to emerge in the 1960s, at least one-third of Victoria's Supreme Court defendants remained unrepresented. Prosecution Project data shows that this had significant impacts on trial outcomes, with represented defendants three times more likely to be acquitted than unrepresented defendants. If sentenced, represented defendants were more likely to receive non-custodial sentences or shorter gaol terms.[43] While the High Court in *Dietrich v The Queen* (1992), expressed the view that legal representation in criminal cases was desirable to ensure a fair trial, the majority of the bench ultimately determined that the right to a fair trial did not equate to a right to counsel at the public expense.[44]

In the absence of defence counsel, twentieth-century accused persons had to defend themselves as best they could. Their ability to do so was profoundly impacted by a change implemented at the turn of the twentieth century in most Australian jurisdictions, allowing an accused person (or their spouse) to give sworn testimony in their own defence. In 1882, South Australia had become the first jurisdiction in the British Empire to allow defendants to give testimony, and New South Wales, Victoria and Queensland followed suit a decade later, all well ahead of England's introduction of such legislation in 1898.[45] Prior to this, an accused could only make a statement at the end of their trial, commonly called a 'dock statement', that could not be cross-examined by the prosecution. The accused's words had been considered inadmissible as sworn testimony on the ground that the temptation to

41 Alana Piper and Mark Finnane, 'Access to Legal Representation by Criminal Defendants in Victoria, 1861–1961' *University of New South Wales Law Journal* 40, no. 2 (2017): 638–63.

42 Judiciary Act 1903 (Cth); Poor Prisoners Defence Act 1907 (NSW); Poor Prisoners Defence Act 1907 (Qld); Poor Prisoners Defence Act 1916 (Vic); Criminal Code Act 1924 (Tas); Poor Persons Legal Assistance Act 1925 (SA); Poor Persons Legal Assistance Act 1928 (WA).

43 Alana Piper and Mark Finnane, 'Defending the Accused: The Impact of Legal Representation on Criminal Trial Outcomes in Victoria, Australia 1861–1961' *Journal of Legal History* 38, no. 1 (2017): 27–53.

44 *Dietrich v The Queen* (1992) 177 CLR 292, 298.

45 Accused Persons Evidence Act 1882 (SA); Criminal Law and Evidence Amendment Act 1891 (NSW); Crimes Act 1891 (Vic); Criminal Law Amendment Act 1892 (Qld); Criminal Evidence Act 1899 (WA); Evidence Act 1910 (Tas).

perjury would be too great. This meant that their self-defence could not legally be given the same weight by the jury as other evidence.[46] Initially, the accused retained the right to make an unsworn statement, but this right was abolished in some Australian jurisdictions in the second half of the twentieth century purportedly in the interest of victims. This outcome is a double-edged sword for the accused – juries might attach a negative inference to an accused not testifying (despite judicial orders not to do so), but undefended, uneducated or vulnerable accused persons may damage themselves under cross-examination. The loss of the unsworn statement has been shown to have been to the disadvantage of Indigenous defendants in particular.[47]

The composition of juries and their role in the criminal justice process also changed dramatically across the twentieth century. At the start of the century, eligibility for jury service in Australia was still based on property qualifications; but starting with Queensland in 1923 and ending with Tasmania in 1957, eligibility for normal jury service was extended to all men on electoral rolls. However, 'special juries' comprised of individuals with greater wealth or from particular educational or occupational backgrounds, most often used in fraud cases or cases where previous juries had failed to reach a verdict, were only gradually abolished, again starting with Queensland in 1923 and ending with Tasmania in 1991.[48] Women campaigned for the right to serve on juries, asserting *inter alia* that women would bring a special understanding to particular types of criminal offences, and be better than men at detecting when female witnesses or defendants were lying. Women slowly started serving on juries, initially through 'opt-in' systems: their inclusion commenced in Queensland in 1923 and was complete in 1965 when they became eligible in South Australia.[49] Aboriginal people were not eligible for jury service until the 1960s. The Australian Law Reform Commission has found that Aboriginal representation on juries today remains limited, even in regions where they comprise a significant proportion of the population.[50]

46 Greg Taylor, *A Great and Glorious Reformation: Six Early South Australian Legal Innovations* (Kent Town: Wakefield Press, 2005).
47 David Brown, 'Silencing the Court: The Abolition of the Dock Statement in New South Wales' *Current Issues in Criminal Justice* 6, no. 1 (1994): 158–62.
48 Alana Piper, 'The Special Jury in Australia' *Criminal Law Journal* 39, no. 4 (2015): 218–20.
49 Sonia Walker, 'Battle-Axes and Sticky-Beaks: Women and Jury Service in Western Australia 1898–1957' *Murdoch University Electronic Journal of Law* 11, no. 4 (2004): 1–33; Kelly Staunton, *The Jury in Theory and in Practice: Serious Crime Trial Decisions, Australia, 1901–1956* (Honours thesis, Griffith University, 2016), 26–7.
50 Australian Law Reform Commission, 'Aborigines and Juries'. Published 18 August 2010, www.alrc.gov.au/publication/recognition-of-aboriginal-customary-

The changing class, gender and racial compositions of twentieth-century juries likely had impacts on the decisions they made about the defendants brought before them. Across the twentieth century, concerns were expressed about the extent to which criminal trial juries followed directives to 'deal with the evidence, and not with the person'.[51] As in the nineteenth century, women defendants were less likely to be convicted by juries, especially of certain types of offences.[52] For instance, given the social mores of the period, single women accused of murder or manslaughter of their infant children were often treated sympathetically by both juries and the press.[53] Indigenous defendants, on the other hand, were disproportionately convicted of the most serious offences, while their non-Indigenous counterparts were found guilty of lesser offences.[54] In the wake of World War I, the 'veteran defendant' emerged as another category that often held a special status in the courts, either because their military service was deemed to indicate that their crimes were out-of-character or because the traumas of war were accepted as having led to some form of diminished capacity.[55] Meanwhile, co-offenders tried together, a category of accused whose appearances increased across the twentieth century, often suffered from a prejudicial 'guilt by association' effect in the minds of juries during joint trials, leading to convictions irrespective of the weight of evidence against each individual. Prosecution Project data suggests, controlling for other factors, that during the twentieth century, being tried with others was more likely to result in a conviction than being tried alone.[56] This factor also significantly affected Indigenous defendants who, in homicide cases, were far more likely than non-Indigenous counterparts to be facing charges committed in company.

laws-alrc-report-31/23-general-issues-of-evidence-and-procedure/aborigines-and-juries / accessed 1 May 2020.

51 D. G. O'Donnell, 'Reminiscences of a Victorian Detective' *Gisborne Gazette*, 24 October 1924, 8.

52 Alana Piper, 'Victimization Narratives and Courtroom Sexual Politics: Prosecuting Male Burglars and Female Pickpockets in Melbourne, 1860–1921' *Journal of Social History* 51, no. 4 (2018): 760–83.

53 Nicola Goc, *Women, Infanticide and the Press 1822–1922: News Narratives from England and Australia* (Farnham: Ashgate, 2013).

54 Mark Finnane and Andy Kaladelfos, 'Race and Justice in an Australian Court: Prosecuting Homicide in Western Australia, 1834–1954' *Australian Historical Studies* 47, no. 3 (2016): 443–61.

55 Arlie Loughnan, '"Society Owes Them Much": Veteran Defendants and Criminal Responsibility in Australia in the Twentieth Century' *Critical Analysis of Law* 2, no. 1 (2015): 106–34.

56 Alana Piper and Lauren Vogel, 'Co-Offenders before the Court: The Joinder Effect in Victoria, 1861–1961' *Law & History* 5 (2018): 111–36.

The twentieth century saw the rapid decline of jury trials as the most common mode of dispensing justice. By the 1990s, juries were used in no more than 1 per cent of criminal cases.[57] For most of the twentieth century, minor infringements heard in the magistrate's courts – a summary jurisdiction with no jury – constituted the majority of the prosecuted offences. These included 'petty' crimes such as traffic offences, gambling offences, and child welfare breaches and offences against good order, such as drunkenness, vagrancy, offensive behaviour and other minor infringements, which led to fines or short periods of incarceration. Together, public order and other petty offences made up more than 85 per cent of twentieth-century recorded crime. A dramatic rise in overall criminal prosecutions from the mid-1950s onwards was propelled by petty offences, especially driving and associated regulatory offences.[58]

The decline of jury trials was also driven by the rise of guilty pleas across all court jurisdictional levels. In the late nineteenth century, guilty pleas accounted for no more than about 15 per cent of indicted defendants. The rate of guilty pleas began to rise during the twentieth century, increasing dramatically in the 1940s and reaching more than 60 or 70 per cent of higher court charges in the 1960s. Today around three out of four defendants charged with indictable offences plead guilty. The increase of property offences as a proportion of crimes mainly drove this change, although other factors were influential, including changes in policing techniques, sentencing changes and the increased presence of defence lawyers (encouraging plea bargaining approaches).[59] This rising guilty-plea rate was necessary for the courts to continue functioning because, while the proportion of criminal cases disposed of through jury trials declined, the length and complexity of trials rapidly increased across the twentieth century. The length of trials may have also fuelled defendants' sense of helplessness and their acceptance of plea bargain scenarios.[60]

57 Michael Chesterman, 'Criminal Trial Juries in Australia: From Penal Colonies to a Federal Democracy' *Law and Contemporary Problems* 62, no. 2 (1999): 69–102.

58 Satyanshu. K. Mukherjee, Evelyn Jacobson, John Walker and R. W. Fitzgerald, *Crime Trends in Twentieth-century Australia* (Sydney: Allen & Unwin, 1981).

59 Lisa Durnian, *The Rise of the Guilty Plea in Australian Supreme Courts: A History* (PhD thesis, Griffith University, 2018).

60 Mark Finnane and Alana Piper, 'The Prosecution Project: Understanding the Changing Criminal Trial through Digital Tools' *Law and History Review* 34, no. 4 (2016): 873–91; Sarah Zydervelt, Rachel Zajac, Andy Kaladelfos and Nina Westera, 'Lawyers' Strategies for Cross-examining Rape Complainants: Have We Moved beyond the 1950s?' *British Journal of Criminology* 57 (2017): 551–69.

The growing complexity of the trial process in the twentieth century was testament to the establishment of the adversarial trial process as the norm, which transformed the courtroom into a less accessible space dominated by contestations, over complex precedents and evidentiary rules, between warring legal professionals. Although national legal scholarship on criminal law and procedure was limited until the mid-twentieth century, legal texts were increasing in their circulation within and across the Australian colonies. Australian lawyers founded the *Australian Law Journal* in 1927, which included judgments, legal opinion and commentary on issues of national and international importance. Smaller specialist journals, such as those on medico-legal studies, were founded in the 1930s.

The growing use of legal practice manuals and printed law reports by practitioners and law-makers to track Australian criminal law developments also coincided with significant changes to media reporting about criminal trials. In the late nineteenth century, Australian newspapers, such as the *Sydney Morning Herald* and the *Argus*, printed sessional law reports that covered the metropolitan, and most of the circuit, court hearings. Even at the start of the twentieth century, these major broadsheets often employed junior barristers as their legal correspondents, with criminal law reports reading almost as transcripts of trial proceedings.[61] However, by the interwar period, media reporting of crime grew more sensationalist and less concerned with the minute details of the trials. The richest reports on criminal cases were often found in cheaper papers, such as the *Herald Sun* and the *Truth*, which were less concerned than the broadsheet law reports with evidentiary and legal matters, and more with whatever scandalous details the trials revealed about the characters of both offenders and victims. During the late twentieth century, journalistic ethics around crime reporting became more established and circumspect; but even in the 1950s it was not uncommon for news reports to include the names of victims and offenders in cases where today these names would be suppressed. In his 1935 memoir, Queensland police officer Michael O'Sullivan lambasted the 'mischief done by newspapers' that reproduced photographs of witnesses, especially female witnesses.[62] As the twentieth century went on, this focus on salacious details rather than legal questions raised in proceedings led to a *decline* compared with a century earlier, in legal literacy and knowledge of the criminal law among ordinary people.

61 P. A. Jacobs, *A Lawyer Tells* (Melbourne: F. W. Cheshire, 1949).
62 Michael O'Sullivan, *Cameos of Crime* (Brisbane: Jackson & O'Sullivan, 1935).

Punishing Offenders

As with the prosecutorial system, significant changes in the processes for punishing offenders, commenced in the nineteenth century, did not reach their full resolution until the twentieth century. In the nineteenth century, the punishment regime of Australia, as in other jurisdictions, was transformed from one focused on disciplining the body to one focused on disciplining and reforming the mind.[63] Settler invasion of Australia by the British in the late eighteenth and early nineteenth centuries brought the continent under the jurisdiction of the 'Bloody Code' that prescribed the death penalty for over 200 offences. The major alternative penalty in England was transportation to the Australian colonies; those prosecuted within the Australian colonies faced sentencing to an even worse colony. The elimination of transportation, the gradual narrowing of the range of offences liable to capital punishment and its increasing disuse, meant that, by the end of the nineteenth century, imprisonment had become the default punishment in both England and the Australian colonies.

However, it would not be until the late twentieth century that 'bloody' forms of punishment were done away with entirely. Until the mid-twentieth century, several Australian jurisdictions retained the death penalty for more crimes than in England.[64] Rape was not removed as a capital crime in New South Wales until 1955, although it had not attracted the death penalty in England since 1841. Conversely, other jurisdictions raced ahead of reforms overseas: in 1922, Queensland became the first place in the British Empire to completely abolish the use of capital punishment. The other Australian jurisdictions followed suit some decades later. By 1985, capital punishment was finally abolished in relation to all crimes throughout Australia, with the last execution having taken place in Victoria in 1967. In 2010, the federal government passed legislation to prohibit its reintroduction. Corporal punishment was retained as a criminal sentence in various Australian jurisdictions until the very last decades of the century. While it had largely fallen into disuse by this point, recent investigation of prison records from Victoria suggests that whippings remained not uncommon into the 1930s and 1940s, used in particular against sexual offenders and serious property offenders.[65]

63 Michel Foucault, *Discipline and Punish: The Birth of the Prison*, translated by Alan Sheridan (New York: Vintage Books, 1995, 2nd edition).

64 Amanda Kaladelfos, 'The Politics of Punishment: Rape and the Death Penalty in Colonial Australia, 1841–1901' *History Australia* 9, no. 1 (2012): 155–75.

65 Piper, 'Digital Crowdsourcing'.

Nevertheless, a prison sentence – or a fine with the alternative of a prison sentence in the case of petty offences – was the default punishment for most indictable criminal acts by the start of twentieth century. Dissatisfaction with the ineffectiveness of prisons in reforming offenders – something that criminological studies continue to demonstrate today – led to various experiments as the century progressed. Sometimes these were aimed at the prison environment: the interwar period produced a growing number of 'prison farms' emphasising vocational training, principally in agricultural and labouring pursuits.[66] Other innovations focused on the length of sentences. Concerns that conventional gaol terms did not provide a sufficient deterrent for offenders already entwined in a criminal lifestyle, led to the introduction of indeterminate sentences under habitual offenders legislation during the first decade of the twentieth century. New South Wales led the way with the Habitual Criminals Act 1905.[67] This meant that defendants judged to be habitual offenders – based on type or number of previous offences or, in some cases, other factors such as having known criminal associates – could be imprisoned indefinitely until the authorities deemed them sufficiently reformed. Conversely, concerns that prisons themselves could foster criminal associations and corrupt individuals not committed to a criminal way of life, caused the expansion of the use of suspended sentences (first introduced in the Australian colonies in the 1880s)[68] from the 1920s onwards.[69] The conditions of suspended sentences were often personalised to the offender, with judges specifying that they refrain from drinking, avoid the company of particular associates or be monitored by the watchful eyes of parents or charitable organisations such as the Salvation Army.

This widening array of punishments affected the processes of discretionary sentencing by judges, who now had to consider not just the length of gaol term appropriate for the defendant before them, but whether alternative punishments or additional conditions might be suitable.[70] Judges considered

66 Finnane, *Punishment in Australian Society*.

67 Habitual Criminals Act 1905 (NSW); Indeterminate Sentences Act 1907 (Vic); Habitual Criminals Amendment Act 1907 (SA); The Habitual Criminals and Offenders Act 1907 (Tas); Criminal Code Act Compilation Act 1913 (WA); Criminal Code Amendment Act 1914 (Qld).

68 Offenders Probation Act 1886 (Qld); Offenders Probation Act 1887 (SA); Crimes Act 1890 (Vic); Probation of First Offenders Act 1892 (WA); First Offenders Probation Act 1894 (NSW); The First Offenders Probation Act 1898 (Tas).

69 Evan Smith, 'Modern Diversion or Colonial Hangover? The History and Development of Suspended Sentences in South Australia' *Australia and New Zealand Journal of Criminology* 49, no. 2 (2016): 240–57.

70 Piper, 'To Judge a Thief'.

a variety of factors in individualising a sentence to an offender. They increasingly heeded juries' recommendations for mercy on account of factors personal to the offender, such as 'youth' or 'provocation'. Such a move towards individualised sentencing also changed the nature of pleas for mitigation. In the nineteenth century, such pleas were made *after* the trial process by petitioning the Executive Council for mercy in capital cases; but by the twentieth century mitigating pleas were made *during* sentencing hearings for all types of offences.

The twentieth century thus witnessed an even greater interest by the police, the courts and prisons in the backgrounds of offenders. Police were set to work not just investigating the offence but profiling the offender, partly in order to prepare detailed character reports, for judges to consider at sentencing, that included interviews with the offender's family, neighbours, employers and co-workers, as well as the offender themselves. Psychological criminal profiling was becoming common internationally, especially in the United States, but the character reports produced by Australian police rarely drew upon psychological claims, instead taking a welfare approach that used social and environmental conceptions of crime. Such pre-sentencing reports had become a standard part of trial briefs by the 1950s and would often be accompanied by a statement from the accused and reports from any other government departments that had had contact with the offender.[71] By the 1950s, to inform sentencing, judges could also order a pre-sentencing mental health screening of convicted defendants by state-appointed psychologists.[72] Moreover, consideration of whether a sentence was appropriate for a particular offender did not always cease after the sentencing hearing. Indeed, by the 1940s and 1950s appeals on sentence were commonly reported and formed a great volume of the appeal hearings in the second half of the twentieth century; later, this led to attempts to streamline sentencing through the introduction of statutory sentencing guidelines, which happened in the 1990s. Building upon the principles of aftercare and attention to individual circumstances of prisoners, parole offices were established around the country in the 1950s and 1960s.

Contest over whether criminal behaviour was reformable framed much of the popular, governmental and intellectual discussion of punishment in the first half of the twentieth century. The push, by some psychologists and progressive judges, for punishment solutions favouring rehabilitation, was criticised by victim advocates, politicians and

71 Ibid. 72 Featherstone and Kaladelfos, *Sex Crimes*.

conservative judges.[73] Rehabilitation was generally not favoured by public advocates or politicians, which helps to explain the long retention of harsher penalties such as corporal and capital punishment.[74] Medical professionals considered the law an inadequate device to deal with the crime problem, which they felt was often a result of a mental disability. Professionals, such as the editors of the prestigious *Medical Journal of Australia*, argued in the interwar period that doctors rather than judges should be in charge of determining why an offence was committed and what should happen to criminals deemed 'mentally defective', pushing for medical rather than legal panels to decide responsibility and punishment.[75] Calls for medical control gained very little traction in Australian police work and the court system, which preferred a social intelligence gathering model to psychological assessment; and judges increasingly expressed wariness about the inconsistency in scientific assessments of criminality. Within prisons and corrections institutions, however, psychology, psychiatry and medicalisation were more influential. Prisons provided not only the capacity to classify and stream detainees according to the latest trends in criminological assessments, but also large numbers of captive persons – ideal subjects for new psychometric testing and research.[76]

The Disappearing Victim?

Occurring in parallel to the adversarial trial system's narrowing focus on criminal identities and their life histories was the disappearance of the formal role of the victim in court proceedings. The twentieth century saw the development of a powerful system of state-led and funded criminal prosecution that was ostensibly governed by principles of impartiality and transparency. Whereas, in the eighteenth century, victims led criminal prosecutions, by the twentieth century a bureaucrat decided whether and how to prosecute a case. While the victim remained a witness, often the primary witness, they had no formal role in proceedings by the twentieth century.

73 Stephen Garton, 'Rise of Therapeutic State: Psychiatry and the System of Criminal Jurisdiction in New South Wales, 1890–1940' *Australian Journal of Politics and History* 32, 3 (1986): 378–88; Kaladelfos, *Crime and Outrage*.
74 Finnane, *Punishment in Australian Society*.
75 Editorial, 'Crime and Criminals' *Medical Journal of Australia*, 5 June 1920: 405–6.
76 See for example, the publication by Sydney prison psychologist John McGeorge, 'Sexual Assaults on Children' *Medical Science and the Law* 4, no. 4 (1964): 245–53.

Victims' lack of a formal position has often been interpreted as signalling the disappearance of victims' rights and power from the criminal justice system.[77] But throughout the twentieth century, victims continued to have a substantive and meaningful role in seeking justice. Perhaps most importantly, policing was reactive: victims' complaints formed the major source of information and initiation of crime detection. Well after the development of the adversarial trial, the criminal justice system remained largely reliant upon victim reports to initiate a police or prosecutorial response. In other words, victims in their hundreds of thousands continued to drive the twentieth-century justice system well after their removal from the formal role as prosecutor, and long before the 1970s victims' rights movements.

However, for twentieth-century victims to file a police report they had to know that an offence had been committed. Visiting courtroom public galleries and consuming newspaper trial reports was a pastime that not only developed legal knowledge of criminal processes but could assist in identifying breaches of the law. For some adult and child sexual assault complainants, the first time they realised they were the victim of a crime was when they read about other sexual assault cases in the newspapers.[78] But reporting to police and testifying at trial came with significant scrutiny and reputational risk. As noted, newspapers routinely printed the names, ages and sometimes addresses of witnesses. The Children's Courts held cases *in camera* by the mid-twentieth century. On the one hand this was a positive change to protect vulnerable children but, on the other, it also limited the transparency of the court. A range of statutory provisions later allowed presiding judges to prohibit the publication of names and details in cases of sexual offences against adults (for example, the Crimes (Amendment) Act 1955 (NSW)). Historically conceived of as a liberal step, the contemporary effects of privacy restrictions were the subject of the national #LetHerSpeak campaign, which sought to remove the 'gag laws' that silenced rape victims from publicly speaking about their experiences.[79] This was not achieved until 2020.

Once victims knew that a criminal offence had been committed, they often decided, perhaps after disclosure to their families and friends, to take the case to the police. In the case of children, victims' mothers generally examined

77 See Paul Rock, 'Victims, Prosecutors and the State in Nineteenth-century England and Wales' *Criminal Justice* 4, no. 4 (2004): 331–54; Tyrone Kirchengast, *The Victim in Criminal Law and Justice* (London: Palgrave, 2006).

78 Kaladelfos, *Crime and Outrage*, 124–5.

79 Nina Funnell, 'Let Her Speak Campaign Aims to Ensure All Victims Can Take Back Their Voices', *ABC News* (Australia), 13 August 2019 www.abc.net.au/news/2019-08-13/let-her-speak-campaign-tasmania-nt/11405050, accessed 2 December 2021.

their children for evidence of assault and called police on their children's behalf. But a system that relied almost wholly upon receiving a report of crime inevitably fails when there are systematic reasons not to report. The economic and psychological dynamics of coercive control made wives reluctant to report their husband's abuse of themselves or their children. In the absence of a working justice system, some women developed ad hoc ways to ensure familial safety, such as never leaving their children home with their husbands, or enlisting the support of other female relatives.[80] Family violence prosecutions, even when women had brought complaints to police, left them very vulnerable. The loss of a husband or breadwinner, at a time when women's wages were less than half that of men and there was no adequate welfare state, was often enough to leave families destitute. This sort of situation would change only after the 1970s.[81]

The other problem, then as now, was that female and child complainants were often not believed. Though false reports have always been few in number, police have long been wary of them, and courts are invariably suspicious of women's and children's motives in reporting offences. In the twentieth century, such beliefs led to the development of statutory and common law requirements for corroboration of three types of testimony: women's sexual assault testimonies, young children's unsworn testimonies, and the testimony of accomplices. All three groups were deemed to have personal interests in the pursuit of a prosecution and a propensity to lie. The year 1933 saw the first use of a common law charge by the Victorian police for making a false complaint.[82] This charge did not involve an offence against a woman, but one against a twenty-year-old man charged with causing public mischief by falsely reporting an assault and robbery and wasting police resources in the investigation process.[83] Even though false complaints were few and far between, a large number of cases reported to police never resulted in charge or prosecution. Records do not allow us easily to identify this 'attrition rate' over time. However, Prosecution Project data has revealed that after a charge was laid, evidentiary factors, such as a judicial

80 Andy Kaladelfos, 'Uncovering a Hidden Offence: Social and Legal Histories of Familial Sexual Abuse', in Alana Piper and Ana Stevenson (eds), *Gender Violence in Australia: Historical Perspectives* (Melbourne: Monash University Publishing, 2019).

81 Michelle Arrow, *The Seventies: The Personal, The Political and the Making of Modern Australia* (Sydney: NewSouth, 2019).

82 This charge was brought in a leading English case in 1932 (*R v Manley* (1932) 1 KB 529), although earlier iterations involved charges of perjury for making false statements.

83 Finnane et al., *Prosecution Project Database*, Trial ID266441; *The Herald*, 5 July 1933; *Kalgoorlie Miner*, 21 July 1933.

assessment of the corroborative potential of witness testimony or the withdrawal of a previous complaint, were the most significant factors in explaining attrition. Both weighed heavily on prosecutions that involved complaints made by women; and the twentieth century saw increasing withdrawals before the case went to the jury.[84]

If a case got to trial and jury verdict, victims' justice-seeking was limited by the creation of an ever-growing list of grounds to exclude witness evidence, notably the lack of corroboration.[85] In some states these included requirements that allegations be corroborated and mandatory judicial warnings to the jury about the dangers of convicting on uncorroborated evidence, alongside statutory limitation periods, which could be as little as fifteen days (Tasmania), to bring a charge to police. Women's bodies were inspected for corroborating forensic evidence; often, this produced inconsistent medical testimony about signs of violence, and women faced fierce questioning without more recent protections against being asked questions about sexual history. Women were regularly accused of promiscuity, lying and immorality for bringing sexual charges against men; puritanical moral codes sometimes also meant that male victims, robbed by sex workers, or defrauded by pretty women, were blamed for their own perceived complicity or naivety.[86] Added to this, the role of the victim was growing ever more limited as a result of the structural changes to the justice system driven by the increasing number of guilty pleas. This meant that victims – who at that stage only appeared to testify at the committal hearing and the criminal trial – were completely absent in cases that proceeded straight to sentence. In the 1980s and 1990s, significant changes to laws of corroboration, removal of judicial warnings, protection of vulnerable witnesses and victim impact statements, were introduced to address these inequities.[87]

Not only did victims themselves continue to use the law to seek justice despite these restrictions, but well-organised campaigns from women's groups throughout the twentieth century sought to change the criminal justice system. From the 1920s onwards, groups of white, predominantly middle-class women, advocated for changes to the criminal law and to

84 Andy Kaladelfos, 'Gender, Victimisation and Prosecutorial Discretion in the Attrition of Sexual Offences' *Law & History* 5, no. 2 (2018): 86–110.

85 Robyn Blewer, *Bringing Little Kiddies into Court: Child Witnesses in Australian Criminal Courts, 1900–2000* (PhD dissertation, Griffith University, 2017); Kaladelfos, 'Gender, Victimisation and Prosecutorial Discretion'.

86 Featherstone and Kaladelfos, *Sex Crimes*; Piper, 'Victimization Narratives'.

87 Patricial Easteal (ed.), *Balancing the Scales: Rape, Law Reform and Australian Culture* (Annandale: Federation Press, 1998).

criminal process. They demanded the presence of women on juries, female magistrates and specialist police for sexual assault cases, but also advocated punitive punishments such as the death penalty, sterilisation, indefinite detention or corporal punishment for offenders.[88] These groups purported to speak on behalf of victims, but their interest was primarily in social order, and they proved just as concerned about juvenile delinquency and youthful morals as they were about offences against children.[89]

The shift from this type of activism to second-wave feminist legal reforms occurred in the late 1970s and brought about major change in the way victimisation and the effect of criminal conduct were viewed.[90] Historically, 'harm' to a victim was framed in terms of physical harm to the body, financial damage, reputational damage (affecting the ability to marry, for instance, or, in the case of children, resulting in illegitimacy), or the wider social harm of commission of crime. One of the key changes brought about by liberal feminism was the shift to a focus on psychological trauma and first-person advocacy. The power of narrating abuse and its role in restorative/transformative justice processes has been one of the most significant changes for victim's rights in the twentieth century.

Conclusion

Criminal law, processes and priorities thus shifted significantly between the start of the twentieth century and its conclusion. However, this was largely the result of slow, incremental changes, seldom introduced in a uniform manner across the different state jurisdictions. The twentieth century also continued trends and approaches evident in the nineteenth century. Perhaps the most important of these was the growth of the penal-welfare state and the proliferation of interacting, overlapping regulatory institutions – at the heart of which sat the criminal justice system. These institutions had to be navigated by individuals, both victims and criminals, who looked to the courts for justice. However, the agency of such individuals within criminal justice processes was, in

88 Finnane, *Punishment in Australia*; Kaladelfos, 'Murder in Gun Alley: Girls, Grime and Gumshoe History' *Journal of Australian Studies* 34, no. 4 (2010): 471–84.

89 For example, NSW Legislative Council, *Report from the Select Committee of Violent Sex Crimes in New South Wales* (Sydney: Government Printer, 1969).

90 Lisa Featherstone, '"Children in a Terrible State": Understandings of Trauma and Child Sexual Abuse in 1970s and 1980s Australia' *Journal of Australian Studies* 42, no. 2 (2018): 164–76.

some ways, limited in the twentieth century, as reliance on legal professionals to conduct criminal cases on both sides became the norm. The legacies of the twentieth-century evolution of Australia's criminal justice system are still being felt today. Accordingly, they deserve more scholarly attention.

27

Indigenous Peoples and Settler Criminal Law

MARK FINNANE

Indigenous peoples in Australia are among the world's most incarcerated populations. The rate of their over-representation in prisons, however, varies between jurisdictions, mapping the uneven transitions of Indigenous peoples from putatively sovereign subjects of their own country in 1788 to colonised subjects of the British Crown a century later. At the time of writing, the highest rate of incarceration is in the Northern Territory, paradoxically the same territory in which 'native title' to land is now most widespread. In the oldest colonised places incarceration differences are less marked. These are jurisdictions along the eastern seaboard where effective dispossession was most complete by the time of Federation in 1901. This chapter explores the reasons for these contemporary phenomena, in so far as their historical conditions lie in the various colonial legal histories of Australia in the nineteenth century. Exploring this intervention we will examine three substantive concerns – legal questions of jurisdiction (much contested in the early decades of many colonies), legal questions of procedure and process (affecting the rights and interests of those appearing in the courts as defendants and witnesses, some of them also victims) and lastly outcomes of trial and sentencing decisions.

To capture the issues involved here let us briefly recall a trial in 1841. In May of that year, two Aboriginal men from the Moreton Bay district, more than a thousand kilometres distant, were tried before judge and jury in Sydney on a charge of murder of a colonial surveyor. One, named in the indictment as Merridio told the court his name was Mullan; the other was a man named Nengavil. As was common in colonial trials, the Aboriginal accused were defended by a barrister, Alfred Cheeke, and the court was assisted by an interpreter, a convict named John Baker who 'appeared to

This chapter draws on research supported by the Australian Research Council (FL130100050 and DP0771492).

speak the prisoners' language with great fluency'. In the challenging task of defending two Aboriginal men against a murder charge, Cheeke confronted the court first with a question about their civil status. Were they 'naturalised', he asked the Attorney General who was prosecuting; if not, then they were entitled under statute to a jury 'half aliens'. Presiding over the trial, Justice William Westbrooke Burton intervened to say that an Act of Parliament had declared that the Aborigines were naturalised by the fact 'that all the laws of England are in force in the colony'. Unbowed by this refusal, Cheeke tried again after the jury had been called, this time 'demanding' a trial by *jury de medietate linguae* [mixed jury], citing Blackstone and English medieval statutes. This time Burton responded at length. The prisoners were not aliens, for whom such a mixed jury might be contemplated, but 'had been naturalised by a general Act of Parliament, under which they were entitled to all the rights and privileges, and subject to all the liabilities, of British subjects'. The colony in any case had its own jury law; but more to the point in Burton's view was that 'some time ago ... it was decided ... that the natives are responsible as British subjects'.[1] The chastened defence counsel, a recent arrival to the colony, responded that he was not aware that the point had been raised before. In subsequent proceedings, the Aboriginal men were convicted of being accessories to murder and sentenced to death.

At play in this 1841 murder trial were issues that continued to trouble the criminal courts across the Australian colonies throughout the nineteenth century and beyond. Statutory and judicial authority as well as government policy mandated the arrest, trial and punishment of Indigenous people who committed offences deemed criminal by the law brought into Australian territories by British colonisers. Burton's dismissal of their alien status recognised the unique standing of Indigenous subjects of the law, whose residence long pre-dated that of colonising settlers, convict or free. But what did it mean to say that such people were entitled to 'all the rights and privileges' of British subjects, as well as bearing liabilities of the same? Attempts, like that of Cheeke, to challenge jurisdiction of the criminal courts were frequently motivated by another colonial discourse, which recognised the startlingly different life-ways, belief, language and culture presented by these Indigenous

1 *Sydney Herald*, 15 May 1841, 2 (the fullest published account of the trial); see also *R v Merridio* [1841] NSWSupC 48 (14 May 1841), http://classic.austlii.edu.au/cgi-bin/sinodisp/au/other/NSWSupC/1841/48.html, accessed 5 November 2019. Burton's reference was to the Court's judgment, which he had drafted, in *R v Murrell* [1836] NSWSupC. For the history of the mixed jury in English and American law see Marianne Constable, *The Law of the Other: The Mixed Jury and Changing Conceptions of Citizenship, Law, and Knowledge* (Chicago, IL: University of Chicago Press, 1994).

subjects of the Crown. The interplay between law's self-image, government policy, settler discourse and Indigenous experience of colonisation – with its elements of dispossession, resistance, rebellion, accommodation and assertion of continuing difference – demands attention in understanding the long history underlying contemporary incarceration rates.

We discover the historical dimension of criminal law's interventions affecting Indigenous lives in three scenarios that find their expression in different measure over time and place. Crimes were variously discovered or reported, investigated, prosecuted and ignored in contexts that pitted Indigenous actors against settlers, settlers against Indigenous people, and Indigenous people against each other. These abstract scenarios can be qualified by other variables, those of intimate and stranger, gender, master and servant, employer and employed, trespasser and defender. The texture of social and individual lives found in these legal encounters can be felt in the words taken down in depositions, in press reports of court proceedings, in the correspondence of police and executive officers as they make decisions about prosecution and punishment. In consequence, the record of criminal law's interventions is a powerful testament to law's power *and* its fragility in dealing with the consequences of settlement on country, on land owned by Indigenous peoples. The weight of this legacy is signalled still by the contemporary unsettling of law's certainty in matters pertaining to criminal and even constitutional jurisdiction pertaining to the conditions and rights of Indigenous people – on the one hand in the attempted prohibition in 2007 of 'cultural' factors in sentencing decisions, on the other in the necessity in 2020 of no less than seven individual judgments in a divided High Court in a matter regarding the 'alien' status of non-citizens of Australian Aboriginal descent.[2]

In outlining the foundational legal conditions of this contemporary situation, this chapter will examine a number of themes in nineteenth-century Australian histories of Indigenous peoples and settler law. First, we consider briefly the assertion of criminal jurisdiction in law and statute in the early nineteenth century, paying attention to some significant differences between the colonies. Second, we look at some elements of criminal trial procedure as they were worked through in the course of implementing the presumption that Indigenous peoples were British subjects, bearing rights, privileges and

2 Northern Territory Emergency Response Act (2007), ss 90–1; Heather Douglas and Mark Finnane, *Indigenous Crime and Settler Law: White Sovereignty after Empire* (London: Palgrave Macmillan, 2012), 207–13; *Love v Commonwealth of Australia*; *Thoms v Commonwealth of Australia* [2020] HCA 3 (11 February 2020).

liabilities. Third, we notice the importance of the criminal justice system's professed concern with the justice due to victims. Finally we consider some evidence about the system-wide impacts of the assertion of criminal jurisdiction over Indigenous peoples, an analysis that underlies the chapter's interest in establishing a framework for understanding contemporary Indigenous experience of the criminal law in Australia.

Jurisdiction

For nearly fifty years after the establishment of the convict settlement at Sydney, the exercise of criminal jurisdiction over Indigenous people accused of crimes was beset with ambiguity. Aboriginal people could be and increasingly were tried for offences committed against convicts and settlers. But what about for those committed against their own people? While beyond the bounds of settlement this was only a hypothetical concern, a recurrent line of thinking in government policy presumed Indigenous autonomy in matters that affected only themselves. In the decision-making around the prosecution of Aboriginal offenders in Sydney and its environs contemporary researchers have discerned a recognition of continuing Aboriginal jurisdiction, a sign of legal pluralism that was later displaced by the assertion of a perfect sovereignty over people and territory.[3] Such pluralism as initially existed was soon put under pressure by the rapid expansion of settlement, which jeopardised any pretence that a strict boundary might be maintained in territory as well as jurisdiction. Indigenous peoples were being dispossessed of exclusive use of their own lands, but they were not always being displaced – and so Indigenous interactions with newcomers, as well as among themselves became the foundation for legal interventions to police disputes or to mete out punishment.

We must exclude from this general picture the experience of Aboriginal Tasmanians, for whom the violence and speed of dispossession proceeded in advance of juridical consideration in criminal cases of their amenability to the introduced law. Indeed such might have been the case in other places, which in their early decades were all marked by armed conflict that bore the character of war rather than policing.[4] But instead we may observe in New

3 Lisa Ford and Brent Salter, 'From Pluralism to Territorial Sovereignty: The 1816 Trial of Mow-Watty in the Superior Court of New South Wales' *Indigenous Law Journal* 7, no. 1 (2008): 67–86.

4 John Connor, *The Australian Frontier Wars, 1788–1838* (Sydney: University of New South Wales Press, 2002); Grace Karskens, *The Colony: The History of Early Sydney* (Sydney:

South Wales (effectively eastern Australia until 1851), Western Australia and South Australia a repeated pattern of criminal jurisdiction in flux over some period of time during the first half of the nineteenth century.[5] The difficulties of communication and the complexities of imperial administration of the colonies provided a space within which the question of the criminal law's application to Indigenous peoples might be raised repeatedly. That is, settlement of the question by judgment in one colony was no guarantee that its terms would be strictly followed either in later prosecutions or in other Australian colonies.

Nevertheless, the judgment of the NSW Supreme Court in the 1836 case *R v Jack Congo Murrell* may still be regarded as foundational, by reason of its frequent citation in case law and policy as well as its historiographical importance.[6] The inclusion of a brief report on this judgment in an 1896 case book signalled its significance, with its heading 'Aboriginals-Jurisdiction of the Court', and its blunt assertion: 'They had no sovereignty.' Prior to *Murrell* the Supreme Court had only once considered whether an Aboriginal person who killed another Aboriginal person was amenable to the criminal law. In 1829 the court declined to hear the case of Bob Ballard, who had been committed by the Sydney magistrates on a charge of killing another Aboriginal man. Two judges agreed in the view that, as Dowling J put it, 'we have a right to subject them to our laws if they injure us, but I know of no

Allen & Unwin, 2009); Stephen Gapps, *The Sydney Wars* (Sydney: NewSouth Publishing, 2018); Mark Dunn, *The Convict Valley* (Sydney: Allen & Unwin, 2019); Grace Karskens, *People of the River* (Sydney: Allen & Unwin, 2020).

5 Mark Finnane, 'The Limits of Jurisdiction: Law, Governance and Indigenous Peoples in Colonised Australia', in Shaunnagh Dorsett and Ian Hunter (eds), *Law and Politics in British Colonial Thought: Transpositions of Empire* (London: Palgrave, 2010); Amanda Nettelbeck, *Indigenous Rights and Colonial Subjecthood: Protection and Reform in the Nineteenth-century British Empire* (Cambridge: Cambridge University Press, 2019); Ann Hunter, *A Different Kind of 'Subject': Colonial Law in Aboriginal-European Relations in Nineteenth-century Western Australia 1829–61* (North Melbourne: Australian Scholarly Publishing, 2012).

6 For example, cited by Plunkett in *The Australian Magistrate* (1866); and included as the only case involving an Aboriginal accused in Legge's NSW cases (1896); cited repeatedly in law reform and policy debates in 1970s and 1980s; and see especially scholarly literature including R. Reece, *Aborigines and Colonists: Aborigines and Colonial Society in New South Wales* (Sydney: Sydney University Press, 1974); Alex Castles, *An Australian Legal History* (Sydney: Law Book Co, 1982); John Hookey, 'Settlement and Sovereignty', in Peter Hanks and Bryan Keon-Cohen (eds), *Aborigines and the Law: Essays in Memory of Elizabeth Eggleston* (Sydney : George Allen & Unwin, 1984); Henry Reynolds, *The Law of the Land* (Ringwood: Penguin, 1987); David Neal, *The Rule of Law in a Penal Colony: Law and Power in Early New South Wales* (Melbourne: Cambridge University Press, 1991); Bruce Kercher, *An Unruly Child: A History of Law in Australia* (St Leonards: Allen & Unwin, 1995); Lisa Ford, *Settler Sovereignty: Jurisdiction and Indigenous People in America and Australia 1788–1836* (Cambridge, MA: Harvard University Press, 2010).

right possessed by us, of interfering where their disputes or acts, are confined to themselves, and affect them only'.[7]

Numerous trials of Aboriginal defendants in the twenty years after 1816 for offences against colonisers, whether free or convict had been decided differently. The assertion of jurisdiction was likely accelerated by the frequency of attacks on settlers that led, in 1835, to numerous prosecutions of Aborigines for a number of crimes including murder, rape and robbery, committed against settlers in the Brisbane Waters region north of Sydney.[8] Acknowledging the increasing reality of an Aboriginal presence within colonised spaces, one that made their disputes *inter se* a matter to be policed, Burton J spoke in *Murrell* for the three judges of the Supreme Court in 'deciding that the aboriginal natives of this Colony are amenable to the laws of the Colony for offences committed within it against the persons of each other and against the peace of our Lord the King'.[9] Murrell had killed Bill Jabingi on the Windsor Road, west of Sydney, in full sight of settler witnesses, 'in our Streets' as Burton noted.[10] So, too, at the Swan River settlement, the critical threshold for judicial decisions determining the amenability of Indigenous accused to criminal trial was their acting within sight of settler witnesses.[11] And while debates about amenability continued into the 1840s, especially in South Australia (as in New Zealand), the notion that offending by any person within the territorial jurisdiction declared by British proclamations and statutes was a matter for the criminal law came to guide policy and policing.[12]

What would follow from this assertion of jurisdiction over conflicts among Indigenous peoples? The judgment was informed by a presumption that the introduced criminal law had a responsibility to protect the interests of victims. Burton thought 'over-rated', the 'difficulties and inconveniences

7 Bruce Kercher, 'R v Ballard, R v Murrell and R v Bonjon', [1998] *AILR* 27; (1998) 3 *AILR* 410, 1998 www.austlii.edu.au/au/journals/AILR/1998/27.html#fnB6, accessed 13 December 2021.

8 Among them *R v Lego'me* [1835] NSWSupC 4 (12 February 1835) www8.austlii.edu.au/cgi-bin/viewdoc/au/cases/nsw/NSWSupC/1835/4.html, accessed 13 December 2021; Ford, *Settler Sovereignty*.

9 Kercher, 'R v Ballard, R v Murrell and R v Bonjon'.

10 For a recent account of the circumstances see Karskens, *People of the River*, 448–51.

11 Hunter, *A Different Kind of 'Subject'*; Heather Douglas and Mark Finnane, *Indigenous Crime and Settler Law: White Sovereignty after Empire* (London: Palgrave Macmillan, 2012).

12 Alan Pope, *One Law for All?: Aboriginal People and Criminal Law in Early South Australia* (Canberra : Aboriginal Studies Press, 2011); Damen Ward, 'Imperial Policy, Colonial Government, and Indigenous Testimony in South Australia and New Zealand in the 1840s', in Shaunnagh Dorsett and Ian Hunter (eds), *Law and Politics in British Colonial Thought: Transpositions of Empire* (New York: Palgrave Macmillan, 2010).

and hardships' likely to arise from the decision in *Murrell*, especially compared to the risk that would flow from a statement that 'our laws are no sanctuary to them'.[13] Judicial assertion, however, was one thing. Giving effect to an ambitious claim that all Aboriginal people lying within the bounds of a vast territorial jurisdiction were now entitled to the protection of British law was quite another. To understand the impact of decisions like *Murrell* we need to consider other changes in policy and practice that lay beyond the court's immediate control. These included statutory and procedural changes that would enable prosecution and shape punishment for Aboriginal people convicted of crimes.

Criminal Procedure and Evidence: Questions of Policy and Practice

Compared with developments in New Zealand, with its variety of institutional experiments addressing Māori difference in the 1840s and after, the Australian colonies have been regarded as less adventurous in their deployment of jurisdiction.[14] Yet as much as the claims of jurisdiction presumed uniformity of laws and equality of protection for victims (in Burton's terms, whether British subjects including Aborigines, or aliens), the development of criminal law constituted a continuing state of exceptionalism for Indigenous accused in different parts of the Australian colonies. Retrospectively, exceptionalism has been recovered as a sign of continuing Aboriginal jurisdiction on the one hand, and of the long existence in Australia of a soft legal pluralism on the other. Looking only at the criminal trial as an instance of this exceptionalism, we note below statutory reforms that enabled the court to hear Aboriginal evidence, judicial approaches to the problem of language in the courtroom, judicial intervention and legal professional performance in prosecution and defence, and penal policy reform that distinguished Indigenous personality as a factor in sentencing and punishment, with a variety of consequences.

Witnessing

The fundamental barrier to Indigenous participation in the criminal trial was the common law presumption that they lacked belief in a god or afterlife. The requirement that evidence be admitted only after a witness had sworn an

13 Kercher, 'R v Ballard, R v Murrell and R v Bonjon'.
14 Shaunnagh Dorsett, *Juridical Encounters: Māori and the Colonial Courts, 1840–1852* (Auckland: Auckland University Press, 2017), part II.

oath to tell the truth was tied to the expectation that the person so sworn was aware of future consequences if they did not tell the truth. This did not require that the witness be a Christian, however much the criminal law and institutions were associated with Christian forms and beliefs. Since the early eighteenth century, judicial tests had been developed to assess whether the witness had the required attributes of belief in an afterlife or a higher justice. As became common in colonial reports of criminal trials, these tests allowed non-Christian witnesses to be heard, including Jews and Muslims, as well as others like Chinese people from a variety of belief traditions. Despite the existence of these tests, courts repeatedly (though inconsistently) rejected the possibility that evidence of an Aboriginal witness could be relied on, or even heard in court.[15]

Colonial conditions by the 1830s heightened the difficulties created by this rejection of Aboriginal evidence. By this time Indigenous defendants increasingly appeared in court on charges for crimes against colonists, especially in New South Wales but also in the Swan River settlement. In these cases, and others which failed to make their way to court, the inability to lead evidence from credible Aboriginal witnesses exposed the law to ridicule. The initiative to recognise Aboriginal evidence through statutory amendment flowed from the judiciary as well as governors. In 1839–40 New South Wales and then Western Australia each enacted evidence statutes, with a view to admitting the unsworn evidence of Aboriginal witnesses. Yet in each case the imperial government rejected the reforms as incompatible with the presumption that all British subjects were equal. In the opinion of the Colonial Office in London, amendments to evidentiary procedure that applied only to Aboriginal subjects threatened the creation of a distinction in law that might 'virtually exclude them from the protection of it'.[16] This metropolitan assumption may have jealously protected the character of a 'British jurisprudence',[17] but it clashed with the realities of administering justice in the very different circumstances of colonies with large Indigenous populations interacting with the settler population. Eventually the Colonial Office relented and imperial legislation in 1843 enabled local legislatures to

15 Douglas and Finnane, *Indigenous Crime and Settler Law*, 55–9; Dorsett, *Juridical Encounters*, 128–32.

16 Russell Smandych, 'Contemplating the Testimony of "Others": James Stephen, the Colonial Office, and the Fate of Australian Aboriginal Evidence Acts, Circa 1839–1849' *Legal History* 10 (2006): 97–143, 127.

17 Ward, 'Imperial Policy, Colonial Government, and Indigenous Testimony in South Australia and New Zealand in the 1840s'.

provide for the use of unsworn evidence by Indigenous subjects of the Crown.[18]

This was scarcely the end of the matter. In the 1840s, both South Australia and Western Australia proceeded to use their new powers to legislate for Aboriginal evidence in the colonial criminal courts. In contrast, New South Wales, failed to address the matter until 1876: consciousness of the threat of Aboriginal evidence to settler interests may have played a role in such delay.[19] In the meantime, pragmatic administration of justice saw the occasional use of Aboriginal witnesses – the Christianisation of some Aborigines in any case enabled some to be regularly sworn as witnesses. Delayed acceptance of unsworn evidence may well have disadvantaged some Aboriginal victims of crime, as discussed later. On the other hand statutory recognition proved its worth in the face of continuing attempts to discount Aboriginal evidence. In a Darlinghurst *inter se* murder trial of an Aboriginal defendant in 1878, two years after the 1876 reform, defence counsel repeatedly sought to discount the evidence of Aboriginal witnesses on the ground of their religious belief. His challenges were to no avail, with the presiding judge three times turning down the objection. The defence then artfully used the evidence of the same witnesses as to the circumstances of the killing to mount a defence of justifiable homicide and the jury acquitted without leaving the box.[20]

Interpreting

A related procedural barrier spoke again to the cultural gap – even were Indigenous people to be heard as witnesses how was the court to communicate with those who had very little or no knowledge of English, the only language of the colonial courtroom? Again, the matter was hardly unique to Australian colonial circumstances, and British courts had long used interpreters. In this crucial test of the fairness of the trial, it was up to judges to decide whether a defendant understood the charges and evidence brought into court. Throughout the century it was very common for judges to discharge an Aboriginal accused if there was no interpreter present. Even when an interpreter was available, their competence remained an issue, there being no professional role or training. Procedural barriers, as well racial prejudice and

18 Dorsett, *Juridical Encounters*; Smandych, 'Contemplating the Testimony'.
19 Nancy E. Wright, 'The Problem of Aboriginal Evidence in Early Colonial New South Wales', in Diane Kirkby and Catharine Coleborne (eds), *Law, History, Colonialism: The Reach of Empire* (Manchester: Manchester University Press, 2001), 140–55.
20 *R v Bob Fly*, NSWSupC 1878: http://app.prosecutionproject.griffith.edu.au/web/public-search/search/88387, accessed 13 December 2021; and see *Sydney Morning Herald*, 14 May 1878, 7.

discrimination, inhibited the use of Indigenous interpreters across a long arc of time. Statutory reform in South Australia in 1849 allowed Indigenous interpreters to be sworn to their role in court. But close study of the South Australian trials in the 1850s shows that their impartiality might be questioned, a vulnerability shared more generally by interpreters, Indigenous or not, and in other jurisdictions.[21] Even as their role became more familiar to the courts of northern Australia, systemic prejudice of the crudest kind interfered with the use of Indigenous interpreters. Hence the protest of a Queensland police officer, after Crown law refused payment to police for the expenses of an Aboriginal man brought in as an interpreter in a Townsville murder trial in 1902 – 'If a European not as competent was employed he would receive at least £1/1/- per day, hence surely the small amount of 12/6 incurred should have been paid.'[22]

Such barriers meant that colonial interpreters more typically included missionaries and philanthropists, but also convicts who had spent time with Indigenous people during periods of escape or after their release from servitude.[23] Moreover the criminal law rested on linguistic protocols at all stages of arrest, interrogation, preparation of indictments as well as admission and examination of evidence in the course of a trial. What did it mean to an accused when asked whether they understood the charges brought against them, in translation or not, or when cross-examined by experienced counsel in the unfamiliar surrounds of a court? Long term, the vulnerability of both accused and witnesses in such spaces as police stations and court-rooms was recognised as a fundamental problem for law and a domain for research. The issue was highlighted famously in a South Australian Royal Commission in 1959 into the conviction of Rupert Max Stuart.[24] But as early as 1846 the South Australian Protector of Aborigines observed that an Aboriginal witness was likely to 'assent or dissent, just as he thinks the Counsel wishes him'.[25] Likewise police interrogation of Indigenous suspects was called into question in the 1881 acquittal in Western Australia of Yingaloo on a charge of murdering a settler. In a Perth court the prosecuting Attorney General was forced to

21 Pope, *One Law for All?*, chapter 5; *R v Next Day* (Meetpoonoong), NTSC, 1949: *Northern Standard* (Darwin), 30 September 1949, 4, http://nla.gov.au/nla.news-article49990702, accessed 13 December 2021.

22 Douglas and Finnane, *Indigenous Crime and Settler Law*, 69–70.

23 Anna Johnston, 'The Language of Colonial Violence: Lancelot Threlkeld, Humanitarian Narratives and the New South Wales Law Courts' *Law & History* 4, no. 2 (2017): 72–102.

24 K. S. Inglis, *The Stuart Case* (Melbourne: Black Inc, 2002).

25 Pope, *One Law for All?*, 47.

question his own witness, a police constable, after it emerged that an alleged voluntary statement could not be verified at trial – the accused could not speak English and the services of a court interpreter proved equally useless. Examining the constable, the Attorney General exposed the strategies involved in extracting a statement from an Aboriginal accused: 'You tell them what to say, and then they say it – is that it?' Both the magistrates who accepted the statement in depositions justifying the committal and the police constable were heavily criticised by prosecutor and judge.[26] In the 1970s the formulation of the so-called Anunga Rules in the Northern Territory sought to protect Aboriginal accused facing police questioning; while linguistic research increasingly focused attention on Indigenous linguistic patterns and cultural dispositions, challenging the law's claim to equal treatment of the subjects before it, and in ways that these nineteenth-century officials had already recognised.[27]

Defenders

Australian colonial settlement took place through a period of fundamental change in common law courts, as lawyers took over the criminal trial. The entitlement of a defendant in a felony trial to a barrister was instantiated in English law in 1836 and was taken up throughout the empire.[28] This important development coincided with the increasing frequency of Aboriginal accused being arraigned at trial. As judges went out on circuit from Sydney and other capitals, barristers accompanied them, both Crown prosecutors and those who would seek briefs from the accused.[29] By the 1840s, although there were exceptions, it was more common than not for judges to assign a barrister to defend an Aboriginal accused, especially those facing capital offences. In some colonies by the end of the century the provision of legal defence for Aboriginal accused was regulated and funded, if not at levels

26 *R v Yingaloo* (also Yungalla) WASC 1881, http://app.prosecutionproject.griffith.edu.au/web/public-search/search/11222, accessed 13 December 2021; see especially the trial report at *West Australian*, 28 October 1881, 3.

27 Diana Eades, *Courtroom Talk and Neocolonial Control* (Berlin: Mouton de Gruyter, 2008); Thalia Anthony, *Indigenous People, Crime and Punishment* (London: Routledge, 2013); Larissa Behrendt, *Indigenous Legal Relations in Australia* (South Melbourne: Oxford University Press, 2009).

28 Prisoners Counsel Act 1836 (Imp); Defence on Trials for Felony Act 1840 (NSW); Greg D. Woods, *A History of Criminal Law in New South Wales: The Colonial Period, 1788–1900* (Annandale: Federation Press, 2002), 176, 142–5.

29 Mark Tedeschi, 'History of the NSW Crown Prosecutors 1830–1901', in G. C. Lindsay and Carol Ann Webster (eds), *No Mere Mouthpiece: Servants of All, Yet of None* (Chatswood: LexisNexis Butterworths, 2002); J. M. Bennett (ed.), *A History of the New South Wales Bar* (Sydney: Law Book Company, 1969), 69–70.

considered adequate by the private bar. By current standards, the conduct of defence was ill prepared, with an assigned barrister being instructed by a solicitor who had himself only just seen the depositions. But the assignation of barristers, who would often be among the leaders of the local bar, provided many Indigenous defendants with a more professional defence than was available to many other accused, especially in the nineteenth century.[30] The court proved to be a place where some displayed their liberal, even radical, thinking, in articulating the colonial 'whispering in our hearts'.[31] 'We had taken their country', defence counsel J. G. L. Innes (later a Supreme Court judge) told an 1872 Bathurst jury during the trial of an Aboriginal man accused of rape; later the same day he explained that the practice of assigning counsel to Aborigines facing serious charges followed the same principle as supplying Aborigines with blankets – 'it was a sort of compensation to them for having taken their country'.[32] By contrast, the availability of such professional counsel in some jurisdictions highlights the historical injustice faced by many other Indigenous people in northern Australia in the later nineteenth century. Especially in the Kimberley (Western Australia) in the later nineteenth century, indictable charges against Aboriginal offenders were very commonly processed in a fashion more characteristic of a magistrate's court, and with no defence lawyer in sight. A consequence was mass transportation of convicted Indigenous men to Rottnest Island or detention in northern prisons with hard labour on public works, helping build roads and railways.[33]

Penalties

Other kinds of exceptional treatment of Indigenous people in the proceedings and institutions of criminal justice were legislated throughout the nineteenth and early twentieth centuries. Their scope is considerable, and found in all jurisdictions.[34] Penal policy was a notable, and especially in Western

30 Alana Piper and Mark Finnane, 'Defending the Accused: The Impact of Legal Representation on Criminal Trial Outcomes in Victoria, Australia 1861–1961' *The Journal of Legal History* 38, no. 1 (2017): 27–53.

31 Henry Reynolds, *This Whispering in Our Hearts* (St Leonards: Allen & Unwin, 1998).

32 *Bathurst Free Press and Mining Journal*, 20 April 1872, 2. See Mark Finnane, '"They Were Subject to Our Laws": Aboriginal Defendants in NSW Courts 1850–1914' *History Australia* 17, no. 3 (2 July 2020): 448–70.

33 Chris Owen, *'Every Mother's Son Is Guilty': Policing the Kimberley Frontier of Western Australia 1882–1905* (Crawley, WA: UWA Publishing, 2016); Mark Finnane and Andy Kaladelfos, 'Race and Justice in an Australian Court: Prosecuting Homicide in Western Australia, 1830–1954' *Australian Historical Studies* 47, no. 3 (2016): 443–61.

34 The major reference point is John McCorquodale, *Aborigines and the Law: A Digest* (Canberra: Aboriginal Studies Press for the Australian Institute of Aboriginal Studies, 1987).

Australia, a very visible instance. Just a decade after the establishment of the Swan River colony, colonial legislation designated Rottnest Island as a prison for Aboriginal people sentenced to transportation or committed for trial – in order, as the statute put it, that 'they may be instructed in useful knowledge, and gradually trained in the habits of civilised life'.[35] A concern that cellular confinement was harmful to their health also informed the Rottnest legislation, as it did some aspects of prison design and prison management in other places. In remote areas of northern Australia, the routinised mass trials of Indigenous offenders on charges of cattle stealing, noted above, was accompanied by statutory provisions for the whipping of Aboriginal offenders in Western Australian legislation in 1849 and 1893. Exceptional penal policy was less evident in eastern Australia, where instead we are likely to find the Aboriginal experience of punishment to be governed more by the infra-legal character of prisons administration than by statute.[36]

Another kind of exceptionalism arose out of some fundamental aspects of trial procedure and judicial sentencing powers. Here the context was a developing discourse of protection that would take many Indigenous people out of civil society altogether. And so, in the Northern Territory in 1918, an Ordinance required that an Aboriginal person might plead guilty at a criminal trial only with the consent of a protector, a provision also legislated in Queensland under a like protection regime. And in the long history of attrition of the death penalty in Australia, we should note the important legal innovation of 1934 by which a judge in the Northern Territory was given discretion over the judicial sentence of death where 'an Aboriginal native is convicted of murder', and in fact after this date no such penalty was ever awarded.[37] That reform had an important interwar context, of debate over the capacity of the prosecution system to recognise the relevance of

35 Mark Finnane and John McGuire, 'The Uses of Punishment and Exile – Aborigines in Colonial Australia' *Punishment and Society* 3, no. 2 (2001): 279–98; At least sixty-seven Aboriginal men were sentenced at Swan River Colony Quarter Sessions (Western Australia) to 'transportation' between 1837 and 1856, at which time the punishment was abolished. This was 46 per cent of the total so sentenced at that court in these years. For Rottnest Island see Neville Green and Susan Moon, *Far from Home, Aboriginal Prisoners of Rottnest Island 1838–1931* (Nedlands, WA: University of Western Australia Press, 1997). For Aboriginal prisoners in early colonial penal settlements see Kristyn Harman, *Aboriginal Convicts: Australian, Khoisan, and Maori Exiles* (Sydney: University of New South Wales Press, 2012).

36 John McGuire, 'Judicial Violence and the "Civilizing Process": Race and the Transition from Public to Private Executions in Colonial Australia' *Australian Historical Studies* 29, no. 111 (1998): 187.

37 Aboriginals Ordinance 1918 (NT); Crimes Ordinance 1934 (NT); Dean Mildren, *Big Boss Fella All Same Judge: A History of the Supreme Court of the Northern Territory* (Annandale: Federation Press, 2011), 149; Martin Kriewaldt, 'The Application of the Criminal Law to

Indigenous 'custom' – leading, in Western Australia, to a short-lived experiment with 'Native Courts'. But the policy interest in system innovation at this level faded in a developing post-war preoccupation with assimilation. An Australian commitment to benign exceptionalism was always half-hearted.[38]

Victims: Questions of Justice

Justification for including Aboriginal people in criminal jurisdiction in the Australian colonies rested not only on the exclusive territorial claims of British imperial authority but on repeated statements by the highest authorities of the justice to which Aboriginal people would be entitled by their subjection to criminal law. We have noted this at the outset in Burton's reference to 'the rights and privileges' as well as liabilities, of British subjects. But how well did the administration of law and criminal justice meet these high standards? The interests of victims were historically a reference point in procedural decisions and sentencing reasons. In *Murrell* Burton J had addressed the interest of victims in justifying jurisdiction – 'serious causes might arise if these people were allowed to murder one another with impunity, our laws would be no sanctuary to them'. Sentencing Aboriginal man Spider, convicted of rape in 1866, Stephen CJ spoke of the necessity of 'dealing with the vagabonds whose object was the perpetration of crime which brought misery to the woman and disgrace elsewhere'.[39] In these ways judges asserted the presumption in play that the criminal law's function was related to the protection of the innocent from harm.

Yet establishing whose interests were in play and to what degree they were protected by criminal jurisdiction is a matter to be considered not in the abstract but with reference to individual victims as well as specific populations – for example, Indigenous victims of non-Indigenous crimes and vice-versa, as well as Indigenous victims of crimes committed by other Indigenous people. From early colonial settlement, criminal prosecutions were brought against Aboriginal people in the Sydney area charged with the killing of settlers or convicts, but also against those settlers who had killed Aboriginal people. The outcomes of these prosecutions followed a colonial

the Aborigines of the Northern Territory of Australia' *University of Western Australia Law Review* 5, no. 1 (1960): 1–50.

38 Douglas and Finnane, *Indigenous Crime and Settler Law*, 108–18; Kate Auty, *Black Glass: Western Australian Courts of Native Affairs 1936–54* (Fremantle: Fremantle Arts Centre Press, 2005).

39 *Spider*, 17 Oct 1866 (executed 26 Nov 1866) http://app.prosecutionproject.griffith.edu.au/web/public-search/search/50742, accessed 14 December 2021.

pattern.[40] Convictions obtained against settlers were rare, especially compared with the likelihood of conviction of an Aboriginal person charged with killing a colonist. Concern over the injustice implicit in such an unbalanced system was evident in the commentary of governors, judges and attorneys-general across the nineteenth century. While, in some cases, prosecutions on behalf of Aboriginal victims foundered on almost insurmountable problems in evidence and identification, in others the outcome was clearly linked to jury nullification. It required a very determined Attorney General to pursue the interests of justice in the face of settler prejudice. The prosecution of a large number of men for the massacres committed at Myall Creek (NSW) in 1838 eventually resulted in the conviction and hanging of seven of them. A first trial foundered on the objections of defence counsel that there was no clear identification of a person killed, or that the human remains discovered were of a person who had been murdered. Famously, the Attorney General, Irish-born and Roman Catholic J. H. Plunkett, brought a new prosecution over the death of an unnamed Aboriginal child and this time succeeded in persuading the jury.[41] The Myall Creek trials were unique in their ambition as well as context; one modern prosecutor has suggested they were 'more akin to modern-day war-crimes trials than to domestic murder trials'.[42]

While nothing on the scale of the Myall Creek trials was again attempted, most jurisdictions record intermittent prosecution of non-Aboriginal perpetrators of violence against Aboriginal people. When juries declined to convict in the face of the strongest evidence, judges could be very critical – their criticism of jury decisions in the Northern Territory in the early twentieth century led eventually to a suspension of trial by jury in all but capital cases.[43] In the face of the strongest evidence of gross and violent mistreatment of an Aboriginal employee that had resulted in his death, a Western Australian jury in 1897 returned a lesser verdict of manslaughter. The Chief Justice was

40 Amanda Nettelbeck, '"Equals of the White Man": Prosecution of Settlers for Violence against Aboriginal Subjects of the Crown, Colonial Western Australia' *Law and History Review* 31, no. 02 (2013): 355–90; Mark Finnane and Jonathan Richards, '"You'll Get Nothing out of It"?: The Inquest, Police and Aboriginal Deaths in Colonial Queensland' *Australian Historical Studies* 35, no. 123 (2004): 84–105.

41 Tony Earls, *Plunkett's Legacy: An Irishmans Contribution to the 'Rule of Law' in New South Wales* (North Melbourne: Australian Scholarly Publishing, 2009), chapter 6.

42 Mark Tedeschi in Jane Lydon and Lyndall Ryan, eds., *Remembering the Myall Creek Massacre* (Sydney: NewSouth Publishing, 2018), 164.

43 [Northern Territory] Observance of Law Ordinance (No. 13, 1921), s 6 (repealed 1930, reinstated 1933 and finally repealed with restoration of trial by jury in 1961); Mildren, *Big Boss Fella All Same*, 59, 69.

dismayed by the decision, which ran against his clear direction, on the evidence, for a murder conviction. He responded in the best way he could by awarding the convicted prisoner the longest possible sentence of penal servitude for life.[44] Facing a rare charge of kidnapping an Aboriginal child in the western New South Wales town of Bourke, two men were cleared by a jury against the run of evidence of both Aboriginal and non-Aboriginal witnesses. The judge thought the verdict inconsistent with the evidence and regarded such a crime as deserving a whipping.[45] Jury acquittals did not always save wrong-doers from other sanctions. A police constable was acquitted in 1872 by a Bathurst jury on a charge of shooting an Aboriginal prisoner in cold blood, but was dismissed from the police service, an outcome observed also in Queensland on a number of occasions.[46] But in another well-known instance, the 1891 acquittal in a murder trial of William Willshire, a mounted constable in charge of the Native Police in Central Australia, failed to bring his police career to a conclusion and he was reassigned to other duties.[47]

The limits of justice to victims exposed by jury trials of non-Aboriginal defendants were less visible in trials of Aboriginal people for offences against others. In spite of the legal obstacles to the conduct of a fair trial, including rules of evidence and corroboration as well as their understanding of proceedings being brought against them, Aboriginal defendants were convicted in considerable numbers throughout the nineteenth century, many of them suffering the death penalty.[48] At an aggregate level then we might say that at least in homicide cases, non-Aboriginal victims enjoyed a higher measure of justice than Aboriginal victims of inter-racial killing. And when non-Aboriginal victims of homicide were left without recompense in the form of conviction of an Aboriginal suspect, the issues at play might be less those of justice to a victim than justice to an accused. In this respect, the position of Aboriginal accused facing serious charges was arguably less exceptional and more consistent with procedural norms. Observant judges could make a difference, and the evidence of non-Aboriginal witnesses also played

44 *West Australian*, 22 December 1897, 3; Ernest Anderson, 20 December 1897, https://app.prosecutionproject.griffith.edu.au/web/public-search/search/1692, accessed 14 December 2021.

45 *Sydney Mail*, 5 November 1881, 794.

46 *NSW Police Gazette*, 1872, 106; for Queensland, see Finnane and Richards, '"You'll Get Nothing out of It"?'.

47 Amanda Nettelbeck and Robert Foster, *In the Name of the Law: William Willshire and the Policing of the Australian Frontier* (Kent Town, SA: Wakefield Press, 2007).

48 Finnane and Kaladelfos, 'Race and Justice in an Australian Court', 443–61.

a role in some Aboriginal acquittals in inter-racial cases. Not guilty verdicts were common enough in trials of Aboriginal defendants in a system that relied on evidence presented in an adversarial contest. Their possibility is captured in the acquittal at Maitland Quarter Sessions of one Jackey in 1861 on trial for the killing of his master. The jury acquitted without leaving the box, after hearing evidence of the master's drunken abuse of Jackey, evidence corroborated by a woman accompanying their bullock drive.[49] Other New South Wales juries both at Quarter Sessions and in the Supreme Court acquitted Aboriginal defendants facing property and personal offence charges after their defending lawyers made good use of rules of evidence and procedure, including corroboration requirements and the rights of individuals to resist unwarranted police interventions. In even the apparently most hopeless cases, like that of Jimmy Governor, convicted after a notorious crime spree, clever lawyers might deploy precedent to challenge the conduct of a trial or the very process of prosecution itself. In that case, Governor's defence counsel challenged his prosecution for murder on the grounds that he had already been convicted in being declared an outlaw under an outlawry statute, the Felons Apprehension Act. While the appeal failed, the case is a reminder of the degree of assimilation into regular proceedings of Aboriginal prisoners in such a jurisdiction.[50]

If the scales of justice weighed unevenly for Aboriginal and non-Aboriginal people as victims in inter-racial crimes (especially in the rarity of prosecutions of non-Aboriginal assailants), how did they balance for Aboriginal victims of offences committed by Aboriginal accused? In this respect it is important to acknowledge that in colonised Australia, the prosecution of Aboriginal people increasingly implied the recognition of Aboriginal victims. The entire significance of judgments like *Murrell* hinges on the policy decisions subsequently taken to prosecute so-called *inter se* offences. So to appreciate the measure of justice afforded Aboriginal victims of Aboriginal crimes we must take account of prosecutions forgone, as well as those that proceeded to trial and conviction or acquittal. Discretion exercised by police and magistrates played a significant role in bringing matters to court and later trial, or not. Subsequently, Attorneys-General and judges presiding over trials also played a crucial role in assessing the interests of victims. Matters of procedure as well

49 *R v Jackey*, *Maitland Mercury*, 11 May 1861, 2, https://app.prosecutionproject.griffith.edu.au/web/public-search/search/163217, accessed 14 December 2021.

50 *R v Jimmy Governor* [1900] NSWLawRp 98; (1900) 21 LR (NSW) 278 (30 November 1900) http://classic.austlii.edu.au/au/cases/nsw/NSWLawRp/1900/98.html, accessed 12 June 2019.

as the quality of evidence were at stake in discretionary decisions that shaped prosecution. Before 1876 in New South Wales doubts about the admissibility of evidence of an Aboriginal witness could see one man arrested twice by police for murder of another Aboriginal person, only to be released each time; while the fact that there were 'only Aboriginal witnesses' was the explanation proffered for the failure to prosecute two men accused of raping Mary Cubby in 1868.[51] Even after 1876 it is apparent that New South Wales police continued to value the need for evidence of a 'European' rather than an Aboriginal witness in judging whether to continue inquiries over an Aboriginal death. But also at play in some *inter se* cases may have been an assertion of Indigenous jurisdiction. When a publican intervened in a fight between Aboriginal men outside an Orange (NSW) pub in 1854, the response from Jemmy Darcy was to tell him 'in a threatening manner that they had better go home, remarking that blackfellows law had nothing whatever to do with English law, and they had better leave the blackfellows to themselves'.[52] Some police and prosecutors appeared to agree. On the other hand, there were some Aboriginal people who used the criminal law as another weapon with which to assert their claims to justice against other Aboriginal people, confessing their anger when their sense of entitlement to punishment of someone who had harmed them was frustrated by an acquittal or early discharge. One Aboriginal witness threatened the accused during a murder trial at Geelong in 1860, 'if he were not hanged he would be killed when he got home'.[53] Such an instance may be read as a reverse kind of assimilation – of Indigenous actors assimilating to their own purposes one of the tools newly available in their changed landscape.

Patterns: Questions of Prosecution and Punishment

As we have seen in this chapter, two questions were asked of British colonisers as they faced Indigenous peoples in the Australian colonies. One was whether there was any jurisdiction at all over Aboriginal people; the second

51 'Naggy, Charged with Murder of Cullenbong Billy', *NSW Police Gazette*, 24 March 1893, 93 (http://nla.gov.au/nla.news-article251750127, accessed 14 December 2021); for the case of Mary Cubby, child rape victim with no prosecution despite arrest of two Aboriginal men see *Sydney Morning Herald*, 13 January 1869: 4 (col. 6) (http://nla.gov.au/nla.news-article13184978, accessed 14 December 2021).

52 *Sydney Morning Herald*, 22 March 1854, 2; and see Paula Jane Byrne, 'The New South Wales Bar and Aboriginal People: Making Aboriginal Subjects c. 1830–1866' *History Australia* 15, no. 3 (2018): 413–29.

53 Douglas and Finnane, *Indigenous Crime and Settler Law*, 63.

question was how that jurisdiction would be exercised? So far we have examined these questions on the evidence of policy and practice found in statutes and case law. In this section we turn to the problem of measuring outcomes. The materials available for doing so are very uneven. Recording the Indigenous identity of accused, victims and witnesses, was common enough in nineteenth-century records, but less frequently aggregated. Indigenous identity was used by police in their investigations into crime, and similarly by prison officials for those who were detained in prisons and jails. Neither of these uses covers comprehensively the information available in court records that are at the heart of the process of criminal prosecution. Nevertheless, archival discovery and triangulation of data enables us to establish some important indicators of Indigenous experience of the criminal justice system, especially at the level of trial and its outcome.[54]

While the available evidence of Indigenous demography limits ready calculation of *rates* of prosecution, the likelihood of significant *numbers* of Indigenous people facing trial was closely linked with transitions from frontier conditions to those of a more colonised and mixed community. So in New South Wales the numbers of prosecutions increased only slowly during the first fifty years of colonisation, but accelerated during the 1840s and 1850s, reaching a peak in the early 1880s. In contrast, in South Australia, close investigation of the first thirty years of settlement shows that the prosecution of Aboriginal people was intense, as also at Swan River through the 1840s and beyond – in both cases the relatively early settlement of the question of amenability for *inter se* crime was the key element.[55] At least one-third of the business of the trial Court of Quarter Sessions in Swan River in the 1840s and 1850s involved Indigenous accused, many of them prosecuted for *inter se* offences, many others for property offences against settlers. In northern Australia in the later decades of the nineteenth and early decades of the twentieth century, court business was very often dominated by the prosecution of Indigenous offenders. This was especially the case for Western Australia's Kimberley region from the 1880s, with the criminal courts being virtually a weapon of war in response to widespread cattle killing.[56] Homicide prosecutions were the other source of frequent Indigenous appearance at northern Australian courts, and again most

54 In addition to references cited below, analysis in this section also draws on materials collected by the Prosecution Project (https://prosecutionproject.griffith.edu.au/, accessed 14 December 2021).

55 Pope, *One Law for All?*; Hunter, *A Different Kind of 'Subject'*.

56 Chris Owen, *'Every Mother's Son Is Guilty'*.

commonly for *inter se* cases.[57] Commonly informing prosecution policy was an expectation that law would be an instrument of pacification and civilisation, complementing the work of missionaries in Christianisation.

A critical test of justice and fairness in an adversarial trial system is the possibility of acquittal, an outcome we have observed in earlier discussion about procedure and victims' justice. When Indigenous people came to court in long-settled districts their conviction rates were higher than those of settlers but not significantly so – and research in New South Wales suggests the gap between Indigenous and non-Indigenous in likelihood of conviction narrowed by the end of the nineteenth century. Conviction, however, appeared always more likely in inter-racial cases involving an Indigenous accused.[58]

Another test of fairness is that of post-conviction outcomes. Two measures are relevant – the kinds of penalty awarded, and the post-sentencing outcomes of those penalties. Much research remains to be done on these measures. With significant numbers of Indigenous accused facing capital charges in which the death penalty was mandatory, the main issue post-conviction is whether Indigenous accused were given the benefit of the limited discretion available in the award of a 'death recorded' sentence, effectively a judicial commutation of a death sentence; or whether their death sentence was commuted by a colonial governor, acting on advice of the executive Council (effectively the ministers of the Crown). In Western Australia where the majority of convictions for murder were of Indigenous people, they were more likely than non-Indigenous people to be awarded the penalty 'death recorded', as well as to receive executive commutation of the death sentence. In Queensland too, where a significant number of Indigenous people were convicted of capital offences, the rate of commutation was higher than for non-Indigenous prisoners.[59] Much work remains to be done on sentencing for non-capital offences, a high proportion of them in the nineteenth century resulting in prison rather than the options introduced late in the period of fine or probation. But analysis of length of imprisonment at sentencing in New South Wales in the second half of the nineteenth century suggests significantly longer sentences for Indigenous prisoners.[60] How this translated into time served is a matter for future research.

57 Finnane and Kaladelfos, 'Race and Justice in an Australian Court'.
58 Finnane, 'They Were Subject to Our Laws'.
59 Mark Finnane and Jonathan Richards, 'Aboriginal Violence and State Response: Histories, Policies and Legacies in Queensland 1860–1940' *Australian and New Zealand Journal of Criminology* 43, no. 2 (2010): 238–62.
60 Finnane, 'They Were Subject to Our Laws', 14.

This brief summary of some prosecution outcomes appears largely consistent with the earlier analysis of the possibilities, limitations and harms of the criminal law system as it came to be experienced by Indigenous people in Australia following the assertion of jurisdiction. What often strikes the historical observer are the disparities among jurisdictions. In some – indubitably in north-western Australia – the criminal law was weaponised as an aspect of frontier politics. Over time, however, there was in most jurisdictions a convergence in experience once people came to trial. What brought Aboriginal accused to trial through police attention in the first place continued to reflect the distinctive and unequal position of Indigenous peoples in Australia.

Conclusion

By the mid-twentieth century, when Elizabeth Eggleston undertook the first major study of Aboriginal people in the Australian criminal justice system, criminal law was a locus of discrimination and disadvantage.[61] A rare judicial officer like Justice Martin Kriewaldt of the Northern Territory Supreme Court in the 1950s reflected on the conditions that made it so and pondered what might be done to mitigate the harms of a system that presumed equality and aspired to fairness without recognising the complexity of conditions that brought an Indigenous person to trial.[62] A prolonged history of Aboriginal protection arguably limited the impact of the criminal law, especially the rate of imprisonment, through the first half of the twentieth century. But changing social policy that removed civil inequalities also exposed greater numbers of Indigenous people to criminal justice interventions, especially to police surveillance in the suburbs and rural towns.[63] The result was a rising imprisonment rate from the 1950s that continues to this day.[64] The conditions

61 Elizabeth Moulton Eggleston, *Fear, Favour or Affection: Aborigines and the Criminal Law in Victoria, South Australia and Western Australia* (Canberra: Australian National University Press, 1976).

62 Heather Douglas, 'Justice Kriewaldt, Aboriginal Identity and the Criminal Law' *Criminal Law Journal* 26, no.4 (2002): 204–22.

63 Gillian Cowlishaw, *Black, White, or Brindle: Race in Rural Australia* (Cambridge/New York/Melbourne: Cambridge University Press, 1988); Heather Goodall, *A History of Aboriginal Communities in New South Wales, 1909–1939* (PhD thesis, University of Sydney, 1982); Chris Cunneen, *Conflict, Politics and Crime: Aboriginal Communities and the Police* (Crows Nest: Allen & Unwin, 2001); Harry Blagg, *Crime, Aboriginality and the Decolonisation of Justice* (Annandale: Hawkins Press, 2008).

64 Roderic Broadhurst, 'Crime and Indigenous People', in Adam Graycar and Peter Grabosky (eds), *The Cambridge Handbook of Australian Criminology* (Melbourne: Cambridge University Press, 2002), 256–80; Roderic Broadhurst, 'Imprisonment of the

for that development, legal, social and cultural, were laid in the dispossessions after 1788 and the associated assertion of a common law jurisdiction. As the blunt instrument of administration of Aboriginal lives, the criminal law too often was an occasion for compounding injustice, expressed today in the reality of mass incarceration. Even where fairness and due process was secured in courts, colonisation exposed the failure of criminal law to secure material justice for Australian Indigenous peoples.

Aborigine in Western Australia: 1957/1985', in Kayleen Hazelhurst (ed.), *Ivory Scales* (Sydney: Allen & Unwin, 1987), 153–89; Don Weatherburn, *Arresting Incarceration: Pathways out of Indigenous Imprisonment* (Canberra: Aboriginal Studies Press, 2014).

28

Civil Wrongs

MARK LUNNEY

This chapter is concerned with the law of civil wrongs in Australian legal history. There is debate at the margins as to what legal actions fall within the definition of 'civil wrongs' but, for this chapter, civil wrongs are taken to comprise the range of actions which do not fall within criminal or public law and have been classified globally as within private law. These include actions in the law of contract and the law of tort as well as actions founded in equity. Land law is not discussed as it is the subject of another chapter.

Plurality and Civil Wrongs

A unifying theme of this collection is the place of pluralism in Australian legal history. As the majority of chapters illustrate, much pluralism in that history lies in the study of the interactions and legacy of the coercive nature of white settlement in Australia. Nothing in this chapter challenges this dominant narrative. But the focus of this chapter is different. Rather, as a consequence of *terra nullius*, the Australian colonists busied themselves in determining how the English common law might apply to disputes between the colonists themselves.[1]

Discussions of the history of civil wrongs in Australia have been significantly influenced by the idea, promulgated by the Judicial Committee of the Privy Council (from 1788 until the second half of the twentieth century the final court of appeal for Australian jurisdictions) that there was 'one common law' for the empire.[2] At the outset it should be recognised that the 'one common law' was always something of a myth. As discussed below, in an empire as heterogeneous as the British it was recognised early in imperial history that divergence made

1 For excellent general legal histories of Australia considering this question see A. Castles, *An Australian Legal History* (Sydney: Law Book Co, 1982) and B. Kercher, *An Unruly Child: A History of Law in Australia* (Sydney: Allen & Unwin, 1995).

2 *Trimble v Hill* (1879) 5 App Cas 342, 345.

necessary through local conditions was acceptable.[3] But the power of the 'one common law' idea in Australian legal history lies in the common law being a constituent part of British race patriotism,[4] a defining feature of one characterisation of Australian identity. To adhere to the common law was to be part of the 'community of culture' at the heart of British race patriotism.[5] As High Court judge Sir Victor Windeyer put it, the English common law was 'not the law of a land but a law of people'.[6]

The common law was the law that applied to civil wrongs. For almost the entirety of white Australian history, the narrative was that the law of civil wrongs in Australia was either a mirror of cognate common law in England or, as time went on, largely derived from that common law.[7] The period before the High Court of Australia in *Parker v R*[8] in 1963 determined that it would not hold itself bound to follow decisions of the Appellate Committee of the House of Lords (then the highest court for most appeals in the UK court system), was thus described as an 'era of deference'.[9] English law *was* Australian law, something that critics attributed to a form of cultural cringe.[10] Many of the works identifying the emergence of an 'Australian' law were written in the shadows of the Australia Acts of 1986, the legislation that formally removed the authority of the United Kingdom Parliament to legislate for Australian jurisdictions and also eradicated the right to appeal to the Judicial Committee of the Privy Council from Australian state courts.[11]

3 P. Mitchell, 'The Privy Council and the Difficulty of Distance' (2016) 36 *Oxford Journal of Legal Studies* 26; more generally, B. McPherson, *The Reception of English Law Abroad* (Brisbane: Supreme Court of Queensland Library, 2007).

4 On its significance in debates about citizenship see Chapter 24 above.

5 N. Meaney, 'Britishness and Australian Identity: The Problem of Nationalism in Australian History and Historiography' *Australian Historical Studies* 32 (2001): 76, 85.

6 V. Windeyer, 'Unity, Disunity and Harmony in the Common Law', in B Debelle (ed.), *Victor Windeyer's Legacy: Legal and Military Papers* (Annandale: Federation Press, 2019), 124. As he made clear, this also included Scots, who despite having their own legal system, had to accept the common law of England perforce when they were overseas.

7 G. W. Paton (ed.), *The British Commonwealth, The Development of its Laws and Constitution: Volume 2 Australia* (London: Stevens & Sons, 1952) xi.

8 (1963) 110 CLR 610.

9 A. Mason, 'The Common Law in Final Courts of Appeal outside Britain' *Australian Law Journal* 78 (2004): 183, 190–1; for private law more specifically see F. Ellinghaus, 'Towards an Australian Contract Law' and H. Luntz, 'Throwing off the Chains: English Precedent and the Law of Torts in Australia' both in M. Ellinghaus et al. (eds), *The Emergence of Australian Law* (Sydney: Butterworths, 1989), chapters 3 and 4; F. Trindade, 'Towards an Australian Law of Tort' (1993) 23 *University of Western Australia Law Review* 74.

10 G. L. Fridman, 'Judicial Independence of a different kind' in N. Mullaney (ed.), *Torts in the Nineties* (Sydney: Law Book Co, 1997) 305.

11 See note 9 above. Appeals on matters of Commonwealth, as opposed to state, law had been largely restricted earlier by the Privy Council (Limitation of Appeals) Act 1968

For too long this narrative of subservience and inferiority has dominated what little academic interest has been shown in the history of the Australian law of civil wrongs. While one struggles to find grandiloquent assertions of Australian independence in Australian law for most of white Australian judicial history, to use the absence of such statements as conclusive evidence for a lack of pluralism in Australian civil law is too crude. As a generalisation Australian courts largely did follow English law where civil wrongs were concerned. Australian judges almost universally said that they did so and to have explicitly refuted English law risked violating the doctrine of precedent. But statements must be read in context, and one of those contexts was the different conception of Australian nationalism that was shared by many members of the legal profession for most of white Australian history, a nationalism based on British race patriotism. While that patriotism brought deference to English pronouncements of the common law, it also brought a willingness to contribute to its development and improvement.[12] This is not to downplay the significance of the demise of the formal constraints on Australian legal creativity in civil wrongs both informally through the demise of British race patriotism in Australia and also through formal changes to the legal rules of precedent that allowed greater freedom for Australian courts to depart from formerly binding English court decisions. Rather, it acknowledges that there is greater continuity than has been recognised.

The Tyranny of Distance – The First Australian Courts

A number of authors have pointed out that notions of rule according to law were inherent in the earliest self-conceptions of the white identity of the penal colony in New South Wales. That rule of law was based on English law, an inheritance that the white settlers in Australia considered a birth right. It was never the case, however, that English law in its entirety applied in a colony, only so much of it as was suitable for the conditions of the colony. As choosing which laws applied largely occurred *ex-post* when deciding cases, the formula of itself gave some scope for ambiguity. In theory, appeals could be taken from Australian judicial decisions to the Privy Council but the practical barriers of time and cost made this an option unavailable to most

(Cth) and appeals from the High Court of Australia were abolished by the Privy Council (Appeals from High Court) Act 1975 (Cth).

12 M. Lunney, *A History of Australian Tort Law 1901–1945* (Cambridge: Cambridge University Press, 2018), chapter 2.

litigants. The result was that early Australian colonial courts had considerable practical flexibility to shape a colonial law that could be different from the formal rules that applied in the metropole.

This capacity has been thoroughly explored by Kercher in his study of the First Court of Civil Jurisdiction in New South Wales.[13] Kercher noted that in many areas of civil law the Judge Advocates took positions that were inconsistent with English law. As he notes, however, there are examples of deviance from English law that seem to go beyond what colonial circumstances might have required.[14] Perhaps the most famous derives from the first civil case to be heard after white settlement in Australia, *Cable v Sinclair* in 1788. The details of this case are discussed in an earlier chapter[15] but what is relevant for present purposes is that the common law of attaint that should have prevented a convict from suing (the plaintiffs were convicts) was ignored in New South Wales in 1788, as it was for most of the early legal history of New South Wales. What this meant for views of the exceptionalism of Australian law has varied with changes in wider Australian historiography. In the 1960s, Windeyer highlighted the case as foreshadowing the commitment of the Australian settlers to the rule of law,[16] a commitment that underpinned cultural links to the United Kingdom that still then had a contemporary resonance. The wilful blindness to attaint receives little attention. By the time Kercher was writing in the mid-1990s, acceptance of an independent, exceptional Australian (as distinct from English) law was long established. The 'rule of law' aspect of *Cable v Sinclair* remains important for Kercher but its deviance from English law is of greater interest as the case was the first example of a Judge Advocate's willingness to innovate in the very different circumstances of the early settlement of New South Wales.[17] Kercher's study highlights how substantive law as well as remedies in civil law were tailored to suit the circumstances of the colony but always in conventional legal forms. In that sense, pluralism formed an integral part of the law of civil wrongs in Australia from the commencement of white settlement, a pluralism that reconciled values internal to notions of the rule of law with the instrumental challenges of a convict colony thousands of miles from England.[18]

13 B. Kercher, *Debt, Seduction and Other Disasters: The Birth of the Civil Law in Convict New South Wales* (Annandale: Federation Press, 1996).
14 E.g. in debt recovery laws: ibid, 211–13.
15 See pages 92–3 above.
16 V. Windeyer, '"A birthright and inheritance": The Establishment of the Rule of Law in Australia' *University of Tasmania Law Review* 1 (1962): 635, 658–64.
17 Kercher, *Debt, Seduction*, xviii–xix; see also Kercher, *An Unruly Child*, 22–3.
18 Kercher, *An Unruly Child*, xx–xxi.

The Long Nineteenth Century

It is tempting to see the period from the 1820s to Federation as the period where the early innovation and deviations from English law were reined in and a more formal administration of justice more closely aligned to England was introduced. It is true that from the creation of the Supreme Court of New South Wales in 1823 Australian courts gradually lost the willingness to see Australian conditions as a reason to explicitly craft a uniquely Australian response. The reasons for this change are complex but reflect greater confidence in the permanence of the settlements and recognition that they could not be regarded simply as penal colonies.[19] Apart from a few notable exceptions, however, this change did not facilitate a band of experienced judges coming to the colonies to help shape its legal future. Though all had legal training from 1810, the remarkable series of biographies of colonial Chief Justices penned by Dr John Bennett reveal a mix of English practitioners with limited opportunities 'at home' and former legal officers of the colonies who made their way from government service to the bench.[20] As Bennett's biographies illustrate, in the newly created colonies legal acumen could run a poor second to the need to navigate the complex political environments of the Australian colonies.

Perhaps for this reason, little detailed research has been carried out on developments in the law relating to civil wrongs in this period.[21] There are at least two reasons for thinking that such a study might reveal more Australian exceptionalism than has traditionally been thought. The first is that there are some well-known examples where nineteenth-century Australian courts did interpret English common (judge-made) law creatively. A good example is *Coultas v Victorian Railway Commissioners* in 1886. The plaintiff was in a buggy with her husband when they approached a railway level crossing in Swan Street, Richmond. Access to the crossing was controlled by a gate opened by an attendant. Without adequately checking for an oncoming train the

19 See further Chapter 5 above.

20 Between 2001 and 2019 Dr Bennett published with Federation Press biographies of the following chief justices: Forbes, Dowling, Stephen, Martin, and Darley (NSW); A'Beckett, and Higinbotham (Vic); Cockle and Lilley (Qld); Pedder, Fleming and Villeneuve Smith (with Ronald Solomon) (Tas); Burt, Wrenfordsley, and Onslow (WA); Cooper (SA).

21 For a notable exception in relation to procedural law, see M. Leeming, 'Fusion-Fission-Fusion: Pre-Judicature Equity Jurisdiction in New South Wales 1824–1972', in J. Goldberg et al. (eds), *Equity and Law: Fusion and Fission* (Cambridge: Cambridge University Press, 2019), chapter X. See also W Swain, 'The Laws of "An Old and Settled Society"? The Law of Contract in New South Wales in the Mid-Nineteenth Century' (2022) https://papers.ssrn.com/sol3/papers.cfm?abstract_id=3963517.

attendant negligently beckoned the plaintiff's husband to cross the tracks where only through urgent evasive action by the plaintiff's husband was a collision avoided. The shock to the plaintiff resulted in psychological harm. Despite a dearth of relevant English authority, the Full Court of the Supreme Court of Victoria held that damages for her 'nervous shock' (the then legal description for her psychological harm) could be awarded in the absence of a plaintiff suffering any other injury, or even the direct application of force, as a result of the defendant's negligence.[22] The case is best known today for the restrictive ruling of the Privy Council on appeal[23] but the Supreme Court decision recognising the case for awarding compensation for shock-induced harm was a creative development of the preceding common law. Another example is the decision of Hanson CJ in the South Australian Supreme Court in *Ward v Taylor*[24] that the defence of fair comment in the law of defamation was available to comments relating to sitting politicians. As Hanson's biographer notes, English authority did not cover the point 'and his judgment was clearly innovatory . . . '.[25]

The second reason why a detailed study of the application of the English common law applicable to civil wrongs in the colonial period may reveal a more complex picture is the parallel presence of quite radical reforming legislation that affected the application of the common law in the Australian colonies. One example from the nineteenth century lies in the statutory amenability of the Crown to civil suit. In England the Crown was immune from civil suit until the Crown Proceedings Act 1947 (UK), and until then an action could only be brought by way of a petition of right (a procedure that effectively required governmental consent).[26] This immunity was abrogated in Australian jurisdictions from the middle of the nineteenth century.[27] Finn argues that the initial impulses to reform related to dissatisfaction with the administration of Crown land[28] but it was also due to the greater involvement of government, both state and local, in the building and operating of key infrastructure, such as railways, in the colonies throughout the nineteenth century.[29]

22 (1886) 12 VLR 895.

23 (1888) 13 App Cas 222. See further P. Handford, '*Victorian Railway Commissioners v Coultas*: The Untold Story' *American Journal of Legal History* 61 (2021): 416.

24 (1873) 7 SALR 103.

25 G. Taylor, *Sir Richard Hanson* (Annandale: Federation Press, 2013), 172.

26 K Oliphant (ed.), *The Law of Tort* (Lexis Nexis, 2015, 3rd edition), para 2.2.

27 Kercher, *An Unruly Child*, 100.

28 P. Finn, *Law and Government in Colonial Australia* (Oxford: Oxford University Press, 1986), 142.

29 S. Kneebone, *Tort Liability of Public Authorities* (LBC Information Services, 1998), 298–9. Similar considerations prompted New Zealand to abolish a blanket Crown immunity

Even when no legislative change was made, recognising that Australian colonies had the power to amend the common law is important when considering arguments of legal subservience. A good example is the common law immunity that applied to highway authorities, the entities responsible for the maintenance of public roads. In Australia, these entitles varied between local councils (only for roads within council boundaries) and state government departments. At common law a highway authority could be liable for carelessness in the construction of a road but not for nonfeasance (usually, the failure to repair a road). While Finn has argued that Australia was in the legal vanguard to remove this immunity as an unwanted imperial appendage, the position is more complex than his portrayal.[30] The highway immunity was never foisted upon an unwelcome Australian community. The Privy Council decision (from a New South Wales decision) which upheld the immunity at common law expressly left open the possibility of legislative reversal.[31] Colonial and state legislatures, however, showed no interest in expressly making government entities responsible for failure to repair highways even though, as noted above, they happily legislated away the general immunity of the Crown. Moreover, when judicial decisions in the late nineteenth and early twentieth century affirmed that existing legislation empowering municipal authorities in relation to roads did not necessarily abrogate the common law immunity, there was no legislative rush to change the law.[32] The highway immunity survived at common law in Australia long after it was abolished in England, and when it was finally overturned by the High Court of Australia in *Brodie v Singleton Shire Council* in 2001,[33] a number of state legislatures reintroduced it in whole or in part.[34] There was some suggestion by members of the High Court in *Brodie* that a more liberal 'Australian' rule departing from the immunity for highway authorities might have been developed but for constraining English case law.[35] However, the Australian case used to support this view – the decision of the High Court in *Miller v McKeon* in 1905[36] – in fact supported the suitability of the immunity for Australia (while not accepting other aspects of English

in 1881: J. McLean, *Searching for the State in British Legal Thought* (Cambridge: Cambridge University Press, 2012), 228.

30 Finn, *Law and Government*, 112.

31 *Municipality Council of Sydney v Bourke* [1895] AC 433, 445.

32 Lunney, *A History of Australian Tort Law*, 152–6.

33 *Brodie v Singleton Shire Council* (2001) 206 CLR 512.

34 M. Lunney, 'Highway Immunity and the Victimisation of Australian Law: Fact or Fiction?' *Tort Law Review* 26 (2019): 83, 94.

35 *Brodie v Singleton Shire Council* (2001) 206 CLR 512, 562.

36 (1905) 3 CLR 50.

highways law that were unsuitable for Australian conditions). To the contrary, Griffith CJ in *Miller* seemed quite content that the highway immunity was a necessary rule for (in his view) a largely uninhabited country in the process of settlement.[37] Both the failure to legislate its abolition, and its judicial acceptance by the High Court in 1905, suggest that, whatever the reasons that founded the rule when it was initially recognised in England, different and more apposite Australian conditions – such as sparse populations, a geographically diverse landscape and a road network vastly more extensive than in the United Kingdom – made it supportable as an Australian rule, albeit one that remains controversial.

While statutory amendment of the common law rules of liability in nineteenth-century Australia was rare, defamation constituted an exception. As early as 1847, New South Wales abolished the distinction between libel and slander, a distinction that remains in the English law of defamation.[38] It also allowed truth as a defence to a defamation action only if the publication of the defamatory imputation was of public benefit.[39] While these reforms had been mooted in England,[40] they had failed but this failure was not thought to be a reason for rejecting them in Australia.[41] Defamation law was also the first body of private law to be codified in Samuel Griffith's Defamation Act of 1889 in Queensland. While his defamation code drew from a mixture of common law sources, his aim in codifying was to improve 'the very general belief that the present libel laws were in an unsatisfactory state'.[42] A prime target was the language used in the tort: civil juries were confused by the legal meanings of ridicule, contempt and express and implied malice. The extent to which the press might be protected in respect of defamatory comments was also uncertain. Griffith aimed to solve these difficulties by 'placing the various matters in logical order' with the result that 'many persons would know a great deal more about the law of defamation than they did at the present time: persons who offended would be more easily brought to justice, and those who did not offend would not be liable to be put to the great expense that they were now in order to defend

37 Ibid, 59–60.

38 Slander and Libel Act 1847 (NSW), s 1. The broad distinction is that libel is defamation in permanent form and slander is defamation in transitory form. The usual exemplars are printed words (libel) and spoken words (slander).

39 Ibid, s 4.

40 P. Mitchell, 'The Foundations of Australian Defamation Law' *Sydney Law Review* 28 (2006): 477.

41 *Sydney Morning Herald*, 10 June 1846, 3 (speech of elected Legislative Council member Richard Windeyer).

42 *Brisbane Courier*, 20 July 1889, 6.

themselves'.[43] Nor did he lack confidence that his codification had improved the situation. When Griffith was later sitting as the Chief Justice of the High Court hearing an appeal relating to his defamation legislation,[44] he gave short shrift to an argument that what he called 'the refinements of English [common] law'[45] should influence the interpretation of the language of the Act: '[t]he English law may be defective on the point, but that is no reason for limiting the meaning of the Statute law of Queensland'.[46] More generally, as Castles points out, nineteenth-century colonial legislative reforms led to important variations in the law applying in various parts of the country.[47] While the extent of the difference among Australian jurisdictions in the statute law that applies to civil wrongs has grown dramatically in the twenty-first century, it is important to recognise that plurality *within* Australian jurisdictions through legislative variance has been a characteristic of the law relating to civil wrongs at least since legislative authority was granted to the colonies. Statutory diversity made the idea of 'one common law', in the sense of a law that applied in all Australian jurisdictions, a legal myth once the capacity to make their own legislation was given to Australian colonies.

The two legislative amendments to defamation law discussed above were passed in eras when the formal rules relating to the freedom granted to colonial legislatures were different. From the formation of the first Legislative Council in New South Wales in 1823 through to 1865, legislative competence was limited by the notion of repugnancy, that is, while some deviation from English law was allowed in adapting that law to local conditions, it could not be 'repugnant' to fundamental principles of that law.[48] In practice, this was a doctrine characterised by its 'utter flexibility', the aim being to keep a 'family resemblance' between English and colonial laws.[49] The uncertainties of the boundary meant there was some latitude for colonial

43 Ibid. The Defamation Code was ultimately incorporated into Griffith's Criminal Code (1899) and this later code was enacted in Western Australia. Tasmania adopted the Defamation Code in 1895. In both jurisdictions there were doubts as to how much the civil law of defamation was altered by the amendments. Other Australian jurisdictions applied the English common law with varying degrees of statutory modification. Victoria retained much of the English common law on defamation throughout most of the twentieth century. See further Lunney, *A History of Australian Tort Law*, 32–3.

44 The provisions of the 1889 Act were incorporated into the Criminal Code Act 1899 (Qld) and the appeal concerned the defamation provisions in this later legislation but the substance of the provisions remained the same as under the 1889 Act.

45 *Hall-Gibbs Mercantile Agency v Dun* (1910) 12 CLR 84, 92.

46 Ibid, 93.

47 Castles, *An Australian Legal History*, 471.

48 Kercher, *An Unruly Child*, chapter 4; Castles, *An Australian Legal History*, chapters 15 and 16.

49 D. Ward, 'Legislation, Repugnancy, and the Disallowance of Colonial Laws: The Legal Structure of Empire and *Lloyd's Case* (1844)' *Victoria University of Wellington Law Review*

legislatures to depart from traditional English rules. However, the cultural constraints around deviations emanating from the colonies – in particular, that too radical a departure from the English common law might be seen as inconsistent with the colonists' identification as members of a common 'British' race – made it less of an issue in practice than it looks in retrospect (at least in the realm of civil wrongs).[50] Perhaps for this reason, the freedom granted to legislatures, as opposed to courts, to depart or deviate from the established position under English common law and statute was enhanced by the passage of the Colonial Laws Validity Act 1865 (Imp), an act of the Westminster Parliament that gave colonial legislatures wide powers to pass legislation, the only limit being that the legislation could not be repugnant to imperial legislation (i.e. passed by the Westminster Parliament) that was expressly stated to apply in the colony.[51] Perceived as a charter for colonial legislative independence,[52] the same cultural factors that limited Australian exceptionalism prior to the legislation remained after it. As far as civil wrongs were concerned, the new legislative freedom was sparingly used and most legislation involving civil wrongs throughout the nineteenth and most of the twentieth century merely reproduced legislative amendments made in England.[53] But whatever the de facto limits, the 1865 legislation was important for providing a firm legal basis for considerable dissonance between English law and the law of the Australian colonies.

The Twentieth Century and the Creation of a National Court

The creation of the High Court of Australia – 'A new court, strictly Australian and national, created for Australian and national purposes'[54] – in 1903

41 (2010): 381, 388–9 (quoting James Stephen, who held a variety of positions, including permanent under-secretary, with the Colonial Office from 1825–47).

50 See e.g., the conflict between the New South Wales Legislative Council and the Colonial Office over the Liens on Wool Act 1843 (NSW): Castles, *An Australian Legal History*, 172–5.

51 Colonial Laws Validity Act 1865 (UK), ss 2, 3.

52 A. Castles, 'The Reception and Status of English Law in Australia' *Adelaide Law Review* 2 (1963): 1, 27; R. Lucy, 'The Division of Powers between the British Empire and Its Australian Self-Governing Colonies, 1855–1900' *Australian Journal of Law and Society* 6 (1990): 83.

53 Such as legislation relating to the survival of actions, contribution between tortfeasors, and contributory negligence.

54 J. Brett, *The Enigmatic Mr Deakin* (Melbourne: Text Publishing, 2017), 271, quoting part of Alfred Deakin's three and a half hour speech in favour of the Judiciary Bill creating the High Court.

presaged further possibilities for diversity between English and Australian law. Under the strict rules of precedent, the High Court was bound only by the Privy Council, although from its early history its members held they would follow decisions of the House of Lords,[55] a position changed by the decision in *Parker* in 1963. Before then members of the High Court never openly disowned decisions of the Privy Council or House of Lords although some judges were adept at giving themselves flexibility by finding inconsistencies between decisions of courts that bound them.[56] At various times, the High Court also held it should follow decisions of the English Court of Appeal in the interests of the 'one common law'.[57] But the dynamics that had prompted this commitment to judicial unity, including an outpouring of imperial fealty during World War II,[58] collapsed in post-World War II Australia, lending a certain inevitability to *Parker*. Before then, however, the incremental development of the common law by judges when deciding cases allowed for some avoidance strategies to be implemented in dealing with what was thought to be unsatisfactory but binding English case authority. Case law, both English and Australian, could be interpreted to produce a new understanding of the law, one formally consistent with but substantively different from what was thought previously to have been the existing law. This established technique of adapting the common law to new circumstances avoided any of the legal or cultural limitations that attended explicit rejection of English case law precedent. It also allowed Australian judges to make contributions to a common law that, as members of the wider British common law community, they felt was their own.

It is impossible in this chapter to detail the many ways in which Australian judges in the twentieth century pre-*Parker* interacted with their common law in an attempt to improve the law relating to civil wrongs for the benefit of the Australian community. A few examples give an indication: the clarification by Griffith CJ of the rules for assignment of choses of action in *Anning v Anning*,[59] the exposition of the legal effect of a wife's disadvantage in terms of establishing undue influence by her husband in relation to the execution of

55 *Brown v Holloway* (1909) 10 CLR 89, 102–3 (O'Connor J).
56 *Lothian v Rickards* (1911) 12 CLR 165, 176 (Griffith CJ).
57 *Sexton v Horton* (1926) 38 CLR 240, 244 (Starke J), 251 (Higgins J).
58 In particular, the decision of *Piro v W Foster & Co Ltd* (1943) 68 CLR 313, holding that the High Court should follow a decision of the House of Lords in preference to a contrary earlier decision of its own.
59 (1907) 4 CLR 1049.

guarantees by Dixon J in *Yerkey v Jones*,[60] and Fullagar J's concise yet rigorous analysis of the effect of one party to a contract being affected by alcohol when signing it in terms of the availability of equitable remedies in *Blomley v Ryan*.[61] More generally, the vast array of Sir Frederick Jordan's judgments in private law provide 'mini-lectures' that did not shy away from pointing out where superior English courts had gone wrong,[62] and Gava has shown that in application Sir Owen Dixon's 'strict and complete legalism' allowed for bounded creativity in engaging with English contract law.[63] But one, largely unrecognised, area where Australian courts had to engage with a common law developed under very different natural conditions from England was liability for damage caused by fire.

By the beginning of the nineteenth century, the English common law relating to liability for damage caused by fire remained uncertain. Earlier authorities had imposed a strict liability (a liability without fault) on an occupier of land for the escape of fire, in some versions extending beyond fires lit by the occupier to fires that began independently through accident or by the act of a third-party over whom the occupier had no control. English legislation from 1774 provided some protection from fires beginning accidentally but there was little definitive authority on what 'accidentally' meant in this context.[64]

Whether the liability of an occupier for the spread of fire from their property was based on the occupier's negligence, or was strict, was of considerable practical importance in Australia where fire was an accepted pestilence with the capacity to cause considerable harm. Equally important was the relative dearth of authority from England: the very few fire cases dealt with urban, domestic or commercial settings, very distant literally and metaphorically from its use in the rural settings which characterised the Australian cases.[65] Australian courts were very much on their own in working out the acceptable risks from the use of fire. An early distinction was

60 (1939) 63 CLR 649. Cf R. Chaudhri, 'Sir Owen Dixon and Yerkey v Jones: Considering the Feminist Implications of Strict and Complete Legalism', in J. Eldridge and T. Pilkington (eds), *Sir Owen Dixon's Legacy* (Annandale: Federation Press, 2019), chapter 10.

61 *Blomley v Ryan* (1956) 99 CLR 362.

62 K. Mason, *Sir Frederick Jordan* (Annandale: Federation Press, 2019), 212.

63 J. Gava, 'When Dixon Nodded: Further Studies of Sir Owen Dixon's Contracts Jurisprudence' *Sydney Law Review* 33 (2011): 157, where earlier articles by the author on the subject are also noted.

64 Fires Metropolis Act 1774 (UK), s 86; *Filliter v Phippard* (1847) 11 QB 347; 116 ER 506.

65 For examples, see *Musgrove v Pandelis* [1919] 1 KB 314; *Job Edwards v Birmingham Navigation Co Proprietors* [1924] 1 KB 341; *Collingwood v Home and Colonial Stores Ltd* [1936] 3 All ER 200.

drawn, without much conviction, between fires deliberately lit and those that started accidentally, there being no action for damage caused by carelessly failing to act to prevent the spread of the latter.[66] The basis of liability for damage caused by the escape of a deliberately lit fire seemed to become less strict when, in 1914, the High Court held that liability for damage caused by the escape of fire fell within the more general principle of strict liability for the escape of a dangerous thing recognised in the English case of *Rylands v Fletcher*.[67] This only applied when there was a non-natural use of land.[68] Hence a fire that was lit for domestic heating or cooking fell outside the situation where strict liability would be imposed; these were 'not non-natural' uses of land. For these categories of fire, liability would only be fault-based. Yet twenty years later, in *Hazelwood v Webber*,[69] the High Court found no difficulty in holding that the burning off in mid-summer of agricultural land for farming purposes was a non-natural use of land and hence the occupier who had lit the fire on his land was strictly liable under *Rylands v Fletcher* when it escaped and caused damage to his neighbour. Whether liability was strict or fault-based thus depended on the question of non-natural use. By making this a legal, rather than a factual, question, the High Court in *Hazelwood* ensured that factual evidence of local practices would not usurp the judicial role of determining, normatively, what ought to be the appropriate balance (in terms of whether liability should be strict or fault-based) between freedom to use fire to advantage on the occupier's land and the risks that imposed on adjoining neighbours.[70] Only when confronted with a decision of the House of Lords in 1947 adopting a very narrow view of what was a non-natural use of land,[71] and indicating that the liability under *Rylands v Fletcher* was exceptional, did Australian courts abandon their earlier approach. This effectively emasculated strict liability for the spread of fire (and it was killed off in 1993 when the High Court abolished *Rylands v Fletcher* as an independent tort).[72]

The Australian fire cases of the first half of the twentieth century reveal the complex interaction between the precedential value of English law and the

66 *Havelberg v Brown* [1905] SALR 1. A later High Court, affirmed by the Privy Council, rejected this rule and imposed a fault-based liability on the occupier: *Hargrave v Goldman* (1963) 110 CLR 40; *Goldman v Hargrave* [1967] 1 AC 64; M. Lunney, 'Goldman v Hargrave', in C. Mitchell and P. Mitchell (eds), *Landmark Cases in the Law of Tort* (Oxford: Hart, 2010), chapter 8.

67 (1868) LR 3 HL 330.

68 *Whinfield v Lands Purchase Management Board of Victoria* (1914) 18 CLR 606.

69 (1934) 52 CLR 268. 70 Lunney, *A History of Australian Tort Law*, 227.

71 *Read v J Lyons & Co Ltd* [1947] AC 156.

72 *Burnie Port Authority v General Jones Pty Ltd* (1994) 179 CLR 520.

need to apply and adapt that law to be meaningful in an Australian environment.[73] These decisions on judicial policy by Australian judges were largely carried out free of interference or even criticism from English judges; indeed it was suggested in an English periodical early in the twentieth century that an Australian case could be a guide for English courts on this issue.[74]

Just as Australia's colonial creativity in liability for negligently inflicted mental harm was demonstrated in the Victorian Supreme Court decision in *Coultas*, its continued pluralism was evident in its quiet resistance to the overturning of that decision by the Privy Council. As noted above, in *Coultas* the female plaintiff suffered shock-induced mental injury due to the buggy she was in almost being hit by a passing train through the negligence of the gatekeeper. On appeal, the Victorian Supreme Court decision was overturned by the Privy Council, which held that harm caused by shock, unaccompanied by any actual physical injury, was not a consequence in the ordinary course of things that would flow from the negligence of the gatekeeper.[75] This precluded Mrs Coultas from recovering and at face value limited the possibilities for future plaintiffs suing for psychological harm caused in this way. But it is striking how little *Coultas* seems to have impeded the development of an Australian law allowing recovery of damages for nervous shock.[76] With impeccable legal logic, Australian courts found that the presence of almost any kind of trivial injury, and in some cases mere impact without injury, was enough to distinguish *Coultas*. And when the legal test for remoteness of damage – which was the legal test applied in *Coultas* – was altered in England,[77] English case law on recovery for pure mental harm applying the new rule was seamlessly absorbed into Australian case law. *Coultas* was rarely cited and never determinative.

When two decisions of the High Court in the 1930s applied the new test for liability – whether nervous shock was a foreseeable consequence of the defendant's negligence – in a restrictive manner,[78] the McKell Labor government of New South Wales proposed legislation to bring New South Wales law into line with what was perceived to be the more liberal English law. Thus far the story is conventional: the less advanced Australian law was to be enhanced by modern English infusion through legislation. But this was turned on its head by a House of Lords' decision in 1942, *Bourhill*

73 Lunney, *A History of Australian Tort Law*, 199–231.
74 (1915) 59 *Solicitors Journal* 785. The case was *Young v Tilley* [1913] SALR 87.
75 (1888) 13 App Cas 222, 225.
76 Lunney, *A History of Australian Tort Law*, chapter 6.
77 *Hambrook v Stokes Bros* [1925] 1 KB 141.
78 *Bunyan v Jordan* (1937) 51 CLR 1; *Chester v Waverley Municipal Council* (1939) 62 CLR 1.

v Young,[79] adopting a more restrictive approach to liability for negligently inflicted nervous shock than had been assumed by the New South Wales legislators. Far from causing retrospection, the McKell government reacted to *Bourhill* by simply pulling the existing bill and introducing a completely different bill, specifying clearly some circumstances where recovery for negligently inflicted nervous shock would be possible. Australian judges and practitioners were intimately involved in this process.[80] When it was passed at the end of 1944, Section 4 of the Law Reform (Miscellaneous Provisions) Act 1944 (NSW) was the first piece of legislation on the subject in the Anglo-Australian legal world. It made clear that recovery was possible if the statutory conditions were met rather than leaving it to the judicial application of more general English common law tests that had (in the legislature's view) unfairly prevented plaintiffs from recovering. English law had gone from being the light on the hill to being discarded in the McKell government's quest to give New South Wales the 'best modern legal developments'.[81]

The same McKell government saw no difficulty in reversing the High Court decision in *Piro v W Foster & Co Ltd*[82] (which had preferred a later House of Lords' decision to an earlier High Court decision) on the effect of contributory negligence in an action for breach of statutory duty. In a High Court decision from the 1920s, *Bourke v Butterfield & Lewis Ltd*, Isaacs J, taking into account the nature of industrial workplaces and the reasons for the introduction of statutory duties in such settings, had denied that the contributory negligence of a worker was a defence to an action for breach of a statutory duty imposed on the employer to provide a particular safety measure for the worker's benefit.[83] The House of Lords later disagreed.[84] When the High Court in *Piro* accepted the later House of Lords' decision, the preferred Australian approach was simply legislatively reinstated by the McKell government.[85] Isaacs was no doubt pleased: he wrote that the House of Lords' decision was a branch of 'static morality' known as judge-made law that stood in the way of a 'public moral obligation' to protect

79 *Bourhill v Young* [1943] AC 92.
80 M. Lunney, 'Unseen Networks: The Legal Professions' Involvement in the *Law Reform (Miscellaneous Provisions) Act 1944* (NSW)' *Australian Law Journal* 92 (2018): 449.
81 W. McKell, 'A Long Overdue Legal Reform', *The Australian Worker* (Sydney) 30 December 1942, 5.
82 (1943) 68 CLR 313.
83 (1926) 38 CLR 354. The other members of the court agreed in result.
84 *Caswell v Powell Duffryn Associated Collieries* [1940] AC 152.
85 Statutory Duties (Contributory Negligence) Act 1945 (NSW).

workers and advocated legislative reform.[86] As for liability for negligently inflicted nervous shock, English authority was not the last word on the subject.

Plurality outside the English Common Law

Throughout white Australian history, England was not the only source of the common law; apart from jurisdictions within the United States, there were an increasing number of decisions from other colonies and later Dominions. During early colonial history, it was common for judges of Australian courts to be peripatetic, moving from one colony to another.[87] Increasing historical interest has been shown in these imperial networks to explain empire as an amorphous whole rather than a series of bilateral relationships.[88]

Whatever the merits of these arguments more generally, there is little explicit evidence of the influence of other networks on the law of civil wrongs in Australia. While it was not unknown for cases from other common jurisdictions to be cited in judicial judgments, precedent and convention dictated a dialogue with England. Attempts to range more widely could attract the wrath of the Privy Council. In *Macintosh v Dun*, an action for defamation involving the defence of qualified privilege for trade protection agencies, both the Supreme Court of New South Wales and the High Court relied, in the absence of English authority, on a decision of the Court of Appeals for the State of New York to reach their decision.[89] When the case reached the Privy Council, Australian courts were reminded that American cases were entitled to the 'highest respect' but that the question had to be decided by English law.[90] As there was no *ex-ante* English law to be had, this comment prompted the newly appointed Victorian Supreme Court judge Leo Cussen to wonder why the help from an obviously relevant case should

86 Papers of Sir Isaac Isaacs 1883–1969, National Library of Australia,2060534, MS2755, Series 6, Box 6, Addresses and Articles, 'Dangerous Machinery'. I have not located if or where this speech/article was made or published. For another example of Isaacs's dislike of 'static morality' and his willingness to deviate from English law, see his dissent in *Wright v Cedzich* (1930) 43 CLR 70 (on a wife's ability to sue for loss of consortium).

87 For notable examples see J. McLaren, *Dewigged, Bothered and Bewildered: British Colonial Judges on Trial 1800–1900* (Toronto: Osgoode Society, 2011), chapters 7 and 8.

88 For a flavour, see D. Lambert and A. Lester (eds), *Colonial Lives across the British Empire: Imperial Careering in the Long Nineteenth Century* (Cambridge: Cambridge University Press, 2006); C. Hall and S. Rose (eds), *At Home with the Empire: Metropolitan Culture and the Imperial World* (Cambridge: Cambridge University Press, 2006).

89 (1905) 5 SR (NSW) 708; (1906) 3 CLR 303.

90 [1908] AC 390, 401.

be dismissed just because it was American,[91] and the New South Wales Legislature almost immediately legislated to reverse the advice of the Privy Council.[92] The 'American snub' may be explained by British concern over rising American influence in Australia at the end of the nineteenth and early twentieth centuries.[93] While American scholars were genuinely interested in some of the progressive legal developments in Australia during this period, such as the resolution of industrial disputes through compulsory arbitration,[94] there is little to suggest any interest on either side in a new bilateral engagement at the level of legal doctrine surrounding liability for civil wrongs. 'Our lady the common law'[95] was a shared resource of the United States and England, an important source for pronouncements of Anglo-Saxon race unity.[96] Even if the settler colony narrative of the Australia–United States relationship excluded the United Kingdom, that did not significantly influence liability for civil wrongs where any American influence was mediated through the historic Anglo-Australian legal relationship.[97]

The End of the Affair

The pluralism of the law of civil wrongs in Australia began to diminish when the normative force of the 'one common law' doctrine began to decline. Apart from wider geopolitical issues associated with the demise of empire, a more specifically legal factor was the creation of an Australian legal academy after World War II and its population by scholars not versed in the legal traditions of British race patriotism.[98] The most important of these

91 L. Cussen, 'A Note on the Case of Macintosh v Dun' *Commonwealth Law Review* 6 (1908–9): 105.

92 Defamation (Amendment) Act 1909 (NSW), s 6.

93 M. Lake, 'British World or New World?' *History Australia* 10 (2013): 36.

94 M. Lake, *Progressive New World* (Cambridge, MA: Harvard University Press, 2019), chapter 4.

95 The expression is Frederick Pollock's: *The Genius of the Common Law* (New York: Columbia University Press, 1912), 2.

96 R Cosgrove, *Our Lady the Common Law: An Anglo-American Legal Community 1870–1930* (New York: New York University Press, 1987).

97 American cases, and even academic literature, were cited in the first half of the twentieth century but only as a buttress rather than the source of authority for the decision and usually only by selected judges: for cases see *Australian Knitting Mills Ltd v Grant* (1933) 50 CLR 387, 441, 445–6; *Cowell v The Rosehill Racecourse Company Limited* (1937) 56 CLR 605, 638–40; *Victoria Park Racing & Recreation Grounds Co Ltd v Taylor* (1937) 58 CLR 479, 509, 518; and for academic literature *Bunyan v Jordan* (1937) 57 CLR 1, 16; *Chester v Waverley Municipal Corporation* (1939) 62 CLR 1, 32–4.

98 Cf T. Pietsch, *Empire of Scholars: Universities, Networks and the British Academic World 1850–1939* (Manchester: Manchester University Press, 2013) where academic lawyers are notably absent.

was Julius Stone,[99] who arrived at the University of Sydney in 1941 and in 1946 published *The Province and Function of Law*, in Australia. One part of this text stressed the fluidity and choice inherent in the application of legal rules, including rules of civil law.[100] German émigrés Wolfgang Friedmann and John Fleming arrived at the end of the 1940s, and while neither stayed long in Australia, their interest in and experience of other legal systems was symptomatic of a change in the legal academy in Australia.[101] Bartie has highlighted how the members of the new academy looked beyond England, particularly to the United States, in their attempts to create an *Australian* legal academy. As she notes, these academics inhabited a different environment from their predecessors, one in which universities grew in student numbers and resources.[102] The possibilities offered to these academic 'pioneers' to create Australian law as an academic discipline, taking the best from other common law jurisdictions but tied to none, would inevitably lessen the attraction of strict adherence to English law at a time when the idea of empire itself was in irretrievable decline.

Judges were bound by more strictures than academics and were understandably slower to embrace the change. Accordingly, when the pronouncement in *Parker v R* was made in 1963, there was no sense of a judicial throwing-off of the imperial yoke. When Sir Victor Windeyer spoke to the New Zealand Law Conference just after the High Court had refused to follow the House of Lords for the first time after *Parker*,[103] he assured his audience of the Australian judicial commitment to the metaphysical aspects of British race patriotism while respectfully pointing out that growing political independence must be mirrored in judicial freedom to depart from English precedents.[104] The first two cases in which the *Parker* ruling was utilised by the High Court were cases on civil wrongs: one involving the award of damages for non-pecuniary loss in personal injury cases where the plaintiff lacked awareness of the injury,[105] and one involving

99 While Stone was born in England and studied there, his postgraduate studies at Harvard gave him a very different perspective; see L. Star, *Julius Stone: An Intellectual Life* (Oxford: Oxford University Press, 1992).

100 J. Stone, *The Province and Function of Law* (Associated General Publications Pty Ltd, 1946), Part 1, chapters VI–VII.

101 M. Lunney, 'Legal Emigres and the Development of Australian Tort Law' *Melbourne University Law Review* 36 (2012): 494; M. Lunney, 'Fleming's Law of Tort: Australian-Made or Foreign Import?' *Australian Bar Review* 36 (2013): 211.

102 S. Bartie, *Free Hands and Free Minds: Pioneering Australian Legal Scholars* (Oxford: Hart, 2019), 35–8.

103 *Skelton v Collins* (1966) 115 CLR 94.

104 Windeyer, 'Unity, Disunity', 123–6.

105 *Skelton v Collins* (1966) 115 CLR 94;

the circumstances when an award of exemplary damages could be made.[106] Neither seem like situations where uniquely Australian factors mandated a change in the law,[107] but when the Privy Council heard an appeal in the exemplary damages case, it justified its refusal to overturn the High Court decision using a version of this argument.[108] In reality, it was not any material difference between English and Australian conditions, but an acceptance that the High Court could decline to follow the House of Lords on the simple basis that it thought the latter wrong, that enlived the freedom granted by the Privy Council to the High Court.

Any hope that this reticence to declare Australian departures from English law misguided might lead to the creation of a 'Judicial Commonwealth'[109] where a new rationale for uniformity might arise was quickly dashed.[110] In 1970, in one of the last appeals from the High Court, the Privy Council allowed, by a 3–2 majority, an appeal in a case involving liability for negligent misstatements causing purely economic losses (i.e. without accompanying physical injury) in tort. The two dissentients had given judgments in the earlier House of Lords' decision (it being the practice for judicial members of the House of Lords to sit also on Privy Council appeals) in *Hedley Byrne & Co Ltd v Heller & Partners Ltd*,[111] which had created this kind of claim, but, despite this support, the majority had no difficulty in rejecting the views of the High Court.[112] The following year a majority of the House of Lords declined to follow the Australian position on awards of exemplary damages, seeing no difficulty in divergence between the two jurisdictions.[113] Shortly thereafter appeals to the Privy Council from the High Court were terminated and the most important vestiges of the legalism of imperialism were effectively removed from the Australian legal system.[114] By then, the truth – made unarguable by the Australia Acts of 1986 – was that the law of civil wrongs

106 *Uren v John Fairfax & Sons Pty Ltd* (1966) 117 CLR 118.

107 G. Barwick, 'Law and the Courts', in A. Madden and W. Morris-Jones (eds), *Australia and Britain: Studies in Changing Relationship* (Sydney: Sydney University Press, 1980), 155.

108 *Australian Consolidated Press Ltd v Uren* [1969] 1 AC 590, 644.

109 D. Jackson, 'The Judicial Commonwealth' *Cambridge Law Journal* 28 (1970): 257.

110 M. Lunney, 'From Parker to the Australia Acts: Sir Victor Windeyer and the Short-lived Triumph of the Independent Australian Britons' *Current Legal Problems*, 74 (2021): 61.

111 [1964] AC 465.

112 *Mutual Life and Citizens' Assurance Co Ltd v Evatt* [1971] AC 793, reversing (1968) 122 CLR 556.

113 *Cassell & Co Ltd v Broome* [1972] AC 1027. See further M. Lunney, 'Uren v John Fairfax & Sons Pty Ltd (1966)', in D. Rolph (ed.), *Landmark Cases in Defamation Law* (Oxford: Hart, 2019), chapter 7.

114 Privy Council (Appeals from the High Court) Act 1975 (Cth).

in Australia was Australian in every sense of the word. While the shared heritage dictated that basic commonalities between English and Australian common law would remain,[115] by the twenty-first century the hidden plurality of the Australian law of civil wrongs had been replaced by an explicit articulation of an Australian law on the subject.[116]

Conclusion

It is tempting to see the history of the law relating to civil wrongs in white Australian history as the intertwining of Whiggish progression with increasing national self-confidence. Apart from displaying racial connotations,[117] for much of its history such a view ignores the contemporary cultural and intellectual milieu which shaped the self-understanding of those who participated in the process of creating and administering the law of civil wrongs. That experience was informed by the transnational concerns of empire in the 'one common law' but was not dominated by them; in Van Duinen's words 'the national was not subsumed by the transnational/imperial but, rather . . . there was an important yet ambiguous dynamic that existed between these spatial ambits'.[118] Only by recognising that this dynamic shaped both conversations about the law[119] as well as the content of the law can we understand the multi-faceted history of the law of civil wrongs in Australia.

115 Barwick, 'Law and the Courts', 161.
116 See, for example, *Trident General Insurance Co Ltd v McNiece* (1988) 165 CLR 107 (consideration in contract law); *Burnie Port Authority v General Jones Pty Ltd* (1994) 179 CLR 520 (abolition of separate tort of *Rylands v Fletcher*).
117 Lake, *Progressive New World*.
118 J. Van Duinen, 'The Borderlands of the British World' *Journal of Colonialism and Colonial History* 15 (2014).
119 P. Mitchell, 'Patterns of Legal Change' *Current Legal Problems* 65 (2012): 177, 201.

29
Labour Law

DIANE KIRKBY

Labour law is usually centred on duties and responsibilities of parties to an employment contract that were first legislated in the later nineteenth century.[1] Labour regulation in Britain, however, is much older – as old as the common law – and the first specific statutory provisions coincided with the emergence of waged labour in the fourteenth century. Legal provisions developed and spread with the expansion of the British Empire, industrialisation and the growth of modern European economies.[2] Australia's labour law history belongs within this frame but has its own distinct features.

Nineteenth-century employment law regulated activity that was, by definition, free and contractual. Labour as penal servitude is excluded. Yet modern Australia began as a colonial penal system of enforced labour and that is where the history of Australian labour law rightly begins. In the earliest decades of the colony, the category of 'employee' first emerged from the category of 'servant' of earlier labour regulation. The penal system blurred the lines between free and unfree labour, a fluidity that continued to underlie the principles and practices of labour law for differentiated groups of workers.

Foundations: Convict and Bonded Labour, the Law of Master and Servant

Australia's foundation as a colony dependent on convict labour meant that labour regulation began as a 'prescriptive and penal regime'.[3] The earliest

1 Breen Creighton and Andrew Stewart, *Labour Law: An Introduction* (Annandale: Federation Press, 1990).
2 Douglas Hay and Paul Craven, *Masters, Servants, and Magistrates in Britain and the Empire, 1562–1955* (Durham, NC: University of North Carolina Press, 2004); B. Hepple (ed.), *The Making of Labour Law in Europe: A Comparison of Nine Countries up to 1945* (Mansell, 1986, reprinted Oxford: Hart Publishing, 2009: B. Hepple (ed.), *The Making of Labour Law in Europe: A Comparison of Fifteen Countries up to 1945* (Oxford: Hart Publishing, 2009)).
3 Michael Quinlan, 'Australia 1788–1902: A Workingman's Paradise?', in Hay and Craven (eds), *Masters, Servants, and Magistrates*, 219–50.

governors were left to their own discretion to find employment for the convicts they had brought to establish a colony. They devised a system of assignment for allocating bonded convict male labourers to civil and military officers needing to clear the land and get farms established, and for binding women convicts to work in domestic service. Hiring out bonded labour was a new idea arising from the reality of the new colony's circumstances (see Figure 29.1). It was subsequently accepted by the authorities back in England but took several years to become an orderly system. In time, assignment moved from being an informal plan 'into a legal covenant between the Government and the employer' that stipulated how the convict should be maintained and for how long.[4] Certain rules were laid down for obtaining the labour, on the hours labourers were to work, and how they were to be treated.

Regulations were also introduced to curtail the masters' powers to punish their assigned labourers, though with little success. Convicts not so assigned remained on the government stores and were put to work in gangs building roads and public buildings. From the beginning, convicts were allowed some free hours to work for themselves or for wages.[5] They accrued some privileges not usually allowed to convicts. This set up a system of partial freedom for convicts to negotiate in a favourable labour market that challenged existing English law.[6] The Australian history of regulating labour from the convict period thus illuminates the fluidity of categories of free and unfree labour. Convicts were wholly subject to the governor's regulations, but on completion of their sentence they, along with non-convict immigrant labourers, were subject to a combination of governor's orders and stipulations under existing employment law.

This was the law of master and servant, a system of regulation by summary action for offences committed within the work relationship that had been in place for centuries. Master and servant legislation set the boundaries of free labour as it effectively criminalised the worker's failure to perform. English manual wage workers were subject to criminal punishment for breach of contract and could be arrested for leaving to change their place of employment. Legislatures and judiciaries in more than 100 British colonies drew upon this law in elaborating the statuses, rights and duties, of unfree, notably 'nonslave', labour.

4 T. A. Coghlan, *Labour and Industry* (Oxford: Oxford University Press, 1918, reprinted Melbourne: Macmillan, 1969), 1: 33.

5 Ibid, 1: 34–6.

6 David Neal, *The Rule of Law in a Penal Colony: Law and Power in Early New South Wales* (Cambridge: Cambridge University Press, 1991).

Figure 29.1: Convict workers in chain gang. Hobart Town Chain Gang by Charles Bruce c.1830, etching printed on orange paper Crowther Library, Hobart. IMAGE number: SD_ILS:177926; shelf number L8 MC3 DR1 iuop. Reproduced with the permission of the State Archives Service, Tasmanian State Library.

Hay and Craven have identified three key principles in these master and servant laws across the empire. First, employment for wages was a matter of private contract between parties differing in their power. That was further widened by the wording used: the employer as master acquired the right to command, and the employee as servant had the obligation to obey. The second principle related to the administration of these private agreements, which was done by magistrates and lay justices of the peace, who were themselves employers. Magistrates were not subject to oversight through appeal to a higher authority, the senior courts, so the provision for summary enforcement was largely unsupervised. The third principle related to discipline: punishment of the disobedient servant or 'uncooperative worker' was not imposed as damages, a remedy for the breach of contract. Instead punishments were inflicted physically – as whipping, forced labour or imprisonment – or in costly fines, the forfeiture of all wages. In the various British colonies, particularly where workers were not of European origin, law 'was often administered in highly oppressive and exploitative ways' that Hay and Craven say demonstrates that master and servant legislation across the empire 'undermines the conventional categories of "free" and "unfree" labor found in most of the economic and historical literature'.[7] US historian Robert Steinfeld contends that, rather than a sharp binary divide, it is more historically accurate to see free and unfree labour as co-existing forms of the labour contract.[8]

English master and servant law with its 'shades of coercion' is usefully described as concerned with an 'intermediate' labour market falling between free and forced labour.[9] The emergence of an industrial economy in the early nineteenth century created new sectors of the economy and revealed the uncertainty that existed in the scope of the existing labour laws, exposing the need for a new legislative regime of regulation appropriate to an industrialising economy. Clarifying the legal relationship between master and servant as employer and employee, however, extended the penal enforcement of labour contracts and increased the number of prosecutions for criminal breach. In twenty years after 1855, in the industrialised regions of northern England,

7 Hay and Craven (eds), *Masters, Servants, and Magistrates*, 1–2, 5; Alessandro Stanziani, *Bondage: Labor and Rights in Eurasia from the Sixteenth to the Early Twentieth Centuries* (New York: Berghahn Books, 2014); Suresh Naidu and Noam Yuchtman, 'Coercive Contract Enforcement: Law and the Labor Market in 19th Century Industrial Britain' *American Economic Review*, 103, no. 1 (2013): 107–44.

8 Robert Steinfeld, *Coercion, Contract, and Free Labor in the Nineteenth Century* (Cambridge: Cambridge University Press, 2001), 9–14.

9 Naidu and Yuchtman, 'Coercive Contract Enforcement'.

there were more prosecutions of servants per year than there were for petty larceny.[10]

In 1823 England passed a new master and servant Act which extended the coverage of the legislation to almost all manual workers.[11] Five years later, the Australian colonies began to pass their own master and servant legislation, starting with New South Wales (including the districts which were later to become Victoria and Queensland and enact their own legislation) and followed by the colonies of South Australia and Van Diemen's Land (in 1837), and the Swan River colony of Western Australia in 1840.[12] Two years later, with the cessation of transportation to New South Wales, the proportion of immigrant labour increased rapidly, especially with the gold rush of the 1850s.

The degrees of freedom that labourers enjoyed, however, rested on the statutory regime of master and servant laws that, in the colonies, reflected the social control objectives of the early penal years and the dominance of pastoralist-employers, politically and economically. With a convict workforce, autocratic governance, military officers as employers, and a garrison of troops for surveillance, these laws – which 'inferred that the rights of a workman were inferior to those of his master' – covered more workers, more harshly, than those in England.[13] Aboriginal people were not drawn into this regulatory regime as 'employees' or 'servants'. While their labour was important, and became increasingly so as the pastoral industry flourished and expanded, where Aboriginal labour was used their payment was usually in the form of European goods, or clothes.[14] Their legal status was administered by the British imperial system of appointing protectors for people not considered able to handle individual freedoms.[15]

Scholars who have studied the enforcement of colonial labour laws in Australia have estimated there were a total of 160,000 prosecutions in the jurisdiction of New South Wales between 1845 and 1930, but from the end of the 1850s there was a steady increase in actions taken by employees/

10 Ibid. 11 Ibid.

12 New South Wales 9 Geo. IV No. 9 1828; Tasmania 1 Vic. No. 15 1837; South Australia 7 Wm, IV No. 3, 1837; Western Australia 4 Vic. No. 2 1840; Victoria 16 Vic. No. 2 1852 and also 18 Vic. No. 16 1855 then 27 Vic. No. 198 1864; Queensland 25 Vic. No. 11 1861; see Quinlan, 'Australia 1788–1902', 224.

13 Coghlan, *Labour and Industry*, 3: 1476; Neal, *Rule of Law in a Penal Colony*, 133–7.

14 Greg Blyton, 'Black Trackers: Labour Contributions of Aboriginal People in the Hunter Region of SouthEastern NSW, 1804–54' *Labour History* no.114 (May 2018): 53–67; Ann McGrath, *Born In the Cattle* (Sydney: Allen & Unwin, 1987); Ann McGrath and Kay Saunders with Jackie Huggins, *Aboriginal Workers, special issue of Labour History* (Sydney: Australian Society for the Study of Labour History, 1995, reissued Liverpool University Press, August 2020).

15 See Nettelbeck, Chapter 20 in this volume.

servants.[16] This rise was a consequence of changes to the magistracy, the formation of trade unions, and a mobile workforce spreading ideas of their rights. Changing demographics with increasing urbanisation, a growing manufacturing workforce and political development prompted steps to broaden the regulation of the employment relationship.[17] Attempts to impose the unequal penalties – of imprisonment for a servant and a fine for a master committing the same offence – led to huge protests from colonists demanding repeal or immediate suspension by the Executive.[18] Amendments were made to the penalties in the New South Wales legislation in 1858[19] similar to those later made in England, but there was no sudden decrease in employer-initiated, or the total number of, cases in New South Wales.

The Australian colonies never repealed colonial master and servant law. Instead the law remained on the books, its demise stretched out: the range of occupations covered by its provisions narrowed, while the acts in various states co-existed with new legislation. Master and servant law remained in place until the 1970s with wage recovery provisions added but the penalty of imprisonment for breach of contract also surviving.[20] There were another 32,000 prosecutions in New South Wales between 1930 and 1963. The South Australian Act was repealed by the Industrial Conciliation and Arbitration Act 1972 and the New South Wales Act by the Industrial Arbitration (Further Amendment) Act 1980. The relevant Acts in Queensland, Tasmania, Victoria and Western Australia still remained in force in the early 1980s.[21] The co-existence of free labour and coercion outlived its convict origins.

Protection: Hours and Wages Legislation with the Growth of Unions

The second major period of Australian labour law came after the mid-nineteenth century, with the emergence and strength of unions and the establishment of a new legal regime. A significant turning point was the 1867 Royal Commission on Trade Unions in Britain. Previously the doctrine of

16 Adrian Merritt, 'The Historical Role of Law in the Regulation of Employment – Abstentionist or Interventionist?' *Australian Journal of Law and Society* 1, no. 1 (1982): 55–86; Rob McQueen, 'Master and Servants Legislation in the Nineteenth-century Australian Colonies' *Law and History in Australia* 4 (1987): 78–110.

17 Miles Goodwin and Glenda Maconachie, 'Minimum Labour Standards Enforcement in Australia: Caught in the Crossfire?' *Economic and Labour Relations Review* 22, no. 2 (July 2011): 55–80.

18 Coghlan, *Labour and Industry*, 3: 1476.

19 20 Vic. No. 28, ss 2 and 4.

20 Quinlan, 'Australia 1788–1902', 247, 250.

21 Merritt, 'The Historical Role of Law in the Regulation of Employment'.

'restraint of trade' had prevented industrial action being taken by organised workers, but the acceptance of trade unions in wage bargaining was spreading and passage of the UK Trade Union Act 1871 gave workers the freedom, and a legal framework within which, to combine. Another Royal Commission followed, which led to more pro-union legislation.[22]

The UK master and servant law was also reformed in 1867, to impose financial penalties whose non-payment led to imprisonment. Its continuing harshness and coercive sanctions provoked more resistance and the law was finally repealed in 1875. This marked the foundational moment of British labour law.[23] Criminal penalties were thus removed from English employment law as it moved towards civil procedure; the new legislation embraced a general theory of contract, where duties and remedies were now to be balanced between the parties.[24] The doctrine of laissez faire was giving way to greater intervention, greater legal protection for employees and a view that industrial stability needed a better balance of power between employers and workers. Though master and servant laws endured, the shift towards collective bargaining was mirrored in Australia. In the Australian colonies a great increase in the number and strength of trade unions was clear by 1869 and spreading to new trades.[25] Employers also began to form associations and no longer refused to deal with union officials. In 1873 the first 'full recognition of collective bargaining as a principle and not an isolated phenomenon' occurred when the coal miners' union was recognised as the representative of the employees 'in every difficulty that might arise'.[26]

In the last quarter of the century state action was oriented towards regulation of what was now a growing urban labour force in the light industrial sector. In 1873, the first colonial factory Act was also passed in the colony of Victoria. Calls for factory legislation limiting the hours of work had begun in Britain with textile workers but only succeeded on grounds of removing harms done to women and children. Thus from 1833 a pattern of first covering trades employing women and children was established, moving from the textile industries to the dangerous trades (mining), then in 1867 to premises employing more than fifty workers. This legislation never regulated the hours of adult males or the wages of any workers but over a period of decades it made intervention by the state acceptable to employers and broke down the doctrine

22 Douglas Brodie, *A History of British Labour Law: 1867–1945* (London: Bloomsbury, 2003), 10.

23 Ibid, 1.

24 Hay and Craven (eds), *Masters, Servants, and Magistrates.*

25 Coghlan, *Labour and Industry*, 3: 1471.

26 Ibid, 3: 1428.

of laissez faire.[27] Australian colonial legislation followed the pattern of first regulating the hours of employment of women, and then passing measures (for the safety of male workers) in the dangerous trades and industries like mining. Legislation passed in Victoria on safety in mines (Regulation of Mines and Machinery Act 1877) made employers responsible for accidents.[28] The Victorian Supervision of Workrooms and Factories Act 1873 which preceded it, and all other colonial laws, limited the hours that women could work, and ensured properly ventilated workrooms, but this was pioneering legislation that contained drafting inadequacies and oversights: it failed to provide for inspectors and it defined a factory in such a way that smaller workrooms and outwork proliferated.[29] Its shortcomings spurred a Royal Commission, a campaign that led to new legislation first in 1885, then most significantly in 1896. This time the law forbade child labour and established an inspectorate as well as a system of wages boards for setting minimum wage rates, an innovation subsequently adopted in England.[30] Other colonies – South Australia (1894), New South Wales and Queensland (1896) and Western Australia (1897) – similarly passed factory acts as manufacturing accelerated and spread.

Protection of labourers against 'the greed of avaricious taskmasters or the evils of uncontrolled competition', was the driving principle of this trend in legislation on industrial working conditions; that the weak (such as 'the weaker sex') should be able 'to look to parliament for protection and assistance', and so too should the 'honest trader' be protected 'against the dishonest'.[31] Protection, however well intentioned, was very problematic and who was actually being protected needs unpacking. Unspoken was the whiteness of this legislation: in defining a factory and specifically including workplaces employing Chinese, it was crafted to afford local manufacturers as well as labour, protection against Chinese competition.[32] Protection as applied to Aboriginal people is covered in

27 Asa Briggs, 'Industrial Relations in Great Britain', in A. Flanders and H. Clegg (eds), *The System of Industrial Relations in Great Britain* (Oxford: Oxford University Press, 1954), 9–10.

28 Coghlan, *Labour and Industry*, 3: 1475.

29 Ibid, 3: 1472; Goodwin and Maconachie, 'Minimum Labour Standards'.

30 J. Hagan, 'Employers, Trade Unions and the First Victorian Factory Acts' *Labour History* no. 7 (November 1964): 3–10; K. Hince, 'Wages Boards in Victoria' *Journal of Industrial Relations* 7 (July 1965): 176; Violet Markham, *Factory and Shop Acts of the British Dominions* (London: Eyre & Spottiswoode, 1908).

31 Hagan, *The First Victorian Factory Acts*, 5, quoting the *Age* (Melbourne) 16 June 1879, 2; Alexander Peacock, MP, when introducing the Factories Act 1896. Victoria, *Parliamentary Debates*, 1896.

32 Coghlan, *Labour and Industry*, 4: 2093–4; Diane Kirkby, 'Honorary Chinese? Women, Whiteness and Labour Legislation in the Early Australian Commonwealth' *Law's Empire, Special Issue of Social Identities; Journal for the Study of Race, Nation and Culture* 13, no. 6 (2007): 801–18.

another chapter. The focus on protecting the weak meant that getting real protections from workplace hazards – in what became Occupational Health and Safety legislation with its own separate history – was very hard for male workers. This emphasis cut both ways. Barring only women from dangerous workplaces, working at night, or from certain tasks such as lifting weights, meant placing and keeping women in a different category of worker, which also protected men's right to work and to be paid higher wages. Women carried the legacy of these 'protective' provisions for another century, and that legacy lingers on even today as a significant issue in the debate over equal rights for women workers.[33] Protective legislation was not unique to England and its colonies but Australia led the way in fixing a minimum wage, first for women workers, and then also extending it to men.[34]

Labour conditions were not only regulated by master and servant law, contract law and factory legislation. Occupational health and safety provisions are often omitted from this history yet the UK Workmen's Compensation Act of 1897 was a major milestone.[35] Legislative provisions covering workers in occupations other than manufacturing should also be considered. One notable example is work behind the hotel bar, performed by both men and women and regulated by licensing laws stipulating hours of trading and the age of employment.[36] In the Australian colonies efforts to exclude women from this employment were highly contested and argued for on the same grounds as gendered protections were for factory workers. Its 'dangers' (excessive hours and unventilated rooms) were from the same cause (women's reproductive capacity). In bars, the protections women supposedly needed were not from machines, or the harms inherent in dangerous work (like underground mining), but from the risks to reproductive health and more specifically morality, of women working in close proximity to men. Intervention had to overcome arguments for 'the liberty of the subject' and 'freedom of contract' that applied to men. It was acceptable to legislatures when the legislation regulated a category of workers, not the employers, and women

33 Rosemary Hunter, 'Representing Gender in Legal Analysis: A Case/Book Study in Labour Law' *Melbourne University Law Review* 18 (December 1991): 305–28; S. J. Kenney, 'Reproductive Hazards in the Workplace: The Law and Sexual Difference' *International Journal of the Sociology of Law* 14 (1986): 393.

34 See Renate Howe, 'A Paradise for Working Men but Not Working Women' in Ulla Wikander, Alice Kessler-Harris and Jane Lewis (eds), *Protecting Women: Labor Legislation in Europe, the United States, and Australia, 1880–1920* (Chicago, IL: University of Illinois Press, 1995); Diane Kirkby, '"The Wage-Earning Woman and the State": the National Women's Trade Union League and Protective Labor Legislation' *Labor History* 28 (Winter 1987): 54–74.

35 Brodie, *A History of British Labour Law*.

36 Diane Kirkby, *Barmaids: A History of Women's Work in Pubs* (Cambridge: Cambridge University Press, 1997).

Figure 29.2: Union float of Breweries Employees. n. d. [c.1900] State Library of Western Australia IMAGE: Number: BA 342/3370. Sourced from the collections of the State Library of Western Australia and reproduced with the permission of the Library Board of Western Australia.

workers consequently carried the burdens of restrictions. By the early twentieth century, a NSW Committee of Inquiry into Factories and Shops said that the state had the power to prohibit work for males under sixteen years of age on 'dangerous machinery', but it had that power to do so for women of all ages in what it deemed 'inappropriate employment'.[37] One Australian jurisdiction (South Australia in 1908) prohibited women's work in hotel bars on that ground, while others only limited access to the work. 'Inappropriate' was a significant, gender-specific conception of workplace hazards.

These decades spanning the end of the nineteenth century only ended bonded labour and gave contractual rights to some workers.[38] Those with the organisational strength of unions or higher bargaining power were better placed to negotiate and campaign to their own advantage (Figure 29.2). The vast majority of workers in the British Empire who were not English and

37 Quoted in ibid, 126. 38 Stanziani, *Bondage: Labor and Rights in Eurasia.*

white have a different history. The concept of British labour law as an employment contract did not allow for indentured or coerced labour, which moved huge numbers of Indian, Chinese and Melanesian labourers within and between colonies during the nineteenth century. Colonies which relied on non-European imported or Indigenous workers invented their own models of coercion and remedy, quite different from those of England.[39] Regulations increasingly distinguished between white Australian and non-white workers. From the 1860s employers in the Australian colonies imported bonded labour from the Pacific islands to work on sugar plantations.[40] Under late nineteenth-century protection legislation, local Indigenous populations were forcibly moved, or confined, according to the labour needs of local industries. The definition of labour law as covering only free and contractual labour is not broad enough to include this history of unfree labour and needs to be expanded to these additional laws regulating and impacting on workers whose experience does not fall into the narrow category of 'employee'.

Aboriginal Australian workers were regulated under a different set of laws, also containing 'protective' provisions. These – usually called Aborigines Acts – were introduced in different colonies from early in the nineteenth century but they accelerated as state governments became active in passing new labour laws. Four years before Victoria passed its first Factories Act in 1873, the state had passed a major new statute on Aboriginal protection.[41] In South Australia Aboriginal labour became very important in the pastoral industry as a system for balancing employment, rations and traditional access to country. The government set no 'meaningful' employment regulations for this labour, instead turning pastoralists (the station owners and managers) into guardians with considerable authority over Aboriginal lives. To safeguard their access and control of this labour, when the South Australian Parliament in 1899 tried to introduce new legislation, pastoralists opposed any changes that were intended to regulate the employment of Aboriginal labour.[42]

'Protection' in labour law may be seen then as less about safeguarding the workers on which it focused (women, Aboriginal people, children) and more

39 Hay and Craven (eds), *Masters, Servants, and Magistrates*.

40 Tracey Banivanua Mar, *Violence and Colonial Dialogue: The Australian-Pacific Indentured Labor Trade* (Honolulu: University of Hawai'i Press, 2007).

41 Aborigines Protection Act (33 Vic. No. 3[49]) 1869 (Victoria).

42 Robert Foster, 'Rations, Coexistence, and the Colonisation of Aboriginal Labour in the South Australian Pastoral Industry, 1860–1911' *Aboriginal History* 24 (2000): 1–26.

concerned with protecting existing labour categories or sustaining vested economic interests. The previous regime of controlling Aboriginal lives gained momentum in the new century as colonies became states following Federation in 1901. States retained the power to legislate on labour and Indigenous populations within their own jurisdictions. The Commonwealth government – 'in stark contrast' to other federal jurisdictions – took responsibility to settle industrial disputes crossing state borders and to set industry-wide minimum standards.[43] Measures to prevent the importation of indentured labour, which started in the 1880s, dominated the legislation and policy framework of immigration, now a Commonwealth responsibility. Racism was nowhere more evident than in restrictions that were imposed on the entry of non-white immigrants, and lasted until the 1960s.[44] Labour law reflected these ideas.

Regulation: Industrial Tribunals and Compulsory Arbitration

By the end of the nineteenth century Australia was leading in enacting progressive ideas, what Victor Clark of Columbia University called 'the progressive betterment of labor' through legislation.[45] Ideas about 'the living wage' for male heads of household and using arbitration in labour disputes were circulating in both England and Australia from the 1870s.[46] While in England 'compulsory arbitration was rejected as impracticable'[47] in New Zealand (in 1894) and Australia, it was embraced. A labour power was formally written into the new constitution and within the first few years of the new nation, legislation established a court of conciliation and arbitration.

Not surprisingly the system for settling industrial disputes established by the Conciliation and Arbitration Act 1904 has dominated the literature and study of labour law and industrial relations in Australia. Written into the Constitution, industrial tribunals and commissions became 'the most

43 David Brody, 'American Labour Law as a Model for Australia? Or, Can You Get Here From There?' *Labour History* No.97 (2009): 189–98.

44 Anthony O'Donnell and Richard Mitchell, 'Immigrant Labour in Australia: The Regulatory Framework' *Australian Journal of Labour Law* 14 (2001): 269; Myra Willard, *History of the White Australia Policy to 1920* (Melbourne: Melbourne University Press, 1923); A. T. Yarwood, *Asian Migration to Australia: The Background to Exclusion 1896–1923* (Melbourne: Melbourne University Press, 1964, reissued 1967); Gwenda Tavan, *The Long Slow Death of White Australia* (Melbourne: Scribe, 2005).

45 Victor Clark, *The Labour Movement in Australasia* (New York: Holt & Co, 1906); Diane Kirkby, *Alice Henry: The Life of an Australian-American Labour Reformer* (Cambridge: Cambridge University Press, 1991).

46 Coghlan, *Labour and Industry*, 3: 1428.

47 Brodie, *A History of British Labour Law*, 60.

powerful institutions in the governance' of Australians' working lives.[48] The awards they made covered all aspects of work, wage rates, job classifications, leave provisions and career structures. At the time the system was finally replaced in the 1990s, 85 per cent of Australia's paid workers relied on these awards for the most significant of their workplace rights.

Despite its legal formalism, the appointment of judges to administer this system and the initial establishment of a court for hearings, the study of arbitration has been mostly undertaken by disciplines other than law.[49] Economists have been most interested in arbitration's role as an instrument of economic management.[50] The precise content of the field of 'labour law' has thus been blurred.[51]

Writing in the 1950s, Orwell de R. Foenander saw working people's welfare as labour law's objective. While fulfilling social objectives of regulating wages, leave and working hours, achieving industrial peace was the overriding objective of a system that was also used as a mechanism of labour market regulation for national economic objectives. By 1960, the subject of 'labour law' or 'industrial law' indicated the relevant parties were federal and state governments, those employed or employing under contracts of employment, and trade unions. The focus was narrowly legal, 'on the various legal rules and institutions which shaped, governed, regulated and impacted upon the relationships between those parties . . . The various statutory provisions and other rules, orders, and awards which ordered and regulated those relationships.'[52] Only by the 1980s were more political economy matters such as 'industrial democracy', 'health and safety', 'discrimination', and 'comparative labour law' also included.

48 Rosemary Owens, 'Women, "Atypical" Work Relationships and the Law' *Melbourne University Law Review* 19, no. 2 (December 1993): 399–430.

49 A point made by Stuart Macintyre and Richard Mitchell, 'Introduction', in Stuart Macintyre and Richard Mitchell (eds), *Foundations of Arbitration: The Origins and Effects of State Compulsory Arbitration 1890–1914* (Oxford: Oxford University Press, 1989), 4.

50 Richard Naughton, 'Early Academic Research in Australian Labour Law: 1920–60' *Australian Journal of Labour Law* 30 (2017): 58.

51 Richard Mitchell, 'The Evolution of the Idea of a Labour Law Subject in Australian Legal Scholarship: (and What Was Regulating "Labour" or "Work" before Labour Law as We Know It)?', Working Paper No. 22, Workplace and Corporate Law Group, Monash University (May 2017); Laura Bennett, *Making Labour Law in Australia: Industrial Relations, Politics and Law* (Sydney: Law Book Co, 1994); Orwell de R. Foenander, *Studies in Australian Labour Law and Relations* (Melbourne: Melbourne University Press, 1952); Orwell de R. Foenander, *Better Employment Relations* (Sydney: Law Book Co, 1954); Mark Perlman, *Judges in Industry: A Study of Labor Arbitration in Australia* (Melbourne: Melbourne University Press, 1954).

52 Ibid, 9.

Historically, the achievement of compulsory arbitration was to validate trade unions and secure their place in setting wages and conditions, enabling them to frame awards and take responsibility for policing those awards among employers. The process of registration, which was required of unions wanting to have their disputes settled, gave unions legitimacy and legal support.[53] This system differentiated Australia (and New Zealand) from the US where judge-made law was 'persistently – and grossly – hostile to trade unions' and anti-union doctrines were much more powerful.[54] The virtue of the awards system was their legally enforceable industry-wide application once decided by the court / commission. Some workers, however, fell outside their application. Only in 1965 did a union finally bring a case for Aboriginal workers in the pastoral industry to be included under an award and granted payment of a proper wage.[55]

The awards system had a complex history for women workers, as feminist scholars have pointed out.[56] Women in other countries have also struggled to achieve the right to work and equal pay, but in Australia they had to do so through the arbitration system, where (chiefly male) unionists put the case before a judge, and which in its very earliest years institutionalised 'the family wage' with its breadwinner model of the paid worker. In the Harvester judgment of 1907 Higgins J decided that 'a fair and reasonable' wage was one that allowed an unskilled worker to support a family – a wife and three children – in frugal comfort.[57] The maleness of the breadwinner was confirmed legally. The breadwinner model assuming there was someone at home, unpaid, to care for the domestic needs of the paid worker, ensured women's dependence, impacted on women's wage rates and structured the labour market. 'If women did work in the paid work force it was assumed that they had only to support themselves.'[58] Their wages were set accordingly.

53 Macintyre and Mitchell (eds), *Foundations of Arbitration*, 16.
54 Brody, 'American Labour Law', 192.
55 Commonwealth Conciliation and Arbitration Commission, Cattle Station Industry (Northern Territory) Award 1951, 7 March 1966.
56 Diane Kirkby, 'Arbitration and the Fight for Economic Justice', in Macintyre and Mitchell (eds), *Foundations of Arbitration*, 334–51.
57 The literature on this is large, and discussed in Kirkby, 'Arbitration and the Fight for Economic Justice'; a foundational work is Edna Ryan and Anne Conlon, *Gentle Invaders: Australian Women at Work, 1788–1974* (Melbourne: Nelson, 1975).
58 Owens, 'Women, "Atypical" Work Relationships and the Law', 407; see also Rosemary Owens, 'The Traditional Labour Law Framework: A Critical Evaluation', in Richard Mitchell (ed.), *Redefining Labour Law: New Perspectives on the Future of Teaching and Research*, Centre for Employment and Labour Relations Law, Occasional Monograph Series No. 3, University of Melbourne, 1995, 3–28.

Figure 29.3: Women meat workers. Women meat workers who brought the first Equal Pay case to the Conciliation and Arbitration Court in *The Bulletin*, 8 February 1969, 29–32. Reproduced with permission of ARE Media.

In regard to the sexual division of labour and classifications of skill, the Court adopted arguments presented by male unionists and male employers in relation to women, which generally positioned women as 'unskilled', doing different work from men. Male workers were able to win for themselves elite supervisory roles and employers were able to afford to pay high margins for skill to the small elite when the bulk of the workforce was on female 'unskilled' rates.[59] Through these awards the Court and commissions constructed the working lives of women both in the paid work force and in the home (Figure 29.3). Breadwinning empowered men within their families. Being made dependent upon men, women were denied economic autonomy, their poverty often only revealed after divorce. Women's family and

59 Kirkby, 'Arbitration and the Fight for Economic Justice'; Raelene Frances, '"No more Amazons": Gender and Work Process in the Victorian Clothing Trades 1890–1939' *Labour History* 50 (1986): 95–112; Laura Bennett, 'The Construction of Skill: Craft Unions, Women Workers and the Conciliation and Arbitration Court' *Law in Context* 2 (1984): 118–32.

domestic responsibilities were dismissed as 'not entailing any legal (that is, real) obligations'.[60] Not entitled by right or convention to participate in the paid work force, women had little access to, or protection of, the full range of rights and benefits of employment relationships that were the substance of a narrowly conceived field of labour law. Feminist scholars also showed that labour law was intertwined with other areas such as social welfare law where entitlements were contingent on labour market participation.[61]

The male focus of Australia's arbitration system is only one part of the gender problem of labour law in Australian history. The relationships surrounding performance of work in the home – the private arrangements in households or between married couples – are still largely ignored by a labour law concerned solely with the paid work force. Indeed, '[f]or many years this law explicitly sanctioned discrimination against women in the paid work force, both by their exclusion from it and by their differential and inferior treatment within it'.[62] The field of labour law as practised and taught, reflected this. When several new books were published in the field in 1990, Rosemary Hunter pointed to their 'un- or barely-acknowledged masculinist orientation of labour law'. They all demonstrated 'an unquestioned acceptance that the subjects of labour law are male workers'. This was a severe limitation in the field: 'a fairly breath-taking dismissal of sixty-seven years of overt wage discrimination against women workers … and also of a great deal of feminist scholarship and energy'. Hunter argued that this conception of labour law ignored the detrimental effects that were still being felt by women workers, their history, and their perpetuation. If 'the information upon which rules are based excludes women, which in turn means that the rules construct men as their subjects and women as "other"', law teaching continued to disadvantage women materially.[63]

Women workers' very long campaign for equal pay was achieved finally in the arbitration court in 1969, but covered so few workers it had to be argued a second and third time (in 1972 and 1974).[64] That date is taken as a turning point in women's labour law history. Since then 'the rhetoric of the worker as breadwinner has all but disappeared'.[65]

60 Owens, 'Women, "Atypical" Work Relationships and the Law', 406.
61 Cora Baldock, 'Public Policies and the Paid Work of Women', in Cora Baldock and Bettina Cass (eds), *Women, Social Welfare and the State* (Sydney: Allen & Unwin, 1983), 20–53.
62 Owens, 'Women, "Atypical" Work Relationships and the Law', 403.
63 Hunter, 'Representing Gender in Legal Analysis', 311.
64 Mary Gaudron and Michal Bosworth, 'Equal Pay?', in Heather Radi (ed.), *In Pursuit of Justice* (Sydney: Hale & Iremonger, 1979), 160–9.
65 Owens, 'Women, "Atypical" Work Relationships and the Law', 407.

Australia's adoption of compulsory arbitration was one exercise of constitutional powers. The powers to pass domestic labour laws were left with the states. Yet there are other powers in the constitution giving direct federal government control over the labour market and workplace conditions. These are not usually recognised as labour law. One was the power to make trade and commerce laws, which could be extended to cover shipping and also railways.[66] It has been put to only minor use to manage labour, but was relied upon heavily in relation to maritime and waterfront employment. Under this power the Navigation Act was introduced alongside the Conciliation and Arbitration Act in 1904 and finally passed in 1912.[67] Its provisions covered methods of employment, apprenticeships, stipulated the age and years of training for ratings and prescribed disciplinary codes to ensure obedience.[68] Other laws were introduced in the early years of Federation to regulate labour; for example, to deport 'non-white' labour that had been brought in from the Pacific islands.[69] At other times over the course of the twentieth century other laws – such as the Trade Practices Act – were extended in their provisions to control trade unionists' ability to take industrial or political action. These too arguably belong within the ambit of twentieth-century labour law.

Being 'compulsory' was a significant component of the Australasian system that marked out its difference from England where 'voluntarism' and collective bargaining were preferred. In the United States, the doctrine of free labour was given constitutional status after the Civil War, in the 13th Amendment ending indentured servitude and slavery, and the United States committed to 'heavily privileging individual over collective rights'.[70] There employers' refusal to engage in collective bargaining, justified as being 'to protect the liberty of their workers', was a 'powerful powerful' argument upheld in the courts.[71] In Australia, arbitration shifted coercion on to employers equally with the unions. It elevated the power of unions but notably compulsion ensured compliance by all the parties. All were legally required to implement the rulings of the Commission. The very fact that the

66 De Foenander, *Studies in Australian Labour Law and Relations*, 7.

67 Australia. Parliament, Acts, Volume XI, 1912.

68 Diane Kirkby, '"The sailor is a human being": Labour Market Regulation and the Australian Navigation Act 1912', in Diane Kirkby (ed.), *Past Law, Present Histories* (Canberra: ANU E Press, 2012), 177–92.

69 Peter Prince, '"Australia's Most Inhumane Mass Deportation Abuse": Robtelmes v Brenan and Expulsion of the "Alien" Islanders' *Law&History* 5, no. 1 (March 2018): 113–41.

70 Brody, 'American Labour Law', 192.

71 Ibid, 193.

Figure 29.4: Striking unionists waiting outside Fremantle magistrates court 1977 *West Australian* 16 June 1977. Acknowledgment: ©*Westpix*.

Commission had this power to compel participation in the resolution of a dispute, and it could impose a decision that was legally binding, was enough to forge industrial agreements without resorting to the use of powers. Industrial tribunals had a key role to safeguard 'the public interest': rather than just bring opposing parties together, the federal Arbitration Commission was responsible for making any agreement they endorsed in the interest of the broader community.[72] Achieving industrial peace is one dimension of 'the public interest' aspect of the labour regulation system (Figure 29.4).

Employer opposition to the arbitration system, which subsided after the first two decades, gained momentum again from the 1970s.[73] Despite widespread public support for its continuance, the election of neoliberal governments at both state and federal levels in the 1990s brought the dismantling of

72 Diane Kirkby, 'Labour, Capital and the Public Interest: The Australian Experiment of Compulsory Arbitration', in Christopher Platt (ed.), *Social Welfare 1850–1950: Argentina, Australia and Canada Compared* (London: Macmillan, 1989), 107–24; Richard Naughton, '"Public interest" in Australian Labour Law – Reshaping an Old Concept in the Enterprise Bargaining Era' *Australian Journal of Labour Law* 27, no. 2 (October 2014): 112–36.

73 David Plowman, 'Forced March: The Employers and Arbitration', in Macintyre and Mitchell (eds), *Foundations of Arbitration*, 135–55.

arbitration.[74] A new system was instituted – of enterprise bargaining and individual workplace agreements – which restored the power of employers that was more akin to the era of master and servant.

Deregulation: The 'New Economy'

As the twentieth century came to an end, labour law hit a crisis in definition with the changes that were occurring in the world of work. Faced with an increased use of temporary and casualised labour; dependence on subcontracting; extensive out-sourcing and restructuring of public sector employment and the return to home-based work, labour law was forced to confront the realities of an unregulated economy. The regime of regulation for full-time waged work now seemed an aberration.[75] A new interdisciplinary approach to labour law-making was called for. Labour lawyers called for extensions to the field to embrace methods of empirical research and areas of law and groups of workers previously excluded that they 'ought to have been interested in from the outset'.[76] They acknowledged that their preoccupation with problems arising out of the legal regulation of employment, 'the factory vision', had generally marginalised broader issues of labour market regulation. They saw new subjects and made connections with historians and other disciplinary fields.

One of those areas which had long been of major importance in Australian labour's history, was immigration. Once Europeans began colonising Australia, immigration became and has remained crucial to providing Australia's labour force, accounting for over half of the additions to the labour force between 1945 and 1981. Today foreign-born labour in Australia is high by OECD standards. Immigration's significance in constituting the size and skills of the labour force has a visible impact on national patterns of employment, and is important to employment contracts, wages and conditions – in short, the regulation of employment relationships.[77] Yet immigration has only recently

74 Creighton and Stewart, *Labour Law*, 38–47.

75 Michael Quinlan, 'Precarious Employment, Ill Health, and Lessons from History: The Case of Casual (Temporary) Dockworkers 1880–1945' *International Journal of Health Services* 43, no. 4 (2013): 721–44; for critiques of the field see chapters in Mitchell (ed.), *Redefining Labour Law*; Andrew Stewart and Shae McCrystal, 'Labour Regulation and the Great Divide: Does the Gig Economy Require a New Category of Worker?' *Australian Journal of Labour Law* 32, no. 4 (2019).

76 Laura Bennett, *Making Labour Law in Australia: Industrial Relations, Politics and Law* (Sydney: Law Book Co, 1994); Mitchell (ed.), *Redefining Labour Law*, xi; Richard Johnstone and Donald McKenzie, 'Empirical Research in Labour Law', in Mitchell (ed.), *Redefining Labour Law*, 150–66.

77 O'Donnell and Mitchell, 'Immigrant Labour in Australia'.

been considered relevant to the field of labour law. Immigration law has followed labour law, in its orientation towards issues of economic efficiency, productivity, competitiveness and regional integration in relation to labour market regulation. Economic changes have undermined 'the very idea of a domestic labour market' with internal labour markets emerging within multinational firms. Hence, the liberalisation of temporary entry procedures for skilled workers has proceeded as 'employers need no longer have direct regard for the employment opportunities of domestic [i.e. local] workers'.[78]

Seafarers are another group of workers whose mobility and diversity exemplify the characteristics of a globalised labour market. Seafarers have always laboured under a separate regime of employment regulation, particular to the industry. Their conditions of harsh discipline and precarious employment lasted long after other workers secured improvements and protections in the late nineteenth century.[79] Seafaring unions consequently turned to international conventions given the difficulties of enforcing national labour laws, in combating the blurring of boundaries between free and unfree labour that continue to plague the industry.

In other sectors, the 'gig economy' has challenged the structure of contracts which had been central in defining labour law. Basic concepts and categories of 'employee', 'employer', and 'employment contracts' are questionable when work is organised through digital platforms which separate the performance of work from the business itself.[80] The new arrangements avoid the usual costs and responsibilities of adhering to legislated standards of employment. Changes in the organisation of work have challenged labour lawyers to broaden the field to include 'all dimensions of law which bear upon human capital deployment'.[81] Leading international scholars called for new categories in ways of representing workers, and to go beyond contract. Labour law's principal concern was now to be with the legal construction and regulation of working experience that lay outside continuous and fixed term employment, i.e. as casual labour, in various forms of contracting, namely labour hire arrangements, or in new forms, like franchising.[82] No longer

78 Ibid, 16.

79 Michael Quinlan, 'Regulating Labour in a Colonial Context: Maritime Labour Legislation in the Australian Colonies, 1788–1850' *Australian Historical Studies* 29, no. 111 (1998): 303–24; Jonathan Hyslop, 'British Steamship Workers, c.1875–1945: Precarious Before Precarity' *Labour History* no. 116 (May 2019): 5–28.

80 Stewart and McCrystal, 'Labour Regulation and the Great Divide'.

81 Brian Langille, 'Labour Law's Theory of Justice', in Guy Davidov and Brian Langille (eds), *The Idea of Labour Law* (Oxford: Oxford University Press, 2011), chapter 7.

82 Stewart and McCrystal, 'Labour Regulation and the Great Divide'.

securely fixed in its place, in the twenty-first century, labour law had become 'an evolving project'.[83]

Being cut adrift from the older categories and ways of thinking compelled a call for change in the conception and normative underpinning of labour law. This was no longer to be confined to preventing unfairness in contract negotiation but to include 'all productive activity', better considered as 'law which regulates the deployment of human capital'.[84] Theorists argued such a conception should be placed at the centre of a policy agenda prioritising values of human wealth and freedom. The more ambitious vision saw an ideal labour law as being 'a system . . . which guaranteed "decent work" for all and upheld the human rights of workers'.[85] As English legal historian Bob Hepple has said 'labour laws are used by people to pursue their own goals . . . and sometimes they need rights such as to a minimum wage or to freedom of association simply in order to survive'.[86] Freedom and human rights have come to the forefront as missing elements of labour law.

Conclusion

Although there are similarities in the issues they confront, labour law regimes are not transferable between jurisdictions. They are experienced in unique configurations of circumstances.[87] Since labour law is the outcome of power relationships and struggles between different ideologies and social actors, law's development and specific features in any jurisdiction must take account of the variety of factors involved. Its history is the specifics of 'why real employers, workers, politicians and judges act as they do in practice'.[88]

The particularities of the Australian experience reveal a history of blurring boundaries on a continuum of freedoms, state intervention, and imperial influence that is complex in balancing competing factors. The colony began with penal unfree labour that allowed some room for waged 'free' work. Indigenous populations were excluded from wages and worked in degrees of unfreedom that extended to slavery. The ideology of 'free labour', and

83 John Howe, Anna Chapman and Ingrid Landau, *The Evolving Project of Labour Law: Foundations, Development and Future Research Directions* (Annandale: Federation Press, 2017).

84 Langille, 'Labour Law's Theory of Justice'.

85 Bob Hepple, 'Factors Influencing the Making and Transformation of Labour Law in Europe', in Davidov and Langille (eds), *The Idea of Labour Law*, 30.

86 Ibid, 30. 87 Brody, 'American Labour Law'.

88 Hepple, *The Making of Labour Law in Europe*, 30; Hepple, 'Factors Influencing the Making and Transformation of Labour Law'.

concepts of 'freedom of contract' and 'the liberty of the subject' were effective weapons in the hands of employers, when the boundaries were contested in, and established by, Parliaments and the courts. As legislation was introduced to alleviate the worst abuses of exploitation and improve health and safety, gender dynamics shaped the labour market and the formalisation of labour standards. Opponents of intervention were keen to limit the power of worker organisations and prevent measures that reduced their own power. The history of labour law exposes these patterns.

30

Place and Race in Australian Copyright Law: May Gibbs's and Albert Namatjira's Copyright

KATHY BOWREY

Copyright laws have been primarily understood in terms of the right of the author, perceived as a universal right that is generally similar in content across the globe, but this view is misleading. From an Anglo-Australian legal perspective the right of the author is not a natural property right. Nor, according to British law, did it survive as a common law right after the passing of the first copyright law, the Statute of Anne 1710.[1] This Enlightenment-era law was enacted with the goal of encouraging learning and securing the employment of printers and booksellers. It imposed limits on the author's intangible property right to secure public interest goals, such as progressing the arts, sciences and education of the masses.[2] One legacy of this is that Anglo-copyright is usually referred to as 'a creature of positive law'.[3]

Following from this logic it might be presumed that a history of Australian law need only trace the technical details of the laws that have applied in Australia since colonial times. However, not only is accounting for these laws complicated, any meaningful history also needs to account for how place and race have affected the significance of Australian copyright. This entails looking beyond the laws of Australian Parliaments to consider their interaction with imperial and international copyright law, and investigate how

This research was supported by the Australian Research Council: DP140100172, Kathy Bowrey and Catherine Bond, *Australian Made: A History of Australian Copyright Law and Creator Success 1868–1968*. With thanks to Professor Irene Watson, Marie Hadley, and Anna Holtby and Erin Butterworth for research assistance, to Diane Giese for permission to access oral history records at Library and Archives NT, and the Northcott Society for permission to access the May Gibbs archive at the Mitchell Library, SLNSW.

1 1710 8 Ann c 21.

2 The leading case is *Donaldson v Becket* (1774) 1 Eng Rep 837; 4 Burr 2408, 98 Eng Rep 257. See Ronan Deazley, *On the Origin of the Right to Copy* (Oxford: Hart Publishing, 2004).

3 Copyright Act 1968 (Cth), s 8.

this complexity affected Australian creators. As colonialism did not end with Federation, there is also a need to explore the situation of Aboriginal creators who have faced additional layers of regulation of their lives, which impacted upon their enjoyment of copyright.

This chapter begins with an overview of copyright legislation, beginning with imperial laws that conferred rights on British subjects living in British Dominions. Australian colonial copyright laws are then discussed in relation both to these laws, and to the Berne Convention for the Protection of Literary and Artistic Works 1886. This international treaty, which Britain entered into on behalf of her dominions in 1886, would lead to Australia setting aside its first Copyright Act 1905 (Cth) and instead, through the Copyright Act 1912 (Cth), enacting the Copyright Act 1911 (UK) in Australia. Accordingly, both before and after Federation, Australian copyright laws were nested within the framework of empire. This situation continued until the passing of the Copyright Act 1968 (Cth).

How the placement of Australian law within empire impacted upon Australian creators is discussed in relation to the artist and illustrator, May Gibbs (1877–1965). Gibbs was unusually proactive in the way she created her own commercial opportunities, maximising the value of her artistic works by establishing a cottage industry based upon 'gumnut babies' Australiana. She is an exemplar of what it was possible to achieve as an entrepreneurial artist protected by Australian intellectual property laws. Gibbs serves as a point of comparison with Aboriginal artist Albert Namatjira (1901–59). Namatjira's experience draws out the relevance of colonialism and race to Australian cultural production in the early to mid twentieth century. When, like Gibbs, Namatjira and other Hermannsburg artists were entrepreneurial in building an infrastructure to commercialise their art, the state responded. As government policy shifted from protection to assimilation, new laws sought to explicitly limit opportunities for cultural expression and the exercise of economic agency by Aboriginal peoples. These included laws designed to limit art sales and assignment of copyright by Aboriginal artists without state approval. The two case studies illustrate how participation in Australian cultural and economic activity has been impacted by the broader historical context of empire and colonialism. This has not only affected the significance of Australian copyright for artists in the twentieth century, it has impacted upon the production and circulation of commodities that helped define Australian culture.

An Historical Overview of Copyright Laws

Nineteenth-century British Laws

Colonisation had an economic and a cultural agenda. The spread of Western civilisation was supported by cultural trade dealing in copyright-protected works. In the British Empire the book trade was imperfectly controlled by London publishers. They came to dominate Anglophone publishing as a consequence of the historical privileges of the Stationers' Company of London, who maintained a register of copyrights and exclusive printing rights to titles that did not offend censorship laws.[4] Seventeenth- and eighteenth-century Enlightenment ideas that informed limits to literary property, especially the idea that there was a public domain of knowledge to be discovered and converted into private property, also served to justify colonialism.[5] Enlightenment philosophy was also instrumental in institutionalising scientific and popular European perceptions of the human race, with numerous writings by Hume, Kant and Hegel articulating Europe's cultural and racial superiority.[6] However, in the nineteenth century, romantic philosophy overtook Enlightenment ideas as the dominant justification for authorial property.[7] This affected how race was constructed in relation to civilisation. Romanticism encompassed highly sentimentalised reimagining of enslaved and Indigenous peoples.[8] However, although Romanticism critiqued industrialisation and encouraged personal reflection upon humanity and nature, it was deeply entangled in cultural imperialism. Nineteenth-century arguments in favour of universal copyright were similarly entangled. For example, in explaining why there was a need to promote the cause of universal copyright through the Society of Authors in 1884, its founder, novelist and historian, Walter Besant (1836–1901), observed:

> There were doubtless more than a hundred millions under the Roman rule round the shores of the Mediterranean, but they spoke many different languages. We have now this enormous multitude, all, with very few exceptions, able to read, and all reading . . . Every day makes it plainer and clearer that we have arrived when the whole of this multitude . . . will very

4 Peter Prescott, 'The Origins of Copyright: A Debunking View' *European Intellectual Property Review* 12 (1989): 453.

5 John Gascoigne, *The Enlightenment and the Origins of European Australia* (Cambridge: Cambridge University Press, 2006).

6 Eze Chukwudi, *Race and Enlightenment: A Reader* (Oxford: Blackwell, 1997), 5.

7 Kathy Bowrey and Jane Anderson, 'The Politics of Global Information Sharing' *Social and Legal Studies* 18, no. 4 (2009): 479.

8 Peter J. Kitson, '"Bales of Living Anguish": Representations of Race and the Slave in Romantic Writing' *English Literary History* 67, no. 2 (2000): 515.

> soon be reading books . . . they will prefer good books to bad. Let the work have a Message. Let it have a thing to say, a story to tell, a Man or Woman to present, a lesson to deliver, clear, strong, unmistakeable.[9]

Advocacy in favour of strengthening copyright protection across the globe was presented as beneficial to humanity and as essential to strengthening empire by ensuring the moral integrity of the cultural messages and values communicated to British subjects.

The first copyright law that explicitly extended copyright protection to the colonies was the Dramatic Literary Property Act 1833.[10] Section 1 provided that the author of unpublished dramatic works held an exclusive property right in any part of the United Kingdom or the British Dominions. The Copyright Amendment Act 1842,[11] which protected books, newspapers, pamphlets, lectures, printed music, printed plays, maps and charts, also explicitly applied to British Dominions.[12] The Act also made it an offence to import a British copyright book into the dominion without the permission of the copyright owner. This measure was designed to prevent the practice of importing cheaper American editions or reprinting works in the British Dominions.[13] Catherine Seville notes, the 'home and colonial markets were very different in their requirements and characteristics . . . British Publishers seemed remarkedly unresponsive to colonial needs' selecting works they thought colonials *should* read, rather than catering for local tastes.[14] In response to largely colonial Canadian objections to the prohibitions in the 1842 Act, the Foreign Reprints Act 1847[15] permitted the rights of British authors to be suspended in the colonies, subject to the local legislature introducing a scheme to compensate affected authors. However, the Australian colonies, concerned at how a departure from British law would be received in London, did not do so.[16]

The 1842 Act did not only confer copyright protection on authors in British Dominions. Rights were granted to 'authors' without further qualification. This meant foreign authors could also obtain a British copyright if they

9 Walter Besant, *The Society of Authors. A Record of its Action from its Foundation* (Incorporated Society of Authors, 1893), 27–8.
10 3 & 4 Will. IV c 15. 11 5 & 6 Vic. c 45.
12 Copyright Law Amendment Act 1842 (5 & 6 Vic. c 45), s 29.
13 Copyright Law Amendment Act 1842 (5 & 6 Vic. c 45), ss 15 and 17.
14 Catherine Seville, *The Internationalisation of Copyright Law: Books, Buccaneers and the Black Flag in the Nineteenth Century* (Cambridge: Cambridge University Press, 2006), 81.
15 10 & 11 Vic. c 95.
16 There were, however, failed attempts to legalise importation of foreign reprints in Australia. See Sarah Ailwood and Maree Sainsbury, 'The Imperial Effect: Literary Copyright Law in Colonial Australia' *Law, Culture and the Humanities* 1 (2014): 10–14.

published their work and registered their copyright at the Stationers' Company in London.[17] A practice emerged whereby some British publishers sought to obtain a British copyright for American titles by arranging for a British, Canadian or West Indian residency for American authors while printing and registering the work in London, then arranging for an assignment of the right to the publisher.[18] However, many British publishers favoured retaining their right to American works in Britain without payment to American authors. The situation was reviewed in *Routledge v Low* (1868).[19] It was determined that copyright only applied to works *first published* in the UK and gaining a British copyright required *residency* in Great Britain. This decision cemented the idea that book publishing was a one-way trade managed from London. By requiring residency and affirming the need for first publication in the UK, the act removed protections from foreign authors. It also meant that works of colonial authors first printed in the colonies were only protected within colonial jurisdictions where copyright laws had been enacted.

With respect to artistic works, the Fine Arts Act 1862[20] extended copyright protection to architecture, photography, sculpture, engraving, painting and drawing, however this law did not confer any copyright in the British Dominions. Residents of the Dominions had to rely upon any protection conferred by colonial laws alone. Conversely, British copyright owners could not rely upon the 1862 Act to extend their rights to the Dominions and had to comply with local requirements for protection, where such laws existed.[21]

Nineteenth-century Colonial Australian Laws

Victoria, which saw itself as the cultural leader of the Australian colonies, was the first to enact a copyright law, the Copyright Act 1869.[22] In terms of

17 Copyright Law Amendment Act 1842 (5 & 6 Vic. c 45), ss 3 and 11.
18 Catherine Seville, 'Authors as Copyright Campaigners. Mark Twain's Legacy' *Journal of the Copyright Society of America* 55 (2008): 283, 298.
19 *Routledge v Low* (1868) LR 3 HL 100. 20 25 & 66 Vic. c 68.
21 See *Graves & Co v Gorrie* (1903) AC 496.
22 33 Vic. No. 350. Minnel refers to the NSW colony as the first to pass a copyright law in 1852. However, the Inventions Registrations Act 1852, 16 Vic. No. 24, pertains to registration of 'inventions or improvements to the Arts and Manufactures' by their authors or designers in view of the difficulty and cost of colonial inventors securing a British patent. There are only design-copyright provisions and none conferring rights on book authors or artists at all. Merilyn Minnel, *A Nation's Imagination, Australia's Copyright Records 1854–1968* (National Archives of Australia, 2003); 'Inventions and Improvements', *Empire* (NSW), 17 July 1852, 2. The terminology of authorship and inventorship was not stable at this time. See Brad Sherman and Lionel Bently, *The Making of Modern Intellectual Property Law* (Cambridge: Cambridge University Press, 1999), 149–52.

taxonomy it differed from British legislation by gathering together protection for different kinds of copyright subject matter in one Act. However, key principles were derived from British legislation. Part 1, which governed copyright in designs, was modelled on the Copyright of Designs Act 1842;[23] Part 2, Literary, Dramatic and Musical works, implemented key provisions of the 1842 Copyright Act; Part 3, Fine Arts, followed the 1862 Fine Arts Act, but with one key innovation. In the colony of Victoria the duration of protection for artistic works was much reduced, from the life of the author plus seven years in the United Kingdom to fourteen years after first publication for paintings, drawings, sculptures and engraving and, to only *three years* for photographs and the negative. There were also additional provisions to secure the aesthetic education of Australians by permitting the imitation and copying of works held in the Melbourne Library and Art Gallery.[24] South Australia and New South Wales waited for another decade to enact a copyright law. Western Australia and Queensland waited for close to two decades and Tasmania chose not to enact a copyright law at all.[25] Overall, the colonial laws conformed to the political priorities established by Britain, ensuring that British publication was preferred to publishing in the colony. As lawyer John Finnamore put it, Australian colonial authors were 'cabined, cribbed, confined, bound in'.[26] Pursuing British publication placed the work before a much larger market, while local publication meant that the work entered the public domain beyond the colony.[27]

International Copyright Laws

Multilateral and bilateral copyright treaties affecting the colonies developed throughout the late nineteenth century. In 1886 Great Britain signed the Berne Convention for the Protection of Literary and Artistic Works.

23 5 & 6 Vic. c 100.

24 See Kathy Bowrey, '"The World Daguerreotyped – What a Spectacle!" Copyright Law, Photography and the Economic Mission of Empire', in Brad Sherman and Leanne Wiseman (eds), *Copyright and the Challenge of the New* (Amsterdam: Kluwer, 2013), 11–42; Sarah Ailwood and Maree Sainsbury, 'An Old Law for a New Literature: Authors, Publishers and the Early Years of the Victorian Copyright Act 1869' *Law, Culture and the Humanities* (online, 2019) https:doi.org/10.1177/1743872119885795, accessed 26 November 2021.

25 Copyright Act 41 & 42 Vic. No. 95 (1878, SA); 42 Vic. No. 20 (1879 NSW); 51 Vic. No. 2 (1887 Qld); 59 Vic. No. 24 (1895, WA).

26 Catherine Bond, '"Cabbed, cribbed, confined, bound in": Copyright in the Australian Colonies', in Isabella Alexander and Tomás Gómez-Arostegui (eds), *Research Handbook on the History of Copyright Law* (Cheltenham: Edward Elgar, 2016), 372.

27 See Kathy Bowrey, 'Imperial Copyright and its Costs', in Kathy Bowrey, *Copyright, Creativity, Big Media &Cultural Value: Incorporating the Author* (Abingdon: Routledge, 2021), 69–110.

Communicating with the Colonial Office by way of telegraph cable, all of the Australian colonial Parliaments consented to be bound by Great Britain's accession to the Convention. In practice, the nature of protection depended upon the terms of existing British laws, with the Convention implemented through the International Copyright Act 1886.[28] Section 8 provided that most works first published anywhere in British colonies would, upon registration in the colony, automatically attract copyright in the United Kingdom, removing the requirement of British residency and first printing in the United Kingdom for a British copyright. Through Berne membership, reciprocal protection was also conferred in other states. Colonial works were simultaneously protected in Belgium, France, Germany, Haiti, Italy, Spain, Switzerland and Tunisia. Works of foreign authors of member states were protected against unauthorised translation for a period of ten years.[29] The United States did not join the Convention, retaining pariah status as a global pirate.[30]

After 1891 it became possible for foreign authors to obtain an American copyright if four technicalities were complied with: (1) registration of the title with the Library of Congress on or before the date of publication; (2) deposit of copies on or before the date of publication with no grace period, although in keeping with previous acts, some late deposit was allowed in practice; (3) the books had to be printed in the United States; and (4) a copyright notice had to be included on all copies.[31] A report by the US Copyright Office from this time notes numerous 'inequalities of exchange' in the internationalisation of rights, including that,

> It is not as easy, for example, for a foreign as for a native author to arrange for the filing of his title page at Washington before publication, and it is obviously a much less difficult matter for an American than for a foreign author to arrange to have his book type-set in the United States before the day of first publication, which may mean for the alien author the burden of a double printing of his work, abroad and in the United States.[32]

The growth of international copyright was viewed enthusiastically in the Australian colonies as it was thought Australians would never be in a position

28 49 & 50 Vic. c 33.

29 International Copyright Act 1886 (49 & 50 Vic. c 33), s 5. Articles in newspapers and periodicals were not automatically entitled to protection.

30 See Adrian Johns, *Piracy: The Intellectual Property Wars from Gutenberg to Gates* (Chicago, IL: University of Chicago Press, 2009).

31 International Copyright Act 1891 (Chace Act), ch 565, 226 Stat 1106.

32 *Report on Copyright Legislation* (Library of Congress, Copyright Office, US Government Printing Office, 1904), 28–9.

to produce any great literature without protection of colonial copyrights in Great Britain and beyond.[33] While it was recognised that Australian authors faced logistical challenges in securing international rights, justifications for international copyright fixated on valorisation of the natural property right of the expressive individual.

> All civilised nations of the slightest pretensions to literary rank, recognise this right, founded as it is on the first principles of natural justice, and in their legislation have provided for its protection . . .. Even supposing [the author] to care nothing for the fair profits of his labour is it likely that he will be equally careless of what is dearer to him perhaps than life itself – his fame? The practice of all civilised nations is, fortunately, entirely against such a supposition.[34]

This rationale transcended national boundaries and diverted attention from the more complicated legislative history of the British literary property right. Most importantly, the militarism and imperialism bound up with the progress of 'civilised peoples' was also effaced. Copyright's focus on a property right located within the interior life of a creative individual helped to distance intellectually those who self-identified as civilised colonials from the grubby violence of ongoing dispossessions and genocides, and from the grasping commercial culture that underpinned the 'progress' of colonial frontiers and port cities.

Australian Legislation

The first Australian Copyright Act 1905 (Cth) included a manufacturing clause. It provided that an author from any country was entitled to protection of their copyright where the work 'was printed from type first set in Australia or published within fourteen days of first publication elsewhere in the world and the copyright was registered'.[35] Customs officers were authorised to seize any works that conflicted with local registration of rights, ensuring that the importation of books was restricted to titles that were not printed in Australia.[36] Following the enactment of the manufacturing clause Angus & Robertson was floated as a public company in 1907.[37]

33 John Finnamore, 'Letter to the Editor: Colonial Author's Copyright', *The Argus*, Melbourne, 10 October 1876, 6.

34 'Colonial copyright', *Freeman's Journal*, Sydney, 21 October 1865, 664.

35 Copyright Act 1905 (Cth), ss 5, 13(2). There is no significant litigation under the 1905 Act. The first, and possibly only, litigation was reported in July 1910. 'Copyright Action. First of its Kind', *Sydney Morning Herald*, Sydney, 6 July 1910, 6.

36 Copyright Act 1905 (Cth), ss 49, 50, 61.

37 Jason Ensor, *Angus & Robertson and the British Trade in Australian Books, 1930–1970* (London: Anthem Press, 2012), 2.

Linking the award of Australian copyright to protection of local publishers went against the spirit, but not the letter, of the Berne Convention in 1905. Given that the United States did not sign the Berne Convention, American manufacturing clauses were accepted by Great Britain in 1891 in order to obtain copyright protection for British authors in that country.[38] However, when Canada sought similar concessions these were strongly opposed by the British Board of Trade, representatives of the Society of Authors and established publisher interests since: 'Copyright will cease to be an imperial principle. The English author will lose control over his property in the colonies and the interests of the London publishers will be seriously affected.'[39] The British-American copyright settlement was predicated on dividing English language book markets into two halves, run from head offices in London and New York that held exclusive control over the supply of major and popular British and foreign-authored works to former British colonies, with importation of titles serviced by local branch offices.[40]

The situation was redressed with revisions to the Berlin Revision of the Berne Convention in 1908. Alongside reform to music copyright, Article 4 precluded copyright formalities such as registration. This left Australia's short burst of 'copyright sovereignty' in support of local publishing non-compliant with the Convention. The quick 'fix' was to repeal the Copyright Act 1905 (Cth) and replace it with the Copyright Act 1912 (Cth), which simply adopted a new Berne-compliant British law, the Copyright Act 1911 (UK).[41] The British legislation had no regard for special protection of Australian interests. It was argued in Australia that this situation was acceptable because 'a man who has copyright in Australia has a copyright over the greater part of the civilised world. He will gain the advantage of a uniform law on the subject, and the further advantage of enjoying the cheapest form of protection which was ever given to a property of this kind.'[42] No consideration was given to how Australia could support a local book publishing industry that had to compete with British and American publishers supported by vastly larger domestic markets, who controlled the copyright attaching to the majority of titles by British, American and other foreign authors that Australians might want to read, and where imported

38 International Copyright Act 1891, ch 565, 226 Stat 1106 (US).

39 'A Copyright Controversy' *The Tribune*, Toronto, 31 July 1895.

40 See Bowrey, 'Imperial Copyright and its Costs'.

41 Section 28 of the Copyright Act 1911 (UK) provided that the law would extend to a British self-governing dominion once declared to be in force by the legislature.

42 Commonwealth, *Parliamentary Debates*, House of Representatives, 30 October 1912, 4861 (W. M. Hughes, Attorney General).

books were exempt from tariffs.[43] In the patriotic climate of Federation, publishing works by local authors was one of the few commercial opportunities open to Australian firms. May Gibbs was one Australian artist and writer who pursued these possibilities.

May Gibbs's Gumnut Babies

Like many Australians with an interest in pursuing a career in the arts, Gibbs went to London for tuition and to enjoy the cultural and social life of one of the world's greatest cities.[44] She attended the Cope and Nichols School of Painting (Pelham Art School) in South Kensington, night school at South Western Polytechnic, Chelsea, and the Henry Blackburn School of Black and White Art.[45] Her choice of educational establishments suggests an interest in understanding the latest technologies being used in book and commercial art production. New photomechanical processes were supporting a boom in illustrated magazines and newspaper publishing and the Henry Blackburn School of Black and White Art was particularly innovative in highlighting the value of linking authorship to illustration, which required rapport between author and publisher. The school promoted simple calligraphic styles over the more traditional Victorian preference for heavily lined, overly ornate works. Artists skilled in these new techniques had improved commercial prospects.[46]

Gibbs's education at Pelham Art School exposed her to the example of bohemian and radical modernist women, including the painters Vanessa Bell (1857–1961) and Nina Hamnett (1890–1956), who had attended the school a few years earlier.[47] She also became involved in the suffragette movement. In 1911 Gibbs produced a number of illustrations for the suffragette weekly, *The Common Cause.* Militant sympathies were demonstrated in 1914 when she

43 Customs Tariff Act 1908 (Cth), Division XXXIII, Paper and Stationery, Item 371.

44 Angela Woolacott, *To Try Her Fortune in London: Australian Women, Colonialism and Modernity* (Oxford: Oxford University Press, 2001).

45 Robert Holden and Jane Brummitt, *May Gibbs: More Than a Fairy Tale* (London: Hardie Grant, 2016), 73–4; Maureen Walsh, *May Gibbs: Mother of the Gumnuts* (Sydney: Sydney University Press, 2007), 44.

46 Gerry Beegan, *The Mass Image: A Social History of Photo-mechanical Production in Victorian London* (Basingstoke: Palgrave Macmillan, 2008), 95–6; Henry Blackburn, *The Art of Illustration* (London: W. H. Allen & Co, 1896), 215.

47 Ruth Brimacombe, 'Cope, Sir Arthur Stockdale (1857–1940)' *Oxford Dictionary of National Biography* https://doi.org/10.1093/odnb/9780198614128.013.107194, accessed 13 December 2021.

Figure 30.1: Portrait of May Gibbs, ca. 1916, National Library of Australia, nla.obj-137405633

protested the gaoling of Emeline Pankhurst outside Holloway Gaol and was fined £10 for dog-whipping a policeman.[48]

While Gibbs's artistic practice, including linking illustration with storytelling for children and producing character-based merchandise, was not dissimilar to Beatrix Potter's (1866–1943), a feminist desire for autonomy and rights-based legal consciousness informed Gibbs's arts practice. Potter looked to older men in her family, her fiancé Norman Warne and, after his death, the Warne company, for general commercial and legal advice and to manage reproductions.[49] On a day-to-day basis, Gibbs mostly sought to manage her own affairs. The Copyright Act 1912 (Cth) was retained among her business

48 'Militant and Dogwhip', *The Bathurst Times*, 14 March 1914, 1.
49 Linda Lear, *Beatrix Potter: The Extraordinary Life of a Victorian Genius* (London: Penguin, 2007).

correspondence. She drafted her own copyright and design registrations, even though registration for a valid copyright was optional after July 1912.[50] She appointed a patent attorney to pursue design registrations in Great Britain and the United States. She also registered her signature as a trade name. Her degree of organisation and foresight is exceptional among artists of this time and even so today.

Gibbs returned to Sydney before the outbreak of World War I and supported herself with commercial and patriotic work, including producing 'gumnut babe' postcards that were sent to diggers by the Red Cross. By 1917 'quite astonishing sales figures were being quoted'.[51] A book contract with Angus & Robertson for *Snugglepot and Cuddlepie* (1919) came on the back of success of the firm printing two 'babies' booklets. Gibbs negotiated to obtain a royalty of 12.5 per cent, which was the same as that achieved by Norman Lindsay for *The Magic Pudding* in 1918.[52] Given the degree of consumer interest in her characters, Gibbs registered a business in her name in 1920, which she managed along with her husband.[53] The pair organised a huge supply of printed matter to businesses across Australia. From 1924 she generated additional, more reliable income from supplying cartoons for Australasian newspaper serialisation based on characters, 'Bib and Bub' and 'Timmy Touchwood'. This was initially so successful she hired an agent, The Special Press, to handle serialisation, but by 1930 newspapers were reducing demand and fees. Gibbs reverted to managing her own affairs as she could not afford the agent's fee, which was 25 per cent of serialisation royalties.[54]

Place-based Limitations

Gibbs's commercial opportunities were limited because she had an Australian publisher, Angus & Robertson. The Copyright Act 1912 (Cth) did not require foreign publishers to print in Australia; and, thus, selling imported books became the most profitable and least risky aspect of the Australian book trade. Angus & Robertson became one of the leading publishers of original Australian works, however the firm had little interest in exporting

50 Copyright Act 1912 (Cth), s 26. For examples see: Applicant, author and owner: May Gibbs. Painting. 'The Gumnut baby', Commonwealth Register of Fine Arts Copyrights, No. 3076, 4 December 1913; 'Gum Leaf Babe', No. 3028, 24 November 1919; No. 4001, 14 August 1922. SLNSW: MLMSS 2048/52-63.

51 Holden and Brummitt, *May Gibbs: More Than a Fairy Tale*, 161, 166.

52 SLNSW: MLMSS 2048/59; MLMSS 3269/394.

53 'May Gibbs' Registered 13 December 1920, Registration of Firms Act 1902 (Cth).

54 Walsh, *May Gibbs: Mother of the Gumnuts*, 123.

books by Australian authors to the big distribution centres in London and New York.[55]

Gibbs investigated publishing opportunities in London, appointing literary agent, A. P. Watt & Son in 1932. However, the British Society of Authors advised that the Australian focus limited appeal and her drawings of babies were 'not pretty enough'. Methuen & Co suggested English editors were prejudiced against images of 'naked children'.[56] However, potential cultural obstacles were not as great as the economic ones produced by international copyright law. George Robertson believed Australian books could find an international audience, but it was not an aspect of his business he felt it prudent to develop. Gibbs took matters into her own hands, distributing Gumnut merchandise in South Africa and, through an American agent, she sought to interest Hollywood in film rights in 1922. However, the decision taken by Angus & Robertson not to arrange for an American copyright left Gibbs's works unprotected in the United States. This would have greatly reduced the prospects of attracting investment in a film title with her participation in the production because, without an American copyright in her books, the story was in the public domain and free for anyone to adapt for film, meaning that no exclusive film audience could be secured.[57]

There was more interest in publishing Australian works in the United States than has been previously assumed. Carter and Osborne estimate that around 11 per cent of Australian novels achieved American editions between 1900 and 1920; 13 per cent the following decade, though less than half were protected by American copyright.[58] This supports George Robertson's view that there was a potential audience for Australian works. However, he was also right to worry about whether obtaining an American copyright was worth the expense. The firm would need to arrange for the printing of a fresh edition newly type-set in the United States, *before publication in Australia* and comply with the other technicalities. They could have exported Australian editions to America; however, this was risky and expensive. These copies could be freely pirated and Australian editions were subject to a 25 per cent customs duty. Robertson argued that the Australian government needed to enact a one paragraph American–Australian copyright agreement requiring reciprocal terms to support local publishing. He anticipated the response would be that 'Copyright is an imperial concern', but '[t]o do it in the British

55 Ensor, *Angus & Robertson*. 56 Walsh, *May Gibbs: Mother of the Gumnuts*, 131.
57 John K. Wells to May Gibbs, 22 February 1922. SLNSW: MLMSS 2048/52.
58 David Carter and Roger Osborne, *Australian Books and Authors in the American Marketplace 1840s–1940s* (Sydney: Sydney University Press, 2018), 114.

fashion, with Royal Commissions, Reports, Blue Books and ten years will not see us righted'.[59]

Gibbs's publishing and her approach to character-based merchandise was very successful on a domestic scale. Acting independently, she likely followed her feminist sensibilities, and demonstrated pragmatism. She would not have survived as a professional author by waiting for interest to come to her. Her entrepreneurship was quite remarkable. Still, it was relatively modest compared to more famous contemporaries such as Beatrix Potter, Australian born 'Felix the Cat' entrepreneur, Pat O'Sullivan or Walt Disney.[60] Her company was a small private firm and there is no evidence she ever considered seeking public investors. The centre of the business remained in Australia. She had no specialist management or legal advice comparable to that available to these others. Her book publisher was no help in engaging a larger trade. In personally managing day-to-day commercial affairs as well as producing her art, her opportunities were limited to businesses servicing proud and enthusiastic Australian consumers. Law played a crucial role in limiting her opportunities. Legal and business infrastructure within Australia was sufficient to support local ambitions, but little more.

Albert Namatjira's Copyright: Race and Economic Agency

National identity is not only created by consumer choices to purchase products that reflect stories and imagery about the place they were made. The state also has an investment in how a nation's culture is presented to its citizens and the world. In the mid-twentieth century, concern over the human rights of Aboriginal peoples and romantic ideas about Aboriginal culture coalesced, leading to new legislation that affected the production and dissemination of Aboriginal art. Displaying artworks by Albert Namatjira in high-end gallery settings was a source of great national pride. However, Aboriginal people engaging in commodification of the same sort undertaken by Gibbs became a target of regulation. Copyright law was not directly amended to restrict the artistic rights of Aboriginal peoples. Rather, this objective was pursued by other laws that targeted the economic opportunities, agency and autonomy enjoyed by Aboriginal artists, excluding them

59 George Robertson to Hon HY Braddon MLC, 2 October 1918. SLNSW: MLMSS 8404/1.

60 See Jose Bellido and Kathy Bowrey, *Adventures in Childhood: Intellectual Property, Imagination and the Business of Play* (Cambridge: Cambridge University Press, 2022).

from a role in developing a growing tourist trade that accompanied increasing public awareness of Aboriginal culture and the place of Aboriginal peoples within the nation. The case study of Namatjira shows how and why this new regulation occurred and explores the implications for Hermannsburg artists who wanted to build an income base from arts production.

The Necessity of Aboriginal Arts Production

Namatjira was educated at the Lutheran-run Finke River Mission established at Hermannsburg in 1877. The nearest large town was Alice Springs. The Lutherans were progressive in translating the Bible into the Aranda language so that its messages could be better understood; and school lessons were also taken seriously.

The mission always struggled to be environmentally and economically viable. The mission was affected by historic tensions with pastoralists, due to massacres. Access to water holes was generally located on Crown land leased to pastoralists. The mission housed fluctuating numbers as Aranda people

Figure 30.2: Albert Namatjira (1952), photographed by M. Lockett, State Library of South Australia, B 36726

came in chiefly in times of drought. This meant that money and supplies purchased from mission resources and earnings by residents were rarely sufficient to support the establishment. Privation was common, leading to reduced rations.[61] In 1927, 85 per cent of the mission children died, including one of Albert and Rubina Namatjira's daughters, from privations related to drought, disease and malnourishment. The mission made multiple attempts to supplement its income. Attempts at growing market gardens failed. Pastoralism, a tannery for kangaroo hides, and production of art and souvenirs such as carvings, poker-art decorated objects and boomerangs, were encouraged.[62] For individuals hunger encouraged arts enterprise.

In the wake of Namatjira's early success as an artist in the early 1930s, art became a particularly promising endeavour. Pastor Albrecht recruited painter Rex Batterbee to teach and support the artists in 1936. By the 1940s the production of art and souvenirs was an organised cottage industry.[63] In 1943 Batterbee's fortnightly report to the Administrator of the Northern Territory noted:

> The boomerang makers and painters have had a harvest and there is still just as big a demand for them as ever. Several of the young men are very keen to be artists and they are getting a good foundation by painting boomerangs, some are painting woomeras now and are showing great improvement in their work. In fact some have advanced so much during the last few weeks that there seems to be no doubt that this place will become known for its Aboriginal artists, they are not going to let Albert Namatjira have it all his own way.[64]

The mission paid wages for physical labour and Hermannsburg artists received income from their art sales. By 1950, of eighteen artists, twelve to fourteen achieved financial independence by selling paintings, with another four individuals working in pastoralism in their own right.[65] Art was not just sold through the artist-run Aranda Arts Council (AAC).[66] Individuals sold

61 Tim Rowse, *White Flour, White Power* (Cambridge: Cambridge University Press, 1998), 84–5.

62 Everard Leske, *Hermannsburg: A Vision and a Mission* (Adelaide: Lutheran Publishing House, 1977), 46, 64–76.

63 Philip Jones, *Ochre and Rust: Artefacts and Encounters on Australian Frontiers* (Adelaide: Wakefield Press, 2007), 307.

64 Rex Batterbee, Report to Native Affairs Branch, 25 August 1943. NAA: F1 1942/286 Pt 2.

65 Review Report for Year 1950. Finke River Mission. NAA: F1 1952/599.

66 The history of the Aranda Arts Council is set out in Tim Rowse, 'Painting from Memory: Art, Economics and Citizenship, 1949–60', in Jane Hardy, JVS Megaw and M Ruth Megaw (eds), *The Heritage of Namatjira: the Watercolourists of Central Australia* (Melbourne: William Heinemann Australia, 1992).

works to businesses and tourists without oversight from government, the mission or AAC involvement. Necessity dictated much of this trade. Mission reports repeatedly note that artists worked 'when and only when inclined', and when funds were exhausted or mission credit was denied. Due to customary obligations 'quite a good proportion of their income is spent on behalf of relations who are disinclined to any useful work themselves'.[67] At times Namatjira asked for income management to help regulate provision of support. He also gifted unsatisfactory paintings to others to sell and signed paintings that were not his, including forwarding some to art publisher, John Brackenreg. As will be discussed below, some of these transactions later came under government scrutiny.[68]

The degree of autonomy enjoyed by Namatjira and other artists was not appreciated outside of the mission. Reports from officials in contact with the artists sought to explain the situation to their superiors:

> cognizance must be taken of the indisputable fact they are, in the majority, educated men who have a fair knowledge of the value of money, and if the policy of advancement is to be maintained must be given an increased say in the management of their affairs, whether or not this is in conflict with mission policy.[69]

Due to their status as wards of the state under the Protection Acts, the artists did not have legal capacity to independently exercise rights such as to enter into binding contracts to sell art or assign copyright. However, until the 1950s, so far as they were able, Namatjira and other artists, with the consent of Pastor Albrecht and Batterbee, ignored these technical limitations in legal status. Namatjira kept several bank accounts, held mining and pastoral leases, invested in war bonds, entered into hire purchase agreements and owned trucks. There was no prohibition in the Crown Land Ordinance to prevent his owning land, but transfers of title had to be approved by an administrator. Ostensibly due to a zoning issue, he was not permitted to build a house at Alice Springs, which would have been more convenient to commercial art partners and Brackenreg (Legend Press) in particular. Officials also alleged that Aboriginal people were camping on Namatjira's land at Morris Soak, and with ready access to cash and cabs willing to supply alcohol, drinking became a problem. Pastor Albrecht preferred that Namatjira move back to the mission and avoid the 'pressures' that would come from his having

67 For example, Review Report for Year 1950. Finke River Mission.
68 Incident associated with Namatjira, 1950-51. NAA: E72/1.
69 Mr McCol, Report to Director of Natives, 17 August 1951, NAA: E743/U63.

freedom.[70] There were concerns that Namatjira remained under 'the sway of tribal law' and spent his money as he saw fit. The significant amounts of 'easy money' that artists received from unregulated cash art sales were increasingly identified as problematic.[71]

Due to the legal and cultural status of wardship, the reality of Aboriginal people having access to money and exercising economic agency perplexed lawyers and bureaucrats. The taxation of Aboriginal wards had long been controversial. In 1921 there was a proposal to legislate a tax exemption to encourage a transition to wage-earning.[72] In Namatjira's case protectors also discussed (with no resolution) the problem that the legal definition of a family and tax dependents was too limited in an Aboriginal context, given the support provided to an extended Aboriginal family.[73] One Commissioner of Native Affairs expressed concerns that while Aboriginal workers paid tax, discriminatory clauses precluded eligibility for old age, widows' and invalid pensions and maternity allowance. Attempts at reforms were unsuccessful.[74] The formal legal status of Aboriginal people was reconsidered in the 1950s when race-based protection legislation shifted to Welfare Acts, in line with the assimilationist objective of transitioning Aboriginal people towards 'full citizenship'.[75]

Perversely, the regulation of the arts industry that emerged in this period was not designed to enhance Aboriginal autonomy. Rather it attacked autonomy. A series of legislative reforms across 1955–7 led to the removal of freedom of contract, including the right to assign copyright, for most Aboriginal artists. The intent of this legislation was not simply to assert control over capable, financially independent artists connected to Country. It was also part of the larger agenda of promoting assimilation through recruiting Aboriginal wards into physical labour, working on terms European employers desired.

70 Namatjira, Albert – Question of ownership of land in Northern Territory. NAA: A431, 1951/1200; Transcript of interview: Harry Giese, 1987–1994. NTRS 226, TS755, Tape 25, 13.
71 'Pot-boilers Ruin Aranda Art' *Adelaide Advertiser*, 16 July 1955.
72 Taxation of Aborigines, NAA: A457, 206/159; NAA: A571, 1922/6553.
73 F. J. S. Wise to the Secretary, Department of Territories, 24 September 1952. NAA: A431, 1951/1200.
74 Annual Report of the Commissioner of Native Affairs, Western Australia (Commonwealth, 1951), 6.
75 The path to citizenship is carefully set out in Julie T. Wells and Michael F. Christie, 'Namatjira and the Burden of Citizenship' *Australian Historical Studies* 31, no. 1 (2000): 110, 120.

Restricting Freedom of Contract

A number of state interventions, exercises of Aboriginal resistance and disciplinary responses led to new restrictions on economic agency. The Crown Law Office questioned the power of wards to conduct business and legal affairs through an Aboriginal-run AAC. The AAC was required to adopt a formal constitution, but the draft produced in consultation with the artists establishing Aboriginal control was rejected.[76] Anticipating the imposition of an undesirable constitution, the artists withdrew from the AAC and the numbers of works handled by it steadily declined from 200 to fourteen from 1954–5.[77] No doubt the number of works sold through Alice Springs businesses and in Sydney to a friend of Namatjira, the travel writer and tax agent, Frank Clune and to Brackenreg increased at this time.[78] Retaliation came in the form of the Police and Police Offenders Amendment Act 1956 (NT). As the Director of Welfare possessed powers over the employment of wards, Harry Geise, requested special provisions to prevent wards, including Namatjira, from selling paintings, especially in light of the collapse of the AAC.[79] Section 53C made it an offence to purchase 'a painting, carving, sculpture or weaving or other article of artistic pretension or merit' from a Aboriginal people[80] or ward without permission of the Director of Welfare or his delegate, the AAC. The penalty was £100 or six-months' imprisonment. Parliament was told the reform addressed the 'problem' of Namatjira selling paintings at 'substantially higher prices' than would have been set by the AAC, and being paid in cash, as well as potentially being underpaid.[81] The 1956 Act was refused assent because the federal Attorney General was concerned that it was too broadly drafted, capturing tourist artefacts like boomerangs and baskets, as well as paintings, and exposing the (white) purchasers of these items to fines and imprisonment if a sale was made without prior permission of the Director of Welfare. There was also

76 Aranda Arts Council, Proposed Constitution: Advising. NAA: E68, DP918.

77 Northern Territory, *Parliamentary Debates*, Legislative Council, 12 April 1956, 150 (Mr Giese).

78 W. McCoy to Harry Giese (Director of Welfare), 24 April 1958. NAA: E743/U63/2; Leske, *Hermannsburg: A Vision*, 72.

79 H. C. Geise (Director of Welfare) to Crown Law Officer, 24 February 1956. NAA: E72 D3642/3 P1.

80 'Aborigine' was defined by Aboriginal Ordinance (1918–1954), s 3. This engaged a descent test and living in accordance with custom. The Director of Welfare could declare a person with an 'aboriginal' ancestor to be an 'aboriginal' if it is in that person's 'best interests' and that person requests the Director to do so.

81 Northern Territory, *Parliamentary Debates*, Legislative Council, 12 April 1956, 147–51 (Mr Giese).

concern that the drafting potentially affected trade between the Territory and a state, infringing Section 10 of the Northern Territory (Administration) Acts 1910–1956.[82]

These problems were redressed in the Police and Police Offenders Amendment Act 1957 (NT). 'Aborigine' was defined as 'an aboriginal native of Australia' without reference to other legislation. Its application was limited to 'paintings or drawings'. Section 53D created the offence of purchasing a painting or drawing from an Aboriginal person or ward and entering into an agreement to do so without the approval of the Director of Welfare or an 'approved institution', namely the AAC. It was possible to apply for retrospective approval of an unauthorised sale, and the application of an AAC trade mark, if the work was presented and the purchaser agreed to pay the price set by the AAC. Section 45E made it an offence to remove Aboriginal paintings and drawings from the Northern Territory without permission.

Copyright Implications

The Director of Welfare requested a separate provision to prohibit copyright assignments by Aboriginal artists. The Crown Solicitor advised that a provision that explicitly dealt with copyright could not be enacted because copyright was a federal matter. However, a work-around was suggested. Where an artwork had been produced by a ward, Section 25 of the Welfare Act 1953 (Cth) permitted the Director to take possession of any property of the ward. As trustee for the tangible property in the painting or drawing, the Director could also take possession of the associated intangible property, that is, the copyright, attached to these works, and dispose of it. Section 70(1)(e) of the Welfare Ordinance 1957 (Cth) also prevented contracts worth more than £10, including copyright assignments, by wards without the consent of the Director of Welfare. It was considered unlikely that any copyright assignment would be for less than £10.[83] Due to these provisions, no further specific amendment to the Police and Police Offences Ordinance was deemed necessary.[84]

82 Crown Law Office, Memorandum: Northern Territory of Australia. Police and Police Offenders Ordinance 1956, 28 September 1956; 19 November 1956. NAA: E72 D3642/3 P1.

83 A restriction focused on contract was thought to sidestep a potential constitutional problem that came from copyright being a right conferred by Commonwealth statute.

84 Paul Hasluck, Minister for Territories, to Mr N. C. Hargave MLC, 29 November 1956. NAA: F1 1955 154.

Namatjira's Copyright

During 1957 it was unclear whether Namatjira was or was not caught by these provisions. Due to his profile and talent, Namatjira had been repeatedly offered an exemption from Aboriginal Ordinances. These he repeatedly denied because '[i]f the application were approved the Director of Native Affairs would declare that Mr. Namatjira should "not be deemed to be an aboriginal". This would . . . have the effect of denying him the right to enter his tribal areas, as these are in an aboriginal reserve.'[85] Yet, a decision was made by the Director of Welfare to exclude his name from the register of wards in 1957. However, the term 'Aborigine *or* ward' in the new legislation could still have encompassed him at the discretion of the Director of Welfare. It was certainly the intention that he return to selling exclusively through the AAC. Further the Police and Police Offenders Amendment Act 1957 (NT) was designed to come into effect the same day Namatjira was exempt from the Welfare Act 1953 (Cth).[86] This puts the significance of Namatjira's rejection of exemption in an entirely new light. It offered him few tangible benefits and exposed him to new risks in maintaining his connection to Country and contact with other artists.[87]

The enactment of the Police and Police Offenders Amendment Act 1957 (NT) and the Welfare Act 1953 (Cth) cast a shadow over the legal status of all Namatjira's former commercial transactions. Namatjira's copyright assignments came into question.[88] This included the exclusive assignment of reproductive rights to Brackenreg. Batterbee concluded:

> It is doubtful if a written assignment given by Albert Namatjira in 1949 would be legally valid. At that time the Director of Native Affairs was, by virtue of the provisions of the Aboriginals Ordinance, legal guardian of all Aboriginals. For this reason, Albert would have been legally incompetent to assign copyright in his painting.[89]

85 Paul Hasluck, Minister for Territories, to Hon. Kim Beazley (Snr), MP Perth, 24 July 1951, NAA: A431, 1951/1200.

86 These provisions were only in force for six months, then subsumed into s 70 and a new Part VA of the Welfare Ordinance 1953–60 (ss 71A–71D).

87 The status had the unfortunate consequence that as a citizen he could be prosecuted for supplying alcohol to his long-standing painting companion, Henoch Raberaba. See *Namatjira v Raabe* (1959) 100 CLR 664.

88 'Alleged Infringement of Namatjira copyrights', 18 April 1957. NAA: F1, 1962/2225.

89 Extract from Rex Batterbee's letter to Legend Press, 1 September,1969. NAA: E460 2001, 1982/108.

Uncertain as to whether or not Namatjira was subject to the Police and Police Offenders Amendment Act 1957 (NT) or the Welfare Act 1953 (Cth), Brackenreg drafted a new exclusive copyright agreement with him for £10 (plus 12.5 per cent royalties on future sales). He only sought AAC advice on how to process royalties due, advising the AAC that Namatjira 'had the right to dispose of property of the kind involved without obtaining the approval of the AAC or the Director of Welfare' because the contract price meant that it was not caught by Section 70(1)(e) of the Welfare Ordinance 1957 (Cth).[90]

Publicly the new restrictions were justified as a necessary intervention to prevent exploitation of the artists. The Director of Welfare, Harry Giese, had earlier placed articles in newspapers advertising this problem.[91] However, upon further investigation, the examples of fraud and exploitation usually turned out to be works Namatjira had sold outside of the AAC at times when there was no prohibition on his doing so. Giese himself noted the bigger problem was that 'they tend to set rather too high a price on their paintings, because of the popularity they have achieved'.[92] It is not the case that there was no exploitation, but this is a relative term, discussed further below. In the numerous files that touch on Aboriginal art, there are a rather small number of references to the potential problem of an oversupply of Aboriginal art. The business conducted through approved institutions, missions and Aboriginal settlements, was largely reactive. There was no actual planning or attempt to grow the market for 'quality' Aboriginal works. The Act did permit businesses to apply to become an 'approved institution' to sell Aboriginal art but these applications were all rejected on the grounds that they did not meet the legal definition of 'institution' or 'look after the interests of Aboriginal artists'.[93]

Though the legislation ostensibly criminalised the buyers of Aboriginal art, there was no campaign at all to advertise the legal change to buyers. Unsurprisingly, the police found the entire proposition of policing tourists problematic. There was some police surveillance of Alice Springs businesses. The main person the Director of Welfare asked be investigated was Frank Clune. This included interviewing an Alice Springs taxi driver, Bert Gardiner,

90 Legend Press to AAC, 8 May 1957. NAA: F1 1962/2225.

91 'Namatjira "Fakes" in Circulation', *Centralian Advocate*, Alice Springs, 15 May 1953, 1.

92 Northern Territory, *Parliamentary Debates*, Legislative Council, 4 April 1957, 102 (Mr Giese).

93 Appointment of Approved Institution, 21 June 1957. E72, D3642/3 Part 2; List of declared institutions, 24 May 1957. NAA: F1, 1957/748.

who had acted as intermediary between artists and Clune.[94] However, Clune's affairs always withstood scrutiny.

Promoting Assimilation through Labour Conditions

The Police and Police Offenders Amendment Act 1957 (NT) that curtailed the autonomy of Aboriginal artists was drafted in view of the implementation of the Welfare Act 1953 (Cth) with the expectation that most Aboriginal people would remain wards. After six months the Territory provisions were subsumed into Section 70 of the Welfare Act 1953 and a new Part VA of the Welfare Ordinance 1953–60. This clarified that the restrictions on selling art were only applicable to Aboriginal wards. The overriding objective of the reforms was assimilation, where 'the tribal structure will gradually be weakened and disappear as the mode of life of the native'.[95] Regulations were drafted to channel Indigenous people into acceptable forms of labour, pastoralism key among them. The Director of Welfare, Harry Geise, and the Minister for the Territories, Paul Hasluck, were the chief designers of the implementation plan, developed in light of negotiations with the Centralists' Pastoralist Association.[96]

The Ordinance regulated labour by listing 'acceptable occupations for wards'. Economic integration was to be supported by manual labour only: pastoralism, agriculture, livestock, mining, pearling, fishing, timber, skins (Buffalo and crocodile), unskilled labour in town and building. Self-employment opportunities included many of the same occupations: mining, pearling, fishing, timber, skins, droving and contracting (fencing and bores).[97] Mostly these occupations were seasonal only, entrenching poverty and welfare dependency. Art production was not listed among them.

The privileging of the interests of the pastoral industry in the implementation of the Welfare Act while interfering with the independence achieved by Hermannsburg artists through enacting the Police and Police Offenders Amendment Act 1957 (NT) was criticised by Clune in the press in these terms:

> The Ordinance, while hypocritically pretending to protect Aboriginal artists from rapacious art dealers, is in reality aimed at preventing the Aboriginal artists from becoming financially independent . . . If Aborigines could make

94 Report of NJ Owens, Sergeant Third Class to Alice Springs Police Station, 26 November 1958. NAA: F133, 1963/446.
95 Report of Conference on Native Affairs, 24–5 February 1955. NTRS: 3548/P1, C1/3E.
96 Ibid.
97 Native Welfare Policy: Tools of Assimilation-Process. NTRS: PAC 33, 34; Transcript of interview: Harry Giese, 1987–1994. NTRS 226, TS755, Tape 24, 7.

> a good living by selling pictures and other art objects such as hand crafted boomerangs to tourists and collectors of art the supply of cheap native labor [sic] for the cattle stations would diminish.[98]

A consideration of the degree of economic independence that had been achieved through art sales, compared to the relevant award for Aboriginal pastoral workers, helps contextualise this allegation. The applicable Aboriginal pastoral award set in 1955 was an in-hand weekly rate of £3 married labourers (£156 per annum), plus rations and tobacco. It did not include a clothing allowance 'because of risk of natives leaving'.[99] Keeping in mind that by 1956 the majority of works were not handled through the AAC, the average income reported through the AAC for tax purposes for 1952–7 for eighteen Hermannsburg artists show roughly 70 per cent of the male artists received more than the full married rate for Aboriginal pastoral workers. Several artists reported annual earnings significantly more than the annual married rate of £156, including Albert Namatjira £1,834, Walter Ebatarinja £409, Otto Paereroultja £396 and Adolf Inkamala £361. One of two women artists, Cordula Ebatarrinja, also averaged £175 per annum over five years.[100]

At this time there was considerable pressure by Northern Territory pastoralists to maintain a separate Aboriginal pastoral award, despite Section 39 of the Welfare Ordinance 1953 (Cth) requiring wards employed under licence to receive the minimum wage. The Wards Employment Ordinance 1953 (Cth) that regulated the actual work and conditions of wards and could be used to hold employers to account was not operational from 1953–9, which meant that during most of the 1950s there were no legally enforceable conditions for Aboriginal employees.[101] Equal pay for pastoral workers was not phased in until 1966–8.[102]

More than economics were at stake, however. Art was an expression of cultural survival and also emerging as a form of protest. In writing about the practice of painting, Yirrkala elder Galarrwuy Yunupingu notes:

> when we paint – whether it is on our own bodies for ceremony or on bark of canvas for the market – we are not just painting for fun or profit. We are painting as we have always done to demonstrate our continuing link with our country and the rights and responsibilities we have to it. Furthermore,

98 Frank Clune, 'Genius in Bondage', *Truth*, Sydney, 4 November 1956, 17.
99 The rate was agreed by the Director of Welfare, Harry Giese, Pastor Albrecht and Minister for Territories, Paul Hasluck. NTRS 3458/ P1, C1/3E.
100 Author's own calculations based upon payments to Aranda Arts Council Artists: NAA: E743, U63/2.
101 Ibid. 102 Rowse, *White Flour, White Power*, 83.

> we paint to show the rest of the world that we own this country, and that the land owns us. Our painting is a political act.[103]

Where tremendously complex legislation was frequently amended to regulate Aboriginal art production, it should not be presumed that 'art' or art industry exploitation was the only or main target. In the 1950s, art sales and copyright became objects of regulatory interest because the Hermannsburg artists, including women, were encouraging others to make a living through art, connected to Country, observing customary law, relatively free from mission and departmental control. Artists were too financially independent, remaining close to culture, minimising the capacity for observation and governance. The consequence of the 'art industry' targeted reforms was significantly to reduce Aboriginal economic autonomy and facilitate greater bureaucratic control over the size, content and participation of actors within the Aboriginal art market.

Reconsidering the Legal Framework of Australian Copyright

Copyright law does not just concern the exclusive property right of an author to their cultural expression as defined by legislation. The significance of copyright, and in particular, how an artist can exploit their right is also profoundly affected by place and race. National laws are situated within an international legal framework that was designed in the late nineteenth century to privilege British Empire and American interests. This impacted upon whose books, plays, art, music and films were produced where they were produced, their distribution and, in turn, the possibilities for artists to communicate with audiences. The exploration of May Gibbs's copyright gives some insight into what one Australian case study of success looks like, as well as highlighting the legal reasons why publishing in Australia limited her prospects. Race is more difficult to account for in Australian copyright history. Here restrictions were embodied in the interface between Australian copyright and multiple other laws and regulations that impacted Aboriginal lives in the early to mid twentieth century. Restricting enjoyment of copyright by Aboriginal people was important because controlling outlets for cultural expression and obliterating the economic autonomy of

103 Alison French, *Seeing the Centre: The Art of Albert Namatjira 1902–1959* (National Gallery of Australia, 2002), 27.

Aboriginal peoples was central to assimilationist policy. And by considering the politics of place and race in connection to Australian copyright law it should be apparent why these laws do more than confer exclusive rights to cultural expressions. Copyright relations are integral to the production of Australian identity and nationhood.

VII

RECKONINGS

31

Indigenous Legal Traditions and Australian Legal Education

NICOLE WATSON

Introduction

It is impossible to imagine life without stories. Stories explain our origins, offer comfort in times of grief and reassurance in a world that can be frighteningly unpredictable. Although stories are of universal importance, they take on even greater significance in Indigenous societies, which rely upon oral storytelling as a means of transmitting vast amounts of knowledge from one generation to the next. Perhaps it was because of the importance of oral storytelling in our culture that I had the great fortune of being born into a family of raconteurs.

The adults of my childhood were strong personalities, possessed formidable wit and delivered their stories with meticulous timing. One of the stories that I have long reflected upon concerned my paternal grandmother's certificate of exemption. This piece of paper shielded its holder from the intrusive provisions of Queensland's protectionist legislation. If one was caught by the tentacles of the legislation, the freedom of movement, the ability to marry and to care for one's children, were wrested away by the shadowy figures within Queensland's Indigenous affairs bureaucracy. The path to freedom was a certificate of exemption, granted to those who could demonstrate an ability to assimilate.

In a soft voice, Nanna said that the certificate had allowed her to 'mix in public with white people'. I do not recall my reaction as a child, but now I struggle to imagine the indignity of having to prove one's capacity to become 'white', in order to exercise the most elementary freedoms. Perhaps

I would like to acknowledge the support of the Australian Research Council in the production of this chapter. Together with Professor Heather Douglas, I am the recipient of a Discovery (Indigenous) grant. I also hold a Discovery Australian Aboriginal and Torres Strait Islander Award ('Bringing Indigenous Voices into Judicial Decision Making' IN180100021).

it was because of the various degradations associated with her certificate of exemption that my grandmother encouraged me to go to law school.

My entry into legal education in the final decade of the twentieth century coincided with momentous developments for Indigenous peoples, such as the Royal Commission into Aboriginal Deaths in Custody and the High Court's watershed decision in *Mabo v Queensland (No. 2)*. The Commonwealth's response to the latter included the enactment of the Native Title Act 1993 (Cth) and with it came a process for the recognition of native title. A few years later, the 'Bringing Them Home'[1] report thrust the stories of the Stolen Generations into the national consciousness.

While the world appeared to be changing, my law school, the T. C. Beirne School of Law, University of Queensland, remained frozen in time. In common with most Australian law schools in the 1990s, the T. C. Beirne School of Law was yet to employ its first Indigenous scholar. Laws that had wrought devastation on Indigenous lives, such as the protectionist legislation, were never mentioned in any of my classes. Likewise, Indigenous legal traditions that were practised for thousands of years before the arrival of the British received no acknowledgment.

Three decades later, there have been some positive changes in Australian legal education. Indigenous legal scholars have broken through the glass ceiling and most law schools offer elective subjects on Indigenous peoples' engagements with settler law. However, the efforts of Indigenous legal scholars to prise open spaces for Indigenous peoples' laws have been largely met with silence by those within our discipline. This chapter will advance one possible means to move forward by engagement with methodologies created by Canadian scholars for the recovery of Indigenous legal orders.

This chapter will be divided into four parts. The first part will provide an introduction to the work of some of the Indigenous legal scholars who are building the foundations of an emerging Indigenous jurisprudence. The second part will unpack some of the hindrances to the inclusion of Indigenous legal traditions. The third part will provide an introduction to methodologies that have been developed by Canadian legal scholars for the revitalisation of Indigenous peoples' law. Finally, in the fourth part, I will advance arguments in favour of reform.

1 Human Rights and Equal Opportunity Commission, *Bringing Them Home: Report of the National Inquiry into the Separation of Aboriginal and Torres Strait Islander Children from their Families* (Canberra: 1997).

Indigenous Jurisprudence

For thousands of years prior to the arrival of the British, Australia was a vast tapestry of Indigenous nations that emerged out of the creation period known as the 'Dreaming'. During this time, ancestral beings created the physical features of the land and Dreaming narratives. As distinct from the laws of the colonisers, Indigenous peoples' laws are not buried in judgments and statutes. They are contained in story, song and art. Law inheres in all living things.

The colonial gaze constructed our ancestors as brutish and lawless. Such representations would have profound and lasting impacts for the recognition of Indigenous peoples' laws. One such impact was the sustained erasure of our legal traditions from the discipline of law. Generations of Australian lawyers have begun and concluded their studies without ever having attended a single class devoted to Australia's oldest and most enduring legal systems. But much like the colonial encounter itself, this absence is being met with resistance by warrior scholars.

In this part I will provide an introduction to the work of some of those who are laying the foundations for an Indigenous Australian jurisprudence. As this chapter critiques the absence of Indigenous legal traditions from the discipline of law, I will confine my discussion to the scholarship of Indigenous legal scholars. However, I acknowledge the important contributions made by scholars who work outside of law schools to the creation of spaces for Indigenous peoples' laws in the Academy.[2]

In *The Land is the Source of the Law*, the Kombumerri and Munaljahlai scholar, Dr Christine Black argued that Indigenous peoples should:

> turn to their ancient narratives rather than taking a D'Artagnan-like musketeer approach of intellectually duelling with the Rule of Law, for I would argue that this approach has actually 'grown up' a whole generation of people who have neglected their own Law stories and succumbed to the 'Rule' stories of legal dualism.[3]

According to Dr Black, such an approach had led to a 'dearth of books and articles on Indigenous jurisprudence and a glut of texts on Indigenous peoples and Western jurisprudence'.[4]

In the years since I read Dr Black's important book I have often reflected upon those passages. I share her view that the number of publications about

2 For example, see Christine Black, *The Land is the Source of the Law: A Dialogic Encounter with Indigenous Jurisprudence* (London: Routledge, 2011).

3 Ibid, 9. 4 Ibid.

Indigenous Australian jurisprudence is outweighed by those that concern how settler law has impacted upon Indigenous peoples. But I would argue that the problem is not so much indifference by Indigenous legal scholars to our own law stories but, rather, the various obstacles that we encounter in our respective institutions. Before identifying some of those obstacles, it is important to acknowledge the ground-breaking work of those who are creating spaces for an Indigenous Australian jurisprudence. Among them is the Tanganekald and Meintangk scholar, Professor Irene Watson.

Professor Watson writes from a standpoint that is grounded in the *ruwe*, that is, the land of her ancestors who hail from the south-east of South Australia.[5] Professor Watson does not claim to speak for all of those who identify as Tanganekald Peoples and, therefore, her work is not a 'master narrative' of their laws. Rather, it is a 'theoretical intervention, which may or may not extend beyond the self in bringing the mob to gather'.[6] Throughout her large body of publications, Professor Watson has reiterated the very questions posed by generations of Indigenous peoples since the arrival of the British – 'by what lawful authority do you come to our lands? What authorises your efforts to dispossess us?'[7]

In her book, *Aboriginal Peoples, Colonialism and International Law: Raw Law*,[8] Professor Watson casts a critical Aboriginal law lens over the colonial project. Drawing from her own language, Professor Watson names the carnage wrought by colonisation as the *muldarbi*, which means 'demon spirit'.[9] It was the *muldarbi* which brought *terra nullius* and created the status of 'native savages': a status that we have been hostage to ever since. Over the past two centuries Indigenous peoples have been subject to 'civilising missions' that have been ostensibly in our best interests but have caused devastation. In recent times those civilising missions have found resonance in policies such as the Northern Territory Emergency Response.[10]

Because the colonial project is built upon inequality between the colonised and the coloniser, it can never offer solutions for our ongoing oppression. Recognition in the form of native title is illusory because it has preserved the

5 Irene Watson, 'Aboriginal Recognition: Treaties and Colonial Constitutions, "We have been here forever . . ."' *Bond Law Review* 30, no. 1 (2018): 7.
6 Irene Watson, *Aboriginal Peoples, Colonialism and International Law: Raw Law* (New York: Routledge, 2015), 23.
7 Irene Watson, 'The Future is our Past: We Once Were Sovereign and We Still Are' *Indigenous Law Bulletin* 8, no. 3 (2012): 12.
8 Watson, *Aboriginal Peoples*.
9 Ibid, 1.
10 Irene Watson, 'Aboriginal Laws and Colonial Foundation' *Griffith Law Review* 26, no. 4 (2017): 469, 473.

power of the *muldarbi* to continue to dispossess Indigenous peoples and cause greater destruction to the *ruwe*.[11] Rather than placing our faith in a system of law that was built upon our annihilation, Indigenous peoples should reject *terra nullius* and restore the authority of our own laws.[12]

Our laws may have been suppressed, but they remain alive underneath the layers of the *muldarbi*. Professor Watson calls this law the 'Raw Law'.[13] As distinct from settler law, which is isolated and inert in judgments and statutes, the Raw Law is all encompassing:

> The law transcends all things, guiding us in the tradition of living a good life, that is, a life that is sustainable and one which enables our grand-children yet to be born to also experience a good life on earth. The law is who we are, we are also the law. We carry it in our lives. The law is everywhere, we breathe it, we eat it, we sing it, we live it.[14]

The laws of First Nations peoples recognise the interconnected relationships between all living things.[15] Indigenous peoples' laws are written in the land, and therefore, they can never be extinguished. This Raw Law provides the 'essential basis of social conduct: respect, reciprocity and caring for country . . . '.[16]

Professor Watson weaves law stories into her writing; stories which have much to teach all of us about how we should live in this beautiful and ancient place. However, Professor Watson adheres to the practice of not referencing stories that are yet to be published, in order to 'keep oral traditions and their interpretation in the hands of the storyteller'.[17]

One story referenced by Professor Watson concerns Gurukmun the Frog. The selfish Gurukmun drinks all of the water in the land before sitting on top of a mountain. Gurukmun refuses to share the water with the other animals. It is only when he is made to laugh by Nabunum the Eel that Gurukmun releases the water.[18] Such stories may be ancient but they continue to be relevant. Today, Gurukmun's behaviour finds resonance in the exploits of those who wreak great harm to the environment in the pursuit of corporate profits.

Other Indigenous scholars are also acknowledging the continuing vitality of Indigenous law in their scholarship. For example, in her book, *Overturning Acqua Nullius: Securing Indigenous Water Rights*,[19] the Wiradjuri Nyemba

11 Watson, *Aboriginal Peoples*, 19. 12 Watson, 'Aboriginal Laws and Colonial Foundation'.
13 Watson, *Aboriginal Peoples*, 12.
14 Irene Watson, 'Indigenous Peoples' Law-Ways: Survival against the Colonial State' *Australian Feminist Law Journal* 8, no. 1 (1997): 39.
15 Watson, *Aboriginal Peoples*, 12. 16 Ibid, 22. 17 Ibid, 14.
18 Watson, 'Indigenous Peoples' Law-Ways', 42–4.
19 Virginia Marshall, *Overturning Acqua Nullius: Securing Aboriginal Water Rights* (Canberra: Aboriginal Studies Press, 2017).

scholar, Dr Virginia Marshall calls for a greater understanding of Aboriginal water rights through engagement with the narratives of Aboriginal peoples. Such narratives 'depict the care and protection for water landscapes within "country" as a legal obligation and a cultural expectation to abide by Aboriginal laws on country'.[20]

The Wiradjuri scholar, Dr Mark McMillan and Anna Dziedzic have also argued for recognition of the age-old constitutions of Indigenous nations. With the constitutional arrangements of the Gunditjmara Peoples and the Ngarrindjeri Nation as their reference points, McMillan and Dziedzic identify common features of Indigenous peoples' constitutions that include a foundation in Indigenous law.[21] Finally, the Palyku scholar, Ambelin Kwaymullina, who hails from the eastern Pilbara region of Western Australia, has written eloquently about the nexus between Aboriginal law and sustainability.[22]

Such work is gradually finding its way in Australia's legal journals. However, the vast majority of those with whom we share a disciplinary background are yet to acknowledge the existence of Indigenous peoples' laws. Below I argue that this sustained erasure is linked to our historical marginalisation in legal education.

The Marginalisation of Indigenous People in Legal Education

Introduction

Many outside Australia, and even those within, are often oblivious to the reality that racism is experienced by Indigenous people as omnipresent. It is manifest in overt forms and subtle gestures and, for some, racism is a wound to the psyche that is endured on a daily basis. The Goenpul scholar, Professor Aileen Moreton-Robinson argues that whiteness is culturally based.[23] The shared beliefs, behaviours and values of white people alone define what is normal and imbue all of our institutions.[24]

20 Ibid, 8.
21 Anna Dziedzic and Mark McMillan, 'Australian Indigenous Constitutions: Recognition and Renewal' *Federal Law Review* 44, no. 3 (2016): 337.
22 Ambelin Kwaymullina, 'Seeing the Light: Aboriginal Law, Learning and Sustainable Living in Country' *Indigenous Law Bulletin* 6, no. 11 (2005): 12.
23 Aileen Moreton-Robinson, 'Witnessing Whiteness in the Wake of Wik' *Social Alternatives* 17, no. 2 (1998): 11.
24 Aileen Moreton-Robinson, 'Unmasking Whiteness: A Goori Jondal's Look at Some Duggai Business' *Queensland Review* 6, no. 1 (1999): 1, 2.

Law schools are microcosms of society and, as such, they reflect and reproduce Australia's racial hierarchy. However, I argue that law schools are especially injurious to Indigenous peoples. This is due to a combination of factors, such as the late entry of Indigenous people into legal education and systemic racism. The sustained invisibility of Indigenous law from legal research and teaching should be contextualised by this story.

A History of Indigenous People in Legal Education

The first generation of Indigenous people to attend law school gained their qualifications in the 1970s; a time when Indigenous political movements had risen to national prominence. Community leaders were also building organisations that would go on to provide medical care, housing and legal assistance to individuals and families who struggled to survive on the margins of Australian society. The burgeoning Aboriginal Legal Services were critical because of the racist policing practices that were rampant in suburbs and townships in which Indigenous peoples congregated. My late father was one of the many activists who contributed to the building of this sanctuary from the unrelenting violence of the men in blue. He would often describe the beatings that he received from members of the Queensland Police Service, and the arbitrary arrests of those Indigenous people who had the temerity to walk in Brisbane's streets at night.

Unsurprisingly, early Indigenous lawyers were motivated to put an end to such violence. Our first magistrate, the Kunjandji woman, Pat O'Shane graduated from the University of New South Wales in 1976. She would work in Aboriginal Legal Services in Sydney and Alice Springs before being appointed as a magistrate in 1986.[25] In a 2017 interview, O'Shane was asked what motivated her to study law.[26] Her answer began with the assault of two Aboriginal women by police officers in Mareeba, West of Cairns. O'Shane observed the subsequent trial of the officers. Although the officers were ultimately convicted, she was deeply affected by how poorly the women were treated and was determined to make a difference.[27]

The Noonucal/Bunjalung man who would become our first judge, Bob Bellear, was also inspired to study law after observing police harassment in

25 Nikki Henningham, 'O'Shane Pat', in *The Encyclopedia of Women and Leadership in Twentieth-century Australia*, www.womenaustralia.info/leaders/biogs/WLE0771b .htm, accessed 11 January 2022.

26 Paul Gregoire, 'A Career of Firsts: An Interview with NSW Magistrate Pat O'Shane', *Sydney Criminal Lawyers*, 22 January 2017 www.sydneycriminallawyers.com.au/blog/a-career-of-firsts-an-interview-with-former-nsw-magistrate-pat-oshane/ accessed 11 January 2022.

27 Ibid.

Redfern. At his swearing in ceremony, the former Attorney General of New South Wales, Jeff Shaw, reflected on Bellear's courage during this dangerous time:

> It was easy for police to arrest Aboriginal people. They had a formula. It was the trifecta, 'unseemly words', 'resist arrest' and 'assault police'. Seeing this injustice repeated week after week hit hard, and there was no way that Bob Bellear was going to sit back and watch it happening.[28]

I do not know what studying law would have been like for those giants who blazed a trail for the rest of us to follow. I can try to imagine how it felt to be among the first of our people to breathe the rarefied air of Australia's sandstone universities, surrounded by peers who had little knowledge of Indigenous peoples' perspectives and historical experience. But I doubt that my imagination would be able to truly capture the challenges overcome by those courageous individuals.

My own experience of law school in the 1990s was characterised by confusion and discomfort. On occasions when we studied cases in which there were Indigenous parties, I would brace myself for the inevitable, offensive comments. The humanity of those whose names appeared in the judgments was seldom acknowledged. Articles written by Indigenous scholars, which might have provided valuable context, were never included in our course reading lists.

It would be many years before I discovered the work of Indigenous legal scholars overseas, such as the Canadian Mohawk scholar, Patricia Monture. During her law studies, Monture experienced a constant feeling that there was 'something missing'.[29] It would take some time before Monture realised that she was not the source of the problem:

> In my first year at law school, I felt it was *my* problem, just as Duncan Campbell Scott, and many others in the 1920's and later, were able to characterize the 'Indian problem' as the sole fault of First Nations. Then the solution rested on changing the 'Indian' into a civilized and assimilated being. In first year, I internalized this characteristic of colonialism and oppression, believing that if I could only change, perhaps fit in a little better, my law school experience would also be rewarding. Since then, I have

28 Peter Manning, 'From the Depths to the Heights', *Sydney Morning Herald,* 17 March 2005 www.smh.com.au/national/from-the-depths-to-the-heights-20050317-gdkyon.html, accessed 11 January 2022.

29 Patricia A. Monture, 'Now That the Door is Open: First Nations and the Law School Experience' *Queen's Law Journal* 15 (1990): 179, 185.

> understood that the greatest obstacle was not myself but the very structure of the institution and the program.[30]

As Patricia Monture was powerfully describing the institutional racism embedded in Canadian law schools, a small number of Australian scholars had begun to cast a lens over Indigenous peoples' experiences of legal education. One early paper by Daniel Lavery was based on a survey of Australian law schools between 1990 and 1991.[31] The survey revealed that of the 11,000 students studying law throughout Australia, only fifty were Indigenous.[32] By that time, a mere twenty-one Indigenous law students had completed their studies.[33]

A few years later, Indigenous legal scholars such as Phil Falk described the numerous obstacles commonly encountered by Indigenous law students, which included onerous community obligations and a lack of financial support.[34] Falk also described the racism frequently experienced by Indigenous law students. Classroom discussions about issues such as native title became platforms for the airing of racist views, and lecturers were often dismissive of the laws and continuing sovereignty of Indigenous peoples.[35] Feelings of alienation and despair were reported by many of the Indigenous law students who contributed to research undertaken by Professor Heather Douglas during the same period.[36] Participants reported feeling 'disorientated by the system' and 'under siege'.[37]

Emerging Indigenous legal scholars also faced barriers. Together with others I described my experiences as a junior academic in a special issue of the *Indigenous Law Bulletin*,[38] which was published in 2005. Reading those articles fifteen years later, one is struck by the harms weathered by virtually

30 Ibid.

31 Daniel Lavery, 'The Participation of Indigenous Australians in Legal Education' *Legal Education Review* 4 (1993): 177.

32 Ibid, 180. 33 Ibid.

34 Phil Falk, 'Law School and the Indigenous Student Experience' *Indigenous Law Bulletin* 6, no. 8 (2005): 8.

35 Ibid.

36 Heather Douglas, '"This is not just about me": Indigenous Students' Insights about Law School Study' *Adelaide Law Review* 20 (1998): 315.

37 Heather Douglas, 'The Participation of Indigenous Australians in Legal Education 1991–2000' *UNSW Law Journal* 24, no. 2 (2001): 485, 490.

38 Nicole Watson, 'Indigenous People in Legal Education: Staring into a Mirror without Reflection' *Indigenous Law Bulletin* 6, no. 8 (2005): 4; Irene Watson, 'Some Reflections on Teaching Law: Whose Law, Yours or Mine?' *Indigenous Law Bulletin* 6, no. 8 (2005): 23; Falk, 'Law School and the Indigenous Student Experience', 8; Hannah McGlade, 'The Day of the Minstrel Show' *Indigenous Law Bulletin* 6, no. 8 (2005): 16.

all of the contributors. Most had experienced ignorance from colleagues and a lack of support. We understood all too well the hurt and disillusionment worn on the faces of Indigenous students, because we too felt isolated in our respective institutions.

Recent analysis by Harry Hobbs and George Williams suggests that while there have been some gains made, there is still a long way to go.[39] Their analysis was based upon the results of a survey completed by thirty-four of Australia's thirty-eight law schools. The authors found that increasing numbers of Indigenous people were enrolling in and completing law courses. However, retention and completion remained problematic.[40] One of a number of hindrances confronted by Indigenous law students was racism:

> A key contributor to the social and academic isolation many Indigenous students experience is racism . . . Racism can be overt and covert. It can take the form of belittling Aboriginal and Torres Strait Islander culture, knowledge and perspectives, or drawing negative stereotypes of Indigenous people, including by identifying defendants as Indigenous where that fact is irrelevant. Racism can also be present in curriculum design, including as to whether Indigenous content is taught in courses, and the manner in which, or assumptions that underlie the way, it is taught.[41]

I would argue that racism within legal education is inextricably tied to the sustained erasure of Indigenous peoples' laws from the discipline of law. Throughout our shared history, Indigenous peoples have been subject to many harmful representations. The first such representation underscored the long application of *terra nullius*. According to that myth, our ancestors were so uncivilised and so lacking in intellect that they did not have legal traditions of their own. This fiction may have been dismissed by the majority of the High Court in the *Mabo* decision. But it continues to lurk within the classrooms of Australia's law schools, where Indigenous peoples' laws are seldom acknowledged.

I appreciate that many non-Indigenous scholars within our discipline are anxious to transform law schools into spaces where Indigenous scholars and students can feel safe. I suspect, however, that we lack agreement on how to move forward. Below, I provide an introduction to methodologies developed by Canadian scholars for the recovery of Indigenous legal orders. This

39 Harry Hobbs and George Williams, 'The Participation of Indigenous Australians in Legal Education, 2001–18' *UNSW Law Journal* 42, no. 4 (2019): 1294.

40 Ibid, 1305. 41 Ibid, 1301.

important research is providing the foundations for the incorporation of Indigenous peoples' law in legal curricula.

Canadian Approaches

Introduction

In Canada there is a burgeoning movement towards a respectful engagement with Indigenous legal traditions. Universities that offer courses on Indigenous law include the University of Victoria, the University of Ottawa, McGill University, the University of British Columbia, Osgoode Hall and Lakehead University.[42] Impetus for this movement was provided by the Truth and Reconciliation Commission of Canada, which recognised the nexus between national reconciliation and the recovery of Indigenous laws.[43] Support for greater recognition of Indigenous law has also been expressed by the Canadian Bar Association and members of the judiciary.[44]

There are a number of arguments in favour of greater engagement with Indigenous law. The revitalisation of Indigenous legal traditions will provide tools to communities to resolve conflicts and strengthen their governing institutions. Greater awareness of First Nations' laws could also enhance judicial decision-making, because judges will become better equipped to grasp the complexities of First Nations societies. Nonetheless, the task of revitalising Indigenous law is problematic. Indigenous laws may not be readily available,[45] and stereotypes that represent Indigenous law as primitive and inferior will need to be overcome.[46] Such hurdles demand rigorous methodologies.

Among those who have responded to this challenge are Professor John Borrows, Canada Research Chair in Indigenous Law, University of Victoria, and Professor Val Napoleon, Law Foundation Professor of Aboriginal Justice and Governance, University of Victoria. Both scholars have been at the forefront of the world's first joint degree program in Canadian Common Law (JD) and Indigenous Legal Orders (JID), which was rolled out in 2018.

42 Val Napoleon and Hadley Friedland, 'An Inside Job: Engaging with Indigenous Legal Traditions through Stories' *McGill Law Journal* 61 (2016): 725, 731.

43 The Truth and Reconciliation Commission of Canada, *Honouring the Truth, Reconciling for the Future, Summary of the Final Report of the Truth and Reconciliation Commission of Canada* (Canberra: 2015), 16–17.

44 Napoleon and Friedland, 'An Inside Job', 731.

45 Hadley Friedland, 'Reflective Frameworks: Methods for Accessing, Understanding and Applying Indigenous Laws' *Indigenous Law Journal* 11 (2012): 1, 8.

46 John Borrows, *Canada's Indigenous Constitution* (Toronto: University of Toronto Press, 2010), 13.

The JID was a direct response to Call to Action #50 of the Truth and Reconciliation Commission of Canada:

> In keeping with the *United Nations Declaration on the Rights of Indigenous Peoples*, we call upon the federal government, in collaboration with Aboriginal organizations, to fund the establishment of Indigenous law institutes for the development, use, and understanding of Indigenous law and access to justice in accordance with the unique cultures of Aboriginal peoples in Canada.[47]

This four-year program enables students to study common law doctrine alongside Indigenous legal traditions. Field schools form a crucial part of the JID. For an entire term in their third and final years of study, students are provided with an opportunity to learn from community experts, observe how Indigenous legal traditions operate in practice and contribute to community legal projects.[48] In the future, the program will be housed in an Indigenous Legal Lodge that will become a national and international forum for critical engagement with Indigenous legal traditions.[49]

It is beyond the scope of this chapter to provide a comprehensive description of the complex and voluminous scholarship of either Professor Borrows or Professor Napoleon.

Therefore, this part will provide a brief introduction to one aspect of the work of each scholar, which is the use of Indigenous stories as cases.

The Single Case Analysis Method

Professor Borrows has developed what Dr Hadley Friedland describes as the 'single case analysis method'[50] as a means of drawing out principles of Indigenous law from stories handed over from generation to generation. An example of the application of the single case analysis method is Borrows's analysis of the story of Mayamaking, who transformed into a '*wetiko*' or '*windigo*'.[51] Within the histories of the Cree and Anishinabek are the *wetiko*; cannibalistic giants or spirits who caused terrible harm to both themselves

47 'World's first Indigenous law program launches with historic and emotional ceremony' University of Victoria, 22 October 2018 www.uvic.ca/news/topics/2018+jid-program-launch+news, accessed 11 January 2022.

48 'JD/JID joint degree program in Canadian common law and Indigenous legal orders', University of Victoria www.uvic.ca/law/assets/docs/jid/JIDBrochureWeb2.pdf, accessed 11 January 2022.

49 Ibid.

50 Friedland, 'Reflective Frameworks', 21.

51 Borrows, *Canada's Indigenous Constitution*, 81.

and others.[52] A person who was turning into a *wetiko* exhibited symptoms that included a lack of self care, refusing food and attempting to hurt others.[53]

An appropriate response to the looming danger posed by someone who was transforming into a *wetiko* was determined according to legal principles and processes embedded in cases such as that of Mayamaking. His story was reported by a Superintendent of Indian Affairs, William Jarvis, in 1838:

> He came among us at the very beginning of last winter, having in most severe weather walked six days, without either kindling a fire, or eating any food.
>
> During the most part of this winter he was quiet enough, but as the sugar season approached got noisy and restless. He went off to a lodge, and there remained ten days, frequently eating a whole deer at two meals. After that he went to another [lodge] WHEN a great change was visible in his person. His form seemed to have dilated and his face was the color of death. At this lodge he first exhibited the most decided professions of madness; and we all considered that he had become a Windigo (giant). He did not sleep but kept on walking round the lodge saying 'I shall have a fine feast.' Soon this (caused) plenty of fears in this lodge, among both the old and growing. He then tore open the veins at his wrist with his teeth, and drank his blood. The next night was the same, he went out from the lodge and without an axe broke off many saplings about 9 inches in circumference. [He] never slept but worked all that night, and in the morning brought in the poles he had broken off, and at two TRIPS filled a large sugar camp. He continued to drink his blood. The Indians then all became alarmed and we all started off to join our friends. The snow was deep and soft and we sank deeply into it with our snow shoes, but he without shoes or stockings barely left the indent of his toes on the surface. He was stark naked, tearing all his clothes given to him off as fast as they were put on. He still continued drinking blood and refused all food eating nothing but ice and snow. We then formed a council to determine how to act as we feared he would eat our children.
>
> It was unanimously agreed that he must die. His most intimate friend undertook to shoot him not wishing any other hand to do it.
>
> After his death we burned the body, and all was consumed but the chest which we examined and found to contain an immense lump of ice which completely filled the cavity.
>
> The LAD, who carried into effect the determination of the council, has given himself to the father of him who is no more: to hunt for him, plant and fill all the duties of a son. We also have all made the old man presents and he is now perfectly satisfied.

52 Hadley Friedland, *The Wetiko Legal Principles: Cree and Anishinabek Responses to Violence and Victimization* (Toronto: University of Toronto Press, 2018), 13.
53 Ibid.

> This deed was not done under the influence of whiskey. There was none there, it was the deliberate act of this tribe in council.[54]

Borrows has emphasised that the death was the outcome of a legal process that was collective and deliberative.[55] The man's deterioration was observed over some time and, when the danger posed by his condition became too great, the decision was made to permanently incapacitate him. Far from being an example of capital punishment, the death was compassionate, being carried out by a loved one. The case also has an element of restitution, with his father receiving support from both the man who killed Mayamaking and the community.

Borrows has identified the legal principles that underpinned the decision:

(1) Wait, observe and collect information;
(2) Consult with their friends and neighbours when it is apparent something is wrong;
(3) Help the person who is threatening or causing imminent harm;
(4) If the person does not respond to help and becomes an imminent threat to individuals or the community, he or she can be removed so that he or she does not harm others (though, to re-emphasize, the act does not involve what the common law has labelled capital punishment);
(5) Help those who rely on that person by restoring what might be taken from them by the treatment; and
(6) Invite both the community and the individual to participate in the restoration.[56]

Today, there would be means other than death to cause permanent incapacitation, and hopefully, compassionate medical treatment for what was likely a grave mental illness. Nonetheless, the legal principles identified by Borrows could be applied in the present day to determine appropriate responses to those who pose a danger to community safety.

Multiple Cases and an Analytical Framework

The approach by Professor Val Napoleon and her colleagues at the Indigenous Law Research Unit (ILRU), University of Victoria, is underpinned by three 'conceptual strands of thought':

> The first strand explores how we hear, see, and experience Indigenous elders using stories as tools for thinking – in their lives, in their talk, and in

54 Jarvis cited by Borrows *Canada's Indigenous Constitution*, 81–2. 55 Ibid, 82. 56 Ibid, 83.

> their written work. The second strand reflects the felt need to shift the discussions about Indigenous legal traditions from broad, generalized, descriptive, or philosophical accounts to discussions about specific principles and legal practices. The third and final strand assesses how effective legal scholarship is for accessing, understanding, and actually being able to apply any law in practice, from an internal and embedded perspective.[57]

The result of the fusion of the three strands of thought is the application to stories of tools used by scholars of common law traditions. It is beyond the scope of this chapter to explore Professor Napoleon's complex method in detail. Consequently, this part will provide an introduction to its core components. The first component is framing the research questions to ensure that research outcomes are useful and applicable to the 'real lives' of communities.[58] The second treats stories as cases that hold crucial information about norms, relationships, obligations and legal processes.[59]

In order to extract such information from stories, Professor Napoleon and her colleagues have adapted the 'case briefing' method designed by the former Dean of Harvard Law School, Christopher Langdell, which remains in popular use.[60] In briefing a case the first step is to ascertain the human problem that it deals with. This is followed by identification of the relevant facts, articulation of the decision and reasons for the decision, both expressed and implicit.[61] Finally, elements of the case that require further information, or are not understood, are bracketed.[62]

Principles of Indigenous law have proven to be consistent over time and, as a consequence, the ILRU engages with stories that are both ancient and contemporary.[63] Napoleon and her colleagues apply the case briefing method to multiple stories. Just as common law doctrine cannot be properly understood by reference to a single decision, rigorous analysis of Indigenous law requires consideration of a significant body of cases.[64]

57 Napoleon and Friedland, 'An Inside Job', 734.

58 Hadley Friedland and Val Napoleon, 'Gathering the Threads: Developing a Methodology for Researching and Rebuilding Indigenous Legal Traditions' *Lakehead Law Journal* 1, no. 1 (2015): 16, 20.

59 Ibid, 22.

60 Napoleon and Friedland, 'An Inside Job', 744.

61 Lori Groft and Rebecca Johnson, *Journeying North: Reflections on Inuit Stories as Law*, Accessing Justice to Reconciliation, 22 https://indigenousbar.ca/indigenouslaw/wp-content/uploads/2014/05/Groft-and-Johnson-Journeying-North.pdf, accessed 11 January 2022.

62 Ibid.

63 Friedland and Napoleon, 'Gathering the Threads', 38.

64 Ibid, 22.

Once completed the case briefs are presented to Elders and other knowledgeable persons, in order to allow for clarification and correction.[65] The analyses are then synthesised into an analytical framework. The analytical framework compels the researchers to focus on specific principles of law rather than broad generalisations. The framework also acts as a powerful reminder that Indigenous legal traditions do not exist in isolation, but belong to a 'comprehensive whole'.[66]

One example of the application of the ILRU methodology is the Secwépemc Lands and Resources Law Research Project. In collaboration with the Shuswap Nation Tribal Council, ILRU researchers set about articulating Secwépemc laws concerning lands and resources[67] through engaging with thirty stories and conversations with twenty-three Secwépemc witnesses.[68] Their work culminated in a report that covered general underlying legal principles, legal processes, legal relationships and the ways in which legal principles are enforced.[69] The stories and the case briefs prepared by the ILRU researchers are contained in the back of the report, together with a thematic index.

In addition to conventional research outcomes the ILRU has created resources that are accessible to a broad audience, including a graphic novel[70] and a teaching guide.[71] Finally, the ILRU methodology is not intended to supplant other tools for the teaching of Indigenous law. As emphasised by Professor Napoleon and Dr Friedland, there are many methods to engage with Indigenous laws.[72]

Arguments in Favour of Reform

Introduction

In a seminal passage in *Mabo (No. 2)*, Brennan J argued that it was imperative that the common law 'neither be nor be seen to be frozen in an age of racial

65 Hadley Friedland, *IBA Accessing Justice and Reconciliation Project: Final Report* (2014), 2 https://indigenousbar.ca/indigenouslaw/wp-content/uploads/2013/04/iba_ajr_final_report.pdf, accessed 11 January 2022.
66 Ibid, 7.
67 Jessica Asch, Kirsty Broadhead, Georgia Lloyd-Smith and Simon Owen, *Secwépemc Lands and Resources Law Analysis* (2018), 1 (available on the ILRU website ilru.au, accessed 11 January 2022).
68 Ibid. 69 Ibid.
70 Val Napoleon, *Mikomosis and the Wetiko* (Indigenous Law Research Unit, University of Victoria, 2013).
71 Emily Snyder, Lindsay Borrows, Val Napoleon and Hadley Friedland, *Mikomosis and the Wetiko: A Teaching Guide for Youth, Community and Post-secondary Educators* (Indigenous Law Research Unit, University of Victoria, 2014).
72 Napoleon and Friedland, 'An Inside Job', 753.

discrimination'.[73] Thirty years after that watershed decision, those within Australia's law schools are yet to acknowledge that like the common law, legal education must also move beyond *terra nullius*. There are a number of compelling arguments in favour of reform.

The first appeals to equality. Indigenous people who are desirous of obtaining a legal education will continue to suffer harm through the perpetuation of stereotypes that underscored the wrongful application of *terra nullius* to Australia, namely the belief that our ancestors were primitive and anarchic. By introducing Indigenous law to the curriculum, our students and scholars will finally see themselves reflected in legal education and, in the long term, law schools will cease to be alienating environments. Furthermore, I believe that all law students stand to benefit from engagement with Indigenous legal traditions. As distinct from the common law, First Nations' laws are rooted in the soil and as such, they must be recognised as a part of Australia's legal heritage.

All Australians can benefit from an awareness of Indigenous legal traditions because they are the only bodies of law that have enabled human beings to live sustainably in this beautiful land. As I completed the first draft of this chapter in the beginning of 2020, Australia was being ravaged by fire. The legacies were catastrophic – millions of animals suffered agonising deaths, families buried loved ones and the nation grieved. Unsurprisingly, there is a growing interest in Indigenous land management practices, such as cultural burning.[74] The success of books such as *Dark Emu*[75] by the Bunurong and Yuin writer, Bruce Pascoe, which celebrate the ingenuity of Indigenous peoples' relationships with their lands, suggests that this interest will continue to grow. Indigenous law is inextricably tied to our land management practices, and as such, it can no longer be ignored.

In moving forward, much can be gained from the work of Professor Borrows and from Professor Napoleon and her colleagues at the ILRU. One of the great strengths shared by both the single case analysis method and the ILRU methodology is the central role of stories. Stories have the potential to create a bridge between Indigenous communities and legal scholars. Writing about the use of stories in American legal scholarship, Scheppele made comments that are equally applicable to Australian legal scholars:

73 *Mabo v Queensland (No. 2)* (1992) 175 CLR 1, 41–2.
74 Victor Steffensen, *Fire Country* (Melbourne: Hardie Grant Travel, 2020).
75 Bruce Pascoe, *Dark Emu* (Broome: Magabala Books, 2014).

> Law comes in cases; cases come with facts; facts are arranged into stories. Our understanding of what the 'law' is in a given case is conditioned powerfully by our understanding of how the facts limit the application of the rule in hypothetical future cases themselves envisioned as having, well, facts. Law is mixed up with facts all the way down. And we arrange facts in stories not in lists.[76]

It follows that we 'can no more do law without stories than we can fly without mechanical devices'.[77]

It is not only a mutual reliance upon the medium of storytelling that can provide a meeting point between Indigenous peoples' law and legal scholars. The means by which principles are drawn out of Indigenous people's stories and applied to resolve conflict finds resonance in the legal reasoning used by scholars of the common law:

> Where a past story is very similar to the problem at hand, judges may follow the decision very closely; where a set of facts (a story) is more novel, judges will look to the principles recounted in past cases and apply these to make a new decision. This process, applying the teachings of stories from the past to conflicts and problems in the present, is the type of legal reasoning that Napoleon and Friedland encourage scholars and interested parties to engage in in order to revitalize Indigenous legal traditions.[78]

Not all Indigenous communities will have an interest in collaborating with legal scholars.

Because of the long nexus between research and colonisation, the former remains 'one of the dirtiest words in the Indigenous world's vocabulary'.[79] Understandably, some will also have concerns about how stories will be interpreted and used once taken into the public domain.

Nonetheless, it is useful to identify possible benefits that could flow from the adoption of the Canadian methodologies in Australia. Firstly, research outcomes, such as those produced by the ILRU in the nature of reports and toolkits,[80] could provide practical tools for communities to resolve internal

76 Kim Lane Scheppele, 'Narrative Resistance and the Struggle for Stories' *Legal Studies Forum* 20 (1996): 83, 84.

77 Ibid.

78 Susanna Quail, 'Yah'guudang: The Principle of Respect in the Haida Tradition' *UBC Law Review* 47, no. 2 (2014): 673, 705.

79 Linda Tuhiwai Smith, *Decolonizing Methodologies: Research and Indigenous Peoples* (London: Zed Books, 2010, 2nd edition), 30.

80 See for example, Hadley Friedland, Jessica Asch and Val Napoleon, *A Toolkit for On-reserve Matrimonial Real Property Dispute Resolution* (Indigenous Law Research Unit, University of Victoria, 2015).

disputes. Such resources could also be used to work through conflicts with government departments, agencies and non-Indigenous land-users. Application of the ILRU methodology could also generate content for courses on Indigenous law, as has occurred at the University of Victoria.

Conclusion

For thousands of years, Indigenous peoples deliberated over, refined and enforced their own laws. While no body of law is infallible, we can assume that those that were practised here before the invasion kept the vast majority of people safe. Those same laws enabled a stewardship of the environment that was so successful that the early colonisers assumed that the land was untouched by human influences. In spite of being shrouded in the mythology of *terra nullius* for two centuries, Indigenous laws endured and have proven to be remarkably resilient.

Today, Indigenous law continues to be lived throughout Australia. Even in areas that suffered the brunt of colonisation, it is likely that remnants of Indigenous legal traditions have survived and therefore, can be recovered. The Canadian experience has taught us that the beginning point for this monumental task of revitalising Indigenous law is legal research. Borrows and Napoleon have demonstrated that the very tools used by scholars of common law traditions can be applied to Indigenous people's stories in order to identify legal principles and processes of legal reasoning.

The arguments in favour of incorporation are persuasive. Law schools will never be level playing fields while Indigenous students and scholars continue to live with the stigma of antiquated stereotypes. Legal education will also be enhanced by the inclusion of legal traditions uniquely designed for the Australian continent, which were thousands of years in the making. Indigenous law is a part of our national story. It is time for this story to be told in its entirety.

32

Reckoning with the Past

SHINO KONISHI

On 9 April 2018 a delegation of Yolngu clan leaders and the Member for Nhulunbuy, Yingiya Mark Guyula, met with Prince Charles in Yirrkala during his official visit to Australia to open the Commonwealth Games. The delegation, convened by Dennis Wanambi and Waka Mununggurr, presented the Prince with a 'letter stick' marked with symbols representing in turn the Yirritja and Dhuwa moieties, the eight provinces of North Arnhem Land, the Yolngu Ngarra Parliament, the six states and two territories of Australia, and the Australian Parliament. The delegation requested that Prince Charles 'accept the letter stick and create a diplomatic passage' to the prime minister of Australia, intervening on the behalf of Yolngu to 'acknowledge our sovereignty and promote a pathway to Treaty'. Upon presenting the letter stick, Guyula reminded Prince Charles that '[w]e are the only indigenous people of a Commonwealth country that does not have the respect or dignity of a Treaty', and asserted that '[t]his here is Yolngu Land, and we are sovereign people and we live by Yolngu law'.[1]

More than two years later, on 6 October 2020, the recently appointed Gunnai and Gunditjmara senator, Lidia Thorpe, entered the Commonwealth Senate chamber wearing a possum-skin cloak with one fist raised in 'an expression of [her] people's strength, resilience and survival'. Significantly, she also carried 'a message stick bearing a single mark for each of the 441 First Nations people who have died in custody since the Royal Commission [into Aboriginal Deaths in Custody] in 1991'. As senator, Thorpe promised she would prioritise calls for a treaty: reiterating the Member for Nhulunbuy's

1 Member for Nhulunbuy, Northern Territory Legislative Assembly, Yingiya Mark Guyula MLA, 'Yolngu Leaders Declare Sovereignty' (Media Release, 9 April 2018), and J. Goff, 'NT leaders stick it to visiting royal', *National Indigenous Times*, 18 April 2018.

assertion that '[w]e're the only Commonwealth country that doesn't have [a] Treaty with its First Nations people'.[2]

Both instances highlight the ongoing need to reckon with Australia's settler legal history and its impact on First Nations people by asserting the continuing legacy of past legal injustices: the myth of *terra nullius* and the consequent failure to treat with Aboriginal and Torres Strait Islander people, as well as past and present discriminatory laws and legal cultures which result in the continued over-policing of Indigenous people and the tragic repercussions of disproportionate incarceration rates. That Guyula and Thorpe were able to use their platform as elected Australian politicians also reveals the gains Aboriginal and Torres Strait Islander people have made in the ongoing struggle for equal political representation and legal rights.

This chapter will explore why and how First Nations people still have to reckon with the myriad colonial and Australian legal histories examined in this collection. *The Cambridge Legal History of Australia* dedicates significant attention to First Nations' legal histories, with a significant minority of chapters specifically focused on Indigenous topics, and many others including discussions of how Indigenous land, people and law were affected by settler/Australian law. Some chapters in this collection have discussed its impact on Indigenous Australians as a people, examining acts and legal discourses and cultures which in turn enabled colonisation and dispossession, disregarded Indigenous sovereignty, and excluded Indigenous people from the Australian political body. Other chapters reveal how such legal histories shaped individual Indigenous lives, from the way laws defined Aboriginality to the ways they circumscribed various aspects of daily life (to differing degrees dependent on time and geography) including one's place of residence and access to Country, freedom of movement, employment terms and conditions, ability to marry and keep one's children, and access to various rights and protections enjoyed by other Australians.

At first glance *The Cambridge Legal History of Australia*'s dedication to First Nations' legal histories seems surprising, for Indigenous subjects are often quarantined to one or two specific chapters in similarly encyclopaedic national history projects. Yet, as the chapters reveal, this attention should not be unexpected because First Nations people were disproportionately

2 M. Hislop, 'Lidia Thorpe makes history as she officially joins Senate: "Determined to work hard for justice in this place"', *Women's Agenda*, 6 October 2020, https://womensagenda.com.au/latest/lidia-thorpe-makes-history-as-she-officially-joins-senate-determined-to-work-hard-for-justice-in-this-place/, accessed 14 December 2021. Tragically, the number of deaths in custody has risen to 475 by 26 May 2021.

impacted by the colonists' law. Australian law emerged from settler law, which, as Bruce Kercher points, began by autocratically and amateurishly adapting British legal customs, and cherry-picking from English legislation to suit the needs of a small colonial population.[3] Significantly, this population was intoxicated by the seeming bounty and opportunities afforded by the wholesale expropriation of Indigenous land (and later the exploitation of Indigenous labour), and pragmatically invested in ensuring that law was complicit in the colonial project. First Nations people have been unduly affected by settler laws enabling the transformation of Aboriginal soil into settler property via the Crown, and (as already mentioned) by laws which governed their lives. Despite settler law's complicity in colonisation, people still turn to Australia's legal system to redress these injustices, constituting new and evolving chapters in the nation's legal history.

This book also seeks to play a role in redressing this history. It is open to exploring Indigenous laws, and a few chapters touch on the subject.[4] But the editors realise this is a fraught endeavour as Indigenous law has also long been marginalised, and attempts to construe it in relation to Western law risk re-enacting colonial processes.[5] Further, Indigenous legal systems are pluralised, each system grounded in the Dreamings and oral traditions of a particular nation: as Palyku legal scholar Ambelin Kwaymullina argues, they represent 'international tradition[s]' which have long determined 'complex networks of relationships' and provided frameworks for negotiating trade, borders, and 'shared law spaces' as well as resolving disputes.[6] Despite this hesitation regarding Indigenous law, the book takes a crucial step in decolonising Australia's legal history by both deconstructing long-standing positivist interpretations of how Australian law developed, and reconstructing such narratives in ways that both highlight the colonial power dynamics inherent in the nation's legal systems and cultures, while remaining sensitive and sympathetic to Indigenous perspectives and concerns.

In service of this decolonising aim, this chapter specifically reflects on how we reckon with the legacy of *terra nullius* and the effects of discriminatory laws. I argue that we still need to reckon with Australia's legal system because

3 See Kercher, Chapter 5 in this volume.

4 See Gover and Cubillo, Chapter 10 in this volume; Kirkby, Chapter 12 in this volume; Kearney, Chapter 15 in this volume; Watson, Chapter 31 in this volume.

5 Cane et al., Chapter 1 in this volume.

6 A. Kwaymullina, 'Aboriginal Nations, the Australian Nation-state and Indigenous International Legal Traditions', in I. Watson (ed.), *Indigenous Peoples as Subjects of International Law* (Abingdon: Routledge, 2017), 5. See also R. Langford Ginibi, 'Aboriginal Traditional and Customary Laws', *Law Text Culture* 8 (1984): 8–12.

settler law denied Aboriginal land title and continues to deny Aboriginal sovereignty. Historically, this denial has had major repercussions. First, it meant that in contrast to other parts of the former British Empire, the settler state failed to treat with Australian Indigenous people, which robbed First Nations people of the seemingly inviolable recognition of their sovereignty. Further, by allowing large-scale dispossession of Indigenous land through legal avenues and overlooking squatting, the denial of First Nations' sovereignty triggered waves of frontier violence, largely blamed on so-called Aboriginal barbarity and construed as crimes rather than resistance or territorial defence, well into the 1930s. Finally, it enabled settler law to deny self-determination, and legitimised inequities and exploitation through a range of discriminatory and paternalistic legal instruments which governed Indigenous lives. These historical denials have had enduring consequences for First Nations people and the state. The absence of a treaty amidst growing calls for one, remains an obstacle towards achieving reconciliation and social justice. Despite attempts to redress dispossession through legislative enactment and the judiciary, we still need to reckon with the issue of land. This is because the recognition of land rights has been uneven and remains inadequate for the majority of First Nations people, and has come at great cost: cultural, social, emotional and financial. We also need to reckon with the legacy of explicitly targeted, discriminatory laws because they enabled the break-up of families, the erosion of languages and cultural practices, and denied individual autonomy and collective self-determination. We need to reckon with these past laws because, in tandem with contemporary laws which continue to unfairly target First Nations people, they have had trans-generational effects that continue to shape Aboriginal and Torres Strait Islander people's experiences.

Reckoning with the Legacy of *Terra Nullius*

The most distinguishing characteristic of Britain's colonisation of Australia was its failure to acquire land by deliberately engaging with First Nations people, either through conquest or cession or, as was the case in North America and New Zealand, by treaty. Before embarking on the expedition which brought him to Australia's east coast in 1770, James Cook had been warned by his sponsor, the Royal Society, that '[n]o European Nation has the right to occupy any part of the country, or settle among them without their voluntary consent. Conquest over such people can give no just title.' With this presumption in mind the Admiralty gave Cook the explicit instruction: 'You are also with the consent of the natives to take possession of convenient situations in the country in the name of the King of Great Britain, or, if you find the country uninhabited take possession for His Majesty.'[7] Cook did take symbolic possession of the eastern portion of the continent, naming it New South Wales, but without obtaining Aboriginal people's consent as instructed. His annexation was later justified as 'discovery': in 1819 the British Attorney General, Samuel Shepherd, and Solicitor General, Robert Gifford, explained that New South Wales had not 'been acquired by conquest or cession, but taken possession of by [His Majesty] as desert and uninhabited'.[8] As Lisa Ford and David Roberts note, this rationale 'grew over time into the doctrine of *terra nullius*'.[9]

Frost and others argue that the failure to treat with Aboriginal people for land was influenced by the likes of Hugo Grotius and John Locke, and was based on ethnocentric British perceptions that Aboriginal people lived in 'a state of nature': that they did not own the land because their populations were sparse, and that they did not appear to enclose the land, practice agriculture, or have any recognisable notion of property.[10] However, an array of scholars has challenged this neat intellectual trajectory. Bill Gammage and Bruce Pascoe have explored the complexity of Aboriginal land management.[11] Henry Reynolds has shown that the intellectual foundations for *terra nullius* are shaky: eighteenth-century jurists, such as Christian Wolff, maintained that nomadic peoples 'could not legitimately be dispossessed simply because their pattern of land use differed from that of agriculturalists'.[12] Reynolds and Banner have shown that colonists recognised Aboriginal land rights, while Banner and Ford have shown that the assumption that Australia had no Indigenous sovereigns or proprietors continued to be challenged into the 1840s.[13] Continuing questions about Aboriginal title were evident in the legislation that enabled the establishment of the colony of

7 Cited in S. Banner, *Possessing the Pacific: Land, Settlers and Indigenous People from Australia to Alaska* (Cambridge, MA: Harvard University Press, 2007), 14.

8 Attorney General Samuel Shepherd and Solicitor General Robert Gifford cited in Banner, *Possessing the Pacific*, 27.

9 Ford and Roberts, Chapter 13 in this volume.

10 A. Frost, 'New South Wales as *terra nullius*: The British Denial of Aboriginal Land Rights', *Australian Historical Studies*, 19, no. 77 (1981): 513–23.

11 B. Gammage, *The Biggest Estate on Earth: How Aborigines Made Australia* (Crows Nest: Allen & Unwin, 2011) and B. Pascoe, *Dark Emu: Black Seeds: Agriculture or Accident?* (Broome: Magabala Books, 2014).

12 H. Reynolds, *The Law of the Land* (Ringwood: Penguin Books, 1987), 16.

13 Banner, *Possessing the Pacific*, 29, 31, 33–4. See also L. R. Hiatt, *Arguments about Aborigines: Australia and the Evolution of Social Anthropology* (Cambridge: Cambridge University Press, 1996), 17–19.

South Australia in 1836. Shane Chalmers explains that the law was 'open ended', since it was essentially framed either to recognise or deny Aboriginal land rights dependent on the views of the colonists themselves. This reveals that the law 'can take form in two ways at the same time'. Thus, while the denial of Aboriginal land rights became the 'law's dominant face' by the 1860s, this denial did not supersede and replace alternative interpretations of the law. Such 'alternates' continue to reside within the law until they are brought 'to life' through the 'actions and discourses' of the law's subjects.[14]

Ultimately, settler criticisms of *terra nullius* petered out in the mid- to late nineteenth century for both pragmatic and cultural reasons. To some, questioning *terra nullius* was a moot point: the fantasy that First Nations people would inevitably die out meant that 'the land would belong to the British soon enough anyway'. Further, as Banner points out, '[r]eversing *terra nullius* would have posed a terrible administrative problem for settlers and their government', as all land title was based on 'purchase from the Crown', and the 'Crown's title to the land rested on the legal fiction that the Crown has instantly become owner' of the land in 1788.[15] Instead, Aboriginal sympathisers agitated for the creation of reserves to which dispossessed Aboriginal people could be removed, and overseen by government-appointed protectors.

The consequence of *terra nullius* and the denial that First Australians 'were ever in possession of their own land' robbed them, as Reynolds argues, of both the 'great legal strength of that position', as well as the right to 'compensation which should have been paid following resumption by the Crown'.[16] As Ford and Roberts illustrate, it allowed the Crown to divide up Indigenous lands. This land grab unleashed waves of frontier violence from the 1790s in New South Wales through to the 1930s in the Northern Territory, as colonies multiplied and expanded. Ford and Roberts assert that '[e]very sphere of expansion . . . was, in varying degrees, murderous', highlighting the crucial role violence played in Indigenous dispossession, through both state-sanctioned violence against First Nations people and through British law's failure to adequately prosecute colonial violence and, in that way, 'help settlers get away with murder'.[17] Such failures were due not only to the pragmatic challenges of policing a 'far-flung' frontier, but also a prevailing

14 S. Chalmers, '*Terra Nullius*? Temporal Legal Pluralism in an Australian Colony' *Social & Legal Studies*, 29, no. 4 (2020): 472–3, 467, and 480–2.

15 Banner, *Possessing the Pacific*, 39 and 43–4.

16 Reynolds, *Law of the Land*, 2.

17 Ford and Roberts, Chapter 13 in this volume.

legal culture, which, as Kercher points out, did not accept 'that the wilful killing of indigenous people was the same as the murder of colonists'.[18]

The scant regard for Aboriginal people's legal rights gave Britain pause in responding to colonists' growing demand for political self-representation from 1835 onwards. In 1854 the Colonial Office worried that settler governments might create 'palpably immoral' laws, 'especially in relation to the unrepresented aborigines'.[19] This was because, as Ann Curthoys and Jessie Mitchell reveal, colonists seeking self-representation rarely believed 'Aboriginal people could possess the same rights, or indeed any political rights at all'. Yet, from the 1840s onwards Aboriginal people asserted their political rights, through sending petitions to the Queen and by demanding compensatory farm land since, as the Maloga petitioners wrote, 'all the land within our tribal boundaries has been taken possession of by the Government and white settlers'.[20] There are countless examples of Aboriginal men and women demanding land throughout much of the nineteenth and twentieth centuries, through moral, political, and legal recourse, and as either small parcels for individuals and families, or collectively through the creation of reserves and the recognition of land rights.[21] As Gumbainggir historian Gary Foley and Tim Anderson assert, there 'has always been a claim by Aboriginal communities for the return of ancestral lands or reparation for dispossession'.[22] Unfortunately, such claims largely went ignored until the 1970s, when land rights were legally recognised.

A key step in the journey towards land rights was the 1963 Yirrkala Bark Petition, which directly preceded Australia's first native title case. This Yolngu petition was a response to the federal government excising more than 300 square kilometres from the Arnhem Land Aboriginal reserve to enable Nabalco to mine bauxite on Yolngu lands. The petition outlined that nearly 500 people resided on this excised land, that it was where they hunted and gathered food 'from time immemorial', and contained sacred sites that

18 Kercher, Chapter 5 in this volume.

19 Cited in Curthoys and Mitchell, Chapter 6 in this volume.

20 Curthoys and Mitchell, Chapter 6 in this volume; H. Goodall, *Invasion to Embassy: Land in Aboriginal Politics in New South Wales, 1770–1972* (Sydney: Sydney University Press, 2008 [1996]), 92.

21 See Goodall, *Invasion to Embassy*, and for early nineteenth-century individual stories see P. Brock, 'Kudnarto (c. 1832–1855)', *Australian Dictionary of Biography*, 2020, https://adb.anu.edu.au/biography/kudnarto-29704/text36776, accessed 30 November 2021; N. Parry, 'Lock, Maria (1805–1878)', *Australian Dictionary of Biography*, 2005, https://adb.anu.edu.au/biography/lock-maria-13050/text23599, accessed 30 November 2021.

22 G. Foley and T. Anderson, 'Land Rights and Aboriginal Voices', *Australian Journal of Human Rights*, 12, no. 1 (2006): 84.

were 'vital to their livelihood'.[23] When the government proceeded anyway, the Yirrkala clans initiated the Gove Lands Rights Case (*Milirrpum v Nabalco*) in 1968. As Kirsty Gover and Larrakia, Wadjigan and Central Arrernte lawyer and legal scholar Eddie Cubillo explain in their chapter, the Yirrkala claimants 'explained the intricacies of the law' passed down from the 'great spirit ancestors' who created the laws and the 'clans as peoples', and secured 'their indelible connection to Country'. In 1971 the court acknowledged that Aboriginal people had occupied the continent prior to British arrival, but Justice Blackburn ultimately decided that 'the people's relationship to land was not a proprietary one', thereby preserving the doctrine of *terra nullius*.[24]

The Yirrkala claim coincided with a nation-wide wave of Aboriginal political protest, sustained partly by increased Indigenous urbanisation (in the wake of assimilationist efforts to move people from government reserves) which resulted in Indigenous-created and controlled services and agencies such as the Aboriginal Legal Service. Large-scale protests, such as the 1972 Tent Embassy, influenced the federal government to introduce the Aboriginal Land Rights (Northern Territory) Act 1976 (Cth) (ALRA).[25] This Act converted Northern Territory reserves into Aboriginal freehold title, enabled the Aboriginal Land Commissioner to grant freehold title to traditional owners who had 'primary spiritual responsibility . . . for the land', and created Land Councils to advocate for, and negotiate on behalf of, traditional owners.[26] The Act did not, however, grant all Northern Territory Aboriginal people equal access to land; Jenny Green and Tim Rowse in their chapter for instance note that the Alice Springs Arrernte did not benefit from the ALRA because 'the only reserve in their country' had 'ceased to be a reserve in 1963'.[27] Such inequities were not limited to the Arrernte. While the ALRA was restricted to the Northern Territory, the Commonwealth hoped that state governments would follow suit; their responses, however, were highly varied. South Australia granted large tracts of land to some desert communities, and New South Wales granted title to some reserves and allocated a proportion of land tax to Land Councils to purchase freehold land.

23 Yirrkala Bark Petitions 1963 (Cth), www.foundingdocs.gov.au/item-did-104.html, accessed 14 December 2021.
24 Gover and Cubillo, Chapter 10 in this volume; F. Merlan, 'The Regimentation of Customary Practice: From Northern Territory Land Claims to Mabo' *The Australian Journal of Anthropology* 6, nos 1 & 2 (1995): 65.
25 Foley and Anderson, 'Land Rights and Aboriginal Voices', 88–92.
26 Gover and Cubillo, Chapter 10 in this volume.
27 Rowse and Green, Chapter 9.1 in this volume.

Queensland, on the other hand, tried to pass laws preventing land claims in the Torres Strait, and Western Australia did not enact any Aboriginal land rights legislation.[28]

This uneven response was not the only issue with land rights legislation; some Indigenous scholars were critical of what land rights vested in legislation as opposed to common law meant. In 1995 Guugu Yimidhirr lawyer Noel Pearson observed that land rights legislation arose from the realisation that 'the common law refused to recognize Aboriginal ownership', and as a 'matter of morality' Australia needed to find another way for creating land rights. Seeing land rights legislation essentially as a remediating endeavour, Pearson pointed out that the ensuing land title was not 'a matter of right', but instead an act of governmental benevolence.[29] Consequently, as Jason Behrendt and Sean Brennan note, land rights measures in each state do not reflect Aboriginal people's inherent rights to land, but instead 'the limits of political will shown by each government in meeting the aspirations of Indigenous people'. Native title, on the other hand, meant to Pearson the recognition of 'an inherent right, an original right that does not need to be granted by the Crown because it arises out of Aboriginal law and custom'.[30]

The successful *Mabo* case was brought by a group of Meriam plaintiffs led by Eddie Mabo, a community leader and unionist aggrieved by the fact that 'Murray Islanders were not the legal owners of land inherited under Meriam custom and tradition, and that instead it was crown land'.[31] In 1981, at a Townsville land rights conference he co-organised, Meriam participants decided to pursue a '"Gove-type" case' against both the Queensland and Commonwealth governments. Launched the following year, the plaintiffs demonstrated that they still followed the 'laws of Malo', proving 'an unbroken line of Meriam succession to private plots of land at Mer' since before Queensland annexed the Torres Strait Islands in 1879.[32] In 1985 the Queensland government tried to quash their case by retroactively abolishing

28 Foley and Anderson, 'Land Rights and Aboriginal Voices', 92; M. Tehan, 'Practising Land Rights: The Pitjantjatjara in the Northern Territory, South Australia and Western Australia' *The Australian Quarterly* 65, no. 4 (1993): 37; Behrendt and Brennan, Chapter 16 in this volume.

29 N. Pearson, 'From Remnant Title to Social Justice', *The Australian Journal of Anthropology* 6, no. 1 & 2 (1995): 96.

30 Ibid, 96; Behrendt and Brennan, Chapter 16 in this volume.

31 N. Loos, 'Mabo, Edward Koiki (Eddie) (1936–1992)' *Australian Dictionary of Biography*, 2016, https://adb.anu.edu.au/biography/mabo-edward-koiki-eddie-16122/text28064, accessed 30 November 2021.

32 N. Sharp, 'No Ordinary Case: Reflections upon Mabo (No. 2)' *Sydney Law Review* 15, no. 2 (1993): 144.

native title without compensation under the Queensland Coast Islands Declaratory Act 1985; but three years later the High Court determined that the Act breached the Racial Discrimination Act (1975).[33] Finally, in 1992, the High Court found in favour of the Meriam, declaring that while Australia was settled under the doctrine of *terra nullius* the land was not in fact an 'uninhabited desert'. The Court determined that the Meriam maintained 'a form of native title which, in cases where it has not been extinguished, reflects the entitlement of the indigenous inhabitants, in accordance with their law and customs to their traditional lands'.[34] The federal government responded to this by enacting the Native Title Act 1993 (Cth), which Behrendt and Brennan describe in their chapter.[35]

The 1992 *Mabo* judgment is often described as the moment when the doctrine of *terra nullius* was finally acknowledged, in the words of William Deane, as a 'travesty of fact and a fallacy of law'.[36] Yet, as Wakka Wakka legal scholar Kevin Williams asserts, '*Mabo* wasn't about terra nullius; it was about recognising rights in land of people that existed prior to the acquisition of [British] sovereignty'. It also marked the point when 'Australia finally caught up to the rest of the common law world', since the 'pre-existing rights of the original inhabitants' had been recognised in the United States, Canada and New Zealand in the eighteenth and nineteenth centuries. For Williams, the *Mabo* decision was deeply affecting: it 'means I am no longer a stranger in my own country'.[37] Yawuru man Tony Lee, a former member of the National Native Title Tribunal, adds that in the early days of the *Mabo* decision Indigenous people believed that 'a fundamental shift in the Australian legal system had occurred' and that it would deliver 'fundamental changes for Aboriginal and Torres Strait Islander peoples'.[38] Pearson, Williams and Lee all illustrate the powerful emotional, symbolic, political, social and cultural implications and promise of the *Mabo* decision, revealing, as Behrendt and Brennan explain in their chapter, that First Nations people do not just want the return of land, but have always sought the 'recognition of traditional laws

33 B. A. Keon-Cohen, 'The Mabo Litigation: A Personal and Procedural Account' *Melbourne University Law Review* 24, no. 3 (December 2000): 893–951.
34 *Mabo v Queensland (No. 2)* (1992) 175 CLR 1, 59–60.
35 Behrendt and Brennan, Chapter 16 in this volume.
36 Cited in T. Lee, 'The Natives are Restless: A Personal Reflection on Ten Years of Native Title' *Studies in Western Australian History* 23 (2003): 30.
37 K. Williams, 'Critique: A Historian Said *Terra Nullius* was an Invention – I'm a Blackfella Lawyer Who Has Serious Concerns about His Lack of Understanding and Knowledge of the Common Law' *Newcastle Law Review* 10, no. 1 (2006): 46, and 41–2.
38 Lee, 'The Natives are Restless', 30.

and customs' and the 'formal recognition by the Australian state as rightful owners of the land'.[39]

Trying to achieve this recognition through the native title process has taken an immense toll on many communities who, as Eve Vincent argues, 'have been inveigled to reimagine and redefine themselves on the state's terms, in order to satisfy the criteria of legislation'.[40] Gover and Cubillo illustrate this in their chapter, revealing that native title claimants are subject to 'prohibitively onerous' and expensive 'evidentiary requirements' in proving they have maintained their connections to Country as a unified group observing laws and customs unchanged by colonisation, including the aforementioned violent dispossession which physically displaced many clans from their Country.[41] Furthermore, as Goenpul scholar Aileen Moreton-Robinson surmises, 'the burden of proof for repossession of our lands is now placed on us, and it must be demonstrated in accordance with the white legal structure in courts controlled predominantly by white men'.[42] Yet even when claimants are able to demonstrate the continuity and co-existence of their laws, Amanda Kearney reveals that Australian and Indigenous legal systems are not regarded equally and 'the greater demand for concession often lies on the side of Indigenous law'.[43] And, needless to say, where native title is deemed to have been extinguished or unproven, the result is not only heart-breaking, but also considered a reassertion of *terra nullius*.[44] Finally, native title discourses have centred on land; yet, as Wiradjuri Nyemba legal scholar Virginia Marshall argues, seascapes and water courses are just as significant to many First Nations people, and it is crucial that Indigenous people's access to water rights be enshrined in law, to recognise their 'special association to water', protect communities'

39 Jason Behrendt and Sean Brennan in their chapter in this collection add that other motivations include the desire to protect important places, perhaps foster new economic opportunities, and spend more time with family on Country. Behrendt and Brennan, Chapter 16 in this volume.

40 E. Vincent, *'Against Native Title': Conflict and Creativity in Outback Australia* (Canberra: Aboriginal Studies Press, 2016), 6–7.

41 Gover and Cubillo, Chapter 10 in this volume.

42 A. Moreton-Robinson, 'Opinion: "Our story is in the land": Why the Indigenous Sense of Belonging Unsettles White Australia', *ABC Religion and Ethics* [online], 9 November 2020, www.abc.net.au/religion/our-story-is-in-the-land-indigenous-sense-of-belonging/11159992, accessed 14 December 2021.

43 Kearney, Chapter 15 in this volume.

44 Here I draw on Tanganekald, Meintangk, and Boandik legal scholar Irene Watson's argument that the 'ongoing effects of terra nullius – the legal dispossession and physical deprivation – [are] still with us today'. I. Watson, 'Re-centring First Nations Knowledge and Places in a Terra Nullius Space' *AlterNative* 10, no. 5 (2014): 509.

access to water, and ensure Indigenous involvement in managing water resources.[45]

While native title has now been recognised in Country comprising 38 per cent of the Australian land mass, represented by 221 Native Title Registered Bodies Corporate, it has not resulted in a 'fundamental shift in the legal system' built on the 'inherent right' of Indigenous law, as was once hoped.[46] In Australia, we have still not fully reckoned with *terra nullius* because its legacies still permeate our legal systems and mainstream culture. Moreton-Robinson suggests its persistence is due to the fact that native title legislation 'creat[ed] in law a hybrid of settlement that diminishes but does not erase *terra nullius*', and that the idea of *terra nullius* still manifests in widespread beliefs that 'white Australians . . . made this country what it is today', as well as the privileges that continue to accrue through the dispossession of Indigenous land.[47]

Reckoning with Discriminatory Laws

In 2005, Aboriginal magistrate Sue Gordon AM, delivered a powerful lecture exploring how the Aborigines Act Amendment Act 1936 (WA) had intruded on her own life since January 1946, when she was first brought to the attention of the Commissioner of Native Affairs. Believing the three-year-old was 'much too light in colour to remain' with her mother at Belele station, she was 'removed to Sister Kate's [Children's Home]', some 750 kilometres south, the following year.[48] Within a week her maternal uncle requested to adopt Gordon, assuring that he would pay for her maintenance, and asserting that he 'liv[ed] under the White Act', meaning he had proved to a magistrate that he had 'severed all ties to extended family and friends', was of 'industrious habits' and had been granted 'citizenship' under the Natives (Citizenship Rights) Act 1944 (WA). Her uncle's request was denied, because as a so-called 'quarter-caste child' Susie was 'entitled to the opportunity to live and be trained as an ordinary white child'. However, the Commissioner

45 V. Marshall, *Overturning Aqua Nullius: Securing Aboriginal Water Rights* (Canberra: Aboriginal Studies Press, 2017), 216–24.

46 Behrendt and Brennan also point out that land rights and native title legislation has opened up possibilities for some traditional owners to leverage their 'finite bargaining power' with government and industry. Behrendt and Brennan, Chapter 16 in this volume; Gover and Cubillo, Chapter 10 in this volume; Lee, 'The Natives are Restless', 30; Pearson, 'From Remnant Title to Social Justice', 96.

47 Moreton-Robinson, 'Opinion'.

48 Cited in S. Gordon, 'The Effects of Early Australian Laws on Aboriginal People – A Personal Perspective' *Flinders Journal of Law Reform* 8, no. 2 (2005): 178.

did not have the authority to remove her, as the 1936 Act only applied to so-called 'quadroon[s] under twenty-one years of age' *if* they 'associate[d]' with so-called 'full blood' persons, which she did not, or *if* they were 'ordered by a magistrate to be classed as a native', which Gordon contends, there is no evidence she ever was. Indeed, in 1956 the department came to the same conclusion, declaring that Gordon was 'not Native under Act', and ceased paying her maintenance at Sister Kate's. Instead of being returned to her family, Gordon was 'declared a destitute child' under the Child Welfare Act 1947–1950 (WA), and made a ward of the Child Welfare Department until she was eighteen years old.[49]

Gordon's heart-breaking story illustrates the legal interventions Aboriginal people faced, sanctioned by both mainstream laws and discriminatory acts targeting Aboriginal people specifically, as well as the authority that the Commissioner of Native Affairs was able to exert beyond his legal powers. Her uncle's story reveals how Aboriginal attempts to comply with these legal intrusions, despite the personal costs, did not guarantee the ostensible 'citizenship' rights promised. Gordon's mother eventually found her, but they had already lost 'over 30 years of birthdays' and 'family life'. Gordon speculates that the 'lack of "due process" in [her] case' might amount to 'negligence or false imprisonment', but acknowledges that pursuing 'legal action' would be prohibitively costly. Gordon's experience reveals how First Nations people were injured by the legal and discretionary discrimination they faced, and the ongoing need to reckon with this history.[50] These discriminatory laws were not limited to child removal, and impacted on First Nations people in myriad ways.

The primary vehicles of the legal discrimination against First Nations people were the Protection Acts introduced by colonial and state governments in the late nineteenth and twentieth centuries, beginning with Victoria in 1869. These acts granted 'wide-ranging powers of control over Indigenous lives', and 'impinged on realms usually defined by Australian society as "private": residence, diet, self-sufficiency, illness, work, education and child rearing' in the service of advancing both segregationist and, as Gordon's story reveals, assimilationist agendas.[51] Yet, as Amanda Nettelbeck reminds us,

49 Cited in ibid, 179–82. Gordon's non-Indigenous father had been forced to pay for her maintenance before this, and upon his death in 1952 the Department pursued her mother to pay for this.

50 Ibid, 183–4.

51 Commonwealth, Royal Commission into Aboriginal Deaths in Custody, *National Report* (Canberra: 1991), 2: 10.5.

protection was originally introduced throughout the empire to 'extend the law's protections to Indigenous people as "new" British subjects'. Appointed protectors were meant to 'monitor the rights and responsibilities' of Indigenous people, and ensure they were treated as 'legal equals'. However, once the colonies achieved self-government, they implemented their own Protection Acts, which were more focused on 'manag[ing] the place of Indigenous people within the white settler state'.[52] This is illustrated by the Aboriginal Protection Act 1869 (Vic), which created 'regulations and orders' governing Aboriginal people's residence, employment, and custody of their children.[53] Other states' legislation enabled protectors to keep full-descent Aboriginal people on government reserves while removing their mixed-descent family members.[54]

The disruption to family lives, especially through the removal of children, was arguably the most devastating effect of protection. Wiradjuri scholar Paul Gray, Katherine Ellinghaus and Teresa Libesman explain that Indigenous children had been taken by settlers from the early days of settlement, occasionally to rescue children orphaned by epidemics and massacres, or as 'experiments' to test whether they could become 'civilised', and often to serve as servants, guides, and companions.[55] This 'extra-legal removal of children' extended into the twentieth century, and left children vulnerable to abuse.[56] Through Protection Acts, governments could take children from their Indigenous parents (either with their consent, usually coerced, or without their consent) and place them in government or church-run children's institutions, or adopt them into Anglo-Australian homes. The 1997 *Bringing Them Home: Report of the National Enquiry into the Separation of Aboriginal and Torres Strait Islander Children from Their Families* found that between one in three and one in ten Indigenous children were removed from their families between 1910 and 1970.[57] Anne O'Brien observes that Indigenous children's experience of removal varied between 'different

52 Nettelbeck, Chapter 20 in this volume.

53 Aboriginal Protection Act 1869 (Vic).

54 Nettelbeck, Chapter 20 in this volume.

55 For an example of this see K. A. Travis Penangke, 'Apma, Undelya (Minnie) (c. 1909–1990)', *Australian Dictionary of Biography*, 2021, https://adb.anu.edu.au/biography/apma-undelya-minnie-30165/text37439, accessed 30 November 2021.

56 Libesman, Ellinghaus and Gray, Chapter 18 in this volume. See also S. Robinson, 'Regulating the Race: Aboriginal Children in Private European Homes in Colonial Australia' *Journal of Australian Studies* 37, no. 3 (2013): 308–9.

57 National Inquiry into the Separation of Aboriginal and Torres Strait Islander Children from their Families, *Bringing Them Home: Report of the National Inquiry into the Separation of Aboriginal and Torres Strait Islander Children from their Families* (Sydney: Human Rights and Equal Opportunity Commission, 1997) ('Bringing Them Home').

jurisdictions': in Queensland they had limited contact with their parents, while in Western Australia they tended to be 'fully separated'.[58] As Ellinghaus, Gray and Libesman explain, this removal was motivated by a range of factors including ethnocentric notions that mixed-descent children would be 'neglected' or 'abandoned' by their mothers, while also serving broader aims of achieving assimilation through either 'biological absorption' or 'cultural integration', depending on the state and the period.[59] Instead of being 'civilised', as the rhetoric maintained, innumerable Indigenous children faced abuse and maltreatment: the 'Bringing Them Home' Report found one in every ten children experienced sexual abuse, and 28 per cent were subjected to severe 'physical brutality'. The head of the inquiry, Sir Ronald Wilson, labelled the removal of children over several generations as 'genocide', because the outcome attempted to eradicate their connection to culture and Aboriginality.[60]

This Report took the first step in reckoning with this history of widespread discriminatory child removal by providing a forum for survivors to voice their experiences and realise the full extent of this systematic policy. Between 1997 and 2017 most Commonwealth and state governments offered packages to provide either 'practical assistance', 'compensation' or 'redress' to those who had been removed. However, such schemes were difficult to access: most were only open for a short time, capped the compensation claimed by individuals, and risked subjecting claimants to further trauma in trying to prove their claims.[61] Such packages could never compensate for the ongoing trauma of removal, nor its transgenerational impact. Some members of the Stolen Generation have pursued redress through the courts. Lorna Cubillo and Peter Gunner were the first, arguing that 'the government was vicariously liable' for their removal under the powers of 'the 1918 Ordinance', and responsible for their 'abuse and lack of care whilst detained'. However, the judge determined that a 'thumbprint' signified Gunner's mother's consent to

58 O'Brien, Chapter 21 in this volume.

59 Libesman, Ellinghaus and Gray, Chapter 18 in this volume. See also A. Moran, 'White Australia, Settler Nationalism and Aboriginal Assimilation' *Australian Journal of Politics and History* 51, no. 2 (2005): 168–93 and R. McGregor, '"Breed out the colour" or the Importance of Being White' *Australian Historical Studies* 33, no. 120 (2002): 286–302.

60 'Bringing Them Home', 163–4, 194 and 266–73.

61 C. Dow, 'Sorry: The Unfinished Business of the Bringing Them Home Report', *Parliament of Australia*, 4 February 2008 www.aph.gov.au/about_parliament/parliamentary_departments/parliamentary_library/pubs/bn/0708/bringingthemhomereport#_ftnref23, accessed 20 December 2021, and J. Korff, 'Compensation for Stolen Generation members', *Creative Spirits*, 14 August 2020 www.creativespirits.info/aboriginalculture/politics/stolen-generations/compensation-for-stolen-generation-members#state-governments-offering-compensation, accessed 20 December 2021.

his removal and that the state did not have a duty of care. Ann Curthoys, Ann Genovese and Alexander Reilly argue that this case reveals 'law's inability to escape its complicity in the colonial project', because it interprets claimants' experiences through 'narrow legal and economic frames', fails to acknowledge the uneven documentary evidence available to the claimants and the state, and remains reluctant to give weight to and fully comprehend oral testimony.[62] As human rights lawyer Julian Burnside concluded, 'suing Governments is brutally hard', and rarely offers a satisfactory means of reckoning with the past.[63]

Protection Acts also gave protectors powers to determine whom Aboriginal people, primarily women, were allowed to marry. As Libesman et al. point out in their chapter, the Western Australia and Northern Territory Chief Protectors, C. E. Cook and A. O. Neville, were particularly 'enthusiastic' in using this power to 'encourage biological absorption' by favouring marriage to Anglo-Australian men and preventing undesirable marriages between Aboriginal women and Asian men. Neville was especially vindictive in prosecuting individuals who circumvented his authority. When Wongatha woman Lallie Matbar began a relationship with Muslim merchant Jack Akbar, Neville had her repeatedly removed to an institution 900 kilometres from home. After the couple eloped to South Australia, Neville had them arrested and extradited to Perth, where they received much public sympathy, forcing the protector to drop the charges. However, he still made them pay a bond, and warned that Matbar would be arrested if she tried to return to Western Australia.[64] Even where state acts did not grant such powers, protectors could still intervene in Indigenous marriages, as Libesman et al. observe, by 'remov[ing] [individuals] from missions and stations and deny[ing] them rations'.[65]

While these legislative intrusions had devastating effects on families, the issue, perhaps, of most concern to protection's architects was Indigenous labour and ensuring its availability to settler interests. Diane Kirkby explains that British labour law did not encompass rights for Indigenous workers, thereby allowing colonists to invent 'their own models of coercion and remedy', including the forcible movement and confinement of Aboriginal

62 A. Curthoys, A. Genovese and A. Reilly, *Rights and Redemption: History, Law and Indigenous People* (Sydney: UNSW Press, 2008), 134–5.

63 Cited in Korff, 'Compensation'.

64 P. Rajkowski, 'Matbar, Lallie (1905–1970)', *Australian Dictionary of Biography*, published online 2020 adb.anu.edu.au/biography/matbar-lallie-30056/text37296 accessed 30 November 2021.

65 Libesman, Ellinghaus and Gray, Chapter 18 in this volume.

people to suit the 'labour needs of local industries'.[66] Despite initial rhetoric to protect First Nations people from exploitation, settler interests eventually won out, and later acts granted greater powers to make Indigenous labour available in the pastoral and pearling industries.[67] As Tanganekald, Meintangk and Boandik legal scholar Irene Watson observes, Indigenous people were forced to provide labour at 'a time when slavery was no longer practiced within the boundaries of "law"'.[68] This was enabled not only through weakening the regulation of employers but also through criminalising Indigenous people's actions that contravened employers' interests: for example by deeming unemployed Aboriginal people vagrants. Instead of prosecuting 'abusive masters' as originally conceived, protectors increasingly policed Indigenous workers.[69] Twentieth-century Protection Acts quarantined Indigenous people away from other populations, curtailing their freedom of movement in order to prevent unionists and activists from agitating Indigenous workers to demand workers' rights.[70] Nonetheless, Indigenous peoples initiated impactful strikes such as the 1936 Torres Strait Maritime Strike (involving Eddie Mabo's father), the 1946 Pilbara Strike and the 1966 Wave Hill walk off.

Protectors were empowered to negotiate employment contracts on behalf of Aboriginal workers, and often negotiated wages substantially lower than that of non-Indigenous employees, and ensured wages were paid to protectors with only 'pocket money' going directly to the worker. Furthermore, a portion could be taken to subsidise missions and government reserves, and the rest held in trust in 'compulsory banking schemes'.[71] Ros Kidd's research found that Queensland protectors expanded this scheme because it defrayed the department's costs. Not surprisingly, Indigenous workers voiced opposition, but were told their money was held for them, even though few had access to transaction records or were made aware of the maintenance funds and taxes.[72] Kidd estimates that in Queensland alone '4,500 to 5,500 Indigenous pastoral

66 Kirkby, Chapter 12 in this volume.

67 A. Curthoys, 'Indigenous Dispossession and Pastoral Employment in Western Australia during the Nineteenth Century: Implications for Understanding Colonial Forms of Genocide', in M. Adhikari (ed.) *Genocide on Settler Frontiers: When Hunter-Gatherers and Commercial Stock Farmers Clash* (New York: Berghahn Books, 2014), 218.

68 I. Watson, 'Sovereign Spaces, Caring for Country, and the Homeless Position of Aboriginal Peoples' *South Atlantic Quarterly* 108, no. 1 (2008): 29.

69 Nettelbeck, Chapter 20 in this volume.

70 See for example, A. Scrimgeour, '"Battlin' for their rights": Aboriginal Activism and the Leper Line' *Aboriginal History* 36 (2012): 43–65.

71 See S. Kinnane, J. Harrison and I. Reinecke, 'Finger Money: The Black and White of Stolen Wages' *Griffith Review* 47 (January 2015): 49–70.

72 R. Kidd, *Trustees on Trial: Recovering Stolen Wages* (Canberra: Aboriginal Studies Press, 2006), chapter 4.

workers may have lost wage entitlements worth more than $500 million between 1920 and 1968'.[73] While 'stolen wages' stories had long circulated in Indigenous communities, Kidd's research sparked similar studies in other states.[74]

So far, the Queensland, New South Wales and Western Australian governments have attempted to reckon with histories of stolen wages through inquiries and redress schemes. Significantly, such inquiries found intrusive governmental control over Indigenous individuals' money impeded their financial literacy and independence and, in many cases, led to 'transgenerational disadvantage' and contributed to ongoing cycles of poverty.[75] Queensland initiated its first redress scheme in 2002 with a $55.6 million package, which, like the Stolen Generation schemes, imposed strict limits on the compensation available ($2,000–$4,000 per person) and severe evidentiary requirements, resulting in '$21 million [remaining] unclaimed'. New South Wales, on the other hand, introduced two schemes in 2006 and 2010 which actually sought to match stolen wages, 'paying $3,521 for every $100 owed, or an $11,000 lump sum' in cases where a total could not be deduced. Finally, Western Australia's 2012 scheme offered payments of only $2,000, despite whistle-blowers reporting that the government knew some were owed up to $78,000.[76] This package was met with 'disbelief and disgust'; Judy Harrison, Isabelle Reinecke and Miriwoong scholar Steve Kinnane explain that it reminded many Aboriginal people of when they were treated as 'non-citizens and were offered payment in sticks of tobacco and finger money (pocket money)'.[77] Some individuals have sought redress through the courts, though only Queensland cases have so far been successful, resulting in a $190 million compensation settlement in 2019. Attempts to reckon with the history of 'stolen wages' have varied: redress schemes differed across the states, and as Thalia Anthony points out, only apply to Indigenous workers whose wages were held in trust, and fail to cover other ways First Nations people were denied their earnings.[78]

First Nations people have also been discriminated against by criminal law. Mark Finnane argues that the ongoing over-representation of Indigenous

73 T. Anthony, 'The new Mabo? $190 million stolen wages settlement is unprecedented, but still limited', *The Conversation*, 11 July 2019.
74 Kinnane et al., 'Finger Money', 52.
75 Stolen Wages Taskforce, *Reconciling The Past: Government Control of Aboriginal Monies in Western Australia, 1905–1972*, Department of Indigenous Affairs, Western Australia, June 2008, cited in Kinnane et al., 'Finger Money', 55.
76 Anthony, 'The new Mabo?'. 77 Kinnane et al., 'Finger Money', 49–50.
78 Anthony, 'The new Mabo?'.

people in prison today is partly an artefact of nineteenth-century 'assertion[s] of common law jurisdiction', which compounded injustice by naturalising Aboriginal people and subjecting them to both the legal responsibilities of British subjects and discriminatory legal processes including the 'inadmissibility of Indigenous evidence in courts', juries' prejudice against Indigenous people, and the lack of interpreters.[79] As Nettelbeck asserts, 'all created obstacles to the possibility of legal redress'. Despite 'supposed equality before the law', First Nations people became 'more regularly subjected to prosecution, incarceration, and execution'.[80] This was especially pronounced during periods of colonial expansion and the ensuing frontier conflict, which, Finnane argues, reveals how criminal law could be 'weaponised'.[81] There is an ongoing wilful blindness regarding criminal law's complicity with colonisation, as Darkiñung legal scholar Mary Spiers Williams highlights, provocatively asking,

> *Can you see how violent colonising-state law and its systems are? Can you see that it is not just ideology, morality, and principles – it is physical. I know you already know that colonisation has damaged and changed our law and everything else that is part of us, especially those who have had contact for longest.*

Have you wondered, though,

> *what has colonisation done to the law that the colonisers transplanted here? How has colonisation affected you? – how you make sense of the world? How has it affected how you see First Peoples and our law?*[82]

Perhaps the most significant attempt to reckon with the ongoing effects of criminal law's colonial legacy was the Royal Commission into Aboriginal Deaths in Custody (1991). Triggered by public outrage, the inquiry was established in 1987, and eventually investigated ninety-nine deaths that occurred between 1 January 1980 and 31 May 1989. In addition to 339 recommendations, which have still not been implemented, the Report emphasised the importance of recognising that history continues to contribute to 'Aboriginal over-representation in custody'. Asserting that few non-Indigenous people know 'the amount of brutality and bloodshed' involved in enforcing the law, the Report pronounces that such laws were 'postulated on the inferiority of the Aboriginal people'.[83]

79 Finnane, Chapter 27 in this volume.
80 Nettelbeck, Chapter 20 in this volume.
81 Finnane, Chapter 27 in this volume.
82 Williams, Chapter 4 in this volume.
83 Commonwealth, *National Report*, 1: 1.4.

The Report focused in particular on police interactions with Indigenous people. While this subject is not explored in detail in this volume, policing has played a crucial role in Australia's legal history, beginning with 'formative experiences of Australia's colonial police' in frontier conflicts in which acts of Indigenous resistance were perceived as 'breaches of the law rather than acts of war'. Significantly, the Report recognised Indigenous law, asserting that 'resistance' might include the execution of Aboriginal law against settlers' transgressions, and arguing that the police thus served as 'the de facto arbiters of two sets of laws in conflict'. However, the greatest impact of police on Aboriginal history is that they 'have acted as the most consistent point of Aboriginal contact with colonial power' because of their unique position in both 'arresting and charging Aboriginal people for "criminal" offences' and 'carrying out "protective" roles'.[84] Police were tasked with enforcing protection and often served as local protectors, interacting with Indigenous people when carrying out a range of duties including issuing rations, expelling 'trouble makers', and removing children. They also policed individuals in possession of alcohol or opium, and those who went to 'prohibited areas' or were seen 'loitering'.[85] Police often served settlers interests, and were instrumental in rounding up Aboriginal people to satisfy demands for labour, especially from pastoralists in northern Australia. Thus, discriminatory protection laws brought First Nations people into contact with the police to a much higher degree than the non-Indigenous population. As Amangu historian Crystal McKinnon asserts, when 'it is reported that we are proportionately the most incarcerated people in the world, in our lives it means that most Aboriginal people have at least one family member who is or who has been incarcerated. Make no mistake, this is the case in every community.'[86]

Recognising this history is integral because, according to the Report, 'it is not surprising that many Aboriginal people avoided and attempted to withhold information from' police, a point echoed in a 2021 coronial inquest into the deaths of two youths fleeing the police.[87] Such tense relationships between Indigenous communities and police helped explain the disproportionate incarceration rates of Indigenous people in the 1980s, and today.

84 Commonwealth, *National Report*, 2: 10.5. See also C. Cuneen, *Conflict, Politics and Crime: Aboriginal Communities and the Police* (Melbourne: Allen & Unwin, 2014).

85 Commonwealth, *National Report*, 2: 10.5.

86 C. McKinnon, 'The Lives Behind the Statistics: Policing Practices in Aboriginal Literature' *Australian Feminist Law Journal* 45, no. 2 (2020): 207–23.

87 Commonwealth, *National Report*, 2: 10.5 and H. McNeill, '"It's no wonder Aboriginal youth run from police": Professor calls out systemic racism at inquest', *WA Today*, 22 March 2021.

Yawuru senator Patrick Dodson pointed out that twenty-five years after the Royal Commission the Indigenous incarceration rate had doubled from 14 to 27 per cent of those in custody; and, as Senator Thorpe's message stick reminded us, the number of Aboriginal and Torres Strait Islander people who have died in custody has grown significantly. Dodson argued that this is because key Royal Commission recommendations, particularly the principle that imprisonment should be a last resort, have not been implemented. Instead, the incarceration rate has been driven up by new 'criminal justice policies', such as mandatory sentencing in Western Australia, paperless arrests in the Northern Territory and the continued criminalising of Indigenous people for minor offences, for example, fine default introduced by governments to satisfy 'law and order' rhetoric that disproportionately affects Indigenous people.[88]

In addition to Protection Acts and criminal law, Australian law has discriminated against First Nations people through the denial of civil rights. Frank Bongiorno explains that in Australia, which lacks a 'bill of rights', rights discourses are often 'framed by a sense of absence'. Consequently, the protection of rights is dependent on the common law, legislative acts and the High Court's interpretation of the Constitution. Despite this lack, however, Australia's colonies were, historically, 'among the most precocious' in recognising 'political rights – of men at first, then of women', and voting rights were awarded very early, as was the right to stand for Parliament. Yet, First Nations people were subject to separate discriminatory laws, and most were denied political rights because they were not deemed 'sufficiently civilised to fulfill the civic responsibilities'.[89]

When the newly federated states debated the Commonwealth Franchise Act 1902, they elected to exclude Indigenous people unless they could vote in their own state. State laws, however, were varied and complex, based on land holdings, exemption certificates, mixed ancestry and military service. Even after the Nationality and Citizenship Act 1948 was passed, the Attorney General confirmed that it did not 'alter the effect of existing' discriminatory protection legislation. A 1961 Select Committee found that 30,000 Aboriginal and Torres Strait Islander people in Queensland, Western Australia and the Northern Territory had been disenfranchised, and in the other states Aboriginal people were 'not aware' they were entitled to vote. Even when Indigenous franchise was not legally

88 P. Dodson, '25 Years on from the Royal Commission into Aboriginal Deaths in Custody Recommendations' *Indigenous Law Bulletin*, 8, no. 23 (2016): 24–6.

89 Bongiorno, Chapter 23 in this volume.

proscribed, racist attitudes saw Indigenous voters turned away. The 1962 Act permitted all First Nations people to vote in Commonwealth elections, although in contrast to non-Indigenous Australians, it was not compulsory until 1984.[90] Both legal and de facto impediments to Indigenous voting rights have contributed to the ongoing belief among many First Nations people that they were excluded from the body politic, and remain outsiders in their own country.

The rights conferred by citizenship, however, are not limited to voting, and in the twentieth century a number of Indigenous organisations such as the Australian Aboriginal Progressive Association (AAPA) and the Australian Aborigines League (AAL) agitated for citizenship rights and the end of discriminatory Protection Acts. They highlighted the moral injustice of such inequality, arguing, for example, that Aboriginal people had served in the wars yet were denied the right to political representation, and that Australia Day was a day of mourning for Aboriginal people because it represented the beginning of colonisation and its ensuing injustices including dispossession, the removal of children and unequal rights. The 1967 Referendum, initiated by a decade-long campaign by the Federal Council for the Advancement of Aboriginal and Torres Strait Islanders to change the Constitution to enable the Commonwealth to legislate on matters pertaining to First Nations people and remove a discriminatory clause which excluded Indigenous people from the census, saw over 90 per cent of voters 'vote yes for Aborigines'. Most people, including many Indigenous people, believed that the Referendum would enable the Commonwealth government to introduce legislation which, unlike state legislation, benefited Indigenous people, thereby inaugurating a great political shift towards equal rights for Aboriginal and Torres Strait Islanders. However, the amended Constitution did not require the 'race powers' to be beneficial, and little changed for First Nations people. The aforementioned Yirrkala native title case, however, did spur Indigenous activists from the 1970s onwards to agitate not for equal rights as earlier campaigners had done, but instead demand specific Indigenous sovereignty rights centred on the return of land and the right to self-determination.[91]

90 Commonwealth Parliament, *Report from the Select Committee on Voting Rights for Aborigines* (Canberra: A. J. Arthur, 1961), 4–5 and J. Chesterman and B. Galligan, *Citizens without Rights: Aborigines and Australian Citizenship* (Melbourne: Cambridge University Press, 1997), 82.

91 See F. Peters-Little, D. Haslem, D. Cheetham and R. Lewis, 'Vote Yes for *Aborigines*' [videorecording] (Canberra: Film Finance Corporations and Denise Haslem Productions, 2007); L. Behrendt, 'The Three Biggest Myths of the 1967 Referendum',

Conclusion: Looking Forward

This chapter has looked back on Australia's legal history, reflecting on why we still need to reckon with the past, and the legacies of historical injustices tied to law's complicity with colonialism. Looking back and evaluating where we have come from is a crucial step in decolonising our disciplines, and decolonising our legal history. It is arguably an aim of this collection, which deconstructs positivist interpretations of the development of Australia's laws and legal cultures, and reconstructs new explanatory narratives which are much more attentive to the colonial dynamics inherent in our legal systems and how they have evolved. This process lays important groundwork for the future: as, one of the delegates from the First Nations Constitutional Convention asserted: 'Our truth has to be told before we can move on from that.'[92] This history needs to be told before the continuing impacts of colonisation and Australia's discriminatory legal systems on Indigenous individuals and communities can be understood. Further, as Botswanan post-colonial scholar Bagele Chilisa explains, this process of deconstruction and reconstruction needs to be undertaken before we can move to the next stage of decolonisation, 'self-determination and social justice'.[93] In the context of legal history, this could mean a deeper engagement with Indigenous laws that does not seek to understand it in relation to Western law, but instead acknowledging, as Irene Watson explains, that 'Aboriginal law is not dependent on Australian law . . . it remains alive within Aboriginal frameworks that exist outside of mainstream legal imaginings'. This would involve a degree of cultural literacy in forms beyond the chirographic, as Chalmers notes, to encompass the ways in which Indigenous laws are 'sung, danced, painted, sculpted or otherwise'. This literacy could only be broached by ensuring, as Murri legal scholar Nicole Watson explains, that Indigenous cultural competency is embedded in Australia's legal education.[94]

ABC News, 26 May 2017 www.abc.net.au/news/2017-05-26/larissa-behrendt-mythbusting-the-1967-referendum/8349858, accessed 20 December 2021; Foley and Anderson, 'Land Rights and Aboriginal Voices'.

92 G. Appleby and M. Davis, 'The Uluru Statement and the Promises of Truth' *Australian Historical Studies* 49, no. 4 (2018): 501.

93 Cited in L. Le Grange, 'Decolonising the University Curriculum' *South African Journal of Higher Education* 30, no. 2 (2016): 3.

94 Watson, 'Sovereign Spaces', 36; Chalmers, '*Terra Nullius*?', 467; Watson, Chapter 31 in this volume.

To conclude this chapter, I would now like to look forward, as Larissa Behrendt, an eminent Eualeyai and Kamillaroi legal scholar, does in her discussion of the promise held out by the recognition of Indigenous sovereignty. Sovereignty encompasses 'a spectrum of claims' including:

> the right not to be discriminated against, the rights to enjoy language, culture and heritage, our rights to land, seas, waters and natural resources, the right to be educated and the right to work, the right to be economically self-sufficient, the right to be involved in decision-making processes that impact on our lives, and the right to govern and manage our own affairs and our own communities.[95]

Broadly these aspirations can be categorised as equal rights which 'all Australians are entitled to'. But, as we have seen, dispossession and government assimilation policies meant that First Nations people have been 'historically denied' rights to 'culture, heritage, language and native title', and the 'dominant culture' is still resistant to Indigenous empowerment rights, or the right to make decisions. Without the enduring legal recognition provided by a treaty or bill of rights, First Nations people's rights are 'dependant on the benevolence and paternalism of government' and remain insecure. Behrendt reassures us that the law has the capacity to balance co-existing sovereignty, as it does every day in regard to Australia's local, state and federal governments; and, thus, recognising Indigenous sovereignty does not pose 'a threat to Australian sovereignty' or bear a cost on non-Indigenous lives.[96] Instead, the legal recognition of Indigenous sovereignty could only be beneficial, by empowering Aboriginal and Torres Strait Islander people to be involved in decision-making processes which affect their lives, Country and laws, a significant departure from Indigenous people having to endure imposed laws which curtailed so many aspects of daily life.

Settler law has been used to deny First Nations' sovereignty and systems of land tenure and law, in order to expropriate land and waters as well as labour, curtail Indigenous autonomy and mobility, withhold citizen rights, and impose a bifurcated legal system which has perpetuated segregation and inequality. Despite settler/Australian law's role as an instrument of dispossession and discrimination, the 1967 Referendum, native title, calls for

95 L. Behrendt, 'Aboriginal Sovereignty: A Practical Roadmap', in J. Evans, A. Genovese, A. Reilly and P. Wolfe (eds), *Sovereignty: Frontiers of Possibility* (Honolulu: University of Hawai'i Press, 2013), 164.

96 Ibid, 163–75.

treaties and the Uluru Statement from the Heart demonstrate that constitutional and judicial law (as opposed to legislative law) nonetheless has been, and continues to be, seen by many First Nations people and their advocates as a promising means to securing enduring, inviolable rights for Indigenous peoples, protection of Indigenous lands and recognition of Indigenous law.

Index

Printed in the United Kingdom by TJ Clays Ltd.